A HISTORY OF ARCHITECTURE

A HISTORY OF ARCHITECTURE

Settings and Rituals

SPIRO KOSTOF

Revisions by Greg Castillo

Original Drawings by Richard Tobias

New York   Oxford 👑 OXFORD UNIVERSITY PRESS 👑 1995

Oxford University Press

Oxford   New York
Athens   Auckland   Bangkok   Bombay
Calcutta   Cape Town   Dar es Salaam   Delhi
Florence   Hong Kong   Istanbul   Karachi
Kuala Lumpur   Madras   Madrid   Melbourne
Mexico City   Nairobi   Paris   Singapore
Taipei   Tokyo   Toronto

and associated companies in

Berlin   Ibadan

Published by Oxford University Press, Inc.,
198 Madison Avenue, New York, New York 10016-4314

Oxford is a registered trademark of Oxford University Press

Library of Congress Cataloging-in-Publication Data
Kostof, Spiro.
A history of architecture : settings and rituals / Spiro Kostof ;
original drawings by Richard Tobias.—2nd ed. / revisions by Greg Castillo.
p.   cm.   Includes index.
ISBN 0-19-508378-4
ISBN 0-19-508379-2 (pbk.)
1. Architecture—History.
I. Castillo, Greg.   II. Title.
NA200.K65   1995   720'.9—dc20   94-38787

9 8 7 6 5 4

Printed in the United States of America
on acid-free paper

(NB) 97-1605
63656-2

PREFACE

This book is something of a compromise. It is a general survey of architectural history that tries to reconcile the traditional grand canon of monuments with a broader, more embracing view of the built environment.

It does so by making no strict distinctions between architecture and building, between architecture and urbanism, between high cultures and low. Hagia Sophia and Versailles are here, but so are igloos and nineteenth-century malt-kilns; the ducal palaces of Urbino and Mantua are discussed within the larger frame of the city-form; the Romans share their chapter with their "barbarian" adversaries, the Dacians, and the tribes of the sub-Sahara. I wanted to tell a story—the epic story of humans taking possession of the land and shaping communities through the act of building.

The aims are set out in Chapter 1. All-inclusiveness is not one of them. I had to confine myself to a relatively small number of sites and buildings in order to be able to look at them in some detail. It was important that this treatment of selective places be full. Architectural style comes in of course; that was the core of my training. But I am as concerned with use and structure and urban process, with motivation and ritual sequence. I would not be at all unhappy if the book were to be seen as an offering of cultural history.

Despite its seemingly ecumenical reach, this cannot claim to be a world history of architecture. That task would entail a fair balance in the account of architectural traditions in all ages and on all continents. We are preoccupied with our own Western tradition. Even with the most permissive attitude, other cultures stand as foils to this perhaps inevitable self-absorption. My limited goal was to resist presenting the Western achievement as if it were an insulated and wholly logical progression. We have always been bound up with other lands;

and the order we have created gains in understanding when it is assessed in the light of alternate orders. As a symbolic recognition of this interdependence, I have avoided discussing non-Western traditions tidily in their own individual chapters. It seemed to me that the excitement of confrontation might outweigh the obvious advantage of separate linear narratives. So I have brought together medieval Florence and Cairo, Palladio and Sinan.

I have also committed one further breach of historical practice. In order to keep the discussion of one place intact, I have introduced some architects ahead of their strict chronological slot. I hope old hands will not be unduly distressed to meet Giulio Romano at Mantua before they meet Bramante in Rome.

Through the years, Richard Tobias has been a steady collaborator. This is as much his book as it is mine. His drawings go beyond mere illustration. They strengthen and clarify the approach of this historical survey, and they convey information far in excess of the limits of the text.

We agreed on some things at the beginning and stayed with them. Except when they remained diagrammatic, all plans would be oriented toward the north. They would also indicate setting—land contours or neighboring structures. Where possible this setting is original to the building. In cases where we could not reconstruct what was there at the time, say for Chartres Cathedral or the imperial külliyes of Istanbul, we settled for the best premodern context we could find. Finally, we wanted to convey the sense of the slow, accretive development of familiar monuments and sites by showing in sequence the principal stages in their planning history. The multipart drawings of Karnak and the Piazza San Marco are examples.

It should be self-evident that a history of this kind reaps the collective effort and

wisdom of scholars in several fields. Since the nature of the book precluded the customary apparatus of notes and extensive bibliographies, I must acknowledge my enormous debt to them all here, a debt which in a number of cases approaches dependence. I must also single out at least some among the many colleagues and friends who offered help at various stages of the project: Marc Treib, Andrew Stewart, Walter Horn, Stanley Saitowitz, Hsia Chu-Joe, and Ian Robertson-Smith. Readers of drafts include Christian Otto, Richard G. Carrott, Osmund Overby, Christopher Mead, and Henry A. Millon. A most patient and sympathetic review came from Elizabeth M. Brown; her scrutiny improved the book tangibly, and I am deeply grateful to her.

The long process wore out several assistants. I will always remember them with gratitude: Wendy Tsuji, Deborah Robbins, Michael Brooder, Carol Silverman, who valiantly tackled the index, and D'vora Treisman. In the final stretch, Mari Adegran and Susan Shoemaker lent their skills to the completion of some of the drawings. To Douglas MacDonald, I owe the most. He has worked long and hard on sources, illustrations, and the glossary, and ably served as liaison with the publisher. On that side, our main ally was Kathy Kuhtz. My fond thanks also to my editors, first, James Raimes, who took the project through its critical starting phase almost ten years ago, and, more recently, Joyce Berry.

To my students, past and future, this book is fondly dedicated: it was written with them foremost in mind.

Berkeley   S.K.
October 1984

PREFACE TO THE SECOND EDITION

In May 1991, Spiro Kostof delivered his last lectures for "A Historical Survey of Architecture and Urbanism"—the long-running course at the University of California at Berkeley that some twenty years earlier had provided a springboard for the first edition of this book. The final lectures, covering the state of affairs from after World War II to the present, had been thoroughly revised a year earlier, and Professor Kostof felt that they were a great improvement. His enduring goal had been to construct an architectural history that avoided "strict distinctions between architecture and building, between architecture and urbanism, between high cultures and low." The closing chapter of the first edition of *A History of Architecture,* written in the early 1980s, fell short of that resolution, having shrunk in scope to a review of "the works of the masters," just the kind of history he had set out to challenge.

In the years following the publication of this book's first edition, Professor Kostof undertook projects that confronted architecture's current events head-on. These included *America by Design,* a 1987 PBS series and a companion publication of the same name, as well as *The City Shaped* and *The City Assembled,* a two-volume study of urban form and its social meanings. Both efforts sent him traveling to sites that embodied the exceptional as well as the ordinary in late-twentieth-century environmental design. The surer footing gained from this research was evident in the updated lectures for Berkeley's survey course, and a revised edition of *A History of Architecture* incorporating these changes was put on the calendar as his next assignment.

In June 1991, Spiro Kostof was diagnosed with cancer. He died six months later at his home in Berkeley. As his research assistant of five years' standing, I was asked to prepare the manuscript of *The City Assembled* for publication. Soon afterward, I decided to take on, as well, Professor Kostof's planned revision of *A History of Architecture.* In both cases, I have attempted to chart a conservative course, limited wherever possible to reconstructing his arguments and the spirited style with which he addressed them.

Professor Kostof's working methods greatly simplified my task. His habit was to prepare complete scripts for his lectures, which he then would commit to memory. These typescripts established the narrative framework and basic text for the final chapters of this edition. Another useful resource was the collection of lecture videotapes now archived at Berkeley's Bancroft Library. Kostof's lectures were recorded in 1990 and 1991, ostensibly for the benefit of students who had missed class, but just as much to give him the opportunity to review and fine-tune his performance. More than one digression from his script, as documented on tape, has found its way into this edition. Nonetheless, the text of a lecture, however polished, is not that of a textbook. Whenever a site or a topic glossed in class demanded more detailed description, I have added it, following the vector and tenor of Kostof's argument to the best of my abilities.

For their help in refining the finished text, I must thank Karl Weimer, as well as Gary Brown, Marta Gutman, Kathleen James, Roger Montgomery, and Steven Tobriner, all at Berkeley's College of Environmental Design. Richard Tobias, Professor Kostof's original collaborator on illustrations for

this publication, again contributed his skills and patience. I also owe a debt of gratitude to Nezar Al Sayyad, Travis Amos, Ken Caldwell, Sam Davis, Diane Favro, Alan Gottlieb, Alan Hess, Carol Hershelle Krinsky, Emily Lane of Thames and Hudson, Nina Libeskind, George Loisos, Christopher Mead, Jean-Pierre Protzen, Maryly Snow and Claire Dannenbaum of Berkeley's Environmental Design Slide Library, Stephen Tobriner, Susan Ubbilohde, Dell Upton, and Fikret Yegul for their help in assembling photographs for this second edition. Kathryn Wayne and Elizabeth Byrne of the Environmental Design Library at Berkeley were, as always, generous with their assistance. And Joyce Berry of Oxford University Press, now a veteran of three Kostof publications, again proved her considerable editorial and diplomatic talents.

Every effort of this sort deserves a dedication. In keeping with my role as the facilitator rather than the author of this volume, I will defer on that count to Professor Kostof, whose meditations were captured on videotape in May 1991 in one of his final public lectures.

Last week was the last lecture of the great Vincent Scully: a terrific mind, a terrific imagination. His course closed after being taught since the early 1940s. He retired unwillingly. He wanted to go on and on until he dies, as most of us do. For whatever it's worth, I dedicate these final lectures to him, my one-time teacher, longtime adversary, and a man who did more for architectural history than most of us put together.

Berkeley   G. C.
October 1994

CONTENTS

CONTENTS

PART ONE

A Place on Earth

Thomas Cole, *The Architect's Dream*, 1840; detail.

1

THE STUDY OF WHAT WE BUILT

The History of Architecture

A history of architecture is both less and more than a grand tour. It does not have the immediacy of walking through the streets and public places of towns as diverse as Isfahan and London, or stepping into covered spaces that range in mood from the dappled, swarming tunnels of Muslim suqs to the single-minded sublimity of the Pantheon in Rome. (Figs. 1.1, 1.2) That is how architecture is meant to be known. As the material theater of human activity, its truth is in its use.

Although a book such as this cannot stand in for "the foot that walks, the head that turns, the eye that sees," as Le Corbusier once described the experience of architecture, it has its own deliberate advantage. For one thing, the book is a compact world. It lets one shift in minutes from Mesopotamia to Peru. Then, it is panoramic. The reader who leafs through it is not unlike the lone figure in this nineteenth-century painting by Thomas Cole entitled *The Architect's Dream*. (Fig. 1.3) The figure reclines luxuriously on top of a column of classical inspiration; before him, past traditions of buildings are composed grandly, like a hybrid movie set. Time is the river that flows toward him, and on its banks are lined the familiar forms of his professional vision: the pyramids, battered walls, and plant columns of Egypt; Greek temples and Roman aqueducts; and closer still, outlined against the glow, the pinnacles and lance-like towers of medieval Christendom. He is an architect, and what he looks upon is the idealized heritage of his craft. He could

draw from this vast and varied wealth, as nineteenth-century architects did, to give shape to contemporary buildings of his own.

Like him, the reader of an architectural history is alone among the built riches of the past, put in order, illustrated, and accounted for. He or she can learn the names of buildings and their makers, and when and how they were made, and other ready information that is not always at our disposal when we travel. A visit to Rome or Istanbul is bound to be confusing. There is so very much to see, and it seems to lie about unsorted, helter skelter. A group of temples from the time before Christ is ringed by recent apartment houses; brick-and-concrete clumps refuse to yield their identity. The historian brings time under control; isolates random scraps and arranges them into a trenchant sequence; sets up relationships among farflung structures, through the hindsight of this day and the collective knowledge of the discipline. What is a ziggurat and how was it used? What sort of people built it? How does it compare with an Old Kingdom pyramid or the stepped platform of a Meso-American temple?

The historian does this, first, by insisting on the recapture of the true physical reality of things built, whether they have since been altered, damaged, or destroyed totally. This is a primary task, akin to archaeology, and makes use of material that is both visual and literary in nature. And then the historian must go beyond this established reality of the buildings to under-

stand what they are, how they came to be, and why they are the way they are.

The Pictorial Evidence
Buildings are often born of images and live on in images. Before there is a foundation trench or a single course of stone, a building has to be conceptualized and its form may be represented in models and drawings. Models of the building in small scale, in clay or wood or plaster, give a full impression in three dimensions of the final product that is being projected. Pictorial views might present the future building's ideal appearance: on commemorative medals, for example, struck at the time of the laying of the cornerstone, or on presentation drawings elaborately rendered in perspective. And there are other, more abstract drawings. *Plans* show in two-dimensional pattern the horizontal disposition of solid parts, like walls and columns, and the voids of entramed or enclosed space. *Sections* slice through the building vertically at some imagined plane to indicate the sequence of rooms in length and the superimposition of floors and roofs in height; they also indicate openings, whether they are physically accessible or not, and so help to explain structure. *Elevations,* using a vertical plane, flatten out one face of the building to indicate schematically the order of its parts.

To the initiate, a ground plan of the church of Hagia Sophia in Istanbul tells at a glance that strings of columns alternate with heavy piers to describe a large square

Fig. 1.1 Aleppo (Syria), suq, or covered market; interior.

Fig. 1.1 Aleppo (Syria), suq, or covered market; interior.

bay and smaller semicircular spaces beyond—the central core of the building. A longitudinal section through this core makes clear that the columns are disposed in two tiers and that, further up, a system of curved roofs over the smaller spaces builds up to the full dome that covers the central square. (Fig. 1.4) Externally, the relationship of the dome to the upper walls of the square and then, in descending order, to a major half-dome, to two minor ones flanking a large semicircular window, to banks of grilled lower windows punctuated by spurs of a buttressing wall, and finally to gates seen through arched recesses at the ground level—all this can be frugally abstracted in an elevation drawing of the west front.

These particular drawings are newly made; but some version of them was undoubtedly prepared in the sixth century by the architects of Hagia Sophia, Isidoros and Anthemios, to convey to their patron, Emperor Justinian, the form of the church he had commissioned. There are extant architectural drawings from as far back as ancient Egypt and Mesopotamia. Indeed, it is hard to see how any structure but the simplest and the most traditional could be built without the benefit of such preliminaries.

Now these devices are formal. In almost every instance they would have been preceded by dozens of sketches and diagrams as the architect's thought developed from an initial conception of the building to the final solution. When they survive, and are properly put in order, such studies help to document the very *process* of design. Look at the plan of Louis Kahn's National Assembly at Dacca, Pakistan; and at another wisp of form in pencil that started it all. They bracket the elusive but fundamental substance of what we call architecture, a complicated course the historian must traverse to make sense of its tangible end, the building itself. (Fig. 1.5)

Fig. 1.2 Rome (Italy), Pantheon, ca. A.D. 118–26; interior, view toward dome.

Fig. 1.3 Thomas Cole, *The Architect's Dream,* 1840. (Toledo Museum of Art, Toledo, Ohio)

The point to remember, then, is that graphic and plastic images are indispensable in the making of architecture—and for its understanding after the fact. They are the conventional language through which the architect communicates with his partners in the act of shaping our daily environment. These are the patron or client who employ the architect to mold their architectural wishes, and the many hands involved in building the structure. That same language assists students of architectural history to get to know structures they have never seen or have seen and not comprehended in full, and one of the earliest tasks for them is to learn to read architectural drawings and models with ease.

Once a building is up it becomes a live presence, to be reproduced at will. It might figure on paintings and sculpture in relief, on prints, maps, or photographs. Models of it might be made to serve as votive offerings to a germane cult, for example, or to be sold as mementoes to visitors or pilgrims. For the history of architecture there is valuable information in all of these reproductions. But we have to be cautious in interpreting the evidence they provide, because the conventions of the various media employed are peculiar to themselves. A photograph is a faithful record that registers all incidents of form, however trifling, that fall within the range of its fixed frame. In the hands of a painter the same building may be pictured less clinically, its mass generalized and rendered in sharp, simple surfaces of shadow and light. (Fig. 1.6) This is testimony of a different kind. Yet it can be just as useful as the photograph; for architectural reality has more to it than stick and stone, and the history of architecture more dimensions than just the categorical.

The Literary Evidence

Literary sources, like images, yield much essential insight for our study of architecture. The birth of most structures of consequence assumes the existence of written documents, some of which may come to be preserved by design or accident. At times, patrons may express their wishes to the architect in writing. The architect, in turn, may have passed on written instructions to subordinates. Legal contracts delineate the precise responsibilities of the parties concerned. The erection of public monuments necessitated administrative committees whose trail can be followed in the minutes of their deliberations, reports, and records of payment. Beyond this immediate context, architectural production would have been affected, directly or indirectly, by the towns' building codes, ordinances of building trades and guilds, theoretical treatises, and manuals of construction.

Again, as with visual representations, the building may live in literary sources long past its completion. First, there is self-serving advertisement after the fact. Patrons often sing the praises of their creation in dedicatory or commemorative inscriptions or tablets. It was the function of court historians to extol the building program of their employer. We also have to heed descriptions of past buildings in old travel accounts or in annals and local chronicles. In all of this, historians of architecture need to borrow the philologist's discipline. But language, the agent of expression, is also the hotbed of ambiguity. And the translation of words into the physical substance of architecture is peculiarly open to contention.

We might illustrate this point by focusing on one monument of antiquity, the famous tomb of King Mausolos of Caria at Halikarnassos that gave us the word *mausoleum.* It was considered one of the seven wonders of the Classical world. It disappeared long ago with hardly a trace except for fragments of its sculptural decoration, now housed in the British Museum in London, and odd bits of the structure that were built into the castle of Bodrum which occupies the site. The Mausoleum of Halikarnassos lived on in memory through mentions of it and its creators in later Latin literature, of which the most detailed is a passage from the *Natural History* of Pliny the Elder.

This is the tomb that was built by Artemisia for her husband Mausolos, the viceroy of Caria, who died in the second year of the 107th Olympiad [351 B.C.]. . . . On the north and south sides it extends for 63 feet, but the length of the facades is less, the total length of the facades and sides being 440 feet. The building rises to a height of 25 cubits and is enclosed by 36 columns. . . . Above the colonnade there is a pyramid as high again as the lower structure and tapering in 24 stages to the top of its peak. At the summit there

5

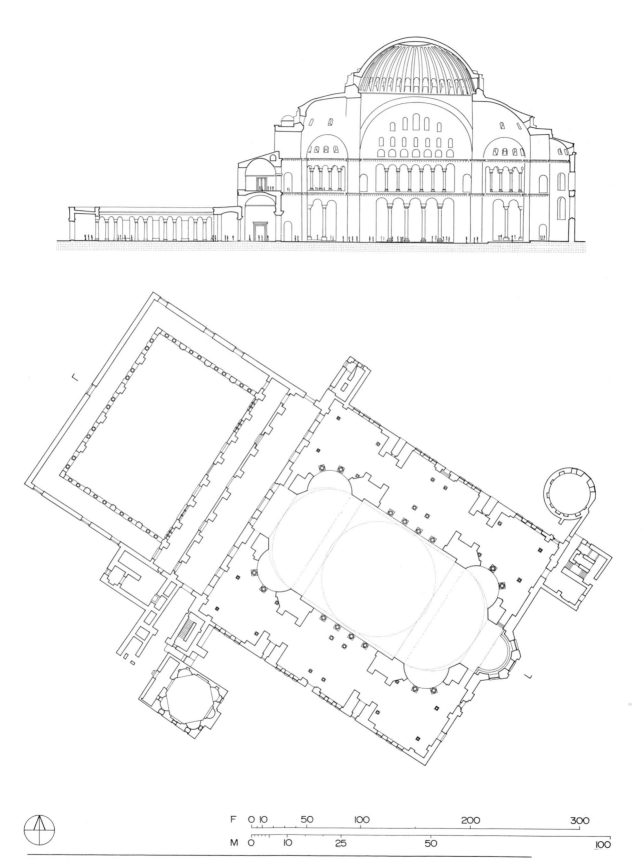

F 0 10   50   100   200   300

M 0   10   25   50   100

Fig. 1.4 Istanbul (Constantinople, Turkey), Hagia
Sophia, 532–37, Isidoros and Anthemios: (**a**)
longitudinal section; (**b**) ground plan.

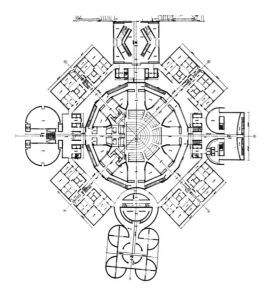

Fig. 1.5 Dacca (Bangladesh), National Assembly Building, 1965–74, Louis I. Kahn: (**a**) ground plan; (**b**) sketch plan, 1963.

is a four-horse chariot of marble, and this was made by Pythis. The addition of this chariot rounds off the whole work and brings it to a height of 140 feet.

Recreating the physical appearance of the Mausoleum on the strength of these words is an exceedingly difficult procedure. First one has to establish the accuracy of the words themselves. Pliny lived two thousand years ago. His book came down to us in various texts, in Latin and Greek; these contain disparities or alternate readings because of different copyists—and the interpretation of modern scholars. This is no trivial matter. Dimensions, whether written in Roman numerals or small letters and accents in the Greek manner, are easily miscopied or misread. And yet they have to be the basis of any reconstruction. Transpose the two initial letters of the word and *altitudinem* becomes *latitudinem*, changing the meaning of "a pyramid as high again as the lower structure" to "as wide"; both readings have their adherents.

There were four centuries between Mausolos and Pliny. The description itself may therefore be inaccurate and Pliny may have erred in writing. At least one scholar believes that, when Pliny gave the width of the north and south sides as 63 feet, he really meant to say cubits, a unit of measurement that is one half of a foot longer: there is no other way in which the dimensions of the original foundations as they have been extracted from the site could be reconciled with such a small figure. And of course the passage in question does not furnish all the particulars. It does not say, for example, how high the pedestal was or how the columns that surrounded the building were arranged.

Historians must juggle all these variables and come up with a building that is a fair interpretation of the literary and archaeological evidence—and a credible form architecturally. They must deduce from the one surviving column the style of the bases and the cornice of the surrounding colonnade, relying on the current knowledge of the general development of Greek architecture. It should not surprise us, then, that two versions of the Mausoleum of Halikarnassos as different as the ones we illustrate could be spawned by the same data. (Fig. 1.7)

The Total Context of Architecture

The effort to establish, through the scrutiny of visual and literary documents, what past architecture really looked like will have already involved us with questions not strictly pertinent to physical form. These might include the identity of the patrons, particulars about the motivation for the buildings commissioned, the identity and careers of the architects, the nature of the materials of construction and their provenance, matters of finance, and so on. But even this is not the outermost limit of the legitimate concern of architectural history. We have to push further still, to the broader frame of general history, for those strands or patterns that illuminate the total setting of architectural production.

Architecture, to state the obvious, is a social act—social both in method and purpose. It is the outcome of teamwork; and it is there to be made use of by groups of people, groups as small as the family or as large as an entire nation. Architecture is a costly act. It engages specialized talent, appropriate technology, handsome funds. Because this is so, the history of architecture partakes, in a basic way, of the study of the social, economic, and technological systems of human history. To understand the Carson Pirie Scott department store in Chicago fully, we must know something of late-nineteenth-century American capitalist enterprise, the philosophy of consumerism, and the business ethic; the urban history of Chicago since the Fire of 1871; corporate financing and land values; the genesis of the department store as a novel concept in commercial architecture; the elevator and the early history of steel-frame skyscraper construction. (Fig. 1.8)

This approach should be kept in the foreground as the ideal way to learn about our built environment. If we are to be satisfied with less, as we must, it should be on the condition that we agree on what the *total context* of architecture is. Every building represents a social artifact of specific impulse, energy, and commitment. That is its meaning, and this meaning resides in its physical form. Neither material reality alone nor general background of culture will suffice to explain the peculiar nature of the building. And the task of the architectural

Fig. 1.6a Jean-Baptiste-Camille Corot, *The Colosseum Seen from the Farnese Gardens*, 1826. (Louvre, Paris, France)

historian, in the long run, can be nothing less than the search for the peculiar nature of those artifacts of place that constitute our architectural heritage.

Let us describe plainly at the outset the thinking that will govern our historical inquiry. It is not a universal approach among architectural historians: it need not be. The selection for emphasis among the many specimens of architecture, the arrangement and interpretation of facts known about them, the personal judgment of each historian, the vantage point of the time and philosophy within which he or she operates—all these variables help create as many histories of architecture as there are historians. In that sense, history is manufactured by historians, and any building or person or event in this process can acquire as much weight as is consonant with each historian's purpose.

There are four premises that underlie the scope and treatment of our survey. First, the material aspect of every building should be looked at in its entirety. Second, the building should be thought of in a broader physical framework and not just in terms of itself. Third, *all* buildings of the past, regardless of size or status or consequence, should ideally be deemed worthy of study. And finally, the extramaterial elements that affect the existence of buildings should be considered indispensable to their appreciation.

1. *The Oneness of Architecture*

The tangible presence of a building is indivisible. The structure that holds it up, the aesthetic refinement of its appearance, its decoration and furnishings are all of one piece. We cannot put aside the mosaic scheme of the interior of a Byzantine church on the grounds that, being inessential to the

Fig. 1.6b Rome (Italy), Colosseum, A.D. 72–80; aerial view.

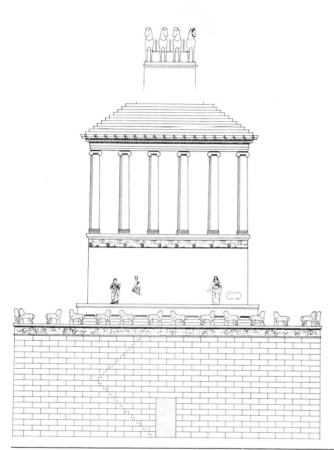

Fig. 1.7 Halikarnassos (Bodrum, Turkey), tomb of King Mausolos, ca. 355–350 B.C., Pythios and Sa- tyros; reconstruction drawings: (**a**) by K. Jeppesen, 1958; (**b**) by J. J. Stevenson, 1896.

architectural frame as such, it is best dealt with independently by *art* historians. Not only are Byzantine mosaics physically inseparable from the architectural frame of their buildings, their placement takes advantage of this frame to set up a ceremonial hierarchy of parts basic to the theater of liturgy housed therein, and their subject informs this theater with precise theological meaning. (Fig. 1.9)

For similar reasons, we cannot divorce the structure of a building from the aesthetic conventions that shape its appearance— what we call its *style*. Buildings are neither primarily structural frames, nor primarily envelopes of form: to write a history of architecture from the perspective of one of these in favor of the other would be pre-

cisely to deny the physical integrity of the buildings. Preoccupation with structure leads to technological determinism, the kind of thinking that is attempted to explain all major characteristics of the form of the Carson Pirie Scott store in terms of the elevator, prefabrication, and the steel frame. The contrary preoccupation with the elements of design—the interweaving of vertical and horizontal members, the rounded corner at the crossing of State and Madison streets, the rich ornamentation of the entrance pavilion—would tend to equate skin with substance and dilute the fact that Louis Sullivan's is not exclusively an abstract mold of visual order but a construction of enormous scale that has managed to stand up and to remain standing.

And yet here, as in many other buildings, the special excitement of architectural intention resides in the tug of war between the structural and formal systems. One or the other at times may seem to take over openly and condition the final effect the building will have on its users. The Eiffel Tower, for example, seems structure triumphant. By contrast, the simple underlying construct of uprights and lintels transforms the Greek temple, at least superficially, into something approaching pure form. But if for the Eiffel Tower the exposed tangle of metal struts is the better part of the form, for the Parthenon on the Athenian Akropolis the clear statement of form, the exterior colonnade with its gabled ends, is also an appropriate diagram of the structure. The two buildings may start from opposite impulses, but they reach the same result. Structure and form are basically one and the same. (Figs. 1.10, 1.11)

In most instances, however, the partnership is more intricate. Look again at the church of Hagia Sophia, and you will notice that the impression it conveys to those within is engendered by means of a strong structural skeleton, purposely obscured by the architects. (Figs. 1.4, 11.28) The heavy-set piers detectable on the plan, to mention only one point, are veiled in three dimensions, at least toward the nave, so that only a thin projection of them is allowed beyond the columnar screen that separates the nave from the aisles. As a consequence, it appears that the great dome rests lightly on the lower structure of the building, soaring without effort; while in reality its full weight presses down on those four tremendous masonry piers. But what under close analysis seems at odds—structural fact and aesthetic intention—is in actuality an integral fabric that cannot be judged but as an entity.

2. *The Setting of Architecture*

No building is an isolated object, sufficient unto itself. It belongs in a larger setting, within a bit of nature or a neighborhood of other buildings, or both, and derives much of its character from this natural or manufactured environment that embraces it. The Parthenon does not exist without the emphatic outcrop of rock called the Akropolis on which it perches and the visible range of mountains beyond, which rings the arid bowl of Attica. The setting of Chartres Cathedral or the Carson Pirie Scott department store is quintessentially urban. (Fig. 1.12) The scale and authority of both buildings depend on the stamp of surrounding construction—small-scale residences in the case of Chartres, tall commercial development in the case of the store. Changes in this urban situation during the course of time will promptly affect the character of the two buildings. We must, then, consider past buildings not as permanent bodies in a vacuum but, instead, components of a variegated arrangement subject to constant change. From this perspective the history of architecture may be said to be, in part, the study of the interaction of buildings with nature and with one another.

Fig. 1.8 Chicago (Illinois), Carson Pirie Scott department store (formerly Schlesinger and Mayer department store), 1899–1904, Louis Sullivan (extension, 1906, Daniel H. Burnham and Co.).

The way we experience architecture also works against the notion of buildings as fixed objects. Tools of design such as models and drawings yield a rigid sense of architecture, a sense furthered by the requisite stability of buildings. But our experience of architecture is not one of static images. We move up to a building and through it and our roving eye registers an infinite number of impressions. We might stumble on the building unexpectedly, or approach it from the back or from the sides. We might catch glimpses of it at sunset or in a winter storm or look down on it from taller structures in the vicinity. Trying to account for this arbitrariness, to be conscious of setting, environmental circumstance, and kinetic vision, brings architectural history within the fold of architectural experience, so that buildings of the past are

Fig. 1.9 Stiris (Greece), monastery of Hosios Loukas, Church of the Theotokos, ca. 1040; interior, view toward dome.

Fig. 1.10 Paris (France), Eiffel Tower, 1887–89, Gustave Eiffel; view from below.

not reduced to neutral relics but manage to keep some of the flavor of their genesis and subsequent use.

How buildings are depicted indicates how they are perceived. To the serious travelers of the eighteenth century, like James Stuart and Nicholas Revett who took it upon themselves to record the legendary remains of Greece for the first time since antiquity, there are two modes of perception: the topical and the archaeological. (Fig. 1.13) To introduce each monument, they resorted to the picturesque tableau. They show the Parthenon at the time of their visit in 1751, when Athens was a sleepy provincial town within the Ottoman Empire and the Akropolis served as the headquarters for the Turkish governor. The temple stands in a random cluster of modest houses; in it we can see a Turk on horseback and, through the colonnade, the vaulted forms of the small Byzantine church that rose within the body of the temple during the Middle Ages. This is what the Parthenon looks like today, the authors are saying; and this depiction carries at once the quaint appeal of an exotic land and that sense of the vanity of things which comes over us at the sight of the sad dilapidation of onetime splendors.

But when they turn from romance to archaeology, the task of showing the Parthenon not as it is now but as it was then, Stuart and Revett restrict themselves to the measured drawing. They re-create, in immaculate engravings of sharp clear lines, the original design of the temple in suitably reduced scale and with a careful tally of dimensions. We are confronted again with the traditional abstractions of the architect's trade. Indeed, those architects who, in subsequent decades, wished to imitate the Parthenon as a venerable form of rich associational value could do so readily from these precise plates of Stuart and Revett, without once having seen Athens for themselves. In nineteenth-century Philadelphia, for example, the disembodied facade of the Parthenon is reconstructed as the Second Bank of the United States in an urban milieu that is completely alien to the setting of the prototype. (Fig. 1.14)

Against the engravings of Stuart and Revett, we might pit two pencil sketches of the Akropolis made by Le Corbusier during his apprenticeship travels in the early years of this century. (Fig. 1.15) The close-up view is neither picturesque nor archaeological. It does not show us the ubiquitous tourists scrambling over the site, for example, nor any other transient features of local relevance. Nor is the sketch a reproduceable paradigm of the essential design of the Parthenon. Instead, we see the temple the way Le Corbusier experienced it, climbing toward it up the steep west slope of this natural citadel, and catching sight of it at a dynamic angle through the inner colonnade of the Propylaia, the ceremonial gate of the Akropolis. The long view shows the building in relation to the larger shapes of nature that complement its form: the pedestal of the Akropolis spur that lifts it up like a piece of sculpture and the Attic mountain chain on the horizon which echoes its mass. And when Le Corbusier draws on this experience later in his own work, it is the memory of the building as a foil to nature that guides his vision. (Fig. 1.16)

Fig. 1.11 Athens (Greece), Parthenon, 447–432 B.C., Iktinos and Kallikrates.

This environmental approach is new to architectural history. It responds primarily to the increasing concern within the architectural profession for a sympathetic coexistence between new structures and the older neighborhoods within which they are planted. The move lately has been toward respecting the built fabric of our communities as it stands; avoiding egocentric forms or monumental gestures that would disrupt its tone and quality; striving for the enhancement of physical continuities in our cities; and, finally, using nature as partner in the act of building rather than as adversary. Such an inclusive concept of the environment carries a double promise: solicitude for older buildings of any period and any style; and tolerance for the presence of humbler stretches in the built fabric. Both hold important lessons for the history of architecture.

3. *The Community of Architecture*
This is what our third premise is all about: that all past buildings, regardless of size, status, or consequence, deserve to be studied. It has not always been so. Historians have chosen for the most part to concentrate on buildings of evident substance—imposing public monuments, religious architecture, and rich, stately residences.

The preference is not hard to understand. It is on such important or grand structures that a culture expends its greatest energy. Built of costly, durable materials, they last longer than their immediate environment because they are meant to. They are associated with notable patrons and architects of rank. They are the subject of comment in their time and later, and thus provide the historian with sufficient raw material to make a case for them.

But there is more to it than that. The historian of architecture has effortlessly come to identify with the architect, and, like him or her, has accepted the traditional distinction between architecture and building. Architecture in this polarity is high art, a conscious creation of aesthetic form that

Fig. 1.12 Chartres (France) Cathedral, 1194–ca. 1230; view in urban setting.

transcends the practical requirements of function and structure. This preeminent quality is what Vitruvius, the Roman architect who wrote around the time of Christ, called *venustas* (beauty); he distinguished it from the other two, matter-of-fact components of architecture, *utilitas* (function) and *firmitas* (structure). This architectural trinity is best known to the English-speaking world in the famous phraseology of Sir Henry Wotton as commodity, firmness, and delight.

Now delight, *venustas,* makes building an art, the art of architecture. Delight is secured through the offices of the architect, a professional person whose training and talent equip him or her to enhance what will be built with aesthetic appeal. To insist on this prerogative, architects distinguished themselves in the modern period from engineers, who lay roads and ford rivers with the primary aim of solving technical problems, as well as from builders, merchants of new construction who are motivated by

profit. In addition, many buildings come about extemporaneously without the benefit of professional counsel, sometimes even as a grass roots production of shelter by the users themselves.

Since delight, in this scheme of things, is a luxury, and since it assumes the sophistication to feel the need for it and the wealth to afford it, architects have traditionally served the highest strata of society—the state, the religious establishment, the upper classes. Thus, in accepting the dichot-

Fig. 1.13 James Stuart and Nicholas Revett, *The Antiquities of Athens*, 1760–1830, Parthenon: (**a**) contemporary view; (**b**) measured drawing.

omy of architecture and building, historians have allied themselves with this aristocratic view of our built world. The history of architecture became synonymous with the history of monuments.

For a number of reasons, this view would seem to be needlessly restrictive. Much of what we build does not qualify as "architecture" in this strict sense; nonetheless, these buildings are often imbued with quality. The grouping of a Nepalese village in its natural setting, farmhouses in New England, the anonymous streetscapes of Mexican towns—these structures can delight us though they are created without the help of qualified architects. (Fig. 1.17) Indeed, we have lately all become increasingly attracted to a wide range of vernacular idioms, what has come to be known as "architecture without architects." Its appeal proves how unwarranted it is to claim that even the humblest of structures is un-

Fig. 1.14 Philadelphia (Pennsylvania), Second National Bank of the United States, 1818–24, William Strickland; view, ca. 1868.

Fig. 1.15 Le Corbusier (Charles-Edouard Jeanneret), sketches of the Akropolis in Athens: **(a)** distant view; **(b)** Parthenon as seen through the Propylaia.

touched by aesthetic concern or devoid of aesthetic appeal. To be sure, this is an innocent sort of visual order. There is no conscious theory behind it, no intellectualized system of form. But it demonstrates that delight is an elusive thing that may apply as readily to the random and unstudied as it does to the calculated designs of the professional.

There is perhaps a more basic consideration for resisting the distinction between architecture and building. The general purpose of architectural history is to examine the constructive impulses of distant and recent cultures. As with all investigations of the past, the belief persists implicitly that, through a proper understanding of the act of making places, this most essential skill of all without which life cannot, literally, exist, we come closer to understanding ourselves. When we exhort historians to be objective, we mean not so much that they should be unfeeling or uncommitted, but that their assessments should be full and representative. And so it would be as improper to evaluate the constructive impulse of a nation exclusively through its literate architecture—public monuments and buildings of prestige—as it would be to determine its social character on the basis of its leading personages alone. To the extent that American society at the time of George Washington depended on slave labor, to pick one random instance, the architectural history of the period must include slave cabins as well as Mount Vernon.

The truth is that modest structures in the periphery of monuments are not simply of intrinsic value; they are also essential to the correct interpretation of the monuments themselves. Slave cabins, outhouses, herb gardens, and water vats complete the meaning of the plantation house. This may seem obvious to us because Southern plantations are a familiar institution of our recent past. If they were not and we subscribed to the aristocratic view of architectural history, the neglect of the subsidiary buildings might well have contributed to the misreading of our focal object, the plantation house itself.

Our appeal, therefore, is for a more inclusive definition of architecture and, consequently, a more democratic view of architectural history. The aim is to put aside the invidious distinctions between archi-

Fig. 1.16 Le Corbusier, sketch of Assembly Building, Chandigarh, India, 1958.

tecture and building, architecture and engineering, architecture and speculative development; to treat buildings with equal curiosity whether they are religious in intent, monumental, utilitarian, or residential; to discriminate carefully among styles or conventions of form without discriminating against any of them; and to have a genuine respect for the architectural achievement of cultures regardless of their place of origin and their racial and theological identities.

The last two observations deserve a further word. If historians have been partial to high-class buildings as the subject of their scrutiny, they have not always been impartial in their treatment of *all* high-class buildings. They have turned on occasion into active champions of one style at the expense of another, justifying their preference in terms of aesthetic, structural, or even moral arguments. At one time or another, Renaissance architecture was extolled over Gothic; Baroque architecture was deprecated as excessively gaudy; and the dominant Beaux-Arts classicism of public buildings in America at the turn of the century was minimized in favor of the occasional unorthodoxy of design that presaged new directions.

The historian must attempt to speak of architecture as it was, not as it should have been. We have no further control over what has happened. We have the duty to understand sympathetically how it was and why it happened. To scold the nineteenth century, say, for what it did or did not do is, for the historian, no more than personal indulgence. To insist that it should not be repeated is useful and the proper function of the critic.

History has no alternative but to accept that matters of quality are not absolute, that the terms of quality are set by each period if not by each building. Ornament, for example, has had wider acceptance at certain times in history than at others, but there is no universal law regarding the propriety of ornament in architecture. Vitruvius devotes a learned chapter in his book to "The Ornaments of the Orders." To Adolf Loos in 1908, "Ornament is crime." We should not have to decide between Classical architecture and the work of Loos on the basis of some presumed immutable principle of "correct" design.

Fig. 1.17 Magar (Nepal), a village.

This is not to say that in writing about the architecture of the past we can forgo the exercise of critical judgment. It means merely that we must first establish the premises that govern a style or the form of a particular building, and then proceed to judge the style or the building in the context of these premises. Whereas the competitive juxtaposition of the Parthenon and Chartres Cathedral would serve no useful purpose, it would be quite legitimate to compare critically the Parthenon with its

exact contemporary in Athens, the temple of Hephaistos which overlooks the marketplace. (Figs. 1.11, 7.14)

What we have just said has special pertinence for our attitude toward non-Western traditions of architecture. In our general scheme of things, these traditions have always held a secondary place. This imbalance is natural given the preoccupation of each culture with itself. But it becomes reprehensible if the relative inattention to non-Western achievement is justified in terms of general worthiness—the mentality that says: If it is not well known, it is because it does not deserve to be. In a popular history of architecture one could still read, as late as 1956, the following characterization of non-Western architecture.[1]

Eastern art presents many features to which Europeans are unaccustomed, and which therefore often strike them as unpleasing or bizzare; but it must be remembered that use is second nature, and in considering the many forms which to us verge on the grotesque, we must make allowance for that essential difference between East and West. . . . These nonhistorical styles can scarcely be as interesting from an architect's point of view as those of Europe, which have progressed by the successive solution of constructive problems, resolutely met and overcome: for in the East decorative schemes seem generally to have outweighed all other considerations, and in this would appear to lie the essential difference between historical and nonhistorical architecture.

Noxious Western chauvinism pervades the tone of this passage. To call the combined effort of China, India, Japan, and the core countries of Islam around the Mediterranean "nonhistorical" is tantamount to removing one-half of civilized architecture from the realm of serious study and relieving us from the burden of understanding it. Among its products, the Eastern world can boast of the Great Wall of China, the *chaitya* at Karli, the imperial mosques of Istanbul—monuments that would surely belie that the East is innocent of good construction. (Figs. 10.25, 10.18, 19.11)

But all this is beside the point. The central purpose of architecture is not victory over matter. Architecture, in the end, is nothing more and nothing less than the gift of making places for some human purpose. Structure in this process is no more essential than texture or decoration or space. The palace of the Alhambra in Granada, as is plain to any student of its fabric, is shoddily built. Nevertheless, by general admission, it ranks among the most alluring of architectural wonders. (Fig. 1.18)

I have tried in this book to do more with

Fig. 1.18 Granada (Spain), palace of the Alhambra, 1354–91, Court of Lions.

1. The book referred to is Sir Banister Fletcher's *A History of Architecture on the Comparative Method*, first published in London in 1896. The passage we quote is omitted in the revised seventeenth edition, published in 1961.

non-Western architecture than the token chapter or two allotted to it in surveys of this kind. Not only is more space devoted to the subject than is customary, but the content of these alien traditions is brought, at least cursorily, into the discussion of Western traditions. Although the architectural interdependence of East and West is far from being documented exhaustively, or even adequately, cross-cultural chapters throughout the book rely on the artless principle of simultaneity to draw together all significant events of architecture in several cultural areas that coincided at specific points in human history. Our esteem for Chartres Cathedral will be more balanced if we were made aware that this masterpiece of medieval Christianity rose during the same decades in which Indochina saw the specter of the great temple complex at Angkor Wat, the empire of Islam undertook the mosque and mausoleum of Sultan Qala'un in Cairo and the great Seljuk caravanserais of Anatolia, and the Meso-American cultures of the Toltecs and the Maya produced enduring monuments of stone like the ball court and observatory of Chichén Itzá.

Fig. 1.19 Giza (Egypt), pyramids of Mykerinos, Cheops, and Chefren (nos. 3, 2, and 1, respectively, on Fig. 4.11), ca. 2570–2500 B.C.; view from southwest.

4. The Meaning of Architecture

The fourth and final premise of this book concerns the meaning of buildings. Buildings are not only physical presences. To study as fully as we can what they are does not exonerate us from asking why they are there, and why they are the way they are. These questions must be answered, or at least asked, and they must be answered in relation to two extramaterial concepts: *time* and *purpose*.

Time implies sequence. Every building is caught in the web of the fourth dimension. Threads extend from it backward and forward, to other buildings whose existence has touched it or been touched by it. Buildings, to say it differently, are based on buildings. As a building goes up it cannot ignore the millennial landscape of form into which it will soon emerge. Once it is up, it will itself be irrevocable, however long its natural life, as a sound is irrevocable once it has been uttered. The building may delight or disgust us; we may grow to revere it or make fun of it, cross ourselves as we go by it or call it by an unflattering nickname. But we get used to it. It becomes

tradition, a fixture in the continuum of form which new buildings are forever replenishing.

This is not to imply a historical determinism of form, whereby each building must be considered the ineluctable offspring of its predecessors. There are many factors that condition sequence, not the least of which is the intention of the patron and the architect. But tradition is there: it is a language, a source, a challenge. It is the great container of architectural experience, and no building can live outside of it. Behind what we call *architectural revivals* lies the desire to emulate the architectural mode of another place and another time, not only to show esteem for the older tradition, but also in order to associate ourselves with the spirit and values that we think were prevalent there and then. The rule of Charlemagne made a conscious return to the architecture of Rome and Ravenna in order to inspire its belief that it was reviving Roman rule; the age of the Renaissance sought to design its own aspirations based on the model of Classical antiquity; and, closer to

our time, the nineteenth century went through a whole series of revivals—the Gothic, the Greek, the Egyptian, the Romanesque, the Exotic—each with its own rationale of form and association.

But there is at least one further motivation for sequence: the sheer competitive drive that prompted patrons of architecture, time and again through the ages, to create monuments that would outshine the splendor or outstrip the size of some legendary masterpiece of the past. What is being recalled in these is not the physical form but the fame of the prototype. There is no evident similarity between the temple of Solomon in Jerusalem, as we might reconstruct it from the description of it in the Book of Kings, and Hagia Sophia in Constantinople. And yet it was this biblical splendor that Emperor Justinian had in mind when he stood in the nave of his new church on the day of its inauguration, 27 December A.D. 537, and said, *Nenikika se Solomon,* "I have surpassed thee Solomon." Six centuries later the abbot Suger, obsessed with the reputation of Justinian's masterpiece which had established itself as the greatest church of Christendom, took this fame as his special challenge in undertaking to rebuild the abbey church of St.-Denis.

Purpose refers to Wotton's commodity, the way in which a building accommodates its prescribed function. Perhaps a better word would be *ritual*, for function tends to undermine and mechanize the concept of purpose. The function of a tomb is to house the dead. But how adequate a purpose is this for the tomb of the Egyptian pharaoh Cheops? Why the stupendous bulk of this pyramid, the megalomaniacal pile of masonry that weighs millions of tons and rises mountainlike to a height of 143 meters (470 feet). Why all this for the tomb of one man? (Fig. 1.19) Why Hagia Sophia, with a dome 33 meters (107 feet) in diameter, swelling to a point some 55 meters (180 feet) above our heads, if all that is really needed is a capacious hall to contain large congregations of Byzantines? (Fig. 11.28)

"All architecture," John Ruskin wrote, "proposes an effect on the human mind, not merely a service to the human frame." Ritual may be said to be the poetry of function: insofar as a building is shaped by ritual it does not simply house function, it comments on it. The pyramid of Cheops ensures the safety and long-lastingness of the pharaoh's corpse and makes tangible to his people the hope that resides in his perpetuity. Hagia Sophia sings the ineffableness of Christian mystery in providing a space of which one user is man and the other user is unseen and unpredictable.

To the extent, then, that architecture is the useful art that lays ready the stage for human activities, the history of architecture is inevitably linked to the pageantry of human endeavors—government, religion, commerce, knowledge and its preservation, justice and its administration. If it is also true that architecture *expresses* human needs as much as it contains the various functions of our daily life, the history of architecture should try, before it is done, to look at buildings as palpable images of the values and aspirations of the societies that produced them.

This final challenge is the most fundamental, but also the most dangerous. It enters the seductive reaches of interpretation where proof is never positive. Reading buildings as the embodiment of the social order that produced them is no easy matter. For one thing, buildings do not always passively reflect society. Sometimes they seek to mould social attitudes, or to spell out what there *ought* to be. Do the pyramids of Giza truly express the absolute power of the pharaoh, or were they built to help create this impression among the Egyptians of the Old Kingdom? For, as Lewis Mumford once observed, it is often the case that "the more shaky the institution, the more solid the monument; repeatedly civilization has exemplified Patrick Geddes' dictum that the perfection of the architectural form does not come till the institution sheltered by it is on the point of passing away."[2]

Architecture is a medium of cultural expression only to the extent that we are able to absorb its messages. And these messages are elicited through the questions that are preoccupying us today. The way we interpret the culture of a period or a nation through its architecture may tell us as much about it as about ourselves.

But this is no grave danger. It is true that for all our quantifiable information about the pyramid of Cheops, for all our knowledge of Egyptian religion and the beliefs of the afterlife, we will never know what that colossus of Tura limestone and granite meant to the pharaoh and his court, to the priests who officiated at his burial rites and his subsequent cult, to the Old Kingdom peasant who tilled the mud banks of the Nile. But we can be sure that they were not indifferent, any more than we are indifferent to the Washington Monument or the Lincoln Memorial.

That much has remained constant in the long history of our built environment: the involvement we feel with the houses we live in, the sanctuaries we pray in, and where we are buried, the quarters of our oppressors and benefactors, the places of our imprisonment and our healing. For this reason if no other, we must conclude the long process of studying the architecture of eras that have gone by with the fundamental and dangerous question: "What did it mean?" In the impossible answer may lie the humanity of past cultures and ours; for it should be "the task of the architectural historian," to quote an architectural historian, "to prove that there is no past in man's concern for the environment of man."[3]

2. Lewis Mumford, *The Culture of Cities* (New York: Harcourt, Brace, 1938), p. 434.

3. Sibyl Moholy-Nagy, *Journal of the Society of Architectural Historians*, vol. XXVI (1967), p. 181.

Further Reading

B. Allsopp, *The Study of Architectural History* (New York: Praeger, 1970).

B. Fletcher, *A History of Architecture*, 18th ed., rev. (New York: Scribner, 1975).

S. Kostof, *The City Assembled: The Elements of Urban Form Through History* (Boston: Little, Brown, 1992).

———, *The City Shaped: Urban Patterns and Meanings Through History* (Boston: Little, Brown, 1991).

———, ed., *The Architect: Chapters in the History of the Profession* (New York: Oxford, 1977).

R. Mainstone, *Developments in Structural Form* (Cambridge, Mass.: MIT Press, 1975).

H. A. Millon, ed., *Key Monuments in the History of Architecture* (New York: Abrams, 1965).

N. Pevsner, *A History of Building Types* (Princeton: Princeton University Press, 1976).

D. Watkin, *The Rise of Architectural History* (London: Architectural Press, 1980).

Avebury (England), Neolithic circle, third millennium B.C.

2

THE CAVE AND THE SKY: STONE AGE EUROPE

The Beginning

Where do we start with a history of architecture? When did architecture begin?

Human beings, in their own distinctive form, have been inhabiting the earth for more than one million years. For most of that time they were unaware of architecture, if by that term we want to understand the ambitious creation of an environment separate from the natural order. But if, as we suggested, architecture describes simply the act of making places for ritual use, it was one of the earliest human needs.

Indeed, architecture may be said to have been there from the beginning, in raw form as it were, in the very arrangement of nature. For only if we conceive of the earth as a vast and featureless plain stretching unendingly in all directions would we have the total absence of architecture. Once there are ridges and rivers to divide this expanse, hills to punctuate it, and caves to gouge it, the business of architecture has already begun. That is what all architecture provides, regardless of its complexity. It marks off one area to distinguish it from others. It raises solid masses that blot out as much space as their bulk. And it rears about our heads barriers, to contain sheltered space.

The last of these is the easiest to see. We are accustomed to thinking of architecture as *shelter:* a home to live in ("a roof over our heads," as we say), offices and shops to work in, cool places of worship to step into from the crowded streets of a hot day. The sense of refuge is instinctive. It seems natural to build to attain it.

But architecture is more than protective

shells. In seeking to bring about places for ritual action, it must set out to define the boundless, that is, to limit space without necessarily enclosing it in all three dimensions. It does this in two specific ways: through circumscription and accent. In the first, it arrests and patterns the flow of ground. This we might call architecture as boundary; examples are a "plot" of land or a walled town. The second way involves the setting up of free structures that, by their very mass and height, might focus an otherwise undifferentiated stretch of open space—architecture as *monument.*

Boundary and monument both imply a determined marking of nature. Humans impose through them their own order on nature, and in doing so introduce that tug of balance between the way things are and the way we want them to be. Now the first human generations lacked such confidence in their own standing within nature. As they moved about in search of tolerable climate and food, the special environments they gave shape to were tentative and unobtrusive, an architecture of shelter contained in the pleats of the earth.

The shelter, for the most part, was there ready to be used, in the caves that had to be wrested from savage predators such as bears, lions, and the giant hyena. We have proof, however, of huts in the open, like the ones at the encampment of Terra Amata, near Nice in southern France, dating back to about 400,000 years ago. (Figs. 2.1, 2.2) But whether shelter was natural or manufactured, the inhabitants transformed it into architecture through purposeful use. They

made of it the stage of their progressively organized life. They turned a spot of earth into a special place.

And here a chief invention, fire, proved to be a great place-maker. It drove the wild beasts from the caves and kept them at bay; it made the home of the moment safe. But beyond this, the burning fire molded an ambience of companionship, a station for the hunter to pause, cook his game, harden his tools, and communicate with his band of fellows. The earliest hearth known to us, at the great cave of Escale in southern France, goes back more than 500,000 years. That may well be our first documented piece of architecture—a bit of nature informed with the daily ritual of *Homo erectus.*

Terra Amata holds the oldest artificial structures of which we have evidence. The site was discovered accidentally in 1966 during construction at the cliff road to Monte Carlo. It was a stone age camp, used for a number of years, it seems, always briefly during the late spring. In a cove by the beach, traces of some twenty huts were found, often disposed on top of one another—on a sandbar, on the beach itself, and on a dune. They were oval in shape and measured about 8 to 15 meters (25 to 50 feet) in length and 4 to 6 meters (13 to 20 feet) in width. Small bands of about fifteen persons built and occupied them for limited hunting forays; the huts then were left to collapse and new huts put up over them, or else nearby, by next year's party.

The huts were made of branches or saplings set close together in the sand as a

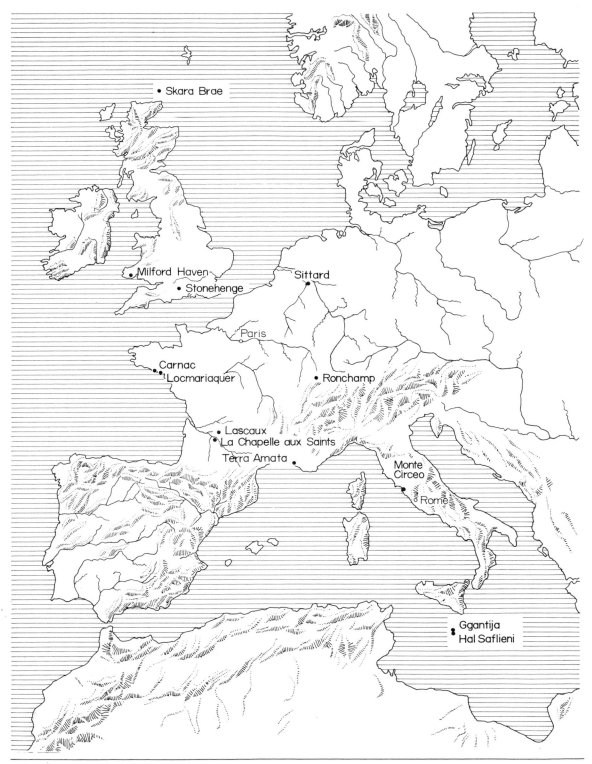

Fig. 2.1 Map: Western Europe, showing Stone Age sites.

- Skara Brae
- Milford Haven
- Stonehenge
- Sittard
- Paris
- Carnac
- Locmariaquer
- Ronchamp
- Lascaux
- La Chapelle aux Saints
- Terra Amata
- Monte Circeo
- Rome
- Ggantija
- Hal Saflieni

Fig. 2.2 Terra Amata (France), prehistoric hut, ca. 400,000 B.C.; reconstruction drawing.

Old Stone Age Architecture

Both building technology and the ritual use of architecture became increasingly so-

palisade, then braced on the outside by a ring of large stones. Within, the long axis was lined with larger posts to help hold up the roof—just how we do not know. We do know something about building tools generally. The digging was probably done with fire-hardened wooden spears; the pruning and trimming, with hand axes made of pieces of flint or limestone.

What is significant is the way in which the hunters made use of the enclosed space. The hearth was in the middle, protected from the prevailing northwest wind by a screen of pebbles. The immediate area around it was free of litter, indicating that there the band must have slept. Further out from this social focus of the hut there were work spaces and, in one case, a kind of kitchen, to judge from the large smooth stone that was marked by tiny scratches, most likely resulting from the cutting of meat. In another hut, fossilized human excrement indicates a toilet area.

phisticated as the millennia went by. During the lifespan of the Neanderthals between 40,000 and 100,000 years ago, and of their successors the Cro-Magnon people, stone tools noticeably improved and now included cutting knives, sharp and easy to grasp. The frame of the huts was sealed against the draft by an exterior sheathing of animal skins. At the same time, the hunters' dealings with nature became formalized into what can only be seen as religious observances. What might have been rites to ensure the hunters' quarry left their mark here and there for us to puzzle over. But the hunters were concerned too with their own related destiny. It was not only surviving day after day that mattered. Death was mysterious and frightening and might not constitute the end.

These anxious thoughts, and the cults that grew up to appease them, complicated the concept of architecture. The role of the shelter was pushed beyond mere housing. The cave became a sanctuary. At its mouth the hunter might still live, but the dark inner recesses came to be reserved for ceremonies of life and death and afterlife. The cave at Monte Circeo, a limestone hill south of Rome, contained a unique chamber

where a single battered skull was stood in a trench along the farthest wall, with stones arranged around it in an oval ring. At La Chapelle-aux-Saints in the Dordogne region of southwestern France, a burial had taken place. The dead man had been laid out in a shallow grave filled with tools and animal bones. On his chest a bison leg had been deliberately placed, perhaps as provision for the world he had slipped into.

Sometime fairly late during this long search for elemental beliefs, the hunters started using art as a tool of expression. It appears likely that, for the communities that produced the splendid cave murals, engravings, and sculpture, the image did more than stand for what it depicted. Art too was reality. It differed from the physical world in that it was free of erratic movement and the biological dictates of growth and death. The mammoth or woolly rhinoceros, fixed to the wall by the artist in a mixture of ground mineral earths and charcoal compressed into bone tubes, stayed there, the sure target of the disabling spear. These images of magic compulsion, if such they were, reinforced the strange power of the cult and quickened its sense of mystery. As ritual use had transformed caves into religious architecture, so art now made tangible a range of meaning in these hidden sanctuaries of the earth.

The Cave at Lascaux

We can see all this in the celebrated cave at Lascaux. It was discovered on a September day in 1940 by five boys from Montignac out rabbit hunting in the woods nearby—the latest and most remarkable of a group of painted sanctuaries that have come to light in the southwest of Europe since the early nineteenth century. They had been created toward the end of the last glacial period. Europe at that time, about 10,000 to 20,000 years ago, had roughly the same Mediterranean coastline, but the great Scandinavian ice sheet reached out to cover most of Ireland, all of Scotland, and the Baltic. There were smaller glaciers in the Alps and the Pyrenees. Hunters followed in the wake of the herds, across the bitterly cold steppes of central Europe and into the milder climate of present-day France and Spain. They brought with them an extraordinary gift for art and put it at the service of a faith that centered on the animal.

The animal, in the hunter's view of the world, must have appeared strong and independent. (Fig. 2.3) The hunter was the dependent and weak one, moving about after his prey—the reindeer and bison, the deer and the horse—in the hope of luring and killing it. The act itself was paradoxical. The animal must be killed to support the hunter. It was the great adversary, deadly in attack and life-sustaining in death. The hunter must prevail; but his success, he knew, would be bound up with defeat. For the more animals he managed to kill, the fewer of them there were left to kill; and therefore the magic that secured the fall of the quarry must also advance its abundance. And so, in these deep caves of France and Spain, the hunter painted the animal truthfully, in the context of this paradox of life and death, of fertility and extinction. Plentiful game was the boon of fertile nature, whom the hunter represented in sculpture as an ample female figure with giant breasts and hips, and comforting recesses like the cave-shelters of the earth. In her hand this mother goddess sometimes holds a horn, the instrument through which the beast's force is expelled. (Fig. 2.4)

This sort of reasoning, we think, must have motivated the makers and users of caves like Lascaux. The paintings convey, across millennia, a striking sense for the build and habits of the animals represented. The attitude toward them seems reverent. According to one school of thought, the caves are sacred repositories of animal spirit, and the hunter's guarantee of participating in the special power of the animal. The painted image is hope and expiation in one—the hope of drawing the animal to the kill, and expiation for having to kill it. Weapons themselves were often carved into animal forms, and men danced in animal masks. At some time, the very eating of the animal came to be a sacrament.

The artists exploited the natural architecture of each cave and conjured an inseparable whole between this and their own images. There was no attempt to change the given configuration, by dropping the floor level, for example, or expanding narrow passages. On the contrary, the difficulties

were scrupulously respected and the artists skillfully set out to complement the peculiar properties of the cave.

At Lascaux, not only were numerous hands busy working on the cave walls, the extensive overlapping of images and the uncertain limits of the cave imply too that the sanctuary was never conceived as a finished thing. We may be dealing with many generations of hunters, each adding its own imprint to the existing design. Both in the making and the presumed benefit of this magical environment, the cave at Lascaux was a community project; and in "community" the present merged with the future and the past.

We enter the cave now, as perhaps one did then, through a hole that was the result of the collapse of a bit of the limestone rock forming the roof of the cave. (Fig. 2.5) About 20 meters (65 feet) in, the path constricts to half its total width, and then opens up dramatically into an oval room, the so-called Hall of the Bulls. A dark ledge here and throughout the cave separates the lower walls from an upper level, which includes the ceiling, and is covered by a thin coat of calcite on which the paint was applied. There was no painting below the ledge.

The far end of the Hall is taken up by a frieze of four immense bulls in thick black outline. Three are in Indian file; the fourth faces them, its huge horns extended across empty space. (Fig. 2.6) The space, in fact, is not altogether empty. Here and all along the remaining walls of the rotunda there is a seemingly random arrangement of smaller animals—horses, deer, and bears. But the confusion is only apparent. It is true that the composition of the walls avoids a single favored focus, and no strict picture frames delineate groupings of images. But there are accents we can detect and visual correspondences even where paintings have been superimposed on others of different date.

The line of the Hall breaks at two points. The first opening, more or less on axis with the entrance, leads into a long gallery that ends in an undecorated tunnel. The floor of this so-called Axial Gallery slopes sharply downward. At one particularly narrow point, a cow of slender build straddles the curved ceiling. (Fig. 2.7) At the farthest end, just before entering the tunnel, a large painted panel shows three horses, one of them

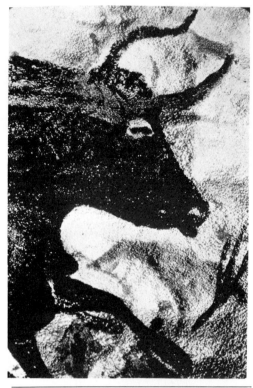

Fig. 2.3 Lascaux (France), prehistoric cave, ca. 10,000 B.C.; interior detail, Axial Gallery.

Fig. 2.4 Laussel (France), prehistoric rock-cut relief, the "Venus of Laussel," ca. 18,000 B.C.; as it would have been seen in its original location. (Musée de l'Homme, Paris)

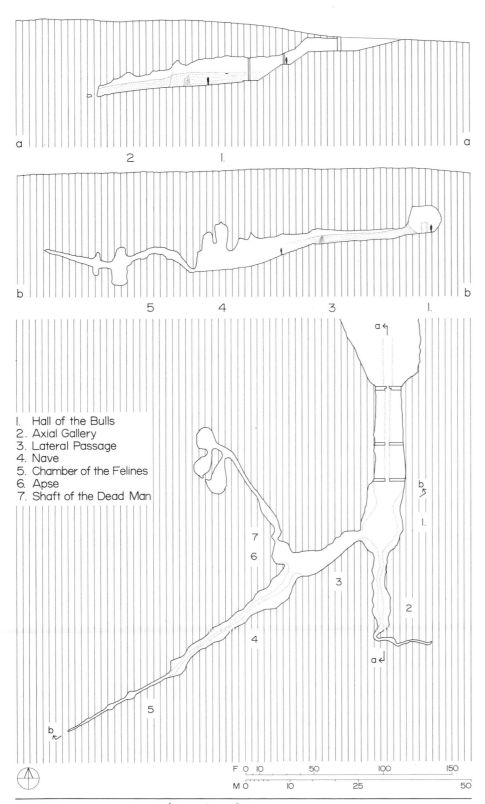

1. Hall of the Bulls
2. Axial Gallery
3. Lateral Passage
4. Nave
5. Chamber of the Felines
6. Apse
7. Shaft of the Dead Man

Fig. 2.5 Lascaux cave: top (**a–b**), sections; bottom, plan.

stumbling over backwards, all four legs in the air. The turn into the tunnel and the exaggerated height of the Gallery at this point heighten the effect of the fall.

The second opening leads to the Lateral Passage. At its farthest end the cave forks. One branch opens out into a vast new gallery, sometimes called the Nave, with a high vaultlike ceiling and a floor that slopes sharply downward toward the back. The animals along the walls have darts depicted on their bodies, but there is no sign of physical pain or collapse. The dramatic skill of the artist and his intimate appreciation of the cave's quirks show to good effect in one corner, toward the Lateral Passage, where a single file of heads of deer in profile is painted just above the ledge. The protrusion of this dark ledge has been worked into the composition. It reads like a body of water through which the beautifully drawn herd is swimming, antlered heads lifted against the current. (Fig. 2.8)

The place of honor belongs to the Shaft of the Dead Man. It lies in the second branch of the Lateral Passage. We come in out of the Passage and into a pouch of the cave called the Apse whose walls are worn through heavy use and marked in every direction. There is a smooth stone at the far end; it forms a lip over a yawning hole, crowned by a small dome. (Fig. 2.9) The bottom of the hole, about 6 meters (20 feet) below the floor of the Apse, must have been reached by means of ropes. The shaft that leads down is too steep to negotiate unaided.

Here, immediately at the base of the shaft, in a small irregular room, there is a painting, the strangest and most affecting of all at Lascaux. (Fig. 2.10) This classic confrontation of man and beast seems to sum up the world view of the prehistoric nomad hunter. The beast is a big wounded bison. The spear is lodged in its strong body; its entrails are coming out. The hunter responsible is himself fatally hurt. He has fallen backwards, gored by the dread horns. He is a small stick figure with a bird's head. Next to him on the ground lie a bird-headed staff and a spear thrower that looks like the ancient Mexican *atlatl*. The hunter, clearly, is the loser in the confrontation. There is nothing pathetic about the beast, which stands proud and triumphant over him even at the point of death.

New Stone Age Architecture

About the time when Old Stone Age hunters were working on the sanctuary at Lascaux, Europe was going through another of the violent changes of climate that had characterized life on the earth since the beginning. It was now a turn of mild weather, a period of warmth that melted the great ice sheets and transformed the European scene of grass- and shrub-covered tundra into stretches of lush forest. The benign climate eased the burden of survival. The hunter slowed down. In many places on the planet, Europe and the Near East among them, he settled and turned to farming and animal husbandry.

It sounds almost too simple in the telling, but what happened was a profound readjustment of humans to nature, and the causes were complicated. To begin with, there were demographic pressures. A swelling population demanded more food than could be secured through hunting and gathering. This meant food production on a systematic basis. To be successful, food production depended on a number of conditions: a settled life, appropriate plant and animal resources, and a technology suitable to the task at hand. Where these conditions prevailed, the new pattern of existence took root. Historians refer to it as the New Stone, or Neolithic, Age.

A fixed place under the sky—that is the Neolithic legacy. The hunter had thought of himself as insignificant in the face of the universal and mystery-filled presence of nature. He was caught up in the flux and flow of life, moving with the herds, courting them, slaying the beasts reverently, and devising magic rituals to ensure their continued abundance. Comfort lay in the depths of the earth. Here, in obscure and womblike caves, the only ray of security in his unpredictable and perilous life was elaborately enshrined. Not security for individuals, or even for single generations, but a kind of timeless unfocused faith in animal spirit, the life-enhancing source.

But the Neolithic revolution shattered this world view, and forged fresh confidence in our ability to tame nature for our own benefit. Humans learned to master the land and the horned beast. The land was marked and tilled, the beast domesticated. There was a new consciousness of the cycles of nature, which is to say of time. The farmer sowed

Fig. 2.6 Lascaux cave, Hall of Bulls.

and reaped and sowed again; the rains came and the cold and then it was warm again and bright and things pushed out of the damp earth and grew, and then once more there came the rains and the cold. Eyes turned upward to the source of moisture and heat. The stars and the moon had patterns that could be recognized and foreseen. Life was stable. In the community each man and woman knew what was expected of him or her, as the community itself had a sense of its specific place in the bigger scheme of things.

Architecture, as we would expect, responded to this basic change in social behavior. The concept of shelter, whether as habitation or sanctuary, persisted of course. But what was revolutionary in general attitude was the readiness to rearrange nature. Farmland began to be divided into individual fields; settlements were similarly circumscribed, if not by walls at least by a simple cattle stockade; sacred ground was distinguished from that of daily life. In addition to this greening interest in architec-

ture as boundary, monuments too made their appearance. Stones were raised upright to mark the open land. (Fig. 2.11) Planted deep in the earth like artificial trees, these tall shafts became signposts of permanence, of civilized life. Architecturally, the cave had been shelter, enclosure, cosmic womb. Now the stone pillars looked up, beyond the elemental comfort of the earth, toward the sky and its knowing patterns of the moon and stars.

The giant stones or *megaliths,* so hard to move and stand up and so striking on the edge of the countryside beyond the farms, must have been proud symbols of community. They spoke of an advanced technology and of group effort. Moreover, they served to focus divinity. Like lightning rods, these markers raised toward the sky brought down on them the sway of deities. We are reminded of Jacob setting up his stone as a permanent Beth El, or house of God.

And Jacob rose up early in the morning, and took the stone that he had put for his pillows, and set it up for a pillar, and poured oil upon the top of

Fig. 2.7 Lascaux cave, Axial Gallery.

it . . . And Jacob vowed a vow, saying "If God will be with me, and will keep me in this way that I go, and will give me bread to eat, and raiment to put on . . . then shall the Lord be my God: and this stone, which I have set for a pillar, shall be God's house. (Genesis 28: 18–22)

Singly or in various combinations, thousands of stone structures were erected throughout Western Europe in the last five millennia before Christ. The megaliths were strewn about in great numbers on the postglacial landscape, along with other debris released by the thawing ice sheets. They could be used on the spot. But the monument builders were not limited to these loose bones of nature. Stone was also laboriously quarried from live rock and sometimes hauled from great distances, by land and by water. The heroic feat was its own reward. It was the utmost the community could do to provide for the sacred.

The Houses

The story of each Neolithic community no doubt began with the search for land suitable for farming and the sustenance of domesticated herds. Often a cultivable patch had to be cleared in the thick of the forest by felling or burning trees. The community would proceed immediately to give itself living quarters and parcel out the farmland.

The settlers normally lived in small individual houses of timber and mud. The timber posts stood in holes dug in the ground and were braced at the top by the roof beams. Boughs were woven through the posts to complete the walls of the house, and the gaps were filled in with mud. The roof was pitched to shed rain and snow, and was covered with thatch or turf. Neolithic villagers along Swiss lakes built their houses on piles, to protect them from sudden floods.

But multiple units of housing were not unknown. Especially in the north, strongly built wooden houses as much as 80 meters (260 feet) long accommodated a number of families, or one extended family, under the same roof. (Fig. 2.12) The hearth was in the middle of the long central space, with a corresponding lantern or louvre cut in the roof overhead to admit light and vent smoke. The aisles on either side of this space were divided into bays and sheltered the animals.

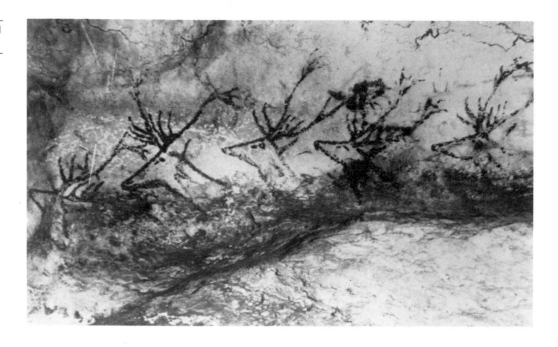

Fig. 2.8 Lascaux cave, Swimming Deer; a detail of the wall paintings in the Nave.

Fig. 2.9 Lascaux cave, Shaft of Dead Man (7 on Fig. 2.5); section.

Fig. 2.10 Lascaux cave, Shaft of Dead Man; detail.

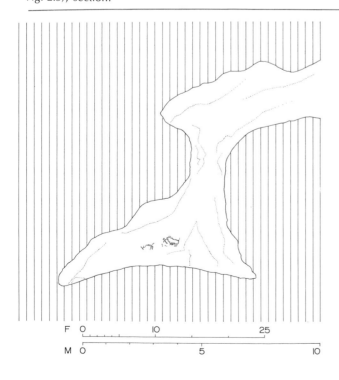

28

Fig. 2.11 Carnac (France), menhir.

Fig. 2.12 Sittard (Netherlands), prehistoric settlement, fifth millennium B.C.; detail of excavation plan showing the post holes and trenches of timber-built long houses.

One instance of multiple housing is unique. In the prehistoric village of Skara Brae, on a small island off the northern coast of Scotland, ten small stone houses linked up by stone alleys form a compact organism. (Fig. 2.13) Each house has a single room with rounded corners. The stone is native, and the builders availed themselves of it for everything, including furniture. The roofs were probably made of animal skins laid on whalebone rafters.

The Monuments
If society in these early villages of farmers and herders had developed a class structure, it left no trace in the pattern of their dwellings. Larger houses were not built for favored people, nothing to call a mansion or a palace. But life may not have been entirely egalitarian. Social distinction seems implied in the fact that monumental tombs honored the remains of some mortals only and not others.

The common dead were disposed of by burning the bodies or simply leaving them on the ground to rot. The burial proper might have taken place in shallow graves, in natural caves, or in long unchambered mounds called barrows. In Malta, the extraordinary rock-cut labyrinth of Hal Saflieni at the top of a hill has tomb chambers arranged on three separate levels for about 7,000 dead. But a privileged few merited lying in state in impressive stone tombs carved with enigmatic designs. With them were buried artifacts—daggers and axes, vessels of various sizes and shapes, both pottery and stone, and personal ornaments in precious materials like gold.

But upended stones, or menhirs, were the simplest form of megalithic monument. The tallest among them, the so-called Grand Menhir Brisé at Locmariaquer in Brittany, once stood up to a height of 21 meters (67 feet) and weighed an estimated 330 tons. Near the town of Carnac, at the northwestern tip of France, more than 3,000 megaliths of local granite line up for several miles in ten to thirteen rows that run east by northeast toward a circle; before reaching the circle they change their angle of direction. (Fig. 2.14) Alignments such as this and circles are two standard compositions for the great megaliths of Europe.

Menhirs, alignments, and circles, unlike tombs, were not intended to enclose space.

Menhirs were objects in mid-space; their height and mass made them visible from a distance and encouraged movement toward them. In this sense they can be characterized as *directional* foci and, as such, they represent our first instance of a principle of organizing space which we will encounter in future chapters under many guises.

At the same time, menhirs are also *rotational* foci. Their form, favoring no one aspect over others, invites us to move around them. This too is a principle of spatial organization. Its object is to give people a reference point as they move about an open space. The central monuments of our city squares—fountains, statues, single commemorative columns—exemplify the same principle.

The stone avenues at Carnac with their circle are the built expression of these two architectural possibilities, the directional and the rotational, inherent in the setting up of a menhir. Alignments and circles, then, outline what is implied. They are examples of architecture as boundary in that they define spatial organization without fully enclosing the spatial forms in question.

But there is more to them than boundary. The large strung stones aggrandize the act of circumscribing. They make of the boundary a monument. In other words, they confound, or rather combine, two of the three classes of architecture with which this chapter began. We can call the alignments of Carnac "monumentalized boundaries," or perhaps even "linear monuments." They afford an intermediate

Fig. 2.13 Skara Brae (Scotland), settlement, third millennium B.C.; plan

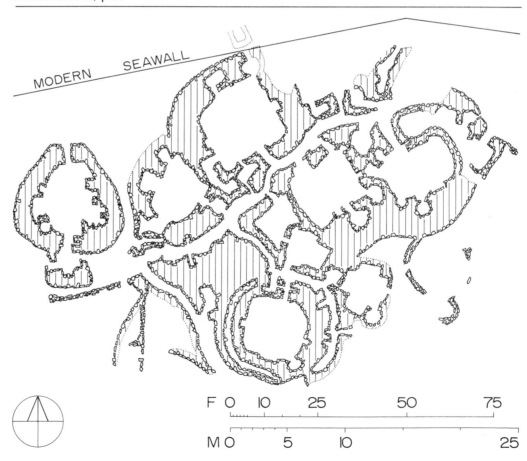

F 0   10   25   50   75

M 0   5   10   25

Fig. 2.14 Carnac, stone alignments, third millennium B.C.; aerial view.

architectural experience between openness and enclosure, between boundless space and a wall. It is an important experience in much of the built environment we will be studying. We might want to think of the stone avenues of Carnac as the conceptual ancestor of the Classical colonnade. (Fig. 12.22b)

The Tombs

In contrast to the menhirs and their groupings, Neolithic stone tombs were designed as closed spaces. The basic form, but not the commonest, is a simple boxlike chamber made up of several upright slabs for walling, with a more or less flat stone on top. (Fig. 2.15) The term *dolmen* should probably be restricted to this type. The other two generally recognized types are more elaborate. The so-called Gallery Grave is a stone corridor closed off by a number of capstones laid in a row. (Fig. 2.16) The bodies were buried along the walls which sometimes converged toward one end in the form of a V. The Passage Grave is similar, but the corridor here culminates usually in a rounded burial chamber. Its walls are made of boulders piled up in irregular courses, a technique called cyclopean masonry. As the structure rises beyond a certain height, successive courses are made to project inward, narrowing the circumference of the chamber until the space is totally sealed off. This is called corbelling. (Fig. 2.17)

Everything else in the construction of the tombs depends on the balancing of large slabs—vertical slabs set on end for the walls and horizontal ones that bridge them across space. The differences between this megalithic technique and cyclopean masonry are evident. The latter relies on the cohesion of many boulders of varying size; it builds by accumulation, and through the careful fitting of the boulders the mason can bring about a fairly tight fabric. Megalithic masonry works with far fewer and larger units. The principle is not unlike building a house of cards, but each "card" weighs tons and the lifting and balancing of it demand massive effort and precise know-how. Moreover, since the fitting of such huge slabs is itself formidable without laborious shaping and dressing, the structure has an uneven mesh, with chinks among the upright slabs and capstones tilting at rakish angles. The

Fig. 2.15 Locmariaquer (France), dolmen, third millennium B.C.

Fig. 2.16 Essé (France), gallery grave, third millennium B.C.; interior view.

Fig. 2.17 New Grange (Ireland), passage grave, third millennium B.C.; interior, view into corbelled vault.

capstones are allowed a generous overhang beyond the edges of the walling.

But in most cases, if not always, the completed tombs would have been submerged under artificial mounds. They mattered, in the main, as interior spaces, houses of stone for the special dead in the ancient embrace of the earth. Exposed, today, they seem to have risen with awkward courage out of the soil and steadied themselves ponderously. In their stark abstraction, they remind us of the primary urge in all architecture, the struggle to stand up against the pull of gravity. Architecture as shelter must encapsulate space in two senses, laterally and in height. The medium of one is the wall, and the wall is the prerequisite for the medium of vertical confinement, the ceiling. The ceiling must be held aloft in defiance of the force of gravity. The heavier the ceiling is, the sturdier the walls must be. Stability in architecture resides in the studied equilibrium of load and support. And the accidental drama of megalithic tombs as they stand denuded in the landscape illustrates stability on the verge of being upset. We have a foretaste here of a standard privilege in architecture, the exaltation of necessary relationships. That is why Le Corbusier's chapel at Ronchamp is a worthy modern successor to a dolmen. (Fig. 28.16) Both gestures of stone celebrate the act, if not the *joy*, of lifting.

Le Corbusier must have known at first hand the megalithic tombs of France. They were real to him as he saw them, deprived of their blanket of earth and battered by time. The inspiration was direct. But if the

tombs help us to see with knowing eyes the bold chapel at Ronchamp, this strong statement of form by an established modern master, unconventional and even jarring for its time, in turn awakens us to the strength of "primitive" architecture such as that made by our prehistoric ancestors. In a parallel way, the formal experiments in the early work of Picasso and Braque seized on the aesthetic provocation of primitive art and through this common language of form taught us to see and value alien things like the masks of Africa and Archaic Greek sculpture.

The Temples of Malta

To conclude our discussion of Stone Age Europe, let us look at two roughly contemporary buildings, one on the small island of Gozo near Malta and the other in the Wiltshire downs of southern England. They are both sanctuaries. Each one took a long time to build because the builders, not content with their initial vision, re-formed and amplified it repeatedly. Taken together, the two sanctuaries illustrate the range of religious expression in Europe by the late third millennium B.C. They typify the complementary impulses of Neolithic communities: reverence for the cave and its ancestral memories on the one hand, and the newfound order of the sky on the other. The double temple at Ggantija speaks eloquently of "chthonic" matters—the earth and its mysteries, the dead and the appeasement they require. Stonehenge, in the

flatland north of Salisbury, charts the heavens.

The complex at Ggantija, or "Tower of the Giants," is not unique. (Figs. 2.18, 2.19) It is one of a number of prehistoric temple structures peculiar to the Maltese islands. They were built of local stone, using a mixture of megalithic and cyclopean techniques, between the early part of the third millennium B.C. and the early second. Their massive walls consist of a double shell filled with earth and rubble. The exterior shell uses coralline, a hard limestone that can withstand weathering. In the hills, coralline fissures both horizontally and vertically, supplying natural building blocks—slabs as well as boulders. The larger pieces among them were brought to the site on rollers, probably spherical balls of limestone. No attempt was made to dress the rough-hewn blocks before they were set up. It is clear that the exterior was considered incidental to the central concern of the temple; it was merely a stout curtain that wrapped itself around the sanctuary without suggesting much of its inner organization.

The experience of the temple was con-

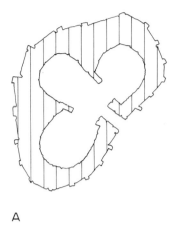

A

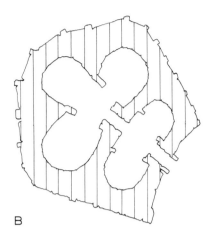

B

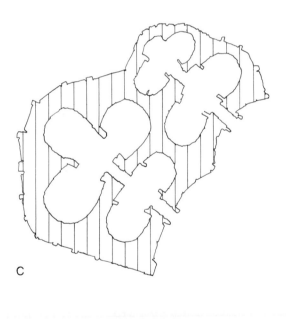

C

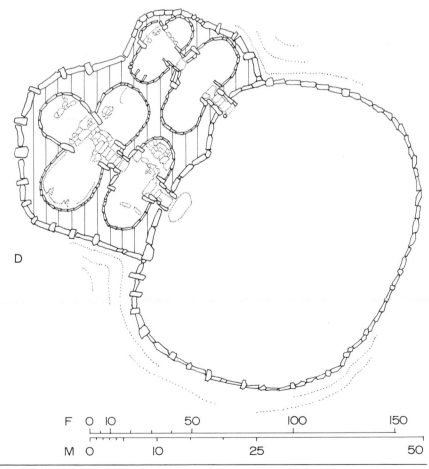

D

F 0 10   50   100   150

M 0   10   25   50

Fig. 2.18 Ggantija (Malta), temple complex, third millennium B.C.; conjectural stages of development: (**A**) beginning phase, large southern temple; (**B**) phase two of large temple, with added pair of curved chambers toward the east; (**C**) the smaller temple added to the original core; (**D**) final plan with circular forecourt.

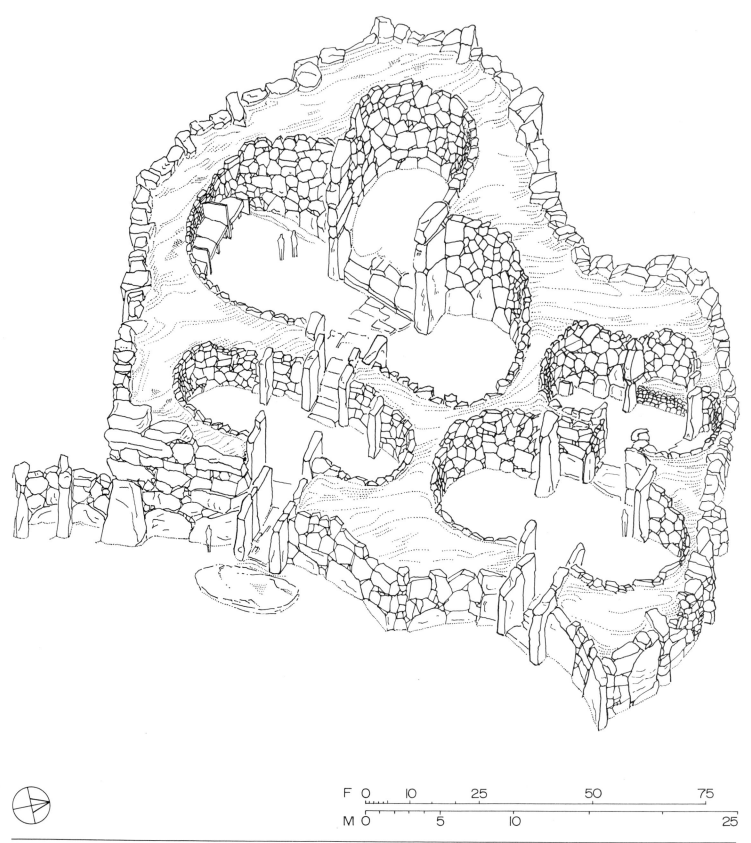

F 0   10   25   50   75
M 0   5   10   25

Fig. 2.19a Ggantija, interior, oblique view; reconstruction drawing.

Fig. 2.19b Ggantija, larger temple, southern apse of west trefoil; interior view. (Cf. Fig. 2.18, D.)

centrated on an enclosed space furnished and decorated in accordance with the needs of an intricate cult. Here the coralline shell was carefully dressed with stone mallets and picks of horn or antler tines. The surface was then finished laboriously by means of small flint blades. Globigerina, a soft warm limestone deep yellow in color, was used for the permanent fittings.

In some ways the Ggantija complex re-enacts Paleolithic cave sanctuaries. From an architectural standpoint, however, there is one notable difference. Lascaux was a natural form, humanized by the art and ritual of its bands of hunters. The sequence of chambers was predetermined and could only be interpreted through the gift of the artist. This was true of each one of the painted caves. They were accepted as they were found, and then defined ritually. There

are, therefore, in one sense, as many different types of Old Stone Age sanctuaries as there are painted caves.

Ggantija is a wholly manmade form, which is to say it is thought out and reproduceable. As such, it is the first true *building type* we are encountering. A building type is an architectural form that is invented for a specific purpose and achieves a general validity, both visual and ritual, through its repeated use. The ziggurat is a building type, and so are the pyramids of Egypt, the Classical temple, the baptistery, the Renaissance palace, the skyscraper, and the railroad station. The list is really relatively small. Although creativity for some people implies the freedom to invent forms, history recognizes a stricter economy of basic forms and, within these limits, a much subtler definition of creative design.

For, of course, there is nothing mechanical or stifling about building types. Their "invention" is neither precipitous nor final. The full form comes about through long experimentation and continues beyond that to be refined, modified, or even purposely perverted. But it remains the basic outline against which the architect works; and being a constant, deviations from it can be judged readily and can become especially meaningful. By reinterpreting the form of the building type one can make a statement about the cultural content with which it is identified.

The cultural content of the Maltese temple as a building type includes the cave of the Old Stone Age hunter. The inwardness of Ggantija, with its staged sequence of constrictions and spatial releases, recalls the passage through Lascaux. The inner shape itself, a double set of curved receptacles, stands as the architectural metaphor for the obese mother goddess of the caves. This lady of fertility continues to be represented in sculpture, as a standard cult image of the Maltese temple. And the horned beast is there, too, again both literally and metaphorically. Animal sacrifice was a main observance of the local cult: remains within the temples and the choice of animals as a subject of temple art testify to that. But, abstractly, the crescentlike facades in front of the double temple at Ggantija suggest great horn gates, a hint strengthened by physical evidence from the larger temple to the south, where below the threshhold slab the horns of a sacrificial bovid were found along with potsherds and an offering bowl.

The other major ingredient in the cultural content of Ggantija is the Neolithic tomb, and specifically the native rock-cut graves for collective burial, like the catacomb of Hal Saflieni. At that catacomb the simplest unit was a kidney-shaped chamber, sometimes subdivided by rock partitions, sometimes joined with others via corridors. These hollowed out pouches undoubtedly inspired the paired curves of Ggantija and its relatives, and did so for a good reason. At some early point it seems likely that the two functions, the burial of ancestors and the propitiation of their spirits, were housed in the same architectural envelope. Elsewhere in prehistoric Europe the separation did not come about; the rites of the dead were celebrated in front of the tomb since the rest was submerged by the burial mound. But at Malta a distinct building type, linked in form to the collective tombs original to the island, absorbed the ritual functions of the ancestor cult, together with related practices, and became a specialized house of worship. (Fig. 2.18)

The Ggantija complex consists of two separate temples of different date enclosed by a continuous outer wall. The larger temple to the south is the earlier, and even that is probably not all of one piece. The west trefoil seems to have come first. This clover-leaf scheme, closely resembling rock-cut tomb formations, must have been the opening stage in the creation of the Maltese temple as a building type. The eastern pair of curved chambers seems to have been an afterthought. When it was added to the initial trefoil, perhaps to accommodate an enlarged repertory of religious practices or bigger crowds of worshippers, the building type assumed this new configuration for its standard design.

Two further changes of consequence took place before the mature temple form was complete; both are illustrated by the smaller temple of Ggantija erected toward the north. First, in terms of size, the order of the two sets of curves was reversed, with the outer set now being the wider. Second, the culminating apse of the trefoil was reduced to a shallow niche in which, at later sites, a single pillar would be enshrined.

The site is a hillside. The temples face downhill. Before their two monumental entrances, the "gates of horn," a circular platform of stone was laid out at some point as a common forecourt, braced by a retaining wall to avoid slippage. Each temple is composed of a long axis, running from the entrance to the back niche and flanked by two pairs of curved chambers of different size. The axis is not of uniform width. Between pairs of chambers, it acts as a small court, its space distinguished from those of the chambers by parapets of globigerina. The narrow points of passage have slabs of fine workmanship and on either side of the one farthest from the entrance two dolmenlike altars are set up. Beyond this point, the south temple picks up a cross-axis. The curved end of one of the lateral chambers is fitted with altarlike slabs and, across the court, at the entrance to the opposite

Fig. 2.20 Salisbury (England), Stonehenge, ca. 2750–1500 B.C.; aerial view.

chamber, a circle of stones must have served as a ceremonial hearth.

Whatever the units of composition, the prevailing sense of Ggantija is one of deep containment. It is the natural quality of curved interior shapes to envelop us totally. In this, Ggantija as an architecture of shelter contrasts with the Gallery Grave as shelter. (Figs. 2.19a, 2.16) There the ceiling is flat and the juncture with the walls is made at right angles. The space is crisp and boxlike. The experience of Ggantija, a folding space that engulfs the user, is different. There is here no strict distinction

between wall and ceiling since the transition from one to another is a curve. The effect is akin to one special feature of Neolithic tombs, the round burial chamber at the end of a Passage Grave. (Fig. 2.17)

Actually, the curved shapes in Maltese temples hold a place midway between the flat-roofed tunnels of megalithic tombs and the round chambers of Passage Graves with their corbelled vaults. The spans at Malta are too wide for complete corbelling. The walls are projected inward at the top, but only up to a certain point; beyond this the gap was bridged, we think, with flat slabs. And since an 8-foot span is the maximum opening a single slab can bridge without the aid of central supports below, of which there is no trace, it is very likely that the culminating portions of the ceilings were fashioned of wood.

In these deep sanctuaries of Malta, a brilliant Neolithic people carried on its sacred rites of pacifying the dead and assuring fertility. The details escape us, but rams and pigs were slaughtered for the gods and libations were poured into holes that maintained contact with the underworld. Here, too, oracles may have been spoken to through tiny windows in otherwise sealed rooms that kept out the profane. The sick and the crippled came to sleep in the wonder-working embrace of the temple, in the hope of being made whole: we have outward signs of their faith in the sculptured figurines of reclining women and the vo-

tive portraiture of hurt or distorted human images. And the earth comforted and healed them until, all of a sudden, about 2000 B.C., the devout culture of Malta was rudely disrupted by invaders, and the temples were abandoned to their ruin.

Stonehenge

Stonehenge, the most famous of Neolithic monuments, is a temple to a different faith. (Fig. 2.20) The haunting circle in the chalk uplands of southern England is not altogether free of the dead. The so-called Aubrey holes just within the bounding earthwork hold proof of cremation burials, for example. But this was probably a secondary function. The early Britons who built and rebuilt Stonehenge over a time span of one thousand years had, from the start, ex-

traterrestrial intentions. Their involvement was with the sun and the moon; their aim, not to communicate with powers of the underworld, but to recognize and celebrate heavenly events. Or so at least many scholars believe.

The final design of Stonehenge is frankly singular. Yet the great horseshoe in the middle was not always there, and the stones that now circumscribe it were not always so disposed. And there was a time at the beginning when there were no central stones at all but only the earth embankment in the midst of the chalk plain of Wiltshire. In these various guises, Stonehenge interlocks with a number of neighboring structures. (Fig. 2.21) There are, first, the large earth circles like the one at Windmill Hill, their circular ditches interrupted by frequent causeways. Were these stockaded cattle pounds, or were they, as their stra-

Fig. 2.21 Map: Southern England, with inset of Stonehenge vicinity.

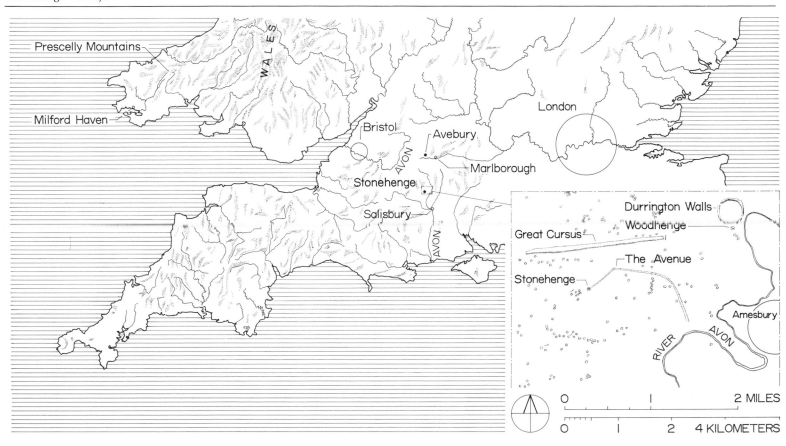

A PLACE ON EARTH

tegic sites would suggest, temporary gathering places for nomadic tribes of herdsmen in times of general celebration? At any rate, they are older than Stonehenge—the oldest surviving structures in England. Then there are circles marked by uprights: either stones, as at Avebury 27 kilometers (17 miles) north of Stonehenge, with two huge interrelated circles; or else wooden posts, as at Woodhenge, closer still, about 3 kilometers northeast. Over 900 stone circles are known today all across the British Isles—in northeast Scotland and Ulster, in Cornwall and Wales.

At Stonehenge, the first stage of building produced the earth circle, 97.50 meters (320 feet) in diameter, that remained constant through all subsequent rebuildings. (Fig. 2.22) It must have been described by an immense compass, probably a stretch of oxhide rope attached to a wooden peg at the circle's center. To mark the circumference, a ditch was dug through the solid chalk, with the usual tools—digging sticks, picks of antler, and shoulder bones of oxen for shovels. The dazzling white earth was piled up on two banks. The circle was broken at one place only, in the northeast quadrant. There, beyond two small uprights that flanked the break in the circle, a tall pillar, of a distinctive grey sandstone from Marlborough called sarsen, was erected. It stood just off the centerline of the break, next to a wooden gateway of four posts, and it stands there still tilted to one side.

The point of this arrangement was first surmised in the eighteenth century. A person standing at the center of the white circle on the morning of the summer solstice, the longest day of the year, and looking in the direction of this so-called Heel Stone, would have seen the sun rise a little to the left of its imposing mass, on axis with the break. It must have been a simple but profound experience, and it happened in a simple but bold-spirited setting of boundary architecture—a round embankment on the broad plateau of Salisbury Plain, at the confluence of many lines of hills along whose ridgeways the people came for the great day.

This seems to have been all that was done in the opening phase of the monument, except for four station stones inside the

chalk palisade that describe a rectangle perpendicular to the axis of the midsummer sunrise, and the ring of 56 Aubrey holes, already mentioned, that may have been meant to hold uprights but were filled up again soon after being dug. The date of this first scheme, known as Stonehenge I, is now thought to be around 2750 B.C.

Then, perhaps several centuries later, the sacred site became the scene of an ambitious new building campaign—Stonehenge II. Pairs of chalk banks, like those of the circle, defined an 8-meter (35-foot) wide avenue along the crucial northeast axis. It ran on straight for a while, and then curved right to reach the river Avon a short distance away. A narrow embanked enclosure about 3 kilometers (1.75 miles) long to the north of the sanctuary seems to belong with the avenue. It is known as the Cursus.

In the middle of the circle a double ring of bluestones began to be set up, with a marked entrance in line with the avenue. What is remarkable about these bluestones is not their size, although they weighed up to 5 tons each, but where they were brought from. As it happens, this particular rock formation is to be found in one place only in all of England, the Prescelly Mountains of Wales. Unless the bluestones were deposited in the area by glaciers, the feat was amazing. The shortest possible route involves a distance of almost 500 kilometers (300 miles). That would entail hauling the bluestones first to Milford Haven in the west of Wales, then moving them by sea to the mouth of the Bristol Avon and, then, by a series of rivers with brief overland hauls in between, reaching the general area of Stonehenge. It seems probable that the avenue of Stonehenge II commemorates the last stretch of portage. (Fig. 2.21)

For all this, the stones were put aside shortly, even before the rings were complete, for a third rearrangement of the precinct—Stonehenge III. Now sarsen megaliths several times larger than the bluestones were brought in from nearby Marlborough, perhaps on a movable track of oak rollers. The naturally irregular blocks had to be cut first, at their place of origin, to uniform size, a procedure that may have included alternate heating and cooling to split the rock along the desired lines.

Within the great chalk circle, the sarsens

were tilted with prodigious effort into a ring of pits, straightened, and stabilized. To consolidate the sarsen circle at the top, curved lintels were placed over each pair of uprights, cut and fitted together so that they would form an integral crown about 6 meters (20 feet) off the ground. The design was completed by a sarsen horseshoe inscribed within, composed of five separate trilithons—that is, groupings of three slabs, two upright ones and the crosspiece that bridges them. The horseshoe opened up toward the avenue and the sacred path of the midsummer sunrise. (Fig. 2.22, C)

The sarsen circle and horseshoe of Stonehenge III are remarkable pieces of architecture. Monumentalized boundaries like the alignments of Carnac differ from them because at Stonehenge the spatial units were cast into total frames through the added definition of the lintels. But the difference is more fundamental. For the builders of Stonehenge III, architecture implies a welding together of units that would read as a single sustained artifact. Of course, Ggantija and the megalithic tombs, too, were complicated assemblages of stones. But as architecture of shelter, they molded interior spaces where incidents of detail were not crucial to the enveloping impact of the stone fabric. The stone core of the tombs let stand imperfections of joining. At Ggantija, dressed stones and slabs of decoration heightened surface appeal as an *applied*, rather than inherent, effect of the structure.

The refinements at Stonehenge belong inseparably to the structure. We have here a skeletal construct, like a stone dance. The care of the detail is important, not so much for its own sake, but for the convincing grace of the construct. For ponderous though the specter of Stonehenge undoubtedly is in the openness of Wiltshire under the vast arc of the sky, the rough-and-tumble look is tempered intentionally with sophistication. The sarsen stones, for one

Fig. 2.22 Stonehenge, plan of four stages of construction: (**A**) Stonehenge I, ca. 2750 B.C.; (**B**) Stonehenge II, later third millennium B.C.; (**C**) Stonehenge III; (**D**) Stonehenge IV, ca. 1500 B.C.

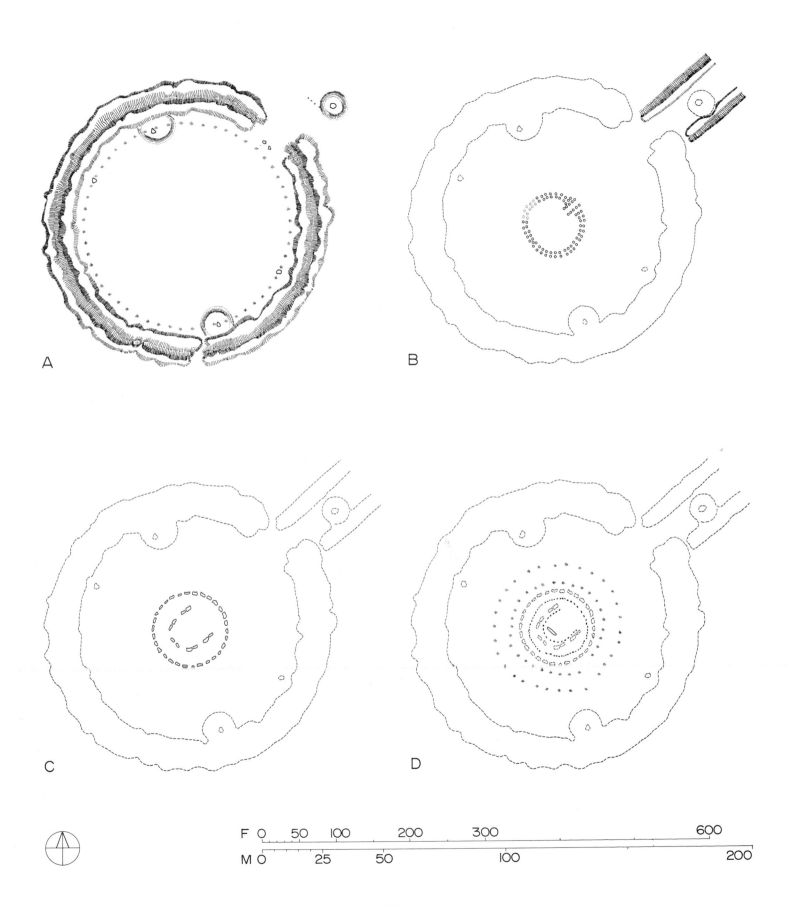

Fig. 2.23 Stonehenge, midsummer sunrise over Heel Stone.

thing, were leveled with heavy stone mauls and smoothed by grinding. Uprights were tapered toward the top, to make them look sprightlier under their burden. For similar visual spruceness, each lintel widened out upward and gently curved inward on the two circumferential surfaces. Those lintels had to be curved along their entire length, so that, joined tightly together as they are in a woodworker's technique known as tongue-and-groove, they would produce a smooth arc both within the circle and without. At the top, the uprights were slightly dished, and the lintels made correspondingly convex, to avoid slipping. Also, a little knob of stone was left projecting at the top of each upright, so that it could be inserted into a matching hole in the lintel. This too is a familiar system of joining used in cabinetmaking, called mortise-and-tenon—perhaps to recall the wooden prototypes of Stonehenge.

The precinct was reorganized one final time. The bluestones, which were already being moved back into the monument during the building of Stonehenge III and set up in front of the horseshoe trilithons, now were also interposed between the horseshoe and the sarsen circle. Further out beyond the circle, two fresh rings of pits were dug, perhaps for holding stones—the so-called Y and Z holes. This last arrangement came about possibly as late as 1500 B.C. (Fig. 2.22, D)

Was Stonehenge, in these final incarnations, solely intent on commemorating midsummer's day? In the opinion of several scholars, it never was. Always, there had been broader cosmic implications. To put it simply, Stonehenge was an open-air observatory where a wide range of astronomical phenomena could be predicted with marvelous precision. So much so that one recent student of the monument refers to it as "a Neolithic computer." According to this theory, the 56 Aubrey holes may relate to the 56 days' difference between five solar years and five lunar years; the 59 Y and Z holes, to the 59 days in two lunar months; the 19 bluestones within the horseshoe, to the 19-year cycle of the moon, crucial for the prediction of eclipses; and so on.

Even were this true—and much of it has been disputed—we must be careful not to confuse our own modern demands on science and the more elemental needs of prehistoric farmers and herders for celestial indicators of the seasons. Furthermore, we must not confuse function and ritual, as we have distinguished these in our introductory chapter. Function in architecture is a prosaic program. It is an abstraction in that it applies to an *activity* without reference to human involvement. Ritual is the transcendence of function to the level of a meaningful *act*.

It may indeed be true that Stonehenge was designed to plot and anticipate some alignments of the sun and the moon. That would be its function. But the meaning of Stonehenge resides in the ritual. It is this that humanizes this calendar of stone and earth in the open countryside; it is this that explains the prodigies of engineering and labor that went into its making. Function did not demand the choice of bluestones and grey sarsens and their transport from long distances away. For the effectiveness of this "Neolithic computer," any convenient stones would have been satisfactory. The materials and the size of the project were urged on these early peoples of the British Isles so that the structure could be a cele-bration of celestial events and not merely a method of predicting them. To this end, the painful sophistication of detail was countenanced—the stamp on uncouth rock of the civilizing will of humans.

Stonehenge was a sacred center of community for the tribes that used it—a monument to their social cohesion apparent both in their spirit of labor, when they toiled together to set up the megaliths, and during their ritual gatherings, when an eclipse or a spectacular rising of the sun, having been predicted by the priestly powers, would summon the community to converge on the precinct to witness the event in unison. (Fig. 2.23) Public architecture at its best aspires to be just this: a setting for ritual that makes of each user, for a brief moment, a larger person than he or she is in daily life, filling each one with the pride of belonging.

Further Reading

R. J. C. Atkinson, *Stonehenge* (Harmondsworth and Baltimore: Penguin, 1960).

A. Burl, *The Stone Circles of the British Isles* (New Haven: Yale University Press, 1976).

G. Daniel, *The Megalith Builders of Western Europe* (London: Hutchinson, 1963).

———, *The Prehistoric Chamber Tombs of France* (London: Thames and Hudson, 1960).

J. D. Evans, *Malta* (London: Thames and Hudson, 1959).

A. Laming, *Lascaux*, trans. E. F. Armstrong (Harmondsworth and Baltimore: Penguin, 1959).

J. McMann, *Riddles of the Stone Age: Rock Carvings of Ancient Europe* (New York: Thames and Hudson, 1980).

Scientific American, *Old World Archeology: Foundations of Civilization* (San Francisco: Freeman, 1972).

P. V. D. Stern, *Prehistoric Europe from Stone Age Man to the Early Greeks* (New York: Norton, 1969).

L. E. Stover and B. Kraig, *Stonehenge: The Indo-European Heritage* (Chicago: Nelson-Hall, 1978).

D. H. Trump, *The Prehistory of the Mediterranean* (New Haven: Yale University Press, 1980).

G. Wainwright, *The Henge Monuments: Ceremony and Society in Prehistoric Britain* (New York: Thames and Hudson, 1990).

Jericho (Israel), wall showing superimposed layers, ca. 7000 B.C. and later.

3

THE RISE OF THE CITY: ARCHITECTURE IN WESTERN ASIA

The Urban Revolution

Behold the bond of Heaven and Earth, the city . . .
Behold Nippur, the city . . .
Behold the kindly wall, the city . . .
. . . its pure river
   . . . its quay where the boats stand
Behold the Pulal, its well of good water
Behold the Idnunbirdu, its pure canal . . .

This is the opening of a Sumerian myth about the moon-god Nanna, and it dates from the beginning of the second millennium B.C.—the time of the third rearrangement of Stonehenge. There are two noteworthy things about this bit of poetry from Mesopotamia. First, it is a written record: a distant culture speaks to us through it directly. This is a very different relationship to the past than the one we had established with the Britons of Salisbury who could reach us only through the mute testimony of their stones. And second, the passage sings rapturously of a thing called the city, set on a river, serviced by canals, blessed with good freshwater.

So at the very same time in history, in two separate corners of the ancient world, different patterns of community were in existence. While Neolithic Europe carried on a stone-using peasant economy well into the second millennium B.C., in two spots of the Near East there were contemporary *literate* cultures that knew how to work metal, organize food production as an industry, and keep written records of their transactions and beliefs. They had left their Neolithic past behind them long before Europe and had gone on to forge a complex society of great technological achievement and ma-

terial wealth. With these two literate cultures, Egypt and Mesopotamia, history proper is said to begin, as distinct from the document-free *prehistory* of the Stone Age. Writing helps us to draw the line between civilized and "barbarous" societies, and for this reason, among others, we have customarily called the Near East "the cradle of civilization."

The word "civilization" derives from the Latin *civitas*, which means city. This gives us the other accepted characteristic of civilized humanity—that it has for its theater of activity an intricate artifact, the city, that sets it apart from the basic life of the village or the pastoral tribe. To be civilized is to be urban; civilization, in this strict sense, is "the art of living in towns." Traditionally, the molding of the city as a social and material concept is credited to the same cradle of civilization that invented writing, specifically to the southern region of Mesopotamia, Sumer, sometime in the early fourth millennium B.C. (Figs. 3.1, 3.8)

If boundary-fixing and stone monuments represent the architectural response to the Neolithic revolution, the ingenious fabric of the city corresponds to the second major upheaval in the human scheme, the urban revolution. How was this fabric wrought? What were its components? Physically, what is it that differentiates the city from the village?

The city is an involved organism under constant change. (Fig. 3.2) In its living mesh, public structures are bonded to the places where people live, and these, in turn, are

bonded to each other, in a rich artifice of contiguity. The city presents us with a new set of environmental ideas, such as the street, the public square, the defensive wall and its gates. It crowds our discussion with a score of building inventions—for example, the canal and the granary, the palace and the bath, the market, the bakery, shops, restaurants, and libraries.

The urban revolution differs from the Neolithic revolution in one essential way. It does not affect the basic relationship of people to nature, as the passage from hunting to food production certainly did. Agriculture and animal husbandry survive as the principal modes of subsistence in the urban period. Even trade cannot be credited exclusively to the rise of cities. Of course, both agriculture and trade were intensified and regimented within an urban economy: the one, profiting from irrigation, crop rotation, and the use of fertilizers, to produce a surplus of food; the other, enlarging its scope to include, besides pottery and stones like obsidian, the metals required by the new urban technology and the consumption of luxury goods. But this is more a matter of disciplined efficiency than a radical turn in the exploitation of nature. The city, above all else, typified a *social* process. The revolution it brought about was embodied in the interaction of people with each other.

Since this is so, we should not be surprised that recent archaeological discoveries have shown the city to have emerged long before the fourth millennium B.C., in areas identified with the Neolithic age. The settlement at Jericho about 9,000 years ago was a well-organized community of about 3,000 people, in contrast to the normal Neolithic village with its population of several hundred. Çatalhöyük in southern Anatolia, a 13-hectare (32-acre) Neolithic settlement of the seventh millennium B.C., with shrines and quarters for specialized crafts, a clever residential layout, and the production of wall paintings, textiles, copper and bone artifacts, patently merits being called a town.

One further corrective should be offered to our thinking about the urban revolution. It is possible to make entirely too much of the city. It appears that in correlating urbanism and civilized history, we have imbued the city with positive qualities the absence of which, at least by implication, has tended to downgrade other social organisms. The term urban has turned into a value judgment; rural or pastoral, in contrast, carry with them a note of regression or conservatism.

This bias is unfair. To hold that civilized life cannot exist outside of cities belittles the genuine achievement of much nonurban culture and may distort the view of a total environmental order where the cities and the countryside are locked in mutually fructifying intercourse. It is not enough to grant the truism that cities, for the most part, could not survive without the sustaining labor of peripheral fields and pasture. There were moments in history when the urban and pastoral modes of life were competing high cultures. There were moments, too, when the collapse of an urban civilization ushered in, after a period of painful adjustment, an equally viable social structure that made do without cities. Because of our preconceptions about the putative superiority of cities, we have too easily seen these nonurban sequels as the inevitable troughs between the peaks of human genius and enterprise. We are given to calling them the Dark Ages. But if we restrain our enthusiasm for the glamor of cities, we might profitably reassess the contribution of the centuries that came after the destruction of Bronze Age city-states in Greece, for example, or the time after the deterioration of Mediterranean urbanism that accompanied the fall of the Roman Empire.

Stirrings of Urban Consciousness

The chemistry of early cities relied on three active properties: people, productive resources, and ambition. The city-form aspired to be compact and versatile. And the future of this proud amalgam of people and buildings could be secured only through faultless defense and aggressive progress.

A city presupposed a concentrated population, beyond the intimate congress of farming homesteads and tribal families. The land it occupied had to be able to do more than feed its crowds. Food surplus ensured a stable way of life against the fitful behavior of nature; it also supplied a source of wealth to pay for importing what the city needed and did not have. Alternatively, the city might derive its strength from some raw or crafted resource, such as animal fur or metal, attractive to markets beyond its lim-

its. In either case, the city proved that it could not, as the village could, remain self-contained. The local interaction among its people, complicated by numbers, was only one dimension of its social mobility. Outside, there were other centers of closely controlled resources that envied it or replenished its wants. To defend itself against the envious and still carry on trade, the city formed a larger sphere of social contact.

The citizenry was forced to organize itself in a way that could contend with the diversified tasks of its supple existence. The population fissured into specialized groups. Besides the great peasant mass, some were trained to fight, others to build. There were full-time craftspeople of metal and stone, as well as priests and merchants. And specialization went hand in hand with social stratification. Some groups administered the urban territory that stretched far beyond the

Fig. 3.1 Map: Western Asia, 8,000–700 B.C.

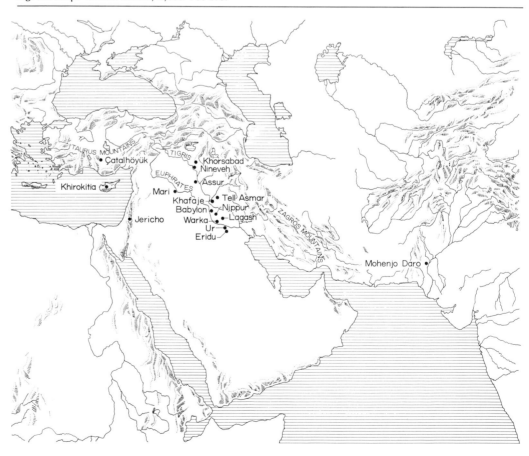

Fig. 3.2 Hamadan (Iran); aerial view.

confines of the city, controlling the principal resources of production. These citizens had a reserve of power that they had come by in the course of time and, through it, they held sway over the rest of the population. But below them the citizenry was not on equal footing. Certain tasks carried less prestige than others. The chance for acquiring wealth was uneven, and the rich

held a definite advantage over those less favored in the social hierarchy.

The city-form, compact and versatile, reconciled the demands of privilege with the pressing need for unity. The powerful must have stages for the ceremonies of their office, and these must be of a scale and level of grandeur that would impress both the citizenry and foreign embassies. For

power manifests itself through architecture perhaps more easily and universally than through anything else. The rich must have residences whose fancy trappings and ampleness in the thick of the urban fabric would plainly bespeak their station. At the same time the city-form contained the human base of this exalted peak and furnished it with a sense of enhanced identity. The gods looked after the entire citizenry, both the humble and the high; the temples solemnized pious community. The ring of walls expressed the fears and the strength of a common fate. Even the opulence of the rich redounded all the way to the simple peasant, for the peasant could boast of belonging to the community that displayed such wealth.

Jericho

Precisely how it all started is unclear. Revolution implies a sudden break, but it may have been in several places at once, and with varying motives, that the idea of the city gradually took root. At this stage of our knowledge, we must assign the origin of the city-form to western Asia; and Jericho would seem to qualify as the earliest surviving town.

The site today is a great mound near the oasis of the modern town, on the left bank of the river Jordan. It holds a series of Jerichos, each built on the ruins of its predecessor. This clinging to a place of birth will prove a durable habit for cities. Time and again until our own day, cities ravaged by conquest or natural disaster will elect to rebuild on their ashes, fully aware that they will be vulnerable anew. In large measure it is tradition, the genius of the place, that accounts for this stubbornness. The ground is hallowed. It has the imprint of time-honored cults and generations of inhabitants. Besides, there is invariably a tangible advantage to the site that prompted occupation in the first place.

In the case of Jericho, this was a reliable source of freshwater that now gushes from the place called Elisha's Fountain. The life-giving value of such a spring, in the desert of the Dead Sea, is obvious. Here by the welling water, where their quarry came to drink, hunters had pitched their tents on bedrock and reserved a small plot of land as a sanctuary; and here, within a thousand years, the transition had occurred to a settled life based on agriculture. The first permanent settlement had solid domed houses of mud-brick, with an entrance porch and curved walls, probably in imitation of the round tents of the nomadic hunters. The floor was sunk below the ground level and was reached by means of wooden stairs. Underneath it, the dead lay buried.

The date of this activity is about 7500 B.C. The settlement covered about 3 hectares (8 acres) and must have therefore been uncommonly populous. (Fig. 3.3) Moreover, once it had reached its optimum spread, the settlement was fortified by a fine stone wall of cyclopean masonry that guarded the people and their precious substance, the spring water, for more than a thousand years. The fort was overseen by a massive round tower, also of stone, built against the inside of the wall. (Fig. 3.4) In its hollow core, a staircase of single stone slabs had been constructed, either to man the tower or else to reach the source of the spring, perhaps both. That water had something to do with the curtain of defense is suggested by the fact that the tower was intimate with a series of mud-brick enclosures, unlike any of the houses, that have been interpreted as water cisterns.

About 6500 B.C., this Neolithic stronghold, perched between eastern nomads and the fertile plains of Palestine, was successfully overrun. The houses were now rectangular, with slightly rounded corners. They were arranged around courtyards where the cooking took place. Each house consisted of several rooms, interconnecting through wide doorways. Sitting among the houses were several buildings set aside for worship; they shared features of residential architecture, such as rounded doorway jambs.

Like the townspeople they displaced, the newcomers were also compelled to use earth as their main building material, but they went to some pains to improve its look. Stone was in short supply; what little could be found within easy portage was used for defenses, the substructure of houses, and for other extraordinary purposes. A shrine in a private house features a dressed pillar of volcanic rock set on a stone pedestal in a semicircular niche. It brings to mind the pillar in the terminal apse of Maltese temples.

The rest had to make do with mud, which has advantages as well as drawbacks. It is of course easier to work with than stone, since it requires no cutting and dressing. But mud has its own problems. Although it is eminently plastic, it has to be shaped somehow and stiffened so that it will stand. Second, it has to be protected from dampness. And because it is a drab material that

yields lackluster surfaces, the urge is keen to do something more with it—whitewash it, liven it with color, or modulate it for effect. One clever expedient is to devise a sheathing that both protects and embellishes—for example, sheathing like tile that will be hard, water-resistant, and colorful. But the invention of tile lies several thousand years ahead in time. The polished reddish plaster of Jericho used on the walls and floors is itself a notable antecedent.

There are several ways to build with earth, all of them ancient. The crudest is to mix together soil, water, straw, reeds, leaves, and whatever else of this sort of material comes to hand and pile it up to form a wall—the technique known as "cob." The wattle-and-daub technique makes use of an upright frame of wattling, on both sides of which the wet mud would be applied. But the two most satisfactory variants of earth

Fig. 3.3 Jericho (Israel), first settlement, ca. 7500 B.C.; site and excavated portion of wall; plan.

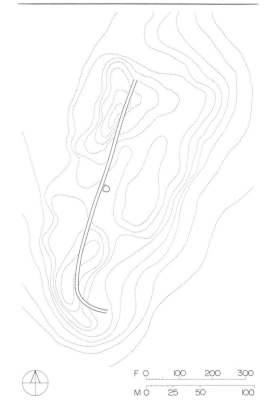

F 0   100   200   300

M 0   25   50   100

Fig. 3.4a Jericho, tower built against side of settlement wall.

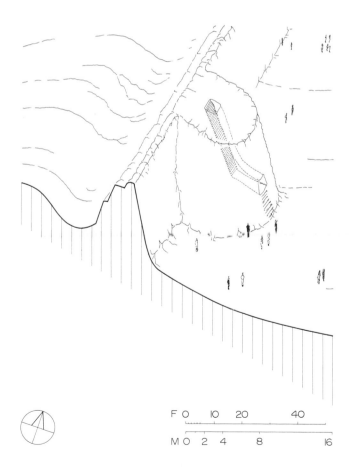

F 0 10 20 40

M 0 2 4 8 16

Fig. 3.4b Jericho, wall and tower; section/perspective view.

construction are *pisé* and mud-brick. In the first case, slightly moist earth is filled into a rigid, movable formwork and is pounded into place, layer on layer, with a rammer. In the second case, the earth is cast into small building units that are then laid in regular courses and bonded together by some kind of mortar.

The mud-bricks of Jericho were molded by hand and were sun-dried. Baking makes bricks more durable, but it requires a great deal of firewood, which affects the cost, and a more advanced system of production. At any rate, both baking and the mechanical shaping of bricks in molds would be perfected later.

Although none, by itself, could be considered decisive, the sizable population, defensive wall, and interweaving of public buildings (cisterns, shrines) and houses are features that point Jericho toward urbanism. If irrigation were in fact practiced, another crucial element of organized life would be present in its structure. For to succeed, irrigation must depend on planning and strict controls. The main and secondary channels must be geared to a rational system of field division. Sluice gates or some other regulating mechanism must be devised. Agreement must be reached on the length of time during the day allowed each farmer to tap the channel he is assigned. The control of sluice gates postulates a community-approved code of behavior; its reinforcement will be entrusted, sooner or later, to some governing board with powers of license and sanction. All this outstrips the social contract of a simple village.

Khirokitia

Curiously, one missing ingredient in the city-form of Jericho is the street. The houses and shrines communicated by means of courtyards, it would seem, and the leftover spaces among buildings. The first true street of which we have a record may be in Khirokitia, a hilltop settlement of the sixth millennium B.C. in southern Cyprus, within the bend of the river Maronioù. (Fig. 3.5) The street runs uphill from the riverbank on the south side of the bend, crosses the settlement, and descends again on the opposite side. In fact, it defines the settlement as emphatically as the walls did the first

Jericho. The principle is of course different. Jericho was a closed town with fixed limits. To grow, it would be obliged to overflow its defensive ring, and either rebuild it further out or else forgo enclosure of the new periphery. The composition of Khirokitia is open. The houses huddle on the two sides of the main street, which gives the settlement a spine of communication

and spectacle. Stone ramps lead down to the houses at regular intervals as tributary lanes. There is no encompassing wall and, therefore, no commitment to a stable size. Growth is linear; it depends architecturally on nothing more than the extension of the main street at either end.

Several points should be made about this main street of Khirokitia. First, it had its

Fig. 3.5 Khirokitia (Cyprus), Neolithic settlement, ca. 5500 B.C.; plan.

practical uses. Built of limestone and raised considerably above ground level, it countered the action of erosion and contributed structurally to the stability of the houses that held onto the hill slopes. Along its paved path, the people of Khirokitia climbed easily from the river, carrying the boulders and the water to build their mud homes.

Beyond this sane utility, the street also implies a sense of design among the Khirokitians that moved them to marshal, through the expediency of a central axis, what might otherwise have been a helter skelter assembly of houses. The formal cohesion promoted the feeling of community. Friends lived up or down the street; sitting in front of your house you saw them pass by and greeted them informally. Halfway up the steepest part of the ascent from the south, the street was widened into a platform about 4.5 meters (15 feet) wide, roughly rounded along one edge and stepped. (Fig. 3.6) This halting place, with its splendid view of the Maronioù Valley and the sea beyond, was the main incident along the ribbon of the public way, and doubtless a special spot at which to tarry and exchange pleasantries. Out of such stages of public congress will evolve the Greek *agora*, the Roman forum, the piazza, and all the other variations of city squares.

Lastly, a thoroughfare such as the one at Khirokitia has organizational and legal consequences. By explicitly defining and articulating an outdoor space for the common good, the people assume a double responsibility: the upkeep of this space and its preservation as public property. A public way, by definition, belongs to everybody;

Fig. 3.6 Khirokitia, village "square"; an oblique view of the area marked as an inset in Fig. 3.5.

F 0   10   25   50   75

M 0   5   10   25

Khirokitia understood this. Steady repair and alteration of the main street during its protracted life show that the community was not innocent of "civic" duty. Again, maintaining their communal artery free of encroachments took vigilance, a general understanding, and social maturity. At the same time, the zealous safekeeping of this public trust tended to sharpen the disparateness between public and private property. The size and shape of the houses at Khirokitia give no hint of a developed social hierarchy; yet *spatial* hierarchies might well be engendered by the design of the community, so that houses right on the main street or adjacent to the halting place might begin to seem privileged and therefore more desirable than others.

Çatalhöyük

Çatalhöyük in the Konya Plain of south Anatolia is the largest and most complex Neolithic settlement to be excavated. And it rests on a new rationale for the city—trade. Besides hunting, a progressive variety of agriculture, and stockbreeding, this town of perhaps 10,000 people would seem to have controlled the trade of a valued commodity, obsidian, the principal sources for which were further north. The black volcanic glass, the best material of the time for cutting tools, fed a brisk local industry and supplied the wherewithal for foreign commerce. The town could afford to obtain numerous luxury items, such as marble, flint, sulphur, pumice, calcite, and alabaster. All of this went to enhance the daily routine and personal appearance of the townspeople.

But there was another important skill present in Çatalhöyük, the working of metal. Lead and copper were shaped into ornaments and small tools such as awls and drills. The raw material was to be found in the Taurus range, the mountain chain that frames the Anatolian plateau on the south side. Prospecting, then, was one of the many activities of the town along with a primitive form of metallurgy, or at least the knowledge of smelting. This is very early indeed for such technical knowledge; metallurgy would not be practiced fully until the cultures of Mesopotamia and Egypt mastered it beginning in the fourth millennium B.C.

The spread of metal has a mixed impact on the history of architecture. The direct application of metal as architectural ornament starts in Mesopotamia; in building construction, not until Classical antiquity. But the indirect effects of metal on the manufactured environment are already evident at Çatalhöyük. The desire to obtain and work this uncommon material could in itself sustain towns that mined it, traded in it, and knew how to fashion it into sumptuous art. To the traditional crafts embraced by the village—stone-carving, pottery, weaving—metal added others that fitted into the nascent townscape with its manufacturing establishments and stalls of sale.

The small part of Çatalhöyük that has so far been excavated covers a residential quarter. (Fig. 3.7) If the rest of the enormous site were to be cleared, one might come across the environmental traces of the intense bustle of its many crafts that left hundreds of artifacts in the soil. There would be the shops of the basketmakers and weavers; of the merchants of animal skin, leather, and fur; the makers of copper mirrors and jewelry. Perhaps there would also be a public market in the midst of the urban fabric, where the townspeople would go to look for stone and shell beads, flint daggers and sickle blades, bone ladles and belt hooks.

The settlement was neither fortified like Jericho nor open like Khirokitia. The buildings were grouped into tight quarters so that a continuous, blank wall of construction faced the countryside: no doors or windows on this side were allowed in the houses. Streets were unknown. The quarter opened up with an occasional courtyard, which also doubled as lavatory and rubbish dump. Entry to the houses was normally through a hole in the flat roof reached by a wooden ladder. Since the hearth and oven were directly below the hole, the entry was also a smoke stack. Small windows below the eaves on at least two sides of the house brought in additional light. The plan is consistent. Each house had one rectangular room, with a narrow storage space along one side and built-in platforms along two walls, one each for the men and women of the household.

The construction method is novel. A timber framework of posts and beams divides the walls into a series of vertical and horizontal panels that are then filled in with mud-brick and plastered. This is the prototype of so-called half-timber construction. In the shrines, laid on the same basic scheme as the houses, the individual panels were decorated with plaster reliefs and paintings dealing with the cult of the mother goddess. The imagery itself looks back on the Old Stone Age past. A bull represents the goddess' constant companion, and stylized heads of bulls and rams in the form of low pillars figure as cult objects. And there is, here and there, a debased version of hunt magic, in lively scenes of animal baiting.

So Çatalhöyük contains it all—it is a telescoped view of human history from the Stone Age hunter to the city dweller. In its ambience, the wildness of the horned beast is at home with no less than three forms of wheat and two of barley; and side by side with the hunter and the sophisticated farmer lives the specialist in metalwork, as well as the merchant with his eyes abroad.

The Cities of Mesopotamia

The stirrings of an urban consciousness that were first felt in Palestine about 7500 B.C. seem to die out by the year 5500. When again we encounter the city some fifteen centuries later, in the "land between rivers" (which is what Mesopotamia means), it shows up in full force and blossoms with unprecedented intensity. (Fig. 3.8) We are now dealing with a concentrated urban culture sustained by a written tradition. So while it is undeniable that the city-form got its start in the Neolithic ambience of the eastern Mediterranean, nothing like the cities of Mesopotamia had ever been seen before in human history.

The history of Mesopotamia is long and tangled. In architectural terms, we are unable to trace a neat, orderly development through the known fragments. As Henri Frankfort, the foremost student of Mesopotamian architecture, has warned us, the story is marked by "promising starts that lead nowhere" and by a tenacious adherence over the millennia to a limited repertory of formal types. In our own brief sum-

Fig. 3.7 Çatalhöyük (Turkey), Neolithic settlement, seventh millennium B.C.; reconstruction view of residential area.

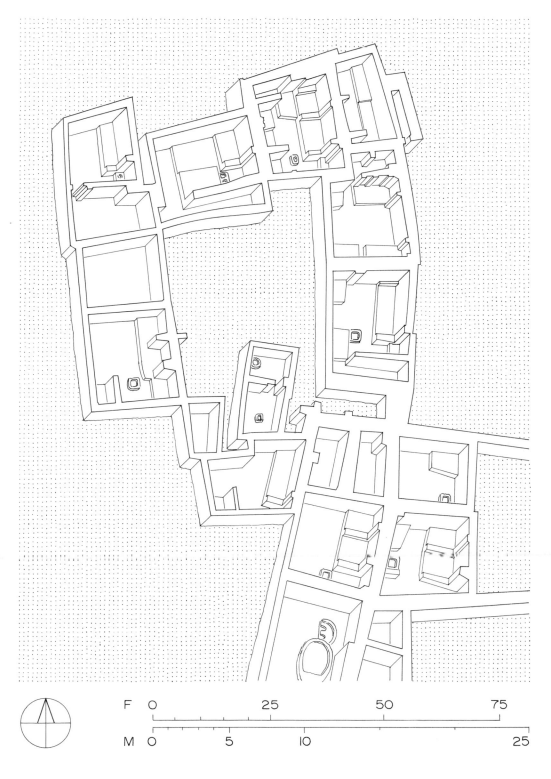

F O   25   50   75

M O   5   10   25

mary, we might therefore suspend a strict chronological account in favor of a few critical environmental contributions that can be isolated for special focus.

Four broad segments of chronology will suffice to govern our discussion.

1. The first is the so-called *Protoliterate Period*, from ca. 3500 to 3000 B.C. During this time, the towns, which had probably evolved from agricultural villages, acquired their battlements of ringwalls; and the temple and the ziggurat began to gain architectural definition. The first written documents made their appearance. Political authority resided in an assembly of male citizens that selected short-term war leaders.

2. When the role of these leaders was retained in times of peace as well, kingship, first elective and then hereditary, became established. With it rose the monumental palace, an administrative center which employed a large retinue of bureaucrats and entertainers and occupied itself with raising and supplying an army and maintaining the defensive system of the city. This period, roughly 3000 to 2350 B.C. is called *Early Dynastic*.

3. The next few hundred years, up to about 1600 B.C., might loosely be referred to as the *later Sumerian* period. This period saw the rise of empire, the collective rule of several city-states through the might of a sovereign king. The first part of the period is dominated by the Third Dynasty of Ur whose prodigious building activity includes the ziggurat of Ur-Nammu, the high point of that building type.

4. One last period is interesting, *the Assyrian*, from about 1350 to 612 B.C. The northern region of the two rivers now flourishes at the expense of lower Mesopotamia. We know the Assyrians by their imposing state reliefs and their palaces, like the one at Khorsabad.

The Layout of Cities

There is not enough at the lower levels of explored mounds to give us a total image of the Mesopotamian city before the Early Dynastic Period. By then, a dozen or so cities containing from 10,000 to 50,000 people prospered, both in lower Mesopotamia or Sumer and further north in Babylonia. The cities were enclosed by a wall and surrounded by suburban villages and hamlets.

(Fig. 3.9) The two monumental centers were the ziggurat complex with its own defensive wall, overseen by a powerful priesthood, and the palace of the king. Lesser temples were sprinkled here and there within the rest of the urban fabric, which was a promiscuous blend of residential and commercial architecture. Small shops were at times incorporated into the houses, but the norm was to have structures devoted exclusively to commercial or industrial use interspersed throughout the city. In the later Sumerian period at Ur, an example of a bazaar was found: a concentration of little booths along a narrow passage, probably sheltered by awnings, with doors at either end that were closed at night. At Tell Asmar, a large building once thought to be a palace has recently been reinterpreted as an industrial complex housing a number of concerns, such as a tannery, a small-scale ironworks, and, at a later date, textile weaving exclusively.

Traffic along the twisted network of unpaved streets was mostly pedestrian. The ass, that classic beast of burden, navigated easily enough. At Ur, one sees on occasion a low flight of steps against a building from which riders could mount, and street corners were regularly rounded to facilitate passage. Street width, at the very most, would be 3 meters (9 feet) or so, and that only for the few principal thoroughfares that led to the public buildings. These would be bordered with the houses of the rich. Poorer folk lived at the back, along narrow lanes and alleys. It is hard to imagine much wheeled traffic in this maze, though both service carts (with solid wheels) and chariots had been in use from an early date. The ill-made tracery of public ways resulted undoubtedly from the ancient occupations of the city sites. Once walled, the land became precious, and the high value of private property kept public space to a minimum. Ample squares or public gardens were very rare.

The houses were grouped into congested blocks, where party walls were common. (Fig. 3.10) In fact, though the constituent unit was the single-family dwelling, it is difficult to see the block as anything but a raveled agglomerate forever adjusting to the pressures of changing use. On the blank face of their tablets, archi-

tects designed perfect house plans, rectangles divided neatly into orthogonal rooms around a central living space. But the reality of a living town played havoc with the conceptual order of the architect. The building lots were not of uniform size. Each house was compelled to fit into a predetermined space, more often than not irregular, in the tangle of its block. Furthermore, it was the custom not to clear an earlier house fully before starting to build over it, but rather to make use of the ruins as a foundation; as a result, the plan of the older

house had a direct bearing on the shape of its replacement, which pushed like a fresh shoot from the older roots in the soil.

The houses, before they collapsed or were abandoned, renewed themselves in various ways as the daily life of their occupants or the rhythm of the streets dictated. Since refuse was dumped in the public space outside the front door, the level of the streets rose perceptibly. At Ur, the townsfolk kept abreast of this phenomenon by raising the threshold of the single door that customarily led into the house and

Fig. 3.8 Map: Mesopotamia.

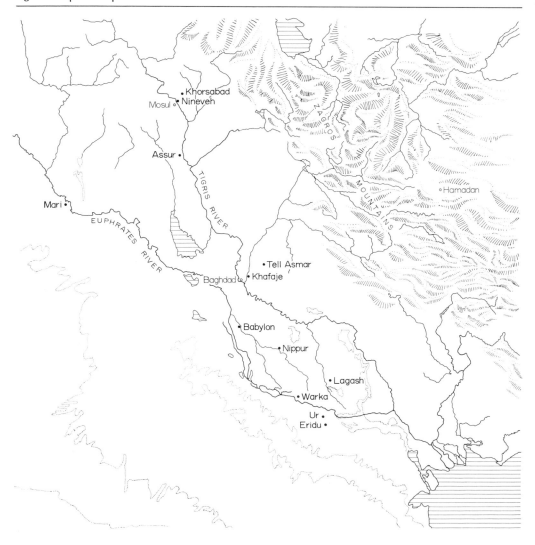

by adding inner steps as required to reach the original floor. When in time the ground storey threatened to be buried below street level, the house would be pulled down to the ceilings of the ground storey, and a new floor would be built on these ceiling beams to match the current height of the street. The replaced ground storey was often pressed into service as a family vault. Furthermore, the house might be altered through suitable remodeling to ready it for a new function, as when Mr. Igmil-Sin of Ur, headmaster of a boys' school, adapted the courtyard and guest room of his house (on what Sir Leonard Woolley has nicknamed Broad Street) into classrooms, or when No. 1 Bakers' Square was entirely redone as a smithy. Nothing about the city-form, in short, was fixed and finished at any time, any more than the human body is fixed and finished at any time during its existence; architectural metabolism constantly transformed the makeup of the cityscape that was held together by the stiffer skeleton of streets and ramparts.

The houses were, for the most part, one-storey structures of mud-brick, with several rooms wrapped around a central court. There were usually no outside windows, no attempt to contribute to a street architecture. The family turned within. The only opening to the outside, the front door, revealed nothing when it was opened but a small vestibule with a blank wall directly ahead. You entered the house proper through a door to one side of the vestibule.

The wealthier classes of Ur lived in ample houses of a dozen or so rooms, arranged on two storeys, and whitewashed inside and out. The ground storey was set aside for the servants, who were generally domestic slaves, and for guests; the family lived upstairs. A typical plan had a wide and shallow reception room on the far side of the court for visitors, a main lavatory on the side of the court facing the guest room, and, next to it, the staircase for the upper floor. (Fig. 3.11) At one corner was the kitchen. The court had four wooden posts at the corners that held up a continuous wooden gallery giving access into the upper rooms. (Fig. 3.12) The roof sloped gently inward, projecting beyond the gallery to protect it from rainwater which was directed, by

Fig. 3.9 Ur (Iraq), schematic plan of city in second millennium B.C.

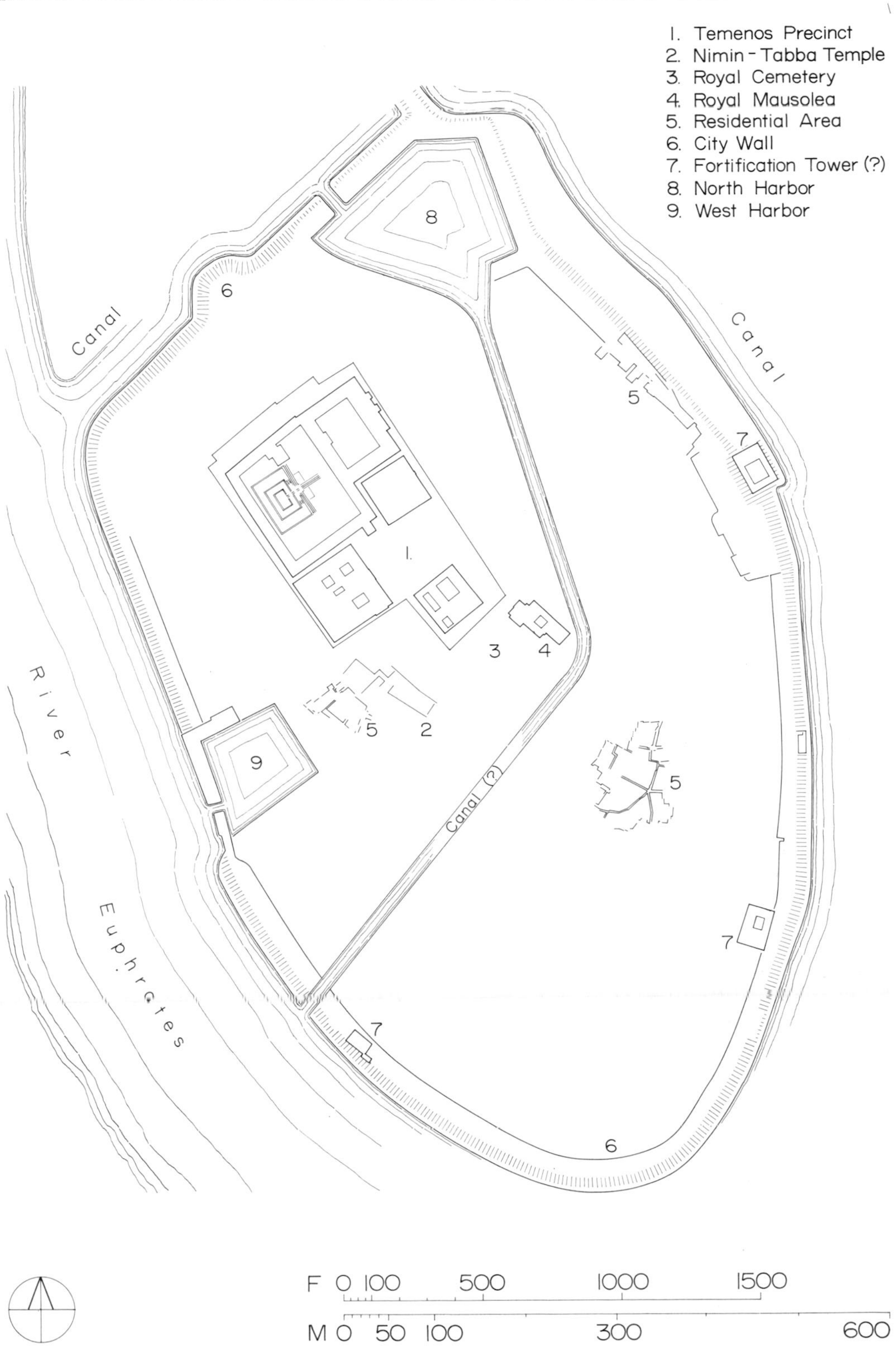
1. Temenos Precinct
2. Nimin-Tabba Temple
3. Royal Cemetery
4. Royal Mausolea
5. Residential Area
6. City Wall
7. Fortification Tower (?)
8. North Harbor
9. West Harbor
Canal
Canal
Canal (?)
River Euphrates
F 0 100 500 1000 1500
M 0 50 100 300 600

means of gutters sticking out of an inner coping, onto the paved court below and from there to the subsoil. These were comfortable, even gracious, houses, with a minimum of simple furniture moved about easily as needed: folding chairs and tables, mattresses, chests of wood or wickerwork to store clothes, colorful rugs on the floors, and plenty of cushions strewn about. The domestic arrangements have much in common with modern Arab houses in the Middle East.

Temples and Ziggurats

A map of Nippur on a clay tablet from about 1500 B.C. gives a graphic rendition of the public aspect of the city. (Fig. 3.13) To the left, the double line of the Euphrates River is evident, the lifeblood of the plain, whose low banks and moderate course made navigation possible and whose flooding, when tamed, turned dust into fertile mud. Alongside it, we can see the double line of the city wall, the crown of sovereignty. In the middle, we find a canal, the imperative of advanced irrigation and the index of an organized and self-reliant community. Then, to the right of the canal, the most important symbol of all, the temple of the god or goddess who watched over the city.

The temple constituted the heart of the Mesopotamian city. Small, freestanding shrines, we know, already existed in the farming villages in preurban days. They had two standard features that were to be retained: a niche of epiphany, perhaps already at this time marked by the statue of the deity or an altar, and a table for offerings. By 3500 B.C. these shrines had become codified into monumental temple forms and fitted into the urban scheme.

One among the many gods ranked supreme, a deity who was thought, quite literally, to own the city. All the townspeople devoted their lives to his or her service, and the ruling powers were thought merely to exercise stewardship over the divine estate. The fields and their produce belonged to the deity. The seeds, draught animals, and implements of tilling were supplied by the temple, and the harvest was stored on its grounds for distribution to the community. Craftsmen, organized in guilds, offered part of their output to the temple,

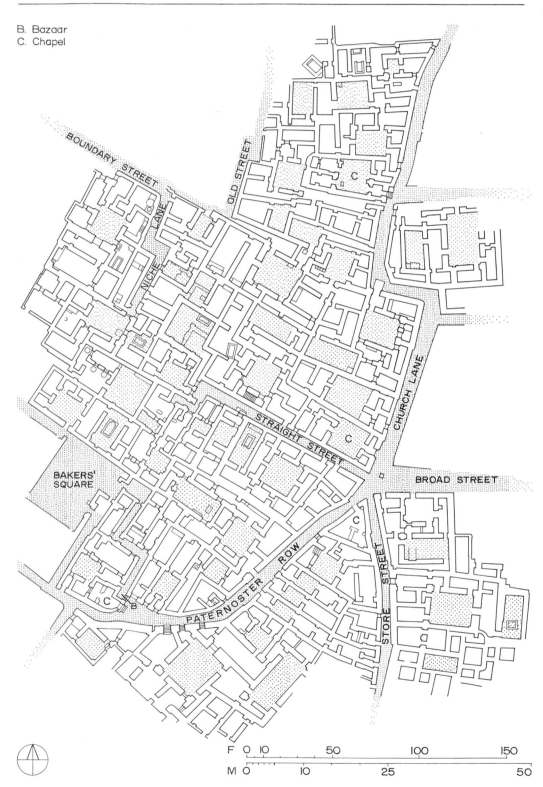

Fig. 3.10 Ur, residential area southeast of the royal mausolea in the twentieth century B.C.; plan.

B. Bazaar
C. Chapel

and so did fishermen with their catch and builders with their labor. The temple complex was the hub of an economic system that has been described as "theocratic socialism." (Fig. 3.14) With its own wall around it, it formed the last bulwark against the city's enemies; when it fell, it was all over for the city, and the patron deity, deprived of a home, would wander aimlessly, as one inscription puts it, like the bird that flies about with no place to alight.

There were two ways in which this temple differed from others in the city. It stood on a tremendous platform called the ziggurat, and being free of the pressures of density in its ample precinct, its form could afford to be both regular and open. It seems that standard temples as well as ziggurat temples grew out of a common archetype. We have a glimpse of this prototype at Eridu, considered in Mesopotamian history to have been the birthplace of kingship. There, a series of temples was built on sand dunes over the years. (Fig. 3.15)

The earliest to leave a trace was a small, thin-walled rectangular enclosure with projecting piers within. Two circular tables for burnt offerings stood outside. When this was overwhelmed by wind-blown sand, or perhaps purposely buried, a similar structure was stood over it, but with some crucial modifications. One side of the rectangle broke out into a projecting bay containing a podium or altar; a second podium, most likely an offering table, stood in the middle. A door led into the enclosure from the side opposite the altar bay.

The next phase was an oblong scheme with a central nave disposed longitudinally and flanked by subsidiary rooms somewhat in the manner of aisles. The corner rooms formed projecting bastions. A cross-axis was set up by an oblong room in the middle of each aisle. These acted as vestibules to doors cut into the long sides of the tem-

1. Courtyard
2. Entry Vestibule
3. Reception Room (Liwan)
4. Private Chapel
5. Kitchen
6. Lavatory
7. Staircase
8. Drain
9. Shop (?)

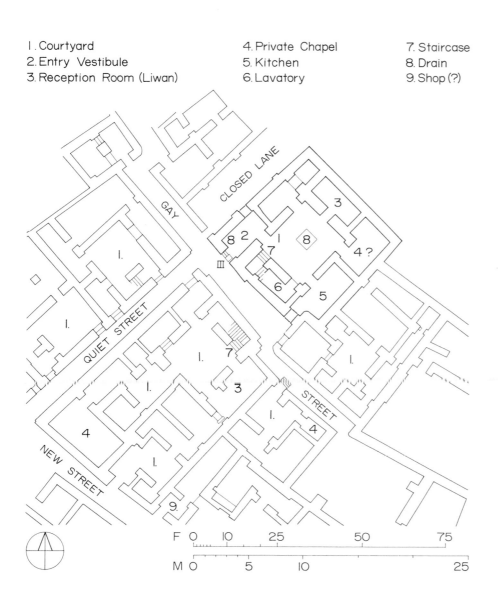

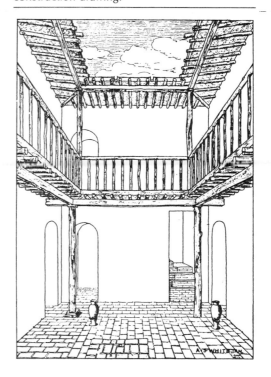

Fig. 3.11 Ur, residential quarter between the ziggurat precinct and the West Harbor; plan. Number III Gay Street is the plan of the upper-class house shown in Fig. 3.12.

Fig. 3.12 Ur, Number III Gay Street, court; reconstruction drawing.

ple, of which one, to the southeast, was approached by a formal stair. There was also a double entrance on the short side opposite the altar. The walls were now thick and buttressed all along the exterior periphery. Inside, spur walls and buttresses were spaced in relation to the ceiling beams and rafters that would rest along the tops of the walls.

At this point the temple form began to diverge. At Warka (Uruk), the biblical Erech, we have an early classical example of the ziggurat temple, while the development of the standard temple can be followed in three successive buildings in honor of the moon-god Sin at the northern town of Khafaje.

At the White Temple of Warka, dating from the Protoliterate Period, the corner bastions were dropped, and the exterior outline was neatly pleated in a uniform arrangement of buttresses that created wall niches and reveals. (Fig. 3.16) Clearly, the initial structural logic of this distinctive feature of Mesopotamian temple architecture had already been transmuted into a system of aesthetics. What started as a support for the mud-brick walls became, in addition, the means of their plastic articulation.

The White Temple sat on an artificial mountain, or ziggurat, of irregular outline, rising 12 meters (40 feet) above the featureless plain. The ziggurat had swelled to grandiose proportions in stages by absorbing the frames of earlier temples, which in accordance with local practice would be filled solid after serving their time, to be used as terraces for the replacement structure. The walls of the ziggurat were sloped and striped with diagonal fluting. Access to the top was by means of a stair and ramp built against the northeast face. The temple stood toward the southwest, unencumbered by parapets. Its four corners pointed toward the main directions of the compass, the standard orientation for religious architecture. Whitewashed and lofty, it would be visible for miles around above the ring of the city walls—a landmark that placed Warka in the vast stretches of fields and marshes and announced its divine patronage.

The case of the urban temple was different. Dedicated to lesser deities, it was built

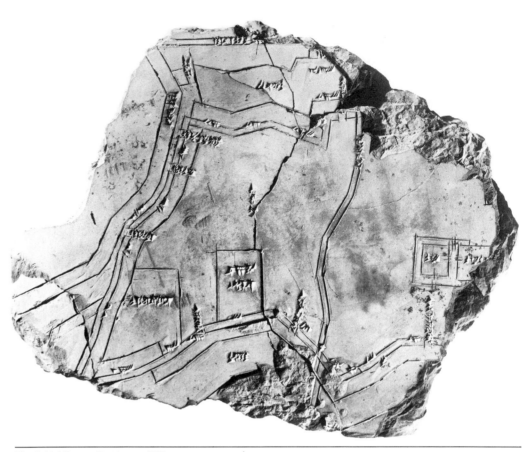

Fig. 3.13 Nippur (Iraq), ca. 1500 B.C.; map on clay tablet.

closer to the living space of the city and was surrounded by common structures. Sin Temple II at Khafaje, roughly contemporary with the White Temple of Warka, illustrates the result of this crowded condition. (Fig. 3.17) The temple proper was sealed tight on three sides and could be entered only through an irregular forecourt. Cult observances carried out in the open air at Warka were here relegated to this odd space. One of the aisles of the tripartite temple plan now housed a narrow staircase leading up to the flat roof, a usable space in the summertime. At Sin Temple V, a later stage of the same building, the stair was removed from this aisle, perhaps to discourage excessive traffic through the temple, and set up outside along one wall of the forecourt. Additional courts con-

tained the bread ovens associated with the daily meals of the deity, and offices and storerooms lined up along the south side.

These practical adjustments to the urban fabric affected the experience of the temple. Rather than being an object in midspace with openings on three sides, as was the White Temple at Warka, the temple now became the innermost of a series of enclosed spaces with a single entrance in one of its long sides. By the time of Sin Temple VIII, in the Early Dynastic Period, the one main entrance to this introverted complex was flanked by massive blocks of masonry and approached by a monumental staircase; the courts were consolidated into one functional space; and the temple was tightened further through the suppression of one aisle and the rigid reordering of the

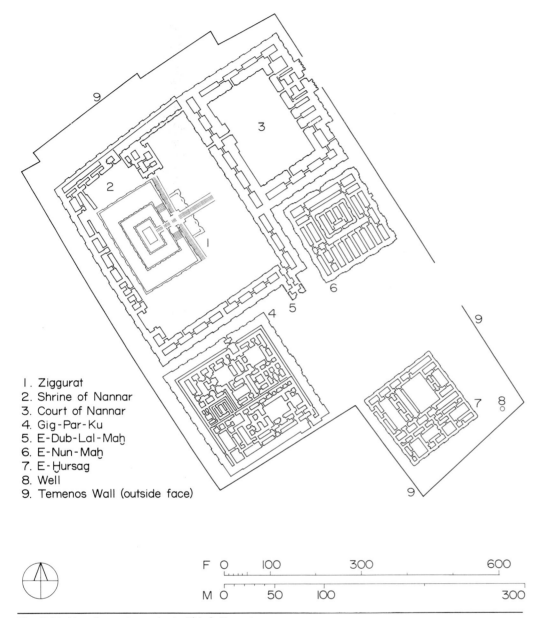

1. Ziggurat
2. Shrine of Nannar
3. Court of Nannar
4. Gig-Par-Ku
5. E-Dub-Lal-Maḥ
6. E-Nun-Maḥ
7. E-Ḥursag
8. Well
9. Temenos Wall (outside face)

F 0   100   300   600
M 0   50   100   300

Fig. 3.14 Ur, ziggurat precinct, Third Dynasty (2113–2006 B.C.) and later; plan.

which had to be entered through a single substantial gate flanked by towers. Here at this fortified gate the transition was made from the profane world of city streets into the sacred world of the temple complex. The worshipper's axial progress moved through the outer and inner courts toward the elevated sanctuary, in a controlled experience of augmenting privilege and sanctity.

The experience of the ziggurat temple, in contrast, rested on reverential climbing. Godhead in the urban temple resided in a remote and guarded sanctum at the end of a planned sequence. In the ziggurat complex, godhead was lifted up above the city, hovering between the heavens and the daily sea. In nature, this intermediate territory was represented by the mountain. It was in the mountain that the earth and the sky were united. Earth deities dwelled inside it, and the deities of the sky could make its summit their halting place. The very form of the mountain suggested a setting of reconciliation between the two prime motives of prehistoric religion, the comfort of the earth and heavenward aspiration. Rooted in the depths of the earth, the cradle of life and death, the mountain thrust upward like solid prayer to a region that the sun's path circumscribed and the stars populated. It married in its shape the dark cave below and the dome of heaven above. It became the traditional stage of communion between gods and chosen mortals. In every religion of the past, processions of pilgrimages make their way up these natural ladders; they were, and still are, among the most elemental rituals of faith.

The ziggurat was conceived as a substitute mountain. (Fig. 3.19) The Sumerians who galvanized the first towns of Mesopotamia had come down from the mountainous north, probably from the area around the Caspian Sea. In the mud plain of the south, the need to re-create the natural architecture of their homeland must have been keenly felt. This atavistic urge is evident in the naming of ziggurats: one of them, for instance, is called "House of the Mountain, Mountain of the Storm, Bond between Heaven and Earth."

The essence of the ziggurat is that it be high. At its skirts will be arrayed the full

other so that it formed a single antechamber to the holy of holies.

The urban temple, now formalized, would retain this program even when, as with the nearby Temple Oval at Khafaje, the demolition of houses opened up a large enough area for a major temple precinct. (Fig. 3.18) The court of the urban temple had a well

and circular basins for ablutions. Workshops, bakeries, and storage rooms arranged themselves on four sides, while the temple was lifted on its own platform at the far end. In front of the court, there was a more public area with the offices of the temple administration to one side. A high wall wrapped around the entire precinct,

panoply of theocratic socialism—store-rooms and workshops, offices and priestly quarters, and a temple where the statue of the deity will stand for his or her epiphany, since the unshielded radiance of divinity is not commonly bearable. Up above, he or she will appear in person to those entitled to witness the deity's full glory. The ziggurat is a ladder, then, as much for the deity's descent into the city as for the ceremonious climb of human servants—the king and the high priest and the pure virgin whom the male god would have chosen for himself and whose union with him would bring about, for one more year, fertility and abundance in the land. The ziggurat temple was, among other things, a marriage bed. We recall the Greek historian Herodotus' description of the ziggurat at Babylon.

On the topmost tower there is a spacious temple and inside the temple stands a couch of unusual size, richly adorned, with a golden table by its side. There is no statue of any kind set up in the place, nor is the chamber occupied by anyone but a single native woman . . . who is chosen for himself by the deity out of all the women of the land. They also declare that the god comes down in person into this chamber, and sleeps upon the couch.

The commission to build the temple came from above. Precise measurements were spoken to the king in secret. We have the account of King Gudea of Lagash and how he first realized that something was expected of him when the Tigris refused to rise during the normal period of inundations; how the god then told him in a dream that he wished to be established, a clear reference to the preurban period when nomads and farmers would consecrate a forest or a mountain or a cavern to the gods in return for the use of the remaining land. When this land was made to carry cities, and the cities became magnificent, a new house for the gods had to be undertaken. We encounter similar feelings in the nomads who

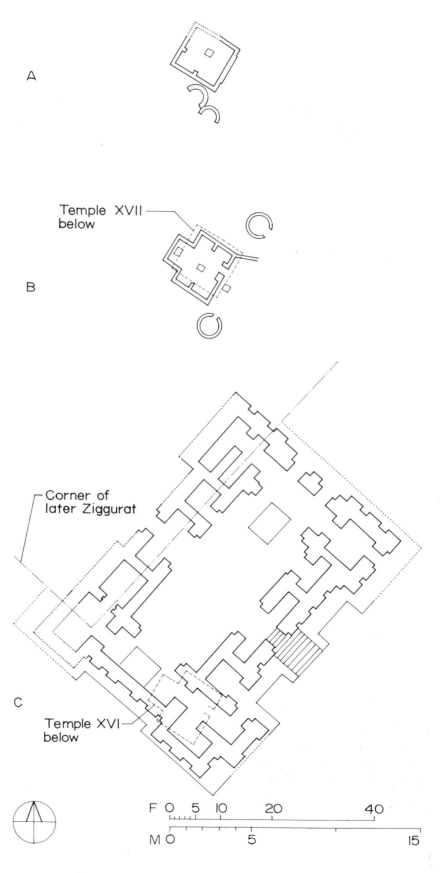

Fig. 3.15 Eridu (Iraq), ground plans of superimposed temples: (**A**) Temple XVII, ca. 5000 B.C.; (**B**) Temple XVI, ca. 4900 B.C.; (**C**) Temple VII, ca. 3800 B.C.

Fig. 3.16a Warka (Erech or Uruk, Iraq), "White Temple," present state.

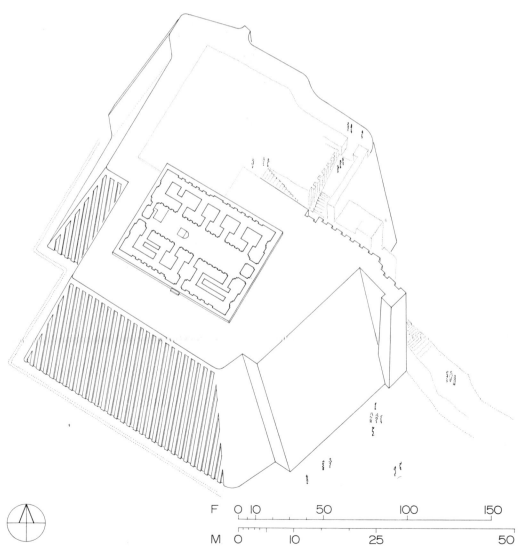

F   0 10   50   100   150

M   0   10   25   50

Fig. 3.16b Warka, "White Temple," 3500–3000 B.C.; axonometric drawing of ziggurat with temple plan.

59

now lived in an architectural environment, as reflected in the Old Testament; King David, to obliterate the deplorable contrast between his luxury and God's houselessness ("See now I dwell in an house of cedar, but the Ark dwelleth within curtains." II Samuel 7:2) announces the founding of a temple that would be a permanent sanctuary for the hitherto portable, peripatetic Tabernacle.

But what form should the house of god take? Gudea was given appropriate instructions. He then alerted his people to gather materials. The city was purified. At the site of the future temple, the soil was swept away until native rock was reached; offerings were laid out; the foundation trenches were filled with purified earth. Then the piling began. The king himself and his family led the community in this ritual of labor. A later Sumerian relief from Ur depicts King Ur-Nammu's involvement in temple architecture. (Fig. 3.20) At the top, the king is pouring libations before an enthroned deity who is shown holding measuring rod and line. In the next register, the king is carrying builders' tools on his shoulders—pick and compasses and mortar basket—assisted by a priest and led by the god. Below this relief the construction of the temple was begun; a ladder remains from the otherwise destroyed scene. We have a late cuneiform tablet that testifies to the king's active role.

The Lord Marduk commanded me concerning Etemenanki, the staged tower of Babylon . . . that I should make its foundations secure in the bosom of the nether world, and make its summit like the heavens. . . . I caused baked bricks to be made. As it were the rains from on high which are measureless or great torrents, I caused streams of bitumen to be brought by the canal Arahtu. . . . I took a reed and myself measured the dimensions. . . . For my Lord Marduk I bowed my neck, I took off my robe, the sign of my royal blood, and on my head I bore bricks and earth.

The word "staged" is accurate. In contrast to the ziggurat at Warka with its single stair, later ziggurats were usually towers

Fig. 3.17 Khafaje (Iraq), ground plans of Sin temples: (**A**) Temple II, ca. 3000 B.C.; (**B**) Temple V, ca. 2900 B.C.; (**C**) Temple VIII, ca. 2750 B.C.

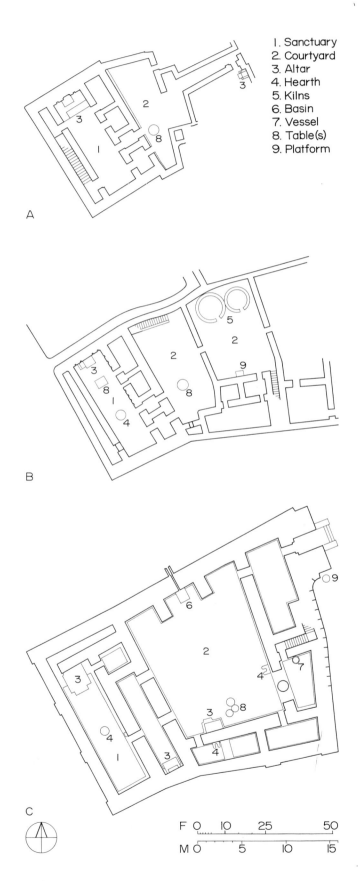

1. Sanctuary
2. Courtyard
3. Altar
4. Hearth
5. Kilns
6. Basin
7. Vessel
8. Table(s)
9. Platform

A

B

C

F 0   10   25   50

M 0   5   10   15

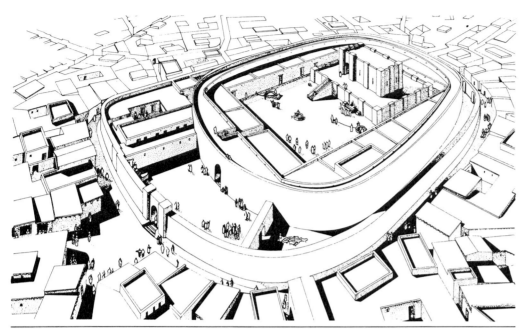

Fig. 3.18 Khafaje, Oval Temple, ca. 2650–2350 B.C.; reconstruction view.

with several distinct terraces. The most famous among them, the great ziggurat of Ur-Nammu at Ur (ca. 2000 B.C.), was a stepped pyramid in three stages. (Fig. 3.21) The core was of mud-brick, and the thick facing of baked brick was set in bitumen mortar. The approach was on the northeast side. Here, three staircases led upward: one of them set at right angles to the building, the other two leaning against the wall. They converged in a great gateway from which a single flight of stairs ran straight up to the door of the temple. None of the lines of the ziggurat is straight. The sloping walls are, in addition, slightly convex. The wall line on the ground plan is similarly curved outward. These calculated diversions were intended to correct the look of stiffness and enervation that strict rectilinearity tends to induce in structures of this size.

We must complete the picture of the Mesopotamian ziggurat with color and some vegetation. At Ur, it seems evident that the upper terraces were planted with trees that formed verdant hanging gardens. Since exposed soil at these points allowed dampness to seep into the core causing the mud-bricks to swell, narrow slits or "weep-holes" were regularly cut through the baked-brick

casing to drain the interior and prevent deformed walls. The color was supplied by tiles. The earliest trace we have of this refinement is at Warka. Glazed bricks come much later; they were widely used in the Assyrian period, the technique having been brought over from Egypt where it had long been known.

Once the ziggurat and its temple were complete, the remaining question was: Would the god be pleased with it and come to reside there? It is the anxiety that King Solomon feels when the Temple he had built was ready for use: "But will God indeed dwell on earth? Behold the heaven and heaven of heavens cannot contain thee: how much less this house that I have builded" (I Kings 8:27). The hope is in rigorously upheld ritual. One false step on the part of the people or their rulers, any gross irreverence or neglect of the proprieties, and god will abandon the city. The Mountain of Heaven, venerated and ascended in humility, will remain a beneficent tower reaching up toward divinity. Used for sinister purposes, to reach the gods rather than reach up to them, it will turn into a tower of enormity. To the inhabitants of Mesopotamian cities, the ziggurat had always

been a ladder of humble reverence, a way to come into contact with the superhuman power that held the secret of their destiny. To the Jews who arrived on the scene with their own jealous Lord God, it was sacrilegious. The ziggurat of Babylon became, for them, the Tower of Babel, an overweening structure that God had no alternative but to interrupt. (Fig. 3.22)

Palaces

This view of the Tower of Babel is of course that of a rival religion that sees in the ruins of the culture it is displacing the just deserts of a wanton community. But internal re-evaluation of the ziggurat in the course of Mesopotamian history is also evident. From being the undisputed center of the city at the beginning, the ziggurat in time lost some physical prominence to other focal points of the urban fabric, the principal one being the palace of the king. At one end of Mesopotamian history, the king lives in the precinct of the god and may in fact be the same person as the high priest. At the other end, during the Assyrian period, the ziggurat becomes a mere adjunct to the king's palace, which now completely dominates the cityscape. (Fig. 3.23)

The stages of such a development are not clear, if indeed they constituted a methodical process. At Ur, the famous ziggurat of the Third Dynasty described above had

Fig. 3.19 A ziggurat as depicted on an Assyrian relief from the palace of Assurbanipal of Nineveh, seventh century B.C. (Fragments in the British Museum, London, and the Louvre, Paris)

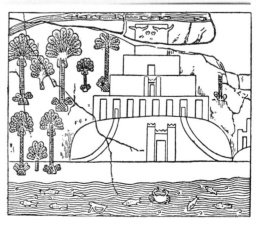

Fig. 3.21 Ur, ziggurat of Ur-Nammu; reconstruction drawing.

Fig. 3.20 Stele of Ur-Nammu (2113–2096 B.C.), from Ur. (University Museum, University of Pennsylvania, Philadelphia)

Fig. 3.22 Pieter Brueghel, *The Tower of Babel*, 1563. (Kunsthistorisches Museum, Vienna)

within its precinct walls two residential buildings. (Fig. 3.14) The larger, called Gig-Par-Ku, seems to have been a priestly residence; it is just below the walled enclosure of the ziggurat proper. The other, further east, is the royal palace, a square building divided into three distinct sections. At Mari, about 1750 B.C., the proportions are reversed. The palace, an enormous building of some 260 rooms and courts, overwhelms the ziggurat complex to its southeast.

The plan at Mari is organized around three main courts. (Fig. 3.24) The first of these, capable of holding hundreds of

Fig. 3.23 Sketch plans showing the relationship of ziggurat and royal palace: (**A**) at Ur, ca. 2000 B.C.; (**B**) at Assur, ca. 1800 B.C.; (**C**) at Assur, ca. 1200 B.C.; and (**D**) at Khorsabad, ca. 700 B.C. The lighter hatching indicates palaces; the darker hatching, ziggurats.

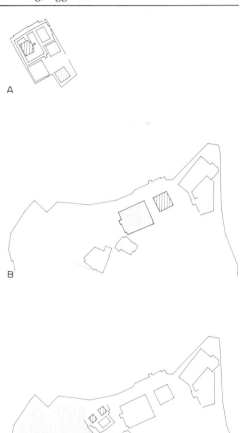

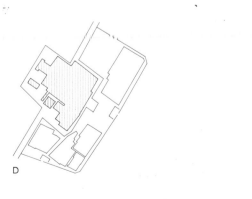

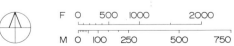

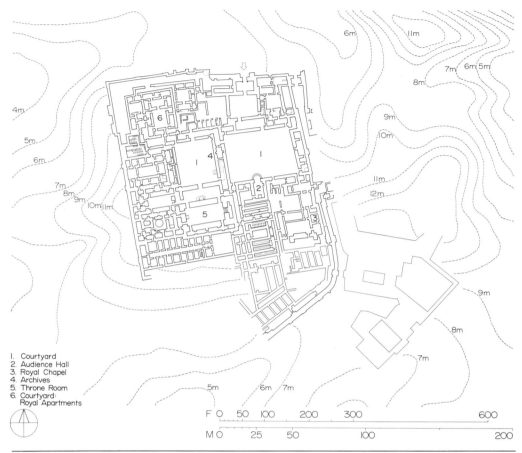

1. Courtyard
2. Audience Hall
3. Royal Chapel
4. Archives
5. Throne Room
6. Courtyard:
   Royal Apartments

Fig. 3.24 Mari (Tel Hariri, Syria), royal palace, ca. 1750 B.C.; ground plan.

functionaries and petitioners, was approached through a devious, nonaxial path from the only outside gate at the northeast corner. Semicircular stairs on the south side of this vast court led up to what may have been an audience hall. The public sector of the palace centered around the second court, immediately to the west. Its walls were decorated with paintings representing scenes of sacrifice and the investiture of the king of Mari by the goddess Ishtar. The palace archives were kept in a room between the two courts. On the south side of the second court was the Throne Room approached by a magnificent set of stairs. The private living quarters of the royal family occupied the northwest section of the palace. Around a small court, with walls painted to imitate marble encrustation, it is possible to recognize bedrooms of lavish design and the king's own hall. Adjacent to these royal apartments was a service wing containing kitchens and bathrooms (one of them displays two terra-cotta tubs and a "Turkish" lavatory), as well as a school for scribes with rows of benches still intact.

It is not difficult to see the layout of the palace as an elaboration of the private house. The organizing principle of a central court surrounded by rooms is the same; so is the tightly sealed periphery with the single door from the outside and the nonaxial entrance path. (Fig. 3.11) But the size, mixed program, and security of the palace limit the comparison. Hundreds of rooms have to have access to natural light. The movement of servants and troups must be kept separate from the royal path; the king's intimate life must be separate from his public presence. And in its frame, the palace must be able to accommodate a variety of functions related to the king's double existence as a family man and head of state. In all this, the palace behaves as a microcosm of the city, with its walls, residences, temples, offices, schools, barracks, workshops, and so on. But it has little of the physical dynamism of the city-form, little of its vital untidiness, little of the social flexibility of streets. It is a regimented city, a vast rectangle divided and subdivided into units of orthogonal geometry, large and small, open and closed, ornate and plain. And the strict relation on paper of one cluster of these units to the next bespeaks a hieratic code of behavior on the part of the thousands of users within. (Figs. 3.10, 3.24)

The next complication in the relationship of ziggurat and palace was that the ziggurat multiplied. At the Assyrian capital of Assur the main ziggurat had stood alone next to the Old Palace. But a double temple to Anu and Hadad (Heaven and Storm) between two square ziggurats rose in time next to the larger New Palace. (Fig. 3.23, B and C) What is more, the ziggurat in Assyrian hands became hard to climb. Means other than stairs and ramps began to be employed, at the cost of the symbolism of the Ladder of Heaven. The two ziggurats of Anu and Hadad were presumably accessible only from the temple roof. At the same time, the classic hierarchy of a deity as the overlord of the city and the king as the steward of the divine estate had been upset as early as 2000 B.C. Some kings, for example those of the Third Dynasty of Ur, were deified in their own lifetime and were adopted as patron deities of vassal cities.

The final debasement of the ziggurat occurs at Khorsabad. This city was a royal Assyrian foundation, begun in 706 B.C., and abandoned, unfinished, shortly afterward. (Fig. 3.25) It covered 2.5 square kilometers (almost one square mile). There were two arched gates on each side of the square, guarded by stone demons in the form of human-headed bulls. On the northwest side one of the gates had been replaced by a

1. Citadel Wall
2. Platform:
   Royal Palace
3. Platform:
   Palace of the Crown Prince (?)
4. Temple(s)
5. Ziggurat
6. Entrance Court
7. Court of Honor
8. Throne Room
9. Ramp Up
10. Unexcavated

F 0   500   1000   2000   3000   4000   MILE

M 0   100   500   1000   1500

Fig. 3.25a Khorsabad (the ancient Dur Sharrukin, Iraq), Assyrian city founded by Sargon II (721–705 B.C.); plan.

bastion that served as a platform for the royal palace. Rather than being surrounded by the fabric of his city, the king now had his back to the city walls. The citadel that contained the palace, ostensibly a point of last defense against an outside enemy as the ziggurat complex once had been, can also be construed as a ring of protection around the ruling monarch to ward against internal uprisings.

The palace at Khorsabad is similar in general layout to that at Mari. The administrative court of honor is here at the top of the plan, with the great Throne Room on the left. The entrance court is associated with a number of temples grouped along the west side. They were all served by a single ziggurat that was like no other example of this Mesopotamian building type. Small and laced with recesses and crenellations, it looked more like a fancy reliquary than the robust manmade mountain

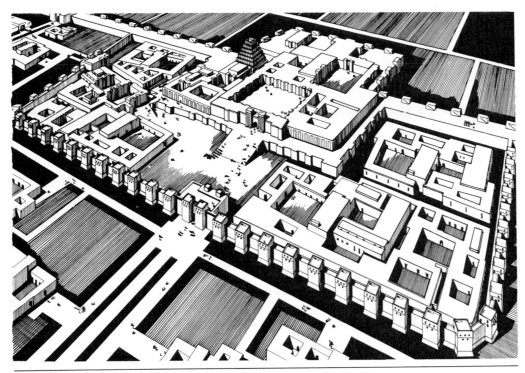

Fig. 3.25b Khorsabad, citadel with royal palace; reconstruction view.

were revetted with stone slabs carved in relief. They showed the king and his courtiers, over life size, all facing toward the Throne Room. Once admitted through one of its three doors, the petitioner or ambassador stood in the brilliantly painted space of an oblong room. The throne, as at Mari, was set against one of the narrow walls. Its base was of stone and carved upon it, as a suitable warning to those within who might contemplate rebellion and to enemies without, was a relief showing King Sargon, the founder of Khorsabad, "in his war chariot above the bodies of the slain while soldiers piled up pyramids of heads before him."

The Throne Room at Khorsabad is a fitting testimonial to the warlike Assyrian kings who had ruthlessly forged an empire out of the city-states of Mesopotamia and struck terror among neighboring people. With the slow erosion of urban integrity and of the allegiance of the city to a single superior deity, the palace as a building type arrives here at its grim apogee. It had started out as an accessory to the ziggurat—the administrative headquarters and official residence of a pious king who supervised grain distribution, the maintenance of dikes and canals, and the preventive rites against floods and outside attacks. But the palace grew at the expense of the ziggurat, as an increasingly autocratic sovereign ruled heavy-handedly over both church and state. And it developed, finally, into a theater of absolute power and intimidation, the symbol of a city whose piety now existed in the shadow of a fierce war machine.

of the cities of the plain. A continuous ramp wound around the exterior, from the base to the summit.

The approach to the palace was through the city, past the citadel gate, and across a large open square. A broad ramp which could accommodate chariots ran up from the square to the main gate of the palace. One passed through it, crossed the first court, and through a small passage at the northeast corner was ushered into the court of honor. This was an impressive, indeed terrifying, waiting room for those who had been granted a royal audience. The walls

Further Reading

J. R. Bartlett, *Jericho* (Guilford, Surrey: Lutterworth Press, 1982).

M. A. Beck, *Atlas of Mesopotamia* (London and Edinburgh: Thomas Nelson and Sons, 1956).

H. Frankfort, *The Art and Architecture of the Ancient Orient* (Harmondsworth and Baltimore: Penguin, 1970).

———, *The Birth of Civilization in the Near East* (Bloomington: Indiana University Press, 1959).

S. Giedion, *The Eternal Present: The Beginnings of Architecture,* vol. II (New York: Pantheon, 1964).

J. Hawkes, ed., *Atlas of Ancient Archeology* (New York: McGraw-Hill, 1974).

P. Lampl, *Cities and Planning in the Ancient Near East* (New York: Braziller, 1968).

S. Lloyd, H. W. Muller, and R. Martin, *Ancient Architecture: Mesopotamia, Egypt, Crete, Greece* (New York: Abrams, 1974).

A. Parrot, *Tower of Babel,* trans. E. Hudson (New York: Philosophical Library, 1955).

C. L. Woolley, *Excavations at Ur* (London: E. Benn, 1955).

Abu Simbel (Egypt), rock-cut temples, ca. 1250 B.C.

4

THE ARCHITECTURE OF ANCIENT EGYPT

The Land of Egypt

The ancient Egyptians were in all likelihood an indigenous people, though they were not as isolated from the rest of the Mediterranean world as it has sometimes been claimed. From the beginning they traded with the communities of Western Asia across the Sinai Peninsula, and with the Libyan tribes to the west across the Delta. They imported cedarwood from Lebanon and exploited the gold mines of Nubia (Ethiopia) to the south.

As in Mesopotamia, the story begins with the village life of farming and animal husbandry, in the highlands above the Nile Valley, which was transformed in time into a sophisticated pattern of river settlements based on controlled irrigation. The political authority that rose in the Land between the Rivers to oversee the network of canals and dykes functioned through a number of independent cities. Neolithic village life along the Nile developed instead into two broad polities: Lower Egypt, which included the whole Delta area until the neighborhood of Memphis, and Upper Egypt, southward from this point as far as Aswan. Each had a separate ruler and a separate capital—Pe (Buto) in Lower Egypt and Nekhen (Hierakonpolis) in Upper Egypt. (Fig. 4.1) Then, at the start of recorded history, King Menes of Upper Egypt invaded the north and unified the country, an event which made a deep impression on the collective memory of the people of the region and became the pivot of political, and hence architectural, symbolism.

This unification and the setting up of a capital at Memphis coincide with the very end of what we had called in the last chapter the Protoliterate Period, that is, about 3000 B.C. By this time some basic schemes had already surfaced in the vernacular idiom of reeds and mud—for example, the battering of walls and plant-based uprights—that will become standard features of the monumental architecture to follow. One of the most characteristic aspects of Egyptian culture is conservatism, or rather the balance it always sustains between innovation and tradition.

During the Early Dynastic Period in Mesopotamia, Egyptian building displayed great advances. Beginning with impressive palaces and tombs in brick which leaned on the vernacular idiom and aggrandized it, the country developed an articulate stone architecture, the great examples of which, at Saqqara and Giza, we soon will be looking at. Egyptologists refer to this stretch of time as the Archaic (or Thinite) Period, roughly 3000 to 2665 B.C., and its sequel the Old Kingdom, down to about 2150 B.C. It is marked by the emergence and consolidation of absolute kingship. The Indestructible monuments that still tower over the riverscape south of modern Cairo were intended to commemorate the rule of the pharaoh, divine and all-powerful, and to ensure the perpetuity of his cult. (Fig. 4.10)

This unchallenged central power was dissipated toward the latter part of the third millennium, but was reinstituted, after a spell of political and social chaos, in a more tempered guise. In the period called Middle Kingdom, about 2250 to 1570 B.C., power was shared by provincial governors, or nomarchs, and the priesthood of important deities. In the bewildering crowd of local gods and goddesses, each with his or her own geographical sphere of authority, the royal cult in the Old Kingdom had stood out as the national religion that absorbed collegiate divinity and transmitted its hope to the masses. Now the pharaoh had to acknowledge the power of some priestly fraternities to act as intermediary between the people and the protagonists of the official pantheon, headed by the sun-god Re and the trinity of the netherworld, Osiris, his wife Isis, and their son Horus. The king's funerary settings came first to accommodate his divine colleagues more generously and, in time, their own temples loomed large on the banks of the Nile.

The actual flourishing of monumental temple architecture in Egypt, as distinct from environments of royal burial and attendant practices, belongs to the so-called New Kingdom, especially between 1600 and 1300 B.C. (Fig. 4.20) This period opened with the expulsion of an alien invasion force, the Hyksos people, out of the Delta, which involved Egypt in a new policy of conquest. A vast Egyptian empire came to embrace much of the Sudan and subject states in Palestine and Syria.

There is no neat correlation in the development of the first two literate cultures of the Near East; no historical coincidence of their high points and nadirs. In the structure of their physical setting, in the building materials they used, in political organization and attitudes toward life and death, the two regions are also not comparable. Although both were river environments disciplined early by a network of canals and dykes, Egypt's single river was never tur-

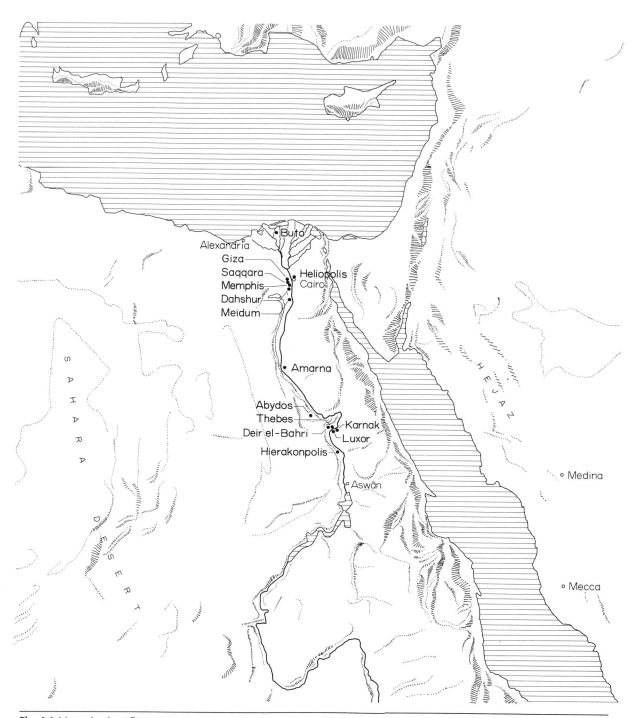

Alexandria
• Buto
Giza
Saqqara
Memphis — Heliopolis
Dahshur Cairo
Meidum

• Amarna

S A H A R A   D E S E R T

H E J A Z

Abydos
Thebes
Deir el-Bahri — Karnak
Hierakonpolis Luxor

° Aswān

° Medina

° Mecca

Fig. 4.1 Map: Ancient Egypt.

bulent like the Tigris and Euphrates. It was a temperate, steady line of water, navigable throughout, and subject to unfailingly regular and benign flooding. From July to October the low-lying banks were inundated, the waters leaving their deposit of rich black silt which could be sowed with little plowing. This narrow strip of valley, the Black Land, was rigidly divided into fields, the boundaries of which had to be re-established after every period of flooding. Egypt's early mastery of geometry and its affinity for the right angle (curved walls or circular buildings are almost unknown in the ancient architecture of Egypt) owe a debt to this annual survey.

The Nile in fact was the great axis. For 500 miles it stretched, the country's liquid spine, a band of blue and arable green hemmed in by parallel lines of cliff in Upper Egypt, and fanning out further north to form the broader frame of the Delta. Beyond, to east and west was the Red Land, the desert, death. Except for the Delta folk, most Egyptians knew no circular horizon. Things ran along the Nile, mostly north and south, or at right angles to it, in the direction of the rising and setting sun. Orthogonal planning came naturally both in the field division of the Black Land and in the design of cities. We have only to compare the tangled layout of later Sumerian Ur with the strictly orthogonal "pyramid city" of Sesostris II (1897–1878 B.C.) at El Kahun, its main streets running precisely north-south, to grasp the difference between Mesopotamian and Egyptian order. (Figs. 3.10, 4.2) This difference is between an organism that grew loosely through time in response to patterns of mixed use, and the predetermined plan of El Kahun, laid down at one time, with standardized buildings grouped into special zones—brick row houses, often

Fig. 4.2 El Kahun (Lower Egypt), the workers' town at the pyramid site of King Sesostris II (1897–1878 B.C.). Top, site plan, with pyramid indicated at the far left and the valley temple with its causeway at the far right, just below the town; middle, plan of the excavated section; bottom, a detail plan of the northwestern strip, showing workers' housing to the left—the darker lines indicate house types—and the ampler quarter for government officials to the right.

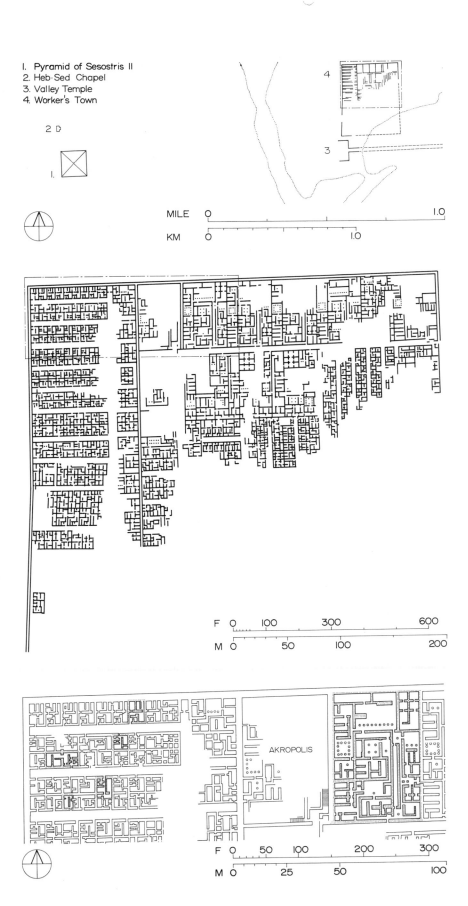

1. Pyramid of Sesostris II
2. Heb-Sed Chapel
3. Valley Temple
4. Worker's Town

back to back, for the workers and crafts-men, a quarter of large mansions for gov-ernment officials, and the enclosed com-pound for the king next to the northern wall.

This is not to say that Egypt was without its organic urban clusters, especially in older cities like Thebes or Memphis, of which unhappily very little has survived. But geo-metric master plans are unique to Egypt at this early date. There were the so-called pyramid cities created by individual phar-aohs, like Sesostris II, to house the work force of their burial complex, the priest-hood of the royal cult, and tenant farmers; and the string of planned fortress towns built in Nubia by the kings of the Twelfth Dynasty. The earliest hieroglyphic sign for "province," or *nome,* was a rectangle di-vided into four by intersecting lines; the sign for "town" showed a circular enclo-sure around an orthogonal street system or a dominant cross-axis. Even a seemingly random arrangement like the capital of King Akhenaten, Amarna, reflects its sensitivity toward the river axis by having three main arteries that run in line with the bank curve. (Fig. 4.3)

The linear stretch of the land is perhaps evoked in one other aspect of the built en-vironment. Egyptian design conceived of major architectural programs as a series of episodes along a predetermined path. The pyramids of Giza appear today like three splendid objects in mid-space at the desert edge. In fact, they were the culmination of an architectural sequence that began at the west bank. New Kingdom temples were themselves channels of passage like the river along which they stood. (Figs. 4.20, 4.22) The great pylons may have encapsu-lated this correspondence by their form—a central trough above the entrance and massive flanking towers, like the rock cliffs that bounded the river valley. The clus-tered columns of the courtyards and halls, with their plant-inspired capitals, conjured up Nile groves.

Once again, the comparison with Meso-potamian temple precincts is instructive. (Figs. 3.14, 4.19) At the ziggurat compound of Ur, a number of independent buildings, each with its own boundary wall, is grouped tidily, but with no unifying axes. The zig-gurat itself has three approach stairs that meet at a single gateway some way up the

northeast slope. At Karnak, the temple of Amon marshals all its component units along a straight path, and a cross-axis that takes off halfway down the middle of the south flank leaves the precinct of this cen-tral group to line up with the Mut complex to the south. Even within the experience of a single temple unit, Khafaje on the one hand and Luxor on the other, the headlong course of an Egyptian axis is distinctive. (Figs. 3.18, 4.18) Not only is the Mesopo-tamian axis bent, but the terminal sanctu-ary space, an oblong transversely laid in relation to the directional line of the ap-proach toward it, slows down the momen-tum of the sequence. At Luxor we are pulled deeper and deeper toward the core of di-vinity as the spaces along the axis constrict beyond the courts and the level rises, heightening through physical means the wonder and privilege of heading toward the holy of holies.

In one sense, everything along the banks was linked to everything else by the Nile axis. That was the major highway of the country. It brought together the villages of Upper Egypt and the cities of the Delta; it carried northward the granite of far-off As-wan, and the fine limestone of Tura upriver to southern building sites; and for the lowly fellah it provided food and also the build-ing material for his house and boatmaking needs—reeds and plants, and silt for daub-ing walls and striking brick. The river's majestic calm and the reliable periodicity of its behavior must have projected a settled, eternal order. The Nile flooded when it was expected to, several crops were raised, then came the dry season, and then, with un-failing regularity, the Nile flooded again, as it had for centuries, and the cycle was re-peated. Such ageless patterns have no foreseeable end and present no choices. It is not surprising that the Egyptians of an-tiquity should stake their all on a belief in unruffled stability, on a world view in which death was not a final thing but merely the passage to another region where, speaking not too metaphorically, the Nile flooded and crops were raised and the dry season came and people did what they always did and had about them what they always had: the pharaoh according to his station, the hum-ble fellah according to his. One's tomb was like one's house, but built to last for eter-nity; its forms logically recalled, through

direct imitation or in symbolic shorthand, the architecture of ordinary residences, palaces, and even city walls. Funerary art, in a literal-minded way, provided magical replicas of the buried person's wants and possessions.

In this, too, Egypt is very different from Mesopotamia. When King Ur-Nammu dies, there is sorrow and weeping throughout the land. The "wail of Sumer" reaches him after many days in the dim and sad netherworld. The walls of Ur which he started are left unfinished; the new palace is unpurified; his wife is left behind and he can no longer press her to his bosom. The Egyptian Book of the Dead has no such worries about death.

Fig. 4.3 Amarna (Upper Egypt), the new capital of King Akhenaten (1379–1362 B.C.), Eighteenth Dynasty; diagrammatic plan of layout, showing the relationship to the Nile and the course of the main streets.

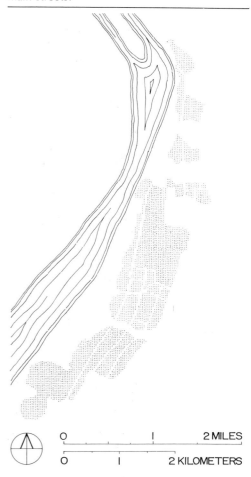

O King N! You are not gone dead, you are gone alive . . . you go in, you come out while your heart is glad in the favor of the Lord of Gods. It so happens that you live again. . . . Your soul will not be kept away from your body. . . . You receive what is upon earth. You have water, you breathe the air, you drink to your heart's content.

Not surprisingly, for the first fifteen hundred years of its existence as a high culture, Egypt was obsessed with the preservation and provisioning of the dead body. It lavished its finest efforts to that end, on the theaters of the afterlife. It put up monumental tombs, often built of lasting stone (which, in contrast once more to Mesopotamia, was plentiful), and decorated them prodigiously. Much Egyptian ritual, as well as the development of a masonry architecture unsurpassed in technical skill and the evasive ingenuity of its design, was motivated by the belief that the corpse must be spared disturbance and its material needs must be supplied, so that it could continue

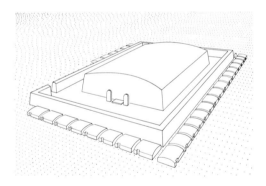

Fig. 4.4a Abydos (Upper Egypt), royal tumulus tomb of First Dynasty (ca. 3100–2890 B.C.); reconstruction drawing.

Fig. 4.4b Saqqara (Lower Egypt), mortuary complex of Queen Herneith, First Dynasty; reconstruction drawing.

to function normally forever. And no corpse was more privileged in this respect than that of the god-king.

The Burial of Kings

At first, after the unification of Egypt and as a consequence of it, the pharaoh was given a double burial. As lord of Upper Egypt, he was buried symbolically at Abydos, 300 miles south of Cairo, a site sacred to the god of the Underworld, Osiris, and the ancestral home of the early kings. The actual body was laid to rest at Saqqara.

The cenotaphs of the early pharaohs at Abydos consisted of a subterranean chamber roofed in timber and topped with a heap of sand contained within a brick shell. (Fig. 4.4) Stelai were set up outside to mark the place for offerings, and beyond a low precinct wall the king's family and members of the court were buried in mastabas, small tumulus graves with a casement of brick. At Saqqara the royal tombs were more complicated. The burial pit, cut into native rock, comprised, in addition to the burial chamber, a number of subsidiary rooms holding the owner's valuable possessions. On this system was erected a large rectangular structure, as much as 9 meters (30 feet) high, with an intricately panelled brick exterior coated with white lime-stucco and painted with geometric designs. This superstructure enclosed rooms where supplies were stored for the use of the deceased. The recessed exterior and the layout of the rooms were meant to stand for the actual palace of the king; consonant with the old Lower Egypt custom, the king was considered buried under the floor of his house.

Two other features make their appearance during the 250-year development of these early dynastic tombs at Saqqara: a small mortuary temple on the north side, and a wooden boat alongside the tomb to carry the pharaoh across the heavens. For everyday he would accompany the sun-god Re on his voyage from east to west and at night in the opposite direction, through the Underworld.

Zoser's Pyramid Complex
The Saqqara tomb of one early pharaoh, Zoser, that dates from about 2680 B.C., is

remarkable in several ways. (Fig. 4.5) It is larger and more elaborate than any before it—a vast scheme, and exceptionally not organized on the Egyptian principle of axial sequence. Its architecture develops the most insistent symbolism of the pharaoh as the sole ruler of Upper and Lower Egypt: there are twin tombs, double-court buildings, matching mock palaces. And all this is done in stone—the first interpretation of the brick, timber, and plant forms of Egyptian architecture in the hard medium of Tura limestone.

The structure actually constitutes a technological revolution. This prodigy of masonry construction seems to have no parents. Tell-tale features announce the infancy of its technique. The blocks used are small throughout, more in the measure of brick than cut stone. Uprights, molded in emulation of tree-trunk pillars or bundles of reeds, are not freestanding but always cautiously engaged to walls, and like them built of regular masonry courses rather than of stacked up drums.

Even so, the achievement was epochal and was credited by antiquity to the architect Imhotep. His name is inscribed in one of the rock-cut galleries of the stepped pyramid where he is referred to as being "first after the king of Upper and Lower Egypt." He was revered later for his great wisdom as an astronomer, magician, and healer, and as healer he was deified. In this we have one more fact that sets Egypt apart from Mesopotamia. We know of no Mesopotamian architect by name. The credit for conceiving public buildings and for supervising their construction went to the king. In Egypt, the execution of sacred or prestigious public works elevated the office of the architect instead of forcing it into obscurity. We know something of his working methods from a handful of architectural drawings that have survived. The design process would appear to have combined a simple overall geometric system and the use of a set module to derive the dimensions of the building.

The stepped pyramid which contained Zoser's body stood on high ground in the middle of a vast rectangular terrace about 550 by 275 meters (1,800 by 900 feet). The high wall with recessed paneling around the terrace and the bastions that imitate towered gateways make it probable that Im-

1. Enclosing Wall
2. Entrance Gate
3. Colonnaded Entry Hall
4. Grand Court
5. Southern Mastaba and
   Offering Room
6. Heb·Sed Court
7. House of the South
8. House of the North
9. Court of the Serdab
10. Serdab
11. Mortuary Temple
12. Step Pyramid
13. Sarcophagus Chamber
14. Mastaba (original)
15. Magazines

Fig. 4.5 Saqqara, mortuary complex of King Zoser, Third Dynasty, ca. 2680 B.C.: (**a**) oblique view;
(**b**) partial plan.

Fig. 4.6 Zoser complex, entry hall (no. 3 on Fig. 4.5); reconstruction drawing.

Fig. 4.7 Zoser complex, dummy chapel in Heb-Sed Court (no. 6 on Fig. 4.5).

hotep wanted to conjure the walled city of Memphis, not just the royal palace.

The only real entrance is at the southeast corner of the enclosure. It leads into a long corridor lined with two rows of half-columns engaged to spur walls. (Fig. 4.6) The columns carry a stone ceiling, cut to resemble rounded logs, which rises higher than the roof of the flanking compartments allowing for clerestory slits. This is probably the earliest known case of clerestory lighting. The shafts of light here may have fallen on statues set in the compartments representing, possibly, head deities of the *nomes* or provinces of Egypt, or Zoser himself, or perhaps double statues of Zoser and a *nome*-god. At any rate, the number of these compartments is so close to the standard number of forty-two provinces that it has been suggested that the central space between the colonnades stood for the Nile, with the sudden doubling of the columns at the end opposite the entrance evoking the spread of the Delta.

Beyond the corridor lies a large court, at the southwest corner of which is a building of nearly solid masonry; it probably served as the offering room for a large mastaba hidden within the western enclosure wall.

This secondary tomb may have represented the usual royal cenotaph at Abydos, or else the actual burial place of the king's entrails, which were customarily removed from the corpse before mummification. Or it may have been a dummy tomb for the symbolic sacrifice of the king during the Heb-Sed, a jubilee festival that celebrated the reconsecration of his reign. This festival included a race that proved the king's renewed vigor and was probably associated with fertility. He ran it accompanied by "the priest of the souls of Nekhen," namely, the prehistoric kings of Upper Egypt, and carrying a flail, the implement that is used to thrash grain. Two hoof-shaped markers in this court may have had something to do with this ritual race.

A second important ceremony, the reenactment of the king's coronation, is provided for in a lower court, north of the entrance corridor. The area is entered skirting an unusual, curved wall. On either side of an oblong court stand dummy chapels dedicated to the *nome*-gods of Upper and Lower Egypt. (Fig. 4.7) As in real life, so too in his death the king would have to obtain their consent, one by one, for a new term of office; he would then be crowned, on separate daises at the short ends of the court, with the cone-shaped white crown of Upper Egypt and the caplike red crown of Lower Egypt.

A pair of smaller courts further north stood before two buildings representing the king's "white" and "red" palaces. The

Fig. 4.8 Statue of King Zoser in *serdab* (no. 10 in Fig. 4.5); now moved to the Egyptian Museum, Cairo.

identification of the two buildings is found in the attached chapels whose columns carry lotus and papyrus capitals, two plants which were the emblems of Upper and Lower Egypt, respectively. The lacing of lotus (or lily) and papyrus plants around a stake driven into the ground was a highpoint of the coronation ceremony.

The stepped pyramid lies to the west of this double palace. Along its north side were the mortuary temple, where the offerings were presented, and the *serdab*, a small room holding a seated statue of Zoser and built of solid masonry except for two holes to enable the image to look out. (Fig. 4.8) This statue and others around the complex were considered reliable substitutes for the dead body in the event of its destruction. The body lay beneath the pyramid, in a granite sarcophagus chamber, or rather a shaft, cut through virgin rock and entered from the top through a circular opening. Initially, a simple stone mastaba was placed over it. This mastaba, enlarged three times in the course of construction, became the lowest stage of a four-stepped pyramid. Then the pyramid in turn was enlarged toward the north and west, and the stages increased to six, bringing the total height to 62 meters (204 feet).

What prompted the transformation of the traditional mastaba into this unique pile of stone? We do not, of course, know for certain. What is obvious is that the object was something more than rendering the tomb securer—the desire to monumentalize the tomb, for example, to have it stand out above the perimeter wall and be scaled against the expanse of the west bank. But these six unequal stages also gave a sense of climbing, of aspiration, an effect visually close to the Mesopotamian ziggurat. The difference is obvious and ritually significant. At Saqqara there were no manageable stairs for human ascent, and nothing at the top—no shrine or architectural climax of any sort to be reached. It was a structure that sublimated the holy person of the king and lifted him heavenward to the realm of the sun-god Re.

The pharaoh's relationship to Re was intimate: that of a son to his father. By the end of the Old Kingdom, the two were completely identified with each other. The main cult center of Re was at Heliopolis, just north of Memphis, and the most sacred relic of his temple there was a pyramid, or cone-shaped stone, the *benben*, symbolizing the primeval mound on which the sun-god first revealed himself at the creation. The conclusion is inescapable that the stepped pyramid stood for this mound of creation whose summit was the resting place of the sun. In addition, it was probably thought of as the staircase of divine ascent, which a spell in the Pyramid Texts says was to be laid out for the king, "so that he may mount up to heaven thereby."

The Pyramids of Giza
To etherialize the staircase and to make the royal tomb a worthy symbol of the sunlight that brings Re and his son the pharaoh together—these aims may have been the cosmic reasons for the subsequent attempts, costly and laborious, to transform Zoser's staged scheme into a true pyramid. The process took time and some experimentation. Zoser's Saqqara complex and the famous pyramids of Giza are separated by more than a century. In between, transitional solutions were tried at Meidum and Dahshur. (Fig. 4.9) An initial stepped pyramid at Meidum, 30 miles south of Memphis, had its sides filled in at some later moment and the whole encased in shining

Fig. 4.9 Map: The distribution of pyramids in Lower Egypt.

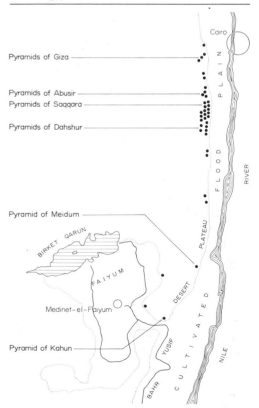

Fig. 4.10 Giza (Lower Egypt), pyramids of Chefren, Cheops, and Mykerinos, Third Dynasty, ca. 2570–2500 B.C.; aerial view from the north. (See also Fig. 1.19.)

Tura limestone. Furthermore, the arrangement of the subsidiary buildings set the pattern for all the later, true pyramids, including those of Giza. This arrangement was now strung along an axis, in contrast to the self-contained layout of Zoser's compound. The mortuary temple was moved to the east side. From here, a sloping causeway reached out to a valley temple closer to the river and connected with it by a canal. The dead body would be brought by boat to this building at the edge of the sown, washed and purified; then it would be embalmed (or perhaps its prior embalmment re-enacted) and subjected to a magic rite called "The Opening of the Mouth" that enabled the king to speak once more and to enjoy offerings. At Dahshur, there were two pyramids, probably built by the same king, Sneferu. Both were planned from the start as true pyramids. One was executed that way; the other, the so-called Bent Pyramid, seems to have been completed in haste after the king's death, with the original 52° angle of incline (which later became standard) reduced abruptly halfway up toward the summit.

At Giza, there are three separate pyramid complexes, the latest, that of Mykerinos, being the smallest. (Figs. 4.10, 4.11) The oldest of the three, that of Cheops, son of Sneferu, has the largest pyramid, 137 meters (450 feet) high at present and another

10 meters originally. But the pyramid complex of Chefren is the best preserved, with its extraordinary valley temple intact, and, next to it, the noble form of the Sphinx, a recumbent leonine body welded to the portrait-head of the king wearing the royal headdress, perhaps the best-known monument in the world. Directly in front of the Sphinx, to the east, was a temple dedicated to Harmakhis, an aspect of the sungod; arranged around a rectangular court paved in alabaster was a continuous cloister that held twenty-four columns, probably an allusion to the sun's daily journey, and two axial niches, east and west, that marked the journey's axis. The temple was entered from the east by two doors.

The same entrance scheme holds for the better-known valley temple next to it. (Fig. 4.12) Between its two doors probably stood the *serdab* for the king's statue. Going in, one encountered, first, a long vestibule and, then, a T-shaped hall set in an enormously thick casement of masonry. It, too, had an alabaster floor which reflected the light that came in through slits set in the upper parts of the walls and the underside of the flat roof. Against the walls stood twenty-three statues of Chefren, representing the deification of individual organs of his body. The walls, which have a pronounced batter, were faced with red granite from Aswan, both inside and out; of granite too were the massive piers and the flat roof they supported. The masonry, for once, does not emulate natural forms or mean anything else, but is content to display its own superb geometry and the clean abstraction of its square uprights and lintels.

From here the body was transferred to the mortuary temple via the covered causeway built on a rock-spur that bridged the depression between the Sphinx group and the pyramid. The walls of the causeway were sure to have been decorated with paintings and reliefs whose subjects, judging from a later example that survived, would include

Fig. 4.11 Giza, the pyramid group: top, general site plan; middle, detail plan of the Chefren complex, showing the mortuary temple, the causeway, the valley temple, and the Sphinx with the attached temple of Harmakhis; bottom, a section through the pyramid of Cheops (the dotted lines indicate stages of construction).

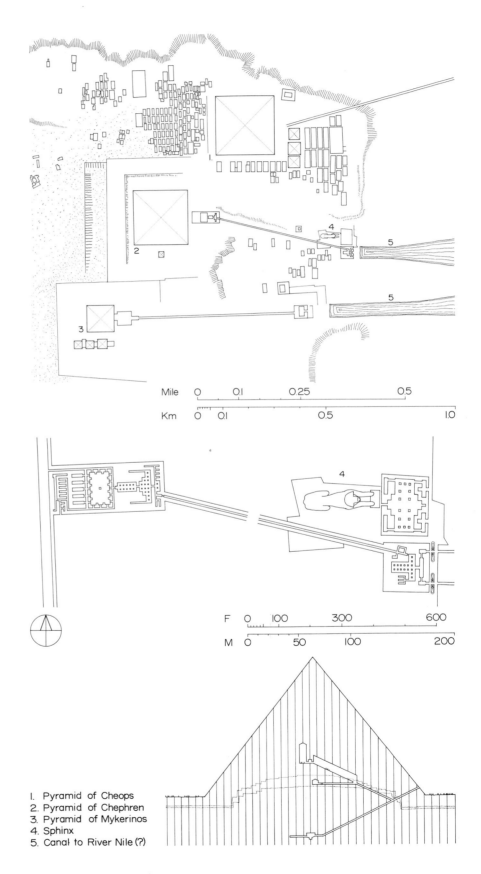

Mile   0   0.1   0.25   0.5

Km   0   0.1   0.5   1.0

F   0   100   300   600

M   0   50   100   200

1. Pyramid of Cheops
2. Pyramid of Chephren
3. Pyramid of Mykerinos
4. Sphinx
5. Canal to River Nile (?)

Fig. 4.12 Giza, valley temple of Chefren; interior.

the actual construction of the project, such as the transport of columns and architraves, the craftsmen fashioning objects of gold and copper, the tilling of the royal estates, processions of servants bringing provisions to the tomb, and hunting and fishing.

The mortuary temple began with a T-shaped entrance hall of two separate units; an open court followed, which was surrounded by a cloister, and on its west side five narrow openings, each with a statue of Chefren, could be counted, possibly representing the five official names assumed by the king on his accession. Beyond this court, which also had statues against the broad piers that defined it, only priests could proceed. At the innermost sanctuary, they would lay down daily offerings for the sustenance of the royal body that lay beyond, in the heart of its stone mountain.

The pyramid of Chefren is relatively simple within. That of Cheops, the Great Pyramid as it is known, has a more ingenious arrangement. It was surrounded by wooden solar boats in pits (one of these boats was found in 1954), three small pyramids for Cheops' immediate family, a mastaba for his mother Hetepheres, and to the east and west of the enclosure wall, an orderly cemetery for his court, the comparatively minute mastabas lined in strict parallel rows like ranks of soldiers at attention.

The entrance into the pyramid is on the north face, a little east of center. (Fig. 4.11) From here a corridor descends through the core and into native rock. It ends in a chamber that was to contain the body before the decision was taken to bury it within the pyramid proper. The Queen's Chamber, a misnomer that endures, was constructed for this purpose exactly midway between the north and south sides, not far from ground level, and the Ascending Corridor was cut to reach it from the initial corridor, beginning at a point about 18 meters (60 feet) from the entrance. Then there was another change of plan, possibly to thwart spoilers and thieves. The Grand Gallery was run as a continuation of the Ascending Corridor, a splendid passage of polished limestone that rises in seven sec-

tions corbelled forward. It led to the King's Chamber, the final resting place of Cheops. Built entirely of granite, this Chamber had a curious superstructure of five compartments above its flat ceiling, to relieve some of the weight that must rest upon it.

There are no extant Egyptian records that tell us of the construction methods of the Giza pyramids, and no scholarly agreement on any aspect of the subject. Did the core rise first, with the aid of a colossal earth ramp, or a system of such ramps, that rose with it, and the casing of Tura limestone applied subsequently, working downward? Or were the casing stones placed first, beveled to the exact incline angle and set on a truly level plane, and this frame then filled with the core blocks? Were hard stones like granite quarried at this early age, or only loose boulders used as they were found lying on the ground? Did the conveying of these blocks, a single one of which might weigh as much as 200 tons, involve wheeled vehicles at all, or only sledges dragged over a way paved with balks of timber?

Whatever the exact details, the feat was epic. It entailed clearing and leveling the site perfectly on the desert bed; surveying this site with measuring ropes of palm or flax fiber to obtain a perfect square; exactly orienting the four faces on the cardinal points without the help of magnetic compasses; quarrying millions of stone blocks and transporting them on the Nile and over land, sometimes for hundreds of miles; lifting them to heights that could exceed 120 meters (400 feet), and this without pulleys; and dressing them meticulously with stone and copper tools.

Then, there is the question of labor. A regular work force of skilled masons and craftsmen and their assistants, housed near the pyramid, was undoubtedly occupied full-time during the span of construction. Additional men were probably levied to transport the blocks between late July and late October, when the Nile flooded and the population was largely idle. But we should refrain from seeing the pyramids as the repressive fruit of slave labor. The satisfaction that ancient communities derived from working on monuments of propitiating and hopeful faith, like Stonehenge or the ziggurats, may be difficult for us to understand in the age of labor unions. It was real nonetheless.

Fig. 4.13 Deir el-Bahri (Upper Egypt), the mortuary temples of Mentuhotep, on the left, ca. 2050 B.C., Eleventh Dynasty, and Queen Hatshepsut, on the right, ca. 1500, Eighteenth Dynasty; view from the northeast.

And the pyramids of Giza were monuments of hope. Today we are fascinated by their size, the precision of their masonry work that eschews the use of mortar, their recondite air. But to the kings of Egypt and the Old Kingdom millions who accepted them as divine, the pyramids were the sole efficacious link between themselves and the realm of the gods, not abstract curiosities. They reproduced architecturally a cosmic truth that called to mind the creation and its eternal guarantee, the rising and setting sun. In several statements of the Pyramid Texts, the earliest preserved body of reli-

gious literature carved on the walls of royal tombs, the pharaoh is described as using the rays of the sun, in place of a staircase, to ascend to Re: "I have trodden these thy rays as a ramp under my feet whereon I mount up to my mother Uraeus on the brow of Re." Heaven strengthened the rays of the sun, we are told, to facilitate this ascent.

It seems likely, then, that the Giza pyramids—these awesome masses of stone—were monuments to something immaterial and gossamer, the rays of the sun. They were the visible proof for the people who

tilled the benign land that the universe was ordered, their well-being and safety vouched for. To us, stripped of their reflective limestone casing and the gold overlay of their capstones, the pyramids seem relentlessly earthbound, broad-based and massive, stone mountains. But to their own audience, they were luminous arrows emanating from, and leading the way to, the sun. More than two thousand years before Christ, these shimmering specters of the desert that focused the long band of water and field that was Egypt proclaimed the truth of the promise: "I am the light of the world. . . . He that believeth in me, though he were dead, shall never die."

The Time of the Gods

The Giza pyramids were never surpassed nor rivaled, since indeed the theocratic absolutism of a Cheops or Chefren remained unreachable. Then, the gods were afraid of the king: "He is the Great Mighty One that has power over the mighty ones. . . . His duration is eternity and his boundary everlastingness." After the term of the three Giza kings, their immediate successors felt it necessary to enhance their pyramid settings at Abusir with separate sun temples in honor of Re. Laid out like the pyramid complex itself, with a small chapel by the water and a causeway, the main feature of these temples was an open court containing an obelisk mounted on a podium, the sacred symbol of the sun-god. While the integrity of the royal tomb that had spoken at Giza of the oneness of Re and pharaoh was thus being sundered, the tomb's scale shrank and the quality of its workmanship deteriorated. At the same time, the mortuary temple was growing bigger and was beginning to compete with the form of the pyramid proper.

In the Middle Kingdom, when stability was restored after a century of social turmoil that undid the old order, the pyramid came to be engulfed by the mortuary temple, if it was there at all. The pyramid did not even hold the real tomb, which had moved elsewhere within the complex. The emphasis had clearly shifted from the visual glorification of the ruler to the pious rites of the burial cult, and these were now dominated more and more by the new chief deity of the national religion, the sun-god Amon who had transcended and absorbed the authority of Re. By the time of the New Kingdom, the pyramid was no longer a royal prerogative. Debased and popularized, it continued to dot the cemeteries for centuries, well into the Christian era.

Deir el-Bahri
We can appreciate how far funerary architecture had evolved since the days of the Giza kings if we look at the arrangement of Mentuhotep's tomb, a Middle Kingdom prince from Upper Egypt instrumental in

ending the civil war and reuniting the country about 2050 B.C. At the time of Mentuhotep, the capital was at Thebes, and the burial compound was within the west bank necropolis, situated against the stately cliff-bay of Deir el-Bahri. (Figs. 4.13, 4.14) The valley temple is now gone, as is the unroofed causeway, lined with statues of the king, which once led to the main group below the bluff. The group consisted of three elements: a large forecourt planted with tamarisks and sycamore figs; a terrace, cut out of the rock, on which the mortuary temple stood; and a narrower unit further west, made up of a court and a hypostyle hall, which was lodged into the cliff.

The temple was a square building faced externally with colonnades, except on the cliff side. It was approached by a massive ramp that cut through a double colonnade; the colonnade masked the terrace embankment on the side that faced toward the forecourt. In the center of this outward-looking temple square was a solid stone platform that probably supported a pyramid; or else the platform itself, without a pyramid, may have emulated a primitive Theban sanctuary of this form believed to have been the primeval hill-abode of the local god Montu. In either case, the king's share of this central space was marked only by a cenotaph. His real tomb lay deep in the cliff, approached by a long underground tunnel that started in the small court behind the temple and ran under the hypostyle hall. The hall was really a remarkable room that held eighty octagonal columns arranged in ten rows. It is the ancestor of the multicolumned transverse hall of the New Kingdom temples in which the central row of columns in line with the longitudinal axis is taller than the rest to admit clerestory lighting.

It is of course significant that cliff burials had been common in Thebes for local nomarchs. It is also significant that the entire scheme of Mentuhotep was oriented toward the newly started temple of Amon across the river in northern Thebes, the modern Karnak. The king's architecture hoped to satisfy the provincial aristocracy and the priesthood of Amon, the partners of his authority.

This landscaped, terrace architecture was adopted in the larger and better-preserved undertaking next to it, that of Queen Hat-

shepsut (1503–1482 B.C.). We are dealing with a much later period, more than five hundred years in fact—a monument of the New Kingdom. Obviously indebted to its older neighbor, it takes the compromised supremacy of the pharaoh a step further. The pyramid is absent from the Queen's funerary complex. The royal person was not less prominent in her own tomb architecture than the divine presence of Amon. Partly this has to do with the special circumstances of Hatshepsut's accession. She was the first woman to wrest the male throne of Egypt, and she held onto it for twenty years. This unusual and precarious position created the added urgency to demonstrate nearness to the gods. Beyond the search for legitimacy, however, the surrender of royal ascendance to the high deity of Thebes, and thus, to a degree, also to his powerful priesthood is unmistakable. By now the temple precinct at Karnak had grown to impressive proportions, as we will soon see. The way to the Queen's funerary complex started there. (Figure 4.15) Indeed, the great god issued from his temple during the Feast of the Valley to visit the mortuary temples of the earthly kings that were now lined up along the west bank facing him. He crossed the river on his barge as the dead came out of their graves to greet him. The mortuary temples were built large, to provide for these divine visits.

Hatshepsut's express instructions to her architect Senmut were to create an earthly palace for Amon reminiscent of the myrrh terraces of Punt, the mythical homeland of the gods. A difficult expedition was sent out to Punt, now probably what we know as Somaliland, to bring back myrrh trees for the terraced gardens of "the paradise of Amon." The story of the expedition is depicted on the walls of the colonnade of the second terrace, between a chapel of the jackal-headed Anubis, lord of cemeteries, and another of Hathor, the cow goddess associated with both love and death. This colonnade consists of two rows of square pillars. Immediately above it is an unusual colonnade, with great painted statues of the Queen in the guise of Osiris standing in front of square pillars. It forms the facade of the temple proper, a large hypostyle hall with an inner sanctuary cut deep into the cliff.

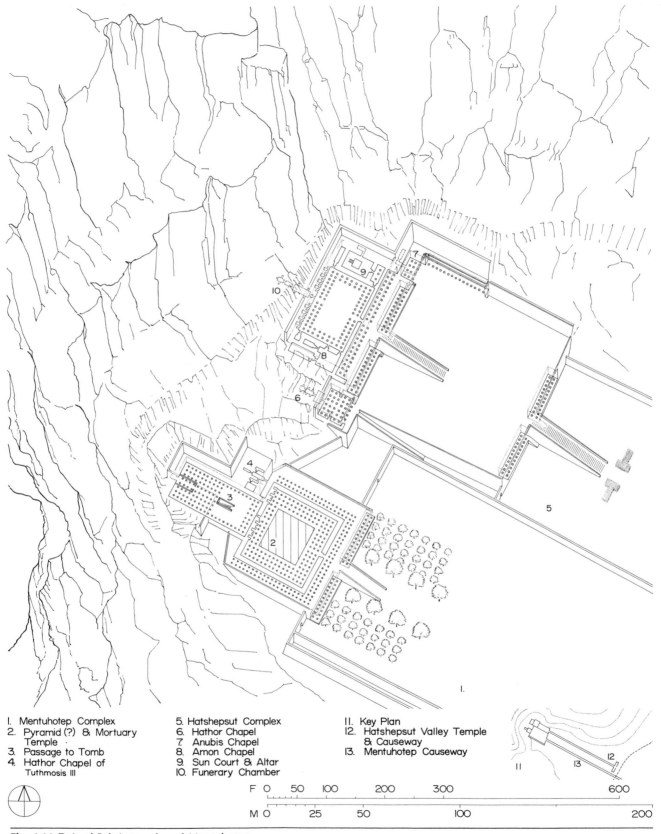

1. Mentuhotep Complex
2. Pyramid (?) & Mortuary Temple
3. Passage to Tomb
4. Hathor Chapel of Tuthmosis III
5. Hatshepsut Complex
6. Hathor Chapel
7. Anubis Chapel
8. Amon Chapel
9. Sun Court & Altar
10. Funerary Chamber
11. Key Plan
12. Hatshepsut Valley Temple & Causeway
13. Mentuhotep Causeway

F O   50   100   200   300   600
M O   25   50   100   200

Fig. 4.14 Deir el-Bahri, temples of Mentuhotep and Hatshepsut; axonometric drawing with plans at selected levels.

Fig. 4.15 Thebes (Upper Egypt); general site plan.

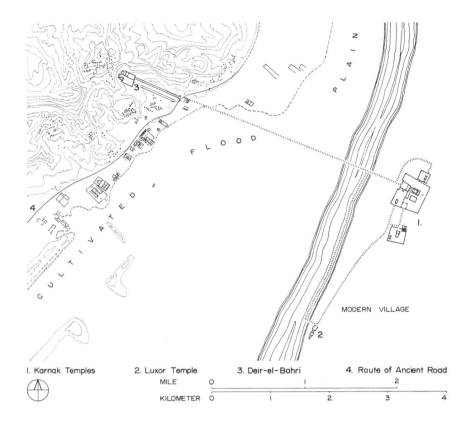

FLOOD PLAIN

CULTIVATED FLOOD

MODERN VILLAGE

1. Karnak Temples   2. Luxor Temple   3. Deir-el-Bahri   4. Route of Ancient Road

MILE   0   1   2

KILOMETER   0   1   2   3   4

Fig. 4.16 Deir el-Bahri, Hatshepsut complex, lower terrace colonnade; detail.

81

The lowest of the three terraces is also faced with a colonnade, this one with an outer row of piers and an inner row of sixteen-sided columns. (Fig. 4.16) A straight axis runs through the entire staged layout, leading from the valley temple to the forecourt first by means of an avenue of sphinxes and then by ramps up the first two terraces. But the effect is hardly one-dimensional. The interest in such terraced architecture lies in how features sink and reappear as one climbs along its axis. The regulating line of Egyptian sequences, often laid out in the flat land, was now made to rise toward the bounding cliff-screen of western Thebes. The Egyptian stone masses grandly set in vast open spaces at Saqqara and Giza—stone-built structures played against the land—were here welded to the rockscape as if nature were an extension of Senmut's design.

Karnak and Luxor

In Thebes itself, "the Mistress of Every City," Amon, was supreme. The New Kingdom capital par excellence, Thebes had raised itself from a modest provincial existence to being the center of government and the national religion. Amon was installed here in splendor as the principal deity of the land and the divine strategist of the policy of expansionism that saw Egyptian armies triumph against the cities of Syria and Palestine and, under Ramses II (1304–1237 B.C.), against their great rival, the Hittites of Asia Minor. War booty and the tribute of subjugated peoples poured into Thebes and was put to use to glorify the name of Amon and his royal wards with a monumental environment worthy of this golden age. The victorious kings continued to build funerary settings for themselves on the west bank and to enlarge the layout of the original Middle Kingdom temples of Amon at Karnak and Luxor on the east bank.

The residential area may have been primarily in the west, between the river and the row of funerary temples. The houses, of varying size and splendor, are not now retrievable, but from representations of them and information gleaned from other excavated sites we have a fair idea of their character. (Fig. 4.17) Modest residential streets held row houses whose main features were a court, a broad hall which

Fig. 4.17 Thebes, a street, ca. 1500 B.C.; reconstruction, perspective drawing.

served as the main living space, and at the rear a kitchen with an independent staircase that led to second-storey bedrooms and the terrace above. Richer families might have a basement for weaving looms and might use the terrace to store grain in bins. Facades were brightly painted and topped by balustrades of interwoven palm fronds; windows had mullions and transoms, and tracery in the lower half. It was an outgoing street architecture, not involuted and street-shy as were the houses of Mesopotamian cities. On the edges of town and the surrounding countryside, villas set on large independent plots had their own gardens

and outbuildings such as granaries and chariot houses. The broad hall, rising higher than the periphery and thus provided with clerestory lighting, was a shared feature of wealthy and more modest houses; so was the shaded portico on the south side of the court taking advantage of the prevalent north breeze.

The two temple compounds on the east bank, Karnak to the north and Luxor which was known as Amon's "southern harem," had their own mud-brick enclosure wall. They were linked with one another by an avenue of ram-headed sphinxes. Between the two enclosures stood the palaces and

administrative buildings. The temple compounds and their dependencies sheltered the attendant staff, thousands of workmen ceaselessly adding and altering, hundreds of thousands of cattle, orchards, boats, and workshops—for these New Kingdom sanctuaries were social and economic centers whose administrators wielded power consonant with the wealth of their holdings.

The great temples at Karnak and Luxor as we see them today were the product of many hundreds of years' work that gradually extended the original axis and enhanced the periphery. Earlier cult temples, which are to be distinguished from mortu-

Fig. 4.18 Luxor, temple of Amon, Mut, and Khonsu; plans of two main stages of its development: left, the temple at the time of Amenhotep III (1417–1379 B.C.); right, with the additions of Ramses II (1304–1237 B.C.).

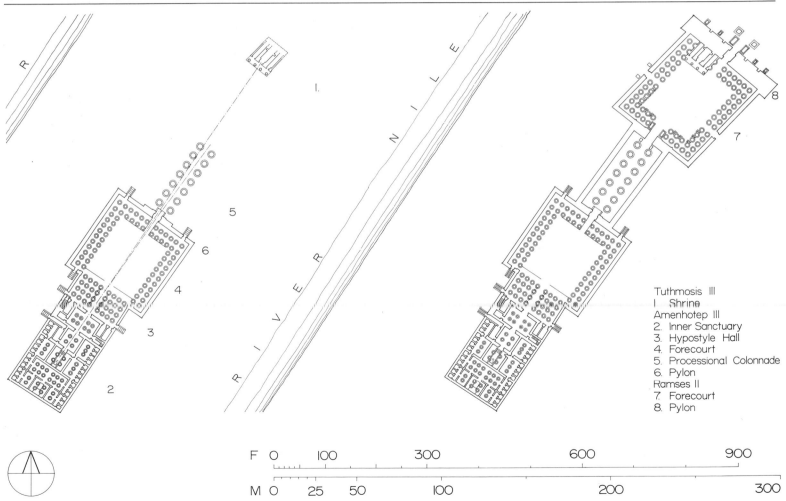

Tuthmosis III
1. Shrine
Amenhotep III
2. Inner Sanctuary
3. Hypostyle Hall
4. Forecourt
5. Processional Colonnade
6. Pylon
Ramses II
7. Forecourt
8. Pylon

F 0   100   300   600   900

M 0   25   50   100   200   300

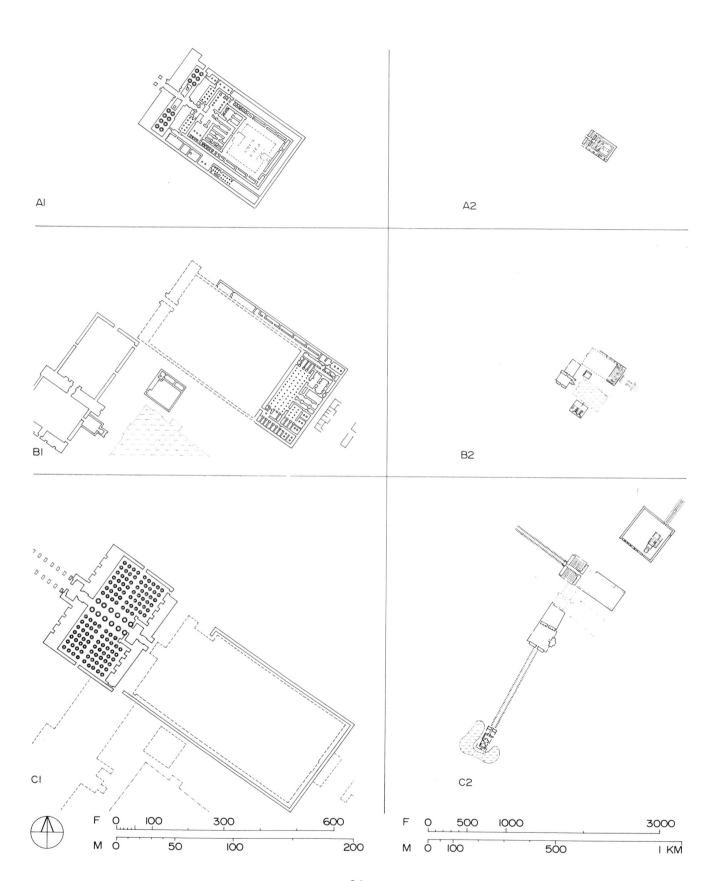

A1

A2

B1

B2

C1

C2

F 0   100   300   600
M 0   50   100   200

F 0   500   1000   3000
M 0   100   500   1 KM

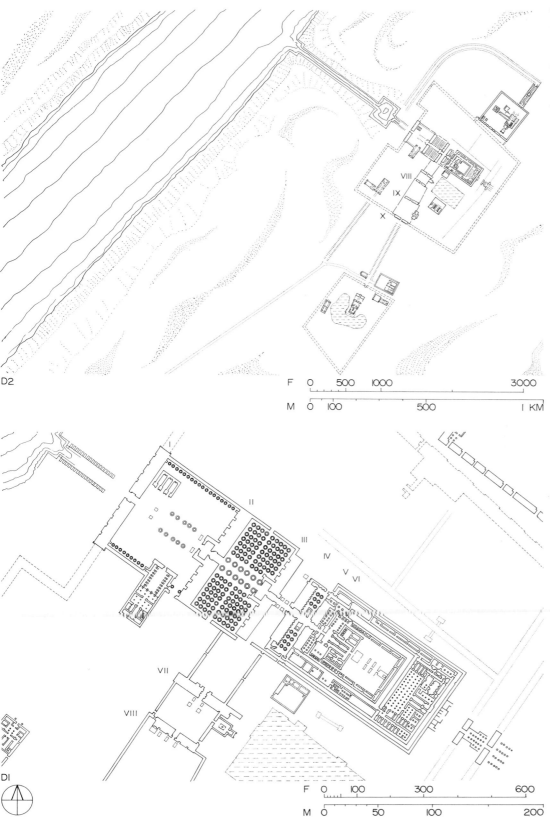

ary temples and the special open-air temples of the sun like those at Abusir, have left scant remains. They were modest in scale and of no standard disposition. They differed from the others in the fact that they invariably housed the statue of a deity, a small wooden figure often sheathed in gold. The Middle Kingdom temples of Karnak and Luxor, impossible to reconstruct today, belonged to this category.

The standard New Kingdom temple may have been originated under Amenhotep III (1417–1379 B.C.) for the first replacement of the early temple at Luxor. The type comprises three parts: the inner sanctuary for the cult statue, the boat that transports it to other temples, and vessels and implements relevant to its care; the hypostyle hall; and an outer forecourt for the public, entered through a pylon. The tripartite scheme is not unlike the layout of the typical Egyptian house, with a reception vestibule and court at the front, the broad living room in the center of the house that parallels the hypostyle hall, and the private apartments at the back that parallel the sanctuary. The New Kingdom custom of honoring the deity by adding to his or her temple came to mean multiple pylons and courts in solemn progression, so that moving along the axes of Amon's temples at Karnak and Luxor one trod both a ritual path, from the most public spaces to the holy of holies, and a historical path, from the most recent reigns, the Ethiopian and Ptolemaic dynasties, through the New Kingdom, to the oldest foundation that marked the site as sacred.

Fig. 4.19 Karnak, temple of Amon (**D1**) and its site (**D2**), at the end of its long history. The main stages of this development can be followed in the preceding drawings. The left-hand column shows the main additions to the temple itself; the right-hand column records the appearance of peripheral structures: (**A**) the complex at the time of Tuthmosis I (1525–ca. 1512 B.C.); (**B**) the addition of the Festival Hall and the small temple to Amon-Re-Herakhty at the time of Tuthmosis III (1504–1450 B.C.); (**C**) additions during the next one hundred years—the new hypostyle hall for the temple of Amon, and the completion of the subsidiary temple groups of Montu (to the northeast) and Mut (to the southwest).

Amenhotep III's temple at Luxor, dedicated to the Theban triad—Amon, his wife Mut, and their son Khonsu—consisted of an elaborate inner sanctuary, a hypostyle hall open in its entire width to a large forecourt, and beyond the pylon of this forecourt, a processional colonnade—two parallel rows of huge papyriform columns, fourteen in all, lining the main approach to the temple. (Fig. 4.18) On axis with the inner sanctuary, some distance to the north of the temple, stood a small shrine in granite built several decades earlier by Tuthmosis III (1504–1450 B.C.). This axis, set by the original Middle Kingdom temple, undoubtedly paralleled the river bank. Beginning with the forecourt of Amenhotep III's temple, however, the axis was noticeably bent eastward, in order to bypass the Tuthmosis shrine and pick up the line of the avenue of sphinxes leading to the northern compound at Karnak.

A century and a half after the completion of Amenhotep's temple, Ramses II added a northern court to it, with porticoes on all four sides. In front of its massive pylon he set up colossi of himself and two obelisks flanking the entrance gate. This court was shaped as a parallelogram to account for the bent axis of the temple, and it incorporated the Tuthmosis III shrine on the inner face of the pylon.

At Karnak the site seems to have been hallowed since the Old Kingdom. Of the Middle Kingdom temple, some remains can be recognized toward the rear of the present complex. (Fig. 4.19) Under Tuthmosis I (1525–c. 1512 B.C.) the architect Ineny enclosed this temple within a perimeter wall; he added an entrance court surrounded by columns and statues of Osiris and preceded by a pylon (V), a hypostyle hall with cedar columns, and another pylon (IV) marked externally by two obelisks. The habit of setting up this ancient symbol of the sun-god Re of Heliopolis, who had now been absorbed by Amon, may have started here. Ineny describes his services in full on the walls of his tomb.

I supervised the great monuments that he caused to make in Karnak, erecting a hall with columns, erecting great pylons on its two faces, in the beautiful white stone of 'Ayn, erecting august flagstaffs at the double doorway of the temple. . . . I supervised the erection of the great doorway "Amon is the One Mighty of strength" whose

Fig. 4.20 Karnak, temple of Amon, the great hypostyle hall.

great door leaf is of Asiatic copper, and upon which is the shadow of Min modeled in gold. . . .

Shortly thereafter, to the east of the new temple, Tuthmosis III constructed a Heb-Sed jubilee complex, the Festival Hall. The long reign of this warrior king had been dominated at its start by his formidable stepsister and wife Queen Hatshepsut. Her stamp at Karnak can still be seen in the two obelisks she had put up in the hypostyle hall of Tuthmosis I, which necessitated the re-

Fig. 4.21 Thebes, the avenue of ram-headed sphinxes leading from the Nile to Pylon I of the Amon temple.

moval of its wooden ceiling. Behind the Festival Hall her husband also provided for a small temple to the rising sun, Amon-Re-Herakhty, with an eastern gate facing the Theban sunrise. The Karnak axis was now a full record of the solar path. The easternmost gateway was "the Upper Door of the Domain of Amon," the station for the rising sun at the first hour. It progressed through the Herakhty temple and across the Festival Hall where two chambers, to the northeast and southeast, housed the terrestrial and solar aspects of the eternal cycle of rejuvenation. At the point in the inner sanctuary of the main temple where Amon's cult boat stood, the sun reached the ninth hour, entering the "Field of Reeds"—the region where those blessed in death lived in perpetual spring. In the transverse hall between Pylons VI and V, the sun was at the tenth hour; at the hypostyle hall, at the eleventh hour. Beyond Pylon IV the daily path was completed with the setting of the sun at the twelfth hour. To celebrate in the open this solar course, Tuthmosis III had a rectangular Sacred Lake dug south of the temple and parallel to it, looked over by a giant granite scarab representing Khepri, the sun growing toward noon.

In the next century the temple axis at Karnak was extended westward with two new pylons (III and II) that held between them a new hypostyle hall, one of the most remarkable achievements of Egyptian architecture. At the same time, two subsidiary temple groups were developed to the north and south of the Amon complex, dedicated to the original local deity of Thebes, Montu, and to Amon's consort Mut, respectively. Between the Amon complex and the northern group of Montu stood a sanctuary to Ptah, the god of the old capital of Memphis, a Middle Kingdom structure of brick and wood rebuilt in stone by Tuthmosis III. The southern group of Mut, with its own trapezoidal girdle wall, was connected with the Amon temple by means of a processional way that entered the central precinct through a pylon in the south enclosure wall and passed through three more pylons before reaching the Amon temple at a point just east of the new hypostyle hall.

The main processional way started at Luxor and ran straight until a point close to the Mut compound. There it forked, with one prong going southeast to the entrance of this compound and the main prong con-

tinuing toward the central group. Where it met the enclosure wall of this group, Ramses III (1198–1167 B.C.) raised a small temple to the remaining member of the Theban triad, Khonsu. One last processional avenue ran from a landing dock on the Nile to the principal western entrance of the Amon precinct.

The purpose of these sphinx-bordered monumental alignments came to the fore during the Feast of Opet when the holy family left their official residence at Karnak for a visit to the "southern harem." The object was the yearly mystical marriage of Amon and Mut. It was a solemn, colorful occasion. The royal house, the priesthood of the various deities, and the common people who arrived from all over participated in a staged pageant which used the river, the temples themselves, and the processional avenues for a peripatetic service that assured the land's fertility. The cult boats of the three gods were taken out of their chapels and carried through the temples to the landing dock where they were loaded on resplendent Nile boats for the short sail to Luxor.

Amon's boat was kept in the central chapel of the Karnak sanctuary, flanked by two courts of offering. After prescribed rites at which the king presided, thirty priests wearing hawk and jackal masks carried the boat on their shoulders, first through the hall of records, passing between two massive granite pillars which were decorated in high relief with the heraldic plants of Upper and Lower Egypt, the lily and papyrus. On Pylon VI, which they crossed next, the warrior king Tuthmosis III was shown worshipping Amon "at the ninth hour." Beyond a transverse vestibule and Pylon V, they passed between the obelisks of Queen Hatshepsut in the old hypostyle hall and then through Pylon IV and its two obelisks that had terminated the initial New Kingdom temple of Tuthmosis I and his architect Ineny.

It was at this point that the congregation may have waited to hail the boat as it entered the great hypostyle hall. (Fig. 4.20) Light filtered through the stone window gratings of the clerestory into the central unit, a nave marked off by huge sandstone columns with papyrus capitals on which the ceiling rested, and two aisles whose lower columns supported the clerestory. The forest of columns on the two sides of this central unit and the boundary walls beyond were decorated with scenes showing the pharaoh in the presence of deities. It was in this hall that New Kingdom pharaohs were crowned, hence its designation as "the Hall of the Two Crowns." But it was also known as "the resting place of the Lord of the Gods . . . the place of appearance . . . at his annual feast."

The sailboats which were to transport the holy family were probably helped along with ropes pulled by members of the procession moving along the avenue of sphinxes. (Fig. 4.21) There were six way stations before Luxor, each marked with a chapel. Upon arriving at the temple, the procession filed through the pylon of Ramses II, passing between the two obelisks (whose alignment with the entrance was not exact, probably in order to conceal their unequal height through the effect of perspective) and two seated colossi of the ruler. (Fig. 4.22) More statues of him were to be seen on the south side of the forecourt. The shafts of the papyriform columns and the walls themselves, both inside and out, were crowded with scenes in sunk relief. On the outside they had a martial character. The famous battle of Qadesh against the Hittites (1300 B.C.) occupied the face of the pylon. Within, the subjects dealt with the Feast of Opet, showing sacrificial scenes and the procession itself—members of the royal family and priests bearing offerings, the sacrificial animals gaily beribboned and painted, and a file of priestesses about to pass through the pylon.

Past the forecourt, the space narrowed and dimmed. Probably leaving behind some of the congregation, Amon's train moved between the two rows of columns towering above it as through a shady grove. (Fig. 4.23) The capitals, in the form of open papyrus, flared out toward the top, at a height of about 15 meters (50 feet) from the floor, enhancing the sense of overhead shelter. The long directional passage and the bright daylight glowing at its end propelled one forward. One emerged into the brilliant sun of the next court as into a clearing. The open space was bordered on three sides with double rows of columns with papyrus-bud capitals, their ceilings painted blue like strips of sky on which were emblazoned the name crests of the pharaoh. The

Fig. 4.22 Luxor, Ramses II pylon. The pylon originally had six colossal statues of Ramses and two obelisks of granite flanking the entrance. The right obelisk was taken to France in the early nineteenth century and now stands in the Place de la Concorde in Paris.

fourth side led directly into the hypostyle hall, its entire facade open toward the court. The trapezoidal shape of the court strengthened the perspective toward this facade. Inside the hall, where thirty-two columns were lined up in four transverse rows, the feeling was of a crowding and closing up.

Once more, as they had started at the inner sanctuary of Karnak, the priests alone now carried the sacred burden beyond the hypostyle hall, leaving it through a single doorway in the rear wall. The ground rose under their feet, the ceiling height fell, daylight was left behind. They passed through a small transverse hall and then through two square rooms one after the other, the southernmost being the repository of the cult boat. The statue of Amon was deeper in, in a room behind the boat chapel and separated from it by a transverse vestibule. A single beam of light fell upon it from a slot in the ceiling. A seated image of enormous proportions, the statue

would be daily administered to by its priesthood, fed and clothed, and appeased ritually. For in the contentment of Amon rested the land's hope for the benevolence of its rulers, the glory of its armies, and the continued plenty of the Black Land.

Survival of the Egyptian Temple

The primacy of Amon and his priesthood was never successfully challenged in the New Kingdom. A religious and political revolution by Amenhotep IV or Akhenaten (1379–1362 B.C.) that attempted to replace Amon with the cult of the sun-disk Aton did not outlast the king's reign. Architecturally this iconoclastic period is famous for the capital of Akhenaten, Amarna, built in neutral territory between Upper and Lower Egypt. A vast and lavish city, it was razed after Akhenaten's death as the setting of heresy. What we can glean from the foundations and the illustrative content of the

Fig. 4.23 Luxor temple; interior view from the forecourt of Amenhotep III, looking back toward the inner face of the pylon of Ramses II.

extraordinary art in its tombs is that the vocabulary of pylons, obelisks, and courts was still relied on, but the main stress now was on a succession of pylon-fronted courts, with open-air altars for sacrifices. Since it was now the sun-disk itself that was worshipped rather than a cult image, no need was felt for inner sanctuaries.

With Amon's restitution, the priesthood grew in strength at the expense of pharaonic supremacy. After the deterioration of the New Kingdom, the pharaoh came to be seen as nothing more than an earthly ruler, the chief of national administration. The priesthood of Amon, on the other hand, became hereditary and extended its dominion beyond religious matters, into the political sphere. In this late period, roughly the first millennium B.C., Egypt was for the most part under foreign domination. The country endured a Nubian or Ethiopian rule for two centuries, and then a century of Persian rule. In the later fourth century B.C. it became part of Alexander the Great's Greek empire and was governed by the house of the Ptolemies, until the arrival of the Romans on the scene.

Through all these changing regimes, public architecture changed little. The New Kingdom temple type continued to be produced, with no significant modification, under the benevolent approval of alien rulers anxious to gain the support of the conservative Amon priesthood. We have a handful of very well-preserved late temples—that of Horus at Edfu, for example, the double temple to Haroeris and the crocodile-god Sobek at Kom Ombo, the Hathor temple at Dendera, and the incomplete temple of the ram-headed god Khnum at Esna. Finely made and predictable, they seem timeless components of a vast setting of ritual. Their very repetitiveness is effective, parallelling as it does what has been called "the grand monotony" of the Egyptian landscape.

It is a passionless, temperate, stately architecture whose premise is the premise of all ancient Egypt: rhythms of faith and nature made permanent and ever durable. The buildings transcend their multiple authorship and the single events their decoration may extol. And since it is single events, single actions, single reigns that time is measured by, these stupendous programs of Upper Egypt create their own immutable order beyond time, an eternal stability imposed on the flow and flux of life. It is only when we identify through captions, among personages in Egyptian costume rendered in the immemorial style of Egyptian art, Julius Caesar or the Emperor Trajan on some Ptolemaic temple wall that we realize how late in history we are, how retardative this architecture is. For by the time of Caesar the Mediterranean world had been reshaped through the force of Classical culture, the benchmark of our Western achievement.

Further Reading

A. Badawy, *Architecture in Ancient Egypt and the Near East* (Cambridge, Mass.: MIT Press, 1966).

———, *A History of Egyptian Architecture*, 3 vols (Berkeley: University of California Press, 1966, 1968).

A. Fakhry, *The Pyramids*, 2nd ed. (Chicago: University of Chicago Press, 1969).

K. Lange and M. Hirmer, *Egypt*, trans. R. H. Boothroyd, 4th ed., rev. and enl. (New York: Phaidon, 1968).

E. B. Smith, *Egyptian Architecture as Cultural Expression* (Watkins Glen, N.Y.: American Life Foundation, 1968).

W. S. Smith, *The Art and Architecture of Ancient Egypt* (Harmondsworth and Baltimore: Penguin, 1958).

I. Woldering, *The Art of Egypt*, trans. A. E. Keep (New York: Crown, 1963).

Alaca Hüyük (Turkey), Sphinx Gate, mid-second millennium B.C.

5

BRONZE AGE CITIES: THE AEGEAN AND ASIA MINOR

Classical culture is the handiwork of Greeks, and the long process of fashioning it begins early, perhaps about 1700 B.C. The Greek-speaking people associated with this initial phase of the story, the Mycenaeans, do not appear to have been a native race. A warlike stock, they moved into mainland Greece and the nearby islands of the Aegean probably from western Asia Minor, and by about 1600 B.C. were in firm control of this region. They built a number of independent citadel towns famous in later legend—Pylos, Tiryns, Mycenae itself—and were using a form of early Greek that modern scholarship has named Linear B.

The exploits of these Mycenaeans were sung by Homer in the *Iliad* and *Odyssey* several centuries after their civilization had ceased to exist. But before their day was over, the Mycenaeans had managed to become an overseas power of consequence. They had trading posts as far away as Sicily and military colonies along the coast of Asia Minor. And when a great Mycenaean force was being assembled to besiege Troy sometime toward the close of the thirteenth century B.C., "eighty black ships," Homer tells us, came from "Crete of the hundred cities." (Fig. 5.1)

Crete, the largest island in the Aegean, had prospered as a high culture for some time prior to the organized presence of the Mycenaeans on the Greek mainland and had influenced the Mycenaean faith and vision before being conquered by them about 1450 B.C. This brilliant Cretan culture was very different from that which took hold in Mycenaean Greece. The language in use, the so-called Linear A, remains undeciphered, but it was certainly not Greek. The settlers who altered the modest Neolithic structure of this important island and produced, around 2000 B.C., an urban pattern dominated by large royal palaces may also have come from Asia Minor. Critically situated in the southern Aegean, Crete became a way-station of the Bronze Age, linking the Greek coastland with Egypt and Mesopotamia.

Asia Minor

It is Asia Minor, then, or Anatolia as it is also called, that has claims to being the first homeland of European civilization. For several thousand years precocious Neolithic settlements like Çatalhöyük (see Chapter 3) had dotted the central plateau of this land-bridge between Europe and Asia and the seaboard that defines it on three sides. The lavish treasures in their tombs betray a level of sophistication not to be expected from the unprepossessing half-timbered houses, a construction technique, by the way, that still persists today and may have always been thought particularly suitable for this earthquake-prone country.

Then, toward the very end of the third millennium B.C., successive waves of an Indo-European people began sweeping into Asia Minor from the west. They mingled with the indigenous population and in time forged a single state out of the scattered Neolithic villages. These people are called Hittites and their best-known capital was Hattusas, the modern Boğazköy, some distance to the east of Ankara. The Hittite state was a great imperial power from about 1600 to 1200 B.C. The towns, some quite large, were forcefully situated in the sere Anatolian hinterland; they had redoubtable defenses, paved streets, monumental public buildings, and drainage channels. A network of good roads welded them together and made possible regular communication with neighboring states. To the southeast, the kingdom of Assyria maintained smooth trade relations facilitated by a string of its own merchant colonies near major Hittite towns. Finally, to the southwest the Hittites dealt with Egypt.

Hattusas

A look at Hattusas will give us a fair idea of the Hittite environment. The strength of their architecture was to accept the raw design of the land as the better part of building. This entailed not only using natural configurations for purposes of defense or advantageous siting, but wresting a kind of manly dignity from the rugged terrain. The image of the fortified city in this martial state mattered as much as the effectiveness of its defensive apparatus. The walls must not only be secure against attack, they must also look formidable so that they would discourage would-be aggressors.

Hattusas sits dramatically on a spur of

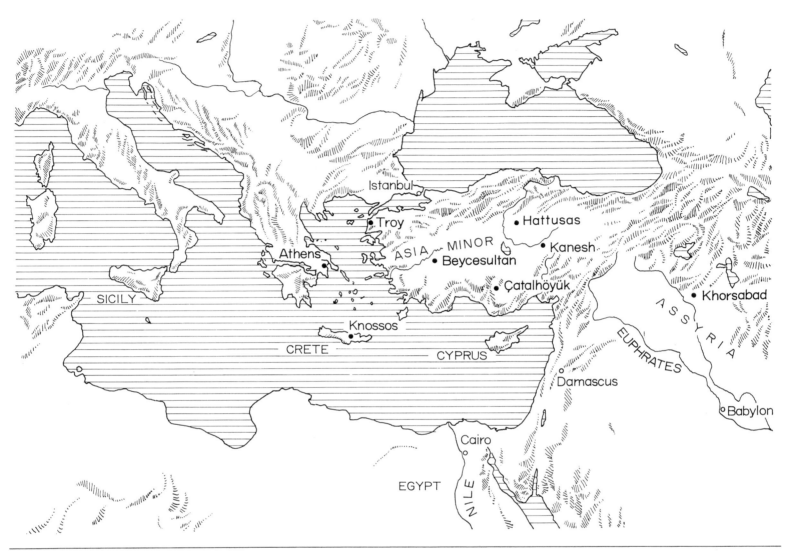

Fig. 5.1 Map: The Mediterranean in the second millennium B.C.

rocky hills at the end of a wide and fertile valley. The original town clung to the north slope overlooking the valley, with a flat-topped rock to the southeast as its citadel. A century or two after it became the Hittite capital, perhaps about 1400 B.C., an enormous new crescent of fortifications was thrown around the exposed hillside to the south, so that the entire circumference now measured about 7 kilometers (4 miles) in length and enclosed an area of over 120 hectares (300 acres). (Fig. 5.2)

Defense and intimidation here were not solely manmade. The very gorges leading to Hattusas, the cliff against which it crouches, were agents of defense. Rocks and boulders were piled up, often unfinished, with such virile effect that it seems as if the city were rooted in the primordial landscape, an extension of the natural order. (Fig. 5.3)

The walls skillfully followed the land contour. They were built on a huge embankment of earth and consisted of a double shell of cyclopean masonry, partitioned with cross-walls and filled with rubble. The superstructure, made of mud-brick reinforced with timber beams, has left no trace.

Both this main curtain and a lower apron wall further down were punctuated by projecting rectangular towers at intervals of about 30 meters (100 feet). Having breached the apron wall, the attacking force would have been confronted by the embankment, which was faced with dressed stones too slippery to scale. This system of smooth artificial slopes, called *glacis* by the Romans, was used to break the momentum of a charge. It was also applied to the ramp that skirted the main wall and forced a lateral approach toward the gates, easily covered by archers placed above. At one point a long tunnel from within the defenses debouched at the very bottom of the embankment, below the apron wall, between two stair ramps that led to a single gate. It was clearly intended for surprise sorties and was lined with huge stones that formed a rudimentary corbelled vault. (Fig. 5.4)

The gates had flanking towers and two portals, the outer set deep within the wall, the inner flush with it on the town side. The portals were made of two monoliths corbelled over so as to form an elliptical archway. On these tremendous jambs of the outer portals animal figures—lions and sphinxes—were carved in very high relief.

The residential arrangement was typical: irregular and contiguous houses grouped around courts. The administrative complex of the citadel was also loosely planned. It consisted of a number of independent buildings strung along the edges of the flat-topped rock, with no discernible formal composition. Some of the buildings were themselves of an irregular outline. This was

Fig. 5.2 Hattusas (now Boğazköy, Turkey), Hittite capital, ca. 1900–1200 B.C.; general site plan and inset of citadel.

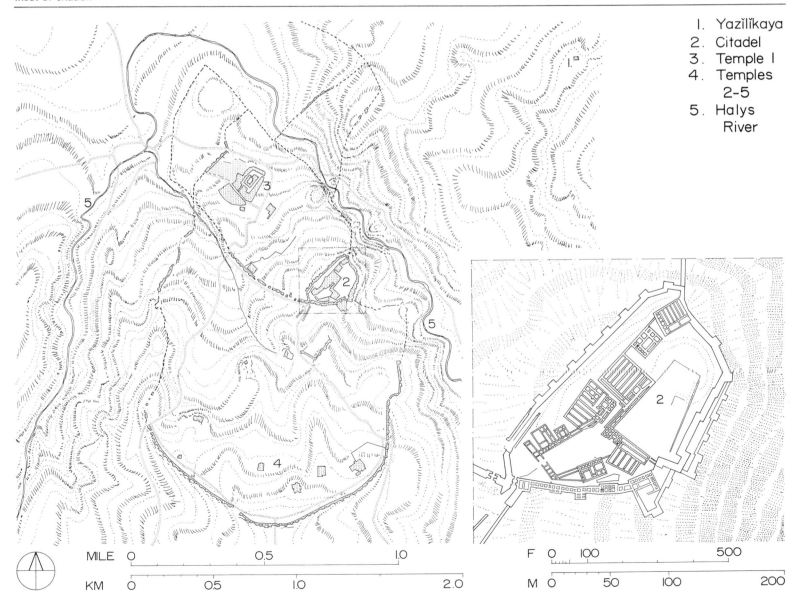

1. Yazīlīkaya
2. Citadel
3. Temple I
4. Temples 2–5
5. Halys River

MILE 0   0.5   1.0

KM 0   0.5   1.0   2.0

F 0   100   500

M 0   50   100   200

Fig. 5.3 Hattusas, the walls along the southwest side of the city, with the Lion Gate, fourteenth century B.C.; close-up view.

Fig. 5.4 Hattusas, underground tunnel leading to a postern gate, fourteenth century B.C.

also true of the temples, the most impressive remains at Hattusas. Four of them, with no standard orientation, seem to have been arranged perpendicularly to a paved main street which wended its way through the new town and may have lined up with a natural sanctuary across the ravine, now called Yazīlīkaya. The fifth and largest temple, known as Temple I and dedicated to the powerful weather-god whose cult was widespread in Anatolia, was in the old town. It was entirely surrounded by storerooms and repositories, many filled with earthenware storage jars. (Fig. 5.5) Hittite temples, like those of Mesopotamia and New Kingdom Egypt, were economic entities. They owned vast estates that they let to farmers for a ground-rent in kind. Yet the layout of the Hittite temple is distinctive and differs from its contemporaries at Thebes or Ur in at least three respects.

First, the court around which the temple was organized was not conceived as a formal space framed by uniform cloisters, in the manner of the Egyptian court. (Fig. 4.18) The column, for one thing, is unknown in Hittite architecture. The standard portico on piers always defined one or two, in some exceptions three, sides of the court, and even then not uniformly. The court, in other words, had four sides of divergent design. Second, the sanctuary was bathed in light that poured through two windows flanking the cult statue and also through side windows. This luminous holy of holies makes a surprising contrast to the dimness and secrecy of the cult chambers in the normal Egyptian temple sequence. In fact, unlike the sealed exteriors of both Egyptian and Mesopotamian temples, the entire periphery wall of Temple I was perforated with ample windows, starting just a few feet above the ground and framed by pilasters. Third, the sanctuary was approached in a roundabout way, through a series of vestibules not directly opening out to the central court. In Temple I the sanctuary is like an annex to the main structure, jutting out

from it off axis. Hittite documents reveal that on important feast days the king sat here, after the proper ablutions in the court, for a ceremonial meal, surrounded by courtiers and priests.

The irregular outline, the asymmetry, the court with the four discrete elevations—these should not be thought of as picturesque effects nor be considered the result of careless accretion. Such buildings differ from the organic tangle of cities like Ur in that their creation did not always stretch over a long span of time and their ownership and pattern of use were much more single-minded than what prevailed in city blocks. But they were no more without a rational order than were organic city plans, and the basis of this order was common to both: the expression of the built structure as the sum total of distinct functions brought together with no concern for the two principles of geometrically ordered compositions, bilateral symmetry along an axis, the principle that governs the design

1. Complex Entrance
2. Temple
3. Temple Sanctuary
4. Residential
   Quarter

F 0   100   300   600

M 0   50   100   200

Fig. 5.5 Hattusas, Temple I dedicated to the
weather-god, ca. 1400 B.C.; ground plan.

of Egyptian temples despite their protracted development, and the strict rectangularity of outline that disciplines the palace of Mari or the city blocks of El Kahun. (Figs. 3.24, 4.2) The crux of the matter is whether an abstract architectural order is given priority and allowed to control, from above as it were, the organization of the general layout, or whether site and function will shape the building, with such outline and elevation as the reality of land contours and the congress of various functional units might produce.

The special quality of Hittite design—its grasp of natural forms and its studied balancing of the civilized and the elemental—is best brought out in Yazīlīkaya, the sanctuary in an outcrop of rocks where a spring must have originally marked, in this dry land, a sacred grove. To reach it you climbed toward the northeast, beyond the ravine, leaving the town and its hubbub behind.

Passing through the gatehouse, you went up two sets of stairs and entered the temple court with its fountain pavilion. The main hall was ahead, but a porch on the left led down to the first gallery, a vast limestone hall open to the sky and paved with turf and flowers. Here a solemn gathering of the Hittite pantheon was taking place. (Fig. 5.6) Two great processions, male divinities on one wall and female ones on the other, converged toward a single isolated rock. On it the great sun-goddess Arinna (Hepatu) was seen standing on the back of a panther, as did her son immediately behind her. (Fig. 5.7) She faced her consort, the elder "Weather-god of Heaven," as he was called in the name-sign he carried. His feet were planted on two mountains that had human form, an image that has a long history going back to Mesopotamia.

A narrow cleft to the right as you faced this awesome rock-theater led into the second gallery, probably the holy of holies. Here a strange dagger-god plunged himself into the rough base of the cliff, and King Tudhaliya IV was shown next to him in the reassuring embrace of his tutelary god Sarumma.

Beycesultan and Troy

Between the Hittites and the Cretan-Mycenaean world lay western Asia Minor—

Fig. 5.6 Hattusas, the open-air sanctuary of Yazīlīkaya northeast of the city (no. 1 on Fig. 5.2), ca. 1350–1250 B.C., main gallery; general view.

a string of principalities of which two have particular interest for our architectural study: a settlement at modern Beycesultan, close to the source of the Meander river; and further north, at the entrance to the Dardanelles, a mound called Hissarlīk, long identified with the city of Troy whose 10-year siege by the Mycenaean Greeks, as told in the *Iliad*, is one of the most celebrated episodes of history. The recently excavated palace at Beycesultan recalls the great palaces of Minoan Crete, while a building form here and at Troy, known in the modern literature by the Homeric term *megaron*, shows up as the central feature of Mycenaean citadels and will form the basis, as we will see in the next chapter, of the later Greek temple.

The main characteristic of these two settlements, as well as of Cretan-Mycenaean towns, is that they lack religious buildings of public scale. Most of the built structure was residential and administrative. Ritual

Fig. 5.7 Yazīlīkaya, main gallery; detail of the rock-cut frieze, showing the sun-goddess Arinna (Hepatu) and her court.

Fig. 5.8 Beycesultan (Turkey), Bronze Age palace, ca. 1800 B.C.; reconstruction drawing.

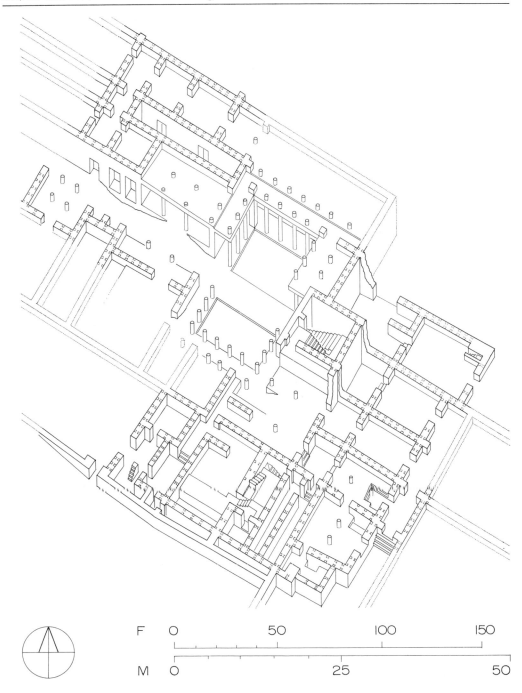

F 0   50   100   150

M 0   25   50

observances were accommodated within these structures and in occasional shrines not very different from ordinary houses, without the need for monumental temples of the sort that still highlighted the archaeological landscape of Mesopotamia, Egypt, and the Hittite empire.

The palace at Beycesultan lies on the eastern of the two summits which the town occupied. It was a large building (some eighty chambers have been excavated), organized around a rectangular court with a surrounding gallery, or a series of balconies, supported on wooden columns. (Fig. 5.8) The half-timbered construction was elaborate, and in some ways peculiar. The fill was rubble at foundation level, mudbrick above. No dressed stone was used anywhere; the dominant craft was that of the carpenter and not the mason. The panels of the half-timbering were strictly rectangular, as would always be the case in Asia Minor until relatively recent times when diagonal struts were introduced to increase the rigidity of the framework.

The practice of strengthening stone or mud-brick walls through the insertion at regular intervals of rows of runner beams, held in position by cross-ties, is quite ancient in Asia Minor. At the palace of Beycesultan the scheme was amplified with rows of vertical posts that enframe the masonry uniformly from the foundations to the roof. In addition, and independently of the thickness of the walls, freestanding posts against the inner wall face were also employed, presumably to support some element of the upper story which contained the principal apartments.

A unique feature at Beycesultan is the system of foundations. The first stones were laid on a bedding of tree trunks lined up traversely to the direction of the wall. The trunks projected beyond the wall faces and became the lower component of a sub-pavement passage on either side of them. This costly device appears to have been intended as a system of ventilation or winter heating, one of the earliest examples of environmental controls in the history of architecture.

The date of the palace is about 1800 B.C. It was destroyed by fire and was overlaid several centuries later by a different palace complex that had extensive stabling facilities—evidence that the horse as a draught animal and mount was greatly valued. The chief residential unit of the palace was now a *megaron*. This term applies to a large, barnlike, single-storey structure comprising a rectangular hall with a circular central hearth and a front porch formed by the prolongation of the side walls. The ends of these walls were specially treated using single, three-quarter columns. Indeed, the megaron had been a standard unit for important residences within the town as far back as the later third millennium B.C.

At Troy, evidence of the megaron is even earlier. The mound of Hissarlīk sits to the north of an ample plain, with Mount Ida in the background. No fewer than nine superimposed cities have been sorted out on the site. We should rather speak of citadels, for the area covered by these settlements was very small, 2 hectares (5 acres) at its most expansive. Unless there was a larger outer town (and some evidence for this does exist), it would be hard to see how archaeological reality could support Homer's account of the great city of Priam and Hector, which was to house an army of 50,000 Trojans and allied troups.

The Homeric city is believed to coincide with the seventh of the nine layers, counting from the bottom up. It was only a little more than a half-century old when it fell to the combined armies of the Mycenaean commonwealth under the command of Mycenae's King Agamemnon.

The first layer goes back to about 3000 B.C. (Fig. 5.9) This earliest settlement, known as Troy I, already had a strong set of walls of sun-dried brick on a massive rubble substructure. The walls had a pronounced batter, the device for buttressing tall masonry planes by raking them which was regularly used in Egyptian architecture. The plan of one complete megaron emerged from the tangle of the dig. It was about 18 meters (60 feet) long, inclusive of the porch, and 7

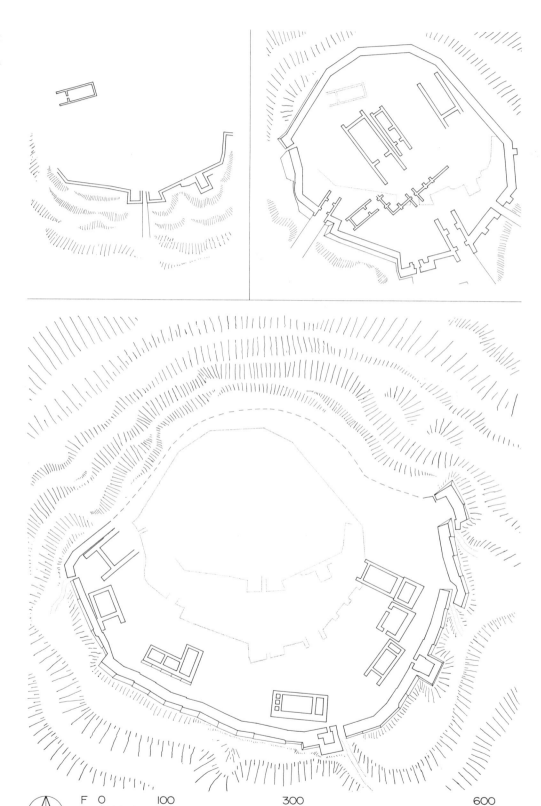

Fig. 5.9 Troy (now Hissarlīk, Turkey), three superimposed levels of occupation, simplified plans: Troy I, ca. 3000 B.C. (upper left); Troy II, ca. 2500–2200 B.C. (upper right); and Troy VI, ca. 1800–1300 B.C. (bottom).

F 0   100   300   600

M 0   25   50   100   200

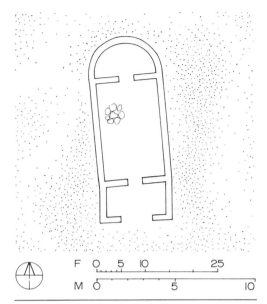

F O 5 10   25

M O   5   10

Fig. 5.10 Korakou (Greece), "hairpin megaron," a house of the first half of the second millennium B.C.; ground plan.

meters (23 feet) wide. The main room contained raised platforms for beds, a stone-paved central hearth, and a smaller hearth for cooking against the back wall. The flat roof was made of small boughs or reeds supporting a coat of clay, and clay was also applied to the inner face of the walls. The floor was raised periodically to cover the accumulated refuse and carpeted in places with rush matting.

The megara of Troy II, including the very large one next to the royal palace which probably served as the council chamber, differed from this norm in one important respect. The side walls were prolonged toward the back as well, forming a shallow back porch to which, however, no access could be had from the main room. The purpose of this false porch was probably to allow the flat roof to extend beyond the back wall face and thus protect the sun-dried bricks from damaging rain. For this same purpose the ends of the side walls were given a wooden facing. It may be from such practical beginnings that the special architectural treatment of these ends developed, leading to the columnar design of them at Beycesultan.

The defensive gateways of the citadel of Troy II have a similar arrangement of front and back porch between which lies a small court enclosed by two sets of doors. A gatehouse of the inner circuit around the palace area dispenses with the court and uses a single set of doors between the deep front porch facing away from the palace and the shallower one at the back. The open space that reaches from here to the council megaron was formalized along two sides by a veranda built against the inner face of this enclosure wall. Spurs of masonry projecting from the wall alternated with wooden columns on stone bases. When seen from the open space, the effect was of a porch of columns and piers reminiscent of later Cretan practice. The conscious planning of this urban corner is remarkably advanced for its time in the context of Asia Minor, although not so in Egyptian or Mesopotamian terms.

Troy VI was the most prosperous phase of the citadel. Its main buildings were informally arranged along the inner periphery of the walls, as in the layout of the citadel at Hattusas with which it is roughly contemporary. But although the walls are of fine construction, Troy was already dated. The single thick line of these walls compared unfavorably with the more advanced system at Hattusas. Furthermore, a curiously retrogressive aspect of Troy VI is that the use of the megaron seems to have been abandoned. The rectangular buildings that take its place all had internal supports and upper stories.

Mycenaeans and Minoans

When we next encounter the megaron, it is on the Greek mainland, as the central feature of Mycenaean palaces. The building probably came to Greece from Asia Minor along with the main Mycenaean stock, but there are sporadic occurrences of it in eastern Europe. At least one related house type of the pre-Mycenaean period in Greece could be considered a native archetype; this is the so-called "hairpin megaron," a U-shaped structure the curved end of which was walled off to make a back room. (Fig. 5.10) The roof, however, appears to have been ridged rather than flat. In the small

settlements of Bronze Age Greece, this type was probably reserved for chieftains; its presence suggests an aristocratic society already at odds with the simpler open village of Neolithic times. The common people lived in houses of several different types, both rectangular and circular, set next to each other indiscriminately. The settlements were at first defenseless. Later, at a time still prior to the arrival of the Mycenaeans, small fortified towns make their appearance, their simple walls buttressed within by the continuous backs of a ring of houses.

The great citadels of Mycenaean lords date from around 1400 B.C., several centuries after the migratory wave that brought this people into Greece. (Fig. 5.11) They represent the first major architectural episode of Greek culture. The preference was for strategically located, defensible eminences with a good supply of water. (Fig. 5.12) At the summit stood the palace of the king. Its defenses took in an open common, to serve in time of danger as shelter for the people of the township who lived for the most part on the unwalled slopes. As in Hittite sites, the fortifications exploited the lay of the land and were built in heavy cyclopean masonry of boulders piled up with rugged effect. Southern Greece is a rough-and-tumble territory of intricate shores and small, rocky, obstreperous mountains—a difficult land where aromatic scrub and the hardy olive tree are the only vegetation to prosper effortlessly. On this raw theater of nature the Mycenaean lords imposed their rule.

The megaron dominated the palace complex in size and determined its axis. (Fig. 5.13) It commonly faced south and was entered through a front porch; between the porch and the hall was a set of guardrooms. In the hall, a large hearth of stuccoed clay focused this ceremonial place. Here libations were poured and sacrificed animals burned. The smoke escaped through the open sides of a lantern with an impervious top over the hearth, an arrangement which also admitted light. The lantern was supported on four columns at the corners of the hearth. Sometimes, as is the case at Pylos, an entire gallery level between the ceiling and the clerestory lantern would surround the hearth opening.

Next to the hearth stood an offering table, and the king's throne was set across the way, in the middle of one of the long sides, flanked by painted guardian griffins. The floor was stuccoed and laid out in squares, each square painted with a different abstract pattern in several colors. On the walls were fresco representations of musicians (it was in such megara that Homer's ancestral bards sang their lays), hunting scenes, and the like.

Pylos

Perhaps the most instructive Mycenaean palace is that of Nestor in Homer's "sandy Pylos." The defensive system of the Mycenaeans, however, is best observed at the citadel of Tiryns, which is planted on an outcrop of limestone rising out of the plain of Argos, like a sturdy ship headed for the nearby sea. And for a sense of the entire Mycenaean community with its gates and tombs and artifacts, none can compete with Mycenae itself. "Well-built Mycenae," Homer calls her, and "Mycenae rich in gold"—two epithets fully confirmed by the excavations that started a hundred years ago with Heinrich Schliemann. It was his discovery of the site and the fabulous gold treasure of its tombs that heralded the exposure of this early Greek culture and the authentication of Homeric myth as history. Something of the initial excitement of Homeric poetry proved true comes across in the jubilant telegram that Schliemann sent to the king of Greece in December 1876:

It is with extraordinary pleasure that I announce to Your Majesty my discovery of the graves which, according to tradition are those of Agamemnon, Cassandra, Eurymedon and their comrades, all killed during the banquet by Clytemnestra and her lover Aegisthus.

To take Pylos first, the older palace was probably the separate building to the southwest of the complex. (Fig. 5.14) The main hall was not a full megaron. The approach was at a right angle from a large entrance hall that had a facade with two wood columns between antae, and one peculiarly placed column within. This orthogonal order of a hall-of-state sequence may have been standard in a first phase of Mycenaean palace design, and its memory may account for the placement of the throne to one side of the otherwise straight axis in the later megara.

In the main palace building at Pylos, the axis begins with a gatehouse consisting of two units; each had a single column in the middle of its open end that aligned with the common entrance in the cross-wall which separated the units. The double gatehouse was followed by an inner court, on the north side of which rose the two-column portico of the megaron proper. A doorway with a sentry box to one side led to a vestibule, and through a second guarded doorway one entered the throne room with its flame-decorated hearth. The axis ended at the blind north wall of this room.

Surrounding rooms were served by a corridor ring around three sides of the megaron. To the right and left of the vestibule, stairs led to the upper floor. These surrounding rooms included three magazines to the north for storing oil, and along the flanks, pantries for dishes and drinking cups. The women's quarter occupied the area above the eastern rooms. The double gatehouse was flanked, to the west, by the archive room where hundreds of Linear B tablets were unearthed, and to the east, by the queen's apartments, these grouped around a large hall with its own hearth and a walled court matching that of the king's immediately to the north. Neither of the

Fig. 5.11 Map: The eastern Mediterranean in the second millennium B.C.

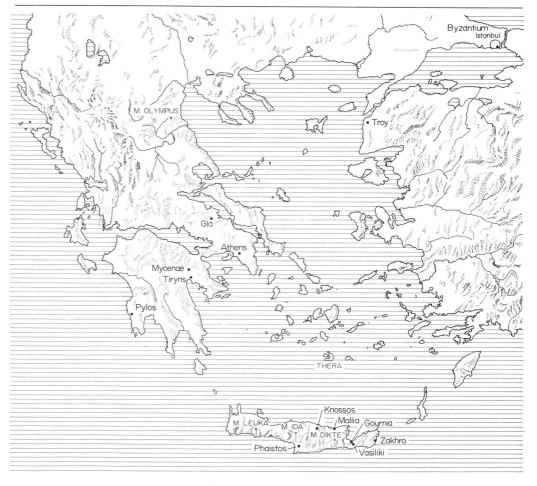

Fig. 5.12 Mycenae (Greece); aerial view from the west.

small courts could be entered from the outside, thus ensuring the privacy of the royal couple. To the east of the courts a main spout delivered the palace water which was carried here by a wooden aqueduct from a spring about one kilometer away across the valley. On the northeast edge of the hill, a large building served as a wine magazine; and to the southeast, a building of several rooms seems to have been the palace workshop where spare parts for

chariots were kept and repairs of metal and leather goods were carried out.

Tiryns

The construction of Mycenaean palaces was of rubble throughout, strengthened by a massive framework of horizontal and vertical timbers. Outside, the principal walls were faced with fine limestone. The practice of using stone as a thin veneer for walls of inferior material might have been learned

from the Cretans who relied on such facing, in their case, alabaster, to produce a sense of opulence.

By contrast, the defensive ring was built of cyclopean masonry. Enormous blocks of irregular shape were packed with smaller stones and clay. The circuit at Tiryns, as it looked after three centuries of revisions and additions, comprised two parts: the close for the commons to the north, entered from the lower town through a gate at the

Fig. 5.13 Pylos (Greece), the main hall or megaron of the palace, thirteenth century B.C.; reconstruction drawing.

Fig. 5.14 Pylos, the palace site; general plan.

1. Old Palace
2. Main Palace
3. Gatehouse
4. Megaron
5. Archive Room
6. Queen's Quarters
7. Wine Magazine
8. Workshop
9. Aqueduct

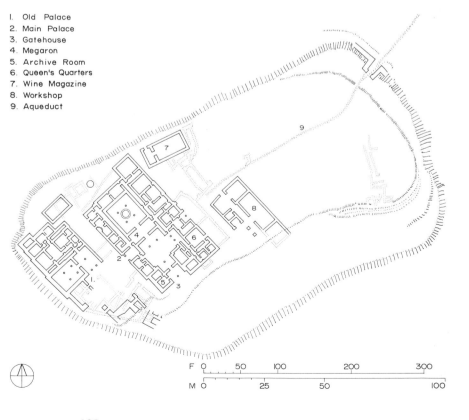

F 0   50   100   200   300
M 0   25   50   100

102

southwest corner; and the palace enclosure, the approach to which was a formidable obstacle course. (Fig. 5.15)

The only access to this enclosure was along the east flank. There was no axial approach from the south, and the postern gate on the west side, overlooked by a huge bastion, led to the main water supply outside the citadel. Hidden spring chambers further north could be reached in times of siege by two tunnellike passages through the west wall of the close. The south and southeast section of the citadel wall contained casemates—a series of rooms, with no lighting of their own, opening off long passages whose tremendous corbel vaults parallel those of Hattusas. In fact, this technique of cyclopean corbelling, where each course overlaps and counterweighs the one below on the cantilever principle until the highest course on each side leans inward against the other, was probably introduced from Asia Minor.

The main eastern access, a narrow slit in the wall, could be gained only by means of a northern ramp that exposed the unshielded right side of enemy troops to bowmen on the parapets. Once in, the hostile force would find itself in a long defile and under fire from the tops of the immense bastions along both sides. Two gateways in this corridor had then to be traversed before reaching the entrance of the palace situated on the western side of a forecourt, just beyond the second gateway. Another right angle turn at the palace court proper and one would finally reach the inner gates of the complex.

Mycenae

The design of the citadel at Mycenae has much in common with that of Tiryns. (Fig. 5.12) Mycenae occupies a hilltop between Mount Zara to the east and Mount Marta to the west. In the background rises Mount Profitis Elias on whose summit there are remains of a Mycenaean lookout post. The position of the citadel commanded the sea approach from Crete and the south Aegean in general, as well as the land road to

Fig. 5.15 Tiryns (Greece), Mycenaean citadel, ca. 1600–1100 B.C.; general plan.

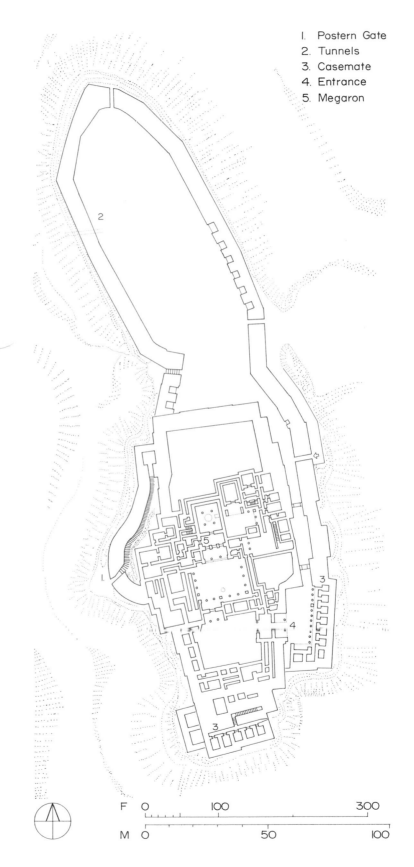

1. Postern Gate
2. Tunnels
3. Casemate
4. Entrance
5. Megaron

F O   100   300
M O   50   100

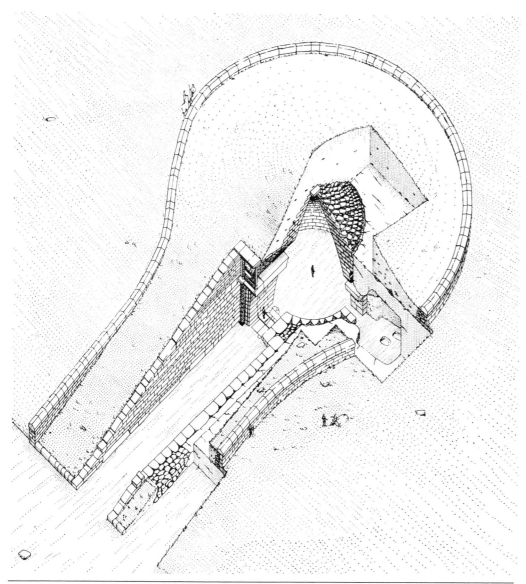

Fig. 5.16 Mycenae, the so-called "Treasury of Atreus," a tholos tomb of the fourteenth century B.C.; isometric view.

Fig. 5.17 Mycenae, "Treasury of Atreus," entrance to the burial chamber; reconstruction drawing.

Fig. 5.18 Mycenae, "Treasury of Atreus," burial chamber; interior view.

Corinth and central Greece beyond. This bold prominence of hard limestone was made even more impregnable by the cyclopean walls, which have a thickness of 6 to 7 meters (20 to 25 feet) and employ boulders that weigh as much as 5 tons each. The water supply was copious. As at Tiryns, an underground cistern (at the foot of the southeastern escarpment) was reached by a stepped secret passage that cut through the wall.

The road from the Argive plain ascended a foothill from the southwest which held a large cemetery. The excavator's pick yielded several finds: pre-Mycenaean burials, rock-cut chamber tombs, and an extraordinary class of buildings called *tholoi*, or "beehive" tombs (Fig. 5.16) These tombs were circular structures with corbelled domes of finely cut stone and an approach causeway, or *dromos*. The oldest among them goes back to 1500 B.C. The form has a gen-

eral resemblance to Neolithic passage graves (see Chapter 2), and circular ossuaries of an earlier date are known in Crete. These ossuaries lacked the dromos, however, and were entered through a simple antechamber; they were built entirely above ground; and when they were vaulted, the stone was finished off in wood. Beehive tombs were subterranean. First, the dromos was cut through a hillslope. Retaining walls were built to secure the two sides of the open passage. Next, a circular area was dug out and the tomb chamber built inside it. The dome, which rose above the ground, was covered up with earth, the mound being supported by a circular buttress wall in line with the haunch of the dome.

The best known and finest beehive tomb is the fancifully named Treasury of Atreus. Its dromos was a full 36.50 meters (120 feet) long and about 6 meters (20 feet) wide. The floor was cemented. The side walls rose in steps toward the two-storey facade of the tomb proper. (Fig. 5.17) The lower story held the doorway which was battered in imitation of an Egyptian pylon. The lintel block extended right across the facade and locked into the dromos walls. The doorway was framed by half-columns of green limestone decorated with bands of zigzag. The downward tapering of these columns and their cushion capitals are clearly of Cretan inspiration. Smaller half-columns stood above them at the second-storey level, the main feature of which was a relieving triangle originally screened with a slab. The purpose of the triangle was to reduce the weight over the lintel. We have already noticed such relieving devices in Old Kingdom pyramids.

The double door of the tomb, as well as the beautifully joined surfaces of the interior, was lined with bronze plaques fixed in place with bronze nails. The curve of the rotunda started at floor level, so that the whole interior described a sweeping arc over the buried prince, made skylike by the bronze rosettes that probably studded it. (Fig. 5.18)

At the Treasury of Atreus, the actual burial took place at a small rectangular chamber to one side of the rotunda, but something of the standard rite can be deduced from evidence on similar tombs. The funeral procession marched down the dro-

mos carrying the bodies of the king and also of his wife and an attendant or two who may have been forced to kill themselves in order to accompany him. The king was lowered into his grave, commonly a pit below the floor, and about him his treasures were arranged—bronze daggers inlaid with gold and electrum, cups of precious materials, ornaments and seals. Logs were stacked up over the opening of the pit, and on this pyre valuable objects and offerings of food and drink in clay pots were burnt. The pyre in the end collapsed into the grave pit. The hole was filled with earth, covering the king and the accompanying bodies laid down by him. Large stone slabs were placed over the grave. The door was closed and secured, and the dromos may have been filled in on the way out.

Beehive tombs were a late form of burial for Mycenaean princes. Earlier on princes were entombed in shaft graves, of which one group, the so-called Circle A group, was incorporated within the citadel during a final enlargement of the walls. The main gate to the citadel, in the northwest corner, is a tremendous structure of monolithic jambs, threshold and lintel; originally it held large wooden doors. (Fig. 5.19) The lintel alone must weigh close to 25 tons. Over its convex top face comes a relieving triangle which here preserves its sculptured screen—a limestone slab showing two lions on either side of a downward tapering column. This is the first piece of large-scale sculpture we have from the Greek world.

We have already encountered beasts as guardians of gates in Assyria and Hattusas. Here at Mycenae the heraldic composition probably stands for the Great Goddess and her beasts. She was portrayed at the rock sanctuary of Yazılıkaya, standing on a panther. (Fig. 5.7) She was also a common image in Crete where small seals depict her on her mountaintop, subduing the wild beasts and insisting on the recognition of her ancient symbol, the horns of consecration. (Fig. 5.20) The rhythmic, small-scale, spruce rendition of the Cretan artist is as eloquent of the fluid vision of that island culture as is the tight, regimented, and powerful relief of the Lion Gate representative of the world of the Mycenaean warlords and their semifeudal society.

Past the Lion Gate, a ramp ascended toward the palace. The unusually oriented megaron is still recognizable, but not much else is, since a Classical Greek temple was built over the palace in later centuries. A path below the ramp led down to Circle A, the site of Schliemann's first spectacular finds. The circular wall around them consisted of two parallel rows of upright slabs, their upper edges cut to receive horizontal roof slabs. The graves were marked by stelai: they have been interpreted as false doors, to let the wandering souls into and out of the tomb. Some of the buried princes wore golden breastplates and face masks with a convincing replication of their features hammered out of the gold sheet.

The concept of shaft graves with false doors, the practice of swathing bodies in bandages and probably mummifying them, and the generous use of gold bespeak direct familiarity with Egypt. Some scholars believe that Mycenaean mercenaries were employed by the pharaohs during the expulsion of the Hyksos from the Delta area in the sixteenth century B.C. If so, Cretan ships may have transported this mainland force.

Knossos

Crete is an island of broad and fertile plains that are defined by tall mountains: Leuka to the west; Dikte to the east; and in the center Mount Ida where according to Greek tradition Zeus was born in a cave and raised secretly, for his father Kronos had taken to swallowing his children as soon as they were born in the hopes that thereby he would thwart the oracle's prophecy that one of his sons would dethrone him. Cretan towns spread out at the foot of these mountains, casual and unfortified. To the Classical world Crete was the Isle of the Blessed: home of the wise King Minos, one of the three judges of the Underworld, home of crafty Daedalus, the architect and inventor, who made wings with which to fly to Sicily, and home of a peaceful, versatile, happy people attuned to the rhythm of the sea and the shaking earth: "There is a land in the midst of the wine dark sea," Homer sings, "a fair and a rich land called Crete, washed by waves on every side, densely peopled and boasting ninety cities."

We have a good image of the builders of this Minoan culture, as it is known from

Fig. 5.19a Mycenae, Lion Gate, thirteenth century B.C.; view.

its legendary king—a race of tall, flexible, narrow-waisted men and women, at home on the high seas in their ships made of the oak and cypress, fir and cedar, trees that then forested the mountain slopes. They lived, so it would seem from their art and built environment, in perfect communion with nature, in a kind of all-embracing pantheism that was never institutionalized into strict religion. In view of most of the ancient civilizations we have studied so far, the extreme rarity of temples (one probable instance is known thus far) and stone statuary is indeed striking. It would seem that there were tree cults, stone pillar cults pregnant of the Neolithic past, and certain rooms in the palace of the king that were set aside for worship. And over it all, over the rising plant and the lapping wave, the Great Goddess ruled from her lofty heights. (Fig. 5.20)

Something of this fluent vision of the world, so different from the preeminent rigidity of Egyptian form, is evident in much of what the Cretans fashioned: in earthen jars, seals, statuettes, murals on the walls of palaces and villas—indeed in the very layout of these buildings and the towns they graced. Marine and plant forms, freshly observed and vividly depicted, figured regularly in the artists' repertory. A large octopus might enliven the surfaces of an oil or wine jar, its writhing tentacles reinforcing the potter's shape. (Fig. 5.21) Flying fish or stalks swaying in the breeze might bring sunny charm into a living room.

Most of these remains date from about 2000 to 1400 B.C. It was at the beginning of this period that a complex urban civilization, based in large measure on overseas commerce, supplanted the existing structure of society. This early society dates back

Fig. 5.20 Minoan seal, showing worship of the Great Goddess, sixteenth century B.C.; line tracing. (Archaeological Museum, Heraklion, Crete, Greece)

to 6000 B.C. when an initial group of immigrants from Asia Minor set up Neolithic communities like those of the homeland. This village-centered culture was galvanized at the turn of the third millennium B.C. by the arrival of metalworking, the development of a flourishing textile industry, and the invention of clay turntables which prefigure the potter's wheel. To this Bronze Age episode belong the large communal ossuaries we mentioned above in the context of the tholos tombs of Mycenae.

By 2000 B.C., the eastern half of the island had attained a startlingly high level of sophistication. Written records and large royal palaces embraced by prosperous towns were the outward signs of this cultural surge. The palaces were designed around a rectangular court; the court elevations reflected the character of the rooms behind, which were grouped according to function—ceremonial, administrative, religious, or domestic. Most of the familiar particulars of Cretan architecture—porticoes with alternating columns and piers, three-aisled hypostyle halls inspired by Egypt, the practice of using large stone slabs at the base of the walls or for framing openings, lightwells and broad flights of steps—all of these were in full use in these first palaces. They were almost completely destroyed around 1700 by what scholars now tend to agree was a devastating earthquake of the kind the Aegean is prone to. The new palaces were built along the lines of the first. Beginning with the spectacular

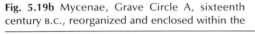

Fig. 5.19b Mycenae, Grave Circle A, sixteenth century B.C., reorganized and enclosed within the citadel in the thirteenth century B.C.; reconstruction view.

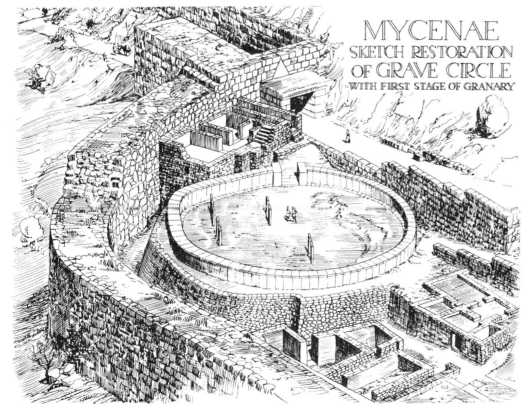

MYCENAE
SKETCH RESTORATION OF GRAVE CIRCLE
WITH FIRST STAGE OF GRANARY

Fig. 5.21 Minoan earthen jar with octopus, from Palaikastro, ca. 1500 B.C. (Archaeological Museum, Heraklion, Crete)

Fig. 5.22 Phaistos (Crete), Minoan palace, ca. 1600 B.C.; view of central court looking north toward Mount Ida.

digging up of Knossos by Sir Arthur Evans, several of them have been sufficiently resurrected to give us a detailed picture of their florid and literate design. (Fig. 5.22)

Despite their small size, the towns themselves, with their public institutions and amenities, were worthy predecessors of the Greek city-state, the *polis*. From the first they made provision for an open place of assembly whose defining wall faces may have supported seats. A network of streets, topographically and functionally determined and retaining the dwelling patterns of the Bronze Age villages on the same site, converged on this town square and the palace. Most were paved. And although in time the palace gained prominence, the sense of a lively community is always unmistakable.

Gournia in the northeast, on the bay of Mirabello, has the best preserved layout. (Fig. 5.23) It had about sixty houses—a very small town indeed in the company of Babylon or Hattusas. But the urban form is cohesive and logical. A tight mesh of streets wrapped itself around the low hill whose saddle held the administrative and ritual focus of the town, the king's palace. Two main streets, one on the hill and one fur-

ther down on the plain to the east, were linked with secondary streets.

The houses were small and densely packed; almost all had upper floors reached by outside staircases. The ground floor was often used as a storeroom, with no entrance from the street. But further up, the facade opened to the outside light by windows, as we can see clearly on a series of tile plaques uncovered at Knossos that depict a Minoan townscape. (Fig. 5.24) These windows of four or six panes must have required a transparent cover of some kind, oiled parchment most likely—an unusually advanced feature for such an early date. To judge from the Knossos plaques, the houses were capped by a lantern or skylight serving as a light well for the interior; or, perhaps, that element should be interpreted as a pent roof or a summer room. The rule seemed to be single-family dwellings. But there were multiresidences too, such as a house from Vasiliki where dozens of rooms were grouped somewhat arbitrarily into

suites on at least two stories along two sides of a paved courtyard. A landed gentry lived in country mansions.

The intricate, seemingly haphazard, plan from Vasiliki is typical of Crete. The Minoan architect did not begin with general frames; he did not think in terms of neat bounding outlines. (Fig. 5.25) Just as the towns themselves were unwalled, so too the larger buildings, the royal palaces especially, were freely circumscribed. True facades, in the main, were ordered toward the court. Indeed, there is reason to believe that the layout was planned from inside out, in units radiating from the central court as their function required. Two sides of the court would be established first by straight lines crossing one another at right angles. The more important units would then be developed in relation to these two baselines and in round numbers of Minoan feet.

In deference to the Goddess who dwelled on mountaintops, and in sharp contrast to the haughty siting of Mycenaean citadels, the palaces occupied slopes or flatland. And the nature of the site was respected, even courted. Hittite and Mycenaean appreciation of natural contours was based on defensive genius. Minoan design celebrated the shape of the landscape even when there was no practical advantage to be derived from it. The meadow's lilt, the skirting hill, the dipping down into valleys, and the climb to ridge-tops—all this was solidified into architecture. The aim, to put it differently, was to open up architectural form toward the prospects that befriended it. This is the same respectful harmony with nature, the same way of accepting things as they are and singing of them, which we noted in the forms of Minoan art and its repertory of animals and plants.

Design is the graph of attitude. Compare a Mycenaean palace like that of Tiryns or Pylos with the royal palaces of Crete, and you will have a truthful image of these two Aegean spheres as functioning societies. (Fig. 5.15) Setting aside the disparate character of their sites, both types of palaces are encompassed within loose outlines. But the heart of the Mycenaean palace is fixed in the megaron, the king's hall at which the gods are given hospitality. It is the largest element of the composition and an axial approach toward it is set up which stiffens the general layout and creates a hierarchy of use that is unequivocal.

Fig. 5.23 Gournia (Crete), Minoan town, seventeenth to twelfth centuries B.C.; general site plan.

Fig. 5.24 Faience plaques showing Minoan houses, from Knossos, ca. 1500 B.C. (Archaeological Museum, Heraklion, Crete)

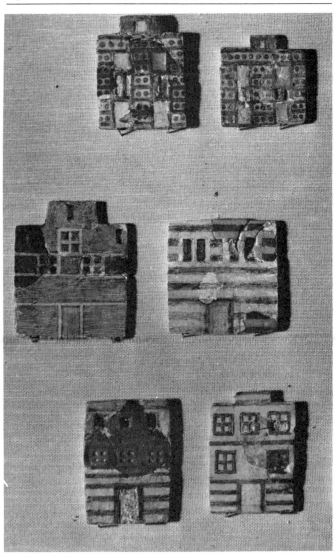

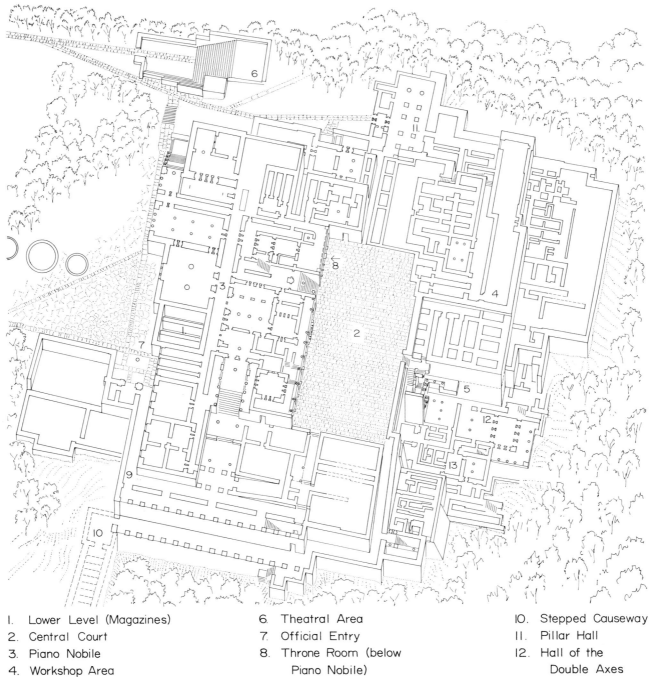

1. Lower Level (Magazines)
2. Central Court
3. Piano Nobile
4. Workshop Area
5. Royal Domestic Quarter

6. Theatral Area
7. Official Entry
8. Throne Room (below Piano Nobile)
9. Corridor of the Procession

10. Stepped Causeway
11. Pillar Hall
12. Hall of the Double Axes
13. Queen's Megaron

F 0   50   100   200   300

M 0   25   50   100

Fig. 5.25 Knossos, the royal palace, ca. 1600 B.C.; axonometric drawing, with plans of major rooms shown at selected levels.

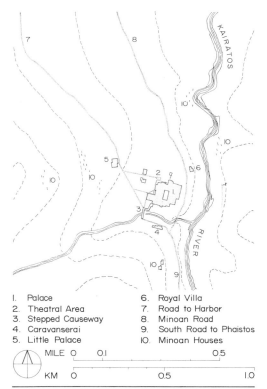

Fig. 5.26 Knossos, general site plan of town.

1. Palace
2. Theatral Area
3. Stepped Causeway
4. Caravanserai
5. Little Palace
6. Royal Villa
7. Road to Harbor
8. Minoan Road
9. South Road to Phaistos
10. Minoan Houses

MILE 0   0.1   0.5

KM 0   0.5   1.0

At Knossos the path is not straight, the goal not predetermined. The heart, if anything, is the all-purpose court. In the surrounding scheme, the functional hierarchy is diffuse, and since this is so, there is no single-minded axis running through the complex. We might picturesquely speak of the design as a labyrinth, and remind ourselves that "labyrinth" is a word of Cretan origin. We see several storeys and half-storeys flexibly stacked up, elevations made up of disparate and accretive elements, rooms arranged in an involved pattern through which pass long corridors of communication with frequent turns and changes of level. Wandering through the remains of Knossos, we recall the story of the Minotaur who resided in the depths of the labyrinth built for him by crafty Daedalus, and of Theseus who went in and killed him but could find his way out only with the help of a guiding thread supplied by the native princess Ariadne. The famous account seems to be Cretan reality made myth.

We should not, of course, exaggerate this mazelike character of the palace. First, a good part of what we see in the plan indicates basement and ground floor rooms; the upper floors where the main state halls were may well have had a more formal organization. Second, there is at Knossos a logic of functional grouping that imposes a conceptual order on the visual irregularities of the composition. The central court and its entrance passages bisect the plan into a western and an eastern half. The western half is in turn bisected by a north-south passage that separates a row of magazines from a higher series of ceremonial rooms, including the famous Throne Room. The eastern half is divided in an east-west sense by a passage, to the north of which lie the workshops of palace craftsmen, and to the south, the domestic quarters of the royal family.

Knossos in its heyday was probably a town of 40,000 inhabitants. (Fig. 5.26) The palace was set on a low rise shielded by gentle hills from any sight of the sea. The knoll slopes sharply on the east and south sides toward the stream of Kairatos. There was a harbor at the mouth of this stream. A main road connected the harbor area with the palace. This road passed by the Little Palace, probably destined for ritual or ceremonial purposes or perhaps for a more intimate summer place; it then ran into the so-called Theatral Area, a public space for some sort of spectacle, with stair-seats along two sides; and finally it reached a gatehouse in the flank of the Pillar Hall, from which a passage of access ran south to the central court.

But there was an equally busy thoroughfare that linked Knossos with the principal town of the south coast, Phaistos, across the Messara plain. Close to the palace this cross-island road went by a resthouse, the so-called Caravanserai. It featured, among other amenities, a footbath for the weary traveler in which water, supplied by a direct pipe, flowed constantly. Beyond that point the road became a stepped causeway or viaduct, crossing the ravine of Kairatos and gaining the south edge of the palace in a series of terraces defined by low side walls supporting a double row of columns and a roof. Along some 90 meters (300 feet) of this covered and stepped causeway, the visitor would have enjoyed both views of the surrounding countryside and the progres-

sively nearer southern prospect of the palace.

The domestic quarters similarly cascaded down the east slope of the knoll and opened up to the outside by airy verandas. Indeed, the purpose of keeping the royal apartments at ground level, while public ceremonial rooms were relegated on the whole to the upper floors, must have been precisely this wish to establish close contact with the land, conceiving of it as an extension of the living spaces.

The official approach was from the west. Here one can truthfully speak of a monumental exterior facade. It overlooked a broad court paved with flagstones. The lower part was blank and composed of upright slabs of alabaster; above this level the facade was punctured by square windows framed in wood. The magazines, with their stone-lined pits for storage and the huge clay jars containing olive oil, the gold of Knossos, lay below this level.

One entered through a single-column porch of the kind we saw emulated at Pylos, past a guardroom, and into the Corridor of the Procession. On the walls of this narrow passage were painted, on two registers, five hundred life-size images of young men and women bearing offerings. The corridor ran south for about 21 meters (70 feet) and then turned left, to arrive at the foot of a broad stair. At the top one discovers a group of small rooms of ritual character. Stairs from here led down to the Throne Room, which could also be entered directly from the central court by means of an anteroom, which housed a shallow prophyry basin for ablutions. (Fig. 5.27) The throne, made of alabaster, survives. It was set against a frieze of griffins and flanked by continuous benches, also of alabaster. Directly opposite the throne was a stone-lined pit for water. For all its formality, this may not have been the most important state room in the palace, which was probably located on the second floor along with the remaining halls of state. The lustral basins and the direct contact with the central court instead indicate that the so-called Throne Room had cult functions associated with the bull dance, the great public celebration of Minoan life.

The domestic wing on the opposite side was built on two stories below the level of the court. Above this, at least two additional stories must have existed originally. The wing was served by a handsome staircase, with a light court to one side of it. (Fig. 5.28) Here, and throughout the palace, the columns were wood and tapered downward; they had cushion capitals, and both shafts and capitals were painted—one black, the other red. The downward taper and the peculiar shape of the shaft, which was often not round in cross section but oval, have never been satisfactorily accounted for. At the foot of this Grand Staircase one came to the Hall of the Double Axes, a room paved with fine gypsum flagging; here the walls were decorated with frescoes of great "figure-eight" shields of bull hide and carvings of two-bladed axes, the sacred symbol of Minoan Crete called *labrys*. This was probably the Men's Hall. Five piers divided the space into two, and sets of double doors between the piers could be drawn shut or pushed aside depending on whether it was desirable to isolate the two compartments or unite them. Above the doors a series of transoms may have been fitted with waxed parchment to let light into the inner compartment when the doors were kept closed. To the east and south the Hall opened out toward the landscape by means of verandas.

A small room just off this Hall is usually referred to as the Queen's Megaron. It was delicately painted with marine scenes and dancing girls, and the ceiling was decorated with an intricate pattern of spirals. There were light wells on two sides, and a small bathroom was attached, with its clay tub still in situ.

The central court absorbed much of the daily activity of the palace. But it was as the setting for the Minoan bull dance that this space came alive. Initially at least, the bull dance was a sacred ritual connected with the cult of the horned beasts which had preoccupied the communal mind since the late Paleolithic period. Sacral horns were set up at certain points in the palaces, and a distant cleft mountain on axis with the court, Mount Jouktas in the case of Knossos, may have evoked this ancient symbol of the earth's active power. (Fig. 5.22)

The audience sat in the porticoes along one of the long sides and at all the openings of the other court facades. Trained men and women were pitted against the charging bull. With agile courage, the partici-

pant would grasp the horns as the bull rushed headlong down the length of the court and would vault over its back, landing on the other side. The grace and lift of this whole maneuver is represented in the painting known as the Toreador Fresco. (Fig. 5.29) The memory of the ritual survives in the later Greek myth of the Minotaur, the creature that was half bull and half man, whose demand of the yearly sacrifice of seven maidens and seven youths from the city of Athens brought Theseus to this spot and made him an immortal hero.

The Closing of the Bronze Age

About 1400 B.C., Knossos and all the other towns of Crete were devastated anew. The palaces collapsed, and the inhabitants moved inland or migrated to Greece. At about this time, perhaps a little earlier, the Mycenaean overlords who had ruled the Greek mainland for two or three centuries extended their sway over the island. But it is doubtful that the Mycenaeans were personally responsible for the ravage. It seems more and more likely that this wholesale

Fig. 5.27 Knossos, royal palace, the "throne room" (no. 8 on Fig. 5.25).

Fig. 5.28 Knossos, royal palace, grand staircase (at no. 5 on Fig. 5.25).

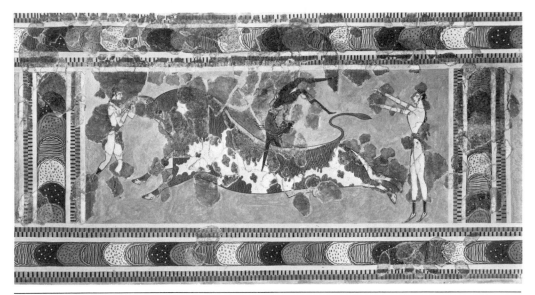

Fig. 5.29 Knossos, royal palace, the "Toreador" fresco, originally in an upper-storey room of the east wing, to the right of no. 4 on Fig. 5.25. (Archaeological Museum, Heraklion, Crete)

destruction of Minoan civilization was the outcome of an upheaval of nature, namely, the violent eruption of a volcano on the island of Thera, which is considerably to the north of Crete, where Santorini now lies. At Thera, a Minoan colony left plentiful remains, including rich wall paintings, which have recently been dug from under the heavy layers of ash that now cover the small cluster of islands in the area. Giant tidal waves and earthquakes occasioned by the eruption wrought havoc as far away as Syria and North Africa. It may be that the apocalyptic texts from Egypt of the Eighteenth Dynasty refer precisely to this disaster. They record a period of prolonged darkness, thunder, floods, a raging plague, and days when "the sun was in the sky like the moon."

Confusion seized the eyes . . . there was no exit from the palace for the space of nine days. Now these nine days were in violence and tempest. None . . . could see the face of his fellow.

So the Minoans who lived by nature may have been brought down by nature. For the next two hundred years Crete functioned modestly in the orbit of Mycenaean Greece. It taught the mainland princes much about nature cults, representational skills and motives, and the art of living graciously. But its own bloom was gone. It carried on a muted existence until a fresh threat to the entire Greek world materialized on the northern borders of the Mycenaean realm.

Linear B tablets from Pylos record emergency preparations. Bronze cult objects were melted down and made into points for spears and arrows. Artisans were assigned to military duties. The coast was hastily fortified. To no avail. Several Greek tribes who had hitherto been left out of the affairs of the mainland, the Dorians among them, now poured in carrying their lackluster iron swords. They systematically sacked every one of the great Mycenaean citadels.

The brilliant Bronze Age was over. The Hittite empire had succumbed to migratory pressures a little while earlier. Groups from mainland Greece spread out onto Aegean islands and the west coast of Asia Minor. On the mainland the newcomers proved no match for the culture they so brutally displaced. They produced no architecture of comparable worth. By 800 B.C. when Homer wrote his poems about the splendid age of the chief prince Agamemnon and his treacherous wife Clytemnestra, of beautiful Helen, of old Nestor, and crafty Odysseus, those giants of epic memory, the contemporary scene about him was dark by comparison.

On the whole he reconstructs the glories and follies of the Mycenaean past knowingly and compassionately. He slips on some details, as when he represents Mycenaean princes cremated rather than inhumed: cremation was introduced into Greece by the Dorians. And when, at one bleak moment of his narrative, he mourns the misery of the human condition, he might be thinking of his own time more justifiably than the golden age of Crete and Mycenae:

> Among all creatures that breathe
> on earth and crawl on it
> There is not anywhere a thing
> more dismal than man is.

Further Reading

E. Akurgal and M. Hirmer, *The Art of the Hittites,* trans. C. McNab (New York: Abrams, 1962).

K. Bittel, *Hattusha, Capital of the Hittites* (New York: Oxford University Press, 1970).

C. W. Blegen, *Troy and the Trojans* (New York: Praeger, 1963).

J. W. Graham, *The Palaces of Crete* (Princeton: Princeton University Press, 1962).

R. Higgins, *The Archaeology of Minoan Crete* (London: Bodley Head, 1973).

J. T. Hooker, *Mycenaean Greece* (London: Routledge & K. Paul, 1977).

S. Lloyd, *Early Anatolia* (Baltimore: Penguin, 1956).

J. G. Macqueen, *The Hittites and Their Contemporaries in Asia Minor* (Boulder, Colo.: Westview, 1975).

S. Marinatos and M. Hirmer, *Crete and Mycenae* (New York: Abrams, 1960).

G. E. Mylonas, *Ancient Mycenae* (London: Routledge and K. Paul, 1957).

P. Warren, *The Aegean Civilizations* (London: Elsevier-Phaidon, 1970).

R. F. Willetts, *The Civilization of Ancient Crete* (Berkeley: University of California Press, 1978).

Persepolis (Iran), royal palace, 518–460 B.C.

6

THE GREEK TEMPLE AND "BARBARIAN" ALTERNATIVES

The Passing of the Bronze Age

The second millennium before Christ had been, for the eastern Mediterranean, a period of prosperous and forward states. Endowed with mobility and technical acumen, these societies built supple environments sympathetic with their political and social aims. Contemporary western Europe by contrast must be seen as backward. Despite the megalithic architecture of Stonehenge, Malta, and some spots on the continent, nowhere did the structure of society hint at the complex patterns of civilized life that were displayed in Egypt and Mesopotamia, the Aegean and Asia Minor. When intrepid Mycenaean sailors hugging the northern shores gained Sicily and the Tyrrhenian in search of metal—the obsidian of Lipari, the copper of Sardinia, and ores from the mines of Etruria between the Arno and Po rivers—this area led a simple pastoral life, innocent of urbanism.

In central and southern Italy, the countryside remained seminomadic; megalithic tombs in Apulia, the peninsula's heel, were probably used as rallying places. Villages took several different forms. Neolithic communities with circular earth ramparts can be spotted throughout Apulia, as well as in southern Etruria. Inside them were smaller circular enclosures with their own individual ditches, each containing dwellings for family groups and their cattle. Further north, in the Po Valley and the Alpine region, we find houses on piles. The river villages were protected against floods by moats, earth ramparts, and even timber constructions. Around the mountain lakes, quadrangular log cabins stood on neatly delineated straight streets paved with planks.

The impact of eastern traders on this rustic world was small but noticeable. We can point to rock-hewn chamber tombs and roughly made beehive tombs in Sicily, an occasional stronghold fortified with stone walls of irregular blocks, and even the remains of an ambitious structure in the wilds of Pantalica above Syracuse, with a touch of the Mycenaean palace about it. All of these indicate a raised architectural consciousness attributable to eastern example. The *nuraghi* of Sardinia are more impressive still. They were watchtowers set on hilltops as part of a system of defense; the oldest among them were in the form of truncated cones that held two or three superimposed circular chambers with corbelled vaults. (Fig. 6.1)

Toward the end of the millennium, massive dislocations of peoples in the eastern Mediterranean unmade the balance of strong states and ushered in a dark spell of several centuries when cultural regression, or at best stagnation, was everywhere evident. Invasions from the northern and western fringes of the civilized sphere brought down established orders, infiltrated native stocks, and caused many residents to migrate. The Bronze Age and its brilliant cities folded. The downfall of the Mycenaean and Hittite empires returned their lands to a general level of low subsistence. For once, cultural parity may have been reached between the retarded West and the formerly progressive cultures of the Aegean and Asia Minor. But with a difference. The collective mind in the eastern Mediterranean had at least memories of a glorious past to fall back on and material remnants of it as proof of its existence.

Recovery was slow. The crucial century was probably the eighth. By then, stabilizing forces both East and West could ensure firm government, an improved standard of living, and an urban setting for the nurture and development of a society. In the East there was a revival, at the center of which stood Greece. The radiant Greek spirit, as expressed in architecture and especially the temple form, is the main concern of this chapter.

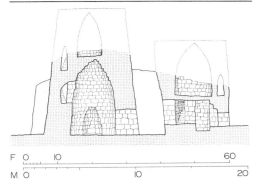

Fig. 6.1 Palmavera (Sardinia), a Bronze Age watchtower (*nuraghi*), ca. 1200 B.C.; elevation.

Fig. 6.2 Map: The Greek commonwealth and its neighbors in the seventh century B.C., with detail maps of Greek Sicily (bottom left), and Greece proper including the mainland, the Aegean islands, and coastal Asia Minor (bottom right).

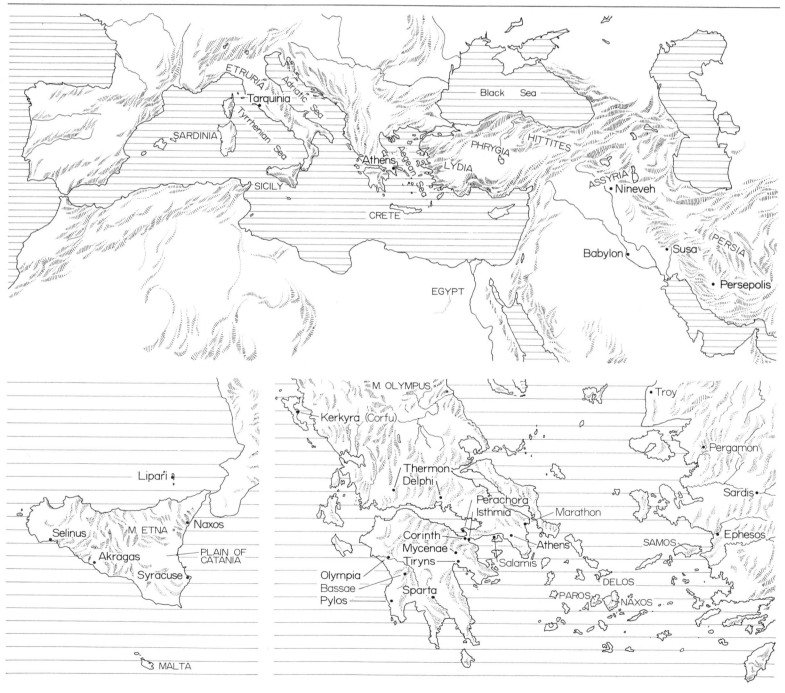

Fig. 6.3 Greek "geometric" vase, with a scene of mourning for the dead, eighth century B.C. (National Museum, Athens, Greece)

But Greece did not blossom miraculously in a cultural desert. In Asia Minor, beyond the coastal strip which it colonized, two small but significant powers, the Phrygians and Lydians, succeeded in upholding the raised hopes of the plateau. Further east the Hittite empire, in reduced but still notable circumstances, roused itself for a sunset career. Assyrians, long locked in a stalemate with their powerful neighbors, resumed an expansionist policy under Tiglath-pileser III (745–727 B.C.) until they were conquered a century later by Medes from the Persian highlands and their capital city of Nineveh was destroyed. Persia itself reacted favorably to the stimulus of an incoming group of Indo-European horsemen, as its fortified towns and wise

exploitation of iron show. At the time of the Achaemenid dynasty, it could boast of an opulent, cosmopolitan culture whose most famous extant theater is the palace of Darius and Xerxes at Persepolis. (Fig. 6.23) In the West, immigrants from Asia Minor (according to the most likely theory) organized northern Italy into a confederation of strong cities. This Etruscan state, under the tutelage of neighboring Greeks who had colonized the southern half of the peninsula and much of coastal Sicily, lifted the sleepy countryside north of the Tiber into a period of heady urbanism; its hallmarks were formal layouts, temples, bridges and aqueducts, and lavishly decorated mound tombs.

The Greek commonwealth stood in the midst of this new order, involved at one or another level with all the young states as well as the venerable antiquity of Egypt. (Fig. 6.2) It considered them all inferior to the self-governed polity of its own city-states. They were all "barbarians," a term which meant both alien and not quite up to Greek standards. But in the universal order of the period, the Greek achievement was only one of several manifestations of cultural vigor, none demonstrably inferior to the others.

The Emergence of Greece

The details of the post-Mycenaean aftermath are unclear. It would seem that the southbound Dorians, having achieved the violent overthrow of the Bronze Age cities in Greece, settled down to a village-centered rural life based on tribal loyalties and the localized authority of chieftains and deities. Land was owned in common. Cremation replaced inhumation as the standard burial rite. The most striking relics of these dim years is in fact of a funerary nature: large stately vases for liquid offerings, decorated with geometric patterns. (Fig. 6.3)

Iron, and not bronze, was now the chief substance out of which weapons and tools were fashioned. The new metal became the physical symbol of the descent from a sparkling past to a lackluster present. Hesiod, the Boeotian poet and rough contemporary of Homer, recounted gloomily in his *Works and Days* the fall from a golden

age to an iron age in which "man will never cease by day or night from weariness and woe." The time of the heroes who had fought at Troy was long gone by—its nostalgic retelling was Homer's subject. Hesiod, on the other hand, looked at post-Mycenaean Greece and the realities of his own time. He put all his faith in the plot of bad land on the slopes of Mount Helikon, which he and his brother Perseus inherited from their father, and cultivated it doggedly.

Community architecture was now simple and of uniform scale. Nothing like the Mycenaean palaces was being attempted. The houses were elliptical at first, then rectangular and apsidal. They were one-room detached structures of mud-brick on a foundation of stones or rubble. Shrines were not much different, except for a small roughly hewn, wooden statuette of the local deity called a *xoanon*. These frequently apsidal chapels might have interior posts—irregularly spaced, or arranged in one or two rows—to facilitate the roofing of the main space. They would also use a triangular truss at the facade end that shaped the tall gable in which a window would be cut, as well as a system of radial poles to support the hip roof over the apse. (Fig. 6.4) The overhanging eaves were sometimes made to rest on posts along the entire length of the struc-

Fig. 6.4 Greek shrine, votive clay model, from Argos (Greece), eighth century B.C.

ture, except at the gabled front, which had its own small porch. The roof, whether pitched or flat, was covered with thatch.

Humble though they were, two aspects of these village chapels foretold of the distinctive character of religious architecture to come in the scheme of the future Greek city-states. First, the chapels were now the only special focus of the built area. The full-grown temple will also figure later as the principal architectural beacon of the cities, and this because no human agency was to seem exalted at the expense of others, as the Minoan-Mycenaean palace had been.

Second, the chapels were intended for the exclusive use of a god or goddess, and not as congregational halls for worshippers or as centers of the community's economic or social structure. This intention, too, will be carried forward into the urban phase of Greek history. There was to be no powerful priestly class in charge of the temple and its rites, along the lines of Egyptian or Mesopotamian practice. The Greeks' relation to divinity was to be an open act around monumental buildings, with laypeople performing priestly duties as part of the responsibility of citizenship. The citizen owed honor to the deities of the land but did not belong to them in the way the citizens of Ur or Warka belonged to their titular deities. The Greeks' allegiance to the city was to be secular, despite the preeminence of religious architecture in the cityscape. The city itself was the faith, and the temple was its banner of fixity, the historic identification of the people with the land vouched for by the immortal beings who preceded human settlement.

The balance of the ancient world is always that tenuous one of the human and the divine. Like two forces that compete but must also complement each other in the structure of life, humans, or their most potent representative the king, and divinities, as they are interpreted by the priesthood, jostle for possession of the land and of communal destiny. Some sort of accommodation is worked out by each culture, depending on that culture's aspirations and outlook. Architecturally, the contest is between the palace and the royal tomb on the one hand, and the temple on the other.

In Mesopotamian city-states, the king was content to serve as the caretaker of the city,

Fig. 6.5 Olympia (Greece), sanctuary of Zeus; general view of site.

which properly belonged to a god. The ziggurat or temple tower loomed in the built environment, and the royal palace rested in its shadow. With the Assyrians, the might of the ruler tended to eclipse the presence of the deity, as we can see from the secondary standing of the ziggurat in the palace district of Khorsabad. (Figs. 3.14, 3.25b)

The progress in Egypt was somewhat the reverse. First came the order of the Old Kingdom when the king *was* god, and the land reflected this one-sided state of affairs by featuring as its most palpable marker the pyramid tomb which announced his central authority. Then came the political change that forced the king, under the New Kingdom, to accept a more modest role among the gods and to allow their ritual setting, the temple, to dominate his land. (Figs. 4.10, 4.22)

In Crete and Mycenae the priesthood was clearly subordinate. There were no major temples. The deities lived in the open, in groves and caves and mountaintops where they originated. Altars and small shrines in these spots focused popular devotion. But,

above all, these deities found hospitality at the king's hearth. (Figs. 5.13, 5.20) Homer makes clear that they had acquired the habit of visiting Mycenaean palaces: "Athena . . . crossed the barren seas, and came to Marathon and the broad streets of Athens, where she entered the strong palace of Erechtheus." With the disappearance of these mighty kings, the predictable happened in Greece. Divinities took over. Being conceived in human form, they were now accommodated architecturally in houses—modest ones at first, and then more and more magnificent ones in the course of time.

Evidence of this transfer of the people's destiny can be found in two architectural facts. First, the basis for the form of the mature mainland temple is the Mycenaean megaron. (Fig. 5.14) There are differences of course. The continuous exterior colonnade of the mature temple was a Greek invention; the orientation of the Mycenaean megaron was north to south, while the temple customarily faced east; and instead of the flat roof of megara, all stone temples

Fig. 6.6 Delphi (Greece), sanctuary of Apollo; general view of site.

had gabled roofs. But the sequence of the columned porch *in antis* and the main rectangular chamber beyond is unmistakable. The shift was in occupancy: the royal hearth was displaced by the statue of the deity.

The second point is topographical. The literary and archaeological evidence shows that at some sites early temples were built on the grounds of a former Mycenaean palace. This was so at the Akropolis of Athens. Sometime during the dark centuries a chapel or shrine dedicated to the goddess Athena was planted in "the strong palace of Erechtheus," overlapping the megaron. Athena who came to visit in the old days was now permanently at home.

Athena and several other major deities of the later Olympian pantheon were known to the Mycenaeans. Whatever deities of their own the Dorians may have brought in, these extant cults were not suppressed. On the contrary, together with a common language they were the chief source of Greek unity. When in the eighth century the Greek commonwealth started in earnest to forge a national identity, this heritage of a holy family helped to transcend the local allegiances of the hundreds of communities that dotted the tough Greek land and its newfangled colonies. Homer's poems sharpened the specific personalities of these gods and goddesses, demystifying them by imparting them with human foibles and weaknesses.

Two cults stood out as particularly important to this Panhellenic effort. At Olympia in southern Greece, Zeus as the father of the holy family was honored by all. (Fig. 6.5) In an ample grove at the foot of a hill sacred to Kronos (the deposed parent of Zeus and his sister-wife Hera), games were instituted beginning in 776 B.C. Every four years, a moratorium would be declared on the bitter rivalries of the Greek communities, and here at the grove athletes would converge to compete on behalf of their fellows and to gain honor from almighty Zeus. A significant complex of buildings grew at Olympia during the next three centuries that included a stadium, a row of treasuries set up by individual Greek cities, and two large temples dedicated to Hera and Zeus.

The other cult was that of Apollo, the overseer of the oracle at Delphi. (Fig. 6.6) Before the setting down of written laws in the sixth century B.C., this oracle had emerged as the general fount of wisdom, the dispenser of binding advice that softened the harsh ancestral morality of tribal living with a new doctrine of moderation and respect for civilized order. The craggy wild of the site testified to the violent struggle between old underworld forces, like the snake Pytho, and the young god who in overcoming these forces trampled basic fear and made reason triumph. There in the tossed land, over the chasm of the earth, Apollo's temple rose as a trumpet call to measure and self-control. Many of the early temples in mainland Greece and abroad were dedicated to the Lord Apollo. Colonies were usually established on the advice of his Delphic oracle.

The Panhellenic community that such a national church encouraged corresponds with the rise of the *polis* or city-state at the regional level. The Greeks embraced urbanism as a matter of choice. The polis did not respond to a major technological advance or the push of commerce. It was not, initially at least, a manufacturing or marketing center; if anything, it remained an overgrown agricultural village dependent on the traditional labor of the countryside. The importance of urban organization lies in the desire to go beyond the common law of tribe and clan, to live under controllable institutions of self-government.

The Greek city was founded on two concepts that typify the turn away from a patriarchal and custom-bound society and its burden of *aidos,* "that vague sense of respect for gods and men," as one scholar describes it, "and shame of wrong-doing before earth and sky." One of these concepts was the right of private property, which spelled the breakdown of the tribal common land. The other concept was individual freedom, the faith in human parity that is the opposite of the self-reducing collectiveness of tribal destiny. The social grouping was now, theoretically at least, one of equals bound by their own decision-making and administered by elected magistrates. The hearth became the city, and every Greek became above all a citizen, there to fight for the city's interests and guide its affairs. There was to be no organized military system, any more than there was an organized priesthood. Each man

carried his own weapons, as each person was ultimately accountable for his or her own good relations with the immortal protectors of the city and its laws.

The Greek Temple

Greek temples served simultaneously as the symbol of a broad union of Greeks—a union predicated upon a common religion, a common tongue, and the belief in a common ancestry—and also as the symbol of each city's special involvement with one of the immortals—Samos with Hera, Ephesos with Artemis, Corinth with Apollo, Athens with Athena. They had, then, both general and particular validity; they distinguished Greek from "barbarian" and one Greek city from the others. The message of the temple to its own audience, from the Tyrrhenian to the Black Sea, was that the same architecture and religious iconography could be used to make very individual statements. The message of the temple to the alien world was that of a free people, subject to neither king nor priest: "The whole folk year by year, in parity of service is our king," as the playwright Euripides was to put it about Athens. In this larger sense, in what it stands for as much as in the way it looks, the temple remains a uniquely Greek achievement.

There were, of course, some borrowings—both in the built form itself and in the art that enhanced it. Already in the eighth century, the geometric style of the funerary vases was being overlaid by a hybrid language of curvilinear designs, plants, and intimidating beasts borrowed from the late phases of Anatolian, Mesopotamian, and Egyptian art. (Fig. 6.7) At the same time, Homer's consolidation of fable into historic memory was finding a visual counterpart in the potter's workshop. It is out of this visual codification of myth, scenes involving Herakles or the wily Odysseus, that the formulae of temple art were to emerge.

In architecture, however, foreign influence went far beyond the importation of specific motifs. The great "barbarian" lesson was monumentality, the power of an architecture of public scale built of cut stone and made pregnant with communicative sculpture: and the great teacher was Egypt,

Fig. 6.7 Greek vase in the "orientalizing" style, seventh century B.C. (Louvre, Paris)

a country with which the Greek world had been in close contact at least since the seventh century. This lesson in architectural expression swept aside the early folk experiments and brought forth the strong, salient form of the Greek temple that we can still see in hundreds of sites throughout the Aegean, southern Italy, and Sicily. It is this luminous stone specter in the landscape

Fig. 6.8 Corinth (Greece), temple of Apollo, sixth century B.C.; view of remains.

that has been, along with Roman law, the Bible, and the plays of Shakespeare, one of the prime staples of the Western imagination.

We should distinguish three overlapping stages in the evolution of the Greek temple.

1. To the first stage belong the apsidal chapels prevalent in the obscure period following the Dorian occupation of mainland Greece. The domestic character of these structures, their literal function as houses of local deities, is evidenced not only in their basic form but also in the fact that some among them included a hearth within the cult room.

2. This initial experimental stage, when the structure of the Greek pantheon was still vague and the Greek nation still unformed, was superseded by a generation of temples noteworthy for two things: their comparatively larger size and the appearance of the peristyle. The period in question, the eighth and seventh centuries, corresponds with the rise and early success of the *polis*, widespread colonization, and the genesis of a common Greek tradition and faith. The apsidal form was now everywhere aban-

doned in favor of strict rectangularity. The cult room, or cella, created a tunnel view toward the statue at the far end. This view could be kept clear only by limiting the width of the room. Ampler proportions usually called for a central row of supports, which either blocked the view or forced the statue to one side of the central axis.

The peristyle made these internal arrangements of minor consequence. (Fig. 6.8) This formal portico that surrounded the entire outline of the cella, including the entrance front, may have been employed first in the temple of Hera on the island of Samos, which was built sometime in the early eighth century.

So far, the temples we have studied in the Near East fall into two classes. They either have cult rooms which are hermetically sealed from the outside, as is the practice in Egypt, or else the temple envelope is perforated with windows that bring in ample light, the solution of Temple I at Hattusas. (Figs. 4.18, 5.5) The effect of the peristyle is very different. Rather than opening up the cella walls toward the light, the Greek builder at Samos chose to enshrine this hall within an architectural screen, and

in so doing he changed the concept of the temple from a tabernacle of the holy image to an external thing, a form that mattered as a mid-space object and had visual validity from all sides. The ring of uniform wooden posts outside prevented the long narrow hall from being read as a simple container and obscured the distinction between the open entrance end and the solid end with the cult statue. The house of the deity was on its way to becoming the monument and talisman for the city. And, in fact, this conceptual advance is what is so revolutionary about these early temples. The continuous portico was never wide enough to provide usable space. The practical advantage of being able to extend the eaves beyond the walls, and thus protect the mud-brick structure from rain, had already been recognized in the first stage. Besides, when a generation or two prior to 600 B.C. stone columns began to replace the wooden posts, and ashlar masonry the mud-brick of the walls, such practical considerations were clearly irrelevant.

3. The shift to permanent materials was completed with the invention of terra-cotta tiles as a new roofing material. Since these tiles were not fastened to the roof but were kept in place by their own weight, the steepness of the roof was moderated to an easy rise, visually more stable and more in tune with the height of the stone columns at the two short ends than the earlier high-pitched gables had been. (Fig. 6.11) These two ends were made to look identical even beyond the peristyle layer by the addition of a false back porch to the main body of the cella, matching the entrance porch of the east front. (Fig. 6.16) In its plan the cella now resembled the megaron type of Troy II. (Fig. 5.9)

Once again, however, it would be perverse to explain the choice of stone columns in the peristyle as the practical requirement for the heavy tiles. Masonry structure and tiles both were the outcome of a new vision that required a new technology and had to do with intangible gains, such as community pride and faith in the city's stability and strength. This mood of confidence that was articulated in the new architecture also accounts for the simultaneous rebirth of large-scale stone sculpture, absent from the Greek scene since the days of Mycenae. Public statues of young men and women singled out for athletic prowess or exceptional virtue began to people the periphery of the temples. (Fig. 6.9) These full-size images were not set up as individual portraits but, instead, existed as civic monuments—generalized presences honoring the city through its choice citizens.

That architecture and sculpture were thought to be integral to this public display of a city's prosperity and glory is suggested by the fact that early architects like Theodoros of Samos were equally well known as sculptors. They were in charge of the total decorative program of the temples which at this time began to include figured panels in painted terra-cotta (a device probably learned from Assyria) and stone reliefs. The spare, almost heraldic, depiction of familiar subjects, the deeds of immortals and half-mortals, completed the statement of the temple, the fabled content of the scenes supplying the citizenry with the archetypes of a shared morality.

The very first stone temples seemed to have appeared in the northeastern corner of the Peloponnesus, at places like Corinth and Isthmia, and in outposts within their cultural sphere, like Thermon in the remote region west of Delphi. It is surely not fortuitous that this sudden show of constructive courage should be staged in the area of the Argolid plain where the ruins of the two greatest Mycenaean citadels, Tiryns and Mycenae, proclaimed past accomplishment and invited revival, even though the stone temples showed little formal and technical similarity to this Mycenaean precedent.

The initial source, for the mechanics of stone-cutting as well as the conventions of large-scale sculpture, was Egypt. Even the Doric column, the central element of the decorative order that was invented on the spot and was adhered to in mainland Greece and the Western colonies for at least three centuries, favored the Egyptian look. The capital itself may well have been inspired by the Mycenaean examples on the triangular relief of the Lion Gate and the facade of the so-called Treasury of Atreus. (Fig. 5.17) But Doric columns did not adopt the peculiarly Minoan-Mycenaean inverse taper; instead, they tapered upward in the

Egyptian manner. At any rate, the borrowed preliminaries were digested within the span of a generation, and the Doric order emerged as a quintessentially Greek system of design. So did the Ionic order, some fifty years later than the Doric, in the Greek cities of the eastern Mediterranean.

The names of their creators have been preserved in the record: Trophonios and Agamedes, the legendary pair associated with the first stone temple at Apollo's Delphi; Theodoros, who worked on the huge temple of Hera at Samos, which superseded the timber structure we spoke of above; Chersiphron, the designer of the temple of Artemis at Ephesos. The task they faced, to embrace a technology that differed fundamentally from the traditional building methods of wood and mud-brick, was comparable to that of Imhotep at Saqqara 2,000 years earlier.

Quarrying and transporting the stone were their principal worries; construction techniques and structural soundness were rudimentary. Beginner's caution probably accounts for the overbuilt forms—the thickly spaced peristyle columns (at times monolithic), heavy superstructures, massive foundations. Chersiphron, we are told, sought the advice of Theodoros of Samos regarding the Ephesian temple's stability on its marshy site; he was instructed to put a layer of ashes (packed charcoal, according to another source) beneath the foundations to keep the stone blocks from sinking. Chersiphron wrote a book about his experiences with the new technology, in which he explained the mechanical device he had used for transporting column drums from the quarry to the site. These were too large to be carried in ox-drawn wagons, so he set them in cylindrical frames of wood that could be pulled along like enormous rollers. (Fig. 6.10)

The general attitude in the ancient world was to submerge the identity of the architect in the person of his powerful patron, the king or minister who commissioned the building. This is the case with Mesopotamian and Hittite architecture. In Egypt, we know a fair number of state architects by name, and we have plenty of evidence that they were held in high esteem and exercised considerable power as supervisors of vast and costly public projects. But their

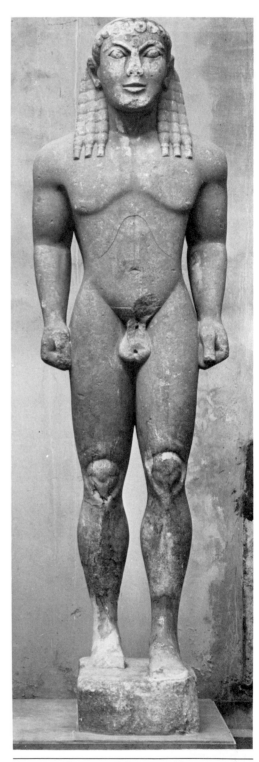

Fig. 6.9 Archaic Greek *kouros*, athlete named Biton, ca. 600 B.C. The statue stands over 2 meters (7 feet) high. (Museum, Delphi)

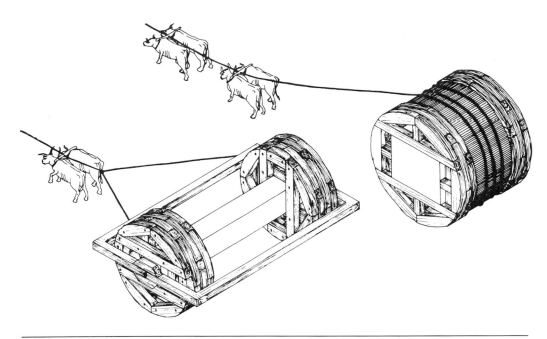

Fig. 6.10 Two ways of transporting stone building blocks in the sixth century B.C., according to ancient Greek sources; reconstruction drawing.

craft was secretive. The architect practiced with the aid of documents, including drawings, that were considered to be divinely inspired and were kept in the archives of temples and other official institutions. He was prominent precisely because of this privileged access to occult sources, since literacy was the exclusive attribute of high courtiers and the priesthood. Senmut, the famous architect and intimate of Queen Hatshepsut, boasted of this distinction on the walls of his tomb: "I had access to all the writings of the prophets; there was nothing which I did not know of that which had happened since the beginning."

The Greek architect was not so exalted, but he was a respected professional whose name was on public record and whose craft was accessible in trade books and treatises. His patron was commonly the city, as represented by its governing bodies. These government agencies set the budget and appointed a building commission to work closely with the architect in procuring the designs and in putting the project out to contract. The contractors were responsible for cutting and shaping the blocks at the quarry and for transporting them safely to

the site. There they would be trimmed down to their final surface for proper fitting. The finishing and assembly of the hundreds of premade units were the most exacting responsibilities of the architect.

The Doric Order

Matters of technique and construction, though obviously important, were not the prime testing ground of Greek architects. The mettle of Greek built form lies in seemly appearance.

Greek thinking is at once typal and specific. It takes on an idea (or a form, which is nothing other than a congealed idea), nourishes and perfects it through a series of conscious changes, and in this way informs it with a kind of universal validity that seems irrefutable. The process is in fact *ideal*, that is, based on "the perfection of kind." It presupposes orderly development and the practicability of consummation. Greek architecture is, by this definition, conservative. It invented little, and invention was slow. License was disciplined, and quality filtered through self-imposed restriction. Every building existed within the limits of its norm and was judged

against other exponents of this same norm. And because this was so, every building could convey precise meaning against a background of familiarity.

The stone temple of mainland Greece and its full decorative panoply, the Doric order, was an ideal invention. It did not constitute, as a mechanistic view would have it, the gradual translation into masonry of conventional timber forms. It seized upon the possibilities of the new technology to restate the principal theme of religious architecture as typified by the first peripteral temples of the eighth and early seventh centuries. In so doing, it *expressed* some of the effects of wood detailing rather than trying to petrify them exactly. It is therefore not very fruitful to seek precise references in timber construction for individual elements of the Doric order, to see triglyphs as beam ends and columns as tree trunks. It is the contrast and not the transference that needs to be stressed. This is plain when we set side by side the reconstructed elevations of the temple of Artemis at Kérkyra (Corfu), about 600 B.C., where the Doric order appeared in full form, and that of the second temple of Hera at Samos from the mid-seventh century, with its flimsy timber armature and its nervous verticality. (Fig. 6.11)

Once launched, this system of design remained fairly stable, except for corrective changes that smoothed out infelicities of form and heightened the expressive impact. This of course is a statement of general fact. The evolutionary process could have been neither entirely systematic nor predictable. Regions marched at a varying pace and offered different solutions to the same design challenges. On occasion a Doric temple—the temple of Zeus at the Sicilian town of Akragas (Agrigento) is a good instance—would take so many extraordinary liberties that it would seem to defy the essential constant of its norm. Finally, we must allow that the results of the evolutionary process could have been very different from what we know them to be. There is no strict determinism in the history of architecture. Tidy accounts of development can be drawn by historians only because they know how it all came out, and they can therefore rationalize a quirky string of choices so that it seems predestined.

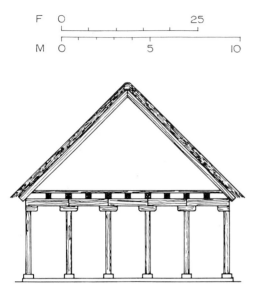

F O 25
M O 5 10

Fig. 6.11a Samos (Greece), the second temple of Hera, mid-seventh century B.C.; conjectural elevation.

Fig. 6.11b Kérkyra (Corfu, Greece), temple of Artemis, ca. 600 B.C.; restored elevation.

Let us now take a close look at the Doric temple. The first thing we should notice is that the temple was a supremely artificial construct—a luminous presence of right angles and sharp geometries. It stood apart in the land, a monument of a vital abstraction, eschewing the studied fusion with the natural site, which was the aim of Minoan-Mycenaean design or the city defenses of Hattusas. Greece is devoid of great sweeps of nature like the Egyptian desert, devoid too of grandiloquent mountain chains or broad navigable rivers. The contrasts are dramatic but on an intimate scale: defiles and precipitous valleys that might become contested boundaries between city-states; small cultivable plains boxed in by naked mountains, which are themselves small but also visually explosive because of the constricted formation of the land; and craggy, wind-battered, inhospitable shores with few natural harbors or easy beaching facilities. It is against all this that the temple stood, its form the very opposite of the agitated landscape. (Fig. 6.6)

This contrast of the natural and the devised is at the heart of Greek religious architecture. It heralds both the separateness of human achievement from the dark ancient forces of the land and the propitiation of these divinely controlled forces

through the act of building. We should neither consider the temple, then, merely as a thing in itself, a beautiful shell independent of its setting, nor should we assume that the setting had primarily picturesque value, as if the land were a neutral element which the builders made use of to add visual interest to their own creation.

For the land was not neutral. Where the temple came to stand was not a matter of arbitrary choice. The choice had been made before any temples were up, by what had once transpired on the land. Here Leto had leaned against a bay tree while giving birth to Apollo; there Athena and Poseidon had fought for the privilege of ruling Attica; here divinity was befriended at the hearth of a Mycenaean king or appeased at some cave or spring source or mountaintop. The hallowed spot was thus predetermined: from the earliest altar set upon it to the latest temple, it would be respected and celebrated. Even where the terrain was extremely unpromising, as at Perachora on the Gulf of Corinth, the temple went up where it did because it had to. (Fig. 6.12)

The first step in the monumental commemoration of the sacred site was the terrace—the element that would horizontally define the space and serve as the pedestal for the structure. The freestanding rectan-

gular shape of this terrace clearly announced that the finished temple would not attempt to blend in with its surroundings. The three continuous steps all around the edge of the terrace would lift the temple above the land and make it equally approachable from all sides. The length and width of the top platform would determine how many columns the temple would have along the flanks and across the two fronts, as well as their spacing.

This spacing depended on two things: the choice of a lower diameter for the columns, which in turn woud dictate their height; and the disposition of the frieze above the peristyle which determined, as we will see, whether the spaces between columns would be of uniform width, or whether there would be variation between the middle range of columns and those at the corners of the rectangle. In other words, the upper parts of the building made precise demands on the lower, and each element was not only proportionally generated but also proportionally keyed to all other elements of the design.

The number of columns for the standard peristyle would be set at 6 by 14, counting the corner columns twice, but early temples sometimes had longer flanks. The columns were stood up along the edge of the

Fig. 6.12 Perachora (Greece), sanctuary of Hera Akraia (Hera of the Cliffs); general view. The archaic temple is in the immediate foreground, with a fourth-century stoa just behind, and further up, beyond the modern structure, the remains of a Hellenistic cistern.

stylobate, the topmost of the three terrace steps, without bases. (Fig. 6.8) The drums were plain and had a hole in the center, so that they could be twisted about a peg as they were piled one on top of the other until they were tightly fitted together. In the sixth century, the height of the shafts measured 4.5 to 5 times the lower diameter; the column was 8 times as high as its capital. The tendency was to make these proportions leaner and more elegant in the course of decades, so that by the fifth century the relation of diameter to shaft was 1:5.5 or even 1:5.75, and the total column stood 11 to 12 times as tall as its capital. At the same time, the upward taper of the columns was also being reduced, so that the flare of the lower member of the capital, or *echinus*, would not be quite as forceful as it had been in the sixth-century temples.

It was this taper as well as the *entasis*, or the slight bulging of the shaft profile, that gave Doric columns a look of vitality and expressed their load-bearing function. The fluting of the shaft also helped to convey this feeling of compression, while at the same time it distinguished the shaft from the smooth background masonry of the cella walls. Fluting was done on the spot, after all the drums of a column were in place. Normally there were twenty flutes per column. This pattern of arrised grooves pulled the individual drums together and created the illusion of flow along the length of the unified cylinder.

The idea of emphasizing the function of lifting by the curved profile and surface treatment of the shaft was an old one. A primitive form of both tapering and entasis had been attempted in the sarsen uprights of Stonehenge. Fluting had been applied to wooden columns in Minoan-Mycenaean architecture, and much earlier in Egypt where entasis was also a common practice. There is in fact a striking resemblance between Doric columns of the sixth and fifth centuries B.C. and some of the attached columns at Zoser's Saqqara complex 2,000 years earlier. (Fig. 4.6)

The Doric capital made the transition from the circular column shaft to the bridging blocks of the architrave above. The capital consists of two parts, a flaring echinus that broadens the circle of the shaft top and brings it in line with the scale of the superstructure, and the square unit of the *abacus* on which the architrave blocks rest. This is a purely geometric cushion of juncture between support and load, with no reference to natural forms like plants or trees. Consequently, we cannot read the column in any literal sense, but must respond to it as an abstraction, or rather as a metaphor.

Perhaps inevitably in the light of their self-awareness, the metaphor of the Greek column has to do with the human body. It is as though we are there bearing the load of the superstructure and would know in our own bodies, empathetically, what is too much or too little for the constitution of the columns. At issue is the *appearance* of a fair balance. The column height and its thickness in relation to the mass of the superstructure are determined with a sense of visual justice, so that both look adequate to their task even if, in the narrow structural context, one or the other, the colonnade or its burden, might actually be overbuilt.

The principle of empathy is central to the understanding of Greek architecture. It comes about intangibly, through the proportional interlocking of the members, which evokes the proportional relationships of a standing human. Proportion, ac-

125

cording to the Classical theorist Vitruvius, "is a correspondence among the measures of the members of an entire work, and of the whole to a certain part selected as standard . . . as in the case of those of a well-shaped man." This description and the fact that the units of measurement themselves are derived from members of the human body—the palm, the foot—are not unique to Greek architecture. But the phrase "as in the case of those of a well-shaped man" implies a physical affinity between user and building so that, for example, the ratio of column to capital could not be too far removed from the ratio of the human frame to its head. It is this affinity that enables us to comprehend the scheme of the peristyle, and what the column is capable of, in terms of our own capabilities. In the end, this humanly inspired reasonableness of built form is what distinguishes the experience of a Greek temple from the crushing gigantism of Egyptian structures. (Fig. 4.20)

The architrave completes the vertical definition of the peristyle. It is a band of stone that separates the colonnade proper from the crowning elements of the temple—the frieze, the gables, or pediments at the two short ends, and the roof (Fig. 6.13) In reality the architrave is not made, as it appears to be, of a line of single blocks bridging pairs of columns but, instead, of two such blocks, one behind the other, extending from the center of one capital to the center of the next. The plain surface of the architrave effectively distinguishes the structural reality of the peristyle from the applied decorative scheme of the frieze, whose component parts, the alternating triglyphs and metopes, repeat schematically the rhythm of alternating columns and voids in the peristyle.

The play between the actual thing and its apostrophe was originally highlighted by the use of color. The colonnade and its architrave were not painted. If a porous stone had been selected, a coat of stucco would ordinarily be applied to cover up the rough texture; marble columns were sometimes waxed so that they would gleam under the strong Greek light. The frieze up above, having no true structural accountability, was painted gaily—blue for the triglyphs, whose grooves echoed the fluting of the actual columns, and red for the background of the

Fig. 6.13 Akragas (Agrigento, Sicily), the so-called Temple of Concord, later fifth century B.C.

metopes against which sculptured scenes stood in relief. We might today be startled by the notion that good limestone or marble should be concealed by bright paint. Faithfulness to the nature of materials is, however, a relatively modern concern. The Greek architect was interested in clarity; he felt no scruples about tampering with the texture and hue of stone for the sake of proper distinctions.

The appropriate place for triglyphs was directly above the columns they recalled, centered over each capital. But since the proportion of mass to void in the peristyle could not be approximated in this way, additional triglyphs were placed in the center of each intercolumniation. The architectural symbolism required that triglyphs occupy the corners of the frieze, since columns defined the four corners of the peristyle. To be flush with the corners, the last triglyphs on each side of the temple had

to be displaced in relation to the corresponding capitals below. This created a wider space between these corner triglyphs and their immediate neighbors than between any other pair of triglyphs. Two solutions were espoused to deal with the problem (Fig. 6.14). One, favored by the Greeks of Sicily and south Italy, involved the progressive stretching of the frieze elements next to the corner. In mainland Greece, the irregularity was offset at ground level by reducing the span of the columns close to the corner, a procedure known as angle contraction. Sometimes a combination of both systems would be used.

The tiled roof and the two pediments formed the crowning unit that projected beyond the line of the frieze. This unit closed off the peristyle screen to create a stone canopy that sheltered the cella building with its cult statue. It seems evi-

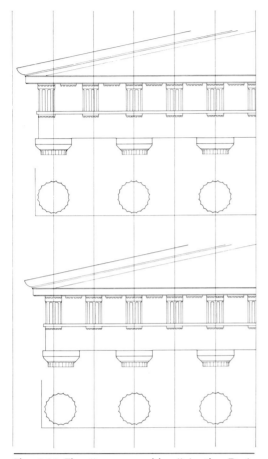

Fig. 6.14 The "corner problem" in the Doric temple. The diagram, with vertical guidelines that are equally spaced, indicates the two alternative adjustments: top, enlarging the width of metopes toward the corner; and bottom, reducing the span between the corner columns, or "angle contraction."

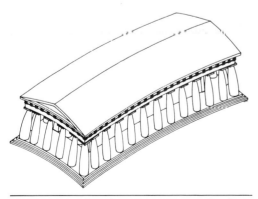

Fig. 6.15 Greek refinements, or visual adjustments in Greek temple design, exaggerated for emphasis; diagrammatic drawing.

dent from temples left unfinished that the cella building was constructed, despite the inconvenience, after the peristyle screen had been set up. It was the screen, then, that mattered most in the expression of the program, both in terms of form and as a religious statement.

The priority of the screen meant that the temple was conceived primarily as an exterior presence. Indeed, it leaned against nothing and had no backdrop except the land shapes around it or the cityscape. It was mid-space architecture par excellence. To stress this point, the screen was made visually continuous. The three steps went all around the terrace; the frieze wrapped itself around the top like a fancy ribbon. There was, in appearance at least, no front and back to the building, no designated entrances. Every approach, ideally, was valid: every intercolumniation could function as a door. To bring home this freedom from a fixed line of access, the path from the precinct gate often cut an oblique line to the temple, so that two sides of the building would be visible at once. (Fig. 6.16)

Meanwhile the architect took pains to have this mid-space object spring forcefully from the ground. To achieve this look of vitality, he incorporated in his design a whole gamut of visual subtleties. (Fig. 6.15) The groundline of the terrace gently curved upward toward the middle of each side. The columns, as we have already observed, tapered and had slightly convex profiles. In addition, the four-corner columns inclined inward and back, and they were also made thicker than the rest. Angle contraction, where it was resorted to for the sake of the corner triglyphs, further strengthened the visual articulation of the temple corners.

These refinements are commonly explained as corrective measures designed, for example, to counter the appearance that the straight lines sag; curving the lines would make them look straight to the naked eye. We had noticed similar adjustments before in the great ziggurat of Ur-Nammu at Ur. Philon of Byzantium in the late third century B.C. wrote that such optical compensation was necessary to prevent things that "were in fact of equal thickness and straight" from appearing not to be so. But actually some of the refinements, for example, the rise of the stylobate and entasis, are easily detected for what they are

if we have been made aware of them. (Fig. 6.13) They are intentional and evident distortions that render the otherwise thoroughly rational design of the temple live and spry. If we do not ordinarily notice them, it is precisely because they are so successful that they become part of the natural image of the Greek temple. "The eye," John Ruskin once wrote, "is continually influenced by what it cannot detect. . . . It is most influenced by what it detects least."

In religious terms as well, the peristyle screen was preeminent. The cult statue in the cella would be glimpsed through the doors that were opened during important observances. The daily intercourse with the godhead took place in the open. At the level of the terrace, the temple was surrounded by statues, mostly of humans—the standing life-size images of nude male youths and draped women set up by their cities as memorials of special excellence. They peopled the sacred precinct and underscored that peculiarly human scale of Greek architecture we spoke about earlier. The metopes and pediments received sculpture too, all of it religious. These sculptures were reared aloft by the columns of the peristyle. Nonetheless, they could clearly and unequivocally be seen by all users of the temple precinct and in the open daylight. The temple, in this sense, was the meeting ground of the human and the divine. At the same time that humans were lifted up by the proud and measured soaring of columns, deities came down to the level of human visibility. (Fig. 7.21)

This, then, is the Doric temple as it matured in Greece during the sixth and fifth centuries B.C. It registered, close up, through the special arrangement and proportions of its parts; and in the distant view, through its interaction with natural elements like the mountains and the sea. There was also an intermediate frame, the holy precinct, defined by a wall that narrowed the landscape at large and that established a fixed boundary within which the temple was played against smaller buildings such as treasuries, altars (and especially the principal altar to the east of the temple on which the open-air ritual focused), and dozens of votive monuments.

Within the precinct, the interplay of the looming mass of the temple and these smaller foils to its visual statement was a

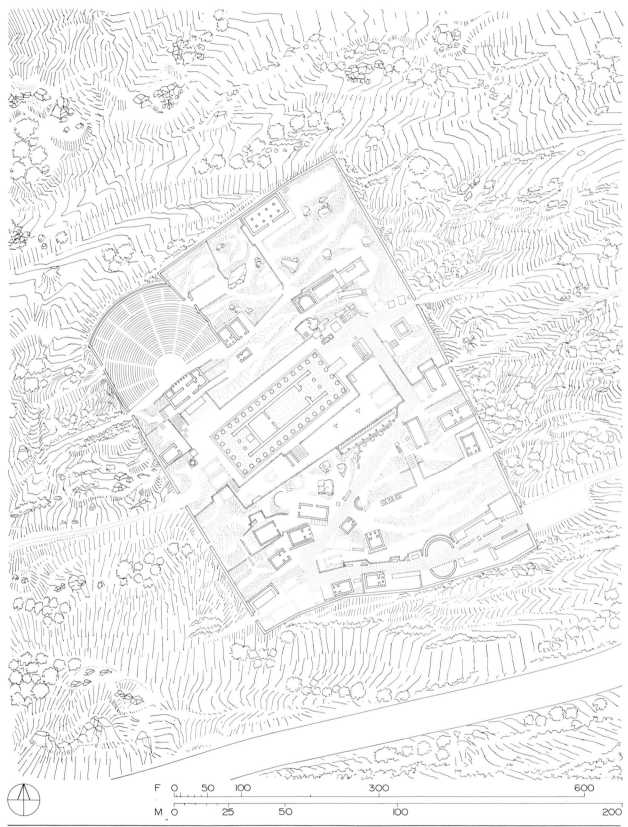

Fig. 6.16 Delphi, the sanctuary of Apollo; general site plan ca. 400 B.C.

vigorous, constantly changing relationship. (Fig. 6.16) First, the buildings and statues were seen according to the way the worshipper moved through the site along time-worn paths. The visual experience of any one building or statue had no fixed value, no single point of view. Treasuries, small replicas of the temple built by individual cities in Panhellenic sanctuaries like Delphi or Olympia, created an unregimented pattern in relation to the sacred way, jostling each other as spectators might during a parade. And second, new structures or monuments were regularly added to the site, and with each addition the relationship of those already present would alter and shift. The site plan, haphazard looking to the modern observer, was keenly reflective of old patterns, the drive of civic competition, and change through time. The temenos was caught in a process of continuous becoming; yet it was also complete at every stage of its growth.

The Temple in the West

A spirited individualism, only partly attributable to local conditions, characterizes the transplanted Doric temple in the Western colonies. At the outset, the strange land in the West posed two unique problems. For one thing, it was not marked, in the way that Greece had been, by a legendary age of pre-Hellenic ancestors. Moreover, the look and feel of the land was alien. The vast, fabulously fertile plain of Catania, the natural harbors and sand beaches, fuming Etna—for these there were no Greek parallels.

To mark this unfamiliar territory with proper, broad-based reverence, and to hold down the extravagant spaces, the religious architecture of Greek Sicily and southern Italy behaved remarkably. The size of the temples was often prodigious. No sixth-century Doric temple in Greece can compete with the heroic bulk of Temple G at Selinus, under construction for more than a century and still unfinished when the Carthaginians destroyed the city in 409 B.C. Such striking monumentality did more than advertise the prosperity of the colonies and their boastful pride: it also overreached in response to the call of the open, un-Greek horizons. The same rationale, coupled with the desire to play host to a fair number of Olympians, must hold for the banding of temples in groups of four or more, as is the case with the group east of the akropolis at Selinus and the other on the akropolis itself, and in the splendid series that dots the southern sea ridge of Akragas. (Fig. 6.17)

Western Greece, although it remained within the Hellenic fold, was in no way subservient to its historic homeland. Its own unique contributions were legitimate regional preferences rather than aberrant provincialisms. We can quickly scan these design peculiarities by looking at one of the most impressive of sixth-century Sicilian temples, the so-called Temple C at Selinus built about 500 B.C. on the highest point of the akropolis and in plain view of the sea.

Temple C was built of local stone. There were no marble deposits in Sicily, and so public architecture relied on local varieties of somewhat friable limestone and sandstone that had to be protected by coats of stucco and terra-cotta revetments. Marble, used for luxury details or heads of sculptured figures, was commonly imported from Greece.

The general plan of Temple C is very elongated. (Fig. 6.17) There are seventeen columns along the flanks in comparison to the standard fourteen. The cella is consequently long and narrow, all the more so

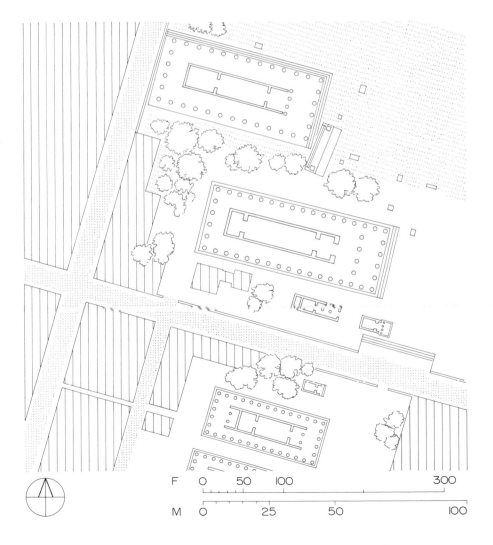

F 0   50   100   300

M 0   25   50   100

Fig. 6.17 Selinus (Selinunte, Sicily), temples at a major intersection of the upper town; ground plan. Temple C, ca. 500 B.C., is in the middle; Temple D is shown to the north; and Temple A to the south. Hatching indicates houses.

in that the architect has chosen to leave an exceptionally wide space between its walls and the peristyle. The cella walls in Greece align with the penultimate columns of the short ends of the peristyle. (Fig. 6.16) Sicilian temples either have cellas that are independent of the lines of the peristyle, or if the walls do align, it is often with the second and not the first intercolumniation. These narrow cellas can be roofed without the aid of interior supports.

Without rejecting the mid-space character of the Doric temple, certain features of Temple C clearly favor the east facade, and therefore an axial approach in the longitudinal sense. Behind the east colonnade of the peristyle, for example, there was a second row of columns that found no equivalent in the west end. There were sculptured metopes over this inner colonnade, but none on the outside in their normal place on the frieze. The terrace had not three but six steps on the east side. Lastly, the cella ended, to the west, in a closed rear chapel, or *adyton,* but lacked the false porch that would equalize the visual status of the two short ends of the cella when seen from the outside.

This incipient axiality of Temple C and a number of other Western Greek temples may bespeak familiarity with Etruscan practice. And there exist less equivocal borrowings in Etruscan temples, indeed in Etruscan architecture and in city planning generally, from their sophisticated neighbors to the south. But the liturgical needs of the two adjoining civilizations, their total outlook toward the world, differed fundamentally.

The Etruscan temple, for long a building of mud-brick and wood brightly painted and clad in terra-cotta, was raised on a high podium that jutted beyond a rectangular precinct. (Fig. 6.18) The only approach was across this formal area and up a broad flight of steps. A deep porch pulled one into its space through two rows of Tuscan columns which, despite their bases and unfluted shafts, owed allegiance to the Doric order. The porch afforded three passages corresponding to the tripartite sanctuary. The central (and broader) passage led into the cella proper; the side passages, into open wings or, in temples dedicated to a triad of deities, into separate cellas. A single, low-pitched roof projected deeply from

Fig. 6.18a An Etruscan temple, according to the description of Vitruvius; modern reconstruction. (Rome University)

the side walls, enveloping the flanks in shadow.

This low, lowering, and strictly axial form, fronting a geometrically oriented public space, is a far cry from the sculptural force of the freestanding Greek temple where enclosed space is of decidedly secondary interest. The basic concept of the Etruscan temple, including its orientation toward the south, seems eastern and not Greek in origin. We should remind ourselves that, in all likelihood, the founding stock of the Etruscan state came to Italy from Asia Minor, and more particularly from Lydia if we are to heed the claim of the Greek historian Herodotus.

Inwardness, along with axial alignment, is a prevailing trait of Etruscan built forms. It is manifested in the Etruscan fondness for the round arch and the circular plan. (Figs. 6.19, 6.20) The origins of the round arch are distant. There are brick, mortared arches in Mesopotamia and Persia, even Egypt, in the second millennium B.C. Even the stone voussoir arch, constructed of precisely cut wedges and dry joints that are locked in place by the keystone, may have had Greek rather than Etruscan parentage.

Fig. 6.18b Orvieto (Italy), the so-called Belvedere Temple, fifth century B.C.; plan. Typical layout of Etruscan temple with enclosed precinct, straight flight of stairs, deep entrance porch, and triple cella.

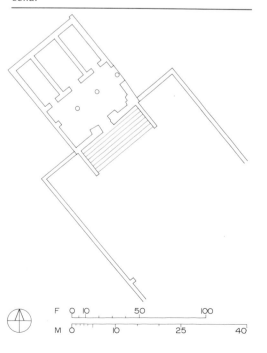

Fig. 6.19 Volterra (Italy), Etruscan city gate, fourth–third century B.C., with later, Roman repairs.

Fig. 6.20 Casal Marittimo (Italy), tholos tomb, ca. 600 B.C.; interior view. (Reconstructed in the Archaeological Museum, Florence, Italy)

Yet even with a handful of Greek examples, it is clear that the arch—and eventually its three-dimensional extension, the true vault—was congenial to the Italic, but not to the Greek, mentality. The Etruscans used corbelled vaulting, and the arch was used singly, in city gates and domestic architecture, rather than in any coherent system of architectural design. It was the Romans who exploited true vaults and arcuated surfaces later. Nevertheless, the Etruscans were nursing the germ of an encapsulating, space-engulfing architecture in these centuries of recovery. And this was a non-Greek phenomenon. Or rather pre-Classical; for the great corbelled tunnel vaults and domes that can still be seen in Etruscan funerary structures are, if anything, a throwback to the era of Bronze Age heroism, to Tiryns and Hattusas.

The same can be said for the most characteristic relics of Etruscan civilization, the mound tombs on handsome circular platforms cut from the living rock in the great cemetery cities of Cerveteri and Tarquinia. Round forms as a whole have an extremely limited appeal in Greek architecture, and interest in the afterlife does not extend to providing for it monumentally. The earth-fast round tombs of Etruscan cemeteries, with their elaborate furnishings imitating domestic environments and equipped for all requisites of a life after death, belong in spirit to the tombs of Egypt and, in form, to Mycenaean pendants like the "Treasury of Atreus." (Fig. 5.18)

The Ionic Order

We must now turn briefly to the second of the Greek decorative systems, the Ionic, which crystallized, somewhat later than the Doric, on the Aegean islands and in coastal Asia Minor. The differences between the two orders are plain enough. The Ionic is a more delicate and more ornate convention. (Fig. 6.21) Vitruvius was to consider it the feminine order, in contrast to the Doric which for him was imbued with "manly beauty, naked and unadorned." And, indeed, the sober abstraction of the Doric is countervailed in Ionic forms by a smack of the organic. Ionic ornamental details favor the curvilinear and freely recall leaf and plant forms.

The column itself is taller and thinner by comparison and rests on an elegantly molded base. The flutes do not meet at sharp arrises as a rule; instead, they are joined with fillets and gathered together at the top of the shaft by neck moldings. The volutes of the capital spread the upward energies of the column laterally along the line of the architrave. The architrave itself is divided into three horizontal strips that reduce the visual impact of the load in appreciation of the slender grace of the supports. The frieze above was often a continuous band of relief, enhancing the sense of a layered elevation that reads very differently from the determined verticality of the Doric.

One of the earliest and greatest Ionic temples was the Artemision at Ephesos of about 560–550 B.C. (Fig. 6.22a) We have mentioned it earlier in relation to the start of stone technology in Greek architecture. It provides us with a good case study for the rising Ionic order as an alternative to the Doric of the mainland. It also demonstrates the peculiar involvement of this order with the non-Greek context of contemporary Asia Minor.

Ephesos was a Greek city, but like most Greek cities of coastal Asia Minor, its affairs were tangled in Anatolian politics. At the time of the construction of the Artemision, it was controlled by the Lydian forces of King Croesus, and his interest in the temple affected the final form. Artemis shared aspects of the Near Eastern great goddess whom we have met in various guises on both sides of the Aegean. The fact that her temple at Ephesos faced west may well reflect liturgical bonds with Asia Minor.

The temple was immense by Greek standards of the time and was rarely surpassed even later. The site was the low ground at the head of a broad bay (today silted up), close by the water's edge. Low marshy sites are as common for Ionic temples as is precipitous high ground for Doric. This setting helped to emphasize the grovelike character of the peristyle that consisted of a double row of columns, eight of them across each short end in the preferred manner of Ionic temples, and had additional columns lining the attenuated front porch. The effect of massing so many columns is almost Egyptian. The cella may have been open to the sky in the middle, forming a monumental stage set around an earlier shrine.

The double peristyle and deep entrance porch filled with columns radically alter the experience of the Greek temple. (Fig. 6.22b) What is lost is the crisp interplay between the single row of peristyle columns and the walls of the cella visible just behind. Also lost is the straightforward relationship of the entrance porch to the colonnade of the east front when viewed head on from the outside—the door slightly higher than the stylobate and standing about half as tall as the framing columns of the porch, which would be partly shielded by the corresponding columns of the peristyle. The entrance to the cella, then, is both keyed to the peristyle and properly set back from it in the next plane. (Fig. 8.5)

At Ephesos the entrance would have been at the end of a long defile, dwarfed by the perspective and buried in the sprawling width of the temple like the promise of a clearing in a forest. The effect would have been one of multiplanar depth, as if the aim were processional penetration. Assuming that the cellas were indeed hypaethral, the pool of light behind the entrance would have enforced this feeling of openness beyond and would have acted as an additional inducement to move toward the core of the building. This prospect is wholly at odds with the obscure depths of a Doric temple where the cult statue would dimly show when the cella doors were thrown open. (Fig. 7.26)

Temple against Palace
One element of the Ephesian monument strikes a curious note. The peristyle columns were a gift from King Croesus of Lydia, and the lower sections of the shafts were carved with figured reliefs that collectively portrayed a grand procession, very probably of the court of Croesus beginning with his divine ancestors. The planting of this dynastic program on the temple of a Greek city-state highlights the peculiar standing of Ionia compared to the structured monarchies of the hinterland, Lydia and Persia in particular, a situation that did not exist for Greece in the West. In these countries, the palace was still the hub of political power. To the extent that the temple competed, it did so in the form of monastic complexes with large landholdings. The Lydian capital of Sardis complemented

Fig. 6.21 Athens (Greece), Akropolis, temple of Athena Nike (Victory), 427–424 B.C., Kallikrates; view of east front. The general form of this commemorative shrine is untypical for an Ionic temple and will be discussed in Chapter 7.

Fig. 6.22a Ephesos (Turkey), temple of Artemis, ca. 560–550 B.C.; reconstruction drawing of west front, close-up view.

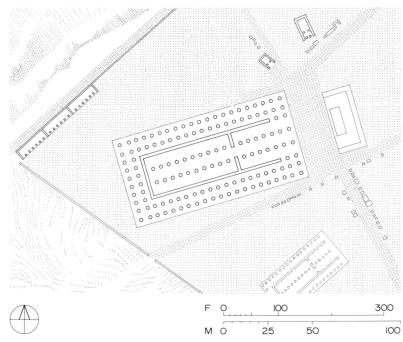

Fig. 6.22b Samos (Greece), third temple of Hera, begun in the late sixth century B.C.; ground plan.

these two traditional components—the palace and temple—with an active agora or public space, but its excuse was principally commercial. It was, in fact, the stage for what may well be the first free market in world history based on a monetary economy, namely, the gold currency made possible by the fabulous mines of the country which made the wealth of Croesus proverbial.

In the Greek cities of Ionia, palaces were rare. The protagonists of urban cohesion were the temple and the agora. The first, as we have seen in this chapter, was as far removed from the temple monasteries in the East as was the Greek view of life from that of pharaonic Egypt or that of the Hittites. The agora, as we will see in the next chapter, existed primarily as an arena for public debate and self-government. In the eyes of the East, it was a theater subversive of the state, an upstart institution to be ridiculed and crushed. "I never feared the kind of men," the Persian king, Cyrus the Great, is said to have remarked disdainfully, "who

have a place set apart in the middle of the city where they get together and tell lies to one another under oath."

With the elimination of Lydia as a buffer state, Persia confronted the Greek commonwealth across the Aegean. The Ionian cities, for the most part, had recognized the suzerainty of the King of Kings and had become constituent members of the Persian empire along with Assyria, Lydia, and Egypt. Whatever the Greek view of absolutism as a political system, this empire, which perhaps for the first time in history embraced peoples of vastly varying tongues and faiths, was distinguished by a prevailing mood of tolerance and decent rule. Its principal belief was the unity of nations under the Achaemenid dynasty. And nowhere is this theme expressed better than in the palace at Persepolis, the ceremonial court of Darius and Xerxes, north of modern Shiraz, on its platform 40 feet above the wide plain of Marv-i Dasht. (Fig. 6.23)

Here every spring, on the day of the vernal equinox, the people came from all

around to attend the festival of Nawruz. They came bearing tribute, bringing the wealth of the empire to Persepolis. They passed through the main gateway, called All Lands, which was reached by means of a splendid, double-reversing stairway in two flights, and moved on to the *apadana* and the throne room, great square halls filled with remarkably tall wood columns, plastered and painted, and opening out on all sides with airy verandas. The stairs that led up to the *apadana* were flanked by a procession in painted relief of guards and representatives of the imperial domain shown carrying their gifts to the King of Kings. (Fig. 6.24)

The palace, too, was viewed as an offering; the symbol of this first modern empire, it was built with the labor and materials that Persian rule could command. A surviving building inscription from the palace at Susa describes this collaborative construction in the words of King Darius.

This is the palace which I erected at Susa. Its ornament was brought from afar. . . . And that the

133

Fig. 6.23 Persepolis (Iran), royal palace, 518–460
B.C.; aerial view.

earth was dug, and rubble was packed, and brick moulded, the Babylonian folk, they did it. The cedar timber was brought from a mountain named Lebanon; the Assyrian folk, they brought it to Babylon; from Babylon the Carians and Ionians brought it to Susa. . . . The gold was brought from Sardis and from Bactria . . . the silver and copper from Egypt . . . the ivory from Ethiopia. . . . The stone cutters who wrought the stone, those were Ionians and Sardians.

Yet the design was also collaborative. Everywhere at the palace of Persepolis the subject nations would have been greeted by motifs of their own invention, absorbed within the general scheme. There were Assyrian monsters and crenellations, Egyptian cavetto cornices, Ionic column bases and volutes. But they were all revised according to the will of the mighty patron and

stamped with the native spirit. Ionic volutes are stacked in two pairs of confronted tiers on top of plant capitals and carry, in turn, crowns of double-headed bulls that take the ceiling rafters. (Fig. 6.25) There is nothing very fearful any more about the Assyrian monsters at the gate, precisely because fear is absent generally from this lighthearted royal environment; the em-

Fig. 6.24 Persepolis, royal palace, staircase with a sculptural frieze representing guards; detail.

Fig. 6.25 Persepolis, royal palace, double "bull" capital from the *apadana,* or audience hall. (Louvre, Paris)

phasis is placed on festive ceremony and the concert of nations.

To compare the palaces of Persepolis and Khorsabad is to acknowledge that dichotomies such as Greek versus barbarian or democracy versus absolutism must remain crude and simplistic. There is benevolent centrism as well as oppressive monarchies; and the authoritarian and highly restricted populism of Sparta is a sinister application of the Greek boast of self-government. Architecture sometimes mirrors these distinctions, and at other times it does not.

Perhaps because of the distance in time and historical identity, the palaces of Persepolis and Khorsabad tell very different stories in their built form. But the temple behaves much the same way in Sparta as at Athens, despite the radical split in their notion of democracy.

A series of seemingly trivial events brought the confrontation of Persia and Greece, the confident centrality of a world power and the disunited but proud congress of city-states, to a boil. The King of Kings and his mighty force crossed over to

Europe to silence the tiny but outspoken neighbor—only to be defeated, against all odds, in one of the great turning points of history. For a time at least, the temple held its own against the palace. It was not until a century and a half after the battles at Marathon and Salamis that Greece and Persia, both victims of Alexander the Great's headlong conquest of the world, found themselves in the same political envelope and were forced to bury the old distinction between Greek and barbarian.

Further Reading

H. Bervé, G. Gruben, and M. Hirmer, *Greek Temples, Theatres and Shrines,* trans. R. Waterhouse (London: Thames and Hudson, 1963).

J. J. Coulton, *Ancient Greek Architects at Work* (Ithaca, N.Y.: Cornell University Press, 1977).

W. B. Dinsmoor, *The Architecture of Ancient Greece,* 3rd ed. (New York: Norton, 1975).

A. W. Lawrence, *Greek Architecture* (Harmondsworth and Baltimore: Penguin, 1973).

R. D. Martienssen, *The Idea of Space in Greek Architecture* (Johannesburg: Witwatersrand University Press, 1958).

V. Scully, Jr., *The Earth, the Temple, and the Gods,* rev. ed. (New Haven: Yale University Press, 1979).

D. Wilber, *Persepolis* (New York: Crowell, 1969).

Athens (Greece), Propylaia, 437–432 B.C., Mnesikles.

POLIS AND AKROPOLIS

Athens and Her Empire

Greece came out of the Persian wars aware and confident, more so than at any other time in her history. The invasion had been sobering for the boastful Greeks. It taught them, for a while at least, the benefits of unity, creating legends of superhuman valor that would sustain generations of Greeks to come. A quickening of spirit and a consciousness of the human frame, what it is capable of physically and bound by morally, were now evident in everything the major cities produced—in art and building, drama and poetry. The public statues of young athletes stood free of the four-square frame that had held them in the sixth century. (Figs. 6.9, 7.1) Leaning now on one leg, the body distributed its weight subtly and unevenly; muscles articulated the vitality of real flesh. The head, instead of staring rigidly ahead, turned to one side and gently inclined forward in a manner that suggested introspection, thought, the mind beneath the stone surface.

Wonders are many [Sophokles sang in his *Antigone*], and none is more wonderful than man. . . . Speech and wind-swift thought, and all the moods that mold a state hath he taught himself: yea, he hath resource for all. . . . Clever beyond all dreams the inventive craft that he hath which may drive him one time or another to weal or ill.

The temple form was civilized. It now had new, svelte proportions and sober sculptural programs in pediments and metopes. Their full impact is felt first in the Panhellenic sanctuary of Olympia, where a splendid temple to Father Zeus rose in the de-

cade of 460 to complement the old Hera temple on the north side of the precinct. It was the first major building effort on the part of the war-ravaged cities.

By mid-century the mood of reconstruction took hold in Athens, the premier Greek city and the acknowledged leader of resistance to Persian hostility. A costly, ambitious building program set about to revive the Akropolis which had been laid waste by the sack of 480. For fifty years, mostly under the general artistic supervision of the sculptor Phidias, marble was quarried at Mount Pentelikon 16 kilometers (10 miles) from the city and transported on carts and timber tracks to the site, columns were fluted and polished, and hundreds of figures carved for pediments and metopes.

This radiant complex of three new temples and a monumental gateway (the Propylaia) on the outcrop of rock that overwatched the bowl of Attica became one of the marvels of the Greek world. (Fig. 7.2) Its theme was uniquely Athenian. It celebrated the divine protectress of the city, the warrior-maiden Athena, and it expressed the rich involvement of worshipper and worshipped, that limit-knowing partnership of humans in the natural order which is one essential aspect of what we mean by the term Classical in reference to fifth-century Greece. And yet, because the Athenian Akropolis was so deeply personal, because it projected its local message so forcefully and finally, it came to be seen as a paragon of Greek achievement—to be coveted, marveled at, emulated.

In the wake of the Persian onslaught, Athens saw herself as the champion of Greece. She presided over the Delian League, a naval alliance of more than three hundred cities bordering the Aegean. Long before the Persians, Athens had subjected the entire district of Attica, dissolving the old boundaries of its four traditional tribes and thereby setting aside local attachments and the power of major landowners. Now under Perikles, the great statesman of the second half of the fifth century, the anti-Persian league was turned into an Athenian empire of tribute-paying cities. Athens kept her own special temples in allied territory and built garrison towns in strategic places as far away as the region of ancient Troy.

To Perikles, Athens was a divine city, the earthly citadel of all Greek gods, and the new Parthenon on the Akropolis was its beacon. It was to surpass all other temples in size and splendor, its shining form of Pentelic marble visible to incoming ships. He had no compunction, therefore, in using moneys from the general treasury of the Delian League for the embellishment of Athens. She was the custodian of Greek might: from her public buildings would emanate a collective pride.

At the time, Athens was not only the most famous Greek city but also the largest. In Piraeus she had the largest and safest natural harbor of mainland Greece. (Fig. 7.3) Her fleet, hastily built after the first Persian invasion, secured a wide sea hegemony. The foodstuffs it carried homeward were transported from Piraeus to Athens within a set of impregnable walls, the so-called Long Walls, built in the decade of 450 to guard against raids by her arch-rival Sparta. The fame and safety of Athens, and the booming construction industry, caused phenomenal overcrowding. Athens alone, not counting the port city and the countryside of Attica, may have had a population as high as 200,000, inclusive of alien residents (metics) and slaves. This was an extraordinary concentration when we realize that a city of 5,000 male citizens (or a total free population of 20,000) was considered large.

The Shape of the Polis

Indeed, the great majority of Greek cities—and there were about seven hundred in the commonwealth—were very small in size and modest in appearance. The older among them had come about through the *synoecism* of several rural settlements sometime around the eighth century. Aristotle later described the process in these words: "When several villages are united in a single complete community, large enough to be nearly or quite self-sufficing, the polis comes into existence." Some few cities, Athens among them, were successors of Mycenaean citadel-towns. For most, agriculture remained the mainstay of the community.

This modest local economy, even when supplemented by some small sea-borne commerce in the case of coastal cities, left little for fancy building. The architecture of the few great cities was often disappointing, outside of a handful of temples and public buildings. A contemporary source describes Athens as

dry and ill-supplied with water. The streets are nothing but miserable old lanes, the houses mean, with a few better ones among them. On his first arrival a stranger could hardly believe that this is the Athens of which he has heard so much.

Greek houses, like those of Mesopotamia, turned inward. They were usually built around a court with a cistern or well in it as well as an altar. (Fig. 7.4) In the more substantial houses the court might have simple porticoes on one or more sides. The rooms were not strictly defined by function. A low, raised platform around its walls

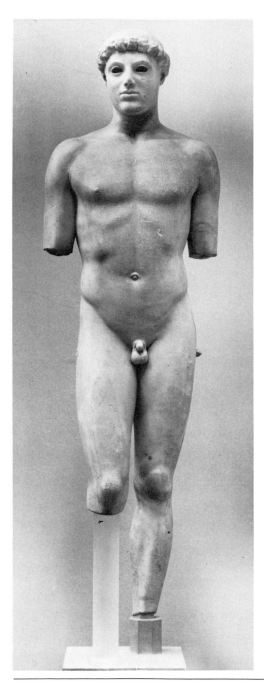
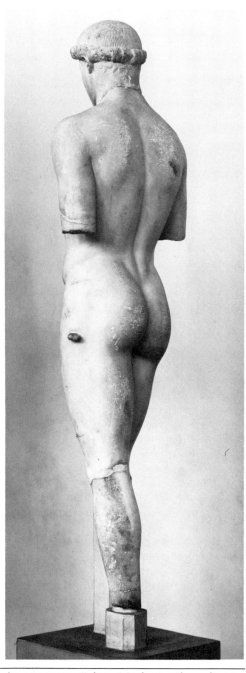

Fig. 7.1 The so-called Kritios boy, Greek sculpture of ca. 490–480 B.C. The height is a little under one meter (2 feet, 9 inches). (Akropolis Museum, Athens, Greece)

138

Fig. 7.2 Athens, Akropolis; distant view from the southwest.

distinguished the main dining and entertainment room, or *andron*. The platform was for the couches on which the diners reclined during meals. The andron was usually found in a corner of the house, so it could receive direct light from two sides. It might also be enhanced with a cemented or pebble floor. All other floors were of hard-packed earth, and the walls of sundried brick would only occasionally be stuccoed and painted. Certain regions featured a well-developed house type whose main peculiarity was a long narrow room north of the court, the so-called *pastas*, extending across the entire width of the house

or nearly so. The megaron has disappeared from the range of residential forms, along with the princely program it once housed.

Orthogonal Planning

In the old cities, the general outlines of both the houses and individual rooms were irregular. Only when a city was consciously planned would the blocks be uniformly rectangular and the houses within more methodically separated. Planned cities were usually colonies imposed on the land at a single stroke. Colonial cities were, at their inception, artificial. They did not come about through the normal growth of an ex-

isting settlement pattern and were therefore not bound by environmental pressures of prior occupancy and use. The settlers took possession of their chosen site directly by imposing on it a rational order. In an unfamiliar terrain, the cityscape had to be diagrammatically intelligible and easy to get used to.

At first this order may have been more hierarchical than strictly geometric. The temples were suitably accounted for. The fire from the state hearth of the mother city, which had been carried along on the journey, would start the colony's own hearth, housed in the *prytaneion*. Then, the agora would be designated—the public open space that would serve as the multipurpose gathering place of the new citizens and their focus of self-government. The leader of the colonial expedition now supervised the division of the remaining land among the settlers, both within the boundaries of the city and for the farmland beyond.

By the seventh century a normative grid began to determine the layout of new colonies and to regulate the form of those already in existence. The grid provided a straightforward way to divide the land, shape the structure of the city, and control its future growth. Too much can be made of the grid, however, as the planning de-

vice of egalitarianism. In the Greek colonies the grid inscribed the social preeminence of a property-owning class, a kind of territorial aristocracy. The first settlers divided the land and thereby ensured themselves the power to govern the affairs of the city. To guard against change, they passed laws that declared property inalienable and

Fig. 7.3 Map: Athens and its region. Left, the walled city of the fifth century B.C.; top right, the relationship of the city to the port of Piraeus; bottom right, the territory of Attica and nearby islands.

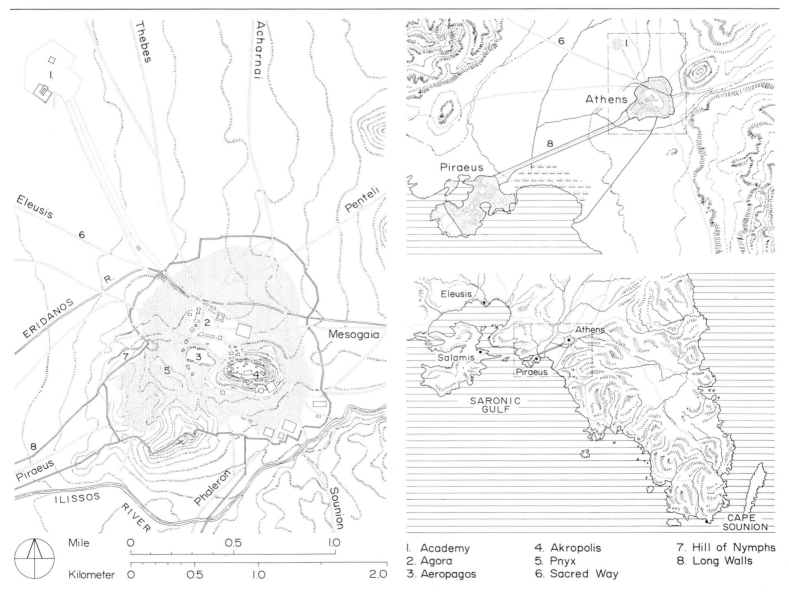

1. Academy
2. Agora
3. Aeropagos
4. Akropolis
5. Pnyx
6. Sacred Way
7. Hill of Nymphs
8. Long Walls

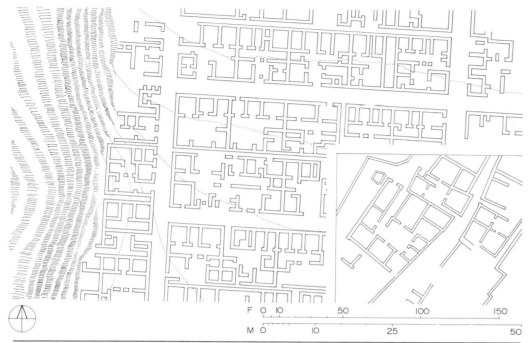

Fig. 7.4a Comparative plans of Greek housing blocks: Olynthos, laid out ca. 432 B.C.; and in the lower right, Athens, houses and workshops west of the Areopagos (no. 3 on Fig. 7.3).

Fig. 7.4b Athens, houses of the fifth–fourth century B.C.; reconstruction views.

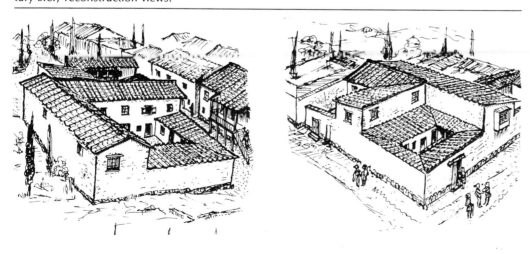

discouraged a land market. Later arrivals constituted the city-dwelling middle class of renters—artisans and also merchants who along with the rank and file of the army constituted the base on which populist regimes might rise from time to time. Demographic or economic pressures within the city could turn this class into the driving force that would set up new colonies further out from the city, creating settlements twice removed from the mother city.

Orthogonal planning is of course as old as Egypt. (Fig. 4.2) But none of the pre-Greek grids can be considered fully coordinated systems of public and residential buildings with coherently organized blocks. That is the achievement of Greece. The preferred Greek variety was the so-called *per strigas* ("by bands") scheme. A small number of broad east-west avenues divided the territory into bands dissected by one or more north-south avenues. The superblocks so delineated were then subdivided by narrow lanes into rectangular blocks, the proportions of which vary considerably from city to city. The blocks were then systematically apportioned into building lots. Once established, the grid determined the size and shape of public buildings as well, temples included.

Miletus
The *per strigas* scheme had seen some obscure pre-Greek applications in Asia Minor, but the major credit should go to the Ionian cities along the Aegean coast of Asia Minor, the birthplace of Greek geometry, and especially to the great town of Miletus. The plan of Miletus must rank as one of the most sophisticated uses of the grid in antiquity. The general layout dates from soon after 479, the year when Miletus was liberated from the Persians who had taken and destroyed it in 490. (Fig. 7.5) But the older city almost certainly also had an orthogonal design. Earlier still, in the Bronze Age and its obscure aftermath, the settlement was centered on the hill to the southwest and the slope in front.

The ruins of Miletus now lie 9 kilometers (5.5 miles) in from the sea. The original site was a triangular promontory oriented northeast-southwest at the mouth of the Meander River. It afforded two natural harbors along one side, the Lion Harbor and the older Theater Harbor. The land was almost level, except for a low eminence between the two harbor bays. The theater took advantage of one of the seaward slopes of this eminence.

The grid was not directed toward the cardinal points but, instead, took best advantage of the configuration of the land so that certain streets could run the length of the peninsula. There were three clusters of housing, about 400 blocks in all which were 30 by 53 meters (100 by 175 feet) on average, a ratio of 4 to 7. Two streets broader than all the rest crossed each other in the southern grid. There may well have been more of these avenues, so that the blocks at the start may have been intended to be more elongated, in the usual early manner of Greek grids.

This grand master plan of Miletus is associated with the name of a local man, Hippodamos. We know of him mostly from Aristotle who says that he discovered "the divisioning of cities," that he laid out the Athenian port city of Piraeus, and that "he was the first man of those not actually involved in politics to make proposals about the best form of constitution." Aristotle does not say, of course, that Hippodamos invented the grid plan, but implies that he advocated a special instance of it and combined it with a social theory of urbanism.

According to Aristotle, Hippodamos conceived of an ideal city of 10,000, with the citizenry divided into three classes—artisans, farmers, and soldiers—and the land into three categories—sacred, public, and private. It seems that the Hippodamian system relied on a theoretical formula of geometry more so than the purely technical (and empirical) practice of architect-planners, and that it was carefully adjusted to the specific demands of the site. If we can judge from the city-form of Piraeus, the system involved the division of the urban territory into sectors, each with its own rectilinear street pattern; the setting aside of public areas for specific public functions (agora, port, etc.); and provision for the placement of individual public buildings. If we can further accept an ancient tradition that attributes the planning of Rhodes to Hippodamos, his geometric system had a triple order of division. (Fig. 7.6) The larg-

est element was a square of which the sides measured about 200 meters (650 feet). Each of these squares was quartered, and each of these smaller squares in turn divided into six parts to form rectangles measuring 30 by 46 meters (100 by 150 feet).

The triple division of Miletus into sectors and the allocation from the very start of public areas for specific functions recall the Hippodamian system. The master plan was laid out for a very large city, clearly with a total population much higher than the 10,000 he found ideal. The huge area of 100 hectares (250 acres) covered by the grid envisioned a brisk and orderly growth.

The old downtown lay between the hill to the southwest and the Theater Bay. Here was the old Athena temple, which under the new plan assumed a different, north-south orientation. In fact, the focus had shifted to the north, the city center now moving close to the Bay of Lions. The earliest agora of the post-Persian city was built facing the bay and aligned in the east with the sanctuary of Apollo Delphinios. A main road of the grid started at this point and ran the length of the peninsula to join the old sacred way, which headed to the great Apollo sanctuary at Didyma about 22 kilometers (14 miles) south. But another agora had already been

Fig. 7.5 Miletus (Turkey), refounded after the Persian sack of 479 B.C.; plan with original coastline.

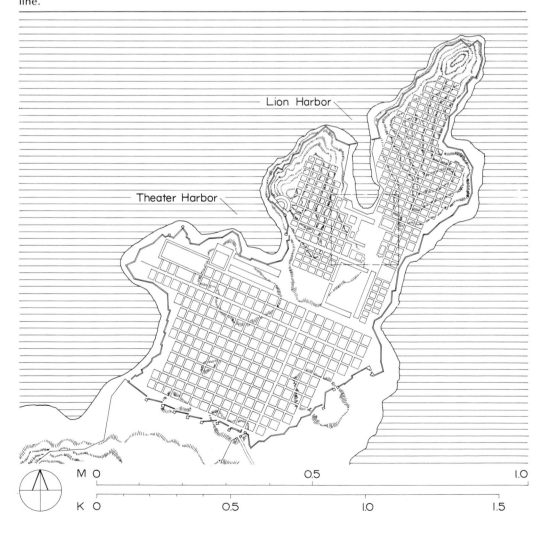

anticipated in the western section, just above the old Theater Harbor, and in the low-lying central area among the three clusters of housing, generous space was allotted for yet a third, the Great Agora.

The Stoa
The word "marketplace" inadequately describes the concept of the Greek *agora*. The agora was the public forum of all the inhabitants and on all days, a bustling place that served as the democratic alternative to the two great organizing foci of non-Greek cities, the temple precinct and the palace complex. It was the scene of public speeches, citizens' assemblies, shows, as well as social and commercial activity. About the marketplace, the public buildings of most consequence for municipal administration tended to gather, as did facilities for shopping and display.

The agoras of Miletus are defined by stoas, at least along two sides. In contrast, the agora of an unplanned city was at first not much more than a level piece of open ground, often with a hillslope on one side which could be used by the attending crowd during spectacles or meetings. (Fig. 7.15) The stoa was one of a number of freestanding buildings that loosely hugged this public space. At Miletus the stoas became elements of a total design, making the open space formal and monumental without enclosing it. (Fig. 7.9)

The stoa is as distinctive a Greek building type as is the temple, and much more flexible in form and function. It came to use about the same time as the full-blown stone temple, in the late seventh century B.C.; and indeed its first role was in the context of sanctuaries. It was a freestanding portico, modest in materials and structure, but able to serve a number of loosely related functions—shelter from the weather, for example, and overnight accommodation for pilgrims and those patients who were brought to the sanctuaries to be healed.

This building type was soon secularized and became a common urban feature. By the fifth century, stoas were substantial stone buildings containing notable programs of public art. New functions came to be identified with them. Public sessions of the courts (and occasionally the city council) might be held there; official banquets given; public notices displayed. The walks around the stoa were frequented by students of human behavior like Zeno whose school of philosophy, Stoicism, owes its name to the architectural setting of his discussions. And quite naturally for a place where people lingered, shopping and browsing became a common aspect of the stoa's varied program.

The external portico, that intermediate space between the indoors and outdoors, was common enough in the Bronze Age Aegean. (Fig. 5.25) But there the feature always functioned as an extension of another building. The continuous colonnade of the peripteral temple is a Greek example of the same practice. But the stoa was a building in its own right, a covered portico of sufficient length and width to be usable by numbers of people. On its own or in conjunction with others of its kind, the stoa gave formal shape to a piece of open space by providing a definite edge that was nevertheless "soft," that is, capable of absorbing some of the public activity of the open space. Stoas constitute some of the finest products of Greek architectural genius. They were a genuinely populist expression of monumental architecture, intended for the common good and were

Fig. 7.6 Rhodes (Greece), founded in 408–407 B.C., school of Hippodamos of Miletus; schematic plan.

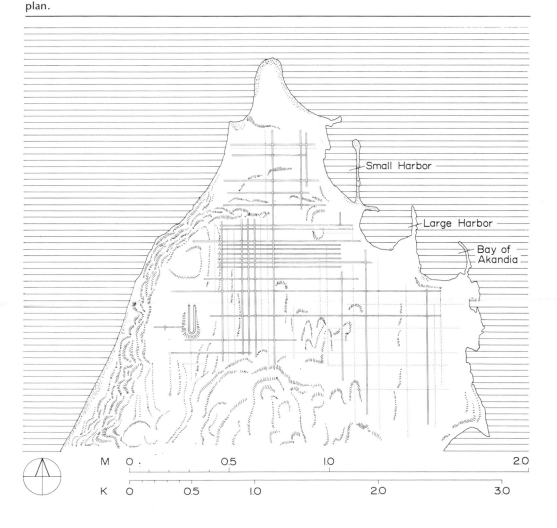

Small Harbor

Large Harbor

Bay of Akandia

M 0.   0.5   1.0   2.0

K 0   0.5   1.0   2.0   3.0

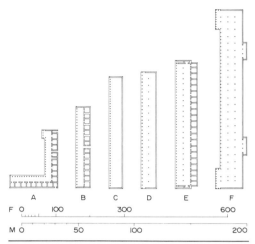

Fig. 7.7 Greek stoa types; diagrammatic plans: (A) L-shaped stoa (e.g., Delos, stoa L); (B) single-aisled stoa with shops (e.g., Delos, south stoa); (C) single-aisled stoa without shops (e.g., Olympia, the first Echo stoa); (D) two-aisled stoa (e.g., Samothrace, stoa J); (E) two-aisled stoa with shops (e.g., Athens, stoa of Attalos, no. 4 on Fig. 8.20); (F) three-aisled stoa with projecting wings (e.g., Megalopolis, stoa of Philip).

often financed through private contribution.

In its simplest form a stoa consists of a long row of posts, a wide aisle behind, and a back wall. (Fig. 7.7) It is covered with a flat or a ridge roof, less commonly with a shed roof. There is no separate ceiling, the interior view being open to the rafters. This basic form was elaborated in several ways. Often the interior space was divided into two aisles by means of an inner row of supports; a line of single-bay shops opened out from the back wall; wings extended at right angles to the two ends; and, by the fourth century B.C., stoas were being built with two usable storeys instead of one, and with L-shaped plans. The supports were columns of the Doric or Ionic order depending on locale, at least until the middle of the fifth century. From then on, Doric was preferred everywhere for the outer colonnade, even in Ionian states. In the case of two-aisled stoas, again until the fifth century, the inner colonnade repeated the order of the outer. It was at Athens where the orders were first mixed, through the use of the Ionic order both for the inner colonnades of stoas and on the Akropolis, in the interior of the Propylaia and the back porch of the Parthenon.

The introduction of the Ionic order in this premier city of the Doric mainland was undoubtedly in part an aesthetic choice. But it must also have been political: Athens claimed leadership over Ionian states as well as peninsular Greece. In two-aisled stoas, an Ionic inner colonnade also responded to architectural convenience. (Fig. 7.8) This colonnade had to be taller than that of the facade in order to reach up and support the roof. The accepted proportions of the Doric order, with the height of the column shaft about 5.5 times the lower diameter in the fifth century, required that an inner row of Doric columns be substantially larger in diameter so that it could reach higher than the outer row, thus inhibiting the usable space; or else, there had to be two superimposed tiers of columns, a system tolerable in temple cellas where the view runs lengthwise, but quite unsatisfactory in stoas where one would encounter the two-storey screen head on. The slenderer proportions of the Ionic order (the column height being 9 to 10 diameters) was clearly a happier solution to the problem of interior height.

The stoa of the earliest agora in the Hippodamian plan of Miletus, the north agora, was single-aisled and L-shaped. (Fig. 7.9) This one distinct architectural corner sufficed to set the scale of the public space and bind it to the harbor. The colonnade afforded an impressive urban frontispiece to incoming vessels. The row of shops was backed by a smaller stoa, also L-shaped, which faced inward toward the city. The L-shaped plan presented two problems: the juncture of roofs at the corner, and the meeting of the two lines of entablature on the corner column. At Miletus the first problem was solved by choosing to use flat roofs, which are easier to reconcile at right angles than ridge roofs. The other difficulty was chiefly aesthetic—the accommodation of two triglyphs over the same column of the re-entrant angle. (Fig. 7.10) It gave rise here to the invention of the heart-shaped pier, made of two half-columns attached to adjacent faces of a square pillar. (Coincidently, this thick pier strengthened the structure at the point where the pressure from the roof is particularly great.) The re-entrant angle will be a recurrent design problem in columnar architecture; for ex-

Fig. 7.8 The two-aisled Doric stoa; sections showing alternative arrangements for interior supports: (A) Ionic inner colonnade; (B) Doric inner colonnade; (C) two-storied Doric inner colonnade.

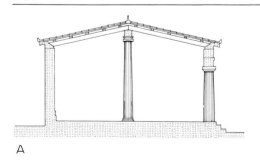

A

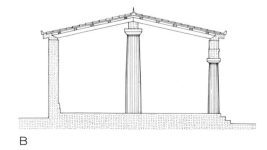

B

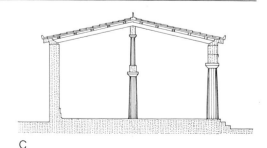

C

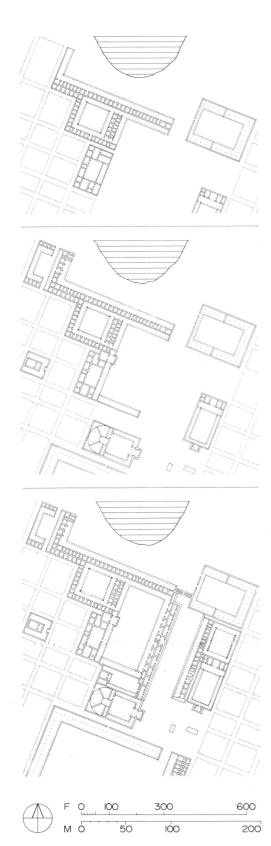

ample, we will meet it again in the inner court of the Renaissance palace in Italy.

Composite forms like the heart-shaped pier are by and large an index of later, Hellenistic practices. The elaboration of the stoa system at Miletus is in fact Hellenistic. (Fig. 7.9) The Hellenistic designs of the Miletian stoa made use of *two* re-entrant angles, either by devising a single stoa with three arms in the shape of the Greek letter P (Π), a type not unknown earlier, or else by facing two L-shaped stoas without actually marrying them. This second arrangement is seen in the Hellenistic duplication of the small L-shaped stoa behind the north agora, which we mentioned above, and in the Great Agora to the south where, in addition to the two matched L-shaped stoas, a straight stoa was run along the fourth side of the space, defining a full rectangle. The plan is in accord with the design sensibilities of this later Greek period which favored the definite circumscription of public spaces by colonnades but eschewed total enclosure.

The final step was taken by the Romans. When they remodeled the Great Agora, they closed off the north-south road that passed between the Π and the eastern stoa of the Hellenistic scheme and turned its stretch within the agora into a colonnade; and again, to the east of the Lion Harbor, they brought the arms of a new, three-sided stoa almost up to the water's edge, using the shoreline as a fourth arm to create the feeling of total enclosure.

Here at Miletus, then, we can follow the three successive stages of Greco-Roman planning. (1) *Classical* Greece understated the architectural definition of civic spaces by merely suggesting enclosure, using the spare presence of colonnaded borders mostly along one or two sides only. (2) In the *Hellenistic* phase, architectural symmetry became important; the space was usually articulated on three or even four sides, but with open access to it from the

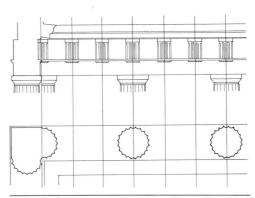

Fig. 7.10 Heart-shaped corner support in the Doric order; elevation and plan.

outside along several points of the architectural envelope. (3) The *Roman* planner, finally, preferred seamless enclosures entered only through formal gates at calculated axes. The public space was thus sealed off from the outside and allowed to stage its own total experience.

Organic Planning
But even in its least restrictive, Classical phase, orthogonal planning sacrifices that dynamic and ever-shifting interrelationship between the open and the built, which is present in older Greek sites like Delphi. (Fig. 6.16) In these sites, the temple would be approached along the flexible path of a traditional sacred way and glimpsed first at an angle; this revealed two of its sides simultaneously and transformed it into a mid-space object. The grid regimented the temple, along with every other aspect of the urban experience. It would now be approached in a straight line. At colonial implants like Selinus or Paestum, several temples might be primly lined up along one main thoroughfare of the city grid. (Fig. 6.17)

The planned Greek city makes several assumptions. First, the entire urban territory is a rational form geometrically conceived at one time. Second, this form governs both private and public buildings. And third, the form is a blueprint for the orderly future development of the city. The polis in this context is at once a work of art, that is, a deliberate and artificial configuration that sets its own internal rules of ar-

Fig. 7.9 Miletus, the north agora at three stages of its development; ground plans: top, the agora in the fifth–fourth century B.C.; middle, in the third–second century B.C.; bottom, in the first century B.C.

F 0   100   300   600
M 0   50   100   200

chitectural behavior, and a controlled experiment, that is, a community with an established growth target and a predetermined, limited setting.

As such, the planned city strains some of the assumptions of the earliest city-states of the Greek world. These were moral and political entities foremost of all, aggregations of free citizens and their dependents. The city was as large as its population of the moment, and this was gauged principally by what the surrounding land would support. When the population came to exceed the tolerance of its countryside, it sent out colonies or tried to advance its area of influence. The small city might aspire to become the center of a group of kindred townships; the center, in turn, might aspire to dominate several, similar clusters, becoming the capital of a state like Macedonia or Thessaly.

The site and its prior sanctities were major conditions of the nongeometric city. Natural paths that led through the terrain and joined villages to each other, or to some ancient citadel-town, continued in use after the official birth of the polis. The choice of the site was itself partly dictated by the convergence of these paths. Some among them had become sacrosanct as the processional ways to shrines. In the case of re-energized Bronze Age towns, the citadel hill, the seat of Mycenaean princes, declined in favor of the agora in the flatland at its feet. The hill was slowly appropriated by the gods and became the *akropolis*, literally the "head of the town." This was not because the gods demanded such lofty premises for the observance of their rites, but because no citizens should presume to set themselves above their fellow citizens.

Aristotle recognized this *symbolic* sense of order when he observed that "An akropolis is suitable for oligarchy and monarchy, level ground for democracy." The premise of democracy is that no citizen is more privileged than any other unless given power for a limited time to do a certain job. To Greek thinking, which is acutely visual, an akropolis invokes a prefixed hierarchy in relation to the plain below, and the only hierarchy that was tolerable in Classical Greece was that between humans who are mortal and the gods who are not.

Athens—"The Eye of Greece"

The city of Athens will serve well as a case study of the old, irregular polis. (Fig. 7.3) Since she had a continuous urban life from Mycenaean times onward, an account of Athens can chronicle the history of settlement from that earliest phase of Greek culture to the Classical period. Enough of her ancient fabric has been revealed through excavation to afford a good chance for us to look at urban arrangements, and at building types other than the temple and the stoa. Finally, a visit to the Periklean Akropolis can summarize the essence of Classical architecture before we move on to later periods, for in that complex of buildings we have perhaps the finest surviving specimen of Greek design and a materialized vision that was considered ageless even in antiquity. "Such is the bloom of perpetual newness, as it were, upon these works of Perikles," Plutarch wrote in his biography of this statesman, "which makes them ever to look untouched by time, as though the unfaltering breath of an ageless spirit had been infused into them."

The Mycenaean City

Athens had not always been famous and great. The Bronze Age citadel on the Akropolis was bypassed by the invading Dorians probably because it was not important or rich enough. The location, however, was superb. The Akropolis rises sheer in the midst of Attica, a bowl-shaped plain that is ringed by mountains all around except toward the south. In that direction it lies open toward the sea, with a spit of land jutting out into the Saronic Gulf that affords excellent harbors. But there is no evidence that Athens was conscious of this advantage, or strong enough to exploit it, until the sixth century B.C. when the spit was first fortified and the port of Piraeus was born.

The Mycenaean city occupied the top of the Akropolis and stretched out and down the south slope, a short way into the plain below. A little further out, on the western cluster of hills—the Pnyx, the Hill of Muses, the Areopagos—small settlements lived in the shadow of the citadel. This agglomeration was hemmed in, to the north and south, by the rivers Eridanos and Ilissos. A ring path (the Peripatos) hugged the base

of the citadel, and a number of roads that utilized the passes of the encircling mountains converged on this central focus of the plain.

The citadel had a strong cyclopean wall around it, from the later thirteenth century, bits of which still survive. A lower outer curtain defended the western approach of the rock, the only side that admitted easy access. At the top were the usual features of a Mycenaean citadel: a fortified gateway at the southwestern tip of the rock, the megaron palace on the north side, and the rock-cut stairway that led from here down to the secret spring outside the walls.

The transition from the Mycenaean citadel-town to the celebrated polis of Pallas Athena is obscure. The citadel lost importance with the passage of the Bronze Age, and by the eighth century a small temple to the goddess had already taken over the prince's palace. At about that time small independent towns in the Attic plain were attached to Athens, which thus became the city-state of a large territory. This consolidation was believed to have been the work of Theseus, the same legendary king of Athens who is also credited with slaying the Minotaur. The fifth-century historian Thucydides described it this way:

[Theseus] abolished the council-chambers and magistracies of the other towns, and merged them all into the present city establishing a single council-chamber and town-hall. Individuals might still enjoy their private property just as before, but they were henceforth compelled to have only one political center, viz. Athens, which thus counted all the inhabitants of Attica among her citizens.

Buildings of Assembly

The word for council chamber in the original Greek of this passage from Thucydides is *bouleuterion,* and for town hall, *prytaneion.* The location of these buildings is uncertain, but it was not far from the agora demarcated by Theseus along the northwest slope of the Akropolis. The city center then, perhaps as a gesture to the incorporated townships, had moved north to face in, toward Attica rather than the sea, while the core residential area continued to be in the south where it had been, between the Akropolis and the Ilissos River.

Fig. 7.11 Athens, agora, the round building called Skias (no. 7 on Fig. 7.15), ca. 465 B.C.; reconstruction view of interior.

In the next two centuries, Athens grew in size and passed, like other Greek cities, from kingship through oligarchy to a full system of democracy. The agora now shifted to a flat open space further north, formerly a major cemetery, which was overlooked on the western side by a low rise. Here it was to stay throughout antiquity. The popular assembly of the Athenian people, or Demos, may have convened in this new agora at first. When the population of free citizens grew too large for the space, the assembly repaired to the Pnyx. But even then some important, mass decisions, such as the vote of ostracism which banished an individual citizen for dishonorable conduct, were taken in the agora. The elected representative council, or Boule, held its meetings in a building on the western rise of the agora. (Fig. 7.15) A complementary structure acted as the prytaneion annex; the actual prytaneion of Theseus, too venerable to relocate, remained where it had always been, somewhere along the north edge of the Akropolis.

At the time of the Persian invasion, both of these administrative structures at the agora, the bouleuterion and the prytaneion annex, called the Skias, had been rebuilt. The Skias was a round building, a very unusual form for post-Mycenaean Greek architecture, which had no fondness for curvilinear design. (Fig. 7.11) Several surviving round buildings, called *tholoi* (*tholos* in the singular), are late for the most part and seem to have served very special functions. Fragmentary evidence points to underground cults and burial. There was a famous tholos at Delphi, and another at Epidauros, connected with the cults of Apollo and the healing-god Asklepios, respectively.

The Skias consisted of a solid, circular wall with a door facing the east, opening toward the agora, and probably a second door on the north side, which communicated with an adjoining kitchen and the bouleuterion just beyond. The tile roof rested on six internal columns spaced in groups of three on either side of the north-south axis

of the tholos. Couches and tables were set up along the inner circumference and perhaps also in the central space defined by the columns. The principal function of the Skias was in fact that of a dining room. Council presidents (or *prytaneis*) took all their meals here during their monthly tenure, joined by a handful of other state officials.

The remaining functions of a normal Greek prytaneion were still housed in the original Theseian building. They included the maintenance of the eternal flame of the city hearth; the convening of a special court that dealt with cases of murder; the enactment of solemn ceremonies such as the induction of Athenian youths into citizenship; the preservation of historic documents and statues of historical and allegorical figures; the official entertainment of foreign ambassadors; and the recognition of prominent citizens and benefactors who were extended daily dining privileges. In its role as home of the communal hearth and state hospitality, the prytaneion appears to have assumed some of the functions of the Mycenaean megaron, as the temple had borrowed characteristic features of its form.

The bouleuterion was rectangular. A partition along one side closed off a vestibule. The inner room held about 700 people. The speakers stood in front of the middle of the partition while the council members spread out on tiered benches parallel to the other three walls. Some version of this basic form, which may have originated with the great hall of mysteries at the sanctuary of the earth-goddess Demeter at Eleusis, a short distance from Athens, was employed in most early assembly buildings. The main design worry was to ensure that the interior posts needed to carry the roof obstructed the sightlines as little as possible.

At the end of the fifth century a new bouleuterion was raised to the west of the existing one. The main innovation here was to fit a semicircular auditorium into the outer rectangle. (Fig. 7.15) This seating arrangement was suggested by the rising ground, which could be cut into to create the benches; in fact, it represented an attempt to bring indoors a formula that had been locally developed during the past hundred years for outdoor assemblies.

The idea of using natural slopes as auditoria is surely ancient. It was at Athens,

Fig. 7.12 Epidauros (Greece), the theater, ca. 300 B.C.

however, toward the end of the sixth century B.C., that the architectural systematization of this simple idea began when the Demos moved its meetings from the agora to the Pnyx. The northern hillside facing the city, which had a gentle incline, was evened off at this time to accommodate the attending membership, and on the north side of this open-air auditorium a straight retaining wall was built to separate it from the speaker's platform, a level place created with land fill. (Not until 403 B.C. was this scheme revised and the direction of the auditorium reversed.)

Meanwhile, on the south slope of the

Akropolis, a similar solution was applied to a different purpose. Here there was the ancient sanctuary of Dionysos, and dances and choral songs were performed as part of the wine-god's festival. It was out of such pious performances that the Greek theater, recalled by the great Athenian names of Aeschylus, Sophokles, and Euripides, eventually emerged. As the literary and technical aspects of the plays became more elaborate, the theater was revised to keep pace. (Figs. 7.17, no. 4; 7.18, nos. 5–6)

There was little at first but the slope itself for the audience and a circular floor of beaten earth at the foot of the hill, called

the *orchestra*, to the south of which stood a semicircular retaining wall and the little temple to Dionysos. In the mid-fifth century a building, which acted at times as part of the set, was put up behind the orchestra primarily for storage. Actors made their entrances and exits on ramps to either side of it. By this time spectators were accommodated on continuous stone seats, and fancy thrones for the priests of Dionysos and other dignitaries ringed the northern hemicycle of the orchestra. Next to the theater, Perikles had an *odeion* erected for musical performances. (Fig. 7.18)

Athens' theater, in use until Roman times,

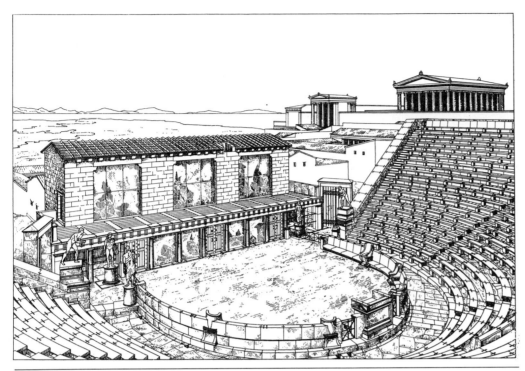

Fig. 7.13 Priene (Turkey), the theater, late second century B.C.; restoration drawing.

underwent constant transformation, but a pure example of the Classical type is the theater at Epidauros, adequate for more than 14,000 spectators, whose remarkable acoustics surprise visitors even now. (Fig. 7.12) Radial staircases divided the stone benches of the auditorium into wedge-shaped segments, and a broad gangway two-thirds of the way up promoted horizontal circulation. This building type remained stable until about 300 B.C. By then the chorus, an integral part of Classical plays, had become detached from the action and assigned independent songs of its own. This separation of actors and chorus was perhaps decisive for the introduction of a new feature into theater design—a high shallow stage where the principal scenes could be elevated above the choral interludes taking place in the orchestra. (Fig. 7.13) The theater of Epidauros itself, built shortly after 300 B.C., had such a stage. It stood just off the circle of the orchestra and had slight projections at the two ends.

The podium of this high stage, called *proscenium*, was usually decorated with attached columns; between them, wooden panels would be inserted with painted scenery suitable for tragedy or the New Comedy of Menander and others. A second storey, the *episcenium*, now formed the backdrop for the acting onstage. With its love for theatrical extravagance, the Hellenistic age will lavish much attention on the design of these two architectural sets, the proscenium and episcenium.

The Classical City

By 400 B.C. the principal lines of the city-form had been fixed. The old town was the Ilissos district, south of the Akropolis, where Mycenaean Athens had its start. Along its north limit, at the edge of the Akropolis slope, stood the theater of Dionysos and the odeion. The densest quarter, the Koile, occupied the Pnyx. Between this hill and the Akropolis, on the Areopagos, open-air jury courts were held. (Fig. 7.3)

The Akropolis itself was entirely dedicated to the gods, and primarily to Athena in her various guises. At the entrance, she was Nike, the securer of Athenian victories. A colossal bronze statue of her just within represented her as Promachos ("the Champion"), in battle gear, the gilded tip of her spear visible all the way from the sea. The two main temples on the hilltop, the Parthenon to the south and the Erechtheion to the north, were dedicated to Athena Parthenos and Athena Polias, two aspects of the goddess as guardian of the city—one an intellectualized presence that personified the hard moral fiber of the polis triumphant, the other a softer, homier, older image of community. The greatest ceremonial moment of this effulgent sacred summit came on the virgin goddess' birthday, the 28th of the month of the Hekatombaion (our own July/August), when the festival of the Panathenaia came to a grand climax as a procession of citizens mounted the Akropolis in pomp to file past her temples.

Public life thrived in the agora. (Fig. 7.14) Near the top of its gentle western rise Athena shared a new temple with lame Hephaistos, the god of fire, the anvil, and the forge. The area southwest of here was largely inhabited by Hephaistos' own craftspeople, the marble cutters and metalworkers who made Athens beautiful and equipped her for war. The temple, which survives almost intact, could be seen unobstructed, and head on from the agora below. On the shelf between the temple and the open space public buildings, both civic and administrative, lined up: the Skias and bouleuterion, and at the northwest corner the Stoa of Zeus, a two-aisled building with short side wings, and the old, very small Royal Stoa, which served as the setting for special trials of impiety and housed the office of the *archon basileus*, a dignitary who had inherited some of the religious functions of the old kings.

There were two other stoas on the north side of the agora of which one, the Stoa Poikile, was famous for its mural paintings of historical and mythological subjects, such as the battle of Marathon and the fall of Troy. (Fig. 7.15) Yet another stoa, along the south side, had a series of dining rooms at the back. This was a very popular rendezvous for Athenian men and underscores once again the special place public dining held in the daily life of Athens. Also on this side was the state mint and the Theseion where the great king was buried in accordance with an old tradition that sanctioned burial within the city walls for the founder of a polis or some other extraordinary local hero. In the middle of the open space, traversed diagonally by the path of the Panathenaic procession, was the orchestra and the *Tyrant-slayers*, a large commemorative sculpture of Harmodios and Aristogiton who had slain the tyrant Hipparchos on this spot in 514 B.C.

Visitors to Periklean Athens poured in by land and sea. Main inland routes included the Sacred Way to Eleusis, which extended beyond the great sanctuary of Demeter to link the city with the Thriasian plain and the Peloponnesus. A ring of distant temples built in the same decades as the Akropolis complex honored old local cults and announced the prospect of Athens. (Fig. 7.3) At Rhamnous on the north coast of Attica a temple to Nemesis, or Fate, perched on a high cliff that plunged to the sea. On a similar, lofty promontory to the south, at Cape Sounion, the sea-god Poseidon was honored with a temple that was the first dramatic beacon of Athena's city for ships sailing in from the east. The main arrival point for overseas vessels was the port of Piraeus, newly laid out in the Hippodamian manner. While cargo and some passengers then proceeded to the city proper within the secure band of the Long Walls, a highway skirted the exterior of the north curtain to join the city on the west.

Whichever the line of approach, the first view of Athens was of its walls. They had been hastily constructed immediately after the Persian wars to replace an older, smaller circuit. They consisted of a dry moat and, in the usual Greek manner, defensive walls made of a brick curtain on a stone base. As with other cities of the commonwealth, the walls wrapped themselves loosely around the urban area without determining its internal organization. Important suburbs remained outside, among them the fashionable later district of the Akademeia, the idyllic site of a gymnasium around which a number of schools and other institutions, including Plato's famous Academy, were established. Such extramural gymnasiums

Fig. 7.14 Athens, agora, temple of Hephaistos (no. 4 on Fig. 7.15), 449–444 B.C., with final details added some twenty years later; general view of site.

set in groves combined in their architecture facilities for athletic contests and classrooms and libraries for the instruction of the mind.

Fifteen gates pierced the walls. The main city gate, called the Dipylon or "double gate," was in the northwest, the area called Kerameikos which the new walls divided into two. Outside lay a large and sumptuous cemetery, including an official burial place for Athenian statesmen and those fallen in war. Here also was a reservoir into which the main sewer of Athens drained; from here, the sewage was conducted through a series of canals to fields near the city. The Inner Kerameikos was the potters' quarter.

It was at the Dipylon that the Panathenaic procession formed on Athena's birthday after several days of contests for athletic skills, chariot racing, music, and the like. Between the gate and the agora, along the line of the Panathenaic Way known as Dromos, were situated cult buildings, including a temple to Aphrodite and the Pompeion, the storage structure for the equipment of the Panathenaia.

These cult buildings coexisted informally with the potters and with the meat, fish, vegetable, and oil markets nearby. The arrangement illustrated that, in the city, religious and secular functions, administrative and commercial, were not neatly segregated. It was only in the later fourth century that Aristotle advocated two separate agoras, far from one another and properly distinguished—one exclusively for public affairs and one for commerce. It was about this same time that in Rome, too, the commercial functions of the original public space, the Forum Romanum, were discontinued and moved to adjacent sites.

The Akropolis

On the appointed day the citizens gathered in the Outer Kerameikos among the tombs of their prominent dead, as if the year's Panathenaic procession was to be the

150

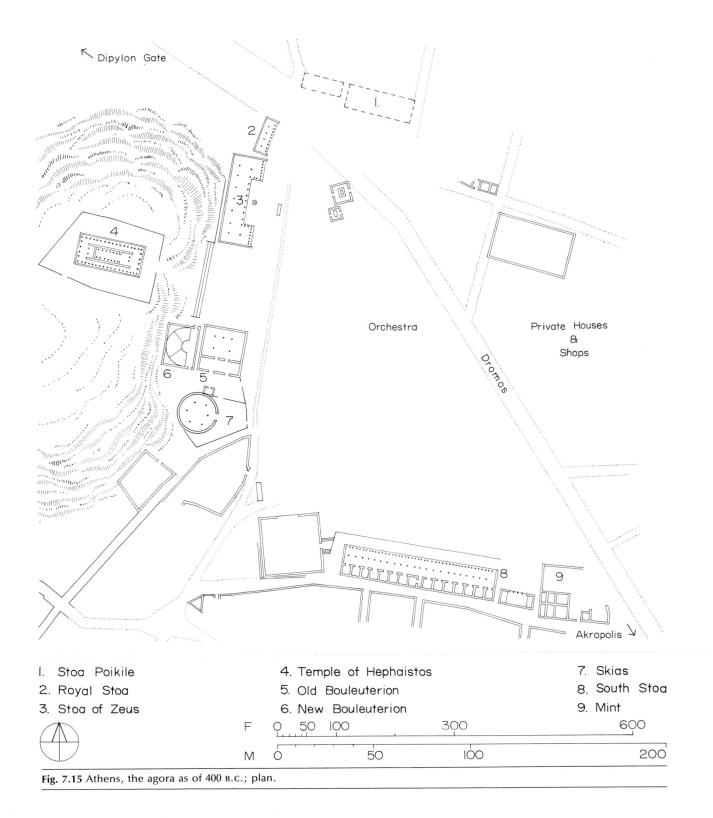

Dipylon Gate

Orchestra

Private Houses
&
Shops

Dromos

Akropolis

1. Stoa Poikile
2. Royal Stoa
3. Stoa of Zeus

4. Temple of Hephaistos
5. Old Bouleuterion
6. New Bouleuterion

7. Skias
8. South Stoa
9. Mint

F 0 50 100   300   600

M 0   50   100   200

Fig. 7.15 Athens, the agora as of 400 B.C.; plan.

vanguard of generations of Athenians, past and recent. A little after sunrise they passed through the Dipylon and onto the wide Dromos that ran directly to the agora. At the head came the *peplos,* Athena's ritual tunic knitted during the year by a select group of the city's maidens and decorated with scenes from the battle of the gods and the giants; it traveled on a cart made to resemble a ship, pinned to the mast like a sail. The Dromos cut diagonally through the agora and then commenced its sharp ascent toard the Akropolis. The procession made a leftward loop to go by the old Theseian agora and the prytaneion, then skirted the Akropolis along the west. Here the ship dropped anchor. The peplos was unhitched and taken over by the maidens who would carry it up the steep slope. They were followed by the cavalry and the charioteers, who would soon dismount; the elders bore olive branches, Athena's own tree; then came musicians, young men with jugs of oil and wine, and the sacrificial animals which included sheep and heifers.

The distance traversed from the Dipylon to this point was about 1,000 meters. All along the processional path, the marble temples displayed their upper mass above the rock, like markers fixing the goal of the ritual advance. As the foot of the escarpment was attained, the temples slowly sank out of sight, to be regained at the top. The maidens now started up the straight ramp, perhaps even a staircase, that had replaced the winding pre-Periklean path: the worshippers had reached their destination. (Fig. 7.16)

To one side, as one gained the gateway or Propylaia, the gleaming silhouette of the temple to Athena Nike could be seen. With four columns only on each of the two fronts and none along the flanks, this tiny elegant Ionic structure acted at once as an abstraction of Victory, the lady who was often represented in the arts alighting in a tentative flurry from above, and as a firm space definer, a wall, for the channeled path that led to the entrance of the Propylaia.

The first altar to Athena as the patron goddess of the Panathenaia was dedicated on this spot in 566 B.C., the year the festival was instituted. A temple was built here shortly after the battle of Marathon in 490, in commemoration of that new and more

Fig. 7.16 Athens, Akropolis; western approach, with the Propylaia seen from below.

spectacular communal victory. In the Persian sack of 480 this small shrine suffered along with the limestone precursors of the Parthenon and the Erechtheion. The new Periklean shrine, by the architect Kallikrates, who also had a hand in an early phase of the Parthenon, was of Pentelic marble. The exaggeratedly pointed corner volutes of the oversized capitals, it has been suggested, were meant to lead the eye toward the sea, toward Salamis, the site of the heroic sea battle against the mighty fleet of Xerxes in 480 that liberated Athens and all of mainland Greece. (Fig. 6.21)

The Propylaia was a very unusual building; it was a clever redoing by the architect Mnesikles of the older gatehouse that had stood at an oblique northeast-southwest angle. (Figs. 7.17, 7.18) One passed, at the top of the broad axial approach ramp, through a forecourt flanked by two un-

equal wings. The north wing, a refreshment station for pilgrims with the usual dining couches, was lavishly decorated with paintings; the south wing was a small chamber that gave access to the Nike temple. Symmetry was probably never intended beyond the Doric facades of the two wings that looked toward the forecourt. The main unit of the Propylaia had a six-column portico, also Doric but of more imposing proportions, with the central opening considerably wider than the rest. This opening led to the middle passageway, while the two doors on either side of it gave way to broad aisles.

Beyond the opening, the scale again changed. The procession filed into a cool, dim interior space that shot upward at the same time that its volume constricted suspensefully. (Fig. 7.19) There was light ahead of the passageway and light at the back. Tall

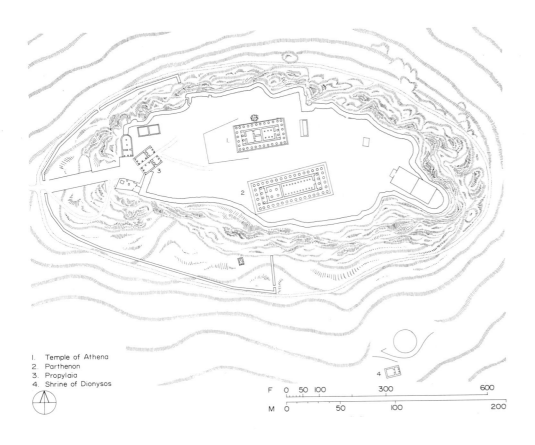

Fig. 7.17 The Athenian Akropolis during the sixth century B.C.; general site plan.

1. Temple of Athena
2. Parthenon
3. Propylaia
4. Shrine of Dionysos

```
F  0  50  100        300                    600
M  0           50            100                 200
```

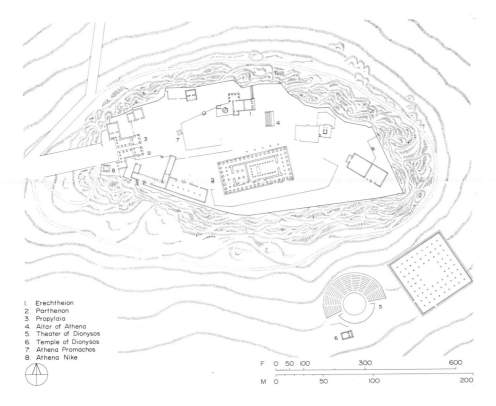

1. Erechtheion
2. Parthenon
3. Propylaia
4. Altar of Athena
5. Theater of Dionysos
6. Temple of Dionysos
7. Athena Promachos
8. Athena Nike

```
F  0  50  100        300                    600
M  0           50            100                 200
```

Fig. 7.18 The Akropolis at the end of the fifth century B.C.; general site plan.

Fig. 7.19 The Akropolis, Propylaia (no. 3 on Fig. 7.18), 437–432 B.C., Mnesikles; view of the central passageway, looking east.

Fig. 7.20 The Akropolis, looking from the east portico of the Propylaia toward the Erechtheion (left) and the Parthenon (right); reconstruction view. The tall statue in the middle ground represents Athena Promachos (the Champion), the colossal bronze image by Phidias, ca. 460 B.C.

slender Ionic columns on either side carried a ceiling of marble beams. At the end of the passage was a porch with a columnar facade matching that of the entrance. The moment of constriction was passed and, once again, with resounding dramatic impact, the procession stood in the blazing sunlight of an Attic August, with the two main temples of the site vying for its attention (Fig. 7.20)

The passage through the Propylaia had purged and altered the worshipping citizens. They were now in a special, open space, different from the one that was left behind at the entrance to the monumental gateway. Directly in front, a little to one side, stood Athena Promachos. Halfway down the void, between the two temples, was the altar of Athena where the animals would be sacrificed; a little to the right and back of this, was the precinct of Zeus where

the axe that killed the beasts would itself be condemned to death.

In the pre-Periklean scheme, the precursors of the Parthenon and the Erechtheion were standard look-alike temples, placed almost parallel to each other, each with a six-column front. (Fig. 7.17) The north temple was the smaller of the two and had a complex cella division, to account for the fact that Athena shared the site with Poseidon, Hephaistos, the legendary King Erechtheus whose palace had once stood in this very place, and the hero Boutes. Otherwise, the two west facades of the temples lined up rather redundantly on either side of the narrow central void.

The Periklean rebuilding changed all this. (Fig. 7.18) The two temples were now quite dissimilar. The Parthenon, which was started before Perikles with typical, six-column facades, developed under the architect Ikti-

nos into a huge looming mass with no fewer than eight columns across the fronts and seventeen along the flanks. The Erechtheion was a delicate structure of a uniquely irregular shape sitting a little to the north of its predecessor and so augmenting the central void. The new Propylaia faced the void rather than favoring either temple. The two natures of Athena were now visually set apart, but one approached both temples nonaxially, adjusting to their varied sequence of view and scale.

The Parthenon was probably the first to be visited by the procession. The rock floor of the Akropolis sloped upward from the Propylaia to the platform on which the mighty temple stood, the result of a vast filling and leveling operation. (Fig. 7.21) Monumental stairs rose to the west front where, on the pediment, Athena and Poseidon fought in the presence of the other

Fig. 7.21 The Akropolis, Parthenon (no. 1 on Fig. 7.18), 447–432 B.C., Iktinos and Kallikrates; near view from the northwest, reconstruction drawing.

frieze was carved in higher relief than the rest, to compensate for the angle of vision and the dimmer light at that height. The background would have been painted blue, and color and metal accessories would have picked out the main accents of the procession.

What was attempted in this long and beautiful frieze was not the representation of any one moment of the procession. Instead, we follow the various stages of the day's activities, arranged in sequence: the preparations, the setting out and gradual acceleration of the pace, the horsemen in the lower city, and those marching on foot. Here they all were: the riders of Athens who, in the words of Sophokles, were

. . . conquered never.
They honor her whose glory all men know,
And honor the god of the sea, who loves forever
The feminine earth that bore him long ago.

Then followed the slow pace of the elders; and behind them the jug-bearing youths and the sacrificial beasts, one raising its head as it were in anticipation of the inevitable blow—"that heifer lowing to the skies," as Keats described it in his "Ode on a Grecian Urn." (Fig. 7.24) And then the maidens with the saffron peplos, marching in pairs, calm and stately in their long tunics like fluted columns. (Fig. 7.25) Then the scene changes, from Athena as a focal point, to Mount Olympus where the gods and goddesses of the Greek world are gathered to hail one of their number.

The worshippers below provided the unity of this episodic composition as they marched along the frieze. They are the human content of the polis, what the polis is made of; Athena is its sacred embodiment. Courageously they chose to portray themselves on the temple of the goddess in the act of doing homage to her because, in a sense, they were the goddess—"Our own dear daughter who is amongst us," as Plato says of her.

To venerate the immortals and to be a member of a polis—these were the covenants of Greek humanity. Nothing that humans achieved or aspired to could be thought of outside this dual covenant. In the gods resided ancient obligations to the forces of nature and the appeasement that was their due. And in the frame of the polis,

gods to determine who would rule supreme over Attica. In the metopes below, eternal adversaries grappled in inextricable pairs: Lapiths and Centaurs, Greeks and Amazons, Greeks and Trojans along the north side in the direction of Troy, Giants and gods on the south. (Fig. 7.22) In many of the metopes the struggle was shown in mid-course: there was no victor, no vanquished. Warring opposites complemented each other in intricate, almost heraldic, groupings—and this is perhaps another essential aspect of the term Classical. It conjures aloofness, a sense of timeless idealism; but involvement, too, and violent involvement at that, is part of the Classical spirit. Yet the artist chooses not to take sides openly, recognizing that the greatness of the victor is directly proportionate to the skill and obduracy of the foe,

that the hero needs the villain to gain his identity, that balance lies in mid-battle.

The procession now moved a little closer, up the west steps of the Parthenon, and a new revelation awaited it. A continuous frieze, running the length of the building along the top of the inner core behind the peristyle, showed, for the first time in Greek history, the citizens themselves on the temple. (Fig. 7.23) The great frieze, probably executed in place, depicted the very procession that had brought them to the Akropolis. The frieze, 160 meters (525 feet) long and 1 meter (3.5 feet) high, started at the southeast corner and progressed in two streams, along the west and north sides and along the south side, ending with a grand gathering of the gods on the east front of the temple's inner core, over the six columns of the pronaos. The top part of the

Fig. 7.22 Parthenon, metope showing a Lapith youth battling a Centaur. (British Museum, London)

Fig. 7.23 Parthenon, Panathenaic frieze, riders. (British Museum, London)

Fig. 7.24 Parthenon, Panathenaic frieze, a sacrificial heifer being led by youths. (British Museum, London)

the citizen found the fulfillment of human life—the realization of moral worth and philosophic, political, and artistic identity. To be cityless was to be lost or to have dwelled with dishonor. Something of all this was being sung in the program of the Parthenon and the eloquent interlocking it attempted of Athena, Athens, and the Athenians.

On the east pediment the birth of Athena was depicted: the maiden goddess who never knew the labor of birth and was not born of the womb, but who sprang fully grown from the brow of her father Zeus. The great east doors of the cella would have been thrown open on this holy day, and the procession would now complete its veneration of one nature of its city's godhead by catching a glimpse, at the end of a tunnel of space lined by two rows of Doric columns, of the tall gold and ivory statue of this warrior maiden, helmeted and with shield and spear in hand. (Fig. 7.26)

The peplos was not meant for this masterpiece of Phidias but for the old wooden cult statue in the Erechtheion. The procession now wended its way toward this other temple, so different from the overwhelming Parthenon that had wrested attention to itself upon entrance to the site, invited approach, and directed the crowd down its flanks. (Fig. 7.27) At the Erechtheion, Athena was another shade of womanhood—warm, refined, domestic. An exquisite Ionic order reflected this character externally and flirted with the masculine severity of the Parthenon across the way.

The layout of the Erechtheion was extraordinary. It was built, like the Propylaia, on several levels. The east front, at the level of the Parthenon, had six columns across. The north side sank along a smooth marble wall and ended in a projecting columnar porch that sheltered the trident mark of Poseidon which was left when he struck saltwater from the rock during his contest with Athena. She retaliated by striking the rock with her spear and producing the olive tree, and an olive tree was always present—and is today—on the irregular west side of the temple. This west elevation climbed in two stages from the north porch

Fig. 7.26 Parthenon, interior of cella with the gold and ivory statue of Athena Parthenos (the Virgin) by Phidias; reconstruction view.

Fig. 7.25 Parthenon, Panathenaic frieze, young women walking in pairs. (British Museum, London)

level up to the level of the Parthenon, along a wall that carried four engaged Ionic columns. A small porch on the south side balanced the tall north porch, but instead of columns it used six sculptured maidens that carried the burden of the entablature on their heads—caryatids as we call them. (Fig. 7.28) They stand there with one leg forward and so begin a cross-axis that runs through the void between the two temples and comes to rest on the north flank of the Parthenon, one-third of the way from the west corner.

There was also a figure of the earth goddess Gaia in this void on the cross-axis, rising from her own soil not far from the altar of Athena. But essentially this empty space belonged to the Athenian. Here he stood,

Fig. 7.27 The Akropolis, Erechtheion (no. 2 on Fig. 7.18), 421–405 B.C., Kallikrates and others; view from the southeast.

the measure of all things, between monuments that immortalized the two natures of Pallas Athena and through her the polis itself. The polis was hearth and it was intellect, tradition and brash invention, security and challenge. The citizen was the bond that locked it all in place. As he filled the center of this devised order on the Akropolis with his own humanity, the Athenian saw to the east and south the spreading city, and beyond the walls the hard-tilled land that sustained it. To the west, he would look toward the Propylaia from where he had entered this proud rock sanctuary, and beyond, the path he took through the agora to reach it. Further out still, the sea and recent memories of triumphs won there against great odds.

This was the physical and temporal frame of the polis, and the built shapes in the immediate periphery—the Propylaia, the Erechtheion, and the Parthenon—held its truth in stone. They stand today much as they did then, a miracle of nothing more than Pentelic marble, the blazing light of Attica upon it, and the concept of the column, reasonable and obvious, a shaft of stone sitting simply upon its stone pavement. This is the secret of Classical art if it can be thought to have a secret: that what is visible is the chief reality; that what is real can be expressed in the simplest and most honest way; that opposites coexist and are interdependent; and that out of such a view of the world comes blooming pride in the achievement of humans, and the corollary of pride is joy. In the words of Aeschylus,

Joy to you, joy of your justly appointed riches,
Joy to all the people, blest
With the Virgin's love, who sits
Next beside her father's throne.
Wisdom ye have learned at last;
Folded under Pallas' wing,
Yours at last the grace of Zeus.

Fig. 7.28 Erechtheion, the Caryatid Porch.

Further Reading

C. M. Bowra, *Periklean Athens* (London: Weidenfeld and Nicolson, 1971).

R. Carpenter, *The Architects of the Parthenon* (Harmondsworth and Baltimore: Penguin, 1970).

F. Castagnoli, *Orthagonal Town Planning in Antiquity,* trans. V. Caldiandro (Cambridge, Mass.: MIT Press, 1971).

J. J. Coulton, *The Architectural Development of the Greek Stoa* (Oxford: Clarendon, 1976).

I. T. Hill, *The Ancient City of Athens, Its Topography and Monuments* (Chicago: Argonaut, 1969).

S. G. Miller, *The Prytaneion, Its Function and Architectural Form* (Berkeley: University of California Press, 1978).

J. Travlos, *Pictorial Dictionary of Ancient Athens* (New York: Praeger, 1971).

R. E. Wycherley, *How the Greeks Built Cities,* 2nd ed. (London: Macmillan, 1963).

———, *The Stones of Athens* (Princeton: Princeton University Press, 1978).

Lindos (Rhodes), sanctuary of Athena, 300–200 B.C.

8

THE HELLENISTIC REALM

The New Order

The crowning age of the polis—the administrative and social unit of the Greek commonwealth—was the fifth century B.C. By then this vigorous institution had begun to leave its mark beyond the Greek sphere. To some degree, the example of Greek Sicily and southern Italy had touched the city-making of the Etruscans even before. Rome itself had come about, in the eighth century B.C., by a process akin to the "synoecism" that Aristotle diagnosed as the agent of early Greek urbanization. In fact, quasi-urban settlements in Spain and in central and northwestern Europe at the time of the polis indicate that Greek practice was now being heeded beyond the coastline of the Mediterranean, in areas where the usual pattern had been one of hill forts.

But at the time when the example of the polis was quickening the rural habits of Europe, its fate in the Greek homeland headed for a decline. Soon after the bitter Peloponnesian War between Athens and Sparta at the end of the fifth century, a sharp rise in the birth rate produced more mouths than the polis could feed. This, coupled with a weak economy, brought on severe unemployment. Colonization as a remedy was by now outmoded. The young man who could not find work now turned professional soldier and was willing to serve anyone. The concept of the mercenary was inimical to the Classical polis which represented, more than anything, a moral entity based on the full commitment of a person to an individual place. And this was only the beginning.

In the fourth century, there was a call to unite the Greek cities into a strong confederation that could push out toward new frontiers. The obvious choice was Asia Minor, the territory held by Persia which also controlled the Greek towns of the Ionian coast. To return past aggression would be a powerful incentive for unity, a holy cause. Rather unexpectedly, the military muscle that could propel this Panhellenic exercise now materialized on the fringes of the Greek world, in the region of Macedonia. This backward kindgom in the northern uplands of Greece rose to prominence toward mid-century under King Philip II. Philip's campaign to unite the Greeks, through force where necessary, was completed by his brilliant son Alexander the Great. (Fig. 8.1) This Macedonian subjection, however noble its ultimate aim, muted the autonomy of the cities, their proudest asset.

Once Greece had been bullied into the semblance of a nation, Alexander set out to liberate Asia Minor. His army swept into the heartland of Anatolia and with uncontainable impetus overwhelmed the traditional states of the Eastern world in the span of a decade, stopping short only at the doorstep of India.

This headlong conquest marked the end of the Classical polis. In the new order the hundreds of coexisting city-states, large and small, that had formed the volatile Greek community found themselves engulfed in a vast political construct that contained old empires like Persia and Egypt. Greek rule was no longer coextensive with the Greek race. Now many Greeks lived among alien peoples, rendering meaningless the age-old duality of Greek and barbarian. So, too, that other grave distinction that fixed the Greek's place in the scheme of things, the relationship between humans and the immortal population of Olympus, lost its power when Alexander, a mere mortal, was deified even before his death. The practice soon became commonplace among the dynasts who carved up this unwieldy empire in the years to come.

A famous image of one of these men, the bronze statue entitled *The Hellenistic Ruler*, is a telling sign of the new order. (Fig. 8.2) In the Classical period such public statues of male nudes were of young triumphant athletes, never of rulers; and the formula of these *kouroi* was to show contained energy at rest or equilibrium—the body aware of its potential without the need to advertise itself. The Hellenistic image is one of sheer brute power, boastful and overpowering. And yet the generalized confidence of the body seems negated by the particular concern of the face, which is often shown worried and frowning. This split between the head and body, and the dependence on the face to characterize the specific humanity of a person, contrasts with the indivisible presence of the kouros, body and head together, representing an individual as the embodiment of something larger than himself, the state that made him.

Classical values were based on the respect of the single individual within the

Fig. 8.2 The so-called *Hellenistic Ruler,* a heroic portrait, bronze statue, later second century B.C. (Museo delle Terme, Rome)

Fig. 8.1 Alexander the Great (336–323 B.C.), a mosaic representation of the Battle at the Issos in 333 B.C., from the House of the Vetii in Pompeii, ca. 100 B.C.; detail. This is a Roman copy of a Hellenistic painting of ca. 330 B.C. (National Museum, Naples, Italy)

framework of the city-state. It was his bigness within the narrow confines of the city that Classical culture celebrated. And it was precisely this that Alexander's fabulous accomplishment destroyed. The state was stretched out formidably to include empires. Even with the more restricted kingdoms that sprang up after his death, the scope of government was enlarged inordinately, and the standing of the individual was correspondingly reduced. (Fig. 8.3) The citizen-soldier unquestioningly defending his own polis when it came under attack yielded to the professional fighting man for whom soldiering was a career. Contending armies seemed now almost interchangeable, and victory became an abstraction. And so inevitably there grew a preoccupation with defeat, and pity toward the vanquished. The professionalization of athletic games similarly annulled the luster of the triumphant kouros. We are now shown tough, leathery pros whose crown of victory is less a godly reward than a hard-won, tangible profit.

The change we are sketching here in broad strokes is more easily evident in sculpture: the rise of portraiture; the depiction of little children and their cute antics, nude women as vehicles of erotic love, and clinically accurate representations of old people; subjects of pain and defeat. (Fig. 8.4) Sculpture itself took on a looser form and became prone to theatricality and vigorous entanglement. The value structure became less rigid. Classical Greece, like youth which it idolized, was high-minded, unyielding, exclusive. Culture seemed to grow old with the enlarged empire and now tended to be permissive, yielding, broadly compassionate.

The Classical hero is above all ethical, and

ethos according to Aristotle is "that fiber in man which reveals choice, what sort of a thing a man chooses or avoids in circumstances where the choice is not obvious." The hero in Classical art is often shown caught in a moment of decision, his dilemma unresolved. It is in the thinking out of it that his humanity is revealed. We feel *empathy* for him because we identify with his stance between opposite ends, because his morality and ours is existential. (Fig. 7.22)

The Hellenistic hero, on the other hand, is not the instrument of choice but its victim. His morality is melodramatic. He is not posed between alternatives, but abandoned to face one. The artists represent him as either gloatingly victorious or else piteously vanquished. The observer is not allowed therefore to remain engaged in the struggle. The image is after effect and is intent on eliciting a predictable response. The message is not implied; it is shouted. We are thus forced into *sympathy*, which means feeling for, not with. (Fig. 8.4)

Precocious Trends
These observations also apply, but rather more abstractly, to architecture. First, though, we must remember that we are charting broad trends over a long period of time. The hinge between the Classical and Hellenistic period is the electrifying reign of Alexander, but political or military events do not always initiate a change of form; they may sometimes merely precipitate it. Remember, too, that a style crystallizes out of conditions and components that reach back beyond the point when it gains general validity. And even after its decisive appearance, a style coexists with older modes that carry on untouched, or touched only in part, by the new vision. What we call Hellenistic architecture in fact had its beginnings before Alexander. The term itself covers three hundred years, from Alexander to the fall of the last of the Alexandrine kingdoms, Cleopatra's Egypt, to the Romans in 31 B.C. Architecture during this extended period was neither static nor uniform across the immense territory involved.

Looking back, we see the seeds of Hellenistic architecture as far back as the fifth century and probably nowhere better than in the Athens of Perikles, the quintessential locus of Classicism. The axial monumentality of the approach ramp of the Akropolis and of the western prospect of the Parthenon presages one of the central themes of Hellenistic architecture, its preference for banked effects and the dramatic use of staircases. (Fig. 7.16) On the west elevation of the Erechtheion the column and the wall, the two hitherto distinct and separate elements of Greek design, are married. The engaged column, which we will return to, is the hallmark of Hellenistic architecture and, along with the pilaster or engaged pier, is the principal component of an exciting range of surface articulation whose distant consequences would be felt all the way to the modern period.

The Parthenon itself looks forward in at least one other important respect—the attention it devotes to the interior layers of its temple form. The public reality of the Doric temple lay in the exterior colonnade and its superstructure; the cella was an interior space of very limited use, a rather straightforward container for the cult image. Two rows of columns in a single or double tier were used to divide the space into three fairly equal aisles, the central one of which tunneled toward the statue. However, in the Parthenon, the placement of the Panathenaic frieze *within* the peristyle, along the exterior walls of the cella, already encourages the user to penetrate the column screen. (Fig. 7.23) Inside, the rows of columns are pushed out toward the lateral walls of the cella, reducing the outer spaces into narrow aisles and aggrandizing the effect of the central nave. Furthermore, the colonnade is brought around and

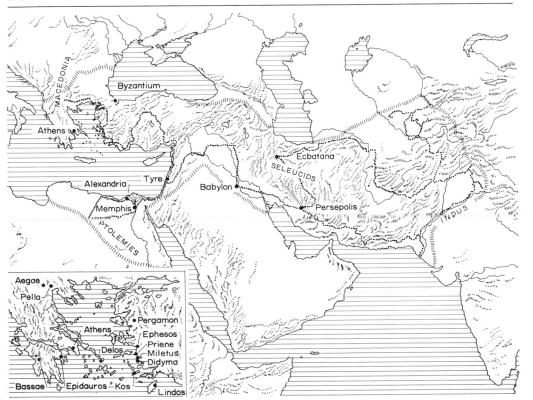

Fig. 8.3 Map: The Hellenistic realm, ca. 330–30 B.C.

behind the statue of Athena Parthenos, framing it fully on three sides. (Fig. 7.26)

It is not clear whether this burgeoning interest in the interior of the temple corresponded to any major change in ritual practice. Whatever the case, the subtler design and fancier embellishment of the cella drew people to enter the temple for reasons other than formal religious proceedings. The temple, which had already at times doubled as a treasury or bank, now started its career as a civic museum. Moreover, architects more and more relied on internal effects to bring out the uniqueness of each deity, most especially in those cults with a potential for drama. Ionic temples (for example, the archaic temple of Artemis at Ephesos) had always been susceptible to architectural elaboration of this kind. Now this concern was becoming general, and temple architecture leaned more and more toward the expressive and theatrical.

The Case of Bassae

The temple to Apollo at Bassae in the wilds of Arcadia is of crucial importance to our discussion. (Fig. 8.5) It was begun roughly at the same time as the Parthenon and is attributed by one ancient source to the same architect, Iktinos, but it probably was not complete before the very end of the fifth century, perhaps even the early fourth. Today it sits in splendid isolation within a tossed, lonely mountainscape not far from the Panhellenic sanctuary of Olympia. Made of the drab grey limestone of its setting, it would compare poorly with the luminous marble form of the Parthenon were it not for the fact that in this remote thunderous site the archaic look and the awkward, rather heavy-handed execution of the temple sculpture seem eloquently appropriate and may well have been intentional. Looking at the design in close detail, we would be justified in suspecting the calculated manipulation of standard conventions of temple architecture for the sake of expressive effects.

To begin with, there is the unusual north-south orientation. (Fig. 8.6) Was Iktinos' idea to have the temple face north toward Delphi, Apollo's chief sanctuary and his favorite dwelling-place on earth? Or was this in-

Fig. 8.4 *Laokoön and His Sons,* a statue in the Hellenistic style, probably a Roman copy, from the first century B.C. or first century A.D., of a mid-second century B.C. original by Hagesandros, Polydoros, and Athanadoros of Rhodes. (Vatican Museums, Rome)

Fig. 8.5 Bassae (Greece), temple of Apollo, late fifth century B.C.; general view of the site.

tended perhaps as a visual device, to get an oblique, three-dimensional view of the building along the original precipitous approach from the town of Phigaleia in the gorge of the Nedda River? Almost certainly, a further advantage was sought in this unorthodox siting for the interior arrangement of the cella. A door along its east wall could bring direct morning sunlight to a small backspace just off the cella where the cult statue may have stood—an appro-

priate tribute to the God of Light who had triumphed long ago over the dark forces of the earth.

Between this room and the cella proper stood a single, extraordinary column. (Fig. 8.7) It is the first surviving instance of a new architectural order, the Corinthian. In later antiquity the Corinthian capital was said to have been invented by a sculptor and metalworker named Kallimachos, a pupil of Phidias. In contrast to the abstraction of the

Doric and the curvilinear grace of the Ionic, this new capital is composed of natural foliage, acanthus, a motif often used on fifth-century funerary stelai. In fact, story has it that it was an offering basket on a tomb enveloped by the leaves of an acanthus plant that had inspired Kallimachos to fashion this architectural novelty. (Fig. 8.8)

The Corinthian order never developed its own distinctive entablature and used the Doric or Ionic themes interchangeably. Its sense was clearly not architectonic. A luxurious plant capital is antithetical to the idea of the column as a load-bearing entity. The deep, shadow-catching, essentially pictorial effects of the carving diffuse the structural logic of the relationship between shaft and architrave. If the Corinthian order indeed started its career here at Bassae, it would seem that the motive was literary rather than functional. It has been suggested that the single, treelike column before the image of the god may have been intended to evoke a central moment in Apollonian myth. When Leto was made pregnant by Zeus, his perpetually jealous and vengeful wife Hera forbade anyone, divine or human, to give the young woman haven for her labor. It was not until Zeus readied the island of Delos that Leto, after her long and desperate wandering, leaned against a laurel tree there and gave birth to Apollo. In commemoration of this event, bronze trees stood outside the temples of Apollo at Delphi and on Delos itself. At Bassae, it seems, the tree was brought within, incorporated in the architecture of the cella, and made the focal point of its deep axis.

This is not the only peculiarity of the temple interior. The sculptural frieze, for the first time in Greek architecture, is brought within the cella proper. The continuous form of the frieze along three sides also tends to centralize the cella and reduce the impact of its axial perspective toward the cult statue. What is more, the manner of the storytelling foreshadows the birth of that tendency toward theatricality, the strongly rendered drama and the controlled appeal to the viewer, which we have already singled out as one visible aspect of the dissolution of the Classical ethos.

The subject is familiar—themes of engagement between Greeks and Amazons, Lapiths and Centaurs. (Fig. 8.9) But the engagement is not concentrated on that midbattle moment, that steady balance of opposing forces, that we have found so potently expressed in the Parthenon metopes. There is a furious abandon here, with the combatants lunging, falling, or fleeing in great agitation. Garments billow as in a strong wind, heads tilt forcefully to convey a variety of emotions, deep-cut eyes set in

pools of shadow hurl glances across intervals of space. Flying drapery, quick action and farflung gestures, the play of deep shadows against highlights, the blurring of planes, bold foreshortening—all the telltale features of a new manner in art are employed in this powerful interior space of Apollo's temple.

The cella seems to have been the target

of the architect's attention and ingenuity, as if its importance were preeminent. The short sides are set unusually far back behind the exterior colonnades as in the archaic temples of Sicily, drawing the worshipper deep inside the temple. The space within expands as one enters, seemingly opening up to engulf a pressing crowd. This feeling of expansion is the result of two

Fig. 8.6 Bassae, temple of Apollo; ground plan.

Fig. 8.7 Bassae, temple of Apollo; interior, looking south, reconstruction drawing.

Fig. 8.8 Epidauros (Greece), tholos, ca. 360–320 B.C., Polykleitos the Younger; detail of the inner, Corinthian colonnade (as reconstructed in the Epidauros museum).

things. There is a single row of tall Ionic columns on either side of the cella (the end columns toward the north may have had Corinthian capitals) instead of the usual arrangement of two superimposed storeys of columns smaller in scale than the exterior order. And these tall cella columns are not freestanding, but are engaged instead to the walls by short spurs of masonry.

The move to unencumber the space of the cella by pushing the columns closer to the walls—and so be able, incidentally to increase the size of the cult statue—was already apparent in the Parthenon. Here at Bassae the side aisles disappear altogether, and the cella becomes one large, unified space with deep niches along the sides. The bases of the engaged columns flare extravagantly, forming more than three-quarters of a circle before they hug their masonry spur. Thus the walls are molded into a rich, plastic tapestry of light and shadow.

The capitals themselves are extraordinary. They are three-sided, with volutes on all three sides joined by full convex lines. We saw the beginnings of these "diagonal" Ionic capitals at the temple of Athena Nike on the Akropolis. There, to define the

corners more precisely and, as suggested, to point away from the body of the temple, the angle capitals were given adjacent volutes. At Bassae, however, the principle goes beyond corner definition. A normal Ionic capital has two legitimate faces with volutes, the lesser lateral faces showing only the cushion connecting the spirals. To the viewer looking along its length, the standard Ionic colonnade would present a receding row of these unsatisfactory side faces. The three-sided arrangement at Bassae obviates this unhappy visual effect. But in the process it also destroys the structural logic of the capital in relation to its architrave, which can no longer be seen resting in the trough between the two high, voluted faces. The capitals now take on a decorative air, looking pretty rather than looking right.

The traditional purpose of cella colonnades was to help support the roof. As these were pushed out toward the cella walls, the central span became too broad to be bridged in stone efficiently. The architect resorted to metal enforcement, and the burden of the roof was shifted more and more to the cella walls. At Bassae the colonnades abandon their load-bearing duties altogether and become mere symbolic attachments at the ends of masonry spurs, which are necessary to buttress the overburdened cella walls. The column, then, surrenders its structural reality for the sake of new visual effects. The Classical unity of structure and appearance begins to come apart. Liberated from its structural role, the column could enjoy a new existence as applied ornament. The one-time tectonic logic was thus overlaid by the pictorial element; the architect was freed to try variations on the columnar tradition for their own sake.

The Hellenistic Temple

About one hundred years after Bassae, a new temple to Apollo began to rise over the ruins of the earlier, Archaic structure at Didyma, the famous pilgrimage site outside of Miletus. (Fig. 8.10) The architects were the Milesian Daphnis and Paeonius of Ephesos. It was a colossal undertaking and construction dragged on into the second century B.C. and beyond without ever being totally completed.

The temple at Didyma illustrates the continuing transformation of this building type in line with the innovations of Bassae. That we encounter this prodigy in the East is no accident. The great eras of architecture in coastal Asia Minor were the seventh and sixth centuries B.C., before Persian suzerainty inhibited the prosperity of Greek cities, and, again, in the Hellenistic period when mainland Greece was eclipsed by the star of Alexander and the initiative passed on to the old Aegean cities set free of their alien yoke, and to the many new towns, like Alexandria and Antioch, founded or Hellenized by Alexander and his successors in the lands of his conquests. Apollo at Didyma spans these two eras of greatness. With its double peristyle and deep entrance porch filled with columns, it retains the formal aspects of the Archaic temples of Ionia, like its predecessor destroyed by the Persians in the early fifth century B.C.,

Fig. 8.9 Bassae, temple of Apollo, interior frieze; detail of the battle between Greeks and Amazons. (British Museum, London)

Fig. 8.10 Didyma (Turkey), temple of Apollo, erected over a sixth-century B.C. structure that was begun in the late fourth century B.C. and was never finished; view from the north.

or the Artemision at Ephesos. But at Didyma the change is revolutionary.

The Ionic order had gone through major adjustments in the fourth and third centuries. A reform of proportions, associated with the architects Pythios of Priene and Hermogenes of Alabanda, made the column taller and slenderer and the spans wider. At Didyma the exterior columns, the height of which is almost ten times their lower diameter or a full 20 meters (65 feet), are the tallest and slimmest of any Greek temple. But it was the decorative possibilities of the Ionic that satisfied Hellenistic taste and made of it the dominant order everywhere. The sterner Doric was less accommodating and was held back by the ever-present "corner problem." After an attempt at modernization that saw it attenuate its proportions, the Doric lost its popularity, "not because it is unlovely in appearance or origin or dignity of form," according to Hermogenes, "but because the arrangement of the triglyphs and metopes is an embarrassment and inconvenience." For the most part, it was now relegated to utilitarian buildings.

There is ample evidence of the decorative enrichment at Didyma. The columns of the east end sat on elaborately carved bases which stood on square plinths whose sides measured 9 Ionic feet each—a module used throughout the building. (Fig. 8.11) The base molding was replaced at times by a set of carved panels that formed an octagon and featured sea animals, dragons, and palmettes. The angle capitals had a bull's head in the center and busts or winged monsters projecting from the corner volutes. Other capitals held heads of Zeus, Apollo, or Leto. This is the start of what are called "historiated capitals," which will enjoy considerable popularity in Roman times and again later in Romanesque churches.

The only approach to the temple was by means of a special flight of stairs cut into the eastern stereobate and through five rows of columns, the three innermost filling the space between the extended walls of the cella. (As in most Hellenistic temples, there was no equivalent back porch.) The central axis terminated in an opening, but passage through it was blocked by a low wall. (Fig. 8.12) To enter one had to use either of two side doors. They gave way to vaulted ramps, dark and narrow, that led down and then emerged, with blinding impact, into a large hall open to the sky.

On three sides, the hall was defined by a very tall podium on which stood pilasters built of ashlar blocks like the wall; so the podium was totally wedded to the wall. (Fig. 8.13) At the top, this interlocking of uprights and wall was expressed by a rich continuous frieze made up of the pilaster capitals, which showed a central acanthus motif flanked by griffins, and linking bands of griffins and lyres. At the end of the hall, where the cult statue would be in a normal cella, sat a miniature prostyle temple, like a play within a play, with other elements of Apollo's oracle sites, such as the spring and the laurel bush, nearby. Only when one had walked toward this chapel, which seems to crystallize the backspace of the Bassae cella, and turned back would the presence of a

Fig. 8.11 Didyma, temple of Apollo; bases of peristyle columns.

magnificent stairway become apparent at the other end of the hall, between the vaulted ramps of access. The stairway led to a platform with two columns that framed the opening one had noticed at the top. This stage was probably used for epiphanies related to the oracular cult, and the opening itself no doubt served a similar purpose for those outside by setting the stage for sacred appearances.

Whatever its relationship in layout to its Archaic predecessor, the Hellenistic temple at Didyma is thus exposed as a theatrical composition that relies on surprise, change of scale and of levels, and an ambivalence in the standing of its various component features. Is the large roofless hall the cella, or an inner courtyard that frames the chapel at the end? Why has it to be approached in such a devious way? What are we doing so deeply drawn into the body of the temple?

The Classical temple was self-contained and active. (Fig. 6.8) It stood in mid-space, a sculptural force complete only in relation to its surroundings, both natural and built, which gave it scale and set it in a dynamic relationship to the approaching worshipper. This vital experience was all—getting to the temple along an often irregular path, moving around it, reading it against distant landscape forms and proximate features of the precinct. The Hellenistic temple tries to be complete in itself. It stages a certain sequence of effects within its own body, to be revealed to the user one by one. It works in only one way: it has secrets to unfold and it is much more than what it seems. The user is not allowed to interact freely with it. The temple becomes, instead, a pattern of staged impressions. The experience is controlled by the architect. We do not make of the temple what we ourselves want, but what the architect wants us to make of it.

Religious Settings

This studied design of the Hellenistic temple extended to its setting as well. This often meant landscaping and terracing, porticoed enclosures and monumental stairways, all arranged along sweeping axes. Nature, once an active participant in the conception and ritual experience of the

temple in its precinct, was now exploited primarily for its pictorial appeal, functioning like a painted backdrop. Remember that it was during the Hellenistic age that artists introduced the Greek world to landscape painting, and that nostalgia for country life and rural scenes became a major theme of literature. All this speaks of the gradual separation of natural from built forms. The size and staged formality of the planned environment so thoroughly predominated now that the precarious balance of Classical times, between what always had been and what humans imposed, was bound to be undone. Nature was neutralized, edited, and made the servant of architectural guile.

The new religious settings affected not only original Hellenistic precincts, but the remodeling of old sites as well. Because of a respect for surviving patterns, but also in order to escape rigidity, the axial layouts

were rarely dogmatic and symmetry became less than perfect. The twin principles of these grand compositions were panoramic succession and architectural unity— that is, the presentation of a series of tableaux, as the user moved upward along the predetermined axis, that afforded progressively more spectacular views and that were capable, because of the uniform design that overshadowed component parts, of being taken in at once. The enclosure for the temple proper, at the end of the sequence, might be an open horseshoe in form, or a Greek letter pi (Π), or some variety of quadrangle. Sometimes the temple stood in the middle of this enclosure, or else it was withdrawn and moved toward, or even engaged in, the surrounding colonnade.

Asklepios at Kos
Two examples should indicate the range of possibilities. The first we look at is a Hel-

Fig. 8.12 Didyma, temple of Apollo; site plan.

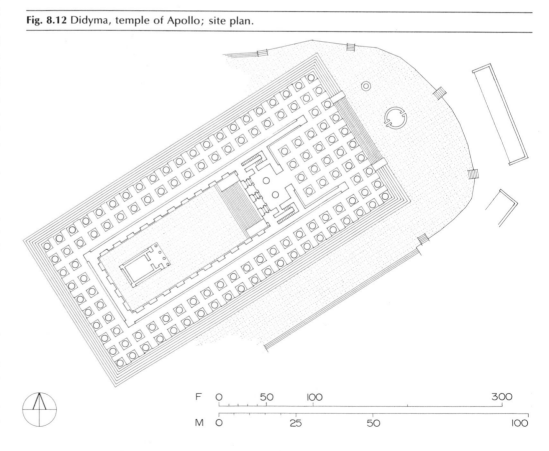

F 0   50   100   300

M 0   25   50   100

170

Fig. 8.13 Didyma, temple of Apollo; interior view looking northeast, with the small temple in the foreground and the stairs to the platform of epiphanies at the rear.

lenistic sanctuary on the Aegean island of Kos, which is sacred to Asklepios, the god of healing. (Fig. 8.14) It stood in the open land, a short distance from the main town, against the gentle slope of foothills rising out of the coastal plain. The second example is the sanctuary of Athena Lindaia, the ancient cult of the akropolis of Lindos, the town along the eastern shore of the island of Rhodes. It was remodeled in several campaigns between the later fourth century and the end of the third. (Fig. 8.17)

The scheme at Kos is calm and contained. Three terraces of easy rise are linked by flights of stairs along an axis that leads to the principal temple at the top. Both the first and last terrace are defined by Π-shaped enclosures facing inward, effectively bracketing the entire complex. The lower enclosure, entered through a formal gateway, contained rooms for the sick who came to wait for the intercession of Asklepios. Along the fourth side were fountains set against the retaining wall of the second terrace and incorporating the two springs that were central to the primitive cult. A small temple with an underground treasury and the main altar of the complex faced each other on either side of the axis at this intermediate level. Then the staircase followed, taking us to the final terrace and bringing us directly in front of the temple of Asklepios.

In fact, going through the complex, at least until the uppermost terrace which is the most formal (and predictably the latest), has something about it of the sacred ways of older Greece, like that of Delphi. (Fig. 6.16) It is as if this kind of naturally organized ascent were stiffened by the novel demands of centralized planning and architectural enframement, and it is precisely the tension between formal control and measured deviation that makes the Kos site so vital.

What is most different is the relationship of the temple to its precinct. It is the climax of the whole composition, but it presides more because of an artificial hierarchy than by its own authority. (Fig. 8.15) Inflexibly frontal, the impact of its peristyle is deflated by the columned frame into which it is visually locked; the temple seems uncommitted, out of the fray, a static image that looks out beyond its place, across the sea, toward the shore of Asia Minor and the cone of Halikarnassos. At Didyma the Greek temple was tamed by absorbing the spirited incidents of a sacred way inside its body. Here at Kos the temple is trapped and put on exhibit by its setting.

Athene Lindaia

At Lindos the temple is even less assertive. It is one of the smallest units of the grandiloquent layout and is caught between the majestic sweep of stairs and column screens through which one must pass to reach it and the sheer drop of its cliff perch which faces the vast open sea.

A temple first marked the craggy spot probably in the sixth century B.C. (Fig. 8.16) The path wound up along the northeast face of the akropolis starting at the harbor below. Pilgrims would have been able to pick out the upper portion of the structure as they climbed the path, confronting the temple directly as it stood clear against water and sky. The design took advantage of the high and unencumbered stance of the temple form against the open horizon—the borrowed bigness of cliff-hung structures.

The new design conjures a different magnitude by starting with an extravagantly scaled terrace, only to narrow down successive elements, until at the scale of the topmost platform the small temple can dominate without effort. (Fig. 8.17) We start out in a huge formal space with a winged stoa ahead of us facing outward. This we reach by a steep and monumental staircase. The central portion of the stoa has been reduced to a single screen of columns, and through this we now see another flight of stairs. We are channeled into a gatehouse not unlike the Propylaia on the

Fig. 8.14 Kos (Greece), the sanctuary of Asklepios, ca. 300–150 B.C.; reconstruction drawing.

Fig. 8.15 Kos, the sanctuary of Asklepios, top terrace with main temple, mid-second century B.C.; frontal view looking southwest, reconstruction drawing.

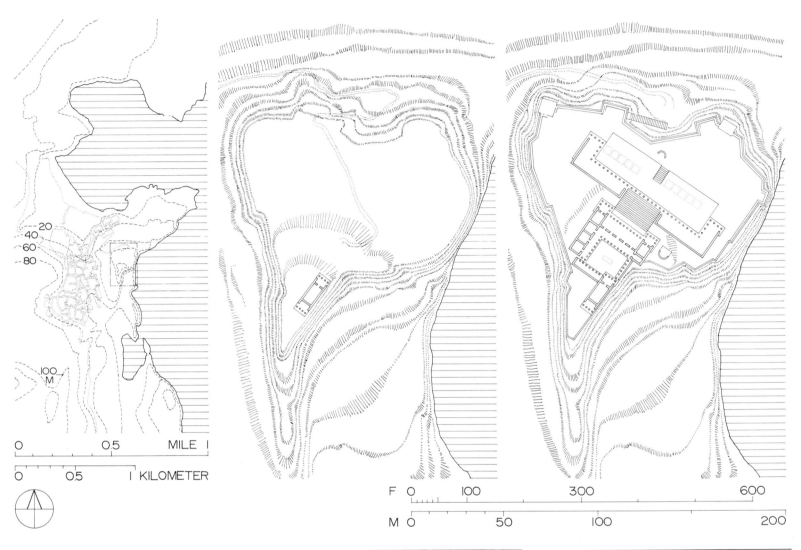

Fig. 8.16 Lindos (Rhodes, Greece), the sanctuary of Athena on the akropolis; plans. Left, the site shown in relation to the modern town and the coastline; center, the site in the sixth century B.C. showing the location of the archaic temple; right, the temple as redone in the fourth century and the additions of the third century.

Fig. 8.17 Lindos, sanctuary of Athena seen from the north; model. The temple is at the upper right; the structures in the lower left are Roman additions and were therefore excluded from the plan in Fig. 8.16.

173

Athenian Akropolis. The inner side of the gatehouse, at the level of the third and final terrace, locks into another system of stoas which defines a small rectangular space. The altar is in the middle and the temple is to the side and back, hugging the cliff-edge to the east.

The contrast between the small, encased temple and this multilevel stage intimates physically the transformed character of the Greek city in the world of Hellenistic kingdoms. The temple and the agora, twin foci of an independent and self-sufficient city-state, were both affected by the princely, centralizing tradition spawned by Alexander's conquests and refined by his successors. Democracy, still thought the ideal form of Greek government, no longer represented real conditions. Royal prerogative touched even the nominally free cities of the Greek homeland. Such august patronage often equated size and ostentation with political prestige. The cities, whether free or subject, began to shape their image in this princely mold. In some ways the Lindos complex is the architectural counterpart of *The Hellenistic Ruler*.

The Noble Metropolis

The fundaments of Hellenistic urbanism were, first, a vastly increased wealth, both corporate and personal, which grew through general trade freshly enhanced by standardized currency and a common language, and second, the willingness of the rich, who monopolized local government, to spend generously for the material betterment of their city. Public funds were set aside for temples, walls, and the planning of municipal services like roads and sewers. But it was mostly civic patriotism that accounted for the evident splendor of most of these cities. Statues of local benefactors were everywhere. The culture that for centuries had declined to commemorate living persons except for victors of the great games now filled sanctuaries, government buildings, and public spaces with rows of wealthy patrons, in bronze or stone or even silver and gold, and even set up special halls of honor for this statuary.

It was now broadly held that respectable cities were invested with noble frames. Self-rule, temples, and a rural territory were no longer enough to make the city. Pausanias in his *Description of Greece* speaks of Panopeus, "a city of the Phocians, if one can give this name to those who possess no government offices, no gymnasium, no theater, no market, no water descending to a fountain . . . ," even though "they have boundaries with their neighbors and even send delegates to the Phocian assembly." The reference to a piped water supply is important. Classical cities with distinguished public monuments, like Athens, could still present a shabby side to visitors because of their lack of public amenities and the rustic look of their residential fabric. The Hellenistic city aspired to be a total work of art.

Determinants of City-Form
The grid continued to be the favorite layout. At the same time a new school of planning introduced a more dynamic organization for hilly sites based on the vertical, three-dimensional alliance of major building groups. The method may have had its origin on the eve of the Hellenistic age in Halikarnassos, the city of King Mausolos, which was disposed like an open-air theater around its bay and was capped by the king's monumental tomb, the famous Mausoleum. (Fig. 1.7) The Attalid capital of Pergamon is the most remarkable product of this school of planning, and we will be looking at it shortly. (Fig. 8.30)

Already a generation or two before Alexander, city walls came to be considered an element of deliberate aesthetic concern, beyond their mere utility. Aristotle in his *Politics* held that "care must be taken that they may be a proper ornament to the city, as well as a defense in time of war." Hellenistic walls have finely turned masonry, often of the "pseudoisotomic" variety that uses alternate courses of differing height; and the introduction of rounded towers should be credited only in part to military advantage. Improved siegecraft and new machines designed on the catapult principle and capable of shooting projectiles at high velocity over considerable distances required larger and more salient towers, as well as an obstructive system of moats and

outworks. The citadel of Epipolai at Syracuse proves how superb, technically and visually, the results could be. (Fig. 8.18) Its most vulnerable western approach was defended by three successive rock-cut ditches, a pointed bastion, and, further back, a massive wall with five huge towers to carry the heavy batteries that came into practice in the late third century B.C. In the ingenious network of tunnels and galleries through which these outworks communicated among themselves and with the inner keep, both rock-cut and masonry vaulting were expertly employed.

Classical Greece by and large showed little affection for the arch and the vault. Interest in this form of spanning increased in the Hellenistic period to the extent that architectural programs now involved special problems that could not easily be resolved with trabeation. These had to do with covered units that sloped; underground buildings, like the tombs in the cemeteries of Macedonia or Alexandria, which had to withstand strong external pressure; and terracing, where hollow vaulted chambers were more efficient in leveling and enlarging usable space than embanked fill. Thus arcuate forms remained essentially utilitarian, although there was some timid flirtation with the arch as a decorative element, especially in the design of monumental gateways. A recoverable example is the eastern gate of the agora in the town of Priene that framed a perspective of stoa colonnades. (Fig. 8.19)

It is probably from the use of the stoa along streets that the idea came for avenues with colonnades down their entire length to shelter pedestrians and turn a public thoroughfare into a stretch of urban pomp. (Fig. 12.22b) In addition, behind these covered walks, city authorities would lease shops. The ceremonial street thus doubled as a kind of linear market.

Colonnaded avenues are a late phenomenon in the Hellenistic realm, but the street had long since come of age as a program of architecture. The best of Hellenistic streets were wide and uniformly paved. Their care and embellishment were entrusted to a body of controllers. A law defining the duties of the office survives; it prescribed a 9-meter (30-foot) width for

Fig. 8.18 Syracuse (Sicily), the Euryalos fort, which culminated the fortification system of the plateau of Epipolai west of the city proper, fourth–third century B.C.; reconstruction drawing.

main highways and 3.5 meters (12 feet) for secondary roads. Officially, paving was the responsibility of householders. In practice, it is likely that they paid their share of the cost to the city which maintained gangs of public slaves for such purposes.

Handsome fortifications, imposing city gates with a court between their two faces, and colonnaded avenues to link the principal ones among them brought the city-form into a larger context than itself. It was to be admired from the outside as well as from within. The city was an incident along a highway, to be approached in a calculated manner, traversed grandly, and bridged decorously to the next incident.

The Persians had already anticipated regional planning in their concept of overland roads, especially the Royal Road from Susa to Sardis which served as the communication axis of their empire, but also in their system of horse-ridden relays with post stops along the way, the choice and placement of the district capitals, and the provision for game preserves and parks in the proximity of springs, lakes, and river waters. The Hellenistic realm was too fragmented for such comprehensive schemes. Nevertheless, landscaping and regional design

should figure in any environmental account of the age.

There is the story about the architect Dinokrates, for example, and the project he submitted to Alexander that proposed to shape Mount Athos into the figure of a man holding a fortified city in one hand and, in the other, a huge vase that would collect the mountain streams and pour them into the sea. We also know that the main extraurban sanctuaries were formally connected by large roads with their cities—Didyma with Miletus, for example, and the Asklepios complex we have analyzed above with the town of Kos. Moreover, the law concerning the office of town controller saw fit to regulate the width of country roads. There are also famous instances of planning ingenuity, like the causeway of the Heptastadion, which brought together Alexandria and Pharos Island, or the lighthouse from which the island derived its name, one of the seven wonders of the Greco-Roman world, which put Alexandria in the arc of the Mediterranean.

Closer at hand the tenets of Hellenistic design dictated how buildings might contribute visually to the principal avenues they fronted on. There were two parallel con-

cerns in this respect. Older buildings were suitably reclothed, and sometimes units of disparate scale and form were pulled together by a common colonnaded front. At the same time entrances to the new public buildings were made into events, with stately gates and forecourts leading in from the street.

A comparison of two plans of the Athenian agora, as it existed in about 400

Fig. 8.19 Priene (Turunçlar, Turkey), eastern gate of the agora, second century B.C.; reconstruction drawing.

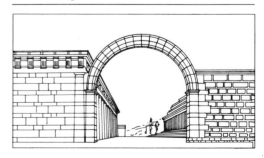

B.C. and again at the end of the first century B.C., demonstrates what Hellenistic design did to inherited patterns. (Fig. 7.15, 8.20) The bent stoa on the south side, yielding to the path of the Panathenaia as it headed toward the Akropolis, has now been straightened, and another stoa further north has pushed back the odd-shaped public space. This constriction was made up for by the removal of private houses and shops east of the *dromos* and the containment of this east side of the agora by a splendid two-aisled stoa, a gift of the Pergamene King Attalos II who had studied at the Athenian Academy in his youth. Before it, a speaking platform or *bema* was set up. On the west side a *metroon* or archive building was built next to the bouleuterion group, and a continuous colonnade masked irregularities of elevation and roofline. In front, across the street from this complex, stood the two-sided base for the statues of the *eponymoi,* the heroes after whom the ten Attic tribes were named. Finally, the two southern stoas were connected by an eastern building and enclosed a formal square which most probably served as a commercial agora, thus segregating this kind of activity from the agora proper, as Aristotle recommended.

The council hall of Miletus was the donation of King Antiochus IV and was built to the north of the Great Stoa between 175 and 164 B.C. (Fig. 8.21) It was of the theater type introduced at Athens in the late fifth century B.C.; but whereas the arrangement of the seats there had been facilitated by the rising ground of the hill to the west of the agora, at Miletus the theater form had to be built up on level ground. Externally, the building was organized in two registers. The lower was treated as a tall plain base. Above this the wall was divided into bays by an engaged order, Doric interspersed with some Ionic details; decorative shields filled the top of alternate bays except on the facade, looking east, where shield bays and bays perforated by windows were grouped in an intricate rhythm. This long rectangular hall on its masonry podium, with its two pediments and the surrounding engaged colonnade, resembled a temple, and in fact temples with the peristyle columns attached to the external cella walls, "pseudoperipteral" as they were called, had made

their appearance in the third century B.C. and would become a favored variant of Roman religious architecture.

But what is perhaps more important about the bouleuterion for the present discussion is that it was designed to occupy one side of a court lined with colonnades and entered on axis through a very ornate gate that held a porch of four Corinthian columns. In the middle of the court was a low and lavishly decorated tomb-shrine (or possibly an altar). The gate, the forecourt, and the attention paid to the design of the exterior surfaces of the council chamber are all Hellenistic gestures toward the decorous and monumental treatment of public spaces and the buildings chosen to grace them.

Fig. 8.20 Athens (Greece), the agora at the end of the first century B.C.; plan.

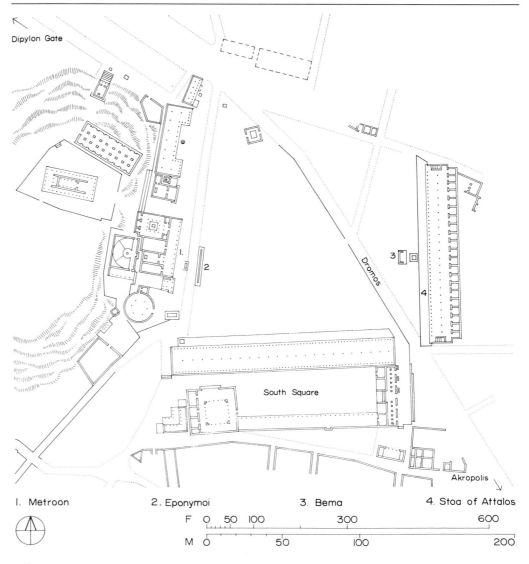

I. Metroon   2. Eponymoi   3. Bema   4. Stoa of Attalos

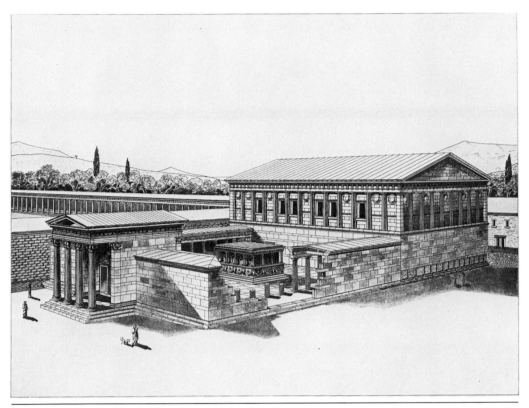

Fig. 8.21 Miletus (Turkey), bouleuterion or council hall north of the Great Agora, ca. 170 B.C.; reconstruction drawing.

perspective vista, and an abundance of luxuriant ornament, Hellenistic architecture approached the freedom of the pictorial arts. And nowhere was this freedom more cavalierly indulged than in theater design where painted scenes of buildings, built scenery, and the functional architecture of seating, stage, storage spaces, and the like coexisted within the same frame.

Although all of the Hellenistic scenery has of course disappeared, we get a fair idea of its virtuosity from wall paintings in wealthy houses where theatrical motifs were very popular. (Fig. 8.23) If the painters could slip into fantasy more easily than the limits of executed architecture would allow, it was obviously on the actual built world that this fantasy was based. Broken, hollow, segmental, and volute pediments; spirally wreathed columns; the mixing, miniaturizing, and attenuating of orders; arched architraves; arcades on columns; the inexhaustible variations of the engaged style; the reliance on landscape features and small pavilions; artificial bowers and grottoes; round *tholoi* in rectangular colonnaded

Fig. 8.22 Alexandria (Egypt), rock-cut Hellenistic tomb, late third century B.C.; interior view of model. (National Museum of the Gold Coast)

Building Types

Like the council hall, the temple, and the stoa, the standard list of buildings in Hellenistic cities was inherited from older Greece; the difference in the Hellenistic era was in the elaboration of each type. Fountains and well-houses were turned into urban showpieces and often worked into the general design of streets and public spaces. Baths, already familiar by the fifth century B.C., acquired the distinctive sequence of cold, tepid, and hot rooms which will characterize Roman baths. Plutocracy and monarchy gave fresh impetus to tombs of a size and lavishness not encountered in Classical times. The underground tombs of Macedonia were often domed structures with impressive funerary programs that included mural paintings and a wealth of precious objects. The tombs of Alexandria contained opulent rooms that imitated, albeit a little fancifully, contemporary domestic interiors. (Fig. 8.22) At Palmyra there were tower tombs of several storeys, with the vaulted lower storey opening to the exterior. And dynastic monuments of burial, like the Mausoleum, could be very grandiloquent indeed.

Perhaps no other Greek building received as much imaginative attention as did the theater. Hellenistic society loved spectacle. The chief preoccupation of its architects was with creating a world of grand display—in the streets, in the agoras, and in the temple precincts. Much of this effort was illusionist, that is, more concerned with surface appearance than structural integrity. In its reliance on highlighting, color,

courts—all these were devices that the painter of architectural scenery and the designer of architectural reality shared between them. (Fig. 8.24)

But beyond the elaboration of standard building types, there were demands for new buildings as well. Setting aside statued settings for choral performances and the like (and also special buildings like the lighthouse in Alexandria or the octagonal Tower of the Winds at Athens), the primary impetus for invention was athletic-educational or commercial.

The principal new building type in the first category included the *gymnasium* and other more specialized institutions like the wrestling school or *palaestra.* The gymnasium housed educational facilities, both of the body and mind. Every Greek or Hellenized city had one or more of these structures, which came to represent civic maturity. The type consisted essentially of a large open space lined with stoas, of which one might serve as the *xystos,* or covered running track. Cloakrooms, anointing rooms, classrooms including lecture halls, and baths usually occupied the units behind the colonnades or were loosely attached to this main core. (Fig. 8.25, nos. 5–9)

Flourishing trade sought its own architecture. For this and similar functions large covered halls were developed which dispensed with exterior colonnades and concentrated on usable interior space. Several examples are found on the island of Delos, an important trading post that became the center of the Aegean grain market when the Romans declared it a free port in 136 B.C.

The so-called Pythion seems to have been built in the third century B.C. to contain a warship commemorating some naval victory. (Fig. 8.26) It was a long narrow hall with a pitched roof, most of it devoted to the ship. A back porch was separated from this main space by two columns engaged to the walls and two others in the middle engaged to piers, which held on their inward sides sculptured capitals of kneeling bulls. They remind us of the bull capitals of Persepolis, but such interchanges between Hellenistic architecture and that of older native traditions were rare. Lindos may have learned from the precedent of Deir el-Bahri, and the main facade of Didyma with presentation window and two flanking doors

Fig. 8.23 Boscoreale (Italy), villa, room with wall paintings of the late first century B.C. (Metropolitan Museum of Art, New York)

may have been influenced by New Kingdom palace facades. But it seems that, despite Alexander's platform of cultural assimilation, the Greek conquerors chose to remain racially aloof, with their architecture pure.

Another Delian example, the so-called Hypostyle Hall, was a mercantile exchange (Fig. 8.27) It was a rectangular building entered from one of the long sides, where much of the wall had been opened up by a Doric colonnade. Internally, there were 44 columns arranged in two concentric rectangles that repeated the shape of the hall, each with a continuous wooden ar-

chitrave, as well as a row of columns along the middle line except for dead center. The eight columns that defined the central square carried a second storey of supports that formed an open lantern above the main roof. This is one of the few demonstrable cases of the Greek use of clerestory lighting. The building proves the limitations of the post-and-lintel system in the creation of large unobstructed interior spaces. This is an architectural task at which Roman technology will excel.

Delos is a prime site for the study of Hellenistic houses. (Fig. 8.28) With the exception of a house type that occurs at Priene where the megaron form reappears as the major room, the affluent Delian house is fairly typical for the age. Its chief element is a peristyle court with marble columns of equal height on all four sides. Sometimes there were two storeys, and in a variation called "Rhodian" the columns of one side of the peristyle would be taller than the rest. Often a cistern beneath this court collected water from the roof. Running water is absent; the latrine emptied into the public drains below street level.

Where these Hellenistic houses differ radically from their Classical forebears is in the richness of their appearance. In the interval, the distinction between public art and private austerity had fallen by the wayside. Fine mosaic floors of colored stones cut to shape replace the earlier, and rather rare, pavement of natural pebbles. Here the walls are stuccoed and painted to imitate marble incrustation, and on occasion there are architectural motifs and other devices drawn from the repertory of theater decoration. The so-called House of Masks displays mosaics with dramatic subjects. One shows a flute player on a rock and a dancing figure; another, Dionysos riding a panther. (Fig. 8.29) The plan incorporates an additional small peristyle that might have been the center of the women's part of the house. The precise function of the rooms is hard to identify, but Vitruvius, in his detailed description of the Hellenistic house, mentions the *oecus magnus* where the family weaving was done, the *andron* or dining room, a lecture room on the east, a picture gallery, a library, a garden with its own dining room, and guest rooms arranged to ensure privacy when it was desired.

Pergamon and Rome

We cannot talk of the Hellenistic world without referring to the Romans, whose attention turned to the kingdoms of Alexander as soon as the main rival in the west, Punic Carthage, had been contained. Rome was not an upstart state; nor was it unfamiliar with things Greek. A republic that had practiced self-rule for three centuries, it had long stood in the shadow of the Hellenized Etruscans and the Greek cities of Sicily and southern Italy. But the tables had been turned: Rome had come to control what it

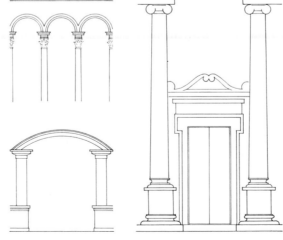

Fig. 8.24 Architectural motifs of the Hellenistic period, including: top left, the twisted column; top right, the engaged column and the broken pediment; bottom center, the arcade on columns and the segmental pediment.

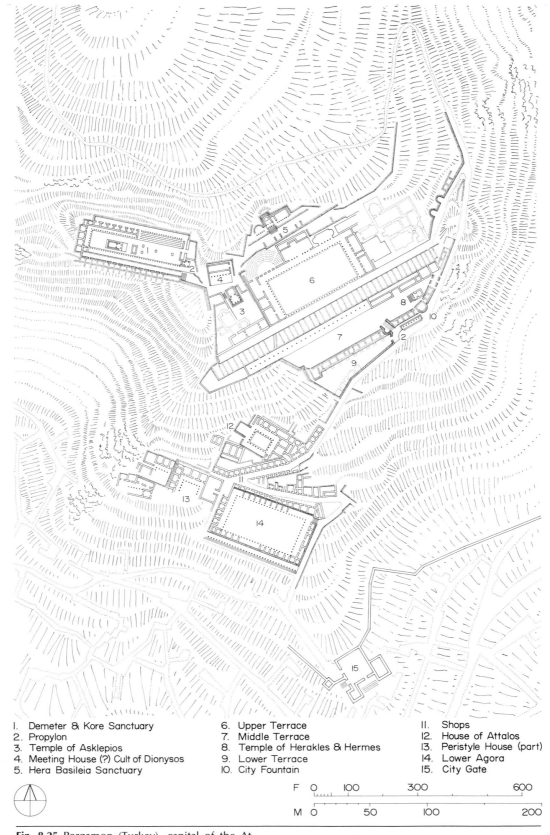

1. Demeter & Kore Sanctuary
2. Propylon
3. Temple of Asklepios
4. Meeting House (?) Cult of Dionysos
5. Hera Basileia Sanctuary

6. Upper Terrace
7. Middle Terrace
8. Temple of Herakles & Hermes
9. Lower Terrace
10. City Fountain

11. Shops
12. House of Attalos
13. Peristyle House (part)
14. Lower Agora
15. City Gate

F 0   100   300   600
M 0   50   100   200

Fig. 8.25 Pergamon (Turkey), capital of the Attalid dynasty, 282–133 B.C., the lower town; plan. Nos. 5–9 are parts of the gymnasium complex.

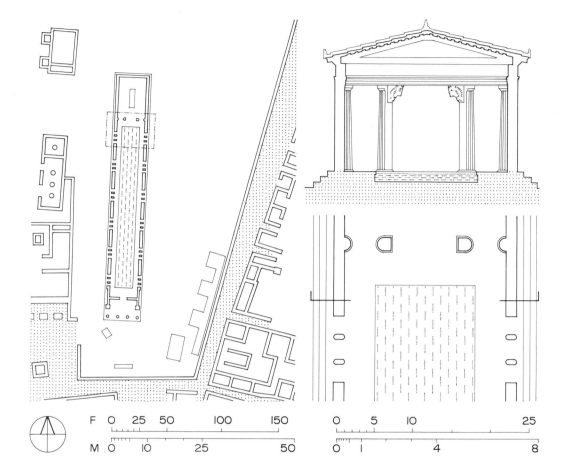

Fig. 8.26 Delos (Greece), Pythion or Sanctuary of the Bulls, exhibition hall for a war galley, probably 306–301 B.C.; ground plan and section.

F 0 25 50 100 150

M 0 10 25 50

0 5 10 25

0 1 4 8

Fig. 8.27 Delos, hypostyle hall, probably a merchants' exchange, ca. 210 B.C.; restored elevation of exterior.

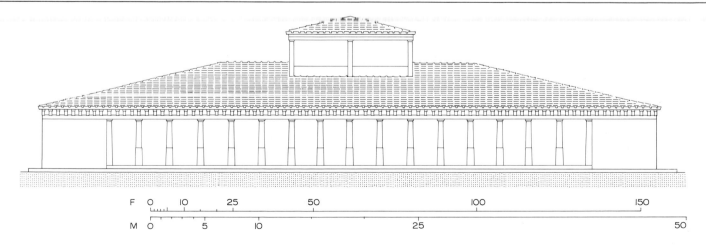

F 0 10 25 50 100 150

M 0 5 10 25 50

had been swayed by. And then, when it was sole master of its side of the Mediterranean, the powerful, austere Roman republic ventured East. In these ancient lands, it immediately clashed head on with two seductive and sinister forces: autocracy and luxury. The lands—Greece, Asia Minor, Syria, and Egypt—were subdued and annexed in less than two hundred years. But "the conquered Greeks," the Roman poet, Horace, confessed, "in turn made captives of the conquerors." Rome succumbed first to the opulence of Hellenistic cities, and in time it imported the other Trojan horse as well, the model of absolute rule for which grand architecture is the common advertisement.

It was an epic confrontation, might against culture. The Romans recognized the difference but refused, for the record at least, to feel inferior. Their goal as a nation lay elsewhere. In the words of Virgil,

Others, no doubt, will better mold the bronze
To the semblance of soft breathing, draw
    from marble.
The living countenance. . . . Remember,
    Roman,
To rule the people under law, to establish
The way of peace, to battle down the haughty,
To spare the meek. Our fine arts these, forever.

But proper Rome, bent on extolling piety and manliness, could not remain immune from the wiles of fashion. Gleaming marble-sheathed buildings, colonnaded avenues, the princely scale of terraces and porticoes, the glitter and sophistication of Hellenistic art—all this worked on their righteous will. First within the private world of the house and then publicly, *virtus*, the republican concept that combined stoic resolve and a sense of virtue, made room for *venustas*, the touch of beauty. And when the repudiation of that old Spartan age was an accomplished fact, it was felt as a poetic loss, an innocence to be vaguely yearned for.

Those were the days [wrote Juvenal] when the
    soldier,
Rough and tough, neither knew nor cared for the
    art of the Greeks
And Jupiter made out of clay,
Undefiled by gold, proved that he cherished his
    people.

The first and most loyal ally of Rome in the East was the Attalid kingdom of Perga-

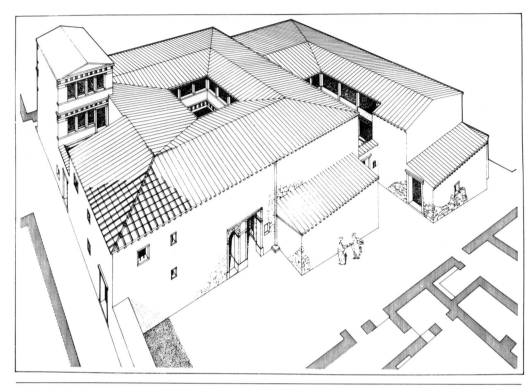

Fig. 8.28 Delos, House of the Comedians, ca. 125 B.C.; reconstruction view.

mon. One of the petty principalities that surfaced in the wake of Alexander's death, Pergamon prospered under an energetic, ambitious dynasty. While extending its authority over most of the Aegean coast, the Attalids turned Pergamon into a showcase of Hellenistic urbanism. With wealth derived from tribute, home industries like animal husbandry and textile manufacture, the pitch deposits of Mount Ida, and state-owned factories manned by slaves and serfs, the rough mountain stronghold was made, in but a hundred years, into a spectacularly terraced and appointed metropolis that exploited its difficult terrain with a flare unparalleled in the Greek world except perhaps in Periklean Athens. (Fig. 8.30)

And it was Athens that Pergamon had set out to emulate. Its home goddess was Athena; its prevalent order, the by now outmoded Doric. Athenian sculptors came to work on the Great Altar of Zeus, and a replica of Phidias' great statue of Athena for

the Parthenon stood in the famous library with its 200,000 volumes mostly of parchment mass-produced locally. In fact, in Pergamon an associative revival of the past was cast in a brash, raw brilliance of architectural and sculptural innovation.

To juxtapose the city-form of Rome and that of Pergamon should bring into focus the two cultural poles of the Mediterranean in the late second century B.C.

Rome was a matter-of-fact city of sensible buildings and sensible mores. Its religion was eclectic. The temples were Etruscan in form, made of mud-brick and timber, and decorated with sculptures of rather garishly painted terra-cotta. The city walls were built of local tufa, porous and dark but ruggedly appropriate for this pragmatic community of several hundred thousand people. (Fig. 8.31)

There had never been a master plan for Rome. The city came about through the merger of several hilltop settlements of

Fig. 8.29 Delos, House of Masks, second century B.C.; mosaic floor panel showing the god Dionysos astride a panther.

Fig. 8.30 Pergamon, view of the city from the west; model. (Staatliche Museen, Berlin)

183

Via Flaminia

Via Salaria

Via Nomentana

RIVER

Via Aurelia

Via Tiburtina

12

Via Tusculana

Via Latina

TIBER

Via Ostiensis

Via Appia

1. Capitoline   4. Caelian   7. Quirinal   10. Circus Maximus
2. Palatine   5. Esquiline   8. Arx   11. Port
3. Aventine   6. Viminal   9. Forum   12. Walls

Mile   0   0.5   1.0   2.0   2.5
Kilometer   0   0.5   1.0   2.0   3.0   4.0

Fig. 8.31 Map: Rome, topography and general layout of the city in the Republican period. The walls shown are of the fourth century B.C.

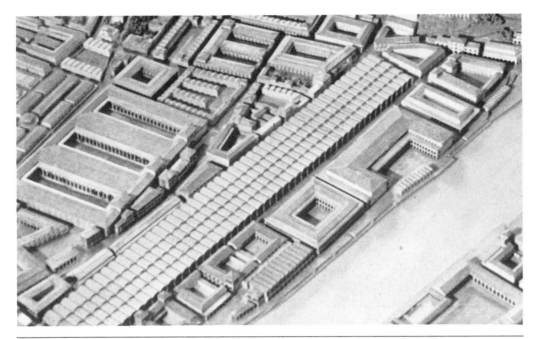

Fig. 8.32 Rome, the Porticus Aemilia, second century B.C.; detail of a model of ancient Rome showing the port area at the foot of the Aven- tine Hill (no. 3 on Fig. 8.31). (Museo della civiltà romana, Rome)

shepherds and farmers, with the valley in between them serving as the common center of government, the Forum. There stood a number of temples; two basilicas or multipurpose assembly halls where law could be administered; and a small, unpretentious brick building for the Senate, the principal arm of republican government. On a rock that towered on the west was the *arx*, or akropolis, with the temple to the Roman trinity: Jupiter Optimus, his wife Juno, and Minerva who was the double of Athena as the others were of Zeus and Hera. On the south side, the Palatine hill was dotted with the houses of the wealthy, each looking inward upon its atrium. In the valley between the Palatine and another hill, the Aventine, lay the Circus Maximus, a course for chariot races.

The port facilities gathered in the strip of alluvial bank between the Aventine and the Tiber. (Fig. 8.32) The grain, oil, and wine from the Roman possessions arrived at the harbor town of Ostia and were then trans- ported on river boats to warehouses at the port. For such utilitarian buildings the Romans employed a new artificial material called concrete, a viscous mixture of sand, lime, and water toughened by an aggregate of rubble. It was poured on wooden formwork and allowed to cure. The shapes so produced were nearly monolithic and fireproof, if inelegant. In the meantime, in the popular quarters of the congested city, people lived in tall tenements of half timber construction, five to six storeys high and prone to raging fires.

Pergamon was a young creation. It was a calculated work of urban design and its aim was to dazzle. All public buildings were framed by porticoes and set on platforms that locked into one another. The building materials were marble and the handsome volcanic andesite quarried locally. The theater in the upper part of town was the only urban element to accept the precipitous land just as it was. The rest was all contrived.

The site of Pergamon is a narrow mountain ridge encircled by river tributaries and backed to the north by the long range of the Madras chain. (Fig. 8.33) The main prospect is toward the south where at the foot of the ridge we see the flatland of the later town, the cemeteries, and, across the valley of the Selinos, a sanctuary of the healer god Asklepios at ease with the calm of the earth as at Kos. The Hellenistic city started at the summit and the easy south slope, some three hundred meters (1,000 feet) above sea level, and spread out through the years to the lower reaches of the west slope and the plain of the Kaikos. By then the city was Roman.

The development of Pergamon should be seen as a downward cascade from the summit where the original stronghold had been in the late fourth century and where the Attalid palaces were later to be built. (Fig. 8.34) On a shelf to the north, just below the summit and totally inaccessible from without, arsenals and storehouses found their proper place. On the next natural level south of the summit, on an emphatic outcrop of rock, the temple to Athena perched early on. The theater was cradled in the steep cavity of the western precipice. This is where the town ended in the first half of the third century, except for a sanctuary of Demeter on a natural terrace that briefly stopped the fall of land southward, a short distance above the riverbeds.

It was this extramural level that occupied Attalos I (241–197 B.C.) and his wife Apollonia. A 90-meter (300-foot) long stoa along the south side of the Demeter precinct at once retained and monumentalized the land shelf and supplied a prototype for all the later interventions that gave Pergamon its matchless appearance. The principles were few and apposite. The architecture was not to violate natural contours but to fortify their inherent design. Terracing was not to be achieved by brutish embankments that offered blank surfaces to the approaching visitor. While the inner face of the stoa at the top of the retaining work opened up its colonnade in the direction of the principal building, the outer face would be similarly cadenced toward the stunning prospects of the south; and below this level an underground gallery lit by windows would exploit the fall of the ground, resting on a

Fig. 8.33 Pergamon; site plan showing the relation of the Attalid city to the modern town of Bergama. The Serapeion (no. 4) is a Roman re- building of the sanctuary in the second century A.D.

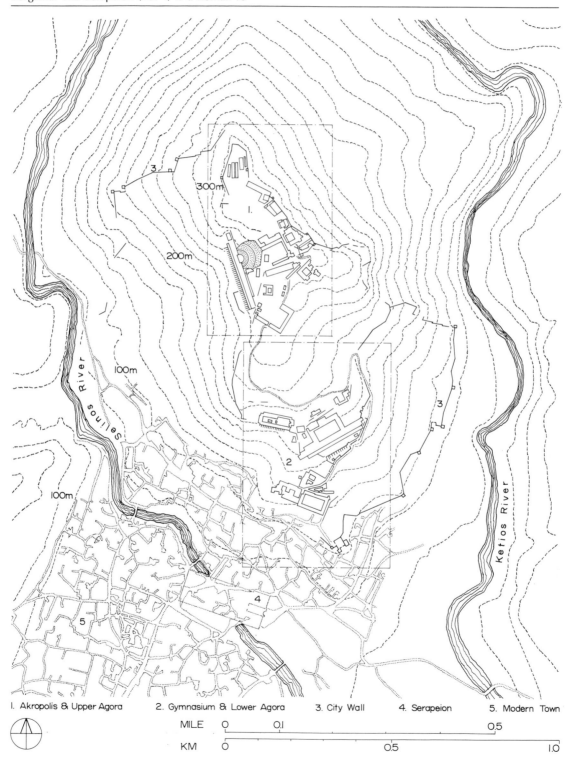

1. Akropolis & Upper Agora   2. Gymnasium & Lower Agora   3. City Wall   4. Serapeion   5. Modern Town

MILE   0   0.1   0.5

KM   0   0.5   1.0

basement level of more mundane utility. The vertical buttresses that reinforced the embankment were to be shaped and spaced purposely in order to articulate the upward rise of the terrain and form panels that might contain monumental sculpture, fountains, and the like. Finally, the roof of this multistoried structure would be kept low enough so that it would not block the view from the stoa on the far side of the same terrace.

This preliminary solution for the Demeter sanctuary sparked the program of Eumenes II (197–159 B.C.) during whose long reign and that of his successor Attalos II (159–138 B.C.), patron of the eastern stoa of the Athenian agora, the city was spectacularly transformed. A gymnasium complex to the east of the Demeter precinct and a lower agora close by indicate the spread of the city at this date. In the upper city, the original agora was encased by stoas, as was the temple of Athena. Between this agora and the temple to Athena, the Great Altar of Zeus and All the Gods sat on its own vast terrace, while at the level above the sanctuary of Athena and its library annex an additional terrace held a cult of now unknown identity, which was buried under the later temple to the Roman Emperor Trajan. This great fan of terraces and buildings was riveted by the theater, and a paved esplanade, which wended its way uphill in sharp bends to follow the natural configuration, linked the lower town with the akropolis.

The esplanade started at the main city gate in the latest ring of walls which hugged the southeastern skirt of the ridge. It was the point toward which the thoroughfares of the Kaikos Valley led. Just within was the lower agora. Then the road passed through rows of shops and skirted the triple terrace of the gymnasium. Access to the intermediate terrace could be gained by means of vaulted stairs to the west of a beautiful fountain at

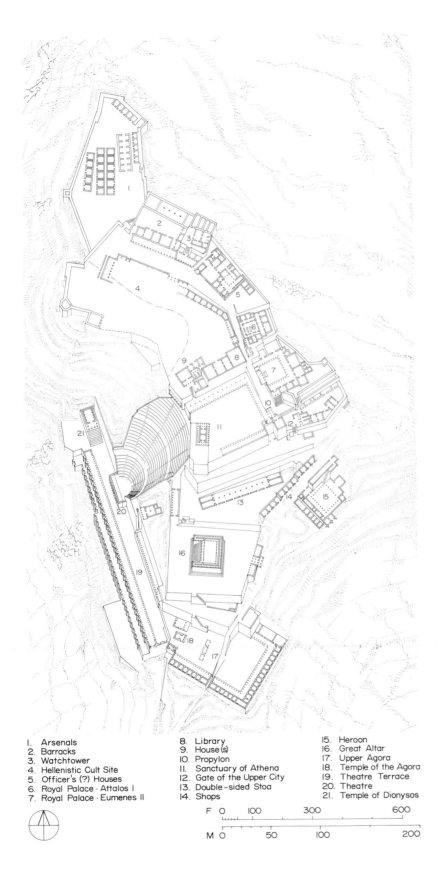

1. Arsenals
2. Barracks
3. Watchtower
4. Hellenistic Cult Site
5. Officer's (?) Houses
6. Royal Palace · Attalos I
7. Royal Palace · Eumenes II
8. Library
9. House(s)
10. Propylon
11. Sanctuary of Athena
12. Gate of the Upper City
13. Double-sided Stoa
14. Shops
15. Heroon
16. Great Altar
17. Upper Agora
18. Temple of the Agora
19. Theatre Terrace
20. Theatre
21. Temple of Dionysos

F 0   100   300   600

M 0   50   100   200

Fig. 8.34 Pergamon, upper town in the second century B.C.; plan. The Romans raised a large temple in honor of Emperor Trajan over the Hellenistic cult site indicated as no. 4.

Fig. 8.35 Pergamon, the Great Altar of Zeus and All the Gods (no. 16 on Fig. 8.34), first half of the second century B.C.; as reconstructed in the Staatliche Museen, Berlin.

Fig. 8.36 Pergamon, Great Altar; detail of the major frieze showing the battle between the Greek gods and the race of giants who challenged them. The towering figure to the left is Zeus. (Staatliche Museen, Berlin)

the tip of the complex, from which the road swung out in a broad loop that headed toward the upper town. The three levels of the gymnasium widened as they rose, and the substructures of each were diversely treated. There were niches destined for statues between the lower and intermediate terraces, and a covered racetrack lodged in the embankment between this terrace and the topmost. As for the high rock-spur that loomed over the complex, it was carved into rooms associated with the program of the gymnasium. At the northwestern point of this richly planned institution, with its baths, palaestrae, and odeion, one found the passage to the long axis of the Demeter sanctuary.

The road, after running past the north edge of the gymnasium and the Demeter sanctuary, entered a residential area that has not as yet been excavated. It crossed the upper agora and then cut obliquely along the east side of the terrace of the Great Altar, and so made its way to the akropolis.

The Great Altar was the showpiece of the royal city and the nub of its triumphal message. (Fig. 8.35) It introduced the sanctuaries that fanned out around the top of the theater, and in a sense served as the altar of them all. The practice of large altars overscaled in relation to their temples and smothered by sculpture was a Hellenistic novelty. At Pergamon the altar was placed in an inner court surrounded by columns and approached from the west by a flight of stairs. The exterior surfaces carried a mighty frieze that represented the god's battle against the giants. (Fig. 8.36) It was an allusion to the victory of Attalos I over the Gauls, Celtic nomads of the interior, and renewed the old duality of Greek and barbarian that had been the main theme of the Classical polis. Within the court a frieze in a different mood, quieter and more delicate, celebrated the legitimacy of the Attalid dynasty through the retelling of the story of Telephos, son of Herakles, from whom the Pergamene kings claimed descent.

The last stretch of the esplanade runs inside the akropolis, between the temples of the gods to the left and the palaces of the kings to the right. (Fig. 8.33) It should be a strong statement, but the meaning of this magnificent urban design is equivocal, just as the culture itself is confused. Pergamon is synthetic, temporary, wistfully revivalist. It speaks with a new language but falls back on old truths. The king's palace is nothing more than a rich version of the peristyle house, yet it sits on the mountain summit like the residence of a Mycenaean prince. The agora is there, but it is the king's personal triumphs that the public art commemorates, his power that the arsenals and barracks shield. This is a royal and Greek city caught in the tail-end nostalgia of a long, legendary era. It is the swan song of Hellenism—that force which toppled empires and was swallowed in the crash. There is something theatrical in the bequest of Pergamon to Rome by the last of the Attalids in 133 B.C., a concluding gesture. Not much is built in the Hellenistic realm in the remaining century of its token existence as Greek culture, and what is built is mostly the result of foreign needs. Delos gets a new agora for its Italian colony, a guild hall for Syrian merchants and shipowners who call themselves the Poseidoniasts of Berytus, and a Jewish synagogue. When the Christian era dawns, the great Greek cities of the East relax in the lulling embrace of the *pax romana*.

Further Reading

T. Fyfe, *Hellenistic Architecture* (Cambridge, England: Cambridge University Press, 1936).

E. V. Hansen, *The Attalids of Pergamon* (Ithaca: Cornell University Press, 1971).

A. W. Lawrence, *Greek Architecture* (Harmondsworth and Baltimore: Penguin, 1957).

M. Lyttelton, *Baroque Architecture in Classical Antiquity* (London: Thames and Hudson, 1974).

J. Onians, *Art and Thought in the Hellenistic Age* (London: Thames and Hudson, 1979).

F. E. Peters, *The Harvest of Hellenism* (New York: Simon and Schuster, 1971).

W. W. Tarn, *Hellenistic Civilization* (Cambridge, England: Cambridge University Press, 1923).

T. B. L. Webster, *The Art of Greece; the Age of Hellenism* (New York: Greystone Press, 1967).

Rome, basilica of Maxentius, A.D. 307–312, and the Colosseum, A.D. 72–80.

9

ROME: *Caput Mundi*

Early Roman Architecture

To hear her later advocates tell it, Rome had known from the start that she was destined for great things. The site, a healthy spot amid infested land, was chosen by the founder, Romulus, far enough away from sea to escape invasion, and yet close enough to reap the benefits of trade: that was Cicero's opinion. To Vitruvius, Italy was ideally situated between north and south, just as Jupiter lay between Mars, which is very hot, and Saturn, which is very cold. Rome, halfway down the Italian peninsula, was set there by divine intelligence "in order that she might acquire the right to rule the world." And Livy recalled how, during the building on the Capitoline of the first Roman temple, a human head was unearthed in the fountain ditch, "with all the features in perfect condition. There could be no doubt that the discovery meant that this place would be at the head of the empire and the world."

These rationalizations long after the fact have tended to obscure the truth about the unspectacular rise of Romulus' city and the considerable element of political luck involved in her subjection of the Italian peoples around her after a period of being subject herself to one among them, the Etruscans. In fact, it was not until the terrible surprise of being sacked by western Gauls in 390 B.C., during her modest post-Etruscan existence, that Rome woke to the call of expansionism and the promise of her favored position at the confluence of the natural avenues of the peninsula, along-

side the easy crossing of the only island in the Tiber. (Fig. 9.1)

Unlike Mediterranean rivers in general, the Tiber—the longest Italian river after the Po—has a stable delta that could be developed as a port. This fact, and the clear passage upriver until the island for transport boats of respectable tonnage, secured Rome's overseas reach. Local traffic was not itself impracticable in the more turbulent upper stretch of the Tiber, and the valleys opened up convenient land routes through the Apennines. With the proper motivation and able military leadership, Rome started to build these assets into a powerful state. A military colony, Ostia, was planted at the river mouth in the late fourth century, the valleys were turned into paved highways beginning with the Via Appia which ran from Capua to Brindisi like a great peninsular spine, and the methodical conquest and colonization of Italy began.

The Sources

At the time, alongside a number of small cultural groups like the Samnites, Ligurians, and the Oscans, the two dominant powers on the Italian horizon were the Etruscans to the north and the Greek cities of southern Italy and Sicily. To account for early Rome, however, in terms of a composite of Etruscan and Greek influence is to oversimplify matters. Etruria, by the time it came to affect the destiny of a fledgling Rome, had already been Hellenized to an

appreciable degree. And there were in Roman environmental thinking native Italic elements (for example, the atrium house) rooted in areas other than Etruria. Pompeii, to many of us the quintessential Roman town, was in fact an Oscan foundation with a long interval of Samnite domination.

Rome's Italic character showed in her irregular city-form that was born, like that of many other towns of early Italy, out of topographical dictates and ancient rituals of town planning. This was the Italy of the eighth century, before the sophisticated urbanism of the Greek colonists in the south had become known in the rest of the peninsula. The Etruscans were the first to avail themselves of the land-surveying techniques of the Greek immigrants in their own efforts to colonize. Rome in her turn adopted orthogonal planning in the new military outposts that secured her conquests and in the expansion of older towns that came under her jurisdiction. Roman centuriation—the division of the territory around a town into great squares measuring 728 meters (2,400 feet) per side, which were known as centuries (*centuriae*) because they were meant to contain 100 small landholdings—was itself inspired by Greek practice. (Fig. 9.2)

The Romans appropriated the geometrical schemes of Greek and Etruscan colonies in various ways. One way was the Roman practice of locating new towns at the meeting point of the main north-south and east-west cross-axes (known as the *cardo* and *decumanus*, respectively), with which centuriation began. The practice of emphasizing this crossing by placing public buildings such as the forum-basilica complex there, was another. Also, the Romans preferred square city blocks over the elongated ones in Greek towns, and Roman town planning was influenced by the pattern of their army encampments, or *castra*, and contributed to them—which is not surprising considering the military nature of early Roman colonies.

But perhaps more important than a geometric layout is the repertory of institutional architecture that distinguishes Roman culture, from its first expansionist phase after the Gallic sack, to the creation of the vast Mediterranean empire under Augustus about the time of Christ, and the subsequent three centuries of its dominion. Architecture was a civilizing mission and a sure means of establishing Roman visibility. In established lands with their own architectural traditions, it was crucial to stamp the Roman seal on the cityscapes through recognizable building types. Occupation armies were actively engaged in the construction of civil buildings. Military architect-engineers became increasingly important under the empire, and the precise assembling of huge and complicated structures like amphitheaters out of thousands of standard units extended the strict discipline of the Roman legions to the construction site. The state became involved in every aspect of construction. It had a monopoly on natural materials like marble, tufa, travertine, and their quarrying, and it manufactured its own bricks in state kilns. Transportation, storage, and manpower were all centrally coordinated. Special issues of coins carried representations of major new buildings, commemorating them as significant public events.

Pure invention is rare in architecture, and originality more commonly manifests itself in the purposeful adjustment of traditional forms. Romans were selective in their borrowings and adapted everything to new specifications. In its own homeland Roman architecture developed techniques of construction and composition that were unmistakably its own. At their apogee, the

Fig. 9.1 Map: Rome and its ports. Right, the relationship of the early city to the Tiber and the river's course to the Tyrrhenian Sea; left, the organization of the Tiber mouth by the second century A.D., with the harbor city of Ostia and the major port facilities to the north along an artificial channel.

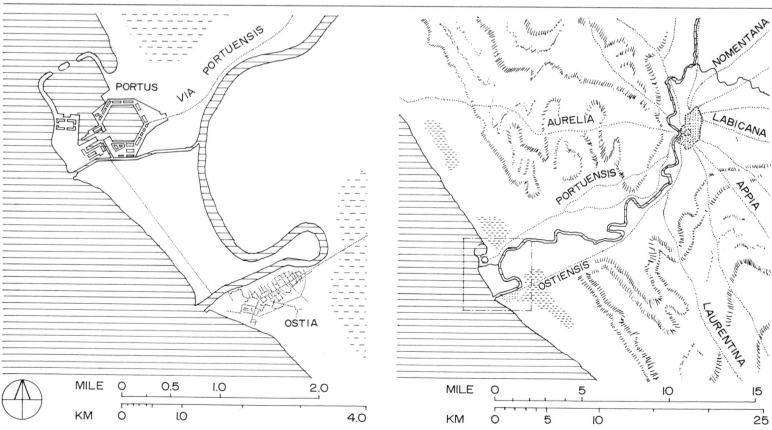

192

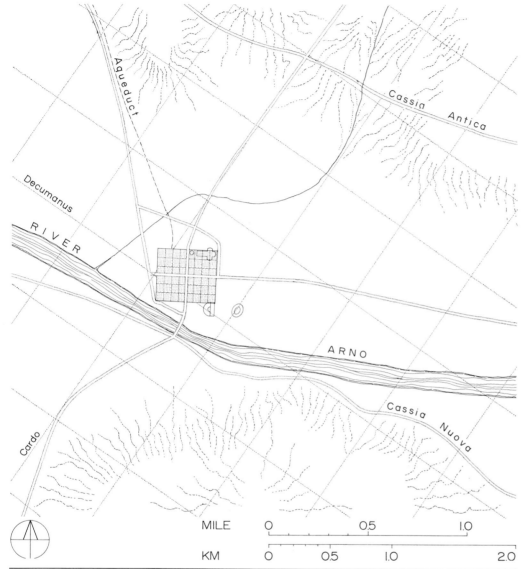

Fig. 9.2 Map: The Roman colony of Florentia (later Florence, Italy) founded in 59 B.C., shown in relation to the ancient highways and the centuriation grid of the territory. The town is oriented toward the four cardinal points; the centuriation is generated by the river course and the land contours. The amphitheater indicated to the southeast of the town dates from about A.D. 130. The cathedral and baptistery at the northeast corner are included to make comparison with the medieval city (Fig. 16.2) easier.

empire and its architecture commanded a uniform vision everywhere, including the traditional Greek territories in the East, even though each province interpreted this imperial program in accordance with local practices.

The Primacy of the Curve
Whatever their Italian origin might have been, the standard buildings of early Roman towns—the forum, the temple, the basilica, and the single-family dwelling—were all aggrandized and enriched by the influence of the Hellenistic East. Still, each one of these conventional trabeated structures bears the Roman stamp; and more to the point is the fact that the true unit of Roman architecture is not the post-and-lintel bay, the colonnade and its stone trabeation, but the arch.

The Romans were preoccupied with the curve—in plan, in elevation, and in the spatial containment of rooms. The premise of the arch is that it enslaves space. Its course is circular and therefore inevitable. In a colonnade the eye, caught anywhere along the length of a column, has the option of going up or down, and at the juncture with the architrave, to continue toward the left or the right. (Fig. 8.27) Each unit of an arcade, however, folds back upon itself; the eye, caught along its path, is inexorably grounded. A series of these units proceeds across space in leaps as if inhaling and exhaling, conquering distances in a way that is alien to the slower and more methodical march of columns. The arch swoops across a river to bridge it, or rises in tiers across a valley to level a tossed landscape at the service of a crossing road or the channel of an aqueduct. (Fig. 9.3) Piled up along the edges of a natural slope, the arch will supply the preparatory formwork for a level platform that extends the usable space at the top.

But the ultimate expression of the arcuated system is in three dimensions, in the encapsulation of interior space. (Fig. 9.4) Extended outward in a straight line, the arch produces a barrel (or tunnel) vault, that is, a curved ceiling that is built on two parallel walls and bridges the rectilinear lower space they define. The intersection of two barrel vaults yields a groin or cross-vault, with four half-cylinders meeting at right angles along ridges called groins. Spun the full 360 degrees, the arch will define a dome.

The word vault comes from the Latin *volvere*, which means to turn about, to roll. Vaulted spaces of any shape are fundamentally different from rectilinear spaces. Flat-roofed rooms are spatially inert. (Fig. 7.26, 8.14) Within their boxlike frame the users have an unchanging relationship to the height of the space wherever they might stand on the pavement. The right angle describes diagrammatically the uncomplicated relationship of load and support. In vaulted spaces an ambiguity is introduced into this relationship because of the tangency of the curved ceiling to the vertical dimension of the walls. (Fig. 9.30b) Since the center of the ceiling stands higher than the periphery, it is as if we are drawn to this invisible central line (or central point in the case of the dome). The space is thus active, reaching upward against the force of gravity. If the image of trabeated architecture in human terms is the caryatid, the standing figure carrying the load of the superstructure on her head, human reach seems to be the proper analogy for vaulted architecture. (Figs. 7.28, 9.5)

Several times in the past we have encountered preliminary experiments with the arch and the vault. The effect of curved ceilings had been achieved in Neolithic tombs and in Bronze Age architecture by means of corbelling. (Figs. 2.17, 5.4) The true arch—that is, one with a semicircular profile—was known in Mesopotamia but, made of brick, it was commonly wedded to a thicker wall that supported it. The voussoir arch, used both by Greeks and Etruscans, supports itself, and so does the true masonry vault, by being built of suitably curved, ashlar units that start the springing from both sides (or all around, in the case of the dome) and span toward the middle where they are locked into place by central keystones. Utilitarian in intention for the most part, the voussoir arch was sometimes exploited for its aesthetic possibilities, as in the agora entrance to Priene or Etruscan city gates. (Figs. 6.19, 8.19) The canopy of the dome probably always carried symbolic connotations in burial architecture, be it in the passage graves of Neolithic Europe, Mycenaean tholos tombs, or the vaulted chambers of Hellenistic cemeteries. (Figs. 2.17, 5.18)

Roman practice stands out in several ways. Vaulting and the arch form are generally pervasive by the first century B.C., instead of being the rare exception. We see them early in a number of building types—shops, warehouses, baths—as well as in the substructures of terraced buildings. The technique of stone- or brick-faced concrete makes vaults single-shelled, comparatively light, and more efficient to build. Moreover, the serial or contiguous ar-

Fig. 9.3 Nîmes (France), Pont du Gard; Roman aqueduct over the Gardon River, late first century B.C.

rangement of vaulted rooms can provide an interesting variety of spaces, as well as mutual buttressing. The warehouse of the Porticus Aemilia in the urban port facilities of Rome, at the foot of the Aventine, has rooms organized in parallel, barrel-vaulted defiles that rise in three levels to introduce clerestory lighting. (Fig. 8.32) In the forum baths of Pompeii, barrel-vaulted shops line the street on the west and south sides of the block, while the bathing establishment proper includes a domed cold room as well as a barrel-vaulted hot room that has a curved end roofed by a semidome. (Fig. 9.17)

Components of a Roman Town: Pompeii

Two famous cities, Pompeii and Rome, looked at in some detail should give us a basic understanding of the early phase of Roman architecture and urbanism and the

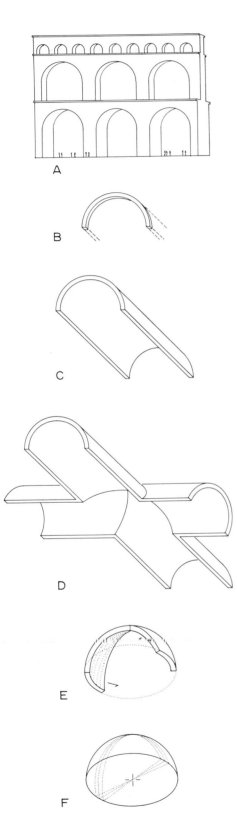

heights they attained in the century or so after the founding of the empire.

Pompeii was a small, comparatively insignificant town with never more than 20,000 inhabitants. Its burial in A.D. 79 under the effusions of Vesuvius preserved its structure intact at a moment in its life before the great changes the empire wrought in cities throughout the Mediterranean had a chance to take hold. As a Romanized town with a distinctive early history of its own, Pompeii also allows us to review the specific qualities that Rome imparted to older communities with some urban sophistication. It is at Pompeii that we meet with the earliest surviving examples of standard Roman building types such as the basilica and the amphitheater, and it is here that excavations have uncovered the most extensive picture of residential patterns in Roman Italy during this time.

This early phase is followed in Rome itself by the magnificent programs of the first emperors who undertook to make of their capital, once a republican city, the paradigmatic setting of a strong and dazzling majesty in the Eastern mold. Here we can return, for the conclusion of this chapter, to look at the theaters in this time of majesty: the imperial residence on the Palatine, the interlocked series of forums created by succeeding emperors in the thick of town, and the places of popular diversion like the imperial baths and the Colosseum.

A General Look

Pompeii sits on an isolated volcanic plateau overlooking the mouth of the river Sarno, a short distance south of Naples—the original Greek colony of Neapolis. (Fig. 9.6) It was always a port town. It served lo-

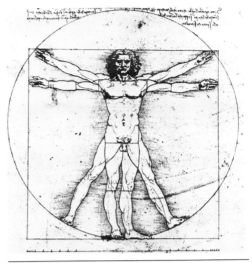

Fig. 9.5 Leonardo da Vinci, *The Vitruvian Man*, ca. 1490. (Accademia, Venice, Italy) This is Leonardo's interpretation of a famous passage in Vitruvius (Book III, chapter 1) which describes how a well-built man, with extended arms and legs, will fit exactly into those most perfect of geometrical figures—the circle and the square.

Fig. 9.4 The arch and its three-dimensional extension into vault forms; structural diagrams. The arch, within a single plane, can be stacked up into several storeys (**A**). Stretched out in one dimension, as shown in (**B**), the arch yields a barrel vault (**C**), which can intersect with another barrel vault to produce a groin vault (**D**). Rotated 360 degrees, as shown in (**E**), the arch produces a spherical dome (**F**).

cal commerce between the communities upriver and the sea traffic of the Bay of Naples; Greeks and Etruscans both used it as their trans-shipment center. Its other base was agriculture, especially vineyards and the cultivation of olives. But Pompeii's beautiful, verdant location made of it, under the Romans, also something of a summering place for the rich.

The walls enclosed about 9 hectares (23 acres) between volcano and sea, in the fertile plain of Campania which stretches back to the Apennine range. The periphery was farmland—small plantations of resident farmers and *villae rusticae* or summer estates of well-to-do citizens with a farm attached. Closer in, just outside the gates, elegant *villae urbanae*, intended primarily for a life of leisure, shared the edges of the highways with cemeteries. At the northern, Vesuvius gate a reservoir collected the waters brought in by an aqueduct from the inland hills. It stood on high ground to ensure adequate pressure and distributed the water by means of lead pipes to the public fountains, the two public baths, and, when the water level was high enough, to some private houses. Just within two of the city gates, visitors could check into quality hotels with ample accommodations, including dining rooms, stables, and parking sheds for wagons.

The main north-south avenue ran between the Vesuvius gate and that called Stabian. It was obliquely intersected by the main east-west avenue (now named Via dell'Abbondanza) which passed through the forum area and headed southwest beyond the walls, toward the Bay. These and all other streets were paved with the easily procurable, dark lava stone. (Fig. 9.7) They had raised sidewalks and stepping stones for pedestrians who wished to cross the streets without soiling their feet in the ever-present refuse piles and overflowed water from the fountains intended to flush the streets. Wheeled traffic, which has left deep ruts in the pavement, was mostly wagons and carts high enough to clear these stones.

The public buildings were grouped in three areas. (Fig. 9.8) The forum and its dependencies in the southwest corner of the city formed the civic and religious center. The baths were close by, one just across the street from the north end of the forum, the other at the crossing of the two main avenues. South of this crossing, just within the city wall, was an entertainment nucleus that consisted of a theater, an odeum, a small palaestra, and sanctuaries to exotic gods. A triangular colonnaded space adjacent to this group contained the oldest temple in the city, which can be dated to the mid-sixth century B.C. Finally, the southeast corner of the city was taken up by the amphitheater and a large palaestra to the west of it. The rest was mostly housing, with inns, fast-food places, fulleries (cloth finishing was an important industry), and brothels sprinkled here and there in the residential fabric.

A quarter of tight, small blocks in the southwest had an irregular configuration. This was the oldest Oscan settlement that seems to have consisted of some 2,000 inhabitants clustered around the forum, then an informal open space. The akropolis was to the east where the Doric temple took advantage of the rise to stand out against the sky, and much later a theater was lodged in the southern slope in the common Greek

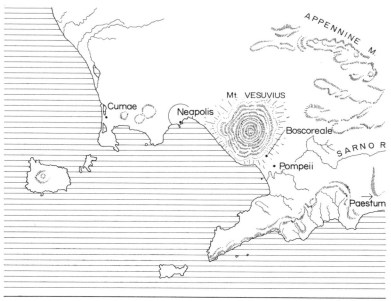

Fig. 9.6 Map: Campania, the district around Naples (ancient Neapolis), with Greek and Roman sites.

Fig. 9.7 Pompeii (Italy); a main intersection (Nola and Stabia streets), with stepping stones.

manner. Beginning in the late fifth century, the inhabited zone was enlarged in several stages, now availing itself of the orderly rectilinear urbanism of Greek neighbors like Neapolis. Each successive addition, however, had its own orientation and block size, so that the overall effect is far from a uniform grid.

The final expansion phase came under the Romans, first in the latter part of the second century B.C. and then after 80 B.C. when Sulla made of Pompeii a colony for veterans of his Eastern campaigns. To this episode belong the final shape of the forum, the remodeling of the baths and of the theater complex, and the building of the amphitheater.

The Doric temple and the original theater were really pure Greek, and the lining of the forum with two-storey colonnades sometime in the second century B.C. represents familiarity with contemporary Hellenistic urban design. The temple of Jupiter on the forum is Italic in its overall disposition, or more particularly Etruscan, but later remodelings gave it a columnar order and decorative veneer inspired by the example of the Hellenistic East. In fact Pompeii, for the greater part of its history, was an architectural crossroads between the Italic north and the Greek south, constantly updating its image with direct infusions from one sphere or the other and with conventions brought in as already hybrid forms.

The Houses
House patterns are a good instance. The earliest, Italic scheme is the single-storey family *domus*—an inward-looking, cool, and quiet house tightly organized around a core space called the *atrium*. (Fig. 9.9) Usually sky-lit, with a corresponding catch basin sunk in the pavement and hooked up to a cistern below, this central room held the shrine of the house gods (*lararium*) and portrait busts of the owner and his ancestors. An entrance vestibule, the atrium, and a main room called the *tablinum* which was open to a back garden were all arranged in a straight line. This axis of alternately light and dark spaces was flanked by symmetrically arranged rooms. The contrast with the looser organization of the Greek house is obvious. (Fig. 7.4) Here we have our first

Fig. 9.8 Pompeii, forum; aerial view. The forum, along with the rest of the city, was destroyed by an eruption of Vesuvius in A.D. 79. The remains of the basilica (see Fig. 9.14) can be seen in the lower left; those of the temple of Apollo are just above the basilica, to the left of the Forum. At the north end of the Forum is the temple of Jupiter, and to the right of it, at the extreme upper right-hand corner, the *macellum*.

1. Entrance
2. Atrium
3. Peristyle
4. Tablinum
5. Garden
6. Shop
7. Cistern

A

B

F 0 10   50   100   300

M 0   10   25   50   100

Fig. 9.9 Pompeii, residential neighborhood northwest of the Forum; plan. Two houses are highlighted: upper left, the House of Sallust, with a section through it shown at (**A**); and, lower left, the House of Pansa, with its section at (**B**). The House of Sallust dates from the pre-Roman phase of the city, in the third century B.C. The House of Pansa, occupying an entire city block, added a peristyle to the original pre-Roman nucleus sometime in the second century B.C.; the market garden at the back, with grapevines, is unusually large for an urban house.

Fig. 9.10a Pompeii, House of Menander, late first century B.C.; interior, looking through the atrium to the peristyle garden at the back.

Fig. 9.10b Pompeii, wall paintings from the House of Ara Maxima, ca. A.D. 70; detail.

indication of two insistent Roman proclivities: a feeling for inwardness and that highly regimented composition that distinguishes Roman layouts from Greek or Hellenistic ones even at their most formal.

When the idea of the peristyle, learned from the wealthy houses of Hellenistic cities, was assimilated in the Pompeiian domus, it was simply added onto the central axis beyond the tablinum. (Fig. 9.10) The catch basin of the atrium was now often marked by four corner columns, and the peristyle also sported columns of Hellenistic inspiration, usually Doric or Ionic. But rather than being paved in the Greek manner, the peristyle absorbed the function of the back kitchen garden, planned formally and with a fountain in the middle. This colorful oasis in the depth of the house would have been evident right from the moment of entering. Again, a peculiarly un-Greek twist is this bringing of nature indoors. For Greeks, nature was there and built things placed themselves in its folds with reverence or, later, dramatic verve.

The practice of stuccoing and painting the walls in imitation of marble incrustation or architectural frames with small figurative scenes was probably derived from Hellenistic mansions. But at Pompeii these painted interiors were splendidly elaborate. The blank walls were covered with architectural fantasies that recall Hellenistic theater sets. Within this simulated depth were placed large mythological subjects, derived from the East but duly Italianized, small daily vignettes, friezes of miniature figures, sacred landscapes, and plain open sky, so that the tight dim ambience of the rooms dissolves into magic panoramas of inhabited nature. Ceiling beams were also painted, gilded, or even inlaid with ivory. The floors were paved in stone or fine mosaic with or without figured representations. Small windows up high, tucked under the eaves, were sometimes fitted with panes of a very thick glass or a translucent material known as *lapis specularis,* but by and large wooden shutters, commonly kept shut against sun or cold air, discouraged communication with the bustling streets.

The exterior of these brick and half-timber houses was stuccoed and painted. Shops flanking the entrance door are a late phenomenon; they coincide with the rising population during the Roman influx. Initially the market was confined to the forum area. Then rental shops—single units with an open front and a living space above, called *tabernae*—began to extend commercial activity into neighboring streets and principally along the Via dell'Abbondanza. Congestion and increased ground rents changed the domus proper into a multiple-family dwelling. Second-storey apartments became frequent. In the busier sections these developments opened up the house exteriors to the street with rows of tabernae, whose goods often spilled onto the sidewalk, with large and often showy house entrances, and with balconies above ground level. Tabernae also lined the edges of public buildings, like the forum baths.

The pressures that were being felt in a country town like Pompeii in the early first century A.D. had long before transformed Rome itself into a city of multilevel tenements. Since there was no adequate mode of transportation, the huge population, perhaps one million by the end of the century, crammed into a narrow space. The domus could be afforded only by the very rich, and the capital turned into a city of renters. The model for the high-rise apart-

Fig. 9.11 Ostia (Italy), an apartment block, second century A.D.; reconstruction model. (Museo della civiltà romana, Rome)

ment block or *insula* may have existed in the more populous of Hellenistic cities. But in Rome tenements probably developed from the simple shop-with-garret scheme, with several storeys of apartments piling up as needed on ground-level tabernae. Often shoddily built of mud-brick or half-timber construction, with wooden floors, stairs, and ceilings, the tenement blocks had no cooking facilities and were, for the most part, appallingly overcrowded. The state attempted to regulate heights and construction methods, especially after the disastrous Great Fire of A.D. 64 which burned down large sections of the downtown, but its success was very limited. Modern insulae, built of brick-faced concrete and facing out onto wide straight streets, can only be seen in Ostia, and they were the result of a determined reconstruction in the second century A.D. and later. (Fig. 9.11)

Most Roman towns of medium density must have stood somewhere between the chaotic crush of the capital and the exemplary order of its renovated port. Pompeii in this respect is atypical. The spread of tabernae and the break-up of family houses were as far as Pompeii's modernization had gone when Vesuvius put an end to its existence in A.D. 79. Even for that period, however, the prevalence of broad peri-

styles and their gardens along downtown streets is exceptional.

Outside the walls, the picture of luxurious domesticity is even more apparent. Terraced houses on the slopes of Vesuvius, along the south flank of the city, had lower floors of cool vaulted rooms. With their larger peristyles and additional produce gardens, these residences were half town house, half country villa. True villas had inward-looking atrium cores, but they were set on artificial platforms and opened up by galleries to face parklands of laurels, pines, exotic shrubs, and clipped hedges of myrtle and flowers. In addition, the order of atrium and peristyle was reversed; the peristyle was seen first as you entered the villa.

The Villa of Mysteries, so-called because of the paintings in one of its rooms dealing with initiation rites for women in a cult of Dionysos, is one of the oldest and best-known examples of this favorite building type of Campania. (Fig. 9.12) It is the product of periodic remodelings over two centuries. A western terrace secured the villa on the hillslope. Inside it ran a vaulted passageway lit by small windows. This *cryptoporticus* is reminiscent of the terracing devices we saw at Pergamon. The top was planted as a formal garden communicating through porticoes with the outer rooms of this west half of the villa, which contained the oldest core. The long axis, starting at the entrance and running through peristyle, atrium, and tablinum, culminated in a spacious niche with a lovely view of the coast and sea. The practice of ending a headlong movement of space in a single room (like the apsed hall in the north wing) or in a linear sequence, with a terminal curve, is typically Roman. Greek designers almost invariably ended axes in a flat wall.

The wine press and cellar at the northeast corner of the peristyle belong to the final remodeling, when this wing was being transformed into a rustic farming unit. A second floor above the entrance vestibule was added at the same time to accommodate the resident overseer. At this stage of its development, just before the holocaust of A.D. 79, this splendid mansion slipped from being a *villa urbana* into being a *villa rustica*.

The villa rustica in its purer form is best represented by a late republican establishment near Boscoreale, a short way north of Pompeii. (Fig. 9.13) A main court with porticoes on three sides is a refinement of the central farmyard around which the villa rustica was habitually organized. One entered directly into the court, passing under an overseer's apartment above the portico. To the left was a large kitchen, an important element in these country farms, stables, a rather fancy bathing complex with the latest fixtures, and some rooms probably for the owner's use during inspection visits or summer stays. To the right was a large court lined with rows of vats for fermenting wine, and across a corridor were the wine press, a hand mill, rooms for producing olive oil, a barn, and sleeping cubicles for attendants. Along the southeast edge of the villa lay the threshing floor. The villa rustica nearby owned by Augustus' grandson Agrippa Postumus had a slave barracks for his agricultural workers. It also contained eighteen cells and a prison with stocks.

Public Buildings

We can now turn to the principal settings of public life at Pompeii, starting at the forum complex. (Fig. 9.8)

In its last phase, the forum was an elongated open space about 150 by 30 meters (492 by 98 feet). It was lined with two-storey colonnades, Doric in the lower order and Ionic above. Fifty statues of prominent personages, some equestrian, stood in front of these colonnades, and behind them, on all sides but the north, a series of large and small buildings opened mostly at right angles to this surrounding portico. The forum was closed to wheeled traffic and, in this late period, it was free of commercial bustle except on market day. Of the surrounding buildings only the *macellum* or food market had a frankly commercial character. The large structure, sponsored by the influential Lady Eumachia, south of the macellum served as headquarters for the clothesmakers' corporation. It is now thought that the basilica, at the southwest corner, absorbed the function of a stock exchange along with its more traditional role as general assembly room and law court. The imposing temple of Jupiter loomed at one end of the prospect. At the opposite end were three small administrative structures. The west side was dominated by the temple of Apollo, placed lengthwise. Between the macellum and Eumachia's building on the east side there nestled an apsed hall, probably the sanctuary of the city

Fig. 9.12 Pompeii, Villa of Mysteries, third century B.C., with later additions; ground plan. The peristyle dates from the late second century B.C., and the semicircular veranda on the west, from the mid-first century A.D.

1. Cellar
2. Wine Press
3. Peristyle
4. Atrium
5. Tablinum
6. Summer Room
7. Cryptoporticus (below)
8. Kitchen
9. Bath

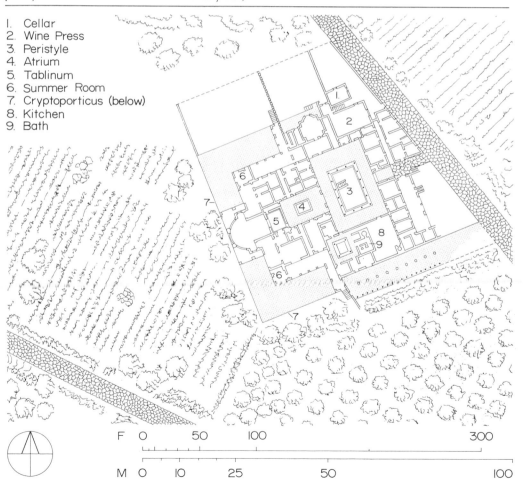

spirits *(lares publici),* and a late addition, the chapel of the imperial cult.

The obvious model for this forum is the Hellenistic agora. The Roman contribution has two aspects to it: the strong sense of axial organization we had noted earlier in the arrangement of the common family house; and the insistence on total enclosure—that is, the preference for interiorized and controlled public spaces whose design, seen from within, would shield undesirable bits of urban fabric or, as is the case at Pompeii, bring uniform order to the irregular massing and elevation of surrounding buildings. Adjustments were made in these buildings so that they and the ground-level portico of the forum would appear to belong to a single master plan. Notice, for example, the way the depth was varied in the row of shops along the west front of the macellum, or the way in which

Fig. 9.13 Boscoreale (Italy), a "villa rustica" or country farmhouse, first century B.C.; ground plan and section. The context is conjectural.

1. Stable
2. Bath Complex
3. Kitchen
4. Bakery
5. Dining Room
6. Sleeping Room
7. Court
8. Wine Presses
9. Fermentation Court
10. Hand Mill
11. Olive Crusher
12. Oil Press
13. Threshing Floor

Fig. 9.14 Pompeii, basilica, ca. 120 B.C.; interior reconstruction.

the piers on the east side of the Apollo temple were reduced in thickness moving from north to south. The object was to bring buildings of different date and orientation together into a total design, something Roman architects and planners were particularly good at.

Forum, temple, and basilica—these were the basic components of the Roman civic center. They were frequently laid out as an articulated complex, ideally with the temple framing the long and narrow space of the forum at one end and the basilica, transversely laid out, closing it off at the other end. This grouping seems to have originated in the towns of northern Italy and then to have moved out to the northern provinces. It was broad planning guidelines of this kind, together with the presence of distinctive building types on a grand scale, like theaters, amphitheaters, and public baths, that gave the Roman stamp to a vast array of towns within the empire

without wholly suppressing local traditions of construction and design. These buildings impressed the townscape by their sheer bulk, by their unique forms that often exploited the sweeping curve, and by their tiered arrangement that created a dramatic sense of architectural height.

The origin of the *basilica* is obscure. Its history started with the Roman Forum, perhaps as a spontaneous invention expanding on the Greek stoa, or with some closer prototype in the Greek towns nearby of which the basilica, and Hellenistic buildings like the Hypostyle Hall of Delos, were the successors. The size of such trabeated halls, whether Roman or Hellenistic, was made possible by the development of the timber truss, a device for roofing broad spans that arranged straight timbers in tension or compression into rigid load-bearing frames. We should not, in our admiration for Roman vaulting systems, forget that timberwork and carpentry improved greatly

too. Even concrete shells demanded master carpenters capable of making the necessary formwork.

The basilica of Pompeii had columns on all four sides and a longitudinal axis running from the entrance on the forum to a tribunal at the other end. Most other basilicas were arranged transversely, with entrances on the long sides. They all had roofs supported on timber trusses and some sort of top lighting. (Fig. 9.14) Two-storey galleries surrounded the central unencumbered space, with outside windows at the upper storey. In formal terms we might view the basilica either as an interiorized stoa or an externalized Greek temple without the peristyle. Functionally, the modern equivalent of this sensible urban meeting place is the spacious arcade of nineteenth-century towns, called *passage* by the French and *galleria* by the Italians.

The *macellum,* a courtyard lined with shops, may well have been inspired by the kind of commercial space enclosed by stoas in the Hellenistic remodeling of the Athenian agora. The difference is that the Romans externalized some of the shops (at Pompeii only those along the south side look out onto the court) and emphasized a formal facade on one outer side. The Roman macellum also featured a round columnar pavilion in the middle of the court (at Pompeii it was probably built entirely of wood) where fish were cleaned before being set out on stalls. The food shops all around sold delicacies and products of quality. This particular scheme seems to have originated in Campania and then spread to the south and east. There is a beautiful specimen with two stone pavilions in the North African city of Leptis Magna, roughly contemporary with the macellum in Pompeii. (Fig. 9.15) But there was another type, current about this time in central Italy, in which the entire arrangement was circular, with the stalls opening off a central circular court.

The macellum was of course only one kind of commercial program. There were always open-air markets in forums and sanctuary sites that hosted fairs. Each city had specialty markets for bread, beef, spices, and so forth. Warehouses, called *porticus* or *horrea,* had special magazines for the deposit of foodstuffs. The Porticus

Aemilia in Rome is rather distinctive. (Fig. 8.32) Most others were simple quadrilateral enclosures with identical storage units all around. The state kept a great number of these in the service of its vast welfare program. The name horrea usually implies private use. Rooms on two sides of a central corridor open to the sky were rented out by the owner who left it up to the tenants to arrange for security. Some horrea floated their floors on small brick or stone piers that allowed the circulation of air underneath and kept the grain and other foodstuffs dry.

This particular system started with Hellenistic *baths*. Called *hypocaust*, or subterranean heating, in Greek, it involved circulation beneath the raised floors of hot air conducted from a furnace. (Fig. 9.16) The advantage over the older system of heating by charcoal braziers that smoked and smelled is obvious. A Roman contribution was to run hollow tubes through the walls, thus carrying the hot steam above floor level. The Romans called private baths in houses and villas *balnea; thermae* referred to public baths, which by the first century B.C. had combined the prescribed series of rooms with a Greek palaestra for outdoor exercise.

The bathing procedure changed hardly at all. At the Stabian baths one walked into the palaestra from Via dell'Abbondanza. Its west side was taken up by a large swimming pool flanked by rooms where one could oil oneself before exercise and scrape off the sweat and dirt afterward. The entrance to the bath proper was at the southeast corner, through a vestibule that gave way to a lavishly decorated dressing room, with wall niches for storing clothes. The *tepidarium* came first. In this room the body began to warm up for the much higher temperature of the *caldarium* and the steam bath it provided. (Fig. 9.17) From there the visitor went out again, by the way of the tepidarium and the vestibule, in order to enter the *frigidarium*, a round room having four semicircu-

Fig. 9.15 Leptis (Lepcis) Magna (Libya), market, 8 B.C.; one of a pair of pavilions enclosed within a rectangular space. An encircling portico, of which some columns can be seen, was added ca. A.D. 35.

Fig. 9.16 Pompeii, hypocaust system of the Stabian baths located east of the Forum area. The baths date from the second century B.C.; the heating system from a renovation of the early first century B.C.

Fig. 9.17 Pompeii, Forum baths, ca. 80 B.C.; the hot room or caldarium in the men's section.

dard Greek temple. Entered on the short south side by means of a steep flight of stairs and a deep porch, the temple had its back to the rear wall of the forum. A perfect specimen, the so-called Maison Carrée, survives at Nîmes in southeastern France; here the porch columns are continued atop the flanks of the podium and are engaged to the cella walls. (Fig. 9.18)

But also present in Pompeii are a number of religious buildings of diverse shape. The temple to the Egyptian goddess Isis north of the theater had a free arrangement seemingly geared to dramatic effects, including an underground tank in which Nile water was kept. On the forum we have already noted the trilobate sanctuary of the public *lares* and the temple to the genius of the emperor (probably Nero). Indeed, Vitruvius is explicit about the fact that temples must not be built "according to the same rules for all the gods alike, since the performance of the sacred rites varies with the various gods."

The placement and grouping of temples within the city also displayed great variety. Several temples—some round, some rectangular—were at times set up in a single precinct. In one particular solution for hilly sites, the temple figured at the top of a theaterlike, semicircular staircase with an orchestra below. These were the settings of religious festivals that featured outdoor performances.

A handful of theater-temples of the late republic rivaled, and even surpassed, in size and richness of conception, the famous Hellenistic sanctuaries like those at Kos and Lindos. Fortuna Primigenia at Praeneste, a small hill town near Rome, still retains its spectacular terracing beneath the modern overgrowth. (Fig. 9.19) It rose above the

lar niches that opened out from the main space, small round windows, and an oculus in its dome for light. Steps led down to a cold bath where freshwater gushed continually from a high spout. The women's section, much simpler in form, was on the other side of the caldarium. It had its own separate entrances and abbreviated the sequence by substituting for the frigidarium a cold-water tub in a corner of the dressing room.

Religious Architecture

Different stages in the life of the Greco-Roman temple form coexist at Pompeii. The Doric temple by the theater represents the Greek phase, as we mentioned. The temple of Apollo on the west side of the forum combines an Ionic peristyle with a frontally approached peripteral temple on a very high podium—a hybrid creation that looks Greek but acts Italian. The Corinthian temple to Jupiter typifies the official Roman temple. It is raised on a podium that contains rooms meant to serve as the public treasury and as storage space for liturgical objects and sacrificial offerings, functions usually served by the *adyton* or back room of the stan-

Fig. 9.18 Nîmes, the Maison Carrée; a Roman temple begun ca. 19 B.C. The order used is Corinthian. The temple type is called pseudo-per-ipteral because the exterior colonnade is not entirely freestanding, but is engaged to the cella walls along the flanks and the back.

Fig. 9.19 Palestrina (the Roman Praeneste, Italy), the sanctuary of Fortuna Primigenia, ca. 80 B.C.; axonometric plan. The sanctuary, famous in antiquity as a place of divination by lots, occupies the hillslope above the forum. The basilica, shown at the bottom left, and the curia or council hall, along its short east side, belong to the forum complex. The sanctuary is separate from this complex and is arranged along seven terraces. The lower terraces contain rows of shops, while the large piazza at the top, surrounded by Corinthian porticoes, was the setting for ritual dances. The semicircular stairs above this piazza are related to these performances. The small circular temple culminates the long axis of the sanctuary.

Fig. 9.20 Leptis Magna, theater, A.D. 1–2; interior.

forum in a crescendo of seven terraces that were resolved in a semicircular recess with a double portico and the round temple of Fortune at the summit. A straight axis ran through the topmost terraces, its forceful course softened in a typically Roman manner by the curve at the top and the countercurve of the temple. Two smaller semicircles flanked the axis at the lower level of the narrow terrace, just below the huge piazza that preceded the terminal curve and the theater it embraced. The columns and the attic that make up the facade of these semicircles conceal coffered barrel vaults of concrete. The trabeated and vaulted systems thus come together in a marriage of opposites. A similarly prophetic blend occurs at the upper level of this terrace where a row of shops is prefaced by a run of arches, each framed by engaged columns. This will become the main unit of facade design, often stacked in several storeys. We will see it applied to the exteriors of theaters and amphitheaters built on flatland, the arches briskly sweeping across the broad curve, while the half-columns, sometimes used in combination with piers, slow down this lateral rhythm and provide the vertical definition for the superimposed storeys. (Fig. 9.22)

Places of Entertainment
The theater proper, a ubiquitous building form in all provinces of the empire, was very close to its Greek prototype. (Fig. 7.12) Many Roman theaters, Pompeii's among them, are in fact remodeled Greek theaters. The differences came in the arrangement of the stage building and the relation of that element to the auditorium or *cavea*. The Roman cavea did not extend beyond a semicircle, and it was united with the stage building to form a single structure. (Fig. 9.20) The Greek *parodoi*, the principal entrances tangent to the stage building, were roofed over by the Romans and boxes situated above them. A portico behind the stage building or, as at Pompeii, a complete colonnaded court acted as a kind of foyer. But the crowds now entered primarily from the outside of the cavea and reached their seats by means of covered passageways. This was especially true of theaters built on flatland, without benefit of a hillside, in which the seating fan rested on vaulted substructures.

Internally, at the top of the cavea, ran a row of freestanding columns which held up a partial roof over the uppermost tiers of seats. The stage building was similarly roofed. Fully covered theaters also exist, the one at Pompeii next to the main theater being an early survivor of the type. They were usually small and specialized in musical events. The stage of a Roman theater was low and deep. The back wall was modulated into a facade with three main entrances, the central one cut into an apse. In some instances this wall was left plain and in front of it was erected a stage set (called *scaenae frons*) in several storeys. This was composed of a remarkable assembly of columns and niches capped by alternating segmental and triangular pediments. The inspiration is Hellenistic stage design, translated into permanent stone frontispieces.

Gladiatorial games, beast fights, and even a spectacle that involved a mock sea battle were sometimes staged at the theaters, in addition to the farcical shows so popular with Roman audiences. For these special purposes the orchestra, which was always paved, was enclosed by a low wall all around. But the amphitheater was the standard building type in those cities that could afford one, or merited that level of state patronage, for gladiatorial combat and *venationes*, the pitting of wild animals against men. The former sport originated in Campania and derives ultimately from the bloody funeral games of the Etruscans. The gladiator contests were held in the forum at first, with improvised bleachers for spectators, and this is the reason, according to Vitruvius, for the long and narrow space of the early forums. *Venationes* are thought to have started with the Second Punic War, when a contingent of Carthaginian elephants were captured by the Romans.

The amphitheater, despite its Greek name which implies two theaters set end to end with the stage buildings removed, was a Roman invention. They are immense stone constructs (though there were probably wooden predecessors) designed to hold anywhere from 15,000 to 80,000 people. Both because of their size and because the type was formalized rather late, they appeared at the edge of town. The elliptical arena, often sunk into the terrain and paved with sand, was surrounded by continuous stone bleachers that sat either on banked mounds of earth held behind retaining walls or on an elaborate maze of radial substructures which housed the circulation system. At Pompeii the amphitheater, the oldest surviving example, is a compromise. (Fig. 9.21) The building is only partly freestanding; half of it, from northeast to southeast, is propped against the city wall, saving much buttressing labor. Outside staircases led to a corridor at the summit where the seats for women were. The best seats, here as well as in the theaters, were at the lowest level. At Pompeii these were reached by vaulted corridors that led directly into the arena and were separated from the rest of the tiered seating by a high balustrade.

Fig. 9.21 Pompeii, amphitheater, first century B.C.; aerial view.

The Look of Empire: Rome at the Millennium

The most famous of Roman amphitheaters, and one of the world's best-known buildings, is the Colosseum, dedicated in A.D. 80. (Fig. 1.6) It was an entirely freestanding structure, 188 meters long by 156 meters wide (617 by 511 feet), in the hollow of three encompassing hills east of the Roman Forum. Eighty arches all around its girth swallowed the more than 50,000 spectators that came to the games—first, into two annular corridors at ground level, and then by means of three storeys of stairs to the different levels of the cavea whose stone seats rested on an immense skeleton of radial walls at a 37-degree incline. (Fig. 9.22) The floor of the arena and the metal barrier around it are now gone, exposing to our view a nightmarish warren of hundreds of subterranean chambers that once housed beasts as well as staff, machinery, and services. The clifflike exterior, of travertine blocks fastened with iron clamps, is composed of three storeys of arches framed by piers and three-quarter columns, and a fourth storey, unprecedented for this type of building, in which bays displayed alternately bronze shields and windows in a manner reminiscent of the bouleuterion at Miletus. (Fig. 8.21) A row of brackets at this level served to moor the awning that shielded the upper third of the cavea. The four storeys employed the principal Roman orders: Tuscan first, which is the ancient Italian variation of Doric; Ionic and Corinthian for the second and third storeys, respectively; and tall Corinthian pilasters for the attic.

This was not Rome's first amphitheater. Its predecessor, the *amphitheatrum Tauri,* stood in the Campus Martius, the flatland in the crook of the Tiber, north of the republican city, where the first emperors continued the tradition of creating buildings of a popular nature: the amphitheatrum Tauri, at least two theaters, an odeum and a stadium, porticuses, two sets of baths, and a circus for chariot races auxiliary to the ancient Circus Maximus in the valley between the Palatine and Aventine hills. (Fig. 9.23) These programs strove to satisfy the insatiable appetite of the populace for diversion during the frequent holidays that accounted for nearly one-half of the year. The vast proletariat, once a self-governing people in theory at least, now had to be appeased and kept under control through bread, circuses, and the presence of an imperial home guard. A fifth of the population, about 200,000 in all, were on the public dole. Real power was in the hands of the emperor and the bureaucracy of appointees that had replaced the old elective offices of the republic. To curry favor with the volatile public and to impress his image on the city, each emperor lavished moneys on places of leisure and public amenities.

The Emperor's Palace

The Colosseum was sponsored by the Flavian emperors (A.D. 71–96), whose dynasty rose victorious after the precipitous end of Nero's rule. Under Nero (A.D. 54–68) this

section of the city between the downtown and the villa-strewn eastern hills, wiped out in the fire of A.D. 64, had been appropriated by a rambling palace, the Domus Aurea or "Golden House." An artificial lake

occupied the hollow of the later Colosseum. Around it, pavilions were erected representing prominent cities of the empire. A 36 meter (120 feet) high statue of Nero as the sun-god stood between this

Fig. 9.22 Rome, Colosseum, amphitheater built under the Flavian dynasty, A.D. 72–80; sections and sectional view (see also Fig. 1.6b).

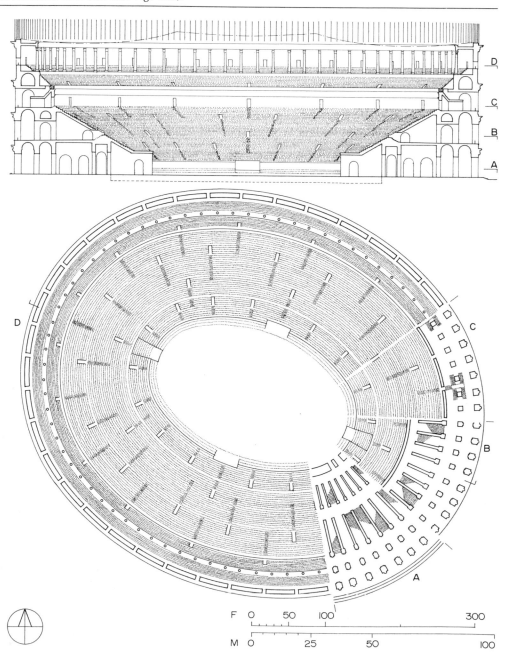

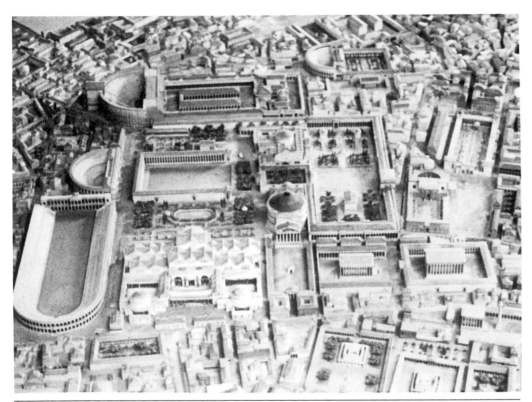

Fig. 9.23 Rome, as it appeared at the end of the imperial period, early fourth century A.D.; detail of a model. (Museo della civiltà romana, Rome) The Pantheon is in the center; to its left are the baths of Nero (A.D. 54–68) as rebuilt in the third century, and further left is the Stadium of Domitian (A.D. 81–96) whose outline survives in the present Piazza Navona (see Fig. 21.7a).

ensemble and the Forum, whose sacred way had been reorganized in this direction into a broad processional avenue lined with multiaisled porticoes. The main residential quarters were on the Palatine and the Esquiline.

A wing of some one hundred rooms has been unearthed on the Esquiline. Its design and structure, credited to Nero's architects Severus and Celer, were of astounding virtuosity. Here for the first time we have the unabashed flowering of vaulted architecture—no longer with the excuse of practicality but as conscious high art. The object was an exciting and mystery-filled drama of inwardness that made use of manipulative lighting, running water, and a gamut of geometric shapes realized in concrete and clad with curtains of color—marbles, painted stucco, and mosaic.

The octagonal hall in the east half of the Esquiline wing should suffice to character-ize this new language. (Fig. 9.24) It lies to one side of a pentagonal court edged with rooms where Nero's fabulous collection of sculpture may have been displayed. The hall, seen from above, consisted of two octagons inscribed one inside the other. Clerestory lighting that came in between them illuminated a series of rooms radially arranged around the central octagon. A viaduct bridging a service corridor that ran behind the hall carried water that was allowed to cascade down into one of these rooms. The central octagon was covered by a dome rising from eight corner piers and pierced by a large oculus. On sunny days a shaft of light moved around this pavilion of concrete, beyond which water fell and pools of indirect light picked out statuary set in the niches of the subsidiary rooms.

It is easy to ridicule the Golden House, along with other excesses of Nero, as the fantasy of an unbalanced mind over-wrought by power. In one sense, however, this bombastic country villa in the center of town must be taken seriously, in spite of its flamboyant rooms that had ceilings of movable parts, which, we are told, changed patterns like a kaleidoscope or opened to sprinkle guests with blossoms, and its banquet hall that "was circular and constantly revolved day and night, like the heavens." Since the first emperor Augustus, the environment of Rome was trying to adjust to a new political reality, a world empire governed by the authority of a single individual in the way of Eastern autocracies. This meant nothing less than the overhauling of a whole system of old values and the creation of new rituals. Just as Alexander had loosened the Classical balance of Greek cities, so less precipitously Augustus and his successors were dismantling the republican ethos of Rome. "The rough simplicity of the past is gone," Ovid wrote, "now Rome is golden."

Gold was the traditional substance of the divine ruler. And Nero's Golden House was, at one level, the idealization of an official residence for a Roman ruler who had begun to assume extrahuman prerogatives. If the Roman Forum had been the focus of republican sentiment, the Golden House posed as the traditional setting of absolutism. It was the stage for ritual ceremonies involving the imperial person. These acts were not altogether different from the duties of an eminent citizen of the republic which would be performed in the setting of his town house or his villa: receiving clients and wards daily, dining in the company of peers, dispensing household justice. But now these acts were transformed into dazzling, operatic performances with an eye toward impressing and intimidating or, more specifically, glorifying the aims and power of the new regime. This, as we have seen before, is a purpose of autocratic states: to equate the extent of their authority with the size and magnificence of their official quarters.

But the effort was too flamboyant and came too soon. Nero was toppled, and the Flavians set out to make amends by burying the Golden House under a populist architecture. The lake was turned into an amphitheater and the colossus of Nero given a new head representing the legitimate deity of the Sun. Over the Esquiline property the emperor Titus erected a small set of baths, overshadowed shortly by the baths of Trajan close by on the famous palace wing. (Fig. 9.25) They became the model for a splendid run of imperial baths in the next two hundred years. The cold, warm, and hot rooms were now arranged on a strict axis and flanked by courts. This core was then placed in a vast enclosure that contained stadia for races, *xysti* or covered gardens, libraries, and refreshment rooms.

The question of the imperial residence still had to be faced. Thirty years after the demise of Nero, the decision was taken to locate it on the Palatine where the imperial family owned considerable property. There were other reasons. The hill, isolated by valleys on all four sides, was the least crowded area in the center of town, having always been the aristocratic quarter where senators and other dignitaries had houses. It was here that the history of Rome began eight centuries earlier with Romulus' furrowed city, and a hut was venerated as his. Augustus lived in a modest *domus* next to it, and his successors until Nero were all involved with building projects in the vicinity. The environmental symbolism was irresistible. The hill towers over the Forum like a banner of imperial dominion over republican rule. It is separated by a mere gap from the Capitoline, the citadel of state religion.

Now under Emperor Domitian (A.D. 81–96) a formal complex was laid out occupying most of the hilltop. (Fig. 9.26) It had facades toward the Forum, where the main approaches were, and toward the Circus Maximus, to which the emperor would repair to attend the major games from his box. The architect was Rabirius. There were two parallel parts to his scheme, both organized along central axes. The *Domus Flavia* was the official residence. A colonnaded facade on the Forum side gave way to three parallel halls: an apsed and barrel-vaulted basilica where imperial justice would be

Fig. 9.24 Rome, Nero's Golden House (Domus Aurea), A.D. 64–68, Severus and Celer; the octagonal room: (**a**) exterior of the superstructure; (**b**) interior. For the plan and section of this remarkable room, see Fig. 11.13.

dispensed, a grand throne room on the central axis, also apsed and with a span of one hundred Roman feet, and a chapel. The next band was mostly taken up by a large peristyle court with walls of Cappadocian marble and an octagonal, maze fountain in the middle. Further back was the state dining room whose lateral walls were opened up by large windows, beyond which were two small courts with oval fountains. The *Domus Augustana* was more private. It was arranged on two levels, that of the Domus Flavia, which held two peristyle courts and some summer rooms, and that of the lower

Augustana with the living quarters of the imperial family, conceived in playful geometries of form around a small court framed by barrel-vaulted colonnades. The facade on the Circus Maximus side was a two-storey concave exedra, and alongside the Augustana stretched a walled, sunken garden made to look like a stadium. (Fig. 9.27)

In the emperors' projects to house themselves we see the evidence of a major architectural revolution, the maturing of what has been called the Roman vaulted style. It combines the most monumental

effects of Hellenistic architecture—columnar facades, peristyles, terraces through which galleries run—and a rich assortment of vaulted spaces, small ones and large, polygonal, circular or directional, which are grouped for maximum surprise and delight. Water, brought within the interior spaces, is relied on as a positive design element that animates inert matter and makes connections through sound and movement. Light is used with dramatic and expressive power: single oculi revolving in closed interiors like mysterious searchlights, indirect diffuse light through distant apertures, the dematerializing of whole walls by banks of windows.

The key aim in all this was the molding of interior spaces that would be juxtaposed by shape, orchestrated through interpenetration, dilated by means of columnar screens and through-views. And the medium was concrete, capable of being made into artful vaulted ceilings—seamless canopies that matched the intricacy of the ground plans. Even though Roman concrete could not, in the manner of modern concrete, simply be poured or used independently of other materials, but had to be applied in layers, it was strong and enormously flexible. Through decades of trial and error, builders had mastered its properties and behavior in warehouses and baths, shops and tenements. They could now sing with it. The basic vault forms were played with, pleated, and warped for effect. The best of them swelled effortlessly like wind-puffed sails, their workings obscured by illusionist devices.

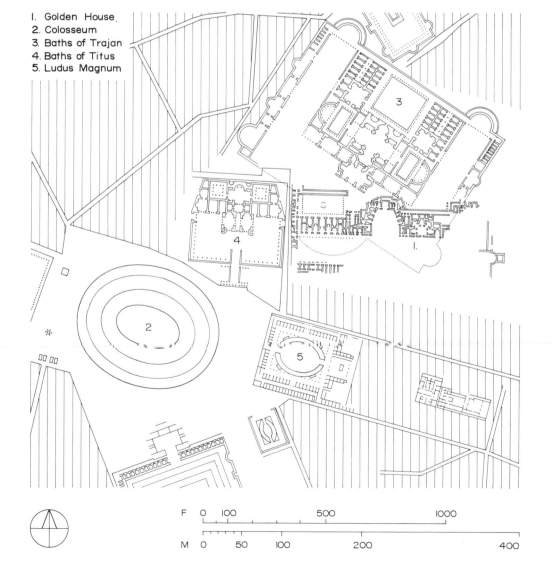

1. Golden House
2. Colosseum
3. Baths of Trajan
4. Baths of Titus
5. Ludus Magnum

Fig. 9.25 Rome, detail of the plan of the imperial city showing the area initially occupied by Nero's Golden House. The Colosseum at the extreme left was built over an artificial lake that was part of the palace. Higher up, on the Oppian hill, the suite of rooms which included the octagonal room (Fig. 9.24) was buried under the baths of Trajan, dedicated in A.D. 109. The smaller baths between these and the Colosseum were built by Emperor Titus (A.D. 79–81). The complex to the right of the Colosseum, with the small amphitheater, is the Ludus Magnum, the training quarters for gladiators.

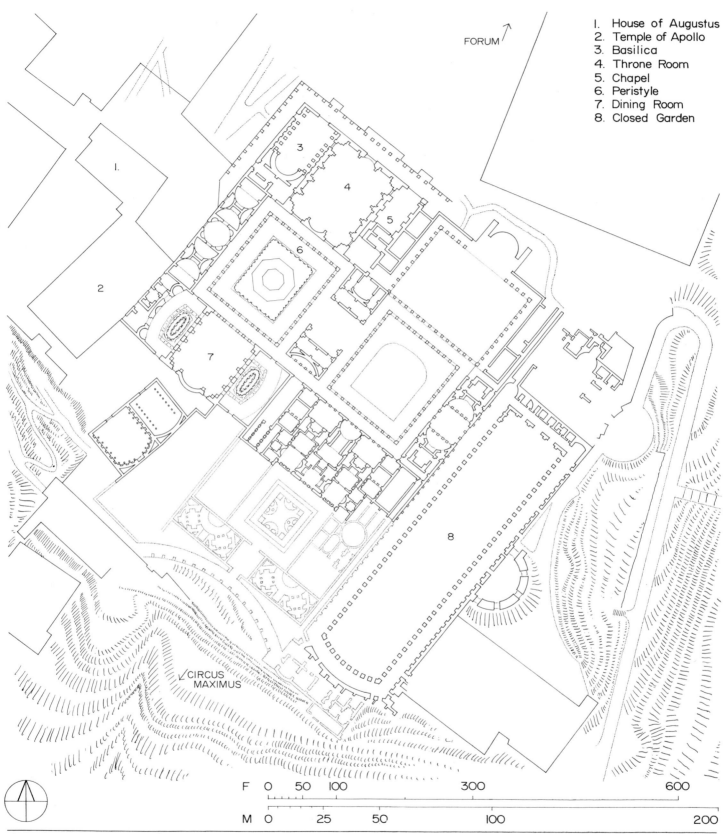

FORUM ↗

1. House of Augustus
2. Temple of Apollo
3. Basilica
4. Throne Room
5. Chapel
6. Peristyle
7. Dining Room
8. Closed Garden

CIRCUS
MAXIMUS

F 0   50 100   300   600

M 0   25   50   100   200

Fig. 9.26 Rome, the imperial palace on the Palatine hill, inaugurated in A.D. 92, Rabirius; ground plan.

The People's Palace

To imperial patrons and their architects, two distinct languages of form were available by the end of the first century A.D. Hellenistic design relying on colonnades, ashlar masonry, and the timber truss still reigned in the Eastern provinces and produced superb results in Rome—for example, in the series of imperial forums that began with Julius Caesar and Augustus as an extension of the congested old Forum. (Fig. 9.28) But the passion of the capital was the Roman vaulted style. To be sure, externally as well as within, the newfangled buildings dressed their walls in Hellenistic decor. Facades were not in the least revealing of interior arrangements, and the surprise of entering into the unconventional spaces that lay behind these familiar screens was the principal reward. And within, the sheathing of functional piers and walls of concrete with Hellenistic trappings gave the vaulted superstructure a feigned advantage of lightness and magic. Concomitantly buildings in the Hellenistic mode freely admitted curves in their plans and the vaulted shells that responded to them. Still each one of the two design options, the heritage of Greece

Fig. 9.28 Rome in the early fourth century A.D., detail of the center of town; model. (Museo della civiltà romana, Rome) The imperial forums stretch from lower left to center; the old Forum continues their line until the Colosseum in the upper right-hand corner. Immediately in front of the Colosseum is the temple of Venus and Rome from the time of Emperor Hadrian (A.D. 117–138), which was rebuilt in the early fourth century.

Fig. 9.27 Rome, the imperial palace on the Palatine; the Hippodrome or enclosed garden (no. 8 in Fig. 9.26).

and the conceit of Rome, conjured fundamentally unique environments.

The contrast was sharper when the Hellenistic courts and timber-roofed halls stood side by side with vaulted buildings of a utilitarian nature that forewent visual luxuries in favor of a columnless frame of brick. This is the case with the markets built by Emperor Trajan (A.D. 98–117) that stand next to his forum complex, the last of the series we mentioned. The structure was extraordinary in many ways. (Fig. 9.29) It was a multilevel, intricate commercial facility steeply terraced on the slope of the Quirinal hill facing the center of town. Three lower storeys of shops, standard barrel-vaulted *tabernae*, were fitted into a semicircular exedra, a concave facade that echoed the curved forms of the forum and basilica of Trajan. The shops on the ground level opened directly onto the street; those of the second storey were set behind an annular corridor which offered through arched windows the prospect of forum activities and the city's center beyond. The third-storey shops turned in toward a street halfway up the slope, the Via Biberatica, on the other side of which rose the irregular mass of the upper market block with three more storeys of shops and an impressive market hall.

This hall, the Aula Traiana, is comprised of a vaulted longitudinal space, something like a roofed street, with tabernae on the two sides arranged in two storeys, the upper ones behind an open gallery broken up into bays by transverse arches. (Fig. 9.30) The vaulting system is very complex. A longitudinal barrel vault over the central space is cut into by six transverse barrel vaults that spring a little higher up on the piers than the main barrel. Since the bays of the cen-

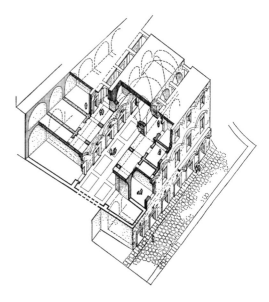

Fig. 9.29 Rome, the Markets of Trajan, ca. A.D. 100–12, Apollodorus of Damascus.

Fig. 9.30 Rome, Markets of Trajan, main market hall: (**a**) axonometric view; (**b**) interior.

tral space are wider than they are long, semicircular vaults raised over them in two directions would not have risen to the same height. By having the transverse vaults spring further up, the architect could attain a continuous and level crown line. The arches flanking this great vault remove some of its thrust, shifting it to the heavy outer walls of the two storeys of shops. The vaulting of rectangular bays and the relieving arches will become central issues again in later medieval architecture, and we will speak of them there in terms of rib vaults and flying buttresses.

This bold architecture of commerce, matched nowhere in the empire, made amends for the demolition of many shops during the necessary land-clearing for Tra-

jan's forum, a process that also entailed the leveling of a spur of land between the Capitoline and the Quirinal, and the drastic reduction of the Quirinal. We must remember that the entire spread of the imperial forums, of which Trajan's was the largest and most resplendent, materialized in the thick of old Rome at the expense of dense neighborhoods. Symbolically the scale and stately order of the redevelopment vividly contrasted an image of imperial magnificence with the congestion and disorder of the Roman Forum and its often squalid environs. The visual contrast, by implication, pointed up the determined control of empire as against the scattered energies of collective government. Functionally, the forums met the urban needs of a phenom-

enal concentration of people in the heart of town whose religious, commercial, judiciary, and cultural activities had long outgrown the provisions made for them under the republic. The individual temples that crowned the forums eased the crush on the sacred precinct of the Capitoline. Porticoes, exedras, the Trajanic basilica, and the great markets absorbed in their noble symmetry various services untidily packed in the older city core—commerce, banking, government business, courts, schools, libraries, and public lavatories.

But the bulk of the demolition necessary for this expansive program affected residential buildings. Thousands of people had to be displaced, but we have no record of their orderly relocation. The state, as often before in the past, condoned hardship for the sake of what it decided was the common good. Individual needs were subsumed under a picture of group affluence: the people were given their own palace, built on an impressive scale and sumptuously appointed, in return for their acquiescence. Whatever else they might profess to be, the forums were boasts of state; they spoke of the might and munificence of rulers whose prerogative it was to reorder and monumentalize urban patterns regardless of adversities and inconvenience.

The overall plan was not the result of forethought or grand design. Each forum rose next to its predecessors as an act of blatant competition and was informed with propaganda relevant to the particular reign that sponsored it. Except for axial or orthogonal relationships, the grouping is neither carefully coordinated from within nor thought about in connection to a broader, improved network of circulation and suitable access. Each complex functioned as an inward-looking entity. It was designed to be bigger than the rest, or at least to look distinctive. Julius Caesar's which started it all was about 10,000 square meters; the last, the forum of Trajan, measured four times that, excluding the markets. Each honored a deity appropriate to the aims of the regime. In addition, each forum commemorated a military achievement of note. The Temple of Peace to the southeast of the Forum Transitorium was inspired by the crushing of the Jewish rebellion in A.D. 79 and the transporting to Rome of the holy objects from the temple of Jerusalem. Trajan's culminating program recalled his triumphs over the Dacians, the campaigns which are depicted on a helical frieze that wraps itself around a triumphal column. (Fig. 10.9) Indeed, the point was made in the accompanying inscriptions that the cost of the forum was defrayed *ex manubiis,* by the spoils of war. The emperor fought against the enemies of the Romans and converted his victories into tangible assets for the public good.

The cost of such immense projects could be staggering. Cicero, who handled land purchase for the forum of Caesar, paid out 100 million sesterces to claimants, perhaps $20 million or so in today's inflated currency—and that was for the smallest of the forums and for the site alone. The custom was to insist that the emperor meet outstanding expenses out of his own pocket. In theory the distinction could be made between the personal wealth of an emperor and the state treasury, but in reality this distinction soon became specious. It was nonetheless of paramount importance to maintain the fiction of personal munificence and to reinforce it with showy gestures. It is likely that the Aula Traiana was the setting for Trajan's *congiaria,* or periodic distributions of public largesse; and it was in the forum of Trajan that Hadrian (A.D. 117–138) at his accession had the notes of debtors to the state burned in a calculated act of magnanimity.

It is important to review the motivations at work in context as we admire the series of imperial forums at Rome, one of the great creations of antiquity. They broke through the Servian walls to marry the republican city with the entertainment quarter of the Campus Martius. They carved out a spacious lung for the choking crowds of the capital. Above all, they developed piecemeal a peerless civic center where, for the resident population, the triumphs of its armies and the genius of its artists could be put on bountiful display; and for the visitor from Syria, Cyrenaica, Britain, Spain, or any other of the far-flung provinces, the might, wealth, and culture of an empire shone through and added substance to the boast of Roman citizenship.

Further Reading

A. Boethius, *Etruscan and Early Roman Architecture,* 2nd ed., rev. (Harmondsworth and New York: Penguin, 1978).

———, *The Golden House of Nero* (Ann Arbor: University of Michigan Press, 1960).

M. Brion, *Pompeii and Herculaneum,* trans. J. Rosenberg (New York: Crown, 1960).

F. Brown, *Roman Architecture* (New York: Braziller, 1965).

T. Kraus and L. von Matt, *Pompeii and Herculaneum,* trans. E. Wolf (New York: Abrams, 1973).

W. MacDonald, *The Architecture of the Roman Empire,* 2 vols. (New Haven: Yale University Press, 1982, 1986).

A. G. McKay, *Houses, Villas, and Palaces in the Roman World* (Ithaca, N.Y.: Cornell University Press, 1975).

E. Nash, *Pictorial Dictionary of Ancient Rome,* 2 vols. 2nd ed., rev. (New York: Praeger, 1968).

L. Storoni Mazzolani, *The Idea of the City in Roman Thought,* trans. S. O'Donnell (Bloomington. Indiana University Press, 1970).

J. B. Ward-Perkins and A. Claridge, *Pompeii A.D. 79* (New York: Knopf, 1978).

Village of Ziou, Burkina Faso (Upper Volta), woman's dwelling unit of the Nankani people; one example of traditional African architecture. It is made of puddled earth clods and painted with an earth pigment of ground laterite.

10

THE WORLD AT LARGE: ROMAN CONCURRENCES

During the reign of Hadrian, the Roman Empire attained the zenith of its material prosperity and the outermost limits of its growth. (Fig. 10.1) The Euphrates formed the natural border in the East beyond which Persia, the long-time adversary of Western ambitions, lived precariously under Parthian rulers. Along the length of North Africa, the Egyptian desert and its continuation determined the width of coastal land subject to Rome, its numerous cities fattened by maritime trade. Hadrian strengthened the most unstable boundary for the empire, the northern frontier, with a system of fortification that included a wall between England and Scotland and strongholds along the Rhine and Danube. Mounted peoples—Sarmatians, Alamanni, Visigoths—ranged restlessly across central and eastern Europe harassing settled agrarian communities and seeking any advantage against their formidable neighbor to the south. Westward the world ended with the Atlantic.

It was a time of peace, a happy time. The provinces were contented and, for the most part, quiet. The troublesome spirit of Jewish independence flared briefly, but their revolt was crushed in 135. Jerusalem, renamed Aelia Capitolina after Hadrian's family name, was disciplined architecturally with a cross-axial scheme, a proper Roman forum, and the usual catalogue of theaters, circuses, and baths.

There were buildings under construction in every corner of the empire. Hadrian himself sponsored hundreds of public structures, most notably in Athens and Ostia. (Fig. 10.2) He traveled around, so an ancient source tells us, with a contingent of "geometers, architects, and every sort of expert in construction and decoration . . . whom he enrolled by cohorts and centuries, on the model of the legions." An amateur architect, he found time to work on his favorite villa at Tibur, the modern Tivoli, a short way east of Rome, and for the capital he oversaw the design of several monuments—among them a temple to his predecessor Trajan, which completed the cycle of the imperial forums, a temple to Venus and Rome, confronting the Colosseum on the west, and a unique creation in the heart of the Campus Martius called the Pantheon. (Figs. 9.28, 10.3, 11.2)

The Roman Cosmos

It is the Pantheon, perhaps, that best stands for the crowning moment of the Roman Empire. It faced north toward the incoming traffic of the coastal highway, the Via Flaminia. The approach was commonplace: a closed forum, long and narrow, at the south end of which rose a standard temple front. But passing through this porch of smooth monolithic columns of Egyptian granite, one entered a mighty domed rotunda, 150 Roman feet (43 meters) both in height and diameter, that enclosed a vast, unobstructed, thoroughly ordered space suffused with the even light that shone through an oculus and the open bronze doors. (Fig. 10.4) The hemispherical concrete dome, with five diminishing rows of coffers verging toward the oculus and harboring gilded bronze rosettes like gleaming stars, rested on a multicolored wall arranged in two storeys. Niches carved in the thickness of the wall, each screened by two columns of colored marble and flanked by pilasters, alternated with small tabernacles or "temple fronts," which stood in front of the wall plane and were crowned by segmental and triangular pediments. At the entrance niche and the apse across the way, the screening columns were omitted. The apse semidome and the barrel vault over the entrance lifted their arc into the second storey. This second storey was actually a broad frieze of blind windows and triplets of tall thin panels patterned with colored marbles. The floor was paved with disks and squares of granite, marble, and porphyry set in a grid that was aligned with the main north south direction of the building and reflected the grid armature of the coffering overhead.

The easy grace of this superb interior is entirely deceptive. Behind the tapestry of Classical niches and precious stones that wraps around the rotunda is a tremendously thick wall, 6 meters or 20 Roman feet across, which is what really supports the approximately 5,000 tons of weight exerted by the dome. The relationship of load and support is not direct. The wall, rather than being solid, has been riddled with stacked chambers. These chambers helped to hasten the drying process of the concrete, and transverse barrel vaults over some among them distributed the weight of the superstructure onto eight points of the perimeter, so that in effect the dome is held up by eight thick piers like some gigantic canopy. The octagonal hall in Nero's Golden House is the logical prototype, but the Pantheon, being free of abutting structures, was forced to resolve its statics wholly within its own big frame. It then proceeded to camouflage the elaborate precautions, so that the user might be duly amazed by the unstrained elegance of this calmly billowing space.

Faultless organization, daring, and a prodigious amount of labor were called for to achieve Hadrian's design, and the effort was thought justified by the uncommon message the building was to convey. The first theme was of course cosmic. This was a temple to all the gods, and the appropriate symbolism was that of the heavens where they resided. The statues of the gods, probably including those of the planetary deities, were arrayed on the edges of the great circle, and the eye of the sun, the central opening in the dome's swell, shone upon them one by one during the course of the day, highlighting their presence.

But the building also had a political content. There were images of Augustus in the entrance vestibule and of the deified Caesar within, and Hadrian held judicial court in the rotunda. The empire, it was being implied, was an analogy for the cosmos, and the Pantheon—like the empire, a structure of many units but one pervading unity—described this analogy in visual terms. The true religion was Romanism, the force that held the Mediterranean world together in a smoothly and reliably functioning order like the harmonious workings of the celestial sphere. Hadrian's, then, was an intellectual statement of what the state was all about. It was his answer to the applied populism of the Colosseum or the billboard swagger of the imperial forums.

As with Persepolis and other central monuments of empire, the Pantheon was also the physical repository of universal tribute from subject lands. It used the granites and porphyries of Egypt, the colored marbles of Africa, the white marbles of the Aegean, pavonazzetto from central

Asia Minor. What held it all together and gave it the authority of a single-minded conception was the Roman vaulted style and its versatile medium, concrete.

In the provinces where this technology was not employable, the effects of the vaulted style were aped in stone and on a small scale, within the predominantly late Hellenistic frame of public architecture. Interiors of Pantheon-like grandeur or interlocked configurations of the playfulness displayed in rooms on the Palatine and in Hadrian's villa at Tivoli were beyond the range of cut stone and wood, and where these enticing cages were modestly and laboriously reproduced they remained massive and earthbound. (Fig. 10.5) A technique of mortared rubble achieved some

limited success in Asia Minor, and plain brick vaults were also experimented with both here and also in Syria and Egypt. But, for the most part, the strength of provincial work drew upon decorative virtuosity, notably in the carving of stone, and theatrical flare and sweep.

Hundreds of cities, large and small, thickly and prodigally dotted the shores of the Mediterranean and lands beyond in the north and east. They were linked by a network of paved highways. Some were old towns rehabilitated by their Roman masters; some were colonies founded by government decree; some had grown around army camps or to exploit a natural resource like a river port or mineral waters (for example, Bath in England). All enjoyed a

Fig. 10.1 Map: The Roman Empire at the time of Hadrian (A.D. 117–138). Dotted lines indicate major land routes.

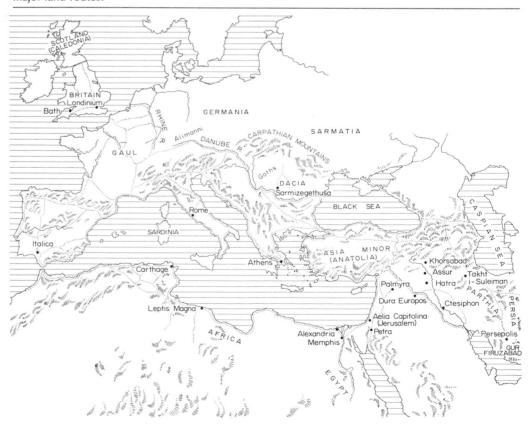

Fig. 10.2 Emperor Hadrian; marble bust. (Vatican Museums, Rome)

measure of local self-government. The majority of towns made do handsomely with agriculture and local trade. A smaller number manufactured goods for distant markets, such as cloth, pottery, and metal objects. In the eastern frontier, towns like Petra, Palmyra, and Gerasa capitalized on the caravan trade that dealt in spices and exotica. Major ports along the shores, equipped with breakwaters, walled basins and docks, handled grain, oil, wine, building materials, and slaves.

By and large cityscapes were not dense. (Fig. 10.6) Skylines were low and the urban fabric generously aired with public spaces and parks. Safe under Roman auspices, towns broke through their walls with large public buildings and affluent suburbs. Luxury villas and handsome funerary monuments lined the highways for several miles beyond city edges. Manors and small efficiency farms blanketed the countryside between towns. The land bore the scars of resounding progress. There were colossal works of agricultural terracing. Dams, canals, tunnels, and aqueducts tamed the natural waterways, carrying fresh spring and stream water to the citizenry and diverting less pure sources to the fields, where pumps and wheels sent it where it was needed. Lakes and marshes were drained and forests felled to extend usable land. Wood was essential for construction and for heating houses, baths, brick kilns, and mines, but logging denuded the mountain slopes. The fact is that several centuries of Greek and Roman urbanization had profoundly transformed the face of the Mediterranean from what it had been at the time of Stonehenge, Knossos, and Troy.

Beyond the Empire

This costly prosperity stopped short at the borders. On the other side, peoples untouched by Roman technology lived simple lives that made only the gentlest demand on natural resources and left the land without permanent markings. That is why it is hard to recover their traces.

Africa

The African continent, outside of the northern littoral, behaved in the traditional ways of the Stone Age. There were hunters and gatherers, pastoral nomads, and farmers. They shaped a broad range of environments depending on the particular geography of a region, its mode of sustenance, its beliefs, and social arrangements. So there was no question of a pervasive pan-African architecture. The earthen round house with its thick insulating walls and soft patterns of shade and shadow was appropriate to the inland savannah; the rectangular house with its light screen walls, raised on a platform and oriented to the cardinal points to catch cross breezes, to the humid rainforests of the coast.

Mud was a prevalent building material. So were poles, brushwood, grass, and loose stones. The variety was seemingly inexhaustible. A recent taxonomy lists thirty-two basic forms for houses alone, from cave houses and underground or semiunderground dug-in buildings to tower houses that consisted of coalescing mud cylinders of one, two, or three storeys. Plans could be round, oval, or rectangular. Roofs might be flat or else conical, trumpet-shaped, or hemispherical with convex, concave, or asymmetrically peaked profiles; or they could be saddle-back or lean-to, hipped, pyramidal, or wagon-shaped. Construction methods ranged from *banco*, a wet-mud process akin to coil pottery, to a frame of poles and skins, which was used in the tents of seminomad tribes of the sub-Saharan belt.

Groupings of homesteads and villages reflected fine nuances of social structure, defining spheres of responsibility, territoriality, and ownership. (Fig. 10.7) Each function of an extended homestead would be allotted its own building: a building for each wife, with a grinding house and granary of her own, the goat house, the stable, the beer store, all arranged in simple constellations and linked by straight walls or embraced by an enclosure wall. In West Africa courtyard houses have abetted speculation about cross-cultural ties. Four buildings, singly or continuously thatch-roofed, faced one another across a courtyard, which in some cases was geared to collect rainwater. This latter feature seems to echo the impluvium in a Roman domus, and there are Egyptian parallels too.

But whatever the balance of indigenous and incursive elements, mainland Africa was the polar opposite of the Roman Empire. Hundreds of self-reliant tribes fended for themselves in the arid zone of the sub-Sahara and the tropical savannah land, in coastal forests, and in benign river basins. They were tied by the same basic verities: "a house, a family and the respect of old age." They built few religious structures. Material permanence was not a fundamental concern. On the contrary, built forms were something that responded to the changing circumstances of daily life and the domestic family cycle; they could be adapted, extended, replaced, or moved. A new wife was entitled to her own addition in the homestead compound; the departing dead and the young who set up their own households reduced the compound. Since no fixed administrative building was thought necessary, the election of a new chief might require the reorientation of the village away from the dead chief's house and toward that of the new chief. The permanence was in the land and its spirits, the generational patterns of self-preservation and reverence. The act of building was a personal right and a collective enterprise. Materials were ready at hand; the labor force was the village.

We should recognize in all this a fundamental premise. Cities are not the only means of claiming stability. Monumental architecture is not the only way people can symbolize their desire to stay together and be remembered. To talk of "savages" or "the unsettled continent" is license for exploitation.

Europe

Although Rome may have known little of this other world, she actively engaged kindred territories of the "uncivilized" world in Europe, England, and the Balkans. For centuries the nomad peoples of the northern steppes, from Hungary to Manchuria, swept in great migratory waves toward regions whose advantage beckoned, or wherever they were forced to move under pressure from others. These restless stockbreeders and herders, who had domesticated the horse and conquered and ruled their vast, fluid empires with their cavalry, had no use for settled permanence except as their last resting place. Under great mounds of earth they would finally lay still, surrounded by their precious objects of gold and their live possessions of servants and horses. In life they spent their time on horseback and in tents—and that, naturally enough, was their architecture. "Having neither cities nor forts," the Greek historian Herodotus wrote of them, "and carrying their dwellings with them wherever they go; accustomed, moreover, one and all of them, to shoot from horseback; and living not by husbandry but on their cattle, their wagons the only houses that they possess, how can they fail of being unconquerable, and unassailable even?"

As long as Rome was strong, these steppe riders preyed on the sedentary belts of agriculture that were comprised of loose tribal aggregations of villages and single homesteads. This was the situation in much of northern and eastern Europe and the British Isles. The rural way of life had taken root over centuries of continuous adaptation and experiment since the Neolithic revolution,

Fig. 10.3 Rome (Italy), the Pantheon, ca. A.D. 120–27; view from the north. The inscription refers to an earlier rectangular sanctuary on the site built by Augustus' great minister Marcus Agrippa, ca. 25 B.C. See also Fig. 9.23

and a stable economy of farming prevailed everywhere, overriding tribal differences. Two distinct outside forces worked on this inveterate European culture. From the south, Greco-Roman urbanization made inroads in search of fresh resources. From the east, invasions of nomadic marauders caused disruptive migration and called for an architecture of defense.

Once again, as in Africa, the same level of existence and social organization did not bring about a uniform building pattern. There were ubiquitous dwelling structures, certainly. The round house with the thatch roof was very pervasive, as it had been in less developed societies everywhere since the days of Khirokitia. Their traces survive all over England and Scotland, and the form lived on in the Christian monasteries of Ireland. But construction methods for them vary, and so do settlement patterns. What is more important, however, is that several other forms—residential, utilitarian, and ceremonial—have left unequivocal remains, as have planned communities other than farming villages. Wooden rectangular houses built on artificial platforms responded to the challenge of the salt mud-

Fig. 10.4 Giovanni Paolo Panini, *Interior of the Pantheon*, ca. 1750. (National Gallery of Art, Washington)

Fig. 10.5a Baalbek (Lebanon), temple of Venus, third century A.D.; view from the south. The temple consisted of a circular cella roofed with a shallow stone dome and encircled by a free-standing colonnade that extended to form a rectangular porch facing the north. This is a provincial attempt to emulate in cut stone the concrete forms of Rome, like the one in Fig. 10.5b below.

Fig. 10.5b Tivoli (ancient Tibur, Italy), Hadrian's villa, ca. A.D.118–134; vestibule of the Piazza d'Oro at the northeast corner of the villa.

Fig. 10.6 Timgad (Thamugadi, Algeria), Roman city founded in 100 B.C.; aerial view. A colony of military veterans laid down a rigid orthogonal plan; the city later developed along the highways outside the gates.

hurl their missiles further downhill than the adversary could send his uphill. Earth was the principal medium in the design of oppida—massively dug ditches, running earth walls. Wooden palisades and stone aprons were secondary.

To see in Roman imperial reliefs representations of bearded, unkempt natives in long bulging pants throwing themselves pell-mell against disciplined rows of legionaries or huddling in fear, one would believe, as the citizens in Rome were doubtless meant to, that the arms of the empire were opening up savage tracts to civilization. (Fig. 10.9) But that of course was

hardly the case. Aside from the land-based order of Iron Age Europe with its satisfying way of life, the design of some oppida belie the notion of rude, uncivilized innocence. Deep in the Carpathian mountain range of modern Rumania, on ably terraced slopes, lie the ruins of Sarmizegethusa, the capital of the Dacians destroyed by Trajan's legions in A.D. 106. The walls of the citadel are 3 meters (10 feet) thick and are made of a rubble and timber core faced with dressed stone. From it issues a partially stone-paved road to terraces that supported the houses of the chieftains of King Decebalus' state as well as a sacred

Fig. 10.7 Yankezia (Ghana), living compound; ground plan. This hamlet of the Konkomba people in northern Ghana was surveyed in 1961.

flats of northwest Europe when they were being occupied a century or two before Caesar's invasion of Gaul. In Scotland, close to the sea, homesteads were built in the shape of circular, drystone-walled citadels of up to three storeys (called *brochs*), with outer defense works like banks and ditches. (Fig. 10.8) In Poland there were great centers of iron-smelting, their furnaces arranged in regular rows like some metallurgical Carnac.

But the most lasting testimony of this European alternative to Romanism are the *oppida* and their defensive systems. These were wartime refuges and centers of tribal gathering. Two natural locations were preferred, for good strategic reasons: hilltops, the commoner by far, and river promontories in deep, precipitous valleys. Some were colossal, enclosing an area of as many as 40 hectares (100 acres). In sling-stone warfare the object was to discourage the attacking force before it had a chance to reach the defenses. A hill-fort gave the upper hand to the occupants, since they could

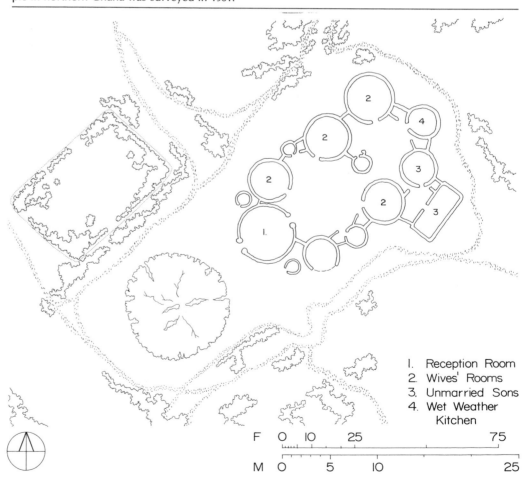

1. Reception Room
2. Wives' Rooms
3. Unmarried Sons
4. Wet Weather Kitchen

F 0 10 25 75

M 0 5 10 25

Fig. 10.8 Mousa (Scotland), broch or walled citadel, ca. 300 B.C.–A.D. 400; reconstruction drawing. The thick walls tapering toward the top had hollow upper levels and the space spanned by flagstones defined superimposed galleries. The form recalls Sardinian *nuraghi* (see Fig. 6.1). About 500 brochs are known in Scotland.

Fig. 10.9 Rome, Column of Trajan, dedicated in A.D. 113; scene representing the Roman army victorious over the Dacians. The 38 meter (125 foot) high marble column was erected as part of Trajan's forum complex to commemorate Trajan's campaigns against the tribes of Dacia, modern Rumania, under the leadership of a chief named Decebalus.

enclosure containing at least five sanctuaries. Three sanctuaries are rectangular buildings, probably open to the sky, and are filled with stone bases on which originally stood wooden columns, no less than sixty in the largest of the temples. The arrangement brings to mind, if anything, the columnar halls or apadana of Persepolis, without the roof.

But more intriguing still is a large circular shrine. (Fig. 10.10) It had an outer ring of stone blocks with a ring of small uprights just inside. There were 180 of these uprights, the number of days in half of the Dacian year. Within this outer frame was a concentric ring of timber stakes, originally sheathed with fine terra-cotta, interrupted by stone blocks at four points on the cross-axes. In the center was a horseshoe of smaller stakes that set the main direction of the complex in a northwest-southeast orientation. All the stakes had iron nails driven through them with terminal rings, from which to hang ornaments and votive offerings. Close by stood a stone sun made up of ten wedge-shaped slabs radiating from a circular slab at the center.

This circular shrine recalls Stonehenge. But we are now no longer in the Neolithic age. The time is the first two Christian centuries; the place, the orbit of the Roman Empire. Decebalus' people, about 1,200 meters (4,000 feet) high in the southern Carpathians, seem to be mooring their state to a solar cosmology just as Hadrian's Romans did with his Pantheon. There is, to be sure, an unbridgeable gap of structural and visual sophistication between the Pantheon and the circle of Sarmizegethusa. But technology and subtle design are not always the proper gauges for assessing the quality of people's views of the world and their place in it.

Persia

In Persia at this time, the circle occurs in two contexts on the land—religious and urban.

Mazdaism, the official faith of the great Achamaenid rulers, which centered on a triad of deities—Ahuramazda the creator, Mithras the sun-god, and Anahita, the Persian equivalent of the mother-goddess of the Near East—was still in force, despite two centuries of Greek occupation that started

with the conquests of Alexander. When the Greek yoke was thrown off in the later second century B.C., a site in the highlands of modern Azerbaijan began to figure as one of the holiest places of Mazdean practice. The object of reverence was a magic lake whose depth could not be plumbed and whose waters held steady even as they were being emptied continually by seven streams. Here, too, burned the sacred fire from which all others were kindled in the fire temples of the land.

The altars, ritual buildings, and annexes of Takht-i-Suleiman, the Throne of Solomon, as this haunting shrine is now called, have disappeared: only the lake and the manmade boundary survive. It is enough. In the midst of a lofty, epic terrain, away from human habitation, the three holy elements of water, fire, and earth, long worshipped in greater Persia, are spectacularly embraced within a circular wall of enormous stones. (Fig. 10.11)

Fig. 10.10 Sarmizegethusa (Rumania), Dacian capital from ca. 100 B.C. to its destruction by the Romans in A.D. 106. This view shows the Stonehenge-like circular sanctuary and the nearby stone sundisk.

Even in Parthian times, the built component of Takht-i-Suleiman was probably modest. Persia's religious worship always took the form of an open-air cult. Lakes and rivers were unrestrained water sanctuaries. In the fields northeast of the Persian Gulf, at Masdjid-i-Suleiman or Badr-i-Nishandah, the oil-rich earth blazed miraculously. The priesthood, the very ancient fraternity of Magi, administered these natural sanctuaries and tended the fire altars that marked assembly places for regular worship. The fire altars were to be found on the roofs of temple towers that were usually square. Later on, the fire would be sheltered in small domed structures open to all four sides by single arches. The only example that might go back to Parthian times, Rabat-i-Safid, stands today on a rugged height southeast of Mashhad. (Fig. 10.12) The construction is rudimentary, but it prefigures an insistent concern of these late Persian builders to place a dome on the walls of a four-sided building.

The transition from the square plan to the circle of the dome was attempted at Rabat-i-Safid by bridging the corners with wooden beams, which in turn supported rather awkward masonry squinches. In Persia full-blown squinches, which are arched or have corbelled corners, must await the Sassanians who displaced Parthian rule in the third century A.D.; but they were hardly new in the history of building. (Fig. 10.13) Hemispherical vaults over square rooms were commonplace in the Roman Empire by this date, and the transition element, rendered in stone, mud-brick, or concrete, was either the squinch or the more polished pendentive, a spherical triangle that continues the curve of the dome down to the four points of the square chamber.

Round cities were known even before the Persians, in Syria and eastern Anatolia, although geometric thinking does not seem to have affected the layout inside. The curve responded for the most part to the hilly topography of the sites and to defensive expedience. In their state reliefs, Assyrian military camps are shown as being round, presumably in flat territory as well as on prominences; and it may have been from this source that Parthians derived their circular cities. Indeed, each one had a purely military origin. Ctesiphon in northern Mesopotamia was built as a camp for the Per-

sian army on the left bank of the Tigris, across from the Hellenistic city of Seleucia. It became in time the Parthian capital and that of the Sassanians after them whose mighty palace, the Taq-i-Kisra, we will look at in a later chapter. Gur-Firuzabad, south of Shiraz, was built as the fortified headquarters of the pretender to the Parthian throne, Ardashir I, who got the upper hand in A.D. 224 and founded the Sassanian dynasty.

Persian kings were indifferent city builders. Capitals, Persepolis included, were equipped with substantial palaces and other accommodations for royal sojourns, but they were surrounded by shanty towns. Central Iran, an arid waste, could barely meet the needs of the nomad. The valleys of the great mountain chains that ring this

majestic, wind-swept plateau with its salt deserts sustained the only settlements. Rainfall, good pasturage, and tilling land encouraged the settlements, and they in turn attracted the trade of major caravan routes. City life proper, however, was mostly confined to old centers in conquered territories. The countryside remained in the hands of a landholding aristocracy, and this ruling class, ensconced in fortified castles, headed a feudal society very like that which we later find in medieval Europe.

In this unsteady political climate where central authority was on the defensive, the Hellenistic cities founded by Alexander and his Seleucid successors played an equalizing role. They provided bureaucrats and an enterprising bourgeoisie, and their reve-

Fig. 10.11 Takht-i-Suleiman (Azerbaijan), Parthian sanctuary, first century A.D.; aerial view. The great circular wall once enclosed the supreme fire called Adhur Gushnasp, which means "fire of warriors" or "royal fire."

Fig. 10.12 Rabat-i-Safid (Iran), fire temple, ca. A.D. 200.

nues enriched the royal coffers. The King of Kings supported the Greek cities, therefore, even after the overthrow of the Seleucid dynasty. Hellenistic grid plans can still be seen in sites like Dura Europos on the Euphrates, founded by the Macedonians in 300 B.C. and occupied by the Parthians about 100 B.C. But the Greek veneer is thin. Private houses revert to the old Mesopotamian solution of irregular rooms grouped around a small courtyard. These coexisted with the native house unit—the columned hall preceded by an open portico. And now under the Parthians a new component was introduced into residential design, which may in fact have been common earlier in the vernacular idiom of eastern Iran. This feature was the *iwan*, a rectangular barrel-vaulted hall open at one end to its full width and height; it was often employed as a triple chamber, the central one usually larger than those on the sides.

The architectural expression of majesty continued to be the ceremonial palace. That at Hatra might be a century later than the Palatine complex in Rome. (Fig. 10.14) A look at its plan will reveal how different it was from the Achaemenid model of Persepolis. (Fig. 6.23) There are no apadana and no monumental staircases, but the new basic unit, the iwan, is used in various combinations. The initial scheme involved two large iwans separated by two-storey sections of smaller rooms. Behind the southern iwan was a temple tower, a kind of vaulted palatine chapel, situated in much

the same way as the ziggurat was attached to Assyrian palaces, like the one at Khorsabad. At Assur, the old Assyrian capital, we encounter the first instance of an extremely influential formula: four cross-axial iwans around a court. This scheme, developed by the Sassanians, will carry over to the Islamic period and will become standard for mosques, schools, and caravanserais alike.

The vaulted forms of the royal palace, at this monumental scale, must have been affected by Roman example. But the only two vault types known to the Parthians were the barrel and the dome. They made no effort to have vaults intersect or to create the kind of spatial sequence and interpenetration characteristic of the Roman vaulted style. They set principal rooms one next to the other, with isolating corridor spaces or bands of auxiliary units between them. Columnar screens, banks of windows, and similar Roman devices to permit the flow of space from one unit to the next are totally absent. Facade design was openly indebted to the Greco-Roman vocabulary of columns and niches, interpreted rather idiosyncratically. (Fig. 10.15) With the rise of the Sassanian dynasty, a nationalist mood began to prevail in architecture. But even then Roman facade conventions lingered like snatches of an old tune.

The Other Ancient World

Parthian Persia stood, Janus-like, between the ancient world that has so far in this book been our chief concern and the equally enduring body of nations in the Far East. (Fig. 10.16) It collected the goods of the Mediterranean at Red Sea ports and transported them from there to the mouth of the Indus; they then traveled upriver as far as

Fig. 10.13 The placing of a dome on a square bay; diagrams. As the basic plan of the bay shows (**A**), the problem is how to make the transition from the cube, defined by the walls, to the circular base of the dome. (**B**) is a diagrammatic plan of the two principal solutions: top left, the pendentive; bottom right, the squinch. The pendentive (**C**) is a spherical triangle. The squinch spans the corner with an arch (**D**), or a series of arches (**E**).

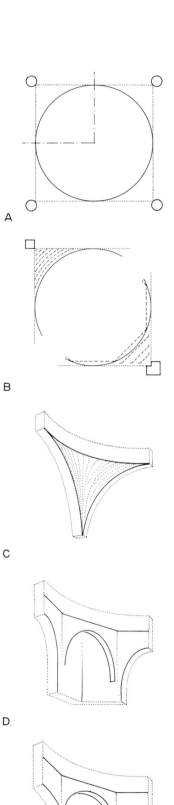

A

B

C

D

E

modern Peshawar, crossed the Hindu Kush and the Pamir range in caravans, and via Chinese Turkestan reached the edges of the broad expanse of China. Special Chinese and Indian commodities found their way to Roman markets along a second, overland, route that made use of the Oxus River, traversed the Caspian Sea, proceeded along the Cyrus (Araks), and after some days'

portage arrived at the Black Sea. Finally, there was the famous Silk Road that passed through Merv, Hekatompylos, Ecbatana, and Ctesiphon and then forded the Euphrates, unloading its precious Eastern cargo into the Roman entrepots of the Syrian coastland.

India in this period had no unified rule. China, by contrast, had been a cohesive empire for more than two centuries under

the Han dynasty (206 B.C.–A.D. 220), whose capital was the city of Ch'ang-an in the Shensi Province of northwest China, by the Yellow River. But for both spheres of continental Asia, these were only the latest episodes of a hoary past. Human life in China goes back one-half million years to the so-called Peking Man. It has continued without interruption ever since. A rich, long

Fig. 10.14 Parthian "palaces," first–second centuries A.D.; ground plans: left, Assur (Iraq), the four-iwan scheme; right, Hatra (Iraq), the parallel-iwan scheme, part of a larger complex now thought to be a sanctuary of the sun.

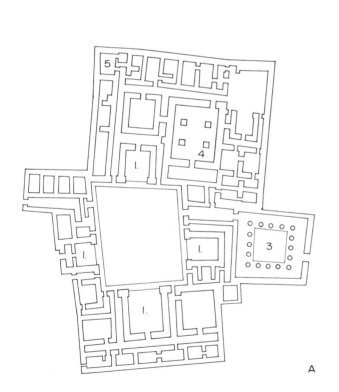

A

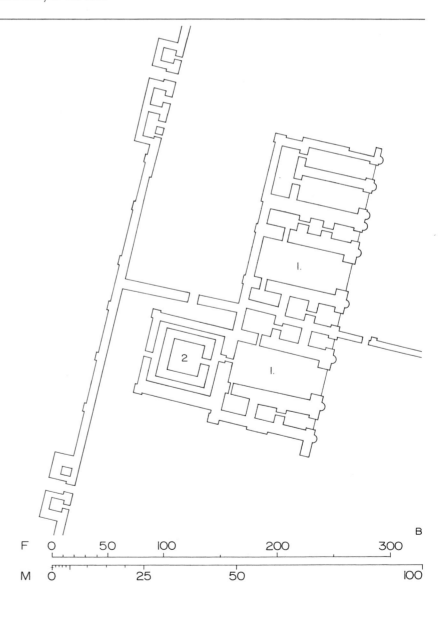

1. Iwan
2. Temple Tower
3. Peristyle
4. Pillar Hall
5. Bath

B

F 0   50   100   200   300

M 0   25   50   100

Neolithic phase is only now being pieced together by archaeologists. And the literate age of the two millennia before Christ shaped many of the environmental attitudes of the Han, which we will be looking at shortly.

Indian prehistory embraces a European-like megalithic culture, with stone avenues and mound-encased dolmens, in the south and central regions of the subcontinent, as well as a brilliant urban culture in the Indus valley that corresponds to the experiment of Mesopotamian city-states. The towns of Harappa and the gridded Mohenjo-Daro were already at least 1,000 years old when they succumbed about 1500 B.C. to an invasion of light-skinned Aryans who enslaved the indigenous Dravidian population and ushered in the tenacious caste system. The new master race brought with it the faith of Brahma, the unimageable ultimate reality on which all things are based. Hinduism, which still has many millions of adherents, evolved out of the idol-loving earthy exuberance of native beliefs and the more purely transcendental idealism of the Aryan overlords.

India

The cerebral aspect of the Indian world view affected architectural theory, especially the design of temples and cities that were considered a diagram of universal order. Vastuvidya, the science of architecture, already constituted a branch of occult knowledge around 1000 B.C. The earth was round, and the circle was its primal form. But an absolute, extramundane order resided in the square in which was manifest the supreme principle, Brahma. The sides of this perfect form, duly fixed by the cardinal points, could be divided by any number up to 32, thus yielding between 1 and 1,024 units or *pādas*. (Fig. 10.17) It was for the priest to select one of these variants or *mandalas* as the basis of a temple design or the layout of a city. Despite the extraordinary surface richness of later Hindu temples, their exterior mass pleated and honeycombed hypnotically with ornament and sculpture, the holy diagram still rules, and every detail is subject to a strict system of canonical proportions. (Figs. 16.26b, 16.27) Early town schemes, if the architectural books are to be believed, conformed to mandalas with as many pādas as there were to be residential quarters, and only within each pāda, which was inhabited by members of a particular professional group, might a looser subdivision of alleys and footpaths be countenanced.

With the architecture of the alternative Indian religion, Buddhism, we slip out of the stern abstractions of the circle and the square and revive the emotional strains of the mountain of god. The Buddha lived in the sixth century B.C., and when he died at the age of eighty at Kushinagara, his body was cremated, and over his relics a mound was raised in the manner traditional in early India for kings and heroes. Out of this primordial symbol of the earth's embrace and the human reach skyward, present in the environmental thinking of old cultures everywhere, the *stupa* was canonized as the most revered monument of Buddhism. Freestanding or rock-cut, single or in numbers, the stupa fixed the permanent havens of families of monks outside of the big towns where the brothers would go begging for half of every day.

The three components of a Buddhist monastery were enunciated quite early. The stupa was the pivot, both reliquary and cosmic egg, atom and universe. On a circular base sat the tall hemisphere of a dome, a cast of the infinite cosmos transfixed to the depths of the earth by an axial pole that ran through it. On the tip of the pole, which showed outside the dome's crown, was hoisted the royal emblem of the umbrella and under it the sacred relic nested, surrounded by a square railing. In addition, there had to be an assembly hall for communal activities like public confession. This hall, called *chaitya*, was often combined with the stupa into a single structure. (Fig. 10.18) The third element was the *vihara*, a large rectangular space entered from the outside along one side and lined on the remaining three sides with dormitory cells.

A whole series of these monasteries can

Fig. 10.15 Assur, Parthian "palace," facade of west iwan; reconstruction model. (Staatliche Museen, Berlin) The facade was originally stuccoed and brightly painted.

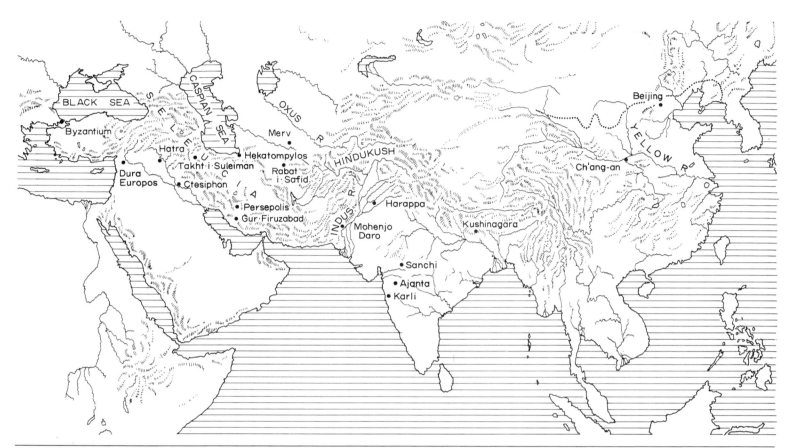

Fig. 10.16 Map: The Middle East and Asia in the second–third centuries A.D.

be seen at Ajanta, in the gorge of the Waghora River which cuts through the plateau of the western Ghats. (Fig. 10.19) They were carved into the rock-cliffs over several centuries starting in the second century B.C. They were accessible from the valley floor by means of narrow flights of rock-cut steps. The stupas here were fashioned in the earth itself and out of its primal rock substance. They were given a protective shell overhead, which was then extended longitudinally to form the barrel-vaulted chaitya. Rows of vertical supports described a continuous U-shaped path along the edges of the hall, behind the stupa, and across the entrance front.

Pilgrims traveled great distances to reach this remote sanctuary, followed the river gorge for a spell, and in files negotiated the difficult path upward to the mouth of the

cave. They probably entered from the left, since the ritual circuit around the stupa was to coil clockwise. They moved slowly between the rock wall of the cave, polished smooth and hospitable to the touch, and the row of receding pillars that were wooden, treelike uprights at their simplest or, in the case of the largest and deepest chaitya of Karli, rock columns with intricately wrought imposts of guardian animals and paired lovers from which sprang a wooden armature of transverse ribs underlying the scooped barrel of the nave. The darkness thickened at each step: the certainties of time and place elapsed. Then, at the edge of the fathomless, the dome of the stupa glowed suddenly, as if the cosmic egg was being unveiled in the heart of the earth.

The source of light was in actuality a hole at the top of the rock shell through which

Fig. 10.17 Indian mandala, the *vastu-purusha;* from an old Indian manual of architecture.

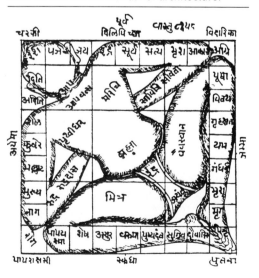

Fig. 10.18 Karli (India), rock-cut chaitya hall of the Buddhist sanctuary, A.D. 100–25; interior.

central Asia Minor, and of course Buddhist monasteries like those at Ajanta and Karli.

These buildings are not inhibited by the force of gravity; problems of loads and thrusts here are negligible. The structure stands intact, as it were, before the carver-builder starts work on it. Columns and vaults are no more than structural symbols liberated from raw matter in the way a sculptor liberates form from a lump of stone.

The Buddhist carver-builders at Karli used pointed chisels and iron mallets, and flat chisels of varying width for the final polish. They scooped out the barrel-vault first, removing the rubble through the sun window. Then they hewed the lower section, probably beginning at the entrance. Next they hoisted the heavy teak ribs, weighing as much as 3.5 tons each, into place and secured them to the polished surface of the vault by strong dowels. The act of sculpturing the chaitya and its holy shrine was regarded primarily as a rite, and no detailed description of the process has survived in the old manuals of architecture.

In the open air, the stupa behaved differently. The subterranean voyage of discovery gave way to the celebration in broad nature of a cosmic trophy; revelation was exchanged for processional homage. Set up on prominences and outlined against the sky, the stupas beckoned magisterially. At Sanchi, a monastery near the important trading center of Vidisha, three stupas were built over a period of about two hundred years, from the second century B.C. to the first century A.D. (Fig. 10.20) The original monastic buildings have disappeared and the stupas have been repeatedly done over. Still, they stand with tremendous presence in the highest point of the plateau, each rivetted to the hillscape by its central mast.

The largest of the three, built in brick and subsequently enlarged and encased in stone, had four cardinal gateways, or toranas, intricately carved with guardian spirits and the miracles of Buddha. The main entrance was probably on the south side. The high balustrade that stands in front of the base of the stupa blocked the stairway within, until one full circle on the ground level brought one to it naturally. The ascent began at this point, and then tightened at the level of the base of the dome. This upper circumambulatory path also has

the builders had first tunneled their way into what was to become the chaitya. This "sun window," functioning like the oculus of the Pantheon in admitting nonworldly light, came first in the process of construction; the Pantheon oculus was instead the final outcome of the laboriously made building. Indeed, the quality of vaulted architecture hollowed out of natural matter sharply differs from that of Roman vaulted forms.

The practice of scooping out an environment in the given forms of nature is more frequent and universal than we might think. There were ancient rock-dwellers in the Red

Sea, Ethiopia, and Armenia. In the vision of Obadiah, the Lord admonishes the land of Edom, "thou that dwellest in the clefts of the rock, whose habitation is high." Rock tombs abound in the Near East. In Sicily whole towns are rock-cut structures: Siculiano, Caltabelotta, Bronte. And in the loess belt of China millions of people have traditionally lived in dwellings hollowed out of the silt that had been formed by the action of the winds in the remote Great Ice Age. In terms of monumental achievement we could point to the Egyptian temples of Abu Simbel, rock-cut Byzantine churches in

Fig. 10.21 Peking (Beijing, China), the Forbidden City; aerial view.

a high balustrade modeled, as are the toranas, on wooden prototypes. Here, on this narrow and paved path, the pilgrims went around the axis of the universe in its domed cosmic shield, touching the source of their faith that would make benign the real world on their way back home.

China

Buddhism was introduced into China under the Han dynasty. By the fifth century A.D., it had begun to bring a note of compassion and devout humanity to the discrepant world view of this ancient people and their inflexible built environment. Unlike their Indian neighbors, the Chinese had little sympathy for the mystical or the infinite. Theirs was basically a secular, intellectual order; unmoved by any need to search for some ultimate truth, they plotted their own precise, clear-cut place on earth. The society at large, dominated by a

ruling class of literate officials, was fundamentally agrarian. But it was in royal walled cities that human hierarchies and values were expressed in codified spatial settings.

Chinese cosmology pictured the heaven round and the earth as a stable cube. Space was conceived as a series of imbricated squares, at the center of which lay the capital of the empire strictly oriented toward the points of the compass. And in its center the palace commanded the main north-south axis, facing southward (as did all important buildings) in the direction of the Red Phoenix of summer and fire. To the east was the region of the Blue Dragon, of spring and growth and the upright tree. In this sector of the capital would be the Temple of the Ancestors. Autumn and its harvest, but also wars, the harvest of men, and memory and regret were all symbolized by the White Tiger of the west, and in the urban layout by the Altar of the Earth. From the north came

cold winter and marauding hordes bent on destruction; its color was black. The emperor faced away from it, and in the northern sector of the city, confined behind the palace, would be situated dubious activities including commerce and its markets.

Rectilinearity and axiality—these were the operative principles of Chinese design. (Fig. 10.21) And with them went the horizontal aesthetic, the conscious preference for a uniform range of heights that shifted the environmental burden of social distinctions to the placement of buildings in the general scheme of the city, the level of the terraces on which they invariably stood, the area they covered, and the degree of their ornamentation. All of these were officially prescribed. Han sources set down the specific code, based on status, that controlled where a house was allowed to be in its *fang* or neighborhood, how big it was to be, and how involved its design.

This system of rigorous discriminations carried over to the frame of the single building or compound. The house, humble or princely, had as its pivot an inner courtyard. (Fig. 10.22) Rooms looked in onto it, their back walls defining the exterior boundary of the household. Or else freestanding pavilions were set within the courtyard and a separate, walled envelope thrown around the compound. The aim always was to screen the intimate world of the house from the bustle of the streets, to observe internal rules of behavior, and to unfold spatial sequences according to what has been called "graduated privacy." The front gate, cut into the perimeter wall, was as far as the peddler or the stranger would be allowed to contact the residents. Friends and relatives came into the courtyard and expected to be entertained in the porched central room (the *ming*), corresponding to the Roman *tablinum*, which sat on its own platform a little higher than the rest of the house. Deeper still were the rooms reserved for the womenfolk and the rituals of family life. The etiquette of the royal palace, with its many courtyards and pavilions, differed only in degree.

Like the Roman domus, the Chinese house had the dual function of a home and a setting for social ceremony, but the patterns of formal behavior were choreographed with unflinching correctness. A

Han dynasty compilation delineates in the greatest detail the movements of a visit, the overriding duty of everyone concerned "to humble oneself in order to honor others." We read:

At each gateway the host must respectfully urge his guest in until they arrive at the door of the inner courtyard. The host excuses himself to enter first so that he may place the mats personally. . . . The host enters the doorway and . . . proceeds to the eastern stairway, while the guest proceeds to the west. . . . As the host lifts his left foot to ascend the eastern stairs, the guest lifts his left foot to ascend the western stairs.

And so it continues.

In Chinese architecture it is the ritual and its diagrammatic plot that endure, not the actual physical structure. Materials were by and large impermanent—rammed earth, mud-brick, timber—and the expected life of any building, public or private, was a generation or so. The structures decayed fast and their material was reused, or they were renewed periodically with or without respect for their original purpose. This recycling was possible because the architectural plans hardly varied: a long and shallow rectangle divided into rows of bays by stone or timber pillars that sustain a superstructure of ceiling beams and a truss roof. Perhaps we should not speak of a truss here in the same way that we speak of the rigid triangles of Western roof construction, with their bracing diagonals. In China the skeletal armature between ceiling and roof pitch consisted of progressively shorter lateral beams and a vertical spine at the top that held up the ridge.

All basic roof types were already present in the Han period: the gable roof with or without overhang, the hipped roof of four slopes, the pointed roof, the so-called "Nine Spines." (Fig. 10.23) The curve of the eaves, so characteristically Chinese, seems to postdate Han practice, but already roofs were being built with a decided change of pitch half way up, as if they had given way under their own weight. The roof covering was tile. The roof, whatever the degree of flare, did not depend on the walls. They were spatial or seclusive panels, little more. The roof, for that reason, appears to float over its building, anchored to its terrace by the skeletal frame of the uprights.

Fig. 10.22 Peking (Beijing), one-courtyard town house; aerial view.

At the juncture of pillar and roof, both externally under the eaves and in the interior space, bracket clusters mushroomed thickly to reduce spans and reinforce joints. In Han buildings these brackets were not yet incorporated in the structural frame, but formed separate supports. The perfection and refinement of the system called *tou-kung*, which entailed both bracketing and cantilever action via members that extended parallel to the rafters directly under the roof, constitute the chief points of interest in later Chinese architecture. (Fig. 10.24)

China built with earth and wood, but not because it had to. There is plenty of architecture in stone to examine from all periods; it is mostly utilitarian—for example, bridges and defensive works. The Great Wall is universally admired. (Fig. 10.25) Some 3,220 kilometers (2,000 miles) long, it wends its way from Tun-huang to the Yellow Sea, shielding Kansu, Shensi, Shansi, and Hopei provinces. The original curtain goes back to the reign of Emperor Shih Huang Ti of the Ch'in dynasty who unified the country in 232 B.C. and to Han rulers who improved on the wall and planted

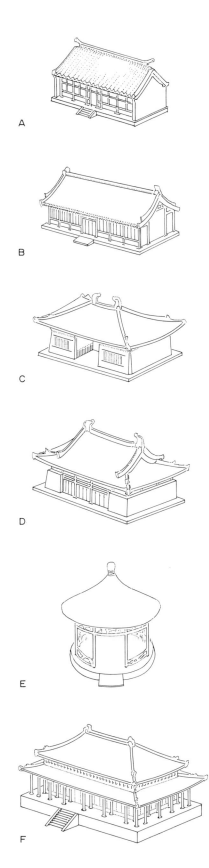

permanent veterans' colonies along its length to control the passage of nomads and regulate their trade, but also to prevent the exit of settled populations.

The permanence and continued enhancement of this official project are, however, exceptional. Chinese rulers usually built for themselves alone and with an almost fatalistic transitoriness in view. In this and in the character of their official building programs their attitude was totally different from that of Rome. They trusted their majestic tombs and the judgment of written history, as revealed in scrupulously kept archives, to carry their name to posterity. Roman emperors built to be remembered. And most of what they built had the public good or leisure activities in mind.

The notion of architecture as public service, or the instrument of the state, or a transmitter of culture was alien to the ruling dynasties of China. Concern for the people might be evinced through gifts to the poor, amnesties, or the remission of some taxes. One did not undertake to supply them with baths, theaters, or forums. Unlike the strong urban legacy of the Roman Empire, there had never been a tradition of independent cities in China attentive to public amenities and civic display. Behind imperial power here was the peasant masses. In the cities the central task of government was social control. Residential grids look to be in the spirit of Hippodamus—on paper. In reality, the blocks were walled individually, to keep the population inside at night and to facilitate census-taking and recruitment for military service and forced labor.

The public image of the city manifested itself in the royal palace alone. The main avenue led directly to the emperor's presence, not to a civic and religious center like

Fig. 10.23 Chinese roof types; isometric diagrams. **(A)** Ying-shan (Ying-shan), without overhanging gables; **(B)** Hsüan-shan (Xuanshan), with overhanging gables; **(C)** Wu-tien (Wu-dien), also called Wu-chi, with five spines and four slopes; **(D)** Hsieh-shan (Xieshan), also called Chiu-chi, with nine spines; **(E)** Tsan-chien (Zanjian), the pinnacle type, shown here on a round structure; **(F)** Ch'ung-yen (Chongyan), with double eaves, an elaboration of type **(C)**.

a Roman forum. No religious architecture competed for attention; no priesthood diverted centralized power. The Temple of Ancestors and the Altar of Earth were palace adjuncts, and so was the Ming-Tan where the emperor performed pious ceremonies for the state. At Ch'ang-an, in the very center of a circular moat that enclosed a square platform was a four-winged structure around a court set on its own circular terrace. (Fig. 10.26) Here the Han emperor adjusted his behavior to nature's cycles, moving from hall to hall as the seasons changed and completing a revolution in the course of the year—the lord of many millions across a wide, expanding land, and the pivot of their universe.

A Continent Alone

Despite their cultural disparity, the continents of Europe, Asia, and Africa were interconnected by trade and war. America stood alone. Contacts with what is collectively called the Old World were superficial. The "Indian" tribes of North America and the more complex states of Central America and the Andes probably developed independently, exploiting what indigenous talent and resources they possessed, with minimal interaction even among themselves.

There had been a time, some 30,000 years ago, when America was in communication with the Old World. (Fig. 10.27) A land bridge existed then between Asia and Alaska, and a Mongoloid race of people moved across it in several waves; and through a glacier-free corridor between the continental ice sheets, they penetrated into the land mass that is now Canada and the United States. They moved mostly on foot, knowing no beasts of burden; they hunted big game, foraged, and in the vast sandstone formations of the Southwest called *mesas* (tables, in Spanish), they practiced rudimentary agriculture perhaps as early as 4,000 B.C. Pit houses partly sunk into the ground for protection against cold and wind were common. But in the Northwest country (British Columbia, Washington, Oregon) foraging tribes mastered a technique of building rectangular, gabled houses of cedar. And in the far north, in the unfriendly frozen tundra of the Arctic circle

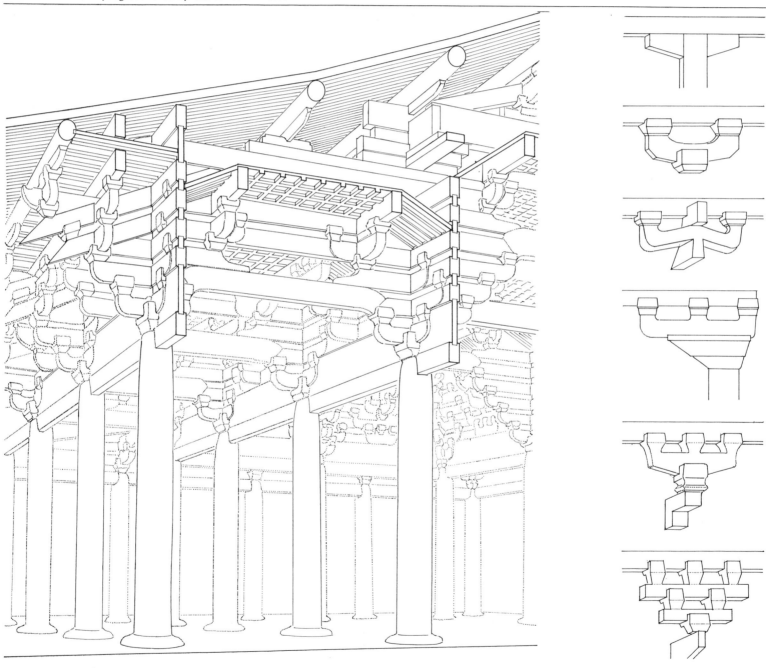

Fig. 10.24 Chinese bracket system, called *tou-kung (dougong)*; diagrams. The right-hand column shows the progressive complication of the primitive bracket. The left-hand drawing is of the main hall of Fo-Kuang Ssu in Wu-t'ai Shan, A.D. 857.

Fig. 10.25 The Great Wall (China), third century B.C. and following. In its present form — rubble faced with stone; a brick-paved roadway on top edged with parapet and battlements — the Wall is substantially a Ming dynasty reconstuction (fourteenth–seventeenth century). Its function as a communication spine through inhospitable mountain regions was from the start as important as its defensive function.

and the areas just below, ingenious responses to the local challenge produced the pit houses of Alaska, with stone domes braced with whalebone and topped by an insulating layer of earth, and the igloo, a house constructed of snow blocks and ice. The Eskimos shaped firm snow as others elsewhere did rocks and earth. The rectangular building blocks of the igloo were arranged in an ascending spiral that closed to form a dome without any need of centering. A window of clear ice placed near the entrance brought in some light.

But shelter has never been the sole objective of built environment, however rude the community. At the time of this survey, defensive, utilitarian, and ceremonial structures had been discovered in several corners of North America. A desert valley in Arizona, occupied by the Hohokam people who were practicing flood irrigation by 100 B.C. was found scored with dikes, ditches, and earth dams having head gates of tightly woven grass mats backed by stakes that could be raised or lowered as needed. But a type of ritual center was also uncovered: a court with an oval playing floor that had stone markers or basins for goals. On the basis of earlier evidence from Central American sites, these must have been fields for a game played with rubber balls that was to have a long history.

More remarkable were the earth works of the Adena or the Hopewell people in the Midwest, who settled along the Ohio Valley. (Fig. 10.28) Here fortified hilltop enclo-sures might have served the same function as the European *oppida*. The main impulse, however, seems to have been a growing mortuary cult. At first it was a relatively modest matter of erecting conical earth mounds over individual burials. Soon groups of these mounds were surrounded by great ridges of piled up earth and approached through earth-enclosed avenues. The Hopewellians were rich and sophisticated. They traded widely; their imports included copper from the Upper Great Lakes region, quartz crystals, mica and schist from the Lower Allegheny, flint from Indiana, and obsidian from as far away as Mexico. They also built lavishly. The earth walls around ceremonial centers described circles and rectangles, were layered self-consciously by alternating sand, earth, and rock, and stretched over an immoderate expanse. The largest center, Newark, covers 10 square kilometers (4 square miles).

We can only speculate: first, that a ruling class managed and manipulated the mortuary cult, and second, that enough agricultural surplus became available to free the manpower to undertake such gargantuan tasks. The model may have been central Mexico or the Gulf Coast where since at least the fifth century B.C. a theocratic system commanded monumental environments for ritual practice, and these in turn fostered limited urbanization. The priests were authorities of the calendar and weather, and intercessors with the divine on behalf of the land-tilling populace. Put mundanely, this means crop management. In return, the farmers shouldered the labor for superlative settings that magnified the religion and the state. The scale of these enterprises impresses manifestly. But the technology in use remains basically Neolithic, deprived of aids like the wheel or the smelting of iron.

The foremost architectural products of this Central Amerrican commonwealth of states were the mounds loosely called "pyramids." One of the earliest, in Cuicuilco in the Pedregal, near the new University of Mexico, is circular. It has four conical stages, the result of two separate campaigns of building, and the earth is faced with stone slabs set in clay. The date of this structure is probably around 500 B.C. On the small island of La Venta, situated

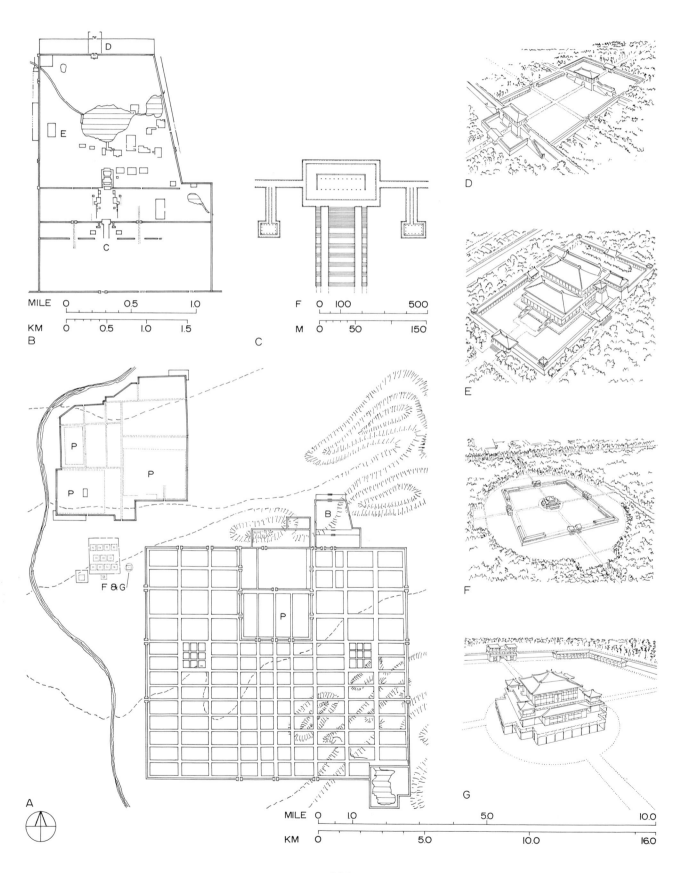

B

MILE 0   0.5   1.0

KM 0   0.5   1.0   1.5

C

F 0   100   500

M 0   50   150

D

E

F

G

A

MILE 0   1.0   5.0   10.0

KM 0   5.0   10.0   16.0

among the mangrove swamps of northern Tabasco, on the Gulf Coast, is a rounded and fluted pyramid that might even be earlier.

These determined pilings were one component of carefully thought out group designs. To the north of the pyramid of La Venta were two adjacent courts, one behind the other. (Fig. 10.29) The first was framed by parallel mounds on the east and west sides; the second was a sunken rectangle paved with colored clays and edged with columns of basalt. Further north another circular mound rose over an elaborate tomb, and beyond this three colossal heads of basalt faced the north like guardian figures. The whole site, about 1.5 kilometers (1 mile) long, was organized on a north-south axis. In addition to the features we have mentioned, it contained a manmade rectangular hill, enormous pits whose bottoms were lined with stone, and monolithic, flat-topped altars.

La Venta was apparently a religious and civic center for villages in the area, with a small resident population of priests and their staff who managed the cult. The labor force may also have been housed on the site. This may well have been the case for early Teotihuacán as well, which became in time the greatest religious nucleus of Middle America and its premier market town. Its ruins lie 40 kilometers (25 miles) northeast of Mexico City in the high, semiarid Valley of Teotihuacán. (Fig. 10.30) This town is a match for the grandest ensembles of the Old World—Giza, Persepolis, the Hellenistic or Roman city-form. The elements of planning were anticipated at La Venta: the pyramid, the court defined by platforms, the north-south regulating axis. But nothing can quite prepare us for the size, conviction, and majesty of Teotihuacán as it first assumed its principal traits between 100 B.C. and A.D. 200.

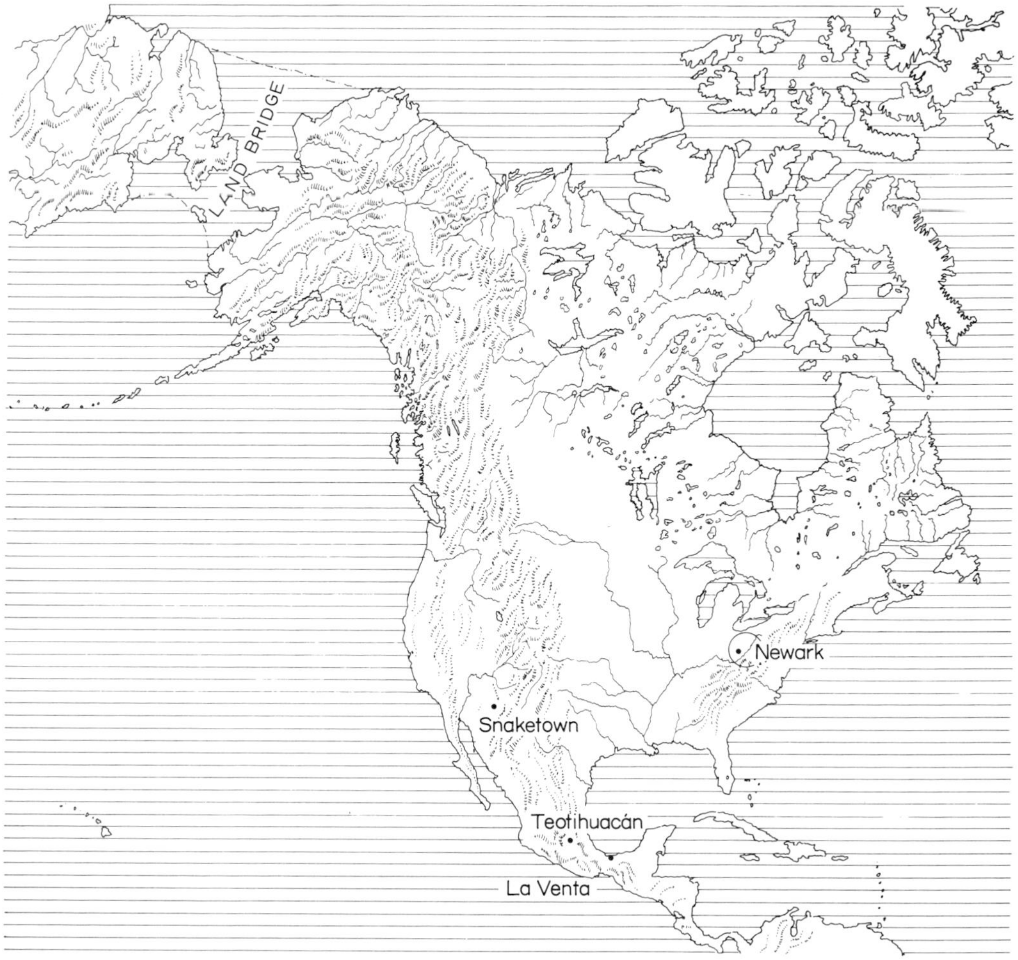

Fig. 10.27 Map: North and Meso-America, up to A.D. 200

The axis at Teotihuacán is a full 5 kilometers (about 3 miles) long. It runs about 15 degrees east of true north, probably to align with the extinct volcano of Cerro Gordo whose springs were a major source of water and whose fertility was celebrated. The ground rises from south to north, and with it the axis—a sunken avenue now called "Street of the Dead." The avenue presses forward in level stretches that are terraced upward, toward the fertile mountain. It is stopped short by the Moon Pyramid that echoes the shape of Cerro Gordo. To the south the avenue concludes without a focus, as if it intended to shoot beyond, inflexible in its direction, toward the southern highlands of Guerrero and the Pacific. Toward this end it is flanked by two generous monumental groups. The Great Compound to the west, which is arranged around a court, appears to have been the city's chief marketplace and administrative center. Across from it is the precinct of Lord Quetzalcóatl, whose stock image as a feathered serpent was popular in mural

Fig. 10.26 Ch'ang-an (China), the cities of the Han and Tang; plans and views. The two cities are shown at the lower left; the smaller of the two is that of the Han dynasty (206 B.C.–A.D 220); the larger, that of the Tang dynasty (618–907). **(P)** refers to administrative palaces. **(B)** is Ta-ming Kung (Daming Gong), a pleasure palace of which the main building, Han-yuan Tien (Hanyuan Dien), is shown in a detail plan **(C)**, and the principal gate complex is shown in a restored view **(D)**. The building shown as **(E)** was a multipurpose component of the palace, used for receptions and some religious rituals. **(F–G)** is the Han dynasty palace, Ming-Tan, described in the text: **(F)** indicates the general layout of the palace complex within its circular moat, and **(G)** a view of the central structure.

Fig. 10.28 Ohio, Serpent Mound of the Adena, ca.
800 B.C. onward; aerial view.

paintings and sculptural ornaments. Halfway between the temple of Quetzalcóatl
and the Moon Pyramid, on the east side of
the avenue, towers the Pyramid of the Sun,
the oldest and largest public building on the
site. It stands over a natural cave and faces
15 degrees north of west, where the sun sets
on the day of its zenith passage (June 21).
It thus unites the sources of the land and
the workings of celestial bodies—twin inducements for the orientation of the master plan and mainsprings of growth for the
community.

Although all major buildings relate directly to the Street of the Dead, there is a

subsidiary cross-axis, where the Great
Compound and the Quetzalcóatl pyramid
are, that helps divide the city into quadrants. Urban settlement began at the
northwest quadrant before the great cruciform layout was decided upon. Part of the
area of this old city was abandoned by A.D.
150 as development shifted to the south and
east. By then the population may have approached 200,000.

The urban fabric was divided into barrios
or neighborhoods, each, it seems, engaged in some dominant craft. Obsidian
work was pervasive, but there were also
potters, painters, masons, merchants, and

of course the priesthood for whom gracious accommodation was provided in the
vicinity of temple precincts. The common
people lived in one-storey apartment compounds, several to a barrio, that were
grouped around patios. A chapel on the east
side faced into the patio, and there were
also one or more barrio temples. The main
urban temples usually occurred in threes;
more than twenty of these three-temple
complexes dotted the sprawling city in the
second century A.D. The Pyramids of the
Sun and the Moon may have been the key
temples of such triads.

The Sun Pyramid still exhibits the old

technique of horizontal layers of clay faced with unshaped stones. (Fig. 10.31) A new technique made its appearance in the Moon Pyramid. The core was now built of tufa piers, the shafts between them filled with rubble. This core was buttressed by fin walls, which also determined the slope of the main terraces. By using a broad axial staircase, five terraces were joined on the side overlooking the Street of the Dead. This complex was linked to a series of platforms that abutted the pyramid, cut into its terrace lines, tempering their enormous scale at the same time as they augmented the general impression of height and monumentality, and set up a rhythmic crescendo of level and rise that is still ineluctable. In these ceremonial platforms of low rise, horizontal projections called *tableros* were cantilevered on stone slabs, their edges vertical to the pyramid slope. The tableros were framed by stone cornices and were the standard repositories of architectural decoration.

But the power of Teotihuacán is hardly conveyed through descriptions of structure and ornamentation. Size comes first: the confident fit of the city in the open flatland with its soft edges that let the city shade away in places. Without the unremitting circumscription of a walled enclosure, the city sits much as the surrounding mountain ranges, low and quietly undulating, dipping to ground level here and there to let the valley floor move on toward distant, hazy counterpoints. The pyramids, which up close appear monumental, are temperate and spreading like the mountains when viewed from afar. They are preceded by lesser platforms and other structures that negotiate the transition to the intimate scale of the urban fabric beyond the banks of the Street of the Dead. More than anything else, these lesser structures are sculptural masses affirming the open volume of the avenue, the plazas, and the precinct grounds. There is no thoughtful shelter, no wholesale enclosure, in the manner of Hellenistic colonnaded avenues or Roman forums. The main pyramid clusters relate to one another in this same volumetric way, without adjacency or axial interlocking. The only axis, the Street of the Dead, is anything but Roman. Shunning bilateral symmetry, its course set by the Sun Pyramid whose own axis fords it like a river, the Street of the Dead serves less as a grand processional way for the Moon Pyramid and its plaza where it terminates and more as a baseline for certain cosmic alignments of the three pyramids and the hundreds of smaller platforms that scan its path.

Once more, then, architecture seeks to apprehend a cosmic order, as it had in the Pantheon, the circle of Sarmizegethusa, the stupas of Sanchi, and the Han capital of Ch'ang-an with its Ming-Tan. Casting a quick

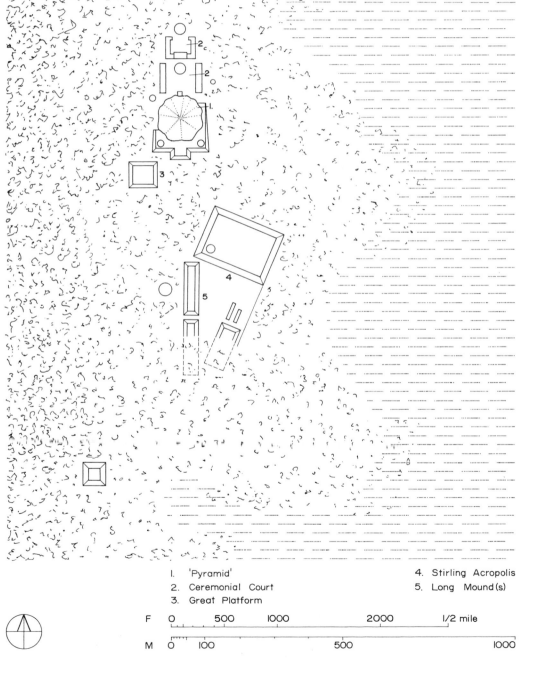

1. 'Pyramid'
2. Ceremonial Court
3. Great Platform
4. Stirling Acropolis
5. Long Mound(s)

F 0   500   1000   2000   1/2 mile

M 0   100   500   1000

Fig. 10.29 La Venta (Mexico), ca. 800–400 B.C.; general site plan.

Fig. 10.30 Teotihuacán (Mexico), first century B.C.– eighth century A.D.; aerial view. (From *Urbaniza-* *tion at Teotihuacán, Mexico,* vol. 1, pt. 1, copyright © 1973, René Millon)

glance around the built world at an arbitrary moment of history verifies what we should have expected: multiformity in every physical detail. Materials run the gamut from earth, grass, and snow to basalt, tile, and concrete. Techniques are just as varied. The buildings are hewn out of native rock, piled up from loose earth and stones, framed by beams or poles, laid in brick, or molded into seamless shapes of concrete. They brood massively and ponderously, inscribe lightly, encase airily, mount, billow, or burrow. They are viewed as ephemeral, renewable, or permanent.

But universal postulates are at work. To chart a place on earth—that is the supreme effort of the built environment in antiquity. Shelter, of course, always takes precedence. But its issue transcends self-preservation and comfort. Shelter engages human alliances and rank, and so it becomes the task of residential architecture to advance the pattern of collective existence. From family to empire, the stages of social and political gradation affect the scope and intricacy of this extendable pattern. But in the end organization only tidies up; it cannot satisfy darker anxieties of being afloat in a mysterious design which is not of our own making. To mediate between cosmos

240

Fig. 10.31a Teotihuacán; platforms as seen from the Moon Pyramid.

and polity, to give shape to fear and exorcize it, to effect a reconciliation of knowledge and the unknowable—that was the charge of ancient architecture.

It is a charge that is no longer pressing, that no longer has meaning. Geomancy had no place in the laying out of New York or Teheran; Buckingham Palace was not planned to be the pivot of the cosmic universe. At some point we chose to keep our own counsel, to search for self close at home. This is the last, modern phase in the history of the built environment. Between antiquity and this modern phase comes a long period of passage which eases us from an ancient, universal wholeness to an all-consuming atomism. This period concentrates the once pervasive and boundless call of earth and sky into a single godhead and invites us to measure up to it. This is the period, of Christ and Muhammed, that we must now turn to.

Further Reading

K. Berrin and E. Pasztory, eds., *Teotihucacan: Art from the City of the Gods* (London: Thames and Hudson, 1993).

M. A. R. Colledge, *Parthian Art* (Ithaca, N.Y.: Cornell University Press, 1977).

S. Denyer, *African Traditional Architecture* (New York: Africana, 1978).

J. Hardoy, *Urban Planning in Pre-Columbian America* (New York: Braziller, 1968).

D. Heyden and P. Gendrop, *Pre-Columbian Architecture of Mesoamerica* (New York: Abrams, 1975).

W. MacDonald, *The Pantheon: Design, Meaning, and Progeny* (Cambridge, Mass.: Harvard University Press, 1976).

W. Morgan, *Prehistoric Architecture in the Eastern United States* (Cambridge, Mass.: MIT Press, 1980).

P. Nabokov and R. Easton, *Native American Architecture* (New York: Oxford University Press, 1988).

M. Pirazzoli-T'Serstevens, *Living Architecture: Chinese,* trans. R. Allen (London: Macdonald, 1972).

A. U. Pope, *Persian Architecture* (New York: Braziller, 1965).

N. S. Steinhardt, *Chinese Imperial City Planning* (Honolulu: University of Hawaii Press, 1984).

A. Volwahsen, *Living Architecture: Indian,* trans. A. E. Keep (New York: Grosset & Dunlap, 1969).

Fig. 10.31b Teotihuacán, temple of Quetzalcóatl; detail view from the south showing tableros and architectural sculpture. The projecting stone heads represent feathered serpents and a cubic, geometric figure, possibly a rain god.

PART TWO

Measuring Up

Istanbul, Hagia Sophia, A.D. 532–37, Isidoros and Anthemios.

11

THE TRIUMPH OF CHRIST

The third century A.D. proved to be a time of general unrest in the Old World. In China, peasant revolts and an intrigue-minded imperial bureaucracy brought down the four-hundred-year-old Han dynasty in 200; partition and civil war followed immediately, starting a long period of bloody disunion. Four years later Ardashir I put an end to the cosmopolitan administration of the Parthians in Persia and established a nationalist state under his own Sassanian house. In 235 Emperor Alexander Severus, the last of an able, vigorous family of North African descent who had managed the affairs of Rome for several decades, was murdered. The end of Severan power plunged the Mediterranean into anarchy.

The Turning Point: Third-Century Rome

The difficulties of Rome were both external and internal. A disorderly succession often engineered by mutinous armies canceled the benefits of one-man rule. Their energies sapped by dissension and the lure of king-making, the once invincible Roman legions could no longer keep predators at bay. The northern border cracked and uncontrollable floods of fringe peoples swept down, at times as far as the Po Valley. Villas and farms were abandoned where incursions went unchecked. Cities, for the first time since the reign of Augustus, were forced to give thought to their own defense. Seventy of them were destroyed

when Franks crossed the Rhine into Gaul in 276.

Rome herself felt vulnerable. The Servian walls of the fourth century B.C. had long since been obsolete. The city had spilled beyond them in every direction since the late Republic. Now, in 270, ten years after the disastrous defeat in the East that left Emperor Valerian and his troups prisoners of the Sassanian government, a strong set of walls was thrown hastily around Rome. (Fig. 11.1) They took less than a decade to build and embraced all of the urban area on the left bank and the popular quarter across the river, Transtiberim (Trastevere). Lower river walls linked up with the main system, enclosing all city bridges except Pons Aelius leading to Hadrian's mausoleum at the Vatican, which had its own bridgehead. The total circuit was about 20 kilometers (12 miles), and in its original form was a solid curtain 4 meters wide and 8 meters high (13 by 26 feet) with a continuous rampart walk at the top protected by a parapet and merlons. Square towers for artillery (ballistae or spring guns) projected at intervals of 100 Roman feet (about 30 meters). There were eighteen main gates. Each gate was flanked by semicircular towers between which ran a windowed gallery that contained the mechanism of the portcullis.

A Change of Mood
The decline of Rome had started even earlier. Throughout the turbulent third century, Italy slipped steadily in relation to the

rest of the empire. Several provincial metropolises vied with Rome in looks and even prestige. Emperors often came from the provinces, beginning with Trajan and Hadrian who were both of Spanish origin, or else they were proclaimed emperor by regional armies. As if symbolic of this shift, the Palatine itself was redirected southward with a fanciful, three-storey marble facade, the Septizodium, framing the perspective of the Via Appia. It was built by Septimius Severus, "so that when his compatriots came from Africa," a contemporary source explained, "a monument to him might at once strike their eyes."

By the end of the century, the supremacy of Rome was only a matter of tradition. The imperial office was now supposed to be shared by four colleagues, each holding court in one corner of the empire. A number of new capitals therefore sprang up, or rather cities in strategic locations were converted to seats of the central government with an appropriate investment in palace compounds, baths, basilicas, and the like. In the East, Thessaloniki in northern Greece and Antioch in Syria were important; in the West, Milan and the town of Augusta Treverorum, modern Trier, on the Moselle just within the Rhine frontier.

But the empire was facing more than a military and economic crisis. Over the long run, the tougher problem was a crisis of the spirit. Perhaps as early as the time of Hadrian, at the height of material prosperity, the gnawing need for spiritual sustenance, the recognition that security, public spectacle, and a high standard of living cannot be all there is, might have surfaced—and in no one more pressingly than the emperor himself. An excellent administrator and responsible head of state, Hadrian was a morose, troubled individual. He looked for and held on to a kind of private world best represented by his villa at Tivoli (the ancient Tibur), a sprawling moody project which occupied him until his death and which he left unfinished, a design in search of a purpose. Closed off by hills to the east and northeast, open on the western side to the view of the Roman countryside, it was a superbly sited collection of units endemic to the tradition of senatorial and imperial villas. (Fig. 11.2) But for all its sparkling, imaginative, light-hearted designs, Hadrian's villa reads like an elegy. It is suffused with the memory of Antinous, a Bithynian youth the emperor loved who drowned mysteriously in the Nile. Statues show him as an unsmiling, contemplative youth. He seems a proper symbol for one aspect of Hadrian's age—a questioning of the standard blessings of life under the Roman sun, of that great comfortable pattern we call civilization. We read in the ruins Hadrian's lonely quest, not for Roman but for human values, a hope for personal salvation, for youth unending. We think of him when we read Marcus Aurelius' *Meditations* a generation later: "They seek for themselves private retiring places, as country villages, the seashore, mountains. . . . A man cannot any whither retire better than to his own soul."

All this would strike one as loosely speculative were it not for the confirmation of subsequent official art. Imperial portraiture that had long supplied ideal images of the sovereign for public consumption, images with a smooth, featureless universality that looked ageless and unruffled, became more intimate after Hadrian (Figs. 10.2, 11.3) The face, focused on the eyes, with pupils now carved out rather than painted, seemed determined to reflect the psychological ambiguities of the subject. The refusal to idealize or glorify the emperor might be thought of in terms of a revival of Republican *virtus*. But this honesty goes beyond pride in the ravaged face as the record of a full and hard life. There is something oth-

Fig. 11.1 Map: Rome (Italy), ca. A.D. 300, showing the line of the walls of Aurelian begun in A.D. 270–71.

1. Capitoline	7. Roman Forum	13. Baths of Trajan	18. Aelian Bridge
2. Palatine	8. Imperial Fora	14. Baths of Diocletian	(Ponte S. Angelo)
3. Vatican Hill	9. Bascilica of Maxentjus	15. Pantheon	19. Mausoleum of Hadrian
4. Republican Walls	10. Temple of Venus and Rome	16. Theater of Marcellus	20. Castra Praetoria
5. Aurelian Walls	11. Trajan Markets	17. Flavian Amphitheater	
6. Circus Maximus	12. Baths of Caracalla	(Colosseum)	

| Mile | 0 | 0.5 | 1.0 | 2.0 | 2.5 |
| Kilometer | 0 | 0.5 | 1.0 | 2.0 | 3.0 | 4.0 |

Fig 11.2 Tivoli (ancient Tibur, Italy), Hadrian's villa, A.D. 118–25; the pool called Canopus with a sanctuary to the Egyptian god Serapis at the far end.

practices of the cult followers supplied the necessary antidote to the proper, undemonstrative, and basically impersonal state religion. Eastern deities were duly tamed and inducted into the Roman pantheon. The difference was that now each cult asserted its exclusive power over the soul of the empire, and depending on imperial patronage, one or the other gained a broadly monotheistic appeal.

Two among these Eastern religions, Mithraism and Christianity, waxed strong in these uncertain decades. Mithras, a member of the holy triad of Persian Mazdaism, was popular in the army. As the invincible god of light, he appealed to the soldiers at the frontiers, and his worship was accorded full official protection. Christianity found its support among the poor. Firmly monotheistic and uncooperative, it was disapproved of by the state and sporadically persecuted. Both were mystery cults, involving initiatory rites that conferred on the individual an indelible, spiritual well-being and the assurance of happiness hereafter. To the initiates, being a Mithraist or a Christian was a way of life; their faith

erworldly about the soulful expression of the upturned eyes that relates, instead, to the contemporary notions of the philosopher Plotinus—his disgust with appearances and his claim that beauty resides not in the body but in the soul and in the soul's yearning toward the universal soul of God. "Ugly is that which has no soul."

Political art is equally anomalous. In the narrative of the column of Marcus Aurelius, set up in commemoration of his victories against Germanic tribes in 172–75, the heroic decisiveness of Trajan's Dacian campaigns is strangely missing. The dominant note is the brutality and futility of war. (Fig. 11.4) The artists dwell on the women and children made victim of hostile circumstance, scenes of wanton destruction, pain. The emperor stoically does his duty from which he now derives only a dismal sadness. He comments in his *Meditations*, with a profound sense of pessimism: "Toys

and fooleries at home, wars abroad: sometimes terror, sometimes torpor or stupid sloth: this is thy daily slavery."

Mystery Cults

The sphere that naturally absorbed and organized these growing doubts was religion. A fresh dissatisfaction with state cults seized the Roman world in the third century. Faith in state cults registered as loyalty to the state. The pious were good citizens, not necessarily good men and women. Provisions for the afterlife were vague. The imperial cult had itself been trivialized by the rapid, bloody turnover. People looked for a deeper faith in strange cults that beckoned from the East.

The attraction of Eastern deities was nothing new of course. Since the black stone of Cybele had been transported to Rome from Phrygia in 203 B.C. and enshrined in a temple on the Palatine, the often orgiastic

Fig. 11.3 Emperor Maximinus Thrax (A.D. 235–38); a portrait bust. (Palazzo Capitolino, Rome)

Fig. 11.4 Rome, the Column of Marcus Aurelius, recording the events of the emperor's Danubian wars of A.D. 172–75; detail. The column still stands in the present Piazza Colonna.

Fig. 11.5 Rome, the sanctuary of Mithras (Mithraeum), early third century A.D. It lies under the church of S. Clemente, to the east of the Col- osseum, and was built into a private house of the first century A.D.

entailed moral rectitude. They gathered for services indoors, away from the public eye– once again in contradistinction to Greco-Roman worship, which took place in public in the open air and which considered the temple a privileged sanctum off limits to popular use.

A tradition deriving from the prophet Zarathustra had it that Mithras, who was miraculously reborn in a cave each year on the 25th day of December, had to be worshipped in dark places in the vicinity of running water. Mithraea were therefore subterranean and vaulted in emulation of a cave, which was in reality the symbol of the celestial vault. (Fig. 11.5) Continuous benches ran along the two flanks, with a sunken trough before them for the draining of the sacrificial blood. The cult image showed Mithras straddling a bull ready to dispatch it. He hunted the noble beast on instructions from the supreme God of Good whose creation it was, captured and overpowered it, and later killed it in the cave to save it from the eternal foe, the God of Evil. From the blood of the animal and the

spinal marrow and tail sprang fresh plants and full ears of corn: out of death rose new life.

Christ had sacrificed himself for the salvation of the world, and He had then risen from the dead. It was His body and blood, symbolized in bread and wine, that constituted the central object of Christian worship. To partake of them at Mass, one had to undergo ritual baptism. Christian architecture had to provide for these two sacraments: Mass and baptism. Indicative of a repressed and plebeian movement, the places of worship were exceedingly modest. Centers for the community were set up in remodeled, outwardly inconspicuous houses.

A good example survives at Dura Europos. (Fig. 11.6) An unexceptional peristyle

house built around A.D. 200 at the edge of town was acquired by a Christian congregation and altered internally in 231. Two rooms in the south wing were merged to accommodate about fifty people. The short east end was raised into a bishop's dais. During services, a large room on the west side of the court adjoining the meeting hall held the as yet unbaptized members who were allowed to hear Mass but not witness the mystery of transubstantiation which was the focal point. When, after a long period of instruction, which took place most likely in the same room, a member was considered ready for initiation, the sacrament of baptism would be conducted in a small rectangular room at the northwest corner of the house where a canopied tub stood against the west wall.

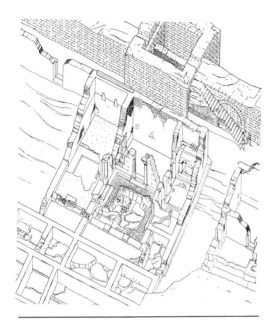

Fig. 11.6 Dura Europos (Salhiyeh, Syria), Christian community house, A.D. 231, converted from a private house of ca. A.D. 200; isometric view. The meeting hall is on the left; the baptistery, on the right, toward the back.

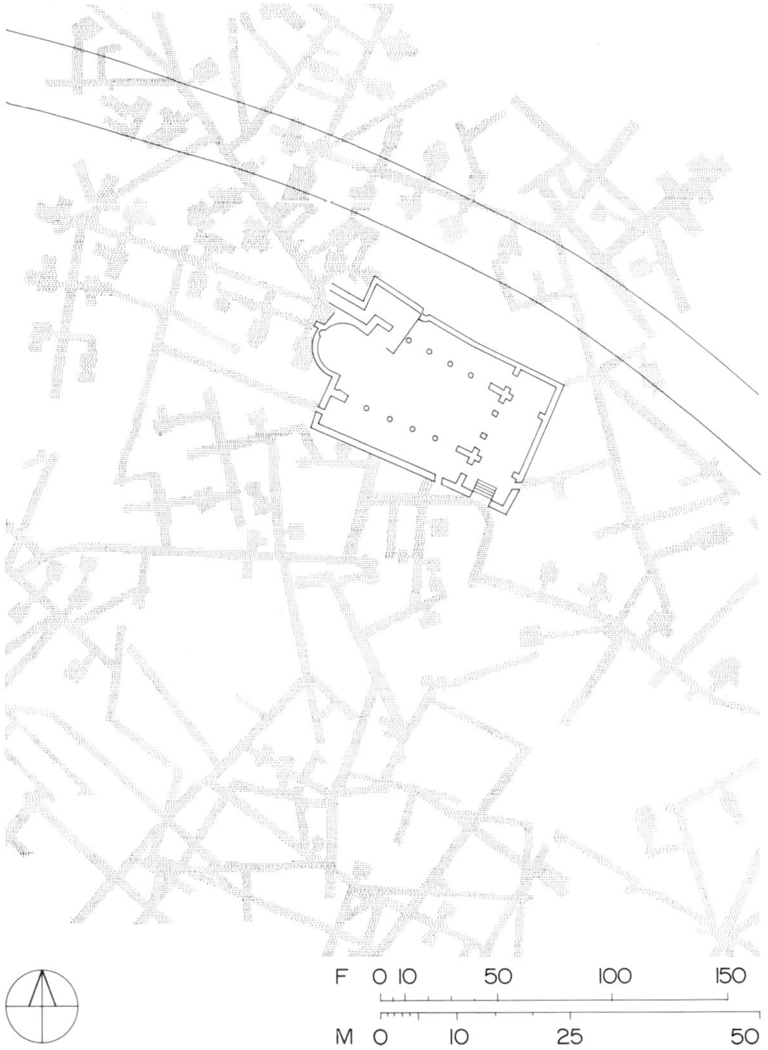

Fig. 11.7 Rome, the catacomb of Domitilla (off the Via Ardeatina, south of the city), in use as a Christian cemetery since ca. A.D. 200; plan of the section under the modern street called Via delle sette chiese. The church was raised over the tombs of Sts. Nereus, Achilleus, and Domitilla, ca. 580–90.

F 0 10   50   100   150

M 0   10   25   50

The only other distinctive quarters of early Christianity were the cemeteries. Here in those sleeping places (that is what the word *coemeterium* means) the faithful awaited the trumpet call of the Second Coming when the evil and the just would receive rewards commensurate with their state of grace. Cremation, the commoner Roman burial, was out of the question, since the raising of the dead was meant literally. By the third century, mixed cemeteries came to be seen as contaminating. The Christian Church now assumed the responsibility of organizing and administering cemeteries for the exclusive use of its own flock. In some cities when the available open-air space had been ex-hausted, Christians followed pagan and Jewish precedent and went underground.

The catacombs of Rome are the best known of these subterranean cemeteries. They started in an orderly fashion—straight rows, orthogonally laid—but with the swelling of the Christian ranks mazelike, multilevel growth took over. (Fig. 11.7) The dismal, nightmarish paths were brightened by lively painted sketches of praying figures, Christ as the Good Shepherd with a lamb draped over His shoulders, and a handful of scenes from the Old Testament like Daniel in the lion's den, Jonah and the whale, and the three youths in the fiery furnace. (Fig. 11.8) These examples of mi-raculous salvation were the visual counter-part of an old prayer called the *Ordo Commendationis Animae* which began: "Deliver, O Lord, the soul of Thy servant as Thou hast delivered Noah from the deluge, Daniel from the lion's den, Jonah from the belly of the whale. . . ." The catacombs, popular belief to the contrary, did not ensconce regular services. They were too cramped for that purpose, and as places of death they were tainted with the impurity that justified long-standing Roman laws against burial within city limits. Only on All Soul's Day or the anniversary of some well-known martyrdom did Christians visit their dead en masse for the observances of the *refriger-*

Fig. 11.8a Rome, catacomb of S. Panfilo, third or fourth century A.D.; view of one gallery. It lies below the old Via Salaria, just outside the city walls.

ium, which involved libations and the partaking of food.

Late Pagan Architecture

These unassuming graveyards and meeting houses of the early Christians are the start of a new building culture that, in the service of an ultimately triumphant Christianity, will encompass the lands of Rome and beyond and over the centuries account for some of the most familiar high points in the history of architecture: Hagia Sophia, Romanesque pilgrimage churches, Gothic cathedrals, St. Peter's in Rome. The prominent monuments of the third century, on the other hand, are the prodigious swansong of the retiring pagan culture.

Yet it is precisely during this last exertion that Roman architecture will sharpen its design identity, distance itself further from Classical commitments, and produce specimens, at once culminating and new, that will be quarried for their lessons by the patrons and architects of the first official

Fig. 11.8b Rome, catacomb of S. Priscilla northeast of the city, below the Via Salaria, in use as a Christian cemetery since the end of the second century A.D.; vault paintings of the third century showing the Good Shepherd in the center; and below, the deceased in a posture of prayer, flanked by a teacher and two students to the left, and a mother and child (possibly the Virgin Mary and the Christ Child) to the right.

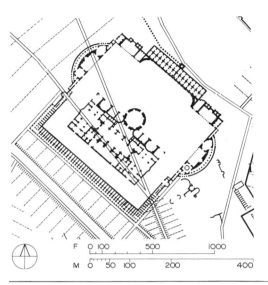

Fig. 11.9 Rome, baths of Emperor Caracalla (A.D. 212–16), known in antiquity as Thermae Antoninianae (no. 12 on Fig. 11.1). (**a**) Ground plan. (**b**) Aerial view from the west; the caldarium is just to the right of center. For a plan and section of the caldarium, see Fig. 11.13. The baths were built over preexisting streets, shown here in the plan.

Christian centuries. The baths of Caracalla and Diocletian and the basilica of Maxentius in Rome, Diocletian's palace at Split (Spalato) and Constantine's at Trier, a string of late antique domed rotundas—here we find the origin of forms and moods that would transfigure the environment of primitive Christianity into a world of state. We can see why one recent scholar is correct in saying that "Classical art became 'medieval' before it became Christian."[1]

In the late imperial baths of Rome, the formula of the first two centuries was enhanced in various ways, as a comparison between the baths of Trajan and Caracalla should indicate. (Figs. 9.25, 11.9) The main block now stands free of the perimeter wall, centered within the huge frame in order to favor the entrance side. In composing the block, a transverse axis running through the frigidarium to the two lateral *palaestrae*, or exercise courts, is as thoughtfully developed as the bather's path of movement through the cold, warm, and hot rooms. To be able to reach the palaestrae directly, the

1. E. Kitzinger, *Early Medieval Art*, 2nd ed. (London: British Museum, 1955), p. 16.

chief entrances to the block are made to flank the swimming pool that introduces the bathing sequence, so that one enters the frigidarium on the transverse axis. This mighty hall does justice to its pivotal post at the intersection of the two axes by balancing the long line of its three cross-vaulted bays (that spring, in appearance at least, from eight single columns) with central recesses in the direction of the swimming pool, the warm room, and the flanking pool niches. These recesses extend the nave space toward the two long sides, and their barrel vaults, at right angles to the big hall, counteract the thrust of its lofty superstructure.

It is this scheme of the frigidarium that was transplanted to the basilica of Maxentius, begun in 307 north of Hadrian's temple to Venus and Rome. (Fig. 11.10) Here the lateral bays communicate with the nave unobstructed, are quite spacious (two-thirds as wide as the nave), and their coffered barrel vaults are kept low enough to permit ample clerestory lighting. The exterior walls make no use whatever of the conventions of Classical facades. (Fig. 11.11) Round-headed windows grouped in threes are ar-

ranged in two storeys and are subsumed under the soaring outline of the barrel vaults. The noncolumnar aesthetic of the markets of Trajan and Ostian apartment houses (Fig. 9.11) is now being celebrated in an official state monument, relying exclusively on the rhythm of voids in the smooth wall plane, and incidentally conveying the disposition of the interior which a traditional Classical facade would have been at pains to screen.

But the taste for banked, round-headed windows and their cadenced progression under an embracing system of arcades extended even to timber-roofed buildings. At the audience hall of the early fourth-century palace at Trier, the startling exterior elevation is wholly arbitrary for the plain rectangular hall. (Fig. 11.12) Setting this elevation next to that of an earlier Roman theater exterior like the Colosseum or the markets of Trajan brings home the novelty of this late-antique design. (Figs. 9.22, 9.29) Even with the two outer service galleries that ran continuously at the base of the windows, the thinking at Trier is vertical and not intent on banding. And, of course, the Classical framing devices of engaged columns and entablatures have vanished without a trace.

From the Aula Traiana in the markets of Trajan (Fig. 9.30) to the frigidarium of the baths of Caracalla and the basilica of Maxentius, we can follow the thread of evolution for the vaulted long hall. A parallel progression for the centrally planned, domed hall would start with the octagonal room in the Esquiline wing of Nero's Golden House and the Pantheon, and go on from there to some units of Hadrian's villa and the caldarium of the Caracalla baths, to the so-called temple of Minerva Medica and a group of late-antique mausolea for members of the imperial family. (Fig. 11.13) Three related trends control this progression: the relish of height, ampler window space, and the opening out of the domed core into semi-independent border spaces.

Worries of stability had restricted direct lighting in the octagon of the Golden House and the Pantheon to the oculus overhead, which suited the intentions of the program nicely. The round caldarium of the Caracalla baths, in part because it is locked for one-third of its circumference into the bracing structure of the larger building, employs instead four large windows just below the level of the dome which free it from the concentration and inwardness of one central opening. For all the niches scooped out of the thickness of its rotunda wall, the Pantheon (or for that matter Nero's octagon) remains a self-enclosed, hermetic world. The caldarium signals the opening up of the centrally planned building of comparable scale, a process that will follow two separate paths.

One of these entails the deployment of an ambulatory and is functionally expedient in mausolea because of the practice in the empire of having a solemn triple procession around the burial spot. At Sta. Costanza in Rome (ca. 350), the mausoleum for the daughter of Emperor Constantine, the dome and its tall drum, perforated by sixteen windows, rest on a circle of twelve pairs of columns which are

Fig. 11.10 Rome, the basilica of Maxentius, A.D. 307–12, completed by Constantine shortly thereafter; reconstruction drawing of the interior showing a perspective of the nave and the north bays.

Fig. 11.11 Rome, basilica of Maxentius; exterior as seen from the Via dei Fori Imperiali.

Housing the Kingdom of Heaven

On 28 October 312, a battle outside Rome between two contending emperors halted the long drift of the Roman ship of state and set it on a most astonishing new course.

Diocletian, who had rallied the empire for a while at the end of the third century, had retired in 305 and had gone to live in his fortified villa at Split on the Dalmatian coast. His senior colleague Maximianus followed suit, withdrawing to family property in central Sicily. The two imperial residences, antithetical in their layout, together summarize the rich experience of the Roman built environment in its heyday. At Maximianus' villa at Piazza Armerina, a basilica, a set of baths, a formal entrance in the shape of a triumphal arch with inset fountains and a semicircular porticoed court beyond, a ceremonial wing with a trilobed main hall, and an oval forecourt are freely composed around a large peristyle. (Fig. 11.17) The picturesque order imitates but tightens the loose assembly of independent units in Hadrian's villa, which was justified there by the spread and shapes of the land.

The palace of Diocletian at Split (ca. 300–6) recalls instead the Roman army camp. (Fig. 11.18) Within a rectangular system of defenses, two colonnaded streets cross at right angles. The residence proper occupies the southern quadrants. Beyond the intersection, past a small temple to the right and the emperor's mausoleum to the left, one crossed a gabled porch (where Diocletian revealed himself to gathered crowds) and a vestibule to arrive at the main wing which took up the entire seaward side of the rectangle. From the sea, the facade presented a continuous, arcaded gallery between two corner towers, a scheme that was becoming widespread in the fortified country estates of late antiquity. The gallery was accented by three pavilions whose pediments, like that of the entrance porch, were cut into by an arch—a peculiarly Syrian touch.

The Conversion of Constantine
The system of four co-rulers, successful under the firm resolve of Diocletian, tottered after his retirement. Dissension broke out among the men who were supposed to

Fig. 11.12 Trier (Germany), the palace of Constantine, early fourth century; exterior view of the audience hall. The palace was in the northeast part of town; the audience hall was originally flanked by low courtyards framed by porticoes.

spanned by arcades. (Fig. 11.14) A barrel-vaulted ambulatory wraps around this well-lighted nucleus; the thick outer wall harbors niches, in one of which, opposite the entrance, stood the porphyry sarcophagus of the princess.

The other path, tried experimentally in some minor rooms of Hadrian's villa, brings us to an early fourth-century pavilion in the Licinian Gardens of Rome, long misnamed the "temple of Minerva Medica." Here the domed cylinder is extended by a ring of projecting apses, the four on the transverse axis being pierced through with triple arches on columns that lead to outer enclosures. Masonry wedges unite the apses and shoot upward, past the drum windows, to support a lightly built dome. (Fig.

11.15) Although of faced concrete, the dome was partitioned by brick ribs into small compartments that facilitated the construction. Brick ribbing went along with efforts to reduce the load of the vault by using light porous fillings or by inserting large empty terra-cotta jars into its fabric. A technique probably invented in North Africa produced vaults made of hollow terra-cotta tubes, fitted one into another, that were laid in concentric courses. (Fig. 11.16) This variant, and vaults constructed of simple brick that had been abroad in the Eastern provinces for some time, came to be depended on more and more in fourth- and fifth-century Italy as the use of concrete declined and was eventually abandoned altogether.

Fig. 11.13 Rome, three centrally planned halls, imperial period; plans and sections: left, the octagonal room in Nero's Golden House (see Figs. 9.24, 9.25); center, the caldarium in the baths of Caracalla (see Fig. 11.9); and right, the so-called "temple of Minerva Medica," a pavilion in the Licinian gardens, from the early fourth century.

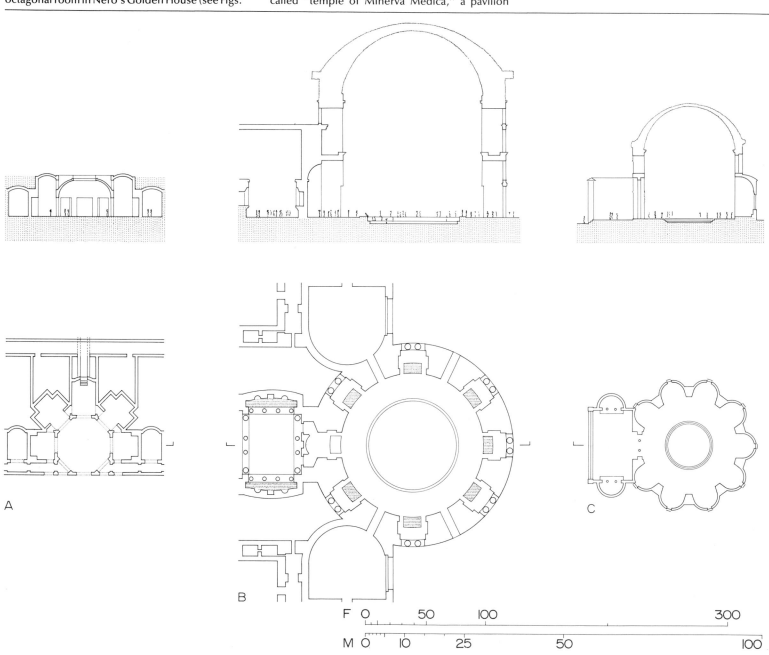

A

B

C

F O   50   100   300

M O   10   25   50   100

Fig. 11.14 Rome, S. Costanza, ca. 350; interior. It was built on the Via Nomentana, northeast of the city, as the mausoleum of Constantia, daughter of Emperor Constantine.

share power. The young Constantine who held the north, with his capital at Trier, precipitated civil war by deciding to march on Rome, which was then in the hands of his rival Maxentius, the son of Maximianus. Hastily the walls were raised higher. But at the last moment Maxentius elected to trust his fate at open battle. The two contenders for the West met at a place north of Rome, where the Via Flaminia crosses the Tiber at the Mulvian bridge. Maxentius lost and his force, caught between the northern legions and the river, was annihilated.

Roman history knew many confrontations of rival generals, and this should have been no more special. But in a momentous and totally unexpected move on the eve of the battle, Constantine had announced his espousal of Christianity, a burgeoning but still illegal Eastern cult whose adherents

within the city constituted a small minority. He now attributed his victory to his new-found faith. Christ was the eternal king, and Constantine was his servant and vice-regent on earth.

The Roman establishment was shocked. The Church was elated—and ready. From the beginning it had spurned any compromise on its central belief that Christianity was the only legitimate religion. The Church fathers had foretold the collapse of pagan Rome, a great whore bedecked with jewels and wallowing in sin. In the social and political disarray of the third century, they had painted Christianity as the spiritual conscience of the empire. "What the soul is in the body," as one of them put it, "that are Christians in the world." At the same time Church hierarchy organized itself into an orderly infrastructure that lodged in the larger body of the state. As the idea took

Fig. 11.15 Rome, the "temple of Minerva Medica"; interior (see Fig. 11.13).

Fig. 11.16 Ravenna (Italy), the Orthodox Baptistery, ca. 400–50; interior view of the dome. The photograph, taken when the mosaic decoration was removed for repairs, shows the method of construction that made use of hollow tubes.

hold generally that Rome was a concept transferable to any city where the emperor was, Rome itself was adopted by Christian apologists as the specific locus of regeneration, the seat of Peter of whom Christ had said, "Upon this rock I will build my church." A disciplined, courageous minority thus patiently laid the ground for what it believed to be an inevitable change of guard. Constantine's conversion accomplished the rest.

The battle of the Mulvian bridge ushered in a fresh, new order of buildings, as it did a new political and social era. The great challenge of forging a monumental setting for the new state religion was both open-ended as well as restricted by Christian precedent and current practice; the architectural results themselves, therefore, were both a break with tradition and yet conservative.

Where major Christian monuments were erected was largely predetermined. The land had been marked with the earthly events of Christ's career and the movements of the Apostles and martyrs. The communal mind recorded the exact place where He was born; where He had lain in death for three days; and the spot of earth on the Mount of Olives, across the valley of Cedron from Jerusalem, which witnessed His ascension. In a public cemetery in Rome, in the extramural region of the Vatican, one knew of St. Peter's tomb since at least the year 125, while St. Paul, the great traveler and preacher of the Word of God, lay buried, fittingly, by the side of the highway that linked Rome to its seaport. These markers were the true beginnings of Christian architecture. Here over these memorials, magnificent architectural complexes would rise because they had to.

But what shape they would take was not itself prescribed by the faith, and therein lay the excitement of innovation. Again, the Christian church might depend on the pagan basilicas of Roman cities as building

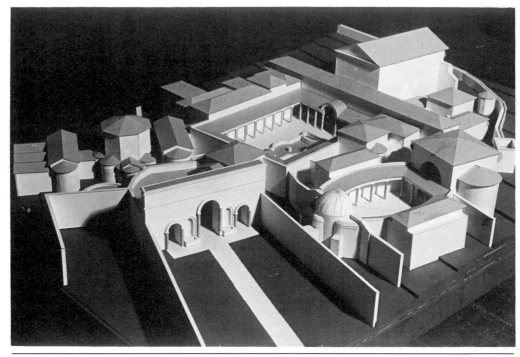

Fig. 11.17 Piazza Armerina (Sicily), the villa of Emperor Maximianus, early fourth century; reconstruction model. To the left, behind a monumental triple entrance, is a bath suite; in the right foreground, a ceremonial wing arranged around an oval porticoed court; further back, a peristyle garden, flanked by living quarters, and an apsed audience hall on the highest ground.

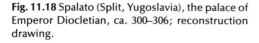

Fig. 11.18 Spalato (Split, Yugoslavia), the palace of Emperor Diocletian, ca. 300–306; reconstruction drawing.

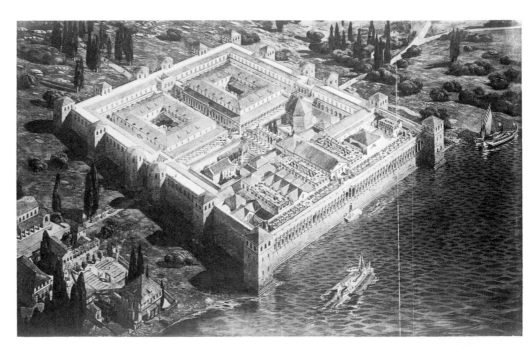

Fig. 11.19 Ravenna, San Vitale, completed 546–48; apse mosaic showing Bishop Ecclesius presenting a model of the church to Christ, Who is seated on the globe and is flanked by angels. He proffers a crown of martyrdom to St. Vitalis, the titular saint of the church, at the extreme left.

low in emulation of the heavenly college painted in the apse vault. Where the apse met the congregational space, or nave, the altar was fixed. To one side of it, a raised pulpit called the *ambo* served for the reading of the gospel. The formula, applied with many variations to newly built churches, made-over meeting rooms of primitive Christianity, or converted pagan buildings, basically involved a rectangular hall, whose longitudinal axis responded to the offertory procession of the faithful, and the apse, where the bread and wine brought by the congregation were transubstantiated at the climax of the service into the body and blood of Christ. (Fig. 11.20)

There were of course spectacular elaborations on this formula, especially with officially sponsored churches in the tradition of pagan basilicas, like the basilica Ulpia attached to the forum of Trajan in Rome. The forum, however, was now in front of the long axis of the building, a colonnaded court called an *atrium* (not to be confused with the atrium of a Pompeiian domus), with a fountain in the middle. The new cathedral of Rome, the predecessor of the present basilica of St. John in the Lateran, built by Constantine immediately following his

types, and for the baptistery and martyrial shrines on the centrally planned forms of Roman bathing compounds or on imperial mausolea. Yet there is nothing in pre-Constantinian Rome quite like the great church of St. Peter's, and the first baptistery of the city at the Lateran, nothing more original than a remodeled late Roman building, was also a genuine invention in the sense that the written word of its inscriptions, the painted images, and the sacramental act molded a specific and consequential ambience that, for all its family resemblance to non-Christian structures, had no true precursors.

The shift to imperial imagery required no hastily devised rationale. The Bible and patristic literature frequently extol the Kingdom of Heaven and allude to its splendor. Even so, the transformation of the humble Shepherd into an enthroned monarch dressed in imperial purple and surrounded

by the Apostles in senatorial garb and attendant angels made a profound impression on the thinking of the Church. (Fig. 11.19)

Congregational and Occasional Architecture

In architectural terms, one feature that distinguished even the simplest of parish churches from pre-Constantinian meeting halls, like the one at Dura Europos, was the apse. In Roman architecture, the apse terminated, most notably, the long axis of halls of state and of temples. It was the canopied stage for the imperial person or his statue, or for the images of the gods in whose ranks the emperor had been admitted beginning with Augustus. Now the apse was made the cusped terminus of the congregational space where Christ, King of Kings, resided with His retinue. The bishop and his presbyters seated themselves be-

Fig. 11.20 Rome, S. Sabina on the Aventine, 422–32; nave.

triumph at the Mulvian bridge over a razed barracks of the Horse Guard that had fought against him, is the earliest example of these imperially sponsored churches. It was situated at the southeastern corner of the city, just within the walls, discreetly removed from the monumental pagan center. It was a five-aisled, timber-roofed basilica with large clerestory windows. The apse was at the west end, a peculiarity shared by most of Constantine's churches. Low wings extended from the body of the church just in front of the apse like a vestigial transept; the cruciform disposition of the whole plan was perhaps already alert to the symbolism of the Cross, always foremost in the Christian's mind. The bare skeleton was resplendently sheathed and accoutered. Gold foil was applied to the beams of the open timber roof and mosaic to the half-dome of the apse. An altar and six offering tables of gold stood in the sanctuary and in the two sacristy wings. The columns of the nave and aisles were of yellow-, red-, and green-veined marbles.

The cathedral availed itself, then, of that rich aesthetic of color and light that had informed the best monuments of the Roman vaulted style, and that had become the benchmark of imperial patronage. Yet it rejected the vaulted style itself, the sailing, overarching spaces of near-contemporaries like the baths of Diocletian and the basilica of Maxentius. It fell back on a dated classicizing design, structurally backward and almost revivalist in form. The intention may have been to dissociate the Church from most of the public activities of the pagan world which took place in vaulted halls, and to stay close to the basilica form which, with the sole exception of the basilica of Maxentius, had remained faithful to a timber-roofed, columnar look.

Whatever the reason, vaulting was avoided in churches for regular worship for a century or more, except for the apse half-dome. In Rome and elsewhere the builders would sometimes project a robust Classicism with files of closely spaced columns, carrying reused capitals and bold marble entablatures. But the principal trend in church architecture moved toward the underplayed Classicism of late antiquity, as we saw it at its most pronounced in the basilica of Trier. (Fig. 11.12) The nave columns carried arcades, their spandrels faced with marble. This flat plane continued upward into the clerestory wall, itself disburdened by a veneer of mural painting in fresco or mosaic. A substanceless cage was thus created, made of flat, flickering surfaces on columns that seemed to alight gently on the paved floor in a free-floating ethereal space.

The facades were rarely imposing. The lower level was obscured by the portico of the atrium; above its tiled pitched roof emerged a smooth gabled wall pierced by windows. Only in the masonry churches of Syria does an interesting facade emerge, one with gabled corner towers and a central entrance whose broad arch is echoed in the round-headed niches that flank it and those that crown a middle-level gallery. (Fig. 11.21) The effect is startlingly reminiscent of later Western medieval facades, as are the heavy stone interiors with their transverse diaphragm arches and clustered piers so reminiscent of Romanesque church interiors.

The sanctuary end was dominated by the apse, which would at times be polygonal externally or, as in Syria, North Africa, and Asia Minor, might be imprisoned in a rectangular frame that often had defensive functions. Two flanking rooms called *pastophories* met the needs of liturgical preparations. They could have their own apses. Rarely, the sanctuary end would be trilobed like the ceremonial hall at the villa of Piazza Armerina. In short, lively regional variation was the rule for the built environment of the empire of Christ, as it had been for its pagan antecedent.

Alongside these regular cult buildings, the Church also required a class of buildings that might be called "occasional." They were intended for specialized rites, like baptism, and as memorial structures or *martyria* over places of special sanctity, like tombs of martyrs or holy spots associated with the origins of Christianity. The goal here was to celebrate a particular object—a tomb, a piece of rock, the baptismal font. To do so, the architect raised a canopy directly above the object, a symbolic dome of heaven that would mark the object as hallowed. In contrast to the directional axis of the church basilica, the axis in martyria

Fig. 11.21 Der Turmanin (Syria), church, ca. 480; reconstruction drawing of principal facade.

Fig. 11.22 Ravenna, the Orthodox Baptistery; interior.

11.22) A modest brick shell conceals an interior space made transcendent by a decorative system of mosaic, painted stucco, colored marbles, and inscriptions that sheaths raw matter from the eye of the worshipper and imposes its own visual and sacred hierarchy over the structural skeleton of loads and supports. In this web of artifice, religious images assert the authority of their own world. Old Testament prophets surround the font in witness. The twelve Apostles, dressed in gold and holding forth their crown of martyrdom, march against a backdrop of paradisiacal blue. In the center is the roundel with the Baptism of Christ. The background is now pure gold. Jordan, the pagan river-god made obsolete, emerges from his waters with a marsh plant in one hand and in the other a green cloth, which he proffers reverentially to the new God Incarnate. This Baptism is the sacred prototype of which the baptism of the neophytes at the font directly below is the reflection. We can imagine the overpowering emotion of the moment when these men and women filed across the threshold of the small unpretentious building next to the cathedral and into a magic realm that must have seemed, after years of spiritual training and anticipation, like a true glimpse of the kingdom of heaven.

The architectural requirements of martyria were different. As centers of pilgrimage they attracted a steady flow of people who would expect to file past or circumambulate the revered spot and to attend services there. One obvious solution was to combine the martyrium with a congregational basilica. Constantine's architects devised a number of serially conceived schemes along these lines for the most prestigious theaters of primitive Christianity in Rome and the Holy Land. In Bethlehem a five-aisled basilica preceded by the usual atrium abutted rather awkwardly on an octagonal martyrium over the grotto of the Nativity, which replaced the apse. Christ's cenotaph at Jerusalem was made the crown of a rigid axial frame that embraces several memorial spots. (Fig. 11.23) The huge five-aisled basilica of the Anastasis, reached from the main north-south street of the city by means of a monumental staircase and an atrium, was built over the cave where Constantine's mother, the sainted Helena, found the True Cross of Christ's

and baptisteries was centrally fixed, and the natural model for these became, as we have said, the centralized rooms and buildings of late pagan architecture. The octagon was the preferred shape for baptisteries because of connotations associated with res-

urrection and rebirth attributed to the number eight.

The beautifully preserved Orthodox Baptistery of Ravenna, from the mid-fifth century, should recall for us the very special nature of these occasional buildings. (Fig.

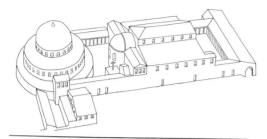

Fig. 11.23 Jerusalem (Israel), the Holy Sepulchre, 328–36; reconstruction drawing.

passion. To the west two landmarks of the great drama—the exact site of the Crucifixion, the Rock of Calvary, and the rock-cut tomb where the body had lain for three days before the Resurrection—were contained within a vast paved court enclosed by porticoes. To secure these memorials, the forum and capitol built there under Hadrian in the aftermath of the Jewish revolt of 135 were now razed. The Rock of Calvary was shaped into a cube, and a giant crucifix was mounted upon it. The Holy Sepulchre itself was sheltered within a centrally planned structure, with an ambulatory that had an upper gallery for the overflow of people. This rotunda, now much changed, was similar to S. Costanza in Rome described above, but the proportions were broader and the dome was made of wood. (Fig. 11.14)

At the other end of the empire, St. Peter was also imperially honored. His modest tomb at the Vatican cemetery became the focal point of an unusual commemorative church. (Fig. 11.24) At the risk of committing a heinous sin, the violation of burials, Constantine had the cemetery leveled and filled with earth, and Vatican hill itself was cut into toward the west. On the immense platform so contrived sat the singular T-shaped church, soon and forever to become the pivot of Western Christianity.

The approach to St. Peter's was through the city, on the opposite side of the Tiber. One crossed by the Aelian bridge at the point where the towering cylinder of Hadrian's mausoleum brooded by the right bank. The new church faced the city. As in Jerusalem, stairs led up to the atrium, beyond which lay the huge basilica, 84 me-

ters long and 58 meters wide (275 by 190 feet). A hundred ancient columns of colored stone—cipollino, breccia, grey and red granite—were used throughout. Those separating the nave from the first pair of aisles carried a strong entablature, broad enough to walk on. The wall above was punctuated by ample clerestory windows; light filtered through grilles of translucent alabaster and softly bathed the prodigious space.

An initial function of this hall was to host the funeral feast on the anniversary of St. Peter's martyrdom, a ceremony that was disallowed in the next century because of its rowdy nature. Tombs of those who wished to be buried next to the prince of the apostles initially crowded the floor. At the western end of the nave Constantine addressed his God across the triumphal arch. "Because under Your guidance the world rose triumphant to the skies," the inscription read, "Constantine, himself a victor, built You this hall." Apparently, the church was meant to celebrate the dual triumph of Christ over death and of the

emperor over his political adversaries, as well as to honor St. Peter's tomb, the martyrium proper. This latter purpose was in fact effected in a unique way. A transept arm was placed at right angles to the direction of the nave and screened off from it, and the tomb was contained within the apse of this arm. In its vault, above five round-headed windows, a sparkling mosaic of Christ enthroned, flanked by Peter and Paul and the palms of Paradise, contrasted with the plain stuccoed walls of the transept.

The Primacy of Constantinople

In the fifth and sixth centuries, some of the most exciting experiments of Christian architecture were directed at fusing the forms of congregational and occasional buildings. The question, put hypothetically, seemed to be: Do standard churches need to be timber-roofed basilicas? Provided they are large enough to hold their congregation, cannot centralized buildings perform as well as basilicas, and even improve on

Fig. 11.24 Rome, Old St. Peter's, ca. 320–30, with later additions to ca. 500; reconstruction drawing.

hand as the symbol of his participation in the sacrament of the Mass, called the Eucharist in the Eastern Church. He is flanked by the army and the religious: he rules by the sword and the book, as Roman emperor and head of the Church. He is responsible alone to Christ who is figured in the apse, enthroned upon the globe and attended by angels and local saints, in the act of receiving from the Bishop of Ravenna a model of this very church as an offering. (Fig. 11.19)

The plan of San Vitale is centrally disposed. (Fig. 11.26) Eight wedge-shaped

Fig. 11.25 Ravenna, San Vitale; view of the sanctuary with the panel of Justinian. (The apse mosaic shown in Fig. 11.19 is off the picture, just to the right.)

Fig. 11.26 Ravenna, San Vitale; interior view toward the sanctuary.

them symbolically? Cannot church design combine the directionality of a long hall that complements the liturgical march toward the apse with the vertical accent of the dome of heaven?

Two of these experiments are outstanding: San Vitale in Ravenna and Hagia Sophia in Constantinople. Both belong to the reign of Emperor Justinian who tried, in the first half of the sixth century, to restore the dwindling assets of the Roman Empire and to return the borders to what they had been in the golden age of Trajan and Hadrian. His capital, Constantinople, was situated on the Bosphorus where Constantine had moved the court in 330.

Ravenna was the seat of the emperor's representative in the west. The church of San Vitale, though sponsored locally, was obviously indebted to Constantinople for some of its ideas and effects. In its sanctuary, a mosaic panel shows Justinian endowed with the imperial purple and diadem as well as the nimbus of a Christian saint. (Fig. 11.25) He holds the paten in his

piers, connected by arches, carry a cupola on a tall drum. This core is set within a second octagon, two storeys high, that reaches up to the base of the drum. This is the basic martyrium scheme as we have encountered it in the rotunda of the Holy Sepulchre at Jerusalem. The novelty of San Vitale was to counteract the sense of focused height with a strong longitudinal path toward the apse, fixed by an entrance atrium and the deep chancel. The nave of this remarkable church was now a luminous centralized space, tall and uplifting, that expanded into the encircling corridor, both at aisle and gallery level, by means of seven niches broken into by triplets of arches. Oblique views prevailed throughout. The rich interlocking of the principal and dependent spaces, the soft banked light, the ubiquitous form of the arch that reverberated, proliferated, and mounted—all this absolved structure of its prose and translated movement into ritual progress.

Hagia Sophia

The building technique of San Vitale is local—simple brick construction and a cupola made of interlinked hollow tubes of terra-cotta—and its general design is allied to the tradition of the West, specifically to buildings like the temple of Minerva Medica. The dependence on Constantinople is attested to by the column shafts and capitals imported from the imperial workshop of Proconnesos and by the inclusion of the emperor in the decorative system of the sanctuary. But, more to the point, it was in the immediate sphere of Constantinople that the most daring essays of the new concept of the domed church were realized a decade or so before the completion of San Vitale.

In the church of Hagia Sophia, dedicated to Christ as Holy Wisdom, the layout of a congregational basilica was married to a vaulted superstructure, but neither was allowed to dominate. (Figs. 11.27, 11.28) The architects Anthemios and Isidoros ensured the flow toward the sanctuary by using screen walls between the nave and the aisles and gallery. But the nave was not closed off with the flat lid of the traditional timber-roofed basilica. Beyond the immediate usable space close to the floor, the church swells into a magnificent system of vaults of mounting height. Four broad arches hold aloft a central dome of brick that hovers some 50 meters (165 feet) above the floor.

Fig. 11.28 Istanbul, Hagia Sophia, 532–37, Isidoros and Anthemios; interior.

Fig. 11.27 Istanbul (Constantinople, Turkey), the area of the Great Palace of the Byzantine emperors; aerial view looking north. Compare with Figs. 11.29 and 11.31. Hagia Sophia is at the top, right of center, overlooking the Golden Horn (modern Haliç). South of Hagia Sophia is the Ottoman mosque of Sultan Ahmed I (Blue Mosque), 1609–17; to its left, the Hippodrome (modern At Meydanï), no. 16 in Fig. 11.29b.

Its base is a band of light made up of forty round-headed windows. To the east and west, lower half-domes reach out toward the sanctuary and the entrance vestibule, respectively. Columned niches of two storeys, like those of San Vitale, allow the bottom edges of these half-domed units to flow into the aisles and gallery.

This complex superstructure is evasive, distant, unattainable. Single individuals count for nothing under it. The immense vaulted space they see from where they stand in the aisles, gallery, or nave is not one that encloses protectively. From here nothing seems solid or definite enough to produce the impression of shelter. Myriad shafts of light, used rhythmically at various heights, serve less to define space than they do to augment the sense of mystery.

The dome of Hagia Sophia was not there to mark an object of veneration, as domes did in martyria. The urge to have relics in churches of standard use never became pressing in the East. It was common to deposit such inestimable treasures in an adjoining structure or in portable reliquaries. In the West, on the other hand, it was made obligatory by the seventh century to consecrate a church through the presence of some relic. The place for it, however, was under the altar (which had since been moved from the juncture of nave and sanctuary to well within the apse), in accordance with the passage in the Apocalypse of St. John the Divine: "And when he had opened the fifth seal, I saw under the altar the souls of them that were slain for the word of God, and for the testimony which they held."

If anything, then, the thought of crowning Hagia Sophia with a dome related to the sanctity of the whole building as an earthly analogue to heaven. The visible universe was concretized in the Byzantine mind as a cube surmounted by a dome. The middle bay of Hagia Sophia can be read without much difficulty as the image of the ideal universe, which had its start with the founding of the Church. So much is in fact admitted in a hymn of the sixth or seventh century in honor of another Hagia Sophia, at Edessa. Justinian's great church expressed this concept through size, light, feel, and niceties of form. It made no use of figurative decoration which might have clarified meaning. The stupendous nave

space projected its own meaning as the clergy led by the patriarch of Constantinople, and the emperor with members of the court, participated in the liturgy of the Eucharist.

To the first generations of believers, the church was where the Christians were. The word *ecclesia,* "church," signified the community of Christ that had no need for prescribed buildings to proclaim its faith and reaffirm its bonds. The people *were* the architecture. In the century or so before Constantine the random gathering places of this primitive Christianity slowly began to be formalized, and with the sudden breakthrough of the imperial conversion, the necessity of a monumental built order to project prestige and authority came to be recognized.

And now, five centuries after the birth of Christianity and two after its legitimization, these premises were being cast in the mold of a surrogate heaven that could be walked into every Sunday and feast day, and stood under. The church was the actual house of God, and so obliged to have an appropriate design. As in the days of King Gudea of Lagash or Solomon and David, it was God who was taking charge of the architecture. This is how Justianian's court historian Procopius described the divine role in the plans of Hagia Sophia:

Whenever one enters this church to pray, he understands at once that it is not by any human power or skill, but by the influence of God, that this work has been so finely turned. And so his mind is lifted up toward God and exalted, feeling that He cannot be far away, but must especially love to dwell in this place which He has chosen.

The Classical concept of beauty, as we have stressed before, rests on physical order—an order whose boundaries are finite and visually within comprehensible reach; whose construction is the logical outcome of the assembly of independent parts; an order furthermore that has relevance in terms of the single user. The effect elicited from beautiful, Classical buildings is that of feeling the architecture as an extension of our limbs.

Not so with Hagia Sophia. We are now in the realm of what modern philosophers will call the *sublime.* It is based on metaphysical order. Parts are completely absorbed into the larger composition and abandon their individuality. The columns, earlier used as supple arbiters of architectural humanism, are now woven into the tapestry of the walls like fancy stitches. With their lacelike

Fig. 11.29a Constantinople in the ninth–eleventh centuries; reconstruction view.

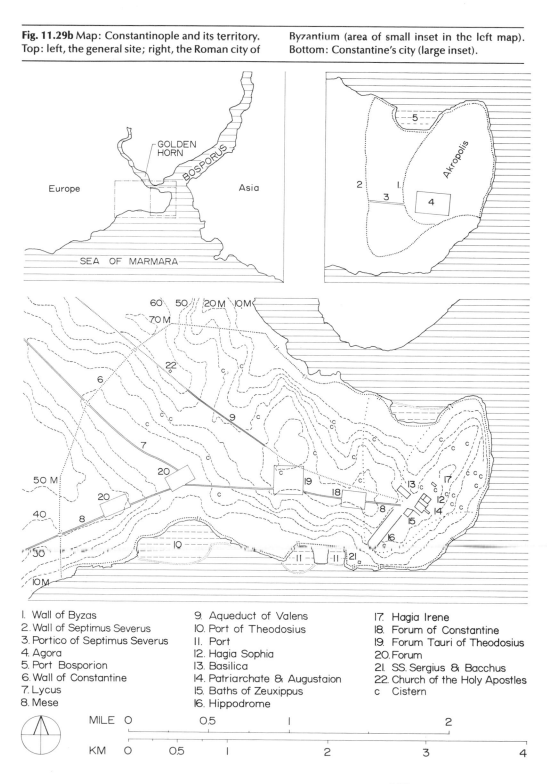

Fig. 11.29b Map: Constantinople and its territory. Top: left, the general site; right, the Roman city of Byzantium (area of small inset in the left map). Bottom: Constantine's city (large inset).

1. Wall of Byzas
2. Wall of Septimus Severus
3. Portico of Septimus Severus
4. Agora
5. Port Bosporion
6. Wall of Constantine
7. Lycus
8. Mese
9. Aqueduct of Valens
10. Port of Theodosius
11. Port
12. Hagia Sophia
13. Basilica
14. Patriarchate & Augustaion
15. Baths of Zeuxippus
16. Hippodrome
17. Hagia Irene
18. Forum of Constantine
19. Forum Tauri of Theodosius
20. Forum
21. SS. Sergius & Bacchus
22. Church of the Holy Apostles
c   Cistern

capitals and insubstantial look, they are neither capable of holding up the building nor of appearing to do so. So too the individual user is absorbed. The scale is theocratic, god-centered, and therefore diametrically opposed to the humanistic scale of Classical architecture. The user no longer feels the building empathetically, with his or her body as it were, but instead is taken up by it, in the very least awed, at best uplifted, elevated.

The Second Rome

Hagia Sophia crowned the extensive site covered by the Great Palace of the Byzantine emperors. (Fig. 11.29) The city was a roughly triangular peninsula surrounded by water except in the west, where it was protected by a formidable triple curtain of walls, 6 kilometers (3.7 miles) long. A low outer wall stood on the city side of a moat that had been subdivided by right-angle spurs. Behind this, there followed a broad terrace called the *peribolos*, and then the high inner circuit that contained 96 towers at regular intervals. At the upper level, the towers communicated by means of a parapet walk, which was reached by ramps and a flight of steps set at right angles to the wall. The construction was a core of rubble faced with alternating bands of brick and ashlar masonry. Of the several principal gates the southernmost, called the Golden Gate, served as the ceremonial entrance to the city. Here the Mese began, the colonnaded avenue that headed eastward to the heart of town and the palace complex at the tip of the peninsula. A series of underground cisterns enabled the city to weather long sieges, of which there were a fair number in its thousand-year history.

These were not the original fortifications of the city Constantine inaugurated in 330. His ran further east and represented at the time a major enlargement of the modest Roman town chosen by the emperor to be the capital of his new Christian state. This earlier town, called Byzantium, clustered around the old akropolis, a hilltop overlooking the narrow inlet of the Golden Horn, and another hill further west. It had the usual trappings of a Romanized provincial center: a forum, a theater, a circus (or hippodrome) for the chariot races, temples, and shrines. What commended it to Constantine, besides its superb location at the crossroads between Europe and Asia, was its obscurity. Free of the millennial pagan tradition that burdened Rome, it could be turned into a Christian showplace more easily and with less offense.

Constantinople was to be the second Rome. The seven hills it spanned and the fourteen regions it embraced were deliberate resemblances, and so was the siting of the imperial palace to one side of the hippodrome, following the model of the familiar relationship of the Palatine and Circus Maximus. The senate met in a nearby basilica on the south side of the old forum, or Augustaion as it was now called. With Constantine, this forum took on the character of an official court between the palace and the first Hagia Sophia, a basilical structure started by the emperor but not consecrated until 360. The new forum, elliptical in shape with a large marble arch at either end and a porphyry column in the middle hoisting aloft the emperor's statue, was the first of several along the length of the Mese.

In the outer city, there were at least two other colonnaded streets directed toward main gates in the land walls. The radial disposition of all the outer streets, a marked shift from the orthogonal pattern of the old town, fit naturally the fan-shaped peninsula. The only notable Christian structure in this outer city was the church of the Holy Apostles, prominently situated on the summit of the fourth hill. It took the form of a cross, at the center of which, beneath a conical roof set upon a well-lit drum, stood the sarcophagus of Constantine being honored as *isapostolos*, the peer of the apostles. (After the emperor's death, his body was moved to a more conventional, circular mausoleum adjoining the church.) The arms of the cross were covered with coffered ceilings until the time of Justinian, when the original structure was destroyed in the Nika riots of 532 that introduced his reign. He rebuilt it with five domes that surmounted the crossing and the four arms and added a two-storey ring of aisles and galleries around the periphery of the building. A sense of the now lost original can be gleaned from a visit to St. Mark's in Venice, which set out to imitate it several centuries later. (Fig. 11.30)

Also burnt down in the Nika riots was the second Hagia Sophia which had replaced Constantine's own foundation shortly after it was destroyed in 404. Justinian's domed church, which took five years to complete, permanently discarded the timber-roofed basilical form of its two antecedents. It was now a principal adjunct of the Great Palace, which had grown since Constantine's day into a sprawling establishment of courtyards, gardens, audience halls, living quarters for court officials, barracks for the imperial guard, armories, textile factories, and workshops for other imperially patronized crafts. (Fig. 11.31) The official entrance was the Chalke or Bronze House, a domed structure decorated with paintings of Justinian's military campaigns. The Augustaion and Hagia Sophia were to the right as one entered; to the left a contingent of the imperial guard, the state silk-weaving looms, and the hippodrome. The central block held the important state rooms, including ultimately a great octagonal hall called Chrisotriklinos and the Triconchos, a trilobed hall like that of the villa at Piazza Armerina. A northern wing surrounded by terraces and gardens communicated directly with the main western prospect of Hagia Sophia. The great church figured critically in that life of fixed ceremonies and slow-moving processions through which, as a late emperor put it, "the imperial power could be exercised in harmony and order and the emperor could thus reflect the motion of the universe as it was made by the Creator." Except perhaps for the reference to a Creator, it is a description of state that would have been at home in Ctesiphon or Ch'ang-an.

Like the church of the Holy Apostles, Hagia Sophia had open courts on all sides. Two baptisteries attached themselves to the outer frame, the more important at the southwest corner. A round sacristy stood at the northeast corner; here the elements were readied for the Eucharist and brought in at the proper moment. On the south side of the church was the patriarch's residence. Four exterior stair ramps provided access to the galleries where the unbaptized followed the service through the reading of the gospel. The empress and her ladies in waiting may also have used the gallery, most likely the section on the west side, over the inner narthex. The emperor's party was accommodated in the south aisle.

Fig. 11.30 Venice (Italy), St. Mark's, begun 1063; nave.

Before the commencement of services, crowds poured in from all parts of the city to this converging point on the first hill. They gathered at the atrium of the church to await the arrival of the patriarch. (Fig. 1.4) The emperor, having arrived earlier from the palace with ceremony, accompanied by court dignitaries, senators, and an honor guard, took his seat at the outer narthex. Here the two men would meet and exchange greetings, cheered on by the crowd. Standing before the Royal Door, the central one of nine doors that led from the inner narthex into the church, they would make a triple reverence, candles in hand. Then, as the crowds were led by the master of ceremonies in the chanting of the *troparion*, patriarch and emperor, preceded by a deacon carrying the gospel and followed by the clergy and the imperial cortège, would enter and traverse the empty nave. Behind this splendid procession the surging crowd of common people would

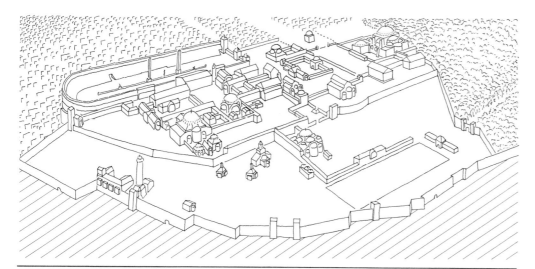

Fig. 11.31 Istanbul, Great Palace of the Byzantine emperors; conjectural perspective view as of ca. 950, looking northwest.

follow chanting and take their place in the western part of the nave and in the aisles. This Lesser Entrance signified the coming of Christ in the person of the patriarch, "and the conversion of those who enter through him and with him," as a contemporary theologian, Maximus the Confessor, tells us—"a conversion from disbelief to faith, from immorality to virtue, from ignorance to knowledge."

The altar, it would seem, was still a little in front of the apse in Justinian's time, and the area around it screened by a low chancel barrier. A passageway with a low wall on either side, called the *solea*, started under the great central dome, linking a large pulpit on an oval or circular platform with the sanctuary. The emperor's honor guard, bearing scepters and standards, lined up on the two sides of the solea as the rest of the procession moved eastward on it to gain the Holy Door of the sanctuary. The patriarch entered first and took his place on the high throne, set against the apse center. The emperor, having followed him into the sanctuary and presented a gift of gold at the altar, withdrew to his own throne in the south aisle.

Readings from the Old and New Testaments and a sermon delivered by the patriarch ex cathedra constituted the first portion of the service. At its conclusion the unbaptized were dismissed; they then left the galleries by the exterior stair ramps without passing through the ground level. The doors of the church were now closed, and the Greater Entrance began with the transport of the Eucharistic bread and wine from the sacristy outside. The emperor put on his purple mantel and crossed the nave to the ambo to greet the procession entering from the opposite side. He was now presented with a lamp, and carrying it he accompanied the deacons who held the paten and chalice, individual veils to place over each one during "the concealment of mysteries," and the *aer* or great veil to spread over them all—the entire retinue headed by candle-bearers and deacons who bathed the elements with incense. At the Holy Door the emperor greeted the patriarch, left his lamp, and returned to his place in the company of his chamberlains and ministers.

The faithful now greeted one another with the Kiss of Peace and recited the Creed of their unity. They then watched the clergy in the sanctuary invoke the central prayer of the liturgy and approach the Holy Door at the end of it to communicate. The emperor was allowed to enter the sanctuary, where he received communion from the patriarch. This done, and the service at an end, the deacon dismissed the people. Finally, in the order in which they had entered, the actors of this magnificent spectacle of faith walked the length of the church, across the two narthexes and the atrium. "And then we go out," the patriarch Eutychius wrote, "each one to his own home"—the patriarch to his nearby residence, the emperor to some corner of his vast palace, and the people fanning out along the radial streets to reclaim their crowded neighborhoods.

With the hall of Holy Wisdom empty again—without celebrants, candles, costumes, and props—the great dome hovered over its vast spaces, incense-sweet and imbued with the aura of celestial hosts. (page 244)

Further Reading

A. Alfoldi, *The Conversion of Constantine and Pagan Rome,* trans. H. Mattingly (Oxford: Clarendon Press, 1969).

H. Kähler, *Hagia Sophia,* trans. E. Childs (New York: Praeger, 1967).

S. Kostof, *The Orthodox Baptistery of Ravenna* (New Haven: Yale University Press, 1965).

R. Krautheimer, *Early Christian and Byzantine Architecture,* 3rd ed. (Harmondsworth and Baltimore: Penguin, 1979).

W. MacDonald, *Early Christian and Byzantine Architecture* (New York: Braziller, 1962).

M. Maclagan, *The City of Constantinople* (New York: Praeger, 1968).

R. Mainstone, *Hagia Sophia: Architecture, Structure, and Liturgy of Justinian's Great Church* (New York: Thames and Hudson, 1988).

T. F. Mathews, *Early Churches of Constantinople: Architecture and Liturgy* (University Park: Pennsylvania State University Press, 1971).

J. Toynbee and J. B. Ward-Perkins, *The Shrine of Saint Peter* (New York: Pantheon, 1957).

F. van der Meer, *Atlas of the Early Christian World* (London: Nelson, 1958).

O. G. von Simson, *Sacred Fortress: Byzantine Art and Statecraft in Ravenna* (Chicago: University of Chicago Press, 1948).

J. B. Ward-Perkins, *Roman Architecture* (New York: Abrams, 1977).

Kairawan (Tunisia), the Great Mosque, ca. 820–36.

12

THE MEDITERRANEAN IN THE EARLY MIDDLE AGES

The Decline of the West

Emperor Justinian died in 565, his dream of restoring Roman rule around the Mediterranean unfulfilled. The Greek-speaking Eastern half of the empire—the Byzantine Empire—lived on for nine more eventful centuries. (Fig. 12.1) The West had been permanently fractured under the steady pressure of Germanic tribes. Goths had run most of Italy for at least a century before Justinian. A new Germanic people, the Lombards, invaded three years after his death and settled in the valley of the Po. The Franks, who had crossed the Rhine first in 276, were now firmly in control of Gaul and on the way to a stable order under the Merovingian house. Vandals held most of North Africa; the Visigoths, Spain. Superficially, they were all united in Christ, having been converted one after another since the fourth century. But a common faith did not engender amity among the Germans, and the particular brand of Christianity espoused by most of them, Arianism, was severely proscribed both by Rome and Constantinople.

The Impact of Islam

Meanwhile, a new and totally unexpected danger to the old Mediterranean commonwealth of Rome materialized in the desert of Arabia in the first half of the seventh century. With phenomenal success, adherents of a religion called Islam put an end, once and for all, to Christian claims on an integral Roman inheritance. Unlike the Germans whose rootless, ruthless vigor jostled the civilized realm without any clear mas-

ter scheme, Islam was the product of a literate, cosmopolitan milieu, the cities of Mecca and Medina. It drew sustenance from a fresh system of belief that posed as an alternative to the old and harried monotheistic religions of the East, Christianity and Judaism. It conquered in the name of this system as put forth in a holy book, the Koran, and immediately organized the conquered territory along the lines of its own view of life. The Muslims established permanent institutions wherever they found themselves, revising the old cities they fell heir to and building new ones.

The great founder of this new religion was Muhammed (570?–632). His mature years had been spent in efforts to convince his countrymen in the cities and deserts of Arabia that he was the last of the prophets of the Lord, and that in him and his book lay the only remaining hope for human salvation. In one shrewd move, he embraced the pagan pilgrimage to Mecca which centered around the Kaaba and its Black Stone, a profitable tradition of long standing, and made it one of the obligatory observances of Islam. (Fig. 12.2) The conversion complete, his followers spilled out of their native isolation only two years after his death and plunged headlong into Byzantine territory. The Fort of Bosra in Transjordania fell in 634; Damascus in 635. In 636 the battle of Yarmok gave them the whole of Syria, a major Byzantine province. A year later Jerusalem opened its gates to Muslim armies. Soon the holiest shrine of Christianity was confronted with the uncompro-

misingly monotheistic message of the Koran that accepted the holiness of Christ but not His divinity, deeming the doctrine of the Trinity polytheism in disguise.

Beyond these victories lay Persia, then under the formidable Sassanian dynasty. This vast realm of the god Ahuramazda and his fire cult—the ancient lands of Mesopotamia and the high, proud plateaus of Iran—was now subjected to the will of Allah. The irrepressible tide rushed westward as well, across the Sinai Desert. Byzantine Egypt succumbed in 641 to the brilliant General Amr. By 670 there was a permanent encampment, and soon thereafter a new city, at Kairawan in Tunisia, built away from the coast to guard against the Byzantine navy. It was Spain's turn next. By 711 an empire that spread across the entire southern half of the Mediterranean, from the Persian highlands to the Atlantic, faced the Merovingian Franks at the Pyrenees.

The impact of all this is obvious. The urban culture of the Roman Empire was rooted in trade, the free trade of the Mediterranean basin and the land routes made safe by the might of Roman armies. Now this trade was interrupted. Southern Europe became landlocked. Much of the subsequent history of the West may be considered in light of the shift away from the inland sea, toward the regions north of the Alps.

The Plight of Cities

We have long been taught to view the period between the fifth and eighth centuries as the Dark Ages, when Western civilization was decimated through the combined onslaught of Germans and Muslims. With long-distance trade stifled, so the story went, the old Roman cities became defunct. The standard of living dropped precipitously. The West turned inward upon itself and tried to adjust to its new Germanic masters. This was an epochal confrontation: on the one hand, an old and venerable culture based on cities, on a humane and civic conception of the world, on human dignity as guaranteed by laws, on monumental architecture and large stone sculpture that celebrated permanence and human achievement; on the other hand, the barbarian's view of things based on the power of tribal and war chiefs, the law of heredity as opposed to the principle of choice, a seminomadic existence that treasured the portable and valuable artifact over anything fixed and monumental, and a visual convention that eschewed the human figure altogether in favor of abstraction and geometric complexity. Through the calamitous instrumentality of this barbarian outlook, ornament submerged human imagery, cities succumbed to the ethic of the countryside, urbanism was displaced by monasticism. This was the first act.

Then came Charles the Great or Charlemagne (742–814), King of the Franks. He conquered vast new territories for his people, brought a semblance of cultural unity and administrative order to much of Europe, and then set about deliberately to revive the Roman Empire and its values. Crowned emperor of the West in Rome on Christmas 800, he presided over a humanistic renaissance in Classical letters, manuscript illumination, and architecture.

However, the restoration was short-lived. Within fifty years of his death, the Carolingian Empire was on the road to decay. Internecine rivalry among his heirs and new waves of invasion from the north and east (Vikings and Magyars, respectively) made a shambles of European cohesiveness. Not until the eleventh century, with the Norse and Magyar invaders converted and settled, will a new faith in the future surge throughout the former lands of the Carolingian Empire, and a burst of large-scale building in the monumental mode called the Romanesque blanket them with feudal castles and imposing pilgrimage churches.

But this scenario of regression and misery temporarily stemmed under Charles overlooks the vigor, resilience, and adaptive imagination of Europe during the long, difficult period in question and underestimates the forces of continuity and cultural process. The cities, for one thing, did not die. It is true that society, from the last stages of the Roman Empire onward, turned overwhelmingly agrarian. Land was now the source of wealth and political influence. With the gradual atrophy of commerce, fluid wealth sharply declined. Real power shifted to landed gentry. Along with imperial patronage, the civic pride that had moved the rich to build lavishly to enhance their city melted away.

Yet the city, diminished and transformed, persisted. *Civitas*, the assembly of citizens, supplanted the more abstruse concept of the Roman *urbs;* "not the stones but the people," as Isidore of Selville wrote. In Italy, especially in the north, an active citizenry continued to function and make its voice heard against bishops and Lombard overlords. Similarly, in Spain the Roman cities pressed on under the Visigoths, so that the Muslim conquerors found them ready to take over and develop.

In the wake of the first invasions, the cities of Gaul had started the process of entrenchment and shrinkage that would make a population of two or three thousand exceptional by the seventh century. Some fifty

Fig. 12.1 Map: The Mediterranean and Western Europe in the ninth century.

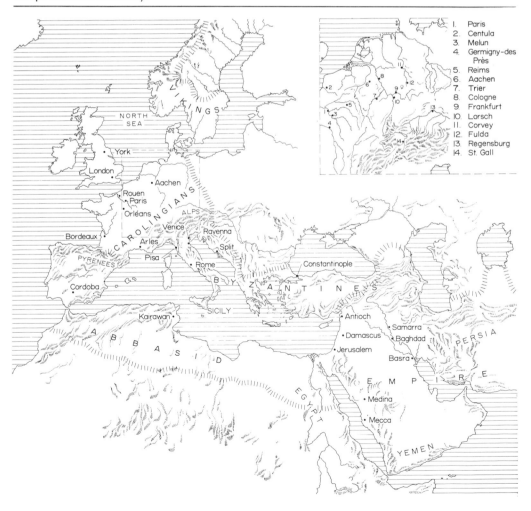

270

Fig. 12.2 Mecca (Saudi Arabia), the Kaaba and its setting today.

dieval Arles moved into its amphitheater; the palace of Diocletian became the town of Split. (Fig. 12.3) In rare instances where the original Roman enceinte continued to protect its city, the inherited fabric within was readjusted to the modest new existence of severely curtailed means. The classic case is Rome herself. For several centuries after the retirement of the court, she dwindled within the heroic curtain of Aurelian's walls, turning the outermost regions into farmland, reusing materials, adjusting large buildings to new uses, and little by little fissuring the grand old pattern of the public areas—the Campus Martius, the imperial forums—into a small-scale, manageable tissue, eloquent of survival and cultural re-evaluation.

Religion was the road to posterity. Towns without bishops faded away. A relic, a saintly person, an apparition could ensure longevity. Rome was saved by her shrines and the authority of her bishop. Pilgrimages and annual fairs bolstered the economy of these holy cities. Otherwise, it was trade or administrative favor that had to be relied on. Paris as the capital of Merovingian rule, Pavia as that of the Lombards, enjoyed some stability. The absence of an organized bureaucracy, of a state apparatus in the Roman tradition, thrust on the kings an itinerant vigilance that profited a number of other towns.

Trade by no means ceased. Until the seventh century maritime commerce between East and West, albeit down to a trickle, was never cut off. When Muslims first staked their claim to the waters of the Mediterranean, river traffic along the Seine, the Loire, and the Po was unaffected, and in the circumstances gained in importance. And it did not take long for enterprising northern Italian towns like Venice and Pisa to engage the "Saracen" clandestinely, even as they joined in the public deprecation of Muhammed as the scourge of God.

The decline of Western cities would probably have come about even without the agency of barbarians. The example of the East shows that under Byzantine rule the great cities lost their independence and civic excellence. Revenues began to be collected by the central government, and even though one-third of the take was ploughed back into the cities to keep them from total collapse, this money was scarcely enough

cities, from the North Sea to the Rhone, all along the Loire Valley, and at strategic approaches to the valley of the Garonne, converted themselves into strongholds. They threw up substantial walls around a small quarter of the city that happened to stand on high ground or had some other natural means of defense. The bulk of the urban fabric and the suburbs were left to crumble. The narrow twisted street we have come to equate with medieval towns was spawned in such stringencies.

Sometimes a single Roman monument contained the reduced citizenry. Early me-for the upkeep of the walls and some public amenities like roads and aqueducts. The rest was allowed to disintegrate. The forums and their dependencies became victims of an outmoded self-government. Theaters, gymnasia, and public baths were obsolete frames for functions condemned by the Church. After a period of reticence, temples were also destroyed, quarried, or converted for Christian use. Only cities of military consequence or those having some special religious association, like the bond of Ephesos to the cult of Mary, justified an emphatic urban posture. So what Islam acquired with its conquest of Syria and Egypt were not the brilliant Greco-Roman cities but their debased shells. Throughout the Middle Ages Constantinople, fabulous and unconquerable, remained in fact "The City" in the ever-diminishing realm of the eastern Roman Empire.

The Strains of Architecture

As far as what was being built in the West between the fall of the Roman Empire and the rise of Charlemagne, we should not expect to see the same continued scale or the same mechanized efficiency and production that governed Roman building operations. State brick kilns, the transport of foreign marbles, inexhaustible slave and army labor were things of the past. Patronage now devolved on the Church, but not exclusively. Barbarian rulers early embraced the notion that involvement in the arts was a princely duty, and a ready passport to prestige. They and their entourage were content to live in Gallo-Roman villas or other requisitioned buildings. But they provided well for their faith. Theodoric's Arian cathedral in Ravenna, with its baptistery, and his stone mausoleum are still there to see. Indeed, it was this enlightened Goth who arrested the physical deterioration of Rome with a series of measures for the repair and conservation of the great imperial monuments. Theodoric's reply to a petitioner seeking leave to put a modern structure over part of the forum of Trajan addresses our own urban dilemma. The petition was granted. It is easy for buildings to become derelict when abandoned, the king explained; keeping them in use forestalls the decay of old age. The history of architecture should entail more than the

Fig. 12.3 Arles (France), the medieval town ensconced within the Roman amphitheater.

chronicling of new construction. How the emerging Europe of the early Middle Ages managed its built legacy from the standpoint of rehabilitation and reuse would make a fascinating, instructive story. The forms of central Florence and Verona are still based on their Roman grids. (Figs. 9.2, 16.2) The mausoleum of Augustus has survived to this day precisely because continuous uses were found for it in line with Theodoric's advice.

The new buildings were primarily religious. The focal point of cities was now the cathedral complex with the episcopal residence. The main church where the bishop officiated was dedicated to the Virgin, while daily services were held in a subsidiary church arranged parallel to the cathedral. Between the two lay the baptistery. Basilicas honoring martyrs' tombs stood at the approaches to cities where the old cemeteries had been. Monasteries also rose near the highways, as well as intramurally.

Monasticism, an early Eastern institution, had reached the West by the late fourth century, through Tours on the Loire and the

island of Lerins off the southern coast of France opposite Cannes; but it was through the efforts of St. Benedict of Nursia that it began to take shape in accordance with his Rule. The first monasteries were doubtless random in layout. Formal planning does not seem to begin until the eighth century. They had walls fortified with towers, guest quarters, one or more churches, a cloister, a refectory, and a bathhouse. They functioned as centers of disciplined communal life, anchors of stability in the fluctuating waters of political and social life, and outposts of missionary work.

Around the extramural basilicas and monastic enclaves sprang communities that led a lively existence. When long-distance trade was successfully re-established, colonies of merchants started setting up their own nuclei outside the walls that would challenge the jurisdiction of the old cities. They are first mentioned about 700. Out of such constellations, medieval towns molded themselves in stages. The countryside was organized economically along feudal lines. The principal institution, at least in Gaul, was the *seigneurie* or *ville*, a large estate with a residence in which the landlord installed himself in perpetuity. Part of the land, the demesne, was cultivated under the immediate direction of the lord or his agents. The rest was alienated to subject settlers in a number of small or middle-sized holdings, called tenures.

The churches were rectangular halls with or without an apse and with or without transepts. They might have open porticoes on the long sides, and sometimes also across the west facade, a device common enough in Roman public buildings. These came to be used as shelter for privileged dead. By and large the buildings were timber-roofed structures. Wooden architecture was more prevalent now, and frame construction common to both church and palace. The standard vernacular form was that aisled and bay-divided long house of the north which we encountered first in prehistoric times, and which had enjoyed a continuous existence since then in Gotland, Iceland, Germany, Belgium, and Holland. This unbroken tradition is confirmed by a number of excavated specimens in these areas, legal and administrative documents of the early Middle Ages, and the literary evidence of Nordic sagas. The long house was a rectangular hall enclosed by dwarf walls of earth and stone. (Fig. 12.4) Pairs of posts rested on stone bases in the earthen floor within; they supported trans-

Fig.12.5 Poitiers (France), the baptistery of St.-Jean, seventh century.

Fig. 12.4 Leicestershire (England), the Great Hall of Leicester Castle, ca. 1150; interior reconstruction.

verse beams that, in turn, held up the pitched roof. This method of construction may have encouraged the northern architect to think in terms of rectangular bays in the process of design, whatever the construction materials he worked with.

Stone architecture and its requisite techniques did not die out. Nor was vaulting forgotten. Local vernacular traditions carried on doggedly, on a drastically reduced scale and level of refinement to be sure, but continuously nonetheless. Northern Italy, Lombardy in particular, kept alive the brick tradition of Ravenna. Lombardy lies in the great alluvial plain of the Po; bricks made of the plentiful river clay bake to beautiful browns and rich reds. Here the Byzantine variety of the oblong brick was retained and walls were built of it without formwork. *Lombardus* came to mean mason. The manufacture of stone capitals and sarcophagi was kept up in Aquitaine, and the celebrated marble quarries there were ac-

tive until the eighth century. What is more, the awesome presence of the old Roman piles everywhere was a steady reminder of what was possible. Old columns, capitals, and stone blocks were regularly reused in new contexts, and these suggestive spoils must have been seen as signs of an unremitting, if hard-pressed, tradition.

A handful of surviving buildings demonstrates the independence and verve of this pre-Carolingian period. Roman evocations are unmistakable, but there is no desire to be loyal to Classical canons. The exterior of the seventh-century baptistery at Poitiers uses Classical themes—pediments, pilasters, cornices—without concern for reading them logically. (Fig. 12.5) To a degree, its aims are akin to the confounding of structural and decorative impulses that we saw in the interior of the Orthodox Baptistery at Ravenna. (Fig. 11.22) But at Poitiers the balance is upset in favor of ornament, of geometric abstraction. Vestigial pediments become fillers for the main pediment, themselves willfully filled with terracotta rosettes.

This abstraction of substance is all too easily credited to barbarian taste. We should recall that Western art had drifted away from naturalism prior to the occupation of Roman lands. An abstract "essence" had been advocated by philosophers like Plotinus and Porphyry in the third and fourth centuries, the debate being between reality or transient appearance and spirituality or universal state. It was this tendency in the West toward abstraction, be it in the treatment of the human figure or in the logic of Classical structure and ornament, that met and welcomed the barbarian's preoccupation with complex patterns and his distaste for empty intervals in the design. The resident talent of the old cities revived small-scale ornamentation to the level of high art, merging it with the memory of Classical forms.

This same disregard for Classical unities in early medieval architecture shows up also in three-dimensions—in the correlation of plans and elevations and in the arrangement of exterior masses and interior spaces. The small but beautifully proportioned churches of pre-Muslim Spain cannot in any way be considered the direct successors of Roman or Early Christian basilicas. Look at San Pedro dela Nave in the province of Zamora, near the Portuguese frontier. (Fig. 12.6) The square sanctuary (with a mysterious, inaccessible room above) and the transept arms are not coherent elements of the total composition but appendages to the main rectangular mass of the church proper. This mass is itself chopped up. Only the western half can be read as a three-aisled, clerestoried basilica. The transept band with the lantern tower over the central bay emphatically distinguishes this congregational space from the choir, a distinction underlined by the shape of windows. Compartmentalization makes vaulting more manageable. But the functional reason for this fragmented interior that displaces Roman respect for spatial cohesion is the increasing separation of the clergy from the faithful, as well as the strict allotment of room for each liturgical activity. In this and in several other features—the crossing tower, the preference for piers over columns, the importance given to transept entrances, the

Fig. 12.6 El Campilo (Spain), San Pedro dela Nave, 680–711.

historiated capitals—San Pedro prefigures later medieval practice.

Carolingian Restoration

The record of the so-called Dark Ages should modify our view of the Carolingian episode in Europe without diminishing its great importance. Instead of a sudden flare in quasi-total darkness, we should think of it as a glimmer that grew strong and bright under Charles. All in all, we are dealing with a period of less than one hundred years, beginning about 790. The order he and his sons were able to bring to the restless and largely unformed energies of central and western Europe was a promising achievement. And it had been immediately preceded by the conscious design of the bishops of Rome to assume political leadership in the West.

By the mid-eighth century the Eastern governorship of Ravenna was inoperative,

the Byzantine emperor's tenuous hold on Italy being restricted to the southern tip and to Sicily. The popes now felt free to pursue a policy independent of Constantinople. They turned north for their support and invited the Franks to defend the seat of Peter against the Lombard kings. At the same time a forged document called the Donations of Constantine sought to prove that this emperor, in giving the Bishop of Rome the Lateran Palace and its dependencies after the battle of the Mulvian bridge, also conferred upon him and his staff in perpetuity the dignities and privileges of the empire in the West. The Lateran now began to be refurbished as an imperial palace, to replace the authority of the abandoned Palatine. The crowning of Charles' father Pepin as King of the Franks in the church of St.-Denis outside Paris in 754 by Pope Stephen II was the prelude to Charles' own coronation in St. Peter's less than fifty years later as emperor of the West. The strong ties between Rome and the Frankish kingdom

274

are proved by the substitution under Pepin of the Roman liturgy for that of the national Gallic church, a move that would have specific architectural consequences—for example, the Western orientation of cathedrals and monastery churches in sympathy with Constantinian practice, and the emulation of the forms of St. Peter's and the Lateran Palace in building programs undertaken by Charles.

The Imperial Example

The point is important. If Charles intended his reign to be a return to the days of the Roman Empire, he understood this age to embrace the first centuries of the triumph of the Church. Architecturally, the Christian monuments of the West, especially those in Rome and Ravenna, mattered as much as the Pantheon or the imperial forums. The agency through which his *renovatio Romae* was to manifest itself was the Church. Religion did not serve only as a means of personal salvation, but also as an instrument that moved and transformed society. Rules of behavior for the clergy and the monks, as well as prescriptions for religious architecture, were formulated in court, there being no difference for Charles between Church and state, any more than there was for Byzantine emperors under the so-called doctrine of caesaropapism which affirmed their supremacy both in political and religious matters.

In real, or at least projected, accomplishment, the Carolingian age ranks with the greatest building eras of Western history. Charles' resources came from his conquests, and they sustained building on a grand scale even beyond his death, at least until 845 when the Norse invasions set in for good. Several palace compounds were created across the realm to satisfy the peripatetic habits of the court. Within the palace the emperor surrounded himself with learned scholars drawn from every subject province: Peter of Pisa and Paul the Deacon from Italy, Theodulf from Spain, the great Alcuin from Northumberland, the emperor's later biographer Einhardt the German. In royal scriptoria ancient manuscripts were copied and illuminated. And this despite the fact that the upper ranks of Carolingian society were unlettered and looked on reading and writing as trades of inferiors. The general revival of letters, at

least for the emperor, coincided with his interest in defining dogma, in getting back to the sources of correct Christian practice.

Monasteries were now state institutions, their hundreds of inmates recruited, indeed conscripted, and their administration entrusted to ranking political figures. Planned expansively, monasteries were in fact urban alternatives; they were fully operational, administrative, economic, and cultural entities planted mostly in the open countryside. Some actual cities—Reims, Frankfurt, Melun, Regensburg—grew confident enough under the Carolingian aegis to tear down their restricting walls and enlarge themselves. Old cathedral complexes were rebuilt in a number of episcopal sees. Slowly majestic groups of buildings replaced Merovingian arrangements, the whole now centered on one church only, which absorbed the functions of the secondary church and the baptistery as well. In these renovations, a new church type was forged that would dominate the scene for a long time to come.

Two characteristics, size and geometric order, allied Carolingian intentions with the example of imperial Rome. At Aachen (Aix-la-Chapelle), the palace and a stately royal church stood at opposite ends of a large courtyard that measured over 200 meters (656 feet) in length. (Fig. 12.7) The entire plan was based on a module of 58 feet, according to one contemporary thesis, or better still, was designed within a grid whose squares had sides of that dimension. A more recent study interprets the layout in terms of a modular base value of a rod or 12 feet. The courtyard was a perfect square with sides of 30 rods or 360 feet. Internally, the square was subdivided into 10 squares, with 7 rods (84 feet) per side. The church stood against the south edge of the courtyard, an apsed audience hall against the north edge. The palace grounds were intersected by two streets, 2 rods (24 feet) broad, that crossed at right angles to divide the site into an inner and outer court. A section of the grounds was named the Lateran, after the papal residence in Rome; and in emulation of the famous equestrian bronze there, believed to be that of Constantine, an equestrian statue of Theodoric was transported from Ravenna to grace the setting of this revived *imperium*.

The palatine church still stands, though altered externally in the Gothic period. It was designed by Odo of Metz and begun in 792. The main building was preceded by a rectangular atrium with two-storey galleries on three sides. The fourth side was occupied by the great "westwork." At ground level, a vestibule led into the church proper. The two corner towers of the westwork contained cylindrical stairs that mounted to the tribune level where the emperor would make appearances and follow the service. The room continued upward into a reliquary chapel that housed Charles' fabulous collection of relics.

From each side of the throne room annular galleries, separated from the octagonal central space by columnar screens, led to a sanctuary directly opposite. (Fig. 12.8) Below this, a ground-storey sanctuary led to two basilical chapels to the north and south. The northern one linked the church with the audience hall on the other side of the courtyard by means of a two-storey passageway. At ground level, an ambulatory opened into the central space of the church through undivided plain arches. The exterior was sixteen-sided. Every other side was joined to one of the eight piers of the core by means of groin vaults, or rather angled-off annular barrel vaults. In the galleries of the second floor the eight square bays were covered by barrel vaults, while an octagonal cloistered vault covered the central space.

The general resemblance of the palatine church to San Vitale in Ravenna has often been noted. It was, no doubt, intended. But the uniqueness of the Aachen structure is more interesting. Setting aside the multi-storied westwork, one of the great inventions of Carolingian architects, the church has much more in common with early medieval design in the West, whose peculiarities we have glimpsed in San Pedro dela Nave, than it does to Byzantine Ravenna or Constantinople. The emphasis on sturdy piers, an interior organization that tends to be multipartite and complex, narrow shaft-like spaces—all these distinguish Odo's work from Justinian's precedent. (Fig. 11.26)

Externally, too, Carolingian massing has little to do with Byzantium. Aachen is now much changed, but a small church at Germigny-des-Prés near Orléans, built by Bishop Theodulf and consecrated in 806, is well known enough to illustrate the comparison. (Fig. 12.9) Its five-domed scheme was to become standard in Byzantine church architecture several decades later. In the East, we have in fact very little to show between the time of Justinian and the ninth century, a period when the rise of Islam and the bloody civil war over holy images, the so-called Iconoclastic Controversy that racked the empire for more than a century, left little room for new construction. When peace was again restored in 843 with the triumph of iconodules, or supporters of images, church architecture settled for a scheme that was to be endlessly repeated in the next five centuries: the cross-in-square design. Basically this scheme was one of nine bays, in which the central one was covered by a dome on a high drum, the corner bays by small cupolas or groin vaults, and the rest, making up the arms of the inscribed cross, were barrel vaulted. The arms opened up the nave space in the direction of the aisles; the longitudinal axis toward the altar was minimized. In the generally very small, centralized form of these new churches, the congregation crowded around and inside the domed square in the middle, which was inscribed at floor level by nothing more substantial than four delicate columns or piers.

We will return to this Byzantine formula. Here we are interested in the contrast with Carolingian centralized buildings. The tall lantern and square belfry tower that culminate the episcopal church at Germigny are perhaps the most notable differences. Great upward-jutting masses are a compositional preference of the Western Middle Ages. This pronounced verticality, the uplifting of the exterior mass beyond the level of the highest roof, has little to do with the Byzantine church that resolves its

amassed volumes at the central dome, relegating bell towers to a corner outside the main building form. (Fig. 12.10)

The arrangement of axial apses at Germigny is also singular. A Byzantine church of the post-Iconoclastic period had three

apses at the east end, the principal sanctuary apse being flanked by those of two chapels to the north and south. The practice of the early Church to allow one and only one altar for the liturgy had been set aside as early as the sixth century. The re-

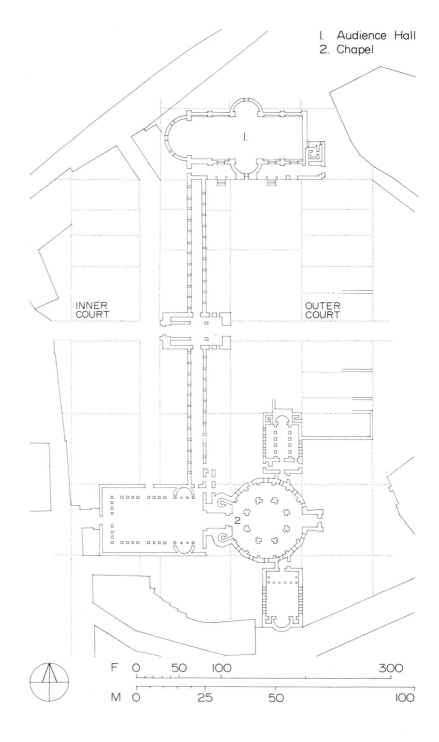

1. Audience Hall
2. Chapel

INNER COURT

OUTER COURT

Fig. 12.7 Aachen (Aix-la-Chapelle, Germany), the palace of Charlemagne, 796–804; site plan of main portion, with conjectural modular grid superimposed. The edge lines belong to the modern fabric. Nothing remains of the palace today except the famous chapel (now the town cathedral) as reconstructed externally in the Gothic period.

Fig. 12.8 Aachen, the palace of Charlemagne, chapel, 796–804, Odo of Metz; interior view.

markable popularity of the cult of relics soon necessitated additional altars in the West too, where the conjoining of altar and relic had become prescriptive. A Carolingian church had to make provisions for as many as twenty altars. These were sheltered in traditional symbolic frames like apses in an expanded multilevel interior, or else partitioned from the principal spaces with parapet screens.

The western apse at Germigny across from the high altar makes of this church a "double-ender"—another of the characteristic formulas of Carolingian religious architecture. This western apse had been required since the early eighth century by the developing nature of Easter services. It forced the abandonment of axial entrances in direct line with the sanctuary and this, coupled with the visual fragmentation which resulted from the parapet screens, hastened that disregard for Classical proprieties that started in pre-Carolingian design.

Basilical Churches
Centrally planned churches in the West remained exceptional. The option was reserved for palatine chapels, paradigms of Jerusalem's Holy Sepulchre, and the baptistery in those few areas, primarily Italy, where it continued as an independent structure. In the Byzantine Empire, the basilica had long since fallen into disuse as a church type, and even the Justinianic, domed basilicas like Hagia Sophia had remained without progeny. The precise steps through which these domed basilicas might have developed into the cross-in-square scheme are unclear, if indeed it was a systematic development. By contrast, Western religious architecture sustained its preoccupation with the basilical layout, and the Carolingian contribution to its continuing revision was of the first order.

There was of course a wide variety of solutions. The simplest retained the pre-Carolingian scheme: a single rectangular hall to which subsidiary units were attached as needed—apse, rectangular choir, axial tower on the entrance front—that communicated with the main hall through small doors only. Low cross arms might form something like a transept, or a number of annexes might be lined up on a single side of the church, on two sides, or even all around. The interiors were richly decorated, the mediums being stucco carvings (a legacy of late antiquity), frescoes, and some mosaic.

But the prestigious churches, episcopal or monastic, were in general aisled basilicas with an atrium in front, from which one entered the building either through a westwork or else, in the case of "double-enders," from one of the two sides of the counter-apse. The overall plan can be reconstructed from the excavations at Fulda and the Romanesque churches of Germany, which held onto the Carolingian shapes much longer than any other part of Europe. (Fig. 12.11) The Benedictine abbey church of St. Vitus at Corvey on the Weser has preserved for us the look of Carolingian westworks. There is also among actual Carolingian remains, the celebrated gateway at Lorsch which originally stood by itself on the west side of the vast atrium that preceded the church of an important abbey there. (Figs. 12.12, 12.13)

The atrium was returning to a Western church design in emulation of Rome—*more romano,* as the Fulda chronicler put it. The phrase probably refers to Constantinian foundations like the Lateran Cathedral and St. Peter's, but the Lorsch gate, set up in the manner of a triumphal arch, also recalls the forum of Trajan where the colonnaded public space was entered via an arch of three openings. (Fig. 9.28) But the Classically inspired orders of the two main facades become wedded at the Lorsch gatehouse to an overall, two-dimensional pattern of stone incrustation; the round staircase turrets at either end and the spacious hall on the upper floor have no parallel in a Roman triumphal arch. A more appropriate model might have been late-antique city gates like those in the Aurelian walls of Rome, where a usable space was to be found at this level between the two flanking towers.

The purpose of this hall, beautifully painted inside with an illusionist architectural decor *all'antico,* is unknown. (Fig. 12.13) It was possibly connected with receptions when the emperor, exercising his prerogatives as founder, came to stay at the abbey. Kings often had living quarters of their own at the entrance to monasteries. Or the room might have served as an audience hall for the abbot, following the old

Fig. 12.9 Germigny-des-Prés (France), the oratory of Theodulf, Bishop of Orléans, consecrated in 806; exterior view. The oratory was originally part of Theodulf's villa; in its present form the church is largely the result of a nineteenth-century rebuilding.

Fig. 12.10 Mistra (Greece), Brontocheion, late Byzantine monastic church, ca. 1300; view from the east.

custom of having the bishop live over one of the gates of his town.

The program of the westwork is also obscure. The surviving specimen at Corvey was built between 873 and 885. (Fig. 12.14) It displays a high facade wall, with a projecting central tract that is flanked by tall towers between which stretches an arcaded bell-house, a later addition. Within, a vaulted space occupied the ground level, while on the second floor a high broad room, now called the Johanneschor, was encircled by two-storey arcades that led into galleries. At the palatine church at Aachen, the corresponding level of the westwork was clearly associated with the imperial throne, and so with the emperor's attendance at services. This may be a clue to at least one use of the Johanneschor.

Symbolically, however, the westwork seems to have figured prominently in the

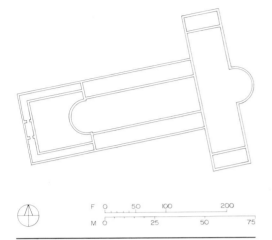

Fig. 12.11 Fulda (Germany), Carolingian church, 802–17; foundation plan. The scheme is based on Old St. Peter's (cf. Figs. 11.24 and 12.15).

Carolingian invention. In earlier instances the secondary apse housed important burials, whereas now it was endowed with an altar and worked in essence as a counterchoir, polarizing the church and encouraging entrance from the long sides.

There is one further difference between St. Peter's and the abbey church at Fulda. The Roman prototype has two parallel nave walls that stand on files of columns. The spacing of these columns bears no modular relationship to the length or width of the church. The design of St. Peter's might have begun, as our drawing shows, with a basic equilateral square whose diagonal was used to determine the length of the longitudinal body of the church (nave and aisles). (Fig. 12.15) The diagonal of the rectangle so formed in turn determined the total length, including the transept. Since the diagonal of a square is in no integer relationship to the sides, dimensions like the width of aisles in relation to the nave, or the positioning

Fig. 12.12 Lorsch (Germany), Carolingian monastery, gatehouse, ca. 800.

conception of the Carolingian basilical complex as an analogue of the Holy Sepulchre in Jerusalem, where the basilica proper would correspond to the aisled church of the Anastasis, the atrium to the court of Calvary, and the westwork to the rotunda over Christ's tomb. The altar in this antechurch, then, celebrated the resurrection of Christ. The tower heights were dedicated to the archangels, guardians of the heavenly Jerusalem. This emphasis on the triumphant in the liturgy would gradually give way to the contemplation of the agonies of the Passion, and by the eleventh century the westwork, reduced to a twin-towered facade, would become obsessively engrossed in its decorative programs detailing the apocalyptic tortures and the rewards of the Second Coming.

Architecturally, the westwork balanced the lateral mass of the transept at the east end, its verticality counterweighed by the tower over the crossing. When the west prospect of the church chose instead to echo the sanctuary apse, the western apse was justified by the fact that the great basilicas of Rome faced east, a peculiarity resulting from a preference of Constantine to whom most owed their start. But in these Roman basilicas there was only one apse, that in the west. In the abbey church of Fulda which purported to copy St. Peter's, there were two at opposite ends of the nave. But the "double-ender" was not a

Fig. 12.13 Lorsch monastery, gatehouse; upper hall.

Fig. 12.14 Corvey (Germany), Benedictine abbey, church of St. Vitus; westwork, 873–85.

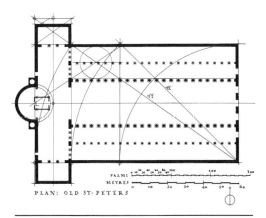

Fig. 12.15 Rome (Italy), Old St. Peter's ca. 320–30; ground plan, with construction diagram superimposed.

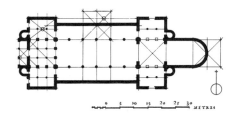

Fig. 12.16 St.-Riquier (Centula, France), abbey church, 790–99; ground plan, with square grid superimposed.

Fig. 12.17 St.-Riquier, abbey, founded in the seventh century, rebuilt by Angilbert, a trusted companion of Charlemagne, in 790–99; as represented in a print of 1612.

of the columns, can have no modular or arithmetical rationality.

The modular basis of Carolingian architecture, apparent in the Aachen palace, introduced into Western church design what Walter Horn has called "square schematism," a principle according to which the constituent parts of the church are calculated as multiples of a standard spatial unit, usually that of the crossing square. At Fulda, for example, the nave consists of three such units; the transept also has three, with two half-squares at the ends. The fully developed system entails three characteristics. First, the nave and transept are given the same width so that they are locked into each other and produce the standard square. (Fig. 12.16) Second, a fixed relationship exists between the width and length of the component spaces of the church—that is, the bays. Third, the placement of the columns or piers that hold up the nave walls is brought into rhythmical alignment with the modular squares instead of being a random file, as is the case in St. Peter's.

This rigorous compositional scheme may be linked to the groin-vaulted bay system in buildings of late antiquity, like the frigidarium of the baths of Caracalla or the ba-

silica of Maxentius in Rome. But it is also very likely that we have here a "Germanic" contribution, one whose source is the wood vernacular of northern cultures, and more precisely the aisled and bay-divided long house in which the concept of modular framing is logical to the timber construction. (Figs. 11.10, 12.4)

Monasteries
The true range of Carolingian architecture comes through in what we know of their monasteries. Again, we have no fully preserved specimen, but documentary information is also absent. The abbey of Centula, the present-day St.-Riquier in northern France not far from Amiens, had an original population of 300 monks, 100 novices, and many serfs and servants. (Fig. 12.17) It

was attached to a small town of 7,000, and together they formed a sort of holy city. Charles' son-in-law, the great writer Angilbert, was the abbot and also mayor of the town, which was regularly planned, with the knights, merchants, and craftsmen living in separate neighborhoods and owing the abbey services in kind. Seven hamlets in the vicinity played a religious part similar to the seven pilgrimage stations of Rome, and processions of monks and laypeople wended their way from one to the other on holy days.

The abbey was dedicated to the Trinity, and the entire layout was given the form of a giant triangle to underline this affiliation. Three churches at the points were joined by walls and porticoes and around the space so enclosed stood subsidiary monastic structures. Services were continuous, each monk being required to say mass daily. In the main church dedicated to the Savior,

Fig 12.18 An ideal Carolingian monastery, as represented in the plan of St. Gall, ca. 820; reconstruction model. The towered church stands out on the left.

three choirs—in the apse, the westwork, and the center of the nave—sang alternating chants day and night. Every detail of the inmate's life was regulated, both by the Rule of St. Benedict and supplementary instructions issued by the court.

The monastery was perhaps the central political institution of Charles' empire. It discharged defensive and economic responsibilities, played host to the visiting court, and served as a school and center of research. The architectural accommodation of this complex program became a principal concern of the court. As state foundations, the monasteries were grandly designed and endowed with land and serfs.

A document of singular interest on this subject has survived to our day and is now preserved in the chapter library of St. Gall in Switzerland. It is the plan of an ideal monastery prepared in court for the guidance of abbots during synods held at Aachen in 816–17. On the basis of this plan the complex has been reconstructed with some degree of accuracy. (Fig. 12.18) The design conforms to a module of 40 feet (or about 12 meters) that is subdivided into 16 units of 2.5 feet, a unit derived through the simple process of continuous halving. It may not be at all fortuitous that the number 40 is rich in biblical associations (particularly those meaningful to a monkish audience)

having to do with periods of expectation and penitence: the forty days of the flood, the forty years the Hebrews wandered in the desert, the forty-day vigil of Moses on Mount Sinai, and so on.

The church, the only stone structure on the site, should by now be familiar—double-apsed and turreted, with vaults at either end and a timber roof for the middle section, the pavement area of nave and aisles cut up by parapet screens into a series of compartments, each furnished with an altar. (Fig. 12.19) An accompanying inscription on this document reduces the length of the church from the 300 feet (91 meters) indicated by the scale of the draw-

Fig. 12.19 An ideal Carolingian monastery church, as represented in the plan of St. Gall; conjectural reconstruction of interior, looking east.

ing to 200 (61 meters). The matter of size had become a bone of contention for the brothers, who were compelled to devote much of their time, and a major portion of the conventual resources, to construction. We know that in 812 the monks of Fulda rebelled against their abbot Ratger, who had designed the new church for the abbey to match the size and shape of St. Peter's, and petitioned the emperor to stop or reduce "these oversized and superfluous buildings." The petition was denied, but under Charles' son Louis the abbot was relieved, and his successor Eigil was admonished by the emperor "to reduce the monastery's building program to normal proportions." The amended plan of St. Gall reflects this conservative trend.

On other disputed issues, the liberal element seems to have emerged victorious in the court synods. The plan allows for a detached abbot's residence, a set of baths, and an outer school to serve the community at large—all matters that met with increasing opposition from influential bishops, abbots, and other policymakers. Beyond the issue of permissible comfort, the overriding concern was the degree to which a monastery was obliged to recognize the outside world. The size of the churches could be explained in part by the fact that they often doubled as parish and pilgrimage churches. To keep the paths of transient worshippers apart from the claustral routine of resident monks was a prime objective of the plan, as was the separation of

the brothers from their serfs and servants who worked in the fields and at other menial jobs without being bound by monkish vows.

And so we find the animal pens, barns, workers' lodgings, and other ancillary functions along the southern edge of the complex. To the north were guest facilities, the abbot's house, and the outer school. All these guest and service buildings used a rectangular unit with a fireplace in the middle and a corresponding lantern or louver in the pitched roof—that is, a variant of the traditional Germanic timber house. The eastern wing held the novitiate, who were assigned their own little church and cloister. This mininucleus was flanked by the infirmary and the cemetery.

The monks reserved for themselves the core of the plan, strictly isolated from these peripheral activities. The dominant elements here, and the principal theaters of their existence, were the church and the cloister on its south side. This arcaded four-square courtyard with cross-paths and a central fountain (the descendant, in form at least, of the Classical peristyle) was exactly 100 square feet (over 9 square meters). It was enclosed on three sides by two-storey buildings: the dormitory, with provisions for 77 beds, situated above a heated day room, the refectory above the wardrobe, and a cellar for the kegs of beer, the bacon, and other "necessities."

The only entrance into this inner *claustrum* was through a small room at the northwest corner, the monks' parlor called the *mandatum*, where the feet of those who were to enter would be washed. Here the brothers passed their days undisturbed, in strict accordance with the Rule of St. Benedict which they read aloud daily, gathered for the purpose in the arm of the cloister adjacent to the church. Here they prayed, attended communal services seven times daily, but, as important, tried to abide by St. Benedict's description of the monkish life, the "Instrument of Good Works":

To watch over the actions of one's life every hour of the day.—To know for certain that God sees one everywhere.— . . . To guard one's lips against uttering evil or wicked words.—Not to be fond of much talking . . . or laughter.—To love chastity.— . . . To show no arrogant spirit.—To reverence the old.—To love the young.

Around this quiet nexus of contemplative piety, at the edges of the monastery and beyond, life surged on all sides. The land was tilled and harvested, the animals fed, children went to school, high dignitaries from the court visited and were entertained by the abbot, and pilgrims found their way from great distances to revere the relics of the church and the sanctity of dead brothers. Further out, cities traded and bickered, the peasantry toiled for its masters and the masters for their overlords, the emperor moved about with his retinue from one royal residence to another, the magnates of the realm—counts, abbots, bishops—attended solemn courts in May and again sometime in the autumn, and the *vassi dominici,* vassals of the royal demesne, administered the provinces with arbitrary wisdom. And beyond the realm, in territories where imperial control wavered, hostile peoples seized advantages, raiding the coast and countryside without fear of a navy or a standing army—neither of which, they knew, existed.

Fig. 12.20 Trelleborg (Denmark), Viking camp, ninth century; reconstruction model.

The Empire of Muhammed

The biggest threat to Carolingian peace lay in the volatile north. Two new branches of migratory peoples, the Vikings and Magyars, attacked at an interval of half a century, and their sustained invasions thereafter unhinged European stability causing depopulation, agricultural decline, and loss of wealth. Already in the 830s, parties of Vikings had begun to winter in the lands they raided and soon they set out systematically to gain control of the urban centers. Cologne, London, York, Bordeaux, and Rouen succumbed by 888. The Magyar invasions from the East, which started about then, might have been stemmed within a reasonable time had Byzantium not been opposed to the missionary activities of the Carolingian church, whose success would have enhanced the Latin West. As it was, the attacks did not abate until the beginning of the eleventh century; by then the Magyars, converted at last, had settled in

Hungary as an established state under King Stephen.

We know little about the environmental order of these peoples but, in the case of the Vikings at least, it was by no means negligible. Their long lithe ships that lashed against the shores of France and England and probed the major rivers and their tributaries were admirably functional. Their camps showed thoughtful planning. The one at Trelleborg in Denmark, on a peninsula at the confluence of streams, consists of two compounds: an outer fortress with a semicircular wall protected fourteen houses whose axes radiated from the center of the wall and an inner fortress with sixteen houses which was arranged in four squares of four houses each. (Fig. 12.20) The streets were paved in wood, and the houses looked like Viking ships. Each could hold 75 men, the total garrison being about 2,300.

Burial grounds by the sea were included in the outer fortress. In general, chieftains were given ship burials, or else they were buried in megalithic analogues of ships, like the still affecting group burial site in Käseberga on the Swedish shore.

The Muslim adversary was more predictable. Leaving aside the regular piratical expeditions and some late gains like Sicily, the empire fashioned by the conquests of the first Islamic century held steady. Charles' campaigns against the splinter kingdom of Umayyad Spain were a failure, and he was soon exchanging embassies with Harun-al-Rashid, the ruling Abbasid caliph of this far-flung nation of Muhammed whose capital was then the newly built city of Baghdad.

Baghdad was a brilliant milieu, on a par with Aachen and the imperial splendor of Constantinople. Inspired by Parthian-Sassanian example, the city was laid out as a perfect circle described by a moat and a double set of mud-brick walls. (Fig. 12.21) The center was devoted to the palace, the great mosque, and the offices of the seven government departments. At the periphery a residential belt was girdled by two encircling streets and was radially subdivided.

The four cardinal rays had gates surmounted by golden domes and named after the main cities and provinces they faced—Kufa, Basra, Khorasan, and Damascus. The population was chosen to represent the major ethnic, tribal, and economic groups of the empire. This was the navel of the

Muslim universe, and in its center sat the caliph in state, under the Green Dome; at its summit stood the statue of a horseman whose lance, so it was believed, always pointed in the direction of the enemies of Islam.

The Place of Architecture
Baghdad, in continuous use since its founding in 762, has swallowed its early past, but Samarra, a temporary capital about 100 kilometers north, also on the Tigris, has been thoroughly excavated. Its palaces expose the tremendous elaboration of courtly life since the early, simple days of the Muslim empire. Friday mosques in Kairawan, Tunisia and Córdoba, Spain attest to the high level of power and sophistication that architecture had gained in the century or so that corresponded to the Carolingian episode and also demonstrate how profoundly different was the Muslim's view of community devotion from that of his Christian contemporaries in Europe and Byzantium.

The land where Islam was born, the Hejaz or middle portion of Arabia, had no monumental buildings. The southern part of the peninsula, Yemen, was early imbued with Hellenism which reached it by way of the caravan trade. We have evidence of temples, palaces, and a conventional tall tower-house. Even so, nothing in the desert homeland could have quite prepared the conquering Muslims for the architectural spectacle of the old Greco-Roman cities or the Sassanian court. And yet within three or four generations, a distinctive Muslim architecture began to materialize that borrowed native forms and talent, and applied

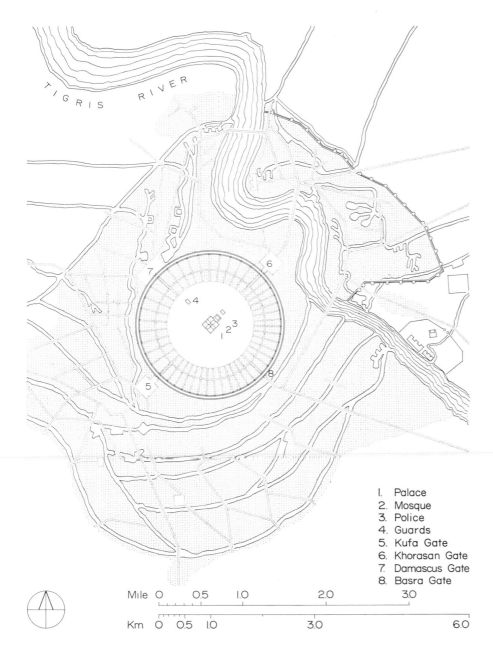

1. Palace
2. Mosque
3. Police
4. Guards
5. Kufa Gate
6. Khorasan Gate
7. Damascus Gate
8. Basra Gate

Mile 0   0.5   1.0   2.0   3.0

Km 0   0.5   1.0   3.0   6.0

Fig. 12.21 Baghdad (Iraq), founded by the caliph al-Mansur in 762–67; plan. The city was located on a site along the Tigris where it comes closest to its twin river, the Euphrates, to the west; a network of canals forms the means of transportation between them. The city broke through its original circular form within a generation and spread out along these canals.

them to its own specific programs, its own way of life.

The training ground was in the adaptation of non-Muslim buildings and in the direct imitation of significant monuments in the conquered lands. The colonnaded avenue of the Classical cities, its bays gradually walled in, was transformed into the characteristic linear markets or bazaars, called *suqs* in Arabic. (Fig. 12.22) The rectangular shell of a pagan temple precinct with corner towers governed the shape of the great mosque of Damascus, capital of the Umayyads, the first ruling dynasty of Islam. The authority of this premier sanctuary in turn imposed its recycled outline on many succeeding examples of the building type. The very first monument of the new faith, the Dome of the Rock in Jerusalem, was a patently competitive enterprise. (Fig. 12.23) It rose on the grounds of the Jewish temple, over the rock of Mount Moriah that had been variously identified in the past as the place of Adam's creation and death, and of Isaac's sacrifice. In substance, the building was a close copy of the rotunda of the Holy Sepulchre. (Fig. 11.23)

The motivation for these decorative religious settings, in the face of Muhammed's known disapproval of costly architecture, is spelled out in a later source by the tenth-century geographer Muqaddasi.

[The caliph] al-Walid beheld Syria to be a country that had long been occupied by the Christians, and he noted there the beautiful churches still belonging to them, so enchantingly fair, and so renowned for their splendor. . . . And in like manner . . . Abd-al-Malik, seeing the greatness of the martyrium [of the Holy Sepulchre] and its magnificence, was moved lest it should dazzle the minds of the Muslims and hence erected above the rock the dome which is now seen there.

Along with the need for impressive buildings, Islam saw from the start the importance of the city. Despite the attractions of nomadic simplicity and mobility ("God made for you of the skins of cattle houses," the Prophet said, "that ye may find them light on the day ye move your quarters and the day when ye abide"), Islam accepted cities as the only ambience in which a full, truly Muslim life could be lived. From the first *amsar*, or garrison towns, to the very end of the Middle Ages, the building

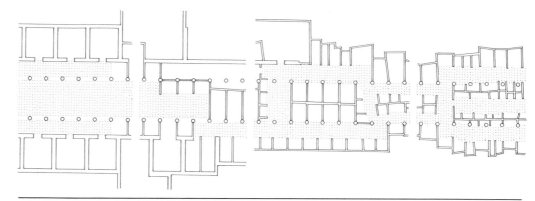

Fig. 12.22a A colonnaded avenue of Classical antiquity (extreme left), like the one seen below, transformed in stages into a medieval linear bazaar; diagrammatic progression from left to right.

Fig.12.22b Timgad (Thamugadi, Algeria), main east-west avenue leading to the Arch of Trajan in the background, second century A.D. (See also Fig. 10.6.)

of cities was deemed a princely act, and many old subject cities carried on under a tolerant regime that countenanced religious and ethnic diversity.

And yet there were no chartered cities in the Muslim empire with independent municipal institutions. The system made few distinctions beyond the individual and the total community (umma). The notables—that is, the learned religious and the merchant class—associated their interests with the city that supplied them with mosques and schools, and offered the possibility of secure commerce. And these benefits issued from the ruler. It was his power that guaranteed safe agriculture in the country to feed the city, as well as safe trade routes to make it prosper.

The Palace
The surviving Umayyad palaces at the edge of the Transjordanian desert were in their time centers of large agricultural estates, in addition to affording a more congenial meeting place than Damascus for the caliphs and the great tribal chieftains with their huge retinues who represented the real strength of early Islam. (Fig. 12.24) The fortified aspect of the palaces was more symbolic than functional. It aped the look of Roman and Byzantine forts (Diocletian's palace at Split is an example we are familiar with) as an expression of power.

The rectangular enclosures contained two storeys of rooms around a central court, an enduring scheme in the Middle East. (Fig. 12.25) The throne room, sometimes situated over the only entrance gate, is recognizable by its formality; the small mosque, which served the extended community as well as the court, is recognizable by the mihrab, a small niche indicating the direction of Mecca. The living quarters were simple, multipurpose spaces, since social mores did not call for special bedrooms or dining rooms. Kitchens are absent; food was prepared outside and brought in, in the manner of present-day bedouins. Also outside the main palace lay the guest houses, a wild game preserve, and baths.

The idea for the baths came from the Roman world. The Muslims kept the entire system except for the tepidarium, which was eliminated. As in Rome, the program went beyond bathing. In the cities, baths had an important social function. They were settings of fellowship and of formal occasions like weddings or circumcision parties. In Umayyad palaces a state room is part of the bathing complex, and in contemporary sources we hear of audiences and poetry readings. Mural paintings show dancers, musicians, athletes, and personifications of the arts. The mixing of ceremonial state functions with physical pleasure will remain characteristic of the Muslim palace. It continued an ancient Near Eastern tradition of transforming pastime and pleasure into formal activities that reflected the greatness of the prince.

The Abbasid palaces of Samarra about one hundred years later are incomparably more involved. The caliph's residence, Jausaq-al-Kharqani, takes up an area of 173 hectares (432 acres) on a cliff overlooking the Tigris Valley. (Fig. 12.26) The rich alluvial land between cliff and river was arrayed with flower gardens and orchards. The grounds included, at the extreme north, barracks with their own small mosques and fortified enclosures for the treasury and the arsenal. Between these and the main complex was a Classical amphitheater. To the south, a mazelike building was probably identified with the harem, the seclusion of women having been introduced into Muslim culture by the Abbasid dynasty.

A single colossal axis ran through the palace proper, from the only public entrance on the river side to the polo grounds at the back. The entrance gate, a great triple-arched facade open to iwans in the Persian manner, was gained by means of a wide stair that led up from an ornamental lake. A gate ceremony inspired by the Roman *adventus*, or Imperial welcoming at city gates, had been inaugurated by the Abbasids and was maintained and embellished in subsequent centuries. The palace gate came to demarcate the point of contact between the people and their ruler, a place where petitions might be presented, justice administered, and admittance to higher authority sought. Names of later palaces like the Ottoman Topkapī or the Ali Qapu of Safavid Isfahan were variations of what the West called the "Sublime Porte."

Beyond the gate, past a succession of five transverse halls in which the public was presumably allowed to circulate, one reached a square court with a fountain. To the north of it were the caliph's apartments; to the south, the restricted access to the harem. An oblong court of honor then led to the cruciform throne room, a domed central unit from which four, T-shaped, aisled basilicas emanated. Further out, beyond a gigantic portico called the "Assembly Hall," the Great Esplanade followed, an open space measuring roughly 350 by 200 meters (1,150 by 656 feet) crossed by canals and a bridge. At its east end was a rock-cut pavilion for hot weather, surrounded by stables and the grandstands from which the caliph and his entourage could watch the horse parades.

The Mosque
By the ninth century the palace had detached itself from the Friday mosque, as the rituals of majesty progressively distanced the ruler from the ruled. In the early decades of Islam the administrative and residential headquarters of governors or the caliph himself stood adjacent to the mosque with direct access from one to the other. The mosque was in fact more than the religious center of the community. It took the place of the Roman forum-basilica core. Prayers inside were led by the ruler or his official representative, and the sermon that followed, the *kutba*, was not a homily tied to Islamic liturgy but a political speech that ended invariably with a show of allegiance by the community.

Unlike the palace, a building type for which a long Mediterranean tradition existed, the mosque perforce was without precedent. The Muslim was enjoined to pray five times a day—this was one of the five tenets of Islam—along with reciting and believing in the *shahada* ("There is but one God and Muhammed is his prophet"), fasting in the month of Ramadan, the ninth month of the lunar year, almsgiving, and the pilgrimage to Mecca. These daily prayers, a fixed number of bows accompanied by a litany, could be performed anywhere, provided that they were preceded by ritual ablution and directed toward Mecca. But when possible, and always for the Friday noon prayer, Muslims prayed as a com-

Fig. 12.23 Jerusalem (Israel), seen from the west. The Temple Mound occupies the foreground: at the extreme left, the mosque of al-Aqsa, built in 705, rebuilt ca. 780 and again in the eleventh century; at the extreme right, the Dome of the Rock (Kubbat-as-Sakhra), ca. 685-90.

Fig. 12.24 Qasr Kharaneh (Jordan), Umayyad palace, ca. 710.

Fig. 12.25 Khirbat-al-Mafjar (Jordan), Umayyad palace, ca. 739–44; ground plan and site plan.

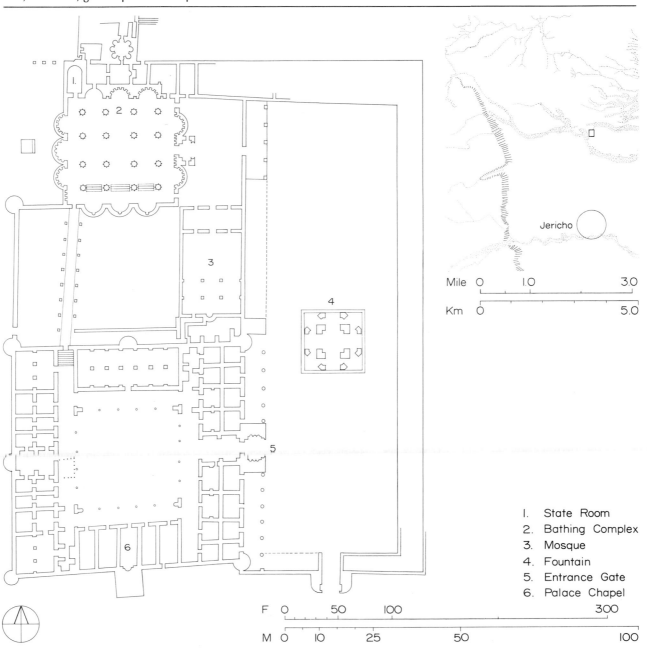

Jericho

Mile	O	1.O	3.O

| Km | O | | 5.O |

1. State Room
2. Bathing Complex
3. Mosque
4. Fountain
5. Entrance Gate
6. Palace Chapel

F	O	50	100		300

| M | O | 10 | 25 | 50 | 100 |

munity under the leadership of an *imam* who stood in front of the lines of worshippers and set the pace for the prostrations.

In contrast to Christian liturgy, Muslim services had no dramatic elaboration whatever. The faith was based on a strict monotheism that excluded a cult of relics or saintly hierarchies. It was free, at least initially, of metaphysical arguments like those regarding the Trinity, the two natures of Christ, or holy images—arguments that precipitated bitter divisions in the Christian world. No priestly oligarchy intervened between the believer and the deity.

Consequently, the mosque had no need of the complicated architectural setting required of the Byzantine Eucharist or Western Mass; no need, that is, of apses and transepts, crypts, westworks, or the symbolic accommodation of heaven. The program was simple: a large space laterally arranged for rows of believers, with an orientation toward Mecca and a fountain for the mandatory ablutions. In theory, then, any architecture could serve as long as these requirements were fulfilled. The first mosque was the Prophet's house in Medina, and it is not difficult to see why for a few decades thereafter large extant buildings of all kinds in the conquered lands were requisitioned as mosques.

The invention of a new building type, and the architectural expression it entailed, came about in areas—the new frontier towns, for example—where there was no extant environment to adapt, or in those cases where the size of the congregation, or the pride of the new religion in subject cities, could not be satisfied with the use of a prior structure. This first generation of mosques embraced two separate categories of form determinants. They sought to monumentalize the simple requirements of the program; and in doing so, they absorbed visual impressions (and sometimes architectural parts) from older buildings of other cultures. Thus the memory of apses, rows of columns, domes, and the like, would be present in the mosque without their precise functional or symbolic meaning. No attempt was made to duplicate either the Kaaba in Mecca or the Dome of the Rock, both occasional buildings of special circumstance.

Fig. 12.26 Samarra (Iraq), the Abbasid palace called Jausaq-al-Kharqani or Bayt-al-Khalifa, ca. 836–37; reconstruction model.

The Great Mosque of Kairawan represents the new building type at its best. Its foundation goes back to 669, but it reached its present shape in the ninth century through several rebuildings. An enclosure wall of tremendous power inscribes an oblong that is divided into two unequal parts. (Fig. 12.27) The eastern part is the congregational space; the western, a marble-paved court lined with arcaded porticoes. The flat roofs over these and the prayer hall are immediately recognizable because of three features—a staged minaret on the western side of the court, from which the call to prayer was intoned, and two domes at the ends of the central one of seventeen aisles that divide the space of the prayer hall. The aisles are defined by arcades on rows of reused Classical columns. These run perpendicular to the end wall, but stop one bay short of reaching it. Here they encounter a transverse corridor running the entire width of the hall. It forms a T-shape with the central aisle, which incidentally is wider than the rest and raised above them by a clerestory.

Fig. 12.27 Kairawan (Tunisia), the Great Mosque, founded in the seventh century, built in its present form in ca. 820-36; aerial view.

The bay at the juncture of the two arms of the T is accorded special treatment. The recess of the mihrab niche is sheathed with marble screens and is framed on the outside by beautiful luster tiles. (Fig. 12.28) To its right stands the wood-carved minbar alternately built of floral and geometric panels. The dome that marks the bay is made up of concave segments, divided by 24 projecting ribs, and sits on an elaborately embroidered drum.

This is the only ornament of the interior. Nowhere else on the walls, or the numerous whitewashed arcades that rise gently and hypnotically from their ancient columns, is any decorative indulgence tolerated. The floor is covered with mats and somehow domesticated. Here the faithful stood, row on row like the columns, equal in their relationship to God as His creatures, ready to perform the set motions and recite the formulas as an expression of their obedience and devotion.

And this ritual of gesture and word was not to be taken lightly. Mecca was before you. The angel of death hovered behind you. On your left side was Hell, vividly individuated in the Koran. One false step and you would be "caught by your sinful lying forelock" and cast into the fire to stay therein forever. You would be fed boiling water and the fruit of the *zakkum,* which resembles the head of the devil and is like molten brass in the belly. And there will be many who will go there. God promises to fill Hell with sinners, but Hell is limitless. "On the last day when we shall say to Hell 'Art thou filled?' . . . Hell shall answer 'Are there yet more?'" But to your right is Paradise, the great alternative. It is the place of flowing rivers, silken couches, heavenly food and drink, dark-eyed virgins, and wives of perfect purity.

So the Muslim stood among the columns, poised on a little spot of earth, caught between eternal damnation and eternal bliss, both within his reach, and the choice left to no agency but his own conscience. (page 268) This is the essence of Muslim prayer: the recurrent display of discipline and unquestioning obedience each day of one's life, and the dream of the sweet reward that may come to be.

Fig. 12.28 Kairawan, Great Mosque; *mihrab* niche and wooden pulpit *(minbar),* ca. 860.

Further Reading

G. Barraclough, *The Crucible of Europe, the Ninth and Tenth Centuries in European History* (Berkeley: University of California Press, 1976).

W. Braunfels, *Monasteries of Western Europe,* trans. A. Laing (Princeton: Princeton University Press, 1973).

K. J. Conant, *Carolingian and Romanesque Architecture: 800–1200,* 2nd ed. (Harmondsworth and Baltimore: Penguin, 1966).

O. Grabar, *The Formation of Islamic Art* (New Haven: Yale University Press, 1972).

J. D. Hoag, *Islamic Architecture* (New York: Abrams, 1977).

W. Horn and E. Born, *The Plan of St. Gall* (Berkeley: University of California Press, 1979).

J. Hubert et al., *The Carolingian Renaissance* (New York: Braziller, 1970).

L. Price, *The Plan of St. Gall: In Brief* (Berkeley: University of California Press, 1982).

P. Sebag, *The Great Mosque of Kairouan,* trans. R. Howard (New York: Macmillan, 1965).

Krak des Chevaliers (Qalaat el Hosn, Syria), 1100–1200.

13

THE BIRTH OF NATIONS: EUROPE AFTER CHARLES

Three separate spheres of political power and cultural outlook ringed the Mediterranean basin in the ninth century.

The Abbasid caliphate centered in Baghdad controlled, at least nominally, the entire Muslim empire except Spain. Here a rival caliph, the descendant of the Umayyads, presided over a florid, cosmopolitan civilization. Its capital Córdoba, once the Roman provincial capital, straddled the Guadalquivir in the vast fertile plain of Andalusia on the ancient route that crossed the peninsula from Cádiz to Narbonne. The Great Mosque, several times enlarged in the course of the ninth-tenth century, survives there still. It differs from its contemporary in Kairawan in its polychromy and decorative brilliance, as seen in the gate panels inserted in the otherwise plain periphery wall, the striped pattern of voussoirs in the two-storey arcades of the prayer hall, and, most flamboyant of all, the mihrab bays elegantly linked by interlaced, scalloped arches that are resolved three-dimensionally in the splendid burst of the domes and their lanterns. (Fig. 13.1)

The mosaicists who contributed to this effulgence came from Constantinople. After the Iconoclastic Controversy, the Byzantine Empire had settled down to a period of renewed strength under the Macedonian dynasty (867–1057). Building resumed. The arts, under tight supervision, returned to selected religious themes. Rendered in fresco or gold-backed mosaic, the subjects were now displayed in the interiors of the new, cross-in-square churches according to a rigid scheme that was intended to correspond to the heavenly hierarchy and the liturgical calendar of the principal feasts. (Fig. 1.9) Christ Pantokrator (the "All-Ruler") figured in the central dome attended by the apostles; scenes of His childhood were arranged in the four pendentives; the miracles and Passion in the upper range of the walls; saints and fathers of the Church below, at eye level; the enthroned Virgin holding the Child and flanked by archangels, in the apse vault. Luxury objects busily manufactured in the palace workshops—enamel plaques and ivory carvings, reliquaries, illuminated manuscripts, and textiles—helped to spread this newfangled imagery.

The Byzantine manner reached the West through such portable treasures, through sketchbooks, and also directly through traveling craftsmen. Byzantine masters were working and training local talent in Córdoba in the tenth century, at the Benedictine abbey of Monte Cassino, Italy, in the eleventh century, and in Norman Sicily throughout the twelfth century. When Venice, the merchant republic with close diplomatic and commerical ties to Byzantium, started to build the cathedral of St. Mark's to hold the relics of the Evangelist brought over from Alexandria in 828, she took for its model the church of the Holy Apostles in Constantinople. And the cross-in-square church passed, along with Eastern Orthodoxy, to the newborn nations of Bulgaria, Serbia, and Russia.

Europe from Charles to Otto

Carolingian Europe was the third sphere. Under Charles an area the size of modern France, Germany, and Italy was united through one ruling class with a similar attitude toward organized life and a strong commitment to an aristocratic, court-sponsored architecture and its supportive arts. This ambitious environment represented a return to the monumentality of ancient Rome, to a large vision that bespoke confidence in the established order and the determination to project stability and permanence. The architectural product, so we tried to suggest in the last chapter, was a temperate amalgam of originality and tradition, of invention and continuity. The art of illustrated manuscripts, and the great painting cycles of church and palace, aspired to a new corporeality that kept the humanist ideal of Classical art alive. And this at a time when Islam insisted on nonfigurative abstraction, and post-Iconoclastic Byzantium continued early Christian predilections for the immaterial in the ascetic, flattened images of its religious iconography and their ethereal, impenetrable gold background.

Fig. 13.1 Córdoba (Spain), the Great Mosque, eighth-tenth centuries; the *mihrab* bay, 962–66.

The Problem of the Western Church

Carolingian society was Church-ridden, clerical. Its constructive cleverness showed best in religious architecture. The new church form, mobilized by Frankish patrons and architects, was to preempt the built environment of the later Middle Ages in the West and, of course, coincidentally, stand for the chief rallying point of the social life in Europe. The Carolingian basilica—St.-Riquier, Fulda, St. Gall—constitutes the first episode in this pervasive architectural story. (Fig. 12.19) Eleventh-century pilgrimage churches, those magnificient anchors of a Europe revivified under the great monastic orders, the Cistercians and the Cluniacs, are the second, the so-called Romanesque, episode; and the filigreed cages of Gothic cathedrals in the hearts of the blossoming cities in the twelfth and thirteenth centuries, the third episode. (Figs. 13.13, 14.15)

There is a kind of logic to the way the Christian church evolved in the West from the late eighth century to the fourteenth, and it is not difficult to see in every stage of this evolution the seedbed of the succeeding stage. But this is only because the story was closed long ago, and looking back on it, we tend to read it in terms of a progression. In truth, despite anticipations and cross-overs, the Romanesque church is very different in form, feeling, and ethos from the Carolingian, and the Gothic from the Romanesque. One might make a case, for example, that in visual terms Gothic cathedrals relate less to their Romanesque forebears than they do to the insubstantial lightness of Early Christian basilicas. (Figs. 11.20, 14.15) And of course it might have come about quite another way, and if it had, we would devise an equally plausible argument to account for it. It is the nature of historical events to happen as they will, and the temptation of historians to explain them as if they could not have happened otherwise.

In reality, the passage from Carolingian to Romanesque was neither smooth nor uninterrupted. The last major undertaking of Carolingian architecture, properly so-called, was St. Vitus at Corvey. We looked at its westwork, built in the 870s, in the last chapter. Even before then, the building fury that had swept the realm with Charles' accession had been spent. The first significant structures to go up thereafter any-where within the empire do not antedate the end of the tenth century, so that when Romanesque churches burgeoned abundantly about the year 1000 they had to pick up an interrupted argument and relearn to some extent the structural and aesthetic lessons of Charles' era.

The Architecture of Anarchy

The hiatus was occasioned by two related conditions. With the death of Charles, the empire was contested among his sons and fell apart. Taking advantage of this political disintegration, Muslim coastal raids and the invasions of Norsemen and Magyars devastated both land and cities. Each segment of Charles' dismembered empire responded in its own way to the unsettling forces of these decades. The nations that emerged in time out of the chaos were correspondingly unique. And beyond their pale, the reorganization of Carolingian lands and the impulse of invasion spurred the cohering of new national entities.

In what is now France, the contest between legitimate Carolingians and the counts of Paris led by 1000 to the establishment of a native royal house, the Capetians. But only with the accession of Louis VI in 1100 did the monarchy really begin to matter. The prime force in post-Carolingian France was feudalism. Long in effect in the countryside as an economic system, feudalism now surfaced as a political device based on protection. The monarchy, unable to defend its territory against the Vikings, was overshadowed by a pattern of local allegiances. The small free peasant class disappeared altogether. There were now only noblemen (distinguished not by birth but the ability to bear arms) and servile dependents. The Church was also forced to become feudal and, in the process, relaxed that direct support of the monarchy that it had extended to the Frankish kings.

England had never been part of the Carolingian Empire. The island suffered more severely from Viking raids than any European territory. In time it was the West Saxon kings, their power resting largely on conquest, who brought forth a remarkable administrative apparatus to withstand the onslaught. A network of hundreds and shires divided the land into manageable units. A

fleet organized by Alfred the Great (871–99), and a string of fortified strongholds called *burhs*, made up the backbone of the anti-Viking defense. By the end of Edward's reign (899–924), the system of fortresses stretched through Wessex and Mercia, and in the mid-tenth century a number of them were already on their way to becoming boroughs in the modern sense—that is, urban settlements and centers of local trade. In England, then, it was the Anglo-Saxon kings who took the initiative in organizing local government instead of leaving it, as in France, to feudal princes.

Germany was the only European state where the legitimacy of Carolingian rule went unchallenged. Feudalism was not an overpowering reality here. Divided into five great duchies, the land was mostly one of peasants. It was also politically strong enough to establish by the later tenth century, under the Ottonian dynasty of the house of Saxony, a new empire that would extend its hegemony to Italy and bolster the

Fig. 13.2 Essex (England), Castle Hedingham; Norman keep, ca. 1140.

Fig. 13.3 Ávila (Spain); city walls, begun 1090.

faltering institution of the papacy. It is, in fact, in Germany and Italy that the first notable post-Carolingian experiments in church architecture—St. Michael's at Hildesheim, the cathedral of Speyer, S. Maria Maggiore at Lomello—are to be seen, while England was busy building a nation and France was submerged in feudal confusion.

In England and France we should be talking about military architecture in this turbulent period of transition, roughly 850–980. In France each county, each valley, was thrown back on self-defense; hundreds of earthworks and forts were built everywhere. Towns repaired their walls as best they could, and in rare cases even incurred the great expense of building new ones. Cathedrals and monasteries raised their own rings of defense, lending substance to the image of the medieval church as the fortified city of God. Western Europe, in short, had armed its peaks and shores, turned over the earth for a cumulative length of hundreds of miles, spiked the countryside with keeps and baronial towers, and grimly tore the skyline with crenellated battlements. It was a great architectural enterprise, but there is alas very little of it now to see.

Wood and earth were the basic materials of defense work in the period of invasions, and techniques included palisades, bastions, and moats, both dry and water-filled. Stone construction is on the whole a later, Romanesque practice. The great *donjons* of Loches and Beaugency, Norman keeps such as Castle Hedingham in Essex, are examples of this masonry defense. (Fig. 13.2) But their ancestor is the early medieval *motte*, a manmade mound surrounded by a bailey and an enclosure ditch, with a timber tower-building standing at the peak of the mound. The tower had a very basic organization: on the ground floor, a storeroom for provisions; then, a large room on the first floor where, to quote an eleventh-century source, "[the] powerful man . . . together with his household, lived, conversed, ate, slept." The cook-house stood a little distance away from the tower to minimize the risk of fire.

The Eleventh Century

By the end of the tenth century the worst was over. The invading heathens decided

Fig. 13.4 Pyrenees (Spain), the high road or *camino* along the pilgrimage route to Santiago de Compostela, eleventh century.

298

Fig. 13.5 Puente la Reina (Spain), bridge over the river Arga, attributed to Queen Urraca, daughter of Alfonso VI of Castile (1065–1109).

scene, emphasizes the religious aspect of this building boom.

Shortly after the year 1000 it came about that churches were rebuilt practically throughout the world, and mainly in Italy and Gaul; and although most of them were very suitable, scarcely needing any alteration, all Christian peoples were seized with a great desire to outdo one another in magnificence. It was as if the world shook and cast off its old age, everywhere investing itself with the white mantle of churches.

But there was much more to the story. Military construction was all-pervasive and it was growing more sophisticated. The once towerless curtains now recovered the cadenced look of the Aurelian walls of Rome and the legendary land walls of Constantinople. (Figs. 11.29a, 13.3) Literally thousands of castles sprang up everywhere, new or reaffirmations in stone of earlier forts. Techniques of siege warfare remained unchanged, and no new weapons would be introduced until a century or two later. Much of the exertion was obviously symbolic, a monumental celebration of power as the great churches now replaced adequate predecessors in a celebration of faith.

The improvement of old continental roads, with the opening up of new ones, presumes regional thinking. The raison d'être for this was pilgrimage traffic as well as trade—interlinked activities in all ages. Charity hospices, inns, and similar lodging facilities proliferated. In towns they tended to be placed outside the walls, so travelers could come and go after the gates were shut at night. Invariably the hospices had a chapel attached, and around them pilgrims' quarters grew up. The "Faubourg St.-Jacques" in many French towns today still retains the name of these quarters which refers to the most popular pilgrimage center of all, the shrine of St. James the Apostle in Castile known in Spanish as Santiago de Compostela.

A good deal of this activity was supervised by the monastic orders, especially the Cluniacs, who controlled the pilgrimages, and the Augustinian canons, and later the two military orders of the Hospitallers and Templars, who ran many of the hospices. They supplied the labor force for building, the materials, and some of the funding from their own considerable resources. But royalty and the landed noble families did their share too. Church building mattered polit-

or were made to settle, embracing Christianity and accepting the principle of nationhood. Magyars, decisively defeated by Otto I on the banks of the Lech in 955, came to rest in Hungary. Bohemia and Poland materialized as new nations, and Russia stirred beyond the steppes through the zeal of the Eastern Church and the prestige of the Emperor of Constantinople. Canute's empire spread across Scandinavia and parts of England. One branch of the restless Norsemen, the Normans, put down roots in northwest France, which was given to them as a fief by the French king. The menace of Islam, too, was receding. The caliphate of Baghdad was increasingly challenged by autonomous provincial governors, and the Umayyad state in Spain had slipped into an irreversible trend of fragmentation. In France the Capetian monarchy gained ground against the feudal nobility. The German empire of the Ottos secured central Europe.

The Building Boom

One outcome of this stability was the quickening of trade. A resuscitated Italy overseen by German imperial might opened up the Mediterranean and set the stage for the phenomenal rise of merchant republics like Pisa, Genoa, and of course Venice. Long-distance exchange with the Far East was re-established for the first time since antiquity, but now through the Baltic by means of the island of Gotland. Relative security and new wealth brought a brimming restorative confidence to the fabric of Europe, and an outpouring of building expressed it tangibly. The famous remark of the monk Raoul Glaber, a witness to the

Fig. 13.6 Autun (France), St.-Lazare, 1120–32; capital.

ically. "We believe," said Otto I (936–73), "that the protection of our empire is bound up with the rising fortunes of Christian worship." At his time Catholicism had not the unwavering loyalty of the common people. Pagan phantoms and odd heresies were abroad, and the heathen invaders had made matters worse. A strong Church was the prerequisite for a strong social order.

But rulers were expected to do more than that. Honorius of Regensburg enjoins them to "equip churches with books, vestments and ornaments, renew destroyed or abandoned churches," but also to "build bridges and streets and thus prepare your way to heaven." If improved communication favored the pilgrim and the merchant, it also tightened the king's grasp over the country. The road from Paris to Bordeaux was the start of the most important pilgrimage route to Santiago; not incidentally it was also indispensable to the Capetians for free passage between their two capitals, Paris and Orléans. The organization of the *camino*, the high road along the Pyrenees which drew together all tributaries of the pious journey on the last leg to the great shrine, was the work of kings Alfonso V (999–1027) and Alfonso VI (1065–1109) whose ambition it was to govern all the Spanish territory recovered from the Muslims. (Fig. 13.4) The project entailed the building of several bridges. (Fig. 13.5)

Bridges were sometimes undertaken by individual lords who were able to set the conditions for their use. In 1035 the Count of Blois and Tours began a 27-arch bridge over the Loire near Tours, "so as not to forfeit his heavenly reward through earthly greed," and he promised free passage to all, "be they foreign or native, pilgrim or tradesman, poor or rich, come they on foot or mount, with burden or without." More often their construction called for some sort of jurisdictional adjustment. In case of conflict higher authority was appealed to. A late example has the citizenry of Saumur address an appeal to the English King Henry II (1154–89), who as lord of Normandy was the ultimate arbiter of the region. At issue was a wooden bridge built by the people for their benefit. The abbot of St.-Florent claimed the right to collect bridge tolls. Henry's decree specified that merchants who used the bridge to transport their wares on beasts of burden be obliged to pay the abbot, but that the knights and burghers of Saumur be allowed to cross free of charge. Furthermore, the monks must pledge to replace the bridge gradually with one in stone, at the rate of one arch per year.

Church Fever

It is the political and economic recovery that should be stressed in discussing the spectacular bloom of religious architecture in the eleventh century—this, rather than the millenniarist relief that is alluded to in the remarks of Raoul Glaber.

It had indeed long been assumed that a thousand years after Christian grace the world would come to an end, the Last Judgment would separate the sinners from the blessed, and the reign of Christ would be over. But there was great confusion about the exact meaning of the millennium. "And when the thousand years are expired," the Apocalypse of St. John the Divine said. Did it mean the year A.D. 1000, or 1,000 years after some event of theological import? What was real was the psychology of fear. The Byzantine church, afraid of the literal belief in the Second Coming and the return of the anti-Christ, had banned the Apocalypse from canonical scripture. In the West, despite official Church efforts to discount the factual reality of this vision, popular fear endured. Extraordinary importance was attached to

falling meteors, and the Church found it necessary to issue frequent edicts against the megalithic monuments of Brittany—the dolmens, menhirs, and alignments of a time before grace—whose powerful presence seemed the natural focus of demonism.

The year 1000 came and went—and nothing happened. The gradual stabilization of the continent, a calmer and more secure daily life, suspended elemental fears, or rather institutionalized them. The devil and the tortures of hell, teratological creatures of all kinds, began to be depicted with great inventiveness within the form of the

Fig. 13.7 Tavant (France), St.-Nicolas, painting in crypt depicting a medieval pilgrim, mid-twelfth century.

new churches that now towered over city and country. (Fig. 13.6) The triumph of the devil was not a universal inevitability. He could be kept at bay indefinitely if the proper refuge was sought in faith. This is what he looks like, the Church was saying, letting her artists freely exploit apocalyptic literature and their own imaginations to blazon monstrous demons on facades and column capitals; this is what may happen to you. But the very frame that carried this terrifying message was also the scene of salvation. There was no need to run or despair. These mighty stone structures, the Church was saying, are your defense, your spiritual insurance, so that you need not fear daily for your fate, and so that you can be certain that at the Second Coming, when-

ever it might arrive as it must someday, you will be on the right side of the great judgment it will bring. If you succumbed to perdition now, it was not because of some impending millenniarist destiny, but through your own wickedness.

Monumental architecture denotes prosperity, or the anticipation of it. This was so in the eleventh century. The land was more and more bountiful. Large tracts of it, thousands upon thousands of acres, were being cleared for the first time for agriculture or reclaimed from abandoned and overgrown farmland; the great forests were cut down and dikes and ditches constructed, to tame the shady realm of knights and monsters and feed a rapidly rising population. On the gained territory new

villages were established by enterprising lords or abbots, in accordance with set plans. The pattern of the houses might be a regular grid, or else a linear strip of house and plot along a newly constructed road, with the fields arranged in herringbone fashion on either side of this spine. Some of these settlements in time would grow into towns.

Land clearance meant colonization. The rooting of new states like Poland and Bohemia set in motion a brisk flow of colonizers from Germany. Spanish rulers in the meanwhile, stubbornly pushing back the Muslim emirates, opened vast new lands for which they attracted settlers from the other side of the Pyrenees with charters that offered generous terms. Then, at the end of the eleventh century, there began a remarkable movement of people across the breadth of Europe to the Near East. Its formal object was the liberation of the shrines of the Holy Land from Muslim control. But these Crusades were actually a massive wave of colonial expansion that implanted Frankish institutions in Asia Minor, Syria, and Palestine, transformed the look of some very old cities and very famous monuments, and liberally dotted the retrieved lands with Romanesque castles and monasteries.

The Pilgrimage

The story of architecture in the eleventh century, then, is much more than the rise and triumph of the Romanesque church. Inns, hospices, rural enclaves, roads, bridges, castles—all these should have their place in the story. And all of them should be seen as working together in one fascinating environmental tapestry, as it would have been experienced by the knight, the traveling court of a high feudal lord, the tradesman, and the thousands of down-at-the-heel pilgrims plodding along the continental tracks of faith toward their distant goals. (Fig. 13.7)

Religious architecture fits into this tapestry. Relics mattered more basically than any other fixture of daily existence. Their

Fig. 13.8 Map: Pilgrimage routes to Santiago de Compostela.

settings, more widespread and lavish than the rest of the built environment, lasted longer. To this day you can feel quite vividly the firm hold of this cult sequence on the land if you retrace the steps of pilgrims on some major routes through France and Spain, and pass by the hundreds of roadside chapels, lonely monastic churches, and urban cathedrals that broke their tedious trudge and spurred them onward. Some of these are now mere wisps of ruin, others rebuilt and modernized piecemeal so that they seem a patchwork of styles and intentions; many are gone for good, victims of some particular malfeasance like the French Revolution, or mindless time. Cluny, the mother church of a tremendous monastic empire that at its height commanded 1,500 priories along with incalculable holdings of land and property, has all but disappeared. But there is enough still untouched, or little changed, to let us marvel at Glaber's white mantle of churches and stand in awe of it.

The practice of touching base with precious relics never ceased in the Middle Ages; it probably gained considerable momentum in the time of Charles the Great. But, for the most part, these were undertakings of local scope. Rome was the only target of long-distance pilgrimages. Large crowds descended on her from the north every year to pay homage to Sts. Peter and Paul, and make the rounds to the other major stations within the city and in the nearby countryside. The pilgrimage route crossed the Alps into Italy at the Great St. Bernard or Mont Cenis pass, joined the Aemilian Way via Modena, met the Cassia at Arezzo, and so reached Rome by way of Viterbo. Many pilgrims stayed on. Already by the early ninth century the Vatican district hosted a number of established national neighborhoods, called *scholae*, each with its own church and hostel.

Two other penitential journeys had high standing. Of these, the Holy Land was practically unattainable until the Crusades. Santiago, closer at hand and on similarly

Fig. 13.9 Conques (France), approach to town with view of Ste.-Foy.

Fig. 13.10 Conques, Ste.-Foy, ca. 1050–1120: top, site plan; bottom, ground plan and transverse section through the nave.

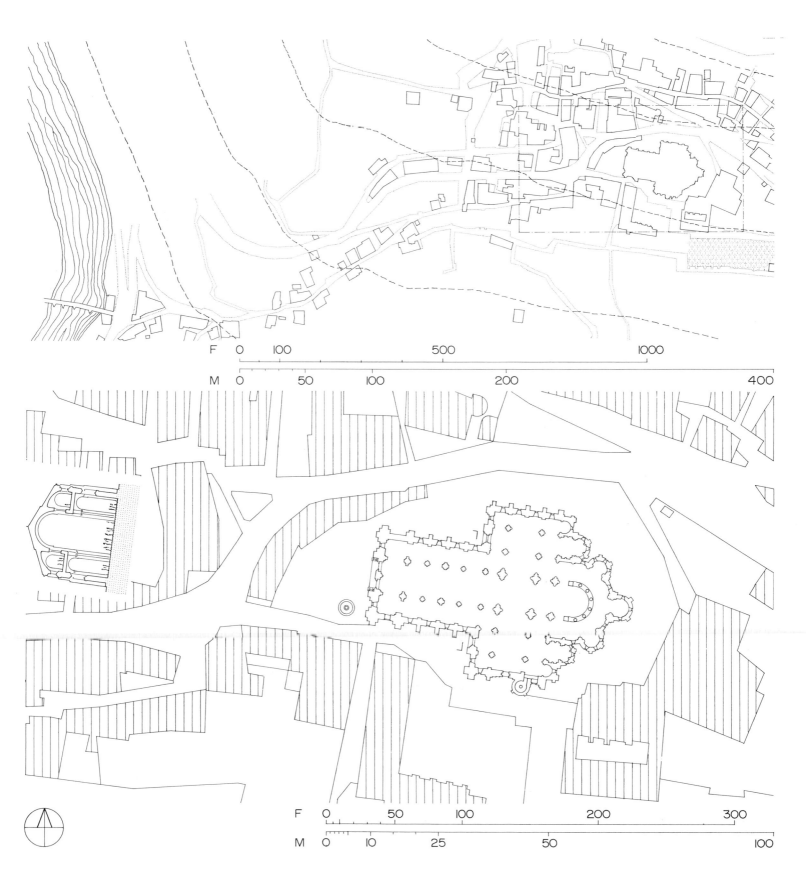

F 0   100   500   1000
M 0   50   100   200   400

F 0   50   100   200   300
M 0   10   25   50   100

303

contested territory which had to be valiantly wrenched from the infidel, was immensely popular even before the vigorous reconquest of northern Spain under the kings of Navarre and Castile. The shrine stood at the rim of the medieval world, at the westernmost promontory of the Iberian Peninsula, a very short way from the Ocean. The pilgrim who reached it after a two- or three-month journey walked down to Padron where the body of the Apostle was supposed to have arrived by sea, and then to the chapel of Nuestra Señora at Cape Finisterre, from the Latin *finis terra*, the end of the earth. Here, between the mists of Galicia and the prospect of an endless sea, with the Muslims kept at bay by Christian knights and the hardships of the long ordeal successfuly endured, it must have seemed to the pilgrims that they were in a chosen spot, a bit of earthly heaven, as close as a humble sinner was likely to get in this life to the promised bliss of the hereafter.

Four main pilgrimage routes crossed France in the first stretch of the way to Santiago. (Fig. 13.8) Three converged at the **pass of Roncesvalles, famous as the site of** one of Charles' battles. One was the Paris route, the official starting point for many pilgrims, French, English, or German. It passed through Orléans and then Tours, where the great church of St.-Martin (c. 1050), of which now only a facade tower and the tower of the north transept are left standing in the old part of the city, may have been the first to enunciate the formula used later at Cluny and Santiago and the prime stops on the other routes: St.-Martial at Limoges, now destroyed, the still intact St.-Sernin at Toulouse, and Ste.-Foy at Conques. Between Tours and Bordeaux, Englishmen who had crossed the Bay of Biscay joined the procession. Past the dread wasteland of the Landes, their ranks were swelled by those who had started the journey at Vézelay in Burgundy, the heartland of Cluniac power, and had traveled due southwest via Limoges and Périgueux. The third route was the shortest. It started in Le Puy in the mountainous region of Auvergne and went through Conques and Moissac.

At St.-Jean-Pied-de-Port, just before the pass, the pilgrims planted the crosses they had been carrying into the ground. Thou-

Fig. 13.11 Conques, Ste.-Foy; view from the east.

Fig. 13.12 Conques, Ste.-Foy; main portal of west facade with tympanum sculpture from ca. 1130.

topical and an international style. Each built specimen is caught in the great currents of influence that flowed along the pilgrimage routes and through the colonizing efforts of monastic orders; but it is also embedded in its local tradition through materials, favored forms and themes, its conservative or progressive spirit.

Ste.-Foy at Conques

For a start we might take Ste.-Foy at Conques (ca. 1050–1120) as a paradigm of the five or six most well-known churches on the Santiago trek. (Figs. 13.9, 13.10) It has the advantage of being early, at least in inception, well-preserved, and pure in the sense of having been spared later updating. Conques is still the village it was when Charles the Great founded a Benedictine abbey in this isolated valley of south Auvergne. The present church was started toward the middle of the eleventh century to replace the Carolingian building that was there. It looms majestic at the end of the steep Rue Charlemagne, an authentic bit of pilgrim's track, scaled more to the bare, sun-burned hills than to the huddle of simple houses with their grey slate roofs. Moissac and Vézelay have better sculpture, St.-Sernin is bigger, a dozen French Romanesque churches are more sophisticated. But none catches quite as well the stark and timeless spirit of the medieval pilgrimage as does Ste.-Foy.

Look at the plan and the overall exterior view together: a nave flanked by two-storey aisles that admit no clerestory lighting; a transept around which the aisles are continued, except along the east side; and a beautifully unfolding sanctuary made up of an apse whose bounding column screen opens out to a semicircular ambulatory, which in turn creates three small curved chapels. Two additional chapels, of unequal size, are attached to either end of the east side of the transept. Two rectangular towers hold down the west end. A polygonal belfry tower pushes out of the crossing where the gable roofs of the nave, the two transept arms, and the bays in front of the apse, all of equal height, come together. From the east, a crescendo of curved shapes: the low radiating chapels reaching up to the high annular shoulder of the ambulatory, and then the tall half-cylinder of the apse, buttressed by the rak-

---

sands could be seen sprouting at any time at this continental gate to Spain. Now the procession, cheered by *jongleurs* who sang epic poems about Charles and his companions to the accompaniment of the hurdy-gurdy, set out on the *camino,* enjoying the luxury of a new roadway. Stretches of it were deeply marked with the steady tramp of feet through the centuries and rutted by the carriage wheels of those who traveled in state. In Puente la Reina where Queen Urraca's bridge carried the road across the Arga, travelers on the fourth French route fell in. These pilgrims had come from Arles along the south of France, passing through Toulouse and crossing the Pyrenees by another pass. The single river of pilgrims covered the last 300 kilometers (200 miles) through recently cleared and still sparsely colonized country, through Burgos and Léon, the capital of the kings of the Asturias, until the last hill before Santiago—Mons Gaudii, Mount Joy.

The pilgrims entered the city from the northeast by one of seven gates. They proceeded along a narrow street lined with hospices and arrived at the north portals of the cathedral. The present building was begun in the 1070s and was not consecrated until 1211. A gilt and jeweled statue of St. James stands above the high altar over the crypt that holds the reliquary. This was the magnet of the epic journey, and it is still a moving spectacle today to see the pilgrim approach the statue from the rear of the altar, embrace it, and place upon its head the pilgrim's hat to which the scallop-shell, the saint's symbol, is affixed.

The Romanesque Church

There is no typical Romanesque church. We rarely mistake the Romanesque character, and yet its strength is in variation, both regional and programmatic. This is at once a

ing blocks of its escort bays and laced by blind arches that lift the eye to the roof, where it encounters and scales the belfry tower. (Fig. 13.11)

The facade is unfinished (and meddled with in the nineteenth century). This is common for Romanesque churches. Moneys often ran out midway in the construction; long delays occurred. It was no use starting small and adding on when you could afford to. Unlike a mosque like that of Córdoba whose serial composition allowed repeated enlargement that kept up with the growing numbers of citizens, the Christian church had an ideal diagram, liturgically so precise, that total rebuilding made more sense than extension. So one had to decide on the basic outline and build from fundament to frill as revenue and private donations permitted. The vessel had to be made functional, perhaps also defensible externally in perilous regions, and towers were necessary for status and visibility. The decorative program came last. Facades were designed to be costly frontispieces, and so they languished.

Some sculpture was evidently considered essential at Conques and was installed above the main portals about 1130. (Fig. 13.12) Indeed by then it was de rigueur for the major churches on the pilgrimage routes to preface the ritual spaces of the interior with a rendition of the Last Judgment in high relief touched up with paint and placed in the arched recess, or tympanum, above the main doorway. Ste.-Foy's is arranged in three tiers. At the top, the cross is held by two energetic angels; two others are blowing the trumpets of the judgment day. In the middle of the next tier, Christ sits enthroned in a star-spangled aureole floating on clouds, a bearded somber figure who raises His right hand to elevate the blessed and lowers His left toward hell. "Come, the blessed of my Father," a banner above His head proclaims, "Take possession of the Kingdom that has been readied for you"; and the other denounces: "Away from me, accursed ones." At His feet the dead are being raised from their graves. After the weighing of their souls, some are led away by angels; others are set upon by hideous demons. The line of the blessed is headed by the Virgin Mary and St. Peter, and includes an abbot and a king. On the

Fig. 13.13 Conques, Ste.-Foy; interior looking east.

306

other side of the tympanum the damned, monks and knights among them, are kept away from the Judge by guardian angels equipped with shield and lance. "Perverse men," the inscription reads, "are thus hurled into the abyss": *Homines perversi sic sunt in tartara mersi.* Below this, two gabled structures contrast the Kingdom of Heaven, where Abraham receives the souls of the just, and the Kingdom of Hell, where the grimacing Lucifer presides over a spirited choreography of horrors.

Chastened by this great cosmic drama, the pilgrim would have entered the church with humility and renewed reverence. (Fig. 13.13) Today Ste.-Foy is naked; photographs of it, unfailingly taken when the church is empty of worshippers, seem determined to impart a textbook recipe of what Romanesque interiors ought to look like. In reality, they were rich and theatrical, alive with bustle and pageantry. Capitals and odd corners were invaded by bizarre and fabulous carvings, a bestiary that is inspired by all the monsters of the ancient world and controlled by a process of design that is both geometrically analytical and protean. As the great French art historian Henry Focillon described them, "The animals are subdivided, reunited, acquire two heads on one body and two bodies for one head, grope one another, devour one another, and are again reborn, all in an indecipherable tumultuous mêlée . . . like the images of some vast collective nightmare." Narrative paintings, Biblical and profane, took over the vaults and nave walls; textiles and tapestries softened the impact of the hard, crisp masonry. On the main altar the treasures of the church would be set out, gleaming drops of goldwork and jewels under the light-filled canopy of the apse vault.

No pilgrimage church matched Conques in this regard. The statue of the saint, one of the oldest pieces of medieval sculpture, is a gem-encrusted fetish of primitive force. (Fig. 13.14) This *Majesté de Ste.-Foy* had a place of honor among other celebrated treasures of the abbey. The chapels had their own attractions, and the pilgrims shuffled down the aisles and around the ambulatory adoring them. In the transept arms, ensconced in stalls and separated from the crossing by low stone balus-

trades, the monks sang the service, their voices echoing in the cavernous spaces and welling up inside the belfry tower. At off hours and special feasts there was also robust music-making in this part of the church, with instrumentalists of all sorts taking part. And at night or in the early morning hours, responsive plainsong ineffably energized this ponderously built, thick-jointed architecture of somber-tinted volcanic rock.

Stripped and void, Ste.-Foy allows us a close look at Romanesque structure. (Fig. 13.13) The central nave is barrel-vaulted, but not in one tunneling sweep. From the clustered piers that define the rectangular bays, single shafts rise the full height of the nave wall to meet arches that run transversely on the underside of the vault. At the crossing the piers are thicker. From them spring four arches that support the two-storey octagonal drum of the tower, with openings in each face, and the octagonal dome with the peaked roof. The aisles have cross-vaulted bays at ground level and, in the galleries, quadrant vaults reinforced by lateral fins reach upward to the nave vault and buttress it along its entire length. But to do so this gallery level, called the tribune, blocks direct light from the nave. Natural light filters across the tribune into the upper nave through twin, round-headed openings, one per bay, and spreads in lengthening bands on the floor across the aisles below. This diffuse illumination enhances height and emphasizes the east end of the church where large windows in the curved walls of the radiating chapels, and others directly below the apse half-dome, conjure a luminous crown that draws us toward itself.

The Precedent
Now we must ask ourselves two questions. In what way is Ste.-Foy at Conques different from the basilical church of the Carolingian period; and what intervening trials, if any, should we be conscious of?

First, the obvious omissions: Ste.-Foy has no atrium, no western counter-apse, no westwork in the sense of a usable multi-level entrance unit. The facade is now a thin screen bracketed by towers that leads directly into the main hall (or in rare instances into a vestibule, one-bay deep, that contains the baptismal font at one end). The

three-part division of this screen vertically corresponds to the internal division of nave and aisles. The full French scheme includes a central arched portal with staggered archivolts, some sort of main window grouping or loggia above, topped by the gable of the nave roof, and side portals at the base of the towers. (Fig. 13.15) This is one solution. In an alternate composition, the gable might control the design by extending over the aisles or rising above their raking roof lines, the corner towers atrophied or left out altogether. (Fig. 13.16)

Major changes are evident in the sanctuary end as well. Where the Carolingian church tried to deal with the need for mul-

Fig. 13.14 Conques, Ste.-Foy; gold-plated statue of the saint, late tenth century.

tiple altars by partitioning the interior with parapet screens, the Romanesque church works out a felicitous architectural answer. A number of individual chapels swing out of the main outline east of the transept. The principal apse is encased by a semicircular ambulatory that runs between it and the easternmost of the chapels. The ambulatory continues the line of the aisles around the high altar, so that the flow of worshippers venerating the preeminent relics of the church would not interfere with ongoing services. These relics were often contained in a spacious vaulted crypt. The idea of an underground chamber and a narrow passage around it, with a window that permitted one to look in, goes back even beyond the Carolingian period. But in contrast to the cramped, cellarlike provision that prevailed until the tenth century, the Romanesque crypt is a multiaisled hall of groin-vaulted square bays, all of equal height in order to support evenly the floor of the church.

To the first generations of users who watched Ste.-Foy and other structures like it replace the old Carolingian churches, the most astounding novelty must have been the tall vaulted naves. We have only to compare the interior of the abbey church of St. Gall with that of Ste.-Foy to appreciate their amazement. (Figs. 12.19, 13.13) In the one, flat nave walls, perforated by neat rows of small clerestory windows, rise from arcades on single columns and support an open timber roof. In the other, thickly grouped cluster piers, branching at three different levels and in three directions, set up a robust stone armature for the vaulting of the aisles, the tribunes, and the nave. Each pier consists of a rectangular core that has pilasters or engaged columns attached to its sides. Two of these, on the east and west sides of the pier, support the nave arcades. From one of the remaining two spring the arches that cross the aisle and the tribune as part of their vaulting system. The last component of the pier, toward the nave, swoops upward the full height of the ground-level arcades and tribune, to the springing point of the transverse arches that prop up a lofty barrel vault. We have not seen any enclosed vaulted space of this power and scale since Hagia Sophia, itself a Christian rendition in brick of the prodigious concrete shells of late Roman build-

Fig. 13.15 Caen (France), Abbaye-aux-hommes, St.-Étienne, begun ca. 1068; west facade.

Fig. 13.16 St.-Jouin-des-Marnes (Poitou, France), church, ca. 1130; west facade.

ings like the baths of Caracalla and the Basilica of Maxentius. And that is what the term Romanesque, that ambiguous concoction of scholars, is meant to suggest in part—sort of Roman.

Two separate developments of the later tenth and early eleventh centuries furnish the elements of transition that take us from Carolingian to Romanesque architecture. One of these developments concerns an architectural language, sometimes called "First Romanesque," that permeated northwest Spain, southern France, and northern Italy. Its source was probably Lombardy which, as we saw in the last chapter, kept alive the brick tradition of early Christian capitals like Milan and Ravenna all through the later centuries. The style is distinguished by an external decoration of blind arcades and pilasters, commonly referred to as "Lombard bands," that trace gable ends and run between storeys. These lighten the otherwise severe massing that characterizes the churches in question, their bold composition often accentuated by the rugged, rocky settings. And within, some of them, especially in Catalonia, have vaulted naves—heavy, with few openings, gloomy and austere. This practice is in keeping with the vaulting tradition of pre-Muslim Spain that produced churches like San Pedro dela Nave. The vault was often an unarticulated half-cylinder, but did use primitive transverse arches at times. The monastery of St.-Martin-de-Canigou (1001–26), on a picturesque spur of French Catalonia, is a perfect example of the First Romanesque. (Figs. 13.17, 13.18)

The other contributor to what we call Romanesque is the religious architecture of Germany built under the Ottonian dynasty. In a deliberate attempt to salvage the prestige of Carolingian days, these kings and their court supported a monumental building program that both conserves and consolidates the forms of the ninth century. The massing is Carolingian; the main roofs are of timber. But particular attention is paid to the design of the interior, where the choice of supports and wall articulation have more to do with visual preference than the structural needs of the roof frame.

At St. Michael's, Hildesheim, built for Bishop Bernward in 1001–33, the Carolingian church plan is advanced and rationalized. (Fig. 13.19) The notion of the "double-

Fig. 13.17 St.-Martin-de-Canigou (France), monastery, 1001–26; view from the south.

Fig. 13.18 St.-Martin-de-Canigou, monastery church; interior looking east.

Fig. 13.19 Hildesheim (Germany), St. Michael's the church of Bishop Bernward, 1001–33; ground plan. The setting indicated is based on a map of the pre-modern period.

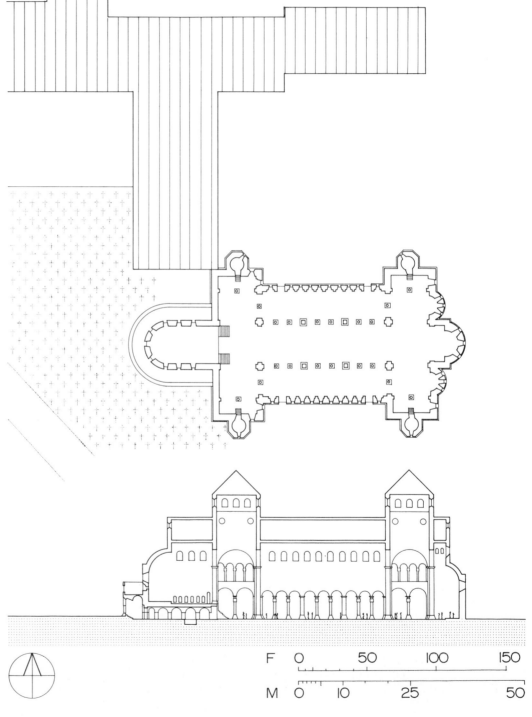

F 0   50   100   150

M 0   10   25   50

310

ender" is played out fully by having not only two terminal apses, but also two matching transepts. The entrances are along the flanks. They line up with the east and west of three squares into which the nave has been divided by piers; these alternate with pairs of columns. The nave walls above the rhythmically varied supports are blank except for clerestory windows. But a cornice line may have run between nave arcades and clerestory, as it does at the nearby church of St. Godehard, where in addition pilaster strips designate the bays on the upper register. (Fig. 13.20)

The first cathedral at Speyer (ca. 1030–61) had a different interior scheme. The wall articulation there was achieved by a colossal order of responds—half-columns that rose from the floor for about 25 meters (80 feet) and were joined at the top by arches. (Fig. 13.21) This bay system subsumed both nave arcades and the round-headed clerestory windows, in a manner reminiscent of the late-antique audience hall at Trier. (Fig. 11.12)

Now at the risk of oversimplifying and of some distortion, we might say that a fundamental feature of Romanesque churches originates from this combination of stone vaults with Speyer-like responds that sweep up and unify the wall surface. Putting the two together means that, unlike Speyer, the visual system will not adhere in a two-dimensional fashion on the plane of the nave wall, but will swing out into the nave space with transverse arches that lock wall and ceiling into one sweeping force. The walls have a tremendous load now that they cannot hold up unaided. They become thicker and more muscular, and they start to register some of the buttressing activity behind them in a new horizontal layering. And the vertical members do double duty as visual organizers and the graph of the structural system, so that they need to proliferate into clusters, with as many subordinate branches as the structural system warrants.

Perhaps the most cautious solution to the problem of propping up the nave vault is that of Conques: tribunes over the aisles. But structural logic will not alone explain the richness of Romanesque design. Form, function, and structure play back and forth from church to church. What makes sense in terms of form, or function, or structure at Conques might be taken up elsewhere for a different reason, toyed with, embellished, and then emulated in this new guise in yet another building. The buttressing aspect of tribunes is obvious enough, and yet tribunes can also occur in timber-roofed basilicas where such supportive needs are doubtful. Again, in terms of function, tribunes behaved as a kind of upper church which nestled extra altars, and so siphoned off some of the crowd of pilgrims and parishioners who filled the church on special days. But, perversely, tribunes might be

Fig. 13.20 Hildesheim, St. Godehard's, 1133–72; interior looking east.

Fig. 13.21 Speyer (Germany), cathedral, first stage, ca. 1030–61; interior looking east, reconstruction drawing.

without floors, that is, unusable, but retained as a register of the nave elevation for aesthetic effect.

This elevation has several variants. (Fig. 13.22) The two-storey elevation at Conques accounts for nave arcade and tribune. With the addition of a clerestory zone at the top, this turns into a three-storey elevation. You might substitute the tribune with a so-called triforium gallery—a narrow, barely negotiable passage animated toward the nave by blind arches or niches, usually three to a bay; hence the name "triforium." This service gallery corresponds to the space between the crown of the aisle vaults and their lean-to roof that must be hooked into a substantial band of masonry between nave arcades and clerestory. Or else you might choose to make do without the triforium, and simply stack up nave arcades and clerestory windows in two roughly equal registers, separated by a cornice. In Bel-

Fig. 13.22a Nevers (France), St. Étienne, ca. 1083–97; interior, showing three-storey nave elevation (nave arcade, tribune, clerestory).

Fig. 13.22b Vézelay (France), Ste.-Madeleine, ca. 1104–32; interior, showing two-storey nave elevation (nave arcade, clerestory).

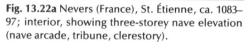

gium the cathedral of Tournai, originally timber-roofed, has a four-storey elevation, with the triforium band running between the tribunes and the clerestory. Finally, in the so-called hall churches, the nave wall disappears altogether by having the aisles as tall as the nave and open toward it to their full height.

What is most striking in all this is that the nature of the wall has changed. At Hildesheim, and indeed since the Early Christian basilica, the wall was a thin defining plane with an applied order of articulation. In Romanesque France it is a massive element that is cut into by deep openings. Sometimes it is even split at the upper levels with a tunnellike cavity big enough for a man to walk through. This double-shell wall can be punctured with windows or arcades that face toward the inside or the outside. The cavity functions as a narrow continuous passageway that, at its most developed form, runs along the facade, down the nave, and around the transept. Such burrows in the thickness of the masonry were of course crucial for the maintenance of these huge, complex buildings.

Construction habits were mostly empirical. At every stage of the erection process, scaffolding, raised from the ground up or suspended from parts of the building, was essential. (Fig. 13.23) It is likely that the passageways we just mentioned played their part during the course of construction in

312

Fig. 13.22c Tournai (Belgium), cathedral; interior from ca. 1110, showing four-storey nave elevation (nave arcade, tribune, triforium, clerestory).

Fig. 13.22d St.-Savin-sur-Gartempe (France), abbey church, ca. 1060–1115; nave. This is an example of a hall church — that is, one in which the aisles rise almost to the same height as the nave. The barrel vault of the nave has a cycle of paintings depicting scenes of the Old Testament.

reducing the need for built scaffolds, and thus cutting down the great expense of timber. Heavy beams were also required to shore up elements of the building against lateral swaying while the permanent super-structure was being worked on. But the most demanding use of timber was for centering, that rigid falsework on which every arch and vault had to be shaped. Mobile units mounted on wheels were probably devised for the banded barrel vaults of churches like Ste.-Foy; the trans-verse arches that are such a prominent fea-ture of these interiors thus had a construc-tional advantage, allowing the vault to be built in sections, as well as having a brac-ing function. Earth formwork supported on platforms that rose to the springing level was sometimes used for nonbanded vaults, like those for the naves of hall churches; and crypt vaults were also built on solid earth embankments filled in from the floor up. None of this was easy; all of it was laborious. But labor was cheap in the Middle Ages. The true cost was in materials.

Italian Counterpoint

In the decades when Ste.-Foy was being built at Conques, the seafaring republic of Pisa, rich with spoils of the Eastern trade and glorying in her fleet's gainful victories over the Arabs in Sicily and Sardinia, had put in hand an ambitious new cathedral in honor of the Virgin, the protectress of the city. (Fig. 13.24, 13.25) Work began in 1063, and the building was dedicated in 1118 by Pope Gelasius II when it was still far from finished. The facade commemorates a certain

Fig. 13.24 Pisa (Italy), the cathedral complex, eleventh–thirteenth centuries; a view from the west. The Baptistery is in the foreground.

Fig. 13.23 Formwork used in Romanesque vaulting; conjectural reconstruction. The drawings apply to the construction of a banded barrel vault—that is, a barrel vault stiffened at intervals by transverse arches (see Figs. 13.22a, 13.22b, and 14.4). Such vaults may have been built with the aid of the rolling scaffolding indicated here. The centering frame is shown in the top drawing. Unit (**A**) and the beam on which the workman is standing were lowered (**D**) when it was time to move the formwork to the next bay(**E**).

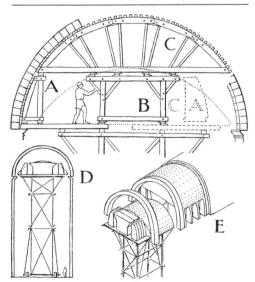

Busketos as the architect. We know nothing about him. But his masterpiece still stands in the large open site at the northeast corner of the city, attended by a round baptistery and a bell tower that has settled unevenly in the course of time and dizzily leans to one side. This lacy marble specter, one of the best-loved groups of architecture in the world, typifies the highest accomplishment of Italy in the Romanesque period. And it looks not in the least like its contemporary at Conques.

Let us take a look first at the freestanding baptistery and campanile. Functions that had long been absorbed within the body of the church in Europe are here allotted their own independent buildings. Then the cathedral itself. (Fig. 13.26) Built outside and in of dressed stone and marble that has weathered beautifully, it is luminous and light-hearted. No towers on the facade or at the crossing, no apocalyptic scare over the portals or on capitals and impost blocks.

The three entrance doors are set in a frieze of blind round-headed arches, and above them run four storeys of open arcaded galleries. The plan is more Early Christian, or Roman for that matter, than Romanesque. A flat coffered ceiling covers the nave, and between it and sets of double aisles are the arcades, resting on reused Classical columns of granite or marble. The transept arms are themselves like smaller Roman basilicas, each with its own apse; a returned aisle at their inward ends coalesces with the inner aisles of the nave. A large ellipsoidal dome is placed at the crossing: a single broad apse at the east end. If this is Romanesque, we have to stop pretending that the great pilgrimage churches of France and Spain are in any way normative, or we should redefine the term so that it can evoke more than clustered piers, banded barrel vaults, and radiating chapels.

Italy has never fit comfortably in a mainstream account of Western medieval archi-

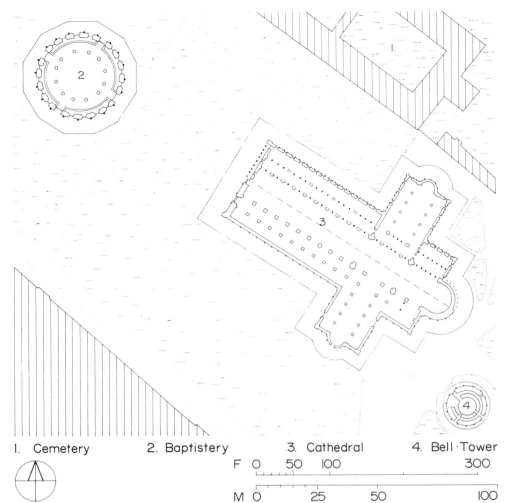

1. Cemetery   2. Baptistery   3. Cathedral   4. Bell·Tower

F O   50   100   300

M 0   25   50   100

Fig. 13.26 Pisa, cathedral; interior view across nave into north transept.

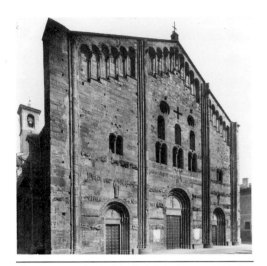

Fig. 13.27 Pavia (Italy), S. Michele, ca. 1110–60; west facade.

Fig. 13.28 Pomposa (Ferrara, Italy), abbey church of S. Maria, with bell tower, 1063.

Fig. 13.29 Rome, S. Giorgio in Velabro, bell tower, twelfth century.

tecture. Here several threads of our story—native Roman-ness, Byzantium, Islam, and transalpine medievalism—get intertwined. The results are some of the most unique and extraordinary structures of the Middle Ages. Medieval architecture in Italy is hybrid and impulsive. It does not easily adhere to purist or logical modes of design—which is why it will not take to Gothic. It

delights in special, wicked effects. It is preoccupied with the elaboration of surfaces. And of course, in the end, its greatest contribution to the medieval environment may be its ability to see the church as the framer of a public space, the town square. (Fig. 13.27) It is not inadvertent that church facades often exceed the volume of the interiors, rising above the roofline in a kind of false front. They are not there only to introduce a religious experience, but also to scale an urban void.

To speak of Italy, however, is a bit misleading. There is no such unified nation, politically at least, until 1870. In the wake of the Roman Empire and the retirement of its Byzantine overseers, Italy coalesced into a number of idiosyncratic territorialities, each with its own political burden, clout, and allegiances. The north never went long without some form of German presence; Venice, independent-minded and enterprising, was the great gate to the East; Tus-cany maintained a fierce loyalty to its Roman past and the Classical concept of the self-governing city; the often stagnant, feudal papal states in the middle of the boot separated all this from the south where Byzantine and Muslim elements came to commingle, in the eleventh and twelfth centuries, with the heritage of the carpet-bagging Normans.

Architecturally, three sources might be singled out as important for the environmental kaleidoscope of medieval Italy, underlying the foreign infusions from Byzantium, Islam, and Germanic Europe.

Working backwards we have, first, the masonry tradition of Lombardy, from Early Christian times to the First Romanesque. This is where surface design (Lombard bands, terra-cotta insets, etc.) and the practice of freestanding bell towers seem to have been nourished. The towers started in ninth-century Ravenna, their shape then being cylindrical and undivided. Soon a rectilinear, multistorey version was settled on, and so they continued with rare exceptions, the leaning cylinder of Pisa chief among them.

Perhaps the most elegant of these early detached bell towers is at the abbey of Pomposa in Ferrara. (Fig. 13.28) It dates from 1063 and has nine storeys. The openings on each side increase from one narrow loophole to four generous arches at the belfry level. The fashion reached Rome by 1100, where some twenty churches were soon accented by these bell towers. They were layered and arcaded, with disks of porphyry and serpentino, and sometimes colored tile, inserted into their warm brick surfaces. (Fig. 13.29) Between storeys ran saw-tooth brick bands and stone cornices on stylish brackets. Visually, which is to say politically, the competition on the spiked skyline of the great city was visible in the defensive towers spawned by feudal factions—bold and brutish and with minimum perforation in their massive form.

Second, there was the legacy of Early Christian architecture, and especially the example of the Constantinian foundations like St. Peter's. Explicit revivals cropped up long past the Carolingian period; the case of the Benedictine monastery of Monte Cassino under Abbot Desiderius (1058–87) is well documented. But also general predilections were always indulged in for features like the atrium (S. Ambrogio in Milan), the basilical plan, or the tall single apse unadulterated by radiating chapels. (Fig. 13.30)

Finally, the legacy of Classical antiquity—never entirely lost here, never purposely thwarted as in the anti-Classical designs of the Frankish world before Charles. This legacy became a sort of native habit, the habit of thinking Roman in the conception of architectural space and its ordering—for example, the preference for the broad proportions of the Classical bay, and the habit of using stone columns in conjunction with

Fig. 13.30 Milan (Italy), S. Ambrogio, tenth–twelfth centuries; view across atrium.

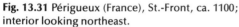

Fig. 13.31 Périgueux (France), St.-Front, ca. 1100; interior looking northeast.

Fig. 13.32 Cambridge (England), the church of the Holy Sepulchre, ca. 1130. Compare with the Holy Sepulchre in Jerusalem, Fig. 11.23.

lintels or semicircular arches, as at Pisa. To this ancient source (and its later incarnation in Byzantium) we should probably assign the abiding fascination with the dome. The survival of the baptistery was a good excuse, but there were also centrally planned churches, and the competitive drive for domed crossings in Tuscany is known to us from the cathedrals of Pisa, Siena, and Florence. In addition, in Byzantinizing areas like Venice and Norman Sicily the dome was perforce catered to. The true cross-in-square scheme appears in Sicily in churches like the Martorana at Palermo dedicated in 1143, complete with its sheath of gold-backed mosaic. St. Mark's in Venice recalls an older prototype, as we have mentioned, namely, the Justinianic church of the Holy Apostles in Constantinople, which it follows closely down to the almost identical dimensions.

The domes of St. Mark's have a tall bulbous shape from the outside, but that is the exotic camouflage of the mid-fifteenth century inspired by Islam. They retain their original shape internally. (Fig. 11.30) The hemispherical rise and the ring of windows at the base recall the dome of Hagia So-

Fig. 13.33 Florence (Italy), the baptistery, eleventh–twelfth century, and the campanile of the cathedral, 1334–57. The campanile was begun by Giotto and completed by Andrea Pisano and Francesco Talenti.

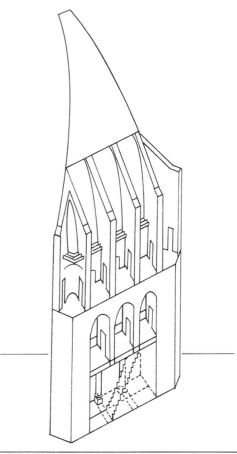

Fig. 13.34 Florence, baptistery; scheme of the wall construction. The transverse partitions transmit the thrust of the dome through the entire lower portion of the building.

phia. But the domes of St. Mark's are actually elliptical in plan, the central one, a bit larger than the rest, approaching an ovoid. The material is brick in both cases, but whereas Byzantine brickwork uses thick mortar layers that make the masonry almost monolithic, at Venice large bricks are held together by very thin mortaring in the Western manner. The domes are supported by sturdy piers that have been cut into; between them run single-storey colonnades and open galleries covered by transverse barrel vaults.

What the interior would have looked like about 1100, before the sheathing of mosaics and marble veneer which is later, we can see at St.-Front in Périgueux, a church that chose to copy St. Mark's using the local chalky limestone of Aquitaine. (Fig. 13.31) Here the galleries and colonnades were suppressed, and only their visual memory was retained in the blind arcading of the main walls. Aquitaine has a number of domed churches, some earlier and some

later than St.-Front. The ultimate inspiration for this unique school of Romanesque architecture is probably Eastern. A vernacular model in the local tradition is the round house covered by a rudimentary dome. At any rate, they have powerful, open, noble spaces, these domed basilicas of Périgord, Gascony, Saintonge, and Poitou, an expansive monumentality that sets them apart from the strongly compartmentalized volume of the familiar French Romanesque interior.

Centrally planned churches, round or polygonal, were often intended as copies of the Holy Sepulchre in Jerusalem. The liberation of Palestine by the First Crusade had guaranteed the direct stimulus that was lacking in previous attempts to recall the great shrine. The general type has a domed central unit, with an ambulatory around it of one or two storeys, and in its execution it often relies on Roman or Early Christian prototypes in the West. There are four Holy Sepulchres in England, those at Northamp-

ton and Cambridge being the oldest (ca. 1100 and 1130, respectively). (Fig. 13.32) Even Denmark has a handful, undoubtedly inspired by the pilgrimage of King Sigurd the Great to the Holy Land about 1100.

Baptisteries, of all domed buildings in the Romanesque period, are uniquely Italian. They too shared the rekindled interest in the Holy Sepulchre. The sacrament of baptism was symbolically allied to death, and baptisteries to tomb architecture. Remember St. Paul in *Romans:* "Know ye not, that so many of us as were baptized into Jesus Christ were baptized into his death? Therefore we are buried with him by baptism into death: that like as Christ was raised up from the dead by the glory of the Father, even so we also should walk in newness of life." There is no doubt that the baptistery at Pisa, begun in 1153, strove to be a fair replication of Christ's tomb—which explains the strange cone that pokes through the hemispherical dome of the fourteenth century. The initial roof was a truncated cone open at the top, to look like the conical wooden dome of the Palestinian paradigm.

Florence's is the largest and grandest of these baptisteries. (Fig. 13.33) Structurally, the baptistery is not innocent of the Pantheon's example, but transforms it significantly enough to point the way to Brunelleschi's dome over the crossing of the Florence cathedral, an early monument of the Renaissance. The baptistery rests on Roman foundations, it would appear. But it is probably an eleventh-century building in essence, and certainly is in the paneling of the exterior, which is the result of the generosity of Countess Matilda of Tuscany, the great patroness of the arts and of learning. In any case, the octagon is made up of a double-shell wall in the hollow of which a system of vertical partitions reaches all the way to the attic storey of the dome. (Fig. 13.34) This is very different from the workings of the Pantheon, where a series of relieving vaults built into the enormously thick rotunda wall adjusts the load onto a number of points along the perimeter. (Fig. 10.3) The present pyramidal roof would not have been there at the start. Beyond an exterior attic that would have masked the springing of the dome, the dome's eight panels would have been visible, simply clothed in brick, and at the crown the graceful, almost Classical lantern which, according to one local source, was set up in 1150 by the Cloth Finishers Guild who had custody of the building.

Three native sources, then, underlie all that we see of "Romanesque" architecture in Italy—the Roman, Early Christian, and Lombard traditions. They colored everything Italian architects borrowed from abroad, and of course these native influences borrowed from one another in a fertile exchange. The "Early Christian" atrium of the late eleventh-century S. Ambrogio in Milan is rendered, like the church exterior and the bell tower, in the familiar surface runs of the First Romanesque. The material changes from brick to stone as we come closer to Tuscany. Here the availability of fine marbles and the sentiment for classi-

Fig. 13.35 Modena (Italy), cathedral, 1099–1184; from the southwest.

cizing form turn the applied Lombard bands into open arcades: Roman superimposed on First Romanesque. Already in S. Michele in Pavia (early twelfth century), still within Lombardy, a clifflike stone facade with a single sweeping gable breaks the density of the thick wall with three sections of arcading under the gable cornice, stepped up like an open stair. (Fig. 13.27) At Modena Cathedral (1099–1184), Lombard geographically, but in fact within the dominions of the Countess Matilda at the time of its construction, a continuous exterior gallery with triple arches in each bay makes the full circuit of the building

except over the main portal. (Fig. 13.35)

When we enter Tuscany proper, the system extends over the entire surface of the church. At S. Michele, Lucca, a giant order of arcading almost free of the wall plane supports a smaller open tier along the flanks and four tiers on the thirteenth-century facade, which is crowned by the statue of the dragon-slaying archangel. (Fig. 13.36) At Pisa, the arcades are blind along the flanks of the cathedral and detach themselves only in the upper range of the apse, at the base of the crossing dome, and of course on the facade, trapping there rich deep shadows that play against the lower relief on the rest of

Fig. 13.36 Lucca (Italy), S. Michele, begun 1143; view from the southwest.

the exterior surface. (Fig. 13.24) In Florence, as we can see on the baptistery and the Benedictine abbey church of S. Miniato (begun 1013) on a hill overlooking the city, plastic effects are spurned in favor of a busy but masterfully controlled surface colorism. (Fig. 13.33) Arcades and a variety of paneling are delineated with a dark green marble on the smooth white-marble sheathing of the wall.

This design of inlays has no exact counterpart in Roman antiquity. Yet its rational order and Classical proportions, and the shorthand of columns, round-headed arches, and pediments, stamped it with the authentic look of that distant past which had never lost its appeal. Within a century or two after they were up, the belief was general that the baptistery and S. Miniato were actual Roman survivals. And it is on this belief that the study and revival of the ancient tradition in architecture were based at first, when restless minds came to think of an end to the Middle Ages and decided to turn back in order to look ahead. Nothing in history is inevitable, but perhaps we could make a good case, after the fact, why Florence and not Paris or Speyer should be the birthplace of the Renaissance.

Further Reading

A. W. Clapman, *Romanesque Architecture in Western Europe* (Oxford: Clarendon Press, 1936).

H. Decker, *Romanesque Art in Italy*, trans. J. Cleugh (London: Thames and Hudson, 1958).

O. Demus, *The Church of San Marco in Venice. History, Architecture, Sculpture* (Washington, D.C.: Dumbarton Oaks, 1960).

H. Focillon, *The Art of the West in the Middle Ages: Romanesque Art*, vol. I, trans. D. King (New York: Phaidon, 1963).

J. W. Franklin, *The Cathedrals of Italy* (London, Batsford, 1958).

H. E. Kubach, *Romanesque Architecture* (New York: Abrams, 1972).

G. Kunstler, ed., *Romanesque Art in Europe* (New York: Norton, 1973).

E. Mullins, *The Pilgrimage to Santiago* (New York: Taplinger, 1974).

R. Oursel, *Living Architecture: Romanesque*, trans. K. M. Leake (London: Oldbourne, 1967).

Chartres Cathedral, 1194–1260; detail of flying buttresses.

14

THE FRENCH MANNER

The Romanesque and *Opus Modernum*

Sometime around 1124 Abbot Bernard of Clairvaux addressed a scathing indictment against Cluny, the powerful monastic order that held sway over Christian Europe. Bernard was the leader of a new reformist order, the Cistercians. Its aim was to step back from the worldly success monasticism had garnered since the subsidence of post-Carolingian disorders and to recover the ancient idealism of St. Benedict's Rule. Stung by the fabulous rebuilding of the Cluniac mother house (Fig. 14.1), with a church that was to prove the largest ever to stand on French soil and the largest of the Romanesque period anywhere, Bernard lashed out at

the immense height of your churches, their immoderate length, their superfluous breadth, the sumptuous decoration and strange images that attract the worshippers' gaze and hinder their devotion. . . . O vanity of vanities, yet no more vain than insane. The church is resplendent in its walls, but its poor go in want; she clothes her stones in gold, and leaves her sons naked; the rich man's eye is fed at the expense of the indigent.

A short while later another prominent abbot, Suger of St.-Denis, undertook a major renovation of his church and proudly entered the praises of this lavish work in a personal account of his years in office. He dwelled lovingly on the treasures and ornaments of the sanctuary (Fig. 14.2) and in response to the qualms of critics like Bernard, justified his actions with these words:

To me, I confess, one thing has always seemed preeminently fitting: that every costlier and

costliest thing should serve, first and foremost, for the administration of the Holy Eucharist. . . . The detractors also object that a saintly mind, a pure heart, a faithful intention ought to suffice for this sacred function: and we too explicitly and especially affirm that it is these that principally matter. [But] we profess that we must do homage also through . . . outward ornaments . . . with all inner purity and with all outward splendor.

Suger was not a Cluniac. His defense was not in support of the form and trappings of the kind of Romanesque church that incensed Bernard. St.-Denis was not in fact a Romanesque structure at all, but a venerable Carolingian foundation. Suger transformed this aging building, for the first time in three centuries, and did so in a manner knowingly different from current usage. To him there was an ineffableness to Godhead that might be conveyed in this material world through richly refractive, light-filled effects—through precious stones, stained glass, and an architecture that reduced matter as much as possible and made the walls transparent.

Each in his own way, therefore, both of these two French prelates were challenging the tenets of the Romanesque church at its Cluniac apogee: one by stripping it of its art and furnishings and its pretentious monumentality, the other by substituting for it a seductive new architecture of the utmost tenuousness and a jewellike quality. In the end, the purist ethic of Bernard and Suger's translucent inventions set in motion the development of a style we call

Gothic. They started from opposite impulses—from plainness and glitter—and reached a common truth: that fundamentals of architecture such as light, proportion, and the handling of building materials can suggest an otherworldly setting as movingly and convincingly as does the applied content of figurative art and surface decoration.

The Cistercian Challenge

To understand the Cistercian revolution, we must highlight the regal ambience of Cluny in its latest guise.

The phenomenal prosperity of the monastery can be explained in part by its location, which was subject neither to the empire nor to the French monarchy. The total allegiance of the order to the pope released it from more immediate feudal pressures. In less than two hundred years, under shrewd abbots like Odo, Hugh of Semur, and Peter the Venerable, the small installation of the early tenth century in the valley of the Grosne in the heart of Burgundy grew into a small town. It amassed a prodigious wealth in real property. It subjected hundreds of once-independent abbeys in every part of Europe, demoting them to priories governed by the mother house. Its inmates, some five hundred strong, left the care of their lands and herds to a lower class of monks, the *conversi*, while they themselves supervised the ceaseless amplification of their home and the affairs of their monastic federation. The remaining time was occupied by long

323

drawn-out services that left little room for meditation, and none for physical labor.

There was no pretense to promote the balanced life prescribed by the Benedictine Rule, with the days divided to accommodate the celebration of the liturgy, the study of the Scriptures, and manual work. In its wealth and world-oriented magnificence, Cluny had also buried the primary monkish urges of withdrawal, poverty, and an existence of humble wants. Cluniacs were not the monks who, in the words of Bernard of Clairvaux, "have cut ourselves off from the people . . . left all the precious and beautiful things of the world for the sake of Christ . . . and in order that we may obtain Christ, considered but dung everything that is fair to see or soothing to hear, sweet to smell, delightful to taste or pleasant to touch." The transformation of a pious community into a socioeconomic instrument of state had already been achieved under Charlemagne. Now the monastery had gone on to become an affluent state unto itself.

The layout of Cluny obeyed, after a fashion, the Benedictine scheme worked out in the councils of Charlemagne. (Fig. 14.1) But some telling points of difference emerge when we compare Cluny with the St. Gall plan for the ideal Carolingian monastery. (Fig. 12.18) Units assigned to farming activities on the St. Gall plan have been eliminated. Cluny farmed through tenants. A wing for the *conversi*, apart from the claustral area, reflects the segregation of menial tasks. The brothers' chief occupation is apparent from the staggering size of the church whose relation to its predecessors on the site can easily be gauged by the two ends of the old church, the choir, and the entrance vestibule, incorporated into the latest cloister. Next to the spared choir is the chapter house—a novelty. The reading of the house Rule, a ritual formerly performed in the arm of the cloister adjacent to the church, has now been given its own building. The place was in fact a council room for the administrative deliberations of the chapter. The building communicated with a small church of its own, the Lady Chapel (so-called because of its dedication to the Virgin Mary), which also served the large infirmary behind it. Both the chapter house and Lady Chapel will become stock

Fig. 14.1 Cluny (France), principal abbey of the Cluniac order, third construction phase, 1095 and following; reconstruction view from the southeast, as it appeared in 1157. The church is on the right, and the infirmary buildings are in the foreground, with the cloister area immediately beyond.

elements of the later medieval monastery and will receive special care, especially in England.

But the glory of Cluny does not reside in its planning. Contemporaries marveled at its appointments, its exquisite art, the psalmody in the main church, the size of the whole which could handle 1,200 monks and *conversi* in its dormitories and dining halls, thousands in the church, and forty noblemen and forty noblewomen in twin palaces. There were twelve bathhouses and a number of fountains, all fed by running water from concealed conduits. The model for such installations was surely Muslim Spain. The church had two transepts and fifteen extruding chapels. Both crossings were marked with towers, and so were the

ends of the westernmost transept and the facade. There was some stained glass in the windows. The choir capitals featured personifications of the nine tones of Gregorian chant. A few of these capitals survive. Their superb quality tells us how much we have lost when the angry crowds of the French Revolution turned their long simmering hatred of churchly privilege against what remained of the legendary abbey which Emile Mâle, the distinguished French scholar, has called "the greatest creation of the Middle Ages."

The church can now be called to memory only in the painstaking reconstructions of Kenneth Conant. The marble cloister and its carved and painted capitals—a boundless array of Old and New Testament scenes, the miracles and martyrdoms of saints, along with creatures of fantasy— might be glimpsed in derivative cloisters at Moissac, Arles, and Toulouse that have come through. (Fig. 14.3) In these you can still see "that marvellous and deformed comeliness, that comely deformity," that Bernard recoiled from:

those unclean apes, those fierce lions, those monstrous centaurs, those half-men . . . those fighting knights, those hunters winding their horns. . . . For God's sake, if men are not ashamed of these follies, why at least do they not shrink from the expense?

The architect of the church at Cluny was Gunzo, a cleric known principally as a musician. Indeed, he was probably thought especially qualified to be an architect because he was a musician. St. Augustine had explained centuries earlier that music was

Fig. 14.3 Moissac (France), Cluniac priory; view of the cloister, ca. 1100.

Fig. 14.2 The chalice of Abbot Suger, mid-twelfth century, originally at St.-Denis. (National Gallery of Art, Washington D.C.) Suger describes it in his writings as being made "out of one solid sardonyx . . . in which . . . the sard's red hue, by varying its property, so keenly vies with the blackness of the onyx that one property seems to be bent on trespassing upon the other."

"the science of good modulation," and that the nature of the science was mathematical. It was based on a system of ratios of which the most important were that of equality—i.e., 1:1—and then the perfect consonances of an octave, fifth, and fourth—1:2, 2:3, and 3:4. These same principles, according to Augustine, applied to the visual arts, architecture included. For the later medieval mind, "musical" numbers were fundamental to the order and stability of the universe. Proportional schemes are of course a function of geometry, and geometry was, like music, an "anagogical" activity—that is, it had the ability to lead the mind from the world of appearances to the contemplation of the divine order. It is not surprising that so much attention should be paid to geometric proportions in later medieval architecture, and that even in its wildest expressive fury Romanesque sculp-

ture should follow in its structure and composition a firm regimen of geometry. Professor Conant has found ample proof for the use of "musical" numbers in the proportions of the church at Cluny, along with a modular unit of five Roman feet (about 1.5 meters).

Bernard was, of course, right. The inordinate, dizzying height of the nave accommodated nothing practical, any more than it did in Hagia Sophia. Stretched beyond belief, the nave piers would have disgusted a Greek and astounded a Roman. This is not a question of size alone: Roman imperial buildings are not inferior in that. It is rather that Romanesque interiors like that of Cluny, or the extant St.-Sernin at Toulouse that resembles it, are single-minded in their spatial celebration of verticality. (Fig. 14.4) Rome worked with both dimensions. It was the spilling of space into

Fig. 14.4 Cluny III, abbey church, 1095–1130; reconstruction of the nave, looking east.

a piling up of curved forms at the two ends and the swooping lateral arch curtains.

In the Romanesque interior the supports shoot up from the floor to the vaults and down to the floor again on the other side, sometimes in a single line, sometimes staggered into storeys. The capital when present is too small, too unpronounced; its load too linear for it to appear as a free noteworthy agent. No distinction is made between lower and upper space; the superstructure is not sufficiently differentiated as in the Roman building, nor hierarchically focused as in Hagia Sophia. The forward drive toward the altar is obsessive, at least until the crossing, and so is the upward pull. The whole is tensile and tense, not particularly peaceful. The worshipper was always a bit on edge, one imagines; the senses heightened; the experience exciting rather than serene.

This then was Cluny. And the Cistercian way was the harsh antithesis. "None of our monasteries is to be constructed in towns, castles or villages," the First Chapter of the order's Institutes reads, "but in places remote from human intercourse." And also from the human jurisdiction of a bishop or lay lord, we might add. From the mother house in the marshes of Cîteaux, teams of twelve monks under an abbot set out in search of out-of-the-way wildernesses in the opening years of the twelfth century. And from this first generation of abbeys new offshoots reached out, with the determination to touch every corner of the Christian world. There were 742 Cistercian monasteries at the end of the Middle Ages, from Ireland to Greece and the Holy Land, and an equal number of nunneries.

The sites lay commonly by a stream in a forlorn valley. To tame a bit of wild nature

ample lateral rooms in buildings like the basilica of Maxentius that produced a balance of height and width. (Fig. 11.10) Also, the vertical supports remained free of the vaults, and it was for the vaults to billow upward from points of concentration as though puffed up by a purposeful wind, free to establish their own reservoirs of space different from that of the hall below. In short, the bays were few and big; the great arches were lateral rather than transverse; and the vertical support was still a column, with a base to stand on, a florid head to wear.

Two hundred years later, the architects of Hagia Sophia had obscured side spaces by column screens. (Fig. 11.28) They had also carried to extremes the distinction between structure and appearance, you will recall, a distinction already present in Roman building where the giant columns seem to do all the work of carrying the vaults, but do not really do so. The purpose in Justinian's masterpiece was a floating dome, toward which the building aspired through

Fig. 14.5 Fontenay (France), Cistercian abbey, 1139–47; the forge and mill building.

through relentless toil was the basic drive; the help of *conversi* never absolved the monk of working the land and raising animals. The order became expert in agronomy, stockbreeding, and forestry. And in the process they grew rich, managing property that included mills, mines, farms, and even villages. But that was not the motive of this ascetic, fanatical movement. It stood for self-sacrifice and hard work, and against display or distraction of any sort. It rejected any scholarly or artistic spur to create. It scorned knowledge, literature, and the production of art works. And the architecture it could not do without was severely restricted in what it could invent or express.

Cistercians took full advantage of the machine-oriented technology of the later Middle Ages and advanced it diligently. They understood water power well. They used the stream that passed through their premises to operate machinery for crushing wheat, sieving flour, fulling cloth, tanning, and probably also for the bellows that kept fires alive under the beer vats. Dams barred the water flow for the more efficient activation of mills. Hundreds of oak piles were rammed into the riverbed to form a series of parallel palisades. The space between them was then filled with earth, gravel, and boulders to make the dam watertight. Cistercian factories, of which some survive, also deserve attention. Every monastery had one, often as large as the church and built just alongside it. (Fig. 14.5) Here iron from nearby mines would be forged into clamps, rods, locks, and nails.

The formula for the monastery grounds never changed. (Fig. 14.6) The church was on the north side, with the cloister immediately to its south. The refectory further south stood at right angles to the cloister walk, to allow for a kitchen between it and the refectory of the *conversi* to the west. Chapter house, common room, and a small room for novices were lined along the east side, and stairs led up to the dormitory that extended over the whole range. This grouping produced impressive rectangular buildings cadenced externally by ground-storey buttresses. There was no bath-house, and no separate abbot's residence. Everything was built of pale, smooth-hewn stones. Even latrines and corridors had stone vaults. Columns, pillars, and windows all rested on one continuous base. Plastering was not allowed, since it was the first step to mural decoration. And for that there was no tolerance whatever: "We forbid there to be any statues or pictures in our churches or in any other rooms of a monastery of ours, because, when attention is paid to such things, the advantages of sound meditation and training in religious gravity are often neglected."

The church conformed to the strict overall rectangularity of the composition. The sanctuary was square. A series of square chapels were created along the eastern side of the transept by means of partitions perpendicular to the transept wall. A door in

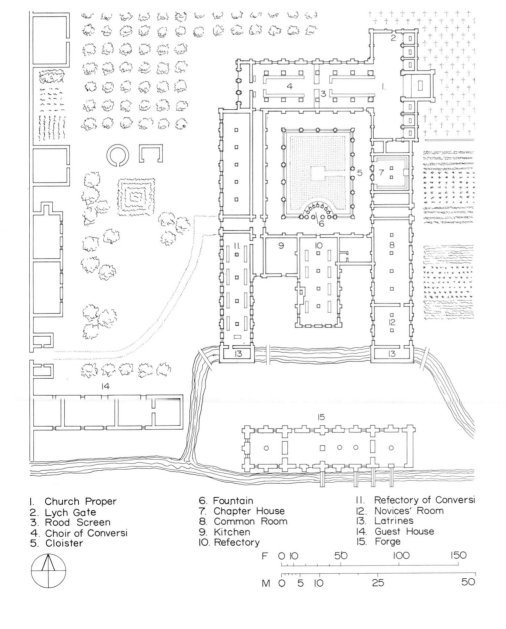

1. Church Proper
2. Lych Gate
3. Rood Screen
4. Choir of Conversi
5. Cloister
6. Fountain
7. Chapter House
8. Common Room
9. Kitchen
10. Refectory
11. Refectory of Conversi
12. Novices' Room
13. Latrines
14. Guest House
15. Forge

F 0 10   50   100   150

M 0 5 10   25   50

Fig. 14.6 Ideal Cistercian monastery; ground plan.

the north transept arm, the so-called lych-gate, was used when bodies were carried to the graveyard after the funeral service. In the south arm, a staircase communicating with the dormitory was for night use. A rood screen separated the monks' half of the church from that of the *conversi,* who arrived through a corridor that ran between the claustral buildings and their own. There was no monumental facade, and no towers could accentuate the outer mass. The windows were to have clear panes. The attraction of the then fashionable stained glass brought a stern warning from the General Chapter of 1182: "Stained glass windows are to be replaced within the space of two years; otherwise the abbot, prior and cellarer are henceforward all to fast on bread and water every sixth day until they are replaced."

What then was left for the architect? What kept the church from looking like the forge or the dormitories? Intellectualized environments of faith, conducive to introspective, abstract spirituality, are not easy to bring off. To make certain they do not look secular or boring or both, one has to rely on beautiful construction with perfect, lucid detailing, a special feel for light, and a sense for architectural proportion which is infallible. Vague words all: beautiful, special, infallible. There is always an element of vagueness in discussing buildings that move us. It is never sheer size that is impressive but the quality of size; never the nature of the materials but their handling. One has rules, of course, and they ensure competent, satisfying buildings. But they alone do not account for the making of eloquent places.

Cistercian architecture had its rules too. St. Augustine's "perfect" ratio of 1:2 controls the elevation and ground plan; for example, the relations of the total length of the church to the width of the transept, the width of the transept to its depth, the width of the nave to that of the side aisles. The bays of the aisles are of equal length and width, and the same dimension is marked off vertically by a string-course on the nave wall; so we have files of spatial cubes on both sides of the nave. The number, size, and location of windows may have been determined more intuitively than accord-

Fig. 14.7 Fontenay, abbey church; interior, looking east.

ing to precise theory. (Fig. 14.7) The general value is muted. Soft spots or tracts of light are made to fall on inky shadows that dissolve the crisp right angles of the masonry. And of course the acoustical properties of Cistercian churches are well attested to. We cannot hope to appreciate the devotional experience of these stripped, stark churches without the limpid echoes of antiphonal song that filled their space for so many hours of the day.

The Gothic Challenge

The abbey of St.-Denis is a stone's throw from Paris. (Fig. 14.8) In the twelfth century this region was at the center of the royal domain. Paris was the Capetian capital—two sandy islands in the Seine enclosed within new walls in the first part of the century,

with a citadel on the right bank and an undefended settlement on the left. At Reims nearby, the kings were crowned and anointed; at St.-Denis, they were buried. In terms of religious architecture the region was unadventurous. The Romanesque had been nurtured by later Benedictine monasticism and its most influential order, Cluny. The unswerving loyalty of the Cluniacs, and in time the Cistercians, to the throne of St. Peter made them as much a threat to the nationalist aims of the royal house as the powerful nobles who had set claim to most of the land. It should not surprise us that an architectural style born to serve monasticism and feudalism would not thrive in the Île-de-France, the territory within a 160-kilometer (100-mile) radius from Paris which was held by the crown.

We should also expect that when the kings came to have the upper hand, they would seek an architectural idiom of their own. The Gothic style was launched in an abbey, but a royal abbey. Suger rose, like Bernard, from the cloister; but he served the French kings first. He busily mediated a national reconciliation between church and crown in the struggle against the feudal nobility on the one hand, and the international ambitions of the empire on the other. From St.-Denis the new style, which contemporary sources would soon baptize the French or modern style (*opus Francigenum, opus modernum*), pushed outward in direct relation to the widening of the king's jurisdiction and influence. Its first, full-blown creations were cathedrals in the cities of the royal domain—Chartres, Amiens, Reims, Bourges. In this respect, too, the Gothic is an affirmation of a national surge, as it came to supersede the style that had primarily catered to an antiurban patronage of monks and lords. These cathedrals, in their financing and iconography, will be the exquisite stage for the political and social contests that will be waged among kings, prelates, noble houses, and merchants and artisans of the aroused cities.

There was of course nothing overtly royal about the Gothic form: the identification was associative. Religion contained all in the Middle Ages. No ruler could hope to gain by opposing it openly or by neglecting its outward adornment. In his writings Suger assesses the novelty of his architectural work in theological terms; the work was after all a new choir and facade for a canonical Christian building. What imparts the political message is the context of the building, its unique relationship to the kings of France.

St.-Denis, the apostle of France, was clearly perfect as the national saint. His church aroused patriotic as well as religious sentiments. It was here that Pepin and Charlemagne had been consecrated kings; here that Pepin and Charles the Bald had

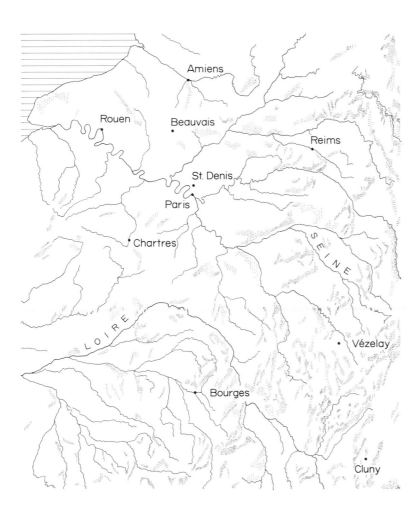

Fig. 14.8 Map: Île-de-France, with the main sites of Gothic churches.

329

been buried. When the emperor, in a dispute with the pope threatened to invade France in 1124, King Louis VI was able to rally the country through an emotional homage to the saint's banner that became from then on the official standard of the royal arms. The king called the abbey "the capital of the realm," and indeed St.-Denis now became the first true religious center of France, and the symbol of the partnership between the royal house and the national church. Louis granted the abbey jurisdiction over the fair held on the feast day of St.-Denis. He also deposited the crown of his father Philip I in the saint's treasury. Prior to the departure of the king's successor, Louis VII, on the Second Crusade, the Royal Assembly chose Suger to be regent of France.

Details of the undertaking, and Suger's own words, leave little doubt that he thought of the rebuilding of St.-Denis as the mystical celebration of a resurgent French monarchy, and of the design as a model for the religious architecture of the realm. To the educated medieval mind things were more than they seemed. Clusters of meaning clung to the bare built forms as they did to banners, odd occurrences, or geometric configurations. These meanings the privileged could expound with erudition, and the common people could intuit vaguely. Perhaps we should not single out the Middle Ages. All public architecture, and we have seen this continually in this story, has significance beyond its mere utility. The user brings to it, and therefore takes from it, much more than the material frame warrants. In the fully developed Gothic cathedral this web of meanings was perhaps more richly spun than for any other building type we have so far considered. And to begin to unravel it, we must heed Suger's view of what it was he thought he had achieved.

St.-Denis was really two different historical people who had been mistakenly fused. The third-century missionary who had converted France thus appropriated the writ-

ings of a fifth-century Eastern mystic, Denis the Pseudo-Areopagite. In these writings, Neoplatonic philosophy blends with Christian theology, especially the gospel according to St. John which espouses the doctrine of Christ as the true Light illuminating the world. Suger shared with a number of his illustrious contemporaries a fascination in the intricate symbolism of light. At the famous cathedral school of Chartres most notably, light was discussed as the noblest of natural phenomena, the least material, the closest approximation to pure form. This aspect of Neoplatonic metaphysics also embroidered into the symbolism a rational, mathematical way of

thinking, which we saw at work both in Cluniac and Cistercian circles, and which went back to St. Augustine's interpretation of the passage from the Wisdom of Solomon, "Thou hast ordered all things in measure and number and weight." The cosmos, in the minds of those at the Chartres school, was a work of architecture designed by God in accordance with a system of mathematical proportions. To Thomas Aquinas and Hugh of St. Victor in the next century, beauty has two main characteristics: consonance of parts, or proportion, and luminosity.

The new emphasis on light is what distinguishes Gothic architecture, aestheti-

Fig. 14.9 St.-Denis (France), abbey church, Suger's choir, begun 1144; ground plan. The plan of the new choir is superimposed on that of the eighth-century Carolingian transept and ninth-century apse extension.

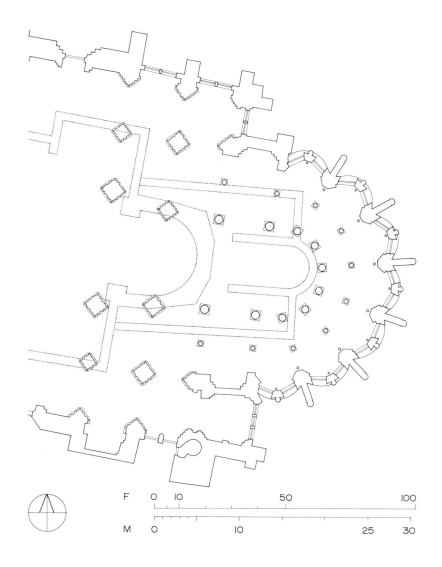

F   0   10   50   100

M   0   10   25   30

Fig. 14.10 St.-Denis, abbey church; interior view of Suger's choir.

cally and theologically, from the Romanesque. For both periods the church stood as an image of Heaven, as the city of God. There are two basic texts that describe what this city is like: the Book of Tobias and the Apocalypse of St. John the Divine. Both stress the terrible, cataclysmic events that will occur before one can enter the city of God, and this is what the Romanesque chose to elucidate in its art. But the descriptive passages invoke a gem-encrusted, translucent, shining vision: "And the building of the wall thereof was jasper and the city pure gold like unto clear glass." That is what the Gothic cathedrals of the Île-de-France will set out to celebrate. And where this crystalline architecture begins is Suger's new choir for St.-Denis.

Look at the plan and compare it to the choir plan of Cluny or Ste.-Foy at Conques. (Figs. 14.9, 13.10) We have a double ambulatory at St.-Denis from which radiate nine chapels. But the outer ambulatory and the chapels actually merge, and the radial alignment of the piers and columns from a single center within the apse makes it possible to bring exterior light to the apse unobstructed. In fact, the curves of the chapels are opened almost in their entirety to the outside. They swing between wedge-shaped piers reinforced by buttresses that continue the radial lines of the columns of the apse and the first ambulatory. Each chapel curve has one more slim pier in the middle—and that is all the solid matter of the choir's exterior outline. (Fig. 14.10) The rest is light, or more accurately many pieces of stained glass that are fitted together into religious paintings. "The entire sanctuary," Suger writes ecstatically, "is thus pervaded by a wonderful and continuous light entering through the most sacred windows."

This is the first point we should remember about the Gothic cathedral. We talk of it as a luminous, light-filled environment and contrast it to the gloomy interiors of Romanesque churches. But, in reality, Gothic interiors were not at all bright. The thick, colored panes of the stained glass glowed only under direct sunlight, and even then it was a muted, chromatic illumination they engendered. It was precisely that rich, deep, encrusted transparency that recalled the bejeweled structure of heavenly

Jerusalem: "And I saw the holy city, new Jerusalem, coming down out of heaven from God . . . having the glory of God: her light was like unto a stone more precious, as it were a jasper stone. . . ."

This then was no ordinary light. It sifted through sacred pictures and was transmuted into something new, the new light, *lux nova,* which is how Suger refers to Christ. We can understand his love of sumptuous treasures in the sanctuary, his belief that the costliest materials were the only ones befitting the holy ritual of Mass. Sensual experience was the elementary step. Our mind rises to the truth with the aid of material things. But rise it must, from the material to the immaterial *(de materialibus ad immaterialia,* in his words), and the diaphanous cage of the church, like the precious fittings of the sanctuary, will release us to this transcendence.

How, then, is this diaphanous aura to be contrived? How can the walls that must be there to hold up the lofty vaults of these

immense stone buildings be displaced by fragile expanses of glass? This is the epic of Gothic technology that has absorbed historians and amazed generations of modern visitors.

At the center of the discussion stand three structural expedients: the pointed arch, the vault rib, and the flying buttress. None is the invention of Gothic builders. Nor for

that matter is stained glass. It is important to emphasize this point, because all too often the Gothic cathedral has been lauded as the triumph of structural logic—the end result of a series of experiments in the pursuit of reduced matter and its elastic distribution. The technology required of such a sprightly armature already existed in pieces in the Romanesque period. But technology

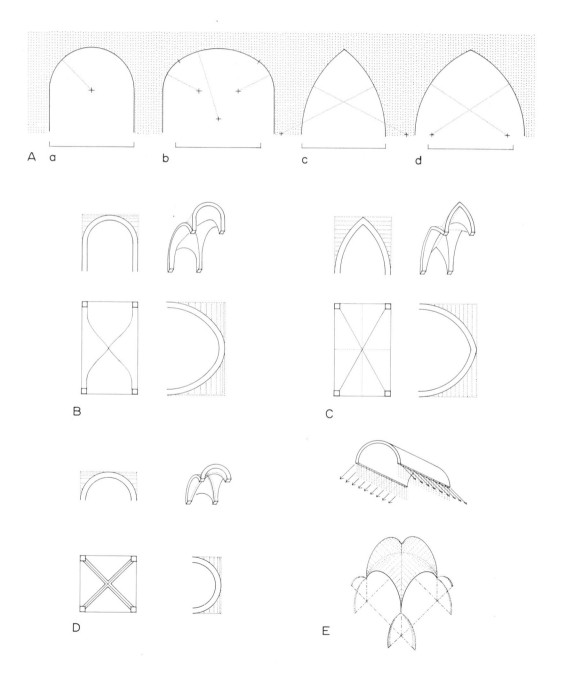

Fig. 14.11 Medieval vaulting; diagrams. The top row (**A**) shows arch elevations in relation to a unit bay represented by the uniform bar. The bay can be spanned using a round-headed arch (**a**), or with a pointed arch struck from two centers that lie outside the bay width (**c**). To span a bay that is wider than the unit, arch (**a**) must be struck from three centers, which flattens and weakens it considerably (**b**); whereas arch (**c**), struck from centers which now fall within the arch span, remains structurally sound (**d**).

These principles are applied here in the diagrams, which show the vaulting of actual three-dimensional bays. A standard square bay (**D**) can take a groin vault generated by four equal round arches. A rectangular bay (**B**) needs round arches of two different widths, in order to reach a common crown line; the arch spanning the broader dimension of the bay, flattened as in (**A–b**) above, will thus be weak. By using pointed arches on a rectangular bay, the architect can eliminate this structural weakness (**C**).

The two sketches at the bottom right (**E**) contrast the thrust of a barrel vault (top), which is continuous along two sides, and a groin vault, whose thrust is concentrated at the four corners of the bay. Therefore, buttressing must be done along the entire length of the barrel vault, but only at the four supports of the groin vault.

needs a vision to become a style; you must want to say something with it before it is inspirited. Roman concrete, long in pedestrian use, was lifted to expressive eloquence by the heady venture of a young empire. Gothic architects put together the principles of the pointed arch, the vault rib, and the flying buttress, marrying these rational links to stained glass, in response to an exultant mysticism of light and the coincident rejuvenation of France under the fresh vigor of her kings.

The pointed arch, which is an arch struck from two adjacent centers, has a double advantage. (Fig. 14.11) It tends to disperse loads more effectively than its round-headed cousin, as Muslim architects appreciated almost from the start; and it is better suited for the cross-vaulting of an oblong bay. This second fact is so, because you can easily vary the degrees of pointing and come up to the same crown line despite the unequal width of the bay sides. With round-headed arches defining the four sides of an oblong bay, the crown line can be held even only by depressing one pair of arches, which in turn would make them more prone to collapse. And why would you want to cross-vault a bay? A barrel vault exerts uniform pressure on its walls. By crossing two barrels at right angles you can conduct the weight of the vault along the groins and concentrate it in four points at the corners of the bay. These points of maximum thrust can then be buttressed individually with half-arches at right angles to them, which is what a flying buttress really is. This is clearly more economical than having to meet the outward push of a barrel vault through some extensive construction along the flanks.

In Cluniac Burgundy, these structural assets were seized on to enliven Romanesque statics. Groin-vaulted aisles were common, although their bays were likely to be square. At places like Autun, the transverse relieving arches of the nave barrels were slightly pointed. Gunzo's church at Cluny had buttressing arches that were visible above the aisle roofs, even if they were being used with a typical Romanesque barrel vault. Norman architects at sites like Caen in northwest France, or Durham just south of the Scottish border, experimented precociously with the third telltale

device of Gothic construction, the vault rib. They used it to reinforce the ridges of groin vaults, and did so over large spans of the nave. Norman vaults are made of rubble and are very heavy. This system of reinforcement distributed this weight more efficiently. The diagonal ribs spanned two of the oblong bays at a time, which together made a square. The issue of holding to a uniform crown line in the sequence of oblong bays was thus circumvented. These two-bay rib vaults are called sexpartite, from the fact that the three transverse and two diagonal ribs subdivide the vault into six curved triangles.

The Gothic advance on this score was to see the potential of the rib as an independent cross-element that could facilitate the construction of the vault by allowing the triangles to be built one by one like webbing, and with minimal centering that would be moved from one triangle to the next. The rib cage was therefore no longer bonded into the masonry of the vault, but rather preceded it. But once freed of the masonry bulk it is supposed to strengthen, and with the pointed arch there to negotiate varying widths, the rib could span bays of any shape, turn corners, proliferate like the branches of a tree.

Look again at Suger's choir from this perspective, and you can forgive him his excitement, his unmonkish boastfulness: single columns launching graceful shoots of masonry; taut, thin vaults distended between them; an even gauze of light hanging softly under this delicate but brisk canopy. Remember, too, that he saw things symbolically, anagogically, that he understood *edification* to mean both the manual labor of construction and the spiritual process of instruction. Columns were apostles and prophets; Jesus, "the keystone that joins one wall to another." He believed also, along with his learned contemporaries at Chartres and elsewhere, in the analogical nature of beauty, that it partakes of a mystical prototype. See it all through his eyes. Then his words will seem not fancy spinnings of a man of letters, but an earnest attempt to explain what to him was a palpable experience.

When—out of my delight in the beauty of the house of God—the loveliness of the many-

colored gems has called me away from external cares, and worthy meditation has induced me to reflect, transferring that which is material to that which is immaterial, on the diversity of the sacred virtues: then it seems to me that I see myself dwelling, as it were, in some strange region of the universe which neither exists entirely in the slime of the earth nor entirely in the purity of Heaven; and that, by the grace of God, I can be transported from this inferior to that higher world in an anagogical manner.

Chartres

The success of Suger's work was immediate in the Île-de-France. Before he had a chance to extend the new manner of the choir and the west front to the rest of this Carolingian church, several neighboring cities raced to capitalize on the structural and aesthetic lessons of St.-Denis and the political prestige that attended the undertaking. Sens Cathedral was probably first; Paris, Noyon, Senlis, and Laon followed in short order. In 1174, thirty years after the glittering dedication ceremonies at St.-Denis, an architect named William from the workshop at Sens was invited to Canterbury to advise on the building of the cathedral choir that had just been destroyed in a fire. The international career of the Gothic style was thus inaugurated. For the next three hundred years the premises of the architectural revolution that started at St.-Denis will be tested, improved on, embellished, pushed to the limits of constructional sanity—and then beyond.

Chartres Cathedral, the noblest and best loved of Gothic churches, epitomizes the classic harvest of early Gothic design. The several campaigns of building from 1130 to the middle of the thirteenth century bring together in one frame several climactic moments in the biography of this *opus Francigenum*, this most consummately French of architectural styles.

Chartres possessed the tunic the Virgin Mary had worn at the Nativity. It was a gift of Charles the Bald, who had obtained it from Constantinople, and it began the association of the royal house of France with this little town on the fringes of the Beauce. The popularity of the sacred garment was such that Chartres had become by 1100 the center of Mariolatry in France, a cult that swept the later Middle Ages. At the famous cathedral school of Chartres, she was extolled as the Seat of Wisdom, the Christian counterpart of the wise virgin of Classical antiquity, Athena. To the people she was the sweet intercessor, gentle and compassionate, a feminine blend of love and suffering. On her feast days, four times a year, great crowds converged upon this hill-town in the midst of its rich grain fields to revere the tunic and take part in lively fairs. (Fig. 14.12)

In the eleventh century a wood-roofed Romanesque church had replaced the original basilica which had burned down and been rebuilt several times since Early Christian times. (Fig. 14.13) Most of the foundation work under the nave of the present cathedral goes back to this church, and so does the basic scheme of the choir with its three radiating chapels. The older church may also have set the proportions of the plan, especially the bays of the aisles and nave and their relative widths. Then, in the 1130s, a campaign of extension and modernization was launched. The money came from the grain trade, the silver mines of the bishops of Chartres and the real property of the chapter, and the city's own revenues from the manufacture of textiles, weapons, and harnesses. A new twin-tower facade was started some distance from the western limit of the Romanesque church as the first step toward extending the nave. The sculpture for this facade was being completed in the very years during which Suger was busy refashioning his church 90 kilometers (55 miles) away.

These Royal Portals, as they are called, represent for the figurative program of the Western church the same shift from the Romanesque that the choir of St.-Denis marks for architecture. The quiet, noble subjects may well be a response to Bernard's condemnation of the lurid repertory of Romanesque sculptors. What is presented is a rational and full commentary on the manifestation of the divine, free of the obsessive Doomsday fears of the Romanesque portals. The emphasis is on the wholeness of the religious experience, on

Fig. 14.12 Chartres (France), the cathedral seen across a grain field.

Fig. 14.13 Chartres Cathedral; ground plans and section. The small plan shows the eleventh-century Romanesque church of Bishop Fulbert as it was in ca. 1100. The present cathedral dates from 1194 to 1260, but the west front is earlier (ca. 1140). In our plan we omit the chapel that was added to the east of the choir in the fourteenth century. The urban context is derived from a pre-modern map.

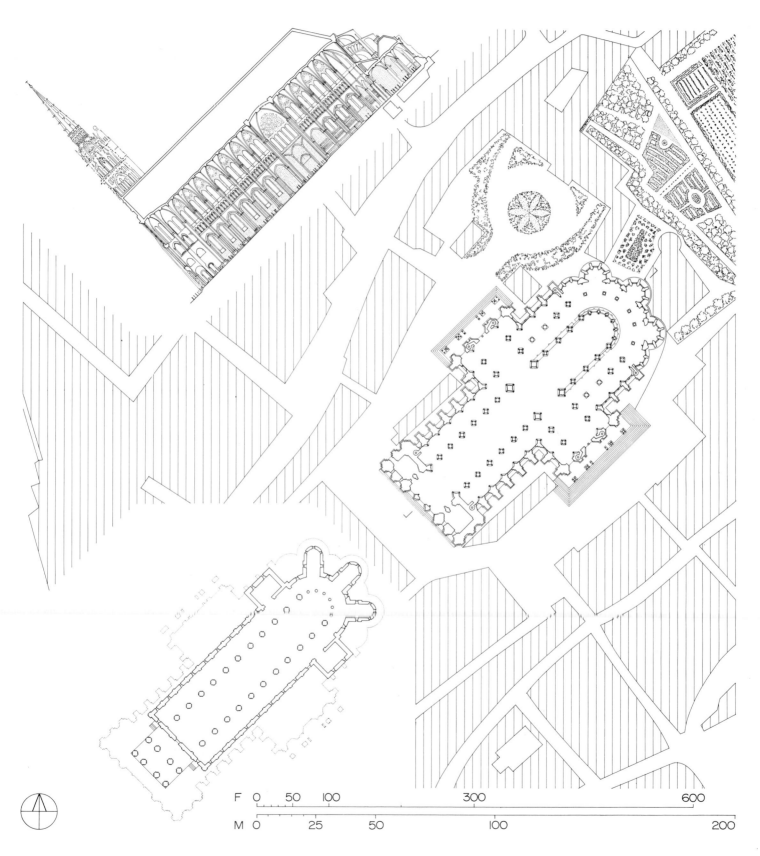

Fig. 14.14 Chartres Cathedral; west facade, Royal Portal, ca. 1145. Compare this with the Romanesque portal sculpture at Conques, Fig. 13.12.

Fig. 14.15 Chartres Cathedral; view of the nave looking west, with the great rose window from the early thirteenth century.

knowledge as a prerequisite of salvation. On the right portal, with diagrammatic clarity, scenes relating to the Incarnation of Christ are displayed; the critical episodes of His childhood culminate in the tympanum, with a large image of the enthroned Virgin holding the Child, surrounded by the seven liberal arts in the framing arches. It is the world of the intellect, with Christ as the ultimate object of all learning. On the left portal the main subject is the Ascension, framed by the signs of the zodiac and the occupations of each month. Christ here is the lord of heaven and earth, of time and its activities. The stress is on menial work, on the eternal cycles of nature and life. In the central portal we see Christ in majesty. (Fig. 14.14) Below him are the apostles; and further down, the columns of the staggered tympanum arches hold in front of them attenuated, columnlike statues of personages from the Old Testament and kings and queens of France in biblical guise. The architectural idea for these statue-columns, which extend to the side portals, was borrowed from Suger's facade at St.-Denis of several years before. The theme is fully in sympathy with his royalist aims—the translation into stone of a prayer that had been part of the coronation rites since Carolingian times, when the Lord was entreated to bestow virtues of Old Testament kings on the anointed rulers of France.

Supported by these regal figures of remote and recent times, and encompassed by apostles, angels, and the twenty-four elders of the Apocalypse who witness His return, Christ sits in an aureole of glory. Heraldically displayed around it are the symbolic beasts of the four evangelists that "rest not day and night, saying, 'Holy, holy, holy, Lord God Almighty, which was, and is, and is to come.' " Nothing is intimated of the punishments and rewards to be meted out at the Second Coming. The worshippers know of these in their hearts. The sculptors choose to celebrate the event itself, gravely and with dignity, to show Christ as the humane Judge from Whom mercy and compassion are to be expected. In a way this recalls the change in ancient Greece from the Archaic ethos to the Classical; here, too, we are at a turning point where fear is brushed aside by awareness.

To know is its own serious burden. To know one's place in the scheme of things is to act with self-respect, to anticipate intelligently, to endure nobly.

The new facade was half complete when disaster struck. The two towers had been raised to a height of three storeys. Between them, corresponding to the Royal Portals, were three lancet windows of stained glass. The lancets lighted a stone-vaulted vestibule that was linked with the Romanesque cathedral beyond. Then, on the night of 10 June 1194, a fire swept through a large part of the town, sparing nothing in its path. The cathedral all but perished and, with it, the gathering crowds tearfully acknowledged, the sacred tunic of the Virgin Mary, the cornerstone of their existence.

But the Romanesque choir and the new facade with its vestibule, vaulted in stone as they were, had withstood the flames. In the crypt, below the choir, the priests found the tunic unharmed and brought it out to the despairing townspeople. The miracle, it was explained to them, could only mean that Mary wished to be reinstalled in greater splendor. Almost immediately building commenced among the charred anchors of the choir and facade. By 1220 Our Lady of Chartres was ready for consecration. And to the brimming congregations of that first year, it must have been apparent that their new cathedral, in the latest style of the region, was itself something of a miracle. Mary "gave Vulcan leave to ravage the church," as the poet Guillaume le Breton put it; and out of its ashes she had made to rise one of the most beautiful churches of Christendom.

The new nave had to remain relatively short. Since the site is intersected by a fault to the east, the choir could not push outward. Instead, an outer ambulatory in the manner of St.-Denis reduced the depth of the Romanesque radiating chapels, making them less obtrusive, more Gothic. The western limit was fixed by the facade with the Royal Portals. But what the new church could not excel in length, it made up for in height. To account for the disparity in height between the towering nave and the facade of an older day, the architect installed a large rose window above the three lancets already there. (Fig. 14.15) This, too, was an invention of Suger for his facade at St.-

Fig. 14.16 Chartres Cathedral; exterior of south transept. The porch was probably begun in 1224.

Fig. 14.18 Chartres Cathedral; flying buttresses on the south side.

Fig. 14.17 Chartres Cathedral; detail, stained glass window, early thirteenth century, showing the signature scene of the carpenters' guild.

Denis. It was both the sun and the rose, a two-pronged symbol of Christ as the new sun and of Mary as the "rose without thorns," in the words of the litany of Loreto. The transept arms were also capped by magnificent roses. Indeed, these arms were now conceived as monumental units that were terminated by façades with porches and triple portals. (Fig. 14.16) They were an irresistible invitation for sculpture, and much was made of the chance. The main scenes explore Christ's relationship to His mother and to the Church which is His bride. Hundreds of single figures fit into the archivolts and the jambs honoring saints and prophets, martyrs and confessors. The jamb figures, still attached to columns, relax their stance, shift their bodies within full, loosely fitting garments, and incline their heads toward us or toward one another. The austerity of the Royal Portals is softened, humanized.

The bustling workshop of masons and sculptors, glassmakers and metalworkers, carpenters and roofers, labored at fever pitch for thirty years. The architect, whose name we do not know, was sensitive to the latest subtleties of the developing Gothic language, using it gracefully and advancing it to paradigmatic heights. The stone was the handsome, shell-bearing limestone of the nearby Berchères quarries. The clients, legally speaking, were the bishop and the cathedral chapter. But it was as much the city's building, with a wider patronage still. It came into being through the alliance of many elements of French society.

The king and his family had blood ties with the county. The Count of Chartres, a member of the still powerful and rich feudal nobility of France, was actively involved. The monument, in fact, was clearly making a social statement. The rapprochement of church and crown was eroding the power of the landed gentry and its feudal institutions, and the bishop was encourag-

ing the merchant class to join in this partnership. This he did by drawing leaders of the trading community into the cathedral family as honorary members of the chapter, and by supporting their attempts to form associations of those crafts and professions not incorporated into the guilds. These groups had begun to organize religious brotherhoods, with the church's blessing. They now emerged as a respectable party of the social contract, to participate in the building of their cathedral.

The windows of Chartres are the most tangible proof of the broad spectrum of community involvement in the construction of this new cathedral. King Philip Augustus is there, and his daughter-in-law Queen Blanche of Castile, the mother of Louis IX, who paid for the entire façade of the north transept with its great rose window, lancets, and portal sculpture, all exalting Mary and her biblical ancestors. Peter of Dreux, Duke of Brittany, sponsored the windows of the south transept. The noble houses of the Île-de-France—the

Montforts, Courtenays, and Montmorencys—were all represented, their coats of arms emblazoned in stained glass beneath the sacred pictures they had chosen to contribute. The guilds signed with scenes of their professional activities—the joiners and wheelwrights, the coopers, carpenters, armorers, and masons, the butchers, the bakers, the wine merchants. (Fig. 14.17)

All this competitive self-advertisement tended to confound the clarity of the overall program, and to work against the kind of disciplined, coherent iconography of the Royal Portals drawn up under the learned direction of the cathedral school. But the jostle acknowledged an important social reality. Gothic cathedrals were community centers as much as they were halls of faith. We hear repeatedly of their being used for town meetings, courts of law, theatrical and musical presentations. The bishop's church, at least in France, no longer trumpeted his feudal prerogatives. It was now both a national monument and the focus of its city, whose prosperity and pride it announced.

This generous sponsorship of the windows at Chartres tells us something about the architecture of this new cathedral. The transparency of Suger's choir had taken over the entire church. The plan alone should indicate the situation at ground level. The heavy lines of masonry along the perimeter are the flying buttresses. You can see these in the photograph of the exterior: staggered masonry spurs that rise solid until aisle level, perpendicular to the course of the wall, and beyond this point bridge the space above the aisles by arched fliers. (Fig. 14.18) These meet the clerestory wall at the springing of the nave vault, and then again at roof level (a later precaution). The plane of the main flier is cut into by small arcades that become daintier in the later bays, and thus displace more of the masonry. In the spaces between this unexampled carapace, the wall has disappeared for the most part. In its place are large aisle windows at ground level, and an ample clerestory that reaches clear up to the vault. Seen from the inside, the wall elevation shows that the nave arcades and clerestory are of about equal height, with a narrow triforium gallery in the middle which, being blind, runs a band of shadow between the two tall but sheer bands of glass.

Fig. 14.19 Beauvais (France), cathedral of St.-Pierre, begun ca. 1225; interior view looking up into choir vaults.

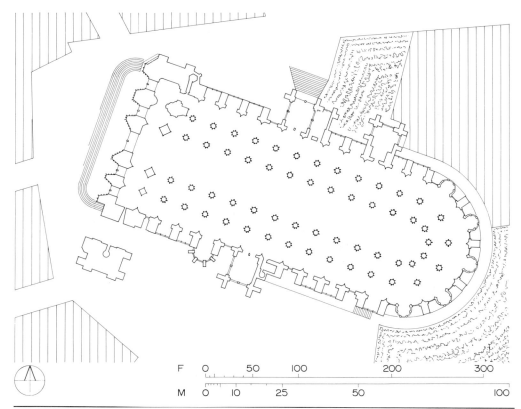

Fig. 14.20 Bourges (France), cathedral of St.-Étienne, 1195–ca. 1250; ground plan.

is free to stand tall, unrestrained as it now is by tribunes above. We look along their height, neatly marked at various levels to respect the horizontal articulation of the wall plane, but are not distracted from their straight course into the clerestory: here our eyes rest on the deep-hued, blue and red carpet of the storied windows. Unseen by us, nimble arches spring over the aisle roofs to stiffen the piers, and to conduct the thrust of the ribbed canopy safely and elegantly down to the ground. Inside and out, all is active energy, seeking and finding its equilibrium.

Gothic Abroad

Reims, Amiens, Beauvais, Bourges—these are the four great sites of the Île-de-France that witness the apogee of the Gothic cathedral beyond Chartres. The critical decades are 1220 to 1270, and a kind of upper limit to High Gothic daringness is signaled by the collapse of the choir at Beauvais cathedral in 1284. These overwhelming structures pushed their competition with Chartres and with one another in a number of ways. Height, surely. The nave vault at Amiens soars to almost 42 meters (138 feet), as opposed to Chartres' 38. The architect of Beauvais strained for more than 45 meters and made it, even if only for ten years. (Fig. 14.19) But this was not, of course, a challenge in the abstract. The Pantheon, after all, is as high; Hagia Sophia higher. The audacity of Jean d'Orbais, Robert de Luzarches, Bernard de Soissons, Hugh Libergier—that new breed of hero-architects who signed their buildings with pride and were prominently buried therein—was to reach ever upward at the same time that they continued to reduce the built mass below the vaults. In the end we can hardly speak of walls at all. The skeleton of clustered piers, rib vaults, and flying buttresses is really all there is of substance—that and the finespun tracery for the glass.

In the plan, the trend is toward an ever more unified space. (Fig. 14.20) Transepts are less pronounced, and they break the body of the church into two almost equal parts: a much enlarged choir area and a

To put side by side the interior views of Chartres and Ste.-Foy, Cluny, or St.-Sernin at Toulouse is to awaken to the profound difference of their vision. (Figs. 13.13, 14.4, 14.15) The time gap is less than one hundred years. The general appearance of these monuments is certainly comparable—they all exhibit tall stone-vaulted naves, layered elevations, and a series of rectangular bays fixed by clustered piers. But where the Romanesque church makes much of these spatial compartments and their heavy march east toward the choir, Chartres avows unity. Where one builds massively and relies on surface ornament to avoid looking oppressive, the other delights in denying the wall its bulk. Where one forgoes clerestory lighting because of the tribune galleries, or else keeps it modest under the mighty barrel vault of the nave so as not to tempt gravity, Chartres glazes each bay with two full windows and reaches for light upward

still with crowning roses. Its fight with gravity is a delicate balancing act. It can hold up better because it has less to hold up. There is no separation at all between structure and appearance. Every visible member does a job and serves also as the linear graph of that job.

The ribs criss-crossing at prodigious heights steady themselves over the nave and let stand lightly upon them thin membranes of masonry. This taut awning uses the nave piers to gain its footing. They are elegant bundles of shafts every one of which conducts a rib down through the clerestory, the triforium, and some of the ground-storey arcade, before it comes to rest on graceful piers that are composed of four slender colonettes attached to an alternately cylindrical and octagonal core. Toward the apse these piers are spaced wider apart to forestall perspective distortion. We look between them at the aisle that

short nave. Bourges has no transept at all. The crypt is gone. In time, the space between flying buttresses tends to be glazed and turned into chapels. Naturalistic ornament blooms on cornices and capitals. It is as if the intellect, long nourished on symbols, were turning to simple observation again. "How great is even the humblest beauty of this world," marvels Vincent de Beauvais; and Thomas Aquinas says he can enjoy natural beauty wholeheartedly even as God Himself rejoices "in all things, because everything is in actual agreement with His being."

As an affirmation of this pantheism, the exterior of the cathedral teems with sculpture of all kinds, biblical as well as mundane. (Fig. 14.21) At its most elaborate, this fertile decoration that fills the portals of the west facade and transepts and spills out onto buttresses, towers, gables, and special niches is an encyclopedic view of knowledge. The desire to be exhaustive is a thirteenth-century trait. Aquinas' *Summa Theologicae* embraced the whole of Christian doctrine; Jacob of Voragine's *Golden Legend,* the lives of saints and Christian festivals. More germane to the reading of cathedral sculpture like the program of Amiens was the *Speculum Majus* by Vincent de Beauvais, a compendium of universal knowledge in eighty books beginning with the natural world, and covering the menial and intellectual arts, virtues and vices, and culminating in the history of humanity from Abel, the first just man, to the modern kings of France.

By mid-century the Gothic style was making inroads in France beyond the crown lands. Le Mans and Coutances gave their cathedrals choirs of the Bourges type; a conservative Burgundian species surfaced at Dijon and Auxerre; and the cathedral of Bayeux in Normandy modernized its Romanesque nave with immense Gothic windows. Chartres spawned Tours and Troyes. But by then the French manner had already been exported widely.

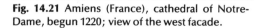

Fig. 14.21 Amiens (France), cathedral of Notre-Dame, begun 1220; view of the west facade.

Fig. 14.22 Winchester (England), cathedral; interior view of north transept, ca. 1080–90.

The Cistercians proved the most effective disseminators. Very early in the game they took for their own a stripped down version of Gothic, without towers, stained glass, and sculpture. Thereafter ribbed vaults sprouted wherever they went as a matter of course. In England, Germany, Spain, and Portugal entire monasteries, from the church to the kitchen and fountain house, proved the versatility of Suger's brainchild. Today the most impressive of the early brood include Poblet Abbey in Catalonia, Eberbach in the Rheingau, and the haunting ruins of Rievaulx and Fountains in England. In France itself, at places like Ourscamp and Royaumont, the order was seduced into coveting the richer effects of Gothic cathedrals with an abandon that would have sent Bernard into a rage. In Greece, on the other hand, opened up to the Latin church by the Fourth Crusade which captured and occupied Constantinople in 1204, they were content with remodeling Byzantine monasteries that were

ceded to them and founding a handful of new ones of very modest proportions.

It was traveling architects who carried the full style of the Île-de-France beyond the French-speaking territories. William of Sens was at Canterbury in 1174; Master Henri at León, Spain, in 1209; and Étienne de Bonneuil in Uppsala, Sweden, in 1287. The buildings themselves speak for the undocumented visits. The cathedral at Toledo belongs to the Bourges family; Cologne Cathedral, not completed until the nineteenth century, mirrors Amiens. Cologne is less interesting than Toledo, because it reproduces its model so ably and wholly. This is the rare exception. More commonly the French manner retouched older churches to make them fashionable. And when Gothic was applied consistently in total rebuilding or new foundations, it was stamped by local preference, construed idiosyncratically, and in this way appropriated. Away from the Île-de-France, the French manner became a license to invent.

To us this is not news. We saw what Sicilian towns did with the Greek temple, how the provinces acknowledged the Roman vaulted style, and what became of the Romanesque style south of the Alps. And we came to take for granted the free spirit of deflection, to see the irrelevance of judging buildings by their fidelity to "pure" models. Reworking fads is an act of imagination. And in any case an architectural paradigm is for the designer only one of several diverse factors that condition the work at hand. Some of the strangest and most memorable buildings are gifts of impurities and mistakes. To look for Chartres in Limburg or Assisi is to miss the joy of two unique contemporaries.

Germany

In examining the Gothic abroad, our first consideration should be the native idiom to which the new style was grafted. Germany, unlike the Île-de-France, had a vigorous home-grown Romanesque that had steered official architecture since the Ottos. The churches combined Carolingian massing with the Lombard bands of the First Romanesque and the elegant planar design of Ottonian interiors like St. Michael's at Hildesheim. In northern Germany and the colonized regions further out, brick was the

favored building material. Here the nationalist resistance to the French manner, so genial a tool for the royal house of France and its growing claims to European leadership, was compounded by the mismatch of brick construction, which is compact and extensive, with the skeletal lightness of Gothic. The Cistercian influx set aside, it was close to one hundred years from the time of St.-Denis until high-style Gothic found acceptance in the German lands—and then only conditionally.

The exteriors remained, by and large, free of sculptural programs, except in direct French imports like the Cologne and Strasbourg cathedrals. Large gabled facades in the brick Gothic of Bavaria and the Baltic cities repudiated carved decoration altogether. Sculpture moved indoors, onto choir screens and as independent statues against the piers. The solidity of the wall mass continued to be respected, and buttresses were cast as single compact blocks of unadorned masonry. Interior elevations, long loyal to the memory of Carolingian and Ottonian precedent, were often visually at odds with the vaulting system, at least in the beginning. Plans varied. The architects and patrons did not abandon centralized church schemes; and there is at least one superb specimen, the Liebfrauenkirche at Trier, that gives us a Gothic update of Charlemagne's chapel at Aachen. St. Elizabeth at Marburg, begun in 1235, has a trefoil choir. It is also a hall church—that is, the aisle and nave vaults are the same height. There were isolated instances of the hall church in France both in the Romanesque and Gothic periods. In Germany it was a favorite.

The inspiration for the hall church may have come from monastic refectories, and it is probably to orders like the Cistercians that we should credit this deritualizing of church layouts. The church to them was a place of prayer, an *oratorium*; it did not pretend to be the model of heavenly Jerusalem or the house of God. And when later generations of Cistercians belied this simple communion with God and opted for the tall radiant choirs of Gothic cathedrals, the mood was captured by the mendicant orders of the early thirteenth century, the followers of St. Dominic and St. Francis of Assisi. For the Dominicans and Franciscans the liturgical pageantry of the choir meant less than the pulpit and the confessional. The high point of services was the long sermon. Gathering about the pulpit to see and hear the speaker mattered enormously. For this, the hall church worked much better than the standard hierarchy of aisles and nave. (Fig. 16.7)

The mendicant orders were especially popular in Germany. Their success naturally left its mark on religious architecture. Transepts, ambulatories, and radiating chapels lost their allure. Even vaults, except in the choir, seemed superfluous to the friars for the purposes of a teaching order. They prefered wood ceilings, and even when the naves were vaulted, the effect was low and broad.

England
England's is a different story. The European Romanesque corresponds here with two eras set apart by the Norman Conquest of 1066. We do not have much from the Anglo-Saxon environment prior to the arrival of William the Conqueror. Odd relics like Earl's Barton, the tenth or early eleventh-century tower in Northamptonshire, have a rustic, elemental look. Norman architecture across the channel was incomparably more sophisticated. The school of Normandy was in fact one of the most advanced of Romanesque regional styles. Its far-sighted experiments included the twin-tower facade and the rib vault. (Fig. 13.15)

The Norman Conquest turned England into a frontier that supported this architectural agility. Stark, massive keeps and churches, some using the imported buff and white limestone of Caen in Normandy, went up within a very short time. The churches have been updated at intervals, but there is enough around to convey their original strength, their virile beauty: St. Albans abbey built of flint and reused Roman bricks from nearby ancient Verulamium, the transept of Winchester Cathedral (Fig. 14.22), and of course Durham Cathedral whose ponderous rib vaults are possibly the earliest anywhere in Europe.

It was in one of these Norman churches, Canterbury Cathedral begun a year after the conquest and consecrated in 1130, that Gothic made its English debut. William of Sens—"a man of great abilities and a most ingenious workman in wood and stone," as

Fig. 14.23 Salisbury (England), cathedral, 1220–58; aerial view.

Gervase of Canterbury describes him—was one of the several architects, French and English, invited in 1174 to inspect the damage of the burned choir at Canterbury. He advised tearing it down for something new:

Dismissing the rest they chose him for the undertaking. . . . Attention was given to procure stones from abroad. He made the most ingenious machines for loading and unloading ships, and for drawing the mortar and stones. He delivered also to the masons models in wood for cutting the stones.

Five years after work began, William was hurt in a fall from the scaffolding and went home to die. An English successor, also called William, was named. So English Gothic, which began with a French design and French materials, was soon naturalized. Thereafter, it became the chief rival of Île-de-France Gothic, just as the English throne was the rival of the French royal house. And after 1250, when France seemed to have exhausted its powers of invention and became absorbed with the belaboring of surface ornament, it was England that took the lead for the next century. This is the time of the cathedrals at Wells and Gloucester, Worcester and York. But the independence of English architects is already quite plain in the decades of the triumph of Île-de-France—at Canterbury, Winchester, Ely, Salisbury, and Exeter.

Let us look at one of these, the Cathedral of St. Mary, Salisbury, built in the first half of the thirteenth century. (Fig. 14.23) One peculiarity of the overall site is that the cathedral has a cloister and chapter house attached to it, as if it were a monastery. Salisbury has never had monks; it has always been administered by a brotherhood of canons under the presidency of its dean. But these monastic adjuncts attest to a strange English practice. In ten of the seventeen dioceses of the country, the bishop resided in a monastery and his cathedral was at the same time a monastery church. Canterbury, Winchester, Ely, and Durham were all cathedral monasteries until Henry VIII's dissolution of monasteries about 1535, at which time the monks were replaced by canons and the prior by a dean. In most cases the monasteries were there first, and the bishops materialized when the community grew large enough to amount to a town.

All this accounts for the characteristic settings of English cathedrals. They are not intimately involved with the town, in the way that Chartres closes in on its cathedral. English cathedrals have ample breathing space. The cloister is on the south side, and other remnants (the gatehouses, for example) sometimes still trace the walled enclosure of the monasteries that originally set them off from the town.

The octagonal chapter house is also an English specialty. (Fig. 14.24) Worcester's was first; the one at Salisbury dates from 1263–84. The design is always the same. A central pier fans out into an umbrellalike vault; the ribs are then gathered again at the corners of the octagon. Except for a low blind arcade just above the benches of the chapter, the walls are glazed with pointed windows of a moderate height. They are comfortable, well-lighted rooms, devoid of the strenuous lift of French Gothic.

Since the bishop had his own palace in which to hold court, the chapter house may well have propped up the dignity of the second in command, the prior or the dean. These men had more daily contact with the cathedral community than did its bishop who, as an important political figure, was often busy with affairs of state. The bishop's primacy in the cathedral was beyond dispute. But his right to preside over the chapter did not always go unchallenged. There is, then, the edge of a power struggle evident in these graceful meeting halls.

The church plan is also quite remarkable

Fig. 14.24 Salisbury (England), chapter house of cathedral, 1263–84; view into the vault.

for a contemporary of Amiens Cathedral. The squared off choir looks early Cistercian; the double transept, Cluniac. Indeed, in eschewing the spatial unity of French Gothic, the cathedral at Salisbury (and this is true of all its peers) builds itself with distinct compartments in the manner of Romanesque design. This is evident in the massing that spreads out placidly, low and generous, with only the somewhat oversized crossing tower for a vertical accent. The west towers are modest. (Fig. 14.25) They are set beside the facade on individual bases, as if they did not quite belong to it. Together they make a richly decorative frontispiece which, despite the three portals that correspond to aisles and nave, has its own life, independent of interior arrangements. The sculptural program is itself meager by French standards. Staying clear of the portals, it layers the facade uniformly all the way to the top.

Inside, we have the same layered effect. (Fig. 14.26) The nave piers carry only their arcades, and the widespread tirforium has its own system of supports. And what to a French architect would have appeared most illogical, the vault ribs take off from brackets shaped into human heads halfway down the triforium band without ever being properly grounded. Color would have stressed the autonomy of the storeys and the vault canopy. The main material is Portland limestone from the quarries at Chilmark 15 kilometers (about 10 miles) west, a fine white stone that weathers to become a light grey. The slender shafts of the nave and the triforium piers are of dark Purbeck "marble." The contrast is tame now, but in the initial design the wall area was decorated with black scroll work on a red ground, capitals and moldings were gilded and painted, and only the vault was left white.

The ribs here describe normal four-part bays. In the early Gothic cathedrals of England, at Lincoln for example, the ribs do not even conform to the bay system. (Fig. 14.27) A ridge rib runs all along the center of the vault and additional ribs, called tiercerons, intervene between the transverse and diagonal ribs of the standard four-part bay. The result is a parade of star-shaped designs. This rejection of French rationalism for the sake of decorative flare is perhaps the most English trait of all.

Fig. 14.25 Salisbury Cathedral; west facade.

We have said enough here to call attention to the uniqueness of early Gothic in England or, more to the point perhaps, to its independence from France. The cathedrals of the thirteenth century were a manifesto of a new national consciousness, just as much as Simon de Montfort's revolt againt the authority of King Henry III and the establishment of the English Parliament. Gothic may have been a French invention, but the English architects, like Elias de Dereham and Nicholas of Ely at Salisbury Cathedral, knew how to harness it to native purposes. And that, after all, is the "English-ness" of English architecture, the "German-ness" of German architecture. The major historical styles have been few. To originate one is no more important in the long run than the gift of being able to make it one's own.

Fig. 14.27 Lincoln (England), cathedral; nave vaults, ca. 1233.

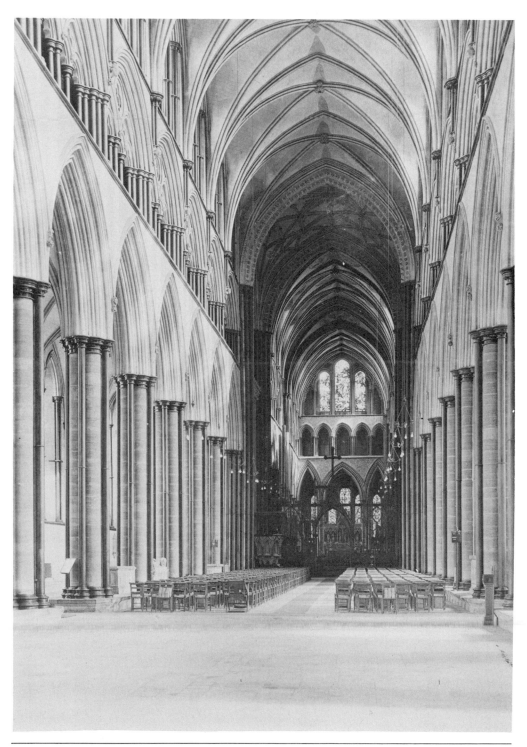

Fig. 14.26 Salisbury Cathedral; nave looking east.

Further Reading

J. Bony, *French Gothic Architecture of the Twelfth and Thirteenth Centuries* (Berkeley: University of California Press, 1983).

R. Branner, *Gothic Architecture* (New York: Braziller, 1961).

H. Focillon, *The Art of the West in the Middle Ages: Gothic Art,* Vol. II, trans. D. King (New York: Phaidon, 1963).

J. Gimpel, *The Cathedral Builders,* trans. C. F. Barnes (New York: Grove Press, 1961).

L. Grodecki, *Gothic Architecture,* trans. I. M. Paris (New York: Abrams, 1977).

J. Harvey, *The Mediaeval Architect* (London: Wayland, 1972).

G. Henderson, *Chartres* (Harmondsworth and Baltimore: Penguin, 1968).

R. Mark, *Experiments in Gothic Structure* (Cambridge, Mass.: MIT Press, 1982).

E. Panofsky, *Suger, Abbot of Saint Denis, 1081–1151,* 2nd ed. (Princeton: Princeton University Press, 1979).

Lavenham, Suffolk (England), merchants' half-timbered houses, fifteenth century.

15

THE URBANIZATION OF EUROPE, 1100–1300

The City Returns

Five archbishops, fourteen bishops, and the king and queen of France attended the consecration ceremonies for the new choir of St.-Denis on 11 June 1144, but not the pope. He could not had he wanted to. Several months before, the people of Rome had rebelled against their bishop. They stormed the Capitol, the seat of the Church-appointed prefect and judges, and "wishing to restore the ancient dignity of the city," Bishop Otto of Freising reported, "set up the order of senators, which had lapsed for a long space of time." Church revenues were confiscated, the houses of cardinals looted, and their towers brought down. The people had risen *contra domum Dei,* a clerical source concluded, against the house of God. They now took charge of their city; their standard stood on the hill that had been the citadel of the pagan republic of Rome. But the surroundings, the fortress ensconced in the ruins of the Tabularium, the ancient record office, were beneath the newly found dignity of the popular government. Thus a grand senatorial palace was built on the site in a hurry. It was the ancestor of the building that now frames the back of Michelangelo's great piazza on the Capitoline. (Fig. 20.8)

In that same year of Roman defiance, 1144, a comparable but milder incident took place in southern France, with a different ending. Long unhappy with their lord the abbot, the people of Montauriol, a small town that had grown up on the Tarn alongside the abbey of St.-Theodard, accepted the invitation of Alphonse, Count of Tou-

louse, to move to an adjoining site and start their own settlement. The land was his to give, and he was ready to issue a formal charter of liberties freeing the settlers from bondage to outside lords. To him they would owe moneys—a modest rent for the building plots; customs from imported wheat, salt, and wine; and tolls from the sale of livestock. But they would not owe him labor or any other form of feudal dues, and should they be called on for military service the count would have no power to requisition supplies. So started the *bastide* of Montauban, the charming little town of brick monuments and terraces a short way north of Toulouse. (Fig. 15.1)

These separate incidents illustrate the two principal ways in which Western urbanism returns for the first time since the decline of Roman civilization. The revolt against the pope is typical of the popular uprisings that galvanized the social and political order of those old cities that survived the earlier Middle Ages as bishoprics, and of others that found themselves in the feudal vise of an abbey or baronial castle. Since the latter part of the eleventh century, the new possessing classes had started organizing themselves to fight this dominant system of Church and nobility. It was a momentous change, and the key word is trade—not the local trade of feudalism, but intermediate and long-distance commerce maintained by a stable professional class of burgesses. For us, the rise of the commune, or self-governing community, means new building types like Rome's senatorial palace. The

Commercial Revolution, as it is sometimes called, brings on its own architecture of guild halls and storehouses, market buildings and shops. But beyond these functional modifications, the city fabric itself undergoes vital inflections. The streets and other public spaces adjust to the centers of the new bourgeois order, the emerging pattern of urban land use affects the old structure of houses and shops, and real estate turns into a major new industry.

This reorganization of old cities is only part of the story. Also important is the planting of new towns, called *bastides* in France and *novi burghi* elsewhere. Something close to one thousand of these towns were started in the later Middle Ages, beginning with Montauban. Many failed; many of the others remained the tiny settings they were at their inception. Others prospered and still live today, either as quaint small stops or else, overtaken by the industrial age, as vastly swollen major cities. In either guise they can be traced all over England and Wales, Spain, southern France, the territory of Piedmont on the Italian side of the Alps, the Low Countries, and Germany east of the Elbe. Their premeditated layouts refute the cliché of the medieval town as the picturesque hilltop cluster of houses along cute crooked streets, huddled about its cathedral church and its seigneurial towers.

The fact is that there is no such thing as "the medieval town." If we think of the Mediterranean at large, the phrase has to include Constantinople, 800 years old at the time of Suger and with a population of perhaps as much as one-half million, as well as the great urban centers of Islam—Baghdad, Cairo, Córdoba—beside which the largest Western cities pale by comparison. And in the Christian West, the range encompasses cities of over 100,000 like Milan and Venice and towns of less than 1,000; it includes royal capitals, episcopal sees, and simple trading posts in rural areas; ports, hill-forts, and mining towns, as well as secured islands, reclaimed lagoons, and crossroads. There are village parishes promoted to towns, and castles forced out of their isolation; ancient *civitates* that had never lost their urban birthright; abandoned Roman *castra* whose skeletons are recharged after centuries (Vienna and Brunswick are examples); and the fresh plantations of the twelfth and thirteenth centuries. There are radial plans, linear cities, and grids. The social and political order, and therefore the morphology, of medieval city-states in northern Italy has features unknown to the industrial centers of Flanders or the German colonies that monopolized commerce on the Baltic and North seas.

The Old Towns
The ground swell of medieval urbanism coincides with the rise and early maturity of the Gothic, from about 1150 to 1300. But the city-form has an earlier history if city liberties do not. Many medieval cities harkened back to Roman times; others to the subsequent period of Germanic kingdoms. We should review the course of these old, established towns to appreciate the scope and intensity of city-making efforts in the era of Chartres, Amiens, and Salisbury. We will leave to the next chapter the paradox of the late Middle Ages, a time that will see the most florid public buildings spring up in cities that had already lost the vitality of their earlier success.

The Roman legacy was imperishable. It left its traces throughout Europe, all the way to the Welsh and Scottish marshes, to the Rhine and the Danube. In the northern cities the public monuments, being of wood, had long since gone. But in the worst of times some cities held onto their street patterns and the remnants of the urban support systems. Otherwise they shrank and improvised, living on the urban carcass

Fig. 15.1 Montauban (France), founded in 1144.

through the clever use of what was there or simply squatting without a fuss. The regrouping was most flagrant in the once populous metropolises, Rome first among them. (Fig. 20.3) The main point is that as prosperity was extinguished, so was autonomy. Survival was hitched to subjection, and the cities in due course came under control either of bishops or powerful seigneurs and crowned heads.

The strength of cities comes from the free exchange of goods and services, a function which bishops and feudal lords did not encourage. Even so, an episcopal or royal palace helped to some extent. Its bureaucracy ran a modest business of administrative and legal services, and consumed products made elsewhere, including luxury items. A small group of merchants attached itself to Charlemagne's palace at Aachen, and town gates here and there hosted similar activities on a very small

scale. Since the Church frowned on profit-making enterprises, this trade was mostly itinerant and therefore episodic. The visiting caravans of merchants were composed largely of Jews, Easterners, and the unscrupulous. Annual fairs, vital to the well-being of towns, were also temporary events. Nevertheless fairs and pilgrimages, increasingly safe after the year 1000, breathed life into stagnant cities. The healthier among them tempted the passing tradesmen to settle for good. These extramural merchant colonies, called *faubourgs* in French, were the beginning of urban expansion.

The faubourgs were just outside the town, in front of one of the gates or across the river, but not part of it until much later. In fact, the greatest source of income for the town, or rather its lord, was drawn from gate tolls charged to those who wanted to enter and use its market. The walls were there to control entry in peacetime, as well

as to safeguard the trading activities of foreigners who paid for the privilege. The
personal safety of the townspeople was only
one aspect of defensive outlays. It was imperative to keep the town small, not only
because walls cost dearly to build and garrison, but also because unlimited expansion reduced the take at the gates and diluted the rights of those within. And there
was another good reason to remain small.
The artisans' and shopkeepers' livelihoods
depended on their being near the marketplace in the center of town. The area around
it was the most desirable; the main streets
that led into it from the town gates the next
best. Even in small towns of 40 hectares (100
acres) or less, the density eased as one
moved away from the center, with a great
deal of open space just within the walls. And
very few towns covered more than 2 square
kilometers.

Under the circumstances, the most sensible layout was the wheel: radial streets
converging on the hub from the gates of a
circular wall. (Fig. 15.2, A) Some variant of
this layout commonly appears in later towns
that grew organically out of villages, abbeys, or forts. In the older Roman grids, on
the other hand, which favored the four arms
of the crossing axes, diagonals might be cut
through the rectilinear blocks, or secondary markets might be established away
from the main marketplace. (Fig. 15.2, B)

The name "city," *civitas,* was reserved
until the thirteenth century for towns of
Roman origin. *Bourg* or *burgus* referred to
the later, organic towns. Their history is
obscure. The castle, that trademark of land-

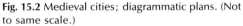

Fig. 15.2 Medieval cities; diagrammatic plans. (Not
to same scale.)

(**A**) Lennep (Germany); the radial scheme.

(**B**) Barcelona (Spain); a modified Roman grid.

(**C**) Olney (England); a borough added to an
older village, ca. 1230; the ribbon-based
scheme.

(**D**) Stia (Italy); the market-based scheme.

(**E**) Villarreal de Burriana (Castellon, Spain); a
new town.

(**F**) Briviesca (Burgos, Spain); a new town.

(**G**) Montségur (France); a new town, founded
in 1263.

(**H**) Montflanquis (France); a new town, founded
in 1256, detail.

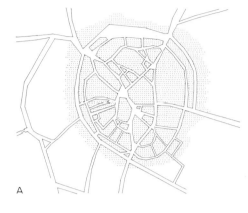

A

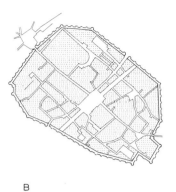

B

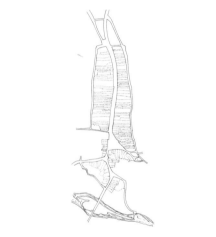

C

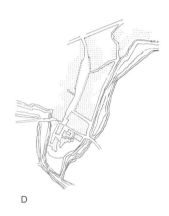

D

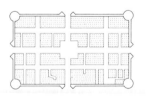

E

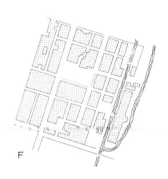

F

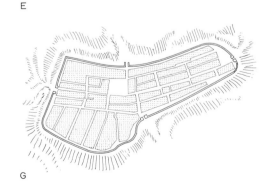

G

H

bound feudalism, would seem to be doggedly antiurban, and the monastery was conceived as the ideal refuge from the evils of the city. And yet some castles and abbeys sprouted towns by tolerating trade at their gates.So did some of the military forts a sovereign might plant along a troublesome border. Forts were not centers of production, and no town linked to them could maintain itself in times of peace without a healthy economy that reached beyond the garrison. Abbeys and feudal castles that did supervise production had to aim for a significant surplus to stimulate a town. Or else they would have to be situated at a particularly favorable site that would bring to it significant trade. Such "natural" towns would be rallying points among the villages of a rural region, according to one theory, collecting and distributing their resources. This clustering of villages is akin to that *synoecism* which Aristotle took to be the origin of the old towns of Greece, as contrasted with the colonial plantations in alien territory.

But the town as the pool of rural resources may be less crucial in the long run than its place within a network of diversified long-distance trade. The inhibiting nature of feudal economy is that it treats the land as a pattern of personal holdings, each one exploited by its lord. This closed system resists a broader outlook of regional or economic integration. It counts on the immobility of capital and labor force, and resents intrusion. Trade, on the other hand, thrives on extraterritoriality and the freedom to come and go. Communities that learned this lesson early on, and were blessed with a geographical location along prevailing or enticeable trade routes, pulled ahead regardless of their rural promise.

Venice is of course the classic case. The people of the Veneto had escaped the Germanic incursions of the early Middle Ages by retreating into the lagoons created by two river mouths, the Po and the Tagliamento. Venice was the most important of a handful of settlements on the islands between the river marshes and the open sea. Spared from Lombard landlubbers because of its site, she professed token subjection to Byzantium and started an astounding career in overseas trade. By the end of the eleventh century, the island city was rich and handsomely appointed; her galleys and citizens were everywhere.

The main lines of her unique city-form were established by 1100 and hardly changed at all thereafter. (Fig. 15.3) A flat rise of land stands in the middle of the lagoon at the confluence of a number of navigable canals. One of them, the Grand Canal, traverses the city in a broad S. The ducal palace, still fortified at this time, and the adjoining cathedral of St. Mark's occupied a large public space at one end of the Grand Canal; the commercial center, or Rialto, was a point halfway along its path where a boat bridge (soon to be supplemented by a wooden bridge that could open at the top to let ships through) united the markets on the two banks. Secondary canals in labyrinthine profusion penetrated into every corner of the land mass. Parish churches and open spaces with cisterns to collect freshwater flecked the dense townscape. On the narrow spit of land in the direction toward the sea was the arsenal, a waterfront of docks and shipyards where it was said twenty-four war galleys could be built or repaired at one time.

The recovery of Europe in the eleventh century underwrote the future of the city. Relative stability in the political structure, the drastic population swell, the Spanish *reconquista*, and the First Crusade which weakened the Muslim hold on the Mediterranean—all worked in its favor. The moral of long Muslim prosperity, the example of Constantinople and Venice, began to sink in. Towns could be gainful for the feudal lord if he were willing to relax his grip on the people and endorse selective liberties. Fairs and foreign merchants on his lands were the first to benefit from this calculated sufferance. And now townsfolk everywhere, increasingly outspoken, began to agitate for their own freedom to travel, to do business, to make and sell goods. The specific franchises sought were control over the market and its buildings, supervision of the trades and regulation of weights and measures, minting coinage, the levy of direct taxes, and jurisdiction over the town's defenses. In return the lord could count on a steady income to do with as he pleased. This required a change in the long-entrenched habit of conceiving of land, and the indentured serfs who worked it, as the

sole source of wealth. The emancipation of towns, a risky deal to be sure, could usher in the lord's own emancipation.

All this took time. Society is set in its ways and fears change. But one by one the towns earned their charters, and with them the right to shape their life. The Po Basin and Tuscany, Flanders, and pockets of France like Normandy, Picardy, Gascony, and the south were the vanguard. Not at all surprisingly. The central axis of European commerce ran from the Low Countries in the north, through the Rhineland, and down the Rhone to northern Italy. From there the galleys of Pisa, Genoa, and Venice extended the axis to the eastern Mediterranean. Intermediate-range traffic in prized commodities like English wool and the wine of Bordeaux revived towns along its path. Transport of goods by water, much preferable to land routes, rivers, and littorals, had the advantage.

The New Towns
But while the older towns fought hard for their liberties, this patently lucrative institution came to be seen as an investment. The kings of England and France, the counts of Toulouse, and an occasional bishop or abbot began to establish new towns. For the royal houses, this activity was an overall strategy to take effective possession of their territory by populating it. The sweetest inducement was personal freedom and the chance to bolt the feudal stranglehold for a life built on personal merits. Since the slate was clean in new settlements, the social disparities of the old towns would not exist for the initial group of settlers. The people, all on a more or less equal footing, would launch an egalitarian community—that, at least, was the theory. In time class

Fig. 15.3 Venice (Italy), conjectural stages of its origin and development: left, the site of the city and its periphery today; right, three moments in the consolidation of the urban form—top, fifth–sixth century (451 is the traditional foundation date of Venice); center, eighth–ninth century; bottom, ca. 1100. The dots indicate parish churches; the dotted lines in the last drawing indicate main canal streets and the present city limits.

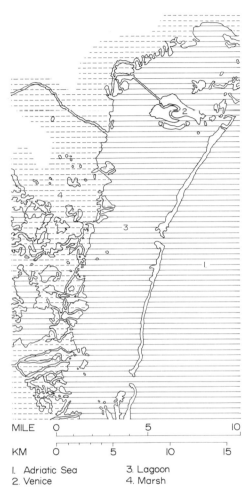

MILE 0   5   10

KM 0   5   10   15

1. Adriatic Sea   3. Lagoon
2. Venice   4. Marsh

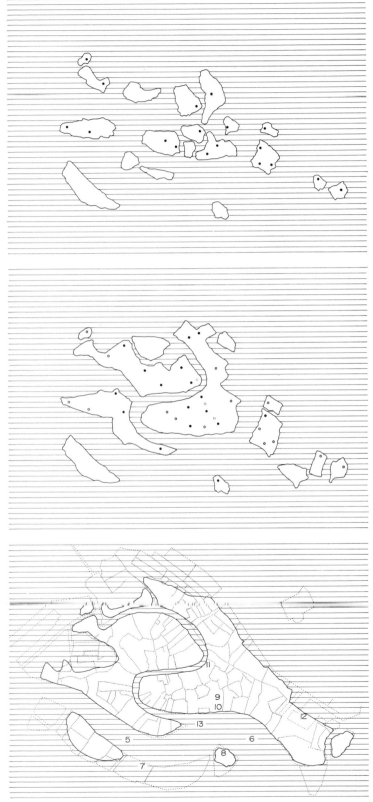

5. Giudecca Canal   10. Doge's Palace
6. Canal of St. Mark 11. Rialto
7. Il Redentore   12. Arsenal
8. S. Giorgio Maggiore 13. Grand Canal
9. St. Mark's

MILE 0   0.5   1.0

KM 0   0.5   1.0   2.0

distinctions materialized of course. These bastides—the name is related to the French verb *bâtir*, to build—are in some ways the forerunners of the colonial cities that were later planted in America and elsewhere by the Spaniards, French, and English. Like them, it is best to think of bastides as a triumph of the middle class, not of democracy.

The towns were always small, at best one kilometer long and one-half kilometer wide. To the founder, the cost was negligible. The return for tilling this land in the old way would be nothing compared to the revenue the town could generate if it were successful. The land, subdivided into burgage plots, was distributed among the first comers. Each man had to build his own house on the plot given him, and had to do so within a stated time, a year at the most. The founder, or *bastidor*, for his part agreed to lay out and level the streets and the marketplace at his own expense. A generous bastidor might offer to contribute a town church, but many plantations are in fact without one. This is mostly because the town was bound to lie in some existing parish, so the bishop concerned would often refuse to consecrate an independent church that would infringe on existing rights and require the redrawing of parish boundaries. A town chapel with no sanctions for burial had to suffice. The bastidor might also provide such facilities as prisons, tollhouses, bake houses, and mills that would pay for themselves in time in the form of fees. Walls were prohibitive. Only kings, with powers to conscript the labor force and to raise revenue or command credit, could afford to defend their towns fully. Perhaps two-thirds of French and English bastides were never provided with walls.

The site was crucial. The town would sink or swim on its ability to attract trade. It had to lie on a major road, with easy access to traffic. The junction of two major roads or a river crossing was an obvious choice. A coastal port, a bridge, a ferry or ford along a river, a seigneurial castle, a royal palace or hunting lodge, a monastery of consequence—all were magnets of human concourse, and so likely prospects to consider for town-making plans. The bastidor would have to negotiate for the land if his terri-

Fig. 15.4 Montpazier (France), a new town founded in 1285; marketplace with *cornières*.

torial holdings did not contain some such safe option. Otherwise, or in addition, he would spend to divert main roads toward his town and in other ways enhance its connections.

Once the site was decided on, the streets and burgage plots were marked out with the help of a length of rope. The envelope was generally rectangular, and so was the plot. This was the simplest way not only to survey the bounds and to draw the streets, but also to divide the area into plots of equal size or at least plots that could be readily measured and evaluated. An orthodox checkerboard was not insisted on. The planners took account of the site contours and demarcated flexibly, especially on hilltops. Our selection of plans in Figure 15.2 is intended to illustrate this sensible variety. The grid seems to have faith in its own ability to people its many blocks, from the market outward to the edges. But many

bastides were less ambitious. In the type called "market-based" by the historian of bastides, Maurice Beresford, the town begins and ends with the plots bordering the long, broad, and level marketplace. In the so-called "ribbon-based" plans, a thin line of plots is arranged for some 500 meters or so on both sides of a main road that may be widened at one point to make the marketplace.

The skills of these planners were probably managerial. The schemes showed good sense topographically, but were hardly revolutionary. Roman towns had kept the grid in the public eye for centuries; it did not have to be reinvented. And the linear principle of "ribbon-based" cities has a history as old as Khirokitia. (Fig. 3.5) When Edward I of England, *rex et bastidor*, ordered twenty-four towns in 1296 "to elect men from among your wisest and ablest who know best how to devise, order and array a new town to the greatest profit of Ourselves and of merchants," he was looking for town-making experience rather than any special training. He had in mind men like Sir Henry le Waleys, a prominent merchant, alderman of the City of London, and mayor of Bordeaux, and the king's seneschal of Gascony, Luke de Thenney. "Devise, order, and array," or "deviser, ordiner, et arrayer" in the French of the original document, imply design. But they are common verbs and may as well have referred to, as Beresford suggests, the selection and procurement of the site, the recruitment of settlers and establishment of their legal privileges, and the allotment to the new town of the "physical accoutrements appropriate for its role." Still, we find that the stock plan is often nicely inflected and may show considerable finesse in the alternation of wide streets and alleys and the regularly shaped marketplace defined by arcaded passages or *cornières*. (Fig. 15.4)

The town having been laid out, a ceremony of some kind was held to announce its birth and invite settlers. In Gascony the founding lord or, in the case of a royal plantation, the king's seneschal dug a hole at the center of town and raised the bastidor's arms on a stake called the *palum*. He then declared the town open and pledged the liberties to be enjoyed within in the name of God, the Virgin Mary, and all the saints. The charter sealed them for the future. And these liberties were exhilarating in a cumbrous world propped on the strictures of feudalism. The charter of Bridgnorth assures its burgesses that "they may come and go throughout our land of England, may do all kinds of trading in buying and selling and bargaining, freely, quietly, well and honorably, in fairs and markets, in cities and boroughs and in all places." At Portsmouth, King Richard I granted that the burgesses "shall be quit and free of toll and pontage and stallage and tallage both by land and sea wherever they may come in all our land." In Newcastle on Tyne, "every burgess can have his own oven and mill."

Who came to these islands of freedom where the townspeople were to be king and the market their palace? The founder hoped for experienced merchants and artisans. The simpler skills of carpenters, bakers, shoemakers, and the like, could be found in the villages. Merchants by and large had to come from older towns. They took the best plots around the marketplace and extended the ground-floor business premises of their houses into the *cornières*. If the home base of a recruit fell within the founder's territory, the transfer was uneventful. But often villeins from a rival's land saw their chance and sought refuge in the new town, to the intense displeasure of their lords. They had to lie low for a while until they were legally beyond danger. "A man," states the charter of Haverford West, "whatever his status may be, who dwells there for a year and a day without being challenged shall be free."

If the town made it, the demand for food helped the countryside. The raw materials for the urban workshops—the wool, metal, charcoal, and stone—were also country-based goods. But a successful bastide had to compete against both other new towns and the old, established towns in whose vicinity it may have been planted. Many bastides never got off the ground. Despite the charter's inducements, the burgesses failed to show up or dragged their feet when they did. The nearness of rival towns, protracted litigation, natural misfortunes, and other similar difficulties shortened the lives of some that were not stillborn. Town-making, the great adventure of the late Middle Ages, proved to be a great gamble.

Bourgeois Architecture, Public and Private

If we now turn from the broad urban canvas to the individual buildings of which it was woven, two general observations ought to preface our brief summary. The first involves the variety of building types; the second, the town as client and user.

Leisure, Health, and Learning

The decline of the urban milieu and the rise of the Christian ethic account for the obsolescence by the early Middle Ages of most building types that had furnished the cities of the Roman world—theaters, amphitheaters, basilicas, forums, administrative buildings of all kinds, warehouses and brothels, baths, and circuses. This major change affected architectural thinking in two ways. Since there was now widespread conversion of Roman structures for purposes other than those they were meant for, a divorce took place between form and function. A building became a hospital because of the sick it sheltered, and not for any specific architectural plan or look. At the same time, new structures of the same basic frame might serve as hospitals or forges without concern for a programmatic image. And conversely, several functions could be served in one shell. A hospital might be also a poorhouse and orphanage, an almshouse, a foundling home, and a halting place for pilgrims and transients.

The reawakening of cities in the twelfth and thirteenth centuries changes all this. It brings with it a diversification of programs and, at a slower pace, endows public functions with an architectural identity. Documents show that in 1262 Toulouse had five hospices for clergy, five homes for unmarried women, seven leprosariums, and thirteen hospitals—a record of evident specialization. Market halls, exchanges, and libraries also develop their own distinctive architecture in time.

The autonomous city also secularized architectural patronage. This meant, first, that civic authorities would commission or tolerate buildings that would have been unthinkable formerly. Town halls and other settings of the commune's sovereignty were of course anathema to prelates and lay lords alike. "Commune! new and detestable name," Abbot Guibert of Nogent wrote. "By it people are freed from all bondage in return for an annual tax payment." But this was not the end of it. The city allowed public baths to operate. A great Roman institution killed by Christianity, except as an adjunct of the cloister, was thus brazenly revived. They were social places, these new baths, as their ancestors had been; people soaked in company, and were served food and drink while doing so. (Fig. 15.5) We know from monastic installations like Cluny that the twelfth century was not ignorant of water systems. A famous drawing of the cathedral abbey of Canterbury shows the underground conduits that were installed to carry water from springs outside the city and feed it to appropriate points on the premises, including the bath-house and the prior's tub. (Fig. 15.6) In the next century or so there were twelve public baths in Nürnberg, and twenty-nine in Vienna. Paris had thirty-two, for men and women, and regulatory statutes set relative prices for a steam bath as distinct from a tub bath.

More important, the city challenged the religious monopoly on critical public services like health and education. The majority of hospitals continued to be built and managed by the monastic orders, especially the brothers of St. John of Jerusalem (commonly called Hospitallers), the Templars, the Augustinians, and the lay order of the Holy Spirit. Divine comfort was obligatory medicine for all within. The stock building was a low, long block crowned by a roof turret. It held within an aisled or aisleless Gothic hall with no partitions, so that the altar could be seen from every bed. (Fig. 15.7) The long axis might terminate in an apse or chapel, or else the chapel might open up to the ward along one side.

But gradually municipal councils moved in, taking over the administration of some extant hospitals and starting new ones. Secular staffs played down the advantage of religion over medicine. "A hospital is not a church," a late document relating to St. Nicholas Hospital in Metz sternly put it. In some, superannuated pensioners who chose to sign over their property to the hospital in return for board, lodging, and medical care, a not uncommon arrangement in the late Middle Ages, expected rooms of their own. Soon the building program was rationalized even further. The pensioners occupied an upper storey, and the main hall on the ground was reserved entirely for the communal life of the sick. Extensions and administrative offices came to be grouped around a court. Civic hospitals usually lay outside the town, in little suburbs of their own, or else they formed the kernel of a quarter within.

Secular learning was more serious. Monasteries and cathedrals had run the schools for centuries. The birth of the university came as a bitter blow. Bologna and Paris were first. And by the thirteenth century there were twenty-two universities in all, one-half of them in Italy. The sons of German burghers studied law at Bologna and Padua, and Paris University whose charter came from the King of France attracted students from all over Europe. The presence

Fig. 15.5 Medieval bathhouse; exterior, in a miniature of the twelfth century.

within the city of this youthful and lively international community with its democratic ways was a social incident of the first order.

Architecturally, the picture is diffuse for a time. There were no permanent buildings; no campus to speak of. The affairs of the university were run by a governing body of students, the Congregation, which preferred to forgo ownership of property and its legal consequences in order to preserve the independent status of the student government in a property-minded urban society. Classes were held in rented rooms or master's houses, and students lodged with the townsfolk. Popular lecturers spoke in

public buildings or in the open air. The "hall" or "hostel," a rented building for residences taken over by groups of students under the direction of a Principal who was elected popularly, was an early development. So was the college—an endowed establishment where students attended classes and lived together according to the founder's statutes, and under the increasingly absolute authority of a Master. The college was a Parisian invention which the English made their own. Merton College at Oxford, founded in 1264 by King Henry III's chancellor, probably was the first on English soil. It provided lodging only to those studying for higher degrees. The quad, that

356

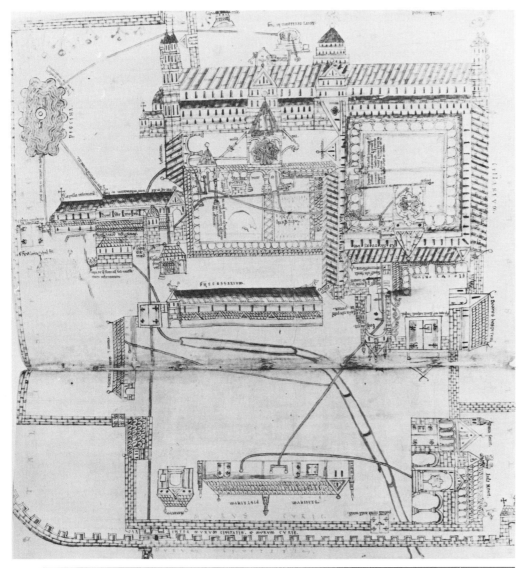

Fig. 15.6 Canterbury (England), Christchurch Monastery; plan of the waterworks, ca. 1165. This is one of two parchment drawings now inserted into the famous Canterbury Psalter (ms. 110) at the Library of Trinity College, Cambridge. The drawings were probably made by Wibert who engineered the waterworks system.

familiar scheme of the English residential college with the buildings arranged on four sides of a courtyard, ample enough to accommodate undergraduates as well, did not emerge until later.

Universities, whether collegiate or of the dispersed continental variety, had need of books. Once again, an institution which had been the privilege of cathedrals and monasteries freed itself of its religious setting. Academic libraries might hold several hundred books, initially kept in cupboards lined along the walls. This is how they were housed in the monasteries if there were enough of them to deserve a separate room, which was rare. More commonly, a niche in the cloister walk next to the church would hold the cupboard or *armarium*. (Fig. 15.8)

Academic libraries were more widely accessible. The best of them, the thirteenth-century library of the Sorbonne, a college of Paris University founded in 1254 by a chaplain of King Louis IX called Robert de Sorbon, had more than a thousand books. It was a sizable, detached building, and it introduced a system that was to prove revolutionary. The books were chained to pairs of lecterns placed back to back, each pair corresponding to one of the nineteen windows along the wall on either side. (Fig. 15.9)

In Italy, where the split between clerical and secular faculties did not exist, monastic libraries served the university community and, in fact, urban monasteries of the Franciscans and Dominicans came close to providing a kind of campus for the homeless student body. The great monastic libraries of the Renaissance, like those of Florence, Padua, and Bologna, should be seen in this light.

City Government and the Guilds
The switch from a feudal to a popular government occurred first in the old bishoprics of northern Italy in the course of the eleventh century. It was neither as precipitous nor as violent as the example of Rome might suggest. Prominent families had always been part of the episcopal administration. When the struggle for free communes began in earnest, the representatives of these families ran the affairs of the city-state, first as consuls and then as an assembly at large called the grand council. A smaller inner council functioned as the executive branch, and an ever-growing number of elected officials saw to the day-to-day operation of the city. The bickering among the old families, grafted to the broader contest between the German emperor and the pope, brought about the office of the *podestà*, an outsider who was engaged to act as impartial arbiter in international disputes. The people, in theory the ultimate sovereigns, asserted themselves in this oligarchical arrangement through the guilds that spoke for occupational groups and the military companies with their own magistrate, the *capitano del popolo*. This, with many variations, was the frame of the urban constitution, and it was made manifest architecturally through new town halls,

where the grand council met, the residences for the *podestà* and the captain of the people, and the market and guild halls.

Early town halls materialized in the immediate vicinity of the cathedral complex which took in the bishop's palace and the open space of the market. This area often corresponded to the site of ancient Roman forums. It enjoyed special immunity; no weapons could be carried within its limits, and unusually severe punishment was meted out for crimes committed there. By electing to be situated in this area, the town hall claimed this old privilege and gave notice of its jurisdiction over the marketplace. So the secular center of the free Italian city-state coincided with the religious center. This is apt, for what was at issue was merely a change of guard. The cities sought to regain temporal powers that, since the early Middle Ages, had been taken over by the bishop's office. Their fight was with the absolutism of the Church, not with religion. The earliest surviving town hall, the so-called Palazzo del Broletto in Como that dates from 1215, was dedicated by the townsfolk "to the honor and glory of St. Abbondio [their patron saint] and the city of Como." (Fig. 15.11) And the cathedral itself was seen as a component of the civic image. The Florentines built their town hall "in honor and reverence of almighty God and the blessed Virgin Mary . . . and for the honor, decorum and adornment of the city." (Fig. 15.10)

The town hall of Como took its place between the old cathedral of S. Giacomo and the church of Santa Maria Maggiore, the precursor of the present cathedral. It is a two-storey building of smooth, striated black and white masonry, interspersed with red. The ground floor was opened up at the front and back by means of arcades on octagonal piers, shortened considerably since by the later raising of the street level. The marketplace spread out in front of the building, and there was additional open space on the east side. Here a freestanding staircase of stone led up to the second floor, which was taken up entirely by one large assembly hall with an open timber roof. In this hall the grand council met to deliberate under the presidency of the podestà, judges had their benches along the walls, and the original copy of the city charter was given reverent safekeeping.

Fig. 15.7 Tonnerre (France), the hospital of Notre-Dame-des-Fontenilles; interior. This sick ward is about 100 meters long and is covered by a wooden barrel vault. The chapel is at the far end.

The ground floor was divided into two aisles by a central row of four supports. This flat-ceilinged room was considered an extension of the marketplace, or rather the administrative premises from which the surveillance of market activities could be conducted and weights and measures regulated. Privileged goods like iron, wine, and herbs, as well as city monopolies like salt, would be sold under the arcades; auctions would be held; jurists, notaries, scribes, and official estimators would have their booths here. A stern bell tower to the left linked the town hall to S. Giacomo. The tocsin rang to summon the council to a session and the people to a town meeting or to battle. But even on ordinary days, the bustle was constant. The town hall was the heart and pride of a commune. A well on the grounds symbolized its vital energy; a caged lion, its sovereignty. The jail was close by for those who had dishonored the town, and blas-

phemers and false witnesses were brought here to be exhibited publicly. "This place," says an inscription on the town hall of Pistoia, "hates, loves, punishes, preserves and honors: laziness, laws, crime, rights, virtue."

The Como formula, generally emulated in northern Italy, is based on the local palace of a bishop or abbot, which in turn reflected the royal or imperial precedent of the earlier Middle Ages. In fact, the town hall was sometimes also a residence; in central Italy, for example, the podestà or the captain of the people used it for that purpose, and officials called *priori* were forced by law to live under its roof during their two-month term. A second formula prevailed in Tuscany. In place of a broad two-storey structure, the town hall in cities like Florence and Volterra is a powerful block of four storeys, akin to the tower houses of the region, with a heavy crown of crenel-

Fig. 15.8 Medieval armorium; illumination in the *Codex Amiatinus*, late eighth century, showing the scribe Ezra at work. (Biblioteca Laurenziana, Florence)

lated machicolation along the top. By now the town hall has been divested of market functions. The ground floor is sealed up and employed as an arsenal and tribunal. Florence's Palazzo Vecchio, the best known example of this type, is a mighty fortress of rusticated masonry. (Fig. 15.10) The bell tower thrusts out of the central block, a little to one side of the main facade, in two unequal stages that have their own crenellations. It is an aggressive building, in tune with the turbulent, internecine politics of the times and the combative attitude toward neighboring cities subjected one by one to Florentine rule.

Fig. 15.9 Cambridge (England), Trinity Hall, ca. 1600; interior. This library illustrates the stall system—a combination of lecterns and shelves that goes back to the thirteenth century.

In northern Europe, town halls are much more varied. New towns like Lübeck that were born of trade and had known no episcopal master, and also older towns like Bruges that began as forts of the counts of Flanders, did not have to play out their sovereignty against the cathedral complex. The religious center here is usually at some distance from the municipal center that can now occupy an extensive area, with several imposing buildings and more than one public space, as it does in Bruges. (Fig. 15.12) But the town hall did not rule the roost, not at the beginning. It was long subservient to the cloth house, that is, the place where cloth was sold. In this monumental facility of the leading group of citizens, the cloth merchants, the council would often meet. Only in the second half of the thirteenth century and later, when the keeping of records gained crucial importance both for municipal government and sedentary trade, did town halls begin to consolidate their simple early structures and extend them in a piecemeal fashion. The result is an amalgam of units of different origin and purpose, embraced at a late date by a monumental envelope and capped by a tower. This is the story of Lübeck, for example, and the mighty town hall of Torun (Thorn) in Poland, which contains a market area, law courts, and shops on the ground floor for the cloth trade—the dominant economic force here as in most major northern cities—haberdashers, potters, soapmakers, and bakers.

We should really be examining the market halls in these cities, like the "Old Hall" of Bruges for the mercers, spicers, and butchers, or the splendid cloth hall at Ypres, which outshine their respective town halls. (Fig. 15.13) But though some of these buildings were started in the thirteenth century, they gained their present form much later than 1300, the terminus we have set for this chapter. The point to be made is that the role of merchants in the governing process of medieval towns, especially in northern Europe, grew steadily, and with it their ambition to express this influence in architectural terms. Theirs was a public statement that went beyond the functional needs of trade. Strictly utilitarian buildings, of no symbolic standing, were there all along. These included warehouses, workshops, and most interestingly the *fondaco*, a large compound organized around an inner courtyard where merchants from a foreign country, under the jurisdiction of their own consul and the spiritual care of their chaplain, lived, traded, stored their goods, and stabled their animals.

The Residential Infill

The medieval house is as varied as the medieval town. The spindling row houses of northern towns like Rouen or Nürnberg with their steeply pitched roofs and spirited half-timbering, which are the end of the line in an evolution of several centuries, are nothing like the medieval streets of Siena or Assisi—their flat planes, exposed brick surfaces, low tile roofs, the late ghost of another line. (Figs. 15.14, 15.15)

More specifically, the house of the twelfth and thirteenth centuries is, first, heir to habits of the past. The Mediterranean regions continued to think of stone and brick as the stuff of neighborhoods, as they had for centuries. There is also a recurrence (or perhaps the survival) of Roman types. One example is the two-bay "strip house" with the ground-floor shop; here the two or three storeys of living premises above were reached by stairs next to the shop. Another type is the Ostian *insula*, the common apartment block with an interior court, rows of shops behind an arcaded portico, and balconies—so the marketplace *cornières* in the new towns of France had recourse to a long memory. Bologna had all its streets lined with porticoes, often in wood. The height of the porticoes was set at 2.66 meters (7 Bolognese feet), so that people could traverse them on horseback. The sturdy tower houses that still bristle in Italian towns like San Gimignano are of a nearer, feudal parentage. In the north, the house had other roots. The timber-framed Saxon barn lived on in the "hall" of the post-Conquest house in England. Half-timbering, and other ancient techniques of building in wood, survived into the late Middle Ages through the period of invasions.

There is, next, the matter of plots. Since street frontage was a critical commodity for tradespeople, streets had to be shared by everyone. This, and the fact that the town boundaries were fixed with no provision for expansion, suggested narrow plots with tall houses. Nonurban activities—and each house still had to carry on a bit of farm-

Fig. 15.10 Florence (Italy), the Piazza della Signoria and the Palazzo Vecchio, 1299–1314, with later alterations and additions. On the right is the public loggia called Loggia della Signoria, Loggia dell'Orcagna, or Loggia dei Lanzi, 1376–82, by Benci di Cione and Francesco Talenti.

Fig. 15.11 Como (Italy), town hall called Palazzo del Broletto, 1215; west facade. There were originally five arches on the ground floor and four windows on the upper floor; the new cathedral cut off one bay from the building in the fifteenth century. This town hall identifies a building type that will endure for several centuries. English market halls, Boston's First Town House, and similar buildings are later examples of the type. (See Fig. 24.11.)

Finally, we should survey the functional and social program. The medieval town house is not only the family home, it is also a manufacturing locale, counting house, store, or shop. Occupancy extends beyond the biological family. The normal seven-year apprenticeship that was specified by artisans' guilds indentured young men to a master with whom they had to live for the duration. Journeymen, the middle grade, though free to move, were still obliged to have the supervision of masters and might lodge with the one they worked for during the period of employment. We have, then, the selling space on the ground floor, which may also be the production space if it is a small business like a shoemaker's or candlemaker's. The family takes up the second floor. Apprentices and journeymen would live on the third floor, which might also have to double as a work area for those industries like weaving or fine handcrafts that need good light. Attics were for the storage of staples, raised from the street by pulley. A merchant's house, in England at least, often had a fireproof basement or "cellar" vaulted in stone, partly sunk below street level.

The wealthy burgher who could afford to build in style built in stone, even in those areas where stone was scarce and therefore expensive, and this gave his house a better chance of surviving than the average timber house. Several have made it to the present in French towns like Cluny, Provins, and Périgueux; several more in England, notably Jew's House, Lincoln, from about 1170–80. (Fig. 15.16) The Jews had come into England with the Conqueror. The guilds were closed to them, since the obligatory oath to the Trinity was out of the question. They concentrated their talents on finance, unaffected by canon law that prohibited Christians from lending money on interest. The two-storey Jew's house was really a bank, a defensible fireproof building where gold and silver, as well as the valuable deeds of loans, would be safeguarded. It had its side to the street and was entered by an ornate doorway. Out of the door hood rose the chimney of the fireplace that heated the hall on the second floor.

This is also the arrangement of the twelfth-century house at Cluny, where a cylindrical chimney rises just above a

ing—were relegated to the back. Here, in a yard adjoining the yard of the house fronting on a parallel street, the few animals, the fruit trees, and the kitchen garden would be tended. The gables were toward the street and the houses were joined broadside, at the eaves. The plot width, at least in the north, was keyed to the maximum size of oak beams that spanned the timber frame, usually 5 or 6 meters. The height of storeys, 2 meters or slightly more, was set by the user. In the so-called "ribbon-based" plan of English bastides, sometimes also referred to as the High Street plan, the single line of plots and the open-ended scheme allowed for houses that were wider than deep, with their eaves toward the street. The back was country; the garden, or garth, could stretch without worry and hold subsidiary structures.

pointed arch that opens into the barrel-vaulted cellar. (Fig. 15.17) Round-headed windows, paired on two sides of the chimney, lighted the hall (*salle* in French), which was the main living space of the family. Often the bedroom or solar took up the third floor. The windows of these two rooms showed the taste of the owner to the townsfolk. They were in the latest Romanesque or Gothic mode and were fitted with oiled parchment to shut out the cold, or sometimes black or green cloth curtains bordered with gold. Ground floor and attic windows made do with wooden shutters. Glass comes into wide use much later.

Inside, the floors would be strewn with rushes. Panels of linen cloth, dyed a solid color or decorated with embroidery, would hang on the walls (tapestries are a four-teenth-century indulgence), and cupboards and benches would stand against them. A long trestle table in the middle of the hall was dismantled after meals. Richer houses might have their walls sealed with wood paneling, or plaster painted with scenes. The solar had a huge canopied bed as its principal piece of furniture, some chairs, a chest or two. Spare spartan furnishings were the rule even in the fanciest of houses.

Ostentation in the timber house was also mostly external. The infilling of the half-timber frame was treated decoratively in a number of ways. In the Alpine lands, the smooth plaster surfaces were painted gaily. In England and northern France they were scored with regular patterns. From the implement used, this design is called "comb-work" in English. In London there were wooden moldings and tile facings. Exposed brick, in northern Germany and Baltic cities, might be enriched by being laid fancifully.

But the carving of framing members inside and out exhibited the freest invention. Alexander Neckam, an observant schoolmaster from Dunstable who journeyed to London and Paris in the 1170s, was quite displeased with these bourgeois exertions. He sounds like the Bernard of domestic architecture in this passage from his *De nominibus utensilium:*

What shall I say about carvings and paintings except that wealth supports stupidity. Roofs that

Fig. 15.12 Bruges (Belgium), view of the city, 1562; detail. In the center is the cathedral. Below the cathedral and to the left is the fish market and the market hall ("Old Hall") with its bell tower. Further left is the Place du Bourg. The large open space at the bottom right is the Friday Market.

keep out the winter should be sufficient. But the destructive luxury of wealth and the deadly vanity of a city have subjected men to the yoke of miserable slavery. . . . Expect superfluous and vain inventions in buildings, clothing . . . and various other furnishings, and you can say with reason: O Vanity, O Superfluity. (Fig. 15.18)

And where in all this riot did the poor live? They lived everywhere, as they had in the Roman cities—in the houses of the rich as servants, in the streets and under the porticoes, at the town gates, and on the bridges. They took refuge in monastic or civic hospices, which were called *domus pauperum.* University students, and others who could afford to, rented single rooms in private houses or shared a room with others. The guilds helped the worse-off workers of their particular trade. The industrial proletariat—wool carders, beaters,

Fig. 15.13 Ypres (Belgium), cloth hall, begun ca. 1200 and not completed until 1620. It included the town hall, law courts, the prison, and a chapel.

mosque. Its name, Fustat, probably derives from the Greek *phossaton,* which means "entrenched camp." Many great Muslim cities started in this way, as temporary army camps, like the earlier urbanization of Roman *castra.*

The future of Fustat was bright. It became the capital of the province of Egypt, first under Umayyad caliphs and then under the Abbasids. But this second dynasty of Islam had to reconquer the town as it chased its rivals across North Africa. This was in 748, and a new encampment, El Askar, was set up for the purpose northeast of Fustat. Fustat now became the old town, and El Askar, the administrative center of the Abbasid governor.

The pattern was prophetic. Again and again in the city's subsequent history, a conqueror would build his headquarters outside the existing urban boundary, the fortified enclosure effectively isolating the new ruling class from the townspeople who likely as not professed to a different and competing Muslim sect. Then it too fell back with the older core, while another citadel rose outside. Thus when a governor of the ninth century, Ahmed ibn Tulun, decided to break with the authority of the Abbasid caliph in Baghdad, he built his very own princely settlement further north with a central complex including a palace and mosque. And when the Shiite Fatimids of Mahdiya in Tunisia marched on the city in 967, they built still another enclosure a kilometer or so further north calling it al-Qahira, "the Victorious," from which we derive the name Cairo. This process of urban expansion is obviously not at all in tune with the bourg-faubourg model of the West where, instead, extramural trading suburbs or other such late residential nuclei are eventually absorbed by the core city in which the administrative apparatus always resides.

Toward the end of the eleventh century, a few years before the First Crusade rolled across Europe, the mud walls of the Fatimid city were retraced in masonry by a Syrian general brought in to quell local disorders. (Fig 15.20) This impressive curtain, one of the finest specimens of military architecture in the Middle Ages, openly avows the building tradition of Greco-Roman and

and combers, for example—were probably housed in buildings owned by their employers, but we have few details. These were usually at the city's edge where property values were the lowest and rents well below downtown levels. Noisome industries like tanning were forced by law to locate in the outskirts also, which thus became the only genuine town slums.

An Urban Contrast: Cairo and Florence

This chapter should not conclude without taking some notice of the Muslim city, the great counterpoint to bastides, *civitates,* and burghs, and in some ways their tutor. To do this briefly, and in the context of our discussion thus far, I have chosen to set side by side sketches of two famous cities, Cairo and Florence, both of Roman origin and with long eventful lives. The purpose is to compare their physical development and where it had brought them by 1300, and thereby bring to light some of the salient points of variance between East and West.

When the young Muslim armies crossed the desert of Sinai in 641 to conquer Byzantine Egypt in the name of Allah, there was only a small insignificant town at the site of the later Cairo, on the right bank of the Nile just north of the ancient capital of Memphis. It was called Babylon and had been a Roman fort once, built by Trajan to guard the western entrance of an important waterway between the river and the Suez. (Fig. 15.19) The Arabs captured it and planted a military encampment outside. This soon grew into a new town around a Friday

Byzantine Syria. The walls are of rubble faced with beautifully cut stone, and they are fortified by massive square towers. The three surviving gateways are masterpieces of defensive planning. Their first two storeys are solid. Behind the third storey is a broad operations platform that could hold enough troops to deal with any attacking party brought over on wheeled siege towers. The space before the entranceway is sloped and paved with highly polished granite to thwart cavalry charges. Whole column shafts are set into the walls a short way above ground as a bond between the rubble core and the outer faces of the dressed stone. They are designed to hold up the gate structure if the lower sections are undermined by battering rams or enemy troops working under the protection of devices called tortoises. The flanking towers of one gate have rounded ends, a form recommended in Vitruvius' ancient treatise in preference to square towers whose corners can be pounded too easily.

In this Fatimid stronghold the ruler lived in great pomp. The general plan was rectangular in shape with cross-axes, as in a Roman *castrum*. The royal residence consisted of twin palaces with a parade ground in the middle. There were barracks for a trustworthy garrison, a mint, and an arsenal, estates for high officers and government functionaries, and two mosques, one of them built against the walls. The other, the mosque of al-Azhar, became the center of a great university.

All learning in Muslim cities until 1100 took place in mosques. Seated against the columns of the sanctuary (and you can still see the practice today), each teacher addressed a circle of students on two kinds of subject matter. (Fig. 15.21) The so-called Muslim sciences dealt with theology, that is, the study and exegesis of the Koran, ritual and canon law, and the Traditions or *hadith*. The other half of all knowledge, and this the Fatimids strongly encouraged, included the sciences of foreign or pre-Islamic origin—philosophy, physics, mathematics, astronomy, and the like—the Sciences of the Ancients, as they were called. The Muslim contribution to some of these fields was far in advance of the West.

As in the Chinese imperial city, this administrative compound was strictly off lim-

Fig. 15.14 Nürnberg (Germany), a medieval street. The large corner house belonged to the artist Albrecht Dürer (1472–1528).

its to the general public. Their city was Fustat, separated from al-Qahira with extensive gardens which were under water during the flooding of the Nile. Communication between the two centers was by donkey or by boat. The old town was frightfully congested, as Cairo is to this day. (Fig. 15.22) Houses clambered to a height of ten storeys and more, and could hold as many as two hundred people apiece. Their balconies and projecting bays, closed in by latticework, almost touched across the narrow streets. Some markets and thoroughfares received no daylight at all; they were illuminated permanently by lamps. The desert dust stormed in and was trapped in blind alleys. The population—Christians, Jews, and Muslims—was intermingled. They

worked together in industry and commerce. They paid the same taxes.

As a rule houses were held in joint ownership, but the shares were calculated in terms of percentages of the overall price rather than as rooms or apartments. It was hard to guarantee regular upkeep under the circumstances, and since labor was expensive, it was more profitable to rent out the premises for as long as one could rather than try to make the needed repairs. Little wonder that the legal documents and inventories speak often of "ruins."

Fustat, an unwalled mosaic of older towns, was totally vulnerable at a time when Crusader castles were going up all over the Near East, the Fatimids had been deprived of their Syrian possessions, and Jerusalem

Fig. 15.15 Siena (Italy), a medieval street (Via Sallustio Bandini).

fostered a Latin kingdom. In 1168 when the Crusaders took Bilbeis and headed toward Cairo, the Fatimid caliph gave the incredible order to set Fustat on fire so as not to risk its capture by the infidel.

The Crusaders never made it. Instead, a shining Muslim knight who engaged them with spectacular success in Syria, Salah ad-Din Ayyubi known to Christians as Saladin, arrived to rescue Cairo—and started by terminating Fatimid rule. The Fatimid palaces were destroyed, the two sexes of the ruling family separated so that the dynasty might become extinct.

The walled city now turned into the commercial center. To the south a redoubtable citadel rose against the arid spur of Muqattam, the stone supplied in part by the pyramids of Giza. (Fig. 15.19) Sitting halfway between Cairo and the ruins of Fustat, it tried to pull the urban fragments together. In the building of it, Crusader prisoners were employed; their presence still shows in the execution of a perfect Gothic detail here and there. Sometimes such features are actual Gothic spoils from Crusader monuments. There is in fact a definite visual affinity at this point between the architecture of Cairo and the Gothic, not the metropolitan Gothic of Europe but the simplified, toned-down version transported eastward by the Crusaders. The two share the use of the pointed arch, attenuated proportions, and a skeletal elegance in the design of facades. The similarity ends in Cairene interiors; they are without the vertical continuities of Gothic, and in place of rib vaults they favor domes and flat ceilings. (Fig. 15.23)

Saladin is also responsible for introducing the *madrasa* to Cairo. This new institution, a theological academy devoted exclusively to the teaching of Muslim sciences, was sponsored officially to stem the influence of nonorthodox sects and the free inquiry of universities, and to produce puritanical administrators and civil servants. Madrasas were endowed by princes or wealthy individuals and were meant to provide for all the needs of their students. In Cairo, they were handsome buildings of two iwans placed axially on either side of a court, a scheme that derives from contemporary Cairene houses. A mosque and the domed mausoleum of the founder are

Fig. 15.16 Lincoln (England), Jew's House, ca. 1170–80. It is sometimes identified with the House of Aaron, Lincoln's most famous Jew, who at the time of his death had on his books as debtors a king of Scotland, five earls, one archbishop, nine Cistercian abbeys, and the towns of Winchester and Southampton.

Fig. 15.17 Cluny (France), twelfth-century town house; reconstruction drawing.

Fig. 15.18 Decorative details of medieval houses: (**a**) 10–14 Place de la Poissonerie, Chartres (France), Maison Saumon, fifteenth century. This is one of three carved posts on the facade; the others depict the Annunciation and a grape vine. (**b**) Saffon Walden, Essex (England), an oriel window of a house and shop, ca. 1500. Decorative mouldings such as this were common on late medieval English houses, whereas representational carving, like that found in (**a**), was less common.

commonly attached, sometimes also a hospital. The tight, small mass is lifted above the surrounding roofscape by a minaret. (Fig. 15.24). The units themselves are oriented toward Mecca, but a high continuous facade screens from the street any necessary tilt in plan.

This then is the city of Cairo in the thir-teenth century. The citadel looms above the flat urban sprawl on the right bank of the Khalīj Misri, Trajan's canal, running parallel to the unstable riverbed. The military and governing elite are concentrated in the Rumailiya quarter at the foot of the citadel; the merchants and artisans, in the former Fatimid stronghold; the lower classes and noxious industries like tanning, in the rubbishy mounds of Fustat around the ninth-century mosque of the upstart governor, Ahmed ibn Tulun. Ethnic and religious groups—Turks, Copts, Jews, Greeks, Nubians, the ruling class of Mameluks—occupy their own quarters; but there is little segregation of land use, except for the ad-

Fig. 15.19 Cairo (Egypt), historical development; schematic plans.

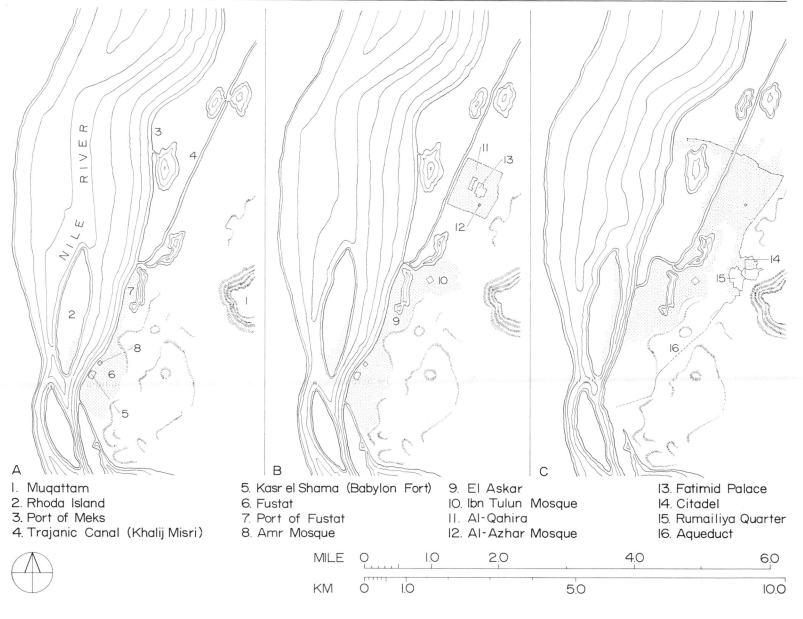

A
1. Muqattam
2. Rhoda Island
3. Port of Meks
4. Trajanic Canal (Khalij Misri)

5. Kasr el Shama (Babylon Fort)
6. Fustat
7. Port of Fustat
8. Amr Mosque

9. El Askar
10. Ibn Tulun Mosque
11. Al-Qahira
12. Al-Azhar Mosque

13. Fatimid Palace
14. Citadel
15. Rumailiya Quarter
16. Aqueduct

MILE 0   1.0   2.0   4.0   6.0

KM   0   1.0   5.0   10.0

Fig. 15.20 Cairo, the walls of the Fatimid minister Badr al-Gamali, 1087–92; detail showing the Bab al-Futuh or Gate of Deliverance, also known as Bab al-Iqbal or the Gate of Prosperity. The walls are the work of three Christian architects from Edessa, the modern Urfa in southeastern Turkey.

Fig. 15.21 Cairo, mosque of Shaikh Malik al-Mu'ayyad, 1415–20; interior view facing the sanctuary, showing classes in session. The *mihrab* is the third bay from the left; the *minbar* is partly visible, immediately to the right. Most of the supports in this mosque are re-used classical columns.

Fig. 15.22 Cairo, the bazaar of the silk merchants; lithograph by David Roberts, 1849. This street market became established between the mosque (left) and the early sixteenth-century tomb (right) of Sultan Qansuh al-Ghuri.

Fig. 15.23 Cairo, the mausoleum of Sultan Qala'un, ca. 1285; interior view looking into the drum of the dome.

ministrative core and the vast cemeteries. The latter are not simply tranquil parks of the dead. Sprinkled throughout are shrines, monasteries, and schools for mystic orders, where the traveler can find free lodging. Family tombs have retainers who live with their dependents in adjacent rooms.

This is in no manner a self-governing city. There is no town hall; no real civic square. Markets and occupational and religious fraternities seek no permanent monumentality. The long crepuscular tunnels of bazaars, crowded and hectic, burrow their way through the urban fabric, especially near the

main thoroughfare of the walled city. Maqrizi, the late medieval historian of the city, mentions 12,000 shops and countless itinerant vendors who block the public way. Each trade and each bit of produce has its own area within the linear market system. Shops also line the street side of *khans*, two-storey inns arranged, in the millennial way, around a court. (Fig. 15.25) In small vaulted cells on the ground floor the beasts and goods are locked up, while the traveler lodges in rooms above, which open off a continuous gallery. The *fondaco* of the Western cities has its prototype here; the very word is Arabic. Add numerous baths, mosques, and madrasas distributed throughout the city, and the survey of public architecture is complete.

A look at the plan of the built-up area may be the most instructive element of comparison with the West. (Fig. 15.26) Open space is at a premium. Streets are uniformly narrow and few of them run clear for any length; and this in the area of the original Fatimid Cairo that had been laid out as a formal, orthogonal palace city. By contrast, in the West, many Roman grids appear to have come through the centuries intact, and even less rigid medieval city-forms than the grid always maintain a co-ordinated public network of principal and secondary arteries. (Figs. 15.2, 20.3) Open spaces may not be independent squares in the manner of the Roman Forum, but they are there nonetheless and they are intimately linked to the streets that flow into them. The Muslim street is rarely seen as a public passage linking one point of interest with another. The maze of dead-end alleys that insinuate themselves like hundreds of inadvertent cracks in the solidly built mass of medieval Cairo are characteristic. At best the few principal thoroughfares might define irregular superblocks, but within these superblocks neighborhood life eats up the public pathways by hundreds of daily encroachments.

A city-form anywhere, at any time, is the battleground between public rights and private interest. In the military feudalism that governed the cities of Islam, there was little room for a municipal organization that would regulate and safeguard the public domain. The care of streets was ultimately the responsibility of those who lived on them and used them. Provided no formal complaint was lodged by neighbors, one could impinge on the open space and get away with it. What is more, the law allowed that owners had preferential access to an easement around their building plots, as well as the air rights over the street. It is

Fig. 15.24 Cairo, the mausoleum and *madrasa* of Sultan Qala'un (1280–90); view from the south-west.

Fig. 15.25 Cairo, the caravanserai of Qansuh al-Ghuri, 1504–5; interior court. Originally, the court had a small prayer hall in the center. The two porticoed lower floors contain storage rooms; the upper floors are occupied by apartments arranged in vertical stacks of three rooms each.

unlikely that a rational system of public ways could remain inviolate against such odds.

The urban history of Florence in the late Middle Ages recounts, from one perspective, the battle of a city to take control of its streets and open spaces. The Roman grid was hardly pristine at the time of the commune's assertion. Thoroughfares, often whole neighborhoods, were obstructed or sealed off by feuding families. Lesser infringements cluttered the city-form as rampantly as they did in Cairo. The charge of the young republic was two-pronged: to unstop urban passageways, weave together all quarters of the city, and thus eradicate pockets of resistance against its authority; and to conceive of the city-form as an intentional design.

The first of these objectives entailed legal constraint, financial settlement, and the use of force. The government adopted a building code and statutes affecting the appearance and care of open space and public works. Officials enforced their provisions which regulated everything from balconies, porticoes, and outer stairs to street traffic and paving. Three classes of streets were recognized: *viae publicae*, or major thoroughfares; *viae vicinales*, or neighborhood streets, often blind alleys; and *viae privatae*, or private streets. The last were slowly purchased from their owners, while critical secondary streets were opened up and widened. The height of feudal towers was systematically reduced, and towers of offending nobles razed altogether.

The city as work of art goes beyond practical amelioration or the presumption of monumentality. It strives for perceivable order, which in turn relies on the ability to see the city as a whole. We have two direct indications of this trend in thirteenth-century Tuscany—the drawing up of town plans, and the appointment of town architects. With a comprehensive and comprehensible image of the way things are, and an adviser alert to formal relationships, the process of urban design—that is, decision-making on how things should be—can get going. The end of this process is to clarify the conceptual priorities of the city's governance, the structure of its society, and the pride of its legend. The means are those tangible interventions that will revise the image in line with these purposes, so that

1. Fustat
2. Giza
3. Bûlâq
4. Rhoda Island
5. Birkat al-Fil
6. City of the Dead
7. Cemetery
8. The Citadel
9. Race Course
10. Mosque of Ibn Tûlûn
11. Sultan Hasan Mosque
12. al-Azhar Mosque
13. Zâhir Mosque
14. Hâkim Mosque
15. Khalij Misiri al Kabir
16. Nasiri Canal
17. Khaur Canal
18. Bâb al-Futûh
19. Bâb al-Nasr
20. Aqueduct

MILE 0 0.5 1.0 2.0 3.0

KILOMETER 0 0.5 1.0 2.0 3.0 4.0 5.0

the city says, to its own people and to visitors, what the commune through its officers has determined it should say. Here attention will center on the walls, the streets, and the public buildings—the chief constituents of the city-form.

Florence thought of her walls as a visual asset. (Fig. 15.27) Private construction was not allowed to abut. Uniform towers at regular intervals were there "for the strength and beauty of the city," writes Giovanni Villani in 1324. Aristotle thought of walls in the same way sixteen hundred years earlier, and indeed it is this Classical precedent that Tuscany looks back on. Wide and straight streets are considered ideal, as they were in Hellenistic and Roman cities. The benefits of rectifying irregularities are said to be health, convenience, and beauty. Public monuments replace humbler forerunners and are coordinated with the guidance of a master plan. In a single year, 1284, in a concerted building campaign directed by the municipal architect Arnolfo di Cambio, the city broke ground for a new set of walls, a new cathedral, and the Palazzo Vecchio, as well as starting the amplification of Orsanmichele, the communal granary and a monument to the city's guilds. Cathedral, town hall, and guild hall were linked by a widened axis, the present Via dei Calzaiuoli, which necessitated that an eleventh-century hospital be demolished.

This was the high point of the city-republic of Florence, and the bold refashioning of its fabric sought to concretize it. The Roman colony had been small, and unimportant. (Fig. 9.2) It had almost disappeared during the Germanic invasions but for a Byzantine garrison that took up residence in the center. The Lombards had bypassed it as the capital of their duchy in favor of Lucca, a creation of their own. The Roman walls were retraced probably in the eleventh century when the city, now the capital of the margraviate of Tuscany under the Countess Matilda, enjoyed its first true bloom since antiquity. Then its struggle for independence began. The rise of the com-

Fig. 15.26 Cairo; map of the city in the nineteenth century. (Compare with Fig. 15.19; no. 4 on that figure corresponds to no. 15 here.)

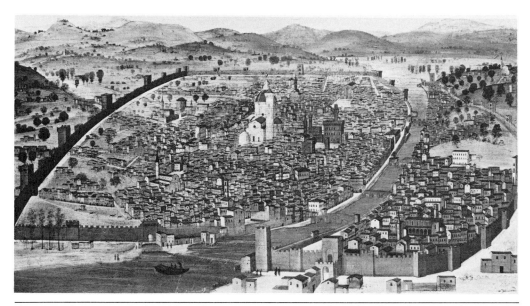

Fig. 15.27 Florence in the late fifteenth century; view painted on a wood panel. The white mass in the center is the cathedral group; the darker mass to the right, the Palazzo Vecchio/Bargello group. (English private collection)

mune paralleled a population swell that stretched the built-up area beyond the old rectangle. A new set of walls embraced this exuberant suburbia in the 1170s, including the communities on the other side of the Arno, along the three roads that emanated from what was then the only bridge. Within, the parish church was already forging neighborhoods and weaning people away from feudal enclaves. Four quarters, focused on the original four gates of the Roman enceinte and organized for purposes of general urban defense, further weak-

ened the hold of feudal factions and the hopeless fragmentation of the city fabric they brought about.

By the early thirteenth century the population had passed 50,000. Landlocked and not ideally situated, the city nonetheless was turning into one of the great economic centers of Europe, thanks to banking and the wool industry. The walls were already too small; the twelve city gates barely able to handle the brimming traffic. Three new bridges were thrown across the Arno. Six streets from the old town converged on the

northernmost of these bridges, and the Piazza S. Trinità at the next bridge acquired the character of a passage-square open to the river. Two new institutions, the guilds and the mendicant orders, brought their own pressure to bear on the city structure. The friars chose to build their monasteries outside the walls—the Dominicans in 1221 to the west, the Franciscans a few years later on the opposite side. A great spiritual cross-axis was thus formed, in a way independent of both Church and state; it appealed directly to the common people beyond parish and gate-company loyalties. Other orders—Servites, Augustinians, Carmelites—followed. By the end of the thirteenth century their monasteries had bred important suburbs, each with its own large square for preaching.

And that is when Florence drew up its master plan. (Fig. 16.2) The new walls that brought the friars inside the city lines, the Palazzo Vecchio and its Piazza della Signoria, the new cathedral of S. Maria del Fiore, and the expansive building program of the orders spilled into the fourteenth century and on into the next. Embedded in all this activity were the mainsprings of change. The plucky, aggressive Tuscan city-state, for reasons still not altogether fathomable, leaped the pale of its time, left behind the elaborately symbolic mind of late Gothic Europe, and edged toward a new age of reason with its concern for the basic dignity of human existence. "Florence," Villani prophesied in 1338, "the daughter and creature of Rome, was in the ascendancy, and destined for great things." There we now follow her.

Further Reading

M. Beresford, *New Towns of the Middle Ages* (London: Lutterworth, 1967).

J. Gies and F. Gies, *Life in a Medieval City* (New York: Harper & Row, 1981).

U. T. Holmes, Jr., *Daily Living in the Twelfth Century* (Madison: University of Wisconsin Press, 1952).

J. H. Mundy and P. Riesenberg, *The Medieval Town* (Princeton: Van Nostrand, 1958).

P. G. Ruggiers, *Florence in the Age of Dante* (Norman: University of Oklahoma Press, 1964).

D. Russell, *Medieval Cairo and the Monasteries of Wadi Natrun, a Historical Guide* (London: Weidenfeld and Nicolson, 1962).

H. Saalman, *Medieval Cities* (New York: Braziller, 1968).

G. Wiet, *Cairo, City of Art and Commerce,* trans. S. Feiler (Norman: University of Oklahoma Press, 1964).

M. Wood, *The English Mediaeval House* (London: Phoenix House, 1965).

Gloucester (England), Gloucester Abbey (now the cathedral);
south walk of cloister, begun 1370.

16

EDGES OF MEDIEVALISM

Florence at the Crossroads

"Destined for great things." (Fig. 16.1) Historians of art and literature have taught us to see Villani's chauvinistic boast about his hometown as a prophecy fulfilled. They recite an honor list of Florentine glory for the fourteenth century: Dante, Petrarch, Giotto, Arnolfo di Cambio. Discussions of Renaissance art and architecture unfailingly begin in early fifteenth-century Florence with the triad of Brunelleschi, Donatello, and Masaccio. Florence is accorded that cultural primacy that Athens held in antiquity, and in these very terms self-satisfied native historians of the time describe their city. In concluding the last chapter I have myself singled her out as a paradigmatic case of medieval urbanism. I spoke of her edging closer to an age of reason and the dignity of human existence.

The bare record of events in this century and a half of Florentine history would seem to mock these judgments. It is a chronicle of belligerence, brutal factionalism, and social unrest. Having already systematically crushed small towns in the area, Florence after 1300 took on rivals of the first rank: Pisa, Milan, the German emperor, the pope and his defenders. The citizenry as bitterly and violently fought with itself—papal-minded Guelfs against Ghibellines, aristocrats against wealthy merchants, the major guilds against the lesser guilds, the working classes against everyone. Vengefulness was the order of the day. The losing side had its leaders banished or cut down; their property was methodically demolished. Dante died in exile. Petrarch, whose father

had suffered the disgrace of banishment in 1302, refused all later entreaties to return. The town hall, or Palazzo Vecchio, stands askew, Villani tells us, to avoid sitting on the land of the razed Uberti property, a Ghibelline family that briefly held power in the 1250s—"which was a great imperfection," he writes with proto-Renaissance solicitude, "inasmuch as the palace should have been given a square or rectangular shape." Florence, like Athens and Rome, accepted slavery and took advantage of the burgeoning trade in Circassians, Serbs, Armenians, and Syrians. The popular Ciompi revolt of 1378 flared up because lower-class workers were forbidden to meet in groups of more than ten, to organize, or to negotiate conditions of employment.

Which, then, is the truth about Florence? Was she enlightened or grim, a united city or the product of contentious energy? Both, really. Her unallayed social ferment had the strength of common action. In the struggle to keep adversaries out of power, every group came to exercise power. Individual quarrels were subsumed under public pride. It was possible to hate and suppress fellow Florentines but love Florence. At a time when the tidier rule of princes was gaining the upper hand generally, Florence resisted the comforts of absolutism. Democracy, however limited, unleashes self-interest, but it also strengthens self-respect. There is no reason to doubt that all social classes, despite the heat of their feuding, were proud to be Florentines. It was in Florence that the thought had been maturing since the late thirteenth century that personal freedom was more than a legal pact: it was a natural right. Reality may have been otherwise, but citizens believed themselves to be free and to matter. However low they might rank on the social lad-

Fig. 16.1 Donatello, *Il Marzocco*, ca. 1420. (Museo Nazionale, Florence, Italy)

der, they were still sons and daughters of a respected, subtle polity with an authentic past, prosperous and subject to none.

The City Center

And it was everybody's city. The very design of the city-form was both cumulative and participatory. A prince would have shaped Florence more sharply, more expeditiously. Her avowed mother, ancient Rome, had been rebuilt by the will of emperors who left it strewn with islands of a grand order like the Palatine and the imperial forums. Even Athens, at its fifth-century peak, was the brainchild of one statesman, Perikles. Florence involved her citizens in an ongoing program of urban design whose broad outline was a matter of selective consensus. There was the estimable Roman ideal—paved streets that were to be "pulchrae, amplae et rectae," as one document puts it, that is, "beautiful, wide and straight." There was the sense that visual order testified to social and political orderliness, that planning must benefit decency and the public good. Finally, there was the determination to provide for the city's magistracy and its faith with competitive grandeur. The proclamation of 1296 for a new cathedral reads:

Since the highest mark of prudence in a people of noble origin is to proceed in the management of their affairs so that their magnanimity and wisdom may be evinced in their outward acts, we order Arnolfo, headmaster of our commune, to make a design for the renovation of S. Reparata in a style of magnificence which neither the industry nor the power of man can surpass.

If the immediate race was against the great rival states of Pisa and Siena, the commune's ambition had also a historical sweep. The new building was to be "so magnificent in its height and beauty that it shall surpass anything of the kind produced in the time of their greatest power by the Greeks and the Romans."

The city relied on the talent of her artists to make good her vaulting aspirations, but the people were an active, vocal clientele. Their taxes and labor went to the building of the walls. Citizens' commissions oversaw street clearance and urban renewal projects. The renovation of the baptistery was entrusted to the Cloth Finishers Guild; general supervision of the new cathedral to the Wool Merchants Guild. A committee of overseers for the latter project appointed in 1318 consisted of three members representing the city, the bishop, and the chapter; only one among them, the last, was to be a cleric. Detailed minutes of the proceedings for the enlargement of the cathedral in the 1350s show the citizenry in the thick of the decision-making process. The first wooden model was judged by a commission of twelve, including nonprofessional members from the Portinari and Albizzi families. At later stages of the design the citizenry at large was invited to pass judgment, and the names of those who testified were entered into the record. And as the group of official buildings in the city center took shape, it remained untouched by the internal scraps and risings. Private property was the customary target of political retribution. No destructive anger was vented by a party or mob on the Palazzo Vecchio, say, whoever the overthrown occupant. In time, even private palaces were seen to enrich the city-form and nurture popular pride.

In the early fourteenth century the city center was an imposing ensemble of new public buildings, among which visual relationships were being clarified step by step. There were: Arnolfo's cathedral across from the baptistery; the Palazzo Vecchio, completed with unusual dispatch by 1310; the still older Bargello, headquarters of the captain of the people (later of the podestà), built during the first popular government in the 1250s in imitation of the very forts of the feudal nobility against which it was to defend the interests of the people; and the showcase of the guilds, the Orsanmichele. (Figs. 16.2, 15.27) All of these buildings lay east of the main north-south artery, or *cardo*, of the Roman city. At the place of the ancient forum was the market whose activity had spread to nearby streets and piazzas with specialized areas for wine, oil, eggs, and the like, and to a new market west of the Palazzo Vecchio.

The distribution was simple and effective. At the two ends of an axis running parallel to the Roman cardo, the Via dei Calzaiuoli, the cathedral complex and the administrative structure of the commune were grouped, not as adversary estates but as pendants of urban identity. In the middle stood the market and the temple of the guilds. The height, mass, and commanding height of the Palazzo Vecchio, with its forcible acuteness of outline which so distressed Villani, clinched a preeminent status among the buildings. In front of the short west side and around the northern corner, where the original main prospect and entrance were, a vigorous public space was carved out of the razed Uberti holdings—the Piazza della Signoria. Its ceremonial worth gained dramatically in the 1370s when a grand loggia was added on the

Fig. 16.2 Map: Central district of Florence, showing the major buildings of the Middle Ages. (Compare with Fig. 16.12.)

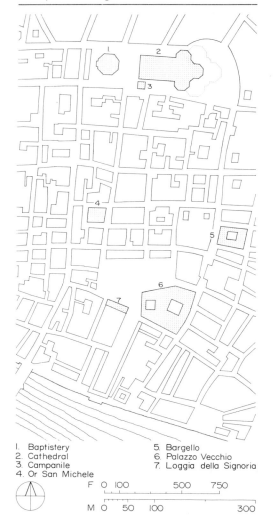

1. Baptistery
2. Cathedral
3. Campanile
4. Or San Michele
5. Bargello
6. Palazzo Vecchio
7. Loggia della Signoria

F 0 100   500   750

M 0 50 100   300

Fig. 16.3 Florence, the Palazzo Davanzati, late fourteenth century: (a) exterior view; (b) the courtyard at ground level. The building is now a museum of furniture and decoration.

south side. This was a generous, open building that stood against the bristling bulk of the Palazzo Vecchio where the public functions of the loggia could complement the intrigue-filled doings of republican government. At the loggia executive officers were sworn in and foreign embassies were received with outward pomp in the name of the citizenry. (Fig. 15.10)

Against this battlemented administrative nucleus, symbol of an alternately strained and festive public life, stood the lifting grace of faith. The general sobriety of this nucleus—the somber masonry, defensive crowns, and rustication—was replaced at the other end of the axis with the bright, luminous cathedral group swathed in a mantle of dazzling polychromy. In the 1330s the painter Giotto, then the city's artistic director, was assigned the task of adding a bell tower to the still unfinished church. (Fig. 13.33) It was to rise, as a native historian tellingly expressed it, "to the honor . . . of a powerfully united, greatly spirited and freely sovereign people"—which does not sound much like an ordinary bell tower. It was in fact a new kind of accent for the city, unique among the towers of the feudal past and the stark piles of communal government. Elegant and marble-encrusted, it soared 89 meters (292 feet), in line with the facade of the cathedral but not attached to it. The traditional Florentine arrangement called for a campanile that was attached to the left flank of the church, usually toward the east end. This was the position that prevailed in S. Reparata, the old cathedral. Giotto's campanile is moved toward the newly hatched city center and is situated conspicuously just off the Via dei Calzaiuoli. To make the point that this is a civic monument, Giotto leaves out the spire required of Gothic bell towers and crowns his building instead with the *ballatoio*, a machicolated cornice of military inspiration employed in earnest on the tower of the Palazzo Vecchio. The same point is brought home at the base where a series of coats of arms heralds Florence, the commune, and the people at large—but not, significantly, the Church.

Palaces

During the first half of the fourteenth century the commune was busy with the ca-

thedral, Orsanmichele, and the latest set of walls begun in 1284 but not completed until 1333. The walls—a colossal undertaking—entailed a circuit over 12 meters (39 feet) high with a total run of 8.5 kilometers (5 miles). As it turned out, these walls overshot the mark. The brisk growth of the city in the preceding period had broken through the late twelfth-century circuit in less than a century, slowed down, and by 1350 stopped altogether. The area between the two walls remained undeveloped, except in the vicinity of the prospering monasteries built by the mendicant orders. Elsewhere single rows of houses fronted the streets that led to the gates, opening out at the back toward gardens and fields. This green belt would not be filled in until the nineteenth century. (Fig. 15.27)

Florence was exceptional in that it did not shrink in size too drastically through the disastrous trials of the fourteenth century. For most of Europe depopulation was universal. Famine, plague, and war bled the continent. The famine of 1315–17 was only the worst of many. In the major cloth towns of the north, which had long outgrown their local food supply, the death rate was appalling. Plagues were recurrent too, but none as general and devastating as the Black Death of 1348–50. It carried off more than a third of the population of Western Europe. The Hundred Years' War between England and France preceded it by a decade. The name is not figurative. Not until the middle of the next century were the English finally dislodged from the vast territories of France that they had conquered at such a frightful cost and held onto tenaciously.

Since Florence had imported two-thirds of her grain supply in the best of times from lands beyond her territorial jurisdiction, all she had to do now was to shift markets opportunely. Money was plentiful. As the recession in the cloth industry became acute, the city converted in part to silk; and even the crash of the 1340s that ruined the great banking families of the Bardi and the Peruzzi proved surmountable. The city's genius for large-scale business was also directed toward the countryside, where wealthy merchants assembled big estates and ran them efficiently. Having a place in the country got to be popular. While the nobility had been compelled to give up its castles since the initial success of the commune and to live within the walls, the better-off bourgeois now sought escape on farms, away from urban pressures and turmoil.

The main structure built on the farm property was probably not much different from the traditional Tuscan farmhouse, perhaps better built and with some swank accessories that would be out of an ordinary farmer's reach. The type is shown in fourteenth-century paintings: a blocky mass built of rough stone, with an arched or trabeated porch or loggia, a balcony, and an outside oven. This is one source of the later, Renaissance villa. The loggia will continue to be the most typical element of the villa, as it was of the farmhouse, only now it will take on Classical airs and be incorporated into the body of the building, often framed by lateral wings. (Fig. 19.32)

The town house was different. It too derived from a traditional type, in this case the tower house we made brief mention of in the last chapter. But by the mid-fourteenth century the type was in the process of civilizing itself, turning into something more urbane, less dour. The Palazzo Davanzati west of the new market is a good example. (Fig. 16.3) It was built originally by the Davizzi family sometime in the second half of the century. It looks narrow and tall still, and a bit stiff, but an open gallery graces its top instead of the aggressive *ballatoio*. Friendly gestures toward the street, like *sporti* or projecting upper storeys, were becoming characteristic of residential architecture. Sometimes the openness came at ground level, with a loggia, where ceremonial affairs, marriages for example, would be intentionally laid bare for the benefit of passersby. The great loggia of the Piazza della Signoria is a public expression of this domestic feature. (Fig. 15.10)

But some things about the Palazzo Davanzati look forward to the urban mansions of the next century. The facade is self-consciously calibrated. The ground floor for shops and storage is distinguished by light rustication. All levels are neatly marked off with string-courses; a fancier cornice at the eaves caps the design. The arched windows are exactly the same, and the floors diminish in size as we move upward. In the interior, the nicety is a small courtyard with

Fig. 16.4a Florence, the Palazzo Medici, 1444–60, Michelozzo di Bartolomeo; (**a**) exterior view. The main change in the exterior design is the filling in of the open ground-level arches at the corner with windows designed by Michelangelo in the early sixteenth century.

an arched loggia that sits on octagonal columns with rich capitals. A nimble stairway unites the three floors of living quarters, each with a main room taking up the whole width of the building and its own lavatory. A well-shaft runs through the floors, the water being raised by bucket.

To the merchant or banker of note who did business with foreign clients, the town house advertised professional prestige. To the city, formal burgher palaces offered a way to lend decorum to the renovated street pattern and to upgrade cluttered neighborhoods. Thus prominent families were encouraged in their efforts to consolidate rambling real estate into monumental

buildings. The commune would agree to the suppression of public space, an alley, or a small piazza, under some accommodation worked out with the family, to allow for the spacious formality of these buildings. The famous urban palaces of the Medici, the Strozzi, the Pitti are not a high-flown Renaissance invention of the fifteenth century. The building type of the Palazzo Medici—with inner court, tiered facade, rusticated ground floor, and a once open loggia—belongs in the later Middle Ages. (Fig. 16.4) What is new in the Medici palace is the grandeur and symmetry, the four-square, mid-space mass, the full cloistering of the courtyard with the staircases tucked

Fig. 16.4b The Palazzo Medici, courtyard.

private wealth and its civic display. As Leon Battista Alberti was to write in his *Ten Books on Architecture*, ''The magnificence of the [house] should be adapted to the dignity of the owner.'' The wealthy merchant could atone for worldly success by supporting pious causes or by contributing to the architectural enhancement of the faith. And one way to honor God and oneself at the same time was to finance a family chapel in the parish church and have it handsomely decorated by a leading artist. This self-serving patronage, which had its start in the fourteenth century, has left many intimate jewels of sacred art, among them Giotto's chapel for the Peruzzi in the church of S. Croce and Michelangelo's for the Medici, and, later in seventeenth-century Rome, Bernini's chapel in S. Maria della Vittoria, for the Cornaro family.

Churches

Church building in late medieval Florence, as we have seen, was in the hands of the commune and the friars. But whether it was the new cathedral or the great churches of the mendicant orders, the architectural language they employed was the same—and it was not that of secular buildings like the Palazzo Vecchio and its loggia or the town houses of the rich. The domestic idiom was indebted to the vernacular of tower houses and farms, as well as the classicizing Romanesque of Tuscany which we have met a while back. Religious architecture leaned toward the more international conventions of Gothic, albeit of a very individual brand.

The style had crossed the Alps into Italy with the Cistercians. The Franciscans and Dominicans in the thirteenth century put it to their own uses. But it is an emblematic acceptance at best—a rose here, a rib vault there, set in an Italian ground that is unmistakable. S. Maria Novella (1278–1350), the Dominican church in Florence, is basically Cistercian in layout, but the bays of the central nave, transept, and choir are square in the tradition of northern Italy; also Italian is the broad opening of the nave onto the tall aisle space. (Fig. 16.5) Flat surfaces prevail. The supporting members are picked out in the cool, gray-green stone of Tuscany called *pietra serena*. In the interior elevation, there is nothing above the nave arches but a single small roundel per bay. The Franciscan church of S. Croce, begun

behind, and of course the heightened appreciation of Classical forms (notice the enormous projecting cornice like a disembodied Classical entablature) and Classical proportions.

Socially, the principal change is in the dramatic expansion of residential space. Contrary to general opinion, these stately premises sheltered a single household that consisted of the immediate family and two or three servants. Little if any room was set aside for the family business, except an office on the ground floor, and space was rarely rented to outsiders. Even the customary shops were gradually excluded. We know that the resale value of these Renaissance palaces hardly ever matched the great cost of putting them up. They were, then, not prudent investments, but conspicuous testimonials to the household of a prosperous businessman and his position in the

city. And in their total outlook they represented a degree of involution unknown to the fluid street life of the later Middle Ages. With the exterior loggias, shops, and lookout towers gone, the palace seals itself off from any interchange with the public sphere of the streets, protecting the privacy of the household behind a noble, expensive, stone curtain.

This indulgent show took hold slowly and hesitantly. The instinct of a banker or merchant runs counter to the nonproductive use of capital. Moreover, Franciscan teaching, especially strong in Florence, extolled poverty. But an enduring image of status was as attractive to these self-made princes of the counting houses and the exchanges, who came to rule the city-states of Tuscany, as it had been for the baron, bishop, or abbot. They were helped by the humanists who devised a moral justification for

Fig. 16.5 Florence, the church of S. Maria Novella, 1278–1350; nave looking east.

in 1294, has an open-trussed, wooden roof in place of rib vaults. (Fig. 16.6) The proportions are quite un-Gothic. With little effort one could replace the prismatic, octagonal piers with Classical columns, round out the points of the arches, and be done with any pretense of a Gothic interior except for the attenuated grace of the apse windows. It does no violence to the exquisite genius of Filippo Brunelleschi (1377–1446) to suggest that that is exactly what his Florentine churches amount to one hundred years later. (Fig. 16.7)

There is of course much more to Brunelleschi's genius than that. The revisions I proposed would also produce a Romanesque church like S. Miniato. Brunelleschi had many ingredients close at hand: round-headed arches on columns, Classical pilasters and cornices, flat ceilings, square bays. But the predisposition of this dressing no more constitutes the style architectural historians call "Renaissance" than the occasional existence of ribs, pointed arches, and

Fig. 16.6 Florence, the church of S. Croce, begun 1295, Arnolfo di Cambio(?); nave looking east.

Fig. 16.7 Florence, the church of S. Lorenzo, 1421–60, Filippo Brunelleschi; nave looking east. The initial design goes back to 1418. This was the parish church of the Medici family; it replaced an earlier church on the site.

flying buttresses within northern Romanesque could blunt the newness of Gothic. A new style, we have said, is the vehicle of a new vision. This is as true of the Renaissance as it was of Gothic. The point we are working toward, however, is this: Whereas Gothic architecture was a bona fide invention, the feat of a region in France that had no logical groundwork for it, and coincided with a strong political message, namely, royalty as the welder of French nationalism, the epiphany of Renaissance architecture that would take place in Florence in the early fifteenth century had long been anticipated locally and carried with it no narrow ideological burden. It was a culmination more than a radical change; it was a cultural maturing, a learnedness and apprehension that had already been in the making locally in the later Middle Ages. As a way of thinking and designing, the differences between the fourteenth and fifteenth centuries in Florence are a matter of degree, not of substance.

The studied poise of a Renaissance church like Brunelleschi's S. Lorenzo or S. Spirito depends on an understanding of the modular basis of Classical architecture—that is, that an initial measurement, often the half-diameter of a column at its base, will determine all other proportions of the building. What matters then is scale, not the largeness of actual dimensions. The smaller the column, the smaller proportionately the rest of the building. All details are keyed to one another, exactly as in a Greek temple, by this arithmetical module. One consequence is that the medieval practice of having a row of chapels attached to the frame of the church, so that all monks could say mass, became a subject of proper modular interlocking. In medieval churches, it was typical for some of these chapels to be very small since there had to be as many of them as there were resident monks, while others, being commissioned by private families for their use, might be arbitrarily sized. S. Croce illustrates all of this. Brunelleschi, however, takes an established type and subjects it to mathematical discipline: all chapels are now uniform or bilaterally matched, and related in proportion to the nave and aisles. (Fig. 16.9)

In his S. Lorenzo (1421–60), some of the larger relationships are self-evident. He began with a square crossing unit and derived the choir and transept by the simple repetition of this unit. So far the procedure reminds us of the "square schematism" of Carolingian architecture. The nave is made up of four squares; the aisles, of squares that are each one-quarter the area of the main unit. But the system is more elaborate. If you take the module to be the half-diameter of the columns, you can show, for example, that the diameter of each coffer in the ceiling is 4.5 modules, and that this measure exactly corresponds to the width of the windows in the clerestory.

And the system does not stay in two dimensions; it applies to elevations as well. Space is articulated in three dimensions, cast into volumetric units. Early Cistercian churches had tested this compositional device three centuries before. Here it is consistently used and, furthermore, fitted into a system of linear perspective. The square pattern of the floor and the grid coffering provide the spatial coordinates of this perspective, and the dark line of the central axis invites the user to move along it so that both nave walls seem to diminish equally toward the vanishing point. In the same way, by standing on the line and looking straight on in the direction of the aisle, a visual recession will be set in motion, through the nave arcade and across the aisle bay, converging in the center of the end wall of the corresponding chapel. (Fig. 16.8)

Brunelleschi was the inventor of one-point perspective. He wanted his buildings experienced as if they were projected on a perspective grid, as if the user were walking into a painted picture—and indeed the difference between architecture and painting in the Renaissance becomes one of artistic medium rather than kind. This of course is fundamentally alien to the experience of Classical architecture which, though modular, is not meant to be conceived in fixed perspective ratios, although obviously any building that progresses in terms of columnar bays will produce the feeling of perspective recession.

In S. Spirito, begun in 1436, the side chapels ended in niches meant to be seen as semicircular protrusions on the outside. (Fig. 16.9) We have something more sculptural here, something approximating the effect, internally, of gouged out spaces in the thickness of the wall characteristic of the

Fig. 16.8 Florence, S. Lorenzo; detail of one nave bay, view looking across the aisle into a side chapel.

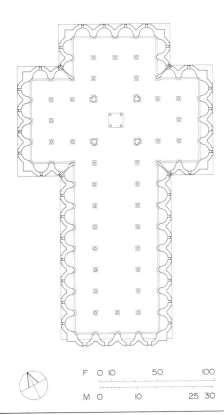

Roman vaulted style, and, externally, of bulging niches in the manner of the so-called temple of Minerva Medica or San Vitale. (Figs. 11.13, 11.15, 11.26) These two structures are of course centrally planned. Brunelleschi tried his hand at one such church, but it was abandoned unfinished. Liturgically, the Latin-cross plan was too firmly entrenched to permit radical departures. Brunelleschi's interest in centrality was more successful in small structures, like adjunct chapels or sacristies, and in the treatment of the east end of his churches. Both S. Lorenzo and S. Spirito have domed crossings from which emanate three arms of equal length; the fourth, longer arm is the nave. The scheme thus combines a longitudinal, three-aisled basilica, the stock Western formula, with a centralized structure for the altar and the clergy.

There was some medieval precedent for this idea. The most relevant case for us is the new cathedral of Florence, S. Maria del Fiore, as redesigned in the second half of the fourteenth century. (Fig. 16.10) Here each of the three equal arms has five sides externally in sympathy with the five chapels within. The altar stood in the center of the octagonal crossing which, quite remarkably, extended the full width of nave and aisles. The sense of focus on a central event, the Mass or an important civic ceremony, with a huge participating crowd packed all around, overwhelmed the customary directional emphasis of the medieval church, as indeed the nave proper was dwarfed physically by this tremendous eastern trilobe.

The only problem was that the central space, over 40 meters (131 feet) across, proved extremely difficult to dome, since its size did not allow for traditional wood

Fig. 16.9 Florence, the church of S. Spirito, begun 1436, Filippo Brunelleschi; ground plan. The church was not finished until 1482; significant changes were made in the plan, including a straight wall around the periphery that concealed the semicircular curves of the side chapels, which Brunelleschi intended to express externally.

Fig. 16.10 Florence, the cathedral of S. Maria del Fiore, begun 1296, Arnolfo di Cambio; dome added by Brunelleschi, 1420–36; ground plan and longitudinal section. The octagonal building indicated to the west of the cathedral is the Baptistery. (See Fig. 13.33.)

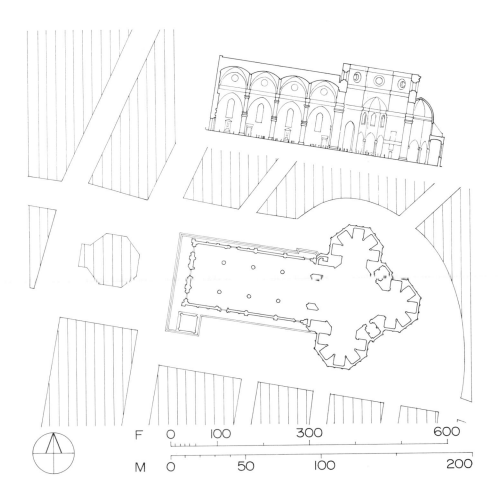

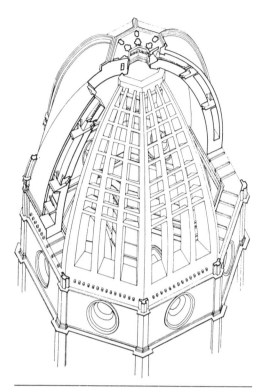

Fig. 16.11 Florence Cathedral, dome, 1420–36; axonometric drawing showing construction.

Fig. 16.12 Florence Cathedral; distant view from the south. The area in this view corresponds to that of Fig. 16.2. The straight street on the left is the Via dei Calzaiuoli, which runs between the Baptistery and, in the foreground, the Piazza della Signoria with the Palazzo Vecchio. (See also Figs. 13.22 and 15.10.)

centering. The octagonal shape was undoubtedly inspired by the baptistery across the way, which has only two-thirds the span. (Fig. 13.33) Construction had proceeded up to the springing of the dome before the end of the century. The drum could have been strengthened by flying buttresses, but was not. They had been omitted probably because of their foreign flavor and their flamboyant use at the time in the cathedral at Milan, the enemy of Florence, whose court was full of Germans. The dome had somehow to be built, then, without centering across a prohibitive span, and given the unbuttressed drum, it had to be very thin, very light. This ultimate challenge confounded the master masons.

Once again it was Brunelleschi, between 1420 and 1436, who brought off this feat. It was a legend at its time and remains one of the great stories in the history of building. The inspiration came from the baptistery, but also from the Pantheon in Rome where Brunelleschi had gone to study "the way the ancients built and their proportions"; as his biographer tells us, "[to observe] closely the supports and thrusts of the buildings, their forms, arches and inventions . . . as also their ornamental detail." (Figs. 10.3, 13.34)

The exact solution, however, was like neither building. Brunelleschi devised a double-shell dome, with each shell made up of eight curved panels joined by strong upright ribs converging at a peak. (Fig. 16.11) The panels were subdivided by more ribs interconnected by several types of horizontal members: rings of sandstone blocks tied with tin-plated iron rods, barrel vaults every 7 meters (23 feet) extending from rib to rib, and wooden tie rings of big oak beams. All this made it possible to build the dome in layers and to reinforce it as it went up. The tie rods and layered construction are Classical expedients; the ribs are Gothic. Between the two shells of the concentric vaults, these ribs worked in fact like hidden flying buttresses for the inner shell, while they protruded powerfully at the corners of the outer shell as part of the visual effect of the dome's mass. For the task was not merely to come up with an engineering device, but also to emblazen the skyline with the city's ultimate symbol. In the description of his model that was submitted to the building commission, Brunelleschi is fully alert to this double motive. He talks of the outer shell, for instance, as necessary to preserve the inner dome from the weather, but adds, "and to vault it in more magnificent and swelling form."

And that the cathedral dome undeniably is—magnificent and swelling. It is sculpture in the round, with every view of it valid—the near and the far, the northeast and the southwest. (Fig. 16.12) With exquisite clarity, its red brick panels stitched by eight ribs of Carrara marble from the native quarries nearby, the dome does more than focus and hold together the widespread town. That it does splendidly, as if the energies of all those decades of building and the sense of community they encapsuled were drawn together and tied at the top by the white strings of marble and the knot of the lantern. But the dome does more. It gathers about itself the *contado,* the jurisdictional territory outside the walls, and the hill range beyond, and creates everexpanding ripples of impact that move toward the distant countryside.

It is no wonder that Florentines abroad will henceforth no longer proclaim themselves homesick, but "sick for the dome." They now possessed, regardless of their social standing, the most perfect standard for their proud city and its aspirations—a city that considered herself in the fifteenth century, under the gentle rule of the Medici, to be the mistress of Tuscany, the mediator of all Italy, and the tutor of Europe beyond.

In one spot of northern Italy, then, the Middle Ages edged closer to the modern era purposely and precociously. Florentines were aware of breaking with other centers of the West and were proud to have recovered those hallowed roots of antiquity that became mongrelized when motley outlanders invaded the Roman Empire. In architecture, the age of the Renaissance in Florence rested on shared cultural attitudes, among them at least three that are central. There was, first, a deep respect for local tradition, for continuities. Some of the foremost efforts of fifteenth-century architects went toward the completion and renovation of extant structure. The new style was a medium of coherence and contextual updating, a middle state between the city of the past and the city of the future. Second, architecture in Florence was a public event; it was everyone's concern. Buildings mattered. They were a source of pride and an exportable commodity of Florentinism, like the currency and the famous cloth. "All the citizens," Alberti says in his book on architecture, "are con-

cerned in anything of a public nature that makes part of the city."

Finally, there grew in fifteenth-century Florence a consistent theory of architecture that assumed, along with the other arts, that the act of design was first a conceptual discipline, and not a craft ruled by techniques of production. Brunelleschi's work defined the underpinnings of this essential change in attitude: there was the relationship of current work to the forms and rules of antiquity, insofar as these were recoverable, and their reinvention where necessary; and there was the indispensability of mathematical perspective as a means of

representing things in space with optical accuracy, and thereby securing that ideal proportionality that engenders Beauty. Alberti will enunciate a third theme, a kind of mysticism that associates architecture, in the final analysis, with a profound spiritual activity.

This point is often overlooked in our haste to paint the Renaissance as a profane style, a language of neopaganism and worldliness, in contrast to what we take to be the close religiosity of the Middle Ages. Geoffrey Scott, in his famous essay of 1914, *The Architecture of Humanism,* pronounced this view when he said: "The Renaissance . . .

Fig. 16.13 Pavia (Italy), the palace of the Visconti (Castello Visconteo), ca. 1360–65.

is an architecture of taste, seeking no logic, consistency or justification beyond that of giving pleasure." But Florence was as religious in the fifteenth century as it had been before. Church and state were separate but thoroughly interdependent, and neither could claim the total allegiance of community spirit. Faith was still the great container, however more erudite and "humanistic" its perception. Renaissance architecture, in the mind of its theorists, was based, to quote one of its foremost students, Rudolf Wittkower, on "a hierarchy of values culminating in the absolute values of sacred architecture."

Europe in the Fourteenth Century

What Florence was rejecting, clearly, was not the programmatic emphasis of contemporary European architecture, but the way this program was generally being expressed. The disparity by 1450 was powerful. For a traveler coming from the north across the Alps, the four-square stone palaces, the boxlike church interiors of S. Lorenzo or S. Spirito, the foundling hospital at the northeastern edge of the city whose facade was composed of a series of identical units crisply detailed to a uniform scaling (Fig. 19.6b), and of course the great dome of the cathedral—all this must have been a wondrous specter. Back home, there was the cumulative tracery of late Gothic monuments, rich and infinitely variegated, the stone filigree of tympanum and rose window, the spiky armature of buttress and finial, the dizzying verticality and the fretwork of ribs that crested the structure internally, the didactic construct of the Christian universe in stained glass and portal sculpture. (Fig. 16.19) Here in Florence: net and measured walls, the single column and the pilaster, temperate bays of uniform march cupping the space to the user's scale, the clear, diagrammatic articulation of horizontal and vertical coordinates, the spare heraldic ornament, and small roundels of terra-cotta neatly contained within the architectural order. (Fig. 16.8)

The lines were sharply drawn. As her cleansing, chaste forms shocked and stirred her contemporaries, Florence showed her contempt of late Gothic. A century after

Fig. 16.14 Paris (France), Ste.-Chapelle, 1243–48; interior of upper hall.

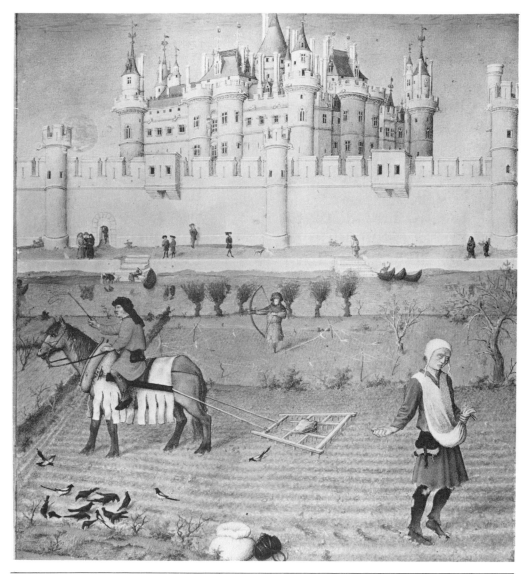

Fig. 16.15 Paris, the Louvre as rebuilt in the 1360s by King Charles V; shown in a miniature from the *Très Riches Heures du Duc de Berry*, a book of hours illustrated by the Limbourg brothers in 1413–16. (Musée Condé, Chantilly, France) For a later site view, see Fig. 21.26a.

Fig. 16.16 Bourges (France), the house of Jacques Coeur, silversmith and merchant, 1443–51; view of the courtyard from the southeast.

ments of a Florentine zealot. The period from 1300 to 1500 has a twofold interest in our story. It is a prolific age of remarkable buildings, both religious and secular, in which the style of Chartres and Salisbury cathedrals embarks on a dazzling adventure of elaborations. Furthermore, changes in the political, social, and economic climate create new conditions for the built environment, new possibilities for patrons and architects.

The Day of Princes

Terrible as the fourteenth century was, it proved a critical time for environmental adjustments. On the negative side, depopulation, the disruption of urban economies, and massive migratory disturbances resulting from famines, the Black Death, and internal warfare weakened the cities of Europe. The concentration of industry and commerce in a handful of centers had already brought about the decline of lesser towns. Now their regression was final. In Flanders only Bruges, Ghent, and Ypres mattered, and they were caught in the vio-

Brunelleschi's experiments with the new style, Giorgio Vasari could write:

On all the facades they build a malediction of little niches one above the other, with no end of pinnacles and points and leaves, so that, not to speak of the whole construction seeming insecure, it seems impossible that the parts should not topple over at any moment. . . . This manner was the invention of the Goths. . . . They turned the arches with pointed segments, and filled all Europe with these abominations. May God protect every country from such ideas and style of building.

All radical movements are intolerant and blind to the achievement of their adversary. Late Gothic Europe is anything but bankrupt, its architectural production hardly dismissed with the jaundiced pronounce-

lent confrontation between England and France. There were very few new towns. The military order of the Teutonic Knights, while busily conquering in the name of the Cross the last heathen stretch of Europe, Prussia, continued to plant walled towns peopled with immigrant burghers in order to control the native population that had been depressed to serfdom. In England only the growth of the cloth industry gave rise to new centers, mainly in the remote areas of East Anglia and Yorkshire where streams were strong and where the resistance to mechanized fulling mills in the old textile towns like Oxford and Lincoln was absent. In Flanders a similar outreach of industry was resisted by the powerful towns collectively; they resorted to the destruction of looms and the tenter frames and vats of fullers. One way to explain the ambitious cloth halls of Ypres, Ghent, and Louvain or the New Hall of Bruges, all of them substantially enlarged or built from scratch at precisely the time of the stubborn recession that set in under competitive pressure from the wool markets of England and Holland, is to see them as monuments of an increasingly restrictionist and monopolistic rigidness on the part of these threatened townships. (Fig. 15.13)

The cities also suffered from financial mismanagement, as well as the internal strife between merchant aristocracies and the working classes. Both of these disorders gave kings grounds to interfere, and even some city charters were suppressed. The swift growth and consolidation of guilds among the lesser, oppressed artisans also worked to the credit of monarchical authority. In France at least, the granting of guild charters began to be considered the prerogative of the king, who then used these enfranchised groups to control the cities.

But the decline of urban autonomy was only one source of the enhanced strength of royal houses in France, England, and Spain. The fourteenth century saw the waning of noble power, the humbling of the papacy, and the dissipation of the German empire. The popes were forced to live in exile at Avignon, a town in southeastern France, from 1308 to 1378. For another half-century thereafter, during the so-called Great Schism, the Church was plagued by

Fig. 16.17 Westminster (England), Great Hall of Westminster Palace, 1397–99, Hugh Herland; interior view.

Fig. 16.18 Ockwells Manor (Berkshire, England), ca. 1450; hall. The house was built for Sir John Norreys, Esquire of the Body to kings Henry VI and Edward IV.

rival claims to the papal title. Feudal nobility had been buffeted about since the twelfth century by the advances of the communes. Now changes in warfare further eroded the prestige of this once mighty class. The introduction of gunpowder and the longbow in the Hundred Years' War spelled the functional obsolescence of the mounted and heavily armed knight. His landed privilege eaten into by the burgher and his military thunder stolen by rapid-fire archers, the nobleman was driven more and more to the service of a princely court.

All this has a bearing on the history of architecture. The papal presence catapults the little provincial town of Avignon to international fame. The fortified papal compound there is a significant late medieval monument, a Gothic Lateran. Gunpowder makes defensive strongholds less secure. This, and the shift in warfare from an emphasis on siege tactics to large professional armies fighting open battles in the field, demotes the feudal castle strategically and, therefore, eliminates it as a serious demand of architectural production. The glories of medieval military architecture, with their baileys, ditches, and keeps, become obstacles to avoid. As seats of baronial state they also fade from the scene as their owners gravitate toward the cities and the princely courts.

Our attention must now shift to royal and princely palaces and the mansions of courtiers. The more chaotic the affairs of Europe turned, the louder grew the demand for one-man rule. "The human race is at its best when under a monarch," Dante argued; "monarchy is necessary for the well-being of the world." Northern and central Italy, which had no legitimate kings, eventually instituted the office of the prince to take charge of diplomacy and war. The fortress-palace of this extraordinary magistrate, who was at first elevated popularly but predictably worked toward family succession, combined the plan of a secure residence with the pomp and bureaucratic needs of the new form of government. It stood at the edge of town, isolated and spacious. Influenced by the town palace on the one hand and the cloister on the other, the building type evolved rapidly into a more or less symmetrical block that enclosed a rectangular courtyard and was reinforced by corner towers. The attraction of these great piles is their calculated balance of force and civility. The Visconti palace at Pavia, from the 1360s, is a case in point. (Fig. 16.13) For all the muscle of the wide, deep moat and the entrance with its double drawbridge, the design of the long south facade is graciously regular under its line of crenellations, and the courtyard sports an elegant loggia on the broad pointed arcades of the ground floor.

In London and Paris, the capitals of the two most important kings of Europe, the royal palaces were old and less orderly. The residence of the French kings, in the western end of the Île-de-la-Cité, dates back to the Carolingian period. If we think of it at all today, it is probably because of the palatine chapel, the Ste.-Chapelle, which survives intact. (Fig. 16.14) This marvel of French Gothic went up in the 1240s to house Christ's Crown of Thorns, which Louis IX had purchased from the Byzantine emperor. A lower chapel was accessible to the public, while the translucent upper chapel, made up almost entirely of stained glass, was at the level of the palace and opened onto it through a porch and gallery. But what is more to the point here is the way the palace compound expanded in stages during the fourteenth century under the last Capetians and the House of Valois. By 1400 this structure was the center of government and the seat of the high courts and the royal treasury. Sheltered within its sprawling grounds were the bicameral Parliament, the *Cour de Comptes*, apartments for numerous courtiers, and quarters for industries that catered to its gilded inhabitants. At the beginning of the next century the royal residence was moved elsewhere, principally to the refurbished thirteenth-century fortress of the Louvre on the right bank and the large manor called Hôtel St.-

Pol. High officials and noblement at the service of the king had in the meantime established their own palatial residences, *hôtels* in French, in proximity to these foci of monarchial government, while members of the royal family dotted the countryside with favorite estates and hunting lodges.

The character of this princely architecture was progressively lighthearted. Defensive apparatus was often subverted to less serious ends. Ramparts were pierced with windows, and at their summit terraces were laid as promenades. (Fig. 16.15) The buildings of the royal palace turned inward onto courtyards and gardens. Crenellations might be demolished, and tall round towers with peaked roofs turned into harmless refinements of a once hostile imagery. The chateaux and the urban *hôtels* had interior courtyards surrounded by porticoes, not dissimilar in type to the Italian fortress-palaces or town houses like the Palazzo Medici, except that they were usually polygonal and of course executed in the late Gothic mode. The sumptuous mansion of Jacques Coeur, financier to King Charles VII, in Bourges is a non-Parisian example. (Fig. 16.16)

The official residence of the English kings was at Westminster, about 3 kilometers west of London. It lay between the river and Westminster Abbey, and like the abbey it was Norman in origin. By the mid-fourteenth century Westminster had become the permanent seat of several government departments, including the Exchequer, the court of Common Pleas, and the Chancery. Assemblies of Parliament met in one of a new range of buildings erected in 1346, the so-called Painted Chamber. Another room was baptized "Star Chamber" from the decoration of its ceiling. Between Westminster and the City of London, prelates and noblement had their mansions. Nothing survives of the palace except for the Great Hall, built between 1394 and 1402 and famous for its hammer-beam roof. (Fig. 16.17) Hammer beams are thick, short, horizontal balks that are used as brackets to project from the wall top and to carry wooden arches that rise all the way to the ridge of the roof or a collar beam just below it. The brackets are themselves supported by curved struts that spring from

Fig. 16.19 Albi (France), cathedral of Ste.-Cecile; interior detail, showing juncture of choir enclosure and rood screen, sixteenth century.

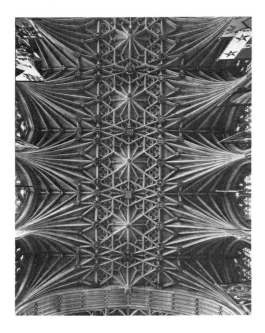

Fig. 16.20 Late medieval vault types: **(a)** Berkshire, Windsor Castle, St. George's Chapel, 1473–1516; **(b)** Wells (England), cathedral choir, first half of the fourteenth century. For a third example, see Fig. 16.22.

short wall posts on corbels. This is one of a variety of timber roofs that are a triumph of late medieval architecture in England. They have no counterpart on the Continent.

Fancy woodwork also graced the houses of magnates, both urban mansions and manors in the surrounding countryside. The traditional domestic components—hall, solar, protruding oriels—carried on, but they came in a variety of shells. A loose palatial arrangement around an open space, in the Continental pattern, was one alternative. Bishop Gower's palace at St. David's in South Wales, which has two halls and two chapels, is an example of this type. The standard residential college with its buildings around a quadrangle, first attempted in 1379 at New College, Oxford, established by William of Wykeham, is obviously related to this type as much as it is to the monastic cloister. Another popular alternative was to build the residence in imitation of castles, with towers, crenellations, and the like, and in doing so project the dignity and power of a previous age.

Ockwells Manor in Berkshire exemplifies the medium-sized country house. (Fig. 16.18) The hall rises the full height of the building. Much of the upper wall area is glazed by multilight windows, exhibiting great heraldic devices in them. One of the two-storied blocks bracketing the hall held the service rooms (buttery, pantry, kitchen); the other, a parlor on the ground level and the solar above. The timber work is exquisitely turned out throughout. The infilling is brick laid in a herringbone pattern. The gabled roofs of the end blocks are at right angles to the main line of the house, and two smaller gables mark the entrance and the oriel that projects at the high table end of the hall, next to the solar wing.

Late Gothic Efflorescence

The Palazzo Medici, the house of Jacques Coeur, Ockwells Manor—three contemporary but very different ways of gracious, stately living. We can add to this list a small number of surviving half-timbered mansions in northern cities. All of them stand at a level of domestic luxury and monumentality remarkable for the European Middle Ages and look to the future. As pri-

vate indulgence, this costly, sophisticated elegance far exceeds the decorative vanity of house frames that so incensed Alexander Neckam. By 1300 Europe had fully converted to a money economy. Wealth was fluid, mobile. Depopulation and the increased mortality rate that resulted from the subsequent disasters of the fourteenth century left people generally richer and anxious to enjoy what they had before it was too late. They turned to luxury goods and manufactured items for their own use or for the adornment of their house. Or else they tried to appease the bustling Prince of Death and court the afterlife. Religious patronage of a selfish sort kept the diminished population of artisans busy on family chapels and chantries, lavish tombs, and devotional art that included portraits of the donors adoring the holy image and exhibiting their piety. The subject matter was emotionally charged and rendered with a good deal of pathos: scenes of Christ's Passion, John the Baptist overcome by grief at the loss of the Savior, or the new and popular theme of the Pietà, Mary mourning the dead Christ in her lap, the tragic late medieval counterpart of the traditional iconography of the Virgin and Child.

This theatrical art is no longer wedded to the public pageantry of universal knowledge that had unfolded majestically on the exterior surfaces of High Gothic cathedrals like Chartres or Amiens. It moves indoors filling corners and edges, standing against the nave piers, crowding choir stalls and chancel screens. The prevalent taste shows a love for narrative wealth and fine detail, and for an elegant stylish lilt that gilds the poignancy and pain of the subject matter. It is a dissolving world that finds its architectural echo in the dissolving of Gothic rationality, in lacelike elaborations that spread with inexhaustible gusto from England to Bohemia, from Flanders to Spain, and that are at once marvels of inventiveness and technical skill but also, perhaps, conceptual dead ends.

In France the initial logic of the style still holds, to the extent that the linear forces of elevations within correspond to ribs in the vaults. But the continued dematerialization of flat surfaces in this so-called Flamboyant phase of the Gothic is very noticeable indeed: in window tracery, in the refinement of flying buttresses, and in facades where whole filigreed cases with great sweeping gables seem to be slipped over the substance of the architecture. The novel decorative twists are the ogee arch with its reverse curves and flamelike motifs called *mouchettes*. (Fig. 16.19) Tracery screens for choirs and rood screens, canopies over tombs, choir stalls—all get the full benefit of this incredibly deft and intricate lacework that pushes stone beyond the limits of its maximum performance.

But it is in England and Germany that any pretension to structural logic is totally abandoned. In naves and aisles the correspondence of wall accents to ribs is ignored, or rather mischievously played with. In England, from very early on, vault webs were not always rationally geared to the bay system and its supports. We saw how Lincoln Cathedral, begun in 1192, had added arbitrary ridge ribs and tiercerons to the structural armature of four-part vaults. (Fig. 14.27) The proliferation of these decorative ribs can be traced through many splendid examples in the next three centuries. (Fig. 16.20) At the same time, the English architects seem fascinated with see-through effects and spatial surprises. Diagonal views are ingeniously set up by the curious strut-bridges under the vaults of Bristol Cathedral, and some sort of climactic whimsy is reached with the magnificent strainer arches at the crossing of Wells Cathedral of 1338, there to support the crossing tower but also obviously taking delight in their improvised exuberance.

Bristol and Wells illustrate the style that in England is called Decorated or Curvilinear and that is characterized by free-flowing forms, notably the sinuous ogee arch, and an almost baroque infatuation with three-dimensional movement in space. (Fig. 16.21) Reaction has already set in by the 1340s. The outcome: the Perpendicular Style that opts for a severe and rigid linearism. (Fig. 16.22) A chief feature of this style is the continuation of the vertical lines of tracery until they meet the curve of the window arch. Rows of tall narrow panels take up entire walls—the flat east wall of a choir, for example. Fan vaulting resumes where chapterhouse vaults with their lily-shaped for-

Fig. 16.21 Wells Cathedral; arches at the crossing ("strainer arches"), 1338.

Fig. 16.22 Gloucester (England); cathedral choir, 1337–67. A notable example of the so-called Perpendicular Style.

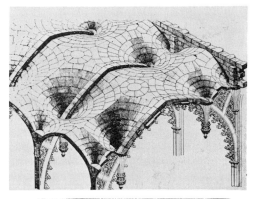

Fig. 16.23 Westminster Abbey, Henry VII's Chapel, ca. 1510, William Vertue; diagram showing the construction of the pendant vaults.

mations leave off. Halves of these lilies are used in series on two sides of a hall space, as in the cloister of Gloucester Cathedral. The bosses are seized as a palette for some spirited carving. The ultimate extension of this preoccupation with the bosses could conceivably be the pendant vaults of Henry VII's chantry chapel at Westminster Abbey, erected between 1503 and 1519 by the architect William Vertue, or the slightly earlier King's College chapel at Cambridge, the work of the master mason Reginald Ely. (Fig. 16.23) The solution is simple but ingenious. Transverse arches provide the structural backbone around which the pendant vault is formed in a series of conoids, each buit around the rigid member of a wedge-shaped voussoir which is extended downward. We should remember that alongside these magic stunts of masonry shines the work of master woodcarvers—on choir stalls and chancel screens, but also more expansively on the great roofs of the fourteenth and fifteenth centuries. (Fig. 16.17)

What is left of the original Gothic skeleton that has not been dissipated, gambled with, made insubstantial? The nave piers? Germany and the East will take care of that. The burgher Gothic of the north starts playing evasive games with the nave piers in cathedrals like that at Landshut, where extremely slender round or polygonal uprights invite the eye to wander diagonally, where the colonettes that were the sup-

Fig. 16.24 Annaberg (Germany), church of St. Anne, begun 1499; nave. This is a hall church, with aisles almost the same height as the nave.

port of vault ribs have been done away with entirely. Sometimes, as at St. Anne in Annaberg, the piers have concave sides as though space were pushing against the stone from all sides. (Fig. 16.24) In Bohemia, piers and ribs are treated as trees and branches, the final romanticizing of structure. At Braunschweig we have twisted piers, and they go beautifully—these growing, living trunks—with the swaying, swinging draperies of statues that play against S-curve axes. One last peculiar turn is taken: the ribs are replaced with deep coffers that have sharp arrises, as though the vault were a meticulously folded paper construction or else the jelling of some fluid poured into a fancy mold.

Aging Traditions Abroad

The florid Gothic sunset has a universal message. Young, tightly encompassed conventions of form, once they have tested the range of their intrinsic effectiveness, are prone to slip into precious habits. Skills that start by solving problems of substance are driven at some point along the way to find excitement in surface challenges. Detail takes over. The forms bask in a flurry of renewal that can only behold a refined virtuosity. Moralists see this cresting as a loss of fiber, irreversible decline, even decay. The immediate audience and later apologists extol the imagination involved, scrutinize subtleties, admire the courage and the mastery.

A number of world traditions, roughly contemporary with the later history of European Gothic, give us coincident proof for this phenomenon of brilliant aging. We would go too far if we were to detect in them all the impact of some general spirit of the times. Each effervesces at its own pace and within a well-fixed cultural predicament. If we bring up some of them here, at the conclusion of this chapter on the late Middle Ages, it is for two innocent reasons: to bring home the point that Gothic has no particular monopoly on our architectural sympathies, and to look comparatively at the very different ways in which building styles stage their evanescence.

Byzantium, the other half of medieval

Fig. 16.25 Gračanica (Yugoslavia), monastery church, 1321. The outer porch is a later addition.

and corner cupolas made more intricate with additional gables, which are semicircular or pointed and leap excitedly upward. This Serbian church is a tense, inspired hyperbole of Byzantine tradition that defies advancing.

Farther afield, in India, a centuries-long epic of complication is written in scores of Hindu temples that celebrate God in the holy figure of the square. The square is the manifestation of the *vastu-purusha* mandala, the geometric form assumed by the world of reality as it was defined by Brahma at the creation. The temple is at once the essence of this absolute godhead and the holy mountain Kailasa, abode of Siva. Architecturally, the epic has two related themes: the proliferating square, and the surface treatment of the mountain. Perhaps we can grasp something of the astonishing richness of what is involved by juxtaposing one of the earliest stone temples, that at Deogarh from about the fifth–sixth century, and the Keshava temple at Somnathpur, built in 1268. (Fig. 16.26) So remote are they from one another in outward appearance that it is hard to believe they are variations of the same basic theme. We are missing the many intermediaries that took the square, the tower that sits over it and lifts it heavenward, the corner towers that accentuate its geometric purity, the axial approach, and the surrounding platform enclosure, and played upon them with the contrapuntal drive of a fugue. Narrow the time span and you will catch the subtler particulars of this transforming fever. In Cambodia where Indian influences prevailed, a brief period of glory came to the indigenous Khmer people in the twelfth and thirteenth centuries. The magnificent temples of Anghor Wat and Anghor Thom were built for the Khmer god-kings by their peasants and artisans during this time of greatness. (Fig. 16.27) They were based of course on earlier examples. I am putting the plan of one of these next to that of the Bayon at Anghor Thom. They are less than two hundred years apart, but it will take one a long time to recount the dispersion and mincing of form that took place along the way.

The most elaborate of these Hindu tem-

Christianity, takes its standard church scheme, the cross-in-square design, and the official dictated hierarchy of mosaic or fresco images that decorate it within, down a gentle path of rarefaction. Late Constantinopolitan art, like the fourteenth-century mural cycles of St. Savior in Chora (Kariye Cami), sparkles with delicate, finespun details and a fresh colorism liberated from the restrictive palette of the post-Iconoclastic periods. Along with this exquisiteness comes narrative wealth, as the artists leap beyond the permissible subject matter and its coded representation, to retell the tale of the Virgin Mother and her divine Son lovingly, with feeling. Not surprisingly, this personalized religious art is the result of private patronage. In its twilight years the great capital of the Byzantine Empire, or what little remained of this state under the

relentless push of the Ottoman Turks, relaxed its centralized production of public works and allowed army officers, rich widows, and courtiers to express a subjective piety.

In terms of building, the fine elongated forms of late Byzantine art meet their aptest analogy in Byzantinized fringe lands like Serbia. Compare the exterior view of the church at Gračanica (1321) with a classic example of the cross-in-square design. (Fig. 12.10, 16.25) The attenuation, the nervous fragility need no laboring. Mass is not subtracted here, in the way of late Gothic; instead, it is drawn out precariously, where drums are pulled to a height of six to eight times their width and window lights are proportionately slenderized. The plan too is compounded, with the basic elements of the central dome, barrel-vaulted cross arms

Fig. 16.26a Deogarh (India), temple of Vishnu, sixth century.

Fig. 16.26b Somnathpur (India), Keshava temple, thirteenth century.

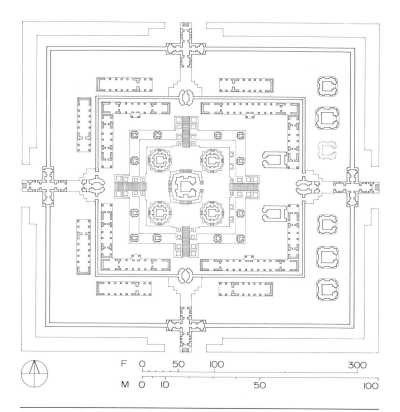

F 0   50   100   300

M 0   10   50   100

Fig. 16.27a Angkor (Cambodia), Temple Mountain of Pre Rup, 961, built by Rajendra varman II; plan.

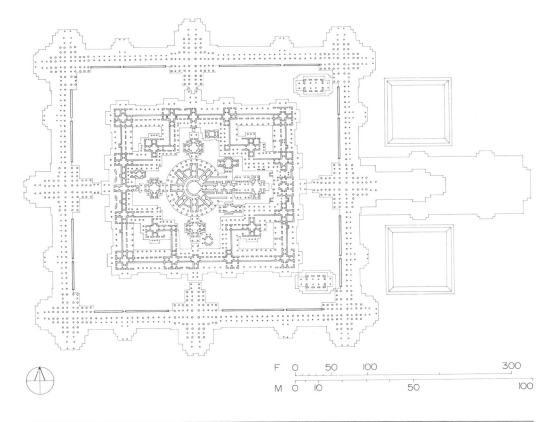

F O   50   100   300

M O   10   50   100

Fig. 16.28a Angkor Wat, 1113–1150, built by Surya Varman II; view of the great temple. The main shrine is in the form of a 215-foot (65-meter) tower, right of center, surrounded by four secondary towers.

Fig. 16.28b Angkor Thom, Bayon Temple; detail. The Bayon Temple is the most complex building on the Angkor site. Its fifty-four towers, one of which is seen here, are decorated with a total of 216 carved faces.

Fig. 16.29 Isfahan (Iran), Masjid-i-Jami (Great Mosque), North Dome Chamber, 1088–89; interior.

ples correspond to the last generations of late Gothic buildings, and there is a kinship of sorts between them if you think of the fragmentation of matter, the bewildering riot of turn and counterturn. But they work differently. Gothic buildings trap space in a glasshouse. The Hindu temple bulges out from what appears to be a tremendous, massive core. This mighty pile of stone is pleated vertically, striated horizontally, and then softened by abundant sculpture. (Fig. 16.28) The curves and easy postures of the multitude of figures break up the pleating and layering without in the least confusing the operative structure. We are impressed at a distance by big strong forms that, close up, prove to have solidified out of myriad bits of matter, carved and mounted with infinite patience.

By the 1300s Islam was an old culture. It was not, however, in any way a spent cul-

ture. The far-flung empire had suffered the Crusades, the much more hurtful Mongol invasion, and, in the West, localized defeats in the North African hinterland and in Spain. But the advent of the Ottomans went a long way toward offsetting these losses, and in the later fifteenth century Islam had spread across eastern Europe and was knocking at the gates of Vienna. By then India, first overrun in 1188, supported several strong Muslim sultanates. So the giant stirred mightily still with some limbs, while others were cut off or withered. Some regional traditions were entering a terminal phase, brief or lingering as the case might be, while elsewhere vigorous offshoots of Muslim architecture waxed strong at the start of some notable careers. The ripe or doomed areas of Islam are where we should expect to find the best instances of those concluding bursts or circumlocutions of late medieval form we have been sampling across the eastern hemisphere: in Mameluke Egypt and Nasrid Spain, for example.

One motif and one place will have to satisfy us. The motif is the stalactite or honeycomb vault known to Arabs as *muqarnas*. The place is the royal palace of the last Muslim principality in Spain, the Alhambra at Granada.

It is pointless to try to fix the origins of the stalactite vault. At some distant remove, we can single out the squinch as the architectural seed. (Fig. 10.13) The first stages of growth may have been motivated by the call of structure. But as squinches multiplied at the corners and fanned outward and up, it is clear that they could be as blithely decorative as Gothic vault ribs. In fact, it is not altogether perverse to see the relationship between the North Dome Chamber that was added to the Friday mosque of Isfahan in 1088–89 and the great stalactite vaults of the Alhambra from the fourteenth century (Figs. 16.29, 16.32) in the same light as we would analyze the vaults of Salisbury Cathedral in relationship to those of, say, York or Gloucester. (Figs. 14.26, 16.22) The later vaults in both the Muslim and the Gothic comparison may seem at first glance wildly licentious, but they are, each one within its own tradition, rationally bred from the visual principles that governed the earlier vaults.

But there is much more in the Alhambra than these incandescent canopies to make it the haunting evensong of Muslim Spain. Perhaps because we know how the story ended, everything about this famous setting atop one of two hills that overlooks the flatlands of Granada on the wide Vega plain seems sweet and sad. (Fig. 16.30) The style of its architecture, called Moorish, had been shaping up for a long while out of the earlier Umayyad brilliance we encountered in the great mosque at Córdoba. This style is responsible, on two sides of Gibraltar, for some of the most intricately spun architectural fantasies in history. Sumptuous and insubstantial, its reality is that of illusion; its goals are escapist. Light is courted with, absorbed. No sharp definition of shades is allowed, and a soft, languid, liquid atmosphere is created where mass is not entirely palpable and the space is not entirely a void. Part of this is due to the texture of the stucco ornament, once gilded and painted, and part to the fact that there are no sharp outlines or right angles possible, since the contours are everywhere tassled with stalactites or lobing, and otherwise blurred. The nature of the burden being so gossamer, the supports become gutless themselves. We get very thin columns, single or paired, with no entasis or fluting to show any sense of compression. Exaggerated impost blocks further isolate the supports from their dainty load. The whole seems not so much constructed as spun, painted, conjured. (Fig. 1.18)

At the Alhambra the main compositional unit is the *rhiad*, a patio framed by architecture. (Fig. 16.31) In the Court of Lions, an open space surrounded by porticoes is crisscrossed with thin water channels that slice through the axial pavilions and enter the rooms behind, like a trickle of life seeking its source. (Fig. 1.18) In the Myrtle Court, water fills up the open space and sets the arches of the porticoes afloat. The slender columns find what mooring they can in this watery stage, their fragile presence devitalized even more in pale, tremulous reflections. Above and behind them, the planes that pass for walls are multicolored tile and plaster casement filled obsessively with carved foliage, abstracted and repetitive, and interlacing designs like stars and lozenges. Today the fountains' spray is too robust. They would have bubbled softly then, as hypnotic as the plaster ornaments around them, sound and sight working together to lull and mesmerize and sadden.

We enter the rooms. The ceilings are gilded honeycombs; the floors opalescent mirrors of marble and tile; the walls invisible behind their embroidered coat, framed in an echoing series of independent cells. (Fig. 16.32) There are no openings at all to the outside world at eye level. The rooms speak to us directly through inscriptions—"I am the very heart of the palace," says the Hall of the Ambassadors—as though buildings were spirits with voices; just so in childhood or in our dreams inanimate objects burst into words. Indeed, it is all the stuff of dreams, an architecture that eschews the loud and the strong for the strange and melancholic. The fortified aspect of the outside, meant in earnest in the eleventh century when the original palace went up, is now a sham. The time of fighting is over. *Wa al-ghalib billah,* as the pithy saying has it that follows us through the rooms: Only God is the Conqueror.

It is impossible to think of this environment of fantasy and introspection, set in an idyllic hilltop amid myrtles, evergreens, and running brooks, as anything other than an earthly paradise. Lines of poetry woven into the texture of the rooms encourage us to think so. They speak of "mouths of boon, bliss, felicity," of constellations and the grandeur of the sun, of beauties both apparent and hidden, of "celestial spheres that are over the glowing pool of dawn." We recall the Koranic descriptions of Paradise, those "pavilions beneath which water flows," and we see them in the channels and hooded porches of the courts. Again, the totally contrived mixture of the natural and architectonic, the verdant fluent patios, raises up the prodigal vision of those great verses:

For those that fear the majesty of their Lord there are two gardens planted with shady trees. Which of your Lord's blessing would you deny?

Each is watered by a flowing spring. Which of your Lord's blessings would you deny?

Fig. 16.30 Granada (Spain), the palace of the Alhambra, thirteenth–fourteenth century; general view from the north.

Each bears every kind of fruit in pairs. Which of your Lord's blessings would you deny?

They shall recline on couches lined with thick brocade, and within their reach will hang the fruits of both gardens. Which of your Lord's blessings would you deny?

They shall dwell with bashful virgins whom neither man nor jinee will have touched before them. Virgins as fair as corals and rubies. Which of your Lord's blessings would you deny?

The sadness we spoke of is circumstantial. This, alas, is not the real Paradise. It is perishable, open to attack, far from eternal. For the Nasrid dynasty which tried to drown harsh reality in this magic refuge called the Alhambra, the end came in 1492. Granada surrendered without a fight to Isabella of Castille and Ferdinand of Aragon. Nearby a new town was built called Santa Fe, or Holy Faith—*their* faith.

The Muslims were not exterminated or banished. They languished, their music filtering through the sounds of Spanish song, their hypnotic ornament flowering on many Christian walls. And their dream architecture continued in North Africa. The once puritanical Muslims of Ifriqya and Morocco had fallen for the charm and lighthearted sophistication of Andalusia two hundred years before the Alhambra. Some of the finest of Moorish fancies—madrasas, palaces, tombs—are in Fez, Taza, Rabat, Marrakesh. And these are the places that cling a little longer to this ephemeral world after the fall of Granada. Then their dream too is over.

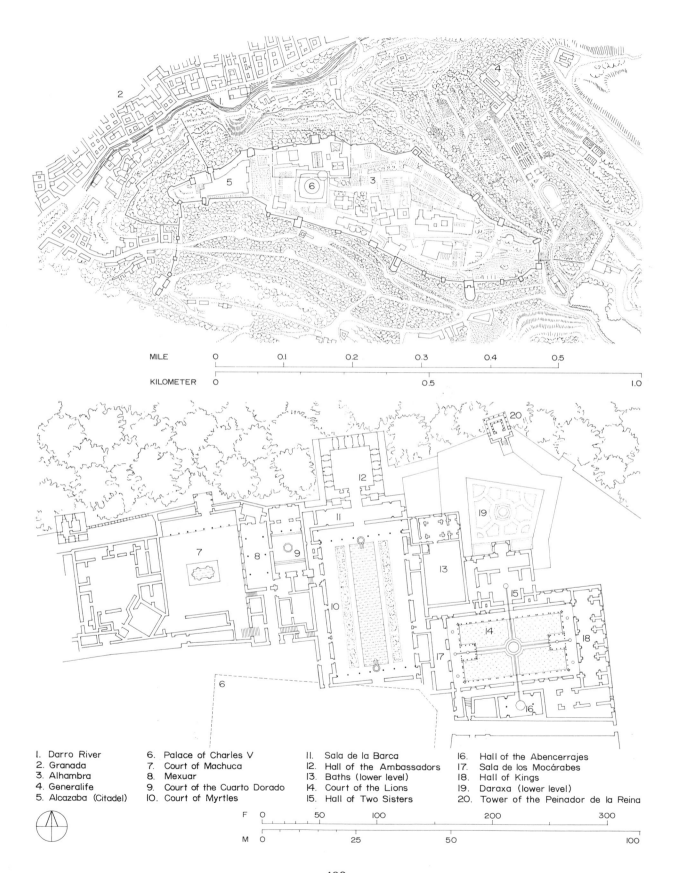

MILE	0 0.1 0.2 0.3 0.4 0.5		
KILOMETER	0 0.5 1.0		

1. Darro River	6. Palace of Charles V	11. Sala de la Barca	16. Hall of the Abencerrajes
2. Granada	7. Court of Machuca	12. Hall of the Ambassadors	17. Sala de los Mocárabes
3. Alhambra	8. Mexuar	13. Baths (lower level)	18. Hall of Kings
4. Generalife	9. Court of the Cuarto Dorado	14. Court of the Lions	19. Daraxa (lower level)
5. Alcazaba (Citadel)	10. Court of Myrtles	15. Hall of Two Sisters	20. Tower of the Peinador de la Reina

F	0 50 100 200 300
M	0 25 50 100

400

Fig. 16.32 Granada, Alhambra, Hall of the Two Sisters, second half of fourteenth century; interior view looking up into the dome.

Further Reading

E. Battisti, *Filippo Brunelleschi* (New York: Rizzoli, 1981).

G.A. Brucker, *Renaissance Florence* (Melbourne, Fla.: Krieger, 1975).

J. L. Cohen and B. Kalman, *Angkor, Monuments of the God-Kings* (New York: Abrams, 1975).

B. Lowry, *Renaissance Architecture* (New York: Braziller, 1962).

H. A. Miskimin, *The Economy of Early Renaissance Europe, 1300–1460* (Cambridge and New York: Cambridge University Press, 1975).

P. Murray, *The Architecture of the Italian Renaissance* (London: B. T. Batsford, 1963).

F. D. Prager and G. Scaglia, *Brunelleschi: Studies of His Technology and Inventions* (Cambridge, Mass.: MIT Press, 1970).

E. Sordo, *Moorish Spain: Cordoba, Seville, Granada*, trans. I. Michael (New York: Crown, 1963).

W. Swaan, *The Late Middle Ages: Art and Architecture from 1350 to the Advent of the Renaissance* (Ithaca, N.Y.: Cornell University Press, 1977).

Fig. 16.31 Granada, Alhambra, plans: top, site plan; bottom, central core of palace.

View of an Ideal City, ca. 1490s, by an anonymous artist
of the Central Italian School.

17

THE RENAISSANCE: IDEAL AND FAD

In the years after the fall of Granada, Spain set out to complete its exorcism of those monuments that testified to the wonder of the long-lived Muslim culture, now permanently displaced. An unobtrusive Gothic chapel had already been inserted into the mosque of Córdoba toward the end of the century. In 1523 the clerics extracted from King Charles V the authorization to build a sizable cathedral in the middle of the Muslim sanctuary. When they were done, the arcades of the multiaisled interior and the reverberating vistas they afforded were rudely cut off. Without, the cruciform domed mass tore its way through the low-pitched roofs that rippled like a gentle swell across the building, from the court to the *mihrab* wall. (Fig. 17.1) The new church was everywhere overlaid by a wealth of ornament that combined Gothic and Classical motifs with the Plateresque—a florid, animated convention perhaps inspired by Moorish taste and as close to a native style as Spain was to field after the reconquest of the peninsula. On his first visit to Córdoba in 1525, Charles was shocked. "If I had known what you wished to do," he is supposed to have said to the bishop's people, "you would not have done it, for what you are carrying out here is to be found everywhere and what you had formerly does not exist anywhere else in the world."

At the Alhambra, the king's intervention was much more considerate. His palace, which was never finished, stands to the south of the patios and honeycomb halls of the Nasrids, set askew, and communicat-

ing with them at one corner of the Myrtle Court. (Fig. 16.31, top) The forms are severely Classical. A circular courtyard, ringed by a two-storey portico, is placed within a square that encases a block of rooms. (Fig. 17.2) On the ground floor, Tuscan columns with a continuous entablature take the thrust of an annular vault behind. Above, the order is Ionic. This academic taste is a far cry from the late Gothic and Plateresque ardor of the cathedral at Córdoba or, for that matter, the majority of Spanish buildings undertaken in the opening decades of the sixteenth century.

The First Advance

Three different architectural styles, then, were abroad in Spain around 1500: the international language of Gothic at the end of its long sojourn, a hybrid local concoction of ornamental motifs applied without regard to the structure of the building, and the newly fashionable design that unearthed and modernized the tradition of ancient Rome.

The source of this third alternative was Italy; its patrons were the courts of Europe, which came to regard it as a means of projecting an enlightened prestige. The sixteenth century was the critical time of transition. The old ways died hard. It had taken generations of architects, patrons, and craftsmen to spread the lure of Gothic, compound its early formulations, and work out local variants that the common people

could take to heart. By now a church meant Gothic vaults and tracery; a castle meant hooded turrets, crenellations, tall multi-lighted windows with lancets and oriels. These were the things the building trades could do. All the skills involved, the architect's included, had been nurtured and institutionalized in the guilds. In these quarters resistance to the Classical wave was strong, and among the common people, too, who do not take to foreign looks easily.

Leon Battista Alberti

The fountainhead of the new architecture, of this new way of thinking, had been Florence. There, the rich merchants and bankers who guided the contentious but brilliant republic had been willing to support Filippo Brunelleschi's experiments in the opening decades of the fifteenth century. The buildings that were to become the generating force of an international movement could not have gone up without this backing. But it was a two-way street. Like good businessmen, the Pazzi, the Medici, the Pitti saw the advantage of a style that allied them with the mood of reawakening, of redefining life, which scholars and artists of their city had put in motion. The excitement, the optimism was palpable. There was a past you could detach yourself from and look at critically. Or rather, there were two kinds of past, the glorious and the mean, and the study of the humanities could help people to recover the strength of the first. It could lead them to a modern

Fig. 17.1 Córdoba (Spain), Great Mosque, eighth–tenth centuries, with the sixteenth-century church inserted into the prayer hall; aerial view from the east. The mosque was first converted into a Christian cathedral in 1238. The planted court on the south side is the Patio de los Naranjos ("Court of Oranges").

life as full and civilized as that of ancient times. Knowledge was not the gift of revelation, but an objective source to be tapped and used. A handful of extraordinary men now sought to breathe life into the dimmed legacy of Greece and Rome, a legacy that was locked in the texts and monuments of these germane cultures. The humanists ransacked libraries everywhere for the written wisdom of Classical antiquity. They worked hard to resurrect the forgotten language of Greek and to restore the purity of Latin.

The renewal of the arts was part of the same effort. Practitioners and scholars alike hunted for gems, coins, and sculpture; they deciphered inscriptions; they measured and drew the strewn relics of the Roman empire. Trips to Rome were now as much for the sake of gazing on ruins as they were to honor Christian martyrs. The popes, rid at last of schism and dissension, sought to harvest this revivalist crop for their own plans of a triumphant Holy See. There were even exploratory visits to Greece. Ciriaco of Ancona traveled in the Greek East just before it was closed off by the Ottoman conquest, copying countless inscriptions and recording buildings and art works. At the Medici villa of Poggio a Caiano, a portico in the form of a Classical temple front recalls his drawing of the west front of the Parthenon. (Fig. 17.3) At the same time, the arts were aided by a mathematical humanism. Research in optics and geometry en-

Fig. 17.2 Granada (Spain), the Alhambra, palace of Charles V, 1527–68, Pedro Machuca; view of the courtyard. The palace is no. 6 in Fig. 16.31. Machuca's design was inspired by the Roman work of Raphael, whose student he apparently was, and of Bramante. (See Fig. 17.14.)

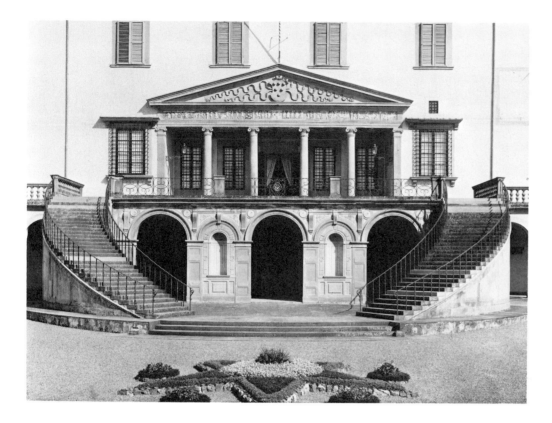

Fig. 17.3 Poggio a Caiano (Florence, Italy), Villa Medici, 1480–97(?), Giuliano da Sangallo; Ionic entrance porch. The villa was designed for Lorenzo de' Medici (the Magnificent).

Fig. 17.4 Naples (Italy), the Arch of Alfonso I of Aragon, ca. 1453–65. This classical triumphal gate was inserted into the northwest corner of the Castel Nuovo, a thirteenth-century castle rebuilt by Alfonso from 1443 onward. The relief over the main arch represents the king's entry into Naples in 1442.

throned linear perspective as the modern muse. She appears among the arts and sciences that surround the bronze effigy of Pope Sixtus IV (1471–84) on his tomb in St. Peter's.

Brunelleschi's application of these antiquarian and scientific studies to the practice of architecture proved decisive. In thirty years he had worked out and demonstrated a full-fledged substitute for Gothic design. Let us remember that a late Gothic building was spun from arcane geometric formulae jealously guarded by the lodge. Gothic architecture functioned according to an abstract system of proportions. Individual elements of the building had no fixed ratios within themselves, or with respect to the overall measurements, but rather depended on internal correlations that followed from the initial geometric choices. A cursory sketch plan was enough to record these choices. All details would be designed on the site and executed individually. The architect supervised every step; he provided templates for every twist of tracery. Improvisation and on-the-spot reversal during the building process were not uncommon.

These entrenched Gothic habits were now thrown out. The architect conceived the building and put it down on a unitary plan, drawn to measure. From this, a building force could proceed to erect the structure without the architect's supervision. This was so because, first, the ratios were simple and keyed to a fixed module of so many *braccia*, the Italian unit of measurement; and, second, the building parts were standardized and could be assembled in a rational, predictable way, much as they were, say, in Greek temples. These parts were of Classical derivation—columns, pilasters, moldings, pediments, round-headed or segmental niches. Their design and correspondence, how they shaped the architectural space or composed the elevations, were learned matters, not workshop skills. The narrow specialization of the guilds

1. Church of Santa Maria
2. Hall of Priors
3. San Francesco
4. Medieval Houses & Gardens
5. Market
6. Town Wall (approximate)
7. Cathedral
8. Palazzo Piccolomini
9. Town Hall
10. Bishop's Palace
11. Palazzo Ammannati

F 0   50   100   200   300

M 0   25   50   100

Fig. 17.5 Pienza (formerly Corsignano, Italy), the square of Pope Pius II, 1459–62, Bernardo Rossellino; plans: top, general site plan; bottom left, the area of the square in the Middle Ages; bottom right, the same area as redesigned under Pius.

would no longer create the architect. He must have a broad education. "Architecture is a very noble science," Leon Battista Alberti wrote, "not fit for every head. He ought to be a man of a fine genius, of a great application, of the best education . . . that presumes to declare himself an architect."

Alberti (1404–72) was describing himself. He was as crucial for the dissemination of Renaissance architecture in the second half of the fifteenth century as Brunelleschi had been for its inception in the first half. But unlike Brunelleschi who had risen through the guild system and conducted his eye-opening search as a practitioner, Alberti was a distinguished scholar who turned to architecture in the latter part of a versatile career as a classicist, playwright, papal secretary, art theorist, grammarian, and social commentator. He had studied at the universities of Padua and Bologna, and moved freely as adviser in a half dozen princely courts in Italy.

In 1452 Alberti completed an early version of *Ten Books on Architecture*. It was the first major architectural treatise since that of Vitruvius, on which it was loosely modeled. Vitruvius had summarized for his contemporaries the cumulative building knowledge of the Greeks; he had been a codifier of past usage. Alberti's interest was with architecture as a component of the new learning. He wrote not so much as a practitioner speaking to other practitioners, but as a humanist explaining to the important and rich people of his day about the exalted profession of architecture and its place in public life.

This was the only class of patrons worth cultivating. "I would have you, if possible," he advises the would-be architect, "concern yourself with none but persons of the highest rank and quality, and those too such as are truly lovers of these arts, because your work loses its dignity by being done for mean persons." Such patrons are not only better judges of taste, they can also afford the best materials. Alberti preferred that they be good people. As a man of his

Fig. 17.6 Pienza; view of the square looking northeast toward the town hall.

Fig. 17.7 Pienza; view of the square, showing the cathedral (left) and the Palazzo Piccolomini (right).

time, albeit a Florentine, he has no objections to authoritarianism, but he draws the line at tyranny. The difference is between a prince who rules through justice and wisdom over willing subjects, and one who is guided by the appetite "to continue his dominion over them, let them be ever so uneasy under it." It is hard for us today to see how some of Alberti's patrons could be called anything other than tyrants, and yet the moralistic tone of the architects was self-propagating. However evil you were in reality, your espousal of the new style made you respectable. There is an aspect of public relations in the popularity of Classical design among the ruling classes of Europe.

Architecture for Alberti, as we said, was not a mere skill or service. Function and its accommodation are mundane things that can easily be taken care of by a builder. The architect, armed with the science of linear perspective and the new mathematics, steeped in the knowledge of ancient sources, becomes the master of a universal law that applies as much to the frame of his buildings as it does to the structure of the natural world. And since nature in Alberti's thought is synonymous with God, the architect in his pursuits approaches the divine. This kind of talk made lodge masons extremely uneasy. They were being demoted by a bookish breed of men who knew Latin and Greek and had gone to Rome to look at ruins overgrown with vegetation, but who could not dress stone or turn a vault. And the contempt was mutual.

But for all his high-sounding rhetoric, Alberti does not rush to repudiate medieval things, nor does he see a world of ideal Renaissance cities. The first half of the fifteenth century, the time of Alberti's matu-

Fig. 17.8 Pienza; the Palazzo Piccolomini from the south. The cathedral is on the right.

Stone age relics are prehistoric records of how humans configured their environment. Although the full range of meanings encoded in these sites is no longer retrievable, our movement among their stones physically reiterates ancient spatial experiences. Right, designs carved into the surface of a passage tomb (third millennium B.C.) at Newgrange, Ireland. Below, some of the more than 3,000 upended stones, or menhirs, aligned into "avenues" near the French village of Carnac (third millennium B.C.).

The twin religious compounds of Luxor and Karnak at Thebes grew from modest cult temples dedicated to the sun-god Amon. Right, ritual processions at Luxor's New Kingdom temple (ca. 1450 B.C.) moved through a hypostyle hall supported by 50-foot sandstone columns in the form of an open papyrus plant. Below, a similar column at Karnak is depicted in a nineteenth-century reconstruction.

Athens's apogee of political influence was celebrated in the reconstruction of the Parthenon, completed in 432 B.C. Below, the temple dedicated to Athena Parthenos took pride of place on the sacred plateau of the Akropolis. Right, Phideas's colossal statue of Athena, faced with ivory and gold around a wooden core, was the temple's towering occupant. It is shown here in a nineteenth-century reconstruction.

Rome's *thermae* provided luxurious public facilities for bathing, swimming, exercising, and dining, as well as a setting for a spectrum of social interaction ranging from intellectual to sexual. Eugène Viollet-le Duc's meticulous drawing, executed in 1867, focuses on Roman construction technique and is thought to have kindled the late nineteenth-century enthusiasm for railroad stations in the form of Roman baths (see color page 13).

New architectural forms heralded the transformation of the provincial Roman outpost of Byzantium into the seat of a resuscitated empire. Left, located beside the Byzantine emperors' palace complex, the church of Hagia Sophia (A.D. 532–37) dissolves the Roman dome's solidity by leaking sunlight through a perforated rim. A thousand years later, as an architectural prototype for an Islamic renaissance, the church inspired a generation of Ottoman mosques. Above, Hagia Sophia's neighboring Byzantine palace was gone by the Ottoman reign. It was replaced by a patchwork of pavilions and leafy courts that made up the sprawling royal residence of Topkapi, sited atop Byzantium's former Akropolis.

Marine commerce built Venice and supported an architecture as exotic and prone to luxury as the cargo of one of the city's galleons. Above, close ties with Byzantium are reflected in the cathedral of St. Mark's (begun 1063), modeled on Constantinople's church of the Holy Apostles. Left, patrician houses like the Ca' d'Oro (1424–36) featured a lower arcade for gondola traffic and elegant upper loggias overlooking the canal.

The French Gothic, launched at the royal abbey of St.-Denis in 1144, spread across Europe as the Middle Age's international style. Inset, workshops at cathedral building sites propagated the new manner through the training of master builders, who typically rose from the ranks of masons. Right, the free-standing veil of tracery across Strasbourg's west front (begun ca. 1275) pushed the limits of dressed-stone construction. It is seen here in a fanciful nineteenth-century reconstruction that fronts the cathedral with an imaginary plaza filled with theatrical pomp.

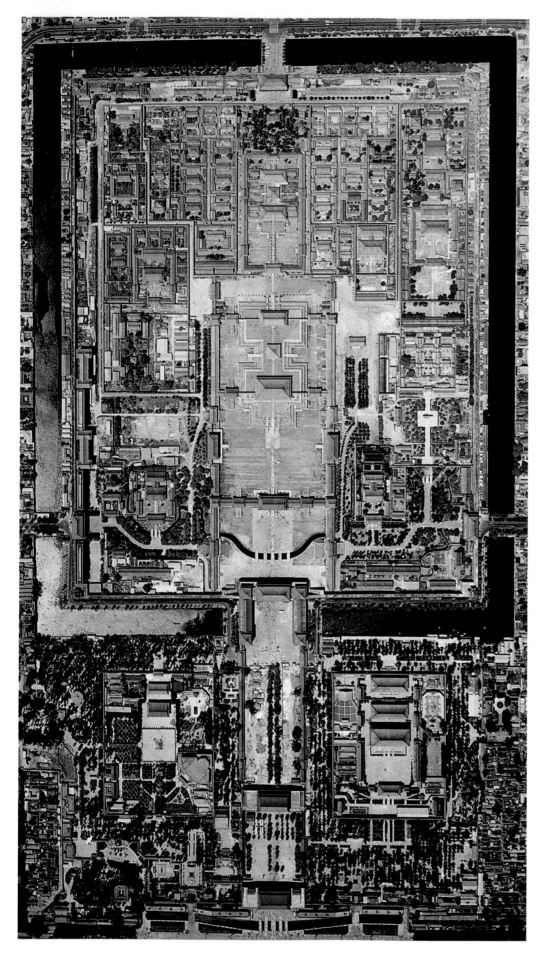

Beijing's Forbidden City, as rebuilt from 1421, reveals a concentric diagram of palace structures focused on the Hall of Great Harmony, a preserve of imperial ritual. Access to the complex is gained along an axial procession route or on one of the bridges that span the surrounding moat.

The architectural legacy of the New World's native cultures includes the abandoned urban matrix of Teotihuacán (far right), a city of 200,000 in A.D. 150, and the monumental ruins of the Inca fortress of Sacsahuaman (top), believed to have been planned by Pachacuti sometime after 1438. The tremendously solid Inca masonry thwarted demolition attempts by the *conquistadores*, who reused the ancient walls for their new city. Illuminated codexes depict a different fate for Aztec sites: upper right, following an unsuccessful attempt to defend the Templo Mayor against Cortés' seige of 1521, the capital city of Tenochtitlán was conquered and ultimately razed; lower right, churches built with native labor replaced the sacred structures of the indigenous state religion.

Below, a detail from Giuliano Bugiardini's *Abduction of Diana* demonstrates two Renaissance passions: for mathematical perspective and for the free-standing, centrally composed building, the latter depicted here as a focal urban monument. Its requisite dome traces a separate formal history, starting (above left) with the structural simplicity of Brunelleschi's sacristy of S. Lorenzo (1421–60) in Florence. Brunelleschi's directness is succeeded by (center) Raphael's rich integration of painting and sculpture at the Chigi Chapel in Rome's church of S. Maria del Popolo (1483–1520), and (right) the complexities of Guarini's chapel of the Holy Shroud (1667–90) in Turin Cathedral.

Right, domical space dissolves in a cascade of Baroque perspective effects in Johan Zeiller's fresco for the Benedictine Abbey (1737–66) in Ottobeuren, Austria. This scenographic sampler of Baroque design motifs includes a broken pediment, staggered pilasters, and Egyptian obelisks.

Above left, Christ Church rises above the ragged edge of Philadelphia's Second Street in this 1799 view.

Below, archeology's appeal to the Neoclassical imagination is depicted in an 1825 watercolor by J. Gandy of John Soane's church design of 1818. The floor plan of the church is depicted as a ruin examined by admiring antiquarians.

Above right, the Pont des Arts in Paris, built in 1801–3 and reconstructed in the 1980s, provided an early urban demonstration of the pragmatic and aesthetic potentials of iron construction.

Right, cast iron was woven into public architecture in Henri Labrouste's Bibliothèque Nationale (1854–75) in Paris. Far right, beneath the patterned terra-cotta cladding of Louis Sullivan and Dankmar Adler's Guaranty Building (1894–96) in Buffalo, New York, is the steel frame of an early Chicago School skyscraper.

Below, New York City's turn-of-the-century urban fabric was composed of standard tenement blocks and punctuated with skyscrapers and monumental facilities like McKim, Mead and White's Pennsylvania Station (1902–11), the focus of this 1910 lithograph commissioned by the architectural firm. The demolition of Penn Station in the early 1960s was decisive in mobilizing the architectural-preservation movement in the United States.

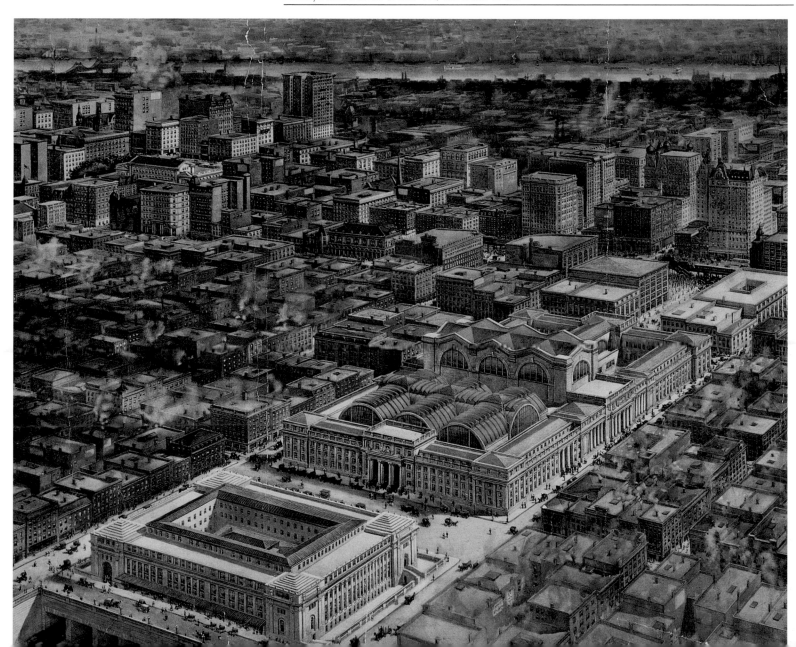

A vocabulary of primary forms and colors unites several strands of twentieth-century Modernism. Above, Le Corbusier's Paris hostel for the Salvation Army (1929–33) is entered through a sequence of free-standing volumes—a hollow cube and a white cylinder—that stand against a glazed backdrop. The colorful window banding is a recent addition. Left, Gerrit Rietveld's Schröder House (1924) in Utrecht, shown here in an interior perspective, marked the first full application of the elementarist philosophy of the De Stijl movement to architectural space. Below, a triptych window by Frank Lloyd Wright from the Avery Coonley Playhouse (1912) in Riverside, Illinois, infuses abstract geometries with playful patriotism. Right, Louis Kahn's Citadel of Assembly (1962–74) at Dhaka, the capital of Bangladesh, sequesters its shaded interiors behind a concrete screen punctured by primary geometries.

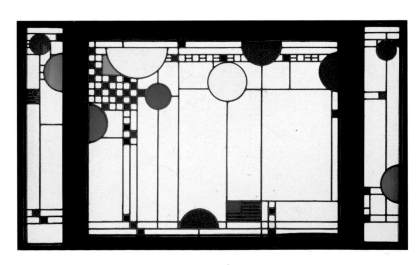

The logic of the freeway makes possible suburban housing patterns like that of Palm City, Florida (left), and provides formal elements to be deconstructed, fractured, and reassembled in Peter Eisenman's design for the Columbus Convention Center (1989–93).

Fig. 17.9 Florence, the Palazzo Rucellai, Leon Battista Alberti; facade. The date is uncertain, ca. 1450–70.

rity, was not propitious for building. Continuing adversities on a European scale and an unstable Italy made major urban interventions, or the planning of new towns, politically and economically unfeasible. The discussion of town planning in *Ten Books on Architecture* assesses positively the experience of medieval practice as we know it from Florence and promotes the new style as an exemplary accent within the old fabric. Renaissance churches and palaces, prominently situated, would ennoble a town; formally conceived high streets with a public purpose—for example, to lead to a princely residence or to a temple (as humanists now called churches)—would set off the winding network of extant streets, which Alberti praises for its visual diversity and military advantage.

Actually, the mid-century saw a stabler climate develop. The fall of Constantinople was a hard blow, but it was not unexpected. More important for the welfare of Europe was the end of the Hundred Years' War, the healing of the papacy, and the suspension of hostilities among Italian states (the Peace of Lodi, 1454). Population was on the rise. A new prosperity, aided by the colonial expansion of the principal monarchies, international capitalism, and the exploitation of the silver and copper mines of central Europe, was beginning to be felt. Renaissance architecture stood to profit from this general convalescence.

Even so, it made very selective progress. The kind of patron Alberti favored was inclined to be satisfied with set pieces, often a partial remodeling of old buildings. Alfonso I of Aragon who conquered the kingdom of Naples from the French in 1442 reconstructed the city fortress, Castel Nuovo, in his native Gothic, but fitted a Classical triumphal arch between the entrance towers. (Fig. 17.4) At Rimini, the tyrant Sigismondo Malatesta had Alberti wrap the medieval church of S. Francesco in a masonry casing *all'antico* to transform it into a memorial for his family and court. The ducal palace at Urbino started as a consolidation and revision of several late medieval buildings on the site. Nicholas V, with more ambitious plans than the secular princes, got little more accomplished.

Nicholas (1447–55) was the first humanist

pope. He knew the value of books and founded the Vatican library. He also knew the value of architecture as a tool of propaganda. The Holy See, secure again after decades of dangerous ferment, required a fit setting to announce its resurgent authority. The pope put it best in a deathbed speech to his cardinals.

The great and supreme authority of the Roman church can be understood only by those who are acquainted with her history through the study of letters. But the common man is innocent of literary matters and devoid of culture; while he often hears it proclaimed by erudites that the authority of the church is supreme and believes it, yet he must be moved by some material work lest his faith fade away with the passing of time. If instead to the teaching of the scholar is added the confirmation of grandiose buildings, of monuments in a certain guise eternal . . . popular faith will be reinforced and stabilized.

Rome herself, run down and depopulated, was beyond total renovation. But the ancient Roman monuments that all Italy now turned to were a priceless asset. They allied the Church with the most progressive phase of modern culture. To match these imperial memories with a contemporary program, Nicholas turned his attention to the Borgo, the papal quarter across the river. The dilapidated Lateran had been given up as the official papal residence. Now the administrative apparatus of the Holy See was moved permanently to the Vatican palace next to St. Peter's. Jointly Alberti and the pope devised a plan for an ideal city of God, which had three aspects to it. The old church was to be enlarged and fortified. The palace was to be overhauled, and its medieval aspect masked. Second, provisions were made for a library, a palatine chapel, a park presumably in line with the formal gardens that were just then being inaugurated in Florentine villas, and a Classical theater. Third, the quarter between St. Peter's and Castel Sant' Angelo, the mausoleum of Hadrian that served as the fortified bridgehead into the Borgo, would be redone in the Albertian manner. Three straight porticoed streets would link the bridge end, with its new square, to the basilica and the palace. A square was to be regularized at that end as well. To the center of this square, on axis with the facade of

St. Peter's, would be moved the obelisk of Nero's racecourse, which had stood since his day on the south side of the basilica. (See Fig. 20.13)

Pienza

This bold stroke for a humanist utopia, unrealized at Nicholas's death, will endure as the blueprint for the marvelous transformation of St. Peter's and the Vatican during the next two centuries. But a papal ensemble did get built in the early Renaissance, far away from Rome, on a hillock south of Siena. It is the first complete, tangible expression of those ideal ambiences that artists of the new school were projecting in paintings, reliefs, and marquetry. The scene is a little town called Corsignano, home of the Piccolomini family, a scion of which ascended the papal throne in 1458 as Pius II. The architect of this site was Bernardo Rossellino. He had worked for Nicholas on St. Peter's and had assisted Alberti at the Palazzo Rucellai in Florence. Indeed, Alberti is clearly looking over Bernardo's shoulder here; the papal palace at Pienza is an almost literal copy of the Rucellai.

But Pius knew exactly what he wanted. If the new community of humanists had raised the architect to the level of lords, it had also given the enlightened patron equal knowledge to interfere professionally. The integrity of the old town that had grown on two sides of a gently undulating spine was respected. But at the crest of the hilly site, on the south side of the spine, Pius had a Renaissance piazza laid out, paved with brick and inscribed in light stone with a perspective grid. (Fig. 17.5) It was enclosed on three sides by a church on the main axis and lateral palaces on the other two sides. These palaces were set on the bias, so that the diverging lines would enhance the monumentality of the church facade and at the same time open the formal space enough to remind us of the vast expanse of sky and valley beyond. (Actually, the trapezoidal arrangement was suggested in part by the original alignment of the old church of S. Maria and the building to the east, which had been the official residence of the prior and other magistrates.) The fourth side, north of the spine, was given a small town

hall east of the approach street with a ground-floor loggia; a cardinal's palace defined the remaining corner of the trapezoid. (Fig. 17.6)

This totally controlled urban ensemble works, and works successfully, on a number of levels. Corsignano stretched lengthwise. The old church was correctly oriented, and so lay parallel to the spine. The prior's building to the east was an old house which Pius bought and handed over to his vice-chancellor "on condition that he should build on the site an episcopal palace and present it to the Blessed Virgin Mary." The new cathedral is made to face north, pulling the stringy town toward itself and transfixing the flow of the spine with a strong counter-axis.

The political diagram is unambiguous. The largest structure, in the plan or from the air, is the Piccolomini palace. (Fig. 17.7) The church has the central place of honor. The town hall, vestigial and politely tucked in one corner, is a symbolic gesture. Behind it is the old marketplace. The remaining palace, the bishop's residence, stands as it does primarily for the sake of the design. At this visual level, seen from within the piazza, the papal block conceals most of itself in order to assure bilateral symmetry. The main eastern entrance shifts to the right of center to relate to the square. The proportions of all three buildings south of the spine are defined and locked in place by the intervening space and its grid. A well at one corner calculatedly offsets the strict balance of the whole and sounds a human note in this thoroughly rational order. It serves as a reminder of basic communal rites, the old ways that intellectualization cannot brush aside.

The well is like a totem of the medieval town of Corsignano, now baptized "Pienza" after its august master. It symbolizes the courteous manner in which the modern age installed itself into a traditional setting. We come upon the piazza along the spine, or along the northern cross-street. Neither has been straightened, widened, or aligned with the Renaissance scheme. On the contrary, the obliqueness of the flanking palaces respects the bend of the spine at the hillcrest. Cardinals who were urged to renovate old houses or to build new ones also

Fig. 17.10 Rimini (Italy), Alberti's original design for S. Francesco (the so-called Tempio Malatestiano); shown on a commemorative bronze medal, after Matteo de' Pasti, 1450.

chose to keep within the old frontages. The deference pays off. The effectiveness of the new is heightened by being reached naturally, without any loud or formal urban announcement. In a similar vein, excessive contrast of scale is avoided between the old and the new. Neither from the valley of the Orcia nor from within do Pius' buildings overwhelm the townscape. Their superiority is expressed in intellectual terms rather than in brute size.

Noble in its public demeanor, the new architecture of Pienza privately indulges the patron. The Palazzo Piccolomini, an urban four-square mass in the Florentine manner that was raised over older houses, had a reservoir on the roof to collect rainwater and distribute it through iron pipes. Filtered through gravel, it filled three cisterns on the premises. "On the very top of the roof," Pius' *Commentaries* tell us, "were built twenty-three tower-like structures ornamented with pinnacles and buttresses and various paintings, which could be seen from a distance and added much to the splendor and charm of the building." On the side facing the valley, the palace block opens out into a formal garden and the view of Mount Amiata beyond, directly on axis. (Fig. 17.8) This south facade consists of three porti-

coes, one above the other, with the sole purpose of taking in the countryside, much in the way Renaissance paintings provide deep naturalistic backdrops for their portraits or religious subjects.

The cathedral is also idiosyncratic. The interior combines a chapelled tribune, reminiscent of the eastern lobes of the cathedral in Florence, with a Gothic, specifically Austrian, nave. Pius had served as legate in that country before he was elevated to the papacy and had admired its hall churches for their openness and luminosity. The broad windows here are of clear glass, however, filled with sky. Suger and his anagogical *lux nova* are in the past. Pius' love of light is direct. The windows "when the sun shines admit so much light that worshippers in the church think they are not in a house of stone but of glass." Wall decoration, like the fresco cycles that covered the surfaces of family chapels in the medieval churches of Italy, is also ruled out. Small detached pictures commissioned from Sienese masters are placed judiciously here and there, leaving the architecture to speak for itself. And Pius wanted his church kept this way forever. A bull of 16 September 1462 orders that "No one shall deface the whiteness of the walls and columns. No one shall draw pictures. . . . No one shall change the shape of the church, either the upper or the lower. . . . If anyone disobeys he shall be accursed."

The facades on the square and its approaches revert to Albertian orthodoxy. The palace scheme improves on the early Renaissance model of Florence, as we saw it at the Palazzo Medici, in one important respect. Vertical dividers have been added between the windows to accentuate the bays. They are stacked up in continuous lines running through the three storeys and are interwoven with the unbroken cornice lines, so that the pattern echoes in elevation the gridded pavement of the square. But even without this obvious urban referent, in Alberti's own Palazzo Rucellai in Florence, the vertical dividers engage the public space directly; they encourage the passerby to turn around and face the building. (Fig. 17.9) The Medici type is layered horizontally. (Fig. 16.4a) It carries the eye along the facade by the perspective

force of the ground line and the cornices, and the unhindered march of the window arcades. The facade passively defines the street volume. Its rhythm is, if you will, the rhythm of a Roman aqueduct. It is in that sense freely extensible. The Rucellai type sets up an active relationship between itself and the street. It has a built-in balance of width and height, not only because of the coordination of vertical and horizontal members, but also because of the subtly differentiated rhythm of the bays, which scans a-a-b-a-a-b-a-(a). (The last bay was never finished.) The facade would suffer from any bold extension without a corresponding adjustment in height and in the volume of the public space it fronts.

But this is only one part of Alberti's scheme. We should also notice something else. The addition of the vertical members brings us closer to a Classical composition, since the cornices no longer seem to float unsupported as they do on the Medici facade. Uprights are requisite in Greco-Roman design, visually if not structurally, to support lintels, entablatures, or their derivatives. The elevation of the Rucellai defers to "correct" models like the Colosseum. Indeed, Alberti gives his uprights capitals of varying orders, like the Colosseum, beginning with Tuscan on the ground floor, then composite (instead of the Ionic used in the corresponding level of the Colosseum), and Corinthian at the top. He also flattens the Roman half-columns into pilasters, smoothly treated to stand out against the principal plane of chaneled rustication.

Alberti considered columns ornamental, unlike Brunelleschi who had used them as load-bearing and space-defining components. Stability and definition for Alberti are the functions of walls. Architecture has two elements that bring about aesthetic satisfaction: beauty and ornament. Beauty is innate. It resides in proportions—"the harmony and concord of all the parts in such a manner that nothing could be added or taken away or altered except for the worst." Ornament is added on. This is where the column and its derivation, the pilaster, come in. Piers, on the other hand, as abbreviations of the wall, can appropriately be made to carry superstructures. Arched forms must rise from piers, or else pilasters; the proper topping for columns is the lintel.

Rossellino disobeys the master in the facade for the church at Pienza by placing arches on columns in the bays of the second storey. His is nonetheless an early attempt to compose a church facade in the new manner. This design problem had not been resolved by Brunelleschi. Neither S. Lorenzo nor S. Spirito was completed externally. Alberti took a first crack at the problem in S. Francesco at Rimini. The Classical temple was the obvious parallel for the Renaissance church, as Pius says it was for his cathedral. But the standard temple front was hard to reconcile with the three-part section of nave and lower aisles. The commemorative nature of the Rimini program may have suggested Alberti's model: a triumphal arch of three openings like the Arch of Constantine in Rome. This took care of the triple partition behind, but could not address the differing height of nave and aisles since triumphal arches have nothing but an attic above their single storey. Alberti's intention, only partly realized, was to repeat the central arch above the doorway, treat it as a window, and flank it with segmental wedges of masonry that would mask the lean-to roofs of the aisles. (Fig. 17.10)

This rather ungainly second storey is treated more successfully in the Florentine facade of S. Maria Novella. (Fig. 17.11) The lower arrangement was conditioned by medieval work. Alberti's giant order of columns broadly frames it and holds up a high attic. A flattened temple front centered above the doorway screens the nave roof, and scrolls fill the corners. As you would expect, simple proportional relationships govern the design. The temple front of the upper storey, including the attic, can be divided by a line running through the center of the doorway. Each of these squares forms one-fourth of the area of a larger square that would circumscribe the whole facade exactly. And so on, with the lesser dimensions.

The general formula of this two-storey facade with its connecting scrolls had a great vogue in Renaissance church architecture. We see it again one hundred years later in the church of the Jesuits in Rome, and one hundred years after that in S. Maria in

Fig. 17.11a Florence, the church of S. Maria Novella, 1460–67; facade as remodeled by Leon Battista Alberti. For the medieval interior of this church, see Fig. 16.5.

Campitelli. (Figs. 17.11b, 21.3, C) Much happens to it of course along the way, but its precept endures. This is the nature of ingenious solutions to pressing architectural problems. They serve so well and look so obvious, we have to remind ourselves that somebody had the sense to invent them.

The Prince and the People: Patronage in Northern Italy

In two other churches he designed, both of them in Mantua, Alberti was able to veer his facades toward a design that resembled the Classical temple front. These were new

Fig. 17.11b Rome (Italy); the facade of the Gesù, the church of the Jesuit order, ca. 1575–84, Giacomo della Porta.

the court had the services of the painter Andrea Mantegna (1431–1506), and after 1524 of Giulio Romano (1499?–1546), the brilliant student of Raphael (1483–1520). Mantegna enjoyed his position as general supervisor of the arts for a while. He was probably responsible for the unusual shape of his own house, a cubic mass aired by a cylindrical courtyard, a miniature precursor of the Alhambra palace of Charles V. Giulio gave Mantua a new law court and a new cathedral, and for his patron Federico Gonzaga he built a suburban villa called Palazzo del Tè. In all these buildings we can see the continuing experimentation of Renaissance architecture and deduce from it one thing clearly. There was to be no single representative manner of dealing with Classical precedent.

The research of Brunelleschi and Alberti had led in different directions. Then, at the turn of the century, a generation of artists tried its hand at a noble summation of these various experiments. Masters like Raphael, Bramante (ca. 1444–1514), and Leonardo da Vinci (1452–1519), working for an elite class that included themselves, sought to stabilize the vigorous, sometimes contradictory, and often hybrid production of several decades. Tolerance of medievalisms diminished. Moving toward an abstract, ideal perfection, they conceived equilibrated worlds of permanence and poise. They preferred freestanding, centrally composed buildings, uniformly enclosed squares, city-forms of immaculate geometry, facades strictly balanced on either side of a central emphasis. The architectural constructs were molded by thick walls which were dug into for sculptural effect, or raised in relief by full or engaged columns, sometimes paired, sometimes attached to or made to alternate with piers. A city plan from a treatise by the Sienese Francesco di Giorgio written about 1480, Bramante's memorial structure, called the Tempietto, over the spot of St. Peter's crucifixion in Rome, and the facade of the "House of Raphael" there, also by Bramante, should suffice to illustrate this hermetic, purist imagination. (Fig. 17.14) (We look at Bramante's work for the popes in Chapter 20.)

Giulio Romano apprenticed in such company. But his artistic activity in Mantua

churches, so he could exercise full control. In S. Andrea, Alberti reduces the full width of the aisled church by means of a high vestibule that can carry his unique version of the temple front. (Fig. 17.12) Four pilasters on tall bases form end bays. Each bay holds a door, then a round-headed niche intended for sculpture, and higher still a round-headed window. Between these bays is a sweeping arch on its own pilasters, rising all the way to the entablature and framing a barrel vault over the main entrance.

This scheme of a deep arched bay flanked by narrow flat strips is carried inside where it defines, on the sides of the barrel-vaulted nave, wide chapels alternating with small service spaces. (Fig. 17.13) The same idea, but on a larger scale, is repeated in the transept, the smaller spaces now being the four piers that hold up the dome of the crossing. Alberti here comes closer

to the spirit of Roman architecture, at least the vaulted style of the empire, than does Brunelleschi in his Florentine churches. Florentine interiors, with their single files of columns and their flat ceilings, have a pristine, light quality, a clear-headed pureness of architectural expression that is almost Greek. (Fig. 16.7) With S. Andrea we think of Roman grandeur—the billowing, interpenetrating spaces of the imperial baths or the basilica of Maxentius. (Fig. 11.10) This invention of Alberti's also had great appeal in the succeeding decades. We could not think of the interior of the Jesuit church in Rome, or of the new St. Peter's, without the remarkable Mantuan prototype of the 1470s. (Figs. 20.23, 21.1)

Mantua

The Mantua of the Gonzagas was a notable center of the Renaissance. Besides Alberti,

Fig. 17.12 Mantua (Italy), the church of S. Andrea, 1470–72, not completed until 1481, Leon Battista Alberti; main facade. The curious vaulted structure above the pediment is a later addition and acts as a hood for the large window that brings light into the nave from the west. To the left of the facade, the late Gothic bell tower is partly visible.

Fig. 17.13 Mantua, S. Andrea; interior looking east.

seems determined to traduce the cool, aloof order installed by his master's circle. In his additions to the ducal palace at Mantua, he whips up a nervous restlessness in the surface through twisted columns, massive effects of rustication, and intentional crowding. At Palazzo del Tè, a gracious garden front of smooth walling, reached by a bridge that spans the moat before it, is contrasted with the rough texture of the main facade which faces the city. Elsewhere, triglyphs are allowed to drop below the line of their frieze, pediments are held up in the air by mere brackets, keystones are grotesquely exaggerated. (Fig. 17.15) In the so-called Hall of the Giants the decoration, a tour de force of illusionist painting, is disquieting, even bizarre. (Fig. 17.16) A huge circular temple floats menacingly in the ceiling above our heads—the setting of an assembly of gods, headed by Jupiter who hurls thunderbolts. The gods rush about to quell the rebellion of the giants who are represented on the walls with terrifying realism, being crushed under enormous boulders and crumbling buildings in a cataclysmic scene that threatens our own security. All of this is

painted without any framing devices, as if to catch the visitor in the chaos of the mythical event. There is no separation between the ceiling and the walls: the whole room is one continuous scene.

This breakdown of Classical decorum admits of at least two interpretations. If we read the design synthesis of the mature Renaissance in terms of stability, permanence, and perfection, its intentional deformity must be seeking to make us uneasy—that is, to project pain or malaise. The infringement of accepted rules can become an expressive tool of psychological tensions and ambiguities. But what is being attempted might also have a lighter purpose—humor, playfulness, variety in place of unity, invention for its own sake. In either case, the moral authority of the Classical revival as Alberti and the generation after him liked to think of it lost ground.

Art historians call this phase of the postmedieval cycle *Mannerism*. It goes beyond

Giulio and affects all of the arts and much of Europe during the sixteenth century. The trend shows that what Brunelleschi and Alberti defined was, after all, an architectural style like all the others—that is, a body of formal conventions open to personal handling and capable of saying as much or little as its managing and consuming public wished it to do. The ideal of some became for others a fad, pure and simple. The tortured depth of a Michelangelo replenished the facile stock of less complicated designers around him, or seemed an interesting "manner" to follow to a contemporary in Flanders or France. There are many manners of Classical architecture that have gripped Western practice from the fifteenth century to the present. All have direct or indirect links to Greece and Rome, a tradition of sufficient wealth to sustain this prodigious issue, and also links with one another. "Every great architect," James Ackerman has said, "finds his own antiq-

Fig. 17.14a Rome, the Tempietto at the monastery of S. Pietro in Montorio, 1504, Donato Bramante.

Fig. 17.14b Rome, Palazzo Caprini (the so-called House of Raphael), ca. 1512, Donato Bramante; shown in a sixteenth-century engraving.

Fig. 17.15 Mantua, the Palazzo del Tè, 1526–34, Giulio Romano; detail of the garden facade.

Fig. 17.16 Mantua, Palazzo del Tè, the Hall of the Giants; mural by Giulio Romano, depicting the battle of the Gods and the Giants.

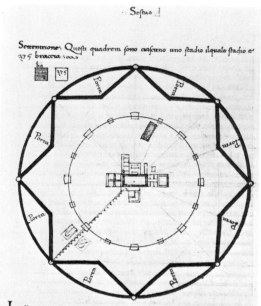

Fig. 17.17 Antonio Averlino called Filarete, the ideal city of Sforzinda, in his treatise on architecture, written ca. 1461–62.

Fig. 17.18 Mantua, the Piazza Sordello (no. 8 in Fig. 17.19); looking northeast toward the Domus Magna.

uity." And the lesser ones move about eclectically in the interstices.

In northern Italy, the uses made of the Renaissance style were both idealistic and faddish. The princes vied for the services of the major artists. It was considered a matter of priority to concentrate this sought-after talent on the princely residence first, and then selectively at the scale of the city. Patronage for public buildings was limited to churches and to rare cases of community welfare like hospitals. But the city-form was also modernized to the extent possible, because the safety and beauty of the prince's seat reflected on himself, but also because the relationship of the prince to the people could be spelled out through interventions at the urban level. One-half of this dialogue was the city; the other half the palace. How the two met and interacted was important. Since the marquis or duke, as supreme authority, sponsored all of this activity, he often found it fruitful to organize the design process and the production

side of things under a single artist. With a suitable court title and the unfettered power that derived from the lord's favor, this person would then supervise everything that was being done in the realm, from the decoration of intimate family apartments on the palace grounds to the statewide system of fortifications.

By 1400 despotism in Italy had become hereditary. Nonetheless, the institution was still ambiguous. The lord, or *signore*, enjoyed no compelling legitimacy like the di-

vine right of kings. His power needed the recognition of the German emperor, the pope, or some superior local prince. Within the city, his intercourse with the bishop and the people had in some measure to be improvised. The tradition of the commune was still potent, its agencies still obtrusively

Fig. 17.19 Mantua; map indicating major Renaissance monuments.

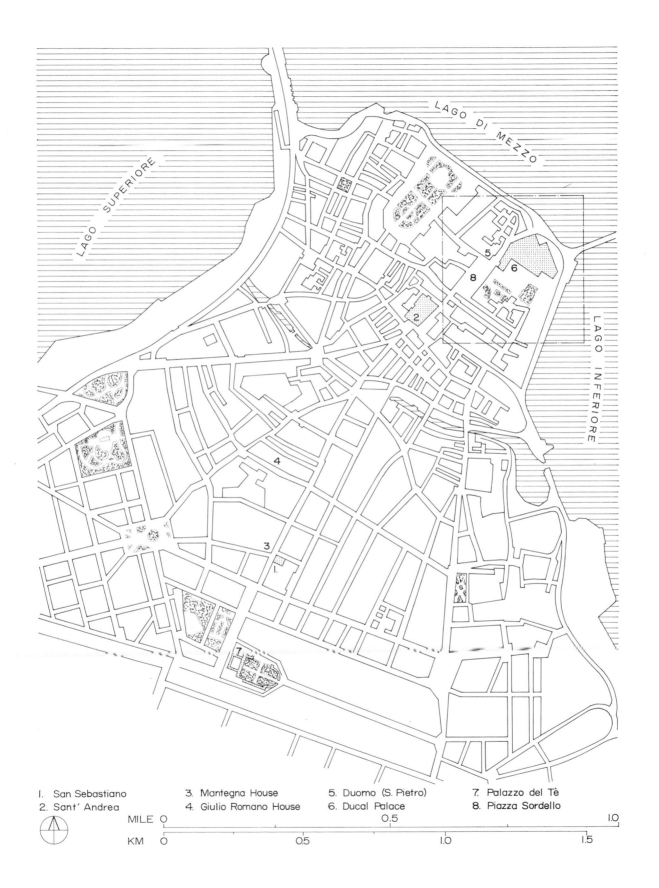

LAGO DI MEZZO

LAGO SUPERIORE

LAGO INFERIORE

5

6

8

2

4

3

1

7

1. San Sebastiano
2. Sant' Andrea
3. Mantegna House
4. Giulio Romano House
5. Duomo (S. Pietro)
6. Ducal Palace
7. Palazzo del Tè
8. Piazza Sordello

MILE 0 _____ 0.5 _____ 1.0

KM 0 _____ 0.5 _____ 1.0 _____ 1.5

417

lodged in the cityscape. Under the circumstances, the architectural expression of the office of *signore* within the fabric of the city could not always be direct or uniform. Theorists like Filarete proposed clear-cut, absolute images. His ideal city of Sforzinda, dedicated to the duke of Milan, Francesco Sforza, was a sixteen-sided star circumscribed by a circular moat. (Fig. 17.17) Sixteen main roads converged on the center where the main square gathered about itself the ducal palace, the cathedral, and the residence of the archbishop. The other public buildings—town hall, prison, mint, and the like—were grouped around two lesser squares. We recognize the urban ideogram of absolutism that had been thought out much earlier for the Abbasid caliph in the round city of Baghdad. (Fig. 12.21)

The perfect form aspires to a utopian view of perfect government. But Sforza and his fellow princes had taken over the reins of very old cities that could not be straitjacketed by symbolic geometry. The origin of their rule may have been the magistracy of the *podestà* or the captain of the people, and the building that had housed it would then be heraldically significant, at least at the beginning, as it was in Mantua. Or else the lord might install his administration in his ancestral home, an old feudal castle somewhere in the city. Urbino, as we will soon see, fits this pattern. But even if a new start was being made with a princely residence located outside the old center of the communal government, as at Milan, one had to decide what it was to look like; what the right sort of political imagery would be.

Again, the theorists had their ideas. Alberti wrote:

The palace of a king should stand in the heart of a city; it should be easy of access, beautifully adorned, and delicate and polite rather than proud and stately. But a lord should have a castle rather than a palace, and it should stand so that it is out of the city and in it at the same time.

But the families that managed Mantua, Urbino, Ferrara, and lesser city-states were increasingly sensitive to the accepted message of towers and battlements—namely, that towers were, as Alberti puts it, "altogether inconsistent with the peaceable aspect of a well-governed city or commonwealth, as they show either a distrust of our

Fig. 17.20 Mantua, the castle of S. Giorgio (no. 8 in Fig. 17.21); looking southwest across the Lago di Mezzo.

countrymen or a design to use violence against them." To advertise coercive rule in the age of humanism was bad politics. At its exemplary best, the residence of the *signore* would project strength and civility, respect for tradition and awareness of the new, localism and worldliness.

In Mantua, the Gonzagas had started their hegemony in 1328 with the overthrow of the Bonacolsi. Under the earlier strongmen the center of government had been a palace called Domus Magna, built about 1300 on the east side of the cathedral square, the present Piazza Sordello, across from the family home of the Bonacolsi. (Fig. 17.18) The city acknowledged this building as the palace of the captain of the people, nominally a municipal post. South of here, on Piazza Broletto, was the town hall and the palace of the *podestà*. The Gonzagas respected these antiquated civic structures, but chose to make their statement in the context of the Domus Magna. The facade of this complex was preserved intact. Behind this emblematic curtain, they began to create a princely residence in the next century, attuned to the precepts of the Renaissance. They backed away from the center of the old city toward the lake front in a se-

ries of buildings and additions that by the seventeenth century would rank as one of the largest and most splendid courts of Europe.

Mantua is a lagoon city like Venice, surrounded on all sides by water. (Fig. 17.19) The island site had been created in the late twelfth century by an extensive program of hydraulic works that formed the three lakes fed by the Mincio. Thereafter, the city grew southward on reclaimed marshland. Alberti's S. Sebastiano and the Mantegna house marked the furthest edge of expansion, and the Palazzo del Tè went up just outside the latest set of walls in this southward direction. The ducal palace took up a good chunk of the original urban core, at the highest point of the site, filling the space between the Piazza Sordello and the water. A long stone bridge connected the city at this point with the opposite bank of the Mincio, where the suburb of S. Giorgio ended the high road from Venice.

Fig. 17.21 Mantua, the ducal palace, fourteenth–sixteenth centuries, four stages of development; plans.

418

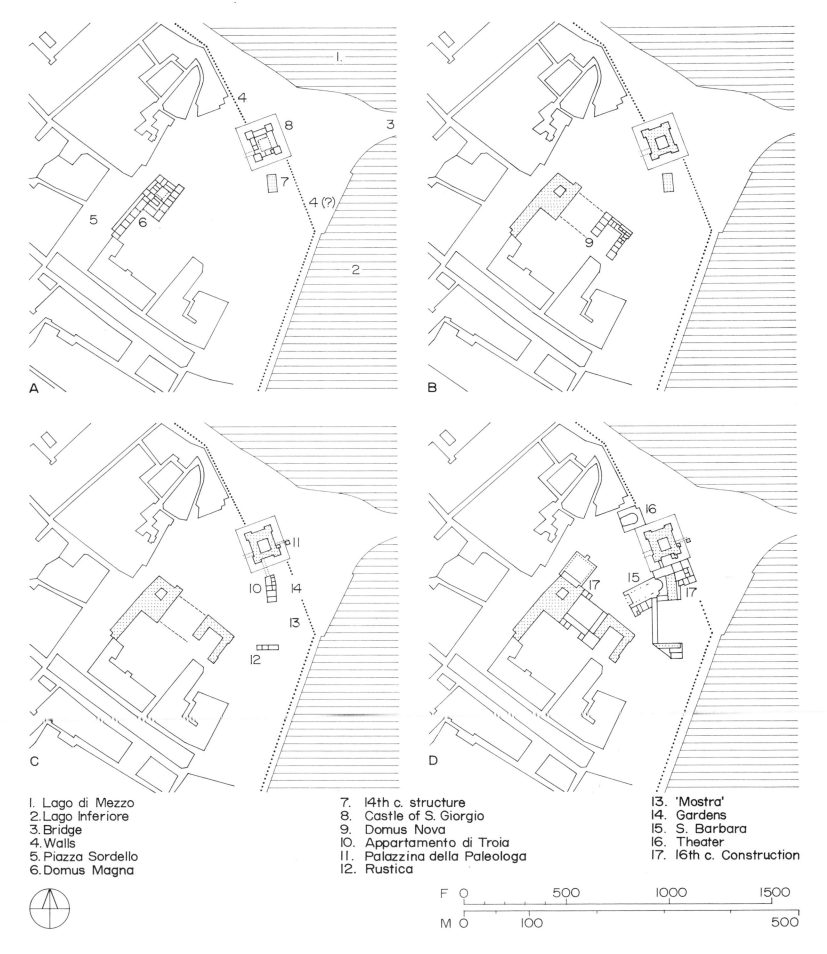

A

B

C

D

1. Lago di Mezzo
2. Lago Inferiore
3. Bridge
4. Walls
5. Piazza Sordello
6. Domus Magna

7. 14th c. structure
8. Castle of S. Giorgio
9. Domus Nova
10. Appartamento di Troia
11. Palazzina della Paleologa
12. Rustica

13. 'Mostra'
14. Gardens
15. S. Barbara
16. Theater
17. 16th c. Construction

F 0   500   1000   1500

M 0   100   500

At the end of the fourteenth century, the fortifications along this vulnerable coast were transformed. The castle of S. Giorgio was built as a formidable bridgehead to defend the palace and the city against attacks from the direction of Venice. (Fig. 17.20) The castle was still very much in the medieval tradition, but its regular plan with four corner towers would not be amiss in a Renaissance design. Here the Gonzagas moved their principal residence. When this proved too small and too forbidding externally for a humanist court, Luca Fancelli was commissioned to build the Domus Nova between the old palace and the castle. (Fig. 17.21) The pairing of storeys between heavy cornices in this building is new for a palace front, and so are the two wings that shallowly project from the facade plane and rise higher than the central block as loggia towers. This feature obviously echoes and updates the elevation of the castle of S. Giorgio. The plan may have followed this disposition of the castle as well—a square block around a court with four salient corner towers—but only three of the wings of the Domus Nova were raised around the court, now the Piazza Paradiso, between 1450 and 1484. What is not clear is whether the fourth wing was intended at all, or whether the castle plan was being brought in line with the new taste, by opening up one side of the Domus Nova toward the city as a gesture of intimacy between the lord and the people.

If that was the case, this relationship to the city did not last long. When Federico was made duke, Giulio Romano undertook the Corte Nova southeast of the castle. In the 1560s the large palatine church of S. Barbara filled the space between this new palace and Fancelli's building, and a theater went up at the west corner of the castle. Closed off by walls that took in a residential section for dependents, the ducal palace turned into a city within a city. The lord drew apart from his people, and the life of the court was distanced by degrees from the life of the streets.

Urbino

The famous ducal palace of Urbino, a small town south of Rimini, built by Federico da Montefeltro during his long tenure (1444–82), typifies a different approach. (Fig. 17.22)

Fig. 17.22 Urbino (Italy), the ducal palace, ca. 1444–82, Luciano Laurana and Francesco di Giorgio; general view from the northwest.

Far from seeking isolation, it draws the city around it on all sides except the southwest corner, where the land plunges into the Valbona ravine. Here in this void, the palace raises an extraordinary front, scaled so that it can be read from the main road approaching the city in this direction, which is the direction of Rome. With this noble device the city is linked with the countryside; the lord with his territory. The palace complex does not brood over the city, then, in the manner of Mantua, but helps to monumentalize it and give it a dignity that transcends its tiny size and the rugged farmland it controls. Better than the big centers of Italy like Milan, Venice, Florence, or Rome, this minor court of the fifteenth century exhibits the humanist ideal of the good prince and the power of the early Renaissance style, undogmatic as yet and still adventurous, to satisfy specific challenges of site and patron.

Federico had his youthful training in Mantua, at the Gonzaga court. The first phase of his palace at Urbino recalls this association in two ways: the retention of earlier structures, and the crenellated facade toward the city which resembles the Piazza Sordello prospect of the Mantuan palace even though it was built more than one hundred years later. To the young Federico, this was what the palace of a *signore* looked like outside.

His ancestors had used two residences in Urbino. The oldest was a rough fort next to the church of S. Maria della Rocca, the tiny predecessor of the later cathedral. This fort was at the top of one of two hills on which the town spread. (Fig. 17.23) About 150 meters (490 feet) to the south, at the edge of the Valbona precipice, Count Antonio had built a four-square castle in the four-

Fig. 17.23 Urbino, ducal palace, stages of its development; plans. Top left, the palace grounds in the later Middle Ages; top right, the first phase of Federico da Montefeltro's palace; bottom, the last phase.

1. Valbona Ravine
2. Porta Valbona
3. Town Walls
4. San Domenico
5. Medieval House
6. Castle (Palazzo Antonio)
7. Castellare
8. Santa Maria della Rocca
9. Cathedral
10. Mercatale
11. Stables & Spiral Ramp
12. Palace

C

F 0   100   300   600

M 0   50   100   200

421

teenth century which the family took as its official residence. Between these two structures there were several medieval houses that Federico now bought, determined to work three of them into his new palace. The point was not of course economy. Older scraps added historical depth to what was being built, in the same way that genealogy buttressed family status. One of the houses became the focus of the first campaign. It was extended at both ends, with some master plan in mind thereby to connect the old fort and Antonio's castle.

The plan apparently envisioned two courtyards behind this long front, a kind of double palace that would abut the castle at its southeast corner and link up with the old fort by a bridge-block. The northern half of this scheme was substantially realized by the early 1460s, at least in the direction of the city. In fact, this was the principal orientation of the palace at this time. The long, intentionally archaic-looking facade turned toward the medieval monuments, civic and religious, that were the focus of this old part of town. An L-shaped piazza next to the cathedral, formed by the north flank of the palace and the bridge-block to the fort, opened out obliquely toward the main traffic route. (Fig. 17.24) This route followed the saddle between the two hills, starting at the Lavagine gate where the road from Rimini came in. (Fig. 17.25) Halfway across town, the main street forked to reach the hilltops. The L-shaped piazza met the left fork, which then passed by the long palace front, and started its southward descent through the ward of S. Polo.

Sometime around 1464, so most scholars on the subject have agreed, Federico's conception of the palace changed. The L-shaped piazza and the new cathedral raised on the site to replace the little church of S. Maria della Rocca may have been the turning point. But what is more striking was the decision to develop the difficult slope at the back, toward the west, into a formal prospect. The main street, extended beyond the point of bifurcation, ended at Valbona gate where the high road from Rome, 200 kilometers (125 miles) to the south, entered the town following the ancient Flaminian Way. Outside this gate a terrace was now created on massive embankments. This became known as the Mercatale. The road

Fig. 17.24 Urbino, ducal palace; view from the northeast. The block seen is no. 12 in Fig. 17.23.

swung along the west side of it, having made a sharp turn at the southwest corner. The palace stood high on the eastern slope, some 30 meters (100 feet) above the Mercatale. The lower part of this drop was negotiated with a long building that housed the stables and was reached from the level of the Mercatale by a spiral ramp inside a huge semicircular tower. The tower was at the northwest corner of the Mercatale, diagonally across the bend of the high road.

Arriving along this road, the visitor's eye would have been caught by this mighty pivot and lifted to the palace mass that now presented a magnificent new face. (Fig. 17.26) Two tall narrow towers rose all the way from the upper level of the stables, their turrets visible above the palace roofscape. Between them a structure of three main storeys opened up at the center in a series of superimposed balconies. The towered front was set at an angle to the

main palace block, directly facing the high road. It pulled together the irregular grouping of the cathedral, fort, and bridge-block to the left, and the jagged ends of the half-finished palace to the right. By means of this unique set piece, the back site of the palace was changed into its chief aspect, so that the town now began to be portrayed from this side rather than the older view from the north.

The transformation was more than the self-indulgent love of the countryside that had induced Pius II to air one side of his palace at Pienza. Italian city-states always depended on a territory that they exploited freely. And yet the city sealed itself from this land with high, towered walls. Advances in miitary technology, as we will soon discuss, will lower these exclusive curtains and point defenses outward into the surrounding country. Urbino itself will renew its defensive circuit in this fashion in the six-

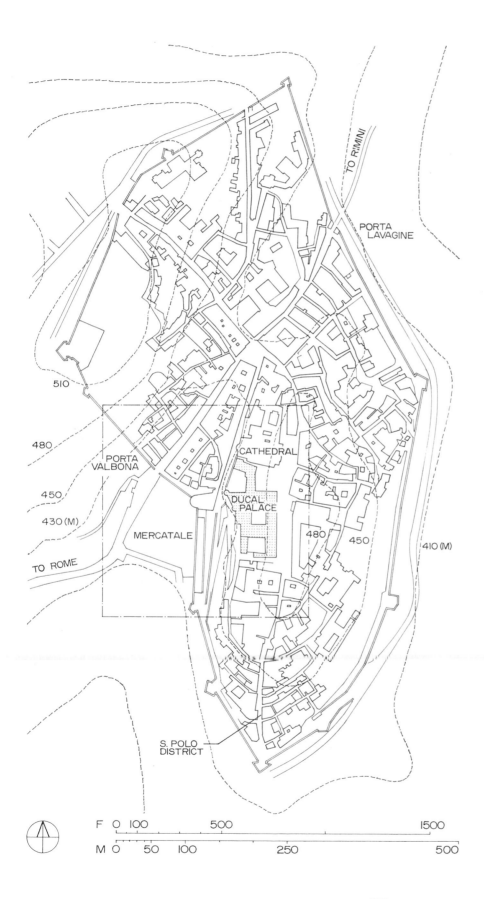

TO RIMINI

PORTA
LAVAGINE

510

480

PORTA
VALBONA

450

430 (M)

CATHEDRAL

DUCAL
PALACE

MERCATALE

480   450

410 (M)

TO ROME

S. POLO
DISTRICT

F O 100   500   1500

M O   50   100   250   500

teenth century. But Federico reaches out to his territory less for practical than symbolic reasons. The palace descends to the valley floor, straddles the walls, and spreads the Mercatale like an inviting carpet at the start of a major southern highway. It is, as Alberti prescribed, "out of the city and in it at the same time."

But the towers of the new facade also strike a military note; they are like banners proclaiming the duke's resolve to defend his patrimony. The better part of this land, including dependent towns like Casteldurante and Gubbio, lay south of Urbino. This was one point to be made with the towered frontispiece. Federico's right to these towns had been affirmed by the popes, whom he served as a feudal knight. It was Sixtus IV who raised his title from count to duke and installed him as Standard-Bearer of the Church and Knight of St. Peter. To turn around and face Rome with an architectural device that has the flare of a triumphal arch was itself a calculated, and inspired, bit of scenography.

In the details of the palace layout, and its decoration, we can follow with finer evidence the rising dignity of Federico's career and the attributes he endowed himself with as a model lord. A comparison of his first study in the long eastern wing and the *studiolo* immediately behind the towered frontispiece of the west is instructive. The stems and warriors on the walls of the earlier room fit his origins. As an illegitimate son, Federico was expected to pursue a career of soldiering—and did. But the art of war was only one skill expected of a Renaissance lord. Arms were nothing without letters, the humanistic study that gave one the virtues needed to govern well. This education Federico had accomplished in Mantua and Venice. His biographers stress that his endowments included wisdom, eloquence, knowledge, benevolence, and the maintaining of "a splendid court and . . . magnificent and splendid buildings."

At the studiolo this full princely iconography is set out with superb taste on the walls of the tiny room in marquetry, the

Fig. 17.25 Urbino; city plan. The inset corresponds to the area shown in Fig. 17.23.

popular new medium of the Renaissance. (Fig. 17.27) In the attic level are painted portraits of famous men of letters, both ancient and modern. The duke is shown among them, dressed in armor and robes of state, reading. In the wood panels that run along the base, cabinets with doors ajar reveal the contents of musical and scientific instruments and books by Classical authors like Cicero, Seneca, and Virgil. In the main panels we see the duke's armor put away, and a full-length state portrait of him holding a spear with the tip down, his life complete. His reward is shown in another panel: a landscape of paradise seen through a Classical arcade. The study offers a memorial exemplum of the virtuous Christian lord whose realm, through wise and just government, lies adjacent to heaven.

The components of the palace have been analyzed in similar terms. The public area is around the L-shaped piazza. A portal in the wing next to the cathedral leads into a loggia and a garden beyond. This is the setting in which the duke met with his people. A contemporary tells us that Federico started the day early with inspection visits to the countryside, then heard Mass, and afterwards went "into a garden with all the doors open and gave audience to all who wished, till the hour of repast." Above the loggia was the hall for entertainments and receptions. In the other arm of the L, over the entrances that led into the main court, was the throne room used for affairs of state that went beyond the realm. The duke's private suite of rooms is fitted between the east end of the throne room and the towered frontispiece that faces toward the countryside. It includes the studiolo, a chapel, and a shrine to the muses. The duchess's apartments are next to the cathedral and communicate with the duke's by means of a walkway across the west enclosure wall of the garden. The second court, never completed, was to have a circular mausoleum in it for the duke, an idea abandoned probably because of the strong tradition against being buried in places other than church grounds.

Ferrara

Federico da Montefeltro died in 1482, and with his death work on the great palace ground to a halt. Pienza had gone back to

Fig. 17.26 Urbino, ducal palace; close view of the western facade.

Fig. 17.27 Urbino, ducal palace; Federico's study (the *studiolo*), immediately behind the towered frontispiece shown in Fig. 17.26.

its quiet country ways earlier, when its native pope was no longer around to promote it. In Rome the epic transformation of the Vatican palace and St. Peter's was not yet started. Building at the ducal palace of Mantua was in a lull, with the Domus Nova of Fancelli left half done and the fury of Giulio Romano's interventions several decades away. The French were making ready to invade Italy by colluding with the Sforza family in Milan, where Leonardo had arrived to work as a military engineer and Bramante was busy on the remodeling of the church of S. Maria presso S. Satiro.

It was in Ferrara, the city of the Este family, that the end of the first Renaissance century was to stage its most ambitious architectural enterprise. The focus here was no longer the princely palace but the entire city. The protagonist, one Biagio Ros-

setti (1447?–1516), was a city planner first and foremost—that is, a man who saw all buildings as incidents that generate specific urban responses. He was not as interested in ennobling the everyday fabric by isolated acts of heroic architecture, as he was in muting the clash between the vernacular and the monumental and in encouraging a general level of decency in the streetscape at large.

Ferrara, a city of Roman origin like Urbino, was a comparatively insignificant place in the Middle Ages, living in the shadow of Venice. (Fig. 17.29) The Este family was established here as early as the thirteenth century, and slowly they gained strength for their little state. By 1400 it was preeminent in the Po plain. With the arrival of the noted humanist Guarino da Verona in 1436, Ferrara entered the age of the Renaissance. The

court attracted some of the same luminaries of the arts who gave Urbino and Mantua their cultural prestige, among them Alberti and Mantegna. The population was rising by the conscious policy of the ruling house whose revenue came from the productive wealth of the city. The medieval city-form was long and narrow, with many canal streets like Venice. Already in the 1450s a planned extension filled the space between the southern edge and the river. The opposite limit was marked by the line of the Giovecca moat, which stretched from northwest to southeast. The Este castle was situated close to the midpoint of this line, with its back to the wall; before it spread the administrative nucleus, the cathedral, and the market.

The flatland north of the Giovecca had received some important buildings linked by a crude system of country roads. One of these roads ran in a straight line from the castle to the suburban estate of the dukes, called Belfiore, about 600 meters (1970 feet) to the northeast. A Carthusian monastery lay east of this axis, and an extensive hunting park still farther out. This area was easily overrun by the Venetians in the war of 1482. To provide a line of defense beyond the city that would protect these establishments was one motivation for the Herculean Addition, the huge new district between the Giovecca and the ducal properties of Belfiore and the hunting park, sponsored by Ercole d'Este and planned and executed by Biagio Rossetti. The other reason for this Addition was the chronic housing shortage which had been made more acute by the emigration since 1480 of large numbers of Jews from Spain. Popular quarters had already sprung up west of the old city and across the river. The Herculean Addition would stop this ad hoc growth with an orderly and walled new town.

Defense was an absorbing interest of the Renaissance. The steady improvement of artillery had antiquated the medieval curtain wall with its high towers and machicolated galleries. Walls could now be breached by cannon from a distance. With the advent of the iron ball at the end of the fifteenth century, the effectiveness of this new method of assault became devastating. To figure out a scientifically appropriate defense and counterattack were pre-

Fig. 17.28 Vigevano (Italy), the ducal piazza, 1492–94, Donato Bramante; view looking west. The castle is on the left.

bastion. This invention, attributed to Giuliano da Sangallo (ca. 1443–1516), was perfected in stages until the familiar arrowhead plan, boldly salient and with slanting wall surfaces, became the norm by the mid-sixteenth century.

Rossetti's defenses for the Herculean Addition are an early instance of the bastioned circuit. The land ramps, the huge terraces, the low, functional, antimonumental ramparts can still be plainly viewed today, and also the bastions, even though these look timid compared to the vastly superior later specimens on the river side. But the telling point is that Rossetti does not allow himself to be tempted by the abstractions of contemporary architects like Francesco di Giorgio (1439–1501) who were beginning to see in the bastioned wall system a modern rationale for their ideal city-forms. The Addition takes in what it must and has defenses where necessary, unconcerned with formal issues of symmetry or the geometric purity of the outline.

And this sensible, pragmatic attitude governs Rossetti's plan for the new quarter as a whole. Radial or gridded shapes are rejected, because they do not correspond to the realities of the site and its antecedent landmarks. The axis between the ducal castle and Belfiore is retained. The longitudinal cross-axis, roughly parallel to the upper wall, joins two important gates but does not align with them. The defensive circuit and the street plan are not locked into each other, because Rossetti sees the street as a directional space that makes sense in the total structure of the city rather than as a finished vista targeted on a worthy focus, like a city gate. Some of the vertical lines of the plan, for example, see to it that streets in the old city are continued across the now filled-in moat of the Giovecca to graft the Addition to the habitual traffic of the downtown.

Perfect geometries in urban design are usually closed patterns. They make no allowance for an evenly distributed growth but, instead, attempt to channel building activity along the high points of the hierarchical diagram. Rossetti's determination to provide incentive for growth in all parts of the Addition comes across in his geometrically impure design. The large new piazza is placed not at the crossing of the

cisely the kind of design problems that, like linear perspective, challenged the rational curiosity of humanist learning.

Earth ramparts were obviously more resistant to artillery fire, as northern Europe had demonstrated. But the Italian preference for stone was a deep-seated, unshakable tradition, symbolically as much as technically. To minimize the impact of artillery on them, the walls now had to be lowered and the towers brought down to the general height of the circuit. Some of this wall mass was further reduced by being

concealed in the broad ditches that were to keep cannon fire at arm's length, and so dull its impact. In order to use the same weapon against the enemy, spacious artillery platforms had to exist at the top of the towers. Earth ramps had to be provided within, for easy access to the platforms. In the event that the attacking force gained the walls, cross-fire from pairs of towers would have to be effected. Polygonal and round towers left dead spots in front that could not be covered from above by the line of fire. The answer proved to be the triangular

main axes where we would expect it, but two blocks further east. This urban focus thus activates the development of the eastern half of the Addition. It also gives the new city a heart of its own, instead of reinforcing the centrality of the prince's residence by fixing the square at the crossroads of the main arteries, and so along the ducal axis.

The institution of the *signore* in the historic cities, as we have observed, had problems of identity vis-à-vis the communal apparatus of self-government which included the marketplace, the people's square. On the whole, princely palaces touched base with this core—whether they were willing to communicate with it freely, as at Urbino, or retreat from it into an isolated enclave, as at Mantua. In at least one striking case, the town of Vigevano which belonged in the realm of the Sforzas of Milan, the whole city center was redesigned about 1490 to create a vast arcaded main square before the castle. (Fig. 17.28) The space of the new square, oversized in the context of the medieval fabric, proclaimed the absolute authority of the prince almost as convincingly as ideal city-forms like Sforzinda would have done had they been built. The uniform arcades that frame the space blocked from view the lively incidents of the earlier governmental setting. The town as a whole thus became the forecourt of the princely residence. This solution, possibly by Bramante, was thereafter imitated in a few other towns.

Ferrara is unusual in that it had the opportunity, with the Herculean Addition that tripled the size of the city, to impose an ideal solution to the issue of princely dominance by subordinating the old center to an unequivocal absolutist statement in the new town. Whether with the conscious assent of the duke, or through Rossetti's clever manipulation of his client, this opportunity was not seized. Rossetti's piazza,

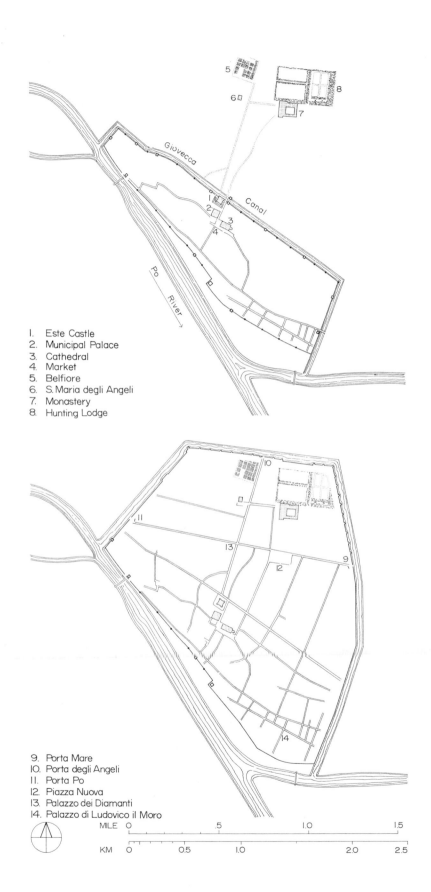

1. Este Castle
2. Municipal Palace
3. Cathedral
4. Market
5. Belfiore
6. S. Maria degli Angeli
7. Monastery
8. Hunting Lodge

9. Porta Mare
10. Porta degli Angeli
11. Porta Po
12. Piazza Nuova
13. Palazzo dei Diamanti
14. Palazzo di Ludovico il Moro

MILE 0   .5   1.0   1.5
KM 0   0.5   1.0   2.0   2.5

Fig. 17.29 Ferrara (Italy), two stages of city growth; plans. Top, the medieval city with the suburban properties of the Este family, and the planned extension along the river; bottom, the city, ca. 1510, with the Herculean Addition and the new walls.

if anything, reinforces the old marketplace, the two being directly linked by a straight street that runs through the Giovecca. There are, furthermore, no important public buildings on the piazza. Its unceremonial character is emphasized by the prosaic design of the surrounding buildings and the fact that the porticoes are not used as a continuous device all around the vast space, but at two points only where the incoming streets are the weakest and the porticoes, lined up with them, help to minimize the contrast betwen them and the vastness of the square. Again, at the crossing of the two main arteries, Rossetti refrains from having four identical or similar corner buildings for the sake of formal harmony. One corner is highlighted by an arresting two-storey palace with diamond-shaped rustication and an ornate corner balcony. The location of the palace at the northwest corner makes it an especially enticing magnet from precisely those approaches to the castle that are most important—coming down from the direction of Belfiore along the north-south axis, and then again from the east where the new piazza lies.

The paradox of the Renaissance street lies in the fact that the emphasis on perspective works to obliterate the individuality of the blocks. Alberti recommended that all facades be uniform, thus condoning the shadow-filled, tunnellike effect of the public space which rushes past the two lines of wall toward its converging point. Rossetti keeps the perspective strong, eschewing frontal compositions and stressing the directional speed of the facades. (Fig. 17.30) But he breaks up the street planes on either side with green spaces and through-views into courtyards and gardens, so that the streets are patched with light and the user gets a feeling for the cross streets and the integrity of the blocks. The special articulation of corners has the same result, to make us conscious that a cross street runs through the perspective tunnel at that point.

But perhaps the most singular aspect of Rossetti's work for Ferrara was his interpretation of Renaissance style as a design language that could be applied to ordinary buildings as readily as to courtly palaces. In place of the uniform array of facade motifs, which in palaces like those of the Medici and the Rucellai give no inkling of what is going on inside, the elevations of Rosset-

Fig. 17.30 Ferrara, Corso Ercole d'Este, which runs from the Este castle to the Porta degli Angeli (nos. 1 and 10 in Fig. 17.28); view looking north.

ti's buildings, both the humble and the rich, play up the functional divisions of the interiors. Totally controlled though it is, a Rossetti facade betrays the variety present in the inner rooms. (Fig. 17.31) It uses round, arched, and rectangular windows, single or paired, spaced with brave nonconformity on the facade plane, and sometimes even defying the division line between storeys. A common device is the *binato*, or double window. This actually marks the juncture of two rooms, with the partition wall corresponding to the line between the two windows. The interior courtyard elevations are equally lively.

The Italianate Craze

From the early works of Brunelleschi to the death of Biagio Rossetti in 1516 we span a hundred years. In that time Italy recovered the architectural leadership of the West that it had lost along with the empire a full millennium before. With a bold start at Florence, a handful of patrons and artists acting in partnership went back to that first period of greatness to find the inspiration for a manner of thinking and designing that would sweep away the phantasmagoric outlook of the Middle Ages.

The movement, restricted to a few cities,

Fig. 17.31 Ferrara, residence on the Via degli Angeli, 1490s, Biagio Rossetti.

or aspirations it means to convey through its language. This is what we might call the politics of the style. And then there is the question of how the style will fit in—whether it will stay aloof and alien waiting for unconditional acceptance, or try in some way to coexist with what is already there. Pienza, Urbino, Mantua, Ferrara—these are some of the experiments of the fifteenth century in which the struggle to establish the Classical viewpoint of the Renaissance was diversely engaged in.

Europe beyond the Alps looked at the goings-on with curiosity. Its tentative sampling of what Italy had wrought was entirely extrinsic. Uncommitted to the premises, away from the struggle, attention focused on the results, the surface look, the visible conventions. These were of several kinds. There was, first, Renaissance decoration, both interior and exterior—artifacts, window frames, Classical motifs. Second, and less accessible, there was the range of building types elaborated by the Italian masters—the urban palace, for example, or the villa with formal gardens, or the bastioned defenses. Finally, there were the Renaissance principles—symmetry, proportional relationships, the balance of parts, those things that underlay the formal construct and accounted for the innate quality of the architecture, the thing Alberti called "beauty." This was the hardest feature of all to appropriate.

The most direct way of importing these Italian ideas—lock, stock, and barrel—was to send for Italian artists. That is the way, you will remember, the French manner had reached out from the Île-de-France three centuries earlier. Already in 1467 the Bolognese architect Aristotele Fioravanti (1415?–86?) had gone to England, and in 1475 he was in Russia where shortly thereafter Pietro Antonio Solari (after 1450–93) from Milan would be working on the fortress walls of the Kremlin and the Diamond Palace, so-called after the pattern of its rustication. The King of Portugal, John II, invited Andrea Sansovino in 1492 through the good offices of Lorenzo de' Medici. A string of major artists and serviceable craftsmen found favor in the French court during the same years. In the Hungary of Mathias Corvinus, magnates of the land followed the example of the humanist king in welcoming Italian talent and ideas.

was deeply reasoned and moralistic. At its loftiest, it sought to advocate a new age of grace. In more practical terms, the task was threefold as it is with any fresh-sprung style. The hardest step is also the most basic: to find an articulate language of form that can

address a variety of problems and that can be handled by both greater talents and lesser. As we saw, this step inevitably affects the systems of production and labor. Initially at least, the novel process of design has to stand for something, have causes

But the success of all these missionaries was limited. No truly Italianate buildings materialized, because neither the patrons nor the local building industries were ready for them. The influx of Italian methods was to be only partial until about the middle of the sixteenth century. Most commonly, building types current in the host country would wear trinkets, or even whole mantles, in the new taste. If locally designed or produced, even this surface ornamentation was likely to be mismanaged, at least in the eyes of an Italian appraiser. Direct imports were simplest. Marble tombs shipped out of the ports of Genoa and Naples stood in church interiors of totally different spirit. Or else the labor could be imported. At the Château de Gaillon in Normandy, the cardinal of Amboise engaged Italian craftsmen to finish in a delicate Classical mode the entrance panel of the essentially medieval castle started in 1501. King Francis I (1515–47) put his Italians to work decorating the interior of his chateau at Fontainebleau and adding a gate lodge, which is an exotic rendering by the local master mason Gilles le Breton of something like the towered frontispiece at Urbino. (Fig. 17.32, 17.26) Chambord, a royal chateau on the Loire begun about 1520, has a riotous roofscape of chimneys, pinnacles, and dormers, all strewn rather incongruously with Classical details. (Fig. 17.33)

But Chambord had the benefit of an Italian architect at the beginning of the design process. It therefore goes beyond decorative affectation, displaying in its totality some sense of Renaissance order. This is a more fundamental susceptibility of Italian tutelage. It makes it possible to interpret familiar medieval structures of all kinds according to Renaissance principles, regardless of correct Renaissance decoration. In this sense Chambord is a Renaissance building; its exact contemporary, Henry VIII's palace of Nonesuch which shows little discipline in its layout or massing, is not.

These changes in attitude that underlie the basic thinking out of design come slowly and with enormous difficulty. They never did take in Russia, and they were cut short in Hungary by the Ottoman conquest. In Europe we will have to wait until the mid-century for the first serious attempts by local exponents to absorb and dissemi-

Fig. 17.32 Fontainebleau (France), royal chateau begun 1528, gate lodge (Porte dorée), Gilles le Breton.

nate the logic of the Italian experience. The education of the building crafts to support a radically altered process would come even later. But that is what had to happen; for no amount of decorative frill alone could move European architecture out of its medieval habits and into the light of humanism.

Fig. 17.33 Chambord (France), royal chateau on the Loire, begun ca. 1520, Domenico da Cortona(?); view from the southeast.

Further Reading

G. C. Argan, *The Renaissance City*, trans. S. E. Bassnett (New York: Braziller, 1969).

L. Benevolo, *The Architecture of the Renaissance*, 2 vols., trans. J. Landry (Boulder, Colo.: Westview, 1978).

A. Chastel, *The Golden Age of the Renaissance, Italy 1460–1500*, trans. J. Griffin (London: Thames and Hudson, 1965).

H. de la Croix, *Military Considerations in City Planning: Fortifications* (New York: Braziller, 1972).

J. Gadol, *Leon Battista Alberti, Universal Man of the Early Renaissance* (Chicago: University of Chicago Press, 1969).

R. Goldthwaite, *The Building of Renaissance Florence* (Baltimore: Johns Hopkins University Press, 1980).

D. Hay, ed., *The Age of the Renaissance* (New York: McGraw-Hill, 1969).

P. Rotondi, *The Ducal Palace of Urbino* (New York: Transatlantic, 1969).

D. Thomson, *Renaissance Paris: Architecture and Growth, 1475–1600* (Berkeley: University of California Press, 1984).

Isleta (New Mexico), mission church of San Agustìn de la Isleta, begun ca. 1613;
seen here as it was remodeled, 1959–60.

18

SPAIN AND THE NEW WORLD

The rediscovery of the Classical past was one of the two great adventures that informed the Renaissance. The other was the exploration and conquest of America.

European colonialism began with the Crusades. When their fast gains were lost and the trade routes to the Far East were permanently blocked by the Ottoman Turks in the fifteenth century, Europe turned elsewhere. The lead nations this time were Portugal and Spain. The targets: Africa, the coasts of South Asia, and the hitherto unknown lands across the Atlantic. Slaves and gold more than any lasting benefit of diversified trade repaid the crowned heads who launched the expeditions. To the colonists fell the chance for a new life. Human and material resources beyond any European measure compensated them for the dangers of settlement. In the long-term tally of human history, unsuspected cultures were unveiled—and destroyed. These newfound cultures should have proved that the worth of Western achievement was only relative, and forced it into fresh channels. They did not. The riches of the conquered New World added nothing to the enrichment of the Christian West except in the material sense.

The Portuguese half of the story is simply told. A tiny outpost at the edge of Europe, caught between a rising Spain and the uncharted expanse of an ocean, Portugal had no option but to look outward. Portuguese seafarers had ventured into this watery realm as far as the Azores and the Madeiras some fifty years before Colum-

bus. They had also traveled down the coast of Africa in the first lap of an undertaking that opened an alternate route to China. Cheap slave labor and exceptionally fertile soil turned the Atlantic islands into major producers of luxury crops like sweet wines and sugar. By mid-century permanent trading stations had been founded on the West African coast, at Arguin and at what is now Agadir. When Elmina on the Gold Coast was settled in 1482, ivory, gold, and pepper enlarged the yield of Portuguese trade. The Cape of Good Hope was rounded in 1486. At the end of the century Vasco da Gama gained India by this route. The west coast of the subcontinent was invaded, and in 1510 the important maritime city of Goa conquered. That was now a year's journey from Lisbon.

The audacious outreach made Portugal wealthy, and its king more powerful than his remote little country would merit. But the cultural profit was negligible. The explorers had no wish to find out what the new lands were like or learn from them. They stuck to the coastline. There was, at any rate, no high civilization in Africa beyond the Muslim north that the European visitor would take seriously. With Goa the picture changed. The Portuguese came face to face with two sophisticated traditions whose monumental architecture was more than a match for theirs—the Hindu state of Vijayanagar, and Delhi which had been a leading Muslim center since the twelfth century. In Goa the Portuguese raised churches next to the existing Hindu tem-

ples, but there was no question of a blend. It was just a matter of time before inevitable fever of conversion set in. The Jesuits arrived in 1542; orders to demolish the pagan temples were issued at the same time.

The urban model everywhere became the Lisbon-like medieval arrangement of hilltop towns, with the trading station down at sea level. Examples are Angra in the Azores and São Paulo de Loanda in West Africa. The Indian possessions did get some modern forts in the later sixteenth century that had a gridded layout and bastioned walls. But colonization was superficial, and beginning about 1600 it was checked by the Dutch initiative. As for the mother country, the excitement of an overseas empire marked its monuments with a strange, expressionist ornament of tropical vegetation, sea creatures, and nautical gear wrapped about windows and doorways of late Gothic structures like the monasteries of Batalha, Tomar, and Belem. (Fig. 18.1)

The American Scene

The greater epic is that of Spanish expansion. (Fig. 18.2) Unified politically in the period of the Catholic kings and ruthlessly strapped to the dictates of the state religion, Spain was ready to assume a strong role in European affairs. American gold vastly improved the odds. For much of the sixteenth century the Iberian kingdom ranked as the premier world power. Seamen of Castile had countered Portuguese

Fig. 18.1 Tomar (Portugal), Convent of Christ, window of the chapter house, ca. 1520, Diego da Arruda.

adventurism from the start. The notion that the earth was round, increasingly popular during the fifteenth century, posed the ultimate challenge. Sailing ever westward, one should be able to reach the mainland of Asia. Columbus tried to sell Portugal on an expedition to prove this argument. When King John II demurred, the Genoese explorer offered his services to their Catholic majesties Isabella and Ferdinand. The first voyage, in 1492–93, took him as far as Cuba, Haiti, and Santo Domingo, which came to be called Hispaniola. John tried to claim these for Portugal, but he had already lost this game. The dispute was resolved with the Treaty of Tordesillas of 1494 in which Pope Alexander VI set down the line of demarcation between Spanish and Portu-

Fig. 18.2 Map: The Spanish and Portugese territories in the Americas, with insets showing the displaced Aztec (left) and Inca (right) states.

Fig. 18.3 Quiriguá (Guatemala), stele E, late eighth century. This sandstone stele stands 10 meters high.

guese jurisdictions in the Atlantic: an imaginary meridian passing 370 leagues to the west of the Cape Verde Islands.

On his fourth and last voyage Columbus hugged the east coast of Central America, and in 1502 landed at Guanaja, one of the Bay Islands off the coast of Honduras. An Indian trading party had also put ashore in a large dugout canoe. They said they came from a land called Maya. No one suspected yet that this land had nothing to do with Asia, that these people were natives of a new, unimagined world. The earth's sphericity was true, but the sphere was much larger than anyone had thought. An enormous continent lay between Europe and Asia. And as Spain persisted, her men now uncovered brilliant, fantastic civilizations with populous cities, stone monuments, and precious works of art. On 9 December 1519 a ship sailed into the harbor of Seville laden with wondrous treasures. They included a sun wheel of gold, a full 2 meters across, covered with designs. This was sterling

proof of the wisdom of expansionism. The lands out there were golden. They must be explored and settled. The gifted pagans, who even had books, must be brought within the Catholic faith.

Not counting lesser entities, the colonists encountered three high cultures in Central and South America—the Maya, the federation of the Aztecs in central Mexico, and the Inca empire that stretched for more than three thousand kilometers along the western coast of South America. Between the founding of Hispaniola in 1493 and the early seventeenth century, more than two hundred towns were planted on American soil, from Lima and Buenos Aires in the south to Santa Fe, New Mexico, and St. Augustine in Florida. We must discuss the nature of this impressive activity and the architecture it produced.

The Maya
Our only prior encounter with this part of the world thus far, in Chapter 10, had culminated with the city of Teotihuacán in the valley of Mexico as it appeared about A.D. 200. This great center of a people called the Toltecs was the noblest creation of Middle America until about 600. At that time it was attacked by a people we do not know and abandoned. But by then the area now occupied by eastern Mexico, Guatemala, San Salvador, and Honduras was in full ascendancy.

This is Maya land. Its settlement history is long, but it rises as a culture of consequence in the early centuries of the Christian era with three telltale features: stone temples with corbel vaults set atop stepped pyramids, stelai inscribed with temporal hieroglyphs, and polychrome pottery. The several millions of Indians who lived here and built the ritual centers of Tikal, Copán, Palenque, and more than a score of lesser ones, first came under the influence of the Toltecs in the heyday of Teotihuacán and then again, in the tenth century, when dissident groups fleeing the new Toltec capital of Tula invaded the lowlands of the Yucatán and took over Chichén Itzá as their center of operations. The time between these two Mexican interventions, about 600 to 900, is the high moment in Mayan civilization. About 1200, the Mayan settlement begins a slow decline. In the century or so

before the Spanish conquest the Maya have become a backwater people, their magnificent old centers abandoned or neglected, their resources wasted, their building skills degenerate. Even so they put up a spirited defense. The last holdout, on an island in the center of Lake Flores, in the torrid jungles of the Petén, would be subdued only in 1697.

The bare outline of Mayan architecture is quickly drawn. The monumental cores of the foremost cities are made up of temple-pyramids, ball courts, and "palaces" arranged around paved public spaces. The inscribed stelai, which were once thought to have ritual import, are probably dynastic monuments set up by rulers and their families whose images they bear. (Fig. 18.3) No consensus has been reached regarding the palaces. These one-storey buildings, of long and shallow shapes, have impractical interiors: files of small windowless rooms, some of them filled almost to capacity with huge platforms. They appear ill-suited for residential functions. They are sometimes grouped to make courts, but the fully cloistered enclosure is resisted.

The temple-pyramid, steep and tall, has a single axial stairway of narrow tread that leads up to the temple at the summit. (Fig. 18.4) Less common are two corresponding stairways, and in one or two rare cases all four sides are staired. The principal sites are studded with such pyramids—some of forbidding height, others clearly secondary. They are assembled with ritual, probably geomantic, purpose. A common formation has a temple-pyramid facing east, and three others across the plaza from it sitting on a north-south terrace. Within, burials are known to have taken place, but it would surely be wrong to think of these imposing piles as monumental tombs like the Old Kingdom pyramids of Egypt. The crowning temple, tiny in relation to its platform, consists of two rooms, one behind the other. The first opens onto the facade by one or three doors; the inner room has built against it a miniature sanctuary using the model of the actual temple itself. Both rooms carry characteristically Mayan corbel vaults, leaving a masonry trough between them. This, in turn, supports the roof comb, a skeletal crest embellished, like the temple facade, with painted stucco reliefs.

The construction is distinctive. The corbel vault aside, we are dealing with a masonry architecture of post and lintel, but with this peculiarity. It uses a lime mortar, so that the walls are monoliths of rubble and mortar with a casing of cut stone. This veneer, often beautifully finished and set, is plastered over, even when the stone has the fine quality of the light-green trachyte we see in Copán, say, or the dolomite of the Usumacinta Valley. Wooden lintels of metal-hard sapodilla play their part during construction, but are then handled decoratively and covered with often exquisite carvings.

But this dry summary is a poor way to suggest the thrill of coming upon Tikal or Palenque in their jungle sea today, of walking into the silent plazas around which temple-pyramids, large and small, and broad, flat-roofed masses of varying level and height are composed with solemn majesty. The scale is imperial; it recalls Egypt and the world of Pergamon and Rome. Few today attempt to climb the harshly battered slopes of buildings like Temple IV at Tikal, which soars to a height of 70 meters (230 feet). The stunted stairs are badly worn, and even in their pristine state, so narrow that they force you to step sideways. The temple is invisible until you are close to the flat crown. Here the fantastically attired priests led their sacrificial victims, racked them on the stone altar before the temple, and with obsidian knives cut out their hearts. American gods were stern, and exacted vital food.

The view out is breathtaking. The gleaming tops of other temple-pyramids emerge from the luxuriant tangle of cedars, towering mahogany trees, sapodillas, palms, *ceibas* sacred to the Maya, all laced with endless loops of the liana vine. The periphery bulges with hillocks that are the as yet unexcavated pyramids claimed by the jungle. Tikal was big. Over 3,000 separate structures have been mapped to date in the central area alone, which in its entirety covers 16 square kilometers (6 square miles). In the city's prime the tide of vegetation was held in check, but even then no fine line divided forest from built fabric.

Mayan cities were unwalled. Causeways of varying width, raised up to 2.5 meters (8 feet) above ground, ran between them,

Fig. 18.4 Tikal (Guatemala), the Great Plaza from the northwest, with Temple I (Temple of the Giant Jaguar) at the far end, Temple II in the foreground, and the North Akropolis on the left, ca. 700; aerial view.

dry-laid and packed with limestone gravel. These whitish lines crossed the outskirts, where the commonfolk lived in huts of withes covered with adobe and vividly painted. The huts stood on rectangular mounds of earth and stone, and had thatched roofs with a high pitch. Merchants and nobles lived in more substantial houses closer to the ceremonial center, the edges and interstices of which accommodated the priesthood and the bureaucrats. This unregimented residential belt, and its arrangement in relation to the center,

mirrored a class society with a hereditary elite at the top. The city loosely hugged the monumental core that comprised several tightly planned ensembles, sometimes linked with covered walkways. Monumental axes on the model of Teotihuacán were avoided. Passage through these ensembles is richly eventful, spatially and visually. Such superb effects of massing and sequence were hardly improvised.

The Toltecs of Tula carried into Maya land an aggressive militarism, and new cults headed by that of the feathered serpent

Fig. 18.5 Chichén Itzá (Yucatán, Mexico), the Temple of the Warriors, twelfth century. This was a replica of Pyramid B at Tula, Mexico.

Fig. 18.6 Tenochtitlán (Mexico), the Aztec capital and predecessor of Mexico City, the ritual center as it appeared in 1519 when the Spaniards arrived; reconstruction view, looking southeast. To the left is the double temple to Huitzilopochtli and Tláloc.

Quetzalcóatl. This thorough reorientation of life we can read in the architectural environment. There is a marked shift, first, from open cities to defensible sites, such as hilltops or tongues of land shielded by deep ravines. The architectural decoration acquires a martial air, and the monumental assemblies include accommodation for the lay functions of the military orders like the Jaguars and the Eagles. The *tableros* of Teotihuacán reappear in platform construction. Architecture, intent on massive design under the Maya, begins to emphasize interior volumes. Columns and narrow piers reduce the denseness of Mayan buildings. A look at the Temple of the Warriors at Chichén Itzá should say it all: the new profile of the platform, the spacious temple, the ranges of colonnades along two sides of the structure, the wall paintings that detail the defeat of the Maya on land and by sea. (Fig. 18.5) The time is the twelfth century. Henceforth we can find nothing as grand to show anywhere in the home territories of the proud Mayan people.

The Aztecs

The sad internal decline of the region, the hardships of its natural ambience, and more to the point, the lack of silver and gold discouraged Spanish exploitation of Guatemala and the Yucatán—which is why we can face the constructive genius of the American Indian here most fully. Mexico was not as fortunate. The Aztec federation was the strong power in Middle America at the time of the conquest. The capital city of Tenochtitlán, a prosperous, dazzling metropolis the size of contemporary London, logically became the chief target of Cortés' expeditionary force. It resisted, lost, and was annihilated. Mexico City now sprawls over it and several other towns that bordered on it on the shores of Lake Texcoco. The cathedral stands on the precinct of the twin temple of Huitzilopochtli and Tláloc on the vast plaza that corresponds almost exactly to the present Zocalo. Where the presidential palace is now the lavish complex of King Montezuma stretched. The modern city has swallowed all the rest—the lakes, the causeways, the aqueducts, the subjects towns of Coyoacán and Chapultepec, Tlacopan and Ixtapalapa. But the

Aztecs were a literary people who left written records, and the train of Cortés could not refrain from boasting in their diaries and letters of the marvels they had made their own. The great *conquistador* himself made a drawing of Tenochtitlán to send his king. So despite events, we know a fair amount about the land of Mexico at the time of its rape.

The Aztecs were latecomers. They moved in from the north and emerged as a tribe about 1200. Toltec hegemony was still powerful then. There were viable states at Monte Albán, Cholula, and Vera Cruz. Free land was scarce. The Aztecs moved to an island in the middle of Lake Texcoco, and there founded Tenochtitlán in 1325. By 1450 they had raised themselves to a position of primacy in central Mexico. They enlarged their city by turning the lake mud into arable land in great containers of wickerwork *(chinampas),* and by annexing the villages and towns on the shores. The rival city of Tlatelolco on an island to the north was subjugated in 1473 and made part of greater Tenochtitlán. It now occupied an area of 1,000 hectares (2,500 acres). The twin temple replaced earlier shrines on the site in the 1480s. When the Spaniards laid siege to it, Tenochtitlán was a young, vigorous city at the head of an empire in the making.

Three causeways led axially into the central plaza area from terra firma. They doubled as levees. The southern entrance alone was fortified. A fourth causeway stopped at the eastern bank of the island where there was a landing place for canoe service to the shore. Most streets were canals spanned by removable wooden bridges. The whitewashed houses, flat-roofed and windowless, faced inward onto patios. The more important among them rose to two storeys. The pattern was orthogonal. Tribal quarters, of which there were twenty, were focused by their temples. Administratively they belonged to one of four main sections into which the city had been divided. There were two downtowns. Tlatelolco had its temple-pyramid and a market plaza bordered by arcades. From the summit of this pyramid, Cortés' entourage surveyed the city in the presence of King Montezuma before the hostilities began. Bernal Díaz del Castillo, who was there, left a vivid description of what they saw. He speaks of the communities along the shoreline, of the

Fig. 18.7 Cuzco (Peru), late Incan masonry wall, ca. 1500.

boats on the lake bringing in foodstuffs and carrying out merchandise, of terrace houses, of the aqueduct coming in from Chapultepec that supplied the city with fresh water (Texcoco itself being a salt lake). Of the market of Tlatelolco, he writes: "There were among us soldiers who had been to many parts of the world, to Constantinople, to the whole of Italy and to Rome, and they said they had never seen a market so well organized and orderly, so large, so full of people."

The stone-paved main plaza of Tenochtitlán measured 160 by 180 meters (525 by 590 feet). On the east side stood the palace compound of Montezuma, a veritable city of administrative and residential buildings including a royal aviary. The west side of the plaza was defined by two-storey houses of dignitaries. A major east-west canal ran along the south side, with the causeway from Coyoacán, which carried a second aqueduct, coming in at the southeast corner, on axis with the plaza entrance to the temple precinct.

This immense ritual core of Tenochtitlán was a walled rectangle at the crossing of the four causeway avenues. (Fig. 18.6) The great twin temple to the Aztec warrior god Huitzilopochtli and to Tláloc, the old rain god of Middle America, stood east of center, facing west. It celebrated the two dominant concerns of the young state—agriculture and conquest. Lesser temples grouped around it honored the gods of subject peoples. The round temple of Quetzalcóatl, cultural hero and god of the winds, was on axis with the double staircase of the main temple, and west of it was the ball court flanked by the premises of officiating priests and the military orders. Skulls of sacrificial victims were on display on a fancy rack. Each temple had its *calmecac,* a monastic college where the cult's priests lived and its acolytes were instructed. The musicians who played at the festivals had their own special quarters.

Aztec architecture is derivative. Even the round temple of Quezalcóatl has a remote ancestry: we saw it, you will remember, in

Fig. 18.8 Nazca Plain (Peru), ground drawings, ca. 500; aerial view.

Cuicuilco in the Pedregal about 500 B.C. The originality comes across in the planning of the capital, which has echoes in other Aztec towns. The walled akropolis in the center of a large residential area is sharply at variance with the diffuse monumentality of Mayan sites. Again, there is no parallel in the Mayan settlements for the forceful way in which axial coordinates intersect at this ritual center and set guidelines for the orthogonal alignment of residential streets. Even Teotihuacán lacks this determined centrality.

One understands the admiration of the Spaniards. Orderly cities of this scale and magnificence did not figure in their experience. The princely forums and avenues of the Renaissance were just then making their European debut, and that in Italy. Cortés and his followers speak of "the great city of Tenochtitlán" in the same breadth as Seville and Córdoba, and when the home context proves too feeble to convey the wonder of this doomed El Dorado, they reach for mythical analogies. "We were amazed," Bernal Díaz writes of their first sight of Montezuma's city, "and said it was like the enchantments they tell of in the legend of Amadis."

The Incas

There is no reason to believe that the Aztecs, the Maya, and other communities of pre-Hispanic Middle America were aware of the empire that flourished contemporaneously with their own in the immense territory occupying all of modern-day Peru, as well as Ecuador and northern Chile. It was the largest Indian state before the conquest, and it was very strong. The Incas, active in the highlands around Cuzco since 1200, launched a massive campaign in the fifteenth century to subdue and unite the disparate groups that inhabited the high Andean plains and the river valleys of the coast. The toughest adversaries were the Chimu whose kingdom spread for hundreds of kilometers northward from Lima. When they submitted, the Inca dynasty at Cuzco found itself the uncontested master of a superbly organized and tightly administered domain, from Quito and Tumbes to Santiago. (Fig. 18.2)

An admirable network of roads welded this long, kaleidoscopic strip of coastal desert, valley oases, and dizzying moun-

439

tain heights. Extensive public works of ir-rigation boosted urban life along the rivers that slash the sand dunes of the western plain. In the mountain region where only a handful of flatlands and basins could sup-port large numbers of people, an equally stupendous enterprise of agricultural ter-racing testified to the resourcefulness of the empire.

Not all of this was new of course. The In-cas have been called the Romans of pre-Columbian America for their ability to take over a motley crowd of prior polities, ex-tricate from them an efficient, centralized structure, and then expand on it. Many In-can towns were old centers of varying age that the new rulers inherited by dint of conquest and suitably outfitted. In fact, se-rious cultural accomplishment is as long-lived and as bounteous in ancient Peru as it is in Middle America. Construction methods go back a very long way. Tapia, or walling of puddled clay in massive cast form, was in continuous use from at least about A.D. 700. Simple adobe brick antedates it by more than two thousand years. The pride of Incan architecture, as we can still ad-mire it in the fortress of Cuzco, Sacsahua-man, is the beautiful polished masonry made up of immense polygonal blocks in-terlocking without mortar. (Fig. 18.7) But the taste for shaping stones of such size is foreshadowed, for example, in the great monolithic gateway of Tiahuanaco, from about A.D. 500, or the masonry units of its pyramid, some among them weighing as much as 100 tons.

Individual buildings are never as impres-sive in the Andean civilizations as are the results of large-scale planning or public works in general. With so much washed away, destroyed, or unexcavated, the best views are often from the air. On the ground, platforms and pyramids do not measure up to the grandeur of Teotihuacán or Tikal. At Cuzco, the famous temple has the plan of a normal house, a number of rectangular rooms around a court, which is wrapped in an enclosure wall. It was the house of god and his attendants; his golden image was carried into the city square for the great public ceremonies. That is something new in the religious architecture of America. The round burial towers called *chullpas* in the area of Tiahuanaco are also unique. The burial is either inside them, or else they

Fig. 18.9 Chan-Chan (Peru), Chimu capital, founded ca. 1000; aerial view of citadel-compounds.

are built solid and the dead laid in the ground beneath. Now and then there are some striking architectural details. We might mention the carved Chimu decoration in mud-plaster, and the Inca preference for doorways with inclined jambs—probably in order to shorten the span of the lintel.

House types are surprisingly varied. The round house is common in the central An-des; the chullpas may reflect this domestic tradition. Cantamarca province has corbel-roofed tower houses of dry-laid masonry. Chiripa, in the southern highlands, ex-hibits rectangular adobe houses with dou-ble walls that shelter those inside from the cold; the space between the walls held storage bins. But even here the more inter-esting aspect is group design—the way dwelling clusters were devised in different

regions and periods. Incan practice ar-ranges houses in a square with a common yard *(cancha)*. The rectangular unit of planned housing enclosed within massive walls is common in the Chimu area and comes into vogue even before the rise of that kingdom. Its introduction has to do with planned communities and the begin-ning of urbanization. This comes about in the latter half of the first millennium A.D., several centuries after the first true cities of Middle America.

A most singular instance of the Peruvian gift for imposing order on the land on a grand scale may antedate the early towns. I am referring to the famous markings on the pampas above the Palpa and Ingenio rivers, in south Peru. (Fig. 18.8) There on the barren, rocky tablelands around Nazca,

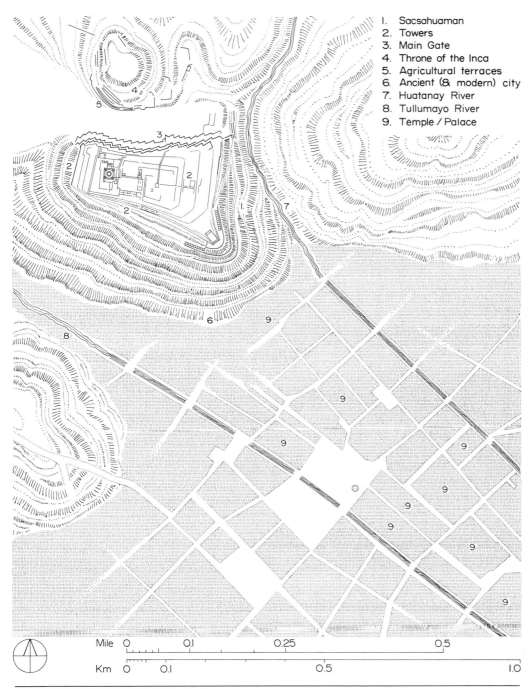

1. Sacsahuaman
2. Towers
3. Main Gate
4. Throne of the Inca
5. Agricultural terraces
6. Ancient (& modern) city
7. Huatanay River
8. Tullumayo River
9. Temple / Palace

Mile 0   0.1   0.25   0.5

Km 0   0.1   0.5   1.0

Fig. 18.10 Cuzco, with fortress of Sacsahuaman to the north, fifteenth–early sixteenth century; aerial view.

over an area of some 90 kilometers (56 miles), a colossal network of lines, geometrical figures, and images of plants and animals has been meticulously imprinted. The yellow sand-and-gravel surface of the plateau is overlaid by a weathered stony crust, dark brown in color. The markings were made by removing this crust and piling the dark stones on the sides. Most likely these are sightings for solstices and the rising and setting of stars that had to do with local cycles of agriculture. The program is that of Carnac, Stonehenge, and Teotihuacán, without their three-dimensional monumentality. The precision is astounding. The perfectly straight lines, which in some places stretch for 8 kilometers (5 miles), cut across the land in every direction, frequently intersect, climb steep slopes, and stop abruptly in the middle of nowhere. And they are enormously affecting.

Towns before the Chimu kingdom are obscure. Irrigation and road systems precede serious urbanization, and so do the *pukios* on the northern coast, a pattern of sunken cultivation that uses plots dug down to the water table. The critical turning point in housing architecture may have been the shift from natural clusters to rectangular-walled compounds of groups of dwellings or small villages. After the year 1000, this trend toward planned communities intensifies and gains urban proportions.

The Chimu capital was Chan-Chan near the modern city of Trujillo. (Fig. 18.9) The ruins today cover an area of 20 kilometers (12.5 miles) and extend to the Pacific coastline. The part that has been excavated shows eleven unequal citadel-compounds assembled with no transparent design. There is also evidence of some building activity in the intermediate spaces. The compounds have high walls of adobe brick, impenetrable except for tiny entrances, and standardized houses on low platforms arranged around rectangular courtyards. A percentage of the land is untouched by buildings, presumably left for cultivation.

Are these palaces, industrial settlements, or restricted quarters for individual clans or specialties? Why the extraordinary measures of isolation? Were new enclosures added as the population grew, or did each represent a different social group? Was there an earlier scheme, perhaps a grid as some of the aerial photographs seem to show? There are no reliable answers now, and the absence of written records of any kind in ancient Peru leaves little hope that we will ever know.

Whatever the logic of this configuration, it left its mark on Incan planners. Cuzco is also dominated by great walled enclosures. In this case we know, through the accounts of Spanish observers, that each was associated with the reign of one emperor; after his death his descendants and their families lived in the enclosure. The old center was on the southern ridge. (Fig. 18.10) The main temple stood here. Pachacuti, who was crowned in 1438 and was the chief architect of the empire, enlarged the city northward with an official quarter that included a huge ceremonial plaza. He also began the fortress of Sacsahuaman. These elements—temple, plaza, fortress—became standard.

Incan cities are without defensive walls, but some are guarded by a fortress nearby. Grids or other geometrical layouts are rare. The central plaza is always present, but it comes in many shapes. At Cuzco two rough trapezoids, unequal in size, are separated by the canalized bed of the Huatanay River. Other plazas are square, rectangular, or polygonal, or just an irregular opening in the thickness of the city-form. This was the stage of public ceremonies, the state-controlled market based on barter, and the administration of justice. It was traversed by one of the imperial highways that connected the major cities.

All roads issued from Cuzco to the four quarters into which the empire was divided. This division did not correspond to the cardinal points of the compass, but to geography. The so-called royal road, about 5,000 kilometers (3,100 miles) long, cut an arduous path through the Andes. The shorter coast road began at the frontier city of Tumbes and followed the bleak desert, keeping to a standard width of about 7 meters (23 feet). Lateral stretches connected the highland cities with the river valleys below. The highway system was not paved. Since draft animals and the wheel were both unknown, this would have been an unnecessary exertion. Low walls on the sides of the road kept out the sand drift along the

coastal artery. In the difficult terrain of the high road, the normal traffic of men and llamas could be accommodated by a much narrower track. The road tunneled through spurs, turned into a staircase to climb sharp ridges, and crossed swamps on stone-paved causeways. Bridges over streams and rivers were simply built, of wood or stone where the spans were reasonable. Suspension bridges were thrown across wider valleys. These were made of great cables of vegetable fiber, secured at the ends to stone towers. At regular intervals were posts for the runners who relayed official messages, and also resthouses for bureaucrats and merchants who traveled on official business.

The Spanish Scene

The collapse of the Inca state was spectacularly sudden, but it was followed by such a long period of local civil wars that colonization was impeded until 1570. By then, the momentum of the Protestant movement had been stemmed in Europe. The militant, implacable Catholicism of the Counter-Reformation tightened its hold on Spain and its American possessions. The old way was shown no mercy. The main Incan cities were destroyed, and rural life similarly disrupted. Irrigated land fell into disuse. The road system was allowed to deteriorate. A number of Spanish cities were planted throughout the vast territory: the work of conversion began in earnest. In architecture Spanish trends were adhered to, but there is little to show before 1600.

The island colonies of the Antilles and the coastline of the Caribbean and the Gulf of Mexico, Spain's first foothold in the New World, also stayed close to the architectural styles of the mother country. The east coast of South America was quite primitive. Here French, Spanish, and Portuguese interests clashed, at least until the end of the century when the crowns of the two Iberian kingdoms were united. Brazil remained basically Portuguese. The few initial towns were allowed to grow without a guiding plan—this in contrast to Spanish American settlements which were generally gridded.

It was in Mexico that European colonialism had the speediest and boldest success. A generation after the conquest most of the native population had been converted. Scores of planned settlements decorously sheltered the tiny Spanish minority and urbanized the largely pastoral Indians. The Mexican landscape was permanently changed with this net of cities, its hydraulic works and looming churches. Transportation, hitherto dependent almost exclusively on human carriers, was revolutionized by the introduction of the solid-wheel cart, draft and pack animals, and the mule train. Also with the settlers came the potter's wheel, woolen cloth, new crops, and Moorish roofs of red tile. A viable society was forged, capable of housing and employing millions, sustaining a diversified industrial structure in the mining and manufacturing towns, and keeping in check transient and nomadic tribes at the edges of the colony.

The architecture of these breathless decades, obstinately European though it remained in essence, was profoundly stamped by local circumstance. The ancient land, lush and fertile and bound to strange cults, only vaguely recalled the tawny hills and pasture lands of Spain. Indian crafts and Indian labor built the cities and the churches. The stones and beams were quarried from the precincts of Huitzilopochtli, Quetzalcóatl, and the maize goddess Tonantzin, who soon faded into the Virgin of Guadalupe. The monasteries and cathedrals sat on Mayan or Aztec platforms. And at least in one specific case, the open-air churches, sixteenth-century Mexico invented a strong new form that answered local needs admirably.

The Cities

Mexico had been settled and converted before the rigors of the Counter-Reformation had set in. The Spanish throne was then occupied by Emperor Charles V whose early reign had humanist pretensions, and the mission of instructing the Indians was assigned to mendicant friars. Twelve Franciscans arrived first in 1524; the Dominicans and Augustinians soon followed. It was this small band of brave, compassionate, enter-

Fig. 18.11 Franciscan activity in the region of Michoacán, Mexico; sixteenth-century drawing.

For their part, however, the friars saw the Indians as a childlike people perpetually needing missionary guidance.

On one issue there was no compromise. Home-grown deities and their observances must be abjured. The building furor ushered in by the conquest had an accompaniment of destruction. The first waves of converts assisted the friars in a thoroughgoing attack on the images and settings of their former cults. Resentful of the divine impotence that permitted their subjugation and anxious to please their new masters, the Indians brought down all religious monuments in the centers that had been active at the time of the conquest. Only sites abandoned earlier, like Teotihuacán, Palenque, and Chichén Itzá, were spared methodical wreckage. By 1531, Bishop Zumárraga could report that 20,000 "figures of the devil" and over 500 "houses of the devil" had already been destroyed.

New cities were sometimes superimposed on the ruins with dramatic symbolism. Mexico City came first of course. Tlaxcala, Texcoco, Cholula were rehabilitated in short order. But preconquest towns were few, and most of the population was rural. It was the countryside that had to be organized. The friars and the Crown were of one mind—that the spiritual welfare of the new subjects presumed urban concentration. For once the colonists' purposes were in sympathy. Cities made political control easier and conveniently pooled the labor force for public and private works. And so massive shifts of population were set in motion.

There was no thought of interracial communities. The Indians were to be isolated in towns of their own where whites were forbidden to reside, or in restricted residential quarters of settlements intended for Spaniards. Mexico City, laid out by a geometer named Alonso García Bravo, held two distinct municipalities. The Spanish capital took over Tenochtitlán proper, with Cortés appropriating Montezuma's palace as his administrative headquarters and the temple of the Sun at the southwest corner of the Huitzilopochtli/Tláloc precinct becoming the platform of a new cathedral. The Indian community had its own government

prising men who planned the towns, built the churches, and governed the communities. (Fig. 18.11) Their ways were firm yet gentle. They were untiring champions of Indian rights against the white colonists whose record of exploitation is appalling.

The system of *encomienda* granted settlers native labor, several hundred subject Indians per *encomendero*. While the friars worked to save their souls and educate them, the civilian masters turned their bodies into profit-producing chattel. The two aims were not reconcilable. Many colonists agreed with eminent authorities like Juan Ginés de Sepúlveda that Indians were an inferior race destined to be the slaves of others. The friars thought otherwise. As a group of Franciscans wrote the emperor in 1533:

How could anyone call them irrational or beasts? How can they be held incapable, with such sumptuousness in their buildings, such subtle exquisiteness in their handiwork? . . . when they are skilled in administering and allocating labor? . . . when they have elective offices, punishment of crime and excess?

and plaza at Tlatelolco, beyond which were the irregularly disposed native *barrios* or wards.

The city was unfortified. Whatever the temporary restlessness of the resident peoples, New Spain had little to fear. Guns and cavalry had demoralized the Indians' fighting spirit, and kept it that way. Only at the "silver frontier" of Zacatecas did Chichimec hostility linger, especially after the mining rush that began in 1546. Along this northern frontier the vice-regal government built a system of defensive towns and posts. Coastal towns were also protected, these against seaborne attacks by fellow Europeans. This accounts for the up-to-date fortifications of Veracruz, Cartagena, Acapulco, and also Havana, Santo Domingo, and Old Panama. (Fig. 18.12) Otherwise Mexican towns were open.

The kernel of a new city was commonly a monastery. It overlooked the plaza, and with it formed the civic center. Around the plaza administrative buildings were put up in time: town hall, jail, hospital, slaughterhouse. In bishoprics, a cathedral took the place of the monastery. The towns were mostly small, but the size varied from a few families to the teeming population of Mexico City, which must have had upwards of 100,000 souls. There were of course many more Indian towns than white, even though a staggering mortality rate resulting from colonial abuse, natural disasters, and above all a string of epidemic diseases pitifully reduced the native stock. The planners moved people around at will. The mines, and administrative centers like Mexico, Puebla, and Oaxaca, required proximate labor, and the friars worked best with large concentrated *congregaciones*. Authorities, uneasy about defensible hilltop communities, drove the inhabitants down to the flatlands where they could be contained more readily and plugged into the main communication channels. It was not uncommon to relocate a town once or twice in the hope of finding the optimum site.

The speed and scope of Mexican urbanization presumed methodical design, as in the similar instances of colonial town-making by the ancient Greeks and Romans and the medieval *bastides*. At the start of their American adventure, the Spaniards had

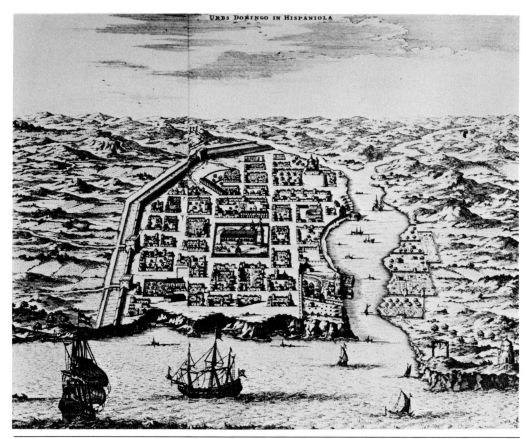

Fig. 18.12 Santo Domingo (Dominican Republic), founded 1496; seventeenth-century view.

been casual about their settlements, much like their Portuguese competitors in Africa and South Asia. With the exception of Santo Domingo, Spanish towns in the Antilles started and grew haphazardly. In Mexico, however, there was a determination at the outset to be orderly. Each town was to have a master plan that incorporated certain standard features. The street pattern was to be a grid, and in the middle a plaza was to be laid out and a church and other public buildings were to stand within it or close to it. But this is only the barest summary. Ordinances issued at intervals addressed finer matters, until the comprehensive Laws of the Indies, dated 13 July 1573, codified a set of 148 articles dealing with every aspect of site selection, planning, and organization.

The Laws say unequivocally that preaching the gospel to the Indians "is the principal objective for which we mandate that these discoveries and settlements be made" (Article 36). But that this Christian ideal was yoked to imperialism is self-evident. The shaping of America in the Spanish mold had to proceed in unison with three directives: a Christian society, an absolute State, and a colonial economy. The State subsumed the other two. A license had to be granted by the king for any discovery and settlement, and all future affairs were to be conducted under direct guidance from Madrid, through the office of the viceroy. Great emphasis in the Laws is placed on colonizing the territories "without injury to the natives," a noble thought honored more in the breach than the observance.

The model location for a new town is summed up in Article 111. It must be

in an elevated and healthy location; with means of fortification; fertile soil and with plenty of land for farming and pasturage; have fuel, timber and resources; fresh water, a native population, ease of transport, access and exit; open to the north-wind; and, if on the coast, due consideration should be paid to the quality of the harbor and that the sea does not lie to the south or west; and if possible not near lagoons or marshes in which poisonous animals and polluted air and water breed.

Proximity to older towns and property is also recommended, so that materials left over from their demolition might be reused.

The town is to be laid out "using cord and ruler." The main plaza is to be the starting point for the city-form. The plaza should be one and one-half times as long as it is wide, because this shape works better for fiestas in which horses are used. The size should be proportioned to the site of the town, making allowances for growth, but the plaza should in no case be less than 61 meters wide by 91 long (200 by 300 feet), nor larger than 162 by 243 meters (532 by 800 feet). From this public space main streets are to issue, as follows: one from the middle of each side, and two from each corner forming a right angle. Around the plaza and along these principal streets, there should be arcades (portales), "for these are of considerable convenience to the merchants who generally gather there." The streets running into the corners of the plaza are not to encounter these arcades, which are to be kept back, so that there is a side walk between the arcades and the public area of the plaza.

The main church has to be near the plaza but not necessarily within it. If the settlement is near the sea, the church should be sited so that it might be seen by incoming and outgoing vessels. Other public buildings specified are the royal council and town hall, the customs house, a hospital, all these grouped around the church, and then farther out slaughterhouses, fisheries, tanneries, and the like. These main buildings

should be allotted full blocks, so that lesser structures do not abut them.

Building plots are to be distributed by lottery, from the plaza outward, and some should be held for late arrivals. No settler is to receive more than five peonias (a peonia being a plot of 15 meters in width by 30 meters in depth, or 50 by 100 feet), or three caballerias (these being house plots of 30 by 60 meters, or 100 by 200 feet). The settlers will be given grain, cereals, and seeds, and also animals. The plots will have closed boundaries. Any settler who has accepted a plot in the new town is obligated to build on it within a short period of time, work the land, and acquire herds and grasslands. Each house must be built so that horses and work animals can be kept therein, and each must have yards and corrals. As far as possible "the buildings [shall be] all of one type for the sake of the beauty of the town" (Article 134). "The town shall maintain a plan of what is being built" (Article 137).

Some of this will sound very familiar to you. We have noted similar dispensations in the charters of medieval bastides. This European experience, in which Spain shared, was the training ground for the colonization of America. The regular plots, the use of the cord, the main square and its arcades—all this was the legacy of the bastidors. On the Iberian Peninsula Villarreal de Burriana at Castellón, founded by Jaime I in 1271, has a central square at the crossing of two major avenues. (Fig. 15.2) The square in the comparable grid of Briviesca, north of Burgos, has the same pattern of emanating streets as that of Spanish American plazas prescribed in the Laws of the Indies. Advocation of the grid plan continued locally in theoretical works of the late Middle Ages—in the description of the ideal city in the writings of the Catalan Franciscan of the late-fourteenth-century Eximeniç, and less than a century later in the work of Rodrigo Sánchez de Arévalo, prelate, ambassador, and statesman. The next generation saw the post-Muslim grids of Santa Fe outside Granada in 1491 and, slightly earlier, Puerto Real on the Bay of Cadiz. By this time Italian Renaissance treatises were slowly becoming known on the other side of the Pyrenees. The Laws of

the Indies show knowledge of Vitruvius, and we can tell for certain that copies of Vitruvius, Alberti, and Sebastiano Serlio had been imported by Mexican booksellers.

Still, this pedigree of orderly town-planning was exceptional. The daily urban experience of Spaniards derived almost universally from tangled towns that, if of Roman origin, had lost their grid during the long Muslim occupation. None could show a planned monumental plaza in the center of the city-form; the first example we can cite is at Valladolid, and that not until 1592. There were market plazas of course, usually outside the gates and, in the downtown, public spaces with a close functional relation to the street pattern developed naturally. Monumental plazas, when they do arrive in Spain, tend to be large closed forums unconcerned with the rhythms of traffic. As you can see, here the plaza mayor, following the codified Laws of the Indies, combines the formal qualities of the monumental plaza with a rigid but functional set of approach and egress streets. It would be obtuse not to recognize that the colonists might have been inspired in this by native example, especially the great center of Tenochtitlán. The cathedral-plaza of Mexico City directly assimilated the Aztec arrangement of a large square that serves as a public court for the religious compound. Cortés' occupation of the Montezuma palace retained the administrative component in this grouping. What transpired in the capital has probably as much bearing on the urban product of New Spain as the European special case of Renaissance theory.

Many drawings of Mexican towns survive; they were executed by Indian artists about 1580 to form part of a great cosmographic survey of the colony undertaken by the court of King Philip II (1556–98). Our illustration shows Cholula, with its rectangular blocks, the plaza mayor at the intersection of principal roads, the large monastery with its walled courtyard, and six churches of barrios, each set next to the ruins of a temple-pyramid. (Fig. 18.13) The plaza has a public fountain, a mayor's house, and an arcaded town hall.

Most of the plans give us a vivid sense of environment. They show streams and highways, and a countryside peopled with villages and ranches. Urban distribution was subject to regional planning. No large towns were allowed near the capital, and when too many monasteries crowded the favorable valleys of Mexico and Morelos, Philip II ordered a minimum limit of 24 kilometers (15 miles) between any two.

The Buildings

There is little trace of the original buildings in Mexico City or Puebla or any of the other principal cities. But even after four hundred years, what these sixteenth-century Mexican towns looked like is not entirely beyond recovery. From the air we can still sense the perfect order of Puebla's grid, and the plaza mayor of Mexico City still reminds us of the magnificent civic area it once was. (Fig. 18.14) Cholula's plaza has kept its *portales*, and Merida's, planted with handsome Indian laurels, retains its original architectural character since the cathedral and the palace of the conquistador Montejo on two of its sides are those of the sixteenth century and the town hall and other buildings, though later, respect the scale and general rhythms of their antecedents. The Moorish-looking tower called *rollo* from which justice was administered survives in Tepeaca's plaza. In hundreds of small towns, in the states of Hidalgo and Oaxaca and most notably the Yucatan, the full aspect of those neat, self-possessed communities planted by the friars in the generous landscape, and the industry and faith they betoken, still come through with a little imaginative effort.

Houses that go back to the beginning we cannot of course hope to find. There were block houses and patio houses, and as in Spain the patio was the privilege of the wealthy city dweller. Other signs of one's station included a picturesquely fortified look, ironwork window grills, and painted ornamentation that included rosettes and edifying inscriptions. In Mexico City roofs were flat, as they were in the Muslim cities of North Africa and in Andalusia. Lavish country houses prefigured the haciendas of the nineteenth century. The minimal, one-room windowless house of the poor Aztecs passed into the Christian era unchanged, reproduced in adobe, wattle and daub, or stone. Town houses incorporated

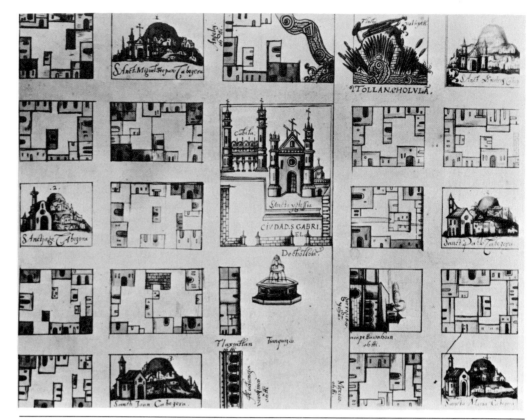

Fig. 18.13 Cholula (Mexico); the town as represented on a drawing of 1580. The artist has captioned the drawing partly in his Aztec language and partly in Spanish.

commercial facilities on the ground floor, and there were shops in the colonnaded porticoes around the plaza with living quarters behind or above. In addition, we know of freestanding, one-storey shop buildings.

Of other building types there is little to be said. The fortification of coastal towns, primarily in the Caribbean, were speeded up at the end of the century, when French and English attacks became more serious. Much of the work was done under Italian military engineers. Aqueducts are spoken of with pride in contemporary documents. (Fig. 18.15) This pride is plainly justified in the remains of the great aqueduct of Zempoala, built by Fray Francisco de Tembleque in the 1540s and 1550s. It carried water for 45 kilometers (28 miles) on a system of arcades whose scale and technology are clearly Roman. The capital excelled in one

other class of buildings, the hospitals. There were about twelve of them in sixteenth-century Mexico City, but none approached the grandeur of the one founded by Cortés in 1524 in the southeast quarter. In its final form, it was to consist of a church and four ranges enclosing two large courts. This is one of two related schemes that were followed in the West by large hospitals in the fifteenth and sixteenth centuries. (Fig. 22.29, A) The origin of both is Italy. The cruciform plan, the first example of which is the hospital of S. Maria Nuova in Florence, had four wards issuing like the arms of a cross from a center, where the altar was placed. The two-court plan may be traced to the Ospedale Maggiore in Milan, designed in the 1450s by the Florentine Filarete for Francesco Sforza. Between two palace blocks is a rectangular court with a church in the middle. The blocks actually frame cruci-

Fig. 18.15 Querétaro (Mexico), Spanish aqueduct, sixteenth century.

Fig. 18.14 Mexico City (Mexico), the main square or Zocalo laid out in the sixteenth century; aerial view. The square corresponds exactly to the ritual center of Tenochtitlán (Fig. 18.6). The cathedral to the left stands over the double temple of the Aztec precinct.

Fig. 18.16 Cholula, the Franciscan monastery church of S. Gabriel, 1549–52 (the top of the tower is later). This is the church shown in the center of Fig. 18.13.

form buildings that leave four small courts between the arms and the exterior envelope. Sixteenth-century Spanish parallels are the Hospital Real at Santiago and the Hospital de la Sangre in Seville, which is closest in layout to Cortés' foundation in Mexico City.

But the Spanish presence is best announced by the churches. The conquest was the last of the medieval crusades and the conversion that followed it, one of the great triumphs of Christian history. The small number of friars who brought off this feat with little coercion and no bloodshed also devised a most appropriate architectural setting for their charges and themselves. The missionaries were untutored builders and that native labor force had to be taught, in a matter of one generation or so, techniques that had taken the Mediterranean hundreds of years to invent and elaborate—things like barrel vaults and Gothic ribs and Renaissance proportional composition. But what overweighed these limitations was the almost intuitive genius of the three mendicant orders, the Franciscans perhaps especially, in achieving a dignified, monumental form without relying on theory or stylistic consistency. They did so by remembering eclectically the moods and modes of Christian architecture, trusting their individual brand of monasticism and their instinct for effective improvisation, and keeping in mind that the situation they were providing for was special, indeed unparalleled.

In the Indian drawings of town plans, the church and the walled courtyard or *atrio* in front were the two features of the monastery pictured prominently. At Cholula we are also shown an imposing turreted building with an open arcaded front, labeled *Capilla*. These three structures—the church, the atrio, and the "Indian chapel"—constituted the public facade of the friars' compound, and the stage for communion with their fold. Their own conventual quarters were modest and unexceptional: cloister, refectory, the anteroom in which the De Profundis was recited before meals, and the kitchen, all on the ground floor; monastic cells and a dormitory for transients were situated on the second floor, perhaps also a library.

By far the commonest type of church is an aisleless hall with a polygonal sanctuary at the east end that has no windows. (Fig. 18.16) The Dominicans, always more ambitious, added along the two sides of the nave a number of shallow chapels between interior buttresses, a practice common in eastern Spain. When resources permit, the church is given a Gothic rib vault, at least over the sanctuary; in the poorer regions, or when scruples against luxury prevailed, there is apt to be a simple barrel vault, more Romanesque than Renaissance in flavor, or simply a timber roof. On the outside the simple high mass, which goes beyond the roofline, is dramatized by more or less regularly spaced pier buttresses, and very likely a run of crenellations along the top. The buttresses act as water conduits, the final collection point being a cistern at the rear of the church. Windows are few and not uniform. They are placed erratically high up in the thick lateral walls, and sometimes, at Actopan for instance, they are cut in a startling variety of abstract shapes like triangles, ellipses, and rhomboids. The facade is treated as an element of the massing. In the early part of the century it is framed by diagonal corner buttresses, which around 1576 gave way to towers.

The military aspect is in keeping with the pioneering venture of conquest and conversion, but also with the strength of faith, the notion of the Lord as a mighty fortress. The austerity is mendicant. Since the thirteenth century the friars' churches had been associated with reform—a demystifying of the central rituals and a stress on the spoken word, on preaching. Furthermore, the mendicant establishments of Mexico were going up at a time of general religious questioning. Protests could be heard throughout Europe against ostentatious services and the practice of celebrating Mass at multiple altars. The spirit of the Refor-

Fig. 18.17 Laguna Pueblo (New Mexico), church of San José, 1699: **(a)** view toward altar; **(b)** view toward entrance.

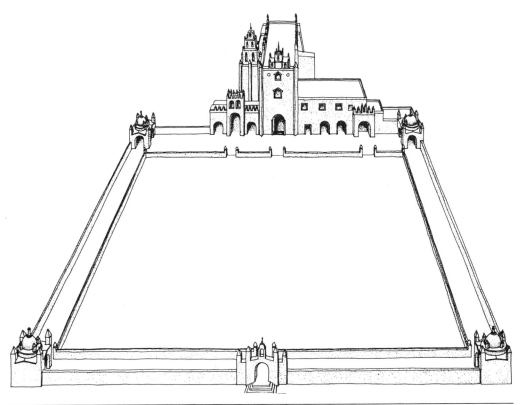

Fig. 18.18 Atlatláuhcan (Mexico), church and *atrio* complex, 1570s; reconstruction drawing. The atrio, about 112 by 810 meters (370×270 feet), is bounded by a flagstone road and has the typical corner *posas*.

Fig. 18.19 Cholula, the *capilla de Indios*, called Capilla Real, 1560s, in an earlier form than that shown in Fig. 18.13. It stood east of the atrio and was covered by nine brick barrel vaults on stone arcades. It was reminiscent, in its lateral spread and in the multitude of supports, of Muslim mosques, like the Great Mosque of Kairawan. (See page 402.)

mation, and the friars' own tradition, stand behind these guileless but strong churches of Mexico.

The interiors are particularly telling. (Fig. 18.17) The unitary volume with an unimpeded view of the altar sets store by a congregation that comes together in the communion of a single service. The walls are bare but for decorative frames around the windows; the flat surfaces are only rarely divided into bays. Sometimes the surfaces are enlivened by didactic black-and-white frescoes, probably with a mind to the elaborately painted walls of Indian temples. In the west end, in the reverse of the facade wall, a deep balcony housed the choir; it spanned the nave, and at times extended over as much as one-third of its space. The balcony was lit by a single window that, along with the ornate doorway and sometimes a crowning espadaña, the typical arcaded belfry wall, was the principal feature of the facade. Music was provided by a harmonium, or in the case of large churches an organ with horizontal trumpet pipes. By way of additional furniture the church had two holy water stoups within the doorway and a baptismal font close by.

At the other end, unobstructed by any choir with its crowd of singers and appurtenances, the altar stood in the apse which was raised a few steps above the level of the nave floor. The altar was a simple stone table set against the glittering backdrop of the reredos or retable. The development of this many-storied fixture with its compartments of panel paintings and gilded sculpture had begun in Spain in the fifteenth century and had brought about the blinding of the richly glazed medieval sanctuary. In the Mexican churches the result is a powerful introversion, a much more tangible emphasis on the altar.

It is hard to know now what use Indians made of the church. In many cases the size would have been too small to hold all qualified converts in the settlement. But a ritual theater of a very different sort was readied for them in front of the church. (Fig. 18.18) This was little more than an open space at first, where the large numbers of natives who were being brought into the fold could gather for services in the presence of the provisional chapel that pre-

449

Fig. 18.20 Fray Diego de Valades, *Rhetorica;* drawing of the Franciscan ideal of the atrio and its activities. In the center, the Church carried by Franciscan monks, led by St. Francis; around the edges, scenes of teaching and the administering of sacraments like baptism and marriage.

ceded a permanent church. The space, called an atrio, was institutionalized because of its practicality, and also because it made sense to the Indians who had always revered their deities in the open air, in front of the temple-pyramids. So the atrio, more than any presumed analogy to the atrium of an Early Christian basilica or the court of a Muslim mosque, should be seen as the acclimatizing of the Aztec religious courtyard.

A wall went around the rectangular space, some stairs climbed up to it from the plaza, and a cross stood in the middle. At the top of the stairs, opposite the church, a gateway of three open arches pierced the wall. The colorful processions, wisely organized by the friars to channel the native love of pageantry, brought in one further component. Four small chapels were placed at the corners of the atrio, and a paved way led from one to another along the edge of the enclosure wall. These *posas,* literally stopping-places, were domed or pyramid-topped rectangular pavilions opened by arches on one or two faces. Before them the processions would halt, and the priest would say special prayers at the altars. They were therefore aligned not symmetrically in relation to the center of the courtyard, but made to turn toward the procession that moved counterclockwise beginning at the church.

Since the friars did celebrate Mass at the atrio, a sanctuary had to exist large enough to contain the celebrants, the altar, and the ritual. This was achieved by the addition of a chapel to one side of the church, open toward the atrio. Contemporary sources often speak of it as the *capilla de Indios,* and it can at times be quite elaborate. One common type consisted of a portico with an apse protruding from the rear wall. This is usually thought to have been the first stage in the creation of a most extraordinary plan that was given to the Indian chapel of San José de los Naturales in Mexico City, and the one at Cholula which their historian John McAndrew rightly calls "a Mexican mosque." (Fig. 18.19) Rows of columns define multiple aisles, and the front toward the atrio is opened along its entire width. At San José a single tower, attached to the rear of the hall, provides an accent very like a minaret.

Was this resemblance conscious? The last mosques were closed in Spain in 1525, and the resisting Muslims forcibly baptized. Yet some of these Moriscos slipped into New Spain. But even without their help, pure-blooded settlers, it seems, were fond of aping Arab manners. This may explain the mosque form. It is also conceivable that the friars saw a kinship in the roughly contemporary conversion of the Moors and the Indians, and sought to suggest it architecturally. At any rate, there is something wonderfully fetching about celebrating Catholic Mass for ex-Aztecs in the columnar hall of an Arab mosque.

The unorthodox ways of early Mexican Christianity were a matter of considerable worry for the official church. Especially after the Council of Trent, which had convened to deal with the Protestant threat and had firmly defined church ritual, the improvised freedom of American observances began to be thought of as inexcusable. The open-air church, with its atrio, posas, and Indian chapel, had no doctrinal authority. It was countenanced probably because it greatly facilitated and hastened the work of conversion. Still, the idea was disturbing. This was particularly so because the same ground was also used for processions and plays that, although ostensibly Christian in content, often developed into dances accompanied by the old instruments and the lusty singing of devotional songs, of *alabados* and *Pasiones* and *Calvarios*. (Fig. 18.20)

The secular clergy of New Spain had never been very pleased with mendicant independence, or the Crown's reliance on the orders for the task of taming millions of heathens across the vast territory subdued by Spanish arms. The friars' phenomenal success, and their exclusive custody of this multitude who seemed overwhelmingly to love and obey them, made matters worse. Increasingly, in the second half of the century, pressure was brought to bear in Madrid to return control of the Indian flock to the priesthood under the ultimate authority of the primate of Mexico, the archbishop of Mexico City, and the bishops of Puebla, Guatemala, Oaxaca, and Michoacán under him. The architecture sponsored by them was pointedly different. The parish churches of the small towns were carelessly built, rudimentary buildings, but in the major cities the cathedrals grew large and ambitious, and from the start stood more in line with prominent European models. The splendid new cathedrals of Mexico City, Guadalajara, and Mérida after 1580 signify the full ascendancy of the secular clergy.

For the bishops indeed prevailed. In 1574 the friars were subjected to the office of the viceroy and the administrative frame of dioceses. Soon their sacerdotal privileges were removed. The building of monasteries stopped. The adjacent open-air churches were deemed to have outlived their usefulness. The friars hastened to civilize new lands further north, and Mexican architecture took its place as a respectable offshoot of European production. Something of promise, perhaps, was lost. And the Indian cause had its most compassionate voice effectively stilled.

Further Reading

G. F. Andrews, *Maya Cities: Placemaking and Urbanization* (Norman: University of Oklahoma Press, 1975).

L. Baudin, *Daily Life in Peru Under the Last Incas* (New York: Macmillan, 1968).

J. Broda, D. Carrasco, and E. M. Moctezuma, *The Great Temple of Tenochtlan: Center and Periphery in the Aztec World* (Berkeley: University of California Press, 1987).

G. H. S. Bushnell, *Peru*, rev. ed. (New York: Praeger, 1963).

M. D. Coe, *The Maya* (London: Thames and Hudson, 1980).

D. P. Crouch et al., *Spanish City Planning in North America* (Cambridge, Mass.: MIT Press, 1982)

G. Kubler, *Mexican Architecture of the Sixteenth Century*, 2 vols. (New Haven: Yale University Press, 1948).

J. McAndrew, *The Open-Air Churches of Sixteenth-Century Mexico* (Cambridge, Mass.: Harvard University Press, 1965).

J.-P. Protzen, *Inca Architecture and Construction at Ollantaytambo* (New York: Oxford University Press, 1993).

J. Soustelle, *Daily Life of the Aztecs on the Eve of the Spanish Conquest* (Stanford, Calif.: Stanford University Press, 1970).

J. E. S. Thompson, *The Rise and Fall of Maya Civilization* (Norman: University of Oklahoma Press, 1954).

M. Treib, *Sanctuaries of Spanish New Mexico* (Berkeley: University of California Press, 1993).

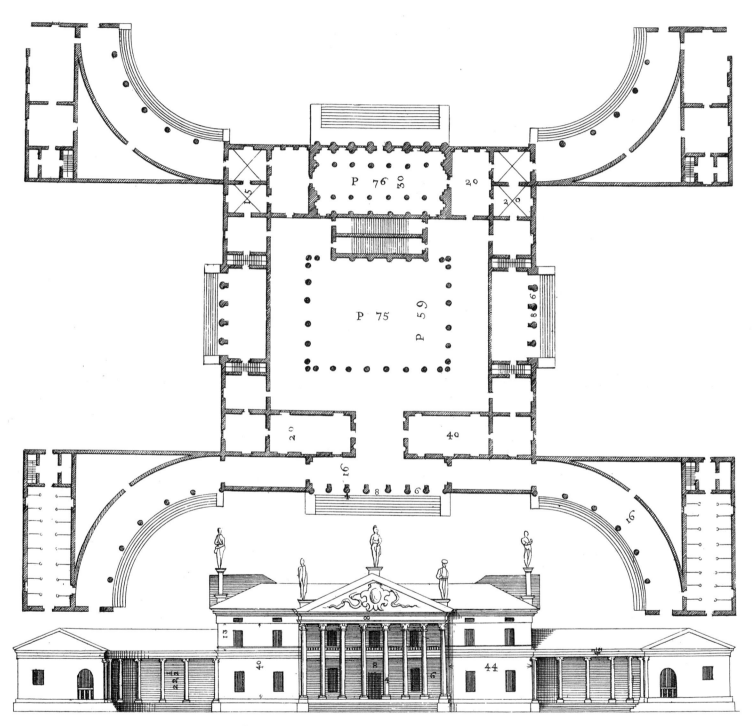

Andrea Palladio, design for a villa from *The Four Books of Architecture*, 1738.

19

ISTANBUL AND VENICE

Tenochtitlán fell to Cortés' conquistadors in 1521. In that same year, the armies of Süleyman the Magnificent, sultan of the Ottoman Turks, captured Belgrade and moved into Hungary. The world in the opening decades of the sixteenth century was not what it used to be. Europe had reached the shores of the Pacific Ocean, and Asia bordered on Austria. Italy, seat of the Renaissance and light of the West, was caught between two superstates that had hardly figured in her plans one hundred years earlier. Charles V, to one side, wore the twin crowns of Spain and the Holy Roman Empire; he ruled Mexico, but also Flanders, Austria, Sicily, and Naples. Süleyman was master of Egypt, Syria, Asia Minor, and the Balkans, keeper of the holy sites of Mecca and Medina, and sole caliph of the Muslim world. He had broken Venetian ascendancy in the eastern Mediterranean. Turkish galleys were active in the Red Sea, at the straits of Otranto, and along the coast of Algeria and Tunisia.

These developments sapped the strength of Europe. Spanish prosperity and Ottoman aggressiveness combined to bring economic and political decline to the Mediterranean. The new trade routes to Asia had given colonial powers mercantile preeminence, and the long reign of the republic of Venice as the mistress of long-distance trade was at an end. Lisbon and Seville were now the great ports of the prodigiously expanded world. What accumulated there through intercontinental traffic found its European market in Antwerp, Augsburg, or

Nürnberg. At the same time, a crisis of another sort threatened the old order throughout Europe. This was the Protestant schism, which became a fact at the Diet of Augsburg in 1530; in its wake the English broke away from Rome in 1534. The story of the sixteenth-century concerns the continent's manifold adjustment to such galvanizing challenges, and others that are less flashy but equally real—a steadily increasing population, runaway inflation, the pervasive commercialization of agriculture, the weakening of urban industries, and the first swell of modern capitalism.

This cursory overview will suggest the breadth of architectural themes that are opened up to the historian. To the East, the Turkish phenomenon recharges an extensive urban and rural environment, formerly in Byzantine or Latin control, with the patterns of a new cultural order. To the North, the Reformation leads swiftly to the remodeling of thousands of medieval churches in Germany, England, Scotland, France, and the Netherlands; and this is only the first step. By the end of the century, new buildings for Protestant worship will exhibit a rich variety of experimental forms. In reaction to these novelties, the architecture of Catholicism will itself enter a period of inventiveness of which the building activity of the Jesuits and Andrea Palladio's Venetian churches are only two testimonials. A more crowded Europe, and the huge influx of people into cities, inevitably affected housing practices. Classical design followed the paths of colonization,

while in Europe it was interpreted, timidly or radically, with a fertile imagination that knew no end.

Two exceptional cities, Istanbul and Venice, will help us experience something of this unfolding Mediterranean world. (Figs. 19.1, 19.3) The choice is of course rather arbitrary, but not without method. Istanbul, capital of the Ottoman Empire from 1453 onward, holds the finest fruit of Turkish architecture. The decision to revive the thousand-year-old city of the Byzantine emperors, a mere shadow of its former self at the time of its conquest by Mehmed II (1451–81), was fully self-conscious. Within a century it would become one of the two most populous cities of the Mediterranean, the other being Naples. How the legendary bastion of Eastern Christianity, the city of Constantine and Justinian, was redesigned as the foremost capital of the Muslim commonwealth is a fascinating story. (Fig. 19.2)

Venice achieves the zenith of its urban form in the sixteenth century, that is, at the start of its long decline. The definitive completion of the Piazza S. Marco ranks as a climatic, and altogether unique, chapter of Renaissance urban thinking. The great architect of Venice and the Veneto in this period, Andrea Palladio (1508–80), has been called "the most imitated architect in history." But beyond this, Venice has one further distinction. It is perhaps the one historic city that has always clearly understood that urban form, in the final analysis, is the inseparable weave of the ordinary and the

Fig. 19.1 Istanbul (Constantinople, Turkey); view in a print of 1635. The European quarter, called Galata or Pera, is in the foreground; the old city, on the other side of the Golden Horn (Haliç), is in the distance.

heroic. This discernment led in Venice to two exceptional attitudes. The establishment accepted it as its duty to provide decent housing for the poor and the helpless. And the professional architect here was willing to lend his newfound dignity to the task of designing the ordinary house. As the native Alvise Cornaro wrote in the 1520s, to justify the attention he was paying in his treatise to residential architecture:

The beauty and comfort of houses, dwellings and abodes of citizens are important, because these are of an infinite number and they make up the city. . . . I am not writing about theaters, amphitheaters and how to make a new city, because this never happens and because these other types of buildings cannot be useful [to the ordinary citizen].

A Turkish Renaissance

The Turks, a tribal people of Central Asia, came to know Islam in the ninth century. They were intrepid fighters and much prized by the early Abbasid caliphs, and other rul-

Fig. 19.2 Map: Ottoman Empire in the sixteenth century. The hatch line marks the Empire's outermost boundaries.

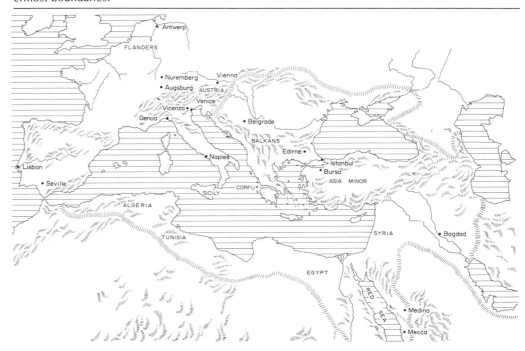

454

Fig. 19.3 Canaletto (Antonio da Canal), *Venice: The Basin of S. Marco on Ascension Day*, ca. 1740. (National Gallery, London) The Doge's Palace is on the right, with the campanile of St. Mark's seen behind it. The entrance to the Grand Canal is left of center, and beyond that are the Dogana (Customs House) and the domes of S. Maria della Salute.

ers later, as private palace guards. But there were independent Turkish states as well, and great ruling houses like the Mamelukes of Egypt and the Seljuks, who took control of Persia about 1000 and engaged the Byzantine Empire in eastern Asia Minor, were of Turkish origin. The founders of the Ottoman state emigrated into Asia Minor in the thirteenth century. They were one of many nomadic, warring tribes deployed by the Seljuk state at the steadily receding frontiers of Byzantium. When the Mongol invasion of 1253 undermined Seljuk power, the Ottoman Turks seized the chance to come into their own. They absorbed their Muslim neighbors and began a brilliant program of conquest that was to deprive the Greeks of what remained of Asia Minor, and then of their holdings in the Balkans, on the European side of the straits. Only Constantinople held on, girded by the sea and her impregnable land walls. Then, on 29 May 1453, she too gave in. Her new master, Mehmed II, the Conqueror, renamed the city "Istanbul" and took it for his capital.

Two other Byzantine cities had previously been converted for use as capitals of the Ottoman state—Bursa and Edirne. Bursa, on the south shore of the Sea of Marmara, nestled in the foothills of Ulu Dağ. (Fig. 19.4) To this day it retains the flavor of a small, traditional Turkish town, with its modest domed mosques and tombs sheathed in beautiful tile, and its light-filled houses on sloping sites, their projecting bays enjoy-

Fig. 19.4 Bursa (Turkey); partial view of the city in an old photograph, showing the character of the original houses.

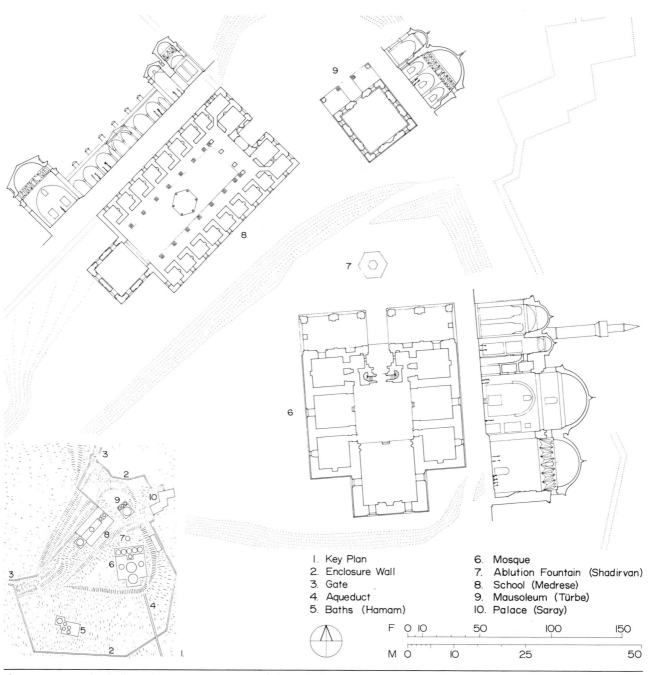

1. Key Plan
2. Enclosure Wall
3. Gate
4. Aqueduct
5. Baths (Hamam)
6. Mosque
7. Ablution Fountain (Shadirvan)
8. School (Medrese)
9. Mausoleum (Türbe)
10. Palace (Saray)

F   O IO   50   100   150

M   O   IO   25   50

Fig. 19.5 Bursa, the külliye of Bayazīd I (called Yīldīrīm, or "Lightning"), 1390–95; site plan, lower left, and plans and sections of the major buildings.

ing the verdant view. Edirne, Byzantine Adrianople, is in Thrace, on the river Tunca. It gave the Turks their first foothold in Europe from which they fanned out into Bulgaria, Serbia, Rumania, and down into Greece.

Neighborhood Planning and Sinan

The chief device of Ottoman city-making was the *külliye.* The word derives from the Arabic word meaning "the whole." A külliye was the functional center of a well-defined neighborhood, identified in these first decades by family bonds, profession, or place of origin. It consisted of an interrelated group of buildings around a mosque, installed and endowed by the sultan as the public nexus of obedient subjects. It is to be distinguished from the administrative center of the town, usually a citadel, and the commercial center of bazaars and khans, which were placed next to the Friday mosque.

The practice starts in Bursa. Here several külliyes were pitched at the outskirts of the old town as the vehicle of urban expansion, and with the aim of promoting the teaching of Islam and the Ottoman way of life. The sites are hilly and the grouping relaxed. The mosque holds the summit, while the other buildings gather about it on lower ground, except in the southeast sector, the general direction of Mecca. Our example shows the külliye of Bayazīd I, built between 1390 and 1395. (Fig. 19.5) A wall wraps loosely around it. From the main entrance a path leads up toward the summit, where three principal buildings, different in size and form and not on the same level, turn toward it; they are the *madrasa* or theological college, the founder's tomb, and the mosque adorned in front by a public fountain. Further out are the alms-kitchen, the baths, the hospital, and a small palace.

The main traits of Ottoman architecture are already present here: cut-stone masonry (grey, rather melancholy limestone in the case of Bursa) and simple, clear forms often used serially. The recurrent unit is the square bay covered by a true dome. The massing relies on the contrast between the cubic shapes of the walls and the full taut hemispheres that rest on them. Variety and emphasis are created by proj-

Fig. 19.6a Edirne (Adrianople, Turkey), külliye of Bayazīd II, 1484–88, Hayrettin; detail of the porch of the lunatic asylum.

Fig. 19.6b Florence (Italy), the Foundling Hospital (Ospedale degli Innocenti), 1419, Filippo Brunelleschi; exterior from the northwest.

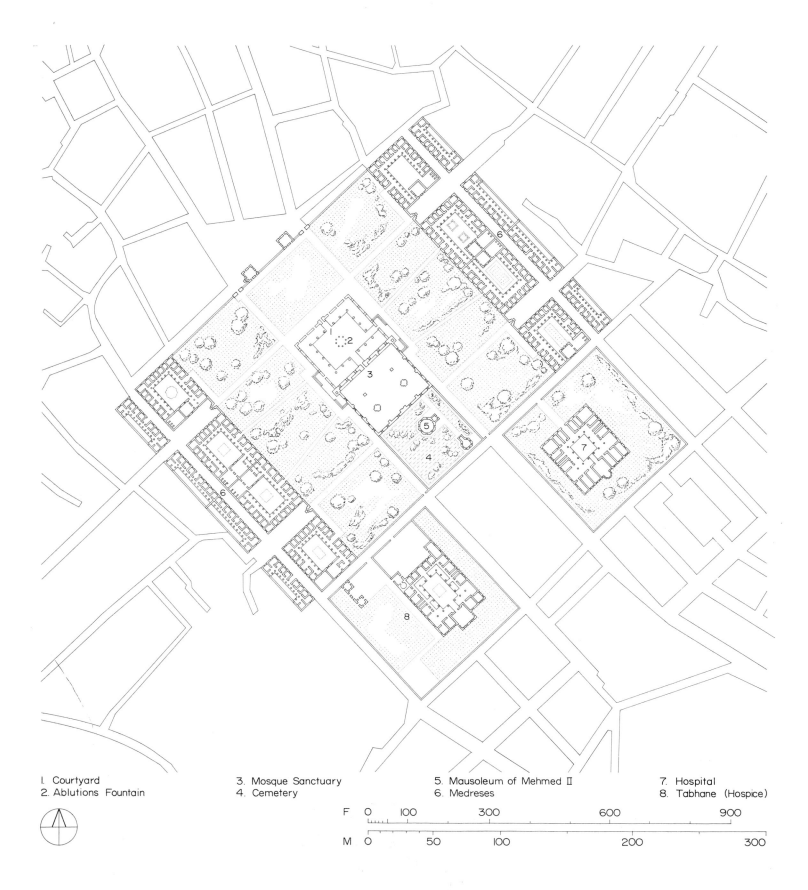

1. Courtyard
2. Ablutions Fountain
3. Mosque Sanctuary
4. Cemetery
5. Mausoleum of Mehmed II
6. Medreses
7. Hospital
8. Tabhane (Hospice)

F 0   100   300   600   900

M 0   50   100   200   300

458

Fig. 19.7 Istanbul, külliye of Mehmed II (called Fatih, or the "Conqueror"), 1463–70, Atĭk ("Old") Sinan; general plan. (The complex is marked as no. 10 in Fig. 19.14.) It was built over the Byzantine church of the Holy Apostles (no. 22 in Fig. 11.29b).

ecting oversized units from the main block and by varying the sizes and levels of the domes. Slender vertical accents lend a touch of buoyancy. A pencil-thin, cylindrical minaret with one or two balconies, called *şerefes*, rise from one corner, or else a pair at the ends of the entrance porch frames the main elevation. In functional buildings, like kitchens or rows of living units, the even line of domes is picked out by pert chimney stacks. The domes sit on their square bays by means of stalactite squinches

Fig. 19.8 Istanbul, the külliye of Mehmed II; seen here in a mid-sixteenth-century engraving by Melchior Lorichs.

or flat triangles, rarely true pendentives. Arches are mildly pointed or round-headed. The flat-topped variety that occurs in the porch of the Bayazĭd mosque is a Bursa specialty. Most commonly, Turkish arcades swing from unfluted columns that carry some form of stalactite capital.

At times the design has a Brunelleschian purity. (Fig. 19.6) The subject of East-West contacts has hardly been scratched by architectural historians, but it may well be that such similarities are not altogether fortuitous. Italian artists were invited to the Ottoman court. Mehmed II spoke their language, along with Greek and Arabic, and there is a beautiful portrait of him painted by the Venetian Gentile Bellini. The Conqueror's own külliye in Istanbul, a little more than a half-century after Bayazĭd I's in Bursa, has a grand composition with strict bilateral symmetry. (Fig. 19.7) Is this the scale and regimentation of empire alone, or

is Mehmed trumpeting his modernism? At any rate, the immense terrace on vaulted substructures that level the hilly site, the marshaling of large cellular structures on either side (the madrasas that made up the university of the new capital, hostels, charitable foundations), the confident proportions of the principal units that suggest a broad module, the courtly axis that runs through the mosque sequences beginning at the main entrance of the complex—all this has the authority of ancient Rome. Nothing so early in the Western Renaissance has this grandeur. We have to remember that Constantinople was originally created as the New Rome. In her the Conqueror inherited the one city that safeguarded the Classical tradition in the eastern half of the Christian world as authentically as Rome did in the West. After the fall of Constantinople, the Turks were well placed to stage their own renaissance.

Let us focus on the mosque for a moment. (Fig. 19.8) It is apparent at a glance that the plan is very different from that of the Bayazĭd mosque in Bursa. (Fig. 19.5) The entrance porch has been amplified into a full courtyard exactly as large as the sanctuary proper. The mihrab bay is not allowed to protrude beyond the rectangular envelope of the sanctuary. Its vault has been reduced to a half-dome, lower than and subsidiary to the great central dome. Three small domed units that echo in miniature the canopy of the central bay on either side of this core extend the space outward. The run of domes that traces the four sides of the courtyard is on a smaller scale still. Lateral stairs bracket the outer juncture of court and sanctuary, and create a cross-axis that acknowledges the extrinsic buildings of the complex and their many inhabitants, as the main axis itself reaches out toward the town. In terms of size, the central dome here is almost twice the span of the Bursa mosque. More important, it bravely dispenses with the support of lateral walls. The dome rests on four piers, two of which are extrusions of the entrance wall, and on small columns halfway along the lateral spans, which also double up as the corner props of the aisle domes.

This novel plan can be explained in part by the difference in programs. Bayazĭd's

building was more than a mosque. The domed bay in the middle is in fact a covered court that serves the prayer hall, as well as two lateral iwans, all raised two steps above it. The iwans in turn are flanked by pairs of rooms. Those next to the prayer hall have plaster shelves built into their walls and hooded fireplaces. The pair closest to the entrance porch is entered through a small lobby from which stairs give access to small, second-storey cells. We have not merely a neighborhood mosque, but a shell that combines a royal chapel with a hostel for pilgrims.

But the matter goes beyond function. In the design of Mehmed's mosque, the vastly enlarged congregations of Istanbul and also the old Turkish proclivity for a unified ground space under the enveloping swell of domes were certainly two main considerations. But why the extraordinary vaulting hierarchy over the prayer hall when the simpler solution of the Friday mosque at Bursa, where files of uniform domes cover the prayer hall, would have done just as well? The answer points inevitably to a self-imposed, architectural challenge, in the abstract sense, and the challenger is plainly Justinian's Hagia Sophia. (Figs. 1.4, 11.27, 11.28) Muslim architecture started off competitively, as the Dome of the Rock in Jerusalem has shown us. Now, in the latest chapter of its distinguished history, it takes on once again the best of the rival faith.

To say this is not to slight the majestic imperial mosques that transformed forever the topography of this ancient city between continents. Hagia Sophia is not an easy model. Were it not for the building technology and the superior organization that Ottoman architecture had garnered in the century and a half before the fall of Constantinople, there would be no question of attempting to match a monument of that scale and complexity. Payment books for the mosque of Süleyman the Magnifi-

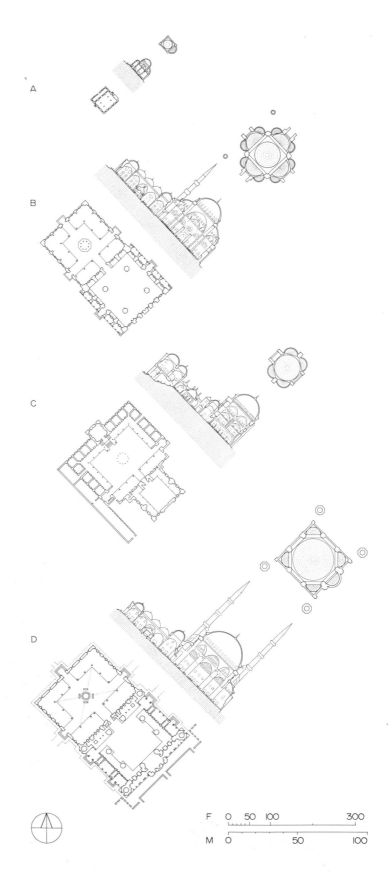

Fig. 19.9 Mosques of the sixteenth century, by the architect Sinan; diagrammatic plans: (**A**) Gözleve (Crimea, U.S.S.R.), Mosque of Mimar Sinan, 1552; (**B**) Istanbul, Shehzade Mosque, or Mosque of the Princes, 1544–48; (**C**) Istanbul, Sokullu Mehmed Pasha Mosque, 1571; (**D**) Edirne, Selim Mosque, 1569–75.

Fig. 19.10 Istanbul, the külliye of Süleyman I (the Magnificent), 1550–57, Sinan; close view of the mosque from the southwest.

cent (1520–66), for example, reveal a highly efficient workshop of thousands of masons, carpenters, glaziers, draftsmen, blacksmiths, sappers, and roofers. The state sponsored hundreds of buildings in the conquered territories, and the capital itself was one immense building site. The court commandeered the best of every craft; the economic and industrial resources of the empire were at the disposal of the architect-in-chief. Construction progressed astonishingly fast. Entire imperial külliyes were completed within a decade. Süleyman's took about seven years.

But the sultans and their viziers were also fortunate in the architectural talent they could call on. The fame of Sinan (ca. 1490–1588), state architect under Süleyman and his son Selim II (1566–74), has overshadowed a number of gifted predecessors and successors, although none equals his fertile mind and broad mastery. After an early army career which took him all over the Near East and the Balkans, he was made head of the empire's corps of architects in 1539 when he was about fifty. His title was Architect of the Abode of Felicity. Sinan, a convert, had gained his standing as a military engineer during the campaigns of Belgrade, Corfu, Puglia, Baghdad, and Persia, and the great number of buildings he is credited with include every conceivable type. But the mosques were his prodigy; Hagia Sophia his obsession. Of his late work, the mosque of Selim in Edirne, he wrote in his autobiography:

Architects in Christian countries may rank themselves above Muslims in technical skill, owing to the failure of the latter to achieve anything approaching the dome of Hagia Sophia. This assertion of insurmountable difficulty has wounded the author of these writings. However, with God's help and the Sultan's mercy, I have succeeded in building a dome for Sultan Selim's mosque which is four ells greater in diameter and six ells higher than that of Hagia Sophia.

It is a human boast, a builder's boast, and rather beside the point. The family of Sinan

mosques, intimate chapels and imperial monuments alike, plays so richly on a range of set themes—some derived from Hagia Sophia, others of his own invention—that it rewards the most exacting scrutiny. But even a casual visit will delight and amaze. In either case it is the originality of this near-contemporary of Michelangelo and Palladio that will come through, rather than the weight of his inspiration. A great dome on true pendentives, with lower half-domed units extended by semicircular niches—this is the bond between the Isidoros-Anthemios team and Sinan. With this he goes to work. Look at his plans first, diagrammatically. (Fig. 19.9) The half-dome stays on one side of the central square, as in the original mosque of the Conqueror; on two opposite sides, as in Hagia Sophia; or else, it spins a four-leaf clover with attendant pairs of niches on all four sides. Now the center is a hexagon and four half-domed volumes open obliquely at the north and south flanks. In Edirne the big half-domes are gone altogether. The dome sits on eight equal arches, fronting niches that are alternately half-domed and barrel-vaulted.

But this is only the opening hand. About this core and in the courtyards up front, Sinan strews his crop of smaller domes which are entirely absent from Hagia Sophia. We see them best in three dimensions, in the composition of the exterior mass. They pile up with contrapuntal rhythms moving toward the mighty lead-coated hemisphere of the central square, as our view of Süleyman's mosque from the southwest shows. (Fig. 19.10) There are triplets of tiny cupolas over the main western entrances, on two sides of the staggered buttresses that carry their own domed caps. Between these buttresses, over the eaves of a two-storey loggia which shelters the ablution fountains, we see the three aisle domes, the central one bigger and taller. Then comes the great arch-wall that brings light to the nave heights, a direct citation from Hagia Sophia; it is flanked by two of the domed buttressing towers placed at the corners of the central square. And so to the all-commanding summit. From the left, close to the ground, march the domed bays of the courtyard porticoes under the galleried shafts of the four minarets. On the right, beyond the south half-dome, sit the domed mausolea of the emperor and his favorite consort, in an underbuilt enclosure of green, dotted by turbaned tombstones.

We enter axially from the north or through four lateral gates. The great space, evenly lighted by hundreds of windows that reach in places down to the pavement, is overwhelming but not mysterious. (Fig. 19.11) From where we stand we can see into every direction freely and to the full height of the perimeter walls. The sanctuary wall is flat, as are the others. Horizontal stresses overall moderate the soaring effect. A mass of lamp wheels, suspended by cords from the vaults, forms a low roof of light just above the heads of the congregation. All around the interior—at the springing line of the pendentives, the half-domes, and the niches—runs a continuous service gallery on handsome consoles. All this has its own design logic, which is to say a cultural outlook that is not Byzantium's. The program of a Muslim mosque, however indebted its shape might be to the geometries of Hagia Sophia, has no use for the clever obscuring of the structural system, the diaphragm walls between nave and aisles, and the theater of the apsed sanctuary which give Justinian's great church its special quality. (Fig. 11.28, and page 244)

And if Sinan rejects the mystical sublimity of Byzantine Constantinople, he is also sufficiently removed from contemporary Renaissance practice, which he was undoubtedly familiar with, to keep his identity as a Muslim architect and a Turkish one. Neither the interior of St. Peter's in Rome nor that of a Palladian church in Venice, both roughly coeval with the Süleyman mosque, strike anything but the most general note of affinity with Sinan's design. (Figs. 19.12, 20.23) In part, it is because we have stalactites, Koranic inscriptions, and other such traditional Islamic motifs in Sinan's mosque, as opposed to the Western use of Classical columns and entablatures, pedimented niches, and urnlike balusters. But more fundamentally, Sinan does not compose with independently articulated parts related to one another in consistent proportionalities. His is a looser approach to design. The volumes are not cast with interlocked architectural members but, instead, are broadly enveloped by shells and walls, which are then punctured by many

Fig. 19.11 Istanbul, mosque of Süleyman (no. 3 in Fig. 19.13); interior looking up into the dome.

windows that have no molded frames. In religious terms, this architecture falls somewhere between the metaphysical theocentricity of Hagia Sophia and the mathematical clarity of the Renaissance— somewhere, that is, between awe and reason.

As planner, on a more neutral level, Sinan is more recognizably allied to advanced European thinking. The layout of Süleyman's külliye, of which the mosque is the stately hub, displays a peerless sense of organization and technical adroitness. (Fig. 19.13) One hundred years earlier, the Con-

Fig. 19.12 Venice, the church of Il Redentore (the Redeemer), 1576–80, Andrea Palladio; interior looking southwest. (See also Figs. 19.27 and 19.28.)

queror's külliye had set the standard for such orderly planning. (Fig. 19.7) But that scheme looks static and mechanically conceived when confronted with the way Sinan exploits his hill site. He has the same respect for symmetry and axial, right-angular composition. The central rectangular compound of courtyard, prayer hall, and cemetery remains unchanged. But Sinan groups the accompanying buildings more intimately around this core. He manipulates changes of level and the incidents of approach with sure-footed invention, giving lively play to contacts with the surrounding neighborhood and the distant prospects.

The hill overlooks the Golden Horn to the east. A portion of the buildings and the park of the old imperial palace, started on this site by the Conqueror before he settled on Topkapï, was left standing on the south slope. Below this, the markets spread. The area to the west, where the modern University of Istanbul now is located, was likely planned as a new district; old maps show a bit of a checkerboard between the külliye of Süleyman and the slightly earlier one, the Şehzade, built by Sinan for the same sultan in memory of a dead crown prince. All told, this adds up to quite an ambitious urban project. North of here were the old quarters, focused by the Conqueror's own külliye and that of Selim I, Süleyman's father, closer to the land walls. Their wooden houses on crooked streets and steep alleys must have heightened the impact of the starchily arrayed stone akropolises that loomed above them.

At the Süleyman complex Sinan keeps all his outlying buildings low, to emphasize the primacy of the mosque. Most are madrasas, meant to extend the original core of the Ottoman university at the külliye of Mehmed II. The two madrasas on the east side sink below the level of the stupendous artificial terrace, so that they would not interfere with the panorama of the Horn and the Bosphorus. A common embankment runs the length of the two buildings, and a garden court lies between them. The plan is basic to all the units of the külliye regardless of function—a courtyard enclosed by cubical domed rooms. In this case the rooms serve as student cells. The schoolroom is on the west side, raised above the courtyard and entered directly from small

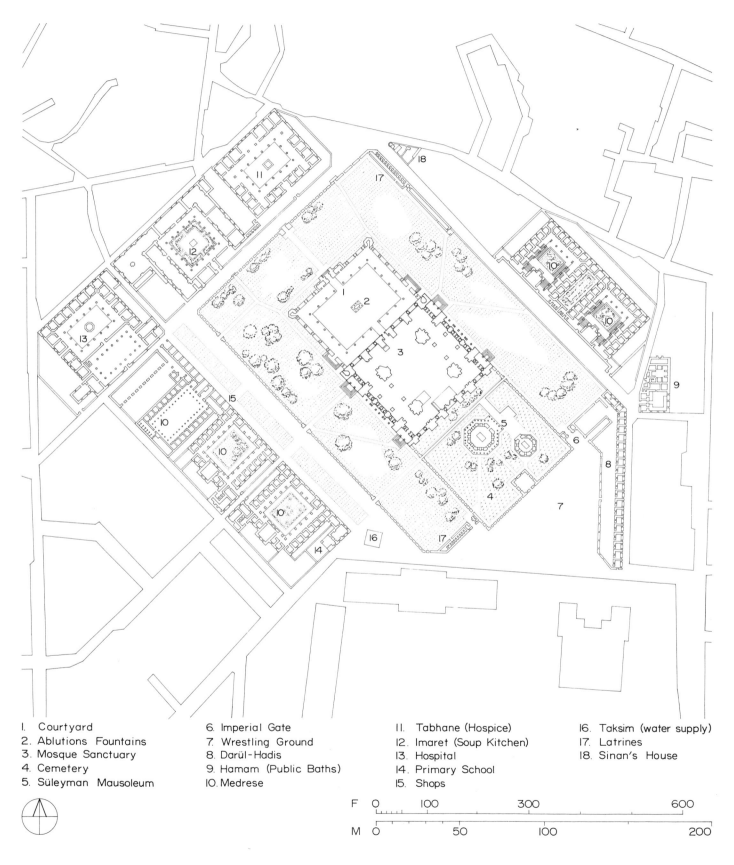

1. Courtyard
2. Ablutions Fountains
3. Mosque Sanctuary
4. Cemetery
5. Süleyman Mausoleum

6. Imperial Gate
7. Wrestling Ground
8. Darül-Hadis
9. Hamam (Public Baths)
10. Medrese

11. Tabhane (Hospice)
12. Imaret (Soup Kitchen)
13. Hospital
14. Primary School
15. Shops

16. Taksim (water supply)
17. Latrines
18. Sinan's House

F 0   100   300   600

M 0   50   100   200

464

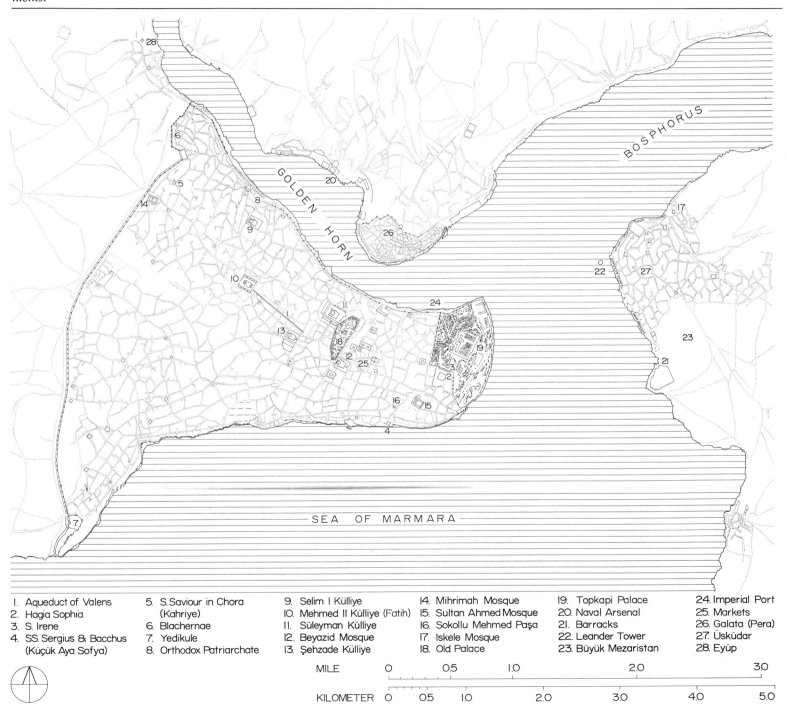

1. Aqueduct of Valens	5. S. Saviour in Chora (Kahriye)	9. Selim I Külliye
2. Hagia Sophia	6. Blachernae	10. Mehmed II Külliye (Fatih)
3. S. Irene	7. Yedikule	11. Süleyman Külliye
4. SS. Sergius & Bacchus (Küçük Aya Sofya)	8. Orthodox Patriarchate	12. Beyazid Mosque
		13. Şehzade Külliye

14. Mihrimah Mosque	19. Topkapi Palace	24. Imperial Port
15. Sultan Ahmed Mosque	20. Naval Arsenal	25. Markets
16. Sokollu Mehmed Paşa	21. Barracks	26. Galata (Pera)
17. Iskele Mosque	22. Leander Tower	27. Üsküdar
18. Old Palace	23. Büyük Mezaristan	28. Eyüp

MILE   0   0.5   1.0   2.0   3.0

KILOMETER   0   0.5   1.0   2.0   3.0   4.0   5.0

gate lodges at the north and south ends of the western perimeter wall. In the vaulted chambers of the embankment, below the eastern cells, Sinan fits a third madrasa—one instance of his imaginative use of substructures that recalls Pergamon and Praeneste.

This half of the complex, the east and south sides to be exact, seizes on oblique streets to relieve the monotony of a grand rectilinear composition. Sinan put his own house on the triangular plot at the northeast corner, with an open mausoleum for himself in the garden. At the opposite corner there is a small bath, and across from it, closing the line of the mosque enclosure and then following the strong diagonal of the street that descends toward the markets, was the *darül-hadis,* the foremost school of prophetic traditions in the empire. Its frame and the south cemetery wall defined a public space which was used once a week for the popular wrestling matches.

This was the direction from which the largest number of the faithful arrived at the mosque. The enclosure gates here, on either side of the cemetery, are therefore the amplest. The eastern gate was reserved for the imperial party, which ascended by means of a ramp and entered the prayer hall near the sanctuary wall. The western, with its attached row of latrines, was used by the people and the caravans that were allowed to pitch tents in this half of the enclosure. The crowd would file in, stop at the ablutions fountains, and then enter the mosque laterally. The formal approach from the north, through the courtyard, was curiously secondary in importance, facing the soup kitchen and the hospice where travelers could lodge free for three days. Next to the kitchen a hospital held the northwest corner. The entire west side was otherwise occupied by colleges, and a small primary school at the south end of the line. The embankment on this side had small shops, the rent from which augmented the revenues of the külliye.

The Ideal Muslim City

The külliye of Süleyman the Magnificent crowned the third hill of the great city. (Fig. 19.14) The Conqueror's was on the fourth hill, over Constantine's church of the Holy

Fig. 19.15a Istanbul, Topkapï Palace, the pavilion of Kara Mustafa Paşa, from the second half of the seventeenth century.

Apostles. Between these two hills ran the fourth-century aqueduct of Valens, with the Şehzade complex on the opposite side of it. On the fifth hill, at the edge of the Golden Horn, stood the mosque of Süleyman's father, Selim (1512–20), part of an incomplete külliye. Just below this, between the mosque and the land wall, there was a heavy concentration of Greeks around the church and residence of their patriarch. In the enduring Koranic tradition of tolerance, Istanbul was to be a world city, as Islam was the superseder and protector of all religions. In the Turkish capital Greeks, Armenians, and Jews lived decently, with a fair degree of self-rule. The prominent külliyes set the Muslim community apart from these alien subjects and announced its dominion over them. Europeans were allowed to settle across the Golden Horn, at Galata, where a Latin mer-

chant colony had long been known under the Byzantines.

Ideologically bridled, Byzantine Constantinople survived nonetheless. The walls, the underground cisterns, the roads were a neutral bequest. The Mese remained the city's spine, although the chain of forums alongside it was all but swallowed up. Churches were mostly converted to mosques; offensive Christian decoration was whitewashed. Much of the Great Palace was built over. The Hippodrome became a horse market. Mehmed definitively settled the Ottoman sultans and their administration further east, on the first hill, where the ancient akropolis of Byzantium had been. (cf. Fig. 11.29) This fortified citadel, called Topkapï, was largely an open, tree-softened space, the buildings themselves being mere incidents, never large enough to dominate. At the center, the palace proper con-

Fig. 19.15b Konya (Turkey); interior of a house.

sisted of a sequence of courts and pavil-ions. The areas of least mass become functionally the most important: porticoes, gates, pavilions placed here and there like measured drops, always in relation to greenery, water, or the view.

In these tiny buildings, mounted on bases which lift them to open light, horizontal bands of windows do away with the solid-ity or confinement of the wall and restate what floors are for—to level the user with the light. (Fig. 19.15) The window line is very low; the space is meant for the sitting or kneeling person. Architecture in this guise is an extension of the ground on which it sits. In it, we relate laterally to what sur-rounds us. There is no call for tall furniture or the blocking of the lower parts of the space we are in—as the West so often does, thinking in terms of the upright figure, its principal gauge of scale. The stress is on the intermediate realm, the passages where the

outside and the inside meet. Even in mos-ques, the banks of windows reach down to the ground. Staged suspense, the revela-tion of depths, the drama of spatial se-quence—this is not the province of the Ot-toman architect. Single spaces, clear, gently and evenly luminous—this is what he is aiming at.

In the congested walled town, the resi-dential pattern favored tall attached houses whose street aspect was governed by lat-ticed bay windows. But up and down the Bosphorus, on both the European and Asiatic sides, the hillslopes teemed with small communities where the indepen-dent, open-plan house was the norm. Along the coastline, the *yalīs* of the wealthy pushed out over the water on wooden brackets, sheltering boat docks under-neath and shading the glazed main cage with broadly overhanging eaves. The hall, *sofa* in Turkish, was the center of these

summer houses and seaside villas. Where the sofa was not glazed, it opened freely to the ancillary rooms, so that space flowed within the house from room to room un-impeded by tight partitions or bulky furni-ture.

Bursa still preserves the model of this airy Turkish house. Commonly it is a two-storey arrangement, although split levels and mezzanines are not infrequent. It takes up one-half of the lot. The other half is de-veloped as a fruit garden. Often one enters the house first through a gate in the gar-den wall and then through a door, deep behind the outer plane, that opens onto a stair hall leading to the upper floor. The ground floor is irregular and holds both kitchen and pantry. The overhanging up-per storey, in wood, is rectangular, with lots of glazing in bands, some of it as bay win-dows. There are two separate living quar-ters, for the male and female inhabitants. In the larger houses these actually occupy separate buildings connected by a covered passageway. The sofa is where the family came together; it is really a wide porch at the top of the stairs above the ground floor. Where possible, the rooms had windows both toward the street and the garden. A second row of fixed windows above these brought in additional light. Between the windows, there were very low sitting couches. The word "sofa" came to be as-sociated with these in English. The floors had colorful rugs and carpets or tiles ar-ranged in rug patterns. Closets and cabi-nets along the walls hid the bedding, which at night would transform a parlor into a bedroom. Others stored low tables which were brought out for meals; the diners would sit on cushions around them. The typical Turkish fireplace was circular and topped by a conical hood of plaster or bronze.

These houses, ignored in the West until this century, prefigure much that has dis-tinguished modern residential design: the open plan, the exterior massing which denies the boxlike arrangement of walls, the horizontal continuities of the window bands and the projecting eaves. These features now strike us as singular because of our present visual memory that links them to Voysey, Frank Lloyd Wright, the Shingle Style, and the open plans of houses by

Bruce Price or the young Charles McKim. We are again reminded that we usually become conscious of vernacular traditions in one of two ways. A modern architect will specifically direct us to a region as the source and inspiration of his work, in the way Le Corbusier singled out the houses of the Greek islands; or else, having absorbed and glorified a certain modern design trend, we will be enthralled by some remote instance that seems, quite by chance, to presage it. The second is the case with the residential architecture of old Bursa and other early Turkish towns.

The Consummation of Venice

The Italian Renaissance was slow to touch the marshlands of the Veneto and its maritime capital. Italy had no strong claims on Venice. She was self-made, an early medieval creation unbeholden to Roman par-

Fig. 19.16 Map: Venice, ca. 1550.

1. La Giudecca	4. St. Mark's	7. Dogana da Mare	10. Il Redentore
2. Grand Canal	5. Rialto	8. Marinarezza	11. S. Giorgio Maggiore
3. Ghetto	6. Arsenal	9. S. Maria della Salute	

| Mile | 0 | 0.5 | 1.0 | 2.0 |
| Kilometer | 0 | 0.5 | 1.0 | 2.0 | 3.0 |

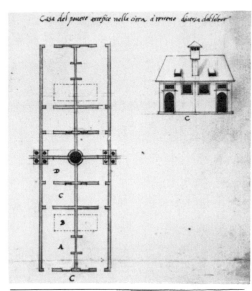

Casa del povere artefice nella citra à'terreno divisa dal decoro

Fig. 19.18 Sebastiano Serlio, artisan's house; plan and elevation, from his book *On Domestic Architecture*, 1541–51. The drawing is labeled "Dwelling for a poor artisan" and is a two-family house type intended to be constructed in rows.

Fig. 19.17 Venice, the Palazzo Centani; courtyard with exterior staircase and well, fifteenth century.

entage. There were no ancient monuments for her to recover; no ancient sentiments to enthrone. Pious yet habitually antipapist, the city had entered the sixteenth century under an official edict of excommunication. Predictably, the active context of the Classical idiom—the authority of an imperial past, mixed with the internationalism of a Catholic present—was not persuasive on the Grand Canal or the quiescent terra firma.

Venice's past was her own; she clung to it proudly. She too was a world center, and her world was the international community of trade. Her inspiration was drawn from ports of call overseas and continental market towns: Byzantium, the Arab countries, Gothic Europe. Her architectural taste was as exotic and as prone to luxury as the cargo of her galleons. Venetian buildings went in for color, precious stones, carved ornament, and lacy frills. This was surface glitter, applied to traditional frames that survived the centuries with little change.

The Classical orders were another such

Fig. 19.19 Venice, the Grand Canal; detail view.

finery. They were taken up sparingly, with no moral commitment. The standard plans and the airy openness of traditional facades were unaffected by them. Even when the city officially imported the Italian style in the person of Jacopo Sansovino (1486–1570), who left Rome for Venice after the Sack of 1527, local patterns persisted, for Sansovino knew how to fit the most advanced architecture of the Renaissance into that gilded fabric—that was the secret of his success. With the native architect Palladio, in the second half of the century, the Ve-

neto invented its own Renaissance: eclectic, empirically functional, adaptable, full of the radiance and lightheartedness that always marked its environment.

Palladio was trained as a stone carver before he fell in with the humanist circle of Vicenza. His *Four Books on Architecture*, published in 1570 and addressed to the professional architect, abounds in sane, practical advice, balanced with erudite commentary. Palladian villas pay lip service to antiquity with temple-front porches, while the rest is a stripped, cubist design

of crisp geometric clarity. His much more scholarly churches for Venice amalgamate into their humanist discourse elements of Byzantine, Gothic, and utilitarian Roman buildings. Their white or cream stucco interiors, lit for soft, subtle modulations, stand apart from the sumptuousness of post-Reformation churches elsewhere in Italy with their frescoed vaults and domes. Civic and private commissions in good part, these churches strike a religious strain halfway between the blare of Romanism triumphant and Protestant plainness.

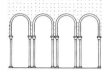

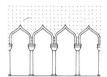

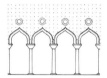

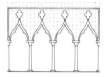

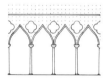

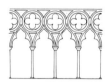

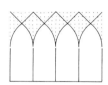

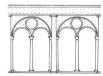

Houses for Everyone

Venice, as we said in a previous chapter, settled the guiding features of her urban form by the twelfth century. Land had been reclaimed from the lagoon, and a number of islands joined together on two sides of a curving waterway, the Grand Canal: this fixed the main mass. (Figs. 15.3, 19.16) The only substantial addition of land until the 1500s came in three areas: in the north, beyond the Ghetto; a triangular bit in the region of the great arsenal; and the extension of the Isola di Spinalonga into a scimitar-shaped strip of land called the Giudecca which, with the island of S. Giorgio at its tip, shielded the city from the long southern lagoon. The sea axis of the Piazza S. Marco ran across to this island and, at the point where the Grand Canal met the much wider "canal" of the Giudecca, there rose the tower of the customs house, the Dogana da Mare, with rows of pitched-roofed warehouses and the monastery of S. Maria della Salute behind it. There were six administrative quarters, and a larger number of neighborhoods, each with its church on an intimate square, announced on the skyline by a tall brick bell tower.

One other public building type figured significantly—the *scuola*. These were centers of confraternities, corporations of artisans, or alien groups that were engaged in charity, social services, and the general welfare of their constituency. The plan was the same for all. On the ground floor of a two-storey rectangular structure one usually found offices, and an altar in front of the door which was on one of the short sides; the upper floor was divided into a meeting hall with a second altar, and a smaller room called the *albergo* where the executive committee deliberated.

The rest of this tightly woven pattern of

water and land was residential. The houses had their principal face toward the water, while the back came to be formalized by the thirteenth century with a court enclosed by a merloned wall. (Fig. 19.17) The robust *pietra di Rovigno* had been in use from the start in noble and upper-class houses and the more notable of public buildings, while rustic brick served the lesser classes, utilitarian structures, and neighborhood churches. There was also a lot of wood in evidence. The external stairs of houses, the terraces at the top, the brackets holding up projecting upper storeys, all were made of wood. The minimal residential unit, from the city's inception onward, was a narrow two-storey house with a shop on the ground floor, or else a vestibule, kitchen, and living room for families who could afford more space. From here a stair, often attached to the back facade, led to the piano nobile of two additional rooms. Other floors would be added in time, though no area quite reached the density of the Ghetto with its houses of six or seven storeys; this, being a restricted quarter, had nowhere to grow but up.

The shared hope was that each family be able to live in its own house. But by the sixteenth century rental blocks and row houses put up through individual bequests, through state initiative or by confraternities and other charitable institutions *amore dei*, accounted for a considerable percentage of the total housing. Even in these there were as many doors and stairs as there were families living within. The usual pattern was to build the rental units around an enclosed *campiello*, which would serve as common court and ensure that daily life would take place mostly outdoors. Alternatively, two blocks of row houses were placed on two alleys running perpendicular to a canal or a main paved embankment street. Toward this access artery the two parallel blocks were united by a bridge-building of some kind. Such marriages across alleys were also favored by fancier houses—one of many instances of the Venetian penchant to have flowing continuities in the built environment echo the fluidity of the traffic net.

Locally the tradition of social housing goes back to the later Middle Ages. But it was in the first half of the sixteenth century

Fig. 19.20 The Venetian window and its transformations through history; elevations. The earliest form is at the top (eleventh–twelfth century); the Gothic form used in the Doge's Palace, Fig. 19.23, is third from the bottom (fourteenth–fifteenth century); and the last in the series, the Renaissance window, can be seen in Fig. 19.21 (sixteenth century).

that an urgent housing shortage loomed in Europe as poor people in the countryside, battered by war, famine, and an economic depression made worse by a much higher birth rate, flocked to the cities in search of jobs, food, and lodgings. Two different remedies came to be applied to those of the urban community who owned no property, a good one-half of the total population in many cities.

One was subsidized housing. Its first instance is the Fuggerei, a walled district of terraced houses, with its own school and church, built by the great banker Jacob Fugger in the 1520s in the suburbs of Augsburg for workers' families. The houses were to be free, with a nominal contribution for maintenance. The beneficiaries, according to the foundation deed, had to be "pious workers and artisans, burghers and inhabitants of the city of Augsburg, who are in need and who are the most deserving." In the same decade, Venice passed a poor law that provided for the construction of temporary shelters to be paid for by a poor tax levied on all citizens and that instructed the Senate to find jobs for those who were able to work. At the same time the state and agencies controlled by it built collective housing for special groups of individuals, like unmarried noble women over thirty, widows with no male offspring, repentant prostitutes, and so on, whose care was considered a matter of civic responsibility. There is a late medieval precedent for this, too—the Beguine houses in the Netherlands and Germany, for example, for single women of the middle and lower classes.

The second approach was more mercenary, and a direct consequence of disposable income. Land and labor were still the chief mainstays of economic institutions, but those with large holdings of capital, individuals or consortia, sought nontraditional outlets. Some of these outlets included the procurement of military, administrative, and judicial offices on the part of the bourgeois nouveau riche; investment in government bonds and annuities, and in shares of joint-stock companies, which come to the fore in the next century as a result of colonial trade; and of course banking. Moreover, the construction of rental real estate now came to be considered a timely venture. In

Venice where rents were extremely high, not only private capital but the state itself entered the business of speculative development. In the large urban concentrations of the Roman empire, apartment dwellings had been a familiar phenomenon. We spoke back then of the *insulae* of ancient Rome and its port, Ostia. This practice now returns, in Paris for example, to remain a fixture of residential arrangements until the present. In Venice, however, speculative houses for the working and middle classes also emerge, and architects begin to supply models for them in their treatises. Sebastiano Serlio (1475–1554), a native of Bologna who worked in Rome and came to Venice after the Sack of 1527, left us a manuscript on housing that includes semi-detached and duplex dwellings for artisans designed for mass production. (Fig. 19.18)

Upper-class and patrician houses had main facades that were cut into by two registers of open arcades framed by towerlike strips. (Fig. 19.19) The ground-level arcade was really a portico for arrivals and departures by gondola, and the unloading and storage of goods. On the next floor a loggia of narrow dainty arches opened the rectangular or L-shaped great hall toward the Grand Canal or a waterway of comparable importance. In more opulent palaces this loggia might be inflated to two storeys. The late antique villa front with a loggia between corner tower-blocks (refer again to the seaward prospect of Diocletian's palace in Split; Fig. 11.18) seems to have enjoyed a continuing vogue in northern Italy and to have been carried into the vernacular of farmhouses. Venice, a product of the early medieval world, might have brought along the type from the mainland and preserved it throughout her deeply conservative building history.

These Venetian loggias were the vehicle of fashion and elegance. We can trace their course from simple, stilted arcades to a pointed variety, which becomes lobed and interlaced in a salute to Islam, and finally to the Classical reinterpretation of the sixteenth and seventeenth centuries. Changes also occur in the accompanying devices over and between the arches—roundels, quadrilobes, and roses. Our drawing sketches a probable sequence—from Byzantine and

Romanesque tastes, through the various stages of Gothic, and from there to the Renaissance. (Fig. 19.20)

The typical Italian palace mass with its central court had no place in a city where land was at a premium and construction often entailed the tedious procedure of driving piles into the waterbed. Rare attempts to reproduce the Renaissance palace facade produced mixed results. The example we illustrate is from the opening decade of the sixteenth century. (Fig. 19.21) It regularizes the fenestration and replaces the spiked roofline with a proper Classical cornice. But you can still see the special treatment of that uninhabitable ground storey, and the traditional division of the facade plane into three vertical segments of which the central one is the widest.

The City as Design at Large

The Piazza S. Marco was the showcase of the republic. The basilica of St. Mark's, the Doge's Palace, and the public space itself received constant and lavish attention. The broad outline of this beloved ensemble had been confirmed by 1400. (Fig. 19.3, 19.22) By then the canal called the Batario that ran west of the campanile had been filled in, and the church of S. Geminiano that straddled it had been taken down and rebuilt at the end of the extended square, across from St. Mark's. This three-sided enclosure, the Piazza S. Marco proper, held the offices of the procurators of the basilica and a thirteenth-century hospice along the south side. Loggias lined all three faces of the enclosure space which, with its long perspective toward St. Mark's, came close to a Roman forum (Pompeii is an example we know; Fig. 9.8) focused toward its temple on the long axis. The moat around the original castle-palace of the doges had also been eliminated long ago, except for the canal that edged the east side. The seaward shelf of land had been widened and extended west, and a strip of buildings in line with the campanile had shaped a shallow square on the east side of the palace, the so-called Piazzetta.

The palace front on this side dates from a revamping of the first half of the fifteenth century. (Fig. 19.23) It is the exemplar of the

Fig. 19.21 Venice, the Palazzo Loredan, later Vendramin-Calergi, on the Grand Canal, begun ca. 1502, Mauro Codussi; main facade. The building is now the winter home of the casino of Venice.

Venetian formula, with the ground-storey portico and the graceful unglazed loggia of the piano nobile. And it was not allowed to change, despite two devastating fires in 1574 and 1577. The interior court with its grand staircase to one side had submitted to Classical taste after an earlier fire, but of a richness to suit the Venetian palate. The most pervasive Renaissance tailoring by far, however, befell the Piazza S. Marco and the Piazzetta beginning in 1537, following the designs of Jacopo Sansovino.

In 1501 a special commission, called The Magistracy of Waters and comprised of three senators and three patricians, took over the direction of all planning activities, conceding leases (gratiae) to private interests to develop parts of the city, but under strict control and approved procedures. At the executive level, the most urgent need was to stabilize the edges of the city-form and bring some order to the internal system of canals and alleys. The old method of ensuring the stability of emersed land had relied on wooden palisades. These were now replaced by stone embankments. At the same time the waterways and streets that ran into the Grand Canal were made perpendicular to its course where it ran more or less straight, and radial where it swerved.

The idea of one primary civic center and a constellation of local subcenters was firmly adhered to. The government rejected a project by Fra Giocondo (1433–1515), inspired by Vitruvius' discussion of the Greek agora, for a unitary design of a commercial quarter at the Rialto. New facilities of a purely functional nature were put up instead, while at the same time the Piazza S. Marco began to be cleared of the more popular businesses that had crowded it with stalls and tables of the money changers. There was to be only one formal square where it had always been, at the point where the Grand Canal met the wider waters of the sea. Two free-standing granite columns at the south end of the Piazzetta framed this distant horizon from within, anchoring the fluid approaches from the outside. This delicate proscenium between the world and the spectacle called Venice bore symbols of her history: the winged lion of St. Mark and the statue of an older patron saint, Theodore, shown atop a crocodile.

Sansovino's challenge was to clarify the design and freshen up the look of a fabulous architectural collection of several centuries at the entrance to the city, including St. Mark's and its campanile, the Doge's Palace, and the heraldic columns. There were two angles to the problem. The Piazza S. Marco and the Piazzetta each had to be reconsidered in terms of the basilica and the palace, respectively, and then ways would have to be found to link the two spaces and make them episodes of the same urban experience. The existing L-shaped concourse allowed each monument to command an open space of different shape, according to its function and axial imperative. The palace had a ground arcade with no central focus. It was a lateral block, a flank really of a building whose principal facade, theoretically, was on the water side. The public court in front of this flank had to be broad and shallow, both to acknowledge its uncentered spread and to funnel traffic toward St. Mark's—to reveal St. Mark's the palace, in effect, pulls back deferentially. This long north-south perspective that began with the heraldic columns was closed off beyond the basilica with a new clocktower over the lofty gateway that formed the entrance to the Merceria, the principal business street that led to the Rialto. The deep, convergent Piazza S. Marco, at right angles to this perspective, set off the glittering church facade and its cluster of bulbous domes, pulling the internal axis of the building far down into the heart of the eponymous city quarter within the south bend of the Grand Canal.

The famous campanile held the corner of the L, across from the junction of church and palace. Here the ceremonial entrance to the ducal apartments began at the Porta della Carta; then the path proceeded along the cloister of the palace courtyard, and up the splendidly decorative Stair of the Giants on the highest landing of which the doges were crowned. The strange position of the

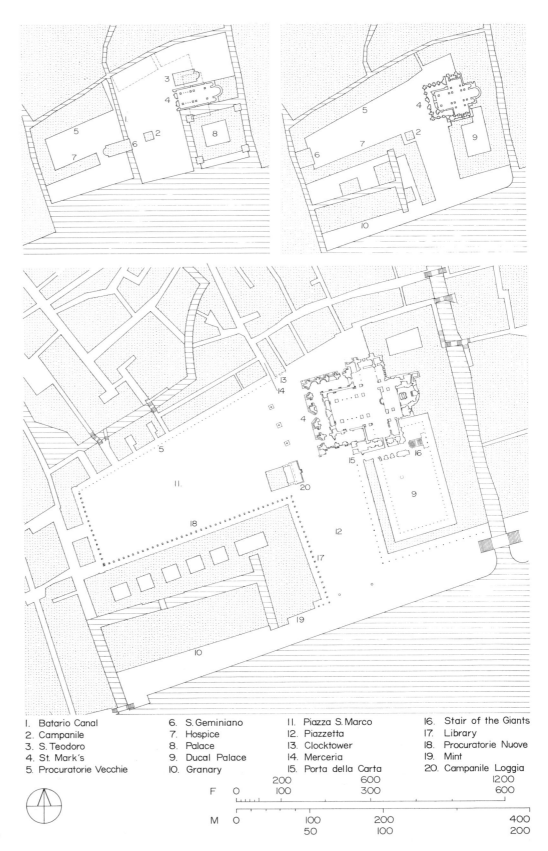

1. Batario Canal	6. S. Geminiano	11. Piazza S. Marco	16. Stair of the Giants
2. Campanile	7. Hospice	12. Piazzetta	17. Library
3. S. Teodoro	8. Palace	13. Clocktower	18. Procuratorie Nuove
4. St. Mark's	9. Ducal Palace	14. Merceria	19. Mint
5. Procuratorie Vecchie	10. Granary	15. Porta della Carta	20. Campanile Loggia

Fig. 19.22 Venice, the Piazza S. Marco, three stages of development; plans. Top left, tenth century; top right, ca. 1400; bottom, ca. 1550.

Fig. 19.23 Venice, the Piazzetta looking north, with the Doge's Palace on the right, the basilica of St. Mark's further back, and the library by Jacopo Sansovino on the left.

campanile precedes the emergence of the L. It was set this far from St. Mark's perhaps in order that it might pull together the basilica, the small church of S. Geminiano, then only a short distance away, and also the palace which the church faced. Sometime before 1400 S. Geminiano had been moved, as we mentioned, and the Piazzetta had materialized. The campanile now found itself joined to both arms of the L, but not quite aligned with either. The porticoed hospice made up the long arm; the shorter arm facing the palace was defined by several nondescript buildings, among them a bakery.

This is what Sansovino had to work with. He began by tearing down the bakery and its adjacencies, and building a new library for St. Mark's with a unified two-storey facade that emphasized a horizontal spread. (Fig. 19.23) The ground storey was designed as a portico; the upper contained the reading room and the stacks. The language of this architecture is a rich version of the mature Renaissance, but the elevation is clearly meant to echo the facade of the Doge's Palace across the way. From the air, the long library block shows two superimposed colonnades. Close up these prove to be a main order of engaged columns between which swing arches—from lower piers in the case of the ground storey, in the manner of the theater of Marcellus in Rome, and from small Ionic columns in the case of the upper window arches. Between these columns and the engaged main order are flat strips crowned by bits of entablature. (Fig. 19.25) If the panels were open, this three-part arched window would be called a Palladian (or Serlian) window—a

Fig. 19.24 Venice, the Piazza S. Marco looking southwest, with the campanile in the foreground (no. 20 in Fig. 19.22) and the library and the Procuratie Nuove (nos. 17 and 18 in Fig. 19.22) on the left side. A porch of the basilica of St. Mark's frames the view on the right.

motif, probably invented by Bramante at the turn of the century, that will enjoy a great vogue abroad because of Palladio's extensive use of it.

The library stopped about 5 meters (16.5 feet) short of the campanile. The three-bay end facing the campanile determined the design of the adjacent Procuratie Nuove, which soon replaced the medieval hospice. The facade of this building was not supported on the old foundations, but was set back in a straight line. Thereby the Piazza S. Marco was widened by about 70 meters (230 feet) on the east side and 50 (164 feet) on the west. This was enough to situate the basilica in the center of the east side of the square, whereas previously it favored the south corner. The campanile, a freestanding monument now, lined up with the critical southwest corner of the L, which almost formed a right angle. A lovely new loggia on the east face oriented it toward the junction of church and palace, on axis with the Porta della Carta. (Fig. 19.24) Finally, a sturdy mint went up next to the library on the water side.

But our description has left out the most vital element of this urban masterpiece: its pageantry. Venice was addicted to public theater. Her painters, celebrated across the breadth of Christendom and beyond, loved to dwell on, with the finest detail, the physical appearance of their city, caught in the shimmer of its watery realm and the velvet glow of its light. They show up the places and the people, the fanfare, the feasts; with the excuse of some religious or historical episode, each paints the city of his own day, the buildings and costumes, all of which is a great help to the modern scholar. It is from Gentile Bellini's painting of the Corpus Domini procession that we learn what the Piazza S. Marco looked like just before Sansovino's intervention. (Fig. 19.26) Dozens of sketches and tableaux of the seventeenth, and especially the eighteenth, century depict the later appearance of the grand complex from all sides and, more important, in daily and festive use. (Fig. 19.3) To see Canaletto's view of the doge setting out from the quai of St. Mark's in a golden ship on Ascension Day, to reenact in the open waters the ancient ritual marriage of Venice to the sea, is to grant once again an old but para-

Fig. 19.25 Venice, Piazza S. Marco, library, begun 1536, Jacopo Sansovino; detail of exterior.

mount truth. No architect, however great, can design a life for the forms he creates. No architecture is grasped without knowledge of the social patterns it has contained.

Palladio in Town and Country
If Sansovino had the honor of orchestrating the ceremonial center of Venice, it fell to Palladio in the second half of the century to transform the city's skyline and to

establish visual responses between the core and the outlying landmass of the Giudecca and the island of S. Giorgio. The occasion was the construction of a pair of churches on this outer landmass, which, along with a third church built one hundred years later in place of the old S. Maria della Salute, did for Venice what Brunelleschi's dome had done for Florence at the start of the Renaissance. Palladio's churches, too, depend on the ability of a dome, properly

476

Fig. 19.26 Gentile Bellini, *Corpus Domini Procession in Piazza San Marco*, 1496. (Accademia, Venice) This view shows the Piazza before it was redesigned by Sansovino (see Fig. 19.22, plan at top right). We are looking west toward the facade of St. Mark's, with the medieval hospice to our right (no. 7 in Fig. 19.22), the campanile and the Doge's Palace immediately behind it, and the Procuratie Vecchie to our left.

scaled and mounted, to confederate urban fragments or give to urban sprawl a sense of purpose and unity. In the Middle Ages the low, flat cityscape afloat in its lagoon was heralded to incoming ships by its many brick church towers, the campanile of St. Mark's supreme among them. Looking out across the open waters which their fleet of galleons plied, the Venetians had no prominent landmark to anchor the distant view. Palladio's churches, domed and with facades of white Istrian stone, stake a middle ground between the city and the far horizon that works from both sides.

These churches—Il Redentore ("Redeemer") built by the Senate as a thanksgiving after the terrible plague of 1575–76 and S. Giorgio Maggiore, on the island of that name, built for the Benedictines—continue Italian efforts to combine a spacious nave with adequate side chapels and a centralized tribune under a great dome. (Fig. 19.27) This had been the Renaissance compromise between the theoretical perfection of the central plan and the dictates of liturgical space. But for Palladio the churches were

also attempts to arrive at a modern civic temple. He experimented to this end with a new kind of interior (we spoke above of the creamy tone that prevailed), and with the enduring problem of rehabilitating the Roman temple front as a church facade. The Redentore interior is shown in Fig. 19.12; here we find the narrowing of the nave at the start of the domed bay and the open screen of columns that forms a half-circle behind the main altar, through which we see the light and hear the sounds from the choir. This screen and all the pairs of engaged columns that hold up the main vaults are kept at the same height and are united by a continuous entablature. Against this major order, a flatter minor order is used exclusively for the side chapels. The semicircular windows are also a Palladian trademark; they are referred to as "thermal" windows because we find them in late Roman buildings, especially the imperial baths.

The facade of Il Redentore shows off Palladio's virtuoso formalism. (Fig. 19.28) It is built up of several different planes or levels of relief, interlocking two separate tem-

ple fronts. The foremost one, corresponding to the major order within, has its pediment set against a rectangular attic, an idea that ultimately comes from the Pantheon. A second temple front, lower and broader, shows through on the two sides, and so accounts for the aisles behind. The buttresses for the nave's barrel vault appear as yet another set of auxiliary half-pediments just behind and below the attic. The whole is raised on a high podium that projects outward along the width of the nave, with a staircase in front of it. The approach, then, is strongly frontal, as in most of Palladio's buildings, and the intricate visual construct of the facade falls into place as we look at it from some distance away. This axiality was made tangible on the feast of the Redeemer, the third Sunday of July, when a causeway would be built across the water on barges, so that the procession of dignitaries could reach the votive monument head on.

The Venetian churches appear somewhat late in Palladio's career. He had begun in mid-century with a new town hall for Vicenza—actually an encasing of the medieval town hall in a two-storied loggia, very reminiscent of Sansovino's library in Venice—and then had gone on to work for wealthy Vicentine patrons on villas and urban palaces.

Vicenza was a tributary of Venice. It had a palace tradition of its own—a block with a ground-storey loggia through which street traffic was allowed to pass, and no interior court. Palladio, an admirer of such medieval porticoes along city streets, gives us a humanist rendition of the theme in the beautiful Palazzo Chiericati (1549–57). (Fig. 19.29) The Doric of the ground-storey loggia and the Ionic of the main floor, which is divided into a central windowed tract and two flanking loggia wings, are of great purity. The loggia also evoked a Classical precedent, for it was originally planned to be continued around four sides of a formal square, in the manner of a Roman forum.

The plan is studiously integrated. (Fig. 19.30) A central axis that runs through the double-apsed entrance hall is attended by two parallel axes that organize the wings. Cross-axes are established through the loggia, through the hall and the adjacent large rooms, and again for the staircases and landings at the back. All of these axes pass through doorways that align and end in windows and fireplaces.

In addition to pulling the plan together with these uninterrupted cross-vistas, the units are locked into each other proportionately. In the wings, the rooms method-ically graduate in size. The front room measures 30 by 18 feet, to use Palladio's unit—or 9 by 5.5 meters. The room behind it retains the depth and reduces the width to the same number. The back room re-tains this latter width, but cuts down the depth to 12 feet (3.65 meters). These num-bers are all multiples of 6 and are in ratios known to correspond to musical harmon-ies which were introduced into architec-ture in some system or other since the Middle Ages. (We touched on this subject in our discussion of Cluny.) Palladio's pro-portions go beyond all precedent in being

Fig. 19.27 Venice, the church of Il Redentore (no. 10 in Fig. 19.16), 1576–80, Andrea Palladio. Left to right: section, ground plan, and site plan.

integrated throughout the building, relating one room to the next, the plan to its elevations, the exterior and the interior.

The Chiericati is far from canonical for Palladio's palaces. In the Palazzo Thiene you will find the full rusticated swagger of Mannerism as we encountered it in Giulio Romano's Mantua. The Palazzo Valmarana (1565–71) uses huge pilasters which run through the floors, from a high podium to the cornice line. (Fig. 19.31) The inspiration, as we will see in the next chapter, is Michelangelo, although Alberti's S. Andrea had started the trend. (Figs. 17.12, 20.9) In the end bays this giant order is abandoned, making it easier to relate the palace to less monumental buildings on either side. The skyline was to be picked out with statues over all the pilasters, a favorite device of Palladio's.

All of these Vicentine palaces are unfinished. The belated mid-century zeal of the noble families to proclaim their humanist credentials and their public status architecturally was hampered by reality. A subject city, at the forefront of land wars against the Venetian republic and a meeting ground of Protestant reformers in Italy, Vicenza's fortunes waxed and waned fitfully. So of the ten or so palaces Palladio undertook here, he rarely got much done beyond the facade. We have to learn of his intentions from the *Four Books*, which is where the rest of the world also went for ideas long after his death.

The villas had another rationale. The events of the first half of the sixteenth century had forced the maritime republic and its allies to reassess their interests. Changing patterns of world trade and the inflationary impact of American gold and silver were straining national prosperity. Industry, especially that of cloth, and agriculture began to have a fresh appeal to the moneyed class seeking stable investment. The state, which had never had trouble in the past procuring its grain supplies, could no longer count on its Adriatic sources to feed a vastly swollen population in excess of 150,000. Necessity and capitalist reason pointed to the terra firma. The task of turning this malarial marshland into a profitable enterprise on a large scale was tremendous. The state took the initiative. It financed land reclamation projects, distributed unused lands among investors who would undertake to cultivate them, and coordinated the private efforts of individual landowners and investment companies. The noble families, long enticed by the heady gains of trade and banking, returned to their estates for a purposeful stay.

For this new race of gentlemen farmers, Palladio invented an architecture that would at once recognize their breeding and function properly as a business establishment. The Palladian villa is therefore not at all like the Renaissance villa elsewhere in Italy. The

Fig. 19.28 Venice, Il Redentore; view from the north.

distinction was always drawn, by Alberti for example, between farms for profit and villas for pleasure, between *negotium* and *otium*. In Florence much was made of balancing the two, but the emphasis was on the contemplative life, on refuge from the grubby, grueling city days. Feudal lords in the late Middle Ages had already started the fashion of hunting lodges and parks. This became an added incentive for *villeggiatura*, and it infected the princes of the Church even though hunting was prohibited to the clergy by canon law. It was in fact papal dignitaries who most enflamed the villa craze. From June to October when the court in Rome was in recess, the cardinals would retire to their superb country estates, designed in emulation of ancient villas and distinguished by rigorously tamed landscape settings and formal gardens.

In the Veneto, it is another story altogether. Not only does Palladio leave nature alone, he brings utilitarian functions into the great house. The long wings that spread out from the main block have no more exalted aim than to harbor animals and farm equipment. The attics serve for grain storage. Fields and orchards are roundabout, the master in residence all year supervising in person the cultivation of his holdings. That is why the plain stucco exteriors, the clean, sharp-edged cubic masses, are as appropriate to the program as are the one- or two-storey porches of the main block and the sometimes lavishly decorated halls. With Palladio the Classical language ranges within the same building program from the aristocratic to the purely utilitarian; in Ferrara Rossetti accomplishes a similar task by democratizing this language at the urban scale. This is a more perspicacious view of Greco-Roman antiquity. As practitioners in ancient Rome could drop the canonical orders when the program was one of utility, so did Palladio. As they were willing, especially in the late imperial era, to abstract the Classical panoply into a system of spare walls and openings even in prestigious buildings (remember the audience hall of the palace at Trier; Fig. 11.12), so was he.

Fig. 19.29 Vicenza (Italy), the Palazzo Chiericati, 1549–57, Andrea Palladio; exterior from the east.

Fig. 19.30 Plan, from the architect's *Four Books*. The measurements are in *palmi*, equal to a span, or nine inches.

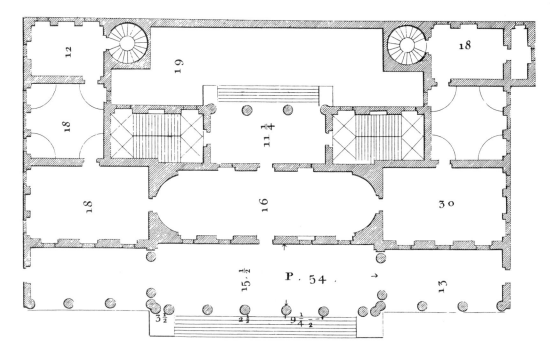

Fig. 19.31 Vicenza, the Palazzo Valmarana, 1565–71, Andrea Palladio; main facade.

Fig. 19.32 Maser (Italy), the Villa Barbaro, 1550s; main prospect.

Fig. 19.33 Vicenza, the Villa Rotonda (Villa Capra), 1560s, Andrea Palladio.

Fig. 19.34a Piombino Dese (Italy), the Villa Cornaro, 1551–53, Andrea Palladio.

A random look at the twenty or so surviving villas will once again bring to mind the versatility of Palladian design. They all have in common a porch in the form of a pedimented temple front, an odd sort of entrance for a house. But Palladio believed that temples and other public buildings of antiquity had probably borrowed this feature from residential architecture. At any rate, he liked the idea because it "added very much to the grandeur and magnificence of the work," and because the pediment came in handy to display the patron's coat of arms.

One major type is represented by the Villa Barbaro at Maser (1550s). (Fig. 19.32) Here the temple front is contained within the central block which has one major storey only. From it, arcaded (or colonnaded) wings extend to small side pavilions which house farming functions. In one case, the Villa Badoer, the wings are curved. The approach is always axial, down an allée, and as in a Classical atrium house, the main hall is in the middle of the plan, just behind the porch, surrounded by lesser rooms. In another type, the porch is placed on a high podium and is reached by stairs from the sides. There are no wings. When the main block is two storeys high, the porch is also doubled. The most famous of the villas has a temple front on each one of the four sides, and a dome over the main hall. This Villa Rotonda (1560s), on the outskirts of Vicenza, was for once not the center of a working estate, but a genuine retreat. (Fig. 19.33) It sits on a gentle hilltop, "and because it enjoys the most lovely views on all sides," Palladio wrote of it, "some screened, others more distant, and others reaching the horizon, loggias were made on each face."

Why does it look so familiar? Why indeed do most Palladian villas not strain American eyes in the way that Alberti or

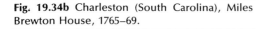

Fig. 19.34b Charleston (South Carolina), Miles Brewton House, 1765–69.

Giulio Romano do? Because country gentlemen of our own South in the eighteenth century found Palladian imagery compatible and had his book to work from. The Villa Rotonda we know as Jefferson's Monticello; the curved arcaded wings of Mount Vernon nod toward the Villa Badoer; the two-storey, pedimented portico of Drayton Hall or the Charleston house of Miles Brewton is American cousin of the Villa Cornaro in Piombino Dese, about as far as one can think to go from South Carolina. (Fig. 19.34)

But the route from Italy to South Carolina was not a direct one, for Palladio had already been domesticated in rural England by the nobility and the lesser gentry who had their own Monticellos and Drayton Halls. To a gentleman of the colonial South with money and cultural pretensions, these villas were a natural model. And there were ways to make it his own, as his black slave labor set it apart economically from English manors or the elegant farms of the Veneto.

Still, what was it about Palladio that made him such a hit in these countries? It is not difficult to say. England and northern Europe opened themselves very late to the full influx of the Renaissance. By then the first phases of Italian classicism looked dated. In the second half of the sixteenth century, two architects had the makings of a universal cult: Michelangelo, whom we will soon review properly, and Palladio. The first proved too moody, too passionate for northern tastes, as did the Baroque of the seventeenth century that leaned so heavily on his genius. This rich Roman tradition appealed to the Catholic countries. For the Protestant world the clean, rational forms of Palladio were far more sympathetic. His adherence to Classical precepts was never fanatically purist. He recognized that erudition must be accessible and responsive to incidents of site, program, and resources. And then there is the fact that Palladio *wanted* to have a wide following. His illustrated treatise made it easy to export his design. But it needs to be said with some force that it was because this design had a fundamental simplicity and clarity about it that so many later architects could translate his intentions within their local context. One doubts that a working book by Michelangelo would have been enough to give him that kind of popularity. Between passion and common sense, a borrowing architect is wise to choose the latter. Nothing is more personal in architecture, less assimilable, than expressive intensity.

Further Reading

J. Ackerman, *Palladio* (Harmondsworth and Baltimore: Penguin, 1966).

M. Brion, *Venice,* trans. N. Mann (New York: Crown, 1962).

G. Goodwin, *A History of Ottoman Architecture* (Baltimore: Johns Hopkins University Press, 1971).

L. Heydenreich and W. Lotz, *Architecture in Italy, 1400 to 1600* (Harmondsworth and Baltimore: Penguin, 1974).

D. Howard, *The Architectural History of Venice* (London: Batsford, 1980).

G. Masson, *Italian Villas and Palaces* (London: Thames and Hudson, 1966).

E. Muir, *Civic Ritual in Renaissance Venice* (Princeton: Princeton University Press, 1981).

G. Necipoglu, *Architecture, Ceremonial, and Power: The Topkapi Palace in the Fifteenth and Sixteenth Centuries* (Cambridge, Mass.: MIT Press, 1993).

D. T. Rice and W. Swann, *Constantinople: Byzantium-Istanbul* (London: Elek, 1965).

A. Stratton, *Sinan* (New York: Scribner, 1972).

R. Tavernor, *Palladio and Palladianism* (New York: Thames and Hudson, 1991).

U. Vogt-Goknil, *Living Architecture: Ottoman* (London: Oldbourne, 1966).

Rome (Italy), St. Peter's; detail of the throne of St. Peter,
cathedra Petri, 1657–66, Gian Lorenzo Bernini.

20

THE POPES AS PLANNERS: ROME, 1450–1650

We define the See of the Holy Apostle and the Roman pope to hold primacy in all the world, and the pope to be the successor of St. Peter, the Prince of the Apostles, and the true Vicar of Christ and head of the universal church and father and teacher of all Christians.

These words from the papal bull *Laetentur Coeli* of 6 July 1439 would seem to recapitulate the stock claims of the papacy. The time of their utterance, however, and the insistence on the priestly sway of the Bishop of Rome make them a manifesto of great importance, as prophetic for Renaissance history as the *Donations of Constantine* was for the Middle Ages. In that forged document of the eighth century, the popes had sought to build a legal case for their inheritance of the authority and privileges of the Roman emperors in the West, and therefore the right to confer office upon rulers chosen by the popes to defend the Roman cause. The stress of temporal power embroiled the papacy in debilitating contests abroad and on the home front. By the end of the Middle Ages the prestige of this redoubtable institution, badly bruised and now installed on French soil, slipped almost beyond deliverance. Rome herself was near-deserted. Most of the area within the ancient city walls had the look of backwoods country in which, preposterously, hulking piles of tremendous broken monuments from an irredeemable time stood side by side with more recent, far from beggarly, buildings of Christian worship. Petrarch described this one-time world capital as "a matron with the dignity of age

but with her grey locks dishevelled, her garments rent, and her face overspread with the pallor of misery." (Fig. 20.1)

Yet this was not to be the end. The popes returned, the citizenry began to pick up the pieces, life surged in the Tiber bend and around the great pilgrimage centers at the frazzled edges of the built-up core and in the desolate tracts within and outside the walls of Aurelian. Papal power and its inveterate seat stood poised for a slow but spectacular recovery. And the bull of 1439 declared that the basis of this recovery was to be the pastoral preeminence of the bishop of Rome in the Christian commonwealth. Transferring the papal government from the Lateran, that imperially sponsored headquarters of the Holy See, to the Vatican, the resting place of Peter, dramatized the shift.

With the fall of Constantinople in 1453, the only venerable contestant of Roman primacy, the Greek patriarch, retired into impotence. The popes now concentrated their struggles against defiance in the ranks and the reformist ferment of the north. It would hardly be true to suggest that they were satisfied with the rewards of spiritual leadership alone. But the tactical switch from blatant imperialism to priestly power is unmistakable. This is what lends perspective to the bitter church councils and the militancy of the Counter-Reformation. And it helps us to understand the long and dazzling campaign to make the basilica of St. Peter's and the adjacent palace the peerless queen of Christian courts—a cam-

paign launched by Pope Nicholas V in the 1450s, as we saw, and pursued almost without pause until the 1650s when Bernini's great Piazza was completed. (Fig. 20.2)

Making the City Whole

But first there was the city. Since the popular uprising of 1144, a municipal administration ensconced on the Capitoline had conducted the affairs of the townspeople, often in open conflict with papal interests. Rome had been a jumble of jurisdictions—feudal, civic, and papal. This carried over physically in the profusion of adversary clusters that rent apart the urban fabric. The noble families were divided in their loyalties, the commune fought to prevail over the conniving barons, and the popes tirelessly worked to regain the control they were forced to relinquish in the twelfth century at the height of the libertarian revolution in Europe. Now it was time to refashion the city of whole cloth, to have one rule, one order. With the nobles brought to heel and communal assertiveness in retreat, the Vatican took over the running of the city in all but name.

The office of planning commissioners, the *maestri di strada*, filled since the thirteenth century by the commune, became an adjunct of the Apostolic Chamber during the fifteenth. In a papal bull of 1480 it was given powers to expropriate and demolish private property, for the public good and the construction of important religious or civic

Fig. 20.1 Rome represented in a miniature of 1447 for an illustrated manuscript, *Dittamondo,* a poem of the mid-fourteenth century by Fazio degli Uberti. (Bibliothèque Nationale, Paris) Rome is shown as an old woman seated next to the Colosseum. She is listening to the poet Fazio who stands outside the city walls, next to the Roman geographer of the third–fourth century, Caius Julius Solinus. North is at the bottom of the miniature where, on the right-hand side, the Castel Sant'Angelo is depicted. The circular building to the left of that, on the other side of the Tiber, is the Pantheon.

buildings. In the early 1500s the financing of new streets and the alignment and widening of old ones came to be derived from a Church-imposed improvement tax exacted from the property owners. When something like a building code was finally drawn up in 1574, it was promulgated as a papal bull. Even the replanning of the municipal center on the Capitoline from the 1530s onward following the designs of Michelangelo was in essence a papal undertaking.

Fig. 20.2 Rome, the Piazza S. Pietro during a papal blessing; aerial view looking southwest.

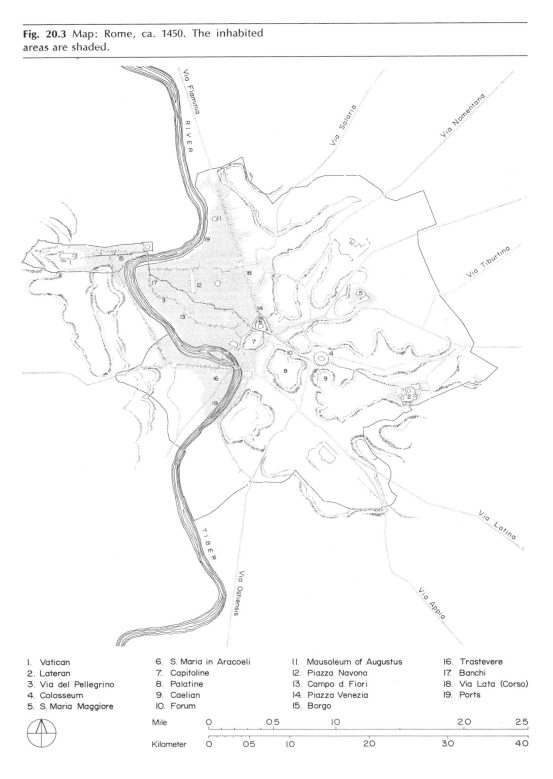

Fig. 20.3 Map: Rome, ca. 1450. The inhabited areas are shaded.

1. Vatican
2. Lateran
3. Via del Pellegrino
4. Colosseum
5. S. Maria Maggiore
6. S. Maria in Aracoeli
7. Capitoline
8. Palatine
9. Caelian
10. Forum
11. Mausoleum of Augustus
12. Piazza Navona
13. Campo d. Fiori
14. Piazza Venezia
15. Borgo
16. Trastevere
17. Banchi
18. Via Lata (Corso)
19. Ports

Mile	0	0.5	1.0	2.0	2.5
Kilometer	0	0.5 1.0	2.0	3.0	4.0

The Reorganization of Old Quarters

In the intention to modernize the city, three principal aims were paramount. The medieval core needed to be aired out and improved, and the contemporary political message of the Church triumphant stamped upon it. New residential areas had to be opened up for a briskly growing population. And lastly, ways had to be found to link widely scattered foci—especially the great basilicas and the quarters that had mushroomed around them—with each other and with the core city.

The limits of the built up area at the time of Nicholas V were set by the river and the straight avenue from the north, the ancient Via Flaminia/Lata now called the Corso, which stopped short at the Capitoline. (Fig. 20.3) South and east of here stretched the graveyard of imperial Rome—the Forum, the Colosseum, the Palatine, the baths. There was little by way of residential neighborhoods past the mausoleum of Augustus on the west side of the Corso, and even less on the east side where the waterless hills climbed toward the walls.

On the right bank two communities, separately walled, were divided by a strip of country—Trastevere and the Borgo. Trastevere was the older by far and was linked to the main town only via the ancient island bridges, at least until 1474 when further upstream the Ponte Sisto was carried across on the piers of yet another ancient bridge. With it, Trastevere was brought closer to the main markets: the produce and livestock market at Campo de' Fiori and the general market, which took place at the foot of the Capitoline in the Middle Ages but was moved in 1478 to Piazza Navona, the open field where Domitian's stadium had been in antiquity.

The Borgo had had its start in the early Middle Ages, you will remember, as a district of aliens attached to St. Peter's. Its bridge, Ponte Sant' Angelo, spanned the river between the fortress of Castel Sant' Angelo (the mausoleum of Emperor Hadrian) and a small square on the left bank where several important streets met. One among them, the Via Papale, ran from the square to the foot of the Capitoline, and then through the ruins of the Roman Forum and past the Colosseum, through the abandonment of the Caelian hill, all the way

487

to the Lateran. This was the processional route of the Middle Ages. New popes traversed it during ceremonies of their installation, and also rulers from the north on the occasion of being crowned emperor at St. Peter's. The urban segment of the route was the closest thing to a spine medieval Rome possessed.

The most important interventions in the old city during the Renaissance took place at the two ends of this spine. At the east end the Palazzo Venezia, built in the mid-fifteenth century below the north slope of the Capitoline, was the earliest of Renaissance palaces in Rome. Michelangelo's Campidoglio, a century later, carried the Via Papale up this hill by a noble stair-ramp, and lowered it again toward the Forum on either side of the Palace of the Senators. At the Tiber end was a knotted district of extreme congestion. Pilgrims moving toward St. Peter's or away from it into the city crowded the Ponte Sant' Angelo, disastrously during the crush of jubilee years. Here in this district northern Italian, mostly Tuscan, and foreign bankers who did business with the papal court had their establishments. Hence its name, Banchi.

It was under Julius II (1503–13) first, at the opening years of the sixteenth century, that a bold plan was put into effect to redevelop Banchi. Julius' thinking was quite venturesome. He proposed, to begin with, the replacement of St. Peter's with a new church and a drastic overhaul of the Vatican. His ideas for Banchi went beyond simple decongestion. They fitted into his grand scheme for a coordinated and magnificent rehousing of papal government that overshadowed the humanist dream of his predecessor Nicholas V. A new bridge a short way downstream from Ponte Sant' Angelo was to be continued by a straight street parallel to the river, the Via Giulia, running due south until it met the Ponte Sisto. (Fig. 20.4) Correspondingly, a street on the right bank would link the Borgo with Trastevere

across open country. The Via Giulia was envisioned as a wholly new creation. Designed by Bramante, it ran counter to the existing street net and was flanked by individual blocks of official buildings and palaces subject to uniform height limitations. Chief among them was the Palace of Justice (no. 10 in Fig. 20.4). It would bring under one roof the most critical secular institution of the papacy, the courts of law, agencies of which were dispersed throughout the Vatican and in prelates' palaces on the left bank. A large formal square in front of this building was to extend all the way to one of these palaces some distance to the

east, along the Via Papale. This immense redevelopment project, planted in the flank of the commercial center, represented a papal attempt to cross over into the administrative jurisdiction of the city, stabilize and unite the legal apparatus of the Church, and challenge the competence of the commune's own tribunals. The Palace of Justice, with its four corner towers and central bell tower, intentionally took after the Palace of the Senators on the Capitoline.

The audacious initiative was dropped after Julius' death. The commune would soon be allowed to have its own glorious showpiece on the Capitoline, which we will ex-

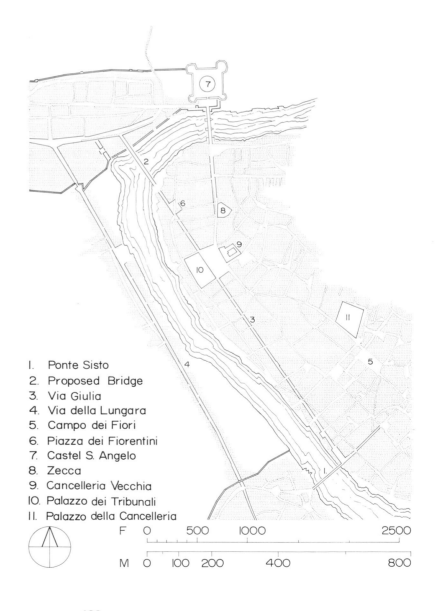

1. Ponte Sisto
2. Proposed Bridge
3. Via Giulia
4. Via della Lungara
5. Campo dei Fiori
6. Piazza dei Fiorentini
7. Castel S. Angelo
8. Zecca
9. Cancelleria Vecchia
10. Palazzo dei Tribunali
11. Palazzo della Cancelleria

Fig. 20.4 Rome, the project of Pope Julius II (1503–13) for the left bank of the Tiber, across from the Borgo; general plan. The architect in charge was Donato Bramante.

Fig. 20.5 Map: Rome ca. 1585, showing major urban interventions undertaken by the popes of the

sixteenth century, from Julius II to Gregory XIII (1572–85).

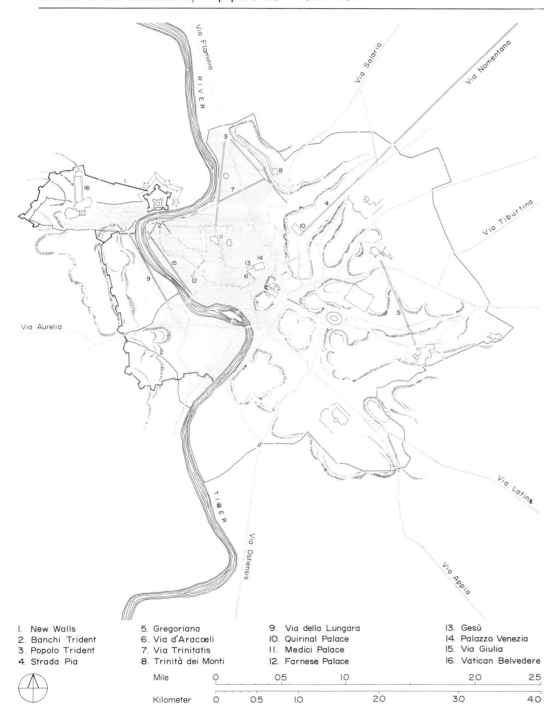

1. New Walls
2. Banchi Trident
3. Popolo Trident
4. Strada Pia
5. Gregoriana
6. Via d'Aracœli
7. Via Trinitatis
8. Trinità dei Monti
9. Via della Lungara
10. Quirinal Palace
11. Medici Palace
12. Farnese Palace
13. Gesù
14. Palazzo Venezia
15. Via Giulia
16. Vatican Belvedere

Mile	0	0.5	1.0		2.0	2.5

Kilometer	0	0.5	1.0	2.0	3.0	4.0

amine shortly. But by then the papal stranglehold on the city was so effective, the communal offices so clearly the secular branch of the Vatican, that the urban distribution could afford to look symbolically bicameral.

Julius' successor, Leo X (1513–21), was a Florentine. To honor his compatriots, who were the dominant element of the Banchi district, he started for them a national church, dedicated to their patron saint John the Baptist, at the upper end of Via Giulia. With Julius' axial bridge unrealized, the new church of S. Giovanni dei Fiorentini was connected to the Ponte Sant' Angelo by a straight line in the 1530s. This short street formed an acute angle with the start of the Via Papale. The purely aesthetic decision to echo this angle on the other side by means of another short street gave shape to a novel urban formula, the trivium, repeated in these same years on a much larger scale at the north entrance to the city, the Piazza del Popolo. (Fig. 20.5)

A trivium is the meeting of three radial streets at a piazza, or if you like, their divergence from one. The central prong is axial, and the side ones run in equal or near-equal acute relationship to it. This formal device is affiliated with Renaissance experiments in radial urbanism, but is less totalitarian and more flexible. It has an enormous potential to concentrate an urban area of variable size on a crucial rallying point. There is no precedent for the trivium in antiquity or the Middle Ages, the closest analogy being more or less regular Y intersections. Nicholas V's proposed scheme for the Borgo (see above, page 409) may have been the first theoretical formulation of the concept in the Renaissance. Once applied at Banchi and Piazza del Popolo, it became popular in the later sixteenth and the seventeenth centuries and spread far beyond Rome. (Figs. 21.29, 23.18)

As head of an absolutist regime, the pope decided how much was to be spent on public buildings and for what particular projects. The fate of unfinished work was in his hands. By and large each incumbent built on the efforts of his predecessors: the city was coaxed into shape by piecemeal adjustments based on earlier initiatives. It was taken as a global imperative to make livable and resplendent the city that Sixtus

V (1585–90) was to call "the home of the Christian religion," and most pontiffs agreed with his predecessor Gregory XIII that "Building too is a form of charity." But individual policies, personalities, family interests, all played a part. The newly elected pope often took his property within the city as the focus of his planning activities. The family palace was enlarged, a piazza carved in front of it, a new road directed on it or an old one ameliorated. The Venetian Pope Paul II (1464–71) systematized the Corso because it ran axially toward his palace, the Palazzo Venezia. Leo X, a Medici, started the arm of the Popolo trivium west of the Corso because it could be made to link up in a straight line with the family palace in the thick of town, between Piazza Navona and the Pantheon. The accession of a Farnese cardinal changed the scope of the Palazzo Farnese, gave the city its first perfect Renaissance square, and saw this monumental interlude connected through conscious design solutions with the Campo de' Fiori in front of it, the Via Giulia behind it, and by means of a bridge, with the family's villa on the opposite bank.

The palaces of the cardinals were themselves nodes of urban order. An incentive to invest heavily in them was the law of the 1470s that exempted immovable property of officials who died while serving at the Roman court from being appropriated into the papal fisc, as was the continuing custom for movable property. Both prelates and other prominent members of the nobility or the monied aristocracy built their palaces along important arteries, old ones like the Via Papale and the Corso and newly planned streets like the Via Giulia. This made economic and ceremonial sense.

The model was the Florentine palace of the fifteenth century—now refined, aggrandized, and given fuller, more plastic detailing. (Figs. 20.6, 16.4) The preexisting medieval cluster of family holdings would be razed for the purpose, or grouped into two or three decorous structures, separate but adjacent. Some "palaces" were still rustic conglomerates behind a polite front; they included stables, barns, and laborers' quarters. We must keep in mind the lingering country flavor of papal Rome, the strange mix of the monumental and the bucolic in its age of grandeur. Cows grazed

Fig. 20.6 Rome, the Palazzo Farnese, 1530–89, Antonio da Sangallo the Younger and Michelangelo; in an early eighteenth-century view by Jan Goerée.

in the Roman Forum, herds of buffalo were kept on the Tiber island to tow boats along the southern port road, and the stockbreeders had the strongest guild in the city.

The modern palace blocks, here as elsewhere in Italy, directly countered the dwelling compounds of the late Middle Ages with their irregular courtyards, gardens, and view towers. By their bulk and regular shape these palaces brought a monumental scale to their neighborhoods and helped to generate orderly streets, squares, and orthogonal city blocks. The four-square mass was the enemy of winding streets; the cornices and regimented storeys the very opposite of picturesque groupings and casual facades. But we should not make these buildings sound more dogmatic than they actually were. They were insinuative and adaptable. They catered to standardized design and production. Windows and doors served as a kind of additive module: it was therefore not essential to fix forever either the height or the width of the palace before construc-

tion began. The uniform bays and binding cornices would cancel out irregularities of plot or street line. The facades were outgoing. A family with a pope in its recent history would invariably have a presentation balcony above the main entrance, benches for staff and passersby would be incorporated at the base of the facade, and the public use of the piazzas with their fountains would not be restricted.

As active concerns, the palaces gave work and housing to many in the lower classes. These were the "mouths" of the owner, and a cardinal of the rank of a Farnese was likely to have two or three hundred such mouths, as census records show us. They lived in the attic and basement, and spent most of their working hours on the ground floor which was taken up by offices, stables, and kitchens. Some of the street-front space might be rented out as dwelling rooms or shops. The piano nobile held large ceremonial rooms and the master bedrooms. On the third floor were guest suites, and quarters for lesser members of the family and the

Fig. 20.7 Rome, the Campidoglio; view ca. 1554–63 by an anonymous artist. The facade of the Palace of the Senators, directly ahead, is shown already undergoing changes according to Michelangelo's scheme, but nothing much else has been accomplished. The palace on the right is the medieval structure that will form the core of the Palazzo dei Conservatori. The approach from the city is still a mound of earth with steep footpaths, soon to be replaced by Michelangelo's great stair-ramp, the Cordonata. (Compare with Fig. 20.9a.)

quarters, carve and define squares in front and sometimes also in the rear of the new establishment, and build rental blocks at the periphery of these squares or on adjacent streets as an investment. Funds permitting, this institutional takeover of medieval neighborhoods would not stop until the group came up against an equally powerful interest like a noble family, another religious order, or elements of the papal bureaucracy.

Campidoglio

In 1536 Emperor Charles V resolved to visit Rome on his way back from a victorious campaign against the Turks in Tunisia. Charles was to arrive like conquering Roman generals of old along the Via Appia, march up the ancient Via Triumphalis until the Colosseum, cross the length of the Forum to the Piazza Venezia, and then by means of the Via Papale he would lead his splendid parade through the inhabited parts of the city to the Ponte Sant' Angelo and from there to St. Peter's. The sitting pope, Paul III (1534–49), ordered the hasty preparation of this three-kilometer long processional route within the walls. In fifteen weeks the "imperial avenue" was cleared, leveled, paved in parts, decorated, and spanned with mock triumphal arches.

At one point, it was decided that the imperial cortège should pass through the civic center on the Capitoline, ascending from the Forum and regaining the Papale south of the Palazzo Venezia. (Fig. 20.7) The site was in a deplorable state. The Palace of the Senators, wrapped about the ancient Tabularium, overlooked the unpaved and unkempt hilltop. On the south side, the old guild hall made an 80-degree angle with the Palace of the Senators. To the north, the space was bounded by the Franciscan monastery of S. Maria in Aracoeli. Michelangelo, then busy on the pope's Palazzo Farnese, was commissioned to systematize the hilltop and its east and west approaches from the Forum and the city, respectively. Because of the lack of time and money, not much besides simple tidying was accomplished before Charles' visit. Also, the bronze equestrian statue of Marcus Aurelius, believed to be that of the first Christian emperor, Constantine the Great, was brought from the Lateran, where it had

more distinguished members of the retinue.

The law favored these large dignified buildings. It provided that neighbors be obliged to sell adjoining property to those who proposed to upgrade an old structure or build one from the ground up. Furthermore, through an arrangement worked out with the *maestri di strada*, in one sense the true planners of the city, a property owner could often barter private for public land in order to adjust the shape of the block, alter the alignment of neighboring facades, and even change the width and direction of streets. This not only made possible the sort of patrician palace complex like the Farnese, it also started the long process whereby the two- or three-storey single family houses of which medieval Rome was composed could be replaced by multistorey apartment blocks. These were put up by private interests, but also, as in Venice, by institutions,

and especially confraternities, congregations, and religious orders.

Most active in this respect were the strong Counter-Reformation groups like the Jesuits or the Oratorians of St. Philip Neri. Their program called for a church, a residence for the secular priesthood and lay brothers, accommodations for musical and preaching events, and the reception of important guests—something of an urban monastery, in short, but much more worldly and liberal.

The group would get a foothold in a residential neighborhood by acquiring an old church or some rundown houses. It would then proclaim its intention to rebuild and would establish orthogonal discipline on the edges of this property, thus reshaping the urban pattern in the area. The demolition and swallowing up of small, private holdings would continue as the group found the means to complete its own ample head-

stood in front of the papal palace all through the Middle Ages like a talisman, and placed in the middle of the Capitoline hilltop facing out toward the city.

But Michelangelo's program was not shelved. It was slowly executed in the subsequent decades and as it stands today is in all essentials his. On the face of it, the design solution was simple. Michelangelo clothed the two existing palaces in Renaissance envelopes, and then duplicated on the opposite side the acute angle they formed by erecting a third block (a screen really, since there was not much room for a full building) before the monastery of the Aracoeli, or rather in front of the long flank of its church which faced the open space. (Fig. 20.9a) This space, already fixed by the equestrian statue, was now paved and striped with a radial pattern emanating from the statue. A stair-ramp, called the Cordonata, negotiated the gentle incline from the city.

In some ways the scheme recalls Pienza. (Figs. 17.5, 17.7) But the similarities are skin deep. We note, first, that the surface of Michelangelo's Piazza del Campidoglio is convex like a shield, and the pavement inscribes an oval within the elongated trapezoid of the open space. Both of these features destabilize the formal perfection that could have been attained through, say, a level circle in a quadrangular piazza. The stellate lines of the pavement, moreover, disperse our attention throughout the space and keep us from reading the design, in the manner of Pienza, as a simple recession toward the principal building at the far end,

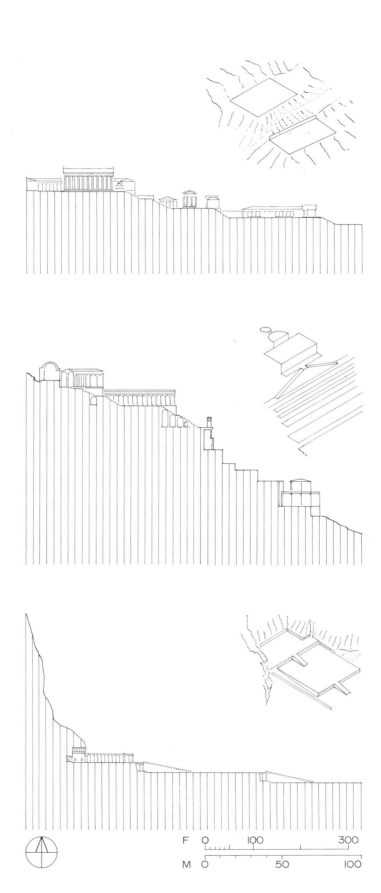

Fig. 20.8 Rome, the Campidoglio compared with other terraced architecture: Hellenistic Kos (Fig. 8.14), Roman Praeneste (Fig. 9.19), and the Egyptian complex of Deir el-Bahri at Thebes (Fig. 4.14). The general site plan of the Campidoglio shows its relationship to the thirteenth-century church of S. Maria Aracoeli (no. 2), the modern monument to Victor Emmanuel II (no. 1), and the Roman Forum (no. 6). The palaces around the oval piazza are the Palazzo dei Senatori (no. 4), the Palazzo Capitolino (no. 3), and the Palazzo dei Conservatori (no. 5). The section is taken through no. 4, showing the facade of the Palazzo Capitolino and the silhouette of S. Maria Aracoeli.

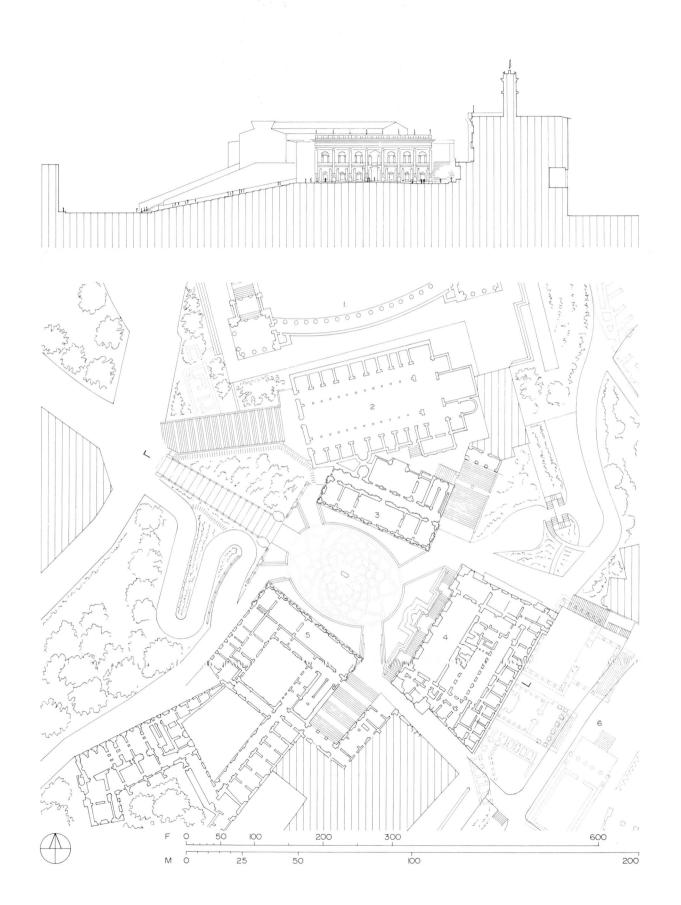

F 0   50   100   200   300   600

M 0   25   50   100   200

in this case the Palace of the Senators. This building is nonetheless made dominant by being raised on a blind basement, against which a triangular stair block forces us to reach the landing of the main portal laterally from either end. In the center of the triangle stands an ancient statue of Minerva touched up to look like the goddess Rome, while at the angles reclining river gods, also from antiquity, represent the Nile and the Tiber. Roman statues of the holy twins Castor and Pollux, excavated near the Capitoline in 1560, frame the middle of the narrow end of the piazza, at the top of the Cordonata. The side palaces are kept low. Their two-storey height, portico below and offices above, is held together by a giant order of pilasters that runs from pavement to cornice line. This giant order incorporating two storeys is a happy invention of Michelangelo's. We have seen it emulated in Palladio's work and, indeed, the formula will become quite common in the next century. (Fig. 19.31)

But the chief novelty of the Campidoglio is that it depends for its full appreciation on the movement of the visitor along a sweeping axis, in the same way that we were expected to move through a Hellenistic temple site like Kos or the Roman complex of Praeneste, or, for that matter, Queen Hatshepsut's funerary compound at Deir el-Bahri. (Fig. 20.8) All of these complexes combine a more or less strict axiality with the staged rise of the architecture that moves toward a climax at the summit, which is also the end of the axis. In this generic situation each achieves its effects uniquely. The broad terraces in the others that work toward relaxing the directional drive upward find no place in the Campidoglio. Again, the enclosure wall, which seals in the ancient examples except along the entrance side, is ruptured in the Campidoglio, at the back corners of the trapezoid, and spills the spatial volume beyond the composition. The stair-ramp of the Cordonata has no exact match in the narrow terrace ramps of Deir el-Bahri, the grand staircases of Kos, or the sharp ladderlike runs of Praeneste. On the other hand, Michelangelo too, like the architects of Kos and Praeneste, uses solid objects and blockages on the line of the central axis to arrest our

Fig. 20.9a Rome, Campidoglio, designed in 1537; view into the piazza from the stair-ramp of the Cordonata. The statues of Castor and Pollux frame the view.

head-on progress and divert us toward the sides.

Kos and Deir el-Bahri are self-sufficient environments set in the vastness of their landscapes, and even at Praeneste, the temple complex of Fortuna Primigenia merely concludes with a titanic burst the intimate statement of the little town below. But Michelangelo's agenda called for a monumental episode to be inserted in the long processional sequence of the Via Papale, and precisely at that point in the sequence where the urban stretch ended and gave way to the heroic romanticism of the ancient ruins. The two facades of the Palace of the Senators fit in with this Janus-like station of the Campidoglio, the rugged Tabularium on its rusticated base looking out toward the forum and the defunct spoils of

an old order, and Michelangelo's advanced classicism on the west front hailing the modern city of the popes.

On this side, a short new street took off from the Via Papale just west of the Palazzo Venezia and broadened into an elongated piazzetta at the foot of the Capitoline. Here the Cordonata began, diverging sharply from the stairs of S. Maria Aracoeli which scaled the hillslope a trifle to the north. This marble staircase was built by vote of the people as propitiation for the plague of 1348. The contrast could not be keener or more eloquent between the steep, demanding ascent to be made by penitents on their knees, and the broad treads of the Cordonata that merely modulate the incline and set a measured pace to start us on the spatial experience ahead.

Fig. 20.9b Rome, Campidoglio; the Palazzo dei Senatori (no. 4 in Fig. 20.8) from the northeast.

As we walk up we see ahead of us, behind the statues of the twins at the top, only the facade of the Palace of the Senators, or rather the portion of it above the basement. These statues guide and sharpen our approach, much like the heraldic columns at the entrance of the Piazza S. Marco. Slowly, as we near them, the flanking palaces and the equestrian statue come into view, while the Palace of the Senators rises ever taller. From the constricted vantage point between Castor and Pollux, as through a triumphal arch, we now take in the whole piazza. (Fig. 20.9a) At that fixed moment we are looking into a perspective box in the way the Renaissance is fond of having one do. But once we step inside, the space opens up, the pavement swells, the imperious presence of Marcus Aurelius impels us toward the edges of the oval, where we turn about to confront the facades of the subsidiary palaces. The oval admirably serves the double purpose of centralizing the space while maintaining the force of the

long axis that has propelled us up the Cordonata and into the square. So we push on.

Beyond this point, with the emperor now behind us, the iconography of the senatorial palace stands before us like a stage set: the seated Rome flanked by rivers, the side elevation of the double-ramped stairs, the bell tower directly above the portal at the level of the first floor, behind the statue-lined balustrade that crowns the full length of the building. We make for the corners of the stair triangle, and we have a new surprise. (Fig. 20.9b) Once more the space opens up; this time into a deep cross-axis with stairs leading off northward to the monastery and south, to a gallery that ends in a park. Now we complete the main sequence by climbing to the portal of the Palace of the Senators. We turn around, as the public speakers would have done, to look down on the square and the people around the statue; then beyond it, following the emperor's outstretched hand, toward the domes and tile roofs of the city, all the way to St. Peter's. (Fig. 20.9c)

The goal of Renaissance urban design was to create a restful visual order, free of tension or unresolved geometry. The control and perfect stability of the design would speak of a serene social system, the sublimation of conflict. The Campidoglio upsets this ideal in urban terms, much as the Mannerism of Giulio Romano had teased Renaissance reason architecturally in the disturbing trickeries of his facades and interiors. The dramatic siting, the compulsive but thwarted axis, the constrictions and releases along the way, the insistence on molding the spatial volume of the piazza as emphatically as the masses that enframe it, perhaps more so, the determination to affect the user—all this takes us away from the serene neutral spaces of Renaissance

Fig. 20.9c Rome, Campidoglio; view facing the city, from the stairs of the Palazzo dei Senatori. The Victor Emmanuel monument is visible at the top right. The prominent dome just to the right of center belongs to the church of the Gesù (Figs. 17.11b and 21.1); the dome of St. Peter's lies left of center, in the far distance.

Fig. 20.10 Rome, the Strada Pia (modern Via XX Settembre); view ca. 1590 from a painting in the Lateran Palace. The street and the gate at the end (Porta Pia) were planned by Michelangelo in 1561.

planning where the building blocks limit the volumes of streets and squares but retain their own individual identity. On the Campidoglio the palaces are drawn into the spatial drama the architect is setting up. They blend into the urban scenography that is being conjured, so that at times—for example, the palace on the church side—they have no practical function beyond helping to create the effect of the group design, like stage flats.

"A Pasture for the Bodily Senses"

We are at a crossroads here in mid-century Rome. Dynamism, impetuous reach, sensate passage through space, the illusionism of theater, sculptural or monumental props —these are the driving motives and devices of the city's planners from this point on. There was something extravagant about Rome; something not quite manageable within the reasoned discourse of the Renaissance. The tumbled, hill-strewn topography, the untidiness of centuries, the vastness of the untamed eastern hills, the call of ruins, all this convulsion and sweep invited a prodigal vision, dramatic gestures, show. The urge was in the air to carry the city to its original gates, to reactivate its dormant stretches. Leo X had started the trend by sending out the straight street

Fig. 20.11a Rome, the master plan projected for the city under Pope Sixtus V (1585–90); wall painting in the library of the Vatican Palace. North is to the left, where the Piazza del Popolo with its newly erected obelisk can be seen. From there the straight line of the Strada Felice runs past Trinità dei Monti (no. 4 in Fig. 20.11), to S. Maria Maggiore (no. 6), and further on to the Lateran in the far distance. The triumphal column in the foreground, just right of center, is that of Marcus Aurelius; the column of Trajan is visible further to the right.

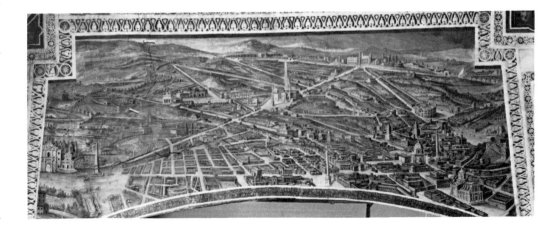

Fig. 20.11b Map: The Rome of Sixtus V. Dashed double lines indicate the projected roads that were never realized.

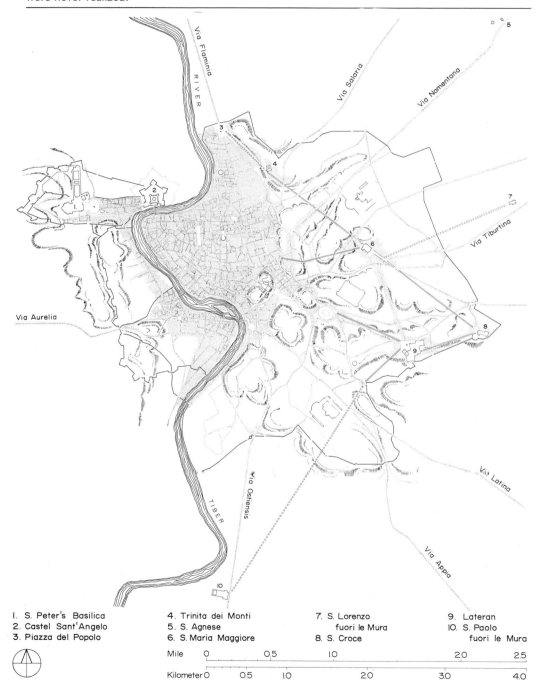

1. S. Peter's Basilica
2. Castel Sant'Angelo
3. Piazza del Popolo
4. Trinita dei Monti
5. S. Agnese
6. S.Maria Maggiore
7. S. Lorenzo
   fuori le Mura
8. S. Croce
9. Lateran
10. S. Paolo
    fuori le Mura

Mile	0	0.5	1.0	2.0	2.5

Kilometer	0	0.5	1.0	2.0	3.0	4.0

along the river (the modern Via Ripetta), past the mausoleum of Augustus, to meet the Corso at the north entrance to the city. Paul III responded with a third prong on the east side, Via Babuino, starting at this northern piazza and shooting off southward through fields and vineyards, below the Pincio and the new French church of Trinità dei Monti, in the direction of the Quirinal at whose summit a summer residence for the pope would soon be put in hand. (Fig. 20.5)

On this hill the next pope ran a straight street of his own, the Strada Pia (today's Via XX Settembre), to the northeastern city gate called Porta Nomentana. (Fig. 20.10) The object was to renovate the ancient highway of the same name beyond the walls as far as the pilgrimage church of S. Agnese, while toward the city the new street would link up with Piazza Venezia by means of an urban staircase, built against the Quirinal slope, like Michelangelo's Cordonata at the Capitoline. The planner was once again Michelangelo, but he was able to complete only the stretch from the hill edge to the gate. Both ends of the perspective were framed artfully. At one end, an ancient sculptural group of Castor and Pollux and their rampant horses was arranged looking in toward the street. At the opposite end, the fortified gate enclosure of Roman date was blocked off by a new inner gate, an indefensible thin brick screen scaled to the vista that the garden walls of villas on either side had closed in.

The solution was momentous. Newly opened streets in Renaissance Rome, like Via Giulia—or, for that matter, in Rossetti's Ferrara—were primarily channels of communication; they facilitated traffic and encouraged the exploration of a quarter, but were not conceived as grand vistas focused on worthy termini. Here the street was now composed as a bifocal prospect, urging the users from either direction to move along its path toward the visual inducement at the point of convergence.

The Master Plan of Sixtus V

This was the prelude to the most ambitious papal project for the design of modern Rome, masterminded by Sixtus V and worked out by an architect named Domenico Fontana (1543–1607). (Fig. 20.11) It was

Fig. 20.12 Rome, the Egyptian obelisk in the Piazza del Popolo, erected in 1589. It was set up at the time of Ramses II at the Temple of the Sun in Heliopolis and was then moved to Rome and placed in the Circus Maximus in 10 B.C. by the Emperor Augustus.

an amazing proposal. Sixtus spurned the sectional approach toward planning practiced by his predecessors. He took the entire city and its extramural periphery as his canvas, and with a broad brush imposed upon it breathtaking avenues that rushed across the empty spaces of the eastern hills and inward to the edges of the built-up core. Each one of these long ribbons of road (or sections thereof) was suspended between two points of interest, be they churches, ancient ruins, or city gates.

The avowed object was to expedite Christian worship, and specifically the pilgrim's penitential round among the seven principal churches. These included—besides St. Peter's, St. John of the Lateran, and S. Croce in Gerusalemme within the walls, and S. Agnese, S. Lorenzo, and St. Paul's outside—the great building on the Esquiline dedicated to the Virgin Mary whose devotion had been ardently reaffirmed by the Council of Trent against Protestant questioning. S. Maria Maggiore, as the church was called, became the hub of this majestic and comprehensive master plan. Pagan monuments that fell within its scope were duly Christianized, or put to some good use. The columns of Trajan and Marcus Aurelius received crowning statues of Sts. Peter and Paul. The Colosseum was slated to be converted into a factory for wool spinning; the baths of Diocletian, into a public laundry.

But Sixtus had other motives besides piety and social welfare. S. Maria Maggiore lay right next to the pope's family property, the Villa Montalto, which stood to gain a lot from the proposed redevelopment. Our sources also make it clear that the seemingly self-fulfilling avenues of the plan were meant to generate new residential quarters. The obvious field of expansion was the hilly terrain east of the Corso, the slopes of the Pincio, the Quirinal, the Esquiline. The prerequisites were two: roads and water. Sixtus sought to provide both.

Private villas had been the first to exploit this undeveloped countryside. Only one of the ancient aqueducts had been kept in continuous operation during the Middle Ages, and this had been the main reason for the gradual shift of the urban population into the crook of the Tiber and the abandonment of the aristocratic suburbs in the once-green hill belt. The aqueducts began to re-emerge after the discovery in 1429 of a manuscript, *De aquis urbis Romae* written by Frontinus, the water commissioner under Trajan, that described in great detail the water system of the capital and its management. Sixtus V was not the first Renaissance pope to give thought to the colossal task of resuscitating it, but the credit goes to him for having the first aqueduct since antiquity rebuilt and operating. This Acqua Felice (the ancient Alexandrina) would prove to be the lifeline of the expanding city core and the estates of the rich.

Sixtus had a series of paintings made for the Vatican library that show vividly how Rome would be transformed by his master plan, and Fontana, the pope's architect and civil engineer, left a good account of their activities. In the paintings and in the words of Fontana we go past the practical and social justifications and catch something of the excitement, something of the formal beauty of this visionary project. (Fig. 20.11a)

Our Holy Father [Fontana writes] . . . has stretched these streets from one end of the city to the other, and not heeding the hills and valleys which they had to cross, but flattening here and filling in there, he has made them gentle plains and most beautiful sites, and along their routes in many places there open views of the lowest parts of the city in varied and different perspectives. Thus beyond the religious purposes these beauties provide a pasture for the bodily senses.

Indeed so. Imagine a road that would begin at S. Croce in the southeast corner of the city, move up the Esquiline in a ramrod span to S. Maria Maggiore, then go straight through the intervening valley to the Quirinal to intersect Michelangelo's Strada Pia, then continue across another valley to the Pincio and the hilltop church of Trinità dei Monti, and on to Piazza del Popolo east of the great trivium. Paved in brick and delimited by high stucco garden walls, this reddish strip of the Strada Felice, laid down with such unswerving confidence on the brown-green country pattern and its rambling paths, covered four urban kilometers and seems capable, in the paintings, of shooting beyond the walls to the distant horizons. What keeps it under control, what cadences its headlong drive, are the architectural accents of the churches and terminal city gates. These slow down the breathless rush onward and break the av-

Fig. 20.13 Map: The Borgo area of Rome at the end of Nicholas V's pontificate, ca. 1455. The transformation of Old St. Peter's, according to the designs of Bernardo Rossellino, is shown in the detailed plan. Lighter lines indicate the subsequent changes in the Vatican Palace and the complex of St. Peter's, including the oval piazza of Gian Lorenzo Bernini.

enue into comprehensible, bifocal frames of the kind first introduced by Michelangelo at the Quirinal street.

But the Sistine design has an added fillip. The frames are not seen as closed, tunnellike perspectives. The accents at the two ends—so the thinking appears to have been—should guide and focus the road space without obstructing or cutting off its flow. Buildings like S. Maria Maggiore were too bulky for this purpose. Thin vertical markers would work best, either by themselves or in front of the more substantial structures. Then, in a brilliant stroke, the pope and his architect hit upon the obelisk.

The form was Egyptian; Roman emperors had transported a number of them to the capital and set them up as exotic trophies in the circuses and other public places. One, belonging to Nero's racetrack

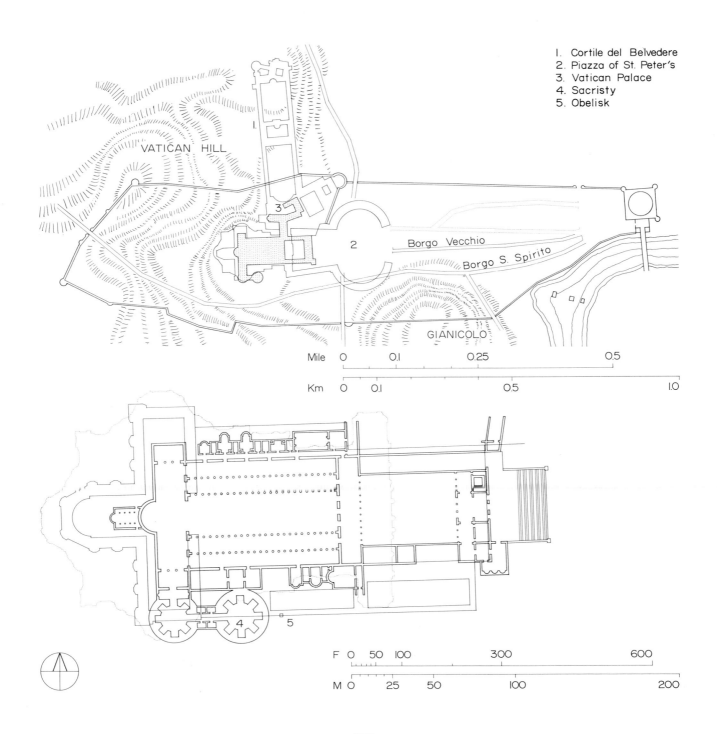

1. Cortile del Belvedere
2. Piazza of St. Peter's
3. Vatican Palace
4. Sacristy
5. Obelisk

in the Vatican district, came through the Middle Ages erect on the south side of St. Peter's. Since the time of Nicholas V, there was talk of moving it in front of the basilica. This monolith of granite stood 25 meters (82 feet) tall and weighed 320 tons; it was no easy job to transplant it intact. Fontana managed the feat in 1586, and was so proud of his success that he wrote a book about it. (Fig. 20.18)

There the obelisk proved that it could perform visually in a number of ways. It was able to hold down a public square, even one as misshapen as that before St. Peter's, giving it a simple cohesion. It also attracted movement toward itself along the Borgo road that led to the basilica from Castel Sant' Angelo. "Rotational" and "directional" principles we had called these spatial properties in talking of menhirs at the beginning of the book. But the obelisk of St. Peter's had a further use. It organized the facade of the church for those approaching it, holding their attention on the entrance and thus forestalling too fine a scanning of its then rather jumbled elevation.

The lesson was quickly learned. Obelisks were ideal anchors for the prodigal mesh of the Sistine plan. One, brought over from the Circus Maximus, now transfixed the north trivium of the Piazza del Popolo; another, the approaches of the rebuilt Lateran. An obelisk from the mausoleum of Augustus erected before the apse of S. Maria Maggiore lightened a critical frame of the Strada Felice. At the summit of each one a globe was mounted and a cross, forcing on these staffs of Egyptian sun worship, once turned trophies of Roman imperialism, yet another message of universal power—the triumph of the Catholic church. (Fig. 20.12)

The Workshop of St. Peter's
Compared to the ebullient freedom of the Sistine plan, Fontana's architecture for the pope is dull. He was in charge of the new summer palace on the Quirinal, major additions to the Vatican, and at the Lateran, the total replacement of the venerable but ruinous papal residence of the Middle Ages. These are all rather dead, uninspired buildings with flat, old-fashioned facades. It is as if the man who knew how to seize upon and bring to a head Michelangelo's

Fig. 20.14 Raphael, *School of Athens;* mural painting in the Vatican Palace in the room called Stanza della Segnatura, 1509–11.

urban experiments was blind to the architectural vigor the master displayed in the Capitoline palaces and in his late work on the new basilica of St. Peter's.

Actually, Fontana was not alone in his conservatism. The shock of the Reformation and the reactionary disciplinarianism of the Council of Trent cooled down the more hotheaded trends in the arts and in architecture for the first decades of the century. Prudery, solemnity, reserve gained the upper hand. It was not until the turn of

Fig. 20.15 Rome, Vatican Palace, the Cortile del Belvedere, begun 1505, Donato Bramante. This view, from an engraving by Étienne Dupérac of 1565, shows the Cortile during a tournament. The large niche at the summit of the court had been added to Bramante's design a few years prior to this event.

the next century that the new spatial mood of the Campidoglio and Sixtus' avenues, the seduction of urban scenography, and the extolling by Counter-Reformation saints of direct religious experience would win over the decision makers; and then the arts would loosen up and forms bubble over in demonstrative, sensuous, exuberant environments.

But let us return for the moment to the Vatican. The program, you will remember, was three-pronged. (Fig. 20.13) First, there was the basilica of St. Peter's. At the time of the popes' return from Avignon, it was over one thousand years old and in serious disrepair. Its outmoded plan, and especially the lack of a proper choir, made it inadequate as the preeminent pilgrimage church of Europe. But there was more. On 25 March 1436 Pope Eugenius IV had consecrated Brunelleschi's cathedral whose great dome, as we saw, had drawn together Florence and its countryside. Papal Rome needed a modern symbol of like force, a spiritual magnet.

Second, the Vatican palace. This too was outmoded. At the end of the Middle Ages it consisted of two interlocked groups of buildings—an old lower palace on the north side of the atrium of St. Peter's (which had never been completed as a fully cloistered

Fig. 20.16b Michelangelo Buonarroti, plan for St. Peter's, begun 1546; an engraving by Étienne Dupérac and Antoine Lafréry of 1569.

Fig. 20.16a Donato Bramante, first project for St. Peter's in Rome, 1506; partial plan. (Uffizi, Florence) What the church would have looked like if built on the basis of this plan can be gleaned from Raphael's *School of Athens* (Fig. 20.14).

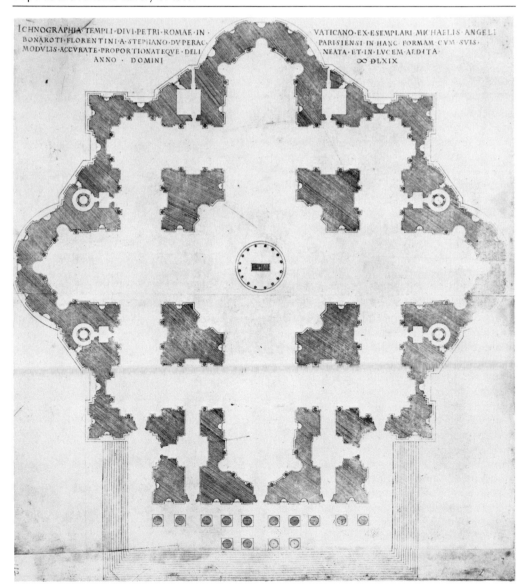

courtyard), and an upper wing on a plateau of the Mons Saccorum, a prominence facing north, built mostly in the thirteenth century. To this new structure, with good views of the city and the countryside, were moved the more intimate functions of papal residence, while the lower palace was remodeled for the administrative machinery of the court. If the palace complex had any great presence at all at the time of Nicholas it was probably a kind of ragged, defensive monumentality, sprouting turrets and laced with crenellations.

Third, there was the Borgo itself which sat between St. Peter's and the Castel Sant' Angelo, a bustling papal town of monasteries, parishes of devout foreigners each with its church and cluster of lodgings, pilgrim's hostels, the houses of curial employees, and the small businesses that catered to this assorted crowd. Nicholas V's plan for the whole area combined Albertian idealism with a matter-of-fact recognition that the papal cause was still not safe. So side by side with the two proposed piazzas and the straight streets between them, the plan also provided for corner towers to strengthen Castel Sant' Angelo, additional defenses for the Vatican palace, and a thorough fortification of St. Peter's to be undertaken at the same time that its choir was being enlarged according to designs by Bernardo Rossellino.

Some of this military reinforcement, several new rooms at the palace, and the start of Rossellino's choir were all that was pushed through of Nicholas' plan after his death. A benediction loggia was tacked onto the church facade, and in the 1480s a small summer house called the Belvedere went up on a rise of land north of the palace, where Nicholas had thought of lodging his theater.

Then entered Julius II, and the mood changed: the hopes for a truly Renaissance ambience soared. The Roman pontiff was by now the mightiest of patrons, the papal court awash with the finest of Italian talent. Raphael was painting spectacular murals in several rooms of the Vatican; the young Michelangelo was busy on forty statues that were to decorate Julius' tomb; architects like Fra Giocondo who had been called from Paris, Giuliano da Sangallo, and the Milanese Bramante were presenting models for

Fig. 20.17 Rome, St. Peter's, 1546–64, Michelangelo, completed in 1590 by Giacomo della Porta; view from the Vatican gardens, looking northeast.

502

Fig. 20.18 Rome, the Piazza of St. Peter's in a fresco at the Vatican Palace. Fontana's obelisk, moved in front of the church in 1586, is shown in place. Michelangelo's dome is incomplete, and Maderno's facade (Fig. 20.22) is not yet there.

the tomb structure that was either to be fitted into Rossellino's choir or was to be treated as an independent chapel.

Along the way, it is not clear how or by whom, the radical idea was conceived to tear down the old basilica and replace it with a centrally planned, domed church. Bramante designed a Greek-cross building for the purpose, with all four barrel-vaulted arms ending in apses. The central dome was to be shallow like the Pantheon's, fully as large, and was to rest on a drum pierced by windows between rings of columns both within and out. Small cupolas over lesser cruciform units were to fill the junctures of the arms, and towers were to mark the corners of a square that enframed the church except for the four apses.

But it seems the project, which might have necessitated moving St. Peter's tomb, proved too arrogant in the end even for Julius. It was decided to compromise and somehow graft Bramante's church onto the Constantinian basilica by sacrificing one of the apsed arms of the cross, that to the east. On 28 April 1506 the cornerstone for this domed basilica was laid, and by 1510 the four dome piers were finished. Both these and the piers of the subsidiary units were deeply cut into by large niches. (Fig. 20.16a) Mass was everywhere reduced in Bramante's intricately proliferating plan, and space allowed to flow from the central bay throughout this perfectly controlled design. We have a pictorial impression of what was intended in the background of Raphael's *School of Athens*. (Fig. 20.14)

In the meantime, Bramante was supervising the opening of the Via Giulia on the left bank and the erection of the Palace of Justice upon it. And at the Vatican he was satisfying Julius' expansive imagination in a number of bold projects that turned it into the most remarkable princely palace since Urbino. First, the east facade toward the city was encased in several storeys of graceful loggias, taking on an inviting, nonmartial look. And then Julius and Bramante, this

ideally matched patron-architect team, considered ways in which the updated medieval core might be connected to the summer house on the northern hill about 300 meters (985 feet) away. They settled on a terraced spatial bridge, the Cortile del Belvedere, which would externalize the palace, enclose a great open space to air out the congested, claustral old buildings, and evoke something of the imperial breadth of the Palatine. (Fig. 20.15) The chosen form recalled, in fact, the walled sunken garden alongside the Domus Augustana that resembled a stadium, or the similar enclosed garden at Hadrian's villa in Tivoli known as the Poikile. (Fig. 9.27)

Those were, however, level sites. In his need to cover the steep grade between the Vatican and the summer house on the north hill, Bramante turned to Roman terraced designs like Praeneste. To the east and west he ran long galleries, beginning three storeys high on the palace end and reduced to two stages further uphill. In this way a level corridor could be effected from the second order of the new loggias, at the east facade of the palace and a comparable point in the west block, to the grounds of the summer house. The space between these galleries was developed in three distinct terraces. The southernmost was the largest and the deepest. It was framed by the three-storey facades of the galleries, of which the second had tall rectangular windows with deep niches on either side, while the third one was an open loggia divided into bays by Corinthian pilasters.

Between this and the short second terrace ran a grand staircase across the full span. The gallery frames of this second terrace were plain, unadorned walls. Access to the third terrace was via two ramps flanking a small nymphaeum. A splendid, semicircular niche with stairs on a double curve terminated this uppermost level and concealed the bias of the summer house. Behind the niche, at the entrance to the house, a statue court now received the Laokoön, uncovered with great emotion in 1506 on the grounds of Nero's Golden House, the Apollo Belvedere, river gods, and other treasures that were to start the famous Vatican collection of antiquities.

Julius died in 1513; Bramante in 1514. Neither the new St. Peter's nor the Cortile del Belvedere had progressed very far, and both were subjected to drastic changes under succeeding popes and architects. Under Sixtus V, for example, Fontana was allowed to cut the great space of the Cortile in two by a library block and to transform the city prospect of the Vatican by closing in Bramante's loggias and turning them into one side of a court for a new clifflike palace block further east. But the architectural impact of the original Cortile, the verve and resourcefulness of its design, set in motion the round of experimentation that produced Michelangelo's Campidoglio, the urbanism of Fontana, and ultimately the scenographic bravura of Baroque Rome. We can see how the Cortile was originally to have been used in a representation of a tournament held there in 1565, showing the gallery facades, the grand stairs, the rooftops full of spectators watching the jousting knights clash. (Fig. 20.15)

It was the great society, those opening decades of the sixteenth century under Julius and Leo X. Rome was the diplomatic capital of Europe. The prime of Italy's first families jostled for position in the hierarchy of the papal court, ruthlessly but in high style, according to the code for noble arrivistes elaborated in Baldassare Castiglione's *Il Cortegiano*. Greek was taught by John Lascaris and other renowned refugees from Byzantium, city magistrates attended history lectures daily on the Capitoline, and courtesans of great beauty with names like Imperia and Isabella de Luna held salons for connoisseurs and literati.

St. Peter's was a continuing story. It was apparent after Bramante's death that the great centralized choir could never be married to the Constantinian nave. The alternatives were to revive Bramante's original Greek-cross plan, and perhaps extend it to the east with a new atrium or roomy vestibule; or else design a new nave in harmony with the spatial grandeur of Bramante's choir. The second solution, more traditional liturgically, became the clear favorite in the recessive, authoritarian decades of the Counter-Reformation. Meanwhile, structural changes in the piers and a general simplification of Bramante's plan shifted the church toward a sturdier, more compact form.

This is the point at which Michelangelo, then an old man, was brought in as chief

Fig. 20.19 Rome, the Ponte Sant'Angelo (the ancient Pons Aelius, second century A.D.), remodeled in 1668–71, Gian Lorenzo Bernini. In the immediate foreground are statues of St. Paul (right) by Paolo Romano, 1464, and St. Peter (left) by Lorenzetto, ca. 1534. In the background is the Castel Sant'Angelo, originally the mausoleum of the Emperor Hadrian.

architect. The year was 1546. In that decisive way he had of marshaling what others had started, he went to work on the messy pile that was held together only by the unchangeable, central concept of a dome on four piers and the trilobe system of apses. First, he cleaned up the intervening areas, abandoning the lesser cruciform units except for their miniscule domed cores. (Fig. 20.16b) This boiled down to having a broad, square ambulatory between the central bay and the three apses. To concentrate on this basic massing, he next eliminated the corner towers and the individual ambulatories of the apses, thereby reducing the total area of the church considerably. Lastly, he wrapped around his structure a vigorously molded wall whose outer and inner faces were independent of each other both in outline and elevation. (Fig. 20.17) The wall externally rose in two registers: a double-

storey giant order with an outstanding cornice band, and a narrow attic. This uniformly pleated and perforated screen was tall enough to submerge the small corner cupolas, which, along with the curtailed periphery, helped to lionize the central dome.

For this crowning feature the immortal paradigm was the cathedral at Florence. (Fig. 16.12) The panels, the ribs, the lantern are all learned from Brunelleschi. But there are notable differences between the two great domes. We have a much more sculptural body at St. Peter's to which the eye is led by the giant order and its extension in the pilaster groups of the attic. (Fig. 20.17) The drum is made prominent by pairs of columns carrying their own bits of entablature, and behind them are sunk windows, with alternately triangular and segmental pediments, that emphasize the high relief.

504

Fig. 20.20 Rome, Ponte Sant'Angelo, figure of angel, 1668–71, Antonio Raggi. This is one of a series of angels placed along the bridge (see Fig. 20.19); each carries an instrument from the Passion of Christ—in this instance, the pillar against which Christ was scourged.

There are twice the number of ribs; they are thicker and the panels between them are not flattened but make up slices of a single spherical surface. Above all, the Florentine polychromy is absent. The dome of St. Peter's was to stand out through its full, resonant shape, its taut solidness, and not on account of chromatic legibility or mere size.

Michelangelo seems to have preferred a perfect hemisphere for his dome. The present, slightly pointed outline is the work of his follower Giacomo della Porta (ca. 1532–1602), the man responsible for building the dome in the 1580s. The east end of the church was also left unresolved at Mi-

chelangelo's death in 1564. To see the dome effectively from this city side, the nave had to be kept short and the facade proportionately low. Michelangelo's plan showed not much of a nave at all. The exterior screen wall was to be continued on this side, which was in fact another apsed arm; a columnar porch with a temple front before it would complete the facade and make clear the preferred axiality. (Fig. 20.16b)

As executed in the end, however, the church was lengthened by three bays with communicating chapels at the two sides, bringing the overall length of the new basilica to 212 meters (695 feet). A stately vestibule was run across the front, and a full-blown facade was raised, incorporating the temple front within the giant order of Michelangelo's exterior elevation, made high enough to conceal the roof of the barrel-vaulted nave. (Fig. 20.22) Both nave and facade were tilted slightly toward the south to line up with the axis of Fontana's obelisk. All this was done following a competition held in 1607 which was won by a nephew of Fontana, an architect named Carlo Maderno (ca. 1556–1629).

In 1612 it was decided to add towers to the facade, and flanking bays were built for this purpose. These proved unable to carry the load of the towers, which were therefore scrapped. But the added bays inflated the facade, blocking any glimpse of what lay behind. Its height also cut off from view the drum of the great dome for those who stood in the open space in front of the church.

The decoration of the interior dragged on a little longer. A new architect was now in charge, Gian Lorenzo Bernini (1598–1680); for the history of architecture he epitomizes a new period. Bernini is to the Baroque what Bramante was to the Renaissance. His work for St. Peter's, which covers every scale from urban approaches and a vast square to interior furnishings, is a kind of manifesto for the artistic culture of the seventeenth century, at least in the Catholic countries.

Bernini's first major assignment was to articulate the crossing of St. Peter's. The apostle's tomb, kept where it had always been, found itself now under Michelangelo's dome. The high altar over it would have been lost in the magnificent vastness of the trilobed choir without some sort of archi-

Fig. 20.21 Rome, the Piazza of St. Peter's, designed in 1667, Gian Lorenzo Bernini; view looking east. The photograph shows the axis of the piazza built up, before Mussolini's demolitions of the late 1930s that created the present Via della Conciliazione.

tectural definition. To begin with, it required a ritual canopy, and this had to be able somehow to hold its own between the sunken area of the tomb, lit by 95 ever-burning lamps, and the dome's remote splendor.

Bernini's bronze baldacchino brilliantly meets these objectives. As tall as a Renaissance palace, it yet alights airily upon the pavement of the crossing, a little west of center. (Fig. 20.23b) Four twisted columns, laced with trailing olive foliage and crowned by angels, hold up a tasseled roof, disingenuously aping the flimsy portable canopies that choir boys hoist over sacred objects during processions. This festive ephemeralness is quite deceptive. The structure is crushingly heavy and the massive foundations for the columns reach deep below the pavement, to the underlying floor of Constantine's church, and lower still into the soil of the ancient cemetery where Peter was buried. The engineering, then, is that of a sizable building; but the form avoids the look of architectural stability and opts for a rippling sculptural energy, full of surface movement and glitter, intended to thrill and dazzle us. And that is the essence of Baroque architecture.

The other side of the Baroque, its expansiveness, its fecund improvisation, the genius for turning odd jumbles of buildings or unintentional urban spaces into exciting tableaux, comes through in Bernini's Piazza S. Pietro. The public space in front of the completed basilica was anything but orderly or grand. (Fig. 20.18) To the north rose the asymmetrical mass of the palace. The south side was taken up by the irregular low buildings of offices connected with the Chapter of St. Peter's. To the east lay the Borgo and the narrow approach streets. In 1657 Bernini, old and of world renown, was given the commission to create an urban concourse worthy of the Renaissance prodigies of church and palace. The program called for a square that would hold the international crowds of many thousands, especially on feast days like Easter when the pope gave his blessing *urbi et orbi* ("to the City and the world") from the benediction balcony over the central portal of Maderno's facade. The square had to convey this guiding idea of ecumenism, and yet be kept low so as not to obstruct or overwhelm the basilica or the Vatican. And the design had

Fig. 20.22 Rome, St. Peter's, main facade, 1606–12, Carlo Maderno; view from the Piazza looking west.

to integrate several prior fixtures, among them the ancient Vatican entrance north of the church facade, Fontana's obelisk, and a fountain to one side of it placed there by Maderno.

After some tentative trials that explored trapezoidal and oval schemes defined by arcades or colonnades, Bernini settled for a three-part composition consisting of an entrance square immediately before the church facade, a huge oval space just a little wider than the church was long, and a small vestibule for this oval in the direction of the city, which was never built. (Fig. 20.2) For his proportions Bernini took the giant order of the facade as a guide. The entrance square is somewhat close to the Piazza del Campidoglio, with the dominant facade at the end and tangent low wings closing in a trapezoidal space. But the wings here are mere corridors connecting the facade with the oval piazza, and unlike the Campidoglio, they do not allow for cross-views at the acute angles they form with the facade plane, the object here being to en-

close the observer totally in a kind of open-air antechamber leading into the church. Two-thirds of the trapezoid were in fact taken up by the cascade of stairs that lifts one to the level of the church entrances.

From the eastern ends of these corridor wings swing two mighty half-circles of Tuscan columns arranged in four rows. They define a covered portico of three avenues, of which the central is wider. At the top of the portico, the entablature of the corridor wings continues, so that the entire piazza complex is tied together horizontally. Above the entablature stand 140 statues of saints. The half-circles end in temple fronts, between which was to go the third arm, what we have called the vestibule. The long axis from here to the church was to have been prolonged in the opposite direction, if Bernini had had his way, as a broad avenue leading to the bridgehead of Castel Sant' Angelo. This part of his design was not realized until the late 1940s.

The worshippers and tourists were to be brought through various parts of the city to

the point at the Banchi district where Ponte Sant' Angelo carries traffic into the Borgo. (Fig. 20.19) Statues of St. Peter holding the keys of Paradise and St. Paul a sword guarded this end of the bridge and welcomed the crowd to the special precinct. From here the yellow-brown bulk of Castel Sant' Angelo could be seen close up, and in the distance Michelangelo's dome was silhouetted against the empty sky.

As it crossed the river, the crowd was escorted along the parapets of the bridge by beautiful stone angels carrying the instruments of Christ's Passion—the column he was scourged against, the crown of thorns, the sponge, the cross. (Fig. 20.20) Past the somber fort, the crowd was forced to take one of two streets that flanked a narrow wedge of blocks, known as the Borgo spine, and walk the kilometer or so to its destination. (Fig. 20.21) Here the dome reappeared, but between it and the small space the people had emerged into, lay the fantastic specter of the piazza. The third arm, had it been built, would have detained them for a brief moment, a few at a time, to take in the entire tableau, before releasing them into the overpowering vastness of the oval. (Fig. 20.2)

The pavement sloped toward the center, fixed by the obelisk, and toward this point also converged the lines of the radial pattern that made the thunderous court with its thick screen of travertine columns, robust and unfluted, and the legion of saints it hoisted up, a little more manageable. The four rows were so arranged along the radii of the half-circles that the forward columns concealed those behind from view at the

centerline, and elsewhere in the court one could not tell how deep the stone forest might be. This centerline, marked by the obelisk, by Moderno's fountain and a matching fountain added on the other side, and by a temple front in the middle of each half-circle, was a strong enough cross-axis to slow down the long directional progress through the Borgo, before it was resumed again west of the line. It gave the crowd a chance to feel the girth of the giant hemicycles which Bernini thought of as the motherly arms of the Church "embracing Catholics in order to reinforce their belief, heretics to reunite them with [her], and agnostics to reveal to them the true faith."

The crowd now climbed the gentle rise of the oval beyond the fountain and the obelisks. At the top of the stair that spills more than 70 meters (230 feet) beyond the church entrances stood Peter and Paul once again, the familiar twins of Christian Rome as Castor and Pollux were of the Classical city. (Fig. 20.22) The dome had now set behind the facade. The crowd flowed through one of the five doors into Maderno's noble entrance porch. Five doors on the west wall of the porch corresponded to those of the facade, but the one on the far north side was sealed except in jubilee years.

The crowd was now in the nave, under the coffered barrel vault. It tunneled toward the pool of light that announced the crossing, with Bernini's baldacchino small and dainty at this distance. (Fig. 20.23a) The piers and the arches that opened into rich side chapels were alive with sculptures and framed reliefs of allegorical personifications, saints, and founders of religious orders: energetic figures that gesticulated and gazed heavenward, or strained to hold up medallions of the first pontiffs, papal stems and tiaras, in defiance of Protestant scruples against papal supremacy.

At the crossing, in niches carved into the dome piers, lodged the ecstatic images of four saints associated with Christ's Passion. With arms outstretched, they drew attention to the attributes that identified them: Longinus with the spear he used to pierce Christ's side at the Crucifixion; Helena, the mother of Constantine, with the True Cross she miraculously uncovered in Jerusalem; Veronica, exhibiting the head-cloth she offered Christ on the way to Calvary to wipe the sweat off His face and on which she

Fig. 20.24 Rome, St. Peter's; view into the dome looking up past Bernini's baldacchino.

afterward found His image impressed; and Andrew, racked on the tremendous X of his martyr's cross. In loggias above them were hidden the genuine relics—the spear, bits of the Cross, Veronica's *sudarium*, and An-

drew's head—displayed with pomp on high festivals. (Fig. 20.23b)

Higher still, in the pendentives, portraits of the four evangelists, and then a frieze of gold at the base of the dome on which, in blue mosaic letters, were written the climactic words from Matthew: *Tu es Petrus et super hanc petram aedificabo ecclesiam meam et tibi dabo claves regni caelorum* ("Thou art Peter, and upon this rock I will build my church . . . and I will give unto thee the keys of the kingdom of heaven"). (Fig. 20.24) And Peter was here at this spot, both above the inscription, in the heaven the dome aspires toward, and below it, under the baldacchino, in a tomb deep down in the bowels of the Vatican hill. He was the rock, and this was the Church Christ had spoken of on the coasts of Judaea.

Still further back, behind the high altar, a final blaze of gold and bronze: the tribune, featuring St. Peter's episcopal throne, the *cathedra Petri,* supported by four doctors of the Church, Augustine and Ambrose from the West and Athanasios and John Chrysostom from the East; and above it, in a burst of angel-filled clouds, the radiant dove of the Holy Spirit (page 484).

Whatever our view of the institution of faith, or our personal affiliation, most of us would probably agree that in the compass of religious architecture surveyed in this book the crossing of St. Peter's has an exalted place. Among Christian churches, certainly, its peers are few—Hagia Sophia, Chartres, the original Holy Sepulchre—and their ways of moving us are very different. Again, as with them, we must imagine the great occasions for which this altar in the round under its bronze canopy was set up. This was not the setting of common services, but of the most magnificent religious spectacles such as canonizations and beatifications, the crowning and funeral of popes, Church councils, and pontifical High Masses. Then the basilica overflowed with ordinary people, and the choir held the ranks of the religious—acolytes, chasubled

friars, abbots, patriarchs of the East, bishops and archbishops of sees in all parts of the world, cardinals in scarlet capes and skullcaps, and the pope brought in upon the gilded *sedia gestatoria,* surrounded by his Swiss and Palatine and Noble Guards in their dazzling uniforms.

Two hundred years after Pope Nicholas V's call to endow the authority of the Roman Church with "the confirmation of grandiose buildings," and one hundred years after the near fatal blow of the Protestant schism, Catholicism now had the tangible proof of its reconstruction ready. St. Peter's was not Rome's cathedral; the Lateran basilica of St. John still filled that function. Nor was it simply a pilgrimage church, albeit a most important one; the city and the rest of Italy had a surfeit of those. St. Peter's was a monument to the boast of a universal Church. Its grandeur and resplendent dress reassured popular faith, as Nicholas knew such things would. The brilliantly orchestrated program trumpeted the power of the Bishop of Rome and dogmatized against all skeptics and dissenters the cause of papal primacy.

Bernini had much to do with the successful visualization of these messages. Bramante's St. Peter's had sought to engender an ideal universality in the perfect hierarchy of the central plan. Michelangelo's intense and forceful molding of form communicated expressive truths, a kind of physical, plastic universality that carried us along without our being able to say for sure what it was we were asked to believe or profess. Bernini absorbs us into a palpable world of devotion, ravishes our senses, persuades us through visual testimony instead of rational argument or abstracted passion. Architecture, painting, sculpture—all the arts and every device of the-

atrical illusion work together to sweep us into a realm of unashamed emotionalism. We see, feel, and believe the pains of our martyrs, the wisdom of the Fathers, the greatness of the Church, the majesty of its pontiffs, much in the same way that St. Ignatius of Loyola, the founder of the Society of Jesus, insisted in his *Spiritual Exercises* that we contemplate sin by *seeing* the flames of Hell, smelling the sulphur, hearing the shrieks of the damned. The initial chill of the Counter-Reformation upon the arts, the dry academicism that was still there in Fontana's architecture, is brushed aside in the seventeenth century in favor of a licentious, exciting environment of persuasion that carries with it a triumphant note and glories in the passions and props of its piety. Bernini's St. Peter's, and all other Baroque churches in Rome, go past apology, doubt, rigid injunction, the seasoned defense of Church prerogatives. Theirs is a jubilant style; it sings paeans to Romanism ascendant, that self-declared champion and sole legitimate interpreter of the Christian faith.

How conditional this optimism was, how deeply rent the tissue of Europe, the history of the seventeenth century makes clear. In our terms, we have only to set side by side a picture of the interior of St. Peter's and one of a contemporary Dutch church like the Nieuwe Kerk in Haarlem to realize that Rome was far from ruling the Christian world, or Bernini and his followers Christian architecture. (Fig. 21.33) St. Peter's was a superb prodigy of pride and affirmation for its own vast community: it is still. But it has not vindicated papal claims or made the body Christian whole. For many Christians the very splendor of this seductive, opulent, assertive environment is an obstacle to an all-healing unity.

Further Reading

J. Ackerman, *The Architecture of Michelangelo,* rev. ed. (Harmondsworth and Baltimore: Penguin, 1970).

S. Giedion, *Space, Time, and Architecture,* 5th ed. (Cambridge, Mass.: Harvard University Press, 1967).

H. Hibbard, *Bernini* (New York: Penguin, 1966).

T. K. Kitao, *Circle and Oval in the Square of Saint Peter's* (New York: New York University Press for the College Art Association of the

United States, 1974).

I. Lavin, *Bernini and the Crossing of St. Peter's* (New York: New York University Press, 1968).

J. Lees-Milne, *Saint Peter's* (London: H. Hamilton, 1967).

T. Magnusson, *Studies in Roman Quattrocento Architecture* (Stockholm: Amquest and Wiksell, 1958).

P. Partner, *Renaissance Rome, 1500–1559*

(Berkeley: University of California Press, 1976).

P. Portoghesi, *Rome of the Renaissance,* trans. P. Sanders (London: Phaidon, 1972).

R. Wittkower, *Gian Lorenzo Bernini, The Sculptor of the Roman Baroque,* 3rd ed., rev. (Ithaca, N.Y.: Cornell University Press, 1981).

A Perspective View of Covent Garden | Vüe de Covent Garden.

J. Maurer, *A Perspective View of Covent Garden*, 1741. The church at the far end
is St. Paul's Covent Garden, 1630–31, Inigo Jones (see also Fig. 21.34d).

21

ABSOLUTISM AND BOURGEOISIE: EUROPEAN ARCHITECTURE, 1600–1750

Europe in the 1600s was a divided continent. Protestant and Catholic forces clashed at every stage of social intercourse and on the battlefield. Although the strength of antipapism lay in the north, the demarcation line was not neatly drawn. Poland, for example, remained staunchly Catholic. In France the Edict of Nantes (1598), which allowed the Huguenots the free exercise of their faith and granted a state subsidy for their troops and pastors, had the effect of creating two legitimate religions side by side. England vacillated all through the century; the German principalities and autonomous Swiss cantons were variously Catholic, Lutheran, or Calvinist. The Thirty Years' War (1618–48) which devastated Central Europe pitted the two religious camps against each other massively, and the century closed with the revocation of the Edict of Nantes and the exodus from France of many thousands, including a large part of her artisan class.

And there were other causes of rivalry, beyond religious differences. Control of international trade engaged England and the Netherlands in a vigorous economic war. Repeatedly the Catholic powers became embroiled in dynastic wrangling that turned violent. Contrasts in the political systems were glaring. Against the absolutist rule of Spain, France, and the Papal States stood the proud and prosperous Dutch republic. Between these two poles, the picture was quite varied. In England civil war had checked the absolutist intentions of the crown. In much of Eastern Europe the

landed nobility continued to administer their large estates autocratically like small kingdoms and made ineffectual any form of centralized government, even that of the German emperor. But in the absolutist states themselves, France especially, urban power still could flex its muscle and resist direction from above. The Paris of Henry IV, Louis XIII, and the absolute monarch par excellence, the Sun King Louis XIV, was shaped by bourgeois energies as much as through court incentive.

The architecture of the seventeenth century reflects all this diversity. The picture here, as in the religious and political alignments, is not neat or clear-cut. The style created by Bernini and others in Rome to celebrate the Church triumphant will spread to Catholic countries, but like other international styles before it, the Gothic and the Renaissance for example, it will be tempered locally. In France some of its basic tenets will be rejected on principle, in favor of a rational reshuffling of the classical repertory to serve the state in its Age of Grandeur. Protestant countries will resist the more representational and emotive side of the Baroque and the bombast of the French *grand goût*, but formal conventions from both will creep into their production in surrender to contemporary taste.

Besides, we should not forget that the argument, architecturally speaking, resides within the one broad tradition that Europe everywhere had embraced by the early 1600s—the forms and dialectic of classicism as constituted both by the legacy of

antiquity and its modern enrichment in the two centuries since Brunelleschi. This tradition was a potent symbolic language, capable of broadcasting strong messages of a political and social nature. It was also the practical way architects had of articulating their buildings everywhere in Europe. The five orders served both Protestants and Catholics in the design of their diverse churches, much as the churches themselves were contestants within the same mother religion. Classical pilasters, pediments, and other such standard motifs were relied on in the houses of wealthy, cultured Dutchmen as well as in the palaces of the Sun King. We are therefore seeking to determine degrees of emphasis, turns of invention, preferred combinations of universal elements—this, rather than radical shifts such as the experimentation of Brunelleschi and Alberti in a late Gothic world.

The Roman Baroque

One such emphatic new trend, the Baroque, we have met already in post-Reformation Rome. If we agree with general opinion to read in this term dynamism, energized form, the preference for the oval, the molding of walls through grouped columns and pilasters, impetuousness of scale, eventful sequences, then the Baroque begins with Michelangelo and the urbanism of Sixtus V. But it was after 1600 when the defensive rigidity of the Counter-Reformation as laid down in the Council of Trent was giving place to the jubilant affirmation of the Church and her renewed vigor that the style found a coherent and contagious voice. Bernini is central to this adventure, but so in a different way is his famous rival Francesco Borromini.

The discussion of St. Peter's has given us a fair impression of Bernini's worth. We saw his magisterial command of site and prior incident, his sense of theater, his love of curves and dramatic lighting, his emotional, or rather sensation-prone, approach to the call of faith and the collaborative use of all the arts to convey its experience. He was the perfect flagbearer of Rome's universal assertiveness—adept equally at sculpture, painting, and architecture, in charge of vast projects and effectively run workshops, and with enough innate gifts, self-confidence, and dash to capture the limelight of a whole age. Urban VIII, one of his foremost patrons, was right to admit: "It is our fortune that master Bernini lives in our pontificate." And the Sun King felt compelled to consult him on the new Louvre, and to see to it that his trip through France was staged like a triumphal march.

Borromini (1599–1667) worked for lesser clients. He was an architect pure and simple, having trained as a stone-carver. And yet in his own introverted, intense way he affected European design just as profoundly. Both masters accepted, of course, the Classical ideal as their guiding authority. But whereas Bernini was a brilliant synthesizer and an innovator who played by the rules, Borromini displayed a personal inventive streak that stretched, if not challenged outright, the permissible restraints of tradition. (Figs. 21.4b; 21.5a) This is most apparent in decorative details. A window or a lantern by Borromini can be a striking novelty, meant to be seen as such. But it is in the thinking that underlies total designs where his originality, so disturbing to contemporaries, is of most consequence. One project, the small monastery of S. Carlo alle Quattro Fontane for the Spanish Trinitarians, should give us a taste for his provocative manner.

Churches

S. Carlo was a Counter-Reformation saint, one of that new breed of canonized heroes, among them Philip Neri, Teresa of Ávila, and the founder of the Jesuit order Ignatius of Loyola, whom the arts rushed to exalt. By the early seventeenth century there were two basic Catholic church types. One was the Jesuit model set by the mother church in Rome, the Gesù. It was designed first in the 1560s by Giacomo Barozzi da Vignola (1507–73), altered in its final execution, and spectacularly redecorated inside a hundred years later. The scheme

Fig. 21.1 Rome, the church of the Gesù; interior, 1568–84, Giacomo Barozzi da Vignola. The church was redecorated in 1669–83.

Fig. 21.2 Rome, the Gesù; view of the nave ceiling, 1669–83, with the painting of *The Adoration of the Name of Jesus* by Giovan Battista Gaulli, and stucco sculptures by Antonio Raggi.

is broken off by heavenly creatures made of stucco who prop up energetically a vision painted in the dizzying, telescopic perspective of the new era, Giovan Battista Gaulli's *Adoration of the Name of Jesus* (1674–79). (Fig. 21.2)

The history of the design of the Gesù spans the expressive and formal progress of the Roman Baroque. The facade stands at the start of the style, or rather belongs with those trends and works in the later sixteenth century that anticipate it. It is easy to show how the same basic scheme was rendered subsequently in richer, more deeply worked, shadow-catching surfaces at churches like S. Maria in Campitelli. (Fig. 21.3, C) The vault fresco, on the other hand, stands at the apogee of an extraordinary opening up of ceiling decoration in churches and palaces—beginning with framed pictures that have their own internal unity, moving on to framed pictures where the perspective is adjusted to the viewer down below and the distance that exists between him and the ceiling, and finally reaching illusionary heights in programs like Gaulli's *Adoration* which spill out of their frames and encompass teeming, vertiginous worlds of paradise and heavenly ecstasy in churches and, in palaces, allegorical reworkings of ancient myths or history.

The second basic Catholic church type of the seventeenth century was the centrally planned church, of which Renaissance architects had been fonder perhaps than their clients. The free, adventurous mood of the high Baroque liberally indulged in this type, and subjected it to a wide variety of solutions. These stress the Greek cross, the oval, the circle, the star, and combinations of two or more, played against the geometry of side chapels. Here the facade has no distributive system of aisles and nave to express, and so it takes off on its own and assumes startling shapes. At Bernini's S. Andrea al Quirinale (1658–70) a single pedimented frame of giant Corinthian pilasters shelters a semicircular porch surmounted by the freestanding coat of arms of the Pamphili family. (Fig. 21.3, B) At S. Maria in Campitelli (1663–67) the facade consists of two fully developed storeys centered on pedimented tabernacles, the whole capped by a powerful broken pedi-

presents a broad, barrel-vaulted nave flanked by a series of clearly subordinate chapels, a shallow transept with a dome over the crossing, and a facade arranged in two storeys, the uppermost narrower and pedimented, and linked by volutes to the ground storey, which is composed in three sections reflecting the inner division of nave and aisles. (Figs. 17.11b, 21.1)

This facade formula goes back ultimately to Alberti's S. Maria Novella (Fig. 17.11a), but is of course no longer developed flatly within a single plane but in various depths of relief culminating toward the center. The rich interior is flooded with light and blanketed with applied decoration. Clustered pilasters form the piers, the cornices move in and out rhythmically, and the ceiling edge

ment. (Fig. 21.3, C) S. Maria della Pace (1656–57) is also two-storied, the upper storey gently curving outward between strongly projecting piers, and the lower, a semicircular columned porch stepping into the public space, through which we read the straight wall of the entrance door. (Fig. 21.3, A)

Borromini's S. Carlo (1638–41) belongs to this group of centrally planned Baroque churches. The plan is basically an oval, with the entrance on the narrow side. (Fig. 21.4b) Four chapels push out the space of the oval, and so yield a configuration that can also be read as a Greek cross with convex corners. In either case, what strikes us looking at the plan is the sinuosity of the outline, the way in which it dips and swells, as if the wall were pliable and subject to external pressures. Baroque plasticity is commonly achieved by the sculptural manipulation of columns and pilasters attached to the plane of the wall, be it curved or straight. Here, instead, the wall plane itself is twisted; the central space and chapels swept into each other.

In three dimensions, too, the main domed core is not separated from the chapels, but they are all made to run smoothly together. (Fig. 21.5b) The order of columns, bulky in relation to the small size of the interior and therefore predominant, goes all around, with varied spacing and some distortion of the elements but with the same beat throughout. It defines the chapel frames as well as the frames of the altar niches within, whose capping pediments sink into the concavity of the radially coffered half-domes. A powerful entablature restates this unity.

Now this of course is wholly at odds with the Renaissance sense of independent static units, each clearly articulated and related hierarchically to a dominant center. Most

Fig. 21.3 Rome, seventeenth-century churches; plans and exterior views:
(A) S. Maria della Pace, 1656–57, Pietro da Cortona;
(B) S. Andrea al Quirinale, 1658–70, Gian Lorenzo Bernini;
(C) S. Maria in Campitellli, 1663–67, Carlo Rainaldi.

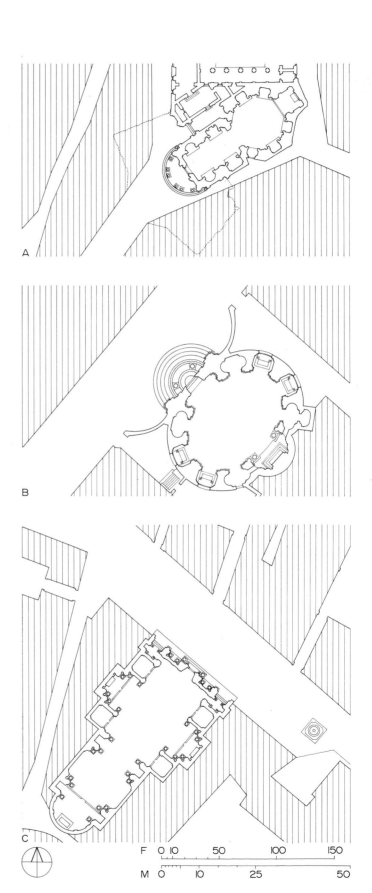

514

A

B

C

Baroque architects respect such an individuation of parts, despite the blustery treatment. At S. Carlo, however, the four apsidal chapels are fragments of small ovals that touch or overlap and are welded into the large nave oval. This unique design results from Borromini's attempt to invent a form based on geometry, symbolism, and the constraints of a cramped site. The repeated reworking of the church plan in Borromini's drawing of the monastery is witness to his persistence. (Fig. 21.4a) Walls move from elongated octagon to oval; the oval shrinks into a rhomboid and moves left. The molding of form and space within the framework of an underlying geometry was one of the most felicitous solutions of architectural history. (Fig. 21.4b)

We had noticed the principle of the undulating line in bits of Roman imperial architecture, for example some rooms at Hadrian's villa at Tivoli. (Fig. 10.5b) And for the oval, the forceful play of concavities, and other devices of Borrominesque Baroque, there were rare recoverable prototypes in tombs, palace architecture, and the stage fronts of theaters. If Borromini sought these isolated examples instead of the more obvious and "purer" inspiration derived by his contemporaries from buildings like the Pantheon, and of course from the writings

of Vitruvius, it is because they conferred legitimacy on his restless inventiveness and proved that what seemed strange in his work was not the product of an irresponsible or rootless imagination. Once again as in the Renaissance, every major architect looked to find his own brand of antiquity.

The oval dome of S. Carlo sits on pendentives above the entablature line. (Fig. 21.5a) It is decorated with deeply incised octagonal, hexagonal, and cross-shaped coffers that decrease in size toward the lantern. There are concealed windows in the lower coffers and the dome area is also lit from above, through the lantern. No painted visions here shooting toward infinity. The architecture stages its own recessive effects, as the even light from lantern and windows falls on the white smoothness of the stone used.

Geometry is clearly central to Borromini's design. Now of course all Baroque architects worked with geometric figures, but once basic choices were made as to shape, the design progressed primarily in terms of a module, the commonest still being the diameter of a column; and both the overall plan and its parts were derived from this module. Borromini's thinking is consistently geometric. His plans are generated

by shapes that are divided into geometric subunits, irrespective of modular proportions. This approach is almost a reversion to medieval practices. At S. Carlo we can show, for example, that the general plan started with two equilateral triangles set base to base to form a lozenge, and two circles inscribed in them. Arcs connecting the circles define the oval of the dome, while the apexes of the triangles fall at the midpoints of the four axial chapels. (Fig. 21.4b)

The facade of S. Carlo, a late work of Borromini, is as full of movement as the interior. (Fig. 21.5b) Concave and convex units answer each other in swaying rhythms, and an undulating entablature runs between the two storeys. Over the door, the saint's image stands in a deep niche with a scrolled gable. In the central unit of the upper storey a painted oval medallion of the saint, carried by angels over a miniature oval temple, pushes into the crowning balustrade and is sheltered by a similar gable. The rocking that is set in motion is picked up by the lantern and the bell tower that holds the corner of the block where the tiny monastery was ingeniously fitted into its cramped site. This corner is beveled and given a river fountain with a bold, semicircular basin that fills at ground level what has been cut back above. The same arrangement is then echoed on the three other corners of the intersection, which is where Michelangelo's street, coming from Porta Pia, meets the Strada Felice—that magnificent backbone of Sixtus V's master plan. So Borromini's exterior treatment of this small church animates an important urban crossroads and locks the Trinitarian community in the larger fabric of Rome.

Scenic Architecture

We should realize with this instance a very important general point. Roman Baroque is an urban style. The curved facades step outward into the street; their gesticulating statues engage the passerby directly. Wings extend from the buildings to encompass a public space. The facade of S. Andrea has short but effective quadrant arms that carve out of the sidewalk an area of individual attention. (Fig. 21.3, B) At S. Maria della Pace large concave wings conceal the extant urban irregularities and help describe a small piazza which dramatizes the projection and scale of the semicircular portico of the lower facade. (Fig. 21.3, A) Architects revel at seizing upon some random open space surrounded by odd bits of city structure and sweeping them into a grand new oneness. Sometimes an overall design is imposed, as was the case at St. Peter's. But mostly one or two features are introduced that energize the space naturally and seem unpremeditated, impulsive, and just. What a brilliant stroke it was, for example, to plant two identical churches at the head of the trivium at the Piazza del Popolo like sentinel buildings at the entrance to post-Reformation Rome, the Catholic counterpart to the triumphal arch. (Fig. 21.6a) How nobly the slope between the western, tribune end of S. Maria Maggiore and the level of Sixtus V's obelisk in the open space below was negotiated with a set of monumental urban stairs that capitalize on the simple outline of the apse curve and the flat wings on either side. (Fig. 21.6b)

Piazza Navona, the stadium of Emperor Domitian that had survived the long stretch of the Middle Ages as a public space, also came in for a grand refurbishing. (Fig. 21.7a) This was thanks to the location on it of the Pamphili palace, a member of which as-

Fig. 21.4a Rome, the church of San Carlo alle Quattro Fontane, 1638–41, in the Monastery of the Discalced Trinitarian Order, 1634–82, Francesco Borromini; plan of the early scheme. (Albertina, Vienna)

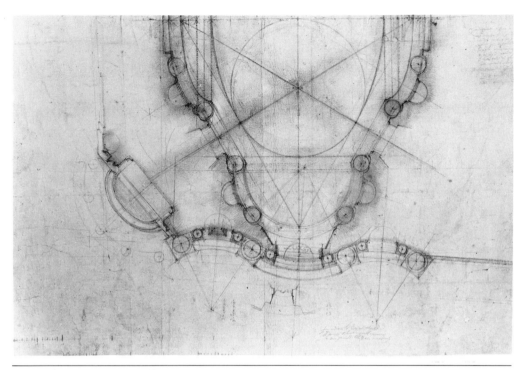

Fig. 21.4b Rome, S. Carlo alle Quattro Fontane; plan of the final scheme, western half of church and facade. (Albertina, Vienna)

the language of spontaneity and wonder is developed which real architecture echoes more permanently. With canvas, wood, wallhangings, and a great deal of paint, and drawing on a prolific imagery of Classical and Christian derivation, architects and painters—who were often one and the same—would throw up whole environments at short notice. The new building interiors and squares were the frame for their fantasies. There were producers, like the Venetian Giuseppe Torelli, who specialized in such spectacles, and learned men who worked out the program of the decoration.

All this had been gaining momentum since the sixteenth century. We spoke of the preparations for the entry of Charles V into Rome in 1536, and Venice's love of staged pageantry. But even so we are not quite prepared for the bravura of Italian festivities in the Baroque age, and the passion with which they were taken up in other countries. The endless fêtes at the French court and the masques of Stuart England blossomed under Italian tutelage. They counted on brilliant sets and machinery for surprise effects and spectacular happenings like storms, conflagrations, or epiphanies.

But in addition to commissioned shows of this kind, there were public displays sparked by religious festivals, civic holidays, and events like coronations and the marriages and deaths of high-ranking personages. Italy was again the first to elevate state funerals to an elaborate art form. Encouraged by the strong stand of the Council of Trent in favor of prayers for the dead, the burials of popes and princes of the Church were turned into theatrical extravaganzas. (Fig. 21.8) Prints of the bedecked church interior that had held the catafalque show mock obelisks and towers; impressions of familiar monuments both ancient and more recent, like the column of Trajan or Bernini's baldacchino; and a wealth of plumes, crests, and shields.

Not surprisingly, the theater re-emerges as a building type during this era. The Renaissance had held its entertainments in palace courtyards, churches, or in the open. The first permanent theaters attempted to reproduce ancient models for an elevated patronage, leaning heavily on Vitruvius'

cended the papal throne in 1644 as Innocent X. Bernini and Borromini were both involved. The church on one of the long sides, S. Agnese, is mostly by Borromini. He exaggerates the scale of the dome and brings it right up to the facade, to compensate for the narrowness of the prospect and to play up to the oblique views that prevail from the various entrances into the piazza. The robustly knit facade with its broad curves is contrasted to the sedate Pamphili palace. But in front of the church explodes Bernini's Fountain of the Four Rivers, one of three fountains that mark the spine of the long U-shaped space. The writhing, gesticulating river gods—the Nile, Ganges, Danube, and Rio della Plata—circle a rock grotto from which their waters spring. (Fig. 21.7b) Over the void of the grotto is raised an Egyptian obelisk topped by a dove—a double metaphor for the Pamphili, whose family arms included the bird, and for the

dove of the Holy Spirit, sign of the Church that had triumphed over four continents.

These zestful urban exhibitions set the stage for public spectacle. The new status symbol of the upper classes was the coach, and here in Piazza Navona coaches would be shown off in the evenings and driven around the horseshoe in single file by liveried coachmen. Temporary installations would transform the area on feast days and special celebrations. Piazza Navona was the scene of festive tableaux when it was flooded in emulation of ancient *naumachiae* or mock sea-battles, but also to evoke the biblical deluge and the story of Noah's ark. On Sundays in August, the aristocrats' coaches did their rounds in two to three feet of water to the strains of instrumental music.

Nothing shows Baroque intentions (and also its boundless imagination) better than these occasional shows. It is in them that

descriptions. Ferrara may have started the breed in 1531, but it is Palladio's Teatro Olimpico (1580–85) at Vicenza for the humanist Academy of which he was a member that is the finest surviving specimen. (Fig. 21.9) Here, the hitherto painted devices of theatrical backdrops were built in earnest. A columnar screen of two storeys with an attic above revives the Roman *scaenae frons*, but it is strikingly opened up toward the rear by scenery showing five city streets of local character built with clever foreshortening to give an effect of them receding into the distance.

This arrangement was not imitated, however. The standard design called for an architectural vista, created pictorially in one-point perspective, and *periaktoi*. (Fig. 21.10, A) These devices were revolving prisms on the wings, set on a raked stage, that made possible a fixed number of scene changes. In contrast, popular theater everywhere adjusted to the needs of its own less learned shows and the social mix of its audiences. The Elizabethan theater, for instance, in which plays like those of Shakespeare were performed, was a circular or polygonal yard, open to the sky initially, onto which looked five tiers of galleries. The wealthier patrons sat in the galleries and on the stage which had a two-storey backdrop; the "groundlings" occupied the pit in front of the platform that extended the stage space.

In the course of the seventeenth century the theater, both popular and courtly, moved toward one, more or less canonical layout. The catalyst was the opera, a new form of musical drama of Italian origin which caught on fast and became the favorite entertainment of cultured Europe. For it the theater reorganized its component parts, so that the auditorium and the stage behind a curtain were now two clearly separate worlds. (Fig. 21.11) The auditorium which could be U-shaped, horseshoed, or bell-shaped was subdivided into two main sections to segregate the lower classes from the wealthy—one taking up the cheaper seats in the orchestra, the other reserving boxes that had replaced the old galleries. On the stage, a principal innovation was the replacement of *periaktoi* by flat scenic wings that moved on grooves on the stage floor, a flexible system that allowed for a multiplicity of quick changes. (Fig. 21.10, B)

Fig. 21.5a Rome, S. Carlo alle Quattro Fontane; interior, view of the dome.

The Baroque in Catholic Countries
The diffusion of the Roman Baroque in the rest of Italy was slow and spotty. It had a limited vogue in Venice where Palladianism was entrenched, and Florence, nourished by her own Renaissance ways, was hardly affected at all. Naples and Sicily, both governed by Spain, waited until the early eighteenth century to respond in any notable way; they did so with an architectural

Fig. 21.5b Rome, facade of S. Carlo alle Quattro Fontane, 1665–67, completed after Borromini's death in 1682; early-twentieth-century photograph.

manner rather independent of Rome, freezing the formal effusiveness of her architects into soberer molds.

Only in Piedmont did the patronage of the House of Savoy, and the talent of a Theatine monk named Guarino Guarini (1624–83), nurture a style that was the immediate successor of Roman design, especially the example of Borromini, and advance well beyond it. Guarini's palace for the Savoy prince, Emmanuel Philibert, in Turin, the Palazzo Carignano (1679), brings the undulating wall to secular architecture. (Fig. 21.12) The great arc of the facade joined to straight wings by concave counterarcs heeds both Bernini's unexecuted first project of 1664 for the Louvre of Louis XIV and the curvilinear intricacies of Borromini. But it is in a series of churches for the Theatine order and the chapel of the Holy Shroud in Turin Cathedral that Guarini outdares his mentors in a new kind of spatial excitement. The plans are exceedingly complex and build up to high skeletal domes. These are constructed on an armature of interlaced arch-ribs, reminiscent of Moorish domes in Spain and North Africa; but there is no interstitial masonry web between the ribs, only the space and light brought in by adroitly placed apertures. (Fig. 21.13)

Beyond Italy, the Baroque entered Central Europe via the Danube. Here the Thirty Years' War, dynastic feuds, and Ottoman pressure from the East kept the area in serious turmoil until the early eighteenth century. Thereafter, however, a great wave of building swept over southern Germany, Austria, and Bohemia, in an effort to mend the frightful war damage and to put ruling princes on a par with absolutist patrons elsewhere in Europe. Whereas the lordly palaces looked to the royal architecture at Paris and Versailles, the churches for the most part continued the story of Italian Baroque of which they are a late but by no means slavish phase.

If we put aside hundreds of rustic parish churches with their characteristic bulbous-topped spires, the bulk of the new churches was undertaken by the monastic orders, still extremely powerful in the German states. The designers, in contrast to the well-traveled court architects with their humanist veneer, were by and large craftsmen from the guilds in a long unbroken tradition of

Fig. 21.6a Rome, the Piazza del Popolo, looking south, with the twin churches of S. Maria di Monte Santo (left) and S. Maria de' Miracoli (right), 1662–79, Carlo Rainaldi and others. This view is from an etching, ca. 1750, by Giovanni Battista Piranesi. (For a view of the obelisk, see Fig. 20.12.)

Fig. 21.6b Rome, the church of S. Maria Maggiore; stairs at the apse end, leading onto the Piazza dell' Esquilino, 1673, Carlo Rainaldi.

Fig. 21.7a Giovanni Paolo Pannini, *Piazza Navona, Flooded,* 1756. (Niedersächsisches Landesmuseum, Hanover) The square was mechanically flooded on summer weekends, and water jousts and historical pageants were held on this improvised lake.

Fig. 21.7b Rome, Piazza Navona, Fountain of the Four Rivers, 1648–51, Gian Lorenzo Bernini; detail. The seated figure with the oar represents the Ganges, and was executed in 1650–51 by Bernini's assistant Claude Poussin. In the background is the facade of S. Agnese by Borromini, 1653–55.

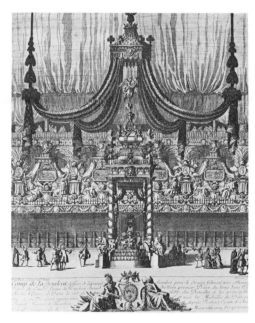

Fig. 21.8 Paris, display for the funeral of the Prince de Condé, 1687, Jean Berain.

521

stuccoists, painters, masons, and carpenters that extended backward to the Middle Ages. Indeed, there is something in the flamboyant artistry of these late Baroque churches that calls to mind the refined, intricate elaboration of late Gothic.

The plans are either centralized or basilical. They are engendered, like Borromini's S. Carlo, of interrelated geometric shapes. The structure is inextricably wedded to a rich decoration of stucco ornament, fresco paintings, and statuary, with a liberal use of gilding. The visual unity of the interior of S. Carlo seems tame and substantial next to the whirling, uncontainable, effervescent rhythms of the Asam brothers, the Zimmerman brothers, Balthasar Neumann (1687–1753), and other such German masters of the first rank. (Fig. 21.14) Everything, from windows and doors to altars, pulpits, and singer galleries, melts together in a seemingly unanalyzable profusion of decorative forces. In the generally pervasive luminosity of white, pink, and gold color tones, the vaulted ceilings are made to intertwine with the lower ranges of the church. These domes and barrel vaults are built of light brick shells, or lath and plaster units that could be cut into or extended below the ring line. Spiral columns, undulating balconies and confessional railings, angels flying in mid-air, and highlighted strands of curvilinear ornament set up an infectious rippling move-

Fig. 21.9 Vicenza (Italy), the Teatro Olimpico, 1580–85, Andrea Palladio; view of the stage. (The garments on the floor are part of the decor of a recent performance.)

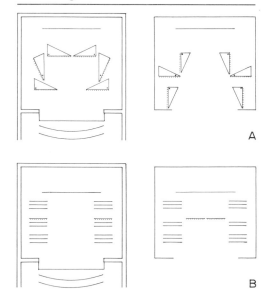

Fig. 21.10 Theater stages and scenery arrangements; diagrammatic plans: **(A)** *periaktoi;* **(B)** flat scenic wings.

A

B

Fig. 21.11 Milan, La Scala theater, 1776–78, Giuseppe Piermarini; interior as shown in an engraving by L. Cherbuin after a drawing by Sidoli.

Fig. 21.12 Turin (Italy), the Palazzo Carignano, 1679–92, Guarino Guarini; facade.

Fig. 21.13 Turin, the church of S. Lorenzo, 1668–87, Guarino Guarini; view into the dome.

ment that flickers along the walls (or rather wall-piers, for load-bearing curtains within are rarely relied on) and leads the eye upward.

Confronted today with what seems to us the licentious sensuality of these interiors, which might enchant or distress us depending on our personal taste, it is easy to miss or to trivialize their artistic worth. The object was delight of course, but there was more at issue than surface glitter. What we see is not the random accumulation of decorative effects, any more than a contemporary piece by Bach is a string of pretty tunes. The comparison is justified. Scholars are right to insist that the conception of this church design is analogous to German fugues and operas of the eighteenth century, to speak of spatial counterpoint or polyphonic elevations. In the same breath we could also mention the work of scientists and mathematicians from Galileo and Descartes to Newton and Leibnitz, not because of any strict correlation between them and Baroque artists, but because of comparable turns in the structure of their thought and a common fascination with ideas of the infinite, of movement and force, and the all-embracing but expansive unity of things. The realms of art and science had drifted apart little by little since the later sixteenth century. Scientists, with increasingly specialized research, were bringing nature under control through rational argument and computation. The artists, thus deprived of the intellectual investigation their efforts encompassed in the Renaissance, shifted to the world of emotions and became arbiters of sensational reality. Nonetheless, late Baroque churches in Central Europe are unthinkable in the earlier, simpler days before projective geometry, calculus, precision clocks, and Newtonian optics.

What we are saying, then, is that a full appreciation of the sacred architecture of eighteenth-century Bavaria or Austria is not

Fig. 21.14 Munich, the church of St. John Nepomuk, begun 1733 and consecrated in 1746, Cosmas Damian Asam and Egid Quirin Asam; interior detail of the apse end.

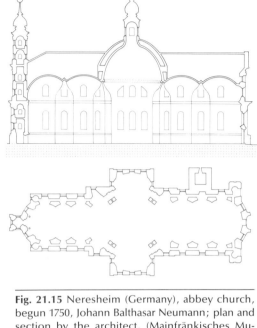

Fig. 21.15 Neresheim (Germany), abbey church, begun 1750, Johann Balthasar Neumann; plan and section by the architect. (Mainfränkisches Museum, Würzburg)

Fig. 21.16 Neresheim, abbey church; interior view of southern nave elevation.

a simple pleasure. It entails and rewards fine analysis. You might want to begin with less ornate, restrained examples, like Neumann's church of the Holy Cross for the Benedictine abbey of Neresheim begun in 1750. The plan is basically a three-aisled church with a transept and a dome over the crossing. (Fig. 21.15) But, on either side of the transept, nave and choir are of equal length, and the oval bay of the crossing, used lengthwise, pushes into both arms. Two smaller ovals set sideways to the direction of this central oval constitute the nave, and two others the choir. Their arcs describe the apse curve at one end and a convex facade at the other, recalling thus across the centuries the Carolingian tradition of "double-enders." These arcs also condition the wedge-shaped inner sides of the nave piers which are defined by diagonally set pilaster clusters. The transept arms too are oval internally. The perimeter wall shows big apertures; the wall plane is in fact everywhere deemphasized, as in Gothic churches, but here the windows have clear glass and the facade itself is opened up by storeys of windows like that of a secular building.

The aisles are too narrow to count as such. They work rather as an outer screen, so that effects of transparency can be achieved. (Fig. 21.16) As you look around, it is clear that the solid parts have been so reduced that the entire space of the church is visible from anywhere you stand. And yet the impression is anything but fixed when you move about. The oval hollows register in the two-storey elevation, but are countermanded by the convex balustrades of the gallery bays. Between the ovals, at the level of the vaults, swing pairs of semielliptical arches that meet at the summit and open out at the point of their springing into ogives, a little like the strainer arches of Wells Cathedral. (Fig. 16.21) The four shallow domes over the nave and choir are thus held up by a sort of freestanding openwork, physically separate from the outer wall, comprised of the piers and these torsion arches. The immense central dome rests instead on four pairs of freestanding columns placed on the cross-axes in front of the piers. The shifting, changing relationships of mass and void are caught in pools of light directed toward them at raked

Fig. 21.17 Seville (Spain), the church of S. Luis, 1731, Leonardo da Figueroa(?); detail of high altar.

angles and absorbed by the cream-white surfaces. All is subtle interchange, sinuous tangencies, and layering.

Only after a review of this kind is it possible to consider the tight interdependence that exists between architecture and the supporting arts, to see the discipline under the frolic. And this, in turn, would make it easier to discriminate between this kind of Baroque and the kind that prevailed in Spain and her colonies, where the decorative gusto is, if anything, more ex-

Fig. 21.18a Neuf-Brisach (France), fortress, 1699, Sébastien Le Prestre de Vauban; aerial view.

treme, but functions mostly independently of any architectural prompting. Strip the fabulous cascades of ornament from the "gilded grottoes" of Mexico, and you will find underneath the standard box of a sixteenth-century church. There is no interest here in the complex spaces and structural forms of Rome, Turin, or Neresheim. In Spain, it is true, the architecture is sometimes swept up in this ornamental fury, but church planning remains conventional by and large. The stone frontispieces of the main west prospect of the church and the great gilded retables, or decorated screens, behind the high altar (and sometimes also the side altars of transept and nave) are the real glories of the religious environment of Baroque Spain and her empire.

The principal components of these fantastic productions are the spiral column, often laced with vines and teeming with putti, and the *estipite,* a pilaster whose surface is broken up by secondary capitals, geometric panels, scroll ornaments, and the like (Fig. 21.17) The inspiration for these motifs, at least in the phase called Churrigueresque after its chief exponent José Benito de Churriguera (1665–1725), is less mainstream Europe than it is the fevered, harsh Mannerism of pattern books that began to appear in the sixteenth century in Flanders and Holland, then part of the dominion of Spain, that featured the kind of ornament known as bandwork or strapwork. The later *Trasparente* is more refined and dissolved, but only comparatively speaking. The design is always controlled, and the virtuosity amazing. The ornamental jungle carved in many different levels of relief is spotted by the application of precious materials and luxury stones like granites and colored marbles, and in it lodge ecstatic holy figures sculptured in the round.

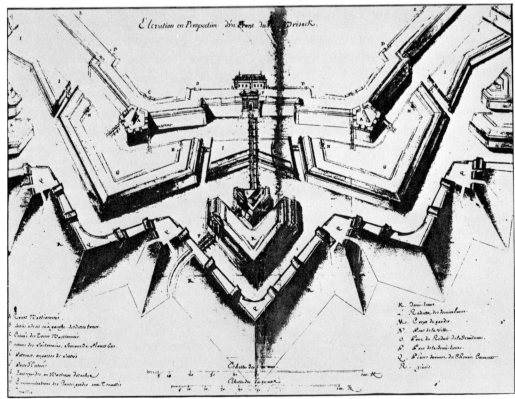

Fig. 21.18b Neuf-Brisach fortifications, perspective detail; eighteenth-century drawing by anonymous artist.

Fig. 21.19 Paris (France), the Place Vendôme, begun 1698, Jules Hardouin-Mansart; engraving by Pierre Le Pautre.

France: The *Grand Siècle*

The seventeenth is the century of France. If Rome was the capital of Catholic Christianity, Paris more than any other city now deserved to be considered the political and social fulcrum of Europe. With that ascendance of the royal house which had begun back in the days of Suger a resounding success at long last, the hereditary nobility impotently yoked to the court, a new enterprising class of administrators and civil servants running the day-to-day affairs of the country, and the huge peasant mass worked and taxed to the limit, France moved to assume an imperial stance of continental domination. Spain's great day of wealth and power was behind her. A politically unstable England reeled internally. The German emperor lacked the practical strength to enforce the prestige of his ancient title. In this general situation, the kings of France were ready to take over. Theirs was not the most modern state economically; it was no

match for Dutch overseas trade, for example, or English laissez-faire industry. But with a population of 20 million it was the largest nation of Europe by far. It commanded, at least for a while, decisive military power. Its gift for centralized administration could harness volatile social forces in closed national systems controlled and manipulated from above.

Architecture ranked as an important sector of public life and was regulated accordingly. It was a state business—and it was run like one. Civil servants, rather than professionals, were in charge. Building workers were subject to the supervision of a state-appointed master general. The guilds, in most respects acting as a governmental agency, were encouraged or compelled to introduce restrictive rules that affected working hours and pay. Their number was greatly increased to strengthen regulatory centralism. Under Jean-Baptiste Colbert, the great minister of Louis XIV, subsidized royal workshops took over the production of ta-

pestries, furniture, and glass. Colbert also attempted the institutionalization of national taste by founding an Academy of Architecture in 1666, on the model of earlier ones for painting, sculpture, and literature. Its charge was to formulate rules for "a unique and perfect beauty which could be followed by all operators and would be accessible to all the public." The Academy ran a school of architecture that replaced traditional training through apprenticeship.

The state administered an extensive program of public works, under three general classes. The residences of the king came first. This was a matter of immense political significance. Given the dependence of the nobility of birth on the person of the king, the royal palace was the symbol of national unity. Where it was and what it looked like were serious affairs of state. The palace was also a means of establishing international visibility.

Expenditure on the magnificence and dignity of the king [the Bishop of Meaux, Jacques Benigne Bossuet, writes] is . . . necessary . . . to maintain his majesty in the eyes of strangers. . . . In our day when a monarch is consecrated . . . the church offers up this prayer: "May the glorious dignity and the majesty of the palace blaze out, for all to see, the splendid grandeur of the royal power, so that, as a stroke of lightning, it sheds light in every direction." All these words are chosen to describe the magnificence of a royal court which is asked of God as a necessary support to royalty.

We cannot hope to understand Versailles, the greatest of European palaces, without this admission.

Public Works

Next came defense. The military muscle of the nation was now professional. This century is a period of large standing armies, modern navies, and vast stockpiles of armaments. To house and provision this national force were architectural tasks of the first order. It was no longer landed nobles who fielded troops at their own expense. The state had all the responsibility. For the first time the wounded, the veterans, and the war widows had to be looked after in a planned way. This is the background of the Chelsea and Greenwich hospitals in England, and the equally monumental Hôtel des Invalides in Paris. (Figs. 21.24b, 22.4)

Old defenses had to be brought up to

date. While Paris, secure behind its spreading empire, was tearing down its walls and converting them to boulevards, strategic towns all across the country beefed up theirs in line with the latest advance in warfare and defense. The towering name in this field is Sébastien Le Prestre de Vauban (1633–1707), Louis XIV's military architect and siege engineer.

The increased range and striking power of artillery were proving Renaissance bastion walls inadequate. These were now superseded by enormous outworks built into a surrounding ditch up to one hundred meters (330 feet) or more wide. Primary defense shifted to the semi-independent units of the outworks—the pincers, lunettes, and ravelins—and the fortified counterscarp. This imposing panoply, reaching far out beyond the city mass, dwarfed the city and in one sense cut it off from its countryside. But in another sense the city-form, fattened by its girth of open space, pointed mighty spearheads toward the distant horizons.

New fortified outposts were also needed along the extended frontiers and as naval bases, especially on the Atlantic coast. Vauban is credited with most of these. Since the old bastions were no longer very important, supplying them along straight access roads lost urgency, and so the radial plan became less popular. Neuf-Brisach on the Rhine (1698), Vauban's best-known stronghold, employs a standard grid inside the monstrous octagonal carapace of the outworks. (Fig. 21.18) The Atlantic ports, of which Rochefort was the first (1665), called for shipyards, rope factories, and cannon foundries. These buildings, as well as the constituent units of the outworks, were designed in a simple, utilitarian style, far apart from the grand high mode of public architecture. This, and the very technical expertise involved, divorced such programs from the repertory of architects and made permanent the distinction between them and civil engineers. But two things bring Vauban and the architects of Versailles together as exponents of the same era: the explosive scale and rational method of planning in what are viewed as single orchestrated works of design, and the subordination of wide tracts of nature under directional systems that open up the infinite dimension.

Here too is the link with the third class of public projects, urban interventions. To the Paris of the *grande siècle* we owe several enduring ideas of city-planning: the square—*place* in French—as a fully integral architectural scheme, the tree-lined boulevard, and the infinitely extendable radiating avenue that starts in a circular, semicircular, or polygonal urban pattern, intersects or joins up with other such patterns along the way, and shoots beyond the edges of town regimenting the countryside. Ver-

sailles itself was one such burst of radiating axes, visually and symbolically reaching out toward Paris and all other directions of the compass. (Fig. 21.27) And Paris sat at the center of a nationwide radial network of highways.

There were models for some of these planning devices. The trivium of Renaissance Rome and Sixtus V's far-reaching avenues are behind the slashing diagonals and convergences of France. But whereas Sixtus started with long-established foci,

Fig. 21.20 Parisian *hôtels;* ground plans: **(A)** the Hôtel Liancourt, 1613–23, Salomon de Brosse and Jacques Lemercier. The main residential quarters run the width of the building before a large rear garden. In the front right is a formal entrance court. On the left is a small court with stables and, behind it, a small garden.

(B) The Hôtel Amelot de Gournay, 1712–14, Germain Boffrand; in a period engraving. The oval grand court is flanked by two smaller courtyards: on the left, for the stables, and on the right, for carriages. This *hôtel* also has a garden in the rear.

1. Stables
2. Carriage Court
3. Kitchens
4. Dining
5. Salon
6. Chambre
7. Cabinet

F 0 50 100 300

M 0 10 25 50 100

Fig. 21.21a Versailles (France), the royal palace, Salon de Diane; typical interior in the style of Louis XIV.

Fig. 21.21b Paris, the Hôtel de Soubise; the oval salon, 1736–39, Germain Boffrand.

Christian basilicas, and monuments of antiquity, and drew his resolute straight lines to connect them, Paris laid out its royal *places* in the thick of town or at critical points of the periphery, and directed arteries from these fresh foci to extend their visual and structural authority to a randomly built-up old district or an open area where urban expansion was being encouraged. Again, we know the planned square from the Campidoglio and the Piazza of St. Peter's, but both of these examples are monumental ensembles. Traditional Roman squares are organized about one outstanding building, a church or a palace, while the rest grows aggregately and changes through

time. The Parisian *places* are residential ensembles. They have uniform facades on all sides, and no monumental highpoint except for the statue of the appropriate king.

The first of these royal squares, Henry IV's Place Dauphine (1599–1606), was a triangle that stiffened the prow of the Île-de-la-Cité, one of the two islands that form the historic core of Paris. (Fig. 21.26a) Directly opposite, on the right bank, was the busiest part of the city's riverfront. The new square acknowledged the city's dependence for food and trade on the traffic of the Seine. The shape accentuated the axis of the great river, and at the tip, where a new bridge was continued by straight streets into the built-up areas north and south, the equestrian statue of the king was put up, facing downstream, in the direction of the Atlantic shores which the Seine meanderingly attains. A second *place*, planned for a canal at the city's eastern edge, also emphasized trade. This one was semicircular, with eight centrifugal spokes; it, however, was not carried through.

Paris the royal capital soon proved more important than Paris the port city. A series of *places* in the next decades opened up new residential areas for the upper class, away from the business district, while the Louvre and other official buildings claimed the riverfront. Place Royale (1604–12), now Place des Vosges, in the quiet aristocratic district of the Marais was a square in shape. Continuous ground arcades and cornices between storeys unified the curtain facades, which were only interrupted by two taller pavilions facing each other on the main access line. At the center stood the equestrian statue of Louis XIII. The Place des Victoires (1682–87) of Louis XIV, in the district to the north of the Louvre, employed a full circle with radial avenues leading toward several important nuclei, both old and new. Finally, the Place Vendôme, also planned under Louis XIV for the new western part of the city, was a rectangular space with beveled corners. (Fig. 21.19) Here the hipped roof too ran continuously, but both the corners and the centers of the long sides were given pediments that broke the steady rhythm of dormers. In all of these squares it was the urban configuration that mattered. The lining buildings lost their individuality within flat screens of a common design. In fact, in some cases these long facades were built first, without any houses behind them, until buyers could be found for each lot.

Domestic Architecture

Between 1550 and 1650, the population of the capital had risen from 130,000 to more than half a million. Among the rich—government officials, suppliers, and tax farmers of the king, that class of the newly elevated bourgeoisie called the nobility of the cloth—speculative building was the preferred type of investment along with fancy houses for one's own use. The parceling of royal domains in and around Paris among trusted courtiers had an early start in the sixteenth century. By now a significant portion of the urban land, progressively broken up through the decades, was in the hands of owners of small lots; their cooperation had to be secured to get royal initiatives like the *places* moving. And along with the new housing developments of the *places* and their avenues, the old houses were being transformed by interior partitioning and the regrouping of rooms. It is at the beginning of the seventeenth century that the classic Parisian bourgeois types came of age: the landlord, the tenant, and the sublessee.

The change from a peripatetic to a fixed court, which we had already seen in Chapter 16, forced secular and church lords to be present in the capital for long periods of time. They took up residence in town mansions called *hôtels*, one of the characteristic building types of the period. Actually, the type is not an invention of the seventeenth century. Since about 1350 it had emerged as the secondary residence of landed gentry, a place to receive and entertain. What happens in the *grand siècle* is that the rural aspects of the program—grain in the attic, hay bundles in the court, the fruit garden—vanish. The *hôtel* becomes a refined setting for the social intercourse of people whom birth in times past would have kept apart. The revised plan that was to become standard surfaces in the 1620s. (Fig. 21.20a) The house, embedded in a continuous block, lacks external regularity. A screen wall detaches it from street life. Behind this is the *cour d'honneur*, a courtyard with access for coaches, flanked by stables and offices. The main residential

Fig. 21.22 Paris, the Louvre; the Square Court (Cour Carrée), begun 1546 by Pierre Lescot. This block was built on the site of the west wing of the old chateau, shown in Fig. 16.15.

Fig. 21.23 Charleval (France), chateau, 1573, Jacques du Cerceau the Elder; as shown in an engraving by the architect.

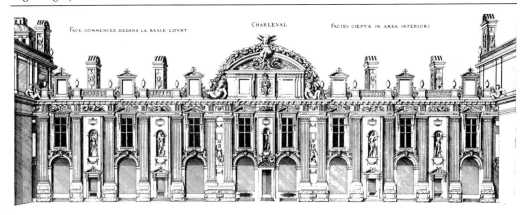

530

Fig. 21.24a Paris, the church of St.-Gervais; facade, 1616, Salomon de Brosse. The church itself dates from the late Gothic period. The facade echoes the scheme used for the entrance to a chateau—three storeys, each featuring one of the Classical orders. (From the bottom, Doric, Ionic, and Corinthian.)

Fig. 21.24b Paris, the Dôme of the Invalides, 1680–91, a church designed by Jules Hardouin-Mansart. The Hôtel des Invalides behind the Dôme was a large establishment designed by Liberal Bruant and built in 1670–77 to house disabled soldiers.

Fig. 21.24c Paris, the church of Val-de-Grâce, begun 1645, François Mansart and Jacques Lemercier.

block is at the back and, space permitting, there is also a more private court and a garden further in.

In the main block, a series of rooms was made to fit on two levels with great ingenuity, connected by a fancy staircase. The two fronts, one toward the cour d'honneur and the other toward the garden, did not always lie on the same axis, although the rooms were arranged symmetrically for each one and their doors often lined up to form an unbroken vista (enfilade). The halves were cunningly interlocked, so that in some later examples a circuit of rooms appeared to wrap around the top-lighted staircase. The rooms were at first rectangular, but oval and polygonal shapes gained quick popularity. (Fig. 21.20b)

The standard sequence was the salon or reception hall, an antechamber next to it, a combination bedroom and sitting room called the chambre, and the most private room of all, the cabinet. This sequence constituted an appartement, and there

would be two or more of these, depending on the pretensions of the owner, unobtrusively linked by service rooms. The arrangement is the same in more sumptuous country chateaux. There the salon is expressed prominently in the middle of the building block and dignified by some kind of frontispiece. The chambres and cabinets of the apartments on either side form terminal pavilions with their own separate roofs, and the antechambers serve as plain bridges between the central motif and the end pavilions. (See Fig. 21.23.)

The interiors of hôtels and chateaux were always rich, but almost never gaudy. (Fig. 21.21a) The walls were sheathed in wood, inlaid marbles, and friezes and panels containing paintings or stucco reliefs. The windows, doors, and fireplaces were framed by Classical motifs, and moldings and dados were also of Classical inspiration. The salon had ceiling paintings of mythological subjects in heavy gilded frames. There was an abundance of furniture. In the chambre, a monumental bed stood in a railed-in recess. The cabinets had delicate, small tables and stools and were filled with small paintings and art objects.

Then, shortly before the death of Louis XIV in 1715, taste started changing. (Fig. 21.21b) By the 1720s a light curvilinear decoration was replacing the heavyset, dignified design of walls and ceilings. The color scheme lightened, mirror surfaces multiplied, angles were softened. A completely new repertory of ornament was invented dependent on natural forms—branches, garlands, acanthus—and the full gamut of abstract sinuosities like scrolls, interlace, and arabesques. This is the style historians called Rococo—an elegant, lighthearted, gay manner that shies away from structural statement or robust, muscular plasticity. It soon affected architecture as well, and spread to Germany and Austria. The eighteenth century church interiors there, which we have talked about above, could be said to belong in this playful taste of the Rococo, a sort of evanescent late Baroque that combines the dynamism and geometric complexity of seventeenth-century Italian architecture with the frilly, frothy decoration emanating from post-Louis XIV France.

But we are ahead of ourselves. The aesthetic task of the age of Henry IV, Louis XIII, and the Sun King was to give substance to an official style of architecture that would convey the dignity and solemn grandeur of the new France. This had to be accomplished against the seductive spread of Roman Baroque and the general dominance of Italian taste. Something in the French character did not take to the flushed ecstasy of a Bernini, or for that matter to Borrominesque whimsy. In the new France the philosophical bent was toward the stoic and didactic. Intellectual life valued reason above fervor. The bourgeoisie and the nobility of the cloth believed in order, dependable regularity, sober good taste. The prevalent architecture had to mirror this national mood while keeping abreast of fresh aesthetic impulses from abroad.

The previous century had left a mixed heritage. There was, on the one hand, a domesticized version of the Italian Renaissance whose beginnings we noted briefly in Chapter 17. This is easy to spot through distinctive details like the pairing and stacking up of columns, extensive use of decorative sculpture, crowning segmental pediments, and sloping hip roofs often broken up by dormers—all of which are present in a new facade for the Louvre designed by Pierre Lescot and begun in 1546. (Fig. 21.22) There too you can see the French compositional preference for a dominant central tract and equivalent end pavilions bridged by recessive wings; this in contrast to the homogeneous mass of Italian palaces, the roughly contemporary Palazzo Farnese for instance. (Fig. 20.6) On the other hand, there were more fashionable, eccentric vogues like Italian and Flemish Mannerism that could produce almost fantastic, anticlassical work, such as Jacques du Cerceau's chateau at Charleval. (Fig. 21.23)

As the century closed with the end of the brutal war of religions and the promulgation of the Edict of Nantes, French design turned away from such exotica. First, it was attracted by the stern conservatism that came out of the Council of Trent; and then, when Rome abandoned this conservatism altogether in the 1620s for the lusty vigor of the Baroque, France responded with a rational, intellectualized interpretation of this new headiness.

The calm, reasoned, and, to some, the rather cold and calculated stability should

Fig. 21.25 Paris, the Louvre; east front, 1667–70, Louis Le Vau, Claude Perrault, and Charles Lebrun.

stand out in several church facades that are grouped in our illustration, especially when they are compared to the group of Roman Baroque churches shown earlier in this chapter. (Figs. 21.24, 21.3) You will notice the basically static, rectilinear composition, the absence of those curves and countercurves that are so beloved of Rome. The articulation is chaste; columns and pilasters are rendered singly or in neat pairs for the most part, instead of being bundled forcefully. As a rule, single elements are not permitted to interpenetrate: they are framed and separated by pristine moldings and cornices. The general forms echo Italian prototypes before Bernini and Borromini. (Figs. 17.11b, 20.22)

Louvre and Versailles

But it is not in religious architecture that the strength of this national manner lies. We think rather of the residential design of *places* and *hôtels,* and of course the royal palaces—the amplified Louvre, Versailles, and its gardens. In the first, and especially the east front by Claude Perrault designed

in 1667, the serene confidence of a settled order comes through. (Fig. 21.25) The famous facade, overlooking the medieval parish church of St.-Germain-l'Auxerrois, is both traditional and new. Typically French is the distinction of the central tract and the end pavilions, the idea of paired columns, the windows with segmental pediments, and the sculptural decoration—all of which recall Lescot's court facade of one hundred years or so earlier. But Perrault subjects the entire front to the pedimented main accent in the middle by denying the pavilions their own crowning features, and by abandoning the traditional hipped roof for a flat roof with an Italianate balustrade. Paired columns scan the full length of the facade and are tied together by a continuous entablature rather than having individual lintels in the manner of the sixteenth century. This slender colonnade is detached from the window plane, and its depth is contrasted to the smooth ground floor on which it is raised as on a podium. It is a superbly controlled design, like the policies of Colbert or an argument of Descartes, and in its un-

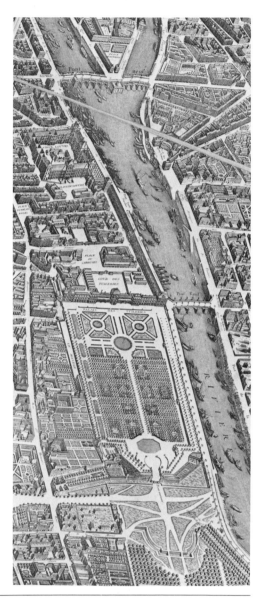

Fig. 21.26 Paris, the Louvre; two stages of its development (a) In 1609, as shown on the plan of Vassalieu (called Nicolay). The Tuileries is already built (lower third, with garden) and connected to the Louvre by the long gallery along the Seine (Grande Gallerie); beyond the Louvre (upper third) is the Île-de-la-Cité, with Henry IV's Place Dauphine (1599–1606) at its tip and the new bridge (Le Pont Neuf) connecting the square to the two banks.

(b) In the 1730s, as shown in the famous map of Michel Étienne Tourgot. The Tuileries gardens have been transformed by Le Nôtre. The Louvre itself has been vastly enlarged. Across from it, on the left bank, is Le Vau's Collège des Quattre Nations. The famous east front, shown in Fig. 21.25, is at the top left-hand corner, facing in the direction of the palatine church of St.-Germain-l'Auxerrois. (For a view of the medieval Louvre, see Fig. 16.15.)

diluted centrality it reads like an elegant graph of the absolutist ethic of the Louis XIV era.

The Louvre had been shaping up for quite a long time as the official royal residence. The palace, in essence still a medieval castle in the early sixteenth century, had been remodeled and enlarged in several campaigns and its relationship to the city altered significantly. The grounds were a vast open workshop for generations. First, under Francis I (1515–47), the central keep was destroyed and the ranges began to be redone by Lescot in the Renaissance style. By the end of the sixteenth century, only the west range and the south range on the riverfront had been completed. (Fig. 21.26) To the east, beyond the royal parish church of St.-Germain, Henry IV's new bridge crossed over to the Île-de-la-Cité where the triangle of the Place Dauphine was under construction. In the meantime, west of the Louvre a large new palace called the Tuileries was started in the 1560s and an Italianate formal garden laid out between it and the city wall. From that moment on, plans to connect the two palaces abounded.

A small gallery, at right angles to the corner of Lescot's Louvre ranges, and the long imposing Grande Gallerie along the river were the first elements of linkage. This work, and the embankments and piers that went with it, externalized the royal residence and promoted the urban quality of the Seine. Then, under Louis XIII (1601–43), the square mass of the Louvre was doubled. The Seine facade was grandly recomposed under Louis XIV by an architect named Louis Le Vau (1612–70) and focused in the middle by a domical feature. On the opposite bank, directly on axis, Le Vau erected a similar dome. It belonged to the church of the Collège des Quatre Nations, an educational institution built through the bequest of Cardinal Mazarin. A connecting bridge planned by the architect was never built, but it is clear that this whole area of the city between the island and the western walls was turning into a superb vista of Baroque scale.

Only the main east approach of the Louvre stood unresolved. To formalize this side and bring unity to the disparate fragments of the last one hundred years was the great achievement of Colbert, and it involved Bernini and the team of Claude Perrault, Le Brun, and Le Vau, whose project included the facade toward St.-Germain discussed above. The project actually entailed doubling the area of the Louvre once again, so that the total block was now four times the size of the medieval castle. And the Tuileries had also kept apace, spreading-out both in the direction of the Louvre and on the western side, where the modest Italianate garden was spectacularly extended along a grand axis up to the city wall and beyond, in the direction of the Bois de Boulogne.

The designer of these Tuileries gardens was André Le Nôtre (1613–1700), a name that more than any other perhaps epitomizes the environmental greatness of the *grand siècle*. His masterpiece is the gardens of Versailles. Hither the attention of the royal workshops had shifted when Louis XIV decided in 1677, against the advice of Colbert, to move the court and the administrative apparatus of the state to this small family chateau some 20 kilometers southwest of Paris. He had had it enlarged once already on the designs of Le Vau in the early 1660s and landscaped by Le Nôtre. Now this pleasance was to be converted into the governing heart of the nation, and at its completion it would house a court of 100,000. (Fig. 21.27) By 1685 a work force of 36,000 was busy on the immense new gardens, and on the additions to the chateau that more than tripled its capacity. To fill the pools and the Grand Canal and keep the many fountains going, Vauban used troops to divert the waters of the Eure by means of an aqueduct over the valley of Maintenon. Royal workshops went into high gear to furnish hundreds of rooms: silk and brocades came from the premises of Lyon and Tours, tapestries and carpets from Gobelins and Savonnerie, mirrors from St.-Gobain, porcelain from Sèvres. Europe had seen no comparable mobilization on a building site since the days of imperial Rome.

The purpose was to create a royal town, but the palace and the gardens were to take

Fig. 21.27 Versailles (France); aerial view.

Fig. 21.28 Versailles, the palace and gardens, ca. 1668; painting by Pierre Patel.

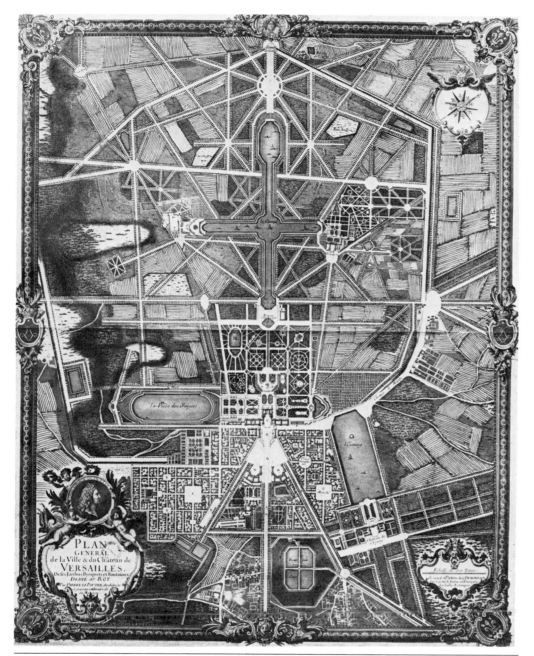

Fig. 21 29 Versailles, the gardens of André Le Nôtre, begun 1660; plan, engraving by Pierre Le Pautre.

Fig. 21.30 Versailles, Grove of the Water Theater, André Le Nôtre, ca. 1680; painting by Jean Cotelle. This was one of several groves created by Le Nôtre in the northern section of the gardens; they have since disappeared, leaving only their sites.

grand perspective on the principal entrance of the palace. Here was the core of the old chateau built by Louis XIII in 1624, a simple brick and stone structure consisting of a court surrounded by three wings. (Fig. 21.28) Le Vau's redoing of the 1660s had preserved the mass, leaving the court as it was but wrapping the outside in the thick envelope of a new building. The new garden front toward the west was a vast block 25 bays wide, with a deep terraced setback in the middle of the second floor. As Perrault would do at the Louvre slightly later, Le Vau abandoned the steep French roof for an Italianate flat roof with balustrade.

The setback was filled in by Jules Hardouin-Mansart (1646–1708), the architect of the principal campaign after 1677, with the famous Hall of Mirrors. To either side of this central block, running breadthways to the north and south, Mansart added tremendous wings. They were to contain ministerial offices, a theater, a chapel, and other secondary premises. The entire garden facade, including the extrusive main block

up most of it. What there was of a town, including the parish church and prefecture, developed in the gridded spaces between the avenues of a great trivium, which headed toward major western suburbs of Paris. Monumental horseshoe-shaped stables filled the tips of the trivium facing toward the palace. The curved lines were picked up by three parapets, rising one above the other, over the slope of the approach hill. The topmost parapet screened a large court with lateral blocks that cut in at the back to lead into a smaller court. This court, constricted in its turn, focused the

that held the royal apartments, now measured 600 meters (1968 feet) in length. This unvaried stone screen masked a myriad of functions and the multiform volumes that sheltered them. And in front of the facade, as far as the eye could see, stretched the amplified gardens of Le Nôtre.

Formal gardens with topiary, clipped hedges, and geometric beds were nothing new. The type had gained currency in the context of Renaissance villas in Italy. In the course of the sixteenth century an element of fun was infused into these strict forms. The perfection of the total design was relieved by hidden delights, surprise changes around corners, diversionary structures and resting places, and passages of free nature that sharpened the appreciation of the prevailing artificiality. All this Le Nôtre inherited. Two aspects of his work were without precedent, however. Italian villas, at least until Domenico Fontana's Villa Montalto for the future pope Sixtus V, tended to exist independently of the spatial organization of their gardens. Even thereafter, the axial relations between villa and gardens are not consistently focused on the main building, which is usually allowed to dominate the partnership. Radial paths fan out from points in the distance toward the facade, for example, instead of converging on it. In all cases the schemes are conceived as closed systems, with a boundary wall and gates that crisply define the edges of the composition.

Le Nôtre's gardens are open-ended. (Fig. 21.29) The perspective does not unfold within a finite frame. With the vanishing point always at the center of the main building, it diverges beyond the limits of the actual garden area. This area, which is immense in relation to the building, graduates from correct formality in the central tracts toward relative ease at the edges, and so avoids a clear dividing line between garden and surrounding country. The scale, then, is at the level of nature at large. The main building itself takes on merely a focal interest, and it has to be sufficiently large or prominent to play even this role in the vastness of its setting. At Versailles, L. Benevolo observes, it is the first time that "a court building assumed the spatial scale and value of the great utilitarian structures—bridges, dykes and aqueducts."

Fig. 21.31 Nieuwerkerk aan de Jissel (the Netherlands), an example of land reclamation and canals; aerial view.

536

Fig. 21.32 Amsterdam (the Netherlands), the Prinsengracht canal. The flanking walkways are now used for parking cars.

Great Galley hung with crimson brocade and edged with fleurs-de-lis. At the west end of the Grand Canal five radial avenues ran into a hunting park, and beyond this point yet another burst of straight lines disappeared into the surrounding countryside.

The composition of the gardens on either side of this great spine was not symmetrical, however. The overwhelmingly geometric layout was relieved by carefully controlled variety. Featured elements were parterres, or stretches of lawn laced with flower beds, limpid basins with fountains, groves and open-air glades actually treated as outdoor rooms, grottoes, statuary of all kinds, and an array of amusements and hideaways. But even here nothing was without calculated effect; no statue or grove without its thematic justification. Indeed, the involved iconography of the state rooms that presented the king as an incarnation of the sun-god Apollo spilled into the gardens. The famous Fountain of Apollo dominated the axis at the head of the Grand Canal. Both within the palace and in the methodical tracings of the gardens, a life of work and play unfolded according to a rigid social code called *etiquette*, inspired by the stultifying formality of the Spanish court. (Fig. 21.30) The luxury of furnishings and the magnificent extravagance of costumes, the pageantry and rehearsed pomp of special galas, set new standards of conduct for all European courts.

But more than anything else, it was Le Nôtre's gardens that impressed royal minds and proliferated. In his old age Le Nôtre was consulted by sovereigns, as Bernini had been before him, and his style was imitated all through the eighteenth century in Spain, Italy, Austria, and other German states, but also in Protestant kingdoms of the north and as far away as St. Petersburg. Princely residences like the Nymphenburg in Munich, the Zwinger in Dresden, the villas of Capodimonte and Caserta near Naples could not exist without Versailles. The lessons of Le Nôtre's intersecting diagonals and radial explosions had been applied contemporaneously to city-planning by the French themselves. These ideas also took root. They colored the extensions or reworkings of major European capitals, and entered North America with Georgian Annapolis and L'Enfant's plan for Washington. (Fig. 24.25)

As with Vauban's outworks and the old cities they surround, we have again a choice of viewpoint in respect to the work of Le Nôtre. We can think traditionally, with the primacy of the built form in mind, and decide that the gardens diminish the substance of the architecture. Or we can view tamed nature, which opens out toward the far horizons, as the triumph of the building and its patron over the environment. In the culture of his own time, Le Nôtre's experiments can be taken as an affirmation of the scientist's redefinition of space as infinite and unfettered by the bodies that occupy it. "Infinite space is endowed with infinite quality," Giordano Bruno (1548–1600) wrote, "and in that infinite quality is lauded the infinite act of existence."

The axis of the gardens at Versailles continued the line of the central avenue of the trivium toward the city. The section close to the garden front of the palace started from water pools and ran through formal flower beds bordered by clipped box hedging. To the south was the orangerie reached by a double descending staircase. Then came a stretch called the Royal Avenue, a green carpet cutting a precise path through a ground colored with fine gravel and crushed brick or slate. Halfway down, the axis turned into the Grand Canal, a broad body of water intersected in its center by a cross-arm. Here Louis XIV kept the flotilla of gondolas, sent to him by the Republic of Venice, and his private fleet of two large gilded galliots, nine shallops, and the

Even after the romantic English garden had offered an appealing alternative to the formalism of Le Nôtre and the city-form had begun to respond to the stresses of the Industrial Revolution, the power of the schemes of the *grand siècle* continued to be felt universally all the way to the near-present. (Fig. 26.7)

The Face of Protestantism

Was there in the seventeenth century a Protestant answer to Versailles? Was there a nonabsolutist environment anywhere in Europe that advanced a national high culture? Can we speak of something called Protestant architecture? The briefest path to this subject is through Dutch planning and Protestant worship. Only Holland among major European nations carried on in the Age of Grandeur the medieval traditions of bourgeois mercantilism, self-government, and the guild system. And only in church architecture, in Holland as well as in Protestant countries run by kings, is the juxtaposition of the two Europes most instructive.

Dutch drainage plans and aerial views of regained land thinly sliced by canals and spotted with windmills—these state the best counterclaim to the sublime cosmos of the gardens of Le Nôtre. (Fig. 21.31) And a practical method of planning cities, free of the drive to impose grand geometries, sets off the Dutch experience from the formal urbanism of the Italians and the French. It is estimated that at the end of the century fully one-half of the population of the confederation of seven states that comprised Holland lived in towns—this compared to France or England, where more than three-quarters of the people were landbound. Commercial and agricultural prosperity was the national goal in Holland only insofar as this goal coincided with the well-being of the towns. Bourgeois efficiency, conservatism, public control, not monumentality or the trappings of grandeur, governed the town-planning process.

The medieval core was respected and extended thoughtfully. Since the city economy heavily favored the waterfront, the main element of expansion was the canal, by means of which the harbor pushed in-

Fig. 21.33 Haarlem, Nieuwe Kerk; interior, looking east, in a painting of 1652 by Pieter Jansz. Saenredam.

land and the cost of waterfront property was kept reasonable. The city's waterways also provided opportunities for the aesthetic enhancement of its form and the unfolding of its public life. The canal was Holland's response to the French boulevard or the Baroque diagonals lunging through space. In the writings of Simon Stevin (1548–1620) this simple principle, combined with the traditional grid and the concept that all public buildings have equal prominence, was refined into a workable theory and had an early impact on the new towns that were being built in the rival kingdoms of Denmark and Sweden on either side of the Sund Strait.

Amsterdam best expresses the Dutch ideal. The original town occupied the two banks of the Amstel; where a dyke blocked its water halfway down the length of the city, there was the central nucleus. After several adjustments occasioned by its growing population, among them the in-

corporation of the peripheral moat as an internal canal, in the late sixteenth century a new semicircular line of walls embraced the city-form. Soon afterward, a master plan for a major additional extension was approved. This entailed the digging of three canals concentric with the semicircle of walls and struck in a broken arc so as to yield more regular building lots. The houses on either side of these canals were not at all like the uniform curtains of the Parisian *places*. (Fig. 21.32) Each facade had its own symmetry, its own individuality. The many kilometers of quays along these new routes bustled with the mercantile rituals of loading and unloading, while behind them, in tree-lined roadways, pedestrians and carriages passed a rhythmic sequence of varied prospects curving gently out of sight.

If Dutch planning has more to do with bourgeois culture than with the Reformation, it is in the design of churches that Protestantism is most explicit as a new

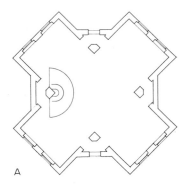

A

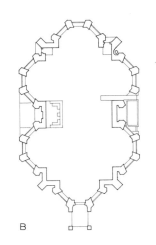

B

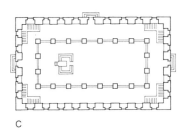

C

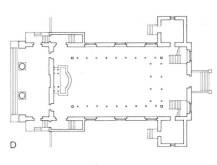

D

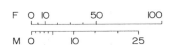

F

M

movement, a new way of life. You should not, even so, expect a full-fledged statement to appear all at once. In countries where Protestantism became the official religion, the existing Catholic building stock was simply taken over and adapted. Rearrangement of the movable furnishings came first, out of which emerged a new concept of the plan and, in due course, a new visual form and decorative scheme. Nor should you expect a consistent viewpoint among those independent-minded peoples across the continent who joined the call of protest and reform—Lutherans, Calvinists, Huguenots, Anabaptists, Mennonites, and others. The richness of Lutheran Baroque in the churches of Germany and Scandinavia warns us against trying to identify too closely a Protestant style of architecture. But there is enough agreement on what constitutes worship to distinguish the buildings in which Protestants of all persuasions prayed from the likes of S. Carlo or Neresheim.

The chief liturgical center is now the pulpit with its tremendous sounding board overhead. (Fig. 21.33) The chancel with its lavish, fixed altar is rejected as quintessentially popish. If old churches are being remodeled, this area is abandoned for purposes of worship, the altars and roods removed or destroyed. In the new churches the people gather about the pulpit and the movable altar, and the minister leads the service from this position "from which the things said may by all present be apprehended abundantly," as Martin Bucer put it.

In architectural terms this means a shift from a processional to an auditorium space, from a longitudinal to a centralizing plan. This centralization is not only horizontal, but vertical as well; that is, it generates the gallery, sometimes successive rows as in an

opera house, drawing in the whole congregation around the focal spot. The floor plan took on a great variety of forms. (Fig. 21.34) It can be L-shaped, T-shaped, polygonal, or round. The "new" Church in the Hague is a dumbbell; the Noorder Kerk in Amsterdam, a Greek cross with beveled corners. The roof was lowered and kept light—by using plaster vaults, for example—so that the supports might be slenderer and the sightlines better. There was no stained glass, sculpture, retable, or other such ornaments, though the organs in the otherwise very austere Dutch church interiors can be quite sumptuous. The internal changes led logically to a new exterior. On the sides, a two-storey elevation was articulated horizontally with string-courses and showed a characteristic fenestration scheme: low windows on the bottom tucked under the gallery, and tall ones above throwing light across the gallery into the nave. The old tripartite section of nave and aisles having been abandoned, the facade could function as a unity, and in England at least the temple front became the norm in time.

The English chapter is a curious one. The breach with Rome came in 1534; the Book of Common Prayer, in 1549. For a good long time there was little need for new churches since Protestantism had inherited a large legacy of reasonably modern churches from the prosperous wool years. Besides, England remained undecided about its Protestantism for about a century. By the 1620s the faint strains of a Gothic revival can be detected in new work, including Perpendicular Style windows, tabernacles, and screens. At the same time the Classical tradition, not as decorative adjunct to medieval buildings as it had been in Elizabethan and Jacobean architecture, but as a mature, coherent language of design, arrived full-blown with Inigo Jones (1573–1652), who bypassed the Roman Baroque and returned to an earlier and a purer vein that drew from ancient Rome and Palladio. While Jones remodeled the west front of St. Paul's Cathedral in London with one of the grandest Classical porticoes in Europe, he also produced an extraordinary church for Covent Garden, the first planned square of London, that seemed to make for the first time since the Reformation a striking Prot-

Fig. 21.34 Protestant church types of the seventeenth century; schematic plans: **(A)** Amsterdam, Noorder Kerk, 1623; **(B)** the Hague, Nieuwe Kerk, begun 1649; **(C)** Paris, the Temple of Charenton, 1623 (to replace the first temple of 1606, destroyed in a fire), Salomon de Brosse; **(D)** St. Paul's, Covent Garden, 1630–31, Inigo Jones.

Fig. 21.35 London, the bell tower of St. Stephen, Walbrook, 1672–87, Sir Christopher Wren.

estant statement of religious architecture. The church was in fact a plain temple form with a Classical portico of detached Tuscan columns, the most basic and unadorned of Classical orders, and the broad eaves were supported by exposed rafter ends. (Fig. 21.34, D and page 510) But the type had no following.

Church building, up until then a very peripheral concern, took stage center after the 1666 Great Fire of London. Eighty-seven parish churches burnt down, and fifty-one of them were replaced with new buildings by the end of the century. In charge of the reconstruction was Christopher Wren (1632–1723), surveyor-general of the King's Works. These were mostly small churches on irregular sites, crowded by adjacent structures: they make no great show externally. But Wren ensures their prominence by tall steeples which take the familiar Gothic

Fig. 21.36a London, St. Stephen, Walbrook; ground plan and section.

tower and recast it with Classical blocks assembled idiosyncratically—a fantasy world of miniature temples, triumphal arches, portals, obelisks. (Fig. 21.35) The variety is dazzling.

The interiors of the churches are wonderfully inventive and unpredictable. With little classical precedent to go on, Wren spun plans that ranged from simple basilicas without galleries, to Greek crosses, even to centrally planned, domed cores fitted into nave-and-aisles schemes. The centrally planned churches are the most adroit, as the plan and view of St. Stephen, Walbrook, suggest. (Fig. 21.36) The rebuilding of St. Paul's also combines a centralized space

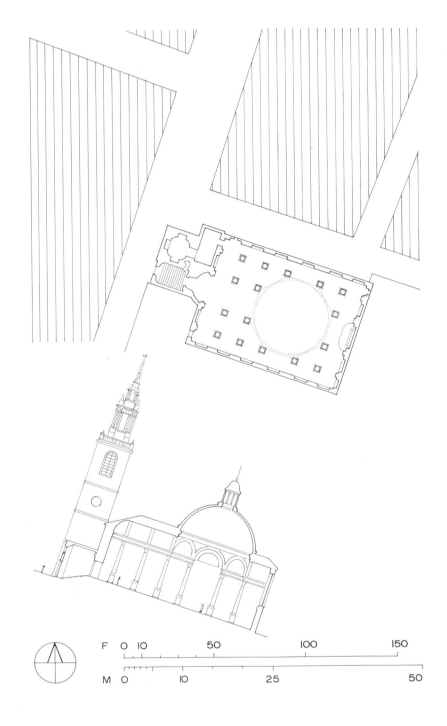

with a plan that is almost medieval. The great double-shell dome, as wide as nave and aisles together, is in the tradition of St. Peter's, but recalls recent French specimens as well. (Fig. 21.37) The coupled columns of the facade derive from Perrault's work at the Louvre; the two flanking towers look openly Baroque. A strange, masterful blend, then, of medieval, Classical, and Baroque sensibilities.

Wren's successors, Thomas Archer (1668–1743) and Nicholas Hawksmoor (1661–1736), are more emphatically Baroque in their churches, but Hawksmoor's is a very personal manner, ponderous and discordant, while Archer is the only English architect to feel at home with the Roman school of Bernini and Borromini, which he apparently knew at first hand. By this time, the Catholic style par excellence could be tapped openly without incurring ideological suspicion. But it is not this second generation of rather eccentric churches that produced the prevailing type of Anglican parish church. That distinction goes to James Gibbs (1682–1754), and especially his design for St. Martin-in-the-Fields on Trafalgar Square (1721–26), familiar to us in this

Fig. 21.37 London, St. Paul's Cathedral, 1675–1710, Sir Christopher Wren; the west facade.

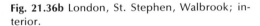

Fig. 21.36b London, St. Stephen, Walbrook; interior.

country from St. Michael's at Charleston, Christ Church in Philadelphia, and the long tradition of congregational architecture in New England which, despite extended interruptions, has lasted into modern times. (Fig. 21.38) The simple rectangular mass of the church is richly decorated externally with pilasters and terminal engaged columns that separate the bays of a two-storey elevation. The steeple for the first time rises from the body of the church, behind the pediment of a colossal Corinthian portico. Inside, the wood and plaster vault suspended from the roof trusses springs from tall slender columns on pedestals, with the galleries running visually through their shafts at the halfway point. Each of the eight columns carries its own entablature. A large Palladian window lights up the chancel wall.

We are now two hundred years from the Reformation, one hundred from the start of the careers of Bernini and Borromini. Protestant worship gets its English masterpiece, as discrete and paradigmatic as the Baroque churches of Rome or Neumann's Neresheim. But there are ironies here typical of the architectural world. Gibbs was a Catholic all his life: architects do not always hold the convictions of their clients. The model of St. Martin's was embraced by non-Anglican denominations in the American colonies, as the First Baptist Meetinghouse in Providence, Rhode Island, proves: clients do not always associate architectural form with its content. As for the sources of this design, they too are varied: Palladio, a hint of Bernini, and a good helping of Wren—that is, pre-Baroque, Baroque and the national English idiom that was spelled out in the London parish churches built after the Great Fire. The new in architecture, as we have found out long ago, is often a reordering of the old.

But to see how Classical architecture in England reaches Gibbs we need to go beyond churches, to other public buildings, palaces, country mansions. With this we may well start the next chapter, since it is in England we will have to tarry for the introduction of themes like the Industrial Revolution, historicism, and the use of new materials—the background, that is, for the subject of the concluding section of this book, the history of modern architecture.

Fig. 21.38a London, St. Martin-in-the-Fields, 1721–26, James Gibbs.

Fig. 21.38b London, St. Martin-in-the-Fields; interior as seen in an engraving from the late eighteenth century.

Further Reading

H. Ballon, *The Paris of Henri IV: Architecture and Urbanism* (Cambridge, Mass.: MIT Press, 1991).

R. Berger, *The Palace of the Sun: The Louvre of Louis XIV* (University Park: Pennsylvania State University Press, 1993).

A. Blunt, *Art and Architecture in France, 1500 to 1700,* 2nd ed. (Harmondsworth and Baltimore: Penguin, 1970).

————, ed., *Baroque and Rococo Architecture and Decoration* (New York: Harper & Row, 1978).

F. H. Hazlehurst, *Gardens of Illusion: The Genius of André Le Nostre* (Nashville, Tenn.: Vanderbilt University Press, 1980).

H. R. Hitchcock, *Rococo Architecture in Southern Germany* (London: Phaidon, 1968).

I. W. Konvitz, *Cities and the Sea: Port City Planning in Early Modern Europe* (Baltimore: Johns Hopkins University Press, 1978).

H. A. Millon, *Baroque and Rococo Architecture* (New York: Braziller, 1961).

C. Norberg-Schulz, *Baroque Architecture* (New York: Abrams, 1971).

C. F. Otto, *Space into Light: The Churches of Balthasar Neumann* (Cambridge, Mass.: MIT Press, 1979).

V. L. Tapie, *The Age of Grandeur. Baroque Art and Architecture,* trans. A. R. Williamson (New York: Grove Press, 1960).

G. Walton, *Louis XIV's Versailles* (Chicago: University of Chicago Press, 1986).

PART THREE

The Search for Self

Chaux (France), the saltworks of Arc and Senans, 1775–79, Claude-Nicolas Ledoux; the house of the director.

22

ARCHITECTURE FOR A NEW WORLD

Europe in Ferment

The history of modern architecture has come to mean two rather different things. If we take "modern" to cover a period of time stretching down to our present day, the history of modern architecture is an account of the major events, ideas, and people that shaped the built environment during this period. But "modern" has also been made to stand for something more specific—an attitude toward the built environment, a contemporary style of design thought to be unique and proper to our age. As such, it developed its own exclusive history. We speak of the Modern Movement in reference to a formalist, functional, and moral streak in the architecture of the last one hundred years, and we reach back as far as the eighteenth century to pluck instances and names that foreshadow it. For this version of the history of modern architecture, much that has happened since 1800 is irrelevant, reactionary, or perverse.

Since in this book we have resisted special pleading for any architectural philosophy and sought to tell a broad story, our sympathy is with the first of these interpretations. But regardless of whether one chooses to be a panoramic chronicler or apologist for a "modern" idiom, there is general agreement that something critical happened in the course of the eighteenth century to jar Western architecture loose from its moorings and set it adrift toward an unpredictable future. There set in a violent reaction to Baroque and Rococo forms, as well as a resistance to the authority of

Vitruvius and classical canons—both ancient and recent. An earnest search was under way for fundamental truths, for a universality more encompassing than that of Greece and Rome. The Golden Age that had supposedly dispersed the primordial gloom at the time of Periklean Athens, bloomed under the aegis of Rome, and bridged the rude Middle Ages, to find new life in the capitals of Renaissance Europe, seemed to be coming to an end. Our heritage was deeper, less tidy than that. The medieval interval might not have been a wasteland, and there was wisdom and beauty to be savored before Greece. The truth had to be extracted and distilled from wilder fruit. A new age, a new vision, was struggling to assert itself.

A Preliminary Look

What are the early signs of this essential reappraisal? Where do we start to look for them? What is there in the architectural scene that hints at revolution, and what deeper causes might be its precipitants?

The architectural historian who reads changes through the analysis of visual form is able to point at certain dislocations of Renaissance and Baroque design precepts—in England earliest of all. Then, toward the mid-eighteenth century, a theoretical position is established in Italy and France for a rigorist, functional architecture, while the past is everywhere rediscovered more accurately and tolerantly. Concrete examples of these attitudes, both buildings and projects, appear and multi-

ply as the century grows older, and there is in them enough clarity of purpose to support the positing of a new style—Neoclassicism.

At the same time, historians concerned with the ways economic and technological forces affect building production and building form place great emphasis on the Industrial Revolution, a major restructuring of the social and cultural order of Europe that has its birth, once again, in England. The phrase applies to the passage in the eighteenth century from an agrarian, handicraft economy to a machine-dominated one, from the home workroom and shop to the mill and the factory. This is not so much a fresh occurrence as it is the acceleration and spread of earlier trends. The technological factors behind it all are mechanized labor, inanimate power and most particularly steam, and an abundance of raw materials at low cost. The classic instance of the last is coal, which substituted in a massive way for the diminished wood supply and was able to feed a substantial iron industry.

A direct outcome of this movement which affects our subject is the increasing use of metal in architecture, and the structural innovations this makes possible. The industrialized production of iron will have spectacular early applications in bridges and in the rail lines. But cast- and wrought-iron also took over as a fire-resistent roofing material, and as early as 1780, cast-iron columns were replacing wooden posts as roof supports in the cotton mills of England. Bricks and timber were produced industrially. Glass, instead of oiled paper, came to be used more and more for windows. Large, many-storied mills, first seen in the previous century in England and northern Italy, were still very few in number, but they, and the remodeling of old buildings to take machines, set the challenge for a nascent industrial architecture.

But more to the point, perhaps, the factories, the abrupt increase in production, the industrial system in general, played fast and loose with long-established patterns of human intercourse. A lower death rate—a result of improved food, hygiene, and medical care—vastly swelled the population of Europe. Peasants abandoning the land in numbers crowded into the big cities. (Fig. 22.1) This landless proletariat—poor, mistreated, and living under constant fear of unemployment—injected a fresh social purpose into architectural thinking. It is the time of housing innovations, model prisons, more humane medicine, and utopian communities. Concurrently, industry found a home in the country, where it could prosper and reap profit unhampered by guilds or government regulations. The cottage and the industrial village emerged as interesting architectural problems.

There were also unforeseen changes simultaneously taking place in the customary channels of patronage. This was the Age of the Enlightenment, and one strong appetite of an enlightened Europe was an all-out attack on the Church. The papacy repeatedly lost ground to national assertions. The Jesuits, that potent and enterprising instrument of the Counter-Reformation, got caught in their own political scheming and were expelled from Portugal, France, Spain, and Naples in short order, beginning in 1759. The combined pressure of the monarchs forced the pope to dissolve the order altogether in 1773. The cloister also came under fire. Monastic privileges were curtailed; monastic land and other property alienated. This was one source of a brisk land market both in cities and the country. In fact, social ferment, capitalism, and new construction methods that weakened the notion of permanence and made the obsolescence of buildings more common helped to give the site on which a building

Fig. 22.1 Paul Gustave Doré, *Over London—by Rail,* 1872.

sat an independent economic value, and so established land as a liquid, negotiable commodity.

But we should also make an accounting of other, less material changes. Morality, in tandem with the challenge of organized religion, was becoming relative. Already in the later seventeenth century, philosophers like John Locke had started defining human action in terms of the pursuit of pleasure and the avoidance of pain. Nature in its raw, untrammeled state was being rediscovered. The awe it now inspired was one of the mainsprings of a new aesthetic concept—the sublime—which was seen as superseding the beautiful. The sublime provided justification for the stronger, more irrational emotions, especially terror and melancholy. "Out of fear pleasure springs," the architect Giovanni Battista Piranesi

wrote, echoing a sentiment that was abroad by mid-century.

Here again England's lead is undeniable. It was her literary figures, Alexander Pope (1688–1744) and Joseph Addison (1672–1719), who first spoke of an unspoiled look in garden architecture, protesting against the regimented designs of Le Nôtre. The *jardin anglais* broke the tyranny of single-minded axes, geometric paths, the clipped hedge, and the shaved tree. Curiosity about our passions, about human psychology, fueled a brand of commentary that upset the polite certainties of good taste. The most famous instance is Edmund Burke's *Philosophical Inquiry into the Origin of Our Ideas of the Sublime and Beautiful,* published in London in 1757. Burke rhapsodized the thrill that comes of danger, darkness and solitude, the noisy vastness of cataracts, the

Fig. 22.2 Rousham House (Oxfordshire, England), 1738, William Kent; a period view of the gardens showing Venus' Vale.

fury of raging storms. Between sublime awe and elegant beauty the century interposed a third aesthetic dimension, the picturesque, to express free and irregular forms, rough textures, indefinite rhythms, the evocative ruin, the quaint mill. (Fig. 22.2)

Finally, our concept of history and our place in it shifted profoundly. The episodic view of *the* Golden Age became untenable as scientific investigation revealed a more distant and widespread antiquity, and the biblical account of human events was no longer held to be sacrosanct. "How old the world is!" Diderot exclaimed in wonder to the painter Hubert Robert. Traders and Jesuit missionaries had discovered China in the late sixteenth century, a venerable culture still prospering after many millennia. Her ancient philosophy was now looked upon as a source of inspiration. The Classical world itself was held under closer scrutiny. The Etruscans were exhumed. Archaeological findings were proclaimed superior to literary sources. Visits to Classical sites, the measurement and systematic presentation of the monuments, and exca-

vation broadened the visual spectrum of this revered antiquity and curbed the time-honored command of Vitruvius and his interpreters. The Greek achievement was individuated and Rome's measured against it, and in each was seen a great variety of idioms, changes through time, sharp turns, and lapses. Excellence too, like morality, was relative.

These are some of the themes, then, that make the eighteenth century a crucial turning point for the history of architecture, as for so much else. It is the end of traditional Europe, that grand "collection of societies composed of princes, aristocrats, peasants and corporate towns." It is a questioning time, fertile but also muddle-headed, and full of contradictory impulses. Nothing goes unchallenged; no institution or dogma is considered immune to dissection. Printing, scholarly academies, and the fraternity of Freemasons give an international circulation to all research. The eye courts both order and disorder. The mind tries to understand and to accept, but also lashes out with rabid intolerance against

faith and traditional privilege. Progress is a central belief, but it is hitched to a retrospective yearning for an innocent, archaic past. Taste embraces both simplicity and variety, high-mindedness, and delight. The individual is extolled, and then neutralized in communistic systems or submerged in collective pride. Virtue and the common good are held up as the noblest of human purposes; private patronage is deprecated for its selfishness. And yet a good part of architectural experimentation takes place through the support of single influential patrons. Revolutionary forms are built for reactionary old regimes. The architecture of the century as a whole has no stylistic coherence, no consistent visual physiognomy. The comfort of a three-hundred-year-old formal syntax is lost, once and for all.

England's Lead

At the most basic, formal level, it is not surprising that the Renaissance and Baroque systems should most easily be shirked in England. The Classical tradition was neither as old there, nor did it unfold as methodically as was the case for Italy or France. There were no outstanding Roman ruins about, and the medieval episode had been very long and idiosyncratic. That was the national style as far back as anyone cared to remember—"Gothic" as it was called inclusively. In the seventeenth century, the English were said to be a "Gothic" people and their laws and government "Gothic" in origin. The Gothic invaders who had settled on the island, it was believed, were a free people, governed by laws made by the people; and that seemed the proper ancestry for a nation that had fought hard against the excesses of absolute rule. This sense of a history outside the Roman mainstream retarded the general acceptance of things classical. It was not until the early seventeenth century, as we have discovered, that the classical language, intelligently understood as an integrated system of design, was introduced by Inigo Jones. Even then it remained a rarefied court taste. We need only look at the white cube of the Queen's House at Greenwich (1616–35) and remind ourselves that it is nearly contemporary with Borromini's S. Carlo, to realize what a chaste, understated classicism Jones' is. (Figs. 22.3, 21.5b) For England this was a strikingly new look—the white balustraded prismatic shapes wholly alien in the midst of those half-timbered or quoined brick buildings, the gables, transomed and mullioned windows, carved barge-boards, and brackets of Elizabethan and Jacobean architecture.

With Christopher Wren the classical language went public and got to be more complicated. It had an eclectic, contemporary character now, borrowing freely from Italy and France but making its own rules as it went along. Wren's Hampton Court, Greenwich Hospital, and of course St. Paul's gave England a taste of the majestic scale of continental Baroque, and a claim to serious international attention. (Fig. 21.37, 22.4) The magnificent dome of St. Paul's climaxed the structural and visual drama that had started with Brunelleschi's dome in Florence and had unraveled with the great experiments of Michelangelo and the Baroque architects of Rome and Paris. The colonnades of Greenwich Hospital are a match for Bernini's colonnades for the square of St. Peter's; the sweep of Hampton Court Palace shares something of the grandeur of Louis XIV's Louvre and Versailles. But it is all quite personal, too—firm and clear-headed, larded with unclassical surprises, more a scientist's architecture than that of an artist locked into theories of codified beauty.

The heirs of this official style of post-Restoration England were Nicholas Hawksmoor (1661–1736) and John Vanbrugh (1664–1726). They are said to represent the height of an English Baroque. But what most attracts our attention is the harshness, the raw strength, the additive congress of solids and spaces, so different from the concatenated, flowing rhythms and spatial dynamics of Baroque Italy. (Figs. 22.5, 21.5b) We are struck by the individualized treatment of parts, the emphasis on elementary geometric forms interlocked ponderously, even clumsily. The rejection of a graduated plasticity in the exteriors and the separateness of the elements, especially the solid round columns, may be closer to France in one sense, (Fig. 21.24a) but not the dissonance of heavy stresses, the composition of big-boned blocks, the iron-handed rustication that often extends to the columns themselves. And the medievalism of Vanbrugh's castellated piles comes through not so much

Fig. 22.3 Greenwich (London, England), the Queen's House, 1616–35, Inigo Jones; view of the south front.

in revived details, but in the pervasive brooding that pushes the classical to the edge of the romantic. (Fig. 22.6). All this is very odd for its day, but strangely prophetic of the so-called revolutionary architects of France, Ledoux especially, who make their appearance at the end of the century. (Fig. 22.25)

Queen Anne died in 1714, and the war of succession ended when a prince of the House of Hanover ascended the throne as George I. This brought the Whig party into power; these were men of the Enlightenment who, in contrast to the conservative Tories, stood for the supremacy of Parliament and the Bill of Rights. This new mood of national freedom and xenophobia worked against the court-centered grand manner of Wren and his disciples. This was the stage for a sudden, unexpected turn of taste, engineered by a small determined group of men led by Richard Boyle, Third Earl of Burlington, who were able to move architecture back in time to Inigo Jones and Palladio.

In 1715 the first installment of a lavish English edition of Palladio's *Four Books of Architecture* appeared in London. In the same year the first volume of Colen Campbell's *Vitruvius Britannicus* reacquainted the public, through superb engravings, with the buildings of Jones. In the preface, Campbell roundly condemns the Italian Baroque. After Palladio "the great Manner and exquisite Taste of Building is lost," except for Jones who takes up and culminates what the Vicentine master had begun. Here we have the groundwork of Neo-Palladianism, the movement that will sweep Georgian England and fashion its architecture, both private and public, for about forty years.

Two prime movers are behind this astonishingly successful movement. The ability and means of its chief patron, Lord Burlington, must come first. His two ancestral homes, the house in Piccadilly (London) and the country estate at Chiswick, were turned into showcases of the new style. Here he surrounded himself with artists and men of letters, including Campbell and the decorator and landscape designer William Kent (ca. 1685–1748). Burlington was a Whig. He dreamed of a universal idiom representa-

Fig. 22.4 Greenwich, the Royal Naval Hospital (now the Royal Naval College), 1696–1716, Sir Christopher Wren, completed by Nicholas Hawksmoor; aerial view looking south. The Queen's House (Fig. 22.3) is at the end of the long axis. The site was that of an abandoned royal palace designed for King Charles II by John Webb and begun in 1664; in the right foreground, the block east (left) of the court belongs to this early program. The western block was added in the early nineteenth century.

tive of liberty that would express the nation's democratic and enlightened present. The simple, reasonable, easily mastered formulas derived from Palladio could disseminate the proper English response to the architecture of absolutism and of the Catholic Church.

And here the phenomenon of the architectural handbook had a decisive part to play. These cheap compact manuals produced by and intended for building craftsmen offered brief, practical explanations of the new style and simple drawings of details such as doors, windows, and the like, that could be copied directly. (Figs. 22.7, 22.8b) The best known of these books are those of the prolific William Halfpenny and Batty Langley. Through them Neo-Palladianism was "made easy for the meanest ca-

pacity," as the title pages often put it. The standardization of house-building in London that came about through various Acts of Parliament promulgated after the Great Fire of 1666 now extended to the trappings of taste. Whole streets were lined with houses that looked almost exactly alike. (Fig. 22.8a) They were most commonly mass-produced by speculative builders from the constructional trades, bricklayers and carpenters especially. The material was brick; the site usually narrow. The house sat on the front portion of this long strip, with a courtyard or garden at the back; a coach house and stable were added beyond for the more substantial clientele. Each floor had two rooms, one behind the other, with a passage and staircase on one side. The stacked up vertical living arrangement was

as typical of London as the horizontal spread was of Parisian *hôtels* with their *appartements*. From the street, steps led up to the front door which had a Palladian frame in wood, usually painted white. The ground floor was handled as a sort of podium, with the main emphasis on the upper floors. These were either articulated by pilasters and attached columns, or else they displayed their simple classicism in the window frames and the top cornice, and of course the proportions. Wooden eave cornices were prohibited by a statute of 1707 and parapet roofs became the trend. At about the same time, casements gave way to sash windows with recessed frames—a Dutch invention.

The set procedure for these developments was for a noble landowner to divide an urban property into lots and lease them at low ground rent, for periods ranging up to 99 years, to people who were willing to build houses on them at their own expense. This activity was coordinated by the speculative builder acting as a middleman. At the end of the lease, the houses reverted to the ground landlord. We should point out that most London estates were entailed in a family, or held in trust by a corporation, and could not be lawfully sold. The system of leasing allowed their development for profit and gave the city neat uniform neighborhoods with a main square, a number of streets, shopping and marketing facilities, and sometimes a church.

The Georgian residential estates stood outside the tight confines of the medieval City of London, in the spacious West End. This area came to be reserved for the nonproductive upper classes, while the City remained securely in the hands of businessmen. The strong appeal of the fashionable quarters triggered the exodus of aspiring merchants from the City, while the quality of life among the increasingly segregated laboring classes and job-seeking migrants deteriorated steadily. Social apartheid between the poor and the well-off, between the run-down urban core and affluent suburbs, became a fact before there was any recourse to legal restraints like zoning.

The public buildings and country mansions in the new style were grander of course, but always deported themselves with that cool reserve and steadfast ortho-

Fig. 22.5 Blenheim Palace (Oxfordshire), 1705–16, Sir John Vanbrugh and Nicholas Hawksmoor; tower of the kitchen court. The palace was built for the Duke of Marlborough.

Fig. 22.6 Seaton Delaval (Northumberland, England), 1720–28, Sir John Vanbrugh.

doxy that characterized the whole Neo-Palladian movement. But we should not think that what was involved was a simple transcription of Palladio. Jones' own reliance on sixteenth-century Italian models had been rather eclectic, and that showed in the work of the architects who now revived him along with Palladio. The new Burlington villa at Chiswick, for instance, is only superficially patterned on Palladio's Villa Rotonda. The plan, arranged around a central octagon, shows contrasting sequences of rooms on the two fronts, and the facades are likewise different. (Figs. 22.9, 19.33) Even the Palladian windows of the garden front, with their embracing outer arches, domesticate this characteristic Venetian motif. The octagonal drum with its thermal windows juxtaposes a strongly extrusive element to the cubic mass below. Internally, the inspiration for the decor of the rooms is Jones, not Palladio.

But most baffling is the fact that Chiswick, and all other Neo-Palladian villas, were meant to stand in parks of an informal design. On the face of it, this seems paradoxical. (Fig. 22.10) How can an architecture of such limpid, doctrinaire formality be reconciled with free, picturesque gardens? We have to remember here that Neo-Palladianism asserted a national, democratic, Protestant ethos against the dual tyranny of Catholicism and absolute rule. If the Baroque advertised the first, the formal gardens of the French reminded Whig aristocrats of princely bombast, of autocracy and its corollary, servitude.

Those parks and gardens, where, his haunts betrimmed
And Nature by presumptuous art oppressed,
The woodland genius mourns . . .

as a poet in Burlington's circle put it. England, a free country, leaves Nature alone—or almost so. Art is content to touch up what is already there, "to dress her mistress and disclose her charms." Classical architecture and the landscape garden, then, are two complementary vehicles through which to express liberty.

The sources of the English garden, according to the commentary of the day, were republican Rome and China. The first was a literary fancy of course. It leaned on Latin pastoral poetry and descriptions of country villas by Cicero, Pliny, and others. The Chinese debt seems stranger. It is the product both of interpretation and fact. Enlightenment belief had it that China was governed wisely by benevolent rulers who had the people's interest at heart, not unlike Plato's model of the philosopher-king. This found confirmation on the environmental level in the carefully bred license of Chinese gardens, with their sinuous rills, dainty bridges, and little islands, of which travelers brought back accounts and, for the first time in 1713, also visual representations. Kent, who laid out what was perhaps the first partly natural garden in England for Burlington's Chiswick villa, shared in this love for the studied irregularity of the

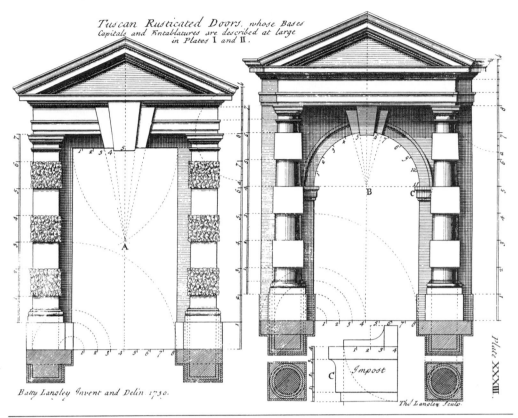

Fig. 22.7 Batty Langley, "Tuscan Rusticated Doors"; a page from his architectural handbook, *Treasury of Designs*, 1745.

Chinese, which the English literati called *sharawagi*.

The decorative fashion called Chinoiserie had started even earlier with a little pleasure house built in the park at Versailles by Louis Le Vau in 1670. Behind this fashion was a fanciful picture of China as the land of brightly painted and latticed garden houses, of tall pagoda towers, upturned eaves hung with carillons of little bells, and lots of jade and porcelain. By the early eighteenth century, Chinese rooms were becoming quite the rage in European palaces. (Fig. 22.11) Their playful, exotic, prettily colored interiors suited the flirtatious mood of the Rococo. These rooms featured porcelain and fretted wood, lacquer paneling, "japanned" furniture, panels with florid Oriental scenes, enamel snuff boxes, and soft-paste porcelain statuettes.

Soon Chinoiserie buildings were being sprinkled in the gardens, especially in England—pagodas called "the house of Confucius," fishing houses, bridges, tea-houses, all made of materials rarely more substantial than fretted wood, *papier mâché*, and painted sailcloth. (Fig. 22.12) By mid-century the poet James Cawthorn could write:

> Our farms and seats begin
> to match the boasted villas of Pekin;
> On every hill a spire-crowned temple swells,
> Hung round with serpents, and a fringe of bells.

A World to Choose From

All this was a little more than curious fancy. The exotic spots in the parkland of country mansions were meant to be evocative of sentiment. The garden was composed to be read as a narrative, like a pastoral romance or poem. Mock temples, pyramids, grottoes, rustic cottages, real or sham ruins, baths, hermitages were carefully planted to be viewed as storied pictures. The statuary included famous men of genius—poets and scientists and playwrights. Guests did the circuit of the grounds on horseback, in carriages, or in lightweight chaises. The most involved circuits in estates like Stowe and Stourhead would feature Turkish tents, temples to Flora and the sun, a Pantheon, a monument to Friendship, antique columns, Chinese houses, a Temple of British Worthies, and a whole range of bucolic buildings associated with country life and agriculture. (Fig. 22.13)

These storied settings had important implications for the future of modern architecture. It is a two-pronged message that comes through. First, architecture is an expressive language, capable of recalling meaningful contexts through association. Second, the building traditions of all times and places merit attention and respect. Both of these attitudes gave a rationale to the architectural revivals—historicism, as it is sometimes called—of the second half of the eighteenth, and most of the nineteenth, century. Moreover, these attitudes bring about a partial liberation from that classical urge for universal canons of beauty.

The associative power of architecture rested, at this initial stage of its formulation, on the ability of ruins to conjure edifying or ruminative memories and on the fascination of cultures other than our own—that is, on our fascination of transferences of time and place. As early as 1709, we find Vanbrugh trying to convince the Duchess of Marlborough to preserve the ruinous old manor house at Blenheim because it would awaken remembrances of things past and provide, with its archaic look, a foil for the splendid palace he had just designed for the family. Ruins brought up "more lively and pleasing Reflections (than History without their Aid can do) On the Persons who have Inhabited them; On the Remarkable things which have been transacted in them, or the Extraordinary Occasions of Erecting them."

The new interest in the passage of time, in spirit-stirring decay, corresponds to that sense of objective history that is characteristic of the Enlightenment. Civilizations were mortal, even the greatest among them, and

Fig. 22.8a London, Bedford Square in Blooms-bury, laid out about 1775; view of the east side with its pedimented central tract.

Fig. 22.8b Farnham (Surrey, England); detail of a Georgian house.

their material remains were useful in re-minding us of this fact. The contemplation of ruins had both a moral and an aesthetic side: moral, in that we were forced to think that all things, our own accomplishments included, must pass, and to accept the vanity of human effort; aesthetic, because ruins were ideal conveyors of picturesque beauty, battered, rough, with intriguing textures and jagged ends—the very oppo-site of the cultivated finish of contempo-rary designs. These responses sprang from the appreciation of ruins for their own sake, in contrast to the interest of Renaissance architects in the monumental relics of an-cient Rome in order to derive from them universal principles of architectural prac-tice. To this class belonged also vernacular

structures—the farmstead and the barn, everyday buildings beyond the concern of serious architects—which communicated spontaneity and timelessness in a similar way.

The attraction of alien traditions was in-evitable after the world was opened up through the voyages and colonization of the sixteenth and seventeenth centuries. But increasingly this exposure to cultures whose operative logic was different from that of Europe raised doubts about the old argu-ments of universality. If there were many valid, sophisticated, and pleasurable archi-tectures across the world, then our way of doing things was not necessarily unim-peachable or best. The built environment too could help us to understand humanity,

if we were open to foreign conventions and mastered them through emulation.

Now came a mounting effort to ascertain the design habits of non-European cul-tures, along with past traditions outside of Greece and Rome. More important, it was realized that this information, to be at all assimilable by architects and decorators, must be presented in graphic form. Visual material now began to appear in travel ac-counts of the Middle East and elsewhere, while scholars like J. B. Villalpanda and Abraham Kircher toiled at fanciful recon-structions of legendary ancient monu-ments such as the Temple of Jerusalem and the Tower of Babel. (Fig. 22.14)

In 1721 an extraordinary book was pub-lished in Vienna that set out to present a world view of architecture through en-graved plates. The author was the Austrian architect J. B. Fischer von Erlach (1656–1723) and his book was quickly reprinted several times, twice with an English translation. Besides the seven wonders of antiquity, Fischer supplied images of the Parthenon, lesser-known Roman buildings like Diocle-

Fig. 22.9 Chiswick House (Middlesex, England), begun 1725, Lord Burlington (Richard Boyle); view of main front. Burlington's inspiration was Palladio's Villa Rotonda (Fig. 19.33).

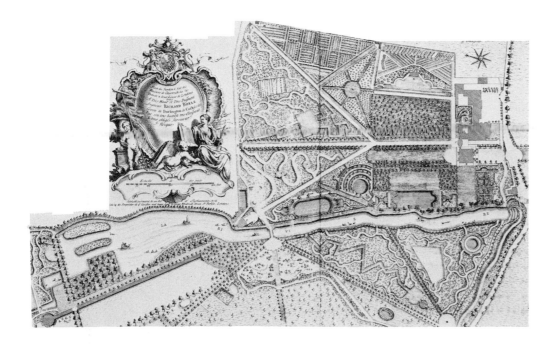

Fig. 22.10 The gardens of Chiswick House, 1736, William Kent; plan. Chiswick House is located at the far right.

tian's palace at Split, and a section entitled "Of Some Arab and Turkish Buildings As Well As about Modern Persian, Siamese, Chinese and Japanese Architecture." This remarkable panorama was supplemented by Fischer's own inventions, including his church of St. Charles in Vienna with a facade that carried allusions of Hagia Sophia, the Temple of Jerusalem, and the triumphal columns of Rome, like those of Trajan and Marcus Aurelius. (Fig. 22.15)

In the meantime medieval architecture, excluded from Fischer's book, was being rehabilitated. Its position was certainly odd. In terms of classical theory, "Gothic" had to be treated as a thousand-year-old deviation from good taste. But the great churches of the Middle Ages in England, France, and Germany were a live legacy, dear to the people; they could not be brushed aside. Admiration for the height of these buildings, their airy grace and technical prowess, was voiced since the seventeenth century. Wren allowed himself to make additions to medieval churches in an approximation of the same style, for "to deviate from the old Form would be to run into a disagreeable Mixture." And of course his famous steeples, and Vanbrugh's castellated mansions, behaved as Gothic structures in classical uniform. (Figs. 21.35, 22.6)

For a while afterward, in a related approach, measures were taken to "correct" Gothic architecture according to classical rules. In 1742, Batty Langley and his brother brought out a book of engravings for country houses and garden buildings called, in the second edition of 1747, *Gothic Architecture, Improved by Rules and Proportions*, in which five orders in the Gothic manner were used to design set pieces for doors, windows, chimneys, and entire rooms. (Fig. 22.16) In France meanwhile, Gothic churches were amended for aesthetic propriety with the removal of those elements—rood screens, altars, stained glass—that had previously given offense to Protestants for religious reasons.

Fig. 22.11 Palermo (Sicily), pavilion in the Villa della Favorita called Palazzina Cinese, 1799–1802, Giuseppe Patricola; game room in the Chinese style.

Fig. 22.13 Stourhead House (Wiltshire, England), the gardens, mid-eighteenth century, Lancelot ("Capability") Brown. The gardens are organized around an artificial lake and are dotted with a number of pavilions, among them, seen in the distance, a pantheon and a rustic cottage.

Fig. 22.12 Kew Gardens (Surrey), Chinese Pagoda, 1763, Sir William Chambers.

Fig. 22.14 Johann Bernhard Fischer von Erlach, "A Chinese Triumphal Arch" from his book entitled *Entwurf einer historischen Architektur (Outline for a History of Architecture),* published in Vienna in 1721. The caption says that many such arches can be seen in the large cities.

Fig. 22.15 Vienna (Austria), the church of St. Charles Borromaeus (Karlskirche), 1716–37, J. B. Fischer von Erlach; drawing by the architect published in his *Entwurf einer historischen Architektur.*

But conversely, some voices were raised in behalf of the positive lessons modern architecture could learn from Gothic churches. The architect Jacques-Germain Soufflot (1713–80) believed that through a serious study of Gothic architecture "we should be able to find the right mean between their style and our own"; and that was what he set out to do in his famous Parisian church of Ste.-Geneviève, to which we will return. In England, on the other hand, public taste came to favor a genuine Gothic revival. It began innocently with garden structures first, but then gained more serious acceptance with Horace Walpole's gothicizing of Strawberry Hill, his country house at Twickenham near London, starting around 1750. (Fig. 22.17)

The central challenge of all this experimentation with exotic and historical modes was to question the absolute validity of classical design. Universal acceptance of certain general rules had ensured a truly astonishing unity of architectural thinking during three centuries. By the mid-eighteenth century this confident sway of classicism no longer went unquestioned. It seemed that the Classical tradition should be considered at best the most worthy of a number of permissible sources for contemporary architecture. It must have been shocking to see public declarations, like Pierre de Vigny's in 1752, that "the productions of all nations and of all centuries must be adopted, brought to perfection and liberated from the tyranny of the antique fashion." But the authority of Greco-Roman culture was not to be shaken off so easily.

Neoclassicism

Even before the pressures built up against them from the outside, classicists had had family quarrels about their aims. In the seventeenth century a lively debate raged in Europe between Ancients and Moderns. Galileo, Francis Bacon, and Descartes, three founders of modern science, had established analytical and experimental knowledge as a substitute for the blind faith in the classics. In architecture, the battle was joined between those who unswervingly upheld the guidelines of antique precedent, and those others who defended the

Fig. 22.16 Batty and Thomas Langley, "The Fifth Order of the Gothick Architecture"; a plate from their book *Gothic Architecture, Improved*, 1747.

The Fifth Order *of the* Gothick Architecture. *Plate* **XIII**.

Batty and Thomas Langley Inv. and Sculp. 1741.

Fig. 22.17 Twickenham (near London), Horace Walpole's house called Strawberry Hill, a cottage enlarged and gothicized, beginning about 1750, on the designs of William Robinson, Richard Bentley, and others. This view is from the south.

right of contemporary architects to vary and amend what Vitruvius and the buildings of Rome prescribed.

The most articulate spokesman of the Moderns was Charles Perrault, the brother of the architect who designed the east front of the Louvre. Without deflecting from the classical faith, Perrault made a rather significant distinction. There were two kinds of beauty, he wrote, positive and arbitrary. The first derived from the use of rich materials, from effective massing, symmetry, grandeur, and fine workmanship. It was obvious to all, and in a sense unarguable. Arbitrary beauty, on the other hand, was a matter of taste, of changing fashion. It depended on ornament, and ornament varied according to local custom and also through time. This was the architect's special province.

Now, to Perrault, the basis of good taste remained the classical language because it enjoyed universal consent. But once the love affair with alternate visual conventions came out into the open, the idea of the architect as style expert took hold. The architect became the artist who applies ornamental dress of various kinds to the immutable substance of architecture—its positive beauty. The rules of design, that is, of surface, did not hinge on absolute values; they merely set down the relative values of what was acceptable at the time. Soufflot put it simply: "Rules are taste and taste is rules . . . taste forms them and they form taste."

But in the first part of the eighteenth century what bothered reform-minded classicists most was not the creeping menace of nonclassical revivals, but the excesses of late Baroque and Rococo architecture—especially the latter, whose precious fragility and curlicued, frivolous ornament catered to an indulgent, sybaritic, self-loving society. In England, the counteroffensive against all of this was Neo-Palladianism, although the serpentine paths and whimsies of its landscape gardens probably owed as much to French Rococo taste as they did to distant China. In France, the reaction took a different turn. By mid-century there was a yearning for the stately, self-possessed taste of the Sun King and his court. It was now generally held that the age of Louis XIV ranked with, and surpassed, the three high points of culture—the days of Perikles (or else Alexander), Augustan Rome, and the Florence of the Medici. The Rococo was an ephemeral deviation from the true path of architecture set down by Le Vau, Mansart, and their associates. Now one had to go back and retrieve the dignity and substance of that culminating achievement. (Cf. the two images of Fig. 21.21.)

In practice, neither the monumentality nor the heavy, rich decoration of the Age of Grandeur was revived. But much of what was built in the decade or two after 1750 favored a clean, purified, crisp look. The most characteristic work in this line is that of Ange-Jacques Gabriel (1698–1782). His elegant Petit Trianon at Versailles says it all— a pristine cubelike mass with sharp clean edges, smooth surface bands for moldings, no domes nor pediments for emphasis, only a polite projection of the central bays in the monochromatic facade plane. (Fig. 22.18) It is not quite Palladian, as a quick comparison with the Queen's House at Greenwich will show, but it shares the same sense of still formality. (Fig. 22.3)

Greece against Rome

And even this amount of reserve did not satisfy a vocal avant-garde of architectural puritanism. There was a movement afoot to deny the ornamental use of the orders, the spirited play of pilasters and applied columns, pedestals, and ornamental pediments—what Abbé Cordemoy pejoratively called "architecture in relief." Columns were working members in the beginning, and that is what they should go back to being. It was Roman architecture that had turned the orders into nonstructural decor, so one had to go farther back in time to regain their true purpose. That meant Greece, whose inventions Rome had absorbed and perfected. And backward still, in the origin of these monuments, one had to acknowledge the wooden structures of which the temples were the petrified transcriptions; and ultimately, one must uncover the primitive hut from which Vitruvius had said all architecture takes its start. To retrace this development would help the modern world to shed all inessential elab-

Fig. 22.18 Versailles (France), the Petit Trianon, begun 1762, Ange-Jacques Gabriel; detail of the exterior.

oration and attain an honest architecture once again.

Advocates of this radical approach were called Rigorists. The most influential names were the Venetian Carlo Lodoli (1690–1761) and Abbé Laugier (1713–69), a lapsed Jesuit, whose *Essay on Architecture,* published in Paris in 1753, had wide repercussions both in France and abroad. Lodoli's was the more extreme stand. His principal contention was that architecture should be thought of as a science, and not as the province of artistic imagination governed by rules of beauty. Lodoli rejected the fixed proportions of the orders. Design was not dependent on ideal models but on (1) *function,* by which he understood how the structure of a building performs in accordance with the use of the building, and (2) *representation,* "the individual and total expression which results from the way the material is disposed according to geometrical-arithmetic-optical rules to achieve the

purpose intended." Ornament could be added once the functional requirements were met, but ornament to Lodoli was not some fancy topping wedded to precedent. It was to be based on the scientific laws that govern the essential building materials, wood and stone, and was thus to become an integral part of the building.

Laugier did not rule out the orders, but insisted that they behave as working members, not as applied decoration. The construction and decoration of buildings must coincide; columns, entablatures, and pediments must *do* the actual work of holding up the building, rather than merely appearing to do so. Without knowing much about real Greek buildings, Laugier advocated a return to Greek architecture when simple structural logic had dictated the form. The Roman contribution had been not so much an improvement but a deceptive elaboration of the principles of statics. Laugier condemned the use of pilasters, arched openings, and pillars, and considered broken pediments, spiral columns, the projection and recession of entablatures, the entire stock-in-trade of Baroque architecture, as intolerable abuses. Freestanding, load-bearing columns and the straight entablatures that bridged them—these were the essence of good architecture.

The singling out for praise of Greek practice destroyed that hallowed unity of the Classical idiom that the orders were supposed to enshrine. Pro-Greek and pro-Roman parties sprang up and fought each other with words and images. Expeditions set out to study and record Greek remains for the first time. The credit of being first goes to the team of James Stuart and Nicholas Revett. For almost three years, between January 1751 and September 1753, they braved the plague, political unrest, and other hazards that resulted from the Turkish occupation and visited ancient sites like Corinth, Delphi, and Delos. But they spent most of their time measuring and drawing the remains of Classical Athens, hoping to rediscover through such accurate fieldwork the lost ideal proportions of Greece. (Fig. 1.13b) The first volume of their beautiful engravings, entitled *Antiquities of Athens,* appeared in 1762. In the meantime the Greek colonial architecture of Paestum

in central Italy was being publicized by others. (Fig. 22.19) These burly, weather-beaten temples bolstered the trend of primitivism, the desire to go back to a rudimentary past in order to begin a new unsullied historical epoch. The Doric order came back into favor.

For its own part, the adversary school amassed evidence to prove the vitality, inventiveness, and bold variety of the Roman tradition. The monuments of distant provinces were lavishly introduced in books such as John Wood's *The Ruins of Palmyra* of 1753 and Robert Adam's *The Ruins of the Palace of the Emperor Diocletian at Spalatro in Dalmatia* of 1764. Meanwhile, the discovery of Herculaneum in 1738 and Pompeii in 1748 opened an exciting chapter of modern excavation.

The most colorful and effective figure of the Roman camp was the architect and printmaker Piranesi (1720–78). Fiercely proud of his country's past and a master of imaginative reconstructions, this hot-headed

Fig. 22.19 Paestum (Italy), the Temple of "Neptune" (Hera II); engraving by G. P. M. Dumont, 1769.

Fig. 22.20a Giovanni Battista Piranesi, imaginary prison interior, from his series of etchings called *Carceri (Prisons)*, ca. 1744 (reissued ca. 1761).

Venetian settled in Rome about 1740 and took on the Rigorists, Grecians, and all others who had joined the chorus against the virtuosity, the inventive vigor, the richness of Roman architecture, both recent and ancient. Piranesi accepted and championed a current theory that the Romans were indebted to the native stock of the Etruscans more than to the Greeks. In architectural terms, he considered the Etruscans the intermediaries between the masonry architecture of Egypt and that of Rome, and one of Piranesi's popular fantasies was a series of fireplaces in the Egyptian manner. At the other extreme stands his series of *Prisons* ("Carceri"), a menacing sinister vision of free-floating interiors where there are no columnar orders of any kind to articulate the space, no fixed architectural climaxes, no boundaries described or implied. These dark inventions that borrowed from the theater, and from underground ruins which Piranesi knew so well, were filled with drawbridges, chains, gaping arched passages, and all sorts of engines and machinery, to create a destabilized world that is the very opposite of classical order—befitting Burke's definition of those terrible and danger-filled sensations that characterize the sublime. (Fig. 22.20a)

But the vast bulk of the more than one thousand etchings of Piranesi is devoted to the visualization of the city of Rome, its monuments and utilitarian structures, its grandeur and decay. (Fig. 21.6a) In rich, inky contrasts of light and dark, he conjures scenes of thrilling gigantism and desolation. He revels in the engineering feats of aqueducts, highways, and densely stacked substructures. (Fig. 22.20b) He uses oblique views and a shaggy windswept atmosphere to suggest immense vistas in which all buildings, old and modern, succumb to the

Fig. 22.20b Giovanni Battista Piranesi, "The Aqueduct of Nero," from the series *Vedute di Roma (Views of Rome)*, ca. 1750.

ravages of time. He catches the scale, the mood, the lighting of that Roman vaulted architecture whose multichambered complexity is much more dramatic in a ruined state than it could have been in actuality. He recorded everything: building fragments, objects, inscriptions, cisterns, fallen vaults, pavings; and from this vast knowledge he put together eclectic and highly literate compositions of his own.

Rome had lost none of her drawing power. On the contrary, she had become in the eighteenth century the obligatory port of call for writers, dilettantes, antiquarians, and aspiring artists—a clearinghouse for new ideas and the showroom of European talent. An English gentleman's education was not deemed complete without the Grand Tour which culminated in Rome. To the French Academy on the Corso came, for a three-year stay, the winners of the Prix de Rome, the highest award of the Academy of Architecture in Paris. They were drawn, these young *pensionnaires,* to the fervid circle of Piranesi whose printing shop was across the way, or else to the circle of Johann Joachim Winckelmann, the chief defender of Greek supremacy.

Since the accession of Pope Clement XIV (1769–1774), antiquarianism was official policy. Ancient statuary was on exhibit in the Palace of the Conservators on the Capitoline and in new rooms at the Vatican built in the 1770s beyond the Cortile del Belvedere. The art museum as a building type, and as an institution of public education, was coming into its own. Private collections at the villa of Cardinal Albani had been similarly installed on the advice of Winckelmann. Distinguished foreigners visited these temples of art and bustled among the ruins, attended by vivacious cicerones. Painters and printmakers obligingly composed the most memorable of the ruins in imaginary views for the visitors to take home with them to London, Munich, or Bordeaux.

The Architectural Harvest
What do we have to show in concrete terms for this new pluralism in European thought? How did the disassembled monument of classicism fall into new formations? Where was the meeting point of Piranesi and Lau-

Fig. 22.21a Osterley Park House (Middlesex), begun 1761, Robert Adam; east portico. This was a remodeling of a sixteenth-century Elizabethan house. The inspiration for the portico is the Erechtheion in Athens (Fig. 7.27).

gier, of revivals and originality, of historicism and modernism?

One thing is certain. Neoclassicism is not a tight, well-defined style like early Gothic or the Rococo. We can tell the product, but the brands are legion. Looking at the more distinctive buildings and building projects of the second half of the century, we can detect several urges at work, singly or in combination. There is, to begin with, an insistence on greater accuracy in the evocation of ancient models, and therefore a wide variety of specific classicisms. Robert Adam's output alone could embrace the

Grecian Ionic order, as displayed in the east portico of Osterley Park, ceilings in the manner of Roman Palmyra, rooms that recapture the design of the baths of Caracalla in Rome, as well as random details taken from Hadrian's villa, the palace of Diocletian, Nero's Golden House, and the Akropolis of Athens.(Fig. 22.21)

In the mind of Neoclassical theorists and artists, this was not a question of direct copying. The aim of the serious architect was imitation. This the painter Joshua Reynolds described as "a perpetual exercise of the mind, a continual invention." One had

Fig. 22.21b Osterley Park House; the fireplace niche in the entrance hall.

and its desire to abstract essences from great buildings wherever they may stand in the pageant of history—these were new and far-reaching attitudes.

An early stage is exemplified by Soufflot's church of Ste.-Geneviève, the patron saint of Paris, begun in 1757. (Figs. 22.22, 22.23) We can notice in the plan its resemblance to St. Mark's in Venice; both have domes over the four arms of the Greek cross. (Figs. 11.30, 19.22) These domes are supported on single columns with straight entablatures, and there are runs of single columns between this inner core and the outer shell. It is probably less easy for us to appreciate, because of later alterations, the extreme lightness of the superstructure, which had to prevail with such a slender support system and which Soufflot intentionally derived through his studies of Gothic statics.

But this interior is still Roman in feeling and rich in decoration. We should compare it to something from the end of the century, Sir John Soane's offices for the Bank of England, for example, to see the true potential of Neoclassicism. (Fig. 22.24) We are struck, first, by the basic geometric shapes of the composition, and then by the flatness of the surfaces. The stress is on crisp outlines, which either have no moldings at all, or else are framed by flat bands of ornament of the architect's own imagining. In fact, the whole Classical apparatus—pilasters, entablatures, coffers—is reduced to a thin, diagrammatic pattern of grooves and fretwork. In these spartan, unalloyed rooms, Piranesi's cavernous spaces with their inky shadows submit to Rigorist discipline. (Cf. Fig. 22.20a)

This is the second component of Neoclassical architecture, then, and perhaps one more important than the accurate imitation of ancient models, which we emphasized at first: a language of abstraction that draws on elementary geometry, sharply cut and unframed openings, and an air or stringency, even a harshness. In terms of mass, this often translates into the use of solid shapes like spheres, pyramids, cones, and cylinders: in terms of the arrangement of parts, juxtaposition rather than fusion prevails. For the Neoclassicist, the attraction of the Pantheon is in its sphericity and the

to know enough about his models, study them thoroughly enough, so that they would become part of his thinking, and so that he would have good reasons to select from among them what he needed for his own designs. The reasons had to do with "character"—that particular quality about every building which expresses its purpose. For architecture was a speaking art, able to convey the moral of its programs and to stimulate sentiments. Prisons had to look austere, for instance, and the severe Doric order might prove the best means to bring out the character of this specific program.

Solemnity, in public buildings at least, was broadly espoused. The target, of course, was the opulent sensualism of the Baroque where illusion, with whatever means secured, had mattered far more than structural or constructional reality. What was being pushed aside now was that rich tradition of applied effects: the plasticity of walls pleated with engaged columns and pilasters, and animated through sinuous rhythms and an abundance of sculptural and painted decoration. The antidote had to be simple, rectilinear wall planes and rows of unattached columns with straight entablatures. We could point to some past instances of such rigor: Bernini's colonnaded arms for the square of St. Peter's, pedimented temple fronts in Palladio's villas, the Protestant simplicity of St. Paul's Covent Garden, and earlier still, Brunelleschi's columnar purity. (Figs. 20.21, 19.32, 16.7) But the erudition of Neoclassical design, the belief that it was recovering some elemental first principles of architecture,

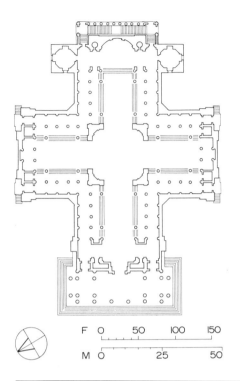

Fig. 22.22 Paris (France), the church of Ste.-Geneviève (renamed Panthéon during the French Revolution), 1757–92, Jacques-Germain Soufflot; ground plan.

Fig. 22.23 Paris, Ste.-Geneviève (Panthéon); interior.

head-on encounter of a temple front with a cylinder. (Fig. 22.25a) A column is primarily a cylindrical shaft, and even fluting would detract from this fundamental truth. The value of the Greek temple lies in its rectangularity, in the play of columnar screens against smooth blank walls.

In the years just before and after the great French Revolution of 1789 that toppled the monarchy, France produced some of the most telling architectural images of Neoclassicism. They are the work of two men, Claude-Nicolas Ledoux (1736–1806) and Étienne-Louis Boullée (1728–99), who both believed passionately in architecture as an expressive language. Boullée built little; his astounding vision soared beyond reasonable means, and that is the way he wanted it. His designs were a form of poetic communication; it mattered little to him if they

Fig. 22.24 London, Bank of England, 1788–1808, Sir John Soane; Old Colonial Office in a period engraving.

Fig. 22.25 Paris, customs toll houses, or *barrières*, 1784–89, Claude-Nicolas Ledoux. There were some sixty of these placed at highway crossings. Despite being hated at the time by ordinary Parisians for representing the oppression of the state's tax collectors, the *barrières* survived the French Revolution of 1789, and remained in service until the mid-nineteenth century when the railways made urban customs borders obsolete.
(a) The Barrière de la Villette. It commanded the harbor of the Ourq Canal in northeast Paris and is one of four of the Ledoux barrières that have made it to our own day.
(b) The Barrière des Bonshommes, north of the Seine.

were ever realized. Ledoux, on the other hand, had an active practice, and much of his early work falls within the limits of conventional taste. But his genius for architectural metaphor took flight when he was chosen to the Academy of Architecture in 1773 and appointed royal architect. In the 1780s he was busy on a series of tollhouses for a customs ring around Paris, and a vast complex for the royal saltworks at Chaux in eastern France. These, and the projects included in his book of 1804, have earned him a special place as a prophet of modernism in the more restricted sense of the word.

Ledoux's tollhouses run the gamut of Neoclassical combinations. (Fig. 22.25) They are basically cubelike and they make use of temple fronts, the arcuated "Palladian"

window, peristyles, domes, and other familiar elements. But what Ledoux does with these is totally unconventional and, to a classical eye at least, jarring if not bizarre. Sometimes a huge cylindrical drum sits crushingly on a square pavilion, or a massive pedimented cube is lifted above ground on small stocky columns. Rustication and ornamental details, disproportionate in scale, obtrusively accent the surfaces. The preferred column is a baseless Tuscan, and in some instances the shafts are broken up by square blocks to create a grating, rusticated order. (See page 546.)

The unexecuted projects, both of Ledoux and Boullée, push abstraction so far that they end up as pure studies of solid geometry. The authors present them with a

sententious moralizing fervor—that belief shared by most Neoclassicists that architecture must be associated with politics and the social condition, and must lead the way to a new and better world. Boullée's monument to Newton, a tremendous hollow sphere, is a metaphorical tribute to the great scientist's work. (Fig. 22.26) The project for a library hall consists of a tunnel-like space defined by walls of stacks and a coffered barrel vault; its crown is slashed by a long skylight. (Fig. 22.27). Between the walls and the vault runs a full-sized colonnade that serves to highlight, by comparison, the vastness of the overall scale. All detail is submerged in the overpowering conception and the strong contrast between broad fields of light and shadow. One understands why Boullée called himself the inventor of "the architecture of shadows."

Form and Reform

The utilitarian side of such architecture was clearly secondary. The projects of Boullée were elevated thoughts expressed in monumental form. He would have agreed with the German philosopher Hegel who defined a public building as the independent, self-justified symbol of a universally valid thought; that is, something conceived for no other purpose than to manifest the highest through itself. Now this would not sit well with ordinary clients who spent money on a building because they had some mundane use for it. The new approach was not popular. It seemed best suited to commemorative structures and also to institutional programs like hospitals, theaters, and prisons which had a social or cultural message to emblazon. But even they had to satisfy functional needs. The ideal, comprehensive forms of the Neoclassical architect were obliged, therefore, to tolerate the logic of use. And since public institutions were under ameliorative review in the rising mood for a new righteous society, form was also seen as the vehicle of social reform.

Reformers wore many stripes: they were economists, intellectuals, philanthropists, and architects. All shared the conviction that the right physical environment had a ben-

Fig. 22.26 Étienne-Louis Boullée, project for a cenotaph for Sir Isaac Newton, 1784; elevation. The drawing was done by the architect. (Bibliothèque Nationale, Paris) There was to be a planetarium inside, with the shrine of Newton at its base. Boullée wrote of this project: "O Newton, as by the extent of your wisdom and the sublimity of your genius you determined the shape of the earth; I have conceived the idea of enveloping you in your own discovery."

Fig. 22.27 Étienne-Louis Boullée, project for the royal library (Bibliothèque du Roi) on Rue de Richelieu, 1788; drawing by the architect. (Bibliothèque Nationale, Paris)

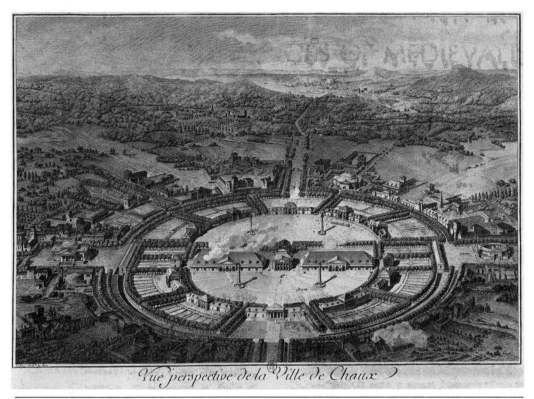

eficial effect on its users, and that bad buildings were capable of doing psychological damage. The ultimate objective was a changed world—more virtuous and egalitarian, nobler, better governed. And the reformers were willing to address pieces of this elusive utopia. Some planned model communities for small groups of like-minded people; others looked at cemeteries, prisons, housing, and the like, with a view to improving them. At the formal level there were proposals for multipurpose buildings, like Jeremy and Samuel Bentham's Panoptikon, a radical scheme applicable to hospitals, schools, and prisons. From the reformist perspective, the appeal of such solutions is in the reflection of total order, in regularity, and in control; for reform is nothing if it is not totalitarian.

The centralized, radial plan, for example, served communal settlements where cooperative and associative living under the benevolent eye of some overseer could be instituted. Ledoux employs this type of diagram for his ideal community of Chaux. (Fig. 22.28). This model country town, realized only in part, was a circle enclosed by a boulevard, with administrative buildings forming a spine across the middle. The various occupations associated with the

Fig. 22.28 Claude-Nicolas Ledoux, model town of Chaux, after 1775. The church is on the left, outside the oval boundary.

Fig. 22.29 Diagrammatic plans of hospital schemes: **(A)** the cross-axial scheme (project for the Ospedale Maggiore in Milan by Filarete, 1460s); **(B)** the radial scheme (project for the Hôtel-Dieu in Paris by Antoine Petit, 1774); **(C)** pavilion scheme (design for a hospital at La Roquette, a suburb of Paris, by Bernard Poyet, 1787).

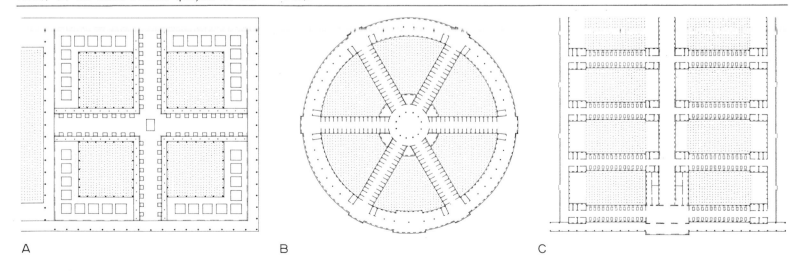

A   B   C

central industry, the saltworks, were to live here in harmony—the charcoal-burners, gunsmiths, and hoopmakers; their morality was sharpened through an educational program revealed by the names of the communal buildings. In the House of Reconciliation, quarrels were to be settled peacefully; in the phallus-shaped Oikema, or House of Love, sexual instruction was to be provided.

The efficacy of the radial plan for prisons and asylums derived from the possibility of central supervision. In hospital planning, the radial scheme was defended on the grounds that it allowed easy access and the maximum accommodation of patients. (Fig. 22.29). The chapel was at the center, and in one famous project it nestled directly beneath an enormous cone-shaped shaft for ventilation. The alternative arrangement was the so-called pavilion type, in which rows of wards flanked a central axis. The advantage of these independent wards was that patients with contagious diseases could be isolated. And Thomas Jefferson, the most well-known Neoclassicist on our side of the Atlantic, adapted the pavilion type to an educational institution, the campus of the University of Virginia, in order to distinguish the various faculties. (Fig. 24.21).

One thrust of the reform movement was to move hospitals out of the city to the cleaner, healthier air of the country and to move cemeteries, prisons, and slaughterhouses out, too, for the sake of the city's physical and moral welfare. The mass graves of the parish burial grounds were a serious threat to public health and an indignity to the memory of the deceased. More and more, informed opinion favored extramural cemeteries where each person could be allotted an individual tomb in a parklike ambience, and where monuments like Boullée's cenotaphs could add a cultural dimension to the grounds. Napoleon's decree of 1804 merely formalized the de facto withdrawal of burials from residential areas in the last decades of the eighteenth century. The detachment of hospitals and cemeteries from the parish church, to which they had long been wedded, could not help but alter the nature of the city core. This may well be the most significant urban response of the new age—this and the imbalance of the age-old relationship be-

Fig. 22.30 Bath (England); aerial view of the crescents. The Royal Crescent is in the middle ground; it dates from 1767–75 and was designed by John Wood the Younger. Higher up, at the top right-hand corner, is Landsdown Crescent (1794, John Palmer).

tween town and country in the wake of the Industrial Revolution.

It is otherwise difficult to categorize a thing called the Neoclassical city. Nonetheless, several points need to be made relevant to eighteenth-century urbanism. There was a genuine concern for the betterment of public thoroughfares and private dwellings. The habit of arranging ordinary town houses as monumental unities, a legacy of the royal *places* of Paris, spread and was made over in three ways. Bath, a sleepy provincial town that rose to great popularity after 1720 as a watering place, illustrates them all. (Fig. 22.30) In the Royal Crescent and in the curving terraces of Lansdown Crescent above it, on the northward slopes, we have majestic testimony of the verve of eighteenth-century planning and its venture into unusual forms. The

great semi-elliptical block of the Royal Crescent will be a hallmark of English urban composition for decades. Lansdown Crescent, even if we account for the magnificent serpentine outline as merely a Baroque survival, stands out for another reason. It is set against the wooded hillside, interpreting an urban space in terms of garden design. This, too, is a notable contribution of the eighteenth century, and it is handled with delightful variety. We find this feature at two other famous sites. The Place de la Concorde in Paris (1755–63) has parks on two sides of it and the river along the third. The present Piazza del Popolo in Rome, conceived in 1794, used a terraced garden on the east side to unite the oval space of the square with the Pincio summit, while the west side was to be free of buildings so that it looked out on a green

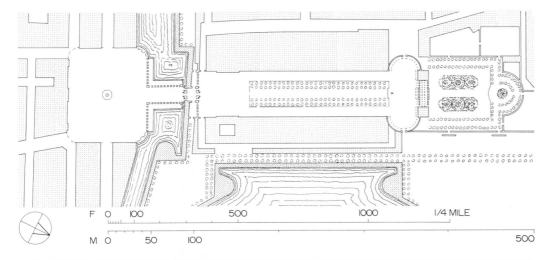

F O   100   500   1000   1/4 MILE

M O   50   100   500

Fig. 22.31 Nancy (France), system of public squares, begun 1752, Emmanuel Heré de Corny. The patron was Stanislas Leczinski, ex-King of Poland, Duke of Lorraine and son-in-law of Louis XV. The system connects the old medieval town on the right with the new town of the seventeenth century on the left. In the new town, the Place Royale (now Place Stanislas) was modeled after royal squares in Paris and featured a statue of King Louis XV in the center. By crossing the moat of the old walls, to the right, and passing through a triumphal arch, we come to the Place de la Carrière—a tree-lined promenade flanked by blocks of housing. It ends in the Hemicycle, a vast forecourt for the Provincial Government Palace (*Intendance*). Behind the palace are formal Renaissance gardens. (The scale is given in *toises*, a *toise* being equal to a fathom, or six feet.)

have guided Europe, but for the rise of Napoleon, is idle to speculate: Where would Greece have ended without Alexander or Rome without Augustus? What happened, happened. The French Revolution spawned an empire, and the high-minded idealism of the eighteenth century was borne away on the wings of a resplendent phoenix that soared for two decades, was consumed, and never quite rose again. While the adventure lasted, the spare stark forms of Neoclassicism fell short of matching the affectations of Napoleonic pomp. The only satisfying model, visually and politically, was the Roman Empire under the likes of Augustus and Trajan. Ornament, opulence, allusions to expansive victory and proud omnipotence—these now swept aside the moralizing severity of Laugier and Ledoux. Piranesi's pride in Roman magnificence now had the edge, but his vision was purified of all that was morbid in it or threatening. Only the confidence, the majesty, and the triumph were retained and celebrated. (Fig. 23.1)

And when the age of Napoleon was over, the European community, architecturally as in every other way, tried to resume the dialogue with history it had bravely taken up during the eighteenth century. For a while yet, its architects would roam through the landscape of the past, leaving their options open and justifying their choices. The time had not come to put away the safe riches of tradition and start altogether afresh. "For although it is difficult for man to learn," as the French architect Viollet-le-Duc explained, "it is much more difficult for him to forget."

area, with a distant view of the dome of St. Peter's on the opposite bank of the Tiber. Third, and last, in Neoclassical urbanism we find a concatenation of squares of different sizes and shapes as a conscious rhythmical progression. At Bath, the conventional Queen Square, the *rond-point* of the Circus, and the Royal Crescent are interconnected by two major thoroughfares that were part of the same grand plan. Similarly, three *places* at Nancy, the capital of Lorraine, stretch in a single line, with a triumphal arch between the first two and a tree-lined avenue between the second and the third. (Fig. 22.31)

Where the Age of Enlightenment would

Further Reading

A. Braham, *The Architecture of the French Enlightenment* (Berkeley: University of California Press, 1980).

W. Doyle, *The Old European Order, 1660–1800* (Oxford: Oxford University Press, 1978).

M. Girouard, *Life in the English Country House: A Social and Architectural History* (New Haven: Yale University Press, 1978).

W. Herrmann, *Laugier and Eighteenth-Century French Theory* (London: Zwemmer, 1962).

H. Honour, *Neo-Classicism* (Harmondsworth and Baltimore: Penguin, 1968).

J. Rykwert, *The First Moderns: The Architects of the Eighteenth Century* (Cambridge, Mass.: MIT Press, 1980).

D. Stillman, *English Neo-Classical Architecture*, 2 vols. (New York: Harper & Row, 1988).

J. Summerson, *Georgian London*, 3rd ed. (Cambridge, Mass.: MIT Press, 1978).

A. Vidler, *The Writing of the Walls: Architectural Theory in the Late Enlightenment* (New York: Princeton Architectural Press, 1987).

D. Wiebenson, *Sources of Greek Revival Architecture* (London: Zwemmer, 1969).

Camborne (Cornwall, England), tin mine winding engine
at the East Pool Mine, 1887.

23

ARCHITECTURAL ART AND THE LANDSCAPE OF INDUSTRY, 1800–1850

A Matter of Styles

In the opening decades of the nineteenth century, European architecture was learning to live with diversity—and even thrive on it.

Classicism was still the leading creed, but it had by now given up all pretense to orthodoxy. A number of readings were current, but none conforming to strict canonical rules. Napoleon's fancy leaned toward the Roman Empire. (Fig. 23.1) A Greek revival, experimentally launched before 1800 in garden "fabricks" and residential architecture, went public with ceremonial city gates and buildings like Downing College at Cambridge by William Wilkins, begun in 1806. (Fig. 23.2) The archaeological savor of this Grecian style came from a spate of new publications, among them the later volumes of Stuart and Revett's *Antiquities of Athens* issued in 1787 and 1794, the team's *Ionian Antiquities,* and Wilkins' studies of Greek temples in Sicily and southern Italy which appeared in *Antiquities of Magna Graecia* (1807). At the same time the Greeks' war of independence against their Turkish masters, a popular cause in Western Europe since the first rising of 1769, enhanced the romantic appeal of the revival.

But both Romanizing and Grecian architects often composed masses and defined volumes in the Neoclassical ways of Ledoux, Boullée, and Soane. If this was partly a question of aesthetic choice for the younger architects, it was also true that archaeological rectitude and contemporary needs and practices were not simply reconciled. For instance, the temple form proved too inflexible an envelope to contain the complicated functions of a bank or a government building. Greek windows, narrower at the top than at the bottom, were not a very fit substitute for modern hinged and sliding windows. So the compositional forms and design pecularities of Greece and Rome, painstakingly documented through fieldwork, had to be amended for the sake of new building programs. It was not at all uncommon, to mention the more obvious departures, that wing blocks would be attached to the Classical temple mass, or that a centralized domed space would be located directly behind a correct Greek temple front that served as the principal facade. Robert Smirke's British Museum in London, begun in 1823, takes both of these liberties, notwithstanding its immaculate adherence to the Ionic order of the Erechtheion in the grand south front of Great Russell Street (Figs. 23.3, 7.27) (It is, however, possible in this case to excuse the salient wings as heeding the precedent of the Athenian Propylaia. See Fig. 7.16.)

But many classically minded architects got around the prim rigidities of their archaeological models by opting for one of two more sensible alternatives. They fell back on the Renaissance, that initial phase of the fifteenth and early sixteenth century acceptable to the purist historicism of the time. Here was the pioneering effort to use antique prototypes with the freedom that contemporary needs called for. (Fig. 23.4) This Renaissance revival, since it could provide the flexibility to suit new building types and programs, became the most popular of all styles in the first half of the nineteenth century. It was used especially for urban residences, hotels, and government offices. In Germany, where countless specimens survive, the preference for the round-headed windows of the fifteenth century explains the local art-historical term *Rundbogenstil,* the "round-arch style." (Fig. 23.5)

The second alternative was to assume the stance of eighteenth-century rationalists and to see classicism less as a bible of aesthetic conventions than a scientific method of responding to the programmatic and structural requirements of modern buildings. The contention here was that architectural form was the direct result of structure and function. So it made sense to reappraise the proportions of the structural elements, which is to say columns and their trabeation, in light of the strength of the materials used and the demands of function. If necessary, columns could be set farther apart than Classical archaeology would condone, and the gap between them could be bridged by a flat arch stiffened with iron, instead of a lintel. It was also permissible in the rationalist doctrine to bend classical principles like symmetry and regularity when use so dictated. Stairs should have their windows correspond to landings rather than be made to obey some uniform facade alignment.

The chief opposition to this congeries of classical modes came from the Gothicists.

In the last chapter we had noted the emergence of medieval partisanship under two separate guises. "Gothick," primarily an English indulgence, referred to a mood-making, wistful recall of the Middle Ages that was inspirited by the picturesque aesthetic and the literary genre we call the Gothic novel. The French, on the other hand, sought to extract from the great cathedrals of the twelfth and thirteenth centuries structural pointers and, specifically, how to transfer thrusts from vaults to outer supports. Soufflot's Ste.-Geneviève is the famous case: it does not *look* Gothic, but it tries to act in the same manner as those great vaulted systems of the past. (Fig. 22.23)

Yet the Gothic revival, properly so named, a fervent and archaelogically rigid movement that stirred public opinion during the 1830s and 1840s, was rationalized as a national and Christian style. In their self-devotion that followed Napoleon's defeat, both England and Germany gleaned from their medieval architecture a message of national identity. The proudest statement of this chauvinism in England was the Houses of Parliament, built when a fire in 1834 had destroyed most of the original buildings of the Palace of Westminster. (Fig. 23.6) For Germany the corresponding display was the fastidious completion of Cologne Cathedral in the High Gothic idiom of the thirteenth century. The Christian exegesis fitted France and the United States as well. In England, it drew strength from the Catholic Emancipation Act of 1829 and the resolve of the Anglican Church, whose authority extended to America, Australia, and New Zealand, to share in the restoration of organized faith by exploiting the mystical ambience of medieval worship. In France, the repair of churches, which had suffered during the Revolution of 1789, and the general program of conserving the nation's medieval heritage kept the Gothic argument alive.

And even this was not the end of it. The taste for things Egyptian, another eighteenth-century affectation, gained the force of a full-fledged revival after Napoleon's campaigns in this province of the Ottoman Empire with the publication of the magisterial twenty-one volume *Description d'Egypte*. The style was especially successful in the United States where it was applied, for a whole train of associations, to

Fig. 23.1 Paris (France), Arc du Carrousel, 1806–8, Charles Percier and Pierre-François-Léonard Fontaine. This triumphal arch, now standing in isolation near the Louvre, was intended to be the main gateway to Napoleon's Paris residence, the since destroyed palace of the Tuileries (see Fig. 21.26).

prisons, medical colleges, libraries, cemetery gates, and even churches and synagogues. The lands of Islam, past and present, cast their spell too. The Moorish monuments of Spain, the Alhambra first among them, were being handsomely set into print. Elsewhere archaeology came in the wake of military invasions. The British Empire absorbed India in the late eighteenth century; Thomas and William Daniell's *Antiquities of India* followed in 1800. A little later the French conquered Algeria and published her heritage.

The plates in these books came alive with such pleasurable settings as Sezincote House in Gloucestershire (1803), designed by Samuel Pepys Cockerell for his brother Charles, a nabob of the East India Company, and John Nash's remodeling of the Royal Pavilion at Brighton (1815–23) for the Prince of Wales, the future King George IV. (Fig. 23.7) Nash (1752–1835), the quintessential genius of the picturesque, also designed Cronkhill, a small residence near Shrewsbury in Shropshire, which started the fad for villas based on the vernacular of the Italian countryside. (Fig. 23.8) This particular style, with its irregular silhouette, asymmetrical towers, and deep eaves, also made it to America where by the mid-century it had extended into public architecture (railroad stations, city halls, etc.).

Nash's example was not unique. Many architects were comfortable in more than

Fig. 23.2 Cambridge (England), the Master's House at Downing College, 1806–11, William Wilkins.

Fig. 23.3 London (England), the British Museum, begun 1824, Sir Robert Smirke.

one style. Versatility, a sign of superior learning and talent, was nothing to be shy about. Clients might sometimes request projects in several different styles for the same job. Cities might favor a collection of assorted buildings for picturesque effect and symbolic propriety. Devonport in Plymouth, England, gathered in one public space a Greek city hall, an Egyptian library, a Roman monument, and the Mount Zion Chapel in "Hindoo," all by the same architect. Intuitively or with some theoretical explanation, subtle amalgams were also tried for the sake of a personal signature or in search of a modern style. The Houses of Parliament are Gothic in detail, but the plan and the facades show all the balance and regularity of a classical composition. (Fig. 23.6)

Still, there were, by and large, two principal schools in the first half of the nineteenth century: the classical and the Gothic. The former dominated the European scene during the first three decades; the latter mounted its challenge during the next two. Let us take a close look at these schools, before we turn to the subject of new building materials and the functionalist environment of the Industrial Revolution.

Napoleonic Interlude

The Napoleonic Wars brought about a general hiatus in building production over much of Europe. In France itself and in the subject lands of the empire during the time of Napoleon's greatness, from his coronation in Paris in 1804 to the battle of Waterloo where he made his final stand in June 1815, only a tiny fraction of the hundreds of grandiose projects that made the rounds were actualized. In Paris the regime is best remembered by two triumphal arches, the church of the Madeleine, the column of Place Vendôme, the Exchange, and several urban schemes like the Rue de Rivoli. For the rest, there was a good deal of remodeling of older buildings. With some justification, in fact, the so-called Empire style is classed more as a decorative than an architectural event.

But the projects are impressive. They countenanced drastic changes in famous old cities from Brussels and Madrid, to Milan, Rome, and Cairo. This seductive paper vision of grandeur underscores two important aspects of the Napoleonic period in France that will affect the future. One has

Fig. 23.4 London, Pall Mall, the Reform Club, 1837–41, Sir Charles Barry. To the left of the Reform Club is the Travellers' Club (1829–32), also by Barry.

to do with a special attitude toward urbanism; the other, with the academic method of design taught in the French professional schools which were reorganized under Napoleon.

"The Emperor," his favorite architect Pierre-François-Léonard Fontaine wrote, "hated to seek the beautiful in anything other than that which was large." The most vocal theorist of the time, Quatremère de Quincy, elaborated:

Physical size is one of the principal causes of the value and effect of architecture. The reason is that the greatest number of impressions produced by that art derives from the feeling of admiration. And it is natural for man to admire size, which is always related in his mind with the idea of power and strength.

Voiced by a culture that conceived Versailles, such sentiments should not surprise us. But there is a difference between the grandeur of Louis XIV and that of Napoleon. Versailles occupied and organized a largely unbuilt area; the royal *places* of Paris did the same. Napoleonic projects condoned massive demolition in the hearts of old cities in order to make room for the public theaters of the regime ("Men are as great as the monuments they leave behind," the emperor declared), but also in order to re-evaluate the great buildings of the past within the scale and scenography imposed on the urban fabric by the new planners.

These prodigious spaces, the wide straight avenues and cavernous squares, would have destroyed once and for all the subtle spatial play between small buildings and large, between the monumental nodes and the unremarkable standard tissue that gives them their status, their impressiveness. In

Fig. 23.5 Munich (Germany), the Ministry of War, 1826–30, Leo von Klenze. A good example of the *Rundbogenstil;* the rusticated arches in accented series recall Florentine palaces such as the Medici (Fig. 16.4).

Fig. 23.6 London, the Houses of Parliament, begun 1835, Sir Charles Barry and Augustus Welby Pugin.

Rome, for instance, many residential blocks were to be torn down around the Pantheon, in front of the Trevi fountain, and around the Colosseum. (Fig. 23.9) The famous landmarks would be isolated and set within monumental perspectives. That struggle of the Baroque to incorporate and galvanize what was there, the calculated huddling of high- and low-style buildings, the dramatic sequence of constricted and open spaces—all this would be sacrificed for the sake of what Pierre Lavedan has called "the beauty of the void."

But there was another, more positive side of Napoleonic urbanism. The emperor, an ex-ordinance officer, had a genius for administration. The planners he trusted tended to be his own prefects and ministers working together with state engineers. Planning was seriously concerned, for the first time, with administrative, economic, and social issues at least as much as urban aesthetics. The highway network was overhauled internally and extended with new stretches outside France, to pull in the strategic centers of the imperial territory. The connection between Paris and Milan through the Simplon Pass, for instance, was opened in 1806. Both in regional and urban planning, land use, circulation, and health were prime considerations.

And education in design as revamped under Napoleon also had mixed consequences. The academic tradition of architecture in France had flourished since the days of Colbert. It rested on the official curriculum of the Academy of Architecture, which was organized around a string of juried competitions; the French School in Rome where the ultimate winners were sent for an extended stay; and a body of theory formulated in the writings and lectures of great teachers like Soufflot, Jacques-François Blondel (1705–74), and Boullée. It was the only formal program of architec-

Fig. 23.7 Sezincote House (Gloucestershire, England), ca. 1805, Samuel Pepys Cockerell.

575

tural education in the West, and when the statute of 1762 admitted foreign students for the first time, they came in increasing numbers, especially from Germany and Russia. The emphasis was on design, on architecture as an art, but history and structure were not slighted. Soufflot studied the resistance to compression of various building materials. Another professor, Antoine Joseph Loriot, invented a new kind of cement derived from slaked lime, which he patented in 1774.

After the Revolution of 1789, when the Academy of Architecture and the Rome School closed down for a time, the system was reactivated, but with two important changes. The Academy's independence ended; it was merged with the Academy of Painting and Sculpture into a new entity, the Academie des Beaux-Arts. Its school was the École des Beaux-Arts. Architecture was thus officially allied with the arts, all of which paid homage to fine drawing. Meanwhile, a technical school called École Polytechnique was founded to train engineers. This gave state recognition to the importance of modern civil engineering.

The move was inevitable. The beginnings of industrialization burdened architecture with technical demands, such as wide-span bridges, fireproof construction, and the scientific handling of environmental controls like heating and ventilation. A corps of technicians now shouldered these new tasks, in France and elsewhere, breeding its own heroes and monuments. Engineers designed a great number of buildings, either because these required mathematical calculation beyond the ken of architects, or because the purely utilitarian nature of industrial structures of all kinds seemed unworthy of an architect's artistic sensibility.

The split between building art and building science has probably been overdrawn. Nineteenth-century architects were not innocent of modern technology, nor were engineers devoid of a formal sense of design. Architects did not dismiss industrial programs out of hand; they merely insisted that these must aspire to something more than simple utility in order to qualify as architecture. The reaction of the German architect Karl Friedrich Schinkel (1781–

Fig. 23.8 Shrewsbury (England), Cronkhill House, 1802, John Nash.

1841) to the factories and mills of Manchester during a visit to England is typical. They are nothing but "monstrous masses of red brick," he wrote in his diary, "built by a mere foreman, without any trace of architecture and for the sole purpose of crude necessity, making a most frightening impression." (Fig. 23.10) He later gave an architecturally sound answer to this problem in the pristine cubic masses of the

Packhof buildings in Berlin, a complex of commercial structures along the Kupfergraben. (Fig. 23.11) And conversely, engineers were not always content to let their technically competent solutions stand without stylistic beautification. There was much that was ugly and unsettling in mechanized industry and transportation. The fury of progress had to be appeased by the established civilities of form; the harsh

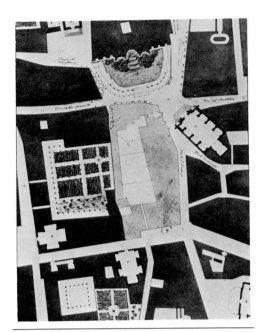

Fig. 23.9 Rome (Italy), project for the enlargement of the piazza in front of the Trevi Fountain, 1812, Giuseppe Valadier; drawing by the architect (Accademia di San Luca, Rome). The fountain is top center; the light gray areas are blocks to be demolished.

contrast between palaces and churches, on the one hand, and railroad stations, factories, and warehouses, on the other, had to be played down.

If architects in hindsight may appear far too conservative with respect to new materials and methods, it is well to distinguish between the launching of innovative practices and their effective commercialization, which may come much later. Until the exploitation of rolled steel on a large scale in the 1880s, metal construction could exert only a limited influence on architectural design. Cast iron was brittle, had little tensile strength, and melted at relatively low temperatures. Wrought iron performed much better, but it was costly to produce. Nor were engineers always interested in addressing the tangible difficulties that faced architects in their vastly diversified practice.

At any rate, in France at least architecture saw itself more and more exclusively as high art—and it was taught that way at the École des Beaux-Arts. The school did have a professor of stereotomy, the applied science of solid geometry relevant to the traditional building methods of masonry and carpentry, and students were given constructional problems regularly. But all this was not integrated with their design studies, and so the impression was created that design and construction were separate disciplines. Still, the Beaux-Arts system rationalized the design process most effectively within a general classical framework and propagated a way of architectural thinking that called forth competent, visually pleasing buildings even from practitioners of modest talent. The process was taught under three headings: elements of buildings, elements of composition, and detailing. And the great guide was Jean-Nicolas-Louis Durand's *Lessons of Architecture,* first published in 1802–5 and reissued regularly until 1840.

Durand (1760–1834), a student of Boullée, became the professor of architecture at the new École Polytechnique. The bias of this association comes across in his insistence that the aim of architecture is not aesthetic. The aim is rather the welfare of users, and fitness and economy are means of reaching it. A building will please if it serves our needs well. The central concern of the architect should be methodically to work out a composition that will satisfy the requirements of the program. Ignoring his teacher's paeans to the symbolic value of architecture and its power of expression, Durand held that "Architects should concern themselves with planning and with nothing else."

The ground plan is, for Durand, the great organizer of composition, and it is guided by major and minor axes and a framework of squares multiplied or subdivided in accordance with the functions to be provided for. (Fig. 23.12a) Do you want a courtyard? Do you want subfunctions accounted for in the main space or given their own subordinate volumes? Having resolved such programmatic claims on the plan, you can then decide how you would like to cover the rooms you have created, choosing between flat ceilings and several kinds of vaults. The elevations, generated by the plan, combine vertically and horizontally architectural elements like columns, arches, and various types of windows in agreeable and historically inoffensive ways. Durand illustrates a number of these combinations. (Fig. 23.12b) They are of Early Christian, Byzantine, Romanesque, and Italian Gothic prompting, as well as the more obvious mutations of the classical family. His book also presents an assortment of standard architectural features like porches, halls, galleries, courtyards, and stairs, and then, in a second volume, designs of buildings according to their functional type, everything from triumphal arches and tombs to lighthouses, treasuries, and barracks.

The Academic Tradition Abroad

French academicism conquered Europe more effectively and lastingly than Napoleon's armies. While students from all over were drawn to Paris to study at the École des Beaux-Arts, French architects were put in charge of major commissions in Finland, Turkey, Russia, and America. From 1806 onward, the Rome Prize projects were collected and published in large, elegant volumes. Durand's *Lessons* circulated widely. The *Rundbogenstil* of Germany and the typology of public buildings in northern Europe in general are plainly indebted to this sensible handbook.

On the subject of town-planning Durand has little to say. At the edges of his city stand hospitals and cemeteries amid trees; the city gates are triumphal arches. These are of course Neoclassical ideas. The rest is standard stuff. The streets are to be straight and lined with porticoes, and for squares one cannot do much better, it seems, than the royal *places* of Paris. But both this Baroque habit of uniform enclosures and the monumentalized voids of Napoleon could be of no practical value to a Europe coming to grips with the political and social harvest of the French Revolution, and the even more ravaging impact of industrialism.

The recession of autocratic rule left states without the power needed to bring off urban intervention on that scale. In the more liberal nations the triumph of capitalism and the bourgeoisie confounded an already circumscribed executive authority. Take, for

Fig. 23.10 A page from the diary of Karl Friedrich Schinkel, dated 16–18 July 1826, with a drawing of factories and mills in Manchester, England. (Staatliche Museen, Berlin)

Fig. 23.11 Berlin (Germany), Lustgarten, Packhof buildings for customs, canal administration, and warehousing, 1829–32, Karl Friedrich Schinkel. (Staatliche Museen, Berlin)

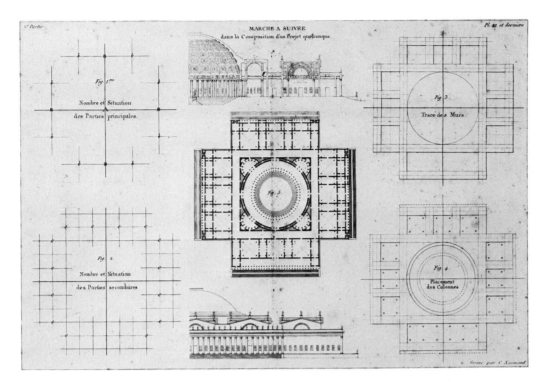

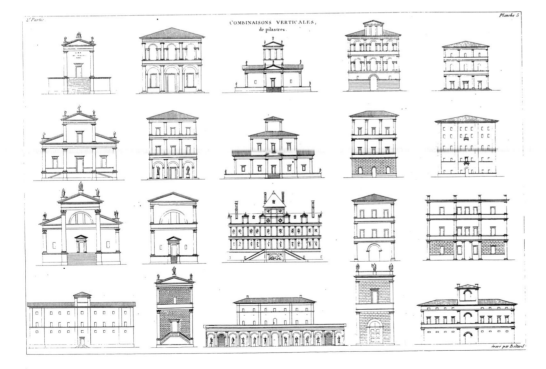

Fig. 23.12 Jean-Nicolas-Louis Durand, *Précis des Leçons d'architecture données à l'École Polytechnique*, 1802–5; two pages. **(a)** Illustrates the sequence of steps for generating an architectural plan; **(b)** shows the variety of facade elevations possible through the stacking up of pilasters.

example, the creation of Regent's Park and Regent Street in London, one of the great urban "improvements" of the early part of the century. (Fig. 23.13) It took Crown property, an act of Parliament, the tenacity and money of the architect John Nash, financing from an insurance company and the Bank of England, and subleasing of all kinds; and even so the final outcome was a bit of a sham. The stately terraces in the picturesque ensemble of the Park, worthy of Bath, are sheer facadism. Behind are identical rowhouses of mean design. Regent Street only *looks* classical. It is, in fact, neither straight nor uniform. Despite the formality of Waterloo Place at one end, Park Crescent at the other, and Oxford and Picadilly Circuses in between, the street was, as John Summerson put it, "an extemporization, a pictorial succession of architectural incident, moulded by luck and persuasion to the uncertain pattern presented by the disposal of sites [and] the speculative market."

But beyond all this, the new bourgeois governments had to face an unprecedented subversion of the environmental pattern of their lands. The industrial fever spawned scores of company towns around country plants. Meanwhile, some of the old cities experienced an industry-related crowding that doubled or tripled their populations in a matter of a decade or so, spilling their peripheries far into the surrounding land. Both of these developments went largely uncontrolled. The private sector, motivated by quick profits and convinced of the sanctity of particularism, met the demand for cheap working-class housing without concern for the long-range consequences of this unreflective sprawl. Soon regional administrations had to cope with nightmarish problems of sanitation and general welfare, brought about by overcrowding, industrial pollution, and the rapid changes in the means and pace of daily transport. In such straits planning in the grand manner was an irrelevance.

With architects uninterested in tackling a messy affair of ever worsening dimensions, two kinds of people took on the challenge of redressing the deterioration of the environment, both built and natural.

First, there were the administrative class, legislators, and the executive organs of cities and counties. Their aim was to ease the plight of the working class, contain the abuses of jerry-builders and profiteers, and check the general decay of cities. Their instruments were poor laws, sanitation ordinances, building codes—in other words, a series of realistic, enforceable controls and, where possible, modest alterations that scarcely aspired to the elegance or formality of architects' perfect devisings.

The reformers made up the second group, and their thinking was utopian. How could industry be humanized? How could model communities be set up as an alternative to the existing chaos of towns? Leaders of this movement were the English industrialist Robert Owen (1771–1858), a hero of the emerging trade unions and co-operative societies, and the Frenchman Charles Fourier (1772–1837) whose experiments enjoyed considerable success in the United States. Both proposed complete ideological systems for small communities of participants, regulating productivity, leisure, and the education of children.

Owen's ideal villages were meant for an average occupation of about one thousand persons. (Fig. 23.14) They were infinitely repeatable squares, each surrounded by a quantity of land, each containing within it a number of communal buildings, such as the public kitchen and messrooms, schools, enclosed gardens for exercise and recreation, houses for the married members of the community along three sides of the square, and, along the fourth, dormitories and apartments for older children and the unmarried. Behind the houses, outside the square, would be gardens bounded by roads, and farther out service buildings like the slaughterhouse, facilities for washing and bleaching, and farming establishments

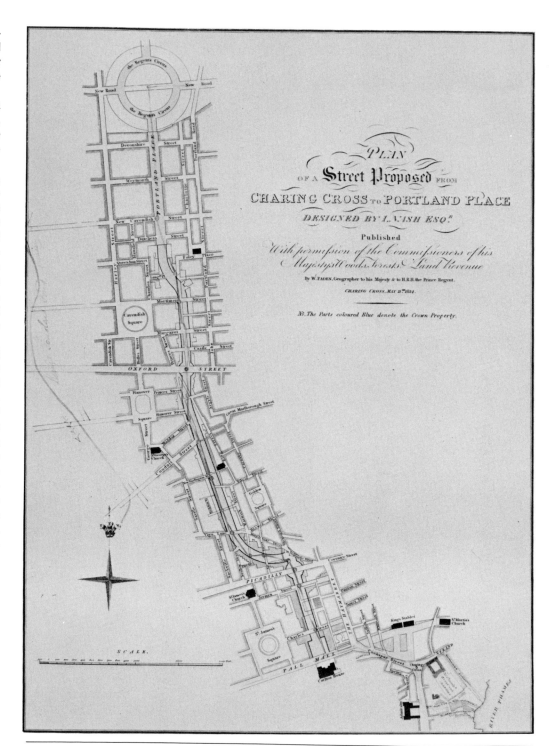

Fig. 23.13a London, Regent Street, in an early project by John Nash, 1814. (British Museum, London) Regent's Park is at the top and the Thames is in the lower, right-hand corner.

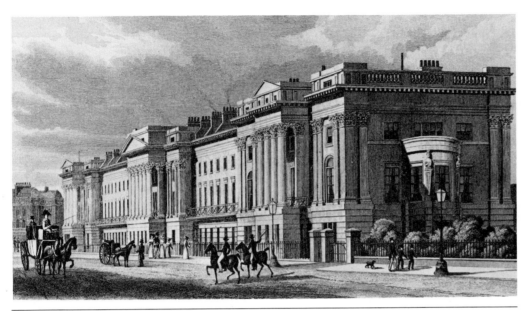

Fig. 23.13b London, Cornwall Terrace, Regent's Park, 1821, designed for John Nash by Decimus Burton and built by his father James Burton. This was the first of the Regent Street terraces; it is shown here in an engraving of 1827.

with corn mills, brewing houses, and the like.

Fourier called his societies "phalanxes." Each was housed in a single building, the Phalanstery, with a central unit for public uses (dining hall, library, post office, chapel, etc.), a wing for workshops, another for a market and other activities that entailed resort with outsiders, and, above all this, multistorey habitations of private apartments opening onto interior streets. The attic floor would be for a visitors' hostel. A small version of the Fourier model built by the industrialist Jean-Baptiste Godin for his iron foundry at Guise on the Oise, northeast of Paris, still survives. (Fig. 23.15) The main difference was that here small glassed-over courtyards took the place of Fourier's interior streets.

These ideal cities belong in the great tradition that begins with the Renaissance. But in their sympathy for the underdog, their determination to bring a humane fullness to the lives of the toiling lower classes, they stand quite apart from the princely designs of Filarete, Fontana, or Mansart. (Fig. 21.27) And if they now seem naive in their confidence that a threatening world could be changed overnight through design, future generations will return to some of the ideas of these utopian reformers. Ebenezer Howard's garden cities will harken back to Owen, and Fourierite phalansteries will resurface in Le Corbusier's *unités d'habitations* and the housing estates of post-World War I Germany called *Siedlungen*.

Was academic town-planning, then, obsolete? Not quite. There were still dynastic regimes around—some old like Russia's; others, like the kingdom of Greece, of recent vintage—and they believed in it. We find ambitious goings-on at Athens and St. Petersburg, Munich, Karlsruhe, and Berlin. But even in these pockets of grandiloquence the mode of operating was neither Baroque nor Napoleonic. Neoclassicism had left a taste for single sculptural building masses that downplayed or ignored lines of

uniform frontage. That is how the neo-Greek monuments of Athens behave. (Fig. 23.16) The plan of the new-laid capital is a Baroque creation—triviums, circles, and all. But the buildings themselves are grouped as separate entities along the broad straight streets, unbeholden to a common line or a continuous facade plane.

St. Petersburg, in existence since 1703 when Peter the Great founded it to be his "window looking into Europe," is a more interesting case. (Fig. 23.17) The story of St. Petersburg has a bearing on the passage of Russia from an inchoate medieval empire to a modern state of the first order. The site is the delta of the Neva River on the Baltic, and it occupies the two banks of the broadest branch and a main island called Vasilevski. First came the Peter and Paul fortress and the arsenal on the right bank, the Admiralty diagonally across the way, and governmental buildings like the Twelve Collegia on the tip of Vasilevski Island. (Fig. 23.18) The city soon established itself on the left bank, behind an imposing plane of continuous facades, especially those of the Admiralty and the Winter Palace to its northeast. A trivium centered on the Admiralty sent its prongs away from the waterfront, the easternmost, Nevski Prospect, connecting the center of the city with the old Novgorod road at the periphery. The monumental core continued to grow around the Admiralty. At the time of Napoleon's invasion, this core included St. Isaac Cathedral, southwest of the Admiralty, attended by the Senate and Holy Synod buildings and the monument to Peter the Great.

In the flush of Russia's victory over the French emperor, this whole area along the Neva front was orchestrated into a magnificent composition of five interrelated squares. And here is where the new attitude of the St. Petersburg planners shows through. Instead of trying to dress up the monumental nodes in a matching design and uniting them with sympathetic curtains of architecture, the planners opted for the effective distribution and visual use of a few main freestanding structures. The Admiralty was rebuilt on a larger scale and three squares systematized along three sides. Two more squares opened out from this spa-

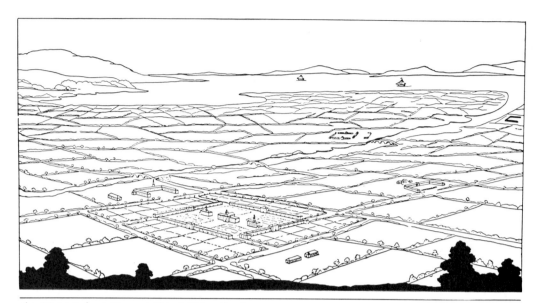

Fig. 23.14 Robert Owens' "Ideal Village"; view attached to his report of 1817 to the Committee for the Relief of the Manufacturing Poor.

Fig. 23.15 Guise (France), the "Familistère," begun 1859, Jean-Baptiste Godin; general view. On the left are the three residential blocks and, facing them in the foreground, the building that houses the schools and the theater. On the right are the factories.

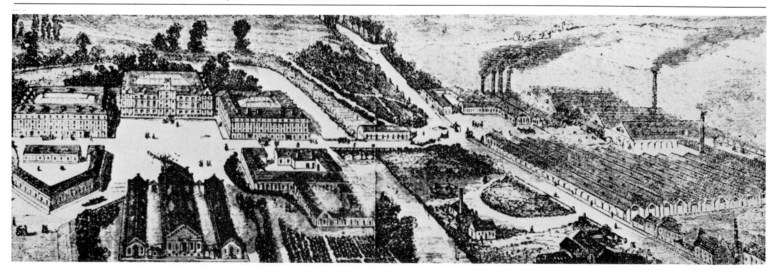

Fig. 23.16 Athens (Greece), public buildings of the nineteenth century. Foreground: the Academy of Science, 1859–87, Theophilus Hansen; cen- ter: the University, 1839–50, Hans Christian Hansen; left: the National Library, 1865–92, Theophilus Hansen.

cious center: one in front of the Winter Palace, the other on the landward side of St. Isaac.

None of the five squares is tightly confined. They spill into each other and interlock in a way that is very different from the serialized public spaces of Nancy or Bath of the preceding epoch. (Figs. 22.30, 22.31) Homogeneity, for the whole constellation or for individual squares, counts for very little. The ornate Baroque bulk of the Winter Palace faces the curve of the General Staff Building whose severe classicism openly announces its early nineteenth century date. But the two are related in a general way and rivetted by the same axis. This axis was fixed by a triumphal column in honor of Czar Alexander I (1801–25). This was also the terminal point of the boulevard that crossed the main square in front of the Admiralty, to arrive at the Senate Square where St. Isaac and the Senate and Holy Synod buildings, unlike structures, coexisted in comparable harmony. The boulevard separated the Admiralty in a forthright manner from the variegated building mass on the other side of the

square, and then turned toward the river along the flanks of the Admiralty to gain the granite quays. Here in this setting militarist Russia could stage its parades and the Orthodox Church its colorful processions, while society strolled or rode along the boulevard, or did its seasonal boating and skating in the basin of the Neva Delta. (Fig. 23.19)

In the Berlin of Friedrich Wilhelm III, the Prussian capital on the Spree, even this kind of formal coordination did not arise. The planned structure of the city, its spines and public spaces, was determined by 1000. The newer section of town, laid out on a grid in the seventeenth century, had a main east-west artery, the famous Unter den Linden. It ran from the old castle-palace of the Hohenzollern and their successors, to the Brandenburg Gate of about 1790, one of the very first examples of civic architecture in the Neoclassical idiom. This was the Prussian *via triumphalis*. On the corresponding north-south artery, Friedrichstrasse, identical rowhouses (based on Dutch prototypes) lined up with that stiff, fanatical discipline that was the rootstock of the national

character. (Fig. 23.20) Even the typical Baroque device of a circular plaza at the south end of the artery, with a kind of trivium emanating from it, was straitjacketed into a tight, restrictive void.

Against this absolutist city-form, we should view the adroitness of Friedrich Wilhelm III's great architect Schinkel. He was not called on to design monumental squares or noble avenues. His commissions were all single buildings: a royal guardhouse, a theater, a museum, the commercial structures of the Packhof we referred to in passing, an academy of architecture. Through the careful siting of each one, and a design that called to its neighbors without forced parity, Schinkel sought to unify the urban environment pictorially. Between his buildings and others around them he set up visual relationships independent of right angles and axial alignments. The blocky mass of each building was raised on a podium and ordered in an abstracted classicism that prefigures some of the visual clarity and structural expression of twentieth-century functionalism. (Figs. 23.21, 28.6) But whereas the pristine cages of a modern master like Mies van der Rohe are conceived in exclusive isolation or within a total scheme of their own making, Schinkel's buildings reached out to the neighborhoods to acknowledge and improve what was there.

The Gothic Revival

From this discussion, three general characteristics of nineteenth-century classicism stand out: its internationalism, its urban bias, and its universal applicability to all classes of buildings. The Gothic revival, on the contrary, is particularistic both as to place and building typology, and when it is not explicitly antiurban, it has no clear position, pragmatic or theoretical, on town-planning.

The serious defense of Gothic architecture and arguments for its adoption began around 1800. The obvious starting point was that Gothic, or rather the broad spectrum of medieval forms, was far more indigenous to northern Europe than the comparatively recent classical layer. Two inevitable claims followed. Gothic expressed a national ethos; it was a truer vehicle of patri-

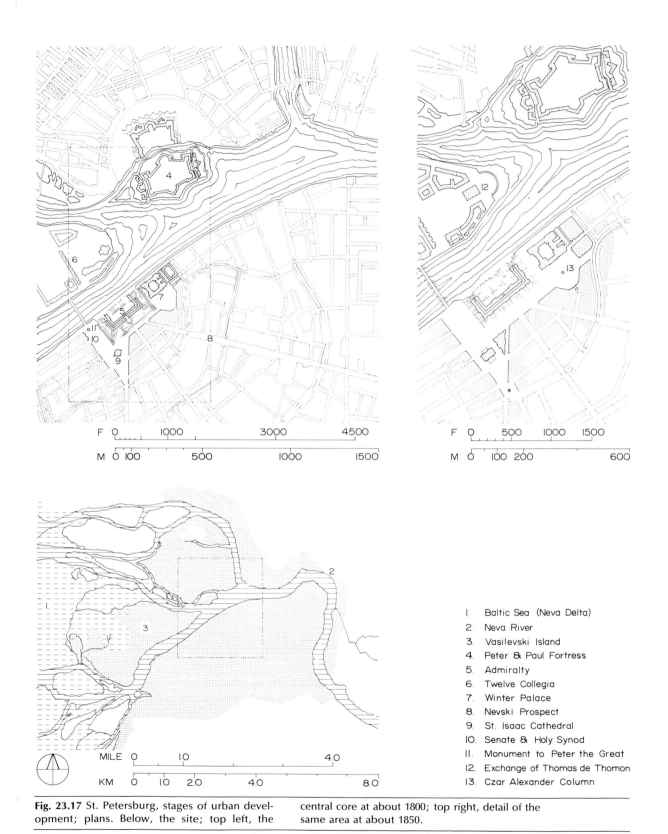

1.	Baltic Sea (Neva Delta)
2.	Neva River
3.	Vasilevski Island
4.	Peter & Paul Fortress
5.	Admiralty
6.	Twelve Collegia
7.	Winter Palace
8.	Nevski Prospect
9.	St. Isaac Cathedral
10.	Senate & Holy Synod
11.	Monument to Peter the Great
12.	Exchange of Thomas de Thomon
13.	Czar Alexander Column

Fig. 23.17 St. Petersburg, stages of urban development; plans. Below, the site; top left, the central core at about 1800; top right, detail of the same area at about 1850.

Fig. 23.18 St. Petersburg (Leningrad, Russia), view of the Neva front, 1761; engraving by M. I. Makhaev. In the left foreground is the second Winter Palace, begun 1716, Georg Johann Mattarnovy and Domenico Tressini. The central tower marks the old Admiralty Building, 1732–38, I. K. Korobov. (See Fig. 23.18, top left, for orientation.)

Fig. 23.19 St. Petersburg, military review, 1829. In the foreground: Dvortsovaia Square, begun 1819, Carlo di Giovanni Rossi; on the left: Rossi's General Staff Building; on the right: his Winter Palace. Further back, beyond the Column of Czar Alexander I, the tower of the new Admiralty can be seen.

otism. And it was also, as a German writer put it in 1804, "the style of building best adapted to a northern climate and a colder zone."

More specifically, Gothic, because of its skeletal articulation and tensile structure, was sympathetic to iron, the new building material. As early as 1803 the landscape architect Humphrey Repton proposed a greenhouse with a cast-iron frame based on octagonal chapter houses like that of Salisbury Cathedral. From the point of view of design, the choice of Gothic permitted the kind of irregular ground plans that might ensue if one really thought in simple functional terms, without worrying about the etiquette of classicism. Such plans were informal, less inhibiting, and therefore ideal for rural residences. This was a timely gloss on a new fashion, the decorated cottage (or *cottage orné*), a second home in the country for the affluent; John Papworth would insist in his *Rural Residences* of 1818 that they "should combine properly with the surrounding objects, and appear to be native to the spot, and not one of those crude rule-and-square excrescences of the environs of London, the illegitimate family of town and country." (Fig. 23.22)

Gothic had its place, then, and should be cultivated in earnest, not to replace classical architecture but as an alternative more congenial to certain classes of buildings. It was the consensus, in England most of all, that the right style for churches and country houses was the Gothic, while the classical language should be confined to public buildings and mansions. Where conformity to surrounding structures or historical constancy made it desirable, in collegiate work for example, the domain of Gothic could be widened.

But the religious argument proved to be the most critical. After the shock of the French Revolution, the English government resolved to strengthen the Church to counter seditious passions. London's population had gone from a million inhabitants at the end of the eighteenth century to about twice that number in twenty years. It was now the largest city in the history of mankind. In 1818 Parliament passed the Church Building Act that allocated one million pounds for new churches, and 612 of

Fig. 23.20a Berlin, the square at the end of Friedrichstrasse, called Das Rondell, and the Hallesche Tor; painting by an anonymous artist, ca. 1735. (Märkisches Museum, Berlin)

Fig. 23.21 Berlin, Altes Museum, 1824–30, Karl Friedrich Schinkel. This museum was part of the reorganization effort for the Lustgarten district and the canals behind. Schinkel's Packhof buildings belonged to the same effort (Fig. 23.11).

Fig. 23.22 John Papworth, *Rural Residences*, 1818; Plate 6 showing a proposal for a "Gothic cottage."

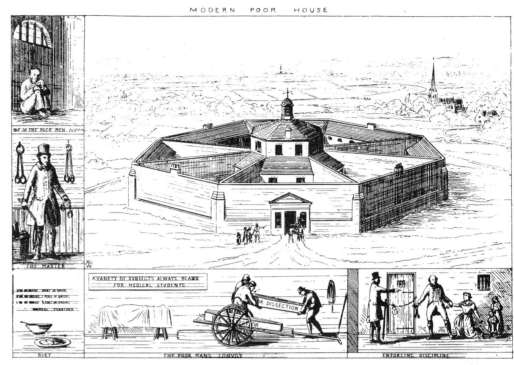

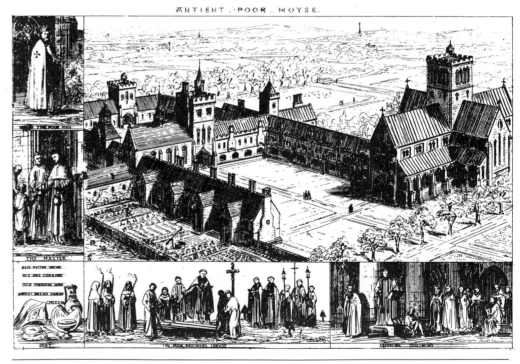

Fig. 23.23 Augustus Welby Pugin, *Contrasts*, 1841; plate contrasting a contemporary poorhouse (above) with a medieval poorhouse (below).

them were built subsequently with accommodation for some 600,000 worshippers in the mushrooming working-class suburbs. Most of these carried on the Classical format—a temple mass with a spire rising just behind the pedimented front portico. But about one in every six new churches was done in what was called Commissioner's Gothic, which was anything but scholarly. The justification was an odd one. Churches in this style were said to come cheaper because they circumvented such costly features as stone porticoes. But the economy was actually achieved by resorting to iron columns and tracery and making the walls of plastered brick, denying, that is, the structural integrity of traditional Gothic masonry.

By the early 1830s the Gothic movement, which had grown markedly contentious, reacted against this state of affairs. Its ad-

Fig. 23.24 Huddersfield (England), Huddersfield narrow canal, opened 1811; and the Huddersfield and Manchester Railway viaduct. In the distance is a late-nineteenth-century mill. This 19 mile (32 kilometer) long canal runs in part through the Standedge Tunnel, slightly over 3 miles (5 kilometers) long. The canal was abandoned in 1944.

herents now fought for two related principles: that Gothic form must be reproduced accurately, and that it must be seen to have devotional relevance. Medieval archaeology had taken long strides ever since the appearance of Thomas Rickman's *An Attempt to Discriminate the Styles of English Architecture from the Conquest to the Reformation* of 1817. Two years later, for instance, William Gunn identified and defined the Romanesque as the style that mediated between Roman antiquity and full-blown Gothic. There were now measured drawings of medieval buildings available in books that did for the Gothic revival what Stuart and Revett had done for the Greek.

One outcome of this erudition was that the medieval doctrine began to acquire as many subheadings as the Classical. There

was a castellated mode, reserved at first for country mansions and extended later, predictably, to prisons. A version of this, the so-called Scottish baronial mode, found favor with the young Queen Victoria, as the private royal residences of Osborne and Balmoral bear witness. The decorated cottage had its own brand of low-style Gothic. Churches and vicarages could choose from among several distinct periods of English medieval architecture.

A parallel interest in medieval worship was institutionalized with the founding of the Oxford Movement in 1833, and of the Cambridge Camden Society in 1839. The invention of mechanical typesetting in 1841 boosted a new industry, the publication of magazines, and the medievalists took good advantage of this popular medium. The

Ecclesiologist, the influential organ of the Camdenites, was launched in that year as a guide to Anglican worship. It dictated in a strong doctrinaire tone matters concerning the design, construction, and furnishings of churches. The goal was the exact imitation of historical models. The fourteenth century was the heavy favorite, and the editors showed a special fondness for the small rural churches of the Middle Ages in an evident mood of antiurban romanticism. Concessions might be made to modern times in technical matters, but not in anything else. The use of iron was grudgingly acknowledged, for example, and even a design was proposed for an iron church that could be prefabricated and shipped to distant outposts of Anglicanism. In the 1840s England was already prefabricating iron dwellings, lighthouses, and warehouses destined for places as far away as Australia, Bermuda, and California. But no all-iron churches were built anywhere in England because bishops made it plain they would refuse to consecrate them.

Internally, the chancel with its high altar was once again the focal point of the church. In fact, the devotional settings and ritual of the Anglicans moved very close to Catholic practice, and intentionally so. The cause of Rome was enjoying fair weather in England since the Catholic Emancipation Act. This phenomenon became knotted to the Gothic revival through the fiery propaganda of one man, an architect named Augustus Welby Pugin (1812–52). The son of a French emigré and a convert to Catholicism, Pugin acquired a learned mastery of medieval architecture when he was still very young. He was Barry's Gothic expert on the Houses of Parliament, the buildings which were to establish the Gothic revival as a contending nineteenth-century option.

In 1836 Pugin published a book entitled *Contrasts, or A Parallel between the Noble Edifices of the Fourteenth and Fifteenth Centuries and Similar Buildings of the Present Day; Shewing the Present Decay of Taste.* The thrust of his argument was this. Not only was late Gothic much superior to anything built in the modern period, it was so because late Gothic society outshined the contemporary industrial world in its humaneness and faith. In paired images, Pugin showed late medieval institutions and their

Fig. 23.25 Ancoats, Manchester, Ashton or Ashton-under-Lyne canal, begun 1794, Benjamin Outram and Thomas Brown, engineers. The main canal and its four branches have a combined length of 16½ miles (28 kilometers) and a total of twenty-five locks, one of which is shown here. The American inventor Robert Fulton worked as a contractor on the excavations through a hill near Woodley, through which this canal runs.

Fig. 23.26 Brighton (England), the Royal Pavilion, 1815–23, John Nash; a view of the kitchen.

Fig. 23.27 Providence (Rhode Island), the Providence Arcade, 1828–29, Russell Warren and James Bucklin.

Fig. 23.28 Paris, the Bon Marché department store, 1876, Louis-Charles Boileau; woodcut, ca. 1880.

modern counterparts to drive home his point. The plate called "Contrasted Residences for the Poor" illustrates the modern poor-house as a grim, radially disposed building, like a Neoclassical prison, stripped of all decoration. In marginal vignettes we see features of an inmate's life: idle boredom, punishment, a diet of gruel, bread, and oatmeal potatoes, and his dead body carted away for dissection. (Fig. 23.23) The "Antient Poor Hoyse" is a cloistered medieval compound watched over by its church and set amidst orchards and vegetable patches. The day is spent in prayer, the overseers are benign brothers, the meals include beef, mutton, ale, milk porridge, and cheese, and in death one finds the comfort of a solemn funeral service and a grave. Bring that style of architecture back, Pugin argued, and you will be on your way to "a restoration of the ancient feelings and sentiments."

Pugin made no bones about averring that "the Roman Catholic Church is the only true

Fig. 23.29a Paris, the Bibliothèque Ste.-Geneviève, 1838–50, Henri Labrouste; reading room. For the exterior view of this library, see Fig. 25.6.

Fig. 23.29b Paris, the Bibliothèque Nationale, 1854–75, Henri Labrouste; reading room.

one, and the only one in which the grand and sublime style of architecture can ever be restored." Others could take the forms without this specific religious affiliation. The *Ecclesiologist* embraced Puginian Gothic, with its emphasis on the reign of Edward I (1272–1307), and canonized it for Anglican use throughout the English-speaking world. And if this is explicable in terms of a Catholicizing trend in the Church of England, the style was taken up equally enthusiastically by non-Anglicans as well. But the Gothic revival made only minor inroads beyond England and the United States. In Germany, native Romanesque forms were preferred and merged in the patterns of the *Rundbogenstil*. The few important neo-Gothic churches in France leaned on earlier, thirteenth-century paragons, while the constructive functionalism of the style was expatiated on, with no religious overtones, by the likes of Viollet-le-Duc, a freethinker.

How can we summarize the contribution of the Gothic revival in the history of modern architecture? First, we must emphasize

Fig. 23.30 London, the Crystal Palace, 1851, Joseph Paxton.

the effect it had of weakening the hegemony of the classical school, in the Anglo-American world particularly. Free plans, asymmetrical massing, varied silhouettes, plasticity, the exploitation of color and texture in its use of local stones—all this was patently anticlassical. Second, its nationalistic perspective led to the discovery of a number of diverse topical idioms from the medieval period—Alpine chalets, Venetian Gothic, and in England Norman, Tudor, and Elizabethan work—which replenished the formal reservoir of Western architecture. And, finally, the insistence of Pugin, the *Ecclesiologist*, the workshop of Cologne Cathedral, and the restorers of medieval monuments on the exact individual detail kept alive a sense of craftsmanship at a time

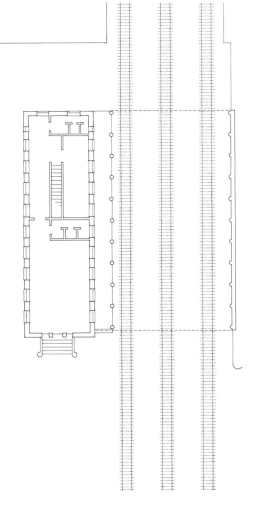

Fig. 23.31 Liverpool (England), Crown Street railroad station, 1830, John Foster II and George Stephenson: (**a**) view in a period print; (**b**) ground plan.

Fig. 23.32 London, Paddington Station, 1852–54, Sir M. D. Wyatt and I. K. Brunel; interior view.

when mass production was beginning to alter the age-old habits of the building industry.

The Iron Age

The battle of styles engaged elevated minds. Ironmasters, millwrights and miners, construction crews of industrial companies, roadbuilders and jerry-builders were in the thick of another kind of environmental drama. This was a frenzied new time, buoyant, brisk, and frightening, and they were giving it shape. The countryside was under siege. (Fig. 23.24) An army of tens of thousands spread out over it, cutting raw swaths through ancient rolling hills, fording, tunneling, lifting monstrous towers of

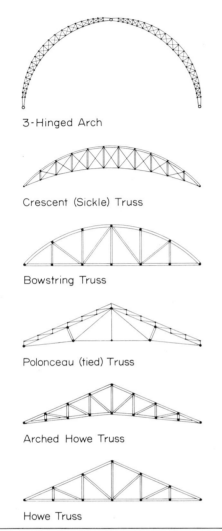

3-Hinged Arch

Crescent (Sickle) Truss

Bowstring Truss

Polonceau (tied) Truss

Arched Howe Truss

Howe Truss

Fig. 23.33 Diagrams of nineteenth-century roof trusses.

Fig. 23.34 London, King's Cross Station, 1851–52, Lewis Cubitt.

prehistoric force where rural churches and princely country houses had brooded over the productive land for centuries. Slag and soil heaps and the refuse of mines were everywhere in evidence like giant stains. Canals were being raised intrepidly above valleys and townships on aqueducts and sent on an uninhibited course laced with locks, wharves, boatyards, limekilns, and warehouses. (Fig. 23.25) In England alone, the Turnpike Acts had authorized by the 1830s more than 32,000 kilometers (20,000 miles) of highway controlled through 1,100 private trusts. The first public railway line was opened in 1825 between Stockton and Darlington, though iron tracks for industrial use and the conveyance of freight and passengers in horse-drawn cars had scarred the earth for some decades. An epic contest now began—to shrink distance and speed up time. The steaming, metal-sleek, unnerving trains bustled along viaducts, through dark and sooty tunnels, across dizzying wide-spanned bridges, calling briefly at small train stations on the way to the great urban terminals that were the pride of engineers and the marvel of their communities. The cities throbbed and heaved as swarms of outsiders converged on them, swelling the old neighborhoods to the limits of endurance or squatting at the edges in bleak settlements of identical, barebone houses.

The New Technology
Two aspects of this brave unquiet world penetrated building practice, both high and low. The increasing use of iron and glass was shaking up traditional construction methods and animating feats of enclosed or traversed space. Not since the Roman in- vention of concrete had a building technology so radicalized architecture. And these new materials went to meet the functional needs of scores of building types—some urban, like banks, government offices, and the fashionable shopping arcades, others industrial. To this second class belong the architectural components of the major transportation systems—everything from tollhouses, docks, and railroad stations to various kinds of bridges, viaducts, and engine houses—and industrial complexes like breweries and maltings, mills, factories, farmeries, and docks with attendant warehouses.

To architects, iron was not quite seemly. In the sort of public building in which they specialized, one concealed it beneath presentable sheaths or, if exposed, stamped it with some stylistic coding. It was impossible not to appreciate its properties, however. Iron was cheaper than stone and more resilient; it withstood fire much better than wood. The casting process was geared to prefabrication in bulk, so that members could be shipped to the site ready-made and assembled with ease. Here one had a natural supporting system, then, for the tra-

Fig. 23.36 Menai Straits (England), Menai Suspension Bridge, 1819–25, Thomas Telford.

Fig. 23.35 Shropshire (England), Coalbrookdale Bridge, 1779, Abraham Darby III and T. F. Pritchard.

ditional masonry and timber architecture. Unseen, iron strengthened walls and floors, formed the armature of stone domes (that of St. Isaac's in St. Petersburg of 1842 is a good early example), and in combination with hollow tiles made for excellent fire-retardant roofs. The novelty of the material fitted in with follies, like the Royal Pavilion at Brighton, where Nash used it frankly for ceiling frames and columns, and for the great kitchen, had it cast into iron palm trees with copper leaves. (Fig. 23.26)

But the potentialities of an iron architecture were best tested in big enclosed spaces that required bright lighting—markets, arcades, libraries, conservatories, and of course train sheds. Here, intricate iron filigrees with glass panes spanned tall ample rooms transparently and often elegantly, and in a sense resumed the story of Gothic dematerialization. In fact, some early metal

and glass structures advertised the relationship openly. Thomas Hopper's conservatory for Carlton House at the south end of Regent Street aped the late medieval fan vaults of Gloucester and Cambridge. But unlike Gothic cathedrals where the vault canopy was itself solid and the walls diaphanous, the modern instance was concerned with even top lighting, glazed domes, and barrel vaults over conventional shells of masonry. Even when iron members reached all the way down to the floor, the logic of the system rarely showed through on the outside; metal skeleton and masonry shell were almost never truly integrated. Still, something of that visual excitement Suger had started with his ambulatory at St.-Denis was rekindled in these nineteenth-century interiors, in their linearism and glow. (Figs. 14.10, 23.29b)

The appearance of metallic canopies in

commercial architecture took place with relatively little fuss. In 1813 the first full iron-and-glass dome was built over the circular granary in Paris, called Halle aux Blés, not far from the Louvre, which had gone up a half-century earlier with a wooden dome. The architect, François-Joseph Belanger, described his creation as "a new conception for the first time, in this genre, which gives Europe the idea." Fifteen years later Fontaine roofed the Galerie d'Orléans in the public garden of one of the palaces in Paris with the first glass barrel vault, and soon this became the favorite way to span these commercial arcades or covered shopping streets for pedestrians, called *galleries* or *passages* in France. Among the most impressive extant specimens are the Providence Arcade (1828) in Providence, Rhode Island, and in France the Passage Pommeraye (1843) at Nantes. (Fig. 23.27)

It was again in France that the new technology was applied to something novel in commercial architecture, the department store. (Fig. 23.28) This was initially a Parisian institution, and a direct result of the freeing of all trade in the Revolution of 1789.

Fig. 23.37 New York, the Brooklyn Bridge, begun 1868, John Roebling. The cable trains were removed in 1944. In the foreground, at the far right, is the Tribune Building, 1873–76, by Richard Morris Hunt.

The first to appear were large shops that sold fabrics and related accessories—lingerie, shoes, millinery—and charged fixed prices. What metal and glass made possible was to open up the entire ground floor and mezzanine to the outside with windows of plate glass and to have a central court with a glazed roof over it.

Public buildings were a more serious matter. When Labrouste dared to work with iron and glass in the library of Ste.-Geneviève in Paris, across from Soufflot's great church, he was roundly ridiculed. (Fig. 23.29a) The main reading room on the second floor is now much admired, precisely because it was so premonitory of things to come. It is divided into two barrel-vaulted naves by a central row of thin iron columns. The barrels are carried on delicately scrolled arches of open-work iron, while the masonry walls that belong to a Renaissance-inspired, but very original, shell have their own ranges of window arches. The scale approaches the visionary interiors of Boullée—we saw his project for a library hall in the last chapter (Fig. 22.27)—and indeed the new technology brought the vast, pure, geometric volumes of Neoclassicism closer to reality. The British Museum library a little later on, with its grand circular reading room, also introduced iron stacks and iron floors. It obviously learned from Labrouste's brave example, but it contributed in turn to his masterpiece of the 1860s, the Bibliothèque Nationale. This has a splendid reading room covered by a series of light terra-cotta domes that rest on thin iron columns and arches and are pierced by oculi. (Fig. 23.29b) It is a sure design, the epitome of metallic elegance and suppleness. But by this time, paradoxically, iron was losing whatever popular favor it had garnered in the first half of the century, especially after the Crystal Palace had amazed and delighted the throngs that visited the Great Exhibition of 1851 in London celebrating the achievement of modern industry.

The Crystal Palace was an astonishing building. (Fig. 23.30) Standing in Hyde Park like a specter, more than 570 meters (1870 feet) long, it was itself a monument to the enterprise and sophistication of English industry in the early Victorian period. It had been assembled within six months from thousands of small prefabricated parts. Sustained by a skeleton of cast- and wrought-iron girders, the five-aisled building was glazed throughout. There was no masonry anywhere—just the iron latticework holding up the uniform sheets of glass framed in wood. A contemporary critic pointed out the common perception that "here the standards by which architecture had hitherto been judged no longer held good." He predicted the rise of a new style. But it did not happen, not for a long while. Metal and glass returned to specialized usage, and public architecture at large reaffirmed its faith in mass and the manuals of history.

Building for Industry
England's most daring adventures with iron were railroad stations and bridges. Crown Street Station, Liverpool, of 1830, the modest forerunner of this building type, had all the basic features in embryo: the vehicle court, anticipating the covered driveways of later stations, a room for ticket-selling and waiting, and the platform where the carriages were boarded under the cover of a

Fig. 23.38 Grand Hornu, Borinage District (Belgium), Grand Hornu, ca. 1820–32, Bruno Renard; aerial view while undergoing restoration.

train shed. (Fig. 23.31) It was the shed, as a special case of wide-span construction, that turned shortly thereafter into a testing ground for modern engineering. By 1854, thanks to the verve of iron, a single clear span of 65 meters (213 feet) was reached in New Street Station, Birmingham, and a triple span with a combined width of almost 74 meters (242 feet) in the second Paddington Station, London. (Fig. 23.32) In the roofing, the Howe truss, based on wooden models, gave way to types more cleverly exploitive of the new material—for example, the so-called sickle-girder, with its curved upper and lower chords connected by cast-iron struts and ties, and the related bowstring truss. (Fig. 23.33)

These great arched spaces were masked from the outside by the palatial fronts of the stations, much as familiar columnar screens had served as a public overture to the billowy interiors of the Roman vaulted style.

The element of wondrous surprise on entering was the same in both cases. While the terminal, not uncommonly combined with a hotel, put on the fashions of the current architectural scene, the smoke- and steam-filled sheds of metal and glass arching over tracks and trains corroborated the coming of the industrial age—its excitement and bluster, but also its disturbing ambiguities. The masonry facades, on the other hand, were comfortingly familiar. It was the duty of railway architecture, as one observer put it, "to reassure the timid traveller." Italianate towers or occasional Egyptian or Moorish features suggested the expectant, festive mood of long-distance travel. Only rarely did the realm of the train shed penetrate into the cityscape. At the London station of King's Cross the two great sheds, one for arrival and the other for departure, are announced in the deep twin arches of the facade and are bracketed with

Fig. 23.39 Stonehouse, Gloucestershire (England), Stanley Mill, 1813; exterior showing weaver's windows.

massive spare stacks of masonry, the central one crowned by the clock tower. (Fig. 23.34)

The drama of metal bridges started earlier, since England's vast network of canals that brought the benefit of cheap bulk transport to areas remote from river navigation had need of them much ahead of the railroads. English engineers, and in particular the great highway expert Thomas Telford (1757–1834), dominate the first phase of bridge building. The oldest iron bridge dates from 1779. It was designed by Abraham Derby III and T. F. Pritchard to cross the flood-prone Severn, near Coalbrookdale at a point some 30 meters (100 feet) wide. The single, nearly semicircular, arch was made up of five cast-iron ribs, each composed of only two members. (Fig. 23.35) Instead of using bolts, the parts were assembled through interlocking joints and wedges. In Sunderland Bridge (1793–96), on the other hand, the ribs of the single arch were constructed out of many cast-iron panels that acted like the voussoirs of masonry arches. The inventor of this system seems to have been the American revolutionary, Thomas Paine (1737–1809).

Telford's distinction was to endow metal bridges with architectural grace. The masonry abutments were designed in one of the current modes of the picturesque tradition; the metal parts enhanced with decorative detail. In the Menai Straits Bridge (1819–25), between North Wales and Anglesey, one mile southwest of Bangar, Telford applied the principle of suspension to an enormous span of 177 meters (580 feet). (Fig. 23.36) The roadbed was hung from wrought-iron chains slung over towers, and was buried deep in rock at either end. To render them rust-proof, the links were treated in boiling linseed oil and stove-dried. Impressive masonry arches anchored the roadbed from below.

Suspension bridges were not new, of course. We encountered them on the Inca high roads, and even the iron-chain version had been tried and patented in New York a decade or so before Menai. Telford's contribution, again, was to approach this as an architectural problem, making it feasible on a large scale. And just as Menai Bridge was being completed, the French engineer Marc Seguin substituted wire ropes for chains in his suspension bridge over the Rhone near Tournon. From this point on the cable principle will be perfected in America; superb later masterpieces—from Roebling's Brooklyn Bridge (begun in 1868) to the Golden Gate Bridge of San Francisco (1933–37)—we live with to this day. (Fig. 23.37)

Along the nerve lines of canals, turnpikes, and railways, at seaports and estuaries, by fast rivers, coal fields, and iron-rich hills, industry arrayed its own building systems. This raw landscape, long neglected by architectural historians, now has a haunting beauty in its abandonment. The trial-and-error advance of this environment is a fascinating story of intelligent response to evolving, technically tough programs; it is a story matched only by the development of military architecture in the Middle Ages and the Renaissance. The architectural forms, spare and commonsensical, are the very model of functional design, which J. M. Richards defines as "the hard-headed relationship of ends and means" and credits with "forthrightness and simplicity, the emphasis on the basic geometry of architecture rather than the ritual of historic styles, the use of building materials in a way that brings out most strongly their intrinsic qualities."

I said "building systems" because it is a mistake to treat the architecture of industrialism, however arresting its remains on land, as if it were another monumental tradition. The industrialist thought in terms of a complete course of operations that embraced production, processing, storage, and marketing. A mining plant was comprised of bellpits and galleries; the dams, water courses, and water wheels that kept the mine dry; derrick towers and dressing floors; smelt mills with their ore hearths; the blowing house of the tin smelter; the local transport system by pony or sled track, road, or tramway; and the final link with a main road or canal. A brewery had to include besides the actual brewhouse, a counting house, cooperage, stables, and the storehouses for the large vats.

And very often there was workers' housing. The employers found it efficient to have the labor force close to the plant, especially in sparsely populated regions, and they built groups of simple dwellings for the purpose. Sometimes this amounted to setting up small towns. In some areas of England, and the Austrasian basin of French Flanders, Wallonia, and the Ruhr, the coal-mining industry totally controlled urbanization. If the employer's pretensions ran high, an architect might be asked to draw up formal designs. The industrial community of Grand-Hornu in Belgium, now being preserved, is an imposing Neoclassical scheme. (Fig. 23.38) A large trapezoid of 425 workers' houses frames the factory, the symbol of economic power.

About the functionalism of industrial architecture we should keep two things in mind. First, buildings like breweries, docks, and workers' housing estates were by no means disdainful of stylistic niceties. And second, the stripped down utilitarian design that did predominate was scarcely peculiar to the modern scene. Every age has its plain style, and I am not talking about folk architecture. Even the Baroque, the age of grandeur, produced large, plain structures like poorhouses, hospitals, and

A

B

Fig. 23.40 Nineteenth-century industrial buildings; **(A)** Wickham Bishops, Essex (England), lucam of a water mill; **(B)** Mistley, Essex, slate-roofed malt kiln; **(C)** Cobham, Kent (England), oast houses; **(D)** Liverpool (England), Albert Docks, 1845, Jesse Hartley, dock engineer, warehouse interior constructed of masonry and iron; **(E)** Stanley Mill, interior showing decorative cast iron frame.

van. But enough survives today of those early decades of the functionalist tradition to indicate the ingenuity and quick imagination of the men who gave it life. A sampling of that wealth should at least touch on the following building types. (Fig. 23.40)

1. Watermills were notable for that bold cantilevered unit called the "lucam," which contains the hoisting machinery.

2. Maltings housed the barley that was converted into malt through a process of arrested germination. The plants have kilns with high pyramidal roofs that break into the skyline and long, low floors with rows of louvred windows.

3. Oast-houses, for drying hops, are distinguished by their kiln-towers—the earliest, cylindrical with a cone roof; the later ones, square. Scores of them, often grouped together, still dot the Kentish countryside like brick hulks of pure geometry. The funnel-shaped kilns of pottery- and glass-works are also quite striking.

4. Breweries were often tall buildings because it was economical, once the malt and the water had been raised to the highest level, to let gravity transfer liquids through the boiler, mushtun, fermenting rooms, and "racking stages" for barreling. The characteristic ground plan of a brewery shows a

the like, with no classicizing detail whatever.

Now often what starts as a utilitarian exigency of function and economy may assume an aesthetic aura and move to influence high architecture. It happened in ancient Rome, for example, where the unadorned brick style of tenements, apartment blocks, and warehouses in time became fashionable. The novel solutions of industrial programs, too, divorced from their original context, frequently become design clichés by later architects. The long horizontal windows of textile and woolen mills, an extension of "weaver's windows" in the earlier cottage industry, stand behind the glazed bands of the Modern Movement. (Figs. 23.39, 27.14) Stacked windows at warehouses, under enveloping arches with no surrounds, look forward to the commercial structures of Louis Sulli-

C

D

E

set of buildings grouped around a yard, with the actual brew-house on the street side and the service facilities at the back.

5. But perhaps the most ubiquitous building type, part and parcel of most industrial enterprises, was the warehouse. Its function was simple. It was a place for storing goods safely, most commonly goods in transit. The requirements stayed basically the same whatever the individual milieu or the goods in question: easy loading and unloading, ample storage space, protection from fire and theft. Architecturally, the features that responded to this program included wide, uninterrupted floors, gable ends that supported cranes and hoists, tiers of loading doors, unvarying rows of windows, and entrances with robust masonry frames. But how unhackneyed their appearance can be, how expressive their banding together on the waterfront of river ports or harbors or at the junction of canals and railroads. Many are grim, gaunt buildings. Others, in southern England most of all, were enlivened by white paint and bold lettering. The vast majority are of brick with stone trim, their surfaces studded with heavy tie-irons. In rare instances the exterior is weatherboarded.

Our example shows the warehouses that encompass St. Katharine's Docks just down river from the Tower of London. (Fig. 23.41) The complex, designed by Telford immediately after the Menai Bridge, consists of two enclosed basins entered through a third, which is itself entered from the Thames through a lock. Here ships loaded and unloaded their wares, unaffected by the rise and fall of tides. The stacks of floors were lifted on sturdy columns flush with the water's edge. At intervals the facades were recessed to allow space for cranes.

The landscape of industry: a scene at once heroic and sad. (Fig. 23.42) We admire the spunk of the first industrialists, their enterprise and vision, their dauntlessness. But more and more as the years go by, and palpably, because of this historical episode we are a living part, we mourn the loss of a way of life, the ravaged land, the blotting out of millennial patterns of life and land. The buildings are stark, stoical, blunt. They impress us with their honesty. But in that honest countenance is etched the record of brutal facts—child labor, the horrifying mortality rate of the mines, the bitter and often violent struggle of employers against workers.

It was all endured in the name of progress, and progress was a faith most everyone embraced in time—bosses and workers alike. The goods produced were for everyone. Industry looked to the steadily expanding middle class to buy its products, but more so to that huge lower class to whom factories and foundries brought cheap abundance. But no class escaped the toll of industrialization; no life, however remote from the colliery, mine, or mill, could stay untouched by what went on there.

We are in the midst of it still. But now, after two hundred years, we have come close to understanding, willy-nilly, that nature is a resource that can be depleted, that every boon has its price, that profit and progress are double-edged. They can diminish and maim us in the long run, while today they might further our material welfare and give us that abstract, unreckonable freedom "to enjoy life," as the saying goes.

Fig. 23.41 London, St. Katharine's Docks, 1826–28, Thomas Telford and Philip Hardwick, who also designed the row of warehouses shown here; their interior structure is wooden. Behind the warehouses were cartways, and then high defensive walls to control looting and pilfering. This photograph was taken in 1979. The warehouses have since been destroyed.

Fig. 23.42 Cornwall (England), abandoned mine engine house. Cornwall once had mines for tin, copper, and coal.

Further Reading

L. Benevolo, *The Origins of Modern Town Planning,* trans. J. Landry (Cambridge, Mass.: MIT Press, 1967).

D. P. Billington, *The Tower and the Bridge: The New Art of Structural Engineering* (New York: Basic Books, 1983).

B. Bracegirdle, ed., *The Archaeology of the Industrial Revolution* (London: Heinemann Educational, 1973).

P. Collins, *Changing Ideals in Modern Architecture* (London: Faber and Faber, 1965).

I. A. Egorov, *The Architectural Planning of St. Petersburg,* trans. E. Dluhosch (Athens: Ohio University Press, 1969).

G. Germann, *Gothic Revival in Europe and Britain,* trans. G. Onn (London: Lund Humphries, 1972).

H. R. Hitchcock, *Architecture: Nineteenth and Twentieth Centuries,* 3rd ed. (Harmondsworth and Baltimore: Penguin, 1968).

F. Loyer, *Architecture of the Industrial Age* (New York: Rizzoli, 1983).

M. McCarthy, *The Origins of the Gothic Revival* (New Haven: Yale University Press, 1987).

H. G. Pundt, *Schinkel's Berlin* (Cambridge, Mass.: Harvard University Press, 1972).

J. Summerson, *The Life and Work of John Nash, Architect* (Cambridge, Mass.: MIT Press, 1980).

B. Trinder, *The Making of the Industrial Landscape* (London: Dent, 1982).

D. Watkin and T. Mellinghoff, *German Architecture and the Neoclassical Ideal* (Cambridge, Mass.: MIT Press, 1987).

Paul Revere, *A View of the Part of the Town of Boston . . .*, engraving, 1768.

24

THE AMERICAN EXPERIENCE

In 1842, several years before the Great Exhibition in London, the famous English novelist Charles Dickens made an extended visit to America, "that vast counting-house which lies beyond the Atlantic." He disembarked at Boston where he spent two weeks, visiting its hospitals and correctional institutions, walking its streets, taking side trips out to Harvard and the textile mills at Lowell. He found the city beautiful, clean, and sparkling, and so slight and insubstantial in appearance that every street "looked exactly like a scene in a pantomine." The houses for the most part were large and elegant—some of brick; others, white wooden houses with green jalousie blinds. The public buildings were handsome; he mentioned specifically the new customs house, the two theaters, and the State House built on Beacon Hill with the green enclosure of the Common sloping down before it.

Later on his trip, in New York, he admired the bustle of Broadway running the length of Manhattan Island. At night it was dotted with bright jets of gas and reminded him of Piccadilly. He stopped at Wall Street and the Egyptian-style prison called the Tombs. From New York, by railroad and two ferries, he attained Philadelphia—"a handsome city but distractingly regular. After walking about it for an hour or two I felt that I would have given the world for a crooked street."

It was a day's journey hence, mostly by steamboat, to Washington. (Fig. 24.1) On the short train ride from Baltimore, he had "a beautiful view of the Capitol, which is a fine building of the Corinthian order, placed upon a noble and commanding eminence." But the actual visit was a disappointment. The President's mansion looked like an English clubhouse. Most of the time it was like being in an abandoned town, or rather one whose residents had left at the end of the season, taking their houses along with them.

[Washington] is sometimes called the City of Magnificent Distances, but it might with greater propriety be termed the City of Magnificent Intentions; for it is only on taking a bird's eye view of it from the top of the Capitol, that one can at all comprehend the vast designs of its projector, an aspiring Frenchman. Spacious avenues that begin in nothing, and lead nowhere; streets, mile-long, that only want houses, roads, and inhabitants; public buildings that need but a public to be complete. . . .

Scrapping an initial plan to go as far south as Charleston, Dickens took in a bit of Virginia instead, saw something of the Midwest, and headed back through Canada. Near Richmond he went to a tobacco manufactory where the workmen were all slaves, and then to a plantation of about twelve hundred acres on the opposite bank of the James River. The planter's house was an airy, rustic dwelling with an open piazza, but the slave quarter was comprised of "very crazy, wretched cabins." Indeed, in Richmond and the surrounding countryside, alongside "pretty villas and cheerful houses," there was everywhere regnant decay: barns and outbuildings moldering away, half-roofless sheds, miserable stations by the railway side. Industrial Pittsburgh had "a great quantity of smoke hanging about it." And St. Louis was busy building. (Fig. 24.2) In the old French quarter the streets were narrow and crooked, the houses quaint and picturesque, of wood, with "tumbledown galleries before the windows, approachable by stairs or rather ladders from the street," and "crazy old tenements with blinking casements, such as may be found in Flanders." But there were also wharves and warehouses, and "new buildings in all directions." The vastness of the prairie did not move him, but the muddy Mississippi did. He traveled fast now through Ohio to Lake Erie, and after brief stops in Toronto, Montreal, and Quebec, he returned to New York where he embarked for England.

It must have been a strange journey, especially for an Englishman. Here was a young nation, barely a half-century old, which had started hesitantly as a British colony only about two hundred years earlier on an uncharted, hostile continent, held on longer than the French, the Dutch, the Swedes, and all those others who had also tried to tame and exploit it, revolted against the authority of the mother country with reckless valor, and was now busy adjusting to a hard-won independence. For a cultured Londoner, an American visit stood the Grand Tour on its head. He made his pilgrimage to the hoary seats of Europe for enlightenment, to feel the impress of Western civilization. But out here, beyond

Fig. 24.1 Washington, D.C., general view in 1850; lithograph by R. P. Smith. The Capitol is in the foreground. The Mall from here to the Washington Monument in the distance has the look of a pasture. The only building of consequence alongside it is the Smithsonian Institution, designed by James Renwick and begun in 1847. The strong line of Pennsylvania Avenue, to the right of the mall, leads out to the White House, not visible in this view.

Fig. 24.1 Washington, D.C., general view in 1850; lithograph by R. P. Smith. The Capitol is in the foreground. The Mall from here to the Washington Monument in the distance has the look of a pasture. The only building of consequence alongside it is the Smithsonian Institution, designed by James Renwick and begun in 1847. The strong line of Pennsylvania Avenue, to the right of the mall, leads out to the White House, not visible in this view.

Fig. 24.2 St. Louis (Missouri), partial view in the early nineteenth century; a detail from the "Panorama" by J. C. Wild, 1840.

the ocean, something raw, untried, and foolhardy was going on; rooted in the Old World to be sure, but also strong-minded and unpredictable for all that. In the open reaches of a heroic landscape, away from the great centers of high culture, a motley people had come together as a nation and was slowly finding itself. Much of its fiber was frontier-rough still, with no historical depth to it at all. But the regional patterns of land occupation were already strongly marked up and down the Atlantic seaboard. The seemingly unbounded hinterland of prairie and river was losing its mystery as official surveyors mapped it and small groups of intrepid adventurers went out to animate hopeful town grids hatched by the score in the awesome wilderness. But at least a handful of decent-sized cities could be assessed in European terms without embarrassment. Chief among them were New York, Philadelphia, and Boston, which, with a population of about 130,000 at the time of Dickens' visit, was one of the largest cities of the United States.

Colonial Dependence

Boston was not the earliest English settlement in America, but it came close. When the Puritan settlers of the Massachusetts Bay Company arrived in the autumn of 1630, led by Governor John Winthrop, to take up residence on the tiny peninsula across the Charles, small communities of their compatriots had been trying to make a go of it on the harsh Atlantic coast for one or two generations. (Fig. 24.3) The Chesapeake tidewater had received the first influx. In 1607 the Virginia Company, a joint-stock enterprise under royal charter, founded Jamestown some thirty miles inland where a narrow isthmus connected the mainland to a near-by island. Hampton, Henrico, and one or two others followed. In the North, Plymouth Plantation was first. Discounting an abortive attempt in 1607, the site was permanently occupied by a self-exiled separatist group of Pilgrims in 1620. A number of small settlements on the bleak shores of Massachusetts and along the Connecticut River came shortly afterward. Boston was among them. Meanwhile, the French had been colonizing the St. Lawrence River valley further north; the Dutch held the Hudson Valley; and the Spaniards, pushing ever upward with their missions, presidios, and pueblos, had gained a firm foothold on the northern arc of the Gulf of Mexico, where St. Augustine was installed at the tip of Florida in 1570 and Santa Fe on the Rio Grande in 1609.

The Dutch had never been keen on permanent and well-administered settlements. Trade was their prime objective. New Amsterdam on Manhattan Island, their only respectable town, lacked governmental or other public buildings. The houses were direct transplants: tall, narrow brick structures fronting the street, with stepped gables and decorations of iron "beam anchors" and the letters and numbers of construction dates. (Fig. 24.4) In the lands between the Hudson and the Delaware riv-

Fig. 24.3 Map: The United States east of the Mississippi ca. 1840. The inset shows areas of European colonization: English in the east; French in the center; Spanish in the west and southeast.

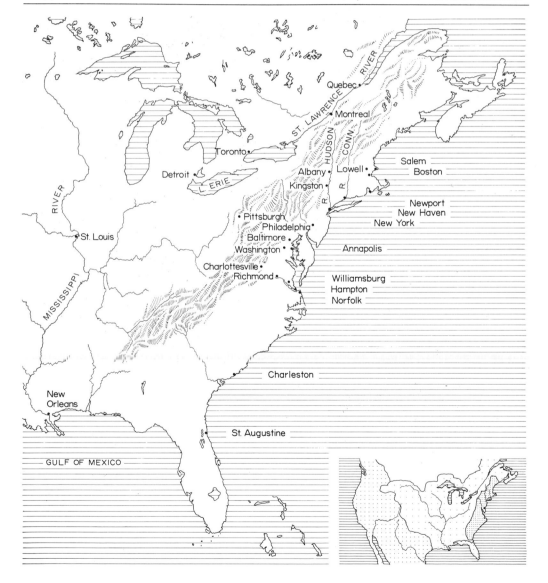

ers, where the patroons had their capacious estates, a peasant house type prevailed. Built of fieldstone, it was one low storey high and one room deep, with an additive plan of two or three contiguous rooms. At any rate, the Dutch episode was brief. New Netherlands was removed as a colonial power in the 1660s, about forty years after the Dutch West India Company had won its exclusive trading charter. And so New Amsterdam became New York, Wiltsyck became Kingston, Beverwyck was renamed Albany. The flat coastal plains of New Jersey and eastern Pennsylvania lay open to British settlement.

This is where the Quaker William Penn will plant the gracious model city of Philadelphia in 1681. This is where waves of German immigrants in the early eighteenth century—Lutherans, Moravians, fundamentalist celibate groups like the Society of the Solitary and the Order of Spiritual Virgins—will harbor their pious, implacably rural, medieval way of life. They will bequeath us the linear village (e.g., Germantown), the outdoor bakeoven, and the stone and log houses of one or two storeys, with

Fig. 24.5a New Roads (Pointe Coupée Parish, Louisiana), Parlange Plantation, main house, 1750. It was built by the Marquis Vincent de Ternant, whose widow married Charles Parlange, a French naval officer. This is a classic example of the French colonial house with its enveloping veranda.

Fig. 24.4 New York, Broad Street in 1831; engraving by J. Archer after Alexander Jackson Davis. The building in the middle is a Dutch house of 1698.

their characteristic central chimneys which open into a kitchen with a single deep fireplace. They also brought us the two-level "bank" barns, which stabled cattle in the basement and used the upper level for hay and grain storage; the bank barn cantilevered out on the barnyard side and was built against a bank or ramp on the opposite side, so that a vehicle could be drawn onto this upper floor.

Paris saw its American possessions not as the refuge of dissidents, but as a royal domain. A decree of 1628, for instance, banned Protestant settlement in New France, which only precipitated the mass emigration of Huguenots to the British colonies. While tough French woodsmen and trappers ventured into the Canadian wilds and into Missouri country, the towns had all the pretense of high culture. The central *place*

d'armes was equipped with the trappings of an administrative headquarters—palaces for governors, bishops, and intendants (the king's trade representatives), barracks, hospitals, and the like. And yet because of foot-dragging on the issue of sending significant numbers of colonists, most of these were hardly viable urban communities. By 1718 when New Orleans was founded, the chain of forts, trading posts, and towns that comprised New France stretched from the Great Lakes to the Gulf of Mexico, but it was an anemic, passive enterprise that survived only in pockets as the success of the Anglo-Americans was sealed. And with Jefferson's purchase of Louisiana from Napoleon in 1803, the French were out of the picture as a colonial power, at least as far as the United States was concerned.

French town-planning in America had

Fig. 24.5b Princess Anne County (Virginia), the Adam Thoroughgood House, ca. 1700–1720.

clear formal precedents at home. Louisburg, intended as the main fortress town in Canada, obeyed the lead of Vauban. Detroit aped the *bastides* of Gascony; its founder, Anthoine de la Mothe Cadillac, was after all a Gascon. The common pattern, however, is represented by Montreal, St. Louis, and New Orleans: a narrow linear grid on a river, with a *place d'arms* close to the water's edge. The typical house of town and country featured an elevated first floor and a veranda that went all the way around when the site permitted, trapping shade and cool breezes. (Fig. 24.5a) These are the "tumbledown galleries" Dickens observed in St. Louis.

Anglo-America in the Seventeenth Century Houses in the English colonies had their own distinctive individuality. They were based on the late medieval vernacular of the homeland, but took on different forms in the North and South depending on the point of origin of the settlers and local conditions. The South commonly built two-storey houses with steep pitched roofs; the chimneys were built externally at each gable end or worked flush within the end walls. (Fig. 24.5b) In the west of England where Virginia and Maryland colonists had their origin external gable-end chimneys were the rule. And the arrangement also made good sense in the hot humid weather of the Chesapeake tidewater, since end chimneys can dissipate the heat generated by summer cooking. The central chimney, on the other hand, was characteristic of the east of England, and so it seemed natural to the homesteaders of Massachusetts and Connecticut who originated there. (Fig. 24.5c)

The huge New England masonry chimney stack went right through the middle of the two-storey frame house, making a

Fig. 24.5c Farmington (Connecticut), the Stanley-Whitman House, begun by Samuel Whitman in 1664; the lean-to at the back was added ca. 1760. The house was fully restored in 1934–35.

ridgepole for the roof impossible. So a system of common rafters was resorted to instead. Here was one of several points of divergence between the New England house and its parent in rural East Anglia. Two others are noteworthy. In late medieval England half-timbered houses most often exposed to the weather both frame and fill. In New England, clapboards nailed directly to the vertical studs, set between the large posts of the frame, sealed the house on the outside, a practice only exceptionally encountered in East Anglia. Moreover, the English thatched roof was changed to shingles here, and the staircase leading to the second-storey sleeping quarters was placed toward the front of the house, as opposed to the English habit of putting it to the rear.

Everything else was traditional enough: the masonry foundation, used either as a low wall or a cellar; the sturdy oak frame, locked together with mortise-and-tenon joints and stiffened by angle braces, chimney girts, and summer beams; the overhanging second floor, fitted on the principal posts with round oaken pins driven in auger holes; the added lean-to at the back that served as "buttery" and "borning-room."

More than seventy of these houses are still scattered across New England. They were not very efficient. The single massive chimney was impractical. The small leaded casement windows may have helped with insulation against the cold in the winter months, but they made the rooms gloomy the year round. The heavy frame was stiff and unalterable. The plan itself showed little elasticity. Of the two main rooms on the ground floor, one was used for family living, cooking, and as work space, too. The parlor was for important guests and religious observances. The family members slept in the two bedrooms on the second floor; the servant in the attic.

Clumsy and scant as the furnishings now look to us in the restored specimens, there was plenty of ornament and color around—intricately carved chairs and tables touched up with paint and inset panels, rich carpets, bright dishes arranged against the plastered wall spans between the corner posts, and pewter. (Fig. 24.6) The Puritan mind, in private, did not banish joy—whatever our fixed notions of the period. Cal-

Fig. 24.6 Ipswich (Massachusetts), room from the house of the tanner Thomas Hart, ca. 1650, as reconstructed in the Henry Francis du Pont Winterthur Museum in Winterthur, Delaware, and furnished with typical furnishings of the time. Another room from this house, the parlor, is now installed in the American Wing of the Metropolitan Museum of Art, New York.

vin himself thought it uncivil to be constrained to "that which is needful," to be denied "the lawful enjoyment of God's blessings."

Public comportment was another matter. The showpiece for this was the meetinghouse. (Fig. 24.7) As the only public building in the town, the meetinghouse, like the Muslim mosque, served multiple functions. It was church, school, forum, social and cultural center. And it was fanatically plain, as a matter of profession. A nondirectional, more or less square building, its peaked roof surmounted by a belfry, the meetinghouse defined a simple integral volume, encompassed by a gallery and focused on a pulpit. These features, along with the box pews and the movable communion table, derived from the Protestant tradition of Europe. But the general shape was native. The clapboarded frame was that of the common dwelling. The interior, bare of any ornament or religious image, rose to the exposed hipped roof. It was supported on enormous trusses, which also held up the platform for the belfry. In this setting Puritan theocracy exercised its stern powers.

The southern church, by contrast, stood compromised in its architecture. The charter of the Virginia Company made it mandatory that the Church of England be the official religion of the colony. What was provided for its practice were simple single-nave brick structures, like the late medieval parish churches of rural England. (Fig. 24.8) The type had a directional plan, a square bell tower on the entrance side,

610

Fig. 24.7 Hingham (Massachusetts), the Old Ship Meetinghouse, 1681, with additions in 1731 and 1755: (**a**) exterior; (**b**) interior looking toward the pulpit.

flying buttresses, and Gothic windows. Some fifty of these churches were built in Virginia Colony in the seventeenth century. Most of them were situated in open country, at a crossroads or in some convenient spot along the banks of a river. This was so because life centered around individual plantations.

The original intention of the colonial enterprise had been to start an urban society. Jamestown, the capital and seat of government, was to be an extension of the commercial world of London merchants. Rowhouses appeared on its streets in anticipation of a serried urbanism. The legislature continued to mandate new towns well into the next century. But the towns never took. Settlement came before a thorough land survey, and the headright

method of land distribution encouraged isolated holdings. Each settler's headright, usually fifty acres, could be taken wherever he chose, and he obviously chose only good land, preferably near a river. The boundaries were irregular and ill-defined; the settlement pattern diffuse. A strong awareness of land values and soil led to the amassing of huge estates and a driving hunger to explore, to search for new land. Then West Indian tobacco was introduced to the Virginia farms, slave labor became available, and the rural character of the region was sealed. Dozens of inlets on the Virginia rivers gave the plantations their own docks, obviating trade centers or a vital harbor economy for Jamestown. London would be Virginia's metropolis.

Country churches were an admission of

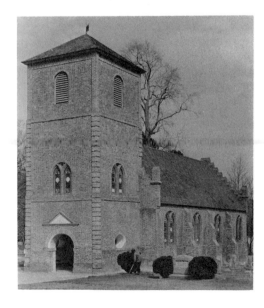

Fig. 24.8 Isle of Wight County (Virginia), St. Luke's Church, ca. 1685.

the failure of tidewater towns. So were courthouse-square compounds. These compounds, usually enclosed within a brick wall, functioned as county centers. Around a tiny square there were, besides the courthouse, a jail, a caretaker's residence, a row of lawyers' offices, and nearby a tavern and inn. They came alive only when court was in session or during sporadic government affairs. The fully blown courthouse town would be exported later to Mississippi and the Ohio country, and wherever Virginians settled beyond the Alleghenies.

New England, conversely, was oriented toward townships from the start, and so it remained by and large even after some coastal settlements—Boston is the prime case—developed into thriving ports run by a canny merchant class. A township was made up of a small covenanted group and its farmland. It aimed to keep small and self-sufficient. The economy was undifferentiated: among them the farmers represented all the skills needed to keep their closed community going.

At the heart of the migration was the church covenant. Each township existed under a commission from God. It could reproduce itself endlessly, looking ahead to the establishment of a utopian Christian commonwealth. The leader was the chosen minister, and the physical symbol of the covenant was the meetinghouse. The community joined forces to clear a common, put a fence around it to prevent grazing livestock from straying, and build the meetinghouse and a home for the minister. Every man then built his own house around the common with the help of neighbors, started a small vegetable and herb garden outside the back door, and cleared his land for farming.

The land for the township had been surveyed ahead of time and delimited. It would be divided according to merit, the size of each allotment reflecting either the relative amount each settler contributed to the initial expense of the enterprise or the extent of his personal property. There was nothing democratic in this procedure, nor in the class hierarchy of proprietors, first settlers, and latecomers to which it gave legitimacy. Even in the meetinghouse a member's social standing was announced in the assign-

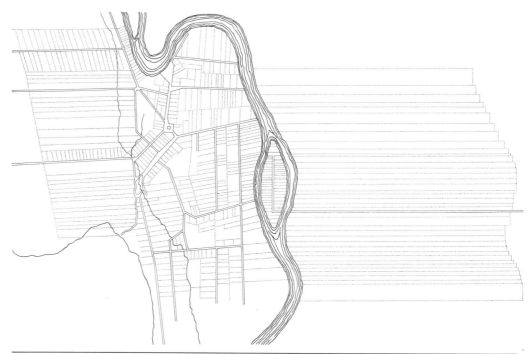

Fig. 24.9a. Wethersfield (Connecticut) at the time of settlement in 1640. The site is a bend in the Connecticut River. The home lots are placed on streets that lead to a central green. Strip fields surround the town.

ment of pews, rank being gauged through how close one sat to the pulpit.

The divided fields were mostly long and narrow. (Fig. 24.9a) Once they were determined, highways and roads were laid out more with the intention of reaching each piece of property than intertown communication. The town itself would be organized either as a nucleated village—that is, a cluster of home lots around the common or along the spine of a single street—or else more formally with an overall geometric frame. New Haven, Connecticut, founded in 1637 on a crystalline plan of nine equal square blocks from which issued an array of straight radial roads, was a rarity even among the more regular towns. (Fig. 24.9b)

Boston: New England's Capital
What Jamestown set out to be, the port of colonial America and London's main respondent, and could not, Boston managed to accomplish in a reasonable northern likeness. Within years of its establishment on the small hilly peninsula that the local

Indians called Shawmut, said to mean "Living Waters," Governor Winthrop's town began to distinguish itself from its sisters. An ironworks with blast furnace, forge, and mill was set up in Saugus before 1650. And earlier still, the leaders of the Massachusetts Bay Colony endowed Harvard College at a village four miles up the Charles River, which they named Cambridge, after the great English university that had educated a good many of them.

The Shawmut Peninsula, surrounded on all sides by water except for the narrow Neck on the south that connected it with the Roxbury mainland, afforded several coves and a good harbor on the east. (Fig. 24.10a) Through the center of the peninsula rose a three-humped high ridge. Of the peaks, only Beacon Hill survives in a much truncated profile. Between this eminent backdrop and the harbor, the town nestled. Its center was pinned naturally where a main road (Great, later King, Street) leading westward from the harbor joined Cornhill Street (now Washington), which

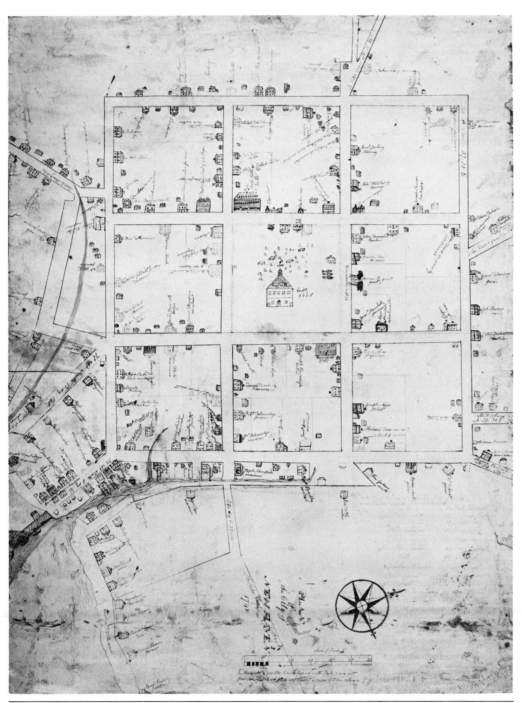

Fig. 24.9b New Haven (Connecticut), plan, 1748. The radial roads that start at the edges of the grid and head to the private fields are still in use today. The central of the nine squares was set aside as common land. The tenth square, set at a diagonal at the juncture of two creeks (lower left), met the harbor. The Long Wharf (center foreground) is now buried under fill.

headed in the direction of the Neck and the mainland. Here was the meetinghouse that fronted the marketplace, with the governor's house nearby, and here in 1657 a town house went up for administrators and merchants alike. With its wharves built into the harbor by merchant owners of waterfront property, Boston was justly described by an early London promoter as "fittest for such as can Trade into England."

On the opposite side of town, in the countryside that sloped toward Back Bay, a piece of land, some forty-five acres of it, was designated as the Common. A law of 1640 declared: "There shall be no land granted either for house plott or garden out of ye open ground or Common field." And so it has endured to this day, a people's place, making it the oldest park in the country. Here the town militia drilled, cattle grazed, and, a visitor named John Josselyn wrote in 1674, "the Gallants a little before Sun-set walk with their Marmalet-Madams, as we do in Morefields, &c till the nine a clock Bell rings them home to their respective habitations, when presently the constables walk their rounds to see good orders kept, and to take up loose people."

By now Boston was "the Metropolis of this Colony or rather of the whole countrey." The north end of the peninsula had grown as a semi-independent district with its own meetinghouse, the road to the Neck had become a crowded spine, and the great program of reclaiming land from the marshes and coves of the watery site had begun. The waterfront was fringed with warehouses, ropewalks, and shipyards. The first houses were of the kind we would expect, but to go with their urban outlook they faced the street with one narrow gabled end and had their chimney at the other. Rowhouses were not unknown, while the wealthier residents had large, free-standing mansions made up of several gabled units picturesquely assembled around a central chimney. The public buildings were also residential in character. The Saugus ironworks was a multiple-gabled house; and so too was the town house, with wooden porches on the long sides that supported the overhanging upper storeys. (Fig. 24.11) The ground floor had open shops for the merchants; in the chambers above, the General Court held its monthly meetings. Here we recognize the European model of the Middle Ages, as we encountered it in the town hall of Como, for example. (Fig. 15.11)

Fires were a recurrent disaster. The growing dependence on brick toward the end of the century was partly a preventive measure. But Boston was also beginning to discover Georgian London. Both New England and the South were becoming more sophisticated as they made an effort to catch up with the recent classical fashions of the homeland. In 1698 the capital of Virginia was moved from Jamestown to Williamsburg, a site on high ground midway between the York and James rivers, where the small College of William and Mary had already introduced the lesser style of Christopher Wren to colonial America. The main Duke of Gloucester Street, a full thirty meters (100 feet) wide, started at the college and terminated at the east end in the new Capitol. Midway was Market Square, through which a tree-lined cross-axis led to the governor's palace. The town plan is credited to Francis Nicholson, an able colonial administrator. He was most probably also responsible for the contemporary plan of Annapolis, the capital of Maryland, which with its two great circles and radiating diagonal streets infused a startling Baroque vision into these still medieval backwaters of the British empire.

The South had always been more in tune with official English culture. Close to Crown and Church, it had heeded English law and emulated the homeland's fashions and social customs. Now the Williamsburg buildings, and a new generation of country houses, furnished an up-to-date stage for a Georgian upper-crust life. The diamond-paned casements, the tall thin group chimneys of Tudor England, the steeply pitched roofs and curved Flemish gables, all this was put aside. A kind of classical vernacular, thin and toylike, took over. Dormers were pedimented, sash windows with white trim lined up in prim symmetry right up close to the brick surface (unlike England, where they were pushed back by law), and oversized white doors at the top of a run of stairs, with classical frames and swan's-neck pediments, accentuated the middle. From the gentler profile of the roofs central cupolas sprouted on tall cylindrical or poly-

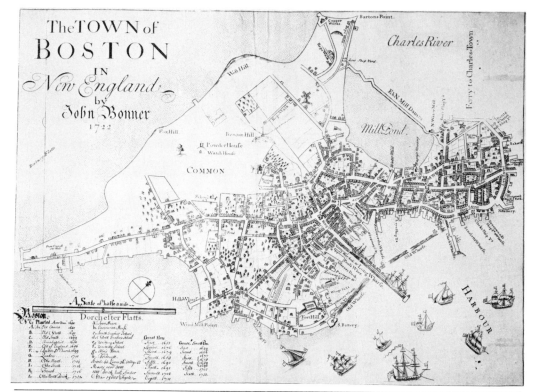

Fig. 24.10 Boston (Massachusetts); plans: **(a)** in 1722; **(b)** opposite page, in 1855.

gonal drums. The plans became adventurous. Stratford, the home of Thomas Lee in Westmoreland County, sits on a raised basement. (Fig. 24.12) Two four-room wings are linked by a central hall reached from either side by means of straight, rather precipitous, flights of stairs. Massive chimneys of four arched stacks lift up and out of the low-pitched hipped roof. A Baroque vigor in short, a little stiff and awkward perhaps, but with clear echoes of Vanbrugh or Hawksmoor. (Figs. 22.5, 22.6)

The pervasive classical mood submerged the regional differences of seventeenth-century colonial America. In the New England towns detached houses, commonly still of wood, imitated rusticated masonry with projecting quoins. The overhang was given up in favor of flat facades. The predominant color was not white, popular belief to the contrary. Sources of the time speak of reds, browns, and yellows. The classical trim

and interior detail were handled ably by a growing class of wood-carvers. In the outlying areas of the upper Connecticut Valley, steadily being engulfed within New England's frontiers, local carpenters fetchingly reworked the orders with an occasional homely twist, like the substitution of tobacco leaves for the acanthus of the Corinthian capital.

Boston, the busy capital of this expanding northern territory, absorbed the Georgian idiom with the versatility to be expected of an English metropolis. And that is what it now was. In 1692 Massachusetts was rechartered as a Royal Province, similar to Virginia. Its governors were no longer to be elected by the colonists, but sent from England by royal appointment. The Province House, where they now resided, was in the South End. This three-storey mansion—with its red stone entrance stairs, the columnar porch surmounted by a presen-

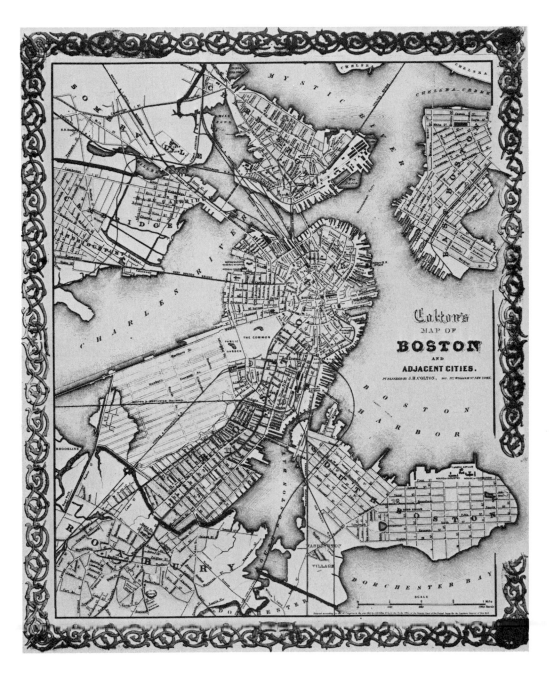

ground floor and simple, shallow arches over the sash windows and the door. Projecting brick string-courses ran between the storeys, and slate was often used as roofing material.

The town center continued to be the crossing of King and Cornhill streets. But the main buildings were all new and elegant, having been stylishly remade after the Fire of 1711. The now brick, Georgian town house sheltered the provincial government, the courts, and the merchant exchange. It faced east toward the harbor at the head of King Street, which had just been extended at the other end for a kilometer (more than half a mile) into the water by the Long Wharf, a broad causeway lined with rows of shops and warehouses. (Fig. 24.10a) Here, at this gateway to America, the largest ships of the time loaded and unloaded their cargo, taking colonial goods home and bringing back articles of fashion and official visitors and troops.

By mid-century the Boston skyline bristled with spired cupolas and towers—and that was something new. Provincial status had ushered in the detested Church of England. The first Anglican church, the wooden King's Chapel, was raised on a corner of the town's burying ground, at the east edge of the Common. Baptists, Quakers, and French Huguenots also opened shop here and there within the city limits, so that the meetinghouses of the Puritan majority, no fewer than six by now, came to keep odd and often unwanted company. The Anglicans, moreover, were attached to their own religious architecture, since it had been updated by Wren first and later Gibbs in the period after the Great Fire of London. In 1723 when the Anglican community of the North End was numerous enough to invest in a church of its own, the Wren model made its first appearance in New England in a simplified, you might say Puritan, version, but defiantly churchy nonetheless. The tower especially, with its thin tall spire that spiked the horizon, must have been irksome to the independent-minded divines and their congregations. In their own defense, they decided to adopt it.

Then King's Chapel went them one better. (Fig. 24.13) In 1749 the original wooden structure was pulled down to make room

tation balcony carrying the royal arms, the cupola on the roof, and the richly paneled and appointed formal rooms within—represented the new residential fashion at its finest. The South End was a suburban area of open fields and large houses, like this one, sitting on spacious lots and attended by stables, sheds, and fruit rooms. From the dormers along the edges of the roomy

gambrel roofs that enveloped the third storey, and from the balustraded decks at the top, one could view Back Bay in the west and the harbor in the east. The rich also ensconced themselves on the high ground at the foot of Beacon Hill, across the Common. The populous and rowdy North End had plainer brick houses, for the merchants and artisans. They had shops on the

Fig. 24.11 Boston, the First Town House, 1657–58; reconstruction drawing. There was an open-walled public market on the ground floor, as in medieval town halls in Europe (e.g., Fig. 15.11); the top floors contained court rooms, a library, an armory, and a meeting room for elders. The hipped roof was of the meetinghouse type. The building was destroyed by fire in 1711. The site is that of the Old State House on King Street (now State Street), originally the second town house, which was freestanding in line with Long Wharf (see Fig. 24.10a); this later building still stands.

for the first stone church in America. The material was local Quincy granite picked from the ground, since no quarries were as yet operative anywhere in the colonies. The model agreed on was Gibbs, and specifically St. Martin-in-the-Fields. (Fig. 21.38) This meant, among other things, a colossal portico, the earliest American temple front. It did get built, but a while later and of wood. Still, the reach was impressive; the whole design set a higher level of learnedness and modernism for colonial architecture.

The man responsible was Peter Harrison (1716–75). We might think of him as our first professional architect, even though he was a merchant and sea captain by occupation and was never paid for his designs. An Englishman born in Yorkshire, Harrison knew firsthand the Neo-Palladianism of Lord Burlington's circle when he settled down at Newport, Rhode Island, and started producing designs for some striking public buildings in this newly prosperous and cosmopolitan port town run by Quakers, Anglicans, and Jews. His works included the Redwood Library, with its monumental Doric portico raised on a podium; the first synagogue in the colonies (internally nothing other than a Neo-Palladian meetinghouse); and the Brick Market, which was based on Somerset House, a royal palace in London attributed to Inigo Jones.

Neo-Palladianism swept America, as it had England, through the agency of pattern books, especially Gibbs' *A Book of Archi-*

Fig. 24.12 Westmoreland County (Virginia), the house of Thomas Lee, called Stratford, ca. 1730–35.

Fig. 24.13 Boston, King's Chapel, 1749–54, Peter Harrison: **(a)** exterior view in the nineteenth century; **(b)** interior. Harrison planned the Ionic porch, but it was not built until 1785–87, and then in wood. The interior is strongly influenced by James Gibbs (see Fig. 21.38b).

tecture, first published in London in 1728. In the domestic field the style was mostly a gloss on the earlier Georgian schemes. This was true at least in the North. The architectural handbooks assured better proportions and more authentic detail, both inside and out. But the most conspicuous changes registered on the main facades of houses. A new monumentality was conveyed through pedimented central pavilions which took the full height of the house. But the flat plane persisted. (Fig. 24.14)

In the South, the central tract projected a bit more forcefully. Sometimes, as in the Miles Brewton House in Charleston, the design was copied directly from Palladio, rather than through Gibbs. (Fig. 19.34) More interestingly, some plantation houses experimented with the three-part plans of Palladian villas with passageways connecting central block to two symmetrically placed dependencies. But unlike Neo-Palladian country houses in England which, as we saw, sat in picturesque grounds, Southern mansions preferred the formal Renaissance or Baroque garden. Middleton Place outside Charleston—with its terraces sloping down to the Ashley River, a canal, pools, and geometric walks—has even a touch of Le Nôtre about it.

Architecture for a Nation

The Revolution started in Boston. In 1774, after the Boston Tea Party, the British closed the harbor. For the next ten years building was at a standstill. With Britain's defeat and the establishment of the United States of America, however, a challenging, fecund period opened up for architecture. Government was the biggest client. The states of the Union, struck with a new sense of pride and self-importance, sought to invest themselves with material symbols of their independence. The federal administration looked for a permanent home, and in 1793 the creation of Washington as a seat of government commenced officially. It was a time for monuments and memorials, for schools, commercial exchanges, and public facilities of all kinds.

It was also the time for the winners in the private sector to show off their good fortune. Misplaced sympathies had forced much of the aristocratic, possessing class into exile. The economic basis of the South was provisionally upset. Merchants and capitalists now found themselves in the lead and were transformed into arbiters of American culture. They were the backbone of the Federal Party, this affluent mercantile aristocracy, and the delicate, refined manner they patronized until about 1820 is known as the Federal style. Its masterpieces survive in Charleston, Providence, New York, and a dozen other cities, but nowhere more conspicuously than in the work of Charles Bulfinch (1763–1844), in Boston, and that of the self-taught woodcarver of Salem, Samuel McIntire (1757–1811).

The Federalists had supported the rebellion against the rule of England, but they had no wish to turn their backs on her cultural guidance. The civilized vision of Bulfinch and McIntire was affiliated with that architecture in England that succeeded Neo-Palladianism, and more precisely the circle of Robert Adam. But the more austere Neoclassicism of Europe, the lofty abstractions of Ledoux and Soane, had a following, too. The formal language was imported by French and British architects familiar with it, people like Joseph-Jacques Ramée (1764–1842) and Benjamin Latrobe (1764–1820) who came to America in search of work and glory. And national leaders impassioned by the French Revolution and its paradigm, the ancient republic of Rome, supplied the impetus.

In this company, Thomas Jefferson (1743–1826) was the great preceptor. Against the Federalist faith in a strong central government reliant on the new moneyed classes, Jefferson championed a democratic society of small landowners, an agrarian utopia. The capacity to give physical shape to this republican environment was locked within the people, he thought, and had only to be released through the proper incitement. The idealism, and the forms that could encap-

Fig. 24.14 Cambridge (Massachusetts), the house of Major John Vassall on Brattle Street, 1759; also known as the Longfellow House because it was occupied by the poet Henry Wadsworth Longfellow for nearly fifty years until his death in 1882.

sulate it, should come straight from the roots, from ancient Greece and Rome—the source that had given revolutionary France her shoring symbols, and could do the same for the United States of America.

The Janus of Neoclassicism
The forte of the Federal style was in residences and decoration. Any of a score of Salem houses by McIntire can attest to the rarefied, sober urbanity of his designs, the chasteness of his ornament. Take the Pingree House, completed in 1805. (Fig. 24.15) The plan breaks with colonial rigidity. There are light touches of the curve, in the central staircase and the entrance portico. The gentle billow of this exquisitely attenuated portico shelters a door with an elliptical fanlight and narrow sidelights, a signature of the Federal style. The facade, a thin taut rectangle of brick, unaccented at the corners, is sliced with stone string-courses in three bands of diminishing height. Simply cut windows, their flaring stone lintels set flush with the wall plane, add little substance to this tight screen that is drawn with mute dignity between the public life of the street and that of the inhabitants. There is no visible roof at all: the balustrade of the late Georgian roof has been moved out to the very edge, to frame the facade like a lacy cornice. McIntire is using his books of course, but such unstrained control has something innate about it, like having a good ear for music.

The more cosmopolitan Bulfinch in Boston matches this understated polish. His houses for the likes of Harrison Gray Otis and Joseph Barrell—with their tree-shaded yards, oval rooms that bow out on the garden side, windows brought down to the floor, wrought-iron balconies of Greek and Japanese designs, and the plaster and carved ornament of the main rooms—were

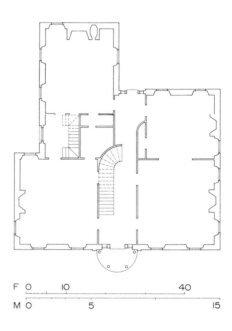

Fig. 24.15 Salem (Massachusetts), the John Gardner House, 1805, Samuel McIntire: **(a)** exterior; **(b)** ground plan. The house is known more commonly as the Pingree House, after its later owners.

paragons of gracious suburban living. But his true strength was to conceive of residential architecture as the agent of street-making. As a serious entrepreneur on the order of British architects like Robert Adam and John Nash, Bulfinch spearheaded the development of Beacon Hill, the edges of the Common, the waterfront north and south of the Long Wharf, and selected spots in the thick of town. In all of these projects, he promoted continuous blocks of uniform design. The long tier of five-storey warehouses on India Wharf civilized a clutter of docks and run-down buildings. The Bathlike Tontine Crescent grouped in a graceful curve sixteen brick houses, painted gray, with the end ones pulled out as bracketing pavilions. (Fig. 24.16) Colonnade Row, nineteen stately town houses on

the south side of the Common across from the tree-lined mall, with a view of the Charles River, was unified by a continuous Doric portico supporting a delicate iron balcony in front of the floor-length drawing-room windows of the second floor. But even on a more modest scale, the Bulfinch tradition was street-enhancing. We need only list experiments with twin houses, bow fronts, sidewalks of brick crossed by cobblestone carriage-ways, and the practice of setting houses back from the street to allow for front lawns with iron fences.

In the public buildings of the Federal style there is the same abstinence from exertive, sculptural mass, the same love for thin, stretched planes. We can see this in the new State House by Bulfinch (1795–97), which Dickens so admired, built high on the Bea-

con Hill side of the Common. (Fig. 24.17) The main shapes of the building block—the two-storey portico, the recessed pedimental unit, the dome—are bravely assembled. But what might have worked as a bold Neoclassical composition is enfeebled with too much small surface detail and the insubstantiating veneer (copper originally, gold leaf later) of the wooden dome on its high drum.

Now look at this same building next to a near-contemporary design with a similar program—Latrobe's revision of a project for the U.S. Capitol. (Fig. 24.18) The constituent elements are the same, but the effect is very different. The shallow cup of the dome rises full and resonant from the general mass, instead of perching lightly on it. Pedimental unit and portico are pulled together into a proper temple front and are integrated with the flight of monumental stairs. The colossal order runs across the entire length in receding emphasis, from the temple front out to the wings. And all of this makes direct visual contact with a podium that gives the building the sturdy ground-line it needs to appear decisive.

Here is the other face of American Neoclassicism—big and firm and conscious of the primary forms of Greece and Rome. Latrobe was the consummate professional. Before coming to America he had substan-

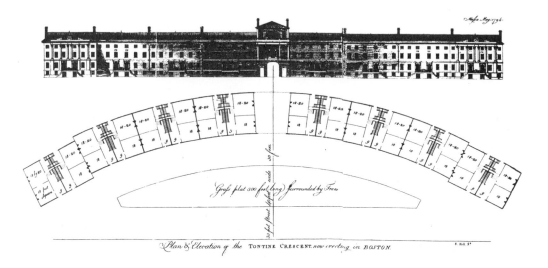

Fig. 24.16 Boston, Tontine Crescent, 1793–95, Charles Bulfinch; a drawing by the architect. An arched passage broke through the center and established communication with the Summer Street neighborhood at the back. A theater, Boston's first, was part of the general scheme.

Fig. 24.17 Boston, the Massachusetts State House, 1795–97, Charles Bulfinch.

Fig. 24.18 Washington D.C., the U.S. Capitol, 1792–1830, William Thornton, Benjamin Henry Latrobe, and Charles Bulfinch; design by Latrobe. (See also Figs. 24.1, 25.13, and 26.6a.)

Fig. 24.19 Philadelphia (Pennsylvania), the pump house for the Philadelphia waterworks, 1799, Benjamin Henry Latrobe; a detail from John Lewis Krimmel's *Fourth of July in Centre Square*, ca. 1810–12. (Pennsylvania Academy of Fine Arts, Philadelphia) The pump house is reminiscent of works by Soane and Ledoux (see Fig. 22.25a). Its site corresponds to the present site of the Philadelphia City Hall.

tial experience as an engineer. He knew the progressive work being done in France, England, and Germany where he had spent much of his youth, and he sympathized with the radical line that was carried down from Laugier to Soane. For this country, this kind of fully qualified designer, familiar with the building of canals and the statics of masonry vaults, fluent in both the classical idiom and the Gothic, was a novelty.

And he arrived at the right time. A country where public architecture had scarcely outstripped domestic scale, where masonry vaulting had never been attempted, now coveted ambitious monuments of European grandeur and needed utilitarian works that presumed mastery of advanced technology. Within months of setting foot in Norfolk, Virginia, in March 1795, Latrobe was being consulted in the construction of the Dismal Swamp Canal, surveying the Appomattox River, and designing the new State Penitentiary in Richmond. He soon moved on to Philadelphia and Baltimore, and through his mentor Jefferson had ended up in Washington in 1803 as Surveyor of the Public Buildings, a post he held until his death in 1820.

Latrobe's presence did much to establish a monumental public architecture of high quality for the young nation. His early projects, like the Philadelphia waterworks with the Ledoux-like pump house, married competent social and mechanical planning with the rationalist doctrine of Neoclassicism. (Figs. 24.19, 22.25) The Ionic temple front and stark cubic stone mass of the Bank of Pennsylvania (1798–1801) gave America its first taste of Grecian design. The type recurs in the Baltimore Cathedral (1804–18), a monument to the rise of Catholicism in the United States. It is a superb masonry building that fronts the street with a proper Greek porch, while behind, a series of interlocked volumes recalls the spatial grandeur of the Roman vaulted style. (Figs. 24.20, 11.10) Incidentally, an alternative design Latrobe presented to his client, the first American bishop, John Carroll, is an early document of the arrival of the Gothic revival on this side of the Atlantic. But perhaps Latrobe's greatest merit was his on-the-job training of native professional architects like Robert Mills (1781–1855) and William Strickland (1788–1854), who were

Fig. 24.20 Baltimore (Maryland), Baltimore Cathedral, 1804–18, Benjamin Henry Latrobe; view into central rotunda.

Fig. 24.21 Charlottesville (Virginia), the University of Virginia, 1817–26, Thomas Jefferson; general view looking east in a lithograph of 1856. The open south end of the mall was filled in with a building by the firm of McKim, Mead & White in 1896–98.

able to give the federal government an architectural image of dignity and poise, on a par with the best of Europe.

Jefferson and an Aspiring Frenchman
No one cared more about a national architecture than Thomas Jefferson; no one did more to direct and promote it. As governor of Virginia, Secretary of State under Washington, and finally as third President of the United States, he had unique opportunities for patronage and made the best of them. He supported the new breed of professional architect, as exampled by Latrobe and his disciples. He tried to influence the course of the new national capital through persuasion, but also direct intervention when it seemed appropriate. But design was something Jefferson could do, as well as talk about. As a young man, he had pored over architectural books and looked critically at the buildings of his native Virginia. His five-year term as minister to the court of France introduced him to the remains of ancient Rome, and the revolutionary work of Neoclassicists like Ledoux that fed on and radicalized its shapes. Jefferson subscribed to the passionate belief current among these men that architecture signified, that it was an expressive language fit for lofty sentiment. The built domain could affect social behavior, could carry a sense of ourselves, what we aspired to be, and should therefore be able to uplift our spirits. Georgian architecture did not measure up to the aspirations of the young republic. It was, for one thing, too prosaic, too naive. The Williamsburg buildings were "rude misshapen piles which, but they have roofs, would be taken for brick kilns." And

Fig. 24.22 Charlottesville, the house of Thomas Jefferson called Monticello, 1768–82; remodeled in 1796–1809.

623

for another thing, these buildings were billboards of colonial dependence. For Jefferson, anti-British sentiment went beyond political differences. Unlike the Federalists, he saw cultural freedom as a crucial aspect of the struggle against the mother country.

So he turned to the only appropriate teacher, Classical antiquity. This of course was the acceptable discourse of his progressive contempories, the only burning issue being the relative superiority of Greece or Rome. Latrobe spoke in favor of the first. The symbolism seemed right on the mark. In 1811 he was telling the Society of Artists in Philadelphia that a new Greece was growing "in the woods of America. . . . Greece was free; in Greece every citizen felt himself an important . . . part of his republic." Jefferson had republican Rome on his mind—that solid *virtus* that excelled in the art of government. It was a common sympathy among his circle, as it had been in the first phase of the French Revolution. The leaders of the War of Independence drew their code of values from the Horatii and Gracchi, from Cato and Cincinnatus, the self-denying Roman heroes of those simple moral days, who put love of country above all else and valued liberty more than their lives. The Senate on the Potomac was the auspicious reincarnation of the Roman senate. Goose Creek there was renamed "Tiber."

In Jefferson's view of things, the first order of business in creating a national taste that would carry the message of this historical destiny was to produce paradigms of Roman architecture in America. The designs he sent from France for the new state capital of Virginia reproduced a Roman temple, the so-called Maison Carrée at Nîmes in southern France, which he had gazed on for whole hours, by his own admission, "like a lover at his mistress." (Fig. 9.18) Legislative, judicial, and executive functions were all fitted inside this Classi-

Fig. 24.23 "The Seven Ranges of Townships," 1796; a plan of the first townships surveyed according to the land ordinance of 1785, in what was then the Ohio Territory.

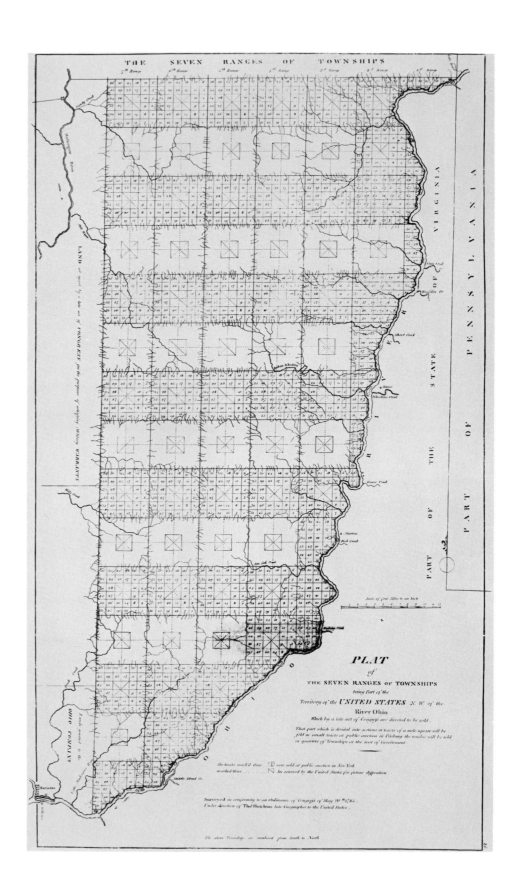

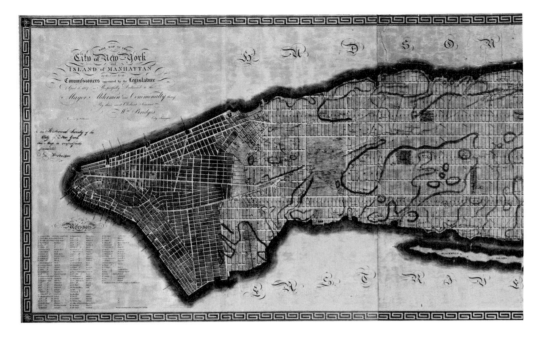

Fig. 24.24 New York, the Commissioners' Plan, 1811; detail.

cal envelope, and the purity of the temple form was preserved on the outside.

In the project for the University of Virginia, the first state university in the country, Jefferson built the Pantheon, at two-thirds of the scale, at the head of a rising mall flanked by interlinked columnar pavilions. (Fig. 24.21) This Rotunda housed the library, while in the pavilions, representing individual disciplines, professors lived and held their classes. Each pavilion demonstrated the correct use of a different Roman order or some variant of it, the campus thus keeping before the students' eyes the full spectrum of Classical design. One pavilion was patterned after Ledoux. There was also in this concept of independent pavilions, formally arrayed in a Neoclassical composition, perhaps something of an analogue for the federal union as Jefferson saw it—self-governing states working together for the common national good.

In Monticello, his house outside Charlottesville, the Pantheon was domesticized in the great tradition of residential Pantheons, which included Chiswick and Palladio's Villa Rotonda. (Figs. 24.22, 22.9, 19.33) Sitting on a hillcrest small enough to be echoed in the swell of its central dome, Monticello had a cross-axial plan like its predecessors, but unlike them stretched itself horizontally, reaching out toward the sweep of its site, while service units were buried underground. So, fixed to the land with its domed core but acknowledging with its out-stretched wings the open-ended expanse, and filled with gadgets of all kinds, Monticello was like the primordial American home—seeking stability but also freedom, respectful of European tradition but insistent on comfort and effort-saving devices, both conventional and one of a kind.

Here Jefferson lived the life of a country squire, the sort of independent farmer he

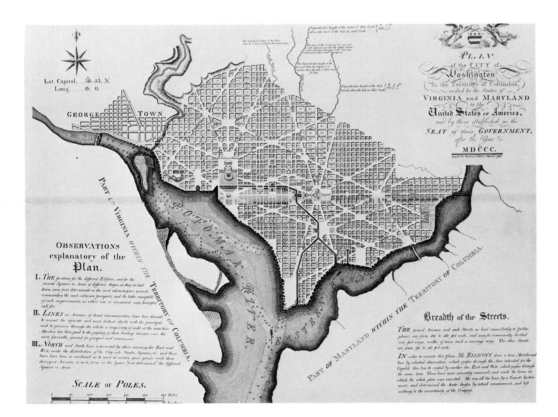

Fig. 24.25 Washington, D.C., plan, 1792, Pierre Charles L'Enfant, as drawn by Andrew Ellicott.

Fig. 24.26 Philadelphia, Girard College for Orphans, 1833–47, Thomas Ustick Walter; engraving by A. W. Graham. The main building, Founder's Hall, is a Corinthian temple externally; it is flanked by four dormitory buildings that are pedimented, but are without columns or pilasters.

was anxious to install as the kingpin of a rural society. He resented centralized urban control and dreamed of an agrarian America of small towns and farms where every white man was his own master and the prodigious land belonged to all the people equally. In 1785, largely through his prodding, the Congress enacted a national land ordinance. The federal government had gained title to western lands all the way to the Mississippi. This new territory was now surveyed uniformly and divided, using geometrically determined parallels and meridians, into square townships measuring 6 by 6 miles. (Fig. 24.23) The townships were subdivided into plots of 1 square mile each, called sections, which in turn were broken up into equal lots. Four sections were reserved for future disposal, one for public schools, and one "for the support of religion." The rest was put up for sale.

The giant regional grid ignored the natural topography. Unlike the example of the thirteen original states (and most of the earth's older settled regions), it subjected four-fifths of the United States to a regular system of land survey that answered the needs of an agricultural economy and could speedily be occupied in a democratic fashion. It was the most extensive region in the world to be taken possession of systematically. The great precedent was Roman centuriation, and its most recent adaptation in the designs of Dutch engineers for reclaimed land. The orthogonal lines of this American network automatically determined the main axes of any new town, and the grid scheme of town-planning became ubiquitous. Other early American models—the nucleated, topography-conscious New

Fig. 24.27 Vacherie (St. James's Parish, Louisiana), the house of the planter Alexander Roman called Beau Sejour, now Oak Alley, 1836, George Swainey, architect.

Fig. 24.28 Boston, Faneuil Hall Market, 1825–26, Alexander Parris. It is better known as Quincy Market because it was built of granite from Quincy, Massachusetts, quarried in bulk about that time. Behind it, in this nineteenth-century view, we can see the towered Faneuil Hall, a civic market hall built in 1740–42 on the designs of the painter John Smibert, and enlarged by Charles Bulfinch in 1805–6.

England towns, the linear German villages in eastern Pennsylvania, the Baroque plans of Williamsburg or Annapolis, the gracious checkerboard of Savannah or Philadelphia, where every few blocks of built-up rectangles were aired with planted squares of open space—these were forgotten.

The dense speculative grid even took over in the old Eastern cities as they outgrew their initial boundaries. Baltimore, Richmond, and Boston embraced rectilinearity, but none more fanatically than New York where a three-member commission of the state legislature covered the whole of Manhattan with identical blocks unrelieved by open public spaces. (Fig. 24.24) The commission's report dismisses "those supposed improvements . . . circles, ovals and stars," and states flatly "that a city is to be composed of the habitations of men, and that strait sided and right angled houses are

the most cheap to build, and the most convenient to live in."

But there was one stunning exception to the rule—Washington. When the heated debate over which city would have the honor of serving as the nation's capital was resolved with the decision to build a new one, Jefferson sketched it as a small grid. The site settled on was a triangle on the Potomac River, at its juncture with the Anacostia. But George Washington, whose Mount Vernon estate was only a few miles away, set his aim higher than the modest proposal of Jefferson. The new capital would be the pivot between the Eastern seaboard and the developing West, cut off from each other by the Allegheny and Appalachian ranges. Washington's hope was to drive a canal across this chain, from the Potomac to the Ohio, diverting inland trade through the capital to the Atlantic ports. At

the same time, the city would play a role in bringing North and South together, a prospect that hinged on the proposed industrialization of Virginia through exploitation of her coal and iron deposits. One had to think big, then. The object was to create not only a fitting home for the governing institutions of the Union but also a viable, prosperous metropolis like London or Paris.

The President called in Major Pierre Charles L'Enfant (1754–1825), the architect Dickens refers to as "an aspiring Frenchman." A volunteer in the American Revolution, L'Enfant combined in himself the skills of an artist (his father had been a court painter at Versailles) and the experience he had gained by working with the engineering corps during the war. Once on the site, he dismissed Jefferson's plan. He noted, in his strained English, that it would "only do on a level plain and where no surrounding object being interesting becomes indifferent which way the opening of streets may be directed." But the truth is that he was thinking of something much more magnificent. He now proceeded to draw up a grand plan which in its tremendous scale and in the conventions of absolutist planning it implied must have made Jefferson very uneasy. (Fig. 24.25)

The plan combined a fine-meshed grid with great slashing diagonals that ran in all directions, intersecting at public squares of various shapes. These swift avenues were conceived magnanimously: roadways of 24 meters (78 feet) with an additional 9 meters (30 feet) on either side "for a walk under a double row of trees" and another 3-meter (10-foot) strip between the trees and the building lots. The diagonals were there to contrast "with the general regularity" and to unite the principal foci that L'Enfant had identified—foremost among them the Capitol, the President's "palace," the national bank, a grand nondenominational church, and the market and exchange—"giving to them reciprocity of sight." In order to encourage rapid settlement across the board, these public buildings were distributed over the whole area rather than being grouped into a monumental core. Jenkins Hill, the most commanding prominence, was reserved for the Capitol. A cascade of water would issue from the base of this building, tumbling down 12 meters (39 feet) and

Fig. 24.29 Wellfleet (Massachusetts), First Congregational Church, 1850 (spire, 1879).

Fig. 24.30 Skagway (Alaska), Broadway, late 1890s. This frontier mining town is preserved to this day almost untouched. Broadway was paved with gravel and had sidewalks of wood under sheltering galleries. The domed building is the Golden North Hotel of 1898. Recent photo.

flowing ultimately into the Tiber. This creek was to be straightened and made part of a mall that extended from the Capitol to the Potomac. At right angles to the mall ran the axis of the presidential compound, and where the two met an equestrian statue of Washington would be set up.

The plan's shortcomings have been pointed out. The juxtaposition of an orthogonal and a radial system of streets yielded too many awkward scraps of space. The failure to establish a prominent site for the third branch of government, the judiciary, weakened the representative logic of the federal program. But the plan was, for all that, a farsighted, complete blueprint for an imposing capital, equal in measure to the current court cities like St. Petersburg, Berlin, or Karlsruhe. In two dimensions, the layout is patently Baroque. But the spacing of monumental buildings as single responsive masses of independent form is alert to contemporary Neoclassical practice.

There is, however, no doubting the princely connotations of L'Enfant's plan—and its ideological inappropriateness for a pridefully self-advertising democracy. Still, it was approved and set in motion. Soon the temperamental Frenchman ran afoul of bureaucracy and lost the chance to oversee his historic design. The miracle is that it came through, almost intact. For a long while it was getting nowhere. The city failed to realize any industrial or commercial distinction. Not many were anxious to settle on the marshes of the Potomac, along the ghostly superavenues that sailed through the near-empty canvas of this "City of Magnificent Distances." Dickens' remarks fifty years later were not undeserved.

But slowly, very slowly, the imperious geometry was fleshed in. The Capitol and the White House came first; they were burned down by the British in the War of 1812, and then later rebuilt. A Navy Yard materialized on the banks of the Anacostia, complete with drydock facilities, and an arsenal at the confluence of the Anacostia and the Potomac. On the spot where L'Enfant

Fig. 24.31 New York, St. Patrick's Cathedral, 1858–79 (spires 1888), James Renwick and William Bodrigue. St. Patrick's is located on Fifth Avenue between Fiftieth and Fifty-first streets. This view is from Rockefeller Center (Fig. 27.27). The later Villard houses (Fig. 26.1) on Madison Avenue can be seen behind the Cathedral at the top of the photograph.

Fig. 24.32 Ironton (Missouri), St. Paul's Church, 1870.

had put his equestrian statue of Washington, a majestic obelisk was raised in his honor, focusing the still ill-defined expanse of the mall in front of the Capitol. The first Treasury Building was replaced after 1836 with a massive colonnaded block of freestone at the convergence of Pennsylvania and New York avenues, obstructing the reciprocal view between the Capitol and the White House. East of it, an equally impressive Patent Office took up the location assigned by L'Enfant to the national church. And the General Post Office took shape during the same years just south of this, in pure white marble. Washington, the capital of the youngest nation in the West, was on its way.

Greece for All Seasons

This federal landscape, masterminded by Latrobe's successor as Surveyor of the Public Buildings, Robert Mills, is one of monumental simplicity. The plans and elevations would not be out of place on the pages of Durand: the detail is all Greek. By 1820 the Roman manner of Jefferson was receding, tainted as it had become through its association with Napoleon's imperialist regime. The eclectic Neoclassicism of Latrobe was being distilled into a purer Grecian mold. As far as government taste went, the shift was unambiguous. In the 1818 competition for the Second Bank of the United States, the program emphatically called for "a chas[t]e imitation of Grecian architecture in its simplest and least expensive form." Latrobe lost to the young William Strickland, who turned in a temple with the facade of the Parthenon. (Fig. 1.14) This design set the trend for government buildings for the next forty years. Internally, iron-reinforced stone

Fig. 24.34 Manchester (New Hampshire), Amoskeag Manufacturing Company, begun 1837: left, a canal building, ca. 1845 with later additions; right, workers' housing, ca. 1845.

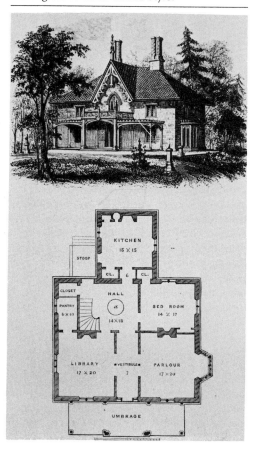

Fig. 24.33 Andrew Jackson Downing, *Cottage Residences*, 1842; page illustrating "A Cottage in the English or Rural Gothic Style."

vaults persisted. The prestige of the Capitol also extended the life of obtrusive domes. But, for the most part, the forms spoke Greek—or were believed to.

And this new taste did not stop at official architecture. The first modern hotels, like the Astor in New York and Tremont House in Boston, donned Greek porticoes, friezes, and windows. Churches exchanged a Gibbsian temple front for a Greek one. Girard College in Philadelphia, built as an unconnected series of temple forms, was only the most conspicuous version of the Hellenized campus, a program where the architectural metaphor was singularly apt since it could reinforce the idealism of a Classical curriculum. (Fig. 24.26) Within the private domain, a "temple" house came into vogue in the North. At its most basic, this was the colonial box painted white, its short

end turned toward the street, and the gable translated into a pediment resting on corner pilasters. But the rich were not beyond insisting on full peristyles or, at the very least, columned facades in a correct order with half-pedimented wings just behind. Southern plantation houses could boast of some of the finest Greek colonnades in America, often without pediments and halved for a second-storey piazza that classicized the French colonial veranda. (Fig. 24.27) A drastic wood vernacular, leaning on builder's guides like those by Asher Benjamin and Minard Lafever, carried the Greek revival to the remote areas of New England and built the gamely opened up West. New towns everywhere called themselves Athens, Sparta, Ithaca, or Troy.

Why was America so taken with Classical Greece? Fashion was part of it of course. An archaeologically aware Greek revival had struck roots in England and Germany even before the Napoleonic Wars; the Treasury Building in Washington is the transatlantic echo of the likes of the British Museum or Schinkel's Altes Museum in Berlin. (Figs. 23.3, 23.21)

Then there was the purity and restraint of Greek architecture, its simple lines and tame decoration, the neat logic of the trabeated structure. "Greek" buildings were easier to build and cost less. Mills was fond of claiming that his buildings "compared with other Public buildings of a like character elsewhere, will show with what *economy* they have been constructed, costing but a *moiety* of other buildings of like dimensions." He also lectured that "we have the same principles and materials to work upon that the ancients had, and we should adapt these materials to the habits and customs of our people as they did theirs."

And, in practice, this is precisely what he and others did. Mills' pioneering essays in fireproof masonry construction, his conception of the auditorium church, the structural module of a groin-vaulted bay used for rows of cellular offices in the Treasury Building—these were solutions spurred by the customs and needs of his country, and not obsessive archaeology. In

Massachusetts, the successful quarrying of Quincy granite gave Alexander Parris (1780–1852) a material that sharply restricted detailing. His Boston buildings make a virtue of this constraint. Quincy Market, built over the filled-in Town Dock and adjacent wharves, is a horizontal two-storey block almost 170 meters long and 15 wide (558 by 49 feet), flanked originally by equally long warehouses. (Fig. 24.28) It has at either end four-columned Doric temple fronts, and in the middle of the long block a saucer dome on a rectangular block; but the envelope is nothing more than a stark trabeated framework of monolithic granite piers and lintels. In wood, Greek forms could be abstracted just as radically. Local carpenters reduced the temple-front church facade into a white diagram; the columns themselves turned into "pilastrades" that only fleetingly suggested Greek antae. (Fig. 24.29) In the Western towns pilastraded porches shaded the boardwalks of the buildings on main street—"the American stoa," Vincent Scully called them. (Fig. 24.30)

But at a deeper level, the Greek revival captured the national ethos of the decades after the second war with Britain, the time of Monroe and Andrew Jackson. The country yearned for a cultured image, something uniquely American, to show itself and

those outside. Colleges were sprouting in the unlikeliest places; small towns supported magazines and debating societies; and there was a general self-consciousness about things aesthetic. Ancient Greece appealed to this adolescent eagerness to appear wordly, independent, and paradigmatic. She was the birthplace of democracy. Her culture, typified liberty, learning, and beauty. This culture, with credentials so unassailable as to be safe, was too universal to be appropriated exclusively by any single party or class. It stood clear of contentious Christianity, a symbolic matter of considerable importance to a nation that professed to be secular, and to its avowedly nonsectarian educational system. For all these reasons, a Grecian architecture seemed the happy vehicle of national expression. A remarkably homogeneous mantle of white spread out from the tip of Maine to the Mississippi Delta and all over the once wild West.

Nothing seriously challenged this arcadian scene up to a decade or so before the Civil War. The Gothic revival, when it made itself felt in the 1840s, could not touch a common cord. It remained alien, exclusive, a bit peculiar. It invaded church architecture, but mostly that of Catholics and Anglicans. In high style, it produced masterpieces like Trinity Church and St. Patrick's Cathedral in New York. (Fig. 24.31) At the folk level, in wood, it sprinkled small towns in New England and the West with churches that used vertical board-and-batten siding and gingerbread tracery that the jigsaw made available. (Fig. 24.32) This carpenter Gothic pushed into residential fashions as well, as part of a picturesque reaction to the Greek towns, led by Alexander Jackson Davis (1803–92) and Andrew Jackson Downing (1815–52). What came of it was a lively tradition of rural residences, and especially two novel types: the villas of the well-to-do and small middle-class cottages. (Fig. 24.33) But perhaps the most lasting impact of Davis and Downing was the introduction of picturesque landscaping as part and parcel of this romantic naturalism.

But the Greek manner would not go away. What belied its idealism and damped its popularity, in the end, was the ease with which it could be made to justify the worst in America along with the best. In the

Fig. 24.35 Mid-nineteenth-century house types; schematic plans: (A) the shot-gun house; (B) the double-pen house, with the chimney at one end (top) and in the middle (bottom); (C) the dog-trot house.

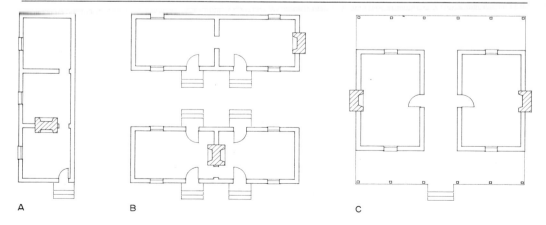

A   B   C

North, in places like Boston, the Greek revival buttressed a humanitarian and intellectual renaissance. It spoke for a society that saw enlightenment in terms of the general welfare of its constituent groups. In the West, Jacksonian democracy embraced the Greek revival to show that rich and poor could share the same vision for a bright future, using it for its burgeoning public school system, its academies, its courthouses and banks, and the false fronts of its often merely basic amenities which coaxed towns out of rough frontier settlements. In the South, that same architectural idiom immortalized a society of masters and slaves.

The South had now recovered from the shock of the War of Independence. Eli Whitney's invention of the mechanical cotton gin in 1794 opened the way to cheap cotton and weaned the economy away from tobacco. The plantation system therefore became firmly entrenched and moved out to new territories in northern Louisiana, Mississippi, Alabama, and western Georgia. The cotton fed the ever-growing textile industry of the North, which in this way tacitly condoned slavery. But the contrast between North and South was sharp enough. Dickens describes Lowell, and there are still several New England mill towns like it to walk about in. (Fig. 24.34) They were well-run, paternalistic communities, thoughtfully planned. They had generous boarding houses for the work force—sturdy farm girls whose decent wages put brothers through Harvard. These rows of boarding houses and the multistoried brick mills, with their characteristic clerestory monitor windows running the length of the raised eaves, were as pure an embodiment of a nation on the move as was Washington, Boston, or the towns of the Ohio River valley.

In the South, there was little of architectural distinction between the elegant Grecian plantation houses and mansions on the one hand, and the slave cabins on the other. The common farmhouse, the so-called double-pen house, was a one-storey, two-room shack with two front doors and a chimney in the center or at one end. (Fig. 24.35) A variant that developed about 1825, the dogtrot house, had two equal units separated by a broad open hall. This rural type that served the poor white or Negro

Fig. 24.36 Portland (Maine), Victoria Mansion, also known as the Morse-Libby House, built as a summer home for Ruggles S. Morse, 1859–63, Henry Austin, architect; exterior view looking north.

farmer, when transferred to the city and stood with its narrow gabled end to the street, became the shot-gun house—one-room wide, with a string of handmade additions tacked onto the rear. Nothing very Greek about any of this. The Greek idiom was not intended to be the common denominator of the society as a whole, but the

preserve of the ruling class. And that class made the idiom its own not because of its power to evoke liberty and democracy, but because it advertised that the institution of slavery no more sullied the cultured Southern aristocrat than it did slave-owning Greeks and Romans.

At mid-century most of the prominent

architects active in the East had eased into a new manner, the Italianate of Nash's invention, that combined classical elements in picturesque compositions. (Fig. 24.36) There was something in it of the Italian Middle Ages (towers for instance) and something of the Renaissance; and indeed the point now was to avoid doctrinaire adherence to individual styles, Greek or Gothic, and so be freed of the loaded symbolism that came with them. The object was to convey a general sense of history, of familiar tradition, without insisting on any specific set of historical associations. The decoration was now lavish, often rather heavy, and the exterior was painted in creamy colors with dark trim. In urban situations, picturesqueness is altogether absent from the facades—in commercial store fronts and offices as well as in residential architecture like the rows of brownstone houses in New York. The facades follow more or less directly the conventions of the Italian Renaissance palace. (Fig. 24.37) Only the South, and government buildings in general, stayed with Greece—the one in defiant glorification of its way of life, the other perhaps through an obstinate faith in a united nation.

And that life, that faith, was to be tried violently when America went to war with itself in 1861.

Fig. 24.37 New York, brownstones at 332–350 West Forty-sixth Street, part of the Astor Estate. The photograph is from 1920; the buildings no longer exist.

Further Reading

L. Craig et al., *The Federal Presence: Architecture, Politics, and Symbols in United States Government Building* (Cambridge, Mass.: MIT Press, 1978).

J. M. Fitch, *American Building: The Historical Forces That Shaped It*, vol. 1, 2nd ed., rev. and enl. (New York: Schocken Books, 1966).

A. Gowans, *Images of American Living: Four Centuries of Architecture and Furniture as Cultural Expression* (New York: Harper & Row, 1976).

J. B. Jackson, *Landscapes*, ed. E. H. Zube (Amherst: University of Massachusetts Press, 1970).

S. Kostof, *America by Design* (New York: Oxford University Press, 1987).

W. Pierson, *American Buildings and Their Architects: The Colonial and Neo-Classical Styles*, vol. I (Garden City, N.Y.: Doubleday, 1970); *Technology and the Picturesque: The Corporate and the Early Gothic Styles*, vol. II (Garden City, N.Y.: Doubleday, 1978).

J. W. Reps, *Town Planning in Frontier America* (Princeton: Princeton University Press, 1969).

V. Scully, Jr., *American Architecture and Urbanism* (New York: Praeger, 1969), 1988.

D. Upton, *Holy Things and Profane: Anglican Parish Churches in Colonial Virginia* (Cambridge, Mass.: MIT Press, 1986).

W. M. Whitehill, *Boston, A Topographical History*, 2nd. ed., enl. (Cambridge, Mass.: Harvard University Press, 1968).

Coupe sur le
Trumeau

Coupe sur les
Baies

ACADÉMIE · NATIO

Paris (France), the Opéra, 1862–75, Charles Garnier;
detail of the main facade, 1880.

25

VICTORIAN ENVIRONMENTS

The Gilded Age

An American of means visiting England after the Civil War would have had his choice of excellent new luxury hotels to stay in. The largest in London would have been the just completed Midland Grand at St. Pancras Station, the main northern entrance into the city. (Fig. 25.1) Of the crop that served the immensely fashionable seaside resorts, perhaps the best known was the Grand in Scarborough, Yorkshire, perched prominently on a wedge-shaped cliffside lot above the North Sea. (Fig. 25.2) Both of these lavish, costly buildings represented the hotel, only recently differentiated as a type distinct from the traditional inn, at its most imposing. Their size and planning reflected the revolution in travel that had started in the eighteenth century with the stagecoach system on the country's turnpike roads and that had heightened dramatically with the coming of the railways. The new hotels had hundreds of rooms, suites with bathrooms, "American bars," "imperial" staircases, and ornate public spaces. Conveniences echoed the latest developments in the United States, the acknowledged leader in hotel design. These included hot and cold running water, private water-closets, and the hydraulic passenger elevator first used by Elisha Graves Otis in New York in 1857.

The organization of the two hotels we mentioned is similar: rows of rooms strung along for many bays and layered in storeys, with no fewer than thirteen on the seaward side of the Scarborough Grand. The resulting visual monotony of the facades is bro-

ken up by slight projections, and there is a busy roofline with dormered attic storeys and towers or towerlike features. But the make of the skin, the style, is very different indeed in the two cases.

This points out one of the peculiarities of the architectural scene in the second half of the nineteenth century. The functional aspects of most building types were worked out rationally, and with the collaboration of a growing number of specialists in heating, ventilation, acoustics, structural engineering, and the like. Architects conceived of their unique task to be the embellishment of the frame that housed the functions of a building, and made use of suitable systems of visual effects. As the architect of the Midland Grand, George Gilbert Scott (1811–78) saw it his job and that of his peers to "decorate construction." And John Ruskin (1819–1900), perhaps the most influential critic of the century in the English-speaking world, proclaimed that "Ornamentation is the principal part of architecture."

On the face of it, there was nothing very new in all this. The stress on ornament as the architect's special province went back to Charles Perrault (see Chapter 22, page 559), and the idea of the architect as style expert able to dress buildings appropriately in a variety of historical costumes had made the rounds for several decades when Ruskin published his *Seven Lamps of Architecture* in 1849. But "ornament" and "style" had been catchwords for dogma in the early phase of modern architecture. Both Neoclassicists and Neo-Gothicists

maintained, a bit disingenuously, that ornament grows in a natural way out of structure. And both defended their particular brand of design in doctrinaire terms, claiming for it rationalist or ethical fitness. For Durand and Grecians like Robert Mills, architectural beauty resided in the logical and economical handling of the building program as expressed through the immutable principles of classicism. For Pugin and the Ecclesiologists, form was a contract of belief, and the correct formal vehicle for a Christian way of life could be no other than the correct restatement of English Gothic. Ruskin shared in these assertive justifications of architectural practice. A confirmed medievalist, he preached against structural deceit and dishonestly obtained effects. And beauty he thought inseparable from virtue: it is only good, virtuous persons who can build beautifully.

But the maturing attitude of the Victorian age, so-called after the great queen who was on the British throne for sixty-three years, tended more and more to shy away from dogma and moral judgment. The habit of the first half of the century of trying to install this or that style of the past out of some purist drive now eased into a more inventive, impure experimentation. Archaeology was pushed aside by a vigorous fancy; dogma, by what mid-Victorians liked to call "sensibility." Most practitioners and theorists agreed that the age must have its own architecture. But modern idiom must be based on what had gone before. You could not gauge progress except on a familiar scale. There was no question of simply inventing something without precedent. The Crystal Palace was a freak, a marvelous creation for a very special moment. It could never be the starting point of a new architecture because it had no ties to the past; it was therefore uncommunicative on a general plane. Its designer, Sir Joseph Paxton (1803–65), went on to build historicist chateaux for the Rothschilds.

But progress also meant improvement, and the way to improve on historical styles was not to resurrect them individually, at some ideal point of their existence or through some respectful distillation of their experience, but to concoct creative assemblages, mixed virtuoso designs. The connoisseur would still detect the sources of the assembled motifs, but the totality would be original and the test of talent would have aesthetic, not rationalist or ethical, criteria.

For us today all this is not without relevance. If we look at mid-Victorian architecture in the abstract, outside of its historical discourse, much of it might strike us as cluttered, overbearing, at times almost perversely ugly. But if we keep in mind the premise under which most practitioners worked, that tremendous outpouring of large public buildings and middle-class housing from the Fifties to the Eighties must be greeted as one of the most exuberant, fertile periods of Western architecture.

Fig. 25.1 London (England), the Midland Grand Hotel at St. Pancras Station (left, in the distance), begun 1861, Sir George Gilbert Scott. King's Cross Station (Fig. 23.34) is partly visible at the extreme right.

The View from London

The exteriors of the two Grands characterize the two major high styles of the mid-Victorian decades. These styles are in a sense the continuation of the classical and Gothic schools of the earlier nineteenth century, but as they have been transformed by that permissive eclecticism we have been speaking of. Cuthbert Brodrick's masterpiece in Scarborough (1863–67), the very image of mid-Victorian substance and assertion, is the tradition of a Renaissance palace—French rather than Italian. It reminds us of sixteenth-century royal chateaux on the Loire and around Paris, but with some exaggerated features. Most notable are the pointed domes that crown the corner pavilions, the staggered dormers on the slanting roof that runs between them, and details like caryatids and the swagged

brackets of the main cornice. These have a more current inspiration; they are French still, but indebted to the New Louvre which Napoleon III, who proclaimed himself emperor in 1852, had built as a showpiece of his regime. (Fig. 25.7) The manner is called "Second Empire" because of this association, the first empire being of course that of Napoleon Bonaparte. It spread abroad and dressed public buildings of all kinds where a certain cosmopolitan sophistication was sought.

Scott's Midland Grand (begun in 1861) is designed in a dazzlingly clever blend of Gothic idioms. There are French details, Dutch or Flemish touches here and there, obvious borrowings from buildings like the Cloth Hall at Ypres (for the tower over the station entrance), and a northern Italian

surface which allows for the even disposition of the windows in an unbuttressed wall. Scott wrote of this style that he had "almost originated" it, and to the extent that the recipe had a strong individuality this is true. But Scott's building actually is in line with the general direction in which the Gothic revival of Pugin was headed after mid-century.

Programmatically, the St. Pancras Hotel exemplifies the determined push of the Gothicists to make their style all pervasive. This meant its secularization of course. Diehard Ecclesiologists drew the line at commercial structures, office buildings, and luxury hotels like the Midland Grand, while they could with clearer conscience condone the use of Gothic in hospitals and schools because of the religious outlook of

Fig. 25.2 Scarborough (England), Grand Hotel, 1862–67, Cuthbert Brodrick. The hotel is built of warm red brick, with rich decorative terra-cotta.

their activities. Governmental agencies were leery of the style, on the other hand, precisely because of its sectarian afflatus. The Houses of Parliament, in the period just before the High Church appropriation of the Gothic, had struck a nationalist chord. The Ecclesiological movement changed all that. In the 1860s the Liberal Prime Minister Lord Palmerston blocked Scott's Gothic design for the Foreign Office and War Office buildings at Whitehall, despite pressure from the Tory party, forcing Scott to produce a new set of designs of Italian Renaissance inspiration. With a few important exceptions, the Law Courts in London (1870–82) by G. E. Street and the Manchester Town Hall (1868–77) by Alfred Waterhouse chief among them, civic and government buildings stayed beyond the reach

of Gothicists. So by and large did terrace housing and the architecture of industry and commerce. But they made up for it elsewhere, most emphatically in churches, schools, and detached houses.

Visually, too, Scott's work falls under the rubric of High Victorian Gothic, which is the art-historical term for those medieval formulas that succeeded the purist dogma of Pugin and the Ecclesiologists. Personal signatures are legion, but the overall trend was to retreat from homegrown versions of Gothic in favor of two foreign traditions. One was the early period of French Gothic, which was preferred for its "muscularity." The other was the medieval architecture of Venice and Tuscany, with its arresting polychromy. The main propagandist for rich Venetian surfaces was Ruskin. With him also

begins the defense of "constructional" or "permanent" polychromy, that is, the creation of colorful planes through the use of bricks and stones of different shades, as opposed to incrustation which conceals the true fabric of the wall.

High Victorian Gothic was an English phenomenon. As an export item it found considerable favor in remote provinces of the British Empire, Canada and India for example, and there is a bit of it to be seen still in the United States. But it never caught on outside the English-speaking world. The style, it is generally agreed, starts with a London church by an architect named William Butterfield (1814–1900), All Saints, Margaret Street, which was being built from 1850 to 1859 on a crowded mid-block site in the thick of a bohemian slum off Regent Street. (Fig. 25.3) It was to be the model church of the Ecclesiologists, and yet it departed radically from their cherished architectural doctrine. The walls externally are both massive and flat. We see a harsh, prismatic assembly of gabled units at the front representing the school and vicarage, and through the narrow yard between them we enter the church on the long side. Just above the entrance porch looms a gaunt tower that at its time was the most conspicuous landmark in central London.

But it was its strident color scheme that really set All Saints apart. On the outside, the red brick planes were diapered and banded with black bricks, and in the church the interior constructional polychromy ran riotous with Aberdeen granite columns carrying capitals of veined alabaster which stood on a floor of patterned tile; the walls were curtains of geometric pattern in several colors and techniques. Contemporary critics, shocked by its garish looks, tried to explain the church as a composite of the medieval architecture of northern Europe and that of the South. (Remember the striped interior of the Cathedral at Pisa; see Fig. 13.25.) They saw in it "a dread of beauty, . . . [a] deliberate preference of ugliness."

While it is easy to make too much of this shrill individualism, Butterfield is prophetic of mid-Victorian culture. His generation has been described as "torn between unprecedented optimism and disorientated despair." It was the best of times, it was the worst of times. England was the strongest and richest nation in the world, full of confidence and aggressive, competitive drive. But it was also riddled with doubt. The industrial age, now a reality, accounted for the country's greatness, but it brought with it a feeling of unease, the feeling that traditional values had slipped irreparably. The landed gentry, the backbone of the social order for centuries, were being pushed against the wall by an ambitious middle class whose wealth came from towns. This class hardly suffered from the near collapse of agriculture in the 1870s under the impact of cheap American corn, a crisis that bled aristocratic wealth. The towns in the meanwhile continued to grow turbulently. The new prosperity was mounted on a rotten armature of human misery. The fear of social upheavals increased when the working class won the vote in 1867. Scientific and biblical scholarship threatened traditional Protestant beliefs, and everybody, rich and poor, looked for a haven in family life and the home.

Something of all this had to come through in mid-Victorian architecture. We should not wonder perhaps that it would show both a blustering confidence, in its massiveness and size, and also confusion in its aesthetic aims. Theoretical strictures seemed incongruous in a laissez-faire world. The association of particular styles with particular building types was losing ground. The purity of stuccoed surfaces or monochrome stone was overwhelmed by the desire for variegated masses and rich, ornate textures through which one sought to resist and counterveil the drab polluting force of industry. Architects overstated the colorful appearance of their projected buildings in large watercolor drawings and presentation models. Noisy, intrigue-filled competitions were held for the major jobs and everyone entered the fray. The big architectural firm employing scores of draftsmen came into its own. "Plan factories" they were called. Scott ran one of them, and it was said that he was sometimes uncertain which buildings then under construction his firm was responsible for.

Industry had drastically affected traditional building methods. Prefabrication turned buildings into shippable commodities. Steam-powered cranes at the quarry and steam-powered saws at the mason's yard were still things of the future, but al-

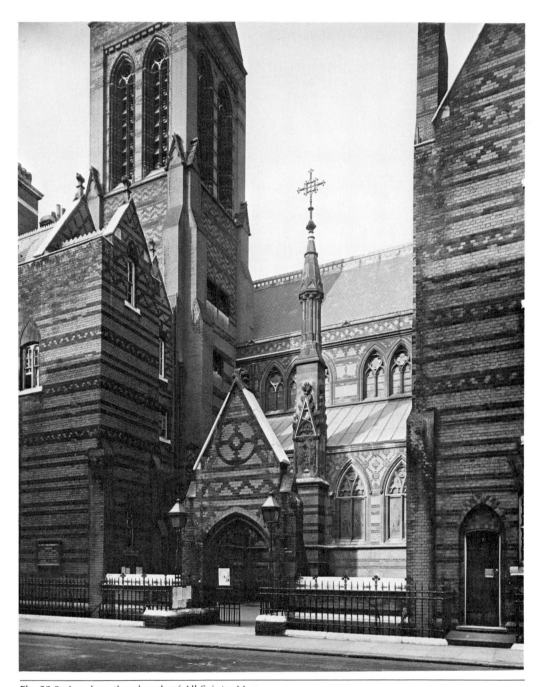

Fig. 25.3a London, the church of All Saints, Margaret Street, 1850–59, William Butterfield; exterior view from the street.

ready machines of all kinds were speeding production and invading the jealously guarded domains of the building trades. The machines also made possible the cheap imitation of those ornaments that once had

indicated status. Serious architects sometimes looked for ways to come to terms with these increasingly sharp lineaments of the new industrial order. Butterfield, for example, was willing to admit exposed cast-

Fig. 25.3b London, the church of All Saints, Margaret Street; interior from the east.

Movement. Art to Morris was "the way in which man expresses joy in his work." And machine manufacture, by taking that joy away, killed art. The firm he started in 1861 was dedicated to the revival of handicraft and to the proposition that good design should affect everything around us. Architecture could not be seen as applied ornament, pure and simple, prescribed by a small band of experts. "Architecture embraces the consideration of the whole external surroundings of the life of man . . . 'tis we ourselves, each one of us, who must keep watch and ward over the fairness of the earth, and each with his own soul and hand do his share therein." The firm hand-produced everything—from carpets and furniture to wallpaper and stained glass.

But Morris was caught in an unresolvable dilemma. The care and cost of craftsmanship worked against his egalitarian, socialist view of life. Only those well off could afford the firm's products. And there really was no way to roll back the Industrial Revolution, to return as he advocated to a world without railways and crowded cities, a world where wind and water were the sole sources of power, where the state was no longer the great controlling force and the craft guild, or cooperative, determined the social organization.

To a younger generation of architects and designers, Ruskin's and Morris's passion for the creative spirit had great appeal, but not their moral thunderings, medieval warp, or socialism. They were willing to live with the machine provided it could be mastered and used as a tool at the behest of the artist. By the 1870s the client middle class had also mellowed. It became fashionable to appear less driven, less righteous. "Sweetness and light" was the key phrase, and it meant the pure enjoyment of beauty and broad enlightenment. Art need have no weightier purpose than to bring pleasure; intellectual curiosity need not be fettered to Christian ethics. Pleasing architectural effects abounded everywhere, in and out of the Middle Ages, in the timeless structures of the countryside, in the West and the Far East. They had only to be combined tastefully. To capture that preindustrial simplicity that Pugin and Ruskin and Morris so fiercely extolled, there was no reason to go back to the time of Edward, or out on the lagoons of Venice, or to seek some inno-

iron girders into the rarified fabric of his church. But for the most part, his generation and Ruskin's recoiled from machine-made ornament and went to battle to keep the crafts, and the spiritual values that were thought to be attached to their handiwork, alive. The role of architecture as social

communication had to be preserved at all costs. Mass production and the inevitable depreciation of quality that came with it were the enemy.

William Morris (1834–96), more so than Ruskin whose disciple he was, spearheaded what we call the Arts and Crafts

cent, utopian "Nowhere." One could travel, sketchbook in hand, on the backroads and town alleys of England and discover both something enduringly English and effortlessly familiar. Out of these sentiments sprang the styles called "Old English" and "Queen Anne." They were the invention of an intimate group of architects, William Eden Nesfield (1835–88) and Richard Norman Shaw (1831–1912) foremost among them, and these styles now became the favored expression of an enlightened middle-class clientele.

Old English leaned on the farmhouse vernacular of the countryside. Queen Anne looked more to low-style Wren and Georgian, but it was not at all a revival in the strict sense. (Fig. 25.4) Georgian details, like white sash windows, figured in houses that were clearly of a Gothic character, with things like prominent roofs, tall chimney stacks, and bay or oriel windows. Tile-hanging, weatherboarding, and half-timbering came back. There was even a touch of Japan, sunflower disks for example, inspired by the Japanese presence at the International Exhibition of 1862. The point was to strive for an artistic confection of such mixed heredity that it would amount, as one practitioner put it, to "an absence of style." The more quaint and old-fashioned it all looked, the better.

So to the disgust of older Gothicists, Nesfield and Shaw assembled in their houses curly Flemish gables and ribbed chimney stacks, plaster coves, wooden cupolas, external shutters and fan lights, wrought-iron railings, and lots of ornamental pargeting. The variety was seemingly inexhaustible, and the style soon went public. The School Board of London, empowered by the Education Act of 1870, applied it to a whole flock of new schools, and Shaw produced at least one masterpiece of commercial architecture, the New Zealand Chambers in Leadenhall Street, London, now gone. (Fig. 25.5) The facade was divided into three gabled bays by emphatic brick piers, and each bay was filled with an ornate oriel that featured small panes framed by thick white sash bars. The off-center door scorned the convention of classical symmetry, and indeed in every other respect the design disclaimed the standard stone-faced palace type for office buildings and warehouses.

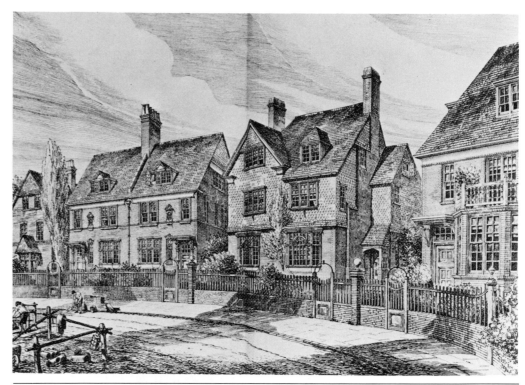

Fig. 25.4 London, Bedford Park; designs for houses by Richard Norman Shaw, published in the *Building News* of 21 December 1877. The suburb of Bedford Park, begun in 1875, is considered to be the first "garden city."

Fig. 25.5 London, New Zealand Chambers on Leadenhall Street, 1871–73, Richard Norman Shaw; drawing by the architect. The building was built as the headquarters of the Shaw Savill shipping line which provided regular service to and from New Zealand. It was destroyed during World War II.

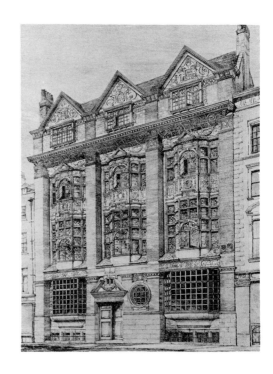

The View from Paris

In France in these same decades, architectural production and the debate that surrounded it were impelled by two forces that had no English counterpart. First, there was the long institutionalized code of architectural behavior. The Academy, and its agency the École des Beaux-Arts, controlled both the education of architects and public patronage. Second, there was Baron Haussmann (1809–91), all-powerful Prefect of the Seine under Napoleon III, and the massive rebuilding of Paris he supervised. This was

Fig. 25.6 Paris (France), the Bibliothèque Ste.-Geneviève, 1838–50, Henri Labrouste. For a view of the reading room, see Fig. 23.29a.

the first total conceptualization of the modern city, and it heralded a technocratically minded, comprehensive approach to town-planning that would bear fruit in Vienna and Brussels, in Mexico City, Melbourne, and Pretoria.

In the opening years of the Second Empire, the École des Beaux-Arts was at the center of a raging controversy. On one side was a band of reformists headed by Viollet-le-Duc who upheld the principles of structural rationalism. Their adversary was the firmly entrenched mainline ranks whose taste was at once academic and romantic. But it would be too simple to think of this as the old nineteenth-century stand-off between Gothic-lovers and classicists. For one thing, Viollet-le-Duc's postulation of Gothic had nothing to do with symbolism or the Christian ethic. He read the style as an utterly rational order in which aesthetic form and structural function were one and the same thing, and he considered it the appropriate field of experimentation in creating a modern architecture. In this he can be said to continue the line of rationalist thought that started with Laugier and the Grecians.

The establishment Viollet-le-Duc challenged, on the other hand, had by now abandoned the hallowed beliefs of classicism—that is, the full adherence to Greco-Roman forms and their Renaissance/Baroque variations, and the reliance on the orders for constructional integrity as well as for the basis of decoration. "Classical" now connoted a general excellence and enduringness, irrespective of style. As Julien Guadet (1834–1908), the chief theorist of the École, was to formulate it later on:

Everything that deserves to become classical is classical, without limits in time, space or school

Fig. 25.7 Paris, the Louvre, the new block added in 1852–57, Ludovico Tullio Joachim Visconti, redesigned and completed by Hector M. Lefuel. The block connected the existing palace with the palace of the Tuileries (cf. Fig. 21.26).

. . . everything which has remained victorious in the struggle of the arts, everything that continues to arouse universal admiration.

This meant Hagia Sophia and Chartres along with the Akropolis and the Pantheon. And by elevating eclecticism as the new liberal doctrine, academic instruction recognized the divorce between form and function. Architecture was no longer the art of constructing decoration, as it were, in the old classical sense, but the art of decorating construction. Here the French academicians sounded like the mid-Victorians in England. Where the two countries differed was in the overwhelming dependence of Beaux-Arts design on classical, Byzantine, and Romanesque rather than Gothic forms and, more critically, in the strict discipline of composition, which still demanded axiality and the balanced distribution of quadrate and circular volumes.

The new liberalism had as a corollary the architect's responsibility to his own imagination, rather than to immutable classical ideals or some truth beyond individuality. Here, too, the French outlook paralleled, indeed anticipated, that shift in Victorian England away from moralism and toward creative improvisation. But again this freedom did not mean quite the same thing on the two sides of the Channel. The spirited collocation of forms indulged in by Queen Anne architects was guided by a simple, unmindful joy. It was art for art's sake, animated by a preference for the quaint, the familiar, the nostalgic. The personalized syncretism of French architects was thought to be inditing an expressive language appropriate to the program, which the public could read. They fused together formal motifs to clothe structure with a rich, signifying mantle of decoration.

The disparity between structure and its ornament, between the real and the fictive, might be said to begin with Labrouste, the first French architect to admit iron frankly into a high-style public monument. His library of Ste.-Geneviève we admire today for the metallic elegance of its reading room; I spoke of it in that context in Chapter 23 (Fig. 23.29a) But far from being a manifesto of structural rationalism, Labrouste's design sought to give literary expression to the building program, a library of the industrial age. (Fig. 25.6) The

Fig. 25.8 Paris, the Opéra, 1862–75, Charles Garnier; the Grand Staircase in an engraving of 1880.

Fig. 25.9 Paris, the "Grand Egout"; an underground sewer line of the mid-nineteenth century, shown in an engraving of 1863.

exposed metal armature, the historicist masonry shell, and the inscriptions were coordinated with this in mind. The intention here is quite at variance with those later projects of Viollet-le-Duc in which metal and masonry are brought together in experimental forms, inspired by the alleged structural logic of Gothic, to propose a rational modern idiom devoid of literary signification.

The regime of Napoleon III and Empress Eugénie had ushered in a new period of opulent grandeur that did its best to forget the realities of industrial society, or rather to keep them separate from the public, ritual life of the country. It is to these aims that both formal instruction at the École and the professional output of its top graduates were directed. And the two Parisian monuments that best reflect the cultural complexion of the age, apart from the magnificent paper architecture of the Rome Prize projects where the grand beauty of Beaux-Arts composition and rendering shines through, are the new Louvre and Charles Garnier's Opéra (1862–75).

The first of these was actually the culmination of long-standing plans to join the Louvre, now principally the home of the national art gallery, with the Tuileries where French rulers usually resided since the Revolution. What concerns us here is the style of the additions. (Fig. 25.7) It recalls of course the architecture of the old Louvre (Fig. 21.22), and since that was by no means unified, having been concocted by a succession of architects as we have seen, the contribution of Napoleon III could be eclectic without qualms.

But complementary to this license to amalgamate artfully, the common urge of the second half of the nineteenth century, the new Louvre exhibits a sculptural braggadocio beyond anything in its past. The effect has been called "neo-Baroque," and indeed it has that plasticity and agitated wall mass we associate with the seventeenth century. But what the new style does is to overstate motifs from that period. Notice especially the bombastic elaboration of the dormers and the profligate height of the slanting roofs over the corner pavilions. This type of roof has a slope in two planes, the lower being longer and steeper. It is called a *mansard roof,* after François Mansart, the great-uncle of the Mansart who designed Louis XIV's Versailles. It was never absent from French practice since the early Renaissance; we already encountered it in some of the royal *places* of Paris. But now in this exaggerated version the mansard roof became the rage. It was the one architectural feature more than any other that distinguished Second Empire taste, as external polychromy distinguished High Victorian taste.

The Opéra brings this showy opulence of the age to the masses. This is their palace, the setting where they can have their chance to glitter, and Garnier (1825–98) spares no effort to ensure its success. The architectural program is not so much the presentation of opera, but the ritual of opera attendance: the arrival, the socializing before the show and during intermissions, the ceremonious departure. Magnificent entrances are provided both for those arriving on foot and for the carriage class. They meet at a grand staircase, the most fabulous part of the building. (Fig. 25.8) Here the audience is on display, showing off and watching others. Garnier writes:

No one used to think that apart from the spectacle of the plays enacted the view of broad staircases crowded with people was a spectacle of pomp and elegance too. But today, luxury is spreading, comfort is demanded everywhere, and there are those who love to see the movement of a varied and elegant crowd. . . . The eyes, as well as the mind, bid for satisfaction and pleasure. It all imposes on the architect broad and monumental arrangements with vast and commodious stairways. . . . By arranging fabrics and wall hangings, candelabra, girandoles, and chandeliers, as well as marble and flowers, color everywhere, one makes of this ensemble a brilliant and sumptuous composition.

Garnier had no faith in rationalism, in engineering, in new materials. His only concession to practical matters was itself a fixture of Beaux-Arts training: circulation, and the clear expression of functions through separate volumes. In this the design is superbly fluent. But it is not this that we are conscious of when we attend. It is the decor. And here the imagination was let loose (the purse too we should add) to invent and compose. Garnier wrote: "Regarding decoration as such, and regarding what ordering and style to adopt, there is no guide other than the inspiration and will of the one who is doing the building." So much for the eternal principles of classicism.

A recent writer called the Opéra a "fantasia of the sumptuous." Its richness is unsurpassed, even in the world of the Baroque. Much of the inspiration we can anatomize. Michelangelo and Claude Perrault's east front of the Louvre would be good places for us to start our analysis. But the regrouping of this material by Garnier, the transmogrifications in scale and ornament, push sources into a cumulatively mnemonic role—nothing more. At best we read a series of tableaux in and around the grand staircase. These are essentially static. Fitted inside the skeletal frame of a giant order in the foreground plane is a secondary system, at a deeper plane, of small-scale columns and perforated wall surfaces. But ornament moves in and out of this static construct, bringing to it Baroque movement. There is a profusion of mirrors in which to adjust our finery and admire ourselves. The color is ravishing. Externally, in a more restrained palette, it helps to articulate the facade so that it would register well from various distances. Inside, the darker shades of gold and brown and harsh splashes of scarlet, blue, and malachite green are intended to come alive in the artificial light of an evening performance.

The Opéra was the focal point of one of Baron Haussmann's new avenues. He had himself selected the site, as he had overseen every detail of the campaign to rebuild Paris, from 1853 when he assumed charge to his dismissal in January 1870, just months before the fall of the Second Empire. In that time he set in motion, and almost concluded, the most thoroughgoing

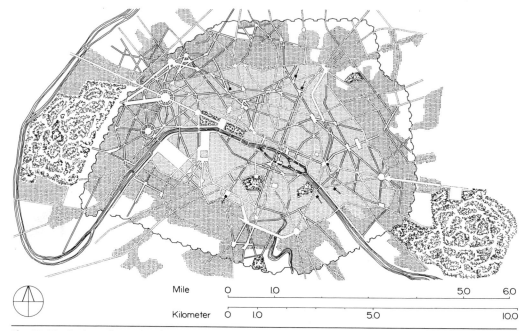

Fig. 25.10a Paris; schematic plan, indicating the interventions of Baron Georges-Eugène Haussmann. New streets are marked by heavy black lines; the cross-hatched areas are new districts; the horizontally shaded areas are the city's two great parks—the Bois de Boulogne in the west and the Bois de Vincennes in the east.

Fig. 25.10b Paris; proposal for the Avenue de l'Opéra, ca. 1850, Baron Haussmann. The bold lines indicate new street boundaries. This new avenue cut through residential holdings expropriated in accordance with the law of 1850. In this plan the Place du Théâtre Français (shown in Fig. 25.11) is at the left; the opera house is just off the plan to the right.

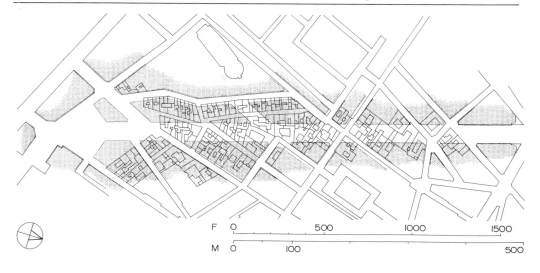

Fig. 25.11 Camille Pissarro, *Place du Théâtre Français, Paris, in the Rain (Avenue de l'Opéra)*, 1898. (The Minneapolis Institute of Arts) Gar-nier's new opera house can be seen in the distance (compare with Fig. 25.10b).

transformation of a European city in history.

The crowded, volatile capital and its mushrooming suburbs had reached a population of close to 2 million. Housing, circulation, water supply, drainage—all of this vital urban structure was critically deficient. Napoleon III's was a bourgeois empire. The real power rested with the newly moneyed upper middle class of merchants, financiers, and manufacturers. Liberal in their business practices but politically right wing, these self-made men demanded law and order, favorable conditions for the conduct of their affairs, nice places to live in, and cultural and recreational centers for their leisure hours. These requirements Haussmann met admirably. He reduced ur-ban unrest by demolishing old popular neighborhoods that were chronic trouble spots. He rationalized and streamlined the street network for rapid communication, weaving into it adequate business facilities like markets, stock exchanges, banks, and an abundant supply of shops and showrooms. The streets, gaslit at night, had standardized furniture—lamp posts, benches, kiosks, pissoirs. The mansarded apartment houses, built of grey stone and holding to an even skyline, provided gracious living for families no longer content with meager flats on side streets but not rich enough to own a town house or *hôtel*. The new Opéra turned public entertainment into a glittering spectacle, and in the western-most of two new parks, the Bois de Bou-logne just off the Champs-Elysées, the same smart crowd could repair daily to ride horses and fancy carriages, stroll along meandering footpaths, and gamble at the racetrack of Longchamps on the edge of a fashionable promenade.

The poorer classes, although not directly catered to, reaped some benefit from this recharging of their superannuated city. The most ameliorative circumstance by far pertained to the overhaul of services. The freshwater supply was more than doubled. Aqueducts worthy of the Romans brought water from sources in the Yonne, Vanne, and Dhuis river valleys as far as 150 kilometers (90 miles) away. Street sewers, working on gravity, emptied into capacious collector sewers that moved drainage northwest, away from the inhabited sector, and disgorged it into the Seine at Asnières, well below Paris. In order to plug into this infrastructure of drains and water mains, new buildings had to submit to some regularity in plan and elevation. In this standardization flashed the genius of the industrial age; we also see it in new constructional methods like ferroconcrete, a cement-based mixture stiffened with metal mesh which its inventor, François Coignet, used in the new sewers, in some public buildings, and in six-storey apartment blocks. (Fig. 25.9) A balanced view of Second Empire architecture must understand the elliptical ferroconcrete collectors of Coignet as the flip side of Garnier's Opéra.

Aesthetically, Haussmann's vision appears more conservative. We are familiar with straight, tree-lined avenues and formal squares framed by uniform frontages as planning principles of the Baroque period. But the similarity is only skin-deep. We are dealing primarily with a very different social system. Despite the prestige of the emperor, political power was neither concentrated at the top nor did it coincide with economic power. Haussmann was ultimately responsible to Parliament and the municipal council. In financing his monumental operations, he was forced to rely on private capital far more heavily than had been the practice in the royal initiatives of the previous two centuries. One of the most astounding feats of his administration, and the most controversial, was precisely the huge success of his intricate financial arrangements which always teetered at the edge of legality. The accomplishment of less than two decades is staggering: 137 kilometers (85 miles) of new boulevards replaced a net of older thoroughfares that was four times as long. (Fig. 25.10) It took an uncanny knowledge of the labyrinthine and pit-filled workings of capitalist society, both its bureaucracy and its profit ethic, to bring about this reforming miracle.

The Baroque city, whatever its explosive vigor, was still a closed city. Its axes achieved finite links between nodes of monumental character that corresponded to a readable scheme of real and symbolic power. They shunned outright destruction and dashed through undeveloped or sparsely built land beyond the finespun urban texture. Haussmann moved with inflexible purpose. He cut through the densest quarters and nearly leveled the Île-de-la-Cité, the ritual core of Parisian history. The cathedral of Notre Dame stood for the first time isolated in open space, and big institutional buildings blocked the area with ponderous regularity: the Palace of Justice built into the old royal palace, the Tribunal de Commerce, the central hospital (Hôtel Dieu), and several barracks.

But there was method in this madness. Haussmann looked at a chaotic city, made in certain respects unlivable by the onrush of technological and social changes, and gave it coherence. He took a patchwork of independent quarters, organized around parish churches, monuments, or orderly residential squares, and made of it a unified organism. The guiding logic was circulation. The grand plan imprinted upon the existing city and the annexed suburbs a general circulatory system. The chief components of this were two interesting axes, the north-south Rue de Rivoli and the east-west Boulevard Sebastopol/St.-Michel, and a double ring of outer boulevards. Within the general framework a number of tributary systems was created, each organized around a public space, a square, that was now seen as nothing more than a traffic node. A main objective was to connect the railway stations with the functioning centers of city life, both extant and devised. The network was so extensive and interlinked,

Fig. 25.12 Newport (Rhode Island), the Griswold House, 1862–63, Richard Morris Hunt. This building now houses the Newport Art Association.

roads and squares so fused into one another, that one now experienced open spaces not as firm enclosures, but as something fluid and unsealed, something defined by crowds and moving vehicles. This is how a new school of painters, the Impressionists, liked to depict Haussmann's boulevards. (Fig. 25.11)

The rationale of Haussmann's work is plausible from the perspective of our own industrial-capitalistic age. But to contemporary witnesses who were reared in the old city, its passing was the cause of painful disorientation or disaffection. Theirs was not the view of planners and technocrats. A sacrilege had been committed. Some mourned the loss of beloved places; many were physically uprooted, their lives transformed overnight. Indeed something fun-

damental had transpired, however short-lived the suffering. The city, that millennial matrix of community, would no longer be the same.

In the past, the city had been the rock of their existence for those who lived within its walls. It was the familiar slow-changing backdrop of generations, the material covenant of spelled-out relationships. One knew it well. It had palpable shapes and hard edges. Real both in fact and faith, it was what commanded deep allegiance and provoked flash uprisings. Now the city behaved erratically. It showed a protean impatience beyond the common will. Waves of immigrants jostled it rudely. It pushed outward messily, shapelessly. It was too big to comprehend, except on paper. It could change its looks jarringly in the course of a

Fig. 25.13 Washington, D.C., the Capitol under construction in the 1860s. Thomas U. Walter's dome is nearing completion, and two end blocks have been added to the building (compare with Fig. 24.1). This sketch was made for *Harper's* magazine from a balloon. Railroad tracks run across what is now the Mall. The Potomac is in the distance.

lifetime. Regularization made only for dissembling permanence: How long before the order of today was deemed obsolescent? One had to seek an anchor elsewhere against the vagaries of human life. The great poet of the era, Charles Baudelaire, said it simply:

> The old Paris is no more; a city's form, alas,
> Changes faster than the human heart.

Victorian America

In the decade before the Civil War, American architecture moved in three rather different grooves. The Greek revival was still respectable in the South and in federal building programs nationwide. But it was the Italianate manner that had gained general popularity. This manner, as we saw briefly at the end of the last chapter, combined picturesque grouping with heavy classical detail. Actually, it had a variety of applications. There were the towered suburban "Italian villas," like Victoria Mansion (Morse-Libby House) in Portland, Maine, with their deep overhanging eaves, varied massing, and thickly framed windows. (Fig. 24.36) And there was the basic Renaissance

Fig. 25.14 Washington, D.C., the State, War and Navy Building (now the Executive Office Building), west of the White House, 1871–75, Alfred B. Mullett. The building is made of granite which was transported from Richmond, Virginia, and the interiors have beautiful marble floors, coffered domes, and eight spiraling cantilevered stairways.

Fig. 25.15 New York, the City Hall Post Office, 1875, Alfred B. Mullett; view looking northeast in a photo of 1938. Broadway is on the left; the Woolworth Building (Fig. 27.25b) is in the left foreground. The tall building on Park Row, behind the Post Office to the right, is the Municipal Building of 1914 by McKim, Mead & White. The Post Office was demolished in 1939 and the site has become part of City Hall Park.

Fig. 25.16 New York, National Academy of Design, 1863–65, Peter Bonnett Wight. Originally at Park Avenue South and 23rd Street; demolished in 1909 and reassembled in modified form as the exterior of a church on West 142nd Street.

revival used in flat-roofed residential row houses like New York's brownstones. (Fig. 24.37) A similar classicizing manner was popular for commercial buildings, including the cast-iron fronts of warehouse districts; it was also relied on, as an alternative to the purer and by now vulnerable Greek revival, in designs that emanated from the Washington office of the Supervising Architect, a position established in 1854.

But something else was also afoot: the new Stick Style. This term refers to domestic architecture in wood, particularly in New England. Since the 1840s, builders' pattern books had been advertising a freely inventive design that translated the picturesque and ethical principles of the Gothic revival into modest, affordable middle-class housing for the suburbs. The stress was on the asymmetrical plan, the lively outline, and,

most important, the articulation of the thin wooden members of the frame. (Fig. 25.12) This last aspect is noteworthy because it stands in sharp contrast to the traditional colonial house, or the Greek house for that matter, where the heavy framing-skeleton was always covered by a skin of clapboarding. The Stick Style, with its insistence on the commonest of all native materials—wood—and on structural honesty, responded to an agrarian, egalitarian, Jeffersonian view of America which was rudely to fall away after the Civil War.

Against this populist carpenter's vernacular, the professional architect began to take a stand. The first serious effort at an organized defense came in 1857, when the American Institute of Architects (AIA) was founded in New York. The moving spirit was Richard Morris Hunt (1827–95), the first American architect to study at the École des

Beaux-Arts. Hunt ran his office like the atelier of an École professor. He and other founders of the AIA pitted the cultured, disciplined procedures of the architect against the free-wheeling creativity of builders whose do-it-yourself philosophy they considered a threat to their status. The new eclecticism advocated by the École also championed the creative imagination, but there it was a scholarly freedom that was involved. One had to be broadly educated, learn strict design principles, and pass through a rigid academic curriculum and professional acculturation. In America, anyone who chose to could call himself an architect and function as such. The centralized, government-supported system of French architecture might be out of the question in this country, but training, accreditation, and overall professionalism could certainly stand some formality. The first school of architecture was started at the Massachusetts Institute of Technology in 1865 on the model of the École, but suitably domesticated. Others soon followed. In 1868 the first architectural journal began publication in Philadelphia.

This fledgling Eastern establishment had to do battle along two fronts. The builders' utilitarian approach, and the populist gospel it was wedded to, had to be exposed as naive. They were mere mechanics incapable of dealing with anything but the simplest of detached houses, the argument went. In the face of large-scale composition, of a public architecture that could hold its own against Europe, these rustics were hopelessly inept.

On this score, the architectural lobby was forced to contend with a much more formidable opponent: the engineer. As an independent expert, the engineer's star had been on the rise for some time now. Technical programs in engineering were ensconced early in American universities, and that is where architecture, the building side of it at any rate, was taught before the advent of architectural schools. The first engineering society was formed in 1852, ahead of the AIA. In Washington, an Office of Construction was set up under the Treasury Department at the same time as the office of Supervising Architect, and an engineer was appointed to head it. In fact, the schism between the "science" of building

Fig. 25.17a New York, house of Mrs. James L. Morgan, Jr., in Brooklyn; the dining room in a photograph of 1888.

Greenough called for "the entire and immediate banishment of all make-believe."

But with the Union secure at last after the ruinous war, it was that make-believe the country needed to build up its image as an aspiring international power. The credible models were the official styles of Paris and London—Second Empire and High Victorian Gothic, respectively. The federal government led the way in the propagation of a boastful public architecture. The business of building Washington resumed in earnest, beginning with the completion of the United States Capitol on orders from President Lincoln. Thomas U. Walter's great dome (1855–65) caught the spirit of L'Enfant's expansive vision. (Fig. 25.13) It was also the first sign of the official preference for the over-wrought classicism of Second Empire Paris. The style suited the ostentatious monumentality now believed necessary to mark the federal presence.

The Supervising Architect of the postwar years, Alfred B. Mullett (1834–90), was perfect for the mood. He had traveled in Europe in the late 1850s, and in all likelihood had been exposed to the rich plastic effects and thick-skinned ornamentation of the New Louvre. His State War and Navy Department to the west of the White House, with its ten acres of floor space and 553 rooms, became the largest office building in the world. (Fig. 25.14) Externally, columned bays of a Roman Doric order were marshalled unendingly in three tiers over a rusticated ground storey; salient pedimented pavilions broke up this massive block, and a high mansard roof crowned it. There was much structural and decorative use of iron, and before its completion in 1888 the latest technological advances, including electric lighting and the telephone, were incorporated. The cost was a staggering $10 million.

This public splendor also extended to the headquarters of the vastly proliferated federal bureaucracy at the state level. Customs houses, court houses, and post offices, as well as army hospitals whose absence was bitterly resented during the war, with facilities for veterans and their dependents, were distributed as federal gifts. They were costly structures far beyond the scale of the barely nascent towns, and they were intended to boost local pride and celebrate devotion to the Union. Many

and the art of design, between technique and ideology, was growing deeper. The debate was joined on the side of engineers by artists like Horatio Greenough and by men of letters like Ralph Waldo Emerson. They preached a brave new world of form that would honestly celebrate function, liberated from the tyranny of historicism. The models for architecture should be ships and locomotives, the metal bridges and useful factories of the industrial present.

Fig. 25.17b Eureka (California), the house of the lumber magnate William M. Carson, 1884–85, Samuel and Joseph Newsome, architects.

went to these towns in the awakening West. During their construction scandals of graft and waste came to light almost yearly.

This was an architecture of obsessive enframement and repetition. (Fig. 25.15) Individual units in themselves were not very different from those of the Renaissance revival, but now the wall plane was obscured by the relentless multiplication of the bays and the stiff, reiterative array of columns, lintels, and cornices that choked the openings and produced the effect of a laborious pile. "Massy" was what the buildings aspired to be. If the end result is seen as "neo-Baroque," it comes about through the inflation of Renaissance means. What is missing is the kinetic flare of the true Baroque that energizes mass and sweeps units into a molded whole. "A broken heap of littleness," an architect of the older generation called Mullett's New York post of-

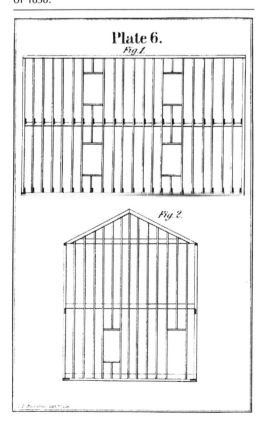

Fig. 25.18 Balloon-frame construction; illustration from William D. Bell's *Carpentry Made Easy* of 1858.

fice, and it is not hard to see what he means.

But rich abundant heaps that took up room and overfilled the eye satisfied the imperial stirrings of the once Arcadian republic—that, and the taste for variety and complication for their own sake. The polychrome medievalism of High Victorian Gothic, fed by the influence of Ruskin's writings, appealed to these same interests. This was the style of the academy and the church. (Fig. 25.16) In the hands of W. A. Potter (1842–1909), who succeeded Mullett as Supervising Architect, Ruskinian Gothic also affected federal building programs for a while.

The time was one of exuberant eclecticism and a lawless, energetic, architectural laissez-faire. Unmindful of even the pretense of archaeological accuracy, buildings were composed as if to prove that all human culture was fair quarry for this triumphant nation. In his *Homestead Architecture* of 1866 Samuel Sloan, having praised St. Mark's in Venice for its blending of the Roman and the Gothic, goes on to say: "Without condemning what has been done . . . we pass sentence on servile imitation as being unworthy of the genius and spirit of the American people." The idea was to range far and wide, to invent and improvise.

Despite the war and the depression of 1873, the country was experiencing an unprecedented boom. Railroads, mines, and steelyards led the way. Bonanza farming in the Midwest turned the production of wheat into big business. Immense fortunes were being amassed, and the power of money was becoming the new idealism. The display of wealth was proof of worth; the absence of restraint was exalted as individuality. Bulk, clutter, conspicuous waste, these are negative readings for what were virtues to Victorians—substantialness, variety, intricacy. They liked rooms densely thrown together, full of ornate furniture and bric-a-brac, framed maxims, and prints of uplifting or sentimental subjects; gaily painted houses with irregular silhouettes, jutting elements and projections, crests, brackets, scrolls, and finials; oversized public monuments of stone and aggregates of curdled ornament, building up to tall mansarded roofs and contumacious towers. (Fig. 25.17)

The irrepressible vigor of this architecture rode the crest of a swelling machine technology. Machines cut up stone and lumber and readied all kinds of milled and metal detail for shipping. Elevators made tall buildings profitable and changed habits of occupancy. The balloon frame, invented in Chicago in the 1830s, could now take off in earnest because of the mass production of dimensioned lumber and machine-made nails, and their prompt distribution by rail. (Fig. 25.18) In this system of construction, studs were vertically continuous from sill to rafters and the floorboards were nailed to their backs. Since members were light and interchangeable and nails dispensed with the fine art of joining, houses could be put up rapidly by relatively unskilled crews. Compared to the heavy rigid frame of colonial days, the balloon frame allowed for greater flexibility in the arrangement of interior spaces, and what was built could easily be modified or added to. The system was popular in the new towns of the Midwest and the mining and trading frontiers further out. It was ideally suited for the big barns that now appeared in the farmlands, with roomy free interior spaces for the storage of large amounts of hay and bulky machinery. The prefabricated house was promoted as the ideal middle-class summer cottage, approximating in form the earlier experiments of the Stick Style.

The View from the East

For all their militant professionalism, architects paid heed to the freedom and inventive improvisation of builders' model homes. In the 1870s they began to design, for wealthy clients of the Eastern seaboard, airy houses with flexible plans spun around a living hall. Entered more or less directly from the outside, this hall had a massive fireplace in it and was open to light through a wall of windows. (Fig. 25.19) The staircase to the upper floor, sometimes fitted with built-in seats, was a formal feature along one side or in a corner. Space flowed freely among rooms that were only minimally separated from each other by mere screen walls, for instance, or very wide sliding doors. And the exterior, perked by gables and turrets, opened out to the garden or lawns with large bay windows and verandas of various shapes and sizes that would often wrap themselves around a portion of the periphery.

What was being cultivated at considerable cost was a self-consciously vernacular look, but this differed from the builder's vernacular in two respects. First, the frame was clothed in shingles rather than being exposed: hence the name Shingle Style. (Fig. 25.20) Here was a shift in emphasis from the skeleton to the surfacing material, from spindly articulation to wraparound continuities. And second, the inspiration was more learned, more sophisticated, than the builder's picturesque fare for that large anonymous audience of middle-class families. It echoed, in general massing and architectural features, the Queen Anne manner of Shaw and Nesfield that had reached the United States through prints published in the new professional journals like *The American Architect and Building News* and *The American Builder*. (Fig. 25.4) But the open plan of Shingle Style houses with its flowing spaces was original; in a Queen Anne house, the rooms remained well-defined separate entities. And the English prototype preferred tile hangings and half-timbering on the outside, often installed over perfectly sound brick walls.

The American penchant for shingles recalled a native source—our own Colonial past. As English architects had turned a decade earlier to the traditional structures of the countryside and the Georgian vernacular of towns, so East Coast architects now rediscovered New England farmhouses and places like Newport, Marblehead, and Portsmouth, which had hardly changed since Colonial days. With the decline of whaling fleets and commercial lumbering, these old port towns were finding new life as summering places for the affluent classes. The memory-laden, nostalgic image of their architecture fed the fashion in the Shingle Style houses for beamed ceilings, leaded casements, and large masonry hearths that had in practice been made obsolete by the spreading use of furnaces and stoves.

There was one additional ingredient in the Shingle Style look: Japan. That country, traditionally sealed off from the West, had been flirting with an open-door policy for a while. Its wood architecture, the norm for almost every kind of building, had been

Fig. 25.19 Newport, the William Watts Sherman House, 1874–75, Henry Hobson Richardson; living hall in a drawing probably by Stanford White, later a partner of the famous architectural firm of McKim, Mead & White.

honed through the centuries into a refined system of structure and design. It was probably the most advanced wood architecture in the world. (Fig. 25.21) The Japanese buildings in the Philadelphia Centennial Exposition of 1876 were a timely stimulus for Shingle Style architects. This was not only because the construction matched their own preoccupation with the wood frame and its sheathing, but also because the spatial organization of the Japanese interiors reinforced the notion of an open plan—an idea central to the purpose of these American designers. One journal said of the Japanese buildings that "at any moment any partition can be taken down, and two or more rooms, or the whole house, be thrown into one large apartment. . . . Doors and windows as we use them, there are none."

So now Shingle Style houses took to suggesting bamboo posts, the *kamoi*, or bracing beams under which white paper screens slide in a Japanese interior, obviating fixed walls, and the elegant latticework screens called *ramma*. In some things, however, this exotic model was not followed. For example, the Japanese house has

all of its joints mortised, tenoned, and pegged; no nails are ever used. Also, all rooms are laid out as multiples of a *tatami*, or floor mat, which measures roughly 1 by 2 meters, and all sliding screens between them have the same height and width.

The Shingle Style was a phenomenon of the suburbs and summer places of New England. It was antimonumental in sentiment and also antiurban. It prided itself on an honest, democratic look. But the mood was escapist. It looked back at those simpler days before industry had changed the world. It ignored the rapid urbanization of America since the Civil War and had little to contribute to the problems of city-building. So it remained a gracious regional effusion reserved for second homes, casinos, and summer hotels of vacationing well-to-do families.

The reality was a lot harsher. The countryside itself was being invaded by industry. Its installations had been spawning mill and factory towns that dwarfed the neighboring Colonial villages. The early paternalistic attitude of the industrialists toward the work force, which had produced model communities like Lowell with its homelike,

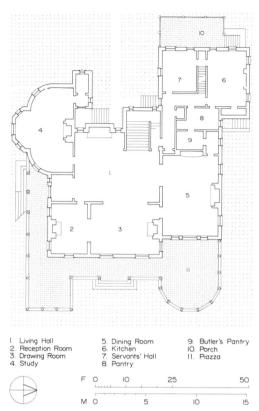

1. Living Hall   5. Dining Room   9. Butler's Pantry
2. Reception Room   6. Kitchen   10. Porch
3. Drawing Room   7. Servants' Hall   11. Piazza
4. Study   8. Pantry

F 0   10   25   50

M 0   5   10   15

Fig. 25.20 Newport, the Isaac Bell House (also known as the Edna Villa), 1881–83, McKim, Mead & White: **(a)** exterior; **(b)** ground plan.

decent living quarters, was becoming a luxury. With the arrival of immigrant labor from abroad in tidal waves, mean shanties were thrown up to house this cheap, disparaged force. In the cities, the immigrant population was crammed into speculator-built tenements (Fig. 25.22) They were a new and abiding urban institution, these tall stacks of flats, five or six storeys high, and they were commonly without plumbing or heating. Their rooms were strung along unlighted corridors, overlooking black airshafts. The only likely median between these wretched slums and the brownstones and Shingle Style summer houses of prosperous businessmen and professionals was represented by the freestanding frame cottages for wage earners in working-class suburbs, which were linked to business districts by streetcars.

In America more so than in Europe, the two fundamental corollaries of the industrial-capitalist era—overpopulation and the separation of workplace and dwelling—traumatized urban culture and dissipated the city-form that is its matrix. From 1860 onward, urban population increased at the rate of 50 percent with each ensuing decade. At the time of the Civil War only 20 percent of the American people lived in cities. This figure doubled by 1900.

In less than thirty years New York reached a population of 3 million, more than twice what it had been when the Civil War started. The oppressive grid spread and filled implacably. Central Park was the only effort to make amends, and that did not come easy. (Fig. 25.23) Even when the long political battles were over and the idea for this open public space was approved, there was no agreement on how it would be used. The upper classes fancied a cultural ambience

sheltering museums and other educational institutions in a sylvan setting. The lower classes would rather have it be for general amusement and sports. We must credit one man, Frederick Law Olmsted (1822–1903), for the fact that neither camp prevailed at the start, and the Park, 800 acres of rock and shrub, survived primarily as natural scenery. Transverse roads, sunk below the surface in deep-walled trenches, let commercial cross-traffic through unobtrusively. Pedestrian walks were carefully separated from paths for horseback riding and roads for recreational vehicles, and these were carried over the crosstown streets on viaducts.

The layout of Central Park was in the English picturesque tradition. (Fig. 22.13) But to Olmsted a park was an idealized rural landscape in the center of town that acted "in a directly remedial way to enable men to better resist the harmful influences of ordinary town life and to recover what they lose from them." No sham ruins, follies, or monuments; just a pastoral picture to be

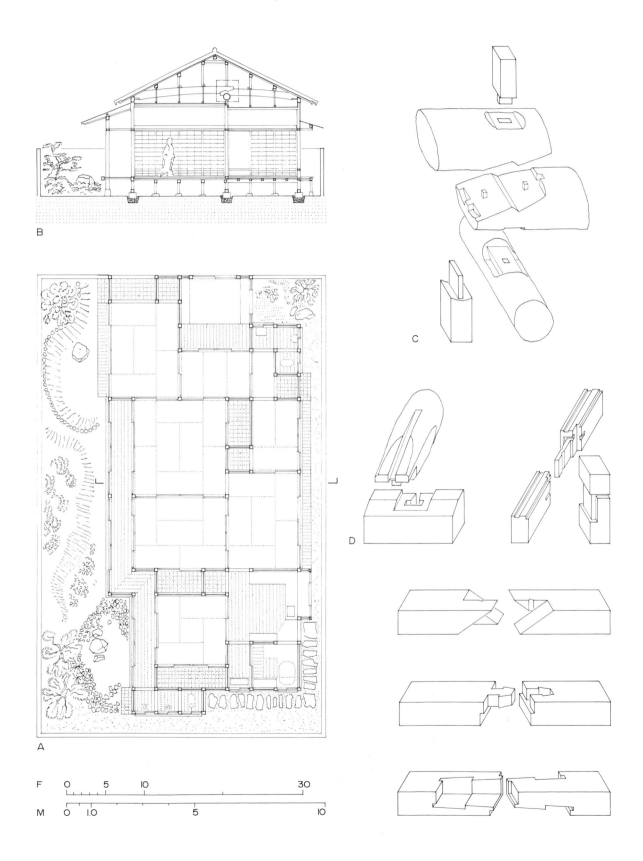

B

C

D

A

F   0   5   10   30

M   0   1.0   5   10

contemplated for relaxation. And Olmsted's tireless exhortations persuaded. The example of the urban park and parkways took hold, and the right of the urban population to insist on them came to be recognized. In the meantime, Olmsted's sinuous lines spread to campus planning, summer resorts, and suburbs all across the country. (Fig. 25.31)

The detached suburban house and the urban park—these are the two architectural themes where a uniquely American contribution was made to the history of architecture in the second half of the nineteenth century. A third theme was the tall office building.

The genesis of this third type is also tied, like the other two, to the dynamics of the changing city. When rapid transportation legitimized commuting, the affluent moved out of the congested city centers to autonomous satellite communities at the periphery where open space and green could still be enjoyed. Working-class people, pushed out by the rising real estate values of a downtown which was becoming exclusively commercial, also took to the edges along the streetcar lines. Each of these suburbs was a residential entity of similar units without an institutional or social focus. Each had a distinct identity—ethnic, religious, or economic. The depleted city center was rapidly claimed by factories, warehouses, and office buildings. In the evenings, life was drained out of it as elevated railways, subways, cable cars, and ferries carried away the working population, to return it in the early morning.

The process was gradual of course, and it affected the big cities more emphatically. The big-city syndrome was itself the child of modern transportation. Decreasing shipping costs due to the railroads and ca-

nals promoted the growth of larger markets. Mail-order business epitomizes this marketplace without boundary. Business and manufacturing firms could now plant their headquarters in a few well-linked commercial centers like New York and Chicago. Since there was only a fixed supply of land in these centers and the demand for it was keen, land values rose precipitately.

And so did the height of buildings. At the end of the Civil War new construction in downtown New York averaged about four storeys; by 1885 seven to eight storeys were common; by the end of the century, twelve to fifteen storeys. This concentration of high-density construction in a small area put severe demands on municipal and transportation services, such as sewer, water, and light rail and underground systems. By contrast, the cores of European cities retained their habits of mixed use; in their new buildings business and residence went together, and before long official limits were set on height.

Free-enterprise capitalism, American style, brooked no interference in these postwar decades that have been christened the Age of Energy. The new business palaces crowded and outsoared one another in a competitive frenzy. Cast-iron fronts were already old hat. Such buildings were quickly and cheaply assembled, and they had well-lit, relatively unencumbered floor space. But widespread fires, like Chicago's of 1871, were proving the vulnerability of the metal frame. The response was twofold. The masonry component regained in importance, to the satisfaction of the stone and brick industry that had felt threatened by the increasing popularity of iron construction. And at the same time methods were sought to make metal fireproof.

Matters were complicated by the question of height. Thanks to the elevator, extra floors of first-class rentable space were now feasible. But the tall building had to stand up safely. It also had to look architecturally plausible, if not distinguished. The professional circles of the East grappled with the aesthetic problem; they worked to induct the tall building into the architectural culture of Europe. Chicago led the technical revolution—and in the end addressed

Fig. 25.22 Jacob A. Riis, *Five Cents a Spot*, ca. 1889. This photograph shows a room in a tenement on Bayard Street, New York. Riis described the scene: "In a room not thirteen feet either way slept twelve men and women, two or three in bunks set in a sort of alcove, the rest on the floor. A kerosene lamp burnt dimly in the fearful atmosphere, probably to guide other and later arrivals to their 'beds,' for it was only just past midnight." The title refers to the price of a "bed" in one of these grim lodging houses.

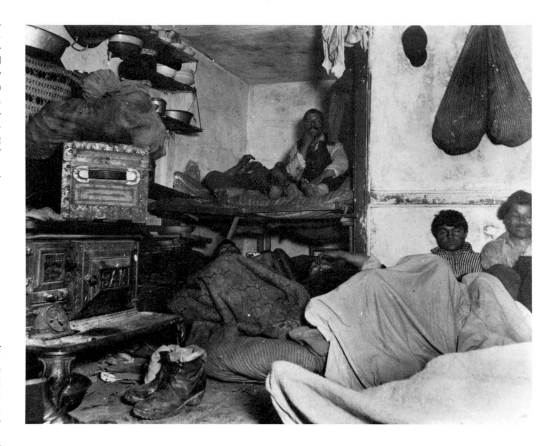

Fig. 25.23 New York, Central Park; map of 1873. This is the revised and extended layout of the park designed by Frederick Law Olmsted and Calvert Vaux in 1857; it was under construction until about 1880. In the middle were the Croton Aqueduct reservoirs that held the city's water supply.

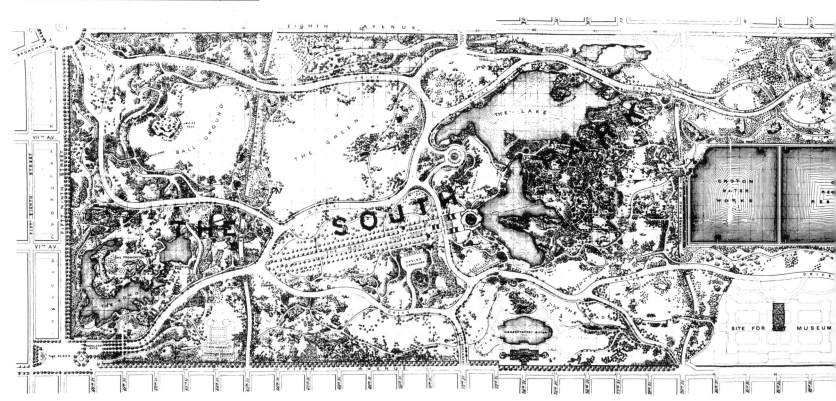

656

issues of form, too, in ways that were exciting, nonacademic, radical.

New York figures very early in skyscraper history, if the term is understood to mean simply an elevator building of exceptional height. The Equitable Life Insurance Building of 1868–70 was the first office structure to install the elevator. It had six storeys, with a seventh tucked in its mansard, and reached a total height of 40 meters (131 feet). Then in 1873 George B. Post (1837–1913) designed the Western Union Telegraph Building, and Hunt the New York Tribune Building. (Fig. 23.37) With these, the skyscraper pushed up to ten storeys and a height of 80 meters (262 feet). All three were metal-using masonry buildings, and their startling bulk was domesticated with historicist detail. They were also traditional in composition. The formula was that classic one for the urban palace: a pronounced ground floor that fixed the visual base of the block, the main body of upper storeys, and the attic with its capping cornice line. In the spirit of the Second Empire a mansard crown sat atop the cornice, and the typical

Victorian tower lifted the mass upward still. But the buildings are not very composed in their unusual height. Hunt groups his storeys into superbays, piling them in two unwedded strata between the open ground floor and the heavy mansarded top. It is a clumsy, gawky invention that does not cohere.

In the next ten years there were many experiments, primarily in New York and Chicago, to make the tall building with masonry walls look less ungainly, to give it a dignified bearing, a style. Should the vertical dimension triumph visually at the expense of the great stack of storeys? How much ornament should be allowed and where should it be concentrated? Is the mansard roof compatible with the new commercial marvel? How could the hundreds of repetitive windows be held together in a bigger, more monumental frame? In short, how could the prodigious spread of the facades be unified?

One of the celebrated solutions was the Marshall Field Wholesale Store in Chicago. (Fig. 25.25) It was designed by a Beaux-Arts

trained Eastern architect, Henry Hobson Richardson (1838–86). Richardson is probably the first major figure of American architecture to be recognized and imitated in Europe. The manner that made him so successful is often labeled Romanesque revival. In fact, Richardson was neither the first to exploit the conventions of that medieval style, nor was his work really very studied Romanesque. His habit of using arched cadences can be traced back to the early part of the century, to the Renaissance revival and the *Rundbogenstil*. (Fig. 23.5) The seeker of sources will also single out in his work, besides regional Romanesque features, more rarefied models like Early Christian churches in Syria. (Fig. 11.21) This is interesting, but not very critical. Richardson's concerns were not in the least archaeological or associative. The argument for him was purely architectonic, and it is the abstract authority of his built statement that engrossed the country.

Richardson took total charge of his buildings, designing everything for them down to furniture and fixtures. His signa-

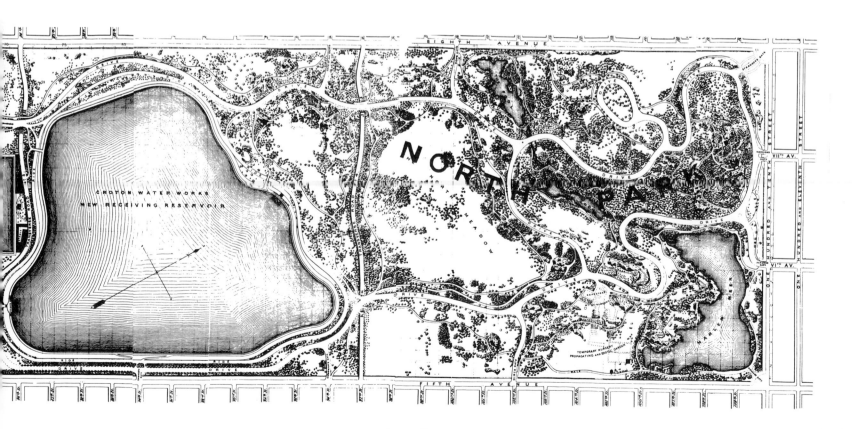

(a)

(d)

(b)

Fig. 25.24 Architectural details by Henry Hobson Richardson:

(a) Quincy (Massachusetts), Crane Memorial Library, 1880–83; eyelid dormer vent.

(b) Pittsburgh (Pennsylvania), Allegheny County Courthouse and Jail, 1884–88; exterior doorway to jail.

(c) Cambridge (Massachusetts), Austin Hall, Harvard University, 1881–83; "Syrian" arch with Byzantine-style capitals. On the right is a round stair turret. (Compare with Fig. 11.21.)

(d) Cambridge, Stoughton House, 1882–83; curving shingle exterior of stairwell.

(e) Boston, Trinity Church, 1873–77; chapel stairway. (See also Fig. 26.3 for a general view of the church's site.)

(c)

(e)

Fig. 25.25 Chicago (Illinois), the Marshall Field Wholesale Store, 1885–87, Henry Hobson Richardson; period drawing. (See also Fig. 25.33.)

Fig. 25.26a Chicago, the Monadnock Building, 1884–92, the firm of Burnham & Root.

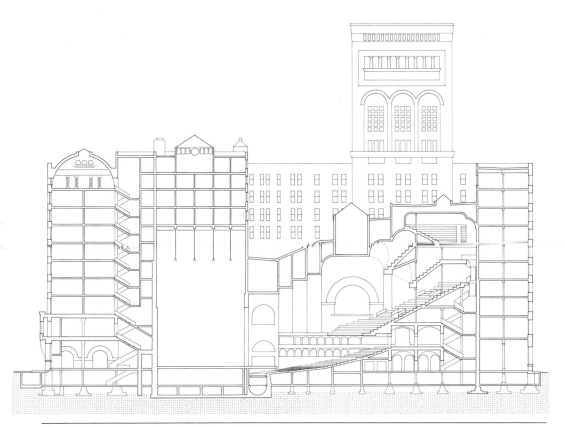

Fig. 25.26b Chicago, the Auditorium Building, 1886–89, the firm of Adler & Sullivan; section.

Fig. 25.26c Chicago, the Rookery on La Salle Street, 1884–86, Burnham & Root Architects; lobby as redesigned by Frank Lloyd Wright for interior court and staircase.

ture was big and strong, rid of fussy frills and clever concoctions. He loved stone, large split-faced blocks, and shaped it into thickset masses. But his sense for materials comes across just as credibly in brick and the masterful taut envelopes of his Shingle Style houses, which are among the first and finest formulations of that genre. And his effects were easy to imitate—the substantial, volume-embracing, generous masonry, the stone-mullioned window walls, the round stair turrets, the "eyelid" dormers, the cavernous entrance arches springing from fat squat stubs of columns or piers, if not directly from the ground. (Fig. 25.24)

Still, for all the hundreds of Richardsonian public buildings in every corner of late nineteenth-century America, his own are unmistakable. They include Trinity Church on Copley Square in Boston's new Back Bay district (Fig. 26.3), a line of small-town libraries, government buildings like the Allegheny County Courthouse and Jail in Pittsburgh, school buildings for Harvard, and commercial structures like the seminal Marshal Field Store, which was senselessly demolished in 1930.

The View from Chicago
In Chicago the Marshall Field building (1885–87) took up a whole city block and filled it with great sobriety. (Fig. 25.25) We might think of a huge Renaissance palazzo, but there is no applied articulation here, no sculptural detail except for the boldly crocketed cornice. Strong pierlike corners, thinly chamfered, firmly hem the block. The facades are ordered entirely by means of window openings. Rows of identical elements move the eye across the facade, while their stacking up and the progressive division of the bay units pull the building together vertically. Above a slightly salient red granite base, broad arches subsume three storeys. Then the arched rhythm doubles for the next three storeys; doubles again, without the arches, in the attic; and the cornice seals the top resolutely in a clean straight line. The wall, for all its thickness and weight, lets us feel the open loft spaces within, and the great run of arched windows speaks of the general uniformity of warehouse floors.

Fig. 25.27 Chicago, the Second Leiter Building, at the corner of State and Van Buren streets, 1888–91, William Le Baron Jenney.

A large, determined, poised building, the Marshall Field Store made a stunning impression in post-fire Chicago. The architect Louis Sullivan found it "an oasis" among the recent buildings of the downtown. "Foursquare and brown, it stands . . . a monument to trade, to the organized commercial spirit, to the power and progress of the age, to the strength and resource of individuality and force of character," he exulted. But it was not the only remarkable sight in that city in those years of heroic reconstruction. There was Burnham & Root's Monadnock Building on West Jackson Boulevard, begun in 1884 and completed in 1892—a stripped, freestanding brick slab with chamfered corners and a curved base, pleated by tall stacks of bay windows. (Fig. 25.26a) The same firm's earlier Montauk Block (1882–83) on West Monroe Street stood firm in the soggy Chicago soil on a "floating-raft" foundation invented by Root; and their Rookery (1884–86) on La Salle Street had a court made of iron and glass throughout, walls and dome alike, and a cast-iron stairway that spiraled dizzyingly from the second to the tenth floor in a semicylindrical glass cage that projected outward from the west court wall. (Fig. 25.26c) Sullivan's own Auditorium Building (1886–90) extended for the entire block along Congress Parkway from Michigan to Wabash Avenue. (Fig. 25.26b) The theater was encased by an office block on the west side and a hotel on the east, which overlooked the lake; in the center of the south front a tower sprouted with several storeys of additional high-rent space.

They were brave, strong-willed concepts all of them, unafraid of history, or rather unmindful of the shifting vagaries of historicism. As Root declared,

Where architects faithfully follow out the logic of a predetermined theory of their building, they have purity of style. . . . To lavish upon [these tall buildings] profusion of delicate ornament is worse than useless. . . . Rather should they by their mass and proportion convey in some large elemental sense an idea of the great, stable, conserving forces of modern civilization.

But while Richardson, Root, and Sullivan thus consolidated traditional architecture, the future asserted itself in another way. A new building technology peremptorily revised the laws of construction and so worked an intrinsic change on facade design. In that sense, Richardson's Field Store was the end of a noble line; William Le Baron Jenney's Second Leiter Building, its exact contemporary, began a new and not fully imaginable architecture. (Fig. 25.27)

Jenney's is also a tightly bound block. It is composed on a rectangular instead of an arcuated matrix. And that seems to be the principal difference visually between his facade and Richardson's. But this undeviat-

ing lattice is not mere design. It confirms a structural system that governs the entire building, inside and out. We have here probably the first instance of true skyscraper construction: a fireproofed metal frame that supports its own weight, as well as all floors and walls that regulate the functional organization of the interior. (Fig. 25.28) There are no bearing masonry walls. There are no walls at all in the proper sense; only a curtain composed of vertical and horizontal bands of masonry, fitted with glass panes, that weatherproofs the building and fireproofs the outermost columns and beams of the metal frame.

The framing members were made of steel now, not iron. This Bessemer steel, named for the man who invented the process in 1856, had been used only in three bridges before 1884 when Jenney introduced it into commercial architecture. It was just beginning to be produced in bulk, by means of a sophisticated open hearth furnace, and sold at acceptable prices. In skyscraper construction the steel members are bolted together with angles, webs, and gusset plates. All portions of the exterior nonbearing curtain rest on metal shelves fixed to the spandrel beams. In this way each outermost girder carries not only its part of the floor, but also one bay of the exterior curtain up to the beam next above it. The steel is fireproofed throughout with insulating hollow tile, and the flooring itself sits on a waffle of flat terra-cotta arches.

The advantage of steel was undisputable. It was superior to iron in matters of compression, tension, and heat. It weighed about one-third as much as bearing masonry for the same number of storeys, a prime asset on this quaggy terrain. Masonry construction had to be massive, especially at ground level where maximum window space was desired most. The thickness of the lower wall had to increase the higher the building climbed. The practice was to allow 1 foot at the base, and then augment this by 4 inches for each additional storey. Ten storeys was more or less the limit for buildings with bearing masonry walls or piers. The only exception, the sixteen-storey Monadnock Building, rests on walls that are a full 2 meters (6 feet) across); it is probably the tallest building

Fig. 25.28 Chicago, the Reliance Building, 1889–95, Burnham & Root; drawings of one bay illustrating skyscraper construction. **(A)** Plan, with three columns of the steel framing, each built up from four standard sections riveted together. **(B/C)** Sections. The girder of the cantilevered bay is marked **(b)**; the exterior cladding is terra-cotta. **(c)** indicates the floor framing system: hollow clay tiles are put together so as to act as arches between the joists (or beams); a layer of concrete is used on top of the tiles, and the wood floor is placed on top of that.

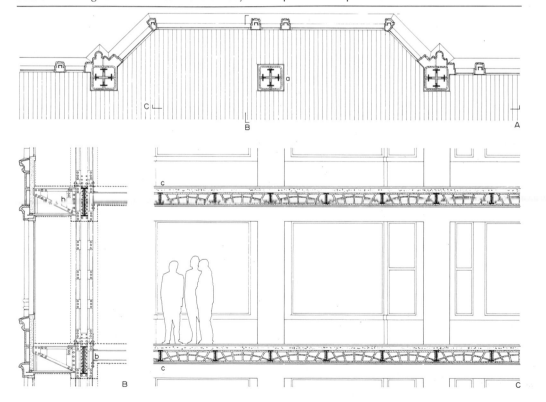

Fig. 25.29 Chicago in the 1850s; a lithograph published by Braunhold & Sonne in 1857.

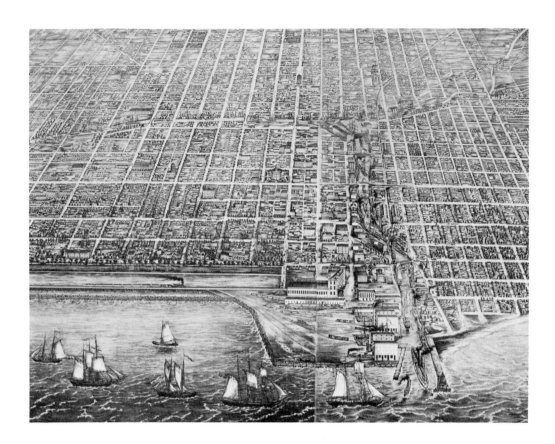

Fig. 25.30 Chicago, the Union Stockyards in 1889.

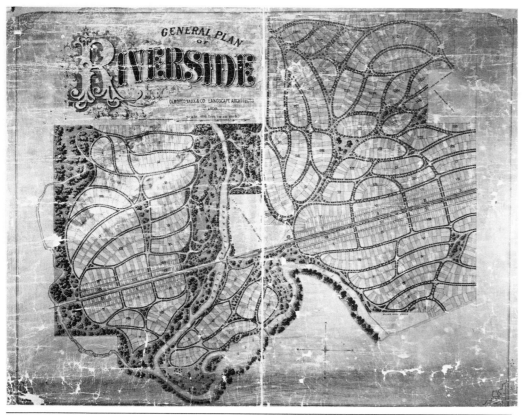

Fig. 25.31 Riverside (Chicago), 1868, Olmsted & Vaux; general plan. The suburb was about 10 kilometers (7 miles) southwest of Chicago; it straddled the Des Plaines River whose edges were left underdeveloped, as a communal park strip.

Fig. 25.32 An ideal kitchen, illustrated in Maria Parloa's *Kitchen Companion* of 1887. Features seen here which Parloa recommends include a hinged table, a sink with a roller for a towel above a grooved draining board, a movable table, and wire screens for the windows. The doors next to the stove lead to the cellar and cold room and to the pantry.

with masonry bearing walls ever constructed. Such a thickset bulk reduced valuable floor space. With true skyscraper construction, on the other hand, the building could rise as high as current technology permitted and still leave the facades free for almost total glazing. The glass cages of our own day—Boston's John Hancock building on Copley Square and the 110-storey towers of the World Trade Center in New York—have their start in Jenney's Chicago.

In principle, skyscraper construction is not unlike the braced wood skeleton of New England or its derivative, the balloon frame, where the sheathing is similarly without supportive duties. (Fig. 25.18) The metal skeleton itself had compiled a brief but plucky story starting with the Crystal Palace. One could even ferret out isolated cases of multistorey commercial structures carried entirely on an iron frame, like the warehouse by one Hippolyte Fontaine for the St. Ouen dock near Paris, completed in 1866. But nothing of this explains away Jenney's breakthrough—the mastery of riveted steel framing. And nothing accounts better for its triumph than his home-ground—that raw, impatient metropolis of Chicago, the instant city with no set traditions of its own.

A frail frontier community at first, nothing more than a collection of cabins on the swamp of a stream's mouth on Lake Michigan, Chicago changed into the nerve center of the West within the lifetime of its settlers. The cutting of the Erie Canal in 1825 opened the way for migration from the East across the Great Lakes. This route was extended to the Mississippi River in 1848, bringing to Chicago the trade previously diverted to St. Louis. This was the beginning. By 1860 Chicago had already grown to a sizable town of 100,000 people. By 1880 the relentless grid had stretched out on the muddy plain to make room for more than 1 million inhabitants. Chicago was now the largest railroad juncture in the nation. It was also the hub of the largest system of inland waterways in the world. (Fig. 25.29)

Lumber trade was a giant business here. It depleted nearby forests in no time and tapped the riches of neighboring states and the Deep South. Along the river vast quantities of pine, ash, walnut, and cypress were piled high. The city was also a principal producer of other materials for the construction industry—brick, stone, plumbing fixtures, and window glass, which before 1875 had been imported, almost all of it from France and Germany. On the West Side, a tract of 64 hectares (160 acres) was given over to steam-boiler factories and metal-processing plants, including those producing steel. Comparable enterprises were devoted to the manufacture of furniture and farm machinery. The mass-produced grain of the Midwest was stored in rows of grain elevators on the lake shore. In the Union Stockyards, laid out in a grid over almost a square mile of land and with pens capable of holding more than 100,000 animals, cattle brought by train from near and far were slaughtered, processed, packed, and shipped out in refrigerated cars. It was the most astounding system of mechanization the world had seen. (Fig. 25.30)

All the while, Chicago was making and remaking itself. The street grade was raised at great pains by as much as 3 meters (10 feet) to escape the inundation of lake water. The streets were widened. A supply tunnel, starting 3 kilometers (2 miles) out from the lake shore, brought in pure drinking water. A fine public park system, conceived by Olmsted and amplified by the local landscape architect Horace Cleveland, slowly came into being. Tree-lined boulevards in the Parisian mold linked the parks to one another and to the center.

Dozens of suburbs were strewn beyond the grid. Their configuration ranged from the casual to the regimented. Olmsted's influence prevailed at Riverside, an early residential suburb in the picturesque manner, with streets curved deliberately despite the level topography, to "suggest and imply leisure, contemplativeness and happy tranquillity"—this in contrast to the ramrod town streets that implied "eagerness to press forward, without looking to the right or left." (Fig. 25.31) Thousands of trees were imported to give the prairie a more forested look.

In the suburbs one could find a different kind of community, that of manufacturing plants which required extensive acreage for the layout of production lines. Some were miniature company towns built with phi-

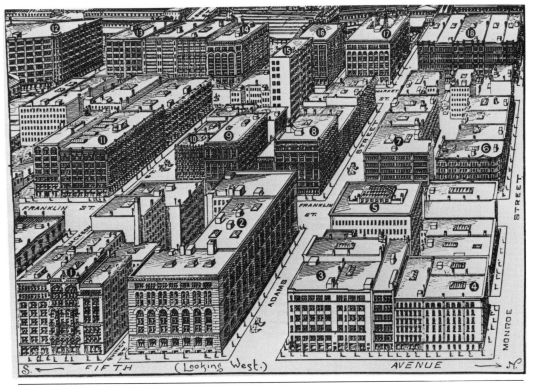

Fig. 25.33 Chicago in 1898, in a view looking west from Fifth Avenue (Wells St.). Number 2 is the Marshall Field Wholesale Store (Fig. 25.25).

lanthropic fanfare by the employer. But management aimed at the total control of workers' lives and made sure that they spent their wages on the premises. The most famous of these was the Pullman Palace Car Company which maintained a 120-hectare (300-acre) site 15 kilometers (9 miles) south of Chicago on the western shore of Lake Calumet, a 40-minute drive by train from downtown. It was organized around a square that served as a retail center where the workforce, about 4,000 strong by the mid-1880s, could do their shopping.

In the city, the housing stock was being replenished at a furious pace. The better houses in the old part of town, converted to rentals as their owners moved further out, were soon derelict. Elegant new town houses stood along the lake on the North and South Sides, and on the West Side just west of the business district. But the high cost of land favored apartment houses and

tenements, mostly three- or four-storey walkups. Perhaps the most telling change in modern American life was the growing acceptance of mass-produced housing, either in the form of an apartment unit or the single-family tract house. At the same time, a correspondingly serious revolution was affecting the traditional program of the American home. Local propagandists like Catharine Beecher and Harriet Beecher Stowe, intent on lessening the burden of the housewife, advocated a centralized core of mechanical services and the efficient organization of storage areas. (Fig. 25.32) These labor-saving reforms for servantless housekeeping entailed changes in the layout of the house, as flush toilets, refrigerators, and central lighting and heating transformed the quality of domestic life.

But it was the business district of Chicago that embodied most trenchantly the image of the future. Packed densely in an area of some sixty blocks called the Loop were urban warehouses, office buildings, department stores, mail-order companies, hotels, all pushing high above the streets and distending their presence by means of telephone lines. (Fig. 25.33) The building activity was frantic and constant. They called it the City of Speed. To build right through the harsh Chicago winter, salt was added to the mortar so that bricks could be laid in freezing temperatures, poured concrete was insulated with straw and tarpaulin, and temporary roofing with electric lights beneath kept crews going in rain or snow. Electric floodlights blazed through the night. They called it the Electric City.

In the absence of height-limiting ordinances, the architect dared to climb higher and higher. Perhaps not since the day of Gothic cathedrals in the Île-de-France had there been such an intense race of boldness and innovation. The technical problems were formidable, and imperfectly understood. Still, the solutions were proffered thick and fast, refined, then discarded for something better. Take foundations. (Fig. 25.34) The stability and equal settlement of the tall building, given the city's weak bearing soil, posed critical difficulties. First came isolated spread footings, in coursed stone, to support individual piers. Then Root's "floating raft," made of concrete reinforced with steel rails, distributed the load over a relatively large area and so reduced the unit pressure delivered by the footings. And finally, caisson foundations in the 1890s used watertight drums to lower massive concrete piers through the boggy topsoil until they touched hardpan clay, letting the reinforced concrete footings rest on these piers. Wind was ignored at one's risk: they called it the Windy City. With no sound scientific calculation of wind loading yet possible, various forms of bracing were tried—double girders, diagonal members across the bays at the basement level where the shearing and bending are most strongly felt, and arches to join the main girders to the columns and so produce a rigid frame.

The cellular facade offered the chance to be inventive with windows. (Figs. 25.28, 25.35) By recessing the spandrels and running the columns in their masonry encasement continuously above the ground storey, the architect could dramatize height. To strengthen the sense of upward lift Sullivan, in skyscrapers for St. Louis and Buffalo, doubled the rhythm with nonfunctional piers interposed between the true supports of each bay. (Fig. 25.35c) Alternatively, by setting the piers wide apart so that the interval between them was more marked than the height of the bay, the architect could stress the horizontality of the metal skeleton, which was nearer its structural truth. Sullivan's Carson Pirie Scott and Co. department store, mentioned in Chapter 1, is a good example—and a sensible thing to do in a building type that requires broad bright horizontal spaces where goods can be displayed. (Figs. 1.8, 25.35b) The intervals here are filled with single sheets of glass, but a commoner solution was the so-called Chicago window. This had a three-

Fig. 25.34 Foundation diagrams of late-nineteenth-century Chicago buildings. **(A)** Isolated spread footing, made of dimensional stone and rubble in alternate courses (e.g., the Home Insurance Building, 1883–85, William Le Baron Jenney). **(B)** Floating raft, made of iron railings and I-sections cast in concrete (e.g., the Monadnock Building). **(C)** Driven long pile, made of wood (e.g., the Public Library, 1893, Shepley, Rutan & Coolidge). **(D)** Caisson system, of poured concrete (e.g., the Stock Exchange, 1893–94, Adler & Sullivan).

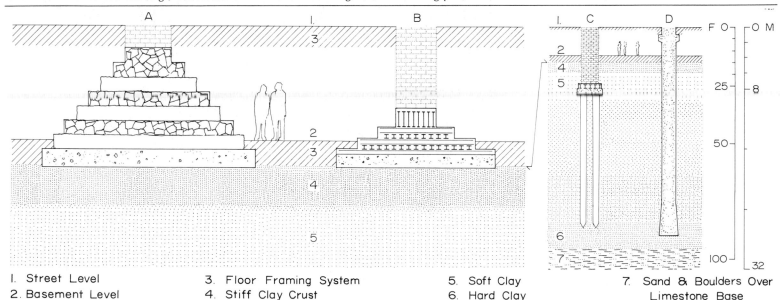

1. Street Level	3. Floor Framing System
2. Basement Level	4. Stiff Clay Crust

5. Soft Clay	7. Sand & Boulders Over
6. Hard Clay	Limestone Base

part division, the central fixed pane of glass being flanked with a narrow movable double-hung sash at the ends, next to the piers. The Chicago window could be bowed, and the movable sash set in the diagonal planes of the projection. (Figs. 25.28, 25.35a)

And so they rose, cheek-by-jowl, the lofty behemoths, from Franklin Avenue to Michigan Avenue, from Congress Avenue northward until the river, all the way into the 1890s. These were the monuments the city was proud of. The Loop caught the mettle of the place, its aggressive thrust, its newness and defiance. It was an unparalleled skyline, and it came about through the coincidence of rare architectural and engineering talent and a tough business clientele who demanded buildings with no frills that would make the best use of their money and bring the best return on their investment. There was no patience here for a battle of styles; no pressure for the latest in European fashion.

In all this, Chicago was turning its back on the architectural establishment of the East. It had started its own journal in 1883, the *Inland Architect and News Record,* and in the next year set up the Western Association of Architects, independent of AIA. Local critics spoke disparagingly of the "gentleman decorators" of the East. More important, they tried to characterize their own accomplishment. Their abnegation, the noncultural, nonhistorical drive forward, had brought out an indigenous manner. A modern architecture was launched, not in Paris, London, or New York, but in the recent wilderness of the reclaimed American continent. It was functional in the way Greenough and Emerson had pressed. It healed the rift between technology and art, and put both at the service of commerce. *Industrial Chicago* called it the Commercial Style. They wrote:

. . . the great airy buildings of the present . . . are truly American architecture in conception and utility. The style is a monument to the advance of Chicago in commerce and commercial greatness and to the prevailing penchant for casting out art where it interferes with the useful. It is a commanding style without being venerable. . . . The commercial style, if structurally ornamental, becomes architectural.

Fig. 25.35a Chicago, the Reliance Building, 1889–91 (and 1894–95), Burnham and Root; exterior detail of Chicago windows used in bays. See also Fig. 25.28.

Fig. 25.35b Chicago, Carson Pirie Scott department store (formerly Schlesinger and Mayer department store), 1899–1904, Louis Sullivan; exterior detail showing large ground-floor display windows and the architect's intricate applied ornament. See also Fig. 1.8 for a general view of this building, showing its horizontal layers of Chicago windows.

Fig. 25.35c St. Louis (Missouri), the Wainright Building, 1890–91, Adler & Sullivan; exterior detail of windows.

Further Reading

C. Condit, *The Chicago School of Architecture* (Chicago: University of Chicago Press, 1964).

R. Dixon and S. Muthesius, *Victorian Architecture* (London: Thames and Hudson, 1978).

A. Drexler, ed., *The Architecture of the École des Beaux-Arts* (New York: Museum of Modern Art, 1977).

M. Girouard, *Sweetness and Light: The "Queen Anne" Movement, 1860–1900* (New York: Oxford University Press, 1977).

G. L. Hersey, *High Victorian Gothic* (Baltimore: Johns Hopkins University Press, 1972).

J. B. Jackson, *American Space: The Centennial Years, 1865–1876* (New York: Norton, 1972).

F. Loyer, *Paris Nineteenth Century: Architecture and Urbanism,* trans. C. L. Clark (New York: Abbeville Press, 1988).

R. Middleton, ed., *The Beaux Arts and Nineteenth-Century French Architecture* (Cambridge, Mass.: MIT Press, 1982).

D. Olson, *The City as a Work of Art: London, Paris, and Vienna* (New Haven: Yale University Press, 1986).

D. H. Pinkney, *Napoleon III and the Rebuilding of Paris* (Princeton: Princeton University Press, 1958).

H. Saalman, *Haussmann: Paris Transformed* (New York: Braziller, 1971).

V. Scully, Jr., *The Shingle Style,* rev. ed. (New Haven: Yale University Press, 1971).

G. Wright, *Moralism and the Model Home: Domestic Architecture and Cultural Conflict in Chicago, 1873–1913* (Chicago: University of Chicago Press, 1980).

Boston (Massachusetts), Boston Public Library, 1887–98,
McKim, Mead & White; period view.

26

THE TRIALS OF MODERNISM

Urban Choices

Then, in 1893, Chicago did an about-face.

The occasion was to be the 400th anniversary of Columbus' discovery of America. A commemorative fair had been in the planning for some time. After much wrangling among would-be host cities, the Congress had voted in favor of Chicago, and locally the undeveloped marshes of Jackson Park on the South Side had been settled on as the fair site. Daniel Burnham was appointed director of the project. This was to be the 15th, and largest, of those popular international exhibitions that started back in 1851 with the Great Exhibition of London. Chicago was determined to rise to the occasion. The nation expected a showcase for its pride. It had survived and reversed the ravage of a civil war. It had staged and completed the most spectacular land conquest in history: the frontier was declared closed as of 1890. Industrially preeminent, strong and rich enough to strike an international pose in politics and trade, it was anxious to overcome its feelings of inferiority in cultural matters.

Burnham invited prominent architects from New York, Boston, and Kansas City to share the work with the Chicagoans. They agreed on two things. They would abandon the metal-and-glass theatrics of past fairs and "suggest permanent buildings—a dream city." And to give unity to this dream city, they would all conform to one binding mode of design—the classical.

On the face of it, this could be judged to be a step backward, at least from the local perspective. In the last twenty years Chicago had given life to an exciting, ahistorical architecture, a modern style all its own.

This was being jettisoned unceremoniously now in favor of hoary pieties. But the move makes sense in retrospect. The commercial style of the Loop, it is easy to see, would be deemed inappropriate for a festive, cosmopolitan affair. Besides the project was vast, the time short, the participating firms numerous and distinct. One had to settle for a common language. In late nineteenth-century America, with many of the leading architects trained in Paris at the École des Beaux-Arts or in native schools modeled after it, the choice was obvious.

The City Beautiful

But the call for uniformity and academic order was also bound up with the national mood. The boisterous individualism of the postwar period, the era of robber barons, land grabs, and unruly urbanization, was beginning to provoke a bridling reaction. More and more after 1885, the country was predisposed toward consolidation and a measure of control. For example, the track gauge for the railroads was now standardized, national time zones were designated, businesses merged into conglomerates, and labor organized to fight for its interests more effectively. The artists also rallied. They caught the stirring sense for a new civic grandeur, for a lofty idealism or at least its display. They coaxed gestures of public patronage from the newly rich and took charge of giving them formal homes in city and country. These self-made men—the Astors, Vanderbilts, Whitneys, and Morgans—now fancied themselves worldly patricians, an aristocracy of money able to carry on the grand tradition of Europe.

In the East, the veering toward a high-minded academic architecture came in the early 1880s, when the Shingle Style was still in vogue, through the agency of some of its best exponents. The firm of McKim, Mead, and White led the way, at first with a much more formal interpretation of Georgian modes. Then, in a group of six rental houses for the railroad financier Henry Villard on New York's Madison Avenue, McKim made a startling return to the Italian Renaissance palazzo. (Fig. 26.1) This was in 1883.

By the decade's end this sort of competent academicism had superseded lingering medieval trends, the Richardsonian "Romanesque," and those native urges in residential design that had nourished the Stick and Shingle styles. The lawless, catch-as-catch-can eclecticism of the Victorian era was stemmed. The regnant high style alleged classical tutelage. Its ingredients—the Roman imperial style, the Renaissance, and more recent French utterances—were brought together with erudite premeditation and rendered in the luxuriant formality of the Beaux-Arts mode.

The term "American Renaissance" now circulated freely, and domestic parallels were labored at every turn. Robber barons were flattered with analogies to the merchant princes of the Renaissance. Art works, bits of architecture, even entire buildings were spirited out of Europe. Americans, the novelist Henry James said, were superior to Europeans in that "[we] can pick and choose and assimilate and in short (aesthetically and culturally) claim our property wherever we find it." And the surge of home-based art was nothing short of amazing. The craftsmanship of furniture, stained glass, ceramics, and jewelry could be superb; architectural ornament, its dependence on mass-produced terra-cotta and fibrous plaster notwithstanding, was often of very fine quality. Painters and sculptors took on elevated themes and handled them fluently. As the harsh truth of the Civil War receded, commemorative works to honor its idealized myth sprang up everywhere. There were grand army plazas, triumphal arches, sailors' and soldiers' memorials, tombs, statues of leaders and heroes. (Fig. 26.2) A public-spirited patronage supported rich civic monuments—libraries, museums, universities, cultural and scientific facilities of all kinds. Within the embrace of these lofty edifices, the arts were brought together in an impressive alliance.

One building of the late 1880s, the Boston Public Library by McKim, Mead, and White, illustrates the power of the American Renaissance to affect the urban scene in the closing decade of the Victorian half-century. (Fig. 26.3) The Library held the west side of Copley Square across from Richardson's Trinity Church. The confrontation could scarcely have been more striking. The rough, brown, medieval pile of the church, massive and picturesque, against an elegant, smooth, light-colored, horizontal block, lifted templelike on a continuously staired platform and inflected in a reserved classicism that derives from Alberti's Tempio Malatestiano and a nearer Parisian prototype, the Bibliothèque Ste.-Geneviève by Labrouste. (Fig. 25.6)

The materials are opulent throughout: light pink Milford granite for the exterior; fine marble paneling, tiled floors, and coffered wood ceilings within. The generous public areas—like the barrel-vaulted main reading room that occupies the entire front, the delivery room, and the stair hall of yellow Siena marble that projects into the arcaded garden court—host (or were meant to) works of monumental art: statues of heroes and patriots, inspirational murals by native and foreign artists, ceiling paintings in the Venetian manner. (Fig. 26.4) The library was to be "a palace for the people," the trustees had specified; the inscription carved into the frieze below the roof declares that it was "built by the people and

Fig. 26.1 New York, the Henry Villard houses on Madison Avenue between Fiftieth and Fifty-first streets, 1882–85, the firm of McKim, Mead & White. Compare with Figs. 17.14b and 20.6.

dedicated to the advancement of learning." Actually, a handful of Boston's first families paid for it. "It will hold its own," the principal patron and president of the trustees Samuel Abbott averred, "beside any of the great works of the great architects of the Renaissance."

It was this sumptuous academic style that Eastern architects now brought to Chicago. And here they were handed a chance to show what it could do for whole environments. The Fair would be a case study for the future look of American cities. The marsh was dredged to create lagoons. The chief buildings, almost all of them white and holding to an even cornice line, were arranged about an axial court of honor. (Fig. 26.5) They were lordly in scale and resounded with the monumental symbols of imperial classicism. At night the scene was floodlighted, and it seemed a specter to the visiting throngs, so remote from the grub-

biness of an industrialized world. Some spoke of it as the promise of what American society could be, a society subject to reforming plans for a higher, common good. The serene ensemble reflected in the still waters of the lagoon stood in total antithesis to the willful vigor of the rest of Chicago, the visual chaos of slums and skyscrapers and its Victorian mansions—with "gables, dormers, minarets, bays, porches, oodles of jiggered woodwork ruthlessly painted, poking in or peeking out of piles of fancified stonework and playing idiotic tricks with each other"—to use the words of one young local architect, Frank Lloyd Wright, who had melioristic ideas of his own.

This was the start of the City Beautiful Movement. Its premise was that overall plans like that of the Fair would bring order to urban America, and that order relied on uniformity. As Burnham saw it,

Fig. 26.2 Brooklyn (New York), Soldiers and Sailors Memorial Arch on Grand Army Plaza, 1889–92, John H. Duncan with McKim, Mead & White. The arch was the principal entrance to Olmsted's Prospect Park and closed the long vista of Flatbush Avenue.

The jumble of buildings that surrounds us in our new cities contributes nothing valuable to life; on the contrary, it sadly disturbs our peacefulness and destroys that repose within us that is the true basis of all contentment. Let the public authorities, therefore, set an example of simplicity and uniformity, not necessarily producing monotony, but, on the contrary, resulting in beautiful designs entirely harmonious with each other.

And he was soon busy touring the great planned places of Europe—Rome, the royal squares and Haussmann's avenues in Paris, Versailles, Vienna, Berlin—in preparation for his plan to improve the nation's capital.

L'Enfant's magnificent scheme for Washington had fallen on bad days. Its centerpiece, the Mall in front of the Capitol, had been ruffled by picturesque interventions and encroached on by railroad lines. (Fig. 25.13) The city looked scattered, scruffy, and unfinished. Henry James described it as "empty, sketchy, fundamentals, however expectant, however spacious, overweighted by a single dome [that of the Capitol] and overaccented by a single Shaft [the Washington Monument]." The commission headed by Burnham now restored the Mall to its intended dignity. It was to be lined with public galleries and museums, and planted with rows of elm trees on either side of a carpet of grass 100 meters (330 feet) wide. The White House axis, marked with fountains, would reach out all the way to the Potomac. The Capitol axis would also be extended, west beyond the Washington Monument, and would terminate at the water's edge with a memorial to President Lincoln set in a *rond point*. A bridge beyond this point would lead to Arlington National Cemetery. Boulevards and parks would encircle the city, and a monumental railway terminal would be built northeast of the Capitol. Union Station, its central portico a Roman triumphal arch, was soon completed. (Fig. 26.6) It set the fashion for great urban entrances, of which the two best-known examples are New York's Penn and Grand Central stations.

The Washington plan was followed by others. They featured symmetrically grouped civic centers with malls and administrative and cultural buildings of a uniform classical design. The most spectacular was Burnham's 1909 plan for his home town. (Fig. 26.7) It called for the redevelopment of the entire Chicago area within a 100-kilometer (62-mile) radius from the center and included a generous system of outer parks, a lakefront park system about 35 kilometers (22 miles) long, an inner harbor, and of course a civic center at the intersection of Halsted and Congress streets. The beautifully rendered views show Haussmannesque boulevards with buildings of identical height and cornice line, as if the jagged cluster of skyscrapers in the Loop which Burnham's firm had furthered was not there.

On closer look, the proposed buildings turn out to be much taller than Haussmann's apartment blocks. Evidently Burnham took exception to the variety of that dramatic Chicago skyline, and not the height of the modern business tower. His Flatiron Building of 1902 in lower Manhattan might be offering us a glimpse of the reconciliation he was working toward between the commercial style and the City Beautiful. (Fig. 26.8) The rounded corner negotiates a triangular site of the kind engendered in Burnham plans by those forceful diagonal arteries that cut through preexisting grids. The two facades of the building are striated definitely, and the edges of the triangle are deemphasized, as if in anticipation of continuous street fronts beyond.

The object of the Chicago Plan, Burnham wrote, was to save the city from "chaos incident to rapid growth, and especially to the influx of people of many nationalities without common traditions or habits of life." Uniform order apparently meant the drilling of a uniform social order, an American order. The same reasoning was then equally applicable abroad in territories where American hegemony now extended. The city Beautiful could be a useful instrument

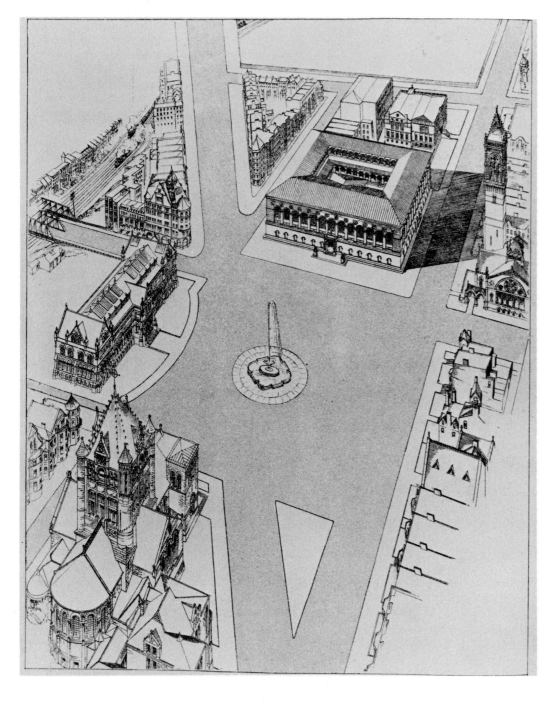

Fig. 26.3 Boston, Copley Plaza, ca. 1890; drawing from the office of McKim, Mead & White. The firm's Boston Public Library occupies the west side of the square, the major open space of the recently developed Back Bay. Across from it, at the lower left corner, stands Henry Hobson Richardson's Trinity Church, 1872–77. To the right of the Library is the New Old South Church designed by the firm of Cummings & Sears and built in 1874. All three buildings are extant. On the south side stands the Museum of Fine Arts by the firm of Sturgis and Brigham, 1871. The sketches over the fountain are part of a firm member's study for completing the square. In the late 1960s the diagonal street was removed and the square was changed to a sunken pedestrian plaza before Trinity Church.

Fig. 26.4 Boston Public Library, 1887–98, McKim, Mead & White; the main stairwell.

Fig. 26.5 Chicago, the World's Columbian Exposition, 1893; the Court of Honor looking west. In the center foreground stands *The Republic* by the sculptor Daniel Chester French; to its left, the Agriculture Building by McKim, Mead & White; and to its right, the Manufactures and Liberal Arts Building by George B. Post. In the distance is the Administration Building by Richard Morris Hunt.

for the empire that was launched with the Spanish-American War, the Panama Canal, the White Fleet, and Teddy Roosevelt's Big Stick. Burnham now supervised City Beautiful plans for Manila and the new summer capital of Baguio in the Philippines. And the same Beaux-Arts layouts were serving French colonialism in countries like Morocco and Vietnam, for those new quarters alongside native towns that kept the European population at a safe distance and afforded it the comforts of the mother country. The British, too, adopted the manner for their own commonwealth, as Edwin Lutyens' plan for New Delhi and Walter Burley Griffin's for Canberra testify up to a point.

The failing of the City Beautiful as an urban remedy for America was that it brushed aside the resistance of a democratic society to imposed solutions. The plans had no legal force. They were not buttressed by any fundamental change in land ownership or administrative control. Beyond the limits of the civic center and the parks, speculation raged on. Not surprisingly, the Burnham school of planners concentrated on the improvement of public facilities, having little to say about the business district or social needs like the housing of the poor. Their vision of the City Beautiful coincided with the Progressive Movement whose concern *was* social reform. The Movement spoke up for municipal ownership of public facilities, women's suffrage, and state control of railroads. Muckraking journalism in the meantime went about zealously exposing the rapacity of modern business

and the corruption of city government. In light of this indictment of urban-industrial America and the invidiousness of social inequities, Beaux-Arts elegance was, if not cynically dissembling, cosmetic at the very best.

By 1905 reaction to the City Beautiful had set in. There was professional debate on neighborhood units, playgrounds, and public housing. But the overriding fear of socialism, the opposition of business to anything that might promote a welfare state, blocked any advance along these lines. The only attempt at state-financed housing, that of the Massachusetts Homestead Commission of 1909, produced only twelve units at Lowell before it collapsed. The only federally sponsored housing was forced on the government by the plight of war-industry workers in World War I. The United States Housing Corporation belatedly pressed forward with a number of building programs, with some distinguished results (Fairview near Camden, New Jersey; Atlantic Heights in Portsmouth, New Hampshire; Buchman in Chester, Pennsylvania; among others), but even these were sold to private interests when the war was over.

As for zoning, a main target of progressive forces, it saw only one early formulation that could withstand challenge in the courts, and that was the New York Ordinance of 1916. Zoning had as its object the preservation of neighborhoods from the steady indiscriminate advance of apartment houses, repair shops, and small factories. The ordinance provided for three categories of use: residential, commercial, and unrestricted; for height limits that were keyed to the width of the adjoining streets; and for area, or bulk, limits having to do with the size of yards and courts. Architecturally its most far-reaching provision was for setbacks in the high-bulk districts, so that the crush of tall buildings would not deprive streets of sunlight. (Fig. 27.26)

Old City/New City
For advocates of the "City Functional," Germany was the place to learn from. In one generation, cities like Frankfurt, Cologne, and Düsseldorf had demonstrated that the common urban-industrial ills need not be thought incorrigible. The key was a fair balance between private rights, above

Fig. 26.6a Washington, D.C., ca. 1920; aerial view looking northeast. We see the monumental center of the capital as realized according to the plans of the Senate Park Commission under Daniel H. Burnham. His Union Railroad Station is at the top, and between it and the Capitol is the Senate Office Building—a fourth side will be added in the 1930s. To the left of this building stand temporary barracks and hotels for civilian government employees, structures necessitated by our entry into World War I.

Fig. 26.6b Washington, D.C., Union Railroad Station, 1903–7, Daniel H. Burnham; the interior of the waiting room in a period photo.

Fig. 26.7 Chicago, the Plan of 1909, Daniel H. Burnham; detail of the Civic Center area with the line of railway depots in the foreground (west of the river, between Canal and Clinton streets) in a drawing by Jules Guerin. The plan was begun in 1906 under the auspices of Chicago's Commercial Club.

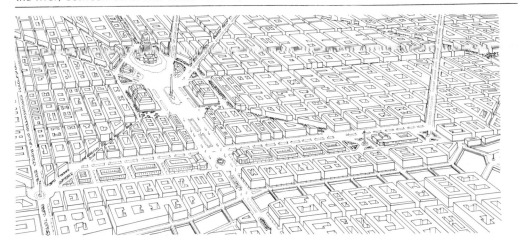

all property and its disposal, and the public good. The German position was succinctly put by the editor of the *Kommunales Jahrbuch* in 1911 to a group of visiting Americans: "The city is far more than a business affair. It is much more than a political agency. It is an agency of social welfare with unexhausted possibilities." German cities owned the street railways, the water and power systems, the docks and harbors. They ran slaughterhouses and pawnshops and exercised the traditional right of home rule—the management of public markets. Zoning was generally adhered to. Property was not only restricted in terms of use, height, and maximum land coverage, it was also taxed on its increased value every time it changed hands—the so-called "unearned increment" tax. This of course dampened speculative ardor.

Urbanization, here as everywhere, caused severe housing shortages. The cities bought land methodically, both inside and outside city limits, in order to be the master of their future development. The municipality of Ulm owned as much as 80 percent of the greater urban area. On this public land, low-rent housing was put up that would remain unaffected by the fluctuations of the free real estate market. State authorities frequently built houses for their own employees. But tax-exempt cooperative building societies also played a big part. Aided by low-interest loans from city and state, they put up housing projects for tenants of limited income. These had a range of amenities, from kindergartens, restaurants, and libraries, to a free public wash in the basement. Workers were protected against injuries, insured, and often enviably housed by their employers. The Krupp empire was exemplary in this respect.

In planning the new quarters of expanding cities, the practice was to purchase the medieval fortifications from the state, pull them down, and create an encircling parkway that would separate the old town from the new. For this, Vienna was the precedent. (Fig. 26.9) On this ring-street rose imposing public structures and monuments. Part of the land was sold to the private sector, but on condition that each building take up only a fixed portion of its site, leaving the remainder as a garden.

Suburban development beyond this point was governed by a long-term plan adopted by the city. To achieve an orderly pattern, the original lot lines were disregarded. When the new scheme was laid out, owners received a share corresponding to the size and value of their holdings. Out of this, they transferred to the city without compensation as much land as was needed for the streets, up to 40 percent of the total area. The city was then responsible for the paving and the installation of sewers and other amenities.

In one other respect Germany stood out during this period of urban upheaval. It pioneered a movement of conservation that is only now sinking in on this side of the Atlantic. It was in Germany and Austria that a strong resistance to Haussmann's urbanism first surfaced. Aesthetically, the rule of geometry—of straight boulevards with uniform frontages, vast formal squares, and monumental vistas—was challenged in an influential book called *The Art of Building Cities* by the Austrian Camillo Sitte, first published in 1889. To Sitte, Haussmannesque design was barren, dehumanizing. He spoke in favor of curving streets, intimate panoramas that could be taken in at a glance like pictures, and interlinked public spaces of dissimilar shapes. (Figs. 26.10, 15.14) These principles he derived from a close study of medieval cities, the common heritage of Central Europe.

Sitte's book underscored the appeal of the historic city core from the standpoint of sensory experience and social compatibility. Public sentiment, at the same time, resisted the manhandling of these areas for strong emotional reasons. The twisting streets and half-timbered houses and public buildings in brick, with characteristic stepped gables, stood for a way of life threatened to be swept away. With deepseated patriotic fervor, the German people resolved to go modern without sacrificing this precious record of who they had been. It was not enough to preserve isolated masterpieces of the past, churches and palaces and castles. The general physiognomy of the place was itself a monument that had to be guarded against radical change.

In accordance with this faith, stringent

Fig. 26.8 New York, the Flatiron (Fuller) Building at the junction of Broadway and Fifth Avenue at East Twenty-third Street, 1902, Daniel H. Burnham; distant view looking across Madison Square.

controls were put into effect. Building regulations at Hildesheim prescribed that in the old center "those parts of any new building which can be seen from any street or public place must be carried out in architectural forms which agree with those in use in Germany up to the middle of the seventeenth century." To maintain the general appearance of neighborhoods, new buildings had to stick to the same materials, "including those used in the roofing and the ornamentation," and to the prevailing color.

We can appreciate how utterly against the tide this was for its day when we review the massive destruction condoned by munici-palities in other countries. Florence, for example, razed a large part of its historic downtown in the 1880s and rebuilt it on a speculative grid. The excuse was always that the volume of modern traffic required proper outlets, and that the old quarters were run down, unhealthy, and conducive to vice. They were in any case of no historic interest. In his memoirs at the end of his life, Haussmann could in earnest challenge his detractors to "cite even one old monument worthy of interest, one building precious for art, curious by its memories" that his administration had allowed to be torn down, while in the same breath he could report without embarrassment that his

Fig. 26.9 Plan: Vienna in 1873, with the Ring-strasse around the medieval core well under way.

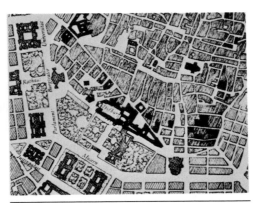

Fig. 26.10 Camillo Sitte, *Der Städtebau (City Building)*, published in 1889; a detail of the plan of central Vienna. The change of scale between the medieval fabric and the new Ringstrasse is quite evident.

1882 came the proposal for a linear city (Fig. 26.11) The author was Arturo Soria y Mata (1844–1920). He questioned the normal expansion of old cities in concentric circles around the original nucleus, proposing instead a ribbon of limited width alongside the cities, infinitely extendable, "from Cadiz to St. Petersburg, from Peking to Brussels." One or more railways would run through the axis, and at the edges of the built-up ribbon the inhabitants would be in direct communication with nature. In the mid-1890s a pilot demonstration was under way in Madrid, but of the 55 kilometers (34 miles) planned as a kind of necklace around the city, only 22 got built before the project was abandoned.

In the opening years of this century the Frenchman Tony Garnier (1869–1948), a native of Lyon, made public a set of drawings for an imaginary industrial city. (Fig. 26.12) The work, published in expanded form in 1917, is a remarkably complete visualization, down to clock towers and house types, and comes across as an amalgam of contemporary and prophetic devices. The general plan fits in the French academic tradition. But the city is placed in a parklike setting, and in this and the informal pedestrian routes Garnier is in sympathy with the English and with Sitte. The public and residential areas are clearly separated, and both are connected to the peripheral industrial cores—including a large metallurgic plant, the mines related to it, and a silk factory—and the railroad station. In line with Garnier's socialist-utopian leanings that harken back to Fourier, there are no religious structures, no jail, no court in his city. Perhaps the most notable aspect of the projected buildings is their use of reinforced concrete, a new and still controversial material at the time. This gives them a stripped, austere, flat-roofed appearance reminiscent of later modernist trends. In the thin, boldly cantilevered roof slab for the station and the planted roof terraces we recognize details that substantiate Le Corbusier's avowed indebtedness to this author of the *Cité Industrielle*.

But this vision of a modern factory town is tame, almost idyllic, compared to the strident pronouncements of a Milanese group called the Futurists who burst upon

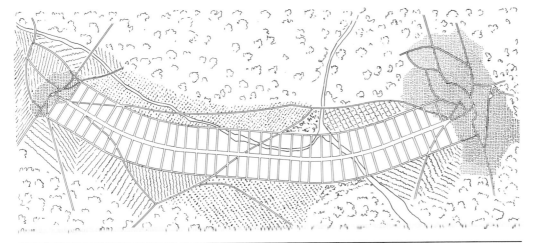

Fig. 26.11 Arturo Soria y Mata, "Linear City," first proposed in 1882. This particular application, from 1913, shows a linear city linking two older towns (at the extreme left and right).

clearances wiped out 19,722 houses in greater Paris, of which 4,349 were in the old core. So oblivious was he to the value of contexts. And the license to destroy in the name of traffic, health, and urban renewal carried into the City Beautiful movement.

Cleveland's civic center rose at the expense of a densely built up urban area, and nobody gave much thought to the relocation of all those misplaced people.

Lone ideas for coping with city growth continued to be advanced. Out of Spain in

Fig. 26.12 Tony Garnier, *Une cité industrielle, étude pour la construction des villes (An Industrial City, Study for the Building of Cities)*, 1917; two views: **(a)** a residential district, and **(b)** the railroad station.

the scene in 1909. With the enthusiasm of new converts, these youthful romantics of a country which had not known industrialization before 1900 exulted in the raw vitality of the industrial city and saw it rebuilt "like an immense and tumultuous shipyard, active, mobile and everywhere dynamic, and the modern building like a gigantic machine." Speed fascinated them; so did engineering triumphs, the power station, airplanes. To the chief architectural spokesman of the group, Antonio Sant' Elia (1888–1916), the city appeared as a multilevel network of transport services. (Fig. 26.13)

In this he was not alone of course. Subways, elevated railways, and other recent forms of metropolitan traffic had already outfaced traditional street patterns and opened up to the eyes of urban residents apocalyptic scenes. (Fig. 26.14) In 1900 the automobile was something to laugh about. By 1910 there were 54,000 automobiles in France alone, most of these in Paris. At least one planner, Eugene Hénard (1849–1923), had started thinking of their movement seriously enough to invent the rotary traffic intersection and the double-level overpass intersection. Hénard also worked on multilevel streets and rooftop landing ports for aircraft, foreseeing the arrival of the helicopter.

But all of these novelties were seen as inevitable revisions of the old cities. The Futurists, on the other hand, had no use for compromise. "Get hold of picks, axes, hammers," one of them urged, "and demolish, demolish without pity the venerated cities." Sant' Elia's *Città Nuova* projects make no reference to any pre-Futurist urban context. They depict skyscrapers with battered walls and canted buttresses, external elevator shafts that stand clear of the upper floors to which they are connected by bridges, and large illuminated skyline advertising, and these buildings are plunged deep into multiple levels of circulation that

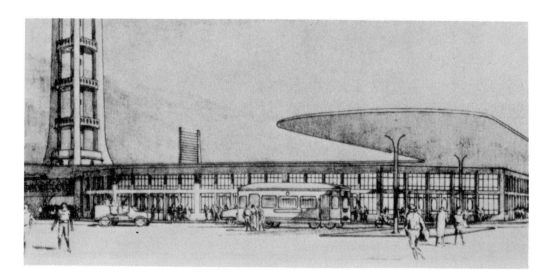

zer Howard (1850–1928) who had spent several years in Chicago in the 1870s. His small book, entitled *Tomorrow: A Peaceful Path to Real Reform*, came out in 1898, and its message was simple. The industrialized metropolis, given the prevailing economic structure, could not be disciplined. One had to try an alternative, a new kind of town, where the root causes of the muddle would be straightened out in advance. The terrible congestion of cities like London or Chicago was the result of one chief predisposing condition: the private ownership of land. This allowed for the exploitation of the center, so that values went up the nearer you were to this downtown. Coincidentally, the concentration of interests led to unlimited sprawl and to what a Howard disciple called "conurbation," or the regional running-together of urban communities. The country was driven ever backward, away from the reach of its citizens.

German municipal practice had no future in England. The cities, far from enjoying full home rule, were under the thumb of Parliament, and Parliament was the near-exclusive instrument of the land-owning noble class. Their monopoly was extensive. One-fourth of the land of the United Kingdom belonged to 1,200 persons who were getting fat on huge rent rolls. Nine estates owned most of the land on which London, with its 7 million inhabitants, was deployed. How unrealistic to expect this all-powerful clan of landlords to pass laws restricting the disposition of private land.

Howard's solution was for a limited company to acquire a tract of land in the country big enough for a community of 30,000 people. The company thereafter would hold the land but leave free buildings, services, and economic activities. Private speculation having thus been eliminated, the buildings would be spread out, open space liberally provided for, and the size of the community always kept small so that the countryside could remain within everyone's reach. (Fig. 26.15) The town would have its industries and businesses, and a ring of farms surrounding it would supply the necessary food. And so the benefits of the town—social life and public services—would be combined with those of the country—the quiet, the healthful air, greenery, fresh produce.

Fig. 26.13 Antonio Sant' Elia, project for a skyscraper, 1914.

include, rather preposterously, airplane landing strips.

Next to the City Beautiful, German social planning, and the very personal efforts of Garnier and Sant' Elia to come to terms with the technological present and celebrate it, what England had to offer to the debate of urban reform, the concept of the garden city, might well be thought to be recessive. And yet perhaps more than any other theoretical position of early twentieth-century urbanism, the garden city left its mark both in Europe and the United States.

The father of the movement was Ebene-

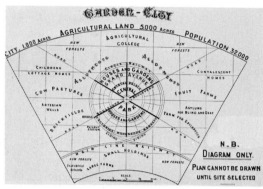

Fig. 26.15 Diagram for a garden city and its territory, 1898, Ebenezer Howard; from *Tomorrow: A Peaceful Path to Real Reform* (later *Garden Cities of Tomorrow*).

Fig. 26.14 New York, Grand Central Terminal on East Forty-second Street between Vanderbilt and Lexington avenues, 1903–13, the firm of Warren & Wetmore; sectional view. The engineer was Colonel William J. Wilgus.

The first garden city, Letchworth, was laid out in 1902 in Hertfordshire, about 130 kilometers (80 miles) from London on the main east-northeast railroad line. The scheme was prepared by the planning team of Barry Parker and Raymond Unwin. Other garden cities followed in time. They were distinguished by an elegant road net, the generous ratio of open space to building ("Twelve houses to the acre" was Parker and Unwin's motto), and a harmonious architecture that aimed to evoke something of the character of the medieval village with its cluster of neat cottages. (Fig. 26.16)

Life was family oriented. Streets were not regarded as a virtue in themselves. "The less area given over to streets," Unwin wrote, "the more chance one has of planning a nice town. To be obsessed with the idea of planning for traffic is a mistake. One rather plans to avoid all needless traffic as far as possible." In these housing patterns, what was being exorcised was the example of the congested, pollution-choked industrial

giants like Leeds and Manchester, with their back-to-back houses built around elongated courts, or yards, many of them several feet below street level; and the supposedly ameliorative new schemes, the so-called bye-law streets mandated in the Public Health Acts of 1872–75, where whatever intimacy the yards possessed vanished in rows of identical houses lining long, wide, and straight prospects—bleak descendants of that formal tradition of the tree-lined avenue with its continuous frontages. (Fig. 26.17) In the garden city, the monotony of street fronts was broken by turning the houses on their lots so that each could command the sunniest and pleasantest view. To get around the awkwardness of irregular sites, the houses were grouped around blind alleys that were frequently T-shaped. The individual variety was kept in check by the narrow repertory of architectural motifs and a common roofing material.

Critics were quick to point out that the

garden city was by its very nature a small-scale affair, hardly an answer to runaway conurbation. They complained that the prototypical plan, with a large green void in the center, negated the vitality of older city cores. For all its insistence on self-sufficiency, they said, the garden city was doomed to be the satellite of the closest metropolis and thus would turn into a mere garden suburb. And that in fact proved to be its widest application. But the original spirit did catch on in parts of the Continent, and in America, after World War I, in the greenbelt towns of the New Deal.

Toward a Twentieth-Century Architecture

The Anglo-American Bid
But we should return for a moment to the beginnings of the garden city, for we have not stressed properly that it drew strength from a deep English commitment to offset the gall of industrialization, a commitment that goes back to Ruskin and Morris. England, we should remind ourselves, was the oldest industrialized nation and the most successful. For this she had reaped a bitter crop. The "progress" that was the boast of industry brought about the despoliation of the countryside, the breakdown of the

Fig. 26.16 Letchworth (Hertfordshire, England), laid out in 1902, Barry Parker and Raymond Unwin; view of a residential street.

family, and an overall decline in human relationships. The great industrial towns in which one-half of England's population huddled were unsurpassed in the ugliness and human misery they abided. A long line of reform-minded artists and architects, from Pugin onward, had one goal in mind: to recapture the wholeness of preindustrial life. They believed in the efficacy of good design to improve mental well-being, and their sympathies were populist.

Similar sentiments were expressed by the people who were involved with the garden city movement. "A decent home and garden for every family . . . that is the irreducible minimum," Unwin insisted. If the garden city came across as rural and folksy and a bit nostalgic, regressive even, it was all those things advisedly. If it kept technology and machinism at arm's length and treasured the crafted look, it was in order to kindle traditional values and build thereby a new humanism. And this humanism had functionalist underpinnings. The spatial and locational planning, the workings of each house, were carefully studied for fitness. Convenience and health determined the forms. Simplicity came first—a clean, pleasant, timeless look.

The residential model of Letchworth was anticipated in the Eighties and Nineties. During that period a group of architects, chief among them C. F. A. Voysey (1857–1941), took up as their special province the modest cottage, and they worked out for it a sensitive nonhistoricist design of great flexibility. The idealization of the small house in the hands of this group made an important statement, both socially and aesthetically. It said that premeditated beauty need no longer be regarded as an upper-class privilege, and that beauty need not be

Fig. 26.17 Birmingham (England), Small Heath, Whitehall Road; a "bye-law street."

BROADLEYS WINDERMERE FOR A CVRRER BRIGGS ESQ

Fig. 26.18 Lake Windermere (England), the A. Currer Briggs House, called "Broadleys," 1898, Charles F. Annesley Voysey; exterior view and plans.

made legitimate through reference to historical detail.

Voysey cottages have free plans, often L-shaped. (Fig. 26.18) They allow for the serializing of related functions (scullery, kitchen, pantry, dining room, drawing room) and for maximum window space. A two-storey hall, reminiscent of the great hall of the Middle Ages, is the pivot of an otherwise horizontal frame that is emphasized by long, mullioned window bands and the overhanging eaves of a hipped slate roof with wrought-iron gutter brackets. The rendered rough-cast walls, a throwback to medieval practice, are scanned with buttresses and chimneys, and there is plenty of plain surface used to good effect. The elevation derives from the plan, unconcerned about symmetry for its own sake. Gables terminate the facade, at one end or both.

Several progressive strands came together in this residential idiom, sometimes called the Free Style. Interest in the local vernacular, you will remember, had started in the 1860s with the Queen Anne architects. But where they tended to echo the forms, the Free Style valued honesty of function and materials and paid attention to barns and stables as functional models. This insistence on what Voysey called "fitness for purpose" was common to most pioneers of modernism, along with the desire to simplify, to eliminate the superfluous. It is paralleled in the skyscrapers of the Chicago School and is captured in Sullivan's famous dictum, "Form follows function."

In England the origin of such an attitude can be traced back to William Morris and the Arts and Crafts Movement he was father to. The indebtedness of the Free Style to this source went beyond functionalism. The premise of the movement was that all objects, even the humble everyday things we use, have artistic potential. The house

in its totality could be made into art, with built-in furniture and other housewares all designed from one point of view by the same hand or sympathetic collaborators. Each person, regardless of class, was entitled to have a house that was beautiful as well as functional.

And there was, lastly, the influence of the American Shingle Style. (Fig. 25.20) That East Coast mode, which had itself been spurred by the English Queen Anne, appealed to the architects of the Free Style on a number of counts: the open plan with its free-flowing space, the breaking up of the house "box," the continuity of the external skin, the asymmetrical elevation, the ground-hugging horizontality and broad deep roof, and the two-storey stair hall, with its various landings that played against the low spread of interior spaces.

Was the Free Style popular in England? Not in the sense of general acceptance, no. On the contrary it was suspected, and the Arts and Crafts mentality as a whole, of being antiestablishment. Ideologically, it was tainted with socialism. Architecturally, taste had shifted toward the academic in the 1880s much as it had in America, and in a

Fig. 26.19 Ilkley (Yorkshire, England), the house called Heathcote, 1906, Edwin Lutyens; close-up of the garden front.

Fig. 26.20 Oak Park (Illinois), Unity Temple, 1904–6, Frank Lloyd Wright; interior.

Americans did not reject machine manufacture. Wright praised the machine as an aid that sharpened the designer's control, but he balked at standardization and mass production that deprived him of his creative birthright. New materials also had their place, again insofar as they bolstered the architect's inborn purpose. In Unity Temple at Oak Park, Wright opted for monolithic concrete. (Fig. 26.20) It was one of the earliest frank uses of this artificial stone in a public building. Yet we feel that the choice was made as much for practical considerations like cost as it was for the fact that slab construction, which is natural to concrete, enhanced Wright's developing cubist design—the flat elements criss-crossing at different levels to shape a thoroughly abstract, three dimensional space. But mostly he preferred brick or wood and plaster, and insisted on their textural expression. He believed, like his Free Style contemporaries, that an architect should design "in the nature of materials."

The Prairie School was by and large very discreet about evoking the past. In contrast to the medieval folk strains of the Free Style, it leaned toward the art of primitive people and remote lands. At one time or another there were nods to exotic sources—the Turkish pavilion at the Chicago Fair, the forms of Japan, the Indian bungalow, and the pre-Columbian architecture of Central America. But the inspiration, in Wright's case at any rate, was of the most fundamental architectural sort, with no concession to decorative recall.

Similarly, he cared little about the urgencies of the present, the social and technological problems of the modern world like industrialization, overcrowding, and the rest. He maintained that there was a core truth to life, something beyond historical circumstances, something "organic"—and that was what the American architect was duty bound to express. Architecture was for him an institutional metaphor, and the institutions he honored were timeless ones. The family remained in his mind the cornerstone of an ideal society, and the detached house was its standard. This was the only allowable center in a democracy. Work ought to be governed by a like-minded intimacy. The commercial style of his home town, Chicago, and what it stood for, had

very similar manner. There it had been McKim, the master of the Shingle Style, who had deserted first; here it was Richard Norman Shaw, the guiding light of the carefree, picturesque Queen Anne. There, with astonishing ease, the installation of the American Renaissance; here in England, the more heedful gathering of classicism that culminated in the Edwardian Grand Manner. (Fig. 26.19) From the 1880s onward, English students in growing numbers were discovering the École des Beaux-Arts. Academic design began to be taught locally in the new architecture programs of the Nineties pioneered by Liverpool and Glasgow. A British School was started in Rome, corresponding to McKim's and Burnham's initiative for an American Academy there. By the turn of the century the Arts and Crafts Movement, never quite at home in public building, was overwhelmed. This century dawned in England, as in most other European countries, with historicism firmly

in the saddle and a plucky pathfinding minority fighting to save the day for style-free modernism.

In America, the resistance was confined mostly to the Midwest—suburban Chicago, Minnesota, Iowa, Wisconsin—and to quiet native ventures in distant California. There were two towering figures: the aging and unreconciled Sullivan and his brilliant pupil Frank Lloyd Wright (1869–1959). Sullivan's career peaked with those classic recapitulations of the Chicago School skyscraper, the Wainwright Building and the Guaranty Building, and the Carson Pirie Scott department store. (Figs. 1.8, 25.35b, 25.35c) Wright and the "Prairie School" that coalesced around him were lively from 1900 to the start of World War I; then, they ground to a virtual halt.

The work of Wright and his school had close ties to England. It shared the Arts and Crafts philosophy of the Free Style architects—with one important reservation. The

no appeal for Wright. The Larkin Building (1904) in Buffalo, a rare commercial project for him, symbolized the kind of American enterprise he favored: small-town, family-controlled, paternalistic, antiunion. (Fig. 26.21) The tall glass-roofed court with the galleries around it, where the offices were located, brought together the whole community of workers, as the house embraced the family. Paradoxically, this conservative view, so divorced from the profit-mongering drive of the Chicago skyscraper, went hand in hand with the extreme modernity of structure and equipment, like the up-to-date ventilation ducts ensconced in the hollow walls of the corner towers or the steel furniture for the offices.

But Wright's greatest invention in this first phase of a long career was the prairie house. (Fig. 26.22) During a ten-year period he developed the type fully in a number of good-sized suburban houses around Chicago. They were built for the sort of individualistic client who prized reason and practicality over East Coast fashions and the prestige of European culture. If there is a precedent for the prairie house, it is the Shingle Style. But Wright takes this native American adventure much farther. The reduction of separate rooms is carried to its logical end, so that the interior flows together as one space, sparingly accented. What holds it firm is axiality: one straight line running through the main dimension of the house, and this countered by a cross-axis visible in plan or, as in the case of the Robie House of 1909, at the level of the roof mass. These axes push out into peripheral elements like verandas and open terraces, and they are riveted by the only thing of substance in that dilating volume, a massive fireplace.

The house is wedded to its flat prairie site by being mounted on a visible foundation platform and by the low cantilevered roofs hovering parallel to the ground. Wright explained that the object was to harmonize the interior with its surrounds by using "light-screens" instead of walls: "no holes cut in the walls as holes are cut in a box." Every feature of the building is clear, precise, and angular. Space is manipulated both horizontally and in stacked interpenetrations, to get a sense of ampleness out of a restricted site on a suburban street. Orna-

Fig. 26.21 Buffalo (New York), the Larkin Administration, 1904, Frank Lloyd Wright. The building no longer exists.

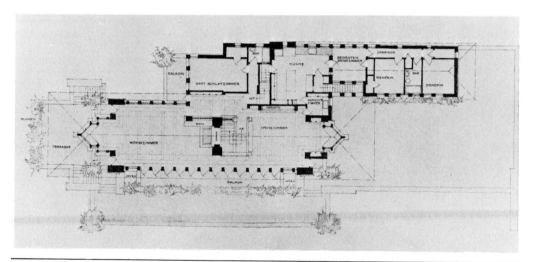

Fig. 26.22 Chicago, the Frederick C. Robie House, 1906–9, Frank Lloyd Wright: **(a)** exterior; **(b)** plan of main floor, from the 1911 Wasmuth edition of Wright's works. On the main floor, the large rooms in the front wing are the living (left) and dining (right) rooms, with a fireplace in between. A balcony runs before both of these and the living room opens onto a terrace. At the rear is a guest bedroom, the kitchen, and servants' quarters.

ment as such we do not find: only the prismatic interlocking of crisp planes and some abstract patterning, most notably in the leaded glass windows. Everything ties together; the house and its furnishings make one design, controlled totally. "Eliminate the decorator," was Wright's parting injunction.

Europe between Tradition and Revolt
Wright's work made little headway at home. But when a German publisher brought out a portfolio of his drawings and a smaller volume of photographs in 1910–11, Europe's avant-garde took to him. The progressive architects of the Old World had been tuned in to America for some time now. For them, it was the sort of virgin territory where the radical had a better chance of germinating. Well before the discovery of Wright, two other American architects, Richardson and Sullivan, had left their impress in Scandinavia, Finland, Holland, Denmark, and Germany. Anonymous industrial buildings, especially factories, coal bunkers, and grain elevators, also roused admiration. In Germany most observably, the English Arts and Crafts Movement contributed yet another ingredient of modernism. From among the recent Continental schools, the legacy of Viollet-le-Duc and his structural rationalism proved enduring to reductive minds. Lastly, there was the powerful Beaux-Arts method that affected almost everyone, traditionalist and usurper, in matters of composition.

Through such mixed inspiration, and the challenges of new materials and new industrial processes, a handful of European architects pushed the search for a modern architecture, while the great bulk of the profession held on to, and even widened, its historicist faith. How firmly entrenched this faith was one can observe from the record of the 1906 international competition for a Palace of Peace—a permanent court of arbitration with a library—to be erected at the Hague. Of the 216 entries worldwide, the overwhelming majority, including the top winners, was blatantly historicist. Many of the projects were quite eclectic, mixing the more familiar classical and medieval modes with strains from Islam and Byzantium and introducing bits of Meso-American and Mesopotamian origin

Fig. 26.23 The Hague (Netherlands), Palace of Peace, 1906; two designs submitted for an architectural competition sponsored by the American steel magnate Andrew Carnegie.
(a) The first-prize entry by L. M. Cordonnier of Lille, France.
(b) Entry by the Dutch architect Hendrik Petrus Berlage.

just then being discovered from recent excavations.

The more innovative designs were themselves simplified versions of some past style, rid of its ornamental load: among these were the fourth-ranked project by Otto Wagner (1841–1918) of Vienna and that of the Dutch Hendrik Petrus Berlage (1856–1934). But we have only to compare the first-prize design with Berlage's to see how crucial the decision was to decorate, or not to decorate. (Fig. 26.23) For the winner, the wall is a prop for sculptural elaboration; for Berlage it is the basic plane that enframes interior space. "Before all else the wall must be shown naked in all its sleek beauty and anything fixed on it must be shunned as an embarrassment," Berlage wrote at the time. A younger Viennese architect, Adolf Loos (1870–1933), put it even more categorically a few years later: "Ornament is crime." To him the decorative panoply of classicism in all its permutations was the tenure of aristocracy. Modern bourgeois culture had no business using it. The houses he built in the early twentieth century were stark white cubes of stucco with the unframed openings cut where the irregular arrangement of the internal plan, indebted to England's Free Style, called for them. (Fig. 26.24)

These three men—Wagner, Berlage, and Loos—along with Auguste Perret (1874–1954) in France and Peter Behrens (1868–1940) in Germany, have been assigned the most prominent place in the formulation of a new twentieth-century idiom. Theirs was actually a second-ditch effort after the earlier Art Nouveau, a movement in which some of them had a hand, failed to consolidate its position. During its short-lived popularity the Art Nouveau had affected young architects throughout Western Europe and shown itself in a number of national guises. It was known as Stile Liberty or Stile Flo-

Fig. 26.24 Vienna (Austria), the Steiner House, 1910, Adolf Loos.

Fig. 26.25 Brussels (Belgium), the Hôtel Van Eetvelde on Avenue Palmerson, 1895, Victor Horta; view of the salon.

reale in Italy, Modernismo in Spain, and had links with those antiestablishment flurries across the Alps called Jugendstil and Sezession. But it remained principally a decorative convention, a surface thing without the impulse to redirect architecture.

Most everyone agrees that the Art Nouveau started in Brussels in the early Nineties with Victor Horta (1861–1947), and that it aspired to that obsessive goal of modernism, freedom from the past. Its signature was a florid, sinuous line suggesting organic growth, the burgeoning of plants. Metal membering, thin and pliant as it was, served the style well, and the frank use of iron now entered domestic architecture for the first time (if we disallow the exotic precedent of Nash's Brighton Pavilion). In the salon of Horta's Hôtel Van Eetvelde in Brussels of 1895, we can observe how these supple Art Nouveau filaments swirl about like tendrils, weaving together walls, ceiling, and supports in a way that recalls the late Baroque of Bavaria. (Figs. 26.25, 21.16) In both cases, the structural and the deco-

rative live inseparably. The other reference would be to late Gothic—the skeletan élan, the transparency, the flicker of ornament. (Fig. 16.19) At the same time in the few successful sallies into public architecture— Horta's Maison du Peuple in Brussels and department stores there and in Paris—the Art Nouveau was matching the audacity of those fair buildings of metal, like the Eiffel Tower and the Gallery of Machines at the Paris fair of 1889, against which Burnham's team in Chicago would turn its back. But more commonly the style had to accept masonry and play its massiveness against the tensile wit of iron, or else cut swaying, whiplash rhythms into the stone. All this, involving as it did an endless round of individualistic, custom-made invention, did not recommend the Art Nouveau to the functionalist wing of modern architecture.

This is the place to bring up the name of the reclusive Catalan master Antoni Gaudí (1852–1926) whose buildings in and around Barcelona go the Art Nouveau one better.

Where Art Nouveau is graceful and calligraphic, Gaudí's restless curvilinearity is but one component of a passionate, bedizened world seemingly in the throes of some primal force. The entire bulk of the Casa Milá (1905–10) undulates convulsively. (Fig. 26.26) Seen from the street, it looks as if it were echoing the serrated profile of the natural landmark near Barcelona, the mountain called Montserrat, or else an ancient, sea-ravaged rock cliff. The thick stone facing in front of the steel structure is hammered and pitted. Into this eroded surface, windows are sunk with the randomness of holes. Balconies are seaweed-strewn; the two entrance courts have the sponginess of grottoes. On the rooftop we are caught in a ground swell. Stairways lead up and down erratically, and bizarre ventilators and chimneys rear menacingly against the sky.

This streak of European antirationalism did not run deep or wide. By 1910, and even earlier, the Art Nouveau and allied modes were played out, and most of their practi-

Fig. 26.26 Barcelona (Spain), the Casa Milá on the Paseo de Gracia, built for Dona Rosario Segimon de Milá, 1905–10, Antoni Gaudí. The building, popularly known as La Pedrera (the Quarry), was meant to carry a gigantic statue of the Virgin Mary on its roof.

tioners had shied away from all that organic exuberance. Individualism, the idea of architecture as personal expression, sustained itself marginally thereafter by invoking the Arts and Crafts belief in the autonomous artist and by poetizing industrial materials like concrete and glass. The programs of these Expressionist architects, as they were later called, tended to be escapist, visionary, or festive. Some seized on the inherent plasticity of concrete to mold space with the flare of imperial Rome.

Gaudí himself had ignored this material except for some of his rooftop creations, even though his architecture, and especially "Catalan" vaults and warped roofs, anticipates very recent forms in concrete construction. Most other architects, since

Fig. 26.28 Breslau (Germany), the Jahrhundert-halle (Century, or Centennial, Hall), 1913, Max Berg. The enormous building, which had a clear span of about 65 meters (213 feet), was built to commemorate the centenary of the rising against Napoleon in 1813.

Fig. 26.27 Le Raincy (France), the church of Notre Dame, 1922–24, Auguste Perret; interior view. The church was a memorial to the soldiers who fell at the battle of the Ourq, one of the most tragic battles of World War I.

the serious emergence of this artificial substance on the building scene in the 1860s, thought of it, if they thought of it at all, as a variant of post-and-beam systems, and this even after the introduction of steel reinforcement, which changed concrete from a heavy inert material akin to stone to a tough resilient one fit for very thin articulation. In the opening years of this century, Ernest Ransome (1844–1917) in the United States had developed a reinforced concrete frame like Chicago's metal frame, which was soon taken up in factory construction. In France, François Hennebique (1842–1921) had used a similar frame visibly, expressing it without embarrassment.

Perret's special distinction was to bring concrete into the mainstream and make it an acceptable alternative for the standard repertory of the architect. (Fig. 26.27) In an apartment building and a garage in Paris, and later on in the early Twenties in a church at Raincy, he perfected a system in which reinforced concrete columns or piers take the place of load-bearing partition walls. Both visually and structurally, in other words, concrete is made to behave in the ways of classical trabeated architecture.

Fig. 26.29 Cologne, the Glass House, a pavilion at the German Werkbund Exhibition of 1914, Bruno Taut; one of the outer stairways. The model factory shown in Fig. 26.31 was built for the same exhibition.

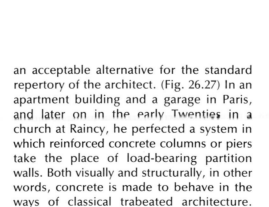

Fig. 26.30 Berlin, the turbine factory for the AEG (Allgemeine Elektrizitäts Gesellschaft), the German General Electric Company, 1908–9, Peter Behrens: **(a)** exterior; **(b)** transverse section.

Only in the work of some engineers, like the bridges of Robert Maillart (1872–1940) or the hangars of Eugène Freyssinet (1879–1962), did the suitability of the new material for arched and vaulted spans come alive. (Fig. 27.3) And now in the second decade of the century a few Expressionist essays pushed in this same direction for nonindustrial programs. Max Berg's Century Hall for the Breslau exhibition of 1913, with its giant ribbed dome on sweeping pendentive arches, is the most dramatic instance. (Fig. 26.28)

The reflective, illusory qualities of a glass architecture also attracted the odd prophet. Touched by a symbolism of rejuvenation, the poetry of a crystal-pure society, this unrealistic bent brought forth at least one masterpiece, Bruno Taut's Glass House of 1914. (Fig. 26.29) It was a gemlike round structure on three levels. Stairs of luxfer prisms rose from the entrance to a room at the top; this was enclosed by a double skin of colored glass and was surmounted by a "gothic" glass dome. From here, a second set of curving stairs descended to an intermediate room whose round wall was of translucent silver glass and stained glass panels. Its conical ceiling, made of red case glass and gilded glass tiles, had an oculus cut into it through which light from the upper room shimmered on the waters of a fountain set in the glass mosaic floor. And from this level, a water cascade strewn with glass pearls fell to a dark basement. A magic, phantasmagoric vision for an incandescent future. "It is not the crazy caprice of a poet," another architect wrote at the cataclysmic end of the Great War, "that glass architecture will bring a new culture. *It is a fact.*"

But the Expressionist's rarefied view competed against a more rational interpretation of European destiny. Its monument was the factory. Its frame of reference was heavy industry—the Krupp armament works in the Ruhr, which supplied forty nations, and the German General Electric Company, or AEG, founded in 1883, which had grown in less than twenty years into a vast

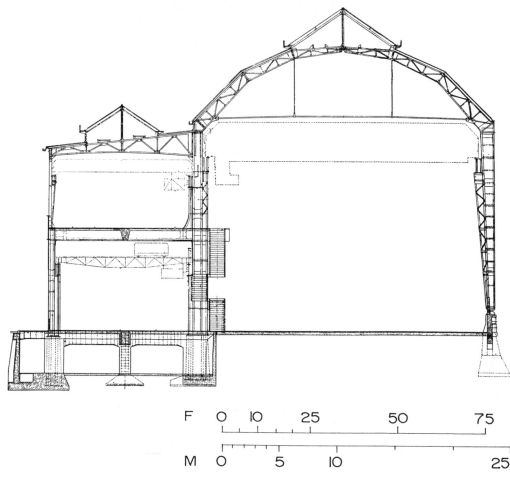

F 0 10 25 50 75

M 0 5 10 25

Fig. 26.31 Cologne, model factory, a building at the 1914 Werkbund Exhibition, Walter Gropius.

Fig. 26.32 Luban (Germany), chemical factory, 1912, Hans Poelzig.

industrial combine manufacturing a wide range of products. In 1907 the AEG appointed Behrens to be its architect and overall designer. In the same year he joined a group of independent artists and craft firms to found the Deutsche Werkbund, an association determined to combat conservative trends in design, and to grapple with the impact of mechanical production on the arts.

The group agreed on one thing: Germany was not as yet the international leader in design craft and industry; it would become so only through some fundamental change in its creative outlook. What kind of change? On this the group was ideologically divided between those, like Taut, who championed the unfettered, autochthonous genius of the artist, and those who stressed the need for *typical* high-quality design handled by large firms with the ability to turn out the products in bulk mechanically and distribute them efficiently. In architectural terms, typical design meant the creation of standard building elements, prefabricated and used generally as basic building units.

Behrens, and the younger Walter Gropius (1883–1969) who got his start with him, ventured out on a middle course. They were ready to embrace the materials and processes of industry, to recognize the inevitability of an industrial culture. But they also reaffirmed the traditional privilege of the architect to give expression to the culture through buildings that solemnized its central institutions. Behrens did just that in designing for the AEG a temple to industrial power. His turbine factory in Berlin of 1908–9 even looks like a temple, one made for machines and of machine crafted materials—concrete, metal, and glass. (Fig. 26.30) The interior of the great hall for the assembly of turbines is a long column-free space with a craneway running the full length and with provision for further swinging cranes along the side walls. The hall is flooded with light pouring in through the side walls that are glazed from a low sill right up to the cornice line, and from a double-pitched skyline over the central portion of the roof.

But externally the building is more than the straightforward statement of this functional space. The iron uprights that hold the glass in place read like the columns of a peristyle, and the corners of the facades are secured visually by strong piers of reinforced concrete constricted with iron bands to suggest rustication. Only the single-ridged roof with pediments that would have completed the temple image has been affected by the demands of the program. To give head clearance to the cranes, the roof profile is described by a three-hinged steel arch that yields a multifaceted gable close to that of a gambrel roof. It comes forward over the battered corner piers and holds the glass screen of the facade like a hanging casement.

In the Fagus shoe-last factory at Alfeld-an-der-Leine two years later, and in the model factory for the 1914 Deutsche Werkbund Exhibition at Cologne near Taut's Glass House, Gropius modified this formula of Behrens by wrapping the glass around the building, without terminal piers of masonry, and showing in these translucent corners spiral staircases. In the model factory, the staircases in their glass cages stand forward of two end pavilions with flat overhanging roofs borrowed from Wright. (Fig. 26.31)

To appreciate how distinctive this clothing of the modern industrial factory truly was, we have only to draw attention to the treatment of the same building type in the hands of the Expressionist wing of the Werkbund. Our illustration is of the chemical plant at Luban by Hans Poelzig (1869–1936), which is an exact contemporary of Gropius' Fagus Factory. (Fig. 26.32) We would be right in associating this unadorned and boldly massed brick building, with its jaunty runs of square and semicircular windows, with England's Free Style—the aesthetic of the Arts and Crafts Movement in contrast to that of the First Machine Age.

And there is yet another gloss on this predominant theme of architecture in the years before the Great War—the factory for the automobile industry in America. (Fig. 26.33) The setting for its appearance is Detroit; the unlikely hero, a conventional architect of residences and clubs, Albert Kahn (1869–1942). The automobile industry got underway in earnest with the founding of the Olds Motor Works in 1899 and the Ford Motor Company in 1903. And what set its architecture apart from the European experience we have just discussed was that the

Fig. 26.33 Detroit (Michigan), the Ford Motor Company Eagle Plant on the Rouge River, 1917, Albert Kahn; the interior of one of five aisles in a photograph of 1918 when the plant was used to build antisubmarine boats. The railroad tracks for the transport of parts and materials, the clerestory lighting, and the steel truss roof are clearly visible.

client, like the client of Chicago's commercial tower earlier, was less interested in a culturally prestigious sheath than the direct meeting of his operational wants. For all its symbolic canonization by men like Behrens and Gropius, the European factory stuck with an old-fashioned layout. It served a fixed production system where operations were performed separately in different sections of the plant, and the assembling was done in large sheds like Behrens' great hall for the AEG turbine factory. The typical multistorey factory of the nineteenth century was still being built; even in Gropius' Fagus factory some units, the workshop block for instance, have multiple floors.

The Detroit phenomenon had three predisposing demands. The factory had to be built for assembly-line operations. It had to be built fast. And it had to be able to undergo indefinite expansion painlessly. These were the things Kahn, and the team of specialists he worked with, tackled in a series of early factories. Speed eventually gave the edge to steel framing, since unlike concrete it required no formwork and no curing time. The prospect of growth at short notice mitigated against a closed, finished shape. It was not for Kahn, then, to worry about elegant corners of matching end pavilions, the temple paradigm. Operationally what was called for was a wide-span, linear format. The standard solution settled on between architect and manufacturer featured a long, one-storey, roof-lit space built on a repetitive cellular unit of steel that could be prolonged horizontally as fast as increased production made it necessary.

Kahn's pioneering plant on this model was the one he designed in 1906 for Geo. N. Pierce Company in Buffalo, New York. That was a small affair in retrospect, over a 6-hectare (15-acre) tract. Two years later the Ford Plant at Highland Park near Detroit for the new Model T took up an area of 92 hectares (230 acres) along Woodland Avenue. The original unit was a four-storey building some 270 meters (885 feet) long, divided into three wide aisles. Then, at the plant on the Rouge River in 1918, Ford made the commitment to a single-storey structure.

America was now a belligerent in the Great War, and Ford proposed to manufacture here, on this vast tract near his home at Fair Lane, the Eagle submarine. Major rail lines passed alongside the plant, and the river linked it with the ports of the Great Lakes. In record time a structure of about 530 meters (1740 feet) had been put up—five immense aisles with clerestory or monitor lighting, of which two carried continuous tracks for the transport of parts and materials, while along the other three, the boats moved through the various stages of production until they emerged complete at the south end and were moved on a transfer table to a launching slip. Ford had introduced the powered moving assembly line at Highland Park back in 1913. But he did not invent the idea—it had been used be-

fore in the meat-packing industry, for example. Here he applied it on an entirely new scale for efficient, large volume production: thereby he revolutionized once and for all the working habits both of people and machines.

The greedy spread of the Ford plant on the Rouge River in the Twenties will remind us that industrial building, for one, did very well in postwar America. So did the commercial tower. Ford's cheap motor cars ushered in the golden age of the suburb, and suburban houses kept many architects happily busy. There were also movie theaters to do, those palaces of the new mass entertainment that let loose a flood of architectural fantasy. All told, except for a short period of inflation brought on by the war, America enjoyed a lively building boom from 1921 until the crash of 1929 and the calamity of the Great Depression.

The situation in Europe was different. The "guns of August" stopped almost all construction for the duration of the conflict. Modernist experiments retreated to the privacy of the sketchbook, while the only real-life target remaining to them were war graves. The younger architects hit the trenches. Some, like Sant' Elia died fighting; others lived to learn that the technology of the First Machine Age served evil as efficiently and dispassionately as it did the humane plans of a progressive society.

When the carnage finally ended, the task of rebuilding was beyond the power of individuals. The long pause in production, the war damage, and the upward swing of population growth precipitated an acute housing crisis. States and public bodies had to assume the responsibility of sheltering Europe. Whole residential districts and large housing estates were now the principal challenge for the practicing architect.

In the defeated countries, Austria and Germany, the modernists moved easily into positions of power within a ruinous social system where the former ruling classes and the designers who catered to them stood discredited. In revolutionary Russia the abstract, history-free avant-garde came up against the didactic needs of the new state, while the disparity of a machine-age architecture which sought its reason in advanced technology, and a backward, primitive building industry, proved irreconcilable. Lenin himself reached the point, before his death in 1924, where modernism seemed antisocial to him, an art for art's sake. The contest of traditionalists and modernists, never innocent of politics, now was turned into an ideological tool under the regimes of Mussolini, Stalin, and Hitler.

Here now, to the twenty-five years between the two world wars, we must take our story.

Further Reading

R. Banham, *A Concrete Atlantis: U.S. Industrial Building and European Modern Architecture, 1900–1925* (Cambridge, Mass.: MIT Press, 1986).

———, *Theory and Design in the First Machine Age*, 2nd ed. (Cambridge, Mass.: MIT Press, 1980).

L. Benevolo, *History of Modern Architecture*, vol. 1, trans. H. J. Landry (Cambridge, Mass.: MIT Press, 1971).

The Brooklyn Museum, *The American Renaissance, 1876–1917* (New York: Brooklyn Museum, 1979).

W. Creese, *The Search for Environment* (New Haven: Yale University Press, 1966).

K. Frampton, *Modern Architecture: A Critical History* (New York: Oxford University Press, 1980).

———, *Modern Architecture, 1851–1945* (New York: Rizzoli, 1983).

T. S. Hines, *Burnham of Chicago, Architect and Planner* (New York: Oxford University Press, 1974).

W. Jordy, *American Buildings and Their Architects: Progressive and Academic Ideals at the Turn*

of the Twentieth Century, vol. III (Garden City, N.Y.: Doubleday, 1976).

V. Scully, Jr., *Frank Lloyd Wright* (New York: Braziller, 1960).

———, *Modern Architecture*, rev. ed. (New York: Braziller, 1974).

P. Selz and M. Constantine, eds., *Art Nouveau*, rev. ed. (New York: Museum of Modern Art, 1975).

R. G. Wilson, *McKim, Mead & White* (New York: Rizzoli, 1983).

Lenoir City (Tennessee), Fort Loudoun Dam, 1940–43, Tennessee Valley
Authority; view while under construction.

27

ARCHITECTURE AND THE STATE: INTERWAR YEARS

The 1920s

The Great War left behind a shattered world. The stable international economy built up in the preceding one hundred years, during which Europe had not known a major war, lay in shambles. Currencies fluctuated wildly. There was a return to protective tariffs and other tactics of self-seeking nationalism. And yet paradoxically, one could see in the dominant socialist mood the desire for universal brotherhood as the war-incited advance in communications dimmed borders and collapsed distances.

Territorial patterns had changed radically. The dismantled czarist nation lost Finland, Poland, and the Baltic states. Three other empires were undone. Ottoman sway, on the decline since the eighteenth century, was rolled back behind the line that now defines modern Turkey. A republic was proclaimed there in 1923, and a new capital started building in the heart of Asia Minor, at Ankara. The Austro-Hungarian empire spawned three nations: the republic of Austria, Czechoslovakia, and Hungary. As for imperial Germany, things could have been worse. Reconstituted as a republic, she managed to hold on to four-fifths of her territory during the peace settlements; her population of 65 million was still the largest in Europe.

The victors had their rewards of course. France swallowed chunks of Africa, won the mandate of Syria, and retained her Indochinese possessions. In countries like Morocco and Vietnam, French administrators and architect-planners found an opportunity to create new settlements free of the restrictions of law, landownership, and custom that held them back at home. They either laid out new quarters alongside the indigenous towns or planted highly visible governmental structures in the old centers. Both the architecture, much of it in the academic tradition of the École des Beaux-Arts, and the geometric street schemes of grids and Baroque diagonals broadcast the presumed cultural superiority of the colonialists.

There were whole new cities, too. England reasserted its hold on the Indian subcontinent with the construction of a new capital near Delhi. Construction began just before the outbreak of war in Europe and continued into the 1930s. New Delhi covered an area of 32 square miles and encompassed some twenty villages. The architect in charge, Edwin Luytens (1869–1944), worked to formulate an Anglo-Indian style, best exemplified in the immense Government House, the viceroy's official residence. (Fig. 27.1) The massive Secretariats flanking the residence formed a set of monumental propylea to the Central Vista, modeled on the Mall in Washington, D.C. (Fig. 26.6a) Despite the gestures toward India's architectural past, the symbolism was uniquely British colonial, and the buildings were fully within the fold of Beaux-Arts classicism.

Construction and Reform

At home, the tasks of architects and planners were formidable. Their scene of operation was now quite different. The defeat of the old regimes had deprived them of high patronage. Private commissions declined generally, and more and more the building industry came to depend on corporate clients, mostly state agencies and public bodies of one sort or another. Enlightened municipalities in Holland and Germany engaged gifted modernists and gave them extensive powers. Willem Marinus Dudok (1884–1974) worked for Hilversum, a fast-growing town about 25 kilometers (15.5 miles) southeast of Amsterdam. Here he applied the same bold idiom to public baths, schools, residences, and the prismatically composed town hall, which opened out to its surroundings with lawns, pools, and gardens. (Fig. 27.2) The more radical Ernst May (1886–1970) was director of all municipal construction at Frankfurt from 1924 to 1930, where he supervised a vast housing program. Bruno Taut (1880–1938) and Martin Wagner (1885–1957) did the same for Berlin.

Dutch and German cities were able, by and large, to plan for and control their development. Elsewhere the picture was less tidy. Overcrowding and urban sprawl kept pace. The migration of rural folk into towns had picked up during the war in response to the expansion of war industries. After the war, boundary revisions

Fig. 27.1 New Delhi (India), the Viceroy's House (now Rashtrapati Bhavan), 1912–31, Edwin Lutyens. The deep cornices that served as sun and rain shades, the sentry boxes with hats and elephants, and the use of red sandstone as a building material are Indian elements.

and other political disturbances forced many people to move, overloading urban centers not ready to absorb this sudden influx of refugees. Vienna, with a population of 2 million, is a case in point. The streetscape had endured elevated trains, streetcar tracks, subways and their stations. Now buses and an increasing number of automobiles were added—and suburbs proliferated. In the major European metropolises like Paris, Brussels, Hamburg, and Manchester, suburbs and planned extensions pushed out toward surrounding towns, merging into huge conurbations. Regional planning was imperative, but not very popular.

The architect, along with every other specialist, had to heed these changed circumstances. There were, for one thing, some new materials, as well as a wider acceptance of concrete, steel, and glass. The standardization of building units and their prefabrication made some progress, notably in housing. But the conception of design as a creative response to an individual architectural problem proved too deep-seated to allow for total mechanization. Each building, even within the same type, was still dealt with as a complex and specific program. Its production could therefore not be reduced to the mere assembly of ready-made parts. Traditional materials persisted, and as Mies van der Rohe put it in 1924, "The nature of the building process will not change so long as we employ essentially the same building materials, for they require hand labor." What is more, the Great Depression with which the decade closed brought on severe unemployment that countered demand for labor-saving construction techniques.

Fig. 27.2 Hilversum (Netherlands), the town hall, 1926–28, Willem M. Dudok.

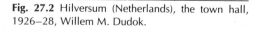

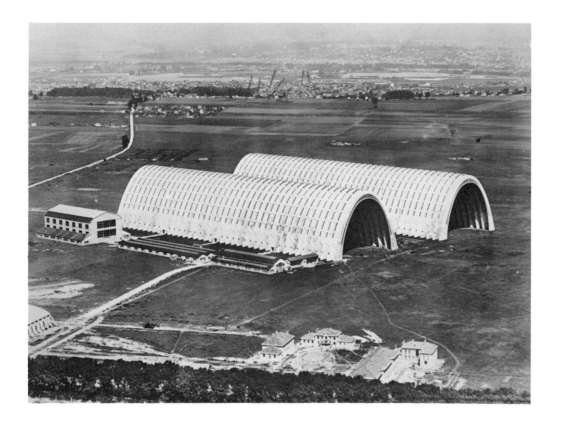

Fig. 27.3 Orly (near Paris, France), airship hangers, 1916–24, Eugène Freyssinet: **(a)** general view; **(b)** structural detail during construction.

There were also the new programmatic demands of the postwar era. The environment of industry required attention. Everywhere industrial plants needed updating. Aviation was young, but an architecture of airports and airship hangars was already on the way. At Orly, near Paris, two strikingly novel hangars went up between 1916 and 1924 to house large dirigibles. Their design, by Eugène Freyssinet, inspired a string of successors. Structurally, he pioneered the so-called space frame, which was to be applied with mounting confidence to a number of building types.

The enormously high structure of the Orly hangars has a parabolic profile. (Fig. 27.3) The walls and vaults are made of elliptical arches over which is stretched a thin skin strengthened by ribs. The whole is an assemblage of prefabricated units of reinforced concrete—a continuous, three-dimensional, load-resistant framework that encloses a space 62.5 meters (205 feet) high and 300 meters (984 feet) long. The inescapable comparison is with the train sheds and exhibition halls of the nineteenth century (Fig. 23.32), but where they used metal frames, this century's vaulted prodigies, starting at Orly, would use reinforced concrete often deployed on the eggshell principle.

The automobile was soon having its own considerable impact on the built environment. Its use changed road design; its storage, the design of the house. Car factories, in which America held the lead, gained prominence. The Fiat works outside Turin, made of reinforced concrete, is as fitting a monument of the 1920s in Europe as any other. (Fig. 27.4) A 24-meter (79-foot) wide track for trial runs on the roof of the factory building celebrates that modern love of speed and mechanical energy that the Futurists had rhapsodized before the war: "A roaring racing car, rattling along like a machine gun, is more beautiful than the winged victory of Samothrace." The other Futurist fascination, the power plant, also took monumental shape now as dependence

Fig. 27.4 Turin (Italy), the Fiat–Lingotto automobile factory, 1916–23, Giacomo Matté-Trucco; aerial close-up view.

on electricity increased steadily. The most famous effort of the decade in this direction was the hydroelectric power station on the new Dnieper dam in Russia, the Dneproges, begun in 1927 as part of a gigantic industrial complex.

But housing came before all else: it is the biggest architectural story of postwar Europe. The shortage was acute. It was not so much the result of war damage—only France had really suffered on this score, having lost 35,000 dwellings along with a large part of her industrial plants. The loss was due to the pause in building activity during the long period of hostilities, the unremitting urban crush, and the rigid system of rent controls that stifled private initiative, at least in Germany.

Even before the war, housing in Europe had taken on the status of a public utility. To a significant degree, the land, construction, and management of low- and medium-cost dwellings were removed from the speculative market. The responsibility was shouldered by municipal councils, cooperatives, and other non-profit societies, and these began to set new standards of decency. They controlled the form and quality of what was built and set the rent for the units. But now the crisis was much more severe, both in terms of numbers and in actual cost. Land crowding and, of course, the aggravated economy brusquely pushed prices upward. Both materials and labor became dearer. Even without any real improvement in quality, the minimal house of 1920 cost a lot more than it did before the war. Massive public aid had to be the answer.

Public subsidies went to labor and consumer groups that were not concerned with a favorable return on investment. This contrasts with the practice in America where subsidies, when tried out at all, took the form of tax breaks on new construction—which ended up fattening the speculators. True "social housing" was exceptional, produced by philanthropic groups or union-sponsored cooperatives and restricted to a few cities, most notably New York. When the federal government became seriously involved with housing about 1932, it did so not as a matter of social policy, but to stem unemployment.

What is more, it insisted on tying housing programs to slum clearance.

Europe had an overall view of the matter that went beyond slum clearance or aid to the poor. In one decade almost 5 million dwelling units were built with public assistance throughout western Europe. In some countries, this amounted to as much as 70 percent of all new housing. An organized working class was responsible for a considerable portion of this total. During the nineteenth century, workers had been housed fitfully through the impetus of philanthropic societies or paternalistic industrialists. Now the societies were founded by the workers themselves or, rather, by that upper layer that corresponded to the traditional artisan class.

Single-family houses accounted for about one-half of all production in Europe as a whole. That was England's preference, and the commonest types there were semidetached and terrace houses. The largest project was Beacontree in Essex, with 25,000 dwellings. On the Continent, the rows of attached houses tended to be longer and the density higher. The norm in any case was not the single-family house, but the apartment.

The units were arranged in a number of ways. The courtyard scheme remained popular, but the small closed courts of the nineteenth century gave way to more spacious, sunnier courts, sometimes open at one end or at the corners. The general plan might be H-, U-, or even T-shaped. Socialist Vienna, one of the cities that is at the forefront of this postwar housing story, has many examples in which uniform apartment blocks are arranged around long courts that serve as gardens and playgrounds. The Karl Marx Hof is a well-known one. (Fig. 27.5) Multistorey tower houses with elevators were still quite uncommon.

In Germany, on the other hand, we frequently encounter the so-called Zeilenbau formation. (Fig. 27.6) Here the ratio-

Fig. 27.6 Frankfurt (Germany), the Am Lindenbaum housing district, 1930, Walter Gropius. This development of nearly two hundred housing units is arranged in parallel low-rise slabs, a format championed by Modernists for its ease of construction and the apartments' reduced exposure to traffic. The rows typically are separated by a green strip for pedestrians, with the blank ends of the rows facing the street.

nale was to eliminate the court altogether, in favor of parallel rows of apartment blocks running approximately north–south and spaced sufficiently apart to get the maximum exposure to the sun. The blocks are single files of apartments, never more than two rooms deep, stacked up on three to five storeys. They turn their narrow ends toward a main traffic street, and between the blocks all cross-traffic is barred. In effect, this arrangement rejects both the traditional city block and the street-defining role of buildings.

Socially, the clearest sense of community derived from the occupational bond in workers' estates. But there were also apartment houses for the elderly and for single women, as well as youth hostels. All of this housing made use, in varying degrees, of public facilities like day nurseries, laundries, libraries, sometimes a post office and shops, even theaters.

A lot of thought was given to the layout of the units and the irreducible minimum of comfort and health. The grouping of the apartments evolved into several flexible schemes. The main distinction was between two groupings: a *linear grouping,* with the apartments flanking a corridor or arrayed along one side of a gallery, and a *direct-access grouping,* with one to four apartments per landing arranged in distinct stacks around an entry and stair hall. (Fig. 27.7)

The style of this European housing varied quite a bit. Much of what was built reworked traditional designs, and the common use of brick helped the new go along with what was there. In Amsterdam, a romantic streak surfaced that took delight in fantasy and arresting form and used them to convey the uniqueness of the place. The precise identity of shape turned each housing complex into a working-class monument—which could be said to fulfill the Marxist doctrine of raising class consciousness. From 1913 onward, the work of Michel de Klerk (1884–1923) for the Eigen Haard housing society was an early high point. (Fig. 27.8) Multipaned windows and ornament rendered in native brick and tile—fragments of an ancestral past—gave the new residential district a dimension of time. These details also reduced the sense of anonymity and made clear that collective units

sheltered individual families. Fanciful as this housing was, it respected the street and contributed to the public presence of the city.

Traditionalists and Modernists
In a way de Klerk belongs to that antirationalist wave we have called Expressionism, which reached for a romantic, soulful symbolization of reality. This remained an interesting undercurrent through the 1920s, mostly as paper architecture. In Germany, at least one architect, Eric Mendelsohn (1887–1953), kept it alive with some buildings that celebrated dynamic form—a streamlined surface continuity that exploited curves and rounded corners. The tamer side of Mendelsohn's output is represented in a series of department stores. But the excitement of his free, fluid lines comes across best in the Ein-

stein observatory tower at Potsdam and in the brilliant preliminary sketches for his buildings. (Fig. 27.9)

The more austere rationalist wing of modernism came through the war convinced that the new order could not be built on dreams, on individual inspiration, on associative recall. Functionalism was its own sufficient beauty. They championed prismatic blocks with flat roofs and a coat of unadorned white stucco, sleekly machined industrial details, efficient interior planning, and up-to-the-minute equipment. In truth, structure was often downplayed, so that the thin flat walls would be unbroken by the structural cage; not much attention was given to site, climate and insulation; and the machined look was painstakingly simulated in handicraft methods.

So there was some dissemblance in this

Fig. 27.7 Apartment types of the 1920s; plans: **(a)** the gallery type as illustrated by an apartment house in St. Gall, Switzerland, designed by H. Hauser; **(b)** the direct-access type as illustrated by the Siemens- stadt housing complex in Berlin of 1929–30, designed by Walter Gropius; two different arrangements are shown in our drawing.

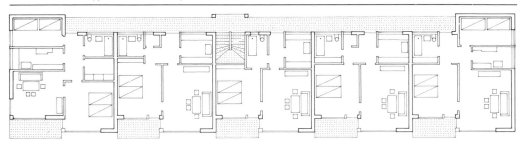

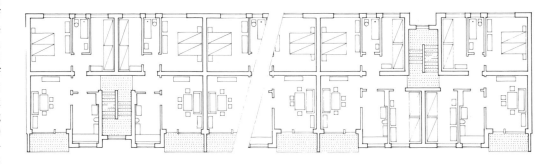

Fig. 27.8 Amsterdam (Netherlands), housing on Hembrugstraat for the Eigen Haard (Our Own Hearth) Society, 1917–20, Michel de Klerk.

rationalist rhetoric. And certainly not everyone in the rationalist confraternity was sold on the idea that the task of design is preordained by sociological and technological determinants. Certainly not Le Corbusier (1887–1965), who held to proportional rules and a very formal, abstract code of composition, not entirely divorced in its basic behavior from Beaux-Arts precepts or broader classical thought. And not Mies van der Rohe (1886–1969), who saw the architect, foremost of all, as an apolitical artist concerned with beauty and Platonic universals.

Nevertheless, whatever their level of commitment to social redress, the architects in this rationalist wing succeeded in creating a distinctive language of design by the decade's end and in finding sponsors in several European countries, most

visibly in Weimar Germany, as well as Russia and the United States. This language had a number of components, reaching back to early experiments with modernism that were cut short by the war. We spoke of some of them in the last chapter: the free plan; new building techniques based on materials like concrete and steel; the visual precedent of Loos's stark white cubes; the functional tradition of the architecture of industry; the influence of Wright and art movements like Cubism that redefined "reality"—what the house should look like on the street, or everyday objects in a painting—by taking it apart, so to speak, and reassembling it to show its constructional truth rather than an image of illusion.

The new postwar synthesis espoused several key attitudes. Architecture was

seen primarily as volume and not mass. So the stress was on the continuous, unmodulated wall surface—long ribbon windows without frames, cut right into the wall plane, horizontally or vertically disposed; flush joints; flat roofs. Corners were not elaborated. Technically, the argument went, materials like steel and reinforced concrete had rendered conventional construction—and with it cornices, pitched roofs, and emphatic corners—obsolete. There would be no applied ornament anywhere, inside or out. Regularity, rather than enforced axial symmetry, would govern the overall design; the phrase sometimes used was "balanced asymmetry." And a machine aesthetic prevailed, underscored by lustrous, machine-made fixtures and the machine analogue. A house was a machine for living, Le Cor-

Fig. 27.9 Potsdam (Germany), the observatory in the Astro-Physical Institute known as the Einstein Tower, 1919–21, Eric Mendelsohn; preliminary sketch by the architect, 1919.

busier provocatively declared in 1923 in his *Towards A New Architecture*, which has proved the most influential book on architecture in this century.

The rhetoric boiled down to two fundamental articles of faith.

First, modernist architecture was antihistoricist, the very antithesis of those "old and rotting buildings that form our snailshell," as Le Corbusier put it. There were two angles to this. One was physical. What was put up must look fresh and immaculate, patina-proof, in no way affecting a natural, mellow look. The other was a spiritual newness from which both picturesque evocativeness and specific historical reference were astringently scrubbed off.

Second, modernist architecture was antimonumental. It rejected durable materials and the concept of permanence. Buildings would be given no firm base; they would sit right on the ground, lightweight volumes appearing to float or else lifted on stilts *(pilotis)* that would free the ground underneath them. Here is Le Corbusier again: "A house will no longer be this solidly-built thing which sets out to defy time and decay . . . it will be a tool as the motor-car is becoming a tool."

The movement was international. Its exponents associated with each other, formed multinational lobbies, published journals, wrote books and pamphlets, and arranged exhibitions in which they showed the public in built form what they had in mind. The leaders were master propagandists. They sought confrontations

with the establishment, especially in the context of world's fairs and design competitions. In three such competitions—for the *Chicago Tribune* building, the Russian palace of labor, and the headquarters for the League of Nations in Geneva—they submitted projects that forced the issue of modernism. Protagonists in four countries—Holland, Germany, Russia, and France—guided the development and dissemination of this International Style, as it came to be called.

In Holland, the De Stijl group was loosely organized around a magazine of the same name, the first issue of which appeared in October 1917. The group, including the painter Piet Mondrian (1872–1944) and the architect J. J. P. Oud (1890–1963), propounded a very theoretical position called Neoplasticism. It had to do with representing a pure reality, antinatural and irreducible. This was to be done through a universal style (*de stijl* means "the style" in Dutch) based on flat rectangular planes of primary color and unequal size relating to each other in a pattern of asymmetrical, dynamic balance.

The group's output was limited. Besides the paintings of Mondrian, there were some interiors, some furniture, and a handful of buildings, among them Gerrit Rietveld's Schröder House at Utrecht (1924) whose interlocking cubic volumes moved Neoplasticism into the third dimension. (Fig. 27.10) But De Stijl's influence was considerable, especially among the avant-garde of Germany and Russia. It was the presence of Theo van Doesburg (1883–1931), a key De Stijl member who was on the faculty of the Bauhaus, that stemmed the initial Expressionist leanings of this revolutionary design school.

The Bauhaus was founded by Walter Gropius and others in 1919 at Weimar as the counterclaim to academic training in the arts. The students were to be trained as both designers and craftsmen and imbued with the democratic collectivity of teamwork. Use, not cultural content or meaning, was to be their guide, and forms were to be derived from what the program and the industrial methods of production dictated.

The new campus at Dessau, where the school moved in 1924, is the built mani-

festo of the Bauhaus system. (Fig. 27.11) In the main building we see the radically simplified cubic masses relieved only by balconies and projecting stairs, connected by bridges, the asymmetrical grouping, the emphasis on clinical, machine-pure surfaces and accessories. In a series of houses for the masters, Gropius could dramatize his belief that the design process must be predicated on mass production.

But for all the insistence on a functional, machine-based, and classless outlook, the new architecture in Germany could be idealized into an abstract manner with no thought of the sociopolitical doctrine that charged its apologists and inflamed its detractors. The Dessau Bauhaus and the vast housing estates of Taut and May were its masterpieces. But so was Mies van der Rohe's German pavilion for the World's Fair of 1929 at Barcelona, a work of rarefied purity. (Fig. 27.12)

Eight freestanding cruciform columns supported the entire weight of the building's sweeping roof slab. Structurally independent of this system, asymmetrically

Fig. 27.10 Armchair, 1917, Gerrit Rietveld. (Museum of Modern Art, New York)

Fig. 27.11 Dessau (Germany), the Bauhaus, 1925–26, Walter Gropius.

placed panes of polished green marble, tinted glass, and translucent onyx sliced through the space. Complemented by reflecting pools, these walls dissolved both material and spatial clarity. Here and in his earlier projects for glass skyscrapers, Mies van der Rohe was replacing the visual dependence of architecture on effects of light and shadow by playing with reflections.

In Russia, too, modernists fell into camps. They squared off against each other in public debate and in Vkhutemas, a school of architecture organized in 1920 along lines parallel to the Bauhaus. "The measure of architecture is architecture," went the motto of one camp. They believed in an unfettered experimentalism of form. A rival camp had a problem-solving orientation. The architect's main mission, in their view, was to share in the common task of achieving the transforma-

tion of society promised by the October Revolution. They were keen on standardization, user interviews, and ideological prompting. They worked on new building programs that would consolidate the social order of communism. These they referred to as "social condensers."

The factory was one of them. The workers' club was another. The term "workers' club" is actually misleading; "cultural center" would be more descriptive. They were places for rest and indoctrination: "workshops for the transformation of men," a contemporary architect called them. (Fig. 27.13)

The most radical social condenser was supercollectivist housing. The intent was to release women from domestic work by providing in the complex "factory kitchens," common dining rooms, child care, and other shared services. (Fig. 27.14) But with a few exceptional examples, such

purpose-built collectives never made it off the drawing board. Until Stalin's rise in the late 1920s, new construction had low priority. Resources were strained, and the construction industry was extremely backward. Even if it had been accepted by the regime and the public, the paper architecture of the young modernists would have been out of the question technically.

After the revolution, the private ownership of land and rented property was abolished. The workers were installed in town houses and apartments once occupied by the bourgeoisie. The debate over whether new towns should be made up of communal houses around industrial plants or whether city life should be forever renounced in favor of a Russia dotted with individual homes of lightweight structure had little bearing on real events. Only in the second half of the decade did new construction take off, and the modernists

Fig. 27.12 Barcelona (Spain), the German pavilion in the International Exposition of 1929, Mies van der Rohe: **(a)** interior; **(b)** ground plan. The chrome and leather chairs, also by the architect, became known as "Barcelona" chairs.

were given a share. Progressive architecture was enjoying its day. Russian modernists were busy with student hostels and industrial compounds, and Ernst May of Germany was designing major parts of the giant industrial city of Magnitogorsk.

But the climate was changing, and not only in Russia. In Germany the reasons for official displeasure were different, but the result was the same. Once installed, the Nazi administration closed down the Bauhaus and attacked it leaders as subversives. Much more mildly but unmistakably, in Italy too, Mussolini's regime withdrew its support of young modernists after 1934 and embraced the rhetorical classicism of Stalin and Hitler.

Under Stalin, Vkhutemas folded, and in 1932, when the competition for the Palace of the Soviets was being judged, the Central Committee of the Communist Party opted for monumentality and a classical style. This was the doctrine of socialist realism, and it brought to an end the brief experimental phase of architecture in the Soviet Union.

We can appreciate the reactionary force of socialist realism if we look at Le Corbusier's scheme for the Palace of the Soviets and compare it with the one the government elected to build. (Fig. 27.15) Le Corbusier was one of several leading European modernists who took part in the competition. The building was proposed in celebration of the achievements of the first Five-Year Plan. It was to go up facing the Kremlin, on the opposite bank of the Moskva, and to be used for political meetings and congresses.

Le Corbusier's scheme for the Palace of the Soviets also illustrates how far the International Style itself had come in the 1920s. The immense curved facades of the two fan-shaped meeting halls, the ramps and platforms between them capable of holding 50,000 participants, and

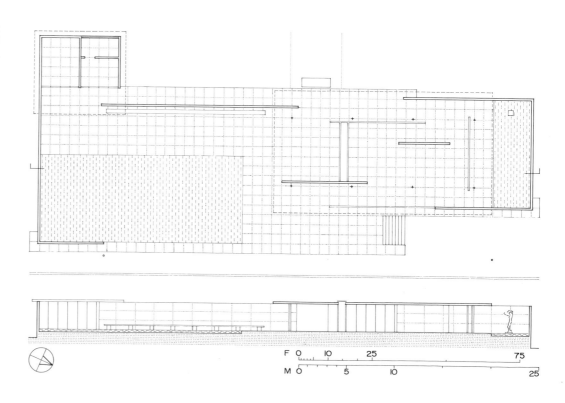

Fig. 27.13 Moscow (Russia), workers' club for the Rusakov factory, 1927–28, Konstantin Melnikov. Workers' clubs were formulated in part as surrogate churches for an atheist society. Events held at the club were modeled on religious ceremonies, including "red weddings" and an "Octobering" ceremony for infants to replace the ritual of baptism. Melnikov's club featured six meeting halls, three of which cantilevered out from the top floor, giving the building its distinctive form. All six were designed to be combined into one large hall through the adjustment of interior partitions.

27.14 Moscow, housing for the People's Commissariat of Finance, or Narkomfin, 1928–30, Moisei Ginzburg and I. Milinis. Built for the officials of Narkomfin, this complex of fifty apartments allowed residents to cook in their own kitchen or to dine in a communal cafeteria connected to the apartment block by a bridge corridor.

the Freyssinet-inspired roofing system of the larger hall with its colossal girders, all this drama and sculptural energy outdistances, if it does not altogether contradict, the prior achievement of the International Style, including Le Corbusier's own share in it.

In truth, Le Corbusier was always, as here, a step or two ahead of his confreres. Since 1915 when he crystalized a modernist idea of the time in his so-called Domino system, this Swiss-born, French master had proved the most protean among avant-garde architects. From the start he was interested in reaching trenchant model solutions with general application. The Dom-ino system, for example, was offered as a prototypical housing solution. (Fig. 27.16) The repeatable unit consisted of two horizontal slabs of concrete supported by columns and connected by stairs. The owner would be expected to purchase prefabricated windows and wall sections and fill in this minimal frame. The columns being recessed with respect to the outer walls, the facade would be structurally independent and could thus be composed freely so as to admit abundant natural light.

This free facade, along with the free plan, pilotis, the roof garden, and elongated windows, became Le Corbusier's syntax. Until about 1930 he applied it to schemes of mass housing, as well as the series of private villas that culminated in the superbly assured Villa Savoye at Poissy. (Fig. 27.17) Controlled by a ground plan that is a perfect square, the villa stands on the familiar Corbusian stilts, in the middle of a field overlooking the Seine valley, with something of the abstract clarity of a Greek temple. A two-staged ramp sweeps up into the raised living area, which is arranged along two sides of the square and then onto a rooftop solarium open to the sky.

More prophetic were Le Corbusier's urbanistic proposals. Characteristically, he took on the city in its totality and not at the level of piecemeal interventions. The historic European town he considered beyond repair. In his alternative model, the urban landscape was one of freestanding skyscrapers lifted above the ground—tall office towers for the business center

Fig. 27.15a Le Corbusier, competition project for the Palace of the Soviets in Moscow, 1932; model.

Fig. 27.15b Moscow, project for the Palace of the Soviets, 1934 revision of the winning design by Boris Iofan; model.

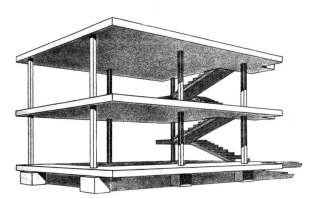

Fig. 27.16 Le Corbusier, Maison Dom-ino, 1915: **(a)** structural skeleton of each unit; **(b)** units arranged in a series, with cladding. The word "Dom-ino" was meant to evoke *domus,* the Latin word for "house," as well as the stacking and standardized look of dominoes. Le Corbusier developed the idea originally in response to the war damage in Flanders; the unit was seen as a housing kit to aid the rapid reconstruction of the area.

Fig. 27.17 Poissy (France), the Villa Savoye, 1928–29, Le Corbusier.

whose supremacy Le Corbusier forcefully reaffirmed—and the residential towers farther out, which passed from being cruciform in the early proposals to being Y-shaped and finally to massive rectangular slabs poised aloft on sturdy pilotis. (Fig. 27.18) A great multilevel transportation spine ran in a straight line through the city and continued beyond its limits as a superhighway. The traditional street with its shopping facilities moved indoors into the residential slabs, and recreation found its place on their roofs. All around and underneath these behemoths was open space and greenery.

This ideal metropolis of modern capitalism is now, of course, commonplace. We are familiar with its towers representing the might of multinational corporations. But for their time, these were astounding inventions. So, too, Le Corbusier's Palace of the Soviets, both as efficient machine and representational symbol, prefigured by two decades the mood of sculptural monumentality that was to seduce modern architecture in the 1950s and 1960s.

The Other Side

Le Corbusier did not get to America until 1935. By then the modern European idiom had made its tentative debut here in some West Coast houses and in at least one public building, the offices of the Philadelphia Savings Fund Society (PSFS), which was designed by George Howe and William Lescaze. Less purely than in these designs, it had started to seep into general practice, fostering crossbred designs of particular originality. But that was not what Le Corbusier cared about most. Like other modernists, he had long been in love with America's silos and skyscrapers. Manhattan was the nearest thing to his vision of the metropolis of tomorrow. "The United States is the adolescent of the contemporary world," he said in an interview in 1932, "and New York is her expression of enthusiasm, juvenility, boldness, enterprise, pride and vanity. New York stands on the brink of the world like a hero."

Jazz-Age America
Until the market crash of October 1929, the 1920s in America had witnessed one

Fig. 27.18 Le Corbusier, urban project entitled "A Contemporary City for Three Million People" exhibited in Paris in 1922. We can see the straight axis of the main transportation spine and the cruciform office towers in the center of town.

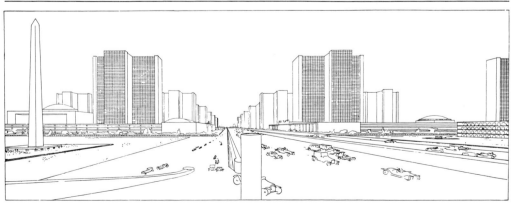

of the biggest building booms in history. It was the time of Art Deco skyscrapers, of fancy suburban homes, of Chinese and Aztec movie theaters. (Fig. 27.19) It was the time when the mass-produced motor car came of age, and with the construction of the first cross-country highway in 1927, the most profound transformation of the American landscape got seriously under way.

There were already more than 20 million automobiles in America. The heyday of the railroads was gone. The West and Southwest thought now almost exclusively in terms of private transportation. Hard-surface, all-weather roads stretched out in all directions at the start of a sensational epic of engineering and design. The new freedom from tracks transfigured urban life as well. Traffic signals were accepted as a standard element of street furniture. All the while, the cluster of cars aggravated downtown congestion, fueling the antiurban sentiment that is never absent from the American mind. The common belief that suburbs are the right place to raise a family was now reinforced; the means to heed it was at hand.

Suburbs no longer had to be strung along rail lines but could sprout anywhere at all. And they could be any size they chose to be. Railroad suburbs had been forced to huddle around the station. They spread out only within walking distance of it, since there was no other way for the arriving commuter to get home. The car canceled this dependency. Huge tracts could now be developed speculatively at the edge of town. Exclusive suburbs for the well-to-do gathered loosely around country clubs and polo grounds, gobbled up green space, and lounged listlessly.

This escapism was reflected in the architecture. Everywhere the preference was for romantic evocations of the past— Moorish villas in Florida, Spanish revival (or "mission") houses in California, neo-Colonial resurrections of Pennsylvania Dutch and Georgian on the East Coast. (Fig. 27.20) We should stress two things about this golden age of the suburb. First, an often deadly physical conformity. For all the love of personalized design and the rich choice of styles, subdivisions typically repeated a single house model planted invariably in unfenced open lots.

Fig. 27.19 Hollywood (California), Grauman's Chinese Theater, 1927, Meyer and Holler.

Second, the matching homogeneity of the population. Tight planning rules subscribed to by developers, real estate brokers, and financing agencies blocked the admission of minority groups like Asians, Blacks, and Jews into suburbs.

While suburbs sprawled complacently, apartment living was gaining acceptance in cities the size of Chicago or New York. Here the skyscraper found one of its specialized uses. Park Avenue in New York was lined with fairly homogenous Neo-Renaissance skyscraper-palaces in brick and limestone. This was New York's answer to the Parisian boulevard, but for all its elegance and Beaux-Arts regularity, the premises were poorly lit and ventilated. A partial answer was garden apartments, U- or H-shaped blocks graced with an interior garden court and set back from the property line to allow for some landscaping in front. In both instances, the units varied from small efficiency apartments that made do with a "kitchenette," to spa-cious duplex or two-floor apartments with private stairways.

But the main role of the skyscraper remained commercial. In the 1920s, the type went national. It symbolized capitalistic success, and most self-respecting cities built at least one, even when the economic justification for it was not there. The structural system had been worked out for the most part by 1900, but the boldly increasing height and the cost and logistics of construction in restricted urban sites did spark several responses. Fixtures and some exterior elements were standardized. New implements thoroughly rejuvenated construction habits. Steam shovels, hydraulic jacks, pile drivers, mechanical cranes, pneumatic hammers, concrete mixers—these were all in use before World War II.

On-site organization advanced in concert. The assembly of the Empire State Building amazed contemporaries. Steel framing members came by train from Pitts-

Fig. 27.20. San Francisco (California), Sea Cliff, 1925, Allen and Co., developer: **(a)** street facades; **(b)** rear elevation as seen from service alley. Historical styles ranging from Spanish revival to an abbreviated Gothic are arrayed side by side in the street facades of this speculative suburban development. Consumer nostalgia gives way to cost-cutting functionalism on the back alley of the same row.

burgh hours after fabrication and were used without delay to obviate storage. Powerful derricks were set up on specially cantilevered platforms. Elevators carried crews and lighter materials where they were needed, and to save time lunch was prepared on the spot at portable kitchens. The workforce counted 3,500 men in all. And the building rose at an average of five and a half storeys a week. The whole enterprise of creating the world's tallest building, from groundbreaking to the moving in of tenants, took no more than a year.

For a corporate client, the skyscraper held two rather conflicting promises—intensive occupancy in a revenue-rich downtown site and the advertising value of visibility on the skyline. One argued for a dense building that could take up all of the land at its disposal; the other pushed toward a tall, strikingly capped building that could stand clear of its neighbors. Since 1900, the freestanding tower with some kind of assertive crown had gained in popularity as one solution to the massing of the skyscraper. This is sometimes called the campanile type. (Fig. 27.21) In an attempt to have it both ways, another solution combined a massive block with a multistoried tower that soared beyond it. This design had the further benefit of admitting more light and air both at street level and for the building's occupants.

The street-level environment was now a major problem in New York. The irresponsible exploitation of space for offices was turning streets into sunless canyons and creating inhuman working conditions within. In part to stop this abuse of overbuilding, the city passed the intricate Zoning Ordinance of 1916 we spoke of in the last chapter. For commercial architecture, it prescribed that after rising sheer from the pavement for a certain height—this depending on the size of the lot and the width of the street—the building had to be pulled back in a series of setbacks. (Fig. 27.22) Only then could a spire be lifted as high as the owner wished, provided each floor's area did not exceed about 25 percent of the total area of the lot.

This restrictive legislation was a tonic for skyscraper design. It meant that the massing, and therefore the profile, of tall buildings could be manipulated for dramatic effect. In predetermining the overall shape as a system of setbacks, the ordinance made it easy to abandon the habit of thinking of the skyscraper as affinitive to the classical column, with a distinctive ground-storey treatment for the base, the uniform office floors for the shaft, and the attic topped by a projecting cornice for the capital. The cornice might be given up altogether or replaced by all manner of fanciful crowning features. Stepped elevations now recalled the ziggurat of old or the craggy, tasseled silhouettes of Gothic cathedrals. The shelflike recessions could be made over as roof terraces or penthouses.

In one spectacular instance, that of Rockefeller Center, the ordinance was brilliantly exploited in a program of group design. (Fig. 27.23) Over three of New York's elongated city blocks, between Fifth and Sixth Avenues, a committee of managers and designers planned several skyscraper slabs of different height around a T-shaped plaza. A superb civic space, this plaza started as shopping promenade and sloped down into a sunken court, which in winter was converted to an ice-skating rink. The long, thin rectangular buildings made possible shallow office space that had maximum contact with window areas.

"Semimodern" is the word sometimes used to describe the external ordering of the Rockefeller Center slabs—semimodern in that the concept at work here stands somewhere between the traditional styles and the "true" modern of the International Style. But in the last quarter of the nineteenth century, as we saw, the first generation of skyscrapers that went up in Chi-

Fig. 27.21 Chicago (Illinois), skyscrapers at the Michigan Avenue Bridge: on the left, the Wrigley Building, 1919–21, Graham, Anderson, Probst and White; on the right, the Chicago Tribune Tower, 1925, Howells and Hood. Hailed as the city's new gateway, these towers and their adjoining traffic plaza were celebrated in their day as an example of Beaux-Arts planning applied to the new building types and traffic patterns of the modern city.

Fig. 27.22 Hugh Ferris, "Evolution of the Set-Back Building—Fourth Stage," a schematic skyscraper design that refers to New York's 1916 zoning restriction on building height and volume, 1929 (from *The Metropolis of Tomorrow*). The form is derived by first sketching the maximum mass permissible for the site under the zoning law. The building rises vertically on its lot lines to a height twice the width of the surrounding streets, above which it slopes inward at specified angles. The original mass is then cut into with "light courts," and the sloping forms are translated into rectangular shapes. The number of setbacks is then reduced in order to make construction more economical. We illustrate the result. Ferriss wrote: "This is not intended of course as a finished and habitable building; it still awaits articulation at the hands of the individual designer; but it may be taken as a practical, basic form for large buildings erected under this type of zoning law."

Fig. 27.23 New York, Rockefeller Center, the firm of Reinhard & Hofmeister, with Harvey Wiley Cor-bett and Raymond Hood; aerial view of 1948, looking west.

cago had settled on a plain ahistorical aesthetic, something that came out of the frank expression of function and the structural frame. This precocious American modernism had fallen victim to the seductive Beaux-Arts formality of the World's Fair of 1893. The tall building went back to wearing historicist garb. This was, broadly speaking, of two sorts. With the City Beautiful movement in full swing, the classical look was to be expected. The Gothic skyscraper, on the other hand, caught on after the popular success of New York's Woolworth Building and was apotheosized in Chicago itself, home of that spartan Commercial Style of Root and Sullivan, in the winning design of the *Tribune* competition of 1922, which was subsequently built on Michigan Avenue. (Fig. 27.21) Since Gothic in its time had stressed the vertical members of its structural skeleton, it was thought a fitting medium with which to convey the expressive height of skyscrapers. The preferred variety was Flemish Late Gothic.

There was little appetite as yet among business giants for the European brand of modernism. For one thing, the International Style had produced no tall buildings of the kind they sought, and what it did produce favored horizontality and a thin exterior skin that emphasized interior volume at the expense of mass. These qualities did not satisfy the corporate image of substantialness, and the open volumes were at odds with the requisite partitioning of rented office space.

Modernity, not modernism, is what corporations plumped for—something less pure, flashier, more popular. And this they got. A decorative craze seized skyscrapers in the 1920s; it was a crowd-pleasing, indiscriminate playfulness that borrowed loosely from a variety of sources, from Cubism and Expressionism, from Mayan forms and Frank Lloyd Wright, from the machine aesthetic of progressive European designers and the 1925 Paris fair, the Exposition des Arts Décoratifs et Industriels, from which the style gets its customary name—Art Deco. In a short time a

Fig. 27.24 New York, Chanin Building, 1927–30, firm of Sloan and Robertson; detail of exterior.

whole repertory of angular and curvilinear forms was developed, none of it related to historical styles. (Figs. 27.24, 27.25) Rendered in metal, terra-cotta, or some other bright veneer, this ornament was woven into the exterior walls, spread out in entrances, lobbies, and elevator areas, piled up into frothy confections for rooftop crestings. But by the early 1930s, the taste for streamlined shapes becomes more noticeable, inspired by the steamlining in transport design. Nautical details from the new luxury liners—curved walls, circular windows or windows with rounded corners, handrails of tubular metal—pass into urban architecture.

Rejection and Renewal
And then there was Wright. He had always been something of an embarrassment to party-line European modernism. Its indebtedness to his early work had been freely acknowledged. But he would have nothing to do with the movement's belligerent socialism. The tensions of industrial society were not his, nor was his faith hitched to the miraculous epiphanies of a machine age. High technology had its place, and so did traditional materials and methods. So Wright continued to speak obscurely of an organic architecture, one that combined modern means with the forms of nature and their growth. He spoke of "shelter not only as a quality of space but of spirit."

Fig. 27.25 New York, Art Deco skyline: on the left, the RCA Victor building, Cross & Cross, 1931; at the center, the Chrysler building, William Van Allen, 1928–30; on the right, a tower of the Waldorf Astoria Hotel, Schulze & Weaver, 1930–31.

Fig. 27.26 Bear Run (Pennsylvania), the Edgar J. Kaufmann house called "Falling Water," 1936–38, Frank Lloyd Wright.

room was meant to be "as inspiring a place to work in," Wright said, "as any cathedral ever was to worship in."

New Deal America

This celebration of the American capitalist enterprise was a little incongruous in the context of the Great Depression. The opening years of the 1930s had plunged the nation into serious trouble. There were farmers' uprisings and hunger marches. More than a thousand home mortgages were foreclosed every day. Cities were going bankrupt. Thirteen million people were out of work. The dispossessed squatted where they could—under bridges, in dumps, in railway yards, and in empty lots. In the big cities hundreds of them lived in improvised shantytowns called Hoovervilles, their shacks made of boxes and scrap metal.

The crisis in the building industry ran deep. In the boom period before the economic breakup of 1929, construction expenses nationally had reached the impressive sum of $12 billion a year, of which three-quarters were spent by the private sector. In 1933 that figure was only $3 billion. As Secretary of the Interior Harold Ickes put it at the time, the situation "showed, on the one hand, relief rolls crowded with the names of building-trade workers, and yards and warehouses filled with lumber, steel and cement; and, on the other, communities with unsanitary housing, inadequate sewer systems and unsatisfactory roads."

With the coming to power of Franklin Delano Roosevelt, the federal government undertook to resolve "this odd conjunction of idle labor and unused material with a desperate need for further public works"—to quote Ickes again. A huge public works program was set in motion that speedily converted the normative finance capitalism of the nation to cooperative capitalism, changing the face of the public landscape everywhere in large ways and small. Teams of thousands were put to work under the new alphabet agencies—the WPA (Work Projects Administration) and PWA (Public Works Administration) and CCC (Civilian Conservation Corps)—on a vast assortment of projects: clearing streams and dredging rivers, ter-

After the fallow 1920s, Wright returned in a typical burst of self-regeneration. In one of two astounding buildings of the 1930s, the house called Falling Water at Bear Run, Pennsylvania, he sends out freefloating platforms audaciously over a small waterfall and anchors them in the natural rock. (Fig. 27.26) Something of the prairie house is here still, and we might also detect a grudging recognition of the International Style in the interlocking geometry of the planes and the flat, textureless surface of the main shelves. But the house is thoroughly fused with its site, and inside, the rough stone walls and the flagged floors are of an elemental ruggedness.

In urban situations the architecture turns inward; Wright, who heeds nature, is in no mood to cater to other people's work. For the central office space of the Johnson Wax Administration Building in Racine, Wisconsin (1936–37), he creates a kind of subaqueous environment by sealing the walls against the day. Externally, right angles melt away in streamlined curvilinearities. (Fig. 27.27a) Inside the Great Workroom, light falls from a ceiling of Pyrex tubing fitted into the interstices of broad disks of concrete supported by hollow "lilypad columns." (Fig. 27.27b) Below, workers sit in Wrightdesigned chairs, at Wright-designed desks with swinging tills instead of drawers. The

Fig. 27.27 Racine (Wisconsin), the Johnson Wax Building, 1936–37, Frank Lloyd Wright: **(a)** exterior; **(b)** interior.

racing land, installing utility systems, and building highways, camps for migrant workers, playgrounds, and athletic fields. From 1933 to 1939, the PWA alone was responsible for 70 percent of the country's new school buildings, 65 percent of its courthouses, city halls, and sewage plants, and 35 percent of its hospitals and public health facilities.

Since the purpose of all this federal activity was to provide employment, speed and efficiency were of no great importance. There was a retreat to primitive technology and crafts methods. The fabrication of the Empire State Building had its flipside in the horse-drawn plows used by WPA road construction crews in the Midwest; the sleek, streamlined machine forms of chrome and formica had their counterpart in the massive handcrafted appearance of New Deal gatehouses and park benches.

Some of the New Deal heritage is still breathtaking in its scope and timeless in its honesty of execution. It is hard not to be impressed by the dams of the Tennessee Valley Authority (TVA) that turned the Tennessee River into a chain of inland lakes. The TVA had a regional structure unhampered by state lines or departmental jurisdictions and so could orchestrate a comprehensive program of rehabilitation that embraced navigation projects, soil conservation, energy resources, land planning, housing, and, with the creation of the model town of Norris, even social planning. Within the first decade of its operation, the TVA replenished the land, started rural industries, and made the region into a major producer of hydroelectric power. And all this was managed in a way that preserved a fine ecological balance.

The biggest construction feat was the system of twenty-one low and high dams over 1,300 kilometers (700 miles) of waterway from the South Appalachians to the Ohio. Built of earth and concrete, the dams turned smooth-sloping faces downstream. Along the top ran a roadway with pedestrian observation points; it was accented by the gantry cranes that operated the sluice gates. (Fig. 27.28) To many, the sight conjured up the majesty of Egyptian pyramids.

Here, it seemed, was a new kind of architecture, modern without being self-consciously modernist, dignified and consequential without the crutch of historical rhetoric. It was an accessible style, as befitted a program that courted public approval. It eschewed the intractable machine-laundered aesthetic of the International Style and yet was able in its own direct functionalism to project what European modernists denied themselves—the symbolic presence of monumentality.

In institutional architecture, this sym-

Fig. 27.28 Powerhouse and gantry of the Kentucky Dam, built by the Tennessee Valley Authority 1938–44, Roland A. Wank, chief architect. This is the largest of the TVA's main river dams.

bolism was even more pressing. Here, if we exempt colleges that heavily favored Gothic, and hospitals and army quarters where regional modes often asserted themselves, faith in the representational powers of the classical remained undiminished. But the question, as always, was, "What kind of classical?" Federal patronage supported two varieties, and they were both on display in Washington. The capital was now the scene of an extensive new building campaign that was advertised as the completion of L'Enfant's plan in its updated Beaux-Arts format of Burnham and his colleagues. And so in a sense it was, except for the elephantine scale commanded by a governmental apparatus that had grown beyond all prior expectation.

One variety was the full-dress classicism of the new Supreme Court Building, the Jefferson Memorial, the National Gallery of Art, and the thickset bureaucratic spread called the Federal Triangle between Pennsylvania Avenue and the Mall. (Fig. 27.29) In these fustian piles of masonry larded with muscle-bound statuary and pious maxims, the recall of traditional imagery was affected both through familiar types—the Pantheon, the buildings of the Place Vendôme in Paris—and the formal syntax of classical architecture. The other variety has been referred to as "starved classicism." (Fig. 27.30) It worked with large expanses of blank wall and rows of shallow unframed window openings. Ornament was simplified into angular accents that receded into the masonry, and all other sculptural featuring, the use of columns included, was held down to a minimum.

Fig. 27.31 Nürnberg (Germany), Zeppelinfeld, 1936, Albert Speer; oblique view.

rationale for what it did. The trumpeting of nationwide physical fitness was one common trait. It explains the outpouring of gymnastic halls and stadiums. Mussolini's urban renewal projects that brought terrible destruction to the historic cities of Italy were as warmly justified in terms of jobs as were the activities of FDR's letter agencies. The rural idyll promoted by many New Deal programs was a popular theme among the dictatorships of the right. This going back to the soil was authenticated through rustic, folk forms. The medievalizing houses of German workers' settlements with their patriotically pitched roofs were meant to be as Nazi as Albert Speer's Party Congress buildings at Nürnberg. (Fig. 27.32)

On the subject of the metropolis, the reasoning was rather tortured. The Soviets rejected decentralization and argued that rural sprawl engendered a socially incohesive and economically wasteful structure. For Fascists and Nazis alike, the modern industrial cities had been destructive of family values and a corrupting influence on a wholesome, fertile race. Mussolini's two-pronged policy involved the thinning out of major urban cores, which his slum-clearance projects did a fair job of accomplishing, and the establishment of new communal agricultural centers geared to the revitalization of productive land. Unadvertised in this move to the countryside, which was equally strong in Germany, was the fear that densely built-up working-class districts within the fabric of the big cities would lead to political unrest.

But if the Duce and the Führer dreaded the big city for its undisciplined social ferment, they were also in need of it, its throngs and frame, to stage celebrations of their rule. The object was to claim the old cities in the name of the regime by pruning out of them undesirable elements, carving into them theaters for programmed mass demonstrations and political events, and building on a scale and magnificence that would prove the comparative worth of the present against the stony testimonials of past glories, native and foreign. All this recalled Napoleon's reign. The grand tradition of urbanism, from the Baroque to the City Beautiful,

The Language of Power

This public architecture of America, uneasy as the thought might be for those who believe that what we build is what we are, looks very much like the public architecture of the 1930s in Hitler's Germany, Mussolini's Italy, and Stalin's Russia. It is in fact a widely current official style that has left its heavy imprint from Madrid and Paris to Rio de Janeiro and Tokyo. Once again, as so often in the past, a convention of forms serves as a receptacle into which states can pour their very different ideologies.

Classical architecture had two distinct advantages: recognition and universality. It was the most familiar of architectural conventions, and it had the ability to transcend narrow symbolism, to mean different things to different users. Most European nations had a classical episode in their architectural past they could point to in defense of this latest revival. Russia

had St. Petersburg, Germany the Neoclassical legacy of Schinkel and his contemporaries, Italy, of course, could claim to be the keeper of the source, one-half of it at least, through the long ancient career of Rome. For all of them the issue was the expression of power, an architecture that would project order, stability, grandeur, enduringness. It was the failure of the International Style to communicate on that level that ultimately disqualified it in the public realm. Regimes, especially authoritarian ones like Franco's or Hitler's, wanted a monumentality that would be both modern and eternal. (Fig. 27.31) So the Nazi architects, for example, would boast of having affected "a harmonious correlation between Hellenic serenity and the austere simplicity of modern functional architecture."

We should not oversimplify matters. Although a general community of forms and concerns prevailed, each country had its own way of going about things, its own

Fig. 27.32 Aachen (Germany), a housing development of the 1930s.

furnished the physical model. And here, there was no disagreement between right and left. So Mussolini, like a latter-day Haussmann, would destroy an entire residential sector of downtown Rome to drive a broad processional avenue in a straight line that began at his Palazzo Venezia balcony and ran through the hastily unearthed complex of the imperial forums to the Colosseum. So Hitler projected a new center for Berlin along an axis that would run from a colossal Arch of Triumph to the Great Hall designed to be the biggest building in the world, with a dome sixteen times the size of St. Peter's. So, too, the 1935 plan for Moscow would feature a monumental axis of some 20 kilometers (12 miles), stretching from Red Square to the Lenin Hills.

It is in such ceremonial urbanism and similar ideologically loaded settings like party headquarters, universities, state museums, and memorials that the official classicism took over. The Doric mode was preferred in Germany; to Hitler it was "the expression of the New Order." Vast, cold, spartan exteriors drew life from the trappings of a quasi-religious nationalism—the swastikas and flag standards and Nazi eagles—set aquiver in the nighttime mass rallies with searchlights and torches.

The Italian specimens of this sort of superarchitecture come late and are in some measure no doubt inspired by the Third Reich, especially after Mussolini's growing involvement with his transalpine ally. More typical in Fascist buildings is a style that derives partly from a generalized Mediterranean vernacular and partly from that Late Antique architecture we spoke about in Chapter 11 whose plain, noncolumnar aesthetic was now becoming known through the excavations at Ostia and ancient Roman colonies in North Africa. (Figs. 27.33, 11.11) The ingredients of this style are primary geometric shapes, largely unadorned, flat unfeatured walls into which are cut unmolded arches or semidomed niches, shallow running bands that are the simple straight-edged

abstraction of proper classical stringcourses, semicylindrical corner towers. With the temple-front motif relegated to doorways and niches only, and the almost total absence of the column and its derivatives either as load-bearing or modulating elements, this Fascist architecture has a very ambiguous scale. It deprives itself of the varied play of light available to most classical styles and stresses instead the stark drama of broad, straight-edged shadows.

In the Soviet Union, classicism had Lenin's blessing. He had never condoned a rupture with the past in matters of art, and the theoreticians of socialist realism could point to the beauty he saw in czarist St. Petersburg. (Fig. 23.19) The Soviet gloss on Russian imperial tradition projected its ensemble design across entire cities. Streets were to be a continuous uniform composition, the paradigm being Moscow's reconstructed Gorky Street (1936–39), the "celebratory highway of the capital." (Fig. 27.34) A new curtain of neo-Renaissance frontages containing apartments and shops defined the channel. This was both the route of mass pageants and the privileged domain of that army of managers charged with coordinating the

Fig. 27.33 Rome (Italy), Palace of Italian Civilization (later the Palace of Labor), 1938–42, Giovianni Guerrini, Ernesto La Padula, and Mario Romano. The building is part of the Esposizione Universale di Roma (EUR), built to commemorate the Fascist regime's twentieth anniversary with a world exhibition and to give Rome a new center rivaling the greatness of the historic city.

Fig. 27.34 Moscow, Blocks A and B on Tverskaya (formerly Gorky) Street, 1937–39, Arkady Mordvinov. These apartment buildings, within sight of the Kremlin, were part of a plan to create a new "celebratory highway" to accommodate mass pageants and parades. Although designed in the neo-Renaissance style popular during the Stalin era, modern techniques like fast-track construction and prefabricated panels were employed.

Further Reading

L. Benevolo, *History of Modern Architecture*, vol. 2, trans. H. J. Landry (Cambridge, Mass.: MIT Press, 1971).

D. P. Doordan, *Building Modern Italy: Italian Architecture, 1914–1936* (New York: Princeton Architectural Press, 1988).

A. Ikonnikov, *Russian Architecture of the Soviet Period* (Moscow: Raduga, 1988).

C. Jencks, *Modern Movements in Architecture* (Garden City, N.Y.: Anchor Press, 1973).

W. Jordy, *American Buildings and Their Architects: The Impact of European Modernism in the Mid-Twentieth Century*, vol. 4 (Garden City, N.Y.: Doubleday, 1972).

S. Kostof, *Third Rome: 1870–1950, Traffic and Glory* (Berkeley, Calif.: University Art Museum, 1973).

C. H. Krinsky, *Rockefeller Center* (New York: Oxford University Press, 1978).

B. M. Lane, *Architecture and Politics in Germany, 1918–1945* (Cambridge, Mass.: Harvard University Press, 1968).

Le Corbusier (Charles Édouard Jeanneret), *Towards a New Architecture*, trans. F. Etchells (London: Architectural Press, 1952).

T. R. Metcalf, *An Imperial Vision: Indian Architecture and Britain's Raj* (Berkeley: University of California Press, 1989).

G. Naylor, *The Bauhaus Reassessed* (New York: Dutton, 1985).

C. Robinson and R. H. Bletter, *Skyscraper Style: Art Deco New York* (New York: Oxford University Press, 1975).

S. von Moos, *Le Corbusier: Elements of a Synthesis* (Cambridge, Mass.: MIT Press, 1979).

A. Whittick, *European Architecture in the 20th Century* (Aylesbury, England: Hill Books, 1974).

W. de Wit, ed., *The Amsterdam School: Dutch Expressionist Architecture, 1915–1930* (Cambridge, Mass.: MIT Press, 1983).

G. Wright, *Building the Dream: A Social History of Housing in America* (New York: Pantheon Books, 1981)

————, *Politics of Design in French Colonial Urbanism* (Chicago: University of Chicago Press, 1991).

formidable machinery of a centrally planned economy.

It was in the communist bloc that the official manner of the 1930s wrote its longest chapter. It reigned unchallenged until 1955 when Nikita Khrushchev, the new ruler of the Kremlin and the architect of de-Stalinization, attacked socialist realism as an instance of Stalinist excess. He faulted it as being wasteful, inflated, and in bad taste. Now came the rush back to modernism, which Russia itself had once helped launch internationally.

In the West, the triumph of modernism was assured with the cataclysmic end of World War II. No democracy could now abide an architecture that had showcased the regimes of the fiendish Hitler and the blustering Mussolini. The break with historicist design was final. Or so it seemed at the time. Perhaps because of this the vindicated masters of the International Style, in their hour of success, took to worrying publicly about their failure to recognize the popular need for celebratory buildings, for monuments. Their chief apologist Sigfried Giedion wrote in 1943, at the height of the war:

Monuments are the expression of man's highest cultural needs. They have to satisfy the eternal demand of the people for the translation of their collective force into symbols. . . . The people want the buildings that represent their social and community life to give more than functional fulfillment.

And so the movement that had lived through one war to proclaim a sentiment-free, antimonumental architecture weathered another to learn that institutional attachment, memory, and pride of place are tangible human urges that rationalism cannot shut away. What we are, in the end, is not all we have been or want to be.

La Jolla (California), Jonas Salk Institute for Biological Studies, 1956–65, Louis I. Kahn;
view across the court toward the ocean.

28

THE ENDS OF MODERNISM

Within the scope of this book, the fifty years since World War II constitute the briefest of episodes. But time slows down as we reach the days we have lived through. Our involvement turns personal and more intense. We are conscious of being witness to the making of history. Flooded by information too recent to digest, our powers of discrimination are taxed. What is enduring? Which are mere flashes in the pan? Where are we headed?

There is no room in such unsettled waters for the cocksure or prophetic. We are confused. The best start is to observe and describe what has been happening: let stories overlap and contradictions go unreconciled. This is the way to come to terms with our confusion and so consign these times to the embrace of history, where we too will find a measure of understanding.

Reconstruction

It is best to begin this summary with the end of World War II. Never in the past had such thoroughgoing destruction of the built environment been countenanced in such a short time. Never had there been such a global need to rebuild. Need we rehearse the terrible statistics? Poland: the loss of 20 percent of its population and 60 percent of that of Warsaw. Germany: 333 square kilometers of urban fabric gone, including 22 square kilometers in Hamburg alone during the holocaust of

firestorms staged in July and August 1943. The near total destruction of Tripoli and Benghazi, of Rijeka and Caen and Saint-Lô, of Mandalay and Stalingrad. If this all is rather abstract, we can think of the actual buildings and note that in Germany 2.5 million housing units were destroyed; in Japan, in Tokyo alone, a total of 710,000 buildings were wholly or partly razed. And so on sickeningly—London and Coventry, Kassel and Essen, Nagasaki and Hiroshima, Chongqing and Hankow.

In the urgent haste to rebuild, the prescriptions of Modernism that had been suppressed by the Nazi and Fascist regimes began to seem reasonable. Bombs had done in more than people and buildings; an entire social order had been shattered. In Europe especially, redemption and reconstruction were in the air, along with a new hope to build the cities *right* this time around. The belief reigned that a brave new world must be designed without sentiment, without a single look backward.

In launching their revolution in the first quarter of the century, the modernists insisted that theirs was an inexorable process, born of the social and technological imperatives of the age. How buildings looked was no longer a matter of choice, they argued. The new architectural language was both exclusive and universally valid. As its early historian Nikolaus Pevsner put it in 1936: "This new style of the twentieth century . . . because it is a genuine style as opposed to a passing

fashion is totalitarian." The term International Style coined in 1932 carried the same message. And the broad acceptance of modernism after the war came to look like destiny fulfilled.

Things were not that simple, of course. The triumph of the modernists was both well earned and providential. On the side of providence, we should count the discrediting of the official neoclassicism of the 1930s as part of the defeat of Germany and her allies. This sudden unpopularity of historicism shored up one of the basic tenets of the modernists: that the International Style cannot in any way be beholden to tradition but must stand solely on its own inflexible logic. Events gave modernists their big chance by midcentury, and they were ready to seize it. All through the lean years of their revolution, when opportunities to build were rare and modest, they had churned out prototypical schemes and grandly unrealistic projects, trained young architects, and fought an apprehensive establishment with crusading fervor. Le Corbusier drew up extravagant plans for Barcelona, for Algiers, and, repeatedly, for his own Paris; lectured in Brazil and helped design a new building for the Ministry of Education; and wrote and sketched tirelessly. His Paris atelier was now a famous halting spot, from which his apprentices carried the gospel to distant corners.

Modernism—history denying, fanatically against memory, and intolerant of traditional institutions and monumental-

Fig. 28.1 Marseilles (France), *Unité d'habitation,* 1946–52, Le Corbusier; exterior view. The *unité* is the single realized fragment of Le Corbusier's larger redevelopment plan for Marseilles. Although this new prototype for collective urban life was meant to be reproduced across the globe, only three other *unités* were built to the architect's designs: one each at Nantes and Briey-en-Forêt in France and one in Berlin, Germany. More widely disseminated was the building's roughcast concrete construction (*béton brut* in French), which inspired the postwar style known as Brutalism (see Figs. 28.17, 28.25, 28.28).

ity—was the perfect vehicle for the post-bellum design of Europe. Images of towers in open green spaces and slabs arranged at right angles to thoroughfares are too familiar to us now to need introduction. (Figs. 27.6, 27.18) Europe's long history of apartment living helped ease the introduction of these towers and slabs. But remember that the traditional apartment house was nothing like the size and scale of the new housing estates and that the apartment house had always been street oriented. Modernism favored an alternative arrangement, with pedestrians removed from streetscapes and housing and commerce subjected to the strictest separation of functions.

The French government, searching for standard housing formulas for its reconstruction program, turned at long last to Le Corbusier and asked him to build a sample of the freestanding residential slab block he called *unité d'habitation.* (Figs. 28.1, 28.2) On a site in Marseilles, he raised a huge reinforced concrete cage holding 337 independent units, ranging from single rooms to capacious apartments opening onto both the front and the rear of the slab. The idea was to ensure a good social mix, for Le Corbusier thought

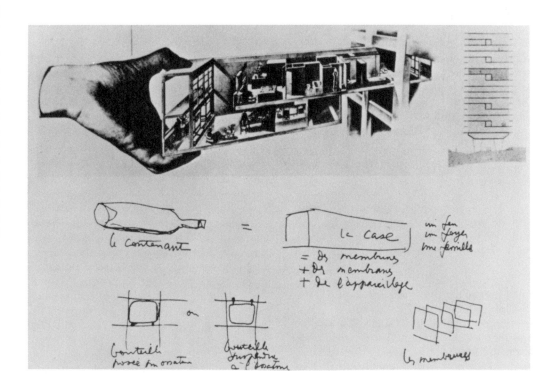

Fig. 28.2 Le Corbusier, sketch depicting an apartment unit in the *unité* as a drawer inserted into the building's structural frame and as a wine bottle resting in a rack (from the architect's *Oeuvre complète,* 1946–52).

Fig. 28.3 Berlin (Germany), the former eastern sector, the Stalinallee (now the Karl Marx Allee), 1952–58, Hermann Henselmann, designer in chief. Proclaimed as "the first socialist street" of East Berlin, this grand boulevard of apartment blocks was modeled on Soviet Socialist Realist prototypes like Moscow's Gorky Street (see Fig. 27.34).

In Germany, where the *Zeilenbau* estates of the 1920s first presented the startling scenography of a Modernist future, a purer version of Gropius's Modernism briefly prevailed. Hans Scharoun, a Modernist, was appointed Berlin's director of planning. There the devastation was so complete that it seemed pointless to resurrect the old lines of the city-form. Modernists thus saw before them the first chance to remake a major European metropolis according to the principles codified in the Athens Charter.

But in 1948 the administration of Berlin was divided, and the mood suddenly changed. Socialist East Germany denounced Modernism. In its place, the "Sixteen Principles of Urbanism" were hammered out in consultation with Moscow and adopted as a formal policy. They presented a radical alternative to the Athens Charter. The notion that planning must heed traffic was rejected, as was the separation of functions. The traditional street and block were reasserted. In 1951, East Berlin announced a competition for an imposing boulevard, the Stalinallee. The winning solution was not far from the old grandeur that sustained the pomp of Mussolini, Hitler, and others before them. (Fig. 28.3) The battle of the styles was now launched in earnest.

Spurred into action, West Berlin in 1953 proclaimed a competition of its own for a high-rise residential quarter called the Hansaviertel. (Fig. 28.4) This showcase of Modernist reconstruction was built in conjunction with an international architecture exhibition called Interbau. The cast of contributors was international and included many of era's most renowned architects: Alvar Aalto, Walter Gropius, Oscar Niemayer, and Le Corbusier. Their freestanding apartment blocks, set in a park landscape, were meant as proof that West Germany had stopped yearning for tradition and was poised to embrace a modern future. All the while, East Germany vigorously pushed its historicist agenda, with its new buildings reflecting, however superficially, its region's golden age: Gothic for Rostock, Baroque for Dresden, Classicism for Berlin. Then this, too, disappeared. With Khrushchev's condemnation of expensive and inefficient

of the *unité* as a self-sufficient neighborhood community that, multiplied in kind, would make up the city. There were interior streets on every third floor and a broad shopping arcade halfway up the slab. A sculptured roofscape harbored playgrounds, a nursery, a gymnasium, and even a stage for improvised shows.

Without its urban implications, the *unité* did catch on, in England and Switzerland, for example, as an archetype of social housing in the welfare state. But the Marseilles block, heroic specimen of postwar architecture that it is, proved too controversial and costly a nostrum for the remaking of French cities. The preferred solution was to plant residential satellites called *grands ensembles* around the old cities. Composed of towers separated by the obligatory open tracts, *grands ensembles* are—in their denial of street continuities and the resolve to bring "nature" to

every habitation—English garden cities built high. By 1964, there were two hundred of these housing estates along the peripheries of Paris and other major French towns.

Sweden was something of a pioneer in this regard. Stockholm's municipal government had been experimenting since the 1930s with high-rise suburban flats. The ten-storey *punkthus*, or "point block," a slim slab that contrasted well with the tossed northern landscape, was the result. By the early 1950s, variants were going up in suburban new towns across Scandinavia and in England as well. There, multistorey flats were interspersed among contrasting low-rise housing in what was known as "mixed development." This version of Modernism was promoted by the London County Council as an alternative to the ever-expanding tracts of suburban cottages.

construction methods, East Berlin did another about-face. The Stalinallee shed its name and in 1959 was finished off in precast concrete slabs. The distance between East and West now shrank, architecturally speaking, illustrating anew the historical truism that the same style can readily accommodate two opposing ideologies.

Postwar America

The International Style had found little sympathy for either its forms or its social message in America before World War II. When the rise of the Nazis had forced leaders of the movement in Germany to emigrate, America took in the lion's share of this Modernist diaspora. In the summer of 1937, Mies Van der Rohe arrived in New York; earlier that year Gropius had joined the faculty at Harvard, ending its long Beaux-Arts tradition and installing Bauhaus training.

Whereas Mies embraced American high technology and monumentalized it, Gropius and his associates were coming to grips with the wood vernacular of New England. In his own house in Lincoln, Massachusetts, Gropius took a first step by introducing into its neo-Bauhaus design, wooden siding painted an abstract white. His partner Marcel Breuer's weekend home leaves the siding natural, but turns some of it on the diagonal to show that the wood has its functional justification in wind bracing. (Fig. 28.5) The house sits off the ground on a masonry pedestal and, despite a strongly projecting terrace, seems crisply detached from its Connecticut countryside.

Suburban Legacies

These attempts at domestication, however, were not enough to sell the International Style to the home-buying public. The vast American home-building industry stayed with the traditional styles, and the domestic ideal remained the roomy, unagitated suburb of detached one-family houses. After World War II, there was a huge market for houses, and a surge in road building put vast tracts of farmland within the commuter's automotive reach.

Fig. 28.4 Berlin, the former western sector, the Hansaviertel, 1953–57, Gerhard Jobst and Willy Kreuer, planners. Modernism's urban ideal of skyscrapers in a park became an icon of the "design of the Free World in all the variety of [its] forms" in this model quarter, built for the Interbau exhibition of 1957.

But more than anything else, a decision in 1934 by the Federal Housing Administration to support low-cost insured loans for single-family houses accounts for postwar suburbia. In concert with generous provisions for veterans—mortgaging the entire value of the house with no down payment—the policy removed risks for buyer and builder alike. Enterprising merchant-builders like Levitt and Sons, Eichler, and Henry J. Kaiser started producing standardized or, rather, "semiprefabricated" houses that were near-perfect replicas of traditional site-built houses. Materials were transported to the site in trucks, and houses were put up in rows in an efficient process that resemled the assembly line. By 1950 Levitt and Sons was producing a four-room house every 16 minutes. Buyers could choose from several models, and built-in appliances, included in the mortgage loan, made the deal even more attractive. On the whole, the East Coast retained traditional styles like the Cape Cod, the saltbox, and the

Colonial, while the West Coast experimented more freely with a modern look.

These thinly spread dormitory communities spawned their own sanitized and disembodied replica of Main Street: the shopping center. (Fig. 28.6) The premise of this most typical of modern American environments is simple: it is a congregation of stores with off-street parking. A number of planning problems were common to all. Shoppers had to have adequate parking facilities isolated from deliveries, and pedestrian traffic had to be kept separate from cars. Strip centers and shopping courts were in use before World War II. The regional shopping mall, pioneered in 1956 by Victor Gruen's Southdale Shopping Center in a suburb of Minneapolis, Minnesota, anchored smaller specialty shops to one or two major department stores. An outer ring road defined the site periphery, with parking restricted to the zone immediately within; mall and plaza areas at the core were devoted strictly to pedestrians.

Fig. 28.6 Livonia (Michigan), Wonderland Regional Shopping Center, 1960, Louis G. Redstone; aerial view looking south. A suburban subdivision can be seen in the background.

Urban Renewal

While the federal government was busy subsidizing home ownership in the suburbs, it was also exercising its powers of eminent domain for the construction of public housing downtown. The steady flight into the suburbs had condemned to decay those older neighborhoods adjacent to the central business district. A new policy was launched with the Housing Act of 1949: urban renewal. This was supposed to free cities "enslaved to the 10- to 25-foot lot," to enlarge the street system, and to run highways into the central business district. At the heart of the program was the government's power to buy vast center-city parcels by exercise of eminent domain.

Modernist solutions for housing and urbanism now seduced planners who had limped along since the days of the City Beautiful without a sweeping and popularly acclaimed model of that kind. With the blessing of municipal authorities and the real-estate industry, they set out to install the Modernist city in American downtowns. Typically, the land was cleared of structures before it was resold or leased to a local redevelopment agency for an approved project, which might be nothing more than a huge parking lot. Connectors from adjacent freeways slashed through the town, cutting it up into fragments and rending its mesh irreparably. (Fig 28.7) Entire neighborhoods were gutted and replaced with commercial towers lapped by vast open spaces where the thick of things had been. Farther out, slabs and cruciform skyscrapers of early Corbusian derivation, grimly executed and with barren parking lots for greenery, were home to those who depended on public housing. (Fig. 28.8) By the 1970s, unsurprisingly, the projects had turned into battlefields of crime and vandalism. Urban renewal had another consequence larger than the simple pref-

erence for a Modernist formal language: the result of gutting often vital neighborhoods and building urban expressways was the further flight of full-time residents from the city.

Modernism Redefined

One approach to installing the Modernist city in America was through the governmental clients that sponsored urban renewal and public housing. The other was private enterprise. It was here that the influence of one of the forefathers of Bauhaus Modernism, Mies Van der Rohe, left its mark on America and changed the look of its cities. Mies ended up in Chicago, at

the Illinois Institute of Technology (IIT), where he was put in charge of creating a new campus, built between 1940 and 1952. This also was the laboratory where he developed the few simple principles of a highly rationalized building method, which the American building industry took up enthusiastically in the 1950s.

The general appeal was in the look of cleanliness, efficiency, and standardization, what William Curtis called "the heraldry of big-business America." Mies's method was based on a modular frame of steel beams with glass or other infill. Because building codes demanded the fireproofing of structural steel, he

Fig. 28.7 Boston (Massachusetts), construction of the central artery (Fitzgerald Expressway), ca. 1956. The street to the right is Atlantic Avenue.

Fig. 28.8 Brooklyn (New York), Farragut Houses—a public-housing project—under construction, 1950. In postwar urban renewal, the apartment towers typically occupied only a small fraction of a site that had been cleared of all previous structures.

sheathed the frame in concrete and welded steel I-beams on the exterior as an organizing veneer. Welded to the outside face of structural piers or made to serve as window mullions, the I-beam was as basic to Miesian architecture in the articulation of wall surfaces as the pilaster or engaged column had been to Renaissance architecture. (Fig. 28.9)

Recourse to such classical analogies is inescapable. In the skeleton of Mies's elegant frames there is the care for clear proportionate relationships, for corners and joints, that informs classical design of any vintage. And yet the means are quintessentially modern—the steel columns, the glazed intercolumniations, the deep steel girders from which the roof is hung. Mies believed that technology is the true vehicle by which each period in history manifests its culture and that "whenever technology reaches its real fulfillment it transcends into architecture."

Mies resolved building programs with two generic solutions: the cellular block or high-rise and the pavilion, with its unobstructed clear span and unitary volume. The second of these recalls the girdered factory spaces of Albert Kahn, as well as Mies's own line of European experiments, best portrayed in his Barcelona pavilion of 1929. (Fig. 27.12) But the shifts are significant—from a fluid plan and asymmetry of wall planes to a fixed, axially organized plan and from cruciform supports kept well behind the edge of the building to the metal frame revealed on the outside. Functions and their individual accommodation held little interest for him, or, to put it positively in the terms he would prefer, the big open space ensured ultimate functional freedom. At Crown Hall (Fig. 28.10), which houses the architecture school, the main studio space is interrupted by nothing more than low, freestanding oak partitions. Activities that require some privacy, like faculty offices and workshops, are put in the basement.

And so it is with his National Gallery in Berlin, its glazed walls defying use as exhibition surfaces, and most functions relegated to the platform structure below.

Mies's second generic type, the reticulated steel skyscraper, took up the work of Jenney, Sullivan, and those other pioneers of the "commercial style," cut short by Beaux-Arts efflorescence. Now early Chicago skyscrapers look labored and apologetic in retrospect. Where they bandage the skeleton with masonry or terracotta, Mies strips it naked and celebrates it. He frees the window from its heavy confinement, stretches the glass taut in front of the structural columns, and gives it substance chromatically.

The paradigm of the Miesian skyscraper, and one of the most influential monuments of this century, is the Seagram tower on Park Avenue in New York, completed in 1958. (Fig. 28.11) By pulling back from the street line, the building could circumvent the setback provisions of the city's code, as well as create its own breathing space—a granite-paved plaza with twin fountains. The rectangular shaft stands regally on two-storey stilts, slightly recessed behind the plane of the window wall and sheltering a glass-enclosed lobby. This wall is a homogeneous mesh of custom-made I-beam mullions of dull, oiled bronze arranged in unbroken runs, matching spandrels in a copper alloy, and dark, amber glass that is in keeping with the overall somber quality. We have here one of those timeless buildings that sums up a running discourse and transcends it, sparking emulation and handicapping all trials in advance.

And emulated he was, this naturalized Chicagoan, from one end of the country to the other—and much beyond. His low temple form led to countless school buildings and shopping centers and spread itself out, in brick-filled concrete or glass-filled metal, for industrial complexes and commercial facilities of all kinds. His skyscrapers were replicated in countless glazed towers with plazas below, most successfully by the firm of Skidmore, Owings and Merrill which proved to be his most competent heir.

If we look at these Miesian clones in

their urban aggregate, it is not difficult to see that Modernism's vow to kill the traditional street was amply redeemed. Even when their alignment respected the street grid, these disenfranchised objects were anchored in a space they could not define, and would not enclose, with anything like public purpose. Inside, neat stacks of open floors rose under banked fluorescent lights—streamlined, modish, monochromatic. (Fig. 28.12) The management of some of these stylish skyscrapers even ruled against adjusting blinds or displaying family photographs, all in the name of preserving the purity of the architectural design.

For the most part, the integrity of Mies's work was diluted in its copies, if not altogether mocked. Whereas Mies's search was to subtract and distill until he reached an architecture that was, as he said, "almost nothing" and then to perfect and polish the essence that was left, his imitators strained for variety. "I don't think every building I put up needs to be different," Mies once said, "since I always apply the same principles. For me novelty has no interest, none whatsoever." But that philosophy ignored the reality of consumer capitalism which thrives precisely on novelty, on quick shifts in taste, on the advertising potential of the package. A society that is impelled to change cars and appliances regularly, whatever their working condition, is not likely to settle for the eternal building.

By the early 1950s, the claim that there was a single legitimate style for the twentieth century was proving illusory. Climate and customs conspired to particularize the International Style. One convincing Americanization came from the West Coast, which nurtured an easygoing residential manner that interwove traditional and Modernist references, most successfully in timber-frame houses. They were wedded to their sites and opened their rooms to terraces and patios and lushly planted gardens—what Breuer dismissed contemptuously as "romantic subsidies." In their structure, the houses often rejected the horizontal slab aesthetic of the International Style for stick verticality, sloping roofs, and unorthodox, view-catching perforations. By the 1960s the

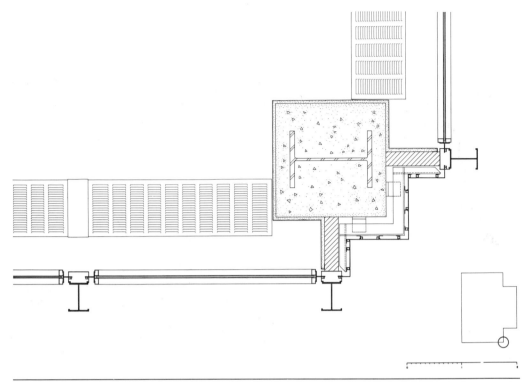

Fig. 28.9 New York, Seagram Building, 1954–58, Ludwig Mies van der Rohe and Philip Johnson; structural plan of one corner, showing the main pier and projecting I-beams.

love of high airy spaces and the exploitation of volumes through height rather than floor area resulted in the vertical, wood-sheathed, shed-roofed Bay Area box. (Fig. 28.13)

Latin American architects like Oscar Niemeyer (b. 1907), touched by the genius of Le Corbusier, let loose exuberant forms that refreshed his purist rigor with the energies of the native Baroque. At Brasilia, the newborn capital of Brazil, Niemeyer was charged with designing the federal buildings bracketing a 200-meter-wide mall. (Fig. 28.14) The legislature complex sits astride the axis, an apparition of two white tower-walls that are the blind ends of the high-rise Secretariat slabs, flanked by two half-spheres, upright for the Senate and inverted for the Hall of Deputies. Moving down the axis, an equally dramatic form, circular and skeletal, rushing up to a spiky crown, represents the cathedral.

Scandinavia, mindful of its bleak winters and its tradition of timber and brick, questioned the wisdom of maximal glazing, flat roofs, and stuccoed planes. Here we need only mention the Finnish architect Alvar Aalto (1898–1976). An early and brilliant convert of the International Style, Aalto had slipped, by the late 1930s, into a lyrical mode that distanced his work from the doctrinaire rationalism of the Germans. His Villa Mairea (1937–38) warmly responds to the dense forest of fir that hugs it. Wood blooms inside and out, in the slatted ceilings, the columns bound by willow withes, the exposed vertical board and batten, and his unique birch plywood furniture. (Fig. 28.15)

After the war, Aalto turned more and more to brick and the billowing or undulating line—in plan, wall surface, and ceiling. In this country, we can catch at its start that sensationally inventive mature phase in the Baker House dormitory

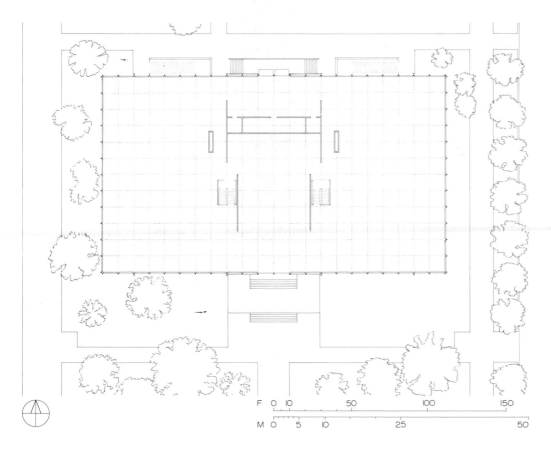

Fig. 28.10 Chicago (Illinois), Crown Hall at the Illinois Institute of Technology, 1950–56, Ludwig Mies van der Rohe: (a) exterior view; (b) ground plan.

Fig. 28.11 New York, Seagram Building, 1954–58, Ludwig Mies van der Rohe and Philip Johnson; exterior view from the northwest.

F 0 10   50   100   150

M 0 5 10   25   50

Fig. 28.12 New York, Union Carbide Corporate Headquarters, 1957–60, Skidmore, Owings and Merrill; interior view of an office floor. This office block is based on a 5-foot × 2½-foot grid, a regulating module that established the dimensions of everything from the structural steel frame of the tower to the desks, overhead lighting panels, and movable partitions of the office space. The continuous view of the luminous ceiling emphasized a unified work environment. All furnishings, from desks to ashtrays, "were scrutinized, adapted, or completely restyled by the architects" to complete the effect.

Fig. 28.13 Sea Ranch (California), Condominium I, 1965–72, Moore, Lyndon, Turnbull & Whitaker, architects; Lawrence Halprin and Associates, planners. Sea Ranch is a short distance north of San Francisco.

Fig. 28.14 Brasilia (Brazil), master plan by Lucio Costa, 1956; view down the monumental axis. Oscar Niemeyer was the architect for the most important federal buildings of the new capital, including the cathedral (right), the series of ministries behind it, and the congress towers, which terminate the axis (left).

Fig. 28.15 Noormarkkhu (Finland), the Villa Mairea, 1937–38, Alvar Aalto; view of the living room. Aalto used polished woods and rough masonry to soften the rigidity of the Modernist design, infusing it with romanticism and a veneration of nature.

(1946–49) at the Massachusetts Institute of Technology, where he taught for a while. (Fig. 28.16) The giant S of the main block was generated by the notion of orienting the student apartments toward long oblique views of the Charles River.

But more so than this serpentine profile of Baker House, it was its coarse brick surface, roughened further by extruding clinkers spaced randomly, that seemed a deliberate affront to International Style sensibilities—right here in New England, Gropius's kingdom in exile. Indeed this forceful building, along with Le Corbusier's own somewhat earlier shift to raw concrete and sturdy detail that led up to the Marseilles block, signaled a redirecting of modern architecture toward traditional concerns: the animation of walls and the earthbound dignity of mass.

Two of Le Corbusier's apprentices, Kunio Mayekawa (b. 1905) and Junzo Sakakura (1904–74), brought his intermediate style to Japan, a country that shone after the war as an important outpost of modern architecture, with the work of a younger generation that includes the prolific Kenzo Tange (b. 1913). (Fig. 28.17)

To maintain the fiction of a monolithic orthodoxy in the face of the vastly differing recent work of Mies, Le Corbusier, and Aalto, two options were open to apologists. They could expand the base of the International Style to include these variant late statements of the masters, along with whatever trends they inspired among younger followers. The purer option was to be stern and to pillory the deviants. Pevsner, who had once purged Gaudí and the Expressionists as irrational diversions, now attacked the new Le Corbusier and his Brazilian brood, among others, for catering to "the craving of the public for the surprising and fantastic, and for an escape out of reality into a fairy world." The premises of industrial society had not changed, Pevsner wrote retrospectively in 1960. "Architects as well as clients must know that today's reality, exactly as that of 1914, can find its complete expression only in the style created by the giants of that by now distant past."

Even so, it was still impossible to dismiss two of those giants, Wright and Le Corbusier, and the later phases of their

Fig. 28.16 Cambridge (Massachusetts), the Baker House dormitory at the Massachusetts Institute of Technology, 1946–49, Alvar Aalto; view of the facade along the Charles River. Communal dining is accommodated in the low pavilion. Above it, the serpentine dormitory slab provides diagonal views across the river from most of the rooms.

long-lasting careers. Wright's divergence from Modernist orthodoxy had been established in the 1930s with works like the Johnson Wax Building. (Fig. 27.27) In his last postwar works, the picturesque abstraction of hexagons and piercing points alternates with circles and sweeping arcs. It is a private, romantic, transcendental vision kept in check to the last through Wright's geometric command and his unfaltering sense of scale. His great swan song, the Solomon R. Guggenheim Museum in New York (1956–59), is a gift of pure architecture or, rather, of sculpture. (Figs. 28.18, 28.19) The museum is a continuous spatial helix, a circular ramp that expands as it coils vertiginously around an unobstructed well of space capped by a flat-ribbed glass dome. As a museum it has problems, at least in the eyes of the museum's curators. Function and con-

text have clearly been subordinated to form. The site on Fifth Avenue across from Central Park could make no restrictive demands on the graduated curves of reinforced concrete smoothed over into a cream-colored, weight-denying surface. Only with the addition of a new museum annex thirty years later did Wright's "quiet unbroken wave" find an appropriately neutral backdrop. Until then, the city grid and its apartment blocks had to live with Wright's building, and not the other way around. The machine age was there to make Wright's fantasies come true.

Le Corbusier's final response to industrial society and the supposed beneficence of machine-age civilization, however, was disillusionment. His buildings—the Chapel of Notre-Dame-du-Haut at Ronchamp and the Capitol triad at Chandi-

Fig. 28.17 Kurashiki (Japan), city hall, Okayama Prefecture, 1958–60, Kenzo Tange; facade facing the plaza.

garh—were now thrown up with a kind of defiant heroism. They sought a basic compromise with nature in their rejection of lightweight machine technology, in their intrepid scale, recalling in them caves and creatures and violent contrasts.

The sagging concrete roof of the pilgrimage church at Ronchamp, with its strong catenary profile, was the crab shell he had picked up on Long Island, he said, that lay on his drafting table. (Fig. 28.20) This dark roof slab bears down on the stippled, whitewashed walls of rough masonry infill rendered over with "gunite" but lifts prowlike at the southeastern corner of the church, where two curving walls meet in a taut, razor-sharp arris. The side chapels send hooded funnels upward to catch the light, and the random pockmark fenestration of the oblique south wall emphasizes its thickness and plastic-

ity. The building both engulfs and resonates, draws us into its hollows, and makes us go around it as we would around powerfully molded sculpture. An extruding pulpit gathers about it large crowds of pilgrims for open-air services. This is the human link between Le Corbusier's shapes and the undulating landscape of the Jura foothills north of the Alps, which they echo in what he liked to call "visual acoustics."

At Chandigarh, the new capital of the province of Punjab occasioned by the independence of India and the partition of 1947 that left Lahore, the old capital, in Pakistan, Le Corbusier had the Himalayas to work with. To the north of the city, between it and the endless, snow-capped ranges, he set three monumental buildings in shifting axial relationships across a vast plaza. (Fig. 28.21) The buildings are

scaled accordingly, with spaces between them hardly negotiable on foot in the searing Punjab sun, even though the whole capitol plaza was indeed conceived as a pedestrian plaza with motor traffic sunk below in trenches leading to parking areas. To complete this cosmic scale, Le Corbusier added an artificial landscape of excavated earth mounds that mimics the real mountain barrier in the distance.

Of the three buildings, the Secretariat is the simplest. An enormously attenuated slab block, it is screened by an irregular pattern of sunbreakers on the long sides, each interrupted by a solid tower that contains circulation ramps. The High Court and Assembly Building also are huge concrete shells, protecting the inner functional cores from the broiling summer sun and the fury of the monsoon rains that break in July. (Fig. 28.22) In the cool cavernous interior of the High Court, beyond the deep entrance portico, ramps and causeways crisscross through space between the courtrooms on one side and the High Court and library on the other. The portico is crowned by a massive concrete overhang of hung vaults. These rest on a series of thin vertical blades that hold up the sunbreaker screen and on three tremendous flattened piers rising sheer for 18 meters (60 feet), each painted a bright color—red, yellow, or green. Across from the High Court, the drama of the Assembly Building breaks through the roof of its shed. Above the mammoth, upward-curving canopy of the entrance portico, which sits on a row of thin flat sections, the assembly chamber pushes out in the shape of a cooling tower, and the smaller rectilinear council chamber emerges into the open with a pyramidal skylight. (Fig. 1.16)

This extravagant, oversized complex, scaled to the empty, monotonous plain and the high mountains, went far beyond specific need. It aggrandized the governing institutions of the newborn Indian nation, just as Lutyens had dignified colonial rule at New Delhi forty years earlier. (Fig. 27.1) But whereas Lutyens could fall back on a long tradition of monumental forms with established cultural meanings, Le Corbusier took it upon himself to invent a whole iconography of power in order to meet the request of his august client, Prime Minister Pandit Nehru, that the city of Chandigarh be "symbolic of the freedom of India, unfettered by the traditions of the past."

The irresistible example of Le Corbusier and Wright opened up a season of unabashed form-giving that carried into the 1960s. This was the coming of age of a second generation of modernists, eager to slough off the preachy rationale of the founding fathers. "Where form comes from I don't know," Philip Johnson (b. 1906) declared, "but it has nothing at all to do with the sociological aspects of our architecture." And again: "Forms always follow forms and not function."

The undoing of the International Style and its content-denying hermeticism obeyed two rather different impulses. There were, first, those who were swept up by the single expressive gesture, the unique shape for each and every program they were commissioned to give shape to. Johnson, a Miesian renegade, is both reminiscent and responsive. His formal inventions are triggered by memories of past buildings—Hadrian's villa at Tivoli, Ledoux, Schinkel—and by the physical realities of neighboring architecture and public spaces. Eero Saarinen's approach was to isolate an idiom or a shape that would be symbolic of the program at hand. He gave General Motors a shiny, sleek headquarters near Detroit, all gleaming metal and thin translucent glass. He gave two new colleges at Yale, where the campus teemed with the literal neogothic of the 1930s, a sort of abstract medievalizing imagery of earthy towers and picturesque paths. The thinking here was akin to the associationism of nineteenth-century revivals. The famous Trans World Airlines terminal (1956–62) at New York's Kennedy Airport, on the contrary, had to suggest flight and did so in its soaring cross-vault roof, spectacularly constructed out of a reinforced concrete shell. (Fig. 28.23) Moving through it, the architecture was supposed to conjure up the experience of this glamorous new mode of public transportation. The analogy now might be with the eighteenth century, the building as poetic metaphor. Only, unlike the projects of Boullée, say,

Fig. 28.18 New York, the Solomon R. Guggenheim Museum, 1956–59, Frank Lloyd Wright; interior. "Here for the first time," Wright later wrote, "architecture appears plastic, one floor flowing into another (more like sculpture) instead of the usual superimposition of stratified layers cutting and butting into each other."

Fig. 28.19 New York, the Solomon R. Guggenheim Museum; exterior. In the foreground is Wright's original design, with its coiled ramp and companion "rotunda"; behind them, the annex (1982–92) by Gwathmey Siegel and Associates. The new backdrop building occupies the site that Wright had proposed for a thin slab housing studios for resident artists.

Fig. 28.20 Ronchamp (France), the pilgrimage church of Notre-Dame-du-Haut, 1950–55, Le Corbusier; view from the southeast. The site is in northeastern France, near Belfort.

Fig. 28.21 Chandigarh (India), the capitol complex, 1951–65, Le Corbusier; left, the Secretariat; center, the Legislative Assembly Building.

Fig. 28.22 Chandigargh, Legislative Assembly Building, 1953–61,Le Corbusier. The main assembly hall is enclosed by the hyperbolic concrete shell on the left, which continues its upward sweep through the roof plane to give the building its monumental silhouette. To the right is the interior open space that Le Corbusier called the Forum: a Piranesian collage of ramps, columns, lighting troughs, and sculptural protrusions. Here delegates can meet spontaneously to relax or exchange views between assemblies.

Fig. 28.23 New York, the Trans World Airlines Terminal at John F. Kennedy Airport, 1956–62, Eero Saarinen: **(a)** street front; **(b)** interior. In 1994, the exterior and much of the interior of Saarinen's expressionist evocation of flight were granted landmark status by New York's Landmarks Preservation Commission.

738

Fig. 28.24 Turin (Italy), Exhibition Hall, 1948–50, Pier Luigi Nervi; interior detail.

which were never meant to be built, for technical reasons if for no other, the versatility of modern structures could now keep up with the architect's fancy.

Structural exhibitionism was, in fact, a good part of this crowd-pleasing imagery. And it tended to annoy resourceful engineers like Pier Luigi Nervi (1891–1979) and Felix Candela (b. 1910) who could produce equally arresting spaces, but did so through the inherent logic of the structure rather than for a figurative purpose. Nervi's vaulted buildings of huge span—exhibition halls, sports arenas, and the like—are based on diagonally intersecting concrete beams, precast and assembled, and held up by massive Y- or V-piers disposed around the periphery like flying buttresses. (Fig. 28.24) He would seek *his* ancestry in Viollet-le Duc, in the trainsheds and fairs of the late nineteenth century, in Freyssinet's airship hangars. (Figs. 23.32, 27.3) Candela uses cleverly folded vaults that are paraboloid, saddle-shaped, or mushroom-shaped. The point is that

they can be applied to churches, factories, and restaurants alike, without sentimentality or interpretative worries.

The second category of form-givers took off from Le Corbusier's robust monumentality. They conceived of their buildings as a collage of parts, thickly cast and boldly fitted together. The method here was to think of elements of construction as expressive architectonic means. The overpowering, if also often overdesigned, exteriors were further dramatized through scored or corroded surfaces and the juxtaposition of contrasting materials. Paul Rudolph (b. 1918) in his Art and Architecture Building at Yale of 1958–62 laboriously flutes the concrete surface and then blunts the ridges. (Fig. 28.25) This "brutalist" corrugation plays up in fine detail the stirring verticality of the mass and particularly the corner piers that hold aloft the upper floors. Between the piers the building is piled intricately. There are seven storeys, but almost forty different levels. Obsessive articulation, or the drive to set up hierarchies of scale, is as characteristic of this group of architects as is the scaleless, single-minded conceit to the likes of Saarinen.

In this heady new freedom that disabled the weak and encouraged the sensation seeker, it seemed now to some that the battles of the old generation had been fought so that the young could make merry and dazzle. The tension drained, social urgency was forgotten, meaning became hard to find. And then a rallying point materialized for those who missed the rigor of some guiding thought in all the indulgent creativity at large. Louis Kahn (1902–74), an older and hitherto lackluster Philadelphia architect, had started to elaborate in the 1950s a building language of artless probity. It went hand in hand with an aphoristic teaching that was determined to go back to the fundamentals of architecture, to rethink the nature of windows and columns. "What does an arch want to be?" he would ask his stu-

Fig. 28.25 New Haven (Connecticut), the Art and Architecture Building at Yale University, 1958–62, Paul Rudolph; exterior from the southwest.

Fig. 28.26 Philadelphia (Pennsylvania), the Richards Medical Research Laboratories at the University of Pennsylvania, 1957–64, Louis I. Kahn.

Fig. 28.27 Fort Worth (Texas), the Kimball Art Museum, 1966–72, Louis I. Kahn; interior. The curved concrete vault filters light through the top and distributes it by means of stainless-steel reflectors. The general feeling is reminiscent of Roman vaulted interiors (see Figs. 9.17 and 9.30).

dents. "The paving block is the grass of the city," he would tell them; "A plan is a society of rooms"; "Order does not imply beauty."

For Kahn, *form* was not wherever we could find it. Rather, it existed in a primal realm as a general conception and had neither shape nor dimension. Once seized, form could be particularized through the demands of *function*. But there was much more to function than mere expediency. The architect's job was not "filling prescriptions as clients want them filled. It is not fitting uses into dimensional areas." We must go beyond the program and probe the nature of human institutions. What does a school want to be? "I think of school as an environment of spaces where it is good to learn." A library's essence: the person who picks up a book and goes to the light. As for *structure,* the third architectural verity, it

would make possible the buildings of particularized form and modify it further as it became necessary. At the same time, structure should itself be perceivable. "The artist instinctively keeps the marks which reveal how a thing is done."

Design, then, was the way the architect went about making form material. It meant finding the spaces for each component activity of the program according to its worth (and in this we catch the bias of Kahn's Beaux-Arts training), organizing them through the structural system, and suffusing them with light. Architecture, the end result of design, was just that: "a harmony of spaces in light."

The struggle and solemnity of design come across in the great Kahn buildings of the 1960s in America—research facilities, museums, libraries—and those he did in India and Pakistan. With total scorn for superficial showmanship, the early work,

compact and ungainly, preserves an almost craftlike care for construction. Kahn's preferred materials are brick and concrete. The composition of the buildings is characterized by a discreteness of parts, bluntly combined. This aggregative growth keeps two things in mind. It intends to break down an institutional identity into human-sized units, and it allows the separation of the primary areas of use from mechanical or support systems, like stairs, elevators, storage rooms, and bathrooms—Kahn's "served" and "servant" spaces. In the Richards Medical Research Laboratories (1956–64) at the University of Pennsylvania, for example, blind utility towers stiffly gather around the main laboratory and office towers, and the horizontal zones of servant spaces below each floor level contain wires, pipes, and ducts. (Fig. 28.26) The cellular solution proceeds from the pavilion concept, here mani-

fested as a square slab on towerlike piers; in the Kimbell Art Museum (1966–72) at Fort Worth, Texas, it becomes a system of flattened concrete vaults. (Fig. 28.27)

They all are buildings of substance, firmly grounded and forthright, and they are progressively involved with layering and an almost mystical sense of light. Like Le Corbusier at Chandigarh, Kahn's encounter with the Asian subcontinent released bursts of deliberate invention. After the partition of 1947, Pakistan was composed of two territorial units separated by 1,500 miles. East Pakistan was determined to build a capital and so in 1962 invited Kahn to preside over its design. He brooded about the program he was given—the assembly and the supreme court, hostels, a school, a stadium, a market—and approached the job as a philosopher of human institutions, set on rediscovering the essence of ritual belonging, government, and community.

Kahn's new capital of Dacca is a diagram of functional dualism: the Citadel of Assembly, where the laws are made and behavior is monitored, and the Citadel of Institutions, where the mind is tutored, the body is flexed, and its unwellness is comforted. An expanse of grass and water separates the two. The Citadel of Institutions includes a hospital, sports facility, and school. The Citadel of Assembly is encircled by subsidiary offices and housing—the servant and the served spaces—and is accented by the mosque. (Fig. 28.28, Fig. 1.5) To shield them against the harsh elements, Kahn encased the buildings within buildings and courted the resultant double wall. "I thought of wrapping ruins around buildings," he said of an earlier project. In Dacca, the ruins are huge freestanding concrete screens pierced by circles, squares, and triangles that soften the outside glare by trapping a curtain of light.

The result is both primal and sophisticated, an act of creation played out with layers of elaborated knowledge. These also are arbitrary, irresponsible, and willful buildings. Like Le Corbusier's monuments for Chandigargh, Kahn's work at Dacca is both supremely cultured and not at all culture specific. Both new capitals

Fig. 28.29 New Gourna (Egypt), 1945–48, Hassan Fathy. Although Fathy's model resettlement village demonstrated that adaptations of vernacular construction techniques could create new housing quickly and cheaply, the town failed to attract its intended residents. It was built as part of a forced relocation of Old Gourna, a village located near the ancient Tombs of the Nobles at Luxor, in order to prevent the illicit sale of antiquities by residents. With a lapse in state surveillance, however, the displaced villagers abandoned the new town and returned to their old homes.

ignore the technological realities attending their postcolonial nations. They are functionalist utopias designed, as Kenneth Frampton observed, "for automobiles in a country where many, as yet, still lack a bicycle."

Perhaps the culminating efforts of Kahn and Le Corbusier took shape in lands where these two had no business building. But, at the conclusion of their professional research and their phenomenal formal development, to expect either to pay attention to the habits, crafts, and cultures of an alien land is unrealistic. That kind of solicitude must probably always come from within, as it does in the postwar work of Egypt's Hassan Fathy (1899–1989), whose reasoned rejection of the cult of high technology and feel for the justness of traditional building practices provides modern vindication for the primordial mud-brick vault and dome. (Fig 28.29)

Kahn's elementarism was not so easily accessible, even in the West. The pasts he distilled so monastically demanded matching reserves to comprehend and enjoy. We like our history to be more declamatory, and so when Modernism stopped denying tradition, we began recalling our most obvious cultural memories. As for the former colonies of the West, their tutelage was short-lived after independence. When they had gotten over the moment of reflective glory, of bringing the choicest designers from the West to give them symbols of renascence, they began to reassert those ancient continuities that colonialism had cut open and bled. For that process of healing, neither the assertive commandments of Le Corbusier nor the aphorisms of Kahn could prevail. To find their way to the future, they had to start walking back, back to times and places before the break.

Further Reading

A. Åman, *Architecture and Ideology in Eastern Europe During the Stalin Era: An Aspect of Cold War History,* trans. R. Tanner and K. Tanner (Cambridge, Mass.: MIT Press, 1992).

D. B. Brownlee and D. E. De Long, *Louis I. Kahn: In the Realm of Architecture* (New York: Rizzoli, 1991).

W. J. R. Curtis, *Le Corbusier: Ideas and Forms* (New York: Rizzoli, 1986).

J. M. Diefendorf, *Rebuilding Europe's Bombed Cities* (London: Macmillan, 1990).

N. Evenson, *Chandigargh* (Berkeley: University of California Press, 1966).

———, *Paris: A Century of Change* (New Haven: Yale University Press, 1979).

———, *Two Brazilian Capitals: Architecture and Urbanism in Rio de Janeiro and Brasilia* (New Haven: Yale University Press, 1973).

K. T. Jackson, *Crabgrass Frontier: The Suburbanization of the United States* (New York: Oxford University Press, 1985).

F. Neumeyer, *The Artless Word: Mies van der Rohe on the Building Art,* trans. M. Jarzombek (Cambridge, Mass.: MIT Press, 1991).

M. Quantrill, *Alvar Aalto: A Critical Study* (New York: Schocken Books, 1983).

J. Steele, *Hassan Fathy* (New York: St. Martin's Press, 1988).

Montpellier (France): on the left, La Place du Nombre d'Or, 1978–84, Ricardo Bofil and the Taller de Architectura. Bofil's concrete-panel housing complex is the first phase of construction of the new town quarter of Antigone. Behind it and to the right are older high-rise towers, a housing type abandoned in the town's new master plan.

29

DESIGNING THE FIN-DE-SIÈCLE

A hundred years ago, during the previous fin-de-siècle, an anxious search was under way in the world of architecture. It was time to clean the slate of all historicist affects and to articulate a modern idiom befitting its own time. The Modern Movement, as we saw, had a mixed parentage—Art Nouveau and the early work of Frank Lloyd Wright and the landscape of industry—but a common aspiration. It staged a spirited fight and became established in a relatively short span, trampling the past, or so it believed, and coming to seem inevitable.

In our own fin-de-siècle, we seem ready to retire that old and compromised revolution, the gospel of Modernism, and are preparing to welcome the millennium. In anticipation of a rebirth, the talk for some time now has been of death and failure. Doomsday books in the last decade or so, with titles like *The Failure of Modern Architecture, Form Follows Fiasco,* and *The Decorated Diagram: Harvard Architecture and the Failure of the Bauhaus Legacy,* have been forging epitaphs, and others have been heralding the advent of Postmodernism. There is uncertainty about where we are, a state that optimists like to call "pluralism," and here and there lone voices of prophecy are announcing an architectural future of liberating novelties—or is it the elegance of defeat? Where are we? What is dying or dead? What wants to be born?

Success and Failure

Let us first take up the issue of the failure of Modernist architecture. What are the charges, and how fair are they? Then we will look at the boasts of its successors.

The most important charge is that Modernism failed to generate social reform. This is true, and it is a failure that the protagonists of the movement invited when they made sweeping promises of social justice, of an unsentimental brave new world reaping the universal benefits of industrial technology. Their claims were immodest, their sense of reality childish, their arrogance supreme. Architecture alone does not bring about social change. Instead, powerful political, economic, and social forces do that, and without a concurrence of these forces the architect is helpless to affect society. With this concurrence, though, change can be accommodated in any kind of architecture.

A magic alliance of form and reform did appear for a few years, in the 1920s in places like Frankfurt, Berlin, Vienna, and Stockholm, where Modernism matched a new outlook and gave it an unforgettable symbolic presence. (Figs. 27.5, 27.6) But once that particular experiment was over, Modernism sold itself to the highest bidder. Le Corbusier tried to find a client for his ideas in every band of the political spectrum, from communists and syndical-

ists to the Vichy government, which collaborated with the Nazis. Mies Van der Rohe, who had once raised memorials to martyrs of the left like Rosa Luxemburg, grew prosperous and famous serving the magnates of capitalism.

A second charge against Modernism stems from its initial assumption that the future held ineluctable new materials and technologies that would buttress its mode of design. Standardization or, better still, prefabrication would prevail, and these new building systems were to be applied globally. Gropius spoke in 1927 of "the impending equalization of life requirements under the influence of travel and world trade." Modernists determined that one architecture, one set of urban solutions, must be valid everywhere.

This agenda enjoyed a fitful success, caused an enormous amount of pain, and, on some of its major items, simply could not deliver. Housing reforms conceived to benefit the masses were based on the needs of a European working class. When promoted as a forced choice between slum dwellings and the architecture of a new way of life, especially outside Europe, Modernist evangelism bore an uncomfortable resemblance to the colonial mission of "civilizing" subject peoples. The new materials—concrete, steel, glass—were installed universally, but primarily for high-style architecture and the landscape of industry and transportation.

Fig. 29.1 Hong Kong, late-twentieth-century skyline: the tallest building in this view is the Bank of China, 1982–89, I. M. Pei; to the left, clad in exterior girders and trusses, is Norman Foster's office tower for the Hongkong and Shanghai Banking Corporation, 1979–85.

Fig. 29.2 San Bernardino (California), suburban single-family homes of the 1980s.

Indeed, they still are too expensive and too sophisticated to serve the common needs of large segments of the world, especially those arrested in a preindustrial state, to which their relevance is negligible. Even highly industrialized societies cling to traditional building materials because of their associations, their sensible properties, their sensual comfort. (Fig. 28.15)

The world did not become one. Differences still exist and are treasured. What surface uniformity we have achieved came about primarily through inventions like the car, the radio, and television and less so through Modernist conventions of form, with urban apartment towers and the corporate landscape being notable exceptions. People were told to forget the past, to sweep away the cobwebs of culture. But nobody willingly does that: societies do not voluntarily erase themselves.

After decades of proscription, for example, the church remained a presence, albeit a muted one, in the communist countries and is now celebrating its own resurrection. If the state, with its overwhelming mechanisms of persuasion, could not eradicate deep-seated patterns of behavior, the designs and mottoes of a group of architects were not likely to do so either.

So it came down to a look, a style, a formal language. Like any other style, Modernism gave us some beautiful buildings and generated its own dross. It created a vernacular of housing estates, public buildings, and the high-rise skyline of the central business district (Fig. 29.1), and it would be foolish to disown all of that. The style found a wonderful fit in structures that do not require a strong representational image and for which many specimens are needed: building types like factories, schools, hospitals, and office buildings.

The language of Modernism was less effective in at least two areas. In the highly decentralized home-building industry of the United States, it proved to be too inflexible and too uncommunicative. American suburbia, enamored at the same time of atomism and tradition, developed without the aid of the International Style—indeed, in most cases without the help of architects. (Fig. 29.2) The other area was representational architecture. Modernism's rejection of monumentality and of ornament did not sit well with institutional landmarks of government and faith. Le Corbusier recognized this and so set out to remedy it, in works like the capitol at Chandigrah and the chapel at Ronchamps. (Figs. 28.20, 28.21, 28.22)

The mention of these late works by Le Corbusier should alert us to a fundamental aspect of Modernism that current rebels push aside. This was a long and versatile movement that continued its research and made adjustments even while standing by its fundamental premises. Today, much of what we like to hold against Modernism is directed against the narrow dogmatism of the 1920s. But despite its own rhetoric, Modernism was far from becoming a homogenized international formula. Rather, its excitement and promise came from restless experimentation, the variations played on a handful of themes. There were strong minds and individually nourished sects, and by the 1950s the sacred Modernist "orthodoxy" had attained a richness that was welcome to all but a handful of mainstream apologists.

The opening challenge came from within the fold. A loosely associated group of young architects called Team X (Team Ten) rejected the establishment guise of postwar Modernism, in which a handful of elders dominated the International Congresses of Modern Architecture (CIAM), setting the official agenda for design practice and theory. Led by Alison Smithson (1928–93), Peter Smithson (b. 1923), Jacob Bakema (1914–81), George Candilis (b. 1913), Shadrach Woods (1923–73), and Aldo Van Eyck (b. 1918), among others, Team X staged a court rebellion stoked by intergenerational conflict. They repudiated the isolated grandeur of Le Corbusier's *unité* and spoke urgently of the need for a new model of urbanity. Their research focused on patterns of human association and the identification of individuals with neighbors and a neighborhood. The term "habitat," which gained currency, sought to convey the bond between the arrangement of living cells and the observable social interaction of the users. The call was for variety, flexibility, and at least the semblance of spontaneity.

The dissidents were willing to retire the Modernist compartmentalization of urban life in four distinct zones—dwelling, work, recreation, and transportation—but they were not yet ready to give up the old faith in the multilevel city, fast traffic, and mass mobility. In contrast with the CIAM ideal of a park landscape punctuated by residential towers (Fig. 28.4), Team X pro-

Fig. 29.3 Alison and Peter Smithson, entry for London's Golden Lane housing competition, 1952; photomontage of the existing neighborhood overlaid with a meandering eleven-storey wall of new housing.

posed an alternative urban order: a network of connected slabs typically arrayed in a loose polygonal pattern.

The Smithsons' 1952 Golden Lane competition project for London, although unbuilt, provided a declaration of goals and a provocative image to go with it. (Fig. 29.3) Here the "interior street" of Le Corbusier's *unité* was recast as an open-sided deck intended to carry the traditional associations and social uses of a village lane. Housing was the organizing web: commercial, educational, and leisure facilities plugged into the system. The concept found application in projects like Sheffield's Park Hill (1957) and the huge urban extension of Toulouse-le-Mirail (1962) by Team X members Candillis and Woods. (Fig. 29.4) In both cases, zigzagging high-rise slabs are linked by an elaborate structure of walkways threaded through blocks at every third level. Ini-

tially hailed as the consummation of Team X's promise, Toulouse-le-Mirail instead proved to be a case study of its frailties. Residents found "streets-in-the-sky" uninspiring as social spaces, particularly when the economic realities of state-financed housing pared them down to the width of a corridor. The interconnection of residential slabs proved to be another fantasy of convenience that went largely unused. Rather than setting the standard for a new urban order, this open-ended matrix of apartment slabs was another inconclusive episode in Modernism's long-standing quest to reinvent the city.

The attempt to resolve the conflict between design and spontaneity, between the large container and the small human incident, led to the megastructure craze. The megastructure was another attempt to create a unitary building type that would encompass all the functions of the traditional city. A massive supporting frame would permit individual variation, frequent and easy change, and continuous extension. These designs were typically submitted for new settlements and extensions of old ones, but were also deemed suitable for institutional communities like universities and corporate centers. At Cumbernauld Center, built during the early 1960s in Scotland, a megastructure even invaded the rarefied intimacy of the English new town with the claim of bringing the garden city up-to-date. (Fig. 29.5)

In the realm of housing, megastructural designs promised to capture some of the visual sparkle of Italian hill towns or Greek island communities through the casual organization and irregular stacking of residential units. Montréal's "Habitat," designed by Moshe Safdie (b. 1938) for an international exposition in 1967, illustrates this point. (Fig. 29.6) The towering hive's precast-concrete boxes are fitted together in a variety of apartment configurations, each with a tiny roof terrace. Each capsule in the dense pileup of units is supported by the walls beneath it, rather than by a load-bearing frame. The picturesque randomness is carefully contrived, its form determined by a rational network of circulation and services.

The British design group called Archigram, founded by Peter Cook (b. 1936), Ron Herron (1930–94), and Mike Webb (b. 1937), among others, also tried to suggest an easy, undogmatic townscape played out on the gargantuan scale of Modernism. Caught up in the social upheaval of the 1960s, Archigram's affinity was with headphones, the cybernetic tower, and the caravan city—"a hundred thousand people on a hilltop turned on by lights and music." This first cousin to Pop Art served up a futuristic collage of tensile structures, inflatable pods, and landing pads as the prerequisites of megastructural urbanity. (Fig. 29.7) Space-age gadgetry and nonstop mobility and mutation were celebrated as icons of human liberation.

The lighthearted side of this technocratic swagger can be enjoyed at the Centre Pompidou (place Beaubourg), a cultural complex completed in 1976 in the heart of Paris. (Fig. 29.8) The designers,

Fig. 29.4 Toulouse-le-Mirail (France), Bellefontaine quarter, construction begun in 1963, George Candilis, Alexis Josic, and Shadrach Woods; view of the apartment slabs from a street deck.

Richard Rogers (b. 1933) and Renzo Piano (b. 1937), eliminated internal columns from the exhibition halls by wrapping them with an external assembly of enormous steel trusses. Tensioning struts, ducts, and escalators are woven through this exoskeletal frame to form an animated veneer. The imagery is industrial, with associations of kit-of-parts assembly from standard components. But the Beaubourg is in fact a custom-made project, costly to both craft and maintain. Its high-tech heroism has tapped a limited market, for the most part composed of global finance corporations, such as Rogers's high-rise headquarters for Lloyd's of London or that designed by Norman Foster (b. 1935) for the Hongkong and Shanghai Bank. (Fig. 29.1) The only populist legacy, if indeed there is one, might be found in recent shopping malls, where the glint of chrome and the glide of escalators simulate the vitality of Main Street through mechanized action and visual gimcrackery.

This attempt to humanize the stern Modernist landscape with touches of the accidental and the whimsical was too little and too late, however. The hue and cry now was about the fate of the old townscape itself, not about its Modernist metaphors. A search was under way to recover the traditional experiences of the street and the rewards of a comfortably familiar architecture.

Recovering the Past

The past, of course, had never been banished. After nurturing the International Style for the future, Europe also found ways of healing the wounds inflicted on its heritage. An act was introduced in France in 1962 with the aim of protecting historic neighborhoods from the onslaught of urban renewal. It was the forerunner of the United States National Historic Preservation Act of 1966 and

Fig. 29.5 Cumbernauld (Scotland), town center, 1962–67, Geoffrey Copcutt; view of the town center over the roofs of row housing. Cumbernauld was built to accommodate the growth of greater Glasgow. The town center, the partial realization of a grander original scheme, is a linear multipurpose building with shops, offices, a hotel and restaurant, and recreational and cultural facilities distributed over eight levels. The strategy of concentrating all of these in a single building is both megastructural and meteorological, as the site is buffeted by 75-mph winds and receives twice the annual rainfall that London does.

Fig. 29.6 Montréal (Canada), "Habitat" at Expo 67, Moishe Safdie; an apartment module is lowered into place by a crane.

Fig. 29.7 Oasis project, 1968, Ron Herron of Archigram. The determinism of the conventional Modernist city is bowled over by Archigram's alternative urbanism in this photocollage. Archigram's notion of a liberating megastructural lifestyle was based on the continual metamorphosis of the city around the needs of its inhabitants, who are envisaged as a species of high-tech nomads.

Fig. 29.8 Paris (France), the Centre Pompidou in the place Beaubourg, 1972–76, Richard Rogers and Renzo Piano; view of the side fronting the place Beaubourg. The building incorporates the Musée de l'Art Moderne, a public library, an audiovisual center, a rooftop restaurant, and generous exhibition spaces.

England's Civic Amenities Act of 1967. Landmark status could now be granted not only for single buildings, but also for entire districts. Communities began to realize that blight could be reversed without massive surgery, that decaying building stock could be rehabilitated slowly, a little at a time. In America, gentrification became an established procedure for this healing, even though its process of social displacement was far from harmless. Where its strategies succeeded, warehouse districts and derelict piers were spruced up as "festival marketplaces," and Main streets were restored.

A related development was the downtown pedestrian mall. The idea was to create areas where foot traffic took precedence over the movement and parking of automobiles. Curbs were eliminated, and street furniture and landscaping were brought in. Water features and wandering musicians were sometimes added, as well, to establish the desired ambiance. Europe embraced the basic premise in postwar reconstruction, an influential prototype being Rotterdam's Linjbaan (1951–53) by J. H. van den Broek (1898–1978) and Team X member Jacob Bakema. European city planners spearheaded movements to close busy shopping streets to vehicular traffic during peak shopping hours, and by the 1960s, cities like Copenhagen, Cologne, and Stockholm had built orchestrated systems of pedestrian streets, shopping arcades, and plazas. In the United States, Victor Gruen (1903–80) was the great exponent of this concept. Combining his extensive experience designing regional shopping centers with an abiding concern for urban renewal, Gruen's Fulton Mall of 1963 became a model to emulate. (Fig. 29.9)

Although it succeeded in Europe without a fuss, the pedestrianized downtown had only limited success in the United States. Because European urban centers had never been abandoned by their middle class, they still had a well-heeled resident population to patronize shops, inhabit promenades, and pay for physical maintenance and public services. In the

United States, on the contrary, the middle class had been escaping to the suburbs since the mid-nineteenth century, draining downtowns of care and capital investment. Europe's unregimented medieval pattern of narrow, twisting streets, moreover, physically resisted automobile traffic. American urban culture, long conditioned to the unfettered experience of the automobile driver, found it hard to accept a Main Street that was anachronistically paved and landscaped for an exclusively pedestrian use.

So why fight it? The bright young architecture and planning team of Robert Venturi (b. 1925) and Denise Scott Brown (b. 1931) relieved the tension by embracing Main Street as it was—cars, tinsel, and all. Their *Learning from Las Vegas* (1972) is a serious analysis of the form and meaning of the Strip, from supermarket parking lots, service stations, and billboards to the

neon marquees of gambling casinos. The moral of the book is an aphorism: "Main Street is almost all right." This means that instead of disdaining the everyday landscape of our towns and highways, we should learn to accommodate it and improve it on its own terms. Venturi had already galvanized the profession with an earlier treatise, *Complexity and Contradiction in Architecture* (1966), in which he argued that the long abstinence of Modernism from associative imagery had been a mistake. He countered the heroic with the ordinary, the purity of "total design" with "messy vitality." This "gentle manifesto" made the case for a rich, ambiguous architecture, one of multiple meanings derived from historical allusion and the use of precedent.

Venturi demonstrated his ideas in buildings like the Guild House of 1962–66, a medium-rise apartment for older adults in Philadelphia. (Fig. 29.10) The thin, cheap-looking facade is made of the same material as its neighbors: brick. The signage and double-hung windows are conventional in format, but inflated and distorted in their use. Here the commonplace is made uncommon in the way that Pop Art during the same years transposed the value of banal objects like Coca-Cola bottles and comic strips. The arched window at the top signals the common room. Above it a gold anodized television antenna—later removed by the building's owners—could be read as abstract sculpture or a logotype for an old age spent watching TV, or both. All this may not make Guild House look much like Las Vegas, but a glance back at Rudolph's Art and Architecture Building (Fig. 28.25) shows just how antimonumental Venturi's design was.

This attack from an obscure architect, a double-barreled blast of populism and historicism, was perfectly aimed. It announced the new revolution at the height of a general antiestablishment mood. A Postmodern or, more accurately, Antimodern regime was quickly installed as architects rushed to taste the forbidden fruit, to throw away the strip windows and the *pilotis* and the talk of functionalism, mass production, social regeneration. Out went the white stucco and exposed con-

Fig. 29.9 Fresno (California), Fulton Mall, 1963, Victor Gruen Associates; Garrett Eckbo, landscape architect. Like many pedestrian street conversions in the United States, Fulton Mall was designed to compete with the new suburban shopping malls that were capturing consumers who had previously shopped downtown.

Fig. 29.11 Portland (Oregon), Portland Public Services Building, 1983–84, Michael Graves.

752

Fig. 29.12 New Orleans (Louisiana), Piazza d'Italia, 1975–78, Charles Moore.

crete, and in came gentle color in building and architectural drawing and an opulence of historical motifs as eclectically mixed as Charles Garnier ever did in his Paris Opéra more than a hundred years earlier. (Fig. 25.8) Pluralism, contexturalism, the decorative and scenographic, and contained volumes—real rooms—were in. Among urban designers, the traditional street, its block structure, and the monumental axis were once again embraced.

Enthusiastic advocates of this architectural upheaval proclaimed the return of architecture as a supple medium of expression. Buildings "talked," their language being ornament and decorative allusion, and we enjoyed this discourse as we used them or passed by them. As many referents to past styles could mingle in a single building as its architect wished. The Portland Public Services Building (1983–84) by Michael Graves (b. 1934) helped define the trend. (Fig. 29.11) Graves's earlier work had revived and refracted the vocabulary of Corbusian Modernism, thereby placing him—along with Richard Meier (b. 1934) (Fig. 29.14), Peter Eisen-

man (b. 1932), Charles Gwathmey (b. 1938), and John Hejduk (b. 1929)—in the ranks of a group dubbed the "New York Five." Graves's civic office building for Portland, Oregon, pushed the strategy of abstraction from Modernist to Classicist referents. A competition version of the design included a penthouse reminiscent of a Tuscan farm complex: an allusion to Neoclassical landscape paintings by Poussin and to the roofscape at Chambord. (Fig. 17.33) Even though that particular folly was cut from the budget, the wedge-shaped pattern of tenant floors survived—a curtain-wall evocation of Mannerist keystones like that of Giulio Romano's Palazzo del Tè. (Fig. 17.15) The result was an exceedingly private communication, witty to insiders and sporadically fun to the common user, but hardly constituting a shared language.

An alternative strategy was straightforwardly referential, recalling and transposing recognizable frames of history rather than their essences. At the Tsukuba Science Center (1983), Arata Isozaki (b. 1931) liberally quotes compositions by Claude-Nicolas Ledoux and Étienne-Louis Boullée in a hotel tower, bank, and concert hall. These buildings front a plaza in which Michelangelo's Campidoglio collides with Japanese-influenced garden elements, yielding something between a European town square and a space for contemplation in the Zen tradition. The spirit of Rome's Fontana di Trevi is injected with campy humor and transplanted to New Orleans in its Piazza d'Italia by Charles Moore (1925–93). (Fig. 29.12) It boasts a fountain shaped like a map of Italy with water running down its Po, Arno, and Tiber Rivers, and twin water-spouting effigies of the architect.

To a new generation of European rationalists, these stylistic games were ludicrous. Nor was Venturi's pandering to the strip and the suburb anything but irresponsible playacting. "There is . . . nothing to be 'learned from Las Vegas' except that it constitutes a widespread operation of trivialization," thundered Leon Krier (b. 1946). For Krier, the ordinary in Continental terms evoked the stone cities of multilayered tradition, now savaged by "unbridled industrialization with no aim but

consumption." Their physical disintegration was aided and abetted by Modernism and its attendant myths: "the separation of functions, the myth of prefabrication, the useless typological works undertaken for themselves in the name of sacrosanct 'creativity.' " Leon Krier's call was to resurrect the preindustrial city. The elements of which it was made—the quarter, the street, the square—would form the basis for reconstruction, and it was to be built using the materials and labor techniques of preindustrial artisanry. (Fig. 29.13)

But we cannot bring back the preindustrial world, even though we might yearn for it. Instead, we must be content with saving as much of it as we can, to know what we once had, and adding our own pieces to this collective artifact. How do we proceed? By obeying typologies, according to Leon's brother Rob Krier (b. 1938). His manifesto, *Urban Space*, was written in the late 1960s and published in English translation a decade later. It rejected remodeling cities as high-speed vehicular promenades, instead proposing earlier building patterns as sources for contemporary urban form. The Rauchstrasse housing complex (1980–87) at the edge of Berlin's Tiergarten is an early application of this concept. Here the layout is governed by a surviving fragment of what was once Berlin's "diplomat's row." The volumetrics of an embassy villa established a compact, five-storey cube as the cardinal building type. Rob Krier's master plan arrayed these freestanding "villas," containing both public housing and private flats, in rows flanking a garden court. A gateway building by Krier separates the court from a busy traffic artery. To infuse the complex with visual variety, each of the villa blocks is the work of a different architect. (Figs. 29.16 e and f)

Another approach to re-creating premodern European urbanism is the attempt by Ricardo Bofill (b. 1939) to install something like the stone artifacts of a monumental city core in the unanchored wastes of France's new towns. (See photo on p. 744) Bofill's specialty is designing housing complexes built of prefabricated concrete. Rather than the monotonous minimalism identified with that construction technique, Bofill's panels are modular

Fig. 29.13 Leon Krier with Francisco Sanin, Insula Tegeliensis, an entry to the competition for the redevelopment of Tegel Harbor, Berlin (Germany), 1980. Krier's project for the Berlin International Building Exhibition (IBA) proposed a romantic resurrection of the ancient city, emphasizing classical architecture and a traditional assembly of streets and squares.

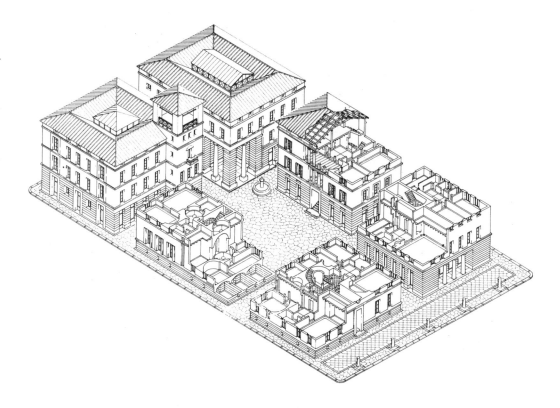

Fig. 29.14 Amiens (France), master plan for rebuilding the cathedral district, begun in 1984, Rob Krier; two perspective sketches. The proposed reconstruction includes a variety of streets, bridges, canal walks, and pedestrian paths, all lined with buildings designed to encourage mercantile and artisan life throughout the district. New construction revives historic building types, with designs for specific sites coming from many architects, to avoid visual monotony.

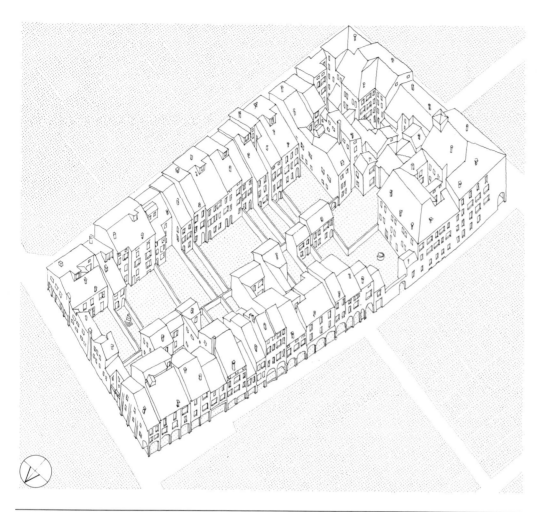

Fig. 29.15 Bologna (Italy), model restoration of one city block, 1973, Pier Luigi Cervelatti. To return the block and its houses to their typological origins, flat-roofed upper-storey additions were removed; the block's; central open space was cleared; and gaps in the street frontage were filled in with new construction based on historical models. These measures relieved the neighborhood's tenement crowding and allowed buildings to be retained rather than demolished.

components of a ponderous and unabashedly scenographic classicism. At Les Arcades de Lac, an apartment slab is configured as a viaduct poised above a lake; at Espaces d'Abraxas, the units are packed into a nine-storey triumphal arch. Each development is conceived as a habitable wall that encloses and embellishes usable public space. These self-assured fragments cannot by themselves create civic organisms, any more than single *unités* could produce the Corbusian city. But before we label Bofill's competent bluster as reactionary, we should compare his work with that of his immediate neighbors, the detritus of several decades of good intentions and radical experiments.

More ambitious are the attempts now under way to create, through managed reconstruction, a diverse functional and social ecology for cities. Rob Krier's master plan for the French city of Amiens, in development since 1982, aspires to re-create the fine-grained mix of residents, merchants, and artisans that was lost when bombing raids during World War II devastated the city's medieval quarter. (Fig. 29.14) New construction is guided by the format of historic building types, with shops at street level, residences above, and block interiors planted out as urban gardens. Much of this agenda was pioneered by Italian architectural workshops like those of Saviero Muratori in Venice and Pier Luigi Cervellati in Bologna. (Fig. 29.15) Each began by identifying archetypal specimens of the city's building stock—that is, the original set of built forms from which the city fabric had developed over the centuries. Blighted neighborhoods were restored by stripping crowded tenements of later accretions to reveal the original building type underneath. Where new construction was inserted, variety was permitted as long as traditional bay widths and floor and building heights were retained. Restored districts retained their visual consistency, and architects kept their originality, without either incongruous novelties or the disingenuous application of "authentic" facades.

Perhaps the best laboratory for recent thought concerning urban structure is, once again, Berlin. Its 1984 International Building Exhibition (Internationale Bauausstellung [IBA]) began as a redevelopment project to upgrade a single district with new offices and luxury housing. But opposition to that plan by citizens' action groups, local politicians, and architects shifted the IBA's emphasis to long-term urban repair, socially integrated housing, and ecological responsibility. Century-old apartment blocks were now spruced up rather than razed, and where the war or later demolition had left vacant lots, they were filled in with new buildings on the scale and pattern of their older neighbors. Accomplishments include the refitting of some 10,000 residential units and the construction of public gardens, day-care centers, and schools, many of them inserted into existing apartment blocks or their courtyards. The IBA commissioned new buildings from an international assortment of architects, just as in the Hansaviertel showcase of the 1950s. (Fig. 28.4) But whereas the Hansaviertel was an isolated collection of blocks executed in a single style, here we have new construction introduced throughout the city, with concepts like "integrative architecture" and "critical reconstruction" prompting as many stylistic responses as there are participants. (Fig. 29.16) In that

(a)

(b)

(c)

(d)

(e)

(f)

(g)

Fig. 29.16 Berlin (Germany), a collection of projects built in conjunction with the IBA of 1987: **(a)** Tegel Harbor Housing, 1982–87, Charles Moore, John Ruble, Buzz Yudell, and Thomas Nagel. **(b)** Residential and commercial building at Checkpoint Charlie, 1982–86, Peter Eisenman and Jaquelin Robertson. **(c)** Apartment house at Lüzowplatz 3, 1985–87, Peter Cook and Christine Hawley. **(d)** House G, Block 33, 1982–86, Arata Isozaki, Eisaku Ushida, and Hans Karil. This residential building, sited in the courtyard of the former Victoria Insurance Building, incorporates as a facade element a war-damaged fragment of the lot's previous occupant. **(e)** Rauchstrasse Housing, Tiergarten, 1982–84, Rob Krier. **(f)** Rauchstrasse Urban Villa no. 8, Tiergarten, Hans Hollein, 1983–85. **(g)** "Firewall" housing, residential development of Fraenkel Embankment, 1979–84, Inken and Hinrich Baller. These Neoexpressionist apartments occupy a site on the interior of one of the city's large, nineteenth-century perimeter blocks, where they back onto the brick firewalls of adjacent older buildings.

a consortium of talented local designers and their international counterparts are engaged in work with social import, to the extent that they believe that healing the physical environment will usher in a communal healing, they should be cheered on. This is what Postmodernism suppressed as it steered architecture to a pure art and put it at the service of eccentric moneybags and image-hungry institutions.

This is the abiding legacy of early Modernism, however poorly it was later managed: that architecture can be a tool for the unempowered as much as for those in power who can afford it; that architecture, whatever private joys it might bring to architect and patron, is a social art that must accommodate, and comment on, human uses, rituals, and needs.

Pluralism is not our problem. All periods of architectural history have been pluralist; it is we who have invented the notion of monolithic visual orders and have anointed styles allegedly appropriate to the prevailing Zeitgeist. The era of Modernism was no more single-minded than are we today.

The death of Modernism is, at any rate, grossly exaggerated. Gropius's house at Lincoln, Massachusetts, may now be a national landmark, and Bauhaus teaching is a thing of the past. But the spirit is alive and well and freely acknowledged by several strands of current practice, not only in the ordinary sphere but also among the superstars. James Stirling (1926–92) held to the technological romanticism of Modernism, at times deforming its pristine volumes to create heretically traditional configurations of public space. Under Stirling's tutelage, Constructivism learned to consort with romantic Neoclassicism in the Neue Staatsgalerie (1977–84), the apex of a trajectory that critic Ada Louise Huxtable described as being "half way between Ledoux and outer space." (Fig. 29.17) Peter Eisenman calls himself not a Postmodernist, but a Postfunctionalist, because he distances himself from the neoeclectic crowd in favor of a hermetic abstraction of form. (Fig. 29.16b) His exercises in pure geometry could not have been conducted independently of the re-

Fig. 29.17 Stuttgart (Germany), Neue Staatsgalerie, 1977–84, James Stirling and Michael Wilford. The program for Stuttgart's new museum stipulated the retention of a pedestrian path that crossed the site. Sterling fulfilled the requirement with an exterior promenade through the museum's hulking, stone-clad mass. The ramped route, marked by gargantuan handrails, begins at the top of this aerial view. It takes pedestrians on a curving descent along the rotunda drum and then down to a terrace café. Constructivist-inspired canopies cantilevered from exterior walls mark the museum's entries.

search of Modernist ancestors. And Richard Meier, whose work still reveals the legacy of the young Corbusier, describes his work as "modernism reconstituted." (Fig. 29.18)

This is as it should be. It would be folly to imitate the first Modernists' contempt for what had preceded them and, in turn, reject and try to throw away three generations of Modernist achievement. Theirs was a formal language of the most articulate and consistent type, and architects, whatever their social and political agenda, must work with formal languages. That is how they say things; that is the specialty they bring to the tasks that shape the built environment.

Of more concern than the choice of language as such is a sobering shift in the architectural profession and the way it has begun to perceive itself since the fall of another Modernist legacy: the illusion of certainty. For a while it convinced us that we had found a formal language inevitable for our circumstances. It is hard not to miss that single-minded message and the purpose and direction it gave to thousands of practitioners for several decades. That message, that purpose, we have now lost, and our freedom to act unfettered by dogma is laced with indecision and bewilderment.

Modernism started with a platform of social regeneration and ended up as a sleek packaging device. In the 1960s, it was challenged with passion along several fronts by those architects who no longer wanted to be standard bearers to the elite, by those who felt improverished without their past and diminished without the wealth of their own individual culture, and by those who saw merit in the life of the sprawl-city and the commercial strip. Now we once again seem to be disengaging. Having convinced ourselves that architecture cannot by itself improve society, we find it simpler not to try at all. "Architecture is made by architects for themselves," Peter Eisenman tells us. "My best work is without purpose. I invent purpose afterwards. . . . Who cares about the function?"

This heady narcissism has found its way into the studio culture of architecture schools and has been joined there by the seductive tours-de-force of Deconstructivism. The name implies an appropriation of both the design vocabulary of Russia's Constructivist avant-grade and the deconstructive literary theory of Jacques Derrida (b. 1930). The art of architecture is said here to lie in the critique of its own semantics and customary meanings. As practiced, the movement has generated a signature of colliding fragments, skewed grids, and warped planes. On occasion, the pained dislocations have a fateful propriety. Such is the case with Daniel Libeskind's (b. 1946) jagged and fractured annex to the Berlin Museum containing exhibits of the city's Jewish cultural heritage, the winning entry of a 1988 competition. (Fig. 29.19) More often, Deconstructivism's formal and verbal hyperbole—with its textual readings of "violations" and "the pleasures of unease," "form-infecting parasites" and "torture from within"—are by turns sensationalistic and inscrutable.

So while paragons of academic design take to the lecture circuit to explain what a particular assemblage really means, the millions without access to architecture are served by profiteers and opportunists or are not served at all. Our cities go about creating themselves in fanciful spurts and joyless routines; the separation of rich and poor becomes consolidated; and some of our best professional talent, incubating in the academy, takes pride in the loftiness and purity of its investigations.

The times are not on the side of the unempowered. In the West, the building of "new towns" for them has stopped, and with specimens like Toulouse-le-Mirail and Cumbernauld coming down the pipeline, it is perhaps as well they did. There is residual bitterness on both sides, in the people for the environment they got and in the architects for what they regard as popular rejection. The people must wait for new initiatives as architects recede to the polite comforts of journals, galleries, and lecture halls, or proffer their gifts to their most appreciative audience, the rich and powerful.

There is plenty to do for that clientele. The central business district still needs showpieces of high-rise splendor, which now keep up with the latest fashion through Postmodern sheaths and toppings. But the mood is increasingly separatist. The magnates who run the information and business world, and the young, upscale crowd that does their bidding want new towns of their own.

"Edge cities" are the new landscape of postindustrial America. (Fig. 29.20) Most started as tract-home suburbs with a regional shopping mall. In the 1980s, hotels and office parks appeared, sensibly close to white-collar patrons, and new cities were born. They rise from open landscapes, 10 or more miles from the edge of town. Examples are the Tech Center near

Fig. 29.18 Atlanta (Georgia), High Museum of Art, 1983, Richard Meier. Among the group of architects known as the "New York Five," Meier has remained the most faithful to the Corbusian vocabulary that initially united their work. The High Museum's strip windows, *pilotis,* and impeccable white cladding reinforced the viability of the traditions of early Modernism at precisely the time these were forsaken by a Postmodern countermovement.

Denver, Cumberland and Buckhead north of Atlanta, and, most impressively, Las Colinas between Dallas and Fort Worth, spread out on more than 18 square miles of land and intended for a maximum population of 150,000.

These instant cities of the countryside have little to do with the dormitory communities that resulted from an earlier and long-lasting abandonment of the old downtown. After the residents had left and the factories and the industrial establishments had been banished by zoning, the heart of the metropolis was still held together, at least in the daytime, by offices, banks, and administrative buildings, symbolically marking it in the way that civic buildings did during an earlier phase of capitalism: the cloth hall (Fig. 15.13) and the *palazzo di podesta* (Fig. 15.11). Now they, too, are leaving, opting for a landscape stripped clean of the centralizing presence of a civic realm. Here there are no poor, no ethnic concentrations. There is no street life in the traditional sense and, of course, no history, except as picturesque vignettes like the pseudo-Venetian canals of Las Colinas, their beautifully rendered old-world facades concealing the parking structures with stairways to the garages housed in campanili.

But the past is not merely a quarry of forms to which we are welcome; it is the vast repository of collective memory that ought to illuminate our borrowings. And architecture is not the carefree manipulation of form; it cannot be practiced without consequences. These, and not exquisite visual divergences, are the overriding issues of the fin-de-siècle.

We have two fundamental challenges in designing the fin-de-siècle. First, we must rediscover our conscience, redirect architecture to social ends, and reaffirm its central purpose as a social art. We must do this without the Modernist hubris, the belief in the inherent healing powers of architecture, but by asserting architecture's role as a mediating instrument for a better-looking and more compassionate environment.

Our second task is to come to terms

Fig. 29.19 Daniel Liebeskind, Berlin Museum Extension and Jewish Museum, 1988 competition model.

Fig. 29.20 Houston (Texas), Greenway Plaza, an edge city with its own office high-rises and condominium housing.

Further Reading

R. Banham, *Megastructure: Urban Futures of the Recent Past* (New York: Harper & Row, 1976).

P. Blake, *Form Follows Fiasco* (Boston: Little, Brown, 1977).

P. Eisenman, M. Graves, C. Gwathmey, J. Hejduk, and R. Meier, *Five Architects* (New York: Oxford University Press, 1975).

R. Fishman, *Bourgeois Utopia: The Rise and Fall of Suburbia* (New York: Basic Books, 1987).

P. Johnson and M. Wigley, *Deconstructivist Architecture* (New York: Museum of Modern Art, 1988).

P. Katz, *The New Urbanism: Toward an Architecture of Community* (New York: McGraw-Hill, 1994).

R. Krier, *Urban Sapce*, trans. C. Czechowski and G. Black (New York: Rizzoli, 1979).

P. Portoghesi, *Postmodern*, trans. E. Shapiro (New York: Rizzoli, 1983).

A. Smithon, *Team 10 Primer* (Cambridge, Mass.: MIT Press, 1968).

A. van der Woud, *CIAM* (Delft: Delft University Press, 1983).

R. Venturi, *Complexity and Contradiction in Architecture,* rev. ed. (New York: Museum of Modern Art, 1977).

R. Venturi, D. Scott-Brown, and S. Izenour, *Learning from Las Vegas,* rev. ed. (Cambridge, Mass.: MIT Press, 1977).

with our past and to take shelter and find pride in the continuities of time and place. This is not alone a professional imperative. All of us—architects and users, environmental policymakers and consumers of such policies—need to become engaged. Informed activism in this realm is as critical as and can be as effective as the pressure we have brought to bear on civil rights, ecology, and the issues of war and peace.

For this, our key resource is the history of architecture, with this critical proviso—that we do not think of this history as an exclusive and uplifting survey of our high artistic achievements, of Gothic cathedrals and Palladian villas and skyscrapers. Instead, we must accept that all buildings,

the standard and the fancy, are worthy of study and that buildings are only the visible tip of a complicated story that encompasses politics and economics, the philosophy of human institutions, and the identity that people of all social levels find in the built environment they inhabit. To foster such an all-embracing, culture-conscious aptitude toward the built domain may yet set us free to spin a judicious architecture of our own. If we continue to regard design as good or bad on the basis of looks alone, we will sprinkle our share of beautiful fragments through our cities and countryside, but we will never install a vital, fair-minded, humane settlement pattern for the fin-de-siècle and the century ahead.

ILLUSTRATION CREDITS

We gratefully acknowledge the following persons and institutions for the photographs and illustrations in this book.

Abbreviations

AR   Art Resource

BFM   Bildarchiv Foto Marburg

BN   Bibliothèque Nationale

CNMHS   Caisse Nationale des Monuments
(SPADEM)   Historiques et des Sites

FU/AAR   Fototeca Unione, American Academy in Rome

HV   Hirmer Verlag

MCNY   Museum of the City of New York

MMA   Metropolitan Museum of Art

MOMA   Museum of Modern Art

NBR   National Buildings Record

NMR   National Monuments Record

RT   Richard Tobias

Chapter 1. Opener, Toledo Museum of Art, Gift Florence Scott Libbey; Fig. 1.1, Werner Forman Archive; 1.2, R. Sheridan; 1.3, Toledo Museum of Art, Gift Florence Scott Libbey; 1.4a & 1.4b, RT, after H. Kähler, *Hagia Sophia*, New York, 1967; 1.5a & 1.5b, *Architecture d'Aujourd'hui*, no. 142, Feb.–Mar. 1969; 1.6a, Musée du Louvre; 1.6b, FU/AAR; 1.7a, K. Jeppesen, "Old and New Evidence of a Reconstruction of the Mausoleum at Halicarnassus," *Paradeigmata*, Vol. IV, 1958, p. 63; 1.7b, J.J. Stevenson, *The Builder*, Vol. 71, Sept. 5, 1896, p. 186; 1.8, Chicago Historical Society; 1.9, R. Sheridan; 1.10, SCALA/AR; 1.11, S. Kostof; 1.12, Editions Houvet; 1.13, J. Stuart and N. Revett, *The Antiquities of Athens*, Vol. 2, London, 1789:(a) chap. 1, pl. IV, Fig. 1, (b) chap. 1, pl. IV; 1.14, Library Company of Philadelphia; 1.15a, from Le Corbusier, *Towards a New Architecture*, London, 1927, p. 206; 1.15b, Le Corbusier, *Creation Is a Patient Search*, New York, Praeger, 1960, p. 34 top; 1.16, *Le Corbusier Sketchbooks*, Vol. 4, 1957–64, New York, The Architectural History Foundation, 1982, Fig. 223, by permission of publisher and of Fondation Le Corbusier; 1.17, C. Jest, Musée de l'Homme; 1.18, G.E. Kidder Smith; 1.19, AIA.

Chapter 2. Opener, West Air Photography; 2.1, RT; 2.2, H. de Lumley, Centre national de la recherche scientifique, Marseille; 2.3, French Government Tourist Office; 2.4, Achille B. Weider; 2.5a & 2.5b, RT; 2.6, Musée de l'Homme; 2.7, Arch. Phot. Paris/SPADEM; 2.8, Musée de l'Homme; 2.9, RT; 2.10, Musée de l'Homme; 2.11, S. Kostof; 2.12, RT, after S. Piggott, *The Neolithic Cultures of the British Isles*, Cambridge, 1954; 2.13, RT, after V. Childe, *Ancient Dwellings at Skara Brae*, Orkney, Edinburgh, 1950; 2.14, JOS Le Doaré Éditions d'Art; 2.15, C.-T Le Roux, Antiquités Préhistoriques de Bretagne; 2.16, JOS Le Doaré Éditions d'Art; 2.17, Commissioners of Public Works, Ireland; 2.18, RT, based on J.D. Evans, *The Prehistoric Antiquities of the Maltese Islands*, London, 1971; 2.19a, RT; 2.19b, Dept. of Museums, Malta; 2.20, Aerofilms, Ltd.; 2.21, RT; 2.22, RT, based on J. Hawkes, "Stonehenge," *Scientific American*, June 1953, and G. Hawkins, *Stonehenge Decoded*, New York, 1966; 2.23, English Heritage, Historic Buildings and Monuments, Commission for England.

Chapter 3. Opener, British School of Archaeology in Jerusalem; 3.1, RT; 3.2, The Oriental Institute, Univ. of Chicago; 3.3, RT, based on J. Hawkes, *Atlas of Ancient Archaeology*, New York, 1974; 3.4a, British School of Archaeology in Jerusalem; 3.4b, RT, based on Hawkes, *Atlas*; 3.5, RT, based on P. Dikaios, *Khirokitia*, London, 1953; 3.6, RT; 3.7, J. Mellaart, "A Neolithic City in Turkey," *Scientific American*, April 1964, p. 121; 3.8, RT; 3.9, RT, based on L. Woolley, "Excavations at Ur," *Antiquaries Journal*, 3(1923), 5(1925) to 13(1934), Woolley, *Excavations at Ur*, New York, 1965, and *Joint Expedition of the British Museum and of the Museum of the University of Pennsylvania to Mesopotamia*. *Ur Excavations* (L. Woolley, Dir.), 4(1956), 5(1939), 6(1965/1974); 3.10, RT, after Woolley; 3.11, RT, after Woolley; 3.12, L. Woolley, *The Buildings of the Third Dynasty*, Ur Excavations: Archaeology, No. 6, 1974, Univ. Museum of the Univ. of Pennsylvania; 3.13, Friedrich Schiller Univ., Jena; 3.14, RT, after Woolley; 3.15, RT, based on *Sumer: Journal of Archaeology in Iraq*, 3:1(July 1947), 4:2(September 1948); 3.16a,

HV; 3.16b, RT; 3.17, RT, after H. Frankfort, *Tell Asmar, Khafaje and Khorsabad*, Chicago, 1933; 3.18, S. Lloyd, *The Art of the Ancient Near East*, Oxford Univ. Press, 1961, p. 264; 3.19, A. Parrot, *Tower of Babel*, New York/Philosophical Library, Inc., 1955, Fig. II, p. 29; 3.20, Univ. Museum, Univ. of Pennsylvania; 3.21, S. Lloyd, *The Art of the Ancient Near East*, Oxford Univ. Press, 1961, p. 265; 3.22, Kunsthistorisches Museum, Vienna; 3.23, RT; 3.24, RT, after A. Parrot, *Mission Archéologique de Mari*, Vol. 2, part 1, *Le Palais: Architecture*, Paris, 1958; 3.25a, RT, after Frankfort; 3.25b, S. Lloyd, *The Art of the Ancient Near East*, Oxford Univ. Press, 1961, p. 275.

Chapter 4. Opener, Bettmann Archive; 4.1, RT; 4.2, RT, based on W.M. Flinders Petrie, *Illahun, Kahun, and Gurob, 1889–1890*, London, 1891, and B. Porter and R.L. Moss, *Topographical Bibliography of Ancient Egyptian Hieroglyphic Texts, Reliefs, and Paintings*, Vol. IV, London, 1934; 4.3, RT; 4.4a, S. Lloyd, *Ancient Architecture*, Abrams, 1974, Fig. 141, p. 78, Electa editrice; 4.4b, S. Lloyd, *Ancient Architecture*, Fig. 143, p. 79, Electa editrice; 4.5a & 4.5b, RT, based on A. Fakhry, *The Pyramids*, Chicago, 1961, and J.P. Lauer, *La Pyramide à Degrés*, *l'Architecture*, Cairo, 1936; 4.6, J.P. Lauer, *La Pyramide à Degrés*, *l'Architecture*, Cairo, 1936, pl. 45; 4.7, B. Balestrini, Electa editrice; 4.8, Egyptian Museum, Cairo; 4.9, RT; 4.10, TWA; 4.11, RT, based on A. Fakhry, *The Pyramids*, Chicago, 1961, and W.S. Smith, *Art and Architecture of Ancient Egypt*, Harmondsworth and Baltimore, 1958; 4.12, HV; 4.13, RT; 4.14, RT, based on J.L. de Cenival, *Egyptian Architecture*, New York, 1964, and H.E. Winlock, *Excavations at Deir el-Bahri, 1911–1931*, New York, 1942; 4.15, RT, based on Giedion, *The Eternal Present: The Beginnings of Architecture*, New York, 1964, and Hawkes, *Atlas of Ancient Archaeology*, New York, 1974; 4.16, Egyptian Expedition, MMA; 4.17, A. Badawy, *History of Egyptian Architecture: The Empire, or the New Kingdom*, Univ. of California Press, 1968, colorplate IV; 4.18, RT, based on A. Badawy, *Ancient Egyptian Architecture and Design*, Berkeley, 1965, and R.A. Schwaller de Lubicz, *Le Temple dans L'Homme*, Cairo, 1949; 4.19, RT, based on A. Badawy, *A History of Egyptian Architecture: The Empire, or the New Kingdom*, Berkeley, 1968, Giedion, *The Eternal Present*, Hawkes, *Atlas*, and Smith, *Art and Architecture*; 4.20–23, HV.

Chapter 5. Opener, Canan Tolon; 5.1, RT; 5.2, RT, after K. Bittel, *Hattusha*, New York, 1970, and Hawkes, *Atlas*; 5.3, HV; 5.4, HV; 5.5, RT, based on R. Boehmer, *Die Kleinfunde aus der Unterstadt von Boğazköy: Grabungskampagnen 1970–78*, Berlin, 1979; 5.6, HV; 5.7, HV; 5.8, S. Lloyd and J. Mellaart, *Beycesultan*, Vol. II, London, British Institute of Archaeology at Ankara, 1965, Fig. A.13, p. 30; 5.9, RT, after C.W. Blegen, *Troy*, 4 vols., Princeton, 1950–58; 5.10, RT, after A.W. Lawrence, *Greek Architecture*, Harmondsworth and Baltimore, 1957; 5.11, RT; 5.12, N. Kontos from *The History of the Hellenic World: Prehistory and Protohistory*, Ekdotike Athenon SA, 1970, p. 244, courtesy J.C. Bastias; 5.13, C.W. Blegen and M. Lawson, *The Palace of Nestor at Pylos in Western Messina*, Vol. I: *The Buildings and Their Contents*, Part 1, copyright © 1966 by Princeton Univ. Press, Photo, p. ii, by permission of publisher; 5.14, RT, based on C.W. Blegen, *The Palace of Nestor*, 2 vols., Princeton, 1966 and 1969, and Hawkes, *Atlas*; 5.15, RT;

5.16, HV; 5.17, A. Wace, *Mycenae*, Princeton Univ. Press, 1949, Fig. 51; 5.18, Erich Lessing/AR; 5.19a, HV; 5.19b, A. Wace, *Mycenae*, Princeton Univ. Press, 1949, Fig. 22, G. Dexter after P. de Jong; 5.20, A. Evans, *The Palace of Minos at Knossos*, 2:2, London, Macmillan and Co., 1928, Fig. 528, p. 809; 5.21, HV; 5.22, HV; 5.23, RT, after H.D. Hawes, *Gournia*, Philadelphia, 1908; 5.24, L. von Matt; 5.25, RT, based on Evans, S. Hood, and W. Taylor, *The Bronze Age Palace at Knossos*, London, 1981; 5.26, RT, based on R. Cadogan, *The Palaces of Minoan Crete*, New York, 1980, and Evans et al., *Bronze Age Palace*; 5.27, HV; 5.28, HV; 5.29, HV.

Chapter 6. Opener, R. Wood; 6.1, A. Boethius and J.B. Ward-Perkins, *Etruscan and Roman Architecture*, 1970, Fig. 5, p. 11, copyright © The Estate of Axel Boethius and J.B. Ward-Perkins, 1970, by permission of Penguin Books, Ltd.; 6.2, RT; 6.3, HV; 6.4, B. Balestrini, Electa editrice; 6.5, HV; 6.6, HV; 6.7, HV; 6.8, HV; 6.9, HV; 6.10 & 6.11a, J.J. Coulton, *Ancient Greek Architects at Work: Problems of Structure and Design*, Fig. 62, p. 142 and Fig. 5, p. 33, copyright © 1977 J.J. Coulton, by permission of Cornell Univ. Press and Granada Publishing Ltd.; 6.11b, G. Rodenwaldt, *Korkyra, Archaische Bauten und Bildwerke*, Vol. II: *Die Bildwerke des Artemistempels*, Tafel I, Berlin, 1939, Gebr. Mann Verlag; 6.12, V. Scully, *The Earth, The Temple and the Gods*, Yale Univ. Press, 1962, Fig. 73, courtesy Vincent Scully; 6.13, HV; 6.14, RT; 6.15, J.J. Coulton, Fig. 44; 6.16, RT, based on J. Pouilloux and G. Roux, *Énigmes à Delphes*, Paris, 1963; 6.17, RT, based on G. Fougeres, *Selinonte*, Paris, 1910; 6.18a, Museo delle antichità etrusche e italiche, Università di Roma; 6.18b, RT, after A. Boethius and J.B. Ward-Perkins, *Etruscan and Roman Architecture*, Harmondsworth and Baltimore, 1970; 6.19, HV; 6.20, HV; 6.21, Deutsches Archäologisches Institut, Athens; 6.22a, F. Krischen, *Die Griechische Stadt*, Berlin, Gebr. Mann Verlag, 1938, pl. 36; 6.22b, H. Walter, *Das Griechische Heiligtum*, Munich, R. Piper & Co., Verlag, 1965, Fig. 60; 6.23, Oriental Institute, Univ. of Chicago; 6.24, RT; 6.25, Musée du Louvre, Antiquitées Orientales.

Chapter 7. Opener, HV; 7.1, HV; 7.2, HV; 7.3, RT, based on C.A. Doxiadis, "Ancient Greek Settlement," *Ekistics* 31:182 (Jan. 1971) 5 and W.R. Shepherd, *Shepherd's Historical Atlas*, 9th ed., New York, 1976; 7.4a, RT, after *The Athenian Agora*, Vol. XIV: H. Thompson and R. Wycherly, *The Agora of Athens*, Princeton, 1972, and *Excavations at Olynthos*, part XII: D.M. Robinson, *Domestic and Public Architecture*, Baltimore, 1946; 7.4b, RT, reconstruction drawing by J. Ellis Jones, Univ. College of North Wales, Bangor; 7.5, A. Von Gerkan, *Griechische Städteanlagen*, Berlin, 1924, Fig. 6; 7.6, RT, after J. Kondis, "Zum Antiken Stadtbauplan von Rhodes," *Athenische Mitteilungen*, 73(1958) and J.B. Ward-Perkins, *Cities of Ancient Greece and Italy: Planning in Classical Antiquity*, New York, 1974; 7.7, RT, after J.J. Coulton, *The Architectural Development of the Greek Stoa*, London, 1976; 7.8, RT; 7.9, RT, after M. Coppa, *Storia dell'Urbanistica*, Rome, 1981, and C.A. Doxiadis, *Architectural Space in Ancient Greece*, Cambridge, Mass., 1972; 7.10, J.J. Coulton, *Ancient Greek Architects at Work*, Ithaca, New York, Cornell Univ. Press, 1977, Fig. 57; 7.11, J. Travlos, *Pictorial Dictionary of Ancient Athens*, Verlag Ernst Wasmuth, Fig. 692, p.

555; 7.12, HV; 7.13, A. Von Gerkan, *Das Theater von Priene*, Munich, 1921, pl. 35; 7.14, RT; 7.15, RT, after J. Travlos, *Pictorial Dictionary of Ancient Athens*, London, 1971; 7.16, Deutsches Archäologisches Institut, Athens; 7.17, RT, after Travlos; 7.18, RT, after A.G. Prokopiou, *Athens, City of the Gods*, London, 1964, and Travlos; 7.19, BFM/AR; 7.20, G.P. Stevens, *Restorations of Classical Buildings*, American School of Classical Studies at Athens, 1958, pl. V, p. 15; 7.21, J. Travlos, *Pictorial Dictionary of Ancient Athens*, Verlag Ernst Wasmuth, Fig. 565, p. 447; 7.22, Greek and Roman Dept., British Museum; 7.23, Deutsches Archäologisches Institut, Athens; 7.24, HV; 7.25, British Museum; 7.26, C. Praschniker, "Das Basisrelief der Parthenos," *Jahreshefte des Österreichischen Archäologischen Instituts*, Vol. XXXIX, 1952, opposite p. 7; 7.27, SCALA/AR; 7.28, HV.

Chapter 8. Opener, B. Balestrini, Electa editrice; 8.1, SCALA/AR; 8.2, HV; 8.3, RT; 8.4, HV; 8.5, HV; 8.6, RT; 8.7, F. Krischen, *Die Griechische Stadt*, Berlin, Gebr. Mann Verlag, 1938, pl. 40; 8.8, Electa editrice; 8.9, Greek and Roman Dept., British Museum; 8.10, HV; 8.11, HV; 8.12, RT, based on Coppa; 8.13, HV; 8.14 & 8.15, R. Herzog et al., *Kos*, Vol. I: P. Schazmann, *Asklepieion*, Berlin, 1932, pl. 40 and pl. 6; 8.16, RT, based on C. Blinkenberg, *Lindos*, 3:1, E. Dyggve, *L'Architecture*, Berlin, 1960, J.P. Bradford, "Fieldwork on Aerial Discoveries in Attica and Rhodes," *Antiquaries Journal* 36(1956), J. Kondis, "Zum Antiken Stadtbauplan von Rhodes," and R. Martin, *L'Urbanisme dans la Grèce antique*, Paris, 1956; 8.17, Dept. of Near Eastern and Classical Antiquities, National Museum, Copenhagen; 8.18, L. Mauceri, *Il castello Eurialo nella storia e nell'arte*, Rome, 1928, pl. II; 8.19, S. Lloyd, *Ancient Architecture: Egypt, Mesopotamia, Crete, Greece*, Abrams, 1975, Fig. 481, Electa editrice; 8.20, RT, after Travlos; 8.21, T. Wiegand et al., *Milet: Ergebnisse der Ausgrabungen und Untersuchungen seit dem Jahre 1899*, Berlin, 1900; 8.22, National Museum of the Gold Coast; 8.23, MMA, Rogers Fund, 1903; 8.24, RT; 8.25, RT, based on *Altertümer von Pergamon*, 12 vols., Berlin, 1885–1978; 8.26, W.B. Dinsmoor, *Architecture of Ancient Greece*, B.T. Batsford Ltd., 1950, Fig. 105; 8.27, A.W. Lawrence, *Greek Architecture*, 2nd ed., 1967, Fig. 157, p. 271, redrawn by D. Bell-Scott, copyright © 1957 Penguin Books, Ltd.; 8.28 & 8.29 École Française d'Archéologie, Athens; 8.30, Staatliche Museen, Berlin; 8.31, RT; 8.32, Museo della civiltà romana, Rome, photo: M. Henry; 8.33 & 8.34, RT, based on *Altertümer von Pergamon*, 12 vols., Berlin, 1885–1978; 8.35 & 8.36, Staatliche Museen, Berlin.

Chapter 9. Opener, L. von Matt; 9.1, RT, based on R. Meiggs, *Roman Ostia*, 2nd ed., Oxford Univ. Press, 1973; 9.2, RT, based on G. Fanelli, *Firenze*, Bari, 1980; 9.3, FU/AAR; 9.4, RT; 9.5, Accademia, Venice; 9.6, RT; 9.7, SCALA/AR; 9.8, Whittlesey Foundation, Inc.; 9.9, RT, based on W.F. Jashemski, *The Gardens of Pompeii*, New Rochelle, New York, 1979, A. Mau, *Pompeii, Its Life and Art*, New York, 1899, and A.G. McKay, *Houses, Villas, and Palaces in the Roman World*, Ithaca, New York, 1975; 9.10a, Alinari/AR; 9.10b, L. von Matt; 9.11, Alinari/AR; 9.12, RT, based on A. Maiuri, *La Villa dei Misteri*, Rome, 1947; 9.13, RT, plan after Mau, *Pompeii*, and McKay, *Houses, Villas, and Palaces;* 9.14, J. Pijoan, *Summa Artis*, 5th ed., 1965, Vol. V, Fig. 206, p. 159, Madrid, Espasa-Calpe, S.A., 1934; 9.15, Deutsches Archäologisches Institut, Rome; 9.16, L. von Matt; 9.17, L. von Matt; 9.18, FU/AAR; 9.19, H. Kähler, "Das Fortunaheiligtum von Palestrina Praeneste," *Annales Universitatis Saraviensis-Philosophie-Lettres*, Vol. VII, Fasc. 3/4, 1958, Saarbrucken, Univ. des Saarlandes, Fig. 3, p. 198; 9.20, Deutsches Archäologisches Institut, Rome; 9.21, FU/AAR; 9.22, A. Boethius and J.B. Ward-Perkins, *Etruscan and Roman Architecture*, 1970, Fig. 93, p. 222, copyright © A. Boethius & J.B. Ward-Perkins, 1970, by permission of Penguin Books, Ltd.; 9.23, M. Henry, Museo della civiltà romana; 9.24a, Soprintendenza per i beni ambientali e architettonici del Lazio, Rome; 9.24b, FU/AAR; 9.25, G. Marinucci et al., "Studi per una Operante Storia Urbana di Roma" map, Rome, Consiglio Nazionale delle Ricerche Roma, 1963; 9.26, RT, after W. MacDonald, *The Architecture of the Roman Empire*, rev. ed., New Haven, 1982; 9.27, FU/AAR; 9.28, M. Henry, Museo della civiltà romana, Rome; 9.29, FU/AAR; 9.30a, A. Boethius & J.B. Ward-Perkins, *Etruscan and Roman Architecture*, 1970, Fig. 97, p. 241, copyright © Estate of A. Boethius & J.B. Ward-Perkins, 1970, by permission of Penguin Books, Ltd.; 9.30b, Barbara Malter, Museo Capitolini, Rome.

Chapter 10. Opener, J.-P. Bourdier; 10.1, RT; 10.2, Vatican Museums, Rome; 10.3, FU/AAR; 10.4, National Gallery of Art, Washington, D.C., Samuel H. Kress Collection, 1939; 10.5a, D.S. Robertson, *Greek and Roman Architecture*, 2nd ed., London, Cambridge Univ. Press, 1969, pl. 19a and T. Wiegand et al., *Ergebnisse der Ausgrabungen und Untersuchungen*, Berlin, 1923, Vol. II, pl. 60; 10.5b, Alinari/AR; 10.6, Dept. of Antiquities, Algeria; 10.7, RT, after L. Prussin, *Architecture in Northern Ghana*, Berkeley, 1969; 10.8, J. Hawkes, *Atlas of Ancient Archeology*, 1974, p. 46, Robert Harding Associates, Rainbird Group; 10.9, P.G. Hamberg, *Studies in Roman Imperial Art*, Uppsala, Almquist & Wiksells Boktryckeri Aktiebolag, 1945, pl. 34; 10.10, H. Daicovicui and I. Miclea, *Rümanien in Frühzeit und Altertum*, Vienna, 1970, pl. 26, Editura Meridiane; 10.11, Oriental Institute, Univ. of Chicago; 10.12, A.U. Pope, *Persian Architecture*, Braziller, 1965, pl. 40; 10.13, RT; 10.14, RT, based on W.A. Andrae, *Das wiedererstehende Assur*, Leipzig, 1938, M. Colledge, *Parthian Art*, Ithaca, New York, 1977, and F. Safar and M.A. Mustafa, *Hatra, the City of the Sun God*, Baghdad, 1974; 10.15, Staatliche Museen, Berlin; 10.16, RT; 10.17, A. Volwahsen, *Living Architecture: Indian*, London, MacDonald, & Co., 1969, p. 4; 10.18, 10.19, & 10.20, A. Volwahsen, *Living Architecture: Indian*, Office du Livre S.A., Fribourg, pp. 22, 30, 34; 10.21, Xinhua News Agency, U.N. Bureau; 10.22, Nelson I. Wu, *Pei-ching Ku-chien-chu*, Peking, 1959; 10.23 & 10.24 RT, source material provided by Chu-Joe Hsia; 10.25, Paul Popper, Ltd.; 10.26, RT, source material provided by Chu-Joe Hsia; 10.27, RT; 10.28, Ohio Historical Society; 10.29, RT, based on I. Bernal, *The Olmec World*, Berkeley, 1969, and *Contributions of the U.C. Archeological Research Facility*, 5(July 1968); 10.30, copyright © René Millon, from *Urbanization at Teotihuacan, Mexico*, Vol. 1, part 1, Fig. 7; 10.31a, RT; 10.31b, G. Kubler and Art Library, Yale Univ.

Chapter 11. Opener, H. Hell; 11.1, RT; 11.2, S. Kostof; 11.3, Musei Capitolini, Rome; 11.4, Museo della civiltà romana, Rome; 11.5, Erich Lessing, Magnum; 11.6, M. Rostovtzeff, *Dura-Europos and Its Art*, Oxford Univ. Press, 1938; 11.7, RT, based on R. Krautheimer, *Corpus Basilicarum Christianarum Romae*, Vol. 3, Vatican, 1967, and G. de Angelis D'Ossat, *La Geologia delle Catacombe Romane*, Vatican, 1943; 11.8a, Benedettine di Priscilla, Commissione Pontificale di Archeologia Sacra; 11.8b, L. von Matt; 11.9a, G. Marinucci et al., "Studi per una Operante Storia Urbana di Roma," map, Rome, Consiglio Nazionale delle Ricerche Roma, 1963; 11.9b, Alinari/AR; 11.10, Papers of the British School in Rome, Vol. 12, 1932; 11.11, FU/AAR; 11.12, Landesmuseum Trier; 11.13, RT; 11.14, HV; 11.15, FU/AAR; 11.16, S. Kostof; 11.17, copyright © 1984 Bernard M. Boyle; 11.18, E. Hebrard and J. Zeiller, *Spalato, Le Palais de Dioclétien*, Paris, 1912; 11.19, HV; 11.20, SCALA/AR; 11.21, M. de Vogüé, *La Syrie Centrale*, Paris, 1865–77, Vol. 2, pl. 135; 11.22, Deutsches Archäologisches Institut, Rome; 11.23, W. MacDonald, *Early Christian and Byzantine Architecture*, New York, Braziller, 1979, Fig. 9; 11.24, K. J. Conant, *Carolingian and Romanesque Architecture*, 2nd ed., Penguin, 1966, pl. 1a, copyright © K.J. Conant and T.C. Bannister; 11.25, HV; 11.26, HV; 11.27, Courtesy of Burak Boysan; 11.28, Erich Lessing, Magnum; 11.29a, D.T. Rice, *Dawn of European Civilization*, McGraw-Hill, 1965, p. 120; 11.29b, RT, based on R. Janin, *Constantinople Byzantine*, Paris, 1964; 11.30, BFM/AR; 11.31, W. MacDonald, *Early Christian and Byzantine Architecture*, New York, Braziller, 1979, Fig. 66, and A. Vogt, *Le Livre des Cérémonies*, Paris, 1935.

Chapter 12. Opener, A. Martin; 12.1, RT; 12.2, *Al-Arabi* magazine, Kuwait; 12.3, A. Corboz, *Haut Moyen Âge*, Office du Livre, Fribourg, 1970, p. 36; 12.4, Courtesy of W. Horn; 12.5, Photo Gallimard, L'Univers des formes; 12.6, A. Corboz; 12.7, RT, after W. Braunfels, *Aachen, Austellung Karl der Grosse*, Aachen, 1965, and W. Horn and E. Born, "New Theses about the Plan of St. Gall," in H. Mauer, ed., *Die Abtei Reichenau*, Sigmaringen, 1974; 12.8, Photo Gallimard; 12.9, J. Feuille, copyright © CNMHS/SPADEM; 12.10, A. Frantz; 12.11, RT, after Horn, "New Theses . . . ," and F. Oswald et al., *Vorromanische Kirchenbauten*, Munich, 1966–71; 12.12, BFM; 12.13, Photo Gallimard; 12.14, BFM; 12.15 & 12.16, W. Horn and E. Born, *The Plan of St. Gall*, Vol. 1, Berkeley, Univ. of California Press, 1979, Fig. 170 and Fig. 168, by permission of the publisher; 12.17, BN; 12.18, courtesy of W. Horn; 12.19, W. Horn and E. Born, *The Plan of St. Gall*, Berkeley, Univ. of California Press, 1979, Vol. 1, Fig. 110, by permission of publisher; 12.20, National Museum, Copenhagen; 12.21, RT, based on A.H. Hourani and S.M. Stern, eds., *The Islamic City*, Philadelphia, 1970, and G. Le Strange, *Baghdad during the Abbasid Caliphate*, 2nd ed., Oxford Univ. Press, 1924; 12.22a, RT, based on Hourani and Stern; 12.22b, FU/AAR; 12.23, copyright © M.E. Newman; 12.24, R. Kawar; 12.25, RT, after R.W. Hamilton, *Khirbat al-Mafjar*, London, 1959, and J.D. Hoag, *Islamic Architecture*, New York, 1977; 12.26, State Organization of Antiquities & Heritage, Baghdad; 12.27, R. Wood; 12.28, A. Martin.

Chapter 13. Opener, A.F. Kersting; 13.1, A.F. Kersting; 13.2, NMR; 13.3, Foto Mas; 13.4 & 13.5, H. Hell; 13.6, Trianon Press, Photo Franceschi; 13.7, H. Hell; 13.8, RT; 13.9, H. Hell; 13.10, RT; 13.11, J. Feuillie, copyright © CNMHS/SPADEM; 13.12 & 13.13, copyright © Arch. Phot. Paris/SPADEM; 13.14, Joubert, copyright © CNMHS/SPADEM; 13.15, BFM; 13.16, copyright © Arch. Phot. Paris/SPADEM; 13.17, Foto Mas; 13.18, BFM/AR; 3.19, RT, based on O. Karpa, *Die Kirche St. Michaelis zu Hildesheim*, Hildesheim, 1965; 13.20, BFM; 13.21, K.J. Conant, *Carolingian and Romanesque Architecture*, 2nd ed., Penguin, 1966, pl. 111a, copyright © K. J. Conant; 13.22a & 13.22b, BFM; 13.22c, J. Roubier; 13.22d, J. Feuillie, copyright © CNMHS/SPADEM; 13.23, J. Fitchen, *Construction of Gothic Cathedrals*, Oxford Univ. Press, 1961, Fig. 13; 13.24, SCALA/AR; 13.25, RT, based on W. Braunfels, *Mittelalterliche Stadtbaukunst in der Toskana*, Berlin, 1953; 13.26. SCALA/AR; 13.27, Alinari/AR; 13.28, Vera Fotografica "Fotoclere"; 13.29, Alinari/AR; 13.30, RT; 13.31, J. Feuillie, Copyright © CNMHS/SPADEM; 13.32, Pitkin Pictorial Ltd.; 13.33, SCALA/AR; 13.34, courtesy of W. Horn; 13.35, RT; 13.36, Brogi/AR.

Chapter 14. Opener, W. Swaan; 14.1, Frances Loeb Library, Harvard Univ.; 14.2, National Gallery of Art, Washington, D.C.; 14.3, Giraudon/AR; 14.4, Frances Loeb Library, Harvard Univ.; 14.5, Arch. Phot. Paris/SPADEM; 14.6, RT, based on W. Braunfels, *Monasteries of Western Europe*, London, 1972, and H. Hofstätter, *Living Architecture: Gothic*, New York, 1970; 14.7, J. Feuillie, copyright © CNMHS/SPADEM; 14.8, RT; 14.9, RT, after S. Mc. Crosby, *Abbaye Royale de St.-Denis*, Paris, 1953; 14.10, J. Feuillie, copyright © CNMHS/SPADEM; 14.11, RT; 14.12, P. Lefèvre; 14.13, RT, based on R. Branner, *Chartres Cathedral*, New York, 1969; 14.14, W. Swaan; 14.15, BFM; 14.16, W. Swaan; 14.17, Y. Delaporte and E. Houvet, *Les Vitraux de la Cathédrale de Chartres*, Chartres, 1926, pl. 182; 14.18, copyright © CNMHS/SPADEM; 14.19, B. Balestrini/Electa editrice; 14.20, W. Blaser, *Drawings of Great Buildings*, Basel, Birkhäuser Verlag, 1983, p. 77; 14.21, W. Swaan; 14.22, BFM/AR; 14.23, Aerofilms Ltd.; 14.24 & 14.25, W. Swaan; 14.26, NBR; 14.27, W. Swaan.

Chapter 15. Opener, W. Swaan; 15.1, Combier imprimeur macon; 15.2, RT; 15.3, RT, based on E. Miozzi, *Venezia nel Secoli*, Venice, 4 vols. 1957–69; 15.4, J. Feuillie, copyright © CNMHS/SPADEM; 15.5, V. Křížek, *Kulturgeschichte des Heilbades*, Leipzig, Edition Leipzig, 1990, Fig. 43; 15.6, MS R. 17.1, ff 284v–285, Master and Fellows of Trinity College, Cambridge; 15.7, Lauros-Giraudon/AR; 15.8, Biblioteca Medicea Laurenziana, Florence; 15.9, NMR; 15.10, Alinari/AR; 15.11, RT; 15.12, Bibliothèque Royale Albert, Brussels; 15.13, Office of Tourism, Ypres; 15.14, BFM; 15.15, Alinari/AR; 15.16, NMR; 15.17, A. Verdier and F. Cattois, *Architecture Civile et Domestique*, Paris, 1864, Vol. 1, opposite p. 74; 15.18a & 15.18b, D. Upton; 15.19, RT, based on J.L. Abu-Lughod, *Cairo: 1001 Years of the City Victorious*, Princeton, 1971, and C.J.R. Haswell, "Cairo, Origin and Development," *Bulletin de la Société Sultanieh de Geographie*, XI (March 1922); 15.20, A.F. Kersting; 15.21, Lehnert & Landrock, Art Publishers, Cairo; 15.22, D. Roberts, *Egypt and Nubia*, 1849; 15.23, B. Balestrini, Electa editrice; 15.24, A.F. Kersting; 15.25, G. Michell, *Architecture of the Islamic World*, New York, William Morrow and Co., Inc., 1978, Fig. 26; 15.26, RT, based on Abu-Lughod, and M. Cleget, *Le Caire*, Cairo, 1934; 15.27, A. Toynbee, *Cities of Destiny*, New York, McGraw-Hill, 1967, Fig. 29, p. 80.

Chapter 16. Opener, W. Swaan; 16.1, Museo Nationale/AR; 16.2, RT, based on E. Detti, *Firenze scomparsa*, Florence, 1970; G. Fanelli, *Firenze, architettura e città*, Florence, 1973; 16.3a, Alinari/AR; 16.3b, Alinari/AR; 16.4a, RT; 16.4b, Anderson/AR; 16.5, Alinari/AR; 16.6, Alinari/AR; 16.7 & 16.8, Brogi/AR; 16.9, L. Benevolo, *Storia della Città*, Rome, Editori Laterza, 1975; 16.10, RT, based on E. Sacriste, *Huellas de Edificios*, Buenos Aires, 1962, and J. White, *Art and Architecture in Italy*, Harmondsworth and Baltimore, 1966; 16.11, P. Murray, *Renaissance Architecture*, New York, 1971, Fig. 22; 16.12, L. Benevolo, *Storia della Città;* 16.13, RT; 16.14 & 16.15, Giraudon/AR; 16.16, Lauros-Giraudon/AR; 16.17, NMR; 16.18, *Country Life;* 16.19, CMNHS/SPADEM; 16.20a, W. Swaan; 16.20b, NMR; 16.21, A.F. Kersting; 16.22, W. Swaan; 16.23, *Transactions of the Royal Institute of British Architects*, I (ii), 1842; 16.24, BFM; 16.25, National Museum, Belgrade; 16.26a, M. Bussagli, *Oriental Architecture*, Abrams, 1973, photo: Federico Borromeo; 16.26b, J.S. Shelton; 16.27a, L.M. Delaporte, *Les Monuments du Cambodge*, Paris, 1914; 16.27b, Groslier, 1961; 16.28a & 16.28b, W. Swaan; 16.29, B. Balestrini, Electa editrice; 16.30, Foto Mas; 16.31, RT, based on J. Goury and O. Jones, *Plans, Elevations, Sections, and Details of the Alhambra*, London, 1842–45, O. Grabar, *The Alhambra*, Cambridge, 1978, and F. Prieto-Moreno, *Los Jardines de Granada*, Madrid, 1952; 16.32, Neg. E-1586, Arxiu Mas, Barcelona.

Chapter 17. Opener, Alinari/AR; 17.1, Foto Mas; 17.2, Lauros-Giraudon/AR; 17.3 & 17.4, Alinari/AR; 17.5, RT, based on A. Schiavo, *Monumenti di Pienza*, Milan, 1942; 17.6, B. Boyle; 17.7, S. Kostof; 17.8, Alinari/AR; 17.9, Alinari/AR; 17.10, National Gallery of Art, Washington, D.C., Samuel H. Kress Collection; 17.11a & 17.11b, Anderson/AR; 17.12, RT; 17.13, BFM; 17.14a, Anderson/AR; 17.14b, Electa editrice; 17.15, RT; 17.16, Alinari/AR; 17.17, Filarete, *Treatise on Architecture*, New Haven, Yale Univ. Press, 1965, Vol. 2, book VI, folio 43r; 17.18, Alinari/AR; 17.19, RT; 17.20, C. Capello, Milan; 17.21, RT, based on G.C. Bascape and C. Perogalli, *Palazzi Privati di Lombardia*, Milan, 1965, and G. Paccagnini, *Il Palazzo Ducale di Mantova*, Torino, 1969; 17.22, R. Ingersoll; 17.23, RT, based on R. Papini, *Francesco di Giorgio, Architetto*, Florence, 1946, and P. Rotondi, *Il Palazzo Ducale di Urbino*, London, 1969; 17.24, Alinari/AR; 17.25, RT, based on G. De Carlo, *Urbino*, Cambridge, 1970; 17.26 & 17.27, Alinari/AR; 17.28, RT, based on B. Zevi, *Biagio*

Rossetti, Torino, Giulio Einaudi editore, 1960; 17.29 & 17.30, RT; 17.31, B. Zevi, *Biagio Rossetti*, Torino, 1960, Fig. 356; 17.32, Giraudon/AR; 17.33, Aero-photo.

Chapter 18. Opener, M. Treib; 18.1, Heyward Associates; 18.2, RT; 18.3, S. Morley, *Guide Book to the Ruins of Quirigua*, Supplementary Publication 16, 1935, Carnegie Institution of Washington, Fig. 17; 18.4, Univ. Museum, Univ. of Pennsylvania; 18.5, Art Library, Yale Univ.; 18.6, I. Marquina, *Arquitectura Prehispanica*, México, Instituto Nacional de Antropología e Historia, secretaria de educación pública, 1964; 18.7 & 18.8, T. Morrison, South American Pictures and Servicio Aerofotografico Nacional, Peru; 18.9, OAS; 18.10, T. Morrison, South American Pictures; 18.11, G. Kubler, *Mexican Architecture of the Sixteenth-Century*, New Haven, Yale Univ. Press, 1948, Vol. 1, pl. 33; 18.12, L. Benevolo, *Storia dell'architettura del Rinascimento*, Bari, Editore Laterza, 1973, pp. 468–69; 18.13, L. Benevolo, *Rinascimento*, Fig. 514; 18.14, Mexicana Aerofoto S.A.; 18.15, Mexican Govt. Tourist Office; 18.16, N. Radetzsky; 18.17a & 18.17b, M. Treib; 18.18 & 18.19, J. McAndrew, *Open Air Churches of 16th Century Mexico*, Harvard Univ. Press, 1965, Fig. 136, p. 291, and Fig. 197, p. 406, by permission of publisher; 18.20, Fay Diego de Valades, *Rhetorica Christiana*, Peabody Museum of Archaeology and Ethnology, Harvard Univ.

Chapter 19. Opener, A. Palladio, *The Four Books of Architecture*, Book II, London, 1738, pl. 58; 19.1, BN; 19.2, RT; 19.3, National Gallery of Art, London; 19.4, A. Gabriel, *Une Capitale Turque, Brousse*, Paris, E. de Boccard, 1958, Vol. 2, pl. IV, no. 1; 19.5, RT, based on Gabriel; 19.6a, U. Vogt-Göknil, *Living Architecture: Ottoman*, New York, Grosset & Dunlap, 1966, p. 28, photo: E. Widmer; 19.6b, C. Yip; 19.7, RT, after B. Ünsal, *Turkish Islamic Architecture*, London, 1970; 19.8, British Library; 19.9, RT, based on O. Aslanapa, *Turkish Art and Architecture*, New York, 1971, G. Goodwin, *A History of Ottoman Architecture*, London, 1971, and U. Vogt-Göknil, *Living Architecture: Ottoman*, New York, 1966; 19.10 & 19.11, U. Vogt-Göknil, *Living Architecture: Ottoman*, p. 34 and p. 40, photos: E. Widmer; 19.12, A.F. Kersting; 19.13, RT, after Goodwin, *Ottoman Architecture*, and Vogt-Göknil, *Living Architecture: Ottoman*; 19.14, RT; 19.15a & 1915b, U. Vogt-Göknil, *Living Architecture: Ottoman*, New York, 1966, p. 159 and p. 167, photos: E. Widmer; 19.16, RT, based on Miozzi; 19.17, A.F. Kersting; 19.18, courstesy of Avery Library, Columbia Univ.; 19.19, RT; 19.20, RT, based on E. Arslan, *Gothic Architecture in Venice*, London, 1972, E. Bassi, *Palazzi di Venezia*, Venice, 1976; 19.21, A.F. Kersting; 19.22, RT, based on Miozzi and G. Samona et al., *Piazza San Marco*, Padua, 1970; 19.23, Alinari/AR; 19.24, M. Treib; 19.25, Marsilio editori; 19.26, O. Böhm, Venice; 19.27, RT, based on *Corpus Palladianum*, Vol. III: W. Timofiewitsch, *La Chiesa del Rendentore*, Vicenza, 1969; 19.28, A.F. Kersting; 19.29, Carol Herselle Krinsky; 19.30, A. Palladio, *The Four Books of Architecture*, Book II, London, 1738, pl. 2; 19.31, M. Treib; 19.32 & 19.34a, S. Saitowitz; 19.33, AR; 19.34b, W. Andrews.

Chapter 20. Opener, L. von Matt; 20.1, F. Ehrle and H. Egger, *Piante e Vedute di Roma e del Vaticano*, Biblioteca Apostolica Vaticana, 1956, pl. 3, no. 3; 20.2, L. von Matt; 20.3, RT, based on T. Magnuson, *Studies in Roman Quattrocento Architecture*, Stockholm, 1958, and Marinucci et al., "Studi per una Operante Storia Urbana di Roma," map; 20.4, RT, based on A. Ceen, *Quartiere dei Banchi*, Ph.D. dissertation, Univ. of Pennsylvania, 1977; 20.5, RT; 20.6, H. Egger, *Römische Veduten*, Vienna, Friedr. Wolfrum & Co., n.d., Vol. 1, pl. 51; 20.7, Cabinet des Designs, Louvre; 20.8, RT, based on *Il Campidoglio di Michelangelo*, Milan, 1965; 20.9a & 20.9b, L. von Matt; 20.10 & 20.11a, Vatican Museums; 20.11b, RT; 20.12, C. D'Onofrio, *Gli Obelischi di Roma*, 2nd ed., Rome, Bulzoni Editore, 1967, pl. 77, photo: C. D'Onofrio; 20.13, RT, based on Magnuson, *Roman Quattrocento Architecture;* 20.14, Anderson/AR; 20.15, BN; 20.16a, Gabinetto Disegni e Stampe degli Uffizi, Firenze; 20.16b, Avery Library, Columbia Univ.; 20.17, L. von Matt; 20.18, Alinari/AR; 20.19, S. Kostof; 20.20, Bibliotheca Hertziana, Max-Planck-Institut; 20.21, Alinari/AR; 20.22, W. Andrews; 20.23a, Bethal Green Museum, Crown copyright, Victoria and Albert Museum; 20.23b, Ed. P. Chauffourier/AR; 20.24, L. von Matt.

Chapter 21. Opener, Byron, *English Bards and Scotch Reviewers*, Vol. III, Print Room, New York Public Library; 21.1 & 21.2, W. Swaan; 21.3a, Anderson/AR; 21.3b, W. Swaan; 21.3c, Anderson/AR, and plans: RT, based on P. Portoghesi, *Roma Barocca*, Cambridge, 1970; 21.4a & 21.4b, Albertina, Vienna; 21.5a, W. Swaan; 21.5b, Alinari/AR; 21.6a, Piranesi, 21.6b, L. von Matt; 21.7a, Niedersächsisches Landesmuseum, Landesgalerie, Hanover; 21.7b, W. Swaan; 21.8, V.L. Tapie, *Age of Grandeur*, New York, Grove Press, 1960, pl. 105; 21.9, M. Treib; 21.10, RT, based on D.C. Mullin, *The Development of the Playhouse*, Berkeley, 1970; 21.11, Harvard Theatre Collection; 21.12, SEF/AR; 21.13, E. Smith; 21.14, W. Swaan; 21.15, Mainfränkisches Museum, Würzburg; 21.16, C. Otto; 21.17, W. Swaan; 21.18a, Combier imprimeur macon; 21.18b, Musée Vauban; 21.19 & 21.20a, C. Norberg-Schulz, *Baroque Architecture*, New York, Abrams, 1971, Fig. 57 and Fig. 308; 21.20b, J. Mariette, *L'architecture française*, Vol. II, 1727, pl. 235; 21.21a & 21.21b, W. Swaan; 21.22, Giraudon/AR; 21.23, J.-A. Du Cerceau, *Les Plus Excellents Bastiments de France*, Vol. 2, Paris, 1870; 21.24a, Giraudon/AR; 21.24b, RT; 21.25, Giraudon/AR; 21.26a, Vassalieu, 1609; 21.26b, Turgot, 1739; 21.27, CNMHS/SPADEM; 21.28, Lauros-Giraudon/AR; 21.29, E. de Ganay, *André Le Nostre*, Paris, Editons Vincent, Freal & Cie., n.d., pl. XVIII; 21.30, Giraudon/AR; 21.31, L. Benevolo, *Rinascimento*, Fig. 932; 21.32, Consulate General, The Netherlands; 21.33, Frans Halsmuseum, Haarlem; 21.34, J.N. Bakhuizen van den Brink, *Protestantsche Kerkbouw*, Arnhem, 1946, and *Vitruvius Britanicus;* 21.35, A.F. Kersting; 21.36a, RT; 21.36b, 21.37, & 21.38a, A.F. Kersting; 21.38b, J. Summerson, *Architecture in Britain, 1530–1830*, 4th ed., Harmondsworth and Baltimore, Pelican, 1963, pl. 146b.

Chapter 22. Opener, Arch. Phot. Paris/SPADEM; 22.1, L. Benevolo, *Storia della Città;* 22.2, M. Jourdain, *The Work of William Kent*, London, Country Life Ltd., 1948, Fig. 109; 22.3, A.F. Kersting; 22.4, Aerofilms, Ltd.; 22.5, A.F. Kersting; 22.6, W. Andrews; 22.7, Langley, pl. XXXIII; 22.8a, A.F. Kersting; 22.8b, F.R. Yerbury, *Georgian Details*, London, E. Benn, 1926, pl. LVIII; 22.9, M. Treib; 22.10, *Vitruvius Britannicus*, London, 1739, Vol. 4, pl. 82–83, in a facsimile ed., Benjamin Blom, Inc., 1967; 22.11, *Great Houses of Italy*, New York, Putnam, 1968; 22.12, M. Treib; 22.13, W. Andrews; 22.14 & 22.15, J. Fischer von Erlach; 22.16, Langley, pl. XIII; 22.17, *Country Life;* 22.18, Giraudon/AR; 22.19, G.P.M. Dumont, *Les Ruines de Paestum*, 1769; 22.20a & 22.20b, Piranesi; 22.21a & 22.21b, W. Andrews; 22.22, J. Rondelet, *Mémoire Historique sur le Dôme du Panthéon Français*, Paris, 1797; 22.23, A.F. Kersting; 22.24, Sir John Soanes Museum, London; 22.25a, Arch. Phot. Paris/SPADEM; 22.25b, M. Raval, *Ledoux*, Paris, Arts et Métiers Graphiques, 1945, Fig. 284; 22.26, 22.27, & 22.28, BN; 22.29, RT, based on (a) Filarete, *Treatise*, 1460s, (b) A. Petit, *Mémoire*, 1774, and (c) J.-N.-L. Durand, *Recueil*, 1801; 22.30, Aerofilms Ltd.; 22.31, P. Patte, *Monuments érigés en France à la Gloire de Louis XV*, Paris, 1765, pl. XXIV.

Chapter 23. Opener, copyright © R. Langenbach; 23.1, RT; 23.2, *Country Life;* 23.3, A.F. Kersting; 23.4, NMR; 23.5, Verlag Georg Dw. Callway, Munich; 23.6, British Tourist Authority; 23.7, W. Andrews; 23.8, E. Smith; 23.9, A. La Padula, *Roma, 1808–1814*, Rome, Fratelli Palombi Editori, n.d., pl. XXV; 23.10, Staatliche Museen, Berlin; 23.11, National-Galerie, Schinkel-Museum, Staatliche Museen, Berlin; 23.12a & 23.12b, Durand, 2e partie, pl. 21, and pl. 5; 23.13a, British Library; 23.13b, J. Elmes, *Metropolitan Improvements*, London, 1829, pl. preceding p. 47, bottom; 23.14, L. Benevolo, *Storia della Città*, and R. Owen, *Report to the Committee for the Relief of the Manufacturing Poor*, 1817; 23.15, L. Benevolo, *Storia dell'Architettura Moderna*, Bari, Laterza, 1977, Fig. 155; 23.16, V. Scully, "Kleanthes and the Duchess of Piacenza," *Journal of the Society of Architectural Historians*, Vol. XXII (Oct. 1963), p. 143; 23.17, RT, based on I.A. Egorov, *The Architectural Planning of St. Petersburg*, Athens, Ohio, 1969; 23.18 & 23.19, G.H. Hamilton, *The Art and Architecture of Russia*, 2nd ed., Harmondsworth and Baltimore, Pelican, 1975, pl. 113; 23.20a, Märkisches Museum, Berlin; 23.20b, Staatliche Schlösser und Gärten, Potsdam; 23.21, Schinkel, *Sammlung architektonischer Entwürfe*, courtesy New York Public Library; 23.22, Papworth, pl. 6; 23.23, Pugin; 23.24, R. Langenbach; 23.25, Manchester Central Library; 23.26, reproduced by permission of the Royal Pavilion, Art Gallery and Museums, Brighton; 23.27, M. Whiffen; 23.28, J.F. Geist, *Passagen*, Munich, Prestel Verlag, 1978, Fig. 41; 23.29a & 23.29b, J. Austin; 23.30, E. Galloway; 23.31a, C. Meeks, *The Railroad Station*, New Haven, 1956, pl. 1, and C.F.D. Marshall, *Centenary History of the Liverpool and Manchester Railway*, London, 1930, opposite p. 64; 23.31b, Meeks, pl. 7; 23.32, The Illustrated London News Picture Library; 23.33, RT; 23.34, National Railway Museum, York; 23.35, R. Langenbach; 23.36, NMR, Wales, Crown copyright reserved; 23.37, MCNY; 23.38, Archives d'Architecture Moderne; 23.39, copyright © R. Langenbach; 23.40a, 23.40b, & 23.40c, NMR; 23.40d, 23.40e, 23.41, & 23.42, copyright © R. Langenbach.

Chapter 24. Opener, Prints Division, Stokes Collection, New York Public Library; 24.1, Library of Congress; 24.2, Missouri Historical Society; 24.3, RT; 24.4, MCNY; 24.5a, W. Andrews; 24.5b, Virginia State Library; 24.6, Henry Frances du Pont Winterthur Museum; 24.7a, G.E. Kidder Smith; 24.7b, Dorothy Abbe; 24.8, M. Whiffen; 24.9a, C.M. Andrews, "The River Towns of Connecticut," *Johns Hopkins University Studies in Historical and Political Science*, Vol. 7 (July-Sept. 1889), p. 4; 24.9b, Beinecke Rare Book and Manuscript Library, Yale Univ.; 24.10a, Stokes Collection, New York Public Library; 24.10b, Library of the Boston Athenaeum; 24.11, Bostonian Society; 24.12, W. Andrews; 24.13a, M. King, *King's Handbook of Boston*, 7th ed., Cambridge, 1885; 24.13b, Society for the Preservation of New England Antiquities; 24.14, J.E. Boucher, HABS, Library of Congress; 24.15a, W. Andrews; 24.15b, F. Kimball, *Mr. Samuel McIntire, Carver, The Architect of Salem*, Portland, Maine, Southworth-Anthoensen Press, 1940, Fig. 242; 24.16, H. Kirker and J. Kirker, *Bulfinch's Boston 1787–1817*, Oxford Univ. Press, 1964, Fig. 8; 24.17, W. Andrews; 24.18, Stokes Collection, New York Public Library; 24.19, Pennsylvania Academy of Fine Arts, Academy Purchase from Paul Beck Estate; 24.20, W.H. Pierson, Jr., *American Buildings and Their Architects*, Doubleday, Fig. 265, p. 366; 24.21, Bettmann Archive; 24.22, Virginia State Library; 24.23, Ohio State Univ. Libraries; 24.24, New York Historical Society; 24.25, Map Collection, Doe Library, Univ. of California, Berkeley; 24.26, MMA, Harris Brisbane Dick Fund, 1924; 24.27, G.E. Kidder Smith; 24.28, Boston Athenaeum Library; 24.29, W. Pierson; 24.30, G.E. Kidder Smith; 24.31, St. Patrick's Cathedral; 24.32, G.E. Kidder Smith; 24.33, Downing, Figs. 9 and 10; 24.34, copyright © R. Langenbach; 24.35, RT, based on H. Glassie, *Pattern in the Material Culture of the Eastern United States*, Philadelphia, 1968; 24.36, HABS, Library of Congress; 24.37, MCNY.

Chapter 25. Opener, C. Garnier, *Le Nouvel Opéra de Paris*, Paris, 1880, Vol. 1, pl. 28; 25.1, NMR; 25.2 & 25.3a, A.F. Kersting; 25.3b, *Country Life;* 25.4, *The Building News;* 25.5, *The Building News*, Sept. 5, 1873; 25.6, J. Austin; 25.7, W. Andrews; 25.8, C. Garnier, *Le Nouvel Opéra de Paris*, Paris, 1880, Vol. 2, pl. 8; 25.9, A. Joanee, *Paris Illustré*, Paris, Libraire de L. Hachette, 1863, p. 997; 25.10a & 25.10b, L. Benevolo, *Storia della Città;* 25.11, Minneapolis Institute of Arts, William Hood Dunwoody Fund; 25.12, B.D. Ray, Newport Historical Society; 25.13, 25.14, & 25.15, Library of Congress; 25.16 & 25.17a, MCNY; 25.17b, G.E. Kidder Smith; 25.18, W.E. Bell, *Carpentry Made Easy*, 1858, pl. 6; 25.19, Avery Library, Columbia Univ.; 25.20a, W. Andrews; 25.20b, RT, based on G.W. Sheldon, *Artistic Country Seats, 1886–87;* 25.21a, RT, based on N. Carver, Jr., *Form and Space of Japanese Architecture*, Tokyo, 1955, and H. Engel, *The Japanese House*, Rutland, 1964; 25.21b, M. Treib; 25.22, MCNY; 25.23, New York City Parks; 25.24a, M. Treib; 25.24b & 25.24c, D. Upton; 25.24d, Boston Athenaeum Library; 25.24e, D.S. MacDonald; 25.25, Chicago Historical Society; 25.26a, Hedrich Blessing; 25.26b, *Inland Architect and News Record;* 25.27, Chicago Historical Society; 25.28, RT; 25.29 & 25.30, Chicago Historical Society; 25.31, New York Public Library; 25.32, M. Parloa, *Miss Parloa's Kitchen Companion*, 1887; 25.33, Rand McNally and Co., *Bird's Eye Views and Guide to Chicago*, 1898; 25.34, RT, based on "History of Building Foundations in Chicago," *University of Illinois Engineering Experiment Station Bulletin*, series 373; 25.35a, G.E. Kidder Smith; 25.35b, MOMA; 25.35c, Missouri Historical Society.

Chapter 26. Opener, *A Monograph of the Work of McKim, Mead and White, 1879–1915*, Vol. II, pl. 100, New York, 1915; 26.1, MCNY; 26.2, Detroit Photographic Co., Library of Congress; 26.3, *American Architect and Building News*, Vol. 23 (June 9, 1888), courtesy Avery Library, Columbia Univ.; 26.4, New York Historical Society; 26.5, Chicago Historical Society; 26.6a, National Archives; 26.6b, Photo Collection, College of Environmental Design, Univ. of California, Berkeley; 26.7, Art Institute of Chicago; 26.8, Bettmann Archive; 26.9, Bildarchiv, Österreich Nationalbibliothek; 26.10, K. Frampton, "Modern Architecture and the Critical Present," *Architectural Design*, Vol. 52 (7/8), 1982, Fig. 2, p. 8; 26.11, G.R. Collins and C. Flores, *Arturo Soria y la Ciudad Lineal*, Madrid, Revista de Occidente, 1968, Fig. 1; 26.12a & 26.12b, Avery Library, Columbia Univ.; 26.13, Museo Civico Storico Risorgimentale; 26.14, C. Meeks, *Railroads*, courtesy Art and Architecture Library, Yale Univ.; 26.15, Howard, Fig. 2; 26.16, First Garden City Museum, Letchworth; 26.17, Bournville Village Trust, Birmingham; 26.18, British Architectural Library/RIBA; 26.19, *Country Life;* 26.20, M. Treib; 26.21, MOMA; 26.22a, H.J. Addison; 26.22b, F.L. Wright, *Ausgeführte Bauten und Entwürfe*, Berlin, 1910, pl. 37, bottom; 26.23, *International Competition of the Carnegie Foundation: The Palace of Peace at the Hague*, London, 1907; 26.24, Loos-Archiv, Graphische Sammlung, Albertina, by permission of Elsie Altmann-Loos and Adolf Opel; 26.25, MOMA; 26.26, FISA, industrias grafica; 26.27, W. Andrews; 26.28, J. Vischer and L. Hilbersheimer, *Beton als Gestalter*, Stuttgart, Julius Hoffmann, 1928, Fig. 86; 26.29, Avery Library, Columbia Univ.; 26.30a, BFM; 26.30b, *Casabella*, Vol. 240 (June, 1960), p. 14; 26.31, J. Joedicke, *Geschichte der Modernen Architektur*, Teulen, Verlag Arthur Niggli, 1958, Fig. 115; 26.32, Plansammlung der UBTUB, Inv. Nr. 2646; 26.33, Henry Ford Museum, Edison Institute, Dearborn.

Chapter 27. Opener, Tennessee Valley Authority; 27.1, *Country Life;* 27.2, Conway Library, Courtauld Institute of Art; 27.3a, Cement & Concrete Assoc.; 27.3b, Vischer, Fig. 199; 27.4, Archiv Burkhard-Verlag Ernst Heyer; 27.5, G. Haberta, ed., *Wonen in Wenen*, Antwerp, Europalia, p. 81; 27.6, Amt für Wissenschaft und Kunst der Stadt Frankfurt am Main, *Ernst May und das Neue Frankfurt, 1925–1930*, Frankfurt, Ernst & Sohn Verlag, 1986, p. 126; 27.7, RT, based on F.R.S. Yorke and F. Gibberd, *The Modern Flat*, London, 1937; 27.8, Nederlands Documentatiecentrum voor do Bouwkunst, Amsterdam; 27.9, D. Sharp, *Modern Architecture and Expressionism*, New York, Braziller, 1966, p. 113; MOMA, Gift of Philip Johnson; 27.11, Bauhaus Archiv, Berlin; 27.12a, Mies van der Rohe Archive, MOMA; 27.12b, RT; 27.13, G. Castillo; 27.14, A. Kopp, *Town and Revolution*,

ILLUSTRATION CREDITS

New York, Braziller, 1970, Fig. 116; 27.15a, SPADEM, Fondation Le Corbusier; 27.15b, Novosti Press Agency; 27.16a, Architectural Publishers Artemis, Zurich; 27.16b, Le Corbusier, *Early Buildings and Projects, 1912–1923,* New York, Garland Publishing, Inc., 1982, p. 21, left; 27.17, W. Andrews; 27.18, Le Corbusier, *Oeuvre complète,* Vol. 1, Zurich, 1929; 27.19, Western History Collection, L.A. County Museum of Natural History; 27.20, The Bancroft Library, University of California, Berkeley; 27.21, Chicago Architectural Photography Co.; 27.22, Ferriss; 27.23, Rockefeller Center; 27.24, D. S. MacDonald; 27.25, Cervin Robinson; 27.26, Ezra Stoller, copyright © ESTO; 27.27a, Werner Schumann; 27.27b, Johnson Wax; 28.28, Tennessee Valley Authority; 27.29, Theodor Horydczak, Library of Congress; 27.30, D. S. MacDonald; 27.31, BFM; 27.32, Otto Hagemann, Berlin; 27.33, G. Castillo; 27.34, *Dreissig Jahre sowjetische Architektur in der RFSFR,* Leipzig, VEB Bibliographisches Institut, 1950, Fig. 8.

Chapter 28. Opener, M. Treib; 28.1, Ezra Stoller, copyright © ESTO; 28.2, Le Corbusier, *Oeuvre complète,* Zurich, Vol. 5, 1946–52; 28.3, G. Castillo; 28.4, G. Castillo; 28.5, P. E. Guerrero, courtesy Gatje, Papachristou, & Smith, Architects; 28.6, Louis G. Redstone Assoc., Inc.; 28.7, L. Benevolo, *Storia dell'Architettura Moderna,* Fig. 484; 28.8, Fiorello H. LaGuardia Archives, F. H. LaGuardia Community College, New York; 28.9, RT; 28.10a, M. Treib; 28.10b, RT; 28.11, Ezra Stoller, courtesy Joseph E. Seagram and Sons, Inc.; 28.12, Ezra Stoller, copyright © ESTO; 28.13, Morley Baer; 28.14, A. Hess; 28.15, Harvas, Museum of Finnish Architecture; 28.16, MIT Museum; 28.17, Cement & Concrete Assoc.; 28.18, R. E. Mates, Solomon R. Guggenheim Museum; 28.19, David Heald, © The Solomon R. Guggenheim Foundation, New York; 28.20, Foto Favatier-Viollet; 28.21, R. Langenbach; 28.22, Rondal Partridge Photography © 1994; 28.23a, Ezra Stoller, copyright © ESTO; 28.23b, Courtesy TWA; 28.24, P. L. Nervi, *Costruire Correttamente Caratteristiche e Possibilità delle Strutture Cementizie Armate,* Milan, Ulrico Hoepli, 1955, Tav. XXVI; 28.25, Ezra Stoller, copyright © ESTO; 28.26, M. Smith; 28.27, M. Treib; 28.28, G. Loisos; 28.29, James Steele, *Hassan Fathy,* New York, St. Martin's, 1988, p. 69.

Chapter 29. Opener, G. Castillo; 29.1, Courtesy Hong Kong Trade and Development Council; 29.2, G. Castillo; 29.3, Alison and Peter Smithson, *Urban Structuring,* New York, Reinhold, 1967, p. 24; 29.4, G. Castillo; 29.5, Reyner Banham, *Megastructure,* London, Thames and Hudson, 1976, Fig. 183; 29.6, Cement & Concrete Assoc.; 29.7, Peter Cook et al., eds., *Archigram,* London, Studio Vista, 1972, p. 79; 29.8, G. Castillo; 29.9, KaiDib; 29.10, D. Upton; 29.11, P. Aaron, copyright © ESTO; 29.12, N. McGrath, courtesy Moore, Ruble, Yudell Architects; 29.13, Leon Krier; 29.14, G. Tagliaventi et al., eds., *A Vision of Europe,* Florence, Alinea Editrice, p. 135; 29.15, RT; 29.16, G. Castillo; 29.17, Tom Jacobi, Black Star; 29.18, Ezra Stoller, copyright © ESTO; 29.19, Daniel Liebeskind; 29.20, G. Castillo.

Color Plates. 1, Jean McMann; 2 (right), Musée d'Orsay, Paris; 2 (below), Photo RMN, Paris; 3, Ecole Nationale Supérieure des Beaux-Arts, Paris; 4, Philippe Berthe © CNMHS/SPADEM; 5 (left), Erich Lessing/AR; 5 (above), Topkapi Palace, Istanbul; 6, SCALA/AR; 7 (inset), Osterreichische Nationalbibliothek, Vienna; 7, Staatliche Kunsthalle, Karlsruhe; 8, University of California, Berkeley; 9 (top), J.-P. Protzen; 9 (far right), D. Upton; 9 (upper right), BN; 9 (lower right), M. Sartor, *Arquitectura y urbanismo en Nueva España, Siglo XVI,* Mexico City, Grupo Azabache, 1992, p. 61; 10 (above), SCALA/AR; 10 (below), Erich Lessing/AR; 11, M. and A. Hirmer, Munich; 12 (above left), Library Company of Philadelphia; 12 (above right), Deidi von Schaewen, Paris; 12 (below), Trustees of Sir John Soane's Museum; 13 (right), E. Revault © CNMHS/SPADEM; 13 (far right), Patricia Layman Bazelon; 13 (below), Collection of the New-York Historical Society; 14 (above), G. Castillo; 14 (left), Centraal Museum, Utrecht; 14 (below), Restricted Gift of Dr. & Mrs. Edwin J. DeCosta and the Walter E. Heller Foundation, 1986.88. Photograph © 1994 The Art Institute of Chicago; 15, Loisos/Ubbelohde; 16 (left), Alex S. MacLean/Landslides; 16 (below), Eisenman Architects, photo Donald Olshavsky, ARTLOG.

Glossary. RT. Doric and Ionic orders from M. Lafever, *The Modern Builder's Guide,* 1883, and Corinthian order from W. Chambers, *A Treatise on Civil Architecture,* 2nd ed., London, 1768.

766

GLOSSARY

abacus The uppermost part of a classical **capital,** often a plain, square slab. (See **order**)

abbey A **monastery** or convent, or its church. (14.1)

adobe Unbaked, sun-dried brick or building block made of a mixture of clay and straw.

adyton The inner room of a temple, situated behind the **cella.** (6.17)

aedicule 1. A wall recess framed by **columns** supporting an **entablature** and **pediment,** and intended as a shrine or as a shelter for a statue; 2. a door, window, or other opening framed by **columns** or **pilasters** and crowned with a **pediment.** (22.7)

agora The open meeting place or market place in an ancient Greek city. (7.15)

aisle A lateral division of a Christian church or an ancient Roman **basilica** parallel to the main central space of the **nave** and separated from it by **arches.** (9.14; 13.22b)

akropolis The upper town or elevated stronghold of an ancient Greek city, containing the chief temples. (7.2)

allée A broad walk flanked by trees.

ambo A pulpit or raised stand used for readings in an Early Christian or Byzantine church.

ambulatory A processional passageway around a shrine or flanking the **apse** of a Christian church. (See **church;** 14.10)

amphitheater A round, semicircular, or oval outdoor arena surrounded by rising tiers of seats. (7.12; 9.21)

andron The men's part, particularly the banqueting room, in an ancient Greek house.

angiportus A narrow road or alley in an ancient Roman city. Called **stenopos** in Greek.

angle brace A bar fixed across a building frame to make it rigid.

angle contraction In the **Doric order,** the reduction of the **column** span near a building's corner to offset irregularity in **column/triglyph** alignment. (7.14)

annular vault See **vault.**

anta The **pier** or **pilaster** created by the prolongation of the side walls of a building, often forming the ends of a **portico** or **porch.**

apadana A columned audience hall in ancient Persian palaces. (See page 114)

appartement A suite of rooms in French residential architecture.

The parentheses following the definition give the figure, if any, that illustrates the term. Boldface words are defined in the Glossary.

apse A vaulted, semicircular or semipolygonal wall recess or extension of a hall, such as on the short side of an ancient Roman **basilica** or at the sanctuary end of a Christian **church.** (See **church;** 11.20)

aqueduct An artificial channel for water, sometimes underground, but often elevated on arches. (9.3; 18.15)

arcade 1. A series of **arches** on **columns** or **piers,** either freestanding or attached to a wall (blind) (11.20); 2. a covered walk with a line of such arches on one or both sides (19.6a/b); 3. a covered walk lined with shops and offices and lit from the top. (23.27)

arch A curved structure, usually made of wedge-shaped stones (**voussoirs**), which spans an opening. An arch across the **nave** of a church with a solid triangular **gable** above and extending upward to the church's pitched roof is called a **diaphragm** arch. A **flat** arch has little or no curve. (9.24b) A **horseshoe** arch is shaped like a rounded or pointed horseshoe and has a diameter at its widest point greater than the opening it spans. An **ogee** arch has an S-shaped **ogee** curve on each side. (16.19) A **pointed** arch consists of two curves and has a point at its top. (14.11) A **strainer** arch is inserted between two walls to keep them from leaning. (16.21)

"architecture parlante" Literally, "speaking architecture," a French phrase that refers to the expressive power of buildings.

architrave The beam that spans a pair of **columns** as the lowest part of an **entablature.** (See **order**)

arris The sharp edge formed by the meeting of two surfaces, as in the **fluting** of columns.

ashlar masonry See **masonry.**

atelier A studio for teaching art or architecture.

atrio The walled courtyard before a Spanish-American church. (18.18)

atrium 1. The main inner hall of a Roman house, with an open roof and a central basin to catch rainwater (9.10); 2. the **colonnaded** forecourt of a Christian church. (11.24)

attic The storey above the main **cornice** in a classical facade. (20.22)

axis An imaginary straight line about which parts of a building or a group of buildings are arranged.

bailey An open court in a medieval fortification.

baldacchino An ornamental canopy over a tomb,

altar, or throne; sometimes portable. (20.23b)

balloon framing A system of light timber-frame construction in which uprights or studs extend the full height of the frame and horizontal structural members are nailed to them. (25.18)

balnea (plural of **balneum**) Ancient Roman baths. (11.9a/b)

balustrade A railing supported by a series of small posts or balusters. (22.18)

banco A wet-mud construction process akin to coil pottery. Commonly used in Africa.

bank barn A two-level barn built against a bank or hillside, with the upper level reached directly from the hill slope.

barrel vault See **vault.**

barrio A district or quarter of a town.

base The lowest supporting part of a **column, pier,** or wall. (8.11)

basilica 1. In ancient Roman architecture, a large meeting hall, often oblong in plan, with a high central space lit by **clerestory** windows; 2. the form of an Early Christian church, oblong, with a high, clerestoried **nave** ending in an **apse,** flanked by two lower **aisles,** and covered with a timber roof. (11.20)

bastide A new town in medieval France, pre-planned and often laid out as an orthogonal grid. (15.2e)

bastion A round, rectangular, or polygonal defensive projection of a fortress wall. (13.3; 21.18b)

batter (battered) The receding slope of a wall as it rises. (4.22)

battlement A low guarding wall or **parapet** with alternating depressed openings (embrasures or crenels) and solid parts (merlons). (13.3)

bay A regularly repeated spatial unit of a building or wall as defined by **vaults, windows, orders,** or other prominent vertical features. (16.8; 22.18)

bay window See **window.**

borough (bourg, burh) A town, larger than a village and sometimes fortified.

boss An ornamental knob or projection at the intersection of **ribs.** (16.20a)

bouleuterion An ancient Greek assembly building or council hall. (8.21)

boulevard An important road, often with a planted strip of trees down its center, or between its curb and sidewalks.

brace frame A system of timber-frame construction using large solid posts the full height of the frame into which horizontal members (girts) are fastened with interlocking joints (**mortise and tenon**).

bracket A projection from a vertical surface providing support under **cornices,** balconies, window frames, and so forth. (16.4a)

broken pediment See **pediment.**

bourg A **borough.**

broch A prehistoric Scottish stronghold in the form of a double-walled round tower with a central court. (10.8)

burh A **borough.**

buttress An additional support projecting from, or built against, a wall (24.8); a **flying buttress** is an **arch** or half-arch that transfers the **thrust** of a **vault** or roof from an upper part of a wall to a lower support. (14.18)

caldarium The hot water room in an ancient Roman bath. (9.17)

campanile A bell tower, usually freestanding. (13.22; 19.23)

campiello A small public space or **square** in an urban neighborhood.

cantilever A structural member supported at one end only. The other end projects beyond its supporting wall or column. (26.12b; 28.20)

capilla (de Indios) A chapel beside a Spanish-American church and open to the **atrio** or courtyard. (18.19)

capital The topmost part of a **column** or **pilaster,** above the **shaft.** A **cushion** capital is a cube with its bottom edges and corners cut away to form a transition from a circular column **shaft** to a square. (25.24e) A **historiated** capital has figural scenes on it. (13.6) **Lotus, palm,** and **papyriform** capitals are the three most common Egyptian capitals, and imitate respectively a lotus bud, the spreading crown of a palm tree, and a group of open papyrus blossoms. (4.23) For **Doric, Ionic,** and **Corinthian** capitals, see **order.**

capstone Any single stone in a protective capping or **coping** on top of a wall or post.

cardo The main north-south street in an ancient Roman orthogonal city grid. (9.2)

caryatid A sculptured, draped female figure used as a **pillar.** (7.28)

casemate A room in a fortress wall with openings (embrasures) for the firing of weapons.

casement window See **window.**

castrum (pl. **castra**) An ancient Roman walled military camp with a gridded rectangular layout (10.6); later a castle, fort, or fortified town.

catacomb An underground system of passages used as a cemetery. (11.8a)

catalan vault See **vault.**

cathedral A bishop's church, usually the principal church in a bishop's jurisdiction. The word comes from cathedra, the bishop's throne.

causeway A raised road or path.

cavea The tiered, semicircular seating area in an ancient Roman theater. (9.20)

cavetto cornice See **cornice.**

cella The main room in a Classical temple, housing the cult statue. (7.26)

cenotaph Literally an "empty tomb"; a monument to a person buried elsewhere. (22.26)

central plan A ground plan that is symmetrical in all directions. (11.13)

centuriation An ancient Roman grid system of land division. (9.2)

chaitya An Indian Buddhist cave temple or shrine carved out of a hillside, aisled, and often richly decorated with sculpture. (10.18)

chamfer The groove or oblique surface made when an edge or corner is beveled or cut away, usually at a forty-five degree angle. (17.15; 25.25)

champlevé An enameling process in which the design is cut out of a metal plate, leaving thin ridges that hold the enamel.

chancel The end of a Christian church that has the principal altar, usually the east end beyond the **crossing.** (See **church**)

chancel screen A screen that separates the altar area, or **chancel,** from the main body of a Christian church.

chapel 1. A small area within a Christian church containing an altar and used for private prayer; 2. a room or building within a larger complex used for religious purposes. A **lady** chapel is one dedicated to the Virgin Mary. A **palatine** chapel is a chapel used by a royal court. (12.8) A **radiating** chapel projects from the curve of an **ambulatory** or **apse.** (See **church**)

chapter house A place of assembly for the business meetings of a monastery. (14.24)

Chicago window See **window.**

chimney girt In **brace framed** construction, one of the heavy horizontal timbers that supports the floor beams.

chinoiserie A Western style of architecture and decoration utilizing Chinese elements. (22.11; 22.12)

choir The part of a church where the choir sits. It is usually the west part of the **chancel,** between the altar and the **crossing,** although the term is sometimes used to mean the same as **chancel.** (See **church**)

chord 1. The main part of a **truss;** 2. the span of an arch.

church The principal Christian religious building, used in public worship. For the parts of a church, see Fig. 1.

Fig. 1

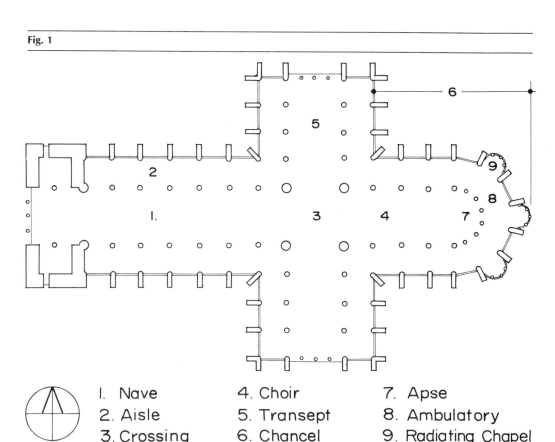

1. Nave
2. Aisle
3. Crossing
4. Choir
5. Transept
6. Chancel
7. Apse
8. Ambulatory
9. Radiating Chapel

churrigueresque A highly ornamented Spanish or Spanish-American style of the early eighteenth century, named after the architect José Churriguera.

circus 1. An ancient Roman roofless enclosure, oblong in shape, with one straight end, and with tiers of seats along both sides and at the other end, which was curved. It was used for horse and chariot races and gladiatorial contests (9.23). 2. In the eighteenth century, a circular or curved range of houses. (22.30)

citadel An elevated fort or stronghold.

City Beautiful A turn-of-the-century American city planning movement based on French academic principles of axiality, monumentality, and bilateral symmetry. (26.7)

Classical architecture The architecture of ancient Greece or Rome; lowercased, the term classical refers to later derivatives of Greek and Roman architecture.

Classicism Ancient Roman and Greek architectural forms and principles or, in lowercase, the revival of these forms in later periods.

claustrum In a **monastery,** the open courtyard surrounded by covered walkways. (14.3)

clerestory The elevated range of windows in a wall that rises above adjacent roofs. (4.10; 11.20)

cloisonné An enameling process in which strips of metal (cloisons) are soldered to a base, forming compartments into which enamel is poured and fused.

cloister A covered walk around a monastery courtyard, or the whole courtyard and walkway complex. (14.3)

cluster housing Suburban, medium-density apartment or row-house complexes. (28.37)

coffer A sunken square or polygonal decorative panel in a ceiling or within an arch. (11.10; 16.7)

collar beam A horizontal member that joins and strengthens rafters of a pitched roof. (12.4)

colonnade A row of **columns** supporting a beam or **entablature.** (4.16; 17.2)

column A cylindrical, vertical support, usually tapering upward and made either in one piece (**monolithic**) or of shorter cylindrical pieces the full diameter of the column (**drums**). In **Classical architecture** a column consists of a **base,** a **shaft,** and a **capital.** (See **order**)

combwork A type of exterior plaster decoration or **pargeting,** often consisting of thin parallel grooves.

common Public land belonging to the community at large.

commune A small administrative district, such as a city and its territory; the inhabitants or government of such a district.

compression The force within a structure that can crush or push together architectural members.

concrete Artificial stone made of a mixture of specific proportions of cement, water, and aggregate, such as crushed stone and sand. **Corrugated** concrete has parallel alternating ridges and grooves. (28.27) **Reinforced** concrete is made by inserting steel rods in the concrete, thus offsetting the weakness of concrete under **tension.**

conurbation A group of towns linked together geographically and possibly by function.

coping A protective capping or cover on top of a wall or post.

corbelled vault See **vault.**

corbelling Parallel masonry layers, each projecting beyond the one below. (6.20)

Corinthian See **order.**

cornice 1. The projecting ornamental **molding** along the top of a building or wall (16.4a); 2. the top, projecting part of an **entablature** (see **order**). A **cavetto** cornice is a projecting molding hollowed in the shape of a quarter circle.

cornières Covered passages around the marketplace of a new town in medieval France. (15.4)

cottage orné A small rustic house of the late eighteenth or early nineteenth century, often with an asymmetrical plan. (23.22)

counter-scarp The area between a fortified wall and the bare slope before it (**glacis**). (13.3)

crenellation A pattern of repeated depressed openings (crenels) in a fortification wall (see **battlement**). (13.3)

crescent A concave, curving row of houses. (22.30)

cromlech A prehistoric circular enclosure made of huge stones. (2.20)

crossing In a church with a cross-shaped plan, the space where the arms of the cross intersect. (See **church**)

cross vault See **vault.**

cross-in-square plan A Byzantine church plan based on a square divided into nine **bays.** The center bay is a large, domed square; the four corner bays are small domed or **groin-vaulted** squares; the remaining four bays are **barrel-vaulted** rectangles. (16.25)

crowstepped gable See **gable.**

cruck construction A construction system using equidistant pairs of large curved timbers (crucks) as the principal framing members in an arched house frame. The crucks serve as both wall posts and roof **rafters** and are joined at the top of the frame where they support a ridge beam.

crypt A room or storey beneath the main floor of a church, sometimes underground, and containing graves, relics, or **chapels.**

cryptoporticus In an ancient Roman house, a covered enclosed passageway with side windows.

cubit A unit of linear measurement, commonly eighteen inches, originally based on the length of the forearm from the elbow to the tip of the middle finger.

cupola A small **dome,** particularly a dome atop a roof or small tower.

cushion capital See **capital.**

cyclopean masonry See **masonry.**

daubing See **wattle and daub.**

demesne A lord's manor; an estate or the land of which the owner is in possession. (See also **seigneurie**)

dike A wall or bank used to contain water.

direct access grouping In an apartment building, one to four apartments per landing, arranged in distinct stacks around an entry and stair hall. (27.7)

dolmen A prehistoric tomb made of large upright stones, capped with a horizontal stone, and originally buried under an earth mound. (2.15)

dome A convex roof of even curvature on a circular or polygonal base (**drum**). (20.17) It can be semicircular, pointed, or bulbous in **section.** An **onion** dome is bulbous with a pointed top. A **saucer** dome has a slight curve and no drum. (24.18) A **semi-dome** is a quarter of a sphere and is used to cover a semicircular area. (19.11) An **umbrella** dome is a hemispherical dome divided into curved wedges by **ribs.** (16.12)

domus An ancient Roman house.

donjon See **keep.**

doric See **order.**

dormer See **window.**

double-ender A medieval church with **apses** at both east and west ends. (12.11)

dromos A long, high-walled entrance to a Mycenean tomb. (5.16)

drum 1. A circular or polygonal vertical wall that supports a **dome.** (25.13) 2. One of the cylindrical blocks of stone that forms a **column.** (See page 136)

Dutch gable See **gable.**

eave The lower part of a sloping roof projecting beyond a wall.

echinus The circular, upward-flaring, lowest part of a **Doric capital,** or the corresponding decorated part of the other orders. (See **order**)

eclecticism The combination of elements from a variety of architectural styles, especially in late-nineteenth-century European and American architecture.

elevation An exterior or interior vertical face of a building, or a drawing of the same as if flattened on a vertical plane. (13.22a–c; 6.11b)

enceinte A fortified, walled enclosure.

entablature The topmost part of a Classical **order;** the elaborated beam that a column supports. It is divided horizontally into the **architrave** (bottom), **frieze,** and **cornice** (top). (See **order**)

entasis The slight convex bulge given to a **column** to offset the optical illusion that it is thinner in the middle. (6.15)

episcenium In an ancient Greek or Roman theater, the upper storey of the stage and scene building, behind the performing area. (7.13)

epistyle The Greek term for **architrave;** the beam spanning a pair of **columns.** (See **order**)

espadaña On a Spanish-American church, the short wall with arched openings in which bells are hung.

esplanade A flat open space used as a walkway.

estipite A **pillar** or **pilaster** whose surface is broken up by secondary **capitals,** geometric panels, scroll ornaments, and so on. Used in seventeenth- and eighteenth-century Spanish and Latin-American architecture. (21.17)

exedra A semicircular or rectangular recess, usually with seats or a bench, and sometimes roofed.

fanlight A semicircular window, usually over a door, with radiating bars suggesting an open fan.

fan vault See **vault.**

faubourg A suburb of a medieval French city, outside the city's walls.

fillet A narrow flat molding, especially between the vertical concave grooves (**flutes**) on a **column shaft.** (See **order**)

finial An ornament that tops a pinnacle, spire, etc., usually pointed and decorated with stylized foliage. (14.21)

fireproof construction A construction system with masonry load-bearing walls, interior iron columns and beams, and masonry arches to support floors; used in nineteenth-century British industrial architecture.

Flemish gable See **gable.**

flute (fluting) A shallow, vertical, concave groove on a **column shaft** or **pilaster;** called **fluting** when in a series. (See page 136; 22.18)

folly A structure, such as a tower or fake ruin, built in a garden or park to highlight a view. (22.13)

forum A public civic and commercial square in ancient Rome. It was usually surrounded by a **colonnade** and included a **basilica** and temple. (9.28)

fresco A wall painting made on wet plaster with water-based colors. (11.8b)

frieze 1. In a Classical **order,** the middle horizontal division of an **entablature.** It is often decorated with sculpture. (See **order**) 2. An elevated, horizontal decorative band on a wall.

frigidarium The room with a cold water pool in ancient Roman baths.

gable The upper, usually triangular, part of a wall below the end of a roof with two sloping sides. (24.5c) The sides are usually straight, but may be stepped (**crowstepped**), curved (**Dutch**), or shaped like scrolls (**Flemish**).

gallerie (passage) A covered walk lined with shops and offices and lit from the top. (See **arcade;** 23.27)

gallery 1. An upper storey open on one side to a building's main interior space or to the exterior. In a church, a gallery runs above an **aisle** and opens onto the **nave.** (13.22c) 2. In secular architecture, a long room on an upper floor, often with windows along one side, used for recreation or the display of paintings.

gallery grave A prehistoric tomb in the form of a roofed stone corridor buried under an earth mound. (2.16)

gambrel roof 1. In the United States, a two-sided roof with two slopes on each side; 2. in Great Britain, a **mansard** roof.

glacis The bare, sloping embankment before a fortification. (13.3)

grange A feudal lord's farmhouse or manor house.

Greek cross A cross with four arms of equal length. (20.16b)

gymnasium In ancient Greece, an architectural complex for exercise, games, physical training, and teaching.

hairpin megaron See **megaron.**

half-timbering A construction system in which a wooden frame is left exposed and filled in with brick or plaster. (See page 348)

hall church A church with side **aisles** as high, or nearly as high, as the central **nave.** (13.22d)

hamlet A small country village without a church, included in the parish of another town.

hammerbeam The short horizontal beam that projects at the top of an interior wall and supports roof braces. (16.17)

headright A land allotment in the southern Anglo-American colonies, usually equal to fifty acres and taken wherever the landowner chose.

henge A circle of upright stones or posts. (2.20)

hipped roof A pitched roof with **gable** ends that slope back.

hippodrome 1. An ancient Greek stadium for horse or chariot racing in the form of an oblong with one curved end; 2. an ancient Roman enclosed garden of the same shape. (9.26; 9.27)

historiated capital See **capital.**

historicism The use of forms from a variety of past styles, either separately or in combination, particularly during the last two centuries. (24.26; 24.31)

honeycomb vault See **vault.**

horreum (pl. **horrea**) A wine storeroom in the upper floor of an ancient Roman house.

hospice A traveler's resort providing lodging and entertainment.

hôtel A French town house.

hundred In England, a division of a county.

hypaethral Open to the sky.

hypocaust An ancient Roman central heating system using hot air ducts in the floors of the building. (9.16)

hypostyle A room with a roof supported by many **columns,** usually in rows. (4.20)

impost A horizontal projection from a wall or post on which an **arch** rests. (6.19; 13.22)

insula An ancient Roman apartment block. (9.11)

intercolumnation The space between adjacent **columns.** (4.16)

Ionic See **order.**

iwan An Islamic vaulted hall, open at one end.

jamb The side of a door or window frame.

jardin anglais An eighteenth-century English garden of irregular plan. (22.10; 22.13)

jubé The French name for **rood-screen;** the carved screen that separates the **nave** from the **chancel** in a church.

kamoi The grooved beam holding the top of a lightweight sliding partition, called a shoji, in a traditional Japanese building.

keep The tower stronghold of a medieval castle, used as a residence in times of siege. Also called a donjon.

keystone The central wedge-shaped stone (**voussoir**) in an **arch,** sometimes decorated. (6.19)

khan An Islamic stopping place for caravans, also called a caravanserai. It was often a rectangular walled complex with a single large portal at one end opening onto a courtyard; along the sides of the complex were accommodations for travelers and animals and, at the end opposite the portal, a covered hall. (15.25)

külliye A Turkish building complex centered around a **mosque** and including educational, charitable, and medical facilities. (19.13)

lady chapel See **chapel.**

lancet window See **window.**

lantern A small, windowed tower on top of a roof or **dome** admitting light to the space below. (20.17; 21.24b)

Latin cross A cross with one arm longer than the other three.

lierne See **rib.**

linear grouping In an apartment building, an arrangement of apartments along one side of a **gallery** or along both sides of a corridor. (27.7)

lintel A horizontal beam or stone that spans an opening. (5.19a)

loggia A roofed **porch** or **gallery** with an open

arcade or **colonnade** on one or more sides. (15.10; 16.3a)

Lombard bands A decorative blind **arcade** on the exterior walls of an early medieval building, often just under the roof. (13.29)

lotus capital See **capital.**

lucam On a watermill, the projecting unit that contains hoisting machinery. (23.40a)

lunette 1. A semicircular window or wall panel framed by an **arch** or **vault;** 2. a freestanding defensive wall before a main fortification, usually in the shape of a projecting angle, with two additional parallel flanks.

machicolation A projecting defensive structure at the top of medieval fortress walls with floor openings through which molten lead, boiling oil, or stones could be dropped on attackers.

madrasa An Islamic theological or law school. (15.24)

mandala In Hindu thought, a magic diagram of the cosmos. (10.17)

manor An estate administered as a unit and worked by freehold tenants. (See **demesne, seigneurie**)

mansard roof A roof with a steep lower slope and a flatter upper slope on all four sides. Also called a **gambrel** roof in Great Britain. (25.7; 25.15)

marquetry Shaped pieces of material, such as wood, fitted together and glued to a surface.

martyrium A site that witnessed events in the life of Christ or His followers, or where the relics of a Christian martyr are deposited. Sometimes **martyrium** is used to refer to the building erected over such a site. (11.23)

masonry Stonework or brickwork. **Ashlar** masonry consists of smooth squared stones laid with mortar in horizontal courses. (16.3a) **Cyclopean** masonry uses huge irregular stones laid without mortar. (5.3) **Pseudoisotomic** masonry is ancient Greek or Roman **ashlar** masonry with courses of nonuniform height. **Quarry-faced** (stone or rock-faced) masonry is composed of squared blocks with rough faces, as if it came directly from the quarry. (25.24e) **Rusticated** masonry consists of blocks separated from each other by deep joints, often wedge-shaped grooves (chamfers). (17.14b)

mass The effect of bulk, density, and weight of matter in space.

mastaba An ancient Egyptian flat-topped, rectangular tomb with sloping (**battered**) sides.

maul A massive wooden hammer or mallet.

megalithic Built of huge, irregular stones. (2.16)

megaron The principal hall of an Anatolian, Cretan, or Mycenaen palace or house. It is rectangular in plan, with a circular central hearth and a front porch formed by the prolongation of the side walls. A **hairpin** megaron is U-shaped, with the curved end walled off to make a back room. (5.10)

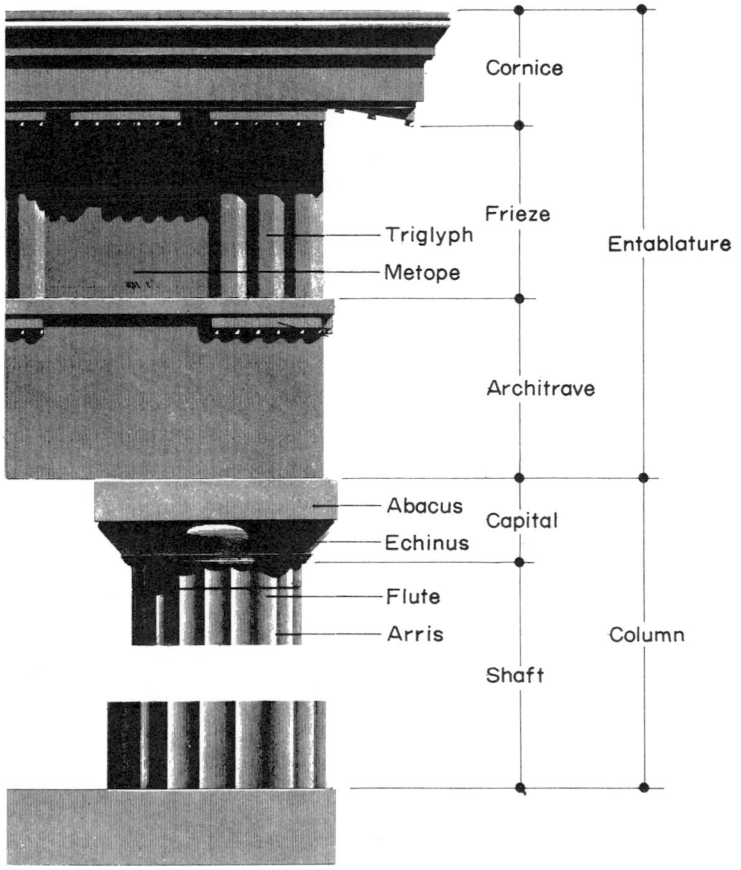

menhir A prehistoric monument in the form of a single, large, upright stone. (2.11)

merlon A solid part in a low protecting wall at the edge of a drop, alternating with depressed openings (**embrasures** or **crenels**). (13.3)

metope The square space, often decorated with sculpture, between the triglyphs of a Doric **frieze.** (See **order;** 7.22)

mihrab A wall recess in a Muslim religious building indicating the direction toward Mecca. (12.28)

minaret A tall slender tower of a **mosque,** from which the faithful are called to prayer. (11.27)

minbar The pulpit in a **mosque.**

mithraeum An underground sanctuary used for the worship of the sun-god Mithras. (11.5)

moat A wide protective ditch surrounding a medieval town or fortress, sometimes filled with water. (16.13)

module A unit of measurement to which parts of a building are related by simple ratios. In **classical architecture,** it is usually the diameter or half the diameter of the bottom of a **column shaft.**

molding A contoured decorative band applied to a wall surface or to the edge of a building part.

monastery The building complex of a monastic order. (14.1)

monolithic Made from a single stone.

mortise and tenon A wood-joining method in which a projecting tongue (tenon) of one member is fitted into a hole (mortise) of corresponding shape in another member.

mosaic Surface decoration formed by small cubes of glass or stone (tesserae) set in mortar or plaster. (11.19)

mosque The principal Muslim religious building. (19.9)

DORIC

Fig. 2A

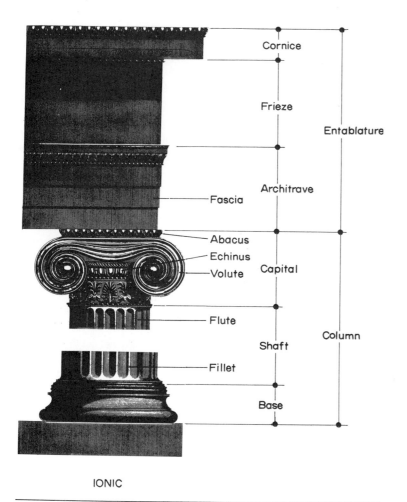

IONIC

Fig. 2B

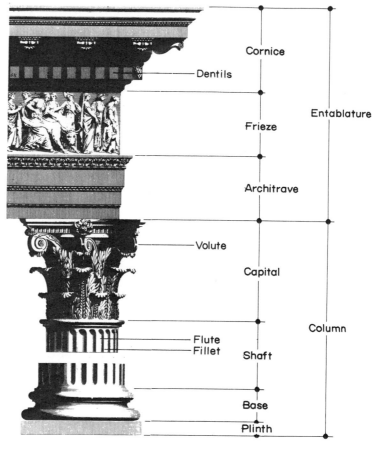

CORINTHIAN

Fig. 2C

---

motte A medieval fortification consisting of a conical earth mound surrounded by a ditch, topped with a wooden wall and tower, and the whole set in an open court or **bailey.**

mouchette A curved, flame-shaped opening in fourteenth-century French Gothic decoration.

mullion An upright that divides windows or other openings set in a series. (23.39)

muqarnas See **vault.**

narthex The interior or exterior transverse **vestibule** of an Early Christian church.

nave 1. In an ancient Roman **basilica,** the taller central space lit by the **clerestory** and flanked by **aisles;** 2. in a Christian church, the middle part of the western arm extending from the entrance to the **crossing** and flanked by **aisles.** (11.20; 13.13)

necropolis Literally, a "city of the dead"; a large, ancient burial ground.

niche A recess in a wall. (22.21b)

nymphaeum A Classical building or room with fountains, statues, and plants, used for relaxation.

obelisk A tall square stone shaft, usually of one piece, tapering upward and ending in a pyramidal tip. (20.12)

oculus A round window, often in a roof. (10.4)

odeion (odeum) A small ancient Greek or Roman theater, often roofed and used for musical performances.

ogee An S-shaped double curve consisting of a concave and a convex part. (16.19)

ogive 1. A pointed **arch;** 2. a diagonal **rib** in a Gothic **vault.**

onion dome See **dome.**

oppidum A Celtic hill-fort in the Roman period.

oratory (oratorium) A small private **chapel** in a church or house.

orchestra In an ancient Greek or Roman theater, the circular or semicircular space before the front row of seats. (7.12; 7.13)

order A classical **column** and **entablature** proportioned and decorated according to accepted modes. The ancient Greeks developed the **Doric, Ionic,** and **Corinthian** orders, and the Romans the **Tuscan** and **composite** orders. The Doric order, the most massive of these five, has a plain **capital,** a **fluted shaft,** and no **base.** The Ionic order is slimmer and its capital has prominent scrolls or **volutes.** The Corinthian order is the most attenuated and richly decorated of the three Greek orders. Acanthus leaves (caucoli) emerge from its capital and are topped by small volutes. The Tuscan order is similar to the Doric, but it has a base and the column shaft is unfluted. The composite order combines in its capital the acanthus leaves of the Corinthian order with the prominent volutes of the Ionic. (See Fig. 2)

oriel See **window.**

outwork Any fortification outside the main line of defenses.

772

pagoda A multistoried Chinese or Japanese tower with elaborately projecting roofs at each storey. (22.12)

palaestra An ancient Greek or Roman building for athletic training.

palatine chapel See **chapel.**

palisade A series of wooden posts with pointed tops set in the ground vertically as a fence or fortification.

palm capital See **capital.**

panoptikon A building with corridors radiating, and observable, from a central point. (23.23)

papyriform capital See **capital.**

parapet A low guarding wall at the edge of a point of sudden drop, such as a roof, terrace, balcony, or bridge. (13.3)

pargeting Exterior plasterwork decorated with low relief designs, often used on late medieval houses.

parodos In an ancient Greek or Roman theater, one of a pair of side entrances between the seats and the stage. (9.20)

parti In the French system of architectural thinking, the basic design concept for a building or group of buildings.

party wall A shared wall on the dividing line between two properties or houses.

pastas A small room before a larger room in ancient Greek architecture.

pastophory In a Christian church, a room near the **apse** for receiving the congregation's offerings and for storing the Eucharist.

pavilion 1. An ornamental building, often in a garden; 2. a prominent projecting subdivision of a larger building.

pedestal A support for a column, statue, or urn.

pediment Originally the triangular **gable** end of an ancient Greek or Roman temple (6.11b); later, any similar crowning feature over a door or window. (17.14b; 22.21a) Its sides may be straight or curved. (21.4c) A **broken** pediment has a gap at its apex or at its base. (22.8b) A **swan's neck** pediment has curving sides that end in scrolls.

pendant vault See **vault.**

pendentive A curving triangular surface or spandrel at the corners of a square or polygonal room that makes a transition from the room shape to a circular **dome** or its **drum.** (10.13; 11.28)

per strigas An ancient Greek system of orthogonal city planning "by bands." Broad east-west avenues divided a territory into bands disected by one or more north-south avenues. The superblocks formed were subdivided into rectangular blocks. These rectangular blocks were then apportioned into building lots.

periaktoi In a theater, the revolving, triangular prisms on either side of the stage used for scenery changes. (21.10a)

peribolos A wall enclosing a sacred area.

peripteral Surrounded by a single row of columns. (8.5; 8.6)

peristyle A roofed, columned porch or **colonnade** surrounding a building or courtyard. (8.5; 9.9)

piano nobile The main floor of a house, usually one storey above the ground floor. (16.4a)

piazza See **square.**

picturesque An aesthetic quality characterized by irregularity, asymmetry, ruggedness, and a variety of texture and form.

pier A solid masonry support, often rectangular or square in plan. (4.12; 20.23b)

pilaster A shallow, flattened, rectangular **column** or **pier** attached to a wall and often modeled on an **order.** (22.18)

piling A group of piles; large, heavy beams driven into the ground to support a structure.

pillar A post or column.

pilotis The French term for pillars or stilts that raise and support a building, leaving the ground floor open. (27.17; 28.3a)

pisé Stiff, packed earth or clay used as a building material.

place See **square.**

plat 1. A ground plan of a building; 2. a map, chart, or plan of a place.

plateia (platea in Latin) A wide street in ancient Greek and Roman towns.

plateresque A sixteenth-century Spanish architectural style characterized by lavish decoration that mixes Gothic, Renaissance, and Moorish motifs.

plaza See **square.**

podium A raised platform or base.

polis A city.

polychromy Architectural decoration using a variety of colors or varicolored materials. (25.3a)

porch A covered entranceway to a building. (14.16)

portal A monumental entranceway to a building or courtyard. (17.4)

portales A Spanish term for **arcade.**

portcullis A massive, movable defensive grating in a fortified gateway.

portico A covered entranceway or **porch** with columns on one or more sides. (22.21a)

porticus A **portico.**

posa Small domed chapels at the corners of an **atrio.** (18.18)

post and beam (lintel) A construction system using vertical supports (posts) spanned by horizontal beams (also called lintels). (2.20; 4.12)

postern 1. An inconspicuous, minor door or gate; 2. the tunnel underneath a city's defenses leading to a secret rear entrance. (5.4)

program A building's uses or activities.

pronaos The **vestibule** of an ancient Greek or Roman temple, with side walls and a row of columns along the front.

propylaia A monumental entranceway to a sacred enclosure. (7.16)

propylon An ancient Egyptian freestanding monumental gateway before the **pylon** of a temple.

proscenium The stage of an ancient Greek or Roman theater. (7.13)

prostyle Having a row of columns before only one face of a building (6.18a)

prytaneion The public hall in an ancient Greek city that housed the sacred hearth and where official and public guests were entertained.

pseudoisotomic See **masonry.**

pseudoperipteral A building with freestanding columns along its front and engaged columns along its back and sides. (9.18)

pylon The monumental entrance to an ancient Egyptian temple; pylon is sometimes used to mean one of the two rectangular, truncated pyramidal towers flanking such an entrance. (4.22)

quad (quadrangle) A rectangular courtyard enclosed by buildings, often within a larger complex.

quarry-faced masonry See **masonry.**

quoin One of a series of stones or bricks used to mark the corners of a building, often through a contrast of size, shape, or color. (24.36)

radiating chapel See **chapel.**

rafter One of a series of sloping beams supporting a pitched roof. (12.4)

ramma In traditional Japanese architecture, a pierced decorative panel between the ceiling and a sliding door frame.

rampart A fortification wall.

ravelin A freestanding fortification wall, with two embankments that make a projecting angle, placed between a curtain wall and a main ditch.

refectory The eating hall in a religious or secular institution.

reinforced concrete See **concrete.**

relief Carved or embossed decoration raised above a background plane. (7.23)

reredos A decorative screen or wall, of wood or stone, behind an altar serving as a frame for carved or painted religious images. (18.17a)

respond A **pilaster** or engaged half-**pier** that supports an arch or a vault rib. (14.7)

retable A painted or carved altarpiece standing at the back of an altar.

reveal On a side of a doorway or window opening, the part visible between the door or glass and the outer wall surface.

revetment A wall-facing or veneer of stone, terracotta, metal, wood, or other material.

revival The use of older styles or forms in new architecture.

rhiad A patio framed by architecture and used as a compositional unit of a complex. (1.18; 16.31)

rib A narrow, projecting band on a ceiling or **vault,** usually structural, but sometimes merely decorative. A **transverse** rib springs from an arch support or **impost** to the impost directly across on the opposite wall, separating the **bays** of a **vault.** A **diagonal** rib crosses a bay diagonally between two main supporting or **springing points.** A **longitudinal** or **transverse ridge rib** runs along the longitudinal or transverse ridge of a vault. A **tierceron** is a secondary rib that rises from a wall pier to the ridge rib, between the main diagonal and transverse ribs. A **lierne** is a small, subordinate rib, usually decorative, that does not spring from a main wall support and connects a diagonal or transverse rib with a tierceron. (See Fig. 3)

ribbed vault See **vault.**

ribbon window See **window.**

rond-point A French circular plaza on which streets converge.

rood-screen The screen, often elaborately carved, that separates the **nave** from the **chancel** in a Christian church.

roof-comb A wall along the ridge of a roof that makes the roof appear higher.

rose window See **window.**

rotunda A round hall or building, usually topped with a **dome.** (10.4; 24.21)

roundel A circular window or window pane.

rusticated masonry See **masonry.**

rustication The separation of regular **masonry** blocks by deeply cut, often wedge-shaped (chamfered) grooves. (16.4a; 17.14b)

sacristy A room in a Christian church where altar vessels and robes are stored.

sally-ports A secret gate or underground passage that links the inner and outer walls of a fortification.

sanctuary The area around the principal altar in a Christian church.

sash window See **window.**

saucer dome See **dome.**

scenae frons In an ancient Roman theater, the decorated front of the scenae, which was the back building behind the stage area. (7.13)

scholae Ethnic communities at the Vatican in the Middle Ages.

section A drawing of a vertical slice through a building at some imagined plane. (1.4b)

seigneurie In the medieval fendal system, a lord's manor consisting of the **demesne** and the

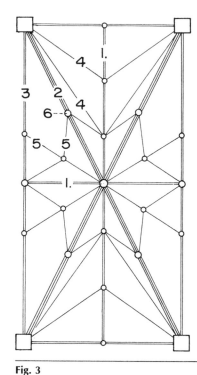

1. Ridge Rib
2. Diagonal Rib
3. Transverse Rib
4. Tiercerons
5. Liernes
6. Boss

Fig. 3

tenements (tenures); small holdings of dependent peasants.

semi-dome See **dome.**

serdab An ancient Egyptian closed statue chamber.

shaft The main part of a **column,** between the **base** and the **capital.** (See **order**)

sharawagi Planned irregularity in a garden or town design. The word was used in mid-eighteenth-century England to describe the irregularity of Chinese gardens.

sofa A living room in a Turkish house. (19.15b)

solar An upper room in a medieval house.

solea In Early Christian and Byzantine churches, the elevated walkway between the raised pulpit or **ambo** and the raised **apse** platform (bema) for the clergy.

space-frame A space-enclosing, three-dimensional framework made of interconnected geometric elements.

spandrel The triangular area between the sides of two adjacent arches and the line across their tops. (19.6a)

springing point The point where the curve of an **arch** begins. (13.22c)

spur wall A short wall that projects at a right angle from a main wall. (4.6; 8.7)

square (piazza, place, plaza) An open area in a city, usually surrounded by buildings or

streets, and paved or landscaped. (17.18; 18.14; 21.19)

squinch A small arch or a series of gradually wider and projecting concentric arches across the interior corners of a square or polygonal room, forming a transition from the room shape to a circular **dome** or **drum** above. (10.13; 16.29)

stalactite vault See **vault.**

stela An upright stone slab marking a grave. (18.3)

stenopos A narrow road or alley in an ancient Greek city. Called **angiportus** in Latin.

stereobate The foundation or platform on which a building or row of **columns** is erected. (8.10; 9.18)

stereotomy The art of cutting stone into shapes or figures.

stoa An ancient Greek, long, roofed **portico** with **columns** along the front and a wall at the back. (7.7)

string-course A projecting horizontal band across an exterior wall of a building. (24.15a)

strut A sloping roof beam at right angles to a pitched roof surface, joining a rafter to a **collar beam.** (12.4)

stucco An exterior plaster building finish.

stupa A Buddhist memorial mound that enshrines relics or marks a sacred site. (10.20)

stylobate   The top or top step of the substructure or platform on which columns stand. (8.10)

summerbeam   In timber frame construction, a horizontal beam supporting a floor or wall.

suq   A linear market-street in Islamic cities. (1.1; 12.22a)

swan's-neck pediment   See **pediment.**

taberna   An ancient Roman shop or booth.

tableros   In Meso-American architecture, a rectangular framed panel **cantilevered** over a sloping wall.

tablinum   In an ancient Roman house, a room with one side open to the central courtyard or **atrium.**

tatami   A straw floor mat used in Japanese architecture.

temenos   A walled sacred enclosure around an ancient Greek altar or temple.

temple front   A building facade or porch, with **columns** and a **pediment,** that resembles an end of a Classical temple. (19.28; 19.32)

tenement   An apartment building.

tensile strength   Strength under **tension.**

tension   The force tending to bend, stretch, or pull apart an architectural member.

tepidarium   The moderately warm room in ancient Roman baths.

terrace   1. A level embankment top, roof, or raised platform adjoining a building, often paved or landscaped for leisure use; 2. a series of attached houses that form a unit. (23.13b)

terra-cotta   Hard, molded, and fired clay used for ornamental wall covering, or roof or floor tile.

thermae   An ancient Roman bath complex. (11.19a/b)

thermal window   See **window.**

tholos   1. A round, corbel-vaulted Mycenaen tomb (5.18); 2. any round ancient Greek building. (6.20)

thrust   Outward or lateral stress on a structure.

tierceron   See **rib.**

tile hanging   A wall covering of overlapping rows of tiles.

tongue and groove   A wood-joining method in which a long, slightly projecting tongue of one member fits into the correspondingly shaped long narrow groove of another member.

torsion   The force tending to twist an architectural member.

tou-kung (dougung)   In Chinese architecture, a cantilevered bracket or cluster of brackets used to support a roof. (10.24)

trabeation   Construction using upright posts and horizontal lintels, not arches or vaults; post-and-beam construction. (6.8)

tracery   A pattern of curvilinear, perforated ornament within the upper part of a medieval window or screen. (16.22)

transept   The transverse arms of a cross-shaped church, crossing the main axis at a right angle. (See **church**)

transom   A horizontal bar across a window.

travertine   A type of limestone.

tribune   1. The apse of a church; 2. the gallery in a church.

triforium   In a medieval Christian church, a shallow arcaded passageway opening onto the **nave** above the nave arcade and below the **clerestory.** (13.22c)

triglyph   A vertically grooved block between the **metopes** in a Doric **frieze.** (See **order**)

trivium   A place where three roads converge. (21.6a; 21.27)

truss   A rigid framework made up of small triangular members and designed to span an opening. (23.33)

tufa   A porous, gray, volcanic building stone.

tumulus   An earth or stone mound over a grave.

tympanum   The segmental space enclosed by the **lintel** or beam over a doorway and the **arch** above it (13.12); the triangular space within the **moldings** of a **pediment.**

umbrella dome   See **dome.**

umbrella vault   See **vault.**

vault   An arched ceiling or roof. An **annular** vault is a continuous, semicircular vault in the shape of a ring. A **barrel** or **tunnel** vault is a continuous, semicircular vault that extends in a straight line. (13.22d) A **catalan** vault is made of tiles laid edge to edge and strengthened with stiffener **ribs.** A **corbelled** vault is a concave roof constructed with **corbelling.** (5.4) A **cross** or **groin** vault is formed by the right-angle intersection of two barrel vaults of the same shape. (9.4D) A **fan** vault is shaped like a concave semicone. (page 374) A **honeycomb, muqarnas,** or **stalactite** vault is an Islamic vault made up of various three-dimensional shapes and corbels. (16.32) A **pendant** vault is shaped like a suspended cone. (16.23) In a **ribbed** vault a web of **ribs** supports, or seems to support, the vault.

(16.20a/b) An **umbrella** vault has ribs fanning out from all sides of the central support below it. (14.24)

vestibule   An anteroom to a larger hall.

viaduct   A series of arches supporting a road or railway. (23.24)

vihara   An Indian Buddhist monastery.

villa   A country house, sometimes including its outbuildings and gardens. (19.32) A **villa rustica** was a villa serving agricultural purposes. (9.13) A **villa urbana** served a recreational purpose and was not a true working farm.

volume   The amount of space occupied by a three-demensional object.

volute   A spiral or scroll. (See Ionic **order**)

voussoir   A wedge-shaped block that is one of the units in an **arch** or **vault.** (8.19)

wattle and daub   A construction system using woven branches and twigs plastered over with mud as filling between the larger members of a wooden frame.

weatherboarding   Overlapping horizontal boards used as a protective wall covering. (24.5c)

westwerk (westwork)   The elaborated west end of a Carolingian or Romanesque church. It consists of an entrance hall with a room above, which opens onto the **nave,** the whole topped with a broad tower. (12.14)

wicket   A small door or gate within a larger one.

window   A wall opening usually admitting light and air. A **bay** window is a projecting window, usually rising from the ground. A **casement** window is hinged at the sides and opens inward or outward. A **Chicago** window consists of a centrally fixed, large window with narrow movable **sash** windows on either side. (25.38c) A window that projects vertically from a sloping roof and has a roof of its own is called a **dormer.** (24.14) A **lancet** window is narrow and is topped with a pointed arch. A medieval window that projects from an upper floor is called an **oriel.** (15.18b) A **rose** window is a large round medieval window with radiating **tracery.** (14.10) A **sash** window opens by sliding up or down. (22.8b) A **thermal** window is semicircular and is divided vertically into three parts. (19.12)

ziggurat   A Mesopotamian temple-tower in the form of a stepped pyramid. (3.21)

zoning   The legal restriction that deems that parts of cities be for particular uses, such as business, housing, and so forth.

Wales, 38, 349, 350

Walls, architectural: Baroque, 514, 519, 523, 525; curtain, 661; diaphragm, 462; Gothic, 323, 340, 341, 343; Islamic, 398, 457, 459, 467; modern, 661, 701, 705, 716, 718, 727, 728, 732, 733, 742, 753, 755; Renaissance, 411, 413, 414; Romanesque, 311

Walls, urban: early medieval, 271; Hellenistic, 174; Hittite, 92–93; Incan, 441, 442; Islamic, 285, 365; medieval, 350–51, 376, 377; Mycenaean, 105; Norman, 298, 299; Renaissance, 425–26; Roman, 182, 217, 275. *See also* Military architecture

Walpole, Horace, 558

Walter, Thomas Ustick, 650, Figs. 24.26, 25.13

Wank, Roland A., Fig. 27.28

Warehouses: in Boston, 613, 615, 619, Fig. 24.28; in Venice, 471; medieval, 359; modern, 577, 589, 595, 601–2, 750; Roman, 185, 194, 203, 600. *See also* Porticus Aemilia

Warka (Uraq, Iraq), White Temple at, 56, 60, 61, 118, Fig. 3.16

Warren, Russell, Fig. 23.27

Warsaw (Poland), 721

Washington, D.C., 537, 618, 627, 647, 671, 716, Figs. 24.1, 24.25, 26.6a; Capitol, 605, 627, 628, 629, 630, 650, 671, Figs. 24.18, 25.13; Department of Commerce building, Fig. 27.29; Federal Triangle, 716; Mall, 629, 671, 695; National Gallery of Art, 716; Smithsonian Institution, Fig. 24.1; State War and Navy Building, 650, Fig. 25.14; Supreme Court Building, 716; Treasury Building, 628, 629, 630, 631; Union Station, 671, Fig. 26.6b; White House, 628, 671, Fig. 24.1. *See also* Jefferson Memorial; Lincoln Memorial; Washington Monument

Washington, George (1732–99), 15, 623, 627, 629

Washington Monument (Washington, D.C.), 19, 629, 671, Fig. 24.1

Water systems, 355, 498, 622, Fig. 15.6. *See also* Aqueducts; Hydraulic works

Waterhouse, Alfred, 637

Wattle-and-daub, 46

Webb, John, 551

Webb, Mike, 748

Wellfeet (Massachusetts), First Congregational Church, Fig. 24.29

Wells Cathedral (England), 345, 525, Fig. 16.21

Werkbund Exhibition (Cologne, Germany), 690, 692, Figs. 26.29, 26.31

Westminster (England), 390; Abbey, 393, Fig. 16.23; Palace, 390–91, Fig. 16.17

Westwork, 275, 279, 280, 307. *See also* Corvey

Wethersfield (Connecticut), Fig. 24.9a

Whitney, Eli, 632

Wibert, 357, Fig. 15.6

Wight, Peter Bonnett, Fig. 25.16

Wilford, Michael, Fig. 29.27

Wilkins, William, 571

William of Sens, 333, 343, 344

William of Wykeham, 391

William the Conqueror (1066–87), 344

Williamsburg (Virginia), 614, 623

Winchester Cathedral (England), 344, Fig. 14.22

Winckelmann, Johann Joachim, 562

Windows: bay, 467, 640; Carolingian, 308, 311; Chicago, 665–66; Cistercian, 327–28; Federal, 618, 619; Gothic, 338, 345; medieval, 362, 391; Minoan, 108; modern, 571, 597, 601, 701, 705, 716, 727, 739, 751, Fig. 29.28; monitor, 632; Ottoman, 462, 467, Fig. 19.5a; Palladian, 475, 542; Portuguese, 434; Queen Anne, 640; Renaissance, 490; ribbon, 701; Roman, 251; Romanesque, 311; sash, 551, 614; Spanish-American, 446, 448; thermal, 477; Venetian, 472, Fig. 19.20; Victorian, 636. *See also* Dormers; Oculus; Rose windows

Windsor Castle (Berkshire, England), Chapel of St. George, Fig. 16.20

Winthrop, John, 607, 612

Wittkower, Rudolph, *cited,* 386

Wonderland Regional Shopping Center (Livonia, Michigan), Fig. 28.6

Wood. *See* Timber

Wood, John, 560

Woods, Shadrach, 747, Fig. 29.4

Woolley, Sir Leonard, 53

Woolworth Building (New York), 711

Worcester Cathedral (England), 345

Work Projects Administration (WPA), 713–14

Workers' clubs, 703, Fig. 27.13

World War I, aftermath of, 695–96, 698

World War II, 721, 724, 755

World's Columbian Exposition (Chicago, Illinois), 669, 670, 683, Fig. 26.5

Wotton, Sir Henry, 13

WPA. *See* Work Projects Administration

Wren, Sir Christopher, 540–41, 550, 555, 614. *See also* Greenwich; London: St. Paul's, St. Stephen, Walbrook

Wright, Frank Lloyd, 467, 670, 683–85, 692, 701, 711, 712, 713, 732, 734, 745, Fig. 27.26; *cited,* 670, 712, 734. *See also* Falling Water; Guggenheim Museum; Johnson Wax Administration Building; Larkin Administration Building; Robie House; Unity Temple

Wrigley Building (Chicago, Illinois), Fig. 27.21

Yale University (New Haven, Connecticut), 734; Art and Architecture Building, 739, 751, Fig. 28.25

Yankezia (Ghana), Fig. 10.7

Yemen, 285

York (England), 284; Cathedral, 345, 398

York and Sawyer, 716

Ypres (Belgium), 387, 388; Cloth Hall, 359, 636, Fig. 15.13

Yucatán (Mexico), 435, 437, 446

Yudell, Buzz, Fig. 29.16a

Zarathustra, 248

Zeilenbau formation, 699, 723, Fig. 27.6

Zempoala (Mexico), 446

Zeno, 143

Zeus, 106, 166, 169, 185. *See also* Agrigento; Olympia

Ziggurats, 3, 35, 54–61, 70, 74, 77, 118, 225, 710. *See also* Assur; Babylon; Khorsabad; Mari; Ur

Zimmerman brothers, 502

Zocalo (Mexico City, Mexico), 437, Fig. 18.14

Zoning, 150, 551, 673, 675, 709. *See also* New York City: Zoning Ordinance

Zoser, pyramid complex of (Saqqara, Egypt), 71–74, 125, Figs. 4.5–8

Zwinger (Dresden, Germany), 537